SAP Transaction Codes – Volume One

A Listing of Every SAP Transaction Code

By Stan X. Kubiyevski

First edition copyright 2017

ISBN: 978-1979740517

SAP Transaction Codes – Volume One

In this series of books you will find a listing of every SAP transaction code in existence, based on SAP ECC6

SAP Transaction Codes

/ASU/MAINTAIN	Maintain ASU XML
/ASU/SHOW_NOTE	Show SAP Note via Web-Browser
/ASU/SSM	ASU Simple Schedule Manager
/ASU/START	Start ASU Toolbox
/ASU/UPGRADE	Start ASU Toolbox in Upgrade Mode
/BDL/SDCC	Service Data Control Center
/BEV1/91000082	Material Sorting 1
/BEV1/91000083	Material Sorting 2
/BEV1/91000084	Material Sorting 3
/BEV1/91000085	Material Sorting 4
/BEV1/91000086	Material Sorting 5
/BEV1/91000098	Billing Types w/o Empties Update
/BEV1/91000099	Valid Empties Fields
/BEV1/91000100	Partner Role in Empties
/BEV1/91000101	Empties Material Types
/BEV1/91000102	Empties Item Categories
/BEV1/91000103	Manage Empties Groups
/BEV1/91000104	Empties Formulas
/BEV1/91000105	Empties material
/BEV1/91000106	Empties Update Sequence Number
/BEV1/91000162	Billing Type for Message Type
/BEV1/91000218	IMG Activity: /BEV1/TSSVARI
/BEV1/BO_MIGERP02	Rebate check report
/BEV1/EM0	Material Sorting Variant
/BEV1/EM1	Form for Material Sorting Variant
/BEV1/EM2	Maintenance of Print Indicator
/BEV1/EM3	Maintenance Empties Material Types
/BEV1/EM4	Maintenance of Empties Materials
/BEV1/EM5	Empties: Assign Item Categories
/BEV1/EMA	Empties Balance
/BEV1/EMB	Archive Monthly Empties Stock
/BEV1/EMC	Reload Monthly Empties Stock
/BEV1/EMD	Archive Empties Update
/BEV1/EME	Reload Empties Update
/BEV1/EMF	Delete Reloaded Empties Records
/BEV1/EMN	Empties Update Number Assignment
/BEV1/EMS	Empties Evaluation
/BEV1/EM_MIGERP01	Empties Migration
/BEV1/NEMB51	Material Document List (w. Empties)
/BEV1/NE_LISTBALPO	Empties Balances in Purchasing
/BEV1/RP_MIGERP01	Migration of Driver Master
/BEV1/RP_MIGERP02	Migration of Loading Units
/BEV1/RP_MIGERP04	Migration of Vehicle Master
/BEV1/RP_MIGERP05	Convert Vehicle Key
/BEV1/RP_MIGERP06	Convert Vehicle Type Key
/BEV1/RP_MIGERP07	Migration of Tour Master
/BEV1/SR0	Enter Sales Returns Analysis
/BEV1/SR1	Display Sales Returns Analysis
/BEV1/SR2	Sales Returns Orders List

/BEV1/TSMA	Part Load Lift Orders
/BEV1/VDT685B	Assi. of Shipment Message/Bill.Type
/BEV2/91000033	Basic Settings for Excise Duty
/BEV2/91000034	Maintain Tax Types
/BEV2/91000036	Maintain Tax-Dep. Material Groups
/BEV2/91000037	Maintain Tax-Indep. Material Groups
/BEV2/91000038	Maintain Procurement Types f. Schema
/BEV2/91000039	Maintain Procurement Types Schema
/BEV2/91000040	Maintain Additional Issues
/BEV2/91000041	Maintain Title Rows of Tax Warehouse
/BEV2/91000042	Assign Storage Loc. to Tax Warehouse
/BEV2/91000043	Maintain payroll units
/BEV2/91000044	Define Tax Warehouse
/BEV2/91000045	Define Actual Shrinkage
/BEV2/91000046	Define Theoretical Shrinkage
/BEV2/91000047	Maint. Warehse Shrink. Rate - St.Loc
/BEV2/91000048	Maint. Warehse Shrink. Rate - St.Typ
/BEV2/91000049	Storage Types for Shrinkage Rate
/BEV2/91000050	Def. of Entries to Post Subsequently
/BEV2/91000051	Mvt Cat for Mvt Type + Cost Center
/BEV2/91000052	Special Partner Type per Cust. Group
/BEV2/91000053	Mvmnt Category per Mvmnt Type
/BEV2/91000054	Excise Duty Movement Categories
/BEV2/91000055	Procurement Types per Block Schema
/BEV2/91000056	Procurement Types Block Schema
/BEV2/91000057	Maintain Print Format Items
/BEV2/91000058	Excise Duty Print Formats
/BEV2/91000059	Replace Stock Ledger Groups
/BEV2/91000060	Properties of Stock Ledger Groups
/BEV2/91000061	Define Stock Ledger Groups
/BEV2/91000062	Obsolete: Do Not Use
/BEV2/91000063	Excise Duty - Print Control
/BEV2/91000064	Excise Duty - Text Modules
/BEV2/91000065	Maintain tax rates
/BEV2/91000066	Excise Duty - Program Control
/BEV2/91000067	ED Form Substitution (SAP Script)
/BEV2/91000068	ED Database Access Optimization
/BEV2/91000069	Exise Duty Error Message
/BEV2/91000070	Excise Duty Report Threshold
/BEV2/91000160	Obsolete: Do Not Use
/BEV2/91000161	Obsolete: Do Not Use
/BEV2/91000185	ED Form Substitution (SmartForms)
/BEV2/91000195	List Types for Archiving
/BEV2/91000196	ED Archiving Parameter
/BEV2/91000198	Define Special Partner Types
/BEV2/91000199	Special Partner Types for GR
/BEV2/91000200	Special Partner Types for Vendors
/BEV2/91000201	Special Partner Types for Cust.Group
/BEV2/91000202	EU: Affiliated Non-EU Countries
/BEV2/ED	IS Beverage: Excise Duty
/BEV2/ED00	IS Beverage Area Menu ED
/BEV2/EDAC	Year-end closing
/BEV2/EDARCMDRELOAD	Reload Documents
/BEV2/EDARCMDSAVE	Excise Duty: Archive Documents

SAP Transaction Codes – Volume One

/BEV2/EDB1	Production Shrinkage (Theoret.) List
/BEV2/EDB2	Production Shrinkage (Actual) List
/BEV2/EDB3	Filling Shrinkage (Theoretical) List
/BEV2/EDB4	Filling Shrinkage (Actual) List
/BEV2/EDB5	Retrograde Shrinkage List
/BEV2/EDB6	Storage Location Shrinkage List
/BEV2/EDC1	Tax Types Definition
/BEV2/EDC10	ED Procurement Type Assignment
/BEV2/EDC2	Tax Warehouse Definition
/BEV2/EDC3	SAP Stor. Loc. for ED Tax Warehouse
/BEV2/EDC5	ED Movement Categories per Tax Type
/BEV2/EDC6	Assignment Mvmnt Types to Mvmnt Cat.
/BEV2/EDC7	Properties of Stock Ledger Groups
/BEV2/EDC8	Print Formats Stock Ledger
/BEV2/EDC9	Movement Categories Maintenance
/BEV2/EDCA	Returns: Order Reasons/Tax Deferral
/BEV2/EDCB	Customer Groups for Special Customer
/BEV2/EDCE	Definition of Movement Categories
/BEV2/EDCF	Excise Duty Units of Measure
/BEV2/EDCG	Assignment Cost Center for ED Type
/BEV2/EDCH	Excise Duty Printer Control
/BEV2/EDCI	Excise Duty Tax Rates
/BEV2/EDCJ	Column Bookable upon Period-End Cls.
/BEV2/EDCK	Returns: Tax Deducting Item Categor.
/BEV2/EDCL	Excise Duty: Basic Settings
/BEV2/EDCM	Header Lines for Tax Warehouse
/BEV2/EDCN	Storage Types for Stock Shrink. Rate
/BEV2/EDCO	Shrinkage Rate Rel. to Tax Warehouse
/BEV2/EDCP	Shrinkage Rate Rel. to Storage Loc.
/BEV2/EDCPROTO	ED: De-/activate Log
/BEV2/EDCQ	Define Theoretical Shrinkage
/BEV2/EDCR	Define Actual Shrinkage
/BEV2/EDCSLX	Stock Ledger Add. Fields: Definition
/BEV2/EDCSLXC	Stock Ledger Add. Fields: Conditions
/BEV2/EDCV	Replace ED Standard Programs
/BEV2/EDCW	Excise Duty - Report Thresholds
/BEV2/EDCX	Excise Duty - Error Texts
/BEV2/EDCY	Define Separator Sheet/Colle. Filing
/BEV2/EDD2	Goods Recipient: General Tax Data
/BEV2/EDD3	Ship-To-Party - EU Special Cases
/BEV2/EDDD	Disregarded Rocuments (General)
/BEV2/EDDEL	Maintain Deleted Documents
/BEV2/EDDS	Start Standard Document Selection
/BEV2/EDFC	Collective Filing/Self-Assessment
/BEV2/EDFE	Maintain Adjustment Documents
/BEV2/EDFF	ED: Additional Functions
/BEV2/EDFK	Spirits Tax Filing
/BEV2/EDIN	Inventory Note (General)
/BEV2/EDIS	Inventory Settlement (General)
/BEV2/EDK1	Vendors: General Tax Data
/BEV2/EDK2	Vendors: EU Special Cases
/BEV2/EDL1	List of Material Master Data
/BEV2/EDL2	List of Tax Warehouse Master Data
/BEV2/EDM1	ED Material Master (Client)

/BEV2/EDM2	ED Material Master (Company Code)
/BEV2/EDM3	Excise Duty Material Master (Plant)
/BEV2/EDMC	Period Closing Month (Beer)
/BEV2/EDMK1	Create Manual Document Adjustments
/BEV2/EDMK2	Change Adjustment Document
/BEV2/EDMKE	Maintain Manual Adjustment Documents
/BEV2/EDP0	Check Master Data
/BEV2/EDP1	Check Material Master Data
/BEV2/EDP2	Check Tax Warehouse
/BEV2/EDP3	Check Movement Types
/BEV2/EDP4	Check Print Parameters
/BEV2/EDP5	Check Movem.Cat./Stock Ledger Group
/BEV2/EDP6	TestProgram Customers/Ship-ToParties
/BEV2/EDP7	Test Program Creditors/Vendors
/BEV2/EDP8	Consistency Check of LIS Structure
/BEV2/EDPP	Define Printing Format Items
/BEV2/EDRD	Maintain Rejected Documents
/BEV2/EDSL	Excise Duty Movement List
/BEV2/EDSLSD	Stock Ledger Entries f. SD Documents
/BEV2/EDT2	Reset ED Document Transfer
/BEV2/EDT3	Excise Duty - Document Evaluation
/BEV2/EDT4	Reset Period
/BEV2/EDT5	Reset Year-End Closing
/BEV2/EDT7	ED: Choice for Document Selection
/BEV2/EDTP	Display Excise Duty Periods
/BEV2/EDTPY	Display ED Year-End Closings
/BEV2/EDTR	Tax Return (General)
/BEV2/EDWA	Set Work Area
/BEV2/ED_ARCDOC_REFR	Update Index Table
/BEV2/ED_CHECK_TOOL	Comparison of Fixed Stocks
/BEV2/ED_CHGLOG_MAT	Material Master Change History
/BEV2/ED_DEL_FIXST	Delete Fixed Stocks
/BEV2/ED_INT_1	ED Documents: Consistency Checks
/BEV2/ED_INT_2	Check ED Document Rel. to MSEG ID
/BEV2/ED_INT_3	ED:Check Stock Ledger Grp Head. Ent.
/BEV2/ED_INT_4	Check MSEG ID Rel. to ED Document
/BEV2/ED_INT_S1	ED Toolbox
/BEV2/ED_INT_S2	Issue ED Internal Log
/BEV2/ED_INT_S3	Express Message for R/3 User
/BEV2/ED_INT_S4	Compress ED Statistics Data
/BEV2/ED_INT_S5	ED: List Transaction Authorization
/BEV2/ED_INT_S6	ED: List Tax Warehouse Authorization
/BEV2/ED_LDS_MNG	ED: LDS Maintenance Dialog
/BEV2/ED_READ_ARCDOC	Read Archived Documents
/BEV2/ED_WRITE_FIXST	Update Fixed Stocks
/BEV4/01000010	IMG Activity: /BEV4/PLDFAUFTRV
/BEV4/77000017	IMG Activity: /BEV4/PLDVKORGZ_V
/BEV4/77000018	IMG Activity: /BEV4/PLDANFVKO_V
/BEV4/77000019	IMG Activity: /BEV4/PLDAUSGABE_V
/BEV4/77000020	IMG Activity: /BEV4/PLDPFAD_V
/BEV4/77000021	IMG Activity: /BEV4/PLAF
/BEV4/77000022	IMG Activity: /BEV4/PLPERIGRP
/BEV4/77000023	IMG Activity: /BEV4/PLPERIRAS
/BEV4/77000024	IMG Activity: /BEV4/PLPERIVIE

SAP Transaction Codes – Volume One

/BEV4/77000025	IMG Activity: /BEV4/PLDPERIOD_V
/BEV4/77000026	IMG Activity: /BEV4/PLDKART_V
/BEV4/77000027	IMG Activity: /BEV4/PLDROLZU_V
/BEV4/77000028	IMG Activity: /BEV4/PLDIFST_V
/BEV4/77000029	IMG Activity: /BEV4/PLDANFBEL_V
/BEV4/77000030	IMG Activity: /BEV4/PLDSTAT_V
/BEV4/77000031	IMG Activity: /BEV4/PLCU
/BEV4/77000399	General Customizing Pendulum List
/BEV4/77000400	Settings PL Requirements
/BEV4/PLAA	Display Sales Request Data
/BEV4/PLAC	Change Sales Request Data
/BEV4/PLAE	Correction of Incorrect Confirmation
/BEV4/PLAF	Aut. Filling of Update Determination
/BEV4/PLAN	New Creation of Sales Request Data
/BEV4/PLCA	Display Customizing Pendulum List
/BEV4/PLCU	Pendulum List Customizing
/BEV4/PLEA	Reported Sales Import
/BEV4/PLER	Manual Entry Confirmation
/BEV4/PLFA	Display Update Determination
/BEV4/PLFC	Change Update Determination
/BEV4/PLFN	Create Update Determination
/BEV4/PLGN	Report Generation of Request
/BEV4/PLKA	Display Assignment Nos Customers
/BEV4/PLKC	Change Assignment Nos Customers
/BEV4/PLKK	Schedule Job Update
/BEV4/PLKM	Update
/BEV4/PLKN	Creation of Assignment Nos Customers
/BEV4/PLPL	Area Menu Pendulum List
/BEV4/PLPQ	Subsequent Output
/BEV4/PLPR	Check Outstanding Sales
/BEV4/PLRS	Cancel Confirmation Pendulum List
/BEV4/PLSF	Create Order for Confirmation
/BEV4/PLSS	Cancelation of a Request Run
/BEV4/PLST	Cancelation Request Pendulum List
/BEV4/PLUA	Display Conversion Extern. Materials
/BEV4/PLUB	Schedule Job: Import Master Data
/BEV4/PLUC	Change Conversion External Materials
/BEV4/PLUD	Schedule Job: Import Sales
/BEV4/PLUE	Import Master Data Ext. Customers
/BEV4/PLUJ	Schedule Job to Generate Request
/BEV4/PLUK	Correction of Incorrectly Read Data
/BEV4/PLUN	Creation for Conversion Ext. Matl.
/BEV4/PLUP	Logs Sales Pendulum Lists
/BEV4/PLVF	Create Orders After Request Termintd
/BOBF/CONF_BO_CHECK	Check BOPF-Configuration of BOs
/BOBF/CONF_UI	BOPF: Business Object Configuration
/BOBF/CONF_UI_RPT	BOPF: Business Object Prototyping
/CUM/ANALYSIS	CU: Compare Plan vs. Actual Costs
/CUM/CM01	CU: Create Construction Measure
/CUM/CM02	Change Construction Measure
/CUM/CM03	Display Construction Measure
/CUM/CM04	CU: Delete Construction Measure
/CUM/CMNR	No. Range Maintnce: /CUM/CMNUM
/CUM/CU01N	Create Compatible Unit

SAP Transaction Codes – Volume One

/CUM/CU02N	Change Compatible Unit
/CUM/CU03N	Display Compatible Unit
/CUM/DESIGN	Compatible Unit Design Builder
/CUM/DESIGN_CHANGE	Change designs
/CUM/DESIGN_LIST	Display designs
/CUM/DESNR	No. Range Maintnce: /CUM/DESNM
/CUM/GEN_CU_CLASS	CU: Generate CU Class Structure
/CUM/SELECTION	Display Compatible Units
/CUM/SELECTION_1	Change Compatible Units
/CWM/CHECK_TRANSIT	Analysis of Stock in Transit
/CWM/IMG	IMG Catch Weight Management
/CWM/MESSAGES	CWM Message Attributes
/CWM/RHU_STOCK_DIFF	Correction of HU Stock Differences
/CWM/STOCK	Stock Overview
/CWM/STOCK_CHECK	Check Stock Variance
/CWM/TCWM	Activate Catch Weight Management
/CWM/VALPROC	Default for Valuation Procedure
/DSD/01002309	IMG Activity: /DSD/VC_CALTYP
/DSD/56000001	IMG Activity: /DSD/SL_CON_RN
/DSD/91000222	IMG Activity: /DSD/HH_DRVTXT
/DSD/91000223	IMG Activity: /DSD/HH_TRADAT
/DSD/91000224	IMG Activity: /DSD/HH_RAARTT
/DSD/91000225	IMG Activity: /DSD/HH_RACKDRS
/DSD/91000226	IMG Activity: /DSD/HH_RADISTYP
/DSD/91000227	IMG Activity: /DSD/HH_RAPAYMNT
/DSD/91000228	IMG Activity: /DSD/HH_RAPROFIL
/DSD/91000229	IMG Activity: /DSD/HH_RAREASON
/DSD/91000230	IMG Activity: /DSD/HH_RATIMTYP
/DSD/91000231	IMG Activity: /DSD/HH_RAVISCOD
/DSD/91000232	IMG Activity: /DSD/HH_RTATYP
/DSD/91000233	IMG Activity: /DSD/HH_TBALCTRL
/DSD/91000234	IMG Activity: /DSD/SL_CLEARSET
/DSD/91000235	IMG Activity: /DSD/SL_CLUSTAT
/DSD/91000236	IMG Activity: /DSD/SL_POSTSET
/DSD/91000237	IMG Activity: /DSD/SL_TBSO
/DSD/91000238	IMG Activity: /DSD/SL_TBSOASSM
/DSD/91000239	IMG Activity: /DSD/SL_TBSOSLTY
/DSD/91000240	IMG Activity: /DSD/SL_TCSTAMAP
/DSD/91000241	IMG Activity: /DSD/SL_TCSTATYP
/DSD/91000242	IMG Activity: /DSD/SL_TIDTAARE
/DSD/91000243	IMG Activity: /DSD/SL_TSLTYASM
/DSD/91000244	IMG Activity: /DSD/SL_TSLTYP
/DSD/91000249	IMG Activity: /DSD/HH_TBALHD
/DSD/91000253	IMG Activity: /DSD/SL_ACTIVETA
/DSD/91000255	IMG Activity: /DSD/SL_SNUM_SLDID
/DSD/91000256	IMG Activity: /DSD/SL_SNUM_FSR
/DSD/91000257	IMG Activity: /DSD/SL_SNUM_SLDEL
/DSD/91000258	IMG Activity: /DSD/SL_SNUM_SLCOC
/DSD/91000259	IMG Activity: /DSD/SL_SNUM_SLINV
/DSD/DE_ENTRY	Tour Data Entry: Entry
/DSD/DE_FUPREC	Tour Data Entry Control
/DSD/DE_SL	Tour Data Entry: Selection
/DSD/DX_AUDIT	Display DEX data for audit purpose
/DSD/DX_CARCHIVE	DEX - Archiving Control

/DSD/GS_DMI_CHK_PAR	Check Customizing Parameters
/DSD/HH_CRED	Send DSD-Specific Credit Data
/DSD/HH_CUST	Send DSD-Specific Customer Data
/DSD/HH_DRIV	Send Driver Data
/DSD/HH_DRVTXT	Send Driver Texts
/DSD/HH_MAT	Send DSD-Specific Material Data
/DSD/HH_PAYM	Maintain Extended Terms of Payment
/DSD/HH_PRINT_BC	Print Bar Code
/DSD/HH_RA_DELE	Route Settlement Deletion Program
/DSD/HH_TEST	Test Route Accounting DB
/DSD/HH_VEHI	Send Vehicle Data
/DSD/ME_CLEANUP	Remove Tour Data
/DSD/ME_CPT	DSD Connector Cockpit
/DSD/PR_PRO_ARCH	Deletion of Deal Conditions
/DSD/PR_PRO_CH	Change Deal Conditions
/DSD/PR_PRO_CR	Create Deal Conditions
/DSD/PR_PRO_DP	Display Deal Conditions
/DSD/PR_PRO_LIST	Display List of Deal Conditions
/DSD/PR_PRO_RESULT	Display List of Result in Orders
/DSD/RP_DYNDISP	Dynamic Transportation Planning
/DSD/RP_TOUR	Maintain Tours
/DSD/RP_VT11	DSD Shipment List
/DSD/SL_AUTOFSR_EXCL	Control Automatic Settlement
/DSD/SL_CLEAR	DSD Clearing: Without Dialog
/DSD/SL_CLEARDIALOG	DSD Clearing: With Dialog
/DSD/SL_CLEAR_APPLOG	DSD: Application Log for Clearing
/DSD/SL_COCKPIT	Settlement Cockpit
/DSD/SL_DIFIAC	Interim Accounts
/DSD/SL_FSR	DSD Final Settlement Run
/DSD/SL_IACFIN	Interim Accounts, Final Difference
/DSD/SL_LIST_DOC_DIF	Differences in Settlement Document
/DSD/SL_MS_PRESALES	Carry Out Presales Processing
/DSD/SL_MS_SETTLE	Perform Final Settlement
/DSD/SL_PMGIAC	General Accounts Driver, Customer
/DSD/SL_PMSIAC	Specific Accounts Driver, Customer
/DSD/SL_RADB	Fill Route Accounting DB
/DSD/SL_SNUM_FSR	Maintain Number Ranges FinalSett.Run
/DSD/SL_SNUM_SLCOC	Number Ranges COCI - Maintain Docs.
/DSD/SL_SNUM_SLDEL	Maintain DSD Del. Doc. Number Range
/DSD/SL_SNUM_SLDID	Maintain Number Range Settlem. Docs
/DSD/SL_SNUM_SLINV	Maintain Number range Ext. Inv. No.
/DSD/SL_TGFIND	Determination Tolerance Groups
/DSD/SL_TGGRP	Tolerance Groups
/DSD/SL_TGSEARCH	Serach Criteria Tolerance Groups
/DSD/SL_TGTYP	Tolerance Types
/DSD/ST_TOUR	Overview of DSD Tours
/DSD/SV_CHECK_CG	Check Counting Groups in material ma
/DSD/SV_LC_ADJUST	Confirm Load Adjustment
/DSD/SV_LC_COUNT	Confirm Load
/DSD/SV_LC_DELETE	Delete Loading Confirmation Data
/DSD/SV_LIST_SHIP	List of Shipments
/DSD/SV_LIST_STOCK	List of Stock on Truck
/DSD/SV_MAN_COR	Reprocess MM Record
/DSD/SV_MR_DEL	Delete Obsolete Movement Record Data

/DSD/SV_RELOAD   Reload
/DSD/SV_RL_RELEASE   Release Final Unloading Document
/DSD/SV_STOCK_AD_CR   Create SV Material Movements
/DSD/SV_STOCK_AD_DP   Display SV Material Movements
/DSD/TCBUS   DSD Loc: Tax Condition Builder USA
/DSD/VC_B_ACC   Access Sequences (Visit List)
/DSD/VC_B_C01   Create Message: Visit List
/DSD/VC_B_C02   Change Message: Visit List
/DSD/VC_B_C03   Display Message: Visit List
/DSD/VC_B_CAT   Field Catalog (Visit List)
/DSD/VC_B_CT1   Create Condition Tables
/DSD/VC_B_CT2   VL Messages - Change ConTab
/DSD/VC_B_CT3   VL Messages - Display ConTab
/DSD/VC_B_MAP   Assignment of Message Schema
/DSD/VC_B_SCH   Message Schema (Visit List)
/DSD/VC_B_TYP   Message Types (Visit List)
/DSD/VC_GEN   Generate Visit Lists
/DSD/VC_GEOCODE   Geocoding
/DSD/VC_MESSAGES   Output Processing
/DSD/VC_RSNAST00   Selection of Messages to Process
/DSD/VC_RSNAST0D   Generic output issue
/DSD/VC_RSNAST0F   Selection of Incorrect Messages
/DSD/VC_SETTLE   Comparison: Deliveries - Visit Lists
/DSD/VC_TEXT_CONTROL   Text Control for DSD Visit Control
/DSD/VC_VL   Maintain Visit List
/DSD/VC_VLRANGE   Maintain Number Ranges: SC Lists
/DSD/VC_VL_DELETE   Delete Visit Lists
/DSD/VC_VL_VIEW   Display Sales Call List
/DSD/VC_VP   Maintain Visit Plans
/DSD/VC_VPRANGE   Maintain Number Ranges: SC Schedules
/DSD/VC_VP_CREATE   Create Sales Call Schedules
/DSD/VC_VP_VIEW   Display Sales Call Schedules
/EACA/CHANGE_TEMPLAT   Characteristics for GL - Templates
/EACA/GLCONTROL   Characteristics for GL - Templates
/EACA/GLPOST_ACCDATA   Post G/L Acct Document to Data Basis
/EACA/GLPOST_ACCSYST   G/L Acct Doc. for Accounting System
/EACA/GLPOST_REFDOC   Enter Sample Documents
/EACA/GLPST_REF_ACCS   Enter Sample Documents
/EACA/GL_BREP   GL Balance Reporting
/EACA/GL_CONFIGURE   Configure xGL
/EACA/GL_DOCNR   GL Document Number Maintenance
/EACA/GL_DOC_DISPLAY   Document Display
/EACA/GL_DOC_JOURNAL   Document Journal
/EACA/GL_IMG   IMG Display for General Ledger
/EACA/GL_MANPOS_VM   Set Up General Ledger Acct Posting
/EACA/GL_MD   GL Master Data: Maintenance
/EACA/GL_POST_ACT   Activate G/L Account Posting
/EACA/GL_PRNTA_SHOW   Display Source Document/Sample Docs
/EACA/GL_REFDOC_SHOW   Display Sample Document
/EACA/GL_REVERSAL   Reverse G/L Acct Posting/Source Doc.
/EACA/GL_REV_DOC   Reverse G/L Acct Posting/Acc. Doc.
/EACA/PMCFACTIV   Activate Profitability Mgt View
/EACA/PMCFSTR_BTAPRO   Configure BTA Profit from PM View
/EACA/PMCFSTR_CR_JR   Struct. Config. of C&R Journal

SAP Transaction Codes – Volume One

/EACA/PMCFVARI	PM: Variant Maintenance
/EACA/PM_CK_GRPS	Char. and Key Figure Grp Maintenance
/EACA/PM_PPR_DISP	Line Item List (Source Document)
/EACA/PM_PPR_LI	Manual Entry of Line Items
/EACA/PM_UR_ADMIN	Execute Assignment Changes (Realgmt)
/EACA/PM_UR_MAINTAIN	Maintain Assignment Changes
/EACC/50000020	IMG Activity: /EACC/SIMG_INST_COMP
/EACC/ACSYST_COPY	Copy Valuation Systems
/EACC/ACTIVATE_AE	Activation of the Accounting Engine
/EACC/ARCHIVE_CONFIG	Document Archiving Maintenance
/EACC/ARCHIVE_RUN	Carry Out Document Archiving
/EACC/CONFIGS	Journal Configurations
/EACC/DMM_COPYTOOL	Copying Map Objects
/EACC/DMM_OBJMAP	BW Objects for Accounting Views
/EACC/DMM_OBJMAP_V	BW Objects for Accounting Views
/EACC/DMON	Monitor Flow Control
/EACC/DM_DEBUG	Activate Breakpoints
/EACC/DOCJOURNALCONF	Configuration of the Doc. Journal
/EACC/DOC_REPORT	Document Display
/EACC/DR_CONFIG	Derivation: Add Source Characterstcs
/EACC/DR_CUST	Derivation: Add Source Characterstcs
/EACC/FOBU	E-Accounting Formula Editor
/EACC/JOURNALCONF	Derivation Test
/EACC/JOURNALCONTENT	Accounting Engine Journals Overview
/EACC/JOURNAL_REPORT	Journal Report
/EACC/KF_CHAR_USAGE	Use of Char/Key Fig for Data Basis
/EACC/READ_REG	Display Characteristic Registration
/EACC/REGIST_01	Char. and Key Figure Registration
/EACC/SARA	EACC-Archiving
/EACC/SHOW_PLIMA	Most Recent Configuration PLIMA
/FSCAA/ADD_SHLP	Additional search helps
/FSCAA/VC_FIELD	Structure Definition and Fld Mapping
/FSCAA/V_IF_2_CLASS	Relation Interfaces and Classes
/FSIH/CNCL	Give Notice on Expired Ins. Policies
/FSIH/DISB	Disburse Insurance Premiums
/FSIH/REPL	Compare Pymnt Plans for Ins. Policy
/GC1/INIT	Garbage Collector: Initial Screen
/GC1/LOG	Garbage Collector: Activities/Logs
/GC1/OVERVIEW	GC: Overview of Obj. Type Relats
/GC1/SCOPE	Overview: Garbage Collector
/GC1/START	Garbage Collector Run
/IBS/95000055	IMG Activity
/IBS/RB_DEVL	RBD: Dev. List Value Adjustment
/IBS/RB_EWB_UPD	RBD: CML Pos. Monitoring: Update Run
/IBS/RB_FILL_GATE	Fill RBD-Gate
/IBS/RB_HINT	RBD: Pos. Monitoring: List of Notes
/IBS/RB_HINTM	List of Notes for Multiple Sce Syst.
/IBS/RB_IAS_FILL	Fill RBD GATE for IAS Proc.
/IBS/RB_IAS_FILL_MIG	RBD: Filling Report IAS/IFRS GATE
/IBS/RB_IAS_POST	Automatic Posting IAS (IVA)
/IBS/RB_IAS_UPD	RBD-IAS: Update Value Adjustment
/IBS/RB_KTO_DIS	RBD Dialog: Display RBD Account
/IBS/RB_KTO_INS	RBD Dialog: Create RBD Account
/IBS/RB_KTO_REACT	RBD: Reactivate RBD Account

SAP Transaction Codes – Volume One

/IBS/RB_KTO_UPD	RBD Dialog: Change RBD Account
/IBS/RB_LOG_POST	RBD: Posting Log
/IBS/RB_PEWB_RFR	RBD:Clearing Actual Recs (Rev. FIVA)
/IBS/RB_PEWB_RFR_SUM	RBD:Clearing Actual Recs (Rev. FIVA)
/IBS/RB_PEWB_RST	RBD: Gen. and Post Plnd Recds (FIVA)
/IBS/RB_PEWB_RSTM	RBD:Create FIVA For Several Sce Sys.
/IBS/RB_PWV_KK	FVA for Consumer Loans
/IBS/RB_PWV_UPD	RND: FIVA with Risk Indicator
/IBS/RB_RBDGATE_FILL	RBD: Fill RBD Gate with Test Data
/IBS/RB_RECLAS	Balance Sheet Transfer RBD
/IBS/RB_REF	RBD: Drilldown Reporting with Ref.
/IBS/RB_VS_SALDO	RBD: Ind. Document Table Source Sys.
/INFATRAN/ZINFABCI	Informatica BCI administration
/ISDFPS/11000002	IMG Activity: /ISDFPS/CUST_TRANS
/ISDFPS/11000003	IMG Activity: /ISDFPS/_FE01
/ISDFPS/11000004	IMG Activity: /ISDFPS/_FE03
/ISDFPS/11000005	IMG Activity: /ISDFPS/_FE04
/ISDFPS/11000006	IMG Activity: /ISDFPS/_FE05
/ISDFPS/11000007	IMG Activity: /ISDFPS/_FE06
/ISDFPS/11000008	IMG Activity: /ISDFPS/_OR01
/ISDFPS/11000009	IMG Activity: /ISDFPS/_OR02
/ISDFPS/11000010	IMG Activity: /ISDFPS/_ORSUP01
/ISDFPS/11000011	IMG Activity: /ISDFPS/_ORMNT01
/ISDFPS/11000012	IMG Activity: /ISDFPS/_CFDP01
/ISDFPS/11000013	IMG Activity: /ISDFPS/_FE02
/ISDFPS/11000014	IMG Activity: /ISDFPS/MB_DELIV
/ISDFPS/11000020	IMG Activity: /ISDFPS/_OPPE02
/ISDFPS/11000021	IMG Activity: /ISDFPS/_OPPE03
/ISDFPS/11000022	IMG Activity: /ISDFPS/_OPPE04
/ISDFPS/11000023	IMG Activity: /ISDFPS/_OPPE05
/ISDFPS/11000024	IMG Activity: /ISDFPS/_OPPE06
/ISDFPS/11000025	IMG Activity: /ISDFPS/_OPPE11
/ISDFPS/11000026	IMG Activity: /ISDFPS/_OPPE13
/ISDFPS/11000027	IMG Activity: /ISDFPS/_OPPE14
/ISDFPS/11000028	IMG Activity: /ISDFPS/_OPPE12
/ISDFPS/11000029	IMG Activity: /ISDFPS/_OPPE15
/ISDFPS/11000030	IMG Activity: /ISDFPS/_OPPESTATUS
/ISDFPS/11000031	IMG Activity: /ISDFPS/_OOVK
/ISDFPS/11000032	IMG Activity: /ISDFPS/_HR_OPPE12
/ISDFPS/11000033	IMG Activity: /ISDFPS/_T77OMTAB
/ISDFPS/11000034	IMG Activity: /ISDFPS/_V_DA04
/ISDFPS/11000040	IMG Activity: /ISDFPS/V_FDPDA5
/ISDFPS/11000041	IMG Activity: /ISDFPS/V_FDPDA6
/ISDFPS/11000042	IMG Activity: /ISDFPS/_FE07
/ISDFPS/11000049	IMG Activity: /ISDFPS/MATMASSRCDET
/ISDFPS/11000051	IMG Activity: /ISDFPS/CIL21SUB
/ISDFPS/11000052	IMG Activity: /ISDFPS/CIL21SUP
/ISDFPS/11000055	IMG Activity: /ISDFPS/V_SA04
/ISDFPS/11000056	IMG Activity: /ISDFPS/V_CPRIO
/ISDFPS/11000061	IMG Activity: /ISDFPS/V_PGRURG
/ISDFPS/11000062	IMG Activity: /ISDFPS/V_PURG
/ISDFPS/11000063	IMG Activity: /ISDFPS/V_PREQ
/ISDFPS/11000064	IMG Activity: /ISDFPS/V_PRILOC
/ISDFPS/11000065	IMG Activity: /ISDFPS/V_PURGSD

SAP Transaction Codes – Volume One

/ISDFPS/11000066	IMG Activity: /ISDFPS/V_PURGPM
/ISDFPS/11000067	IMG Activity: /ISDFPS/PRIO
/ISDFPS/11000068	IMG Activity: /ISDFPS/VSTAACT
/ISDFPS/11000069	IMG Activity: /ISDFPS/VSTACHGC
/ISDFPS/11000070	IMG Activity: /ISDFPS/VSTASUCC
/ISDFPS/11000071	IMG Activity: /ISDFPS/VSTASUA
/ISDFPS/89000007	Maintain Distributed Sys. Landscape
/ISDFPS/99000002	IMG Activity: /ISDFPS/ME_MM_REQ
/ISDFPS/ACCCORATES	Send CO Plan Prices
/ISDFPS/ACCHIERCOPY	Copy CO Standard Hierarchy
/ISDFPS/ACCHIERGEN	Generate CO Standard Hierarchy
/ISDFPS/ACCHIERPREP	Prepare CO Hierarchy in Operation
/ISDFPS/ACCHIERREST	Replace CO Standard Hierarchy
/ISDFPS/ACCMDGEN	Generate CO Account Assignment Objs
/ISDFPS/ALE_CRE_CCMS	Generate CCMS Nodes for System
/ISDFPS/ALE_IN_PROC	Start Inbound Processing
/ISDFPS/ALE_SYS_MAIN	Maintain DFPS System Landscape
/ISDFPS/BD11	DFPS Request Material Master
/ISDFPS/BD87N	DFPS ALE Status Monitor
/ISDFPS/BDXE	DFPS Create Customizing Transport
/ISDFPS/BERID_AEND	Change MRP Areas
/ISDFPS/BERID_ANLE	Create MRP Areas
/ISDFPS/BERID_ANZE	Display MRP Areas
/ISDFPS/BERID_DELE	Delete MRP Areas
/ISDFPS/BERID_GET	Selects MRP Area for Stor. Loc.
/ISDFPS/C02WM1	Maintain WM Addnl Attributes (Basis)
/ISDFPS/CALLRBDAPP01	Start RBDAPP01
/ISDFPS/CALLRBDMIDOC	Start RBDMIDOC
/ISDFPS/CALLRBDSTATE	Start RBDSTATE
/ISDFPS/CALLRSARFCSE	Start RSARFCSE
/ISDFPS/CALLRSEIDOC2	Start RSEIDOC2
/ISDFPS/CALLRSEOUT00	Start RSEOUT00
/ISDFPS/CALLRSNAST00	Start RSNAST00
/ISDFPS/CALL_TRANS	Transaction Call with Memory Export
/ISDFPS/CBSART_CS	Cust.: Assign Receiver PO Doc. Type
/ISDFPS/CFDP01	Structures Workbench: Customizing
/ISDFPS/CFRGKZ_CS	Cust: Release ID f. Synchronization
/ISDFPS/CHANGE_PARTY	Open Docs for Supply Relationship
/ISDFPS/CHA_TBL_LOG	Activate DFPS Table Logging
/ISDFPS/CIL21SUB	Hist. Insts: Customiz. Field Sel.
/ISDFPS/CIL21SUP	Hist. Inst. Locs: Cust. Field Sel.
/ISDFPS/CLEANUP_HR	DFPS Delete HR Master Data
/ISDFPS/CLMASCL	Cust.: Confign Cd Classes to Mod. ID
/ISDFPS/CLMCAP	Customizing: Controlled Usage Rate
/ISDFPS/CLMCUS	Customizing: Controlled Usage Rate
/ISDFPS/CLMEXSTA	Cust.: Master Equipment Sts Objects
/ISDFPS/CLMFLAUF	Customizing: Flight Types
/ISDFPS/CLMFLSTA	Customizing: Flight Status Objects
/ISDFPS/CLMIAST	Customizing: Order Type Tech. Status
/ISDFPS/CLMIMST	Cust.: Notification Type Tech. Sts
/ISDFPS/CLMISE	Cust.: Activate Intersession Events
/ISDFPS/CLMMDID	Customizing: Model IDs (WS)
/ISDFPS/CLMSFCT	Customizing: Status Function
/ISDFPS/CLMSTAD	Cust.: Technical Status Semantics

/ISDFPS/CLMSTB	Cust.: Status Board Transactions
/ISDFPS/CLMSTIC	Customizing: User Status Icons
/ISDFPS/CLMUPRI	Customizing: Usage Rate
/ISDFPS/CMP_AGR_TABS	Comparison of the AGR Tables
/ISDFPS/CPMGOS1	Activate Gen. Obj. Srvc "Chg Auth."
/ISDFPS/CREL	Maintain Relocations/Reloc. Steps
/ISDFPS/CREL01	Maintain Relocation
/ISDFPS/CREL02	Maintain Relocation Steps
/ISDFPS/CREL03	Maintain Weight Groups
/ISDFPS/CREL04	Maintain Relocation Types
/ISDFPS/CREL1	Maintain Relocation
/ISDFPS/CREL2	Maintain Relocation Steps
/ISDFPS/CRWBD	Replication Workbench - Enhanced
/ISDFPS/CUA_SWITCH	Switches the CUA Connection
/ISDFPS/C_CID	Number Range Mainten.: /ISDFPS/CM
/ISDFPS/C_CS_CMD	Cust:Cust: Cross-System Commands
/ISDFPS/C_CS_SYS	Cust.: Assign Log.Syst. to Plnt/SLoc
/ISDFPS/C_MM_CS	Cust.: Cross-System Basic Settings
/ISDFPS/DISP_EQU_SIT	Display Equipment Level
/ISDFPS/DISP_INITSUP	Display Initial and Subs. Supply
/ISDFPS/DISP_MATSTAT	Display Initial Supply Status
/ISDFPS/DISP_MAT_SIT	Display Material Situation
/ISDFPS/DSP1	NCG Planning Workbench
/ISDFPS/EPA_HU	Processing of HUs from EPA
/ISDFPS/EXPO_TEST	Test Explosion FOX for FORCE
/ISDFPS/EXT_BATCHES	Create External Batch Usage
/ISDFPS/EXT_BATCHES3	Display External Batch Usage
/ISDFPS/FDP1	Log. Operations Planning & Execution
/ISDFPS/FDP2	Log. Operations Planning & Execution
/ISDFPS/FDP_START	Structures Workbench
/ISDFPS/FDP_SUPPLY	Execute Initial Supply Run
/ISDFPS/FDP_VSTEL	Create/Change Shipping Points
/ISDFPS/FE01	Organizational Areas
/ISDFPS/FE02	Structure Levels
/ISDFPS/FE03	Structure Types
/ISDFPS/FE04	Branches
/ISDFPS/FE05	Readiness
/ISDFPS/FE06	Classification of Armed Forces
/ISDFPS/FE07	Material Indicators
/ISDFPS/FORCE_CD_DIS	Display Change Documents
/ISDFPS/GEOLOC1	Change Geolocation
/ISDFPS/GEOLOC2	Display Geolocation
/ISDFPS/GIS1	GIS
/ISDFPS/GIS2	GIS
/ISDFPS/GNR_CHECK	Check Global Number Ranges
/ISDFPS/GNR_MAINTAIN	Definition of Global Number Ranges
/ISDFPS/IE11	List Display of Alt. Equip. History
/ISDFPS/IL07R	Multi-Level Reference Location List
/ISDFPS/IL21	Extended Equip. History (Hierarchy)
/ISDFPS/INFRAMAT_ALL	Overview of Infrastructure Material
/ISDFPS/INFRAMAT_RET	Post Infrastruc. Matl to Prior Per.
/ISDFPS/INFRA_COMP	Auth/Actl Comp. Infra.Matl LocMgmtFE
/ISDFPS/INIT_SUPPLY	Trigger Initial Supply Run
/ISDFPS/LA01	Maintain WM Addnl Attributes Online

SAP Transaction Codes – Volume One

/ISDFPS/LA02	Maintain WM Addnl Attributes in List
/ISDFPS/LA03	Display WM Addnl Attributes in List
/ISDFPS/LMACC1	Enter Aircraft Accident
/ISDFPS/LMCUS1	Start Controlled Usage Rate
/ISDFPS/LMER01	Add/Change Operational Role
/ISDFPS/LMER02	Display Operational Role
/ISDFPS/LMFL01	Create Flight
/ISDFPS/LMFL02	Change Flight
/ISDFPS/LMFL03	Display Flight
/ISDFPS/LMFLM1	Change Mission
/ISDFPS/LMFLP1	Flight Overview
/ISDFPS/LMIE01	Create Equipment (Operation Equip.)
/ISDFPS/LMIE02	Change Equipment (Operation Equip.)
/ISDFPS/LMIE03	Display Equipment (Operation Equip.)
/ISDFPS/LMSI01	Change or Add Site
/ISDFPS/LMSI02	Display Site
/ISDFPS/LMSTB1	Status Board (Change Mode)
/ISDFPS/LMSTB2	Status Board (Display Mode)
/ISDFPS/LMTST1	Overview of Technical Status
/ISDFPS/LN01	Create Warehouse Structure
/ISDFPS/LN02	Change Warehouse Structure
/ISDFPS/LN03	Display Warehouse Structure
/ISDFPS/LN04	Delete Warehouse Number
/ISDFPS/LPL1	Material Categories Planning
/ISDFPS/LPL2	Material Categories Planning
/ISDFPS/LSP1	Logistical Mission Support
/ISDFPS/LSP2	Logistical Mission Support
/ISDFPS/MATMAS_COPY	Copy Material Master Data
/ISDFPS/MAT_ASSIGN	Material Assignment
/ISDFPS/MAT_COMP	Auth./Actl Comp. w. Matl Container
/ISDFPS/MB52	Material Stock List for MPO/MC
/ISDFPS/MCHG	Mass Changes
/ISDFPS/MCHG_SUP_REL	Support Relationships Mass Change
/ISDFPS/ME_BSART	Maintenance View for BSART
/ISDFPS/ME_BWB	Maintain View Cluster for BWB
/ISDFPS/ME_BWS	Maintain View Cluster for BWS
/ISDFPS/ME_HR_TAHDM	Maintain Preselection of HR Objects
/ISDFPS/ME_HR_TCTPM	Maint. of Usage Types Rel. for MA
/ISDFPS/ME_IDOC00	Maintenance: Program Object CP1
/ISDFPS/ME_IDOC01	Generation of Initial IDocs
/ISDFPS/ME_IDOC02	Generation of Deletion Record IDocs
/ISDFPS/ME_IDOC03	Call BD21 for Delta Download
/ISDFPS/ME_IDOC04	Generate Change Pointers (DB Log)
/ISDFPS/ME_REQ	Maintain View Cluster for REQ
/ISDFPS/MM_CS_EXLST	Purchase Requisition Exception List
/ISDFPS/MM_RL01	Create Return Delivery PReqs
/ISDFPS/MM_TRANS_DEL	Transport in the Event of a Transfer
/ISDFPS/MPA1	Process Provisions Packages
/ISDFPS/MPA2	Display Material Packages
/ISDFPS/MPANR	Material Package Number Range
/ISDFPS/MPO	Auth. Materials and Material Pkgs
/ISDFPS/MPONR	Material Planning Obj. Number Range
/ISDFPS/MPO_COMP	Authorized/Actual Comparison of MPO
/ISDFPS/MPO_MIG	Migration Data for iPPE Workbench

/ISDFPS/MPO_PLAN	Scheduled Material Planning Objects
/ISDFPS/MPO_SUB	Remove Material Planning Objects
/ISDFPS/NR_CL_UNUSED	Create New Fiscal Year for NR
/ISDFPS/NR_NEW_YEAR	Create New Fiscal Year for NR
/ISDFPS/NR_SYS_CLEAN	Clean Up GNR Data for System
/ISDFPS/OIUO	Multi-Level R.P. List: Ref. Meas. Pt
/ISDFPS/OIX2	Multi-Level R.P. List: Ref. Location
/ISDFPS/OIX8	Multi-Level R.P. List: Class
/ISDFPS/OIX9	Multi-Level R.P. List: Char.
/ISDFPS/OIXA	Multi-Level R.P. List: Document
/ISDFPS/OM_REF	Structure Evaluations
/ISDFPS/OPC_CF	Op./Ex. Calendar - Force Provider
/ISDFPS/OPC_LR	O/E Calendar - Cmd Responsibility
/ISDFPS/OR01	Assgmt: Relationship - Basic Type
/ISDFPS/OR02	Customizing Usage Types
/ISDFPS/ORMNT01	Maintenance Relatshps: Damage Types
/ISDFPS/ORMNT_MMDOCS	Open MM Docs for Maint. Relationship
/ISDFPS/ORMNT_PMDOCS	PM Documents for Maintenance Rel.
/ISDFPS/ORSUP01	Supply Relatshps: Ext. Matl Groups
/ISDFPS/ORSUP_DOCS	Open Docs for Supply Relationship
/ISDFPS/OVXC	Assignment of Shipping Pt to Plant
/ISDFPS/PERS1	Personnel Categories Planning
/ISDFPS/PERS2	Personnel Categories Planning
/ISDFPS/PLBA	Log Display f. Local User Administ.
/ISDFPS/PMCP1	Forward Change Authorization
/ISDFPS/PMCP_OBJ	Objects with Change Auth. in System
/ISDFPS/PMDIS2	Generic Maintenance Obj Distribution
/ISDFPS/PMDISRUN1	Distribution Factory Monitor
/ISDFPS/PMRELOC1	Technical Object Relocation Monitor
/ISDFPS/PMRELO_INT	Int. Call: Forward Change Authoriz.
/ISDFPS/PMRUECK1	Maintenance Data Redistribution
/ISDFPS/PORT_SWITCH	Switch Ports for ALE Partner Profile
/ISDFPS/POSGEN	Position Generator: HCP
/ISDFPS/POS_GEN	HCP Position Generator
/ISDFPS/PRELOC1	Relocation Planning
/ISDFPS/PRELOC2	Relocation Planning
/ISDFPS/PRPLB	Background: Prioritized Matls Plng
/ISDFPS/PRPLD	Dialog: Prioritized Materials Plng
/ISDFPS/PRPLL	Document Processing Log
/ISDFPS/PUWNR_U	Change Declaration Planning Scope
/ISDFPS/PUWNR_V	Display Declaration Planning Scope
/ISDFPS/RELOC1	Relocation Execution
/ISDFPS/RELOC2	Relocation Execution
/ISDFPS/RES_TBL_LOG	Reset DFPS Table Logging
/ISDFPS/RFFMKBHA	Commitment Item: Expenditure View
/ISDFPS/RFFMKBHE	Commitment Item: Revenues View
/ISDFPS/RIC1	Change Reportable Item Code
/ISDFPS/RIC2	Display Reportable Item Code
/ISDFPS/ROLE_MANAGER	Role Generator
/ISDFPS/SET_OFFLINE	Set System to Offline Mode
/ISDFPS/SET_ONLINE	Set System to Online Mode
/ISDFPS/SLG1	Show Application Logs
/ISDFPS/SREL1	Support Relationships
/ISDFPS/SREL2	Support Relationships

SAP Transaction Codes – Volume One

/ISDFPS/STATE_CHECK	Check Organizational Structures
/ISDFPS/STOCK_RELOC	Plan Relocation for Complete FE
/ISDFPS/STOCK_RETURN	Disband Force Element in Operation
/ISDFPS/SWITCH_PP_I	Switch Mode of ALE-PV (In)
/ISDFPS/SWITCH_PP_O	Switch Mode of ALE-PV (Out)
/ISDFPS/SYSTEM_MON	Monitor Partner System
/ISDFPS/SYSTEM_STATE	Display Connection Status
/ISDFPS/SYSTEM_SYNC	Synchronization with Partner System
/ISDFPS/T024D_U	Create/Change MRP Controller
/ISDFPS/T024D_V	Display MRP Controller
/ISDFPS/T313Y_U	ILN for SSCC-Gen. at StorLoc Level
/ISDFPS/T313Y_V	ILN for SSCC-Gen. at StorLoc Level
/ISDFPS/T630L_U	Shpg Deadline - Chg. Ldng Time Info
/ISDFPS/T630L_V	Shpg Deadline - Disp. Ldng Time Info
/ISDFPS/T630R_U	Shpg Deadl- Chg. Pick/Pack Time Info
/ISDFPS/T630R_V	Shpg Deadl-Disp. Pick/Pack Time Info
/ISDFPS/TA_PSPMAT	Exclusion Objs Auth./Actl Comparison
/ISDFPS/TOB1	Assignment of Technical Objects
/ISDFPS/TOB2	Assignment of Technical Objects
/ISDFPS/TOE1	Organizational Structure and Tasks
/ISDFPS/TOE2	Organizational Structure and Tasks
/ISDFPS/TOEACC1	Accounting Organizational Basis
/ISDFPS/TOEACC2	Accounting Organizational Basis
/ISDFPS/TOEFU1	Command and Control Support
/ISDFPS/TOEFU2	Command and Control Support
/ISDFPS/TOELOG1	Logistics Organizational Basis
/ISDFPS/TOELOG2	Logistics Organizational Basis
/ISDFPS/TOEM1	Material Organizational Basis
/ISDFPS/TOEM2	Material Organizational Basis
/ISDFPS/TOEP1	Personnel Organizational Basis
/ISDFPS/TOEP2	Personnel Organizational Basis
/ISDFPS/TORG1	Task Organization
/ISDFPS/TORG2	Task Organization
/ISDFPS/TVKOL_U	Picking _ Change Stor.Loc. Determin.
/ISDFPS/TVKOL_V	Picking - Display Stor.Loc.Determin.
/ISDFPS/TVLA_U	Change Loading Points per Shpg Point
/ISDFPS/TVLA_V	Display Loading Points per Shpg Pt
/ISDFPS/TVSTZ_LGORTU	Change Shpg Pt Determination (SLoc)
/ISDFPS/TVSTZ_LGORTV	Disp. Shpg Pt Determination (SLoc)
/ISDFPS/TVSTZ_U	Change Shpg Pt Determination (Plant)
/ISDFPS/TVSTZ_V	Disp. Shpg Pt Determination (Plant)
/ISDFPS/UPD_ORG_LEVB	Update the Org. Level Fields
/ISDFPS/UPD_ORG_LEVS	Comparison of Organizational Levels
/ISDFPS/UPD_ORG_LEVT	Update the Org. Level Fields
/ISDFPS/UPLN1	Execute Material Plans
/ISDFPS/UPS	ALE Distribution Units - Enhanced
/ISDFPS/UPS01	Create ALE Distr. Unit - Enhanced
/ISDFPS/UPS02	Change ALE Distr. Unit - Enhanced
/ISDFPS/UPS03	Display ALE Distr. Unit - Enhanced
/ISDFPS/UPS04	Copy ALE Distr. Unit - Enhanced
/ISDFPS/UPS_FORCE	Structures Workbench
/ISDFPS/USER_DISTRIB	User Distribution
/ISDFPS/VLV1	Deliveries for Relocation
/ISDFPS/VLV2	Display Relocation Deliveries

/ISDFPS/VLVBE	Complete Relocation Purch. Orders
/ISDFPS/VLVET	Carry Out Own Transport
/ISDFPS/VLVLS	Mass Change of Log. Syst. in FEs
/ISDFPS/VPA_INTERN	Internal Transaction for PPA
/ISDFPS/V_024_U	Create/Change Purchasing Group
/ISDFPS/V_024_V	Display Purchasing Group
/ISDFPS/V_V2	Rescheduling for Defense
/ISDFPS/WF_ACC	Structures Workbench
/ISDFPS/WF_CUST	Workflow Tree Customizing
/ISDFPS/WF_EPA	Structures Workbench
/ISDFPS/WF_EXT	Structures Workbench
/ISDFPS/WF_EXU	Structures Workbench
/ISDFPS/WF_KST	Structures Workbench
/ISDFPS/WF_MAP	Structures Workbench
/ISDFPS/WF_MAT	Structures Workbench
/ISDFPS/WF_MATPLAN	Structures Workbench
/ISDFPS/WF_MC	Structures Workbench
/ISDFPS/WF_PER	Structures Workbench
/ISDFPS/WF_PERPLAN	Structures Workbench
/ISDFPS/WF_RH_TASK	Used for Customizing Tree
/ISDFPS/WF_RIC	Structures Workbench
/ISDFPS/WF_SE16	Call SE 16 for Workflow
/ISIDEX/54000037	IMG Activity: /ISIDEX/_00001
/ISIDEX/54000038	IMG Activity: /ISIDEX/_00002
/ISIDEX/54000039	IMG Activity: /ISIDEX/_00003
/ISIDEX/54000040	IMG Activity: /ISIDEX/_00004
/ISIDEX/B001_U02_01	Create IDEX EDM Factory Calendar
/ISIDEX/B001_U10_01	IDEX DEREG Define Service Types
/ISIDEX/B001_U11_01	IDEX DEREG Define Service Types
/ISIDEX/B001_U12_01	IDEX DEREG Define Service Types
/ISIDEX/B001_U22_01	IDEX CoS: Define Periods/Deadlines
/ISIDEX/B001_U24_01	IDEX CoS: Define Periods/Deadlines
/ISIDEX/B001_U26_01	IDEX CoS: Define Periods/Deadlines
/ISIDEX/B001_U32_01	Maintain Main and Subtransactions
/ISIDEX/B001_U34_01	Maintain Main and Subtransactions
/ISIDEX/B001_U36_01	Maintain Main and Subtransactions
/ISIDEX/B002_U02_01	IDEX EDM: Define Season Types
/ISIDEX/B002_U10_01	IDEX DEREG Define Deregulation Swtch
/ISIDEX/B002_U11_01	IDEX DEREG Define Deregulation Swtch
/ISIDEX/B002_U12_01	IDEX DEREG Define Deregulation Swtch
/ISIDEX/B002_U24_01	IDEX CoS: Define Checks
/ISIDEX/B002_U26_01	IDEX CoS: Define Checks
/ISIDEX/B002_U32_01	Account Determination ID f. Supplier
/ISIDEX/B002_U34_01	Account Determination ID for Distr.
/ISIDEX/B002_U36_01	Account Det. ID for Contract Account
/ISIDEX/B003_U02_01	IDEX EDM: Define Season Groups
/ISIDEX/B003_U10_01	IDEX DEREG Define Control Parameters
/ISIDEX/B003_U11_01	IDEX DEREG Define Control Parameters
/ISIDEX/B003_U12_01	IDEX DEREG Define Control Parameters
/ISIDEX/B003_U22_01	IDEX CoS Exception Handling per View
/ISIDEX/B003_U24_01	IDEX CoS: No. Range for Switch Doc.
/ISIDEX/B003_U26_01	IDEX CoS Exception Handling per View
/ISIDEX/B003_U32_01	Account Assgt for Main Transaction
/ISIDEX/B003_U34_01	Account Assgt for Main Transaction

/ISIDEX/B003_U36_01	Account Assgt for Main Transaction
/ISIDEX/B004_U02_01	IDEX EDM: Define Day Types
/ISIDEX/B004_U10_01	IDEX DEREG Verify WF Customizing
/ISIDEX/B004_U11_01	IDEX DEREG Verify WF Customizing
/ISIDEX/B004_U12_01	IDEX DEREG Verify WF Customizing
/ISIDEX/B004_U22_01	IDEX CoS: No. Range for Switch Doc.
/ISIDEX/B004_U24_01	IDEX CoS: Act. Event Cat. Coupling
/ISIDEX/B004_U26_01	IDEX CoS: No. Range for Switch Doc.
/ISIDEX/B004_U32_01	Account Assignment for Transaction
/ISIDEX/B004_U34_01	Account Assignment for Transaction
/ISIDEX/B004_U36_01	Account Assignment for Transaction
/ISIDEX/B005_U02_01	IDEX EDM: Define Day Groups
/ISIDEX/B005_U22_01	IDEX CoS: Act. Event Cat. Coupling
/ISIDEX/B005_U24_01	IDEX CoS: Define Type of SPA
/ISIDEX/B005_U26_01	IDEX CoS: Act. Event Cat. Coupling
/ISIDEX/B005_U32_01	Define Payment Frequency
/ISIDEX/B005_U34_01	Specs f. Posting Aggr. Inc. Bills
/ISIDEX/B005_U36_01	Specs f. Posting Aggr. Inc. Bills
/ISIDEX/B006_U02_01	IDEX EDM: Define Time-of-Use Types
/ISIDEX/B006_U10_01	IDEX DEREG Define Supply Scenarios
/ISIDEX/B006_U11_01	IDEX DEREG Define Supply Scenarios
/ISIDEX/B006_U12_01	IDEX DEREG Define Supply Scenarios
/ISIDEX/B006_U22_01	IDEX CoS: Define Type of SPA
/ISIDEX/B006_U24_01	IDEX CoS Exception Handling per View
/ISIDEX/B006_U26_01	IDEX CoS: Define Type of SPA
/ISIDEX/B006_U32_01	Define Payment Classes
/ISIDEX/B006_U34_01	Data Exchange Process
/ISIDEX/B006_U36_01	Define Payment Frequency
/ISIDEX/B007_U02_01	IDEX EDM: Define Time-of-Use Group
/ISIDEX/B007_U10_01	IDEX DEREG Setup MD Templates
/ISIDEX/B007_U11_01	IDEX DEREG Setup MD Templates
/ISIDEX/B007_U12_01	IDEX DEREG Setup MD Templates
/ISIDEX/B007_U22_01	IDEX CoS: Define Data Exhange Proc.
/ISIDEX/B007_U24_01	IDEX CoS: Define Data Exhange Proc.
/ISIDEX/B007_U26_01	IDEX CoS: Define Data Exhange Proc.
/ISIDEX/B007_U32_01	Define Data Exchange Processes
/ISIDEX/B007_U34_01	Maintain Service Provider Agreements
/ISIDEX/B007_U36_01	Define Payment Classes
/ISIDEX/B008_U02_01	Define IDEX EDM Profile Roles
/ISIDEX/B008_U22_01	IDEX CoS: Maintain Switch Views
/ISIDEX/B008_U24_01	IDEX CoS: Maintain Switch Views
/ISIDEX/B008_U26_01	IDEX CoS: Maintain Switch Views
/ISIDEX/B008_U32_01	Service Provider Agreement Types
/ISIDEX/B008_U34_01	Bill Check (Part 1)
/ISIDEX/B008_U36_01	Data Exchange Process
/ISIDEX/B009_U22_01	IDEX CoS: Define Front Office Proc.
/ISIDEX/B009_U24_01	IDEX CoS: Define Front Office Proc.
/ISIDEX/B009_U26_01	IDEX CoS: Define Front Office Proc.
/ISIDEX/B009_U32_01	Define Reason Codes
/ISIDEX/B009_U34_01	Basic Settings for Bill Check
/ISIDEX/B009_U36_01	Maintain Service Provider Agreements
/ISIDEX/B010_U22_01	IDEX CoS: Assign CIC Profiles
/ISIDEX/B010_U24_01	IDEX CoS: Assign CIC Profiles
/ISIDEX/B010_U26_01	IDEX CoS: Assign CIC Profiles

SAP Transaction Codes – Volume One

/ISIDEX/B010_U32_01	Parameters for Distr. Aggr. Payments
/ISIDEX/B010_U34_01	Check Parameters for Bill Check
/ISIDEX/B010_U36_01	Define Process Control (Part 1)
/ISIDEX/B011_U22_01	IDEX CoS: Maintain Action Box
/ISIDEX/B011_U24_01	IDEX CoS: Maintain Action Box
/ISIDEX/B011_U26_01	IDEX CoS: Maintain Action Box
/ISIDEX/B011_U32_01	Algorithms for Interpr. of PAN Items
/ISIDEX/B011_U34_01	ID of Bill/PAN Parts
/ISIDEX/B011_U36_01	Maintain Permitted Bill/PAN Lines
/ISIDEX/B012_U22_01	IDEX CoS: Asssign Action Box Config.
/ISIDEX/B012_U24_01	IDEX CoS: Asssign Action Box Config.
/ISIDEX/B012_U26_01	IDEX CoS: Asssign Action Box Config.
/ISIDEX/B012_U32_01	Define Process Control (Part 1)
/ISIDEX/B012_U34_01	Define Payment Medium Format
/ISIDEX/B012_U36_01	Check Parameters for Bill Check
/ISIDEX/B013_U22_01	IDEX CoS: Switch Doc. Entry Dialog
/ISIDEX/B013_U24_01	IDEX CoS: Switch Doc. Entry Dialog
/ISIDEX/B013_U26_01	IDEX CoS: Switch Doc. Entry Dialog
/ISIDEX/B013_U32_01	Basic Settings for Bill/PAN Proc.
/ISIDEX/B013_U34_01	Note to Payee Type for Pymt Medium
/ISIDEX/B013_U36_01	ID of Bill/PAN Parts
/ISIDEX/B014_U22_01	IDEX CoS: Required Field Definition
/ISIDEX/B014_U24_01	IDEX CoS: Required Field Definition
/ISIDEX/B014_U26_01	IDEX CoS: Required Field Definition
/ISIDEX/B014_U34_01	Define Payment Method
/ISIDEX/B014_U36_01	Define Payment Medium Format
/ISIDEX/B015_U22_01	IDEX CoS: PoD Identification
/ISIDEX/B015_U24_01	IDEX CoS: PoD Identification
/ISIDEX/B015_U26_01	IDEX CoS: Min. Duration of Contract
/ISIDEX/B015_U32_01	ID of Bill/PAN Parts
/ISIDEX/B015_U34_01	Specs for Responsible Company Code
/ISIDEX/B015_U36_01	Note to Payee Type for Pymt Medium
/ISIDEX/B016_U24_01	IDEX CoS: Min. Duration of Contract
/ISIDEX/B016_U26_01	IDEX CoS: PoD Identification
/ISIDEX/B016_U32_01	Account Balance Transactions AG27
/ISIDEX/B016_U34_01	Define Form for Payment Advice Note
/ISIDEX/B016_U36_01	Define Payment Method
/ISIDEX/B017_U32_01	Specs for Reset Clearing AG27
/ISIDEX/B017_U34_01	Process Control (Part 2)
/ISIDEX/B017_U36_01	Specs for Responsible Company Code
/ISIDEX/B018_U32_01	Specs for Clearing Item AG27
/ISIDEX/B018_U36_01	Define Form for Payment Advice Note
/ISIDEX/B019_U32_01	Alloc. Function Modules for Dunning
/ISIDEX/B019_U34_01	Define Reason Codes
/ISIDEX/B019_U36_01	Parameters for Distr. Aggr. Payments
/ISIDEX/B020_U32_01	Def. CA Items for Communication
/ISIDEX/B020_U34_01	Complaint Notification Form
/ISIDEX/B020_U36_01	Algorithms for Interpr. of PAN Items
/ISIDEX/B021_U32_01	Process Variants for Identifying PoD
/ISIDEX/B021_U34_01	Define Reversal Reasons
/ISIDEX/B021_U36_01	Def. of Account Balance Transactions
/ISIDEX/B022_U32_01	Use of Process Var. to Identify PoD
/ISIDEX/B022_U34_01	Allocate Register Type
/ISIDEX/B022_U36_01	Specifications for Reset Clearing

SAP Transaction Codes – Volume One

/ISIDEX/B023_U34_01	Allocate Units of Measurement
/ISIDEX/B023_U36_01	Specifications for Clearing Item
/ISIDEX/B024_U34_01	Process Variants for Identifying PoD
/ISIDEX/B024_U36_01	Define Complaint Modules
/ISIDEX/B025_U34_01	Use of Process Var. to Identify PoD
/ISIDEX/B025_U36_01	Definition of Reason Codes
/ISIDEX/B026_U34_01	User-Defined Meter Reading Type
/ISIDEX/B026_U36_01	Define Complaint Notification
/ISIDEX/B027_U36_01	Define Reversal Reasons
/ISIDEX/B028_U36_01	CA Item for Communication
/ISIDEX/B029_U36_01	Process Variants for Identifying PoD
/ISIDEX/B030_U36_01	Use of Process Var. to Identify PoD
/KJRTAX01/ATMIGALVD	Display Trans. Data - Delete (JP)
/KJRTAX01/ATMIGDEL	Delete Asset Transaction Data (JP)
/KJRTAX01/ATMIGINS	Insert Asset Transaction Data (JP)
/KJRTAX01/MIG_PRDCD	Migration of Add. Dep. Code (JP)
/KJRTAX01/PDEL	Delete Data Migr. from Last Yr (JP)
/KJRTAX01/PINS	Data Migration - Last Year (JP)
/KJRTAX01/PUPLOAD	Upl. Migrat.- Data from LY XML (JP)
/KJRTAX01/RINS	Migrate RAJPVERM to Result Tab. (JP)
/KYK/ME53N	Display Purchase Requisition
/KYK/MIGO_GI	Post Goods Issue
/KYK/MIGO_GR_OTHER	Goods Receipt Other
/KYK/MIGO_MB01	Post Goods Receipt - Purchase Order
/KYK/MIGO_MB03	Display Material Document
/KYK/MIGO_MB11	Post Goods Movement
/KYK/MIGO_MB1A	Goods Issue Order
/KYK/MIGO_MB31	Post Goods Receipt for Prod Order
/KYK/MIGO_MBRL	Post Return Delivery for Material Do
/KYK/MIGO_MBST	Cancel Material Document
/KYK/T_CANCEL_GI	Cancel Goods Issue
/KYK/T_COMPL_CMR	Create Credit Memo Request
/KYK/T_COMPL_DMR	Create Debit Memo Request
/KYK/T_COMPL_IC	Create Invoice Correction
/KYK/T_COMPL_RE	Create Returns
/KYK/T_ME81N_01	Analysis of Order Values
/KYK/T_OKKS	Set Controlling Area
/LIME/42000001	Determine Node Width
/LIME/86000063	Process Type
/LIME/86000064	Maintain Index Tables
/LIME/86000065	Hierarchy
/LIME/86000066	Grouping Parameter
/LIME/86000067	Types for Quantity Calculation
/LIME/86000068	Supply categories
/LIME/86000069	Virtual Stock Indicator
/LIME/86000070	Special Stock
/LIME/86000071	Reason for movement
/LIME/86000083	Negative stock qty
/LIME/86000084	Control Dispatcher
/LIME/86000088	BAdI Builder /LIME/CUST
/LIME/86000097	Filter Determination for Dispatcher
/LIME/86000098	Locations Business Key
/LIME/86000099	Loc.-Index Tables Generation
/LIME/86000100	Generate Index Tables Code

/LIME/86000101	HU Business Key
/LIME/86000102	HU Index Tables Generation
/LIME/86000103	Stocks Business Key
/LIME/86000104	Stocks Index Tables Generation
/LIME/86000105	Set Filter Values BAdI Dispatcher
/LIME/86000106	Document Number
/LIME/86000107	Determine Stock Type R/3
/LIME/86000108	Settings Movement Type
/LIME/86000109	Determine Movement Type for R/3
/LIME/86000110	Determine Special Stock Indicator
/LIME/GEN_CODE	Generation of LIME Source Code
/LIME/SNUM_DIEX	Internal LIME Number Range
/LIME/SNUM_EXDO	External LIME Number Range
/LSIERP/MATURITY	TCode for Maturity Payments Report
/LSIERP/PROCEEDS	Process Payment Items
/NFM/ANARM	Rate Analysis, MM
/NFM/ANARS	Rate Analysis, SD
/NFM/BSLM	Exchange Key, Vendor
/NFM/BSLS	Exchange Key, Customer
/NFM/CONVM	Currency Conversion for Rates, MM
/NFM/CONVS	Currency Conversion for Rates, SD
/NFM/COVM1	Maintain Coverage, MM
/NFM/COVM3	Display Coverage, MM
/NFM/COVS1	Maintain Coverage, SD
/NFM/COVS3	Display Coverage, SD
/NFM/C_BASIC	Basic Settings for NF Metals
/NFM/C_BOESL	Maintain Exchange Keys
/NFM/C_CO	Assign CtrlArea/Origin to NF Keys
/NFM/C_COVHM	Number range maintenance: /NFM/COVHM
/NFM/C_COVHS	Number range maintenance: /NFM/COVHS
/NFM/C_KBB_MM	Maint. Mvt Types in Matl Provision
/NFM/C_KBB_SD	Maint. Mvt Types in Matl Provision
/NFM/C_NES	Maintain NF Keys w. Base Quantities
/NFM/C_NES_EKO	Different NF Key, Purch. Org. Level
/NFM/C_NES_VKO	Different NF Key, Sales Org. Level
/NFM/C_NFM	Maintain Rate Determination Modules
/NFM/C_NFR	Maintain Rate Determination Routines
/NFM/C_NFS_MM	Maint.Rate Determination Keys for MM
/NFM/C_NFS_SD	Maint.Rate Determination Keys for SD
/NFM/C_NKTYP_MM	Cond. Type - Cond. Cat/NF Key, MM
/NFM/C_NKTYP_SD	Cond. Type - Cond. Cat/NF Key, SD
/NFM/C_NORG_MM	Number Range Maintenance: Purchasing
/NFM/C_NORG_SD	Maintain Number Range in SD
/NFM/C_PROHM	Number range maintenance: /NFM/PROHM
/NFM/C_PROHS	Number range maintenance: /NFM/PROHS
/NFM/C_RATEREF	NF Rate Reference PurchOrg --> SOrg
/NFM/DEFDS	Different Rate Determination, SD
/NFM/DEHM1	Maintain Default Value Header, MM
/NFM/DEHM3	Display Default Value Header, MM
/NFM/DEHS1	Maintain Default Value Header, SD
/NFM/DEHS3	Display Default Value Header, SD
/NFM/DEPM1	Maintain Default Value Item, MM
/NFM/DEPM3	Display Default Value Item, MM
/NFM/DEPS1	Maintain Default Value Item, SD

SAP Transaction Codes – Volume One

/NFM/DEPS3	Display Default Value Item, SD
/NFM/DNEBM1	Maintain default base key
/NFM/DNEBM3	Display default base key
/NFM/DNEBS1	Maintain default base key
/NFM/DNEBS3	Display default base key
/NFM/GRAFM	NF Rates Graphic, MM
/NFM/GRAFS	NF Rates Graphic, SD
/NFM/MM	NF Metals - Purchasing Menu
/NFM/MM_IM_PROVMOV	NF Provision Posting on GR
/NFM/NEBM1	Materials: Maintain Base Key, MM
/NFM/NEBM3	Materials: Display Base Key, MM
/NFM/NEBS1	Materials: Maintain Base Key, SD
/NFM/NEBS3	Materials: Display Base Key, SD
/NFM/POSLM	List NF Data from Purchasing Docs
/NFM/POSLS	List NF Data from Sales Documents
/NFM/PROM1	Create Provision Master, MM
/NFM/PROM2	Change Provision Master, MM
/NFM/PROM3	Display Provision Master, MM
/NFM/PROM4	Reprocess Provision Posting, MM
/NFM/PROS1	Create Provision Master, SD
/NFM/PROS2	Change Provision Master, SD
/NFM/PROS3	Display Provision Master, SD
/NFM/PROS4	Reprocess Provision Booking, SD
/NFM/RAPM1	Maintain Rates for Provision, MM
/NFM/RAPM3	Display Rates for Provision, MM
/NFM/RAPS1	Maintain Rates for Provision, SD
/NFM/RAPS3	Display Rates for Provision, SD
/NFM/RATM1	Maintain Rates, MM
/NFM/RATM3	Display Rates, MM
/NFM/RATS1	Maintain Rates, SD
/NFM/RATS3	Display Rates, SD
/NFM/SD	NF Metals - Purchasing Menu
/NFM/VGWM1	Maintain Charge Weights for Vendor
/NFM/VGWM3	Display Charge Weights for Vendor
/NFM/VGWS1	Maintain Charge Weights for Customer
/NFM/VGWS3	Display Charge Weights for Customer
/OLC/REBUILD_COSTS	Rebuild PM/CS order operation costs
/OSP/CLIENTCOPY_TOOL	OSP Client Copy Tool
/OSP/SLD	SLD for Duet
/OSP/TR_RP_ERROR_LOG	Error Log for administrator
/OSP/TR_TP_REPORT	List of Reports Scheduled for TP
/PLMB/DISP_PARAM	Display all nav settings parameter
/PLMU/FRW_CHECK_CUST	Customizing Check
/RWD/ZF0	RWD Frontend Toolkit
/RWD/ZF1	RWD Utility - Auto Msg Utility
/RWD/ZF10	RWD Message Utility
/RWD/ZF11	RWD Utility - Server Class
/RWD/ZF12	RWD Utility 5.0 version
/RWD/ZF13	RWD CSH Sub Menu utility
/RWD/ZF14	RWD Upload Utility
/RWD/ZF15	RWD Utility HelpInfo Upload Initial
/RWD/ZF16	RWD Utility HelpInfo Upload online
/RWD/ZF17	RWD Utility Server Upload batch
/RWD/ZF18	RWD Utility Messages Upload batch

/RWD/ZF19	RWD Utility Custom Messages batch
/RWD/ZF2	RWD LSVR2PSVR Table Maintenance
/RWD/ZF20	RWD CSH Release Adjustment
/RWD/ZF21	RWD CSH Statistics Backup Initial
/RWD/ZF22	RWD Utility - Auto_Alert Note Maint
/RWD/ZF23	RWD Utility - Alert Note Maint
/RWD/ZF24	RWD Utility -Alert Initial
/RWD/ZF25	RWD Utility - AutoNote Batch
/RWD/ZF26	RWD Utility - Auto Note Maint
/RWD/ZF27	RWD Utility -Auto Initial
/RWD/ZF28	RWD Utility - Server Assign Batch
/RWD/ZF29	RWD Utility - Server Assign Initial
/RWD/ZF30	RWD Utility - Server Assign Maint
/RWD/ZF31	RWD CSH create url utility
/RWD/ZF32	RWD Logon Message Routine
/RWD/ZF33	RWD Logon Message Routine
/RWD/ZF34	RWD Logon Message Routine
/RWD/ZF35	RWD Batch Logon Utility
/RWD/ZF36	RWD CSH MAC user command utility
/RWD/ZF37	RWD CSH Language Monitor Initial Scr
/RWD/ZF38	RWD CSH Language Monitor Maint Scr
/RWD/ZF39	RWD CSH Infopak Help Checker
/RWD/ZF40	RWD CSH - Sync Utility
/RWD/ZF41	RWD CSH - ActiveX routine
/RWD/ZF42	RWD CSH - Language Utility
/RWD/ZF43	RWD CSH - Load Special Characters
/RWD/ZF44	RWD Alert Child Routine
/RWD/ZF5	RWD Utility - Calendar utility
/RWD/ZF6	RWD Utility - Distribution List Utl
/RWD/ZF7	RWD CSH Screen Parameters
/RWD/ZF8	RWD CSH Configuration Utility
/RWD/ZF9	RWD CSH StatisticsUtility
/RWD/ZF90	test
/RWD/ZF99	RWD Convert A/ert/Notification Msgs
/SAPAPO/FCSTOUTL	Outlier Correction Settings
/SAPBOQ/AC0X	Composite of Service Master Records
/SAPBOQ/MESSAGE	Specify system messages
/SAPBOQ/SES	Service entry sheet Transaction
/SAPBOQ/SES1	Create Service Entry Sheet
/SAPBOQ/SES2	Change Service Entry Sheet
/SAPBOQ/SES3	Display Service Entry Sheet
/SAPBOQ/SES_NR	Number Assignment for Document
/SAPBOQ/SI	Sub Item Enable Transaction
/SAPCEM/12000436	IMG Activity: /SAPCEM/PIVARLV
/SAPCEM/12000437	IMG Activity: /SAPCEM/VARPI
/SAPCEM/12000439	IMG Activity: /SAPCEM/WF_EQUI
/SAPCEM/ABRLISTE	Settlement List
/SAPCEM/BDNUM	Number Range Maintenance: /SAPCEM/BD
/SAPCEM/BD_CHNG	Requirements Overview: Change
/SAPCEM/BD_SHOW	Requirements Overview: Display
/SAPCEM/BEDARF01	Create Requisition Note
/SAPCEM/BEDARF02	Change Requisition Note
/SAPCEM/BEDARF03	Display Requisition Note
/SAPCEM/BESTAUF	Location Setup from J_3GTBEST

SAP Transaction Codes – Volume One

/SAPCEM/BESTKON	Stock Control
/SAPCEM/CI	Transfer of Catalog Data
/SAPCEM/EINSAT	Usage Statement
/SAPCEM/EL	Entry List for Settlement Calendar
/SAPCEM/FP_LGBELEG	Release PBE Documents
/SAPCEM/IND_CAP_CRE	Create Individual Capacities
/SAPCEM/INVENTUR01	Enter Stock in Inventory
/SAPCEM/INVENTUR02	Change Stock in Inventory
/SAPCEM/INVENTUR03	Display Stock in Inventory
/SAPCEM/INV_ABGLEICH	Inventory: Compare Differences
/SAPCEM/INV_AIB	Inventory: Stock in Inventory
/SAPCEM/INV_AUSBUM	Inventory: Reset Multipart Equi.
/SAPCEM/INV_BEST	Inventory: Stock List
/SAPCEM/INV_CHECK	Inventory: Check
/SAPCEM/INV_DIFFLIST	Inventory: List of Differences
/SAPCEM/INV_MENGE	Inventory: Quantity Determination
/SAPCEM/INV_OHNEEQUI	Inventory: Items W/O Equi. Master
/SAPCEM/INV_RUECK	Inventory: Reset Gen. Stock Diff.
/SAPCEM/INV_STAMM	Maintain Table /SAPCEM/INV01
/SAPCEM/INV_VERW	Maitain Table /SAPCEM/V_INV02
/SAPCEM/LAYDEB	Debtor ETM Master Data
/SAPCEM/MCI_TCO	Total Equipment Costs
/SAPCEM/MCK0	Plant Maintenance Information System
/SAPCEM/MCT_1	ETM Settlement
/SAPCEM/MCT_2	Construction Site Stock Values
/SAPCEM/ML	Display Material Assignment
/SAPCEM/MZ01	Create Material Assignment
/SAPCEM/MZ02	Change Material Assignment
/SAPCEM/MZ03	Display Material Assignment
/SAPCEM/MZ04	Delete Material Assignment
/SAPCEM/PI_CSS	Price Information for Constr. Site
/SAPCEM/PRIE	Price Information for Equipment
/SAPCEM/PRIR	Price Info. for Recipient/Equipment
/SAPCEM/PT01	ETM Planning Board - Change Mode
/SAPCEM/PT02	ETM Planning Board - Display Mode
/SAPCEM/SARA_BOM	Archiving: PBE Document
/SAPCEM/SARA_CAT	Archiving: PBE Document
/SAPCEM/SARA_COND	Archiving: Condition Records
/SAPCEM/SARA_INS	Archiving: Insurance Data
/SAPCEM/SARA_PB	Archiving: PBE Document
/SAPCEM/SARA_REQ	Archiving: Requisition Note
/SAPCEM/SARA_SHIPDOC	Archiving: Shipping Document
/SAPCEM/SCS	Catalog Structure Display
/SAPCEM/SDL	List of Shipping Documents
/SAPCEM/SD_PROT	Log for ETM SD Settlement
/SAPCEM/SD_PROT1	Log for ETM SD Settlement
/SAPCEM/SHOW_BOM	BOM Display in Control
/SAPCEM/VKVE	Conditions: Procedure for A V
/SAPCEM/VS_CREATE	Create Shipping Documents - Require.
/SAPCND/43000002	Set Up Usage
/SAPCND/43000003	Set Up Application
/SAPCND/43000004	Set Up Task
/SAPCND/43000005	Set Up Condition Maintenance Context
/SAPCND/68000184	BADI Impl. /SAPCND/ROLLNAME

/SAPCND/68000405	Condition Types
/SAPCND/68000406	R/3 Compatability
/SAPCND/68000633	Access Seq.
/SAPCND/68000635	Impl. for /SAPCND/MNT_CHECK
/SAPCND/68000636	Condition Tables
/SAPCND/68000637	Field Catalog
/SAPCND/68000688	IMG Activity: /SAPCND/V_GROUP
/SAPCND/68000744	MaintenanceGrp
/SAPCND/68000747	Assign Group to Context
/SAPCND/68000927	Det. Procedure
/SAPCND/83000118	Assign Group to Context
/SAPCND/89000018	BAdI for /SAPCND/ARC_CHECK
/SAPCND/ARC1	Archiving of Condition Records
/SAPCND/ARC2	Deletion of Archived Cond. Records
/SAPCND/ARC3	Displaying of Archived Cond. Records
/SAPCND/ARCC	Control for Archiving
/SAPCND/CONTEXT_GCM	GCM with context
/SAPCND/CTCT	Maintain Condition Tables
/SAPCND/CTFC	Maintain Field Catalog
/SAPCND/CT_ACC_SEQ	Maintenance of Access Sequences
/SAPCND/CT_CNTXT_GR	Assignment Maint. Groups to Contexts
/SAPCND/CT_COND_TYPE	Maintain Condition Types
/SAPCND/CT_DET_PROC	Determination procedure maintenance
/SAPCND/CT_GCM_GRP	Assign Maintenance Groups to GCM
/SAPCND/DD_CUS	Configure Information Determination
/SAPCND/DD_MNT	Maintain Information
/SAPCND/GCM	Condition Maintenance
/SAPCND/MASS_GEN	Mass Generation
/SAPCND/UEASS	Userexits: Assignments
/SAPCND/UELIB	Userexits: Library
/SAPCND/UERNG	Userexits: Ranges
/SAPCND/UE_DEV	Development of Cond. Tech. Userexits
/SAPDII/T_CAPPID	Maintain Application Id
/SAPDII/T_CAPPROP	Maintain Application Property
/SAPDII/T_CAPPSET	Maintain Application Set
/SAPDII/T_CCOMPID	Maintain component Id
/SAPDII/T_CCOMPSET	Maintain component Id
/SAPDII/T_CDOCPROF	Maintain Document Profile
/SAPDII/T_CDOCPROT	Maintain Document Type Texts
/SAPDII/T_CDWBAC	MAp Frontend actions Backend action
/SAPDII/T_CDWBACT	Front End Text Maintenance
/SAPDII/T_CDWB_ACC	Actions Changing Vehicle
/SAPDII/T_CDWB_ACM	Maintain Dealer Action Master
/SAPDII/T_CDWB_DST	Text of Dealer Status
/SAPDII/T_CDWDBS	Dealer Status
/SAPDII/T_CEXINTID	Value Table for Ext Interface ID
/SAPDII/T_CEXTINT	External Interface
/SAPDII/T_CIMGMANT	Image Maintenence
/SAPDII/T_CPRSYSM	Partner to System Mapping
/SAPDII/T_CSYSRFCM	Logical sys to RFC Dest Mapping
/SAPDII/T_CUSPRMAP	User To Partner Mapping
/SAPDII/T_CWTYSTAT	Map Frontend toBackend Status
/SAPDII/T_CWTYWBST	Frontend Status
/SAPDMC/LSMW	LSM Workbench: Initial Screen

SAP Transaction Codes – Volume One

/SAPHT/DRMAGRRECON	Agreement Reconciliation
/SAPHT/DRMAGRWL	DRM Agreement Negotiation Worklist
/SAPHT/DRMBUDR	DRM Bill up
/SAPHT/DRMBUMS	DRM Bill up
/SAPHT/DRMCDMS	Descrepancy of Ship and Debit Claims
/SAPHT/DRMCLCAL	DRM Close Calendar
/SAPHT/DRMCLDR	DRM Ship and Debit
/SAPHT/DRMCLMS	DRM Ship and Debit
/SAPHT/DRMCNWL	Ship-and-Debit Contract Worklist
/SAPHT/DRMCONTSTAT	Send Contract status
/SAPHT/DRMDR00	DRM Main Screen - DR Side
/SAPHT/DRMDRBUSMET	Business Metrics
/SAPHT/DRMDRSLBUSMET	DR Side Sell In Business Metrics
/SAPHT/DRMDS_SLIN	DRM Drop Ship Matching of sellins
/SAPHT/DRMEXPXMN	Xmns received and not received
/SAPHT/DRMFIFOROLL	FIFO Rollback
/SAPHT/DRMIADR	Invalid Ship and Debit Agreements
/SAPHT/DRMIMRCN	DRM Inventory Mgmt Reconciliation
/SAPHT/DRMIRMS	Inventory Reconciliation
/SAPHT/DRMIUDR	Web User Management for Distributor
/SAPHT/DRMIUMS	Web User Management for Manufacturer
/SAPHT/DRMIVDR	Transfer of DRM Inventory Data
/SAPHT/DRMIVMS	Inventory Report at MS Side
/SAPHT/DRMLMDR	Manual Lot Maintenance
/SAPHT/DRMLMMS	Manual Lot Maintenance
/SAPHT/DRMMS00	DRM Main Screen - MS Side
/SAPHT/DRMMSBUSMET	Business Metrics
/SAPHT/DRMPCDR	Price Protection Correction Report
/SAPHT/DRMPCMS	Price Protection Correction Report
/SAPHT/DRMPEMS	Partner Validation Report
/SAPHT/DRMPPDR	DRM Price Protection
/SAPHT/DRMPPDR_C	DRM Price Protection : Create
/SAPHT/DRMPPDR_D	DRM Price Protection : Display
/SAPHT/DRMPPDR_P	DRM Price Protection: Change/Process
/SAPHT/DRMPPMS	DRM Price Protection
/SAPHT/DRMPPMS_C	DRM Price Protection : Create
/SAPHT/DRMPPMS_D	DRM Price Protection : Display
/SAPHT/DRMPPMS_P	DRM Price Protection: Change/Process
/SAPHT/DRMPRFDEF_D	DRM Tracking Partner Profile - MS
/SAPHT/DRMPRFDEF_M	DRM Tracking Partner Profile - MS
/SAPHT/DRMPRFRL	Define Inbound and stg validns - DR
/SAPHT/DRMPRRUL	DRM Tracking Partner Profile - MS
/SAPHT/DRMR3DR	DRM R/3 Transactions
/SAPHT/DRMR3MS	DRM R/3 Transactions
/SAPHT/DRMRL11	Condition create
/SAPHT/DRMRL12	change condition
/SAPHT/DRMRL13	Display Condition
/SAPHT/DRMRLAS	Access sequences: Cross-selling
/SAPHT/DRMRLC1	Create Condition Table (DRM Rule)
/SAPHT/DRMRLC2	Change Condition Table (DRM Rule)
/SAPHT/DRMRLC3	Display Condition Table (DRM Rule)
/SAPHT/DRMRLCA	DRM Rule: V_T681F for W H1
/SAPHT/DRMRLCT	DRM Rule: V_T685 for W H1
/SAPHT/DRMRLDB	RLDB Maintenance

/SAPHT/DRMRLH1CR	DRM: Complex Rule definition
/SAPHT/DRMRLH1CSR	DRM: Complex Schema Relation
/SAPHT/DRMRLH1SC	DRM: Schema definition
/SAPHT/DRMRLH1SCR	DRM: Simple Complex Relation
/SAPHT/DRMRLH1SR	DRM: Simple Rule definition
/SAPHT/DRMRLH2CR	DRM: Complex Rule definition
/SAPHT/DRMRLH2CSR	DRM: Complex Schema Relation
/SAPHT/DRMRLH2SC	DRM: Schema definition
/SAPHT/DRMRLH2SCR	DRM: Simple Complex Relation
/SAPHT/DRMRLH2SR	DRM: Simple Rule definition
/SAPHT/DRMRLH3CR	DRM: Complex Rule definition
/SAPHT/DRMRLH3CSR	DRM: Complex Schema Relation
/SAPHT/DRMRLH3SC	DRM: Schema definition
/SAPHT/DRMRLH3SCR	DRM: Simple Complex Relation
/SAPHT/DRMRLH3SR	DRM: Simple Rule definition
/SAPHT/DRMRLH4CR	DRM: Complex Rule definition
/SAPHT/DRMRLH4CSR	DRM: Complex Schema Relation
/SAPHT/DRMRLH4SC	DRM: Schema definition
/SAPHT/DRMRLH4SCR	DRM: Simple Complex Relation
/SAPHT/DRMRLH4SR	DRM: Simple Rule definition
/SAPHT/DRMRLH5A	DRM: Assign Rule to Partner Profile
/SAPHT/DRMRLH5B	DRM: Assign Rule to Partner Profile
/SAPHT/DRMRLH5CR	DRM: Complex Rule definition
/SAPHT/DRMRLH5CSR	DRM: Complex Schema Relation
/SAPHT/DRMRLH5SC	DRM: Schema definition
/SAPHT/DRMRLH5SCR	DRM: Simple Complex Relation
/SAPHT/DRMRLH5SR	DRM: Simple Rule definition
/SAPHT/DRMRLH6A	DRM: Assign Rule to Partner Profile
/SAPHT/DRMRLH6CR	DRM: Complex Rule definition
/SAPHT/DRMRLH6CSR	DRM: Complex Schema Relation
/SAPHT/DRMRLH6SC	DRM: Schema definition
/SAPHT/DRMRLH6SCR	DRM: Simple Complex Relation
/SAPHT/DRMRLH6SR	DRM: Simple Rule definition
/SAPHT/DRMRLPR	Conditions: Procedure for W H1
/SAPHT/DRMRL_C	DRM: Rules
/SAPHT/DRMRUH111	Condition create
/SAPHT/DRMRUH112	change condition
/SAPHT/DRMRUH113	Display Condition
/SAPHT/DRMRUH1AS	Access sequences: DRM Sample Rules
/SAPHT/DRMRUH1C1	Create Condition Table (DRM Rule)
/SAPHT/DRMRUH1C2	Change Condition Table (DRM Rule)
/SAPHT/DRMRUH1C3	Display Condition Table (DRM Rule)
/SAPHT/DRMRUH1CA	DRM Rule: V_T681F for W H1
/SAPHT/DRMRUH1CT	DRM Rule: V_T685 for W H1
/SAPHT/DRMRUH1PR	Conditions: Procedure for W H1
/SAPHT/DRMRUH311	Condition create
/SAPHT/DRMRUH312	change condition
/SAPHT/DRMRUH313	Display Condition
/SAPHT/DRMRUH3AS	Access sequences: DRM PP Rules
/SAPHT/DRMRUH3C1	Create Condition Table (DRM Rule)
/SAPHT/DRMRUH3C2	Change Condition Table (DRM Rule)
/SAPHT/DRMRUH3C3	Display Condition Table (DRM Rule)
/SAPHT/DRMRUH3CA	DRM Rule: V_T681F for W H3
/SAPHT/DRMRUH3CT	DRM Rule: V_T685 for W H3

SAP Transaction Codes – Volume One

/SAPHT/DRMRUH3PR	Conditions: Procedure for W H3
/SAPHT/DRMRUH411	Condition create
/SAPHT/DRMRUH412	change condition
/SAPHT/DRMRUH413	Display Condition
/SAPHT/DRMRUH4AS	Access sequences: DRM PP Rules
/SAPHT/DRMRUH4C1	Create Condition Table (DRM Rule)
/SAPHT/DRMRUH4C2	Change Condition Table (DRM Rule)
/SAPHT/DRMRUH4C3	Display Condition Table (DRM Rule)
/SAPHT/DRMRUH4CA	DRM PP Rules: V_T681F for W H1
/SAPHT/DRMRUH4CT	DRM Rule: V_T685 for W H3
/SAPHT/DRMRUH4PR	Conditions: Procedure for W H3
/SAPHT/DRMSLSROUT	DRM Sales Report - 867 Outbound
/SAPHT/DRMSMMS	DRM Samples
/SAPHT/DRMSTGDR	DRM Staging Area
/SAPHT/DRMSTGMS	DRM Staging Area
/SAPHT/DRMTXRPT	Transmission Report
/SAPHT/DRMXMRPT	Transmission Report
/SAPHT/DRM_C01	Define new transaction codes
/SAPHT/DRM_C02	Map Sls Doc. & Item Ctgry to Tran Cd
/SAPHT/DRM_C03	Define DRM Relevant condition types
/SAPHT/DRM_C04	Define Sales Document types
/SAPHT/DRM_C05	Define Billing Document types
/SAPHT/DRM_C06	Define Reroute condition
/SAPHT/DRM_C07	Define Validation Rules
/SAPHT/DRM_C08	Asgn Validations to Validation rules
/SAPHT/DRM_C09	Asgn validation rule to tran. codes
/SAPHT/DRM_C10	Convert Ext.l To Int. Partner Number
/SAPHT/DRM_C11	Assign Customer/Vendor To Sales Org.
/SAPHT/DRM_C12	Map Pur Doc. & Item Ctgry to Tran Cd
/SAPHT/DRM_C13	Map Gds Mvmt to DRM Tran for Assemb.
/SAPHT/DRM_C14	Define Purch. Document Type
/SAPHT/DRM_C15	Define DRM Relevant condition types
/SAPHT/DRM_C16	Define Drop Ship settings
/SAPHT/DRM_C17	Define fields assoc. with error code
/SAPHT/DRM_C18	Maintain WEB Personalization info
/SAPHT/DRM_C19	Define DRM Relevant condition types
/SAPHT/DRM_C20	Define Dropship relevancy for Orders
/SAPHT/DRM_C21	Define individual validations
/SAPHT/DRM_C22	Assign Validations to Manf/ Dist.
/SAPHT/DRM_C23	Define Ship and Debit Rejection Rsn
/SAPHT/DRM_C24	Assign DRM rej reason to R/3 Rej rsn
/SAPHT/DRM_C25	Define Validation Rules(Distributor)
/SAPHT/DRM_C26	Assign Validations to Rules
/SAPHT/DRM_C27	Assign Validations to Rules
/SAPHT/DRM_C28	Prepare agreement Negotiation
/SAPHT/DRM_C29	Assign Agreement Status
/SAPHT/DRM_C30	Assign logical system for Agreement
/SAPHT/DRM_C31	Map canc. trans. to DRM transaction
/SAPHT/DRM_C33	Define Reroute condition
/SAPHT/DRM_C41	Define transaction codes
/SAPHT/DRM_C42	Map canc. trans. to DRM transaction
/SAPHT/DRM_C43	Map Sls Doc. & Item Ctgry to Tran Cd
/SAPHT/DRM_C44	DRM global settings (MS/DR ind.)
/SAPHT/DRM_C45	DRM end customer type

/SAPHT/DRM_C46	Reference Customer for EC Aliasining
/SAPHT/DRM_C47	Validation Class : Basic Definition
/SAPHT/DRM_C48	Validation: Assign Validation Types
/SAPHT/DRM_C49	Assign DRM text id
/SAPHT/DRM_C51	MS DR SETTINGS
/SAPHT/DRM_C52	Cond. Type for Cond.Rec. creation
/SAPHT/DRM_CUST	DRM View Maintenance
/SAPHT/DRM_PRF	DRM Tracking Partner Profile
/SAPHT/DRM_PRFCP	DRM Tracking Partner PRofile
/SAPHT/DRM_PRFD	DRM Tracking Partner Profile - DR
/SAPHT/DRM_PRFM	DRM Tracking Partner Profile - MS
/SAPHT/DRM_TRKPTNR	Define Tracking Partner
/SAPHT/MESCL30	Batch Characteristic Search
/SAPHT/MESZMLG	Batch Genealogy
/SAPHT/MESZPRM	Formula parameter dynamic generation
/SAPHT/SPCZQ02	QM: SPC Review Control Chart.
/SAPHT/SW_TVAKZ	Contract availability customizing
/SAPMP/97000078	IMG Activity: /SAPMP/LESHPLBA3
/SAPMP/97000079	IMG Activity: /SAPMP/LESHPLBA4
/SAPMP/BN2M	Maintain N:M Batch Assignments
/SAPMP/CHARACT	Assignment of MillCa Characteristics
/SAPMP/COCA	Transfer MillCa Chars. in Logon
/SAPMP/CUST_LGPR	Rental Fees as a Percentage
/SAPMP/LEIHG	Returnable Packaging Settlement
/SAPMP/LE_LBA_LIST	Selection and Display: DTUC Worklist
/SAPMP/MIGC	Migration Cable -> DIMP: Status
/SAPMP/MIGPV	Mig. Cable -> DIMP: Prod. Version
/SAPMP/OATRKZ_PLA_OC	Work Center for Order Combination
/SAPMP/OTATRKZ_OB_OC	Original Batches for Add. Orders
/SAPMP/PP_COHV	Mass Processing of Production Order
/SAPMP/PP_FHM_WC	Link from PRT to Work Center
/SAPMP/RTSQMT	Maintenance of Reel Type Sequence
/SAPMP/SEROU	Send Routing
/SAPMP/STOCK	Batch-Based Packaging Overview
/SAPMP/TOOL_POOL_CHK	Comparison PRT Pool<->Assigned WkCtr
/SAPMP/TOOL_REPLACE	Replace PRT in Order
/SAPMP/VERPART	Weight Allowances for Packing Type
/SAPMP/VERSART	Weight Allowances for Lagging Type
/SAPMP/WEHB	PO History with Characteristics
/SAPMP/WEHF	GR History of Production Order
/SAPNEA/01001951	IMG Activity: /SAPNEA/SUBCON_002
/SAPNEA/FORMSW	Switch Between PDF and SAPScript
/SAPNEA/JSCR04	Price List of Chargeable Components
/SAPNEA/JSCR05	List of Components at Subcontractor
/SAPNEA/JSCR06	In-Out History List
/SAPNEA/JSCR11	Create Chargeable Invoice
/SAPNEA/JSCR12	Percentage-Based Offsetting
/SAPNEA/JSCR16	Output for delivery vendor
/SAPNEA/JSCR19	Consumption-Based Offsetting
/SAPNEA/JSCR2	Subcontractor List
/SAPNEA/JSCR21	Start/Stop Charging for Components
/SAPNEA/JSCR22	Changing component history
/SAPNEA/JSCR23	SCC - Change Component Price
/SAPNEA/JSCR24	SC: Change Valuation Class

SAP Transaction Codes – Volume One

/SAPNEA/JSCR3	Notification of Payment Terms
/SAPNEA/JSCR30	Create Invoices Shrinkage in Phy Inv
/SAPNEA/J_SC00	Area menu for Subcontracting Managem
/SAPNEA/J_SC_OMESCJ	Activate SCC at Client Level
/SAPNEA/MR3_SODT	Discount rate maintenance
/SAPNEA/MRCH	Enter Deductible Payables
/SAPNEA/ROWA	data migration /sapnea/rowa -> rowa
/SAPPCE/06000010	Cust.
/SAPPCE/06000011	Cust.
/SAPPCE/06000013	Cust.
/SAPPCE/0VJVAPROF	JVA master data profile
/SAPPCE/12001093	DP Chains: Change Chain Types
/SAPPCE/12001094	Down Payment Chain Number Ranges
/SAPPCE/12001095	DP Chains: Change Retention Amounts
/SAPPCE/12001096	DP Chains: Change Verifications
/SAPPCE/12001097	DP Chains: Change Assmnt/Addtl Costs
/SAPPCE/12001098	DP Chains: Change Contractual Penlty
/SAPPCE/12001099	DP Chain: Special G/L Transactions
/SAPPCE/12001101	IMG Activity: /SAPPCE/PNVNUM
/SAPPCE/12001104	IMG Activity: xxx
/SAPPCE/12001108	IMG Activity: /SAPPCE/TPNV08
/SAPPCE/12001109	IMG Activity: /SAPPCE/V_TPNV03
/SAPPCE/12001112	IMG Activity: /SAPPCE/PNV_V_T100C
/SAPPCE/12001113	DP Chains: BAdI Implementations
/SAPPCE/12001114	DP Chains: BAdI Implementations II
/SAPPCE/12001115	DP Chains: Change Payment Block
/SAPPCE/12001116	IMG Activity: /SAPPCE/TPNV04
/SAPPCE/12001118	IMG Activity: /SAPPCE/V_TPNV03
/SAPPCE/12001120	IMG Activity: /SAPPCE/TPNV06
/SAPPCE/12001121	IMG Activity: /SAPPCE/BADI_PNV02
/SAPPCE/12001152	IMG activity: /SAPPCE/ORG_01
/SAPPCE/12001162	IMG activity: /SAPPCE/ORG_02
/SAPPCE/24000002	IMG Activity: /SAPPCE/V_TPNV11
/SAPPCE/24000003	IMG Activity: /SAPPCE/V_TPNV13
/SAPPCE/24000004	IMG Activity: /SAPPCE/PNVPSP
/SAPPCE/24000005	IMG Activity: /SAPPCE/BADI_PNV01
/SAPPCE/24000006	IMG Activity: /SAPPCE/TPNV08
/SAPPCE/24000008	IMG Activity: /SAPPCE/BADI_PNV03
/SAPPCE/24000010	IMG Activity: /SAPPCE/TPNV15
/SAPPCE/24000011	IMG Activity: /SAPPCE/DPC_BADI3
/SAPPCE/24000012	IMG activity: /SAPPCE/DPC_MESSAGE
/SAPPCE/DPCD01	Debit-Side Down Payment Chains
/SAPPCE/DPCK01	Credit-Side Down Payment Chains
/SAPPCE/DPCNKR	Number Range Maintenance: /SAPPCE/DP
/SAPPCE/DPC_LIST_C	Credit-Side Down Payment Chains-List
/SAPPCE/DPC_LIST_D	Debit-Side Down Payment Chains-List
/SAPPCE/DPC_TAX	Tax Comparison Report
/SAPPCE/DPC_TAX01_C	Cred. DP Chains - Tax Rate Change
/SAPPCE/DPC_TAX01_D	Deb. DP Chains - Tax Rate Change
/SAPPCE/DPC_TAX02_C	Cred. DP Chains - Delete Payt Block
/SAPPCE/DPC_TAX02_D	Deb. DP Chains - Delete Payt Block
/SAPPCE/JVA_ECP_ACT	Equity Change Management (Actual)
/SAPPCE/JVA_ECP_PLN	Equity Change Management (Planned)
/SAPPCE/JVA_PART	Edit Joint Venture Partners

31

/SAPPCE/JVA_VENCH	Change Joint Venture
/SAPPCE/JVA_VENCR	Create Joint Venture
/SAPPCE/JVA_VENDIS	Display Joint Venture
/SAPPCE/OIC	Debit-Side Open Items
/SAPPCE/OIGL	G/L Account Open Items
/SAPPCE/OIV	Credit-Side Open Posts
/SAPPCE/ORG01	Create Enterprise Structure
/SAPPCE/ORG02	Change Enterprise Structure
/SAPPCE/ORG03	Display Enterprise Structure
/SAPPCE/ORGCK	Check Enterprise Structure
/SAPPCE/ORG_JVA_DEMO	Call Demo Report
/SAPPCE/PNV01	Create Construction Progress Report
/SAPPCE/PNV03	Display Construction Progress Report
/SAPPCE/PNV04	Display construction progress report
/SAPPCE/PNV05	Create and Change CPR
/SAPPCE/PNV07	Create and Change Remaining Plan
/SAPPCE/PNV08	Create and Change CPR via Org. Unit
/SAPPCE/PNV09	Display CPR via Organizational Unit
/SAPPCE/PNV11	Remaining Plan via Org. Unit
/SAPPCE/PVNNUM	Number Range Maintenance: /SAPPCE/PN
/SAPPO/26000047	BAdI Additive Authorization
/SAPPO/26000050	Software Components
/SAPPO/26000051	Software Components:Attribute Assgmt
/SAPPO/26000053	IMG Activity: /SAPPO/BAPI_PROCESS
/SAPPO/26000058	Define Worklists
/SAPPO/72000176	Tab Pages in Order Area
/SAPPO/72000177	Business Processes
/SAPPO/72000178	Assignment of Business Processes
/SAPPO/72000179	Business Processes: Priorities
/SAPPO/72000180	Dialog: Authorization Change
/SAPPO/72000181	Assign Worklist to Processes
/SAPPO/72000182	Root Organizational Unit
/SAPPO/72000183	Object Types
/SAPPO/72000184	Object Type Attributes
/SAPPO/72000185	Processing Methods
/SAPPO/72000186	Function Assignment
/SAPPO/72000187	Tab Page: Object Area
/SAPPO/72000188	Filter Attributes
/SAPPO/72000189	Permit Object Types
/SAPPO/72000190	Server Groups
/SAPPO/72000244	Redirection to Software Components
/SAPPO/72000315	Retry Groups
/SAPPO/AUTOCORRECT	PPO Autocorrector
/SAPPO/CLOSE_ORDERS	Complete Postprocessing Orders
/SAPPO/DELETE_ORDERS	Delete Postprocessing Orders
/SAPPO/LOGSYS	Logical Systems
/SAPPO/LOGSYS_AS	Assign RFC Destination
/SAPPO/PPO	Postprocessing Office
/SAPPO/PPO2	Edit Postprocessing Order
/SAPPO/PPO3	Display Postprocessing Order
/SAPPO/RESUBMIT	Retry Postprocessing Orders
/SAPPO/SYS_VAL_DISP	Display System Settings
/SAPPO/USER_REMOTE	Cross-System User(s)
/SAPPO/WL_CHANGE	Change Worklist Assignment

SAP Transaction Codes – Volume One

/SAPPO/WL_DISPLAY	Display Worklist Assignment
/SAPPSPRO/11000047	Incremental Funding: Change Msg Ctrl
/SAPPSPRO/POPAYMH	PO Payment History
/SAPSLL/98000023	IMG Activity
/SAPSLL/ALRGDA_DSPR3	Display Pref. Agreement Determin.
/SAPSLL/BANK_DIST_R3	Transfer Bank Master to GTS
/SAPSLL/BANMAS_DIRR3	GTS: Initial Transfer - Customers
/SAPSLL/BL_DOC_MM_R3	GTS: LCI: Blocked MM Docmts
/SAPSLL/BL_DOC_RS_R3	GTS: LCE: Blocked SD Documents
/SAPSLL/BL_DOC_SD_R3	GTS: LCE: Blocked SD Documents
/SAPSLL/BOMMAT_DIRR3	GTS: Initial BOM Transfer
/SAPSLL/BWHIDP_R3	Initial Transfer of Duty-Paid Stock
/SAPSLL/CREMAS_DIRR3	GTS: Initial Transfer - Vendors
/SAPSLL/DEBMAS_DIRR3	GTS: Initial Transfer - Customers
/SAPSLL/DS_D_MM0A_R3	GTS: Transfer MM Purch. Ord. to GTS
/SAPSLL/DS_D_MM0C_R3	GTS: Initial Transfer of GR to GTS
/SAPSLL/DS_D_SD0A_R3	GTS: Transfer SD Orders to GTS
/SAPSLL/DS_D_SD0B_R3	GTS: Transfer SD Deliveries to GTS
/SAPSLL/DS_D_SD0C_R3	GTS: Transfer SD Billing Docs to GTS
/SAPSLL/DS_I_MM0A_R3	GTS: Purchase Order Object Index
/SAPSLL/DS_I_RORG_R3	GTS: Reorganize Object Index
/SAPSLL/DS_I_SD0A_R3	GTS: Order Object Index
/SAPSLL/DS_I_SD0B_R3	GTS: Delivery Object Index
/SAPSLL/DS_I_SD0C_R3	GTS: Billing Docmt Object Index
/SAPSLL/DS_P_MM0A_R3	GTS: Follow-On Funct.: MM Purch.Ord.
/SAPSLL/DS_P_SD0A_R3	GTS: Follow-On Function: SD Order
/SAPSLL/DS_P_SD0B_R3	GTS: Follow-On Funct.: SD Outb.Del.
/SAPSLL/KMATBOM_DIR3	Transfer of Configurable Materials
/SAPSLL/KMATWLR3_03	GTS: Display and Transfer KMAT WList
/SAPSLL/MATMAS_DIRR3	GTS: Initial Transfer of Materials
/SAPSLL/MENU_CUS_R3	GTS: Menu: Basis Customizing
/SAPSLL/MENU_LEGALR3	GTS: Global Trade Services Area Menu
/SAPSLL/PERTMVAR_R3	GTS: Period. Transfer: Variant
/SAPSLL/PRCMAT_DIRR3	Initial Transfer: Material Price
/SAPSLL/PRECIP_R3	Initial Transfer of Prod. Attributes
/SAPSLL/PREF_AGR_R3	Replicate Pref. Agreement Determin.
/SAPSLL/PRPARC_DIRR3	Initial Transfer: Vendor Material
/SAPSLL/PRPARV_DIRR3	Initial Transfer: Vendor Material
/SAPSLL/PSD_INIT_R3	Perform Init. Transf. of Procmt Ind.
/SAPSLL/RES_INV_R3	GTS: Create Restitution Invoice
/SAPSLL/SAKE_DLV_MON	Inbound Deliveries in Storage
/SAPSLL/SAKE_LOG_DIS	Display Error Logs
/SAPSLL/SAKE_MTH_R3	Choose Method for Storage
/SAPSLL/SAKE_XMON_R3	Manually Process Temporary Storage
/SAPSLL/SD0C_RIMAR3	GTS: Transfer Bill. Docs to Risk Mgt
/SAPSLL/SWN_RTR_R3	GTS: Retransfer Commodity Code
/SAPSLL/T000_R3	GTS: Assign Logical System
/SAPSLL/T000_SPI	Assign Logical System
/SAPSLL/TBDLS_R3	GTS: Define Logical System
/SAPSLL/TBDLS_SPI	Define logical system
/SAPSLL/TECOR3	Assignment of Custms ID to Plnt/SLoc
/SAPSLL/TIVDR3	GTS: Ctrl f. Vend.-Based VD Worklist
/SAPSLL/TLER3	GTS: Call Global Trade Services
/SAPSLL/TLER3B	GTS: Call GTS: Document Types

/SAPSLL/TLER3_B_R3	GTS: Control: Call GTS
/SAPSLL/TLSDST	SLL: Assgmt Server Legal Services
/SAPSMOSS/IQS1	Create notification
/SAPSMOSS/IQS2	Change notification
/SAPSMOSS/IQS3	Display Notification
/SAPSMOSS/M00	SAP Notifications
/SAPSMOSS/M01	SAP Notifications
/SAPSMOSS/M02	SAP Notifications
/SAPSMOSS/O01	SAP add-on system installation
/SAPSMOSS/O02	SAP add-on system release
/SAPSMOSS/O03	SAP database system
/SAPSMOSS/O04	Frontend for SAP operating system
/SAPSMOSS/O05	SAP installation
/SAPSMOSS/O06	SAP operating system
/SAPSMOSS/O07	SAP release
/SAPSMOSS/O08	SAP system type
/SAPSMOSS/O09	SAP system type
/SAPSMOSS/QM10	Change list of R/3 notificatiions
/SAPSMOSS/QM11	Display list of R/3 notifications
/SAPSMOSS/QM12	Change list of tasks
/SAPSMOSS/QM13	Display list of tasks
/SAPSMOSS/QM19	List of R/3 notifications, multilvl
/SAPSMOSS/QM50	Time line display:R/3 notifications
/SAPSMOSS/U01	Updating R/3 notifications
/SAPSMOSS/U02	Update job planning
/SAPSMOSS/U03	Update job overview
/SAPTRX/68000157	IMG activity
/SAPTRX/68000158	IMG activity
/SAPTRX/68000159	IMG activity
/SAPTRX/68000160	IMG activity
/SAPTRX/68000161	IMG activity
/SAPTRX/68000162	IMG activity
/SAPTRX/68000163	IMG activity
/SAPTRX/ASAPLOG	Appl. system log for event handling
/SAPTRX/ASC0AO	Define App. Object and Event Types
/SAPTRX/ASC0AP	Define application parameters
/SAPTRX/ASC0SCU	Assign Scenario to Users
/SAPTRX/ASC0SD1	Define Solution / Scenario
/SAPTRX/ASC0SD2	Define Solution / Scenario
/SAPTRX/ASC0TC	Define EM Relevance Conditions
/SAPTRX/ASC0TE	Define EM extraction
/SAPTRX/ASC0TF	Define EM Interface Functions
/SAPTRX/ASC0TO	Define Business Process Types
/SAPTRX/ASC0TS	Define Event Managers (Engines)
/SAPTRX/ASEHVIEW	EH list of shipments
/SAPTRX/DISP_LINK	Show the link to SAP System
/SAPTRX/TRACKING_MON	Display Event Handler Status (old)
/SAPTRX/TSC0GBPT	Global Business Process Types Def.
/SAPTRX/TSC0SCR	Assign Scenarios to roles
/SAPTRX/TSC0SCU	Assign Scenario to Users
/SAPTRX/TSC0SO	Define Solution / Scenario
/SAPTRX/TSC0SO1	Define Solution / Scenario
/SAPTRX/TSC0SO2	Define Solution / Scenario
/SCMB/DF_CHAIN	Definition of Maximum Chains in Flow

SAP Transaction Codes – Volume One

/SCMB/DF_CUST	Document Admin. in Flow (Custom.)
/SDF/E2E_TRACE	SAPGUI based E2E trace
/SDF/EXTRACTOR_GEN	Extractor Generation
/SDF/MON	Schedule Monitoring Set
/SPE/ASN01	ASN cancelling in returns process
/SPE/ASN02	Compensating transaction for ASN cn.
/SPE/CDMON	Transportation Cross-Docking Monitor
/SPE/COPY_CHAR	Copy fixed characteristics to logon
/SPE/CRM_QUOT	Report for monitoring quotations
/SPE/CVAL01	Define Validation Routines
/SPE/DELTA01	Delta Report : Start dialog program
/SPE/EGR	Planlieferungen anlegen
/SPE/OL19	Generate Distr. Model ERP => EWM
/SPE/REDIR	ID redirecting dialog
/SPE/REGISTER_NAVI	Register Navigation from Queue
/SPE/RETINSPNO	Number range maintenance: /SPE/RETIN
/SPE/RETINSP_DISPLAY	Display Inspection Outcomes
/SPE/VL10CUC	Create Profile - Delivery
/SSF/AB	Analysis browser & Download
/SSF/PB	Project browser & test environment
/VIRSA/ALERTGEN	Activity Monitoring
/VIRSA/FFARCHIVE	Log Data Auto Archive
/VIRSA/FFCHNGLOGS	Configuration Change Log
/VIRSA/MICCONFIG	Virsa MIC User mapping Configuration
/VIRSA/ORGUSRMAPPING	Maintain ORGUSERS table
/VIRSA/RE_DNLDROLES	Role Expert 4.0
/VIRSA/VFAT	Superuser Privilege Management
/VIRSA/VRMT	Role Expert
/VIRSA/ZRTCNFG	Risk Terminator Configuration
/VIRSA/ZRTDELLOCK	Delete Role Lock
/VIRSA/ZRTRGLOG	Risk Terminator Role Generation Log
/VIRSA/ZVFAT_U02	FirefightId Log summary
/VIRSA/ZVFAT_U03	Reason/Activity report
/VIRSA/ZVFAT_U04	FirefightId Transaction Usage
/VIRSA/ZVFAT_U05	Invalid Firefighter Ids/Owners/Cntrl
/VIRSA/ZVFAT_U06	SOD Conflicts in Firefighter
/VIRSA/ZVFAT_U07	Data Migration from Master to Text
/VIRSA/ZVFAT_V01	Log Report
/VIRSA/ZVFAT_V02	Log Report
/VIRSA/ZVFAT_V04	List of Idle Firefighter ID sessions
/VIRSA/ZVRAT	SAP Compliance Calibrator
/VIRSA/ZVRATBAK1	Update data for Mgmt Graphical View
/VIRSA/ZVRAT_C01	Security & Controls Policies
/VIRSA/ZVRAT_COVN	Conversion of CC tables, Old to New
/VIRSA/ZVRAT_D01	Download Spool Requests by Job Name
/VIRSA/ZVRAT_L01	Conversion Utility for CC Text Table
/VIRSA/ZVRAT_L02	Conversion Utility for Long Texts
/VIRSA/ZVRAT_M01	Upload/Download CC tables
/VIRSA/ZVRAT_M02	Where Used list of Mit. Control Id/M
/VIRSA/ZVRAT_M03	Analyze disabled SOD TCode & Object
/VIRSA/ZVRAT_M04	Optimizer for SOD Data Table
/VIRSA/ZVRAT_M05	Where Used list of Control Id/Monit
/VIRSA/ZVRAT_MG1	Management Cockpit
/VIRSA/ZVRAT_P01	Display changes to Profiles

/VIRSA/ZVRAT_R01	Count authorizations in roles
/VIRSA/ZVRAT_RB2	Rule Architect
/VIRSA/ZVRAT_RB3	Rule Architect Conversion
/VIRSA/ZVRAT_S01	Monitor Conflicts & Critical Trans.
/VIRSA/ZVRAT_S021	Monitor Conflicts & Critical Trans.
/VIRSA/ZVRAT_S03	Download Objects for Tcodes
/VIRSA/ZVRAT_S04	SOD Conflicts for TCodes and Objects
/VIRSA/ZVRAT_S05	SOD Rule Wizard
/VIRSA/ZVRAT_S06	SOD Rule Validation Tool
/VIRSA/ZVRAT_S07	Non Reference Report
/VIRSA/ZVRAT_S08	User Access Report
/VIRSA/ZVRAT_S09	Comparing diffrent SOD Matrices
/VIRSA/ZVRAT_S10	Tcodes by Roles/Profiles, never exec
/VIRSA/ZVRAT_S11	Authorization object by Roles/Profs
/VIRSA/ZVRAT_S12	Transactions executed by Users
/VIRSA/ZVRAT_S13	Comparing Critical Tcode Matrices
/VIRSA/ZVRAT_S14	Comparing SOD Authorization Matrices
/VIRSA/ZVRAT_S15	Compare Sod Tcode & Authorization
/VIRSA/ZVRAT_S16	Comp.Calibrator Data Maintenance
/VIRSA/ZVRAT_U01	Count authorizations for Users
/VIRSA/ZVRAT_U02	Analysis of called trans in Cus.code
/VIRSA/ZVRAT_U03	Management Report
/VIRSA/ZVRAT_U05	Expired and Expiring Roles for Users
/VIRSA/ZVRMT_U01	Check Role Status
/VIRSA/ZVRMT_U02	Check Tcodes in Menu & Authorization
/VIRSA/ZVRMT_U03	Compare Users Roles
/VIRSA/ZVRMT_U04	List roles assigned to a user
/VIRSA/ZVRMT_U05	Where used list for roles
/VIRSA/ZVRMT_U06	List roles and transactions
/VIRSA/ZVRMT_U07	Create/Modify Derived Roles
/VIRSA/ZVRMT_U08	Analysis of Owners Roles and Users
/VSO/91000206	IMG Activity: /VSO/P_V_PRTYP
/VSO/91000207	IMG Activity: /VSO/P_V_F_PRTYP
/VSO/91000208	IMG Activity: /VSO/M_ACT_STAT
/VSO/91000209	IMG Activity: /VSO/M_PLT_TP
/VSO/91000210	IMG Activity: /VSO/R_V_TVTK
/VSO/91000211	IMG Activity: /VSO/M_PROFIL
/VSO/91000212	IMG Activity: /VSO/M_PALVCL
/VSO/91000213	IMG Activity: /VSO/M_PKG
/VSO/91000214	IMG Activity: /VSO/M_PACKTYP
/VSO/91000215	IMG Activity: /VSO/M_PKG_PKTYP
/VSO/91000216	IMG Activity: /VSO/M_PKGPAL
/VSO/91000219	IMG Activity: /VSO/B_SUBVCL_FT
/VSO/91000245	IMG Activity: /VSO/M_VSO_SETUP
/VSO/91000246	IMG Activity: /VSO/R_DPOINT
/VSO/91000247	IMG Activity: /VSO/P_V_HU_CRT
/VSO/91000248	IMG Activity: /VSO/M_PROF_W_S
/VSO/91000250	IMG Activity: /VSO/M_BAY_CAT
/VSO/M_REORG	Reorganize VehicleSpaceOptimization
/VSO/M_STACK	Maintain Overstackability
/VSO/M_VHMPGR	Maintain Pack.Mtls.Prop.for Pack.Grp
/VSO/M_VHMVCL	Assign Allowed Pack.Mtls to Vehicle
/VSO/P_PICK	Picking According to VSO
0000	Dialog Box for Customizing

SAP Transaction Codes – Volume One

00_PTSPPS_INCLUPD	Activate Functionality
0100	Messages: Disp. CondTab: Pur. Order
0184	Delivery item category determination
0817_CHG	Change Object
0817_CUST	SAP ArchiveLink: Bar Code Entry
0817_DIS	Display Object
0817_INS	Create Object
0CJBQ1	Customizing Billing Plan Ps
0DIS01	Distribution profile
0FIEHGF001_01	Define Handling Methods
0FIEHGF002_01	Retrieval of Object Data
0FILA	Customizing LAE Initial Screen
0FILA000R	Reasons for Changes
0FILA000R_1	Define Reasons for Change
0FILA001CE_1	Change Processes Rest. NEWL
0FILA001CE_2	Define Adjustment Processes
0FILA001CE_3	Change Processes Rest. UPGR
0FILA001CE_4	Change Processes Rest. ROLL
0FILA001CE_5	Change Process Rest. BLEX
0FILA001CE_6	Change Process Rest. CONT
0FILA001CE_7	Change Processes Rest. RNEW
0FILA001S_1	Subprocesses
0FILA001_2	Define Adjustment Processes
0FILA003CF_1	Assign Pmnt Schedule to $CASHPREV
0FILA003MV_1	Value Determ. Using Value Determin.
0FILA003M_1	Value IDs for Later Use
0FILA003_1	Value Determ. Using Formula Interp.
0FILA003_10	Value Determ. Using Value Determin.
0FILA003_11	Determine Accrual Postings Balance
0FILA003_13	Value Determination Using Transfer
0FILA003_14	Net Book Value at Retirement
0FILA003_15	Overview of Defined Value IDs
0FILA003_16	Value Determ. Using Value Determin.
0FILA003_2	Value Determ. by Assign.Constants
0FILA003_3	Value Determination By Value Support
0FILA003_4	Value Determ. Using Value Determin.
0FILA003_5	Value Determ. Using Value Determin.
0FILA003_6	Value Determ. Using Value Determin.
0FILA003_7	Value ID of Inbound Predecessor
0FILA003_8	Value Determination Using Method
0FILA003_9	Value Determination By Derivation
0FILA004_1	Assignment of Trans. to Trans. Types
0FILA005_1	Assign Structure for Acct Assignmt
0FILA006_1	Assign Company Code/Grouping Key
0FILA007CF_1	Definition of Payment Schedules
0FILA007C_1	Add Value ID to Basis Payment Sched.
0FILA007VC_1	Value Determination by Calculation
0FILA007_1	Value Transfer from Condition Types
0FILA008G_1	Definition of CoCd Grouping Key
0FILA008_1	Assign Company Code/Grouping Key
0FILA00970	Specifications - Post Retirement
0FILA009F_1	Dates for Postings
0FILA009F_2	Data for Payment Schedule Definition
0FILA009V_1	Value Transfer from Contract Item

0FILA009V_2	Value Transfer from Material Master
0FILA009V_3	Value Transfer from Classification
0FILA009V_4	Value Transfer from Customer Master
0FILA009V_6	Value Transfer from LAE_CRM_CLASS
0FILA009_1	Data for Pmnt Schedule Def. frm IDs
0FILA009_10	Fill Basis Struct. for Fin.Class.
0FILA009_11	Fill Basis Struct. for Validations
0FILA009_12	Fill Bas.Struct.for Deriv. UseflLife
0FILA009_13	Specifications- Post Acquisition
0FILA009_15	Specifications for Posting APC Adj.
0FILA009_16	General Info for Asset Transactions
0FILA009_17	Specifications- Set Deprec. Terms
0FILA009_19	Fill IDAT Structure for Control
0FILA009_2	Fill Basis Struct. for Substitution
0FILA009_20	Fill IDAT Structure for Control
0FILA009_21	Change Specifications- Deprec. Terms
0FILA009_22	Fill Structure for Changing Asset
0FILA009_23	Fill Structure Using Value IDs
0FILA009_24	Fill Structure Using Value IDs
0FILA009_3	Fill Basis Struct. for Derivation
0FILA009_4	Fill Structure for Creating Asset
0FILA009_5	Specifications- Set Deprec. Terms
0FILA009_6	Specifications- Post Acquisition
0FILA009_7	Specifications- Post Retirement
0FILA009_8	Assign Structure for Acct Assignmt
0FILA009_9	Fill Basis Struct. for Valid.Determ.
0FILA011_1	Option IDs
0FILA110_1	Value Determ. Check Sequences/Steps
0FILA110_2	Validation Check Sequences/Steps
0FILA110_3	Classification Check Sequences/Steps
0FILAACCRULE_1	Acct Principles for Classif. in CRM
0FILAALOG_01	Process list
0FILACHECK_01	Process list
0FILACHECK_02	List of Subprocesses
0FILACHECK_03	Where-Used List for Methods
0FILACHECK_04	Value IDs Customizing
0FILACHECK_05	Method Customizing
0FILACOMPSET	LAE: Specify Application Component
0FILACREATE_01	Generate Table Entries
0FILAFA001_1	Assignment of Trans. to Trans. Types
0FILAFA002_1	Assignment Acct Princ. to Dep. Area
0FILAFA003_1	Upgrade Specifications
0FILAHELP_01	Control List of FILAE-MSGNOs Used
0FILAHELP_02	Where-Used List Error Numbers in LAE
0FILAHELP_03	Where-Used List Error Nos. in FIAA
0FILAHELP_04	List of Parameter Transactions
0FILAIMG	Customizing LAE Initial Screen
0FILAIMG_ADJ	Jump to IMG for Customer Customizing
0FILAIMG_CLASS	Jump to IMG for Financing Classif.
0FILAIMG_CUST	Jump to IMG for Customer Customizing
0FILAIMG_SYST	Jump to IMG for System Customizing
0FILAIRCM_1	Assign Company Code/Grouping Key
0FILALAYOUT	Tabstrip Explorer/Adjustments
0FILALAYOUTADMN	Tabstrip Explorer/Adjustments

SAP Transaction Codes – Volume One

0FILALC001_1	Definition Financing Classif.Group
0FILALC002TO_1	Upgrade Specifications
0FILALC002_2	Definition of Financing Classes
0FILALC003_1	Assign Structure for Classification
0FILALDB000_01	Struct. of Selection Cond.-Component
0FILALDB000_02	Assign Val.IDs to Fields of Log. DB
0FILALDB000_03	Struct. of Selection Conditions-Hdr
0FILALDB001_01	Specify Determination of Data Basis
0FILALDB001_02	Specify Determination of Data Basis
0FILANDURDET	Determine Asset Useful Life
0FILASTRUC_ACCDET	Leasing: Acct Determ. for Accrual
0FILASTRUC_ACINF	Structure Enhancemt for Substitution
0FILASTRUC_DATES	Param. Classification Financing
0FILASTRUC_DEPPARM	Determine Asset Normal Useful Life
0FILASTRUC_LCS_PARAM	Param. Classification Financing
0FILASTRUC_LDB_ITEMS	Struct. Adjustment Flds of Log.DB
0FILASTRUC_LVS_PARAM	Validation Parameter
0FILASTRUC_NDURDET	Determine Asset Normal Useful Life
0FILASTRUC_POINF	Structure Enhancemt for Substitution
0FILASTRUC_VALSUP	Structure Enhancemt for Substitution
0FILASTRUC_VSRDET	Struct.Adjustmt Valid./Subs. Determ.
0FILASUBST0	Substitution
0FILASUBST1	Financing Classification
0FILASUBST3	Rules for Value Determ. via Subst.
0FILAVAL1	Validation Processing Steps
0FILAVSRDEF	Derivation of Check Sequences
0FILAVSRDEF_CLAS	Derivation of Check Sequences
0FILAVSRDEF_VALI	Derivation of Check Sequences
0FILAVSRDEF_VALU	Derivation of Check Sequences
0FILA_CALL_FM	Customizing LAE Initial Screen
0FILA_EXPL_001	Hierarchy Steps of Leasing Explorer
0FIOTP001_1	Acct Determ. Document Grouping
0FIOTP003_1	Posting Control for One-Off Postings
0FIOTPKOFIDEF	Maintain Account Determination
0FMCA_FORMNUM	Number range maintenance: FMCA_FORM
0FPM001	Define Standard Texts for Carry/Fwd
0FPM002	Import Logo for Reporting
0K01	List of Costing Variants
0KE0	EC-PCA: Transfer prog. for act. data
0KE1	EC-PCA: Delete Transaction Data
0KE2	EC-PCA: Del. Profit Ctr Master Data
0KE3	EC-PCA:Delete Transaction Data(Bkgd)
0KE4	EC-PCA: Update settings
0KE5	EC-PCA: Controlling Area Settings
0KE5_WIZARD	Activate Profit Center Accounting
0KE6	EC-PCA: Average Balance Ledger
0KE7	EC-PCA: Maintain Time-Based Fields
0KE8	EC-PCA:Maintain Summarization Fields
0KEA	EC-PCA: Maintain report tree
0KEB	EC-PCA: Generate reports
0KEH	EC-PCA: Report List
0KEJ	Account Determination PC Allocation
0KEK	EC-PCA: Account Determination
0KEL	EC-PCA: Substitutions

0KEM	EC-PCA: Maintain substitutions
0KEMD_46C_UPGRADE	EC-PCA: Upgrade PrCtr MstData <= 46B
0KEN	Special handling, PrCtr goods mvmt
0KEO	Activities in Profit Center Accountg
0KEP	EC-PCA:Transport Environ/Master Data
0KEQ	EC-PCA: Transport Master Data
0KER	EC-PCA: Transport Planning
0KES	EC-PCA: Transport Actual Settings
0KET	EC-PCA: Transport Information System
0KEU	EC-PCA: Transport Cycles
0KEW	EC-PCA: Conv. RW reports 2.x -> 3.0
0KEX	EC-PCA: Conv. totals recs 2.x ->3.0
0KEX1	Easy Execution Services
0KEX2	Customizing Execution Profile
0KEX3	Customizing Execution Profile
0KEX4	Detail Control Execution Services
0KEX_ROLE	Workflow: Role Customizing
0KEX_TASK	Workflow: Task Customizing
0KEY	EC-PCA: Conv.act.line items 2.x->3.0
0KEZ	EC-PCA:Conv.plan line items 2.x->3.0
0KM1	CO Variant Maintenance: Cost Centers
0KMV	List Variants, CCA/ABC Master Data
0KW1	CO Area Settings, Business Processes
0KW2	Change Business Process Attributes
0KW3	CO Variant Maintenance: CO-OM-ABC
0KW7	Master Data Report: Cost Objects
0KW9	Import Business Process Reports
0KWD	Delete Business Processes
0KWL	CO-OM-ABC: Change Process Category
0KWM	Activity Based Costing: Customizing
0KWN	Display Process Category Customizing
0KWO	Maintain Search Help for Bus. Proc.
0KWP	Display Search Help for Bus. Proc.
0KWT	CO-OM-ABC: Transport Customizing
0MEC	Settings for B2B Sched. Agreements
0PEG01	General Settings
0PEG02	Allowed Movement Types
0PM3	Define Career Groups and Texts
0PMDIKEY	Distribution Keys
0REP	Start of program, etc. from IMG
0SHP	Customizing for delivery types
0TBLP01	Customizing - TBLP
0VI1	Maintain selection variants calc.
0VI2	Maintain selection variants settl.
0VI3	Selec.var. coll. run shipment costs
0VI4	Selec.var. coll. run shipment costs
0VLK	Customizing for delivery types
0VLKAIP	Customizing: Del. Type Determin. AIP
0VLP	Customizing/deliv.item categories
0VLPAIP	Customizing: Del.Itm.Cat.Determ. AIP
0VRF	Definition of Route Determination
0VSD	Stat. Groups: Trans. Service Agent
0VSE	Units of measmnt. for Transp. stat.
0VSF	Statistics Update: Shipment

0VSH	Customizing Global Shipping Param.
0VST	Statistics Groups: Shipment Types
0VSU	Assign Statistics Group/Shipmnt Type
0VT0	Maintain Selection Variants
0VT1	Maintain PersInChargOfShip SelectVar
0VT2	Maintain Tranport.Process. SelectVar
0VT3	Maintain Selection Var. Registration
0VT4	Maintain Selection Variant Registr.
0VT5	Maintain utilization select.variants
0VT6	Maintain free capacity sel. variants
0VT7	Maintain Selection Variant F4 Help
0VT9	Maintain Selection Variant F4 Help
0VTA	Customizing Shipping Types
0VTB	Customizing Modes of Transport
0VTC	Route definition
0VTCFP	Set Freight Planning for Fwdg Agents
0VTCR	Define routes
0VTD	Def. of Transp. Connection Point
0VTE	Multiple Maintenance Route Stages
0VTG	Cumulation of Materials in TPS
0VTGC	Cumulation of Matl (Freight Plng)
0VTH	Insert Material Cumulation to TPS
0VTI	Copy Material Cumulation to TPS
0VTK	Customizing Transport Types
0VTKT	Assign deadlines to shipment types
0VTL	Activity Profiles for Shipment Types
0VTP	Tr.Planning Pos.ext. Planning System
0VTR	Route limits ext. Transport. Planng
0VTRC	Route Limitation f. Freight Planning
0VTS	Copy TPS Route Restrictions
0VTT	Create TPS Route Restrictions
0VTW	Special Processing Indicator
0VU0	Tracking Operations and Events
0VU1	Tracking: Partner code types
0VU2	Tracking: Tracking ID code types
0VU3	Tracking: Location code types
0VU4	Tracking: Route type code types
0VVT	Set Up Express Delivery Company
0VVT_TVSHP	Activate Exp. Dlv. Company Globally
0VVT_VC_VXSIQ	XSI: External Qualifier
0VVT_V_VLBLTD	Service Agnt as Express Dlv. Company
0VVT_V_VXSI	Express Dlv. Company's Master Data
0VVT_V_VXSI1	Tracking Status Details
0VVT_V_VXSI2	Express Dlv. Company - Routing Info
0VVT_V_VXSIFN	Exp. Dlv. Cmpany - Function Modules
0VVT_V_VXSIQ	Express Delivery Company Qualifier
0VVT_V_VXSIR	Express Dlv. Company-Service Codes
0VVT_V_VXSIT	Express Dlv. Company's Master Data
0VVT_V_VXTD	XSI Carriers
0VVU	Packing Table
0VVW	Item Category Usage
0VX0	Maintain Selection Variants - Japan
0VX1	Maintain Selection Variants MITI
0VX2	Selection variants - Customs decl JP

0VX3	Selection variants - Customs decl JP
1KE0	EC-PCA: Transfer prog. for plan data
1KE1	EC-PCA: Analyze Settings
1KE3	EC-PCA: Rebuild matchcodes
1KE4	EC-PCA: Customizing monitor
1KE6	EC-PCA: Maintain Matchcode
1KE8	Post FI data
1KE9	Post Data SD -> EC-PCA
1KEA	Post Selected Data CO -> EC-PCA
1KEC	Post MM data to EC-PCA
1KED	Transfer Statistical Key Figures
1KEE	EC-PCA: Plan Statistical Key Figures
1KEF	EC-PCA: Parameter acutal postings
1KEG	Callup view maintenance with COArea
1KEH	EC-PCA: Transfer Material Stocks
1KEI	EC-PCA: Transfer Assets
1KEJ	EC-PCA: Transfer Work in Process
1KEK	EC-PCA:Transfer Payables/Receivables
1KEL	EC-PCA: Create Document
2KE0	PrCtr: Field usage assessment
2KE1	PrCtr: Data control assessment
2KE2	PrCtr: Field group definition
2KE3	PrCtr: Field group texts
2KE4	PrCtr: Field usage distribution
2KE5	PrCtr: Data control distribution
2KE6	PrCtr: Field usage assessment
2KE7	PrCtr: Data control assessment
2KE8	PrCtr: Field group definition
2KE9	PrCtr: Field group texts
2KEA	PrCtr: Field usage distribution
2KEB	PrCtr: Data control distribution
2KEE	Profit Center: Totals Records
2KEL	EC-PCA: Display Profit Center Doc.
2KEM	EC-PCA: Account Valuation Variances
2KES	Profit center: Balance carr'd forw.
2KET	EC-PCA: Allow Balance Carryforward
2KEU	Copy Cost Center Hierarchy
2KEV	Copy cost centers
3KE1	EC-PCA: Create Actual Assessment
3KE1N	EC-PCA: Create Actual Assessment
3KE2	EC-PCA: Change Actual Assessment
3KE2N	EC-PCA: Change Actual Assessment
3KE3	EC-PCA: Display Actual Assessment
3KE3N	EC-PCA: Display Actual Assessment
3KE4	EC-PCA: Delete Actual Assessment
3KE4N	EC-PCA: Delete Actual Assessment
3KE5	EC-PCA: Execute Actual Assessment
3KE6	EC-PCA: Actual Assessment Overview
3KE7	EC-PCA: Create Plan Assessment
3KE7N	EC-PCA: Create Plan Assessment
3KE8	EC-PCA: Change Plan Assessment
3KE8N	EC-PCA: Change Plan Assessment
3KE9	EC-PCA: Display Plan Assessment
3KE9N	EC-PCA: Display Plan Assessment

SAP Transaction Codes – Volume One

3KEA	EC-PCA: Delete Plan Assessment
3KEAN	EC-PCA: Delete Plan Assessment
3KEB	EC-PCA: Execute Plan Assessment
3KEC	EC-PCA: Plan Assessment Overview
3KEG	EC-PCA: Transfer Stat. Key Figures
3KEH	EC-PCA:Addit. Bal. Sheet/P+L Accts
3KEI	Derive Default Profit Center
3KEJ	Activate representative materials
3KEK	Choose representative materials
3KEL	Acct determination for prod.variance
3KOV	Cycle Overview
4KE1	EC-PCA: Create Actual Distribution
4KE1N	EC-PCA: Create Actual Distribution
4KE2	EC-PCA: Change Actual Distribution
4KE2N	EC-PCA: Change Actual Distribution
4KE3	EC-PCA: Display Actual Distribution
4KE3N	EC-PCA: Display Actual Distribution
4KE4	EC-PCA: Delete Actual Distribution
4KE4N	EC-PCA: Delete Actual Distribution
4KE5	EC-PCA: Execute Actual Distribution
4KE6	EC-PCA: Actual Distribution Overview
4KE7	EC-PCA: Create Plan Distribution
4KE7N	EC-PCA: Create Plan Distribution
4KE8	EC-PCA: Change Plan Distribution
4KE8N	EC-PCA: Change Plan Distribution
4KE9	EC-PCA: Display Plan Distribution
4KE9N	EC-PCA: Display Plan Distribution
4KEA	EC-PCA: Delete Plan Distribution
4KEAN	EC-PCA: Delete Plan Distribution
4KEB	EC-PCA: Execute Plan Distribution
4KEC	EC-PCA: Plan Distribution Overview
4KED	EC-PCA: Supplement Allocation Cycles
5NZI	Number range maintenance: RP_IRCERT
5NZL	Leave View Transaction
5NZT	New Zealand Terminations
6KEA	Profit Center: Display Changes
7KE1	Change Plan Costs/Revenues
7KE2	Display Plan Costs/Revenues
7KE3	Change Plan Inventories
7KE4	Display Plan Inventories
7KE5	Change Plan Statisitcal Key Figures
7KE6	Display Plan Statisitcal Key Figures
7KEA	Create Planning Layout for Costs/Rev
7KEB	Change Planning Layout for Costs/Rev
7KEC	Display Planning Layout for Cost/Rev
7KEF	Create Planning Layout for Inventory
7KEG	Change Planning Layout for Inventory
7KEH	Display Planning Lyt for Inventory
7KEI	Transport Planning Layouts
7KEJ	Import Planning Layouts
7KEK	Create Stat. KF Planning Layout
7KEL	Change Stat. KF Planning Layout
7KEM	Display Stat. KF Planning Layout
7KEO	Correction of Plan Bals with PCA

7KEP	Set Planner Profile
7KEQ	EC-PCA: Reorganize Long Texts
7KER	Call Up Planning with Initial Screen
7KES	EC-PCA: Carry Forward Plan Balance
7KET	Execute Formula Planning
7KEV	Copy data to plan
7KEX	Flexible Excel Upload
7KEY	Log: Flexible Excel Upload
7KEZ	Planning:Maintain Variable Attribute
8AS5	PCA: Balance Carryforw.Field Transf.
8KAL	Controlling Areas: ALE for PCA
8KE1	PCA: Rollup: Create Field Assignment
8KE2	PCA: Rollup: Change Field Assignment
8KE3	PCA: Rollup: Display Field Assignmnt
8KE4	PCA: Rollup Substitution
8KE5	PCA: Rollup Substitution
8KE6	PCA: Delete Rollup Field Assignment
8KEA	Create Cond. Table (Price/Prof. Ctr)
8KEB	Change Cond. Table (Price/Prof. Ctr)
8KEC	Display Cond.Table (Price/Prof. Ctr)
8KED	Access: Pflegen (Profit Center)
8KEE	Condition:Sheet for Transfer Pricing
8KEF	Maintain Condition Types
8KEG	Create Condition List
8KEG_02	Change Pricing Report
8KEG_03	Display Pricing Report
8KEG_16	Execute Pricing Report
8KEH	Condition Exclusion:Sheet Assgt TP
8KEI	Maintain Exclusion Group (TP)
8KEJ	Maintain CElem for Excl. Grou (TP)
8KEK	Maintain Transfer Price Variants
8KEL	Trans.Pr.:Allowed Flds for Cond.Tab.
8KEM	Currency and Valuation Profiles
8KEN	Acct Det. for Charg. Off Val. Diff.
8KEO	Assign Representative Material
8KEP	Activate Cur.+Val. Profile in COArea
8KEP_WIZARD	Activate Transfer Pricing
8KEQ	Assign Cur. + Val. Profile to COArea
8KER	Derive Partner Profit Center: Sales
8KES	Derive Partner Profit Center: Purch.
8KET	Derive Costing Key
8KET1	Maintain Stock Change Accounts
8KET2	Maintain Stock Change Accounts
8KET3	Define Costing Key
8KET4	Opening Balance for PCA Costing
8KET5	Valuation for Calculation Base
8KET6	Enter Accts for Quantity Based Plang
8KET7	Set up Profit Planning
8KEU	Deactivate C&V Profile in CO Area
8KEV	CO-PA Pricing
8KEW	EC-PCA/CO-PA Pricing
8KEX	Conversion of condition vals for TP
8KEY	Company Code Field Transfer Rule
8KEZ	EC-PCA Transfer Pricing

SAP Transaction Codes – Volume One

9KE0	Create Profit Center Document
9KE1	Change Cost/Revenue Balances
9KE2	Display Cost/Revenue Balances
9KE3	Change Balance Sheet Accnt Balances
9KE4	Display Balance Sheet Accnt Balances
9KE5	Change Statistical Key Fig. Balances
9KE6	Display Statist. Key Figure Balances
9KE7	Change Actual Document
9KE8	Display Actual Document
9KE9	Display Profit Center Document
9KEA	Create Layout for Cost/Revenue Bals
9KEB	Change Layout for Cost/Revenue Bals
9KEC	Display Layout for Cost/Revenue Bals
9KED	EC-PCA: Reverse Local Actual Doc.
9KEF	Create Layout for Stock Balances
9KEG	Change Layout for Stock Balances
9KEH	Display Layout for Stock Balances
9KEI	Transport Layout
9KEJ	Import Layout
9KEK	Create Layout for Entering ActStatKF
9KEL	Change Layout for Entering ActStatKF
9KEM	Display Layout for Entering AcStatKF
9KEN	Create Layout for Doc. with Stat. KF
9KEO	Change Layout for Doc. with Stat. KF
9KEP	Display Layout for Doc. with Stat.KF
9KEQ	Reorg. of Actual EC-PCA Long Texts
9KER	Reverse Local Actual Documents
9KES	Create Layout for Actual Doc. Entry
9KET	Change Layout for Actual Doc. Entry
9KEU	Display Layout for Actual Doc. Entry
9KEX	Flexible Actual Excel Upload
9KEY	Log for Flexible Actual Excel Upload
AAA_1_IMG	AAAI in IMG
AAA_2_IMG	AAAI in IMG
AACCOBJ	Display Active Acct Assgnmt Elements
AARC	Archiving Asset Accounting
AART	Reading of Archive Data
AATENV1	Create Data Collection
AATENV2	Create Test Cases
AATENV3	Execute Test Cases
AAVN	Recalculate base insurable value
AB01	Create asset transactions
AB02	Change asset document
AB03	Display Asset Document
AB08	Reverse Line Items
ABAA	Unplanned depreciation
ABAD	Asset Retire. frm Sale w/ Customer
ABAD0	Derivation: Initial Screen
ABAD_OLD	Asset Retire. frm Sale w/ Customer
ABAKN	Last Retirement on Group Asset
ABAO	Asset Sale Without Customer
ABAON	Asset Sale Without Customer
ABAPDOCU	ABAP Documentation and Examples
ABAPHELP	ABAP Documentation

45

SAP Transaction Codes – Volume One

ABAP_COEN	SAP Enterprise Tomograph
ABAP_DOCU_SHOW	Call ABAP Keyword Documentation
ABAP_ENGINEER	SAP Enterprise Tomograph
ABAP_INTRO	Enterprise Introspector
ABAP_SEARCH	ABAP Search
ABAP_TRACE	ABAP Objects Runtime Analysis
ABAV	Asset Retirement by Scrapping
ABAVN	Asset Retirement by Scrapping
ABAW	Balance sheet revaluation
ABAWN	New value method
ABB1	Correction of Asset Accounts
ABCO	Adjustment Posting to Areas
ABF1	Post Document
ABF1L	Post Document in Ledger Group
ABGF	Credit Memo in Year after Invoice
ABGL	Enter Credit Memo in Year of Invoice
ABIF	Investment support
ABMA	Manual depreciation
ABMR	Manual transfer of reserves
ABMW	Reverse asset trans. using doc. no.
ABNA	Post-capitalization
ABNAN	Post-Capitalization
ABNC	Enter post-capitalization
ABNE	Subsequent Revenue
ABNK	Subsequent Costs
ABNV	Number range maint: FIAA-BELNR
ABSO	Miscellaneous Transactions
ABSO_OLD	Miscellaneous Transactions
ABST	Reconciliation Analysis FI-AA
ABST2	Reconciliation Analysis FI-AA
ABT1	Intercompany Asset Transfer
ABT1N	Intercompany Asset Transfer
ABUB	Transfer between areas
ABUM	Transfer From
ABUMN	Transfer within Company Code
ABUZSM	Maintain Line Item Schema
ABZE	Acquisition from in-house production
ABZK	Acquisition from purchase w. vendor
ABZO	Asset acquis. autom. offset. posting
ABZON	Acquis. w/Autom. Offsetting Entry
ABZP	Acquistion from affiliated company
ABZS	Enter write-up
ABZU	Write-up
ABZV	Asset Acquis. Posted w/Clearing Acct
AC00	Service Master
AC01	Service Master
AC02	Service Master
AC03	Service Master
AC04	Service Master
AC05	List Processing: Service Master
AC06	List Display: Service Master
AC08	Send service
AC10	Class Hierarchy with Services
ACACACT	Calculate and Post Accruals

SAP Transaction Codes – Volume One

ACACAD   ACE Account Assignment
ACACADCONT01   Accrl Acct Detmn: Mntn Entry Area 01
ACACADCONT02   Acct Determntn: Mntn Entries Area 02
ACACADMETA01   Acct Determntn: Define Rule Area 01
ACACADMETA02   Acct Determntn: Define Rule Area 02
ACACADMETASGL   Act Dtmn: Define Simple Set of Rules
ACACAD_MAIN   Acct Determination: Maintain Entries
ACACAD_META   Account Determination: Rule Definitn
ACACARCHPREP   Preparation of the Archiving Run
ACACCARRYFORWARD   Balance Carryforward
ACACDATADEL   Deletion of Data in the Accrl Engine
ACACDATATRANS   Example: Data Transfer to ACE
ACACDSITEMS   Reporting Accrual Objects ACAC
ACACDSPARAMS   Reporting ACE Object Parameter ACAC
ACACFIRECON   Accrual Engine / FI Reconciliation
ACACFISCYEAR   Open/Lock Fiscal Years in ACE
ACACIMG   Accrual Accounting IMG
ACACPPLOG   Display Periodic Posting Runs
ACACPSDOCITEMS   Display Line Items in ACAC
ACACPSITEMS   Display Totals Values in ACAC
ACACREVERS   Reversal of Periodic Accrual Runs
ACACTRANSFER   Transferral of ACE Docs to Accnting
ACACTRANSFERCUST   Settings for data collection
ACACTREE01   Create Accrual Objects
ACACTREE02   Edit Accrual Objects
ACAC_ACEPS_APPLLOG   Number Range Maintenance: ACEAPPLLOG
ACAC_NUMOBJ   Number Range Maintenance: ACAC_OBJ
ACB1   Compact Account Balance Display
ACBD   Display Shared Buffer: ATP Check
ACC01   Account Maintenance FI-AA
ACCESS_SEQ_CRM_FG   Access Sequences for Free Goods
ACCESS_SEQ_CRM_PD   Access Sequences for Product Determ.
ACCMAP   Convert Depreciation Areas
ACCR   Personal Menu Volker Hofmann
ACCR01   Create Accrual/Deferral Document
ACCR02   Change Accrual/Deferral Document
ACCR03   Display Accrual/Deferral Document
ACCR04   Execute Accruals/Deferrals
ACCR05   Display Accruals/Deferrals Log
ACCR06   Delete Accruals/Deferrals Log
ACCR07   Reverse Accruals/Deferrals
ACC_CHECK   Accessibility Checktool CRM PC UI
ACC_CUST_CALL   Call Customizing Transaction
ACC_DATABASIS_SET   Set Data Basis
ACC_PERIOD   Open and Close Periods
ACC_SYSTEM_SELECTION   Accounting Selections
ACC_SYSTEM_SET   Set Accounting System
ACEACM   Accrual Methods
ACEADET   Accrual Engine: Acct Determination
ACEADETCUST   Accrual Engine: Acct Determination
ACEADETCUST_D   Accrual Engine: Acct Determn Display
ACEADETCUST_DISP   Accrual Engine: Acct Determn Display
ACEADET_D   Accrual Engine: Change Acct Detrmntn
ACEADET_DISP   Accrual Engine: Change Acct Detrmntn

SAP Transaction Codes – Volume One

ACEARCHPREP	Preparation of the Archiving Run
ACEC	Accrual Engine - IMG
ACECOMP	Components Setup
ACEDATADEL	Deletion of Data in the Accrl Engine
ACENAVIGATOR02	Change ACE Navigator
ACENAVIGATOR03	ACE Navigator Change Mode
ACEPP	Accrual Engine - Periodic Postings
ACEPS	Posting Schema for Accruals
ACEPSAD	ACE Account Assignment
ACEPSADCONT01	Acct Determntn: Maintn Entry Step 01
ACEPSADCONT02	Acct Determntn: Maintn Entry Step 02
ACEPSADFILA1	ACE Acct Determination: FILA Area 1
ACEPSADFILA1CUST	ACE Acct Determination: FILA Area 1
ACEPSADFILA2	ACE Acct Determination: FILA Area 2
ACEPSADFILA2CUST	ACE Acct Determination: FILA Area 2
ACEPSADMETA01	Acct Determntn: Define Rule Step 01
ACEPSADMETA02	Acct Determntn: Define Rule Step 02
ACEPSADMETASGL	Acct Detrmn: Define Single-Step Rule
ACEPSAD_MAIN	Acct Determination: Maintain Entries
ACEPSAD_META	Acct Determination: Define Rules
ACEPS_ACEDOCNR	Number Range Maintenance: ACEPSDOCNR
ACEPS_APPLLOG	Number Range Maintenance: ACEAPPLLOG
ACEPS_AWREF	Number Range Maintenance: ACE
ACEPS_RUNID	Number Range Maint: ACE Posting Run
ACEPS_RUNID_TST	Number Range: Test Posting Run ACE
ACEPS_TRANS	Transfer ACE Documents to Accounting
ACEREV	Reverse Postings
ACE_CHECKOFF	Extended Data Checks off
ACE_CHECKON	Extended Data Check on
ACE_COMP_SET	Set the Component in Accrual Engine
ACF_WHITELIST_SETUP	ACF Sicherheitsliste installieren
ACLA	Define Archiving Classes
ACNR	No. Range Maintenance: Ext. Service
ACO1	Activities for Authorization Check
ACO2	Authorization Check Object Types
ACO3	Allowed Activities per Object Type
ACO4	Change Documents for ACO Objects
ACOMPXPD	Progress Tracking Evaluations
ACPTOOL	for admin cock pit sanity check tool
ACSET	Maint.Acct Types for Acct Asgmt Obj.
ACTEXP_APPR	Approve Working Times and Trips
ACTEXP_APPR_LITE	Approve Working Times and Trips
ACTIVATE	Activation of DDIC Object
ACTL	INTERNAL: Work List
AD08	Enter G/L Account Posting
AD0M	New A&D functionality
AD1T	Clear down payment requests
AD20	Search help maintenance (for IMG)
AD21	Matchcode maintenance (for IMG)
AD31	Plan data handling
AD32	Costs-to-complete evaluation
AD3P	Plan data handling profile
AD3V	Version type and text maintenance
AD43	Assessment Preprocessor with rollup

SAP Transaction Codes – Volume One

AD4P	Customize assessment: stat.key figs.
ADAA	Activity Allocation Conversion
ADA_COCKPIT_LVC	liveCache im DBA Cockpit
ADA_COCKPIT_VOL	liveCache Volumes in DBA Cockpit
ADA_GOTO_ALERT_MONIT	Alert Monitor
ADA_SQLDBC	SQLDBC_CONS
ADBOS01	SD-SRV Reporting: Quantity Flow
ADBOS02	SD-SRV Reporting: BOS w. Hierarchy
ADBOS03	SD-SRV Reporting: BOS w/o Hierarchy
ADBT	ORF: Stock Calculation (Batch)
ADCO99	Closure of SM Orders
ADCPL1	Maintain CMC FFFC Parameters
ADCPL10	Display CMC UserStatus Setup
ADCPL2	Display CMC FFFC Parameters
ADCPL3	Maintain CMC Settings
ADCPL4	Display CMC Settings
ADCPL5	Maintain Inventory Group Customizing
ADCPL6	Display Inventory Group Customizing
ADCPL7	Maintain CMC Profile
ADCPL8	Display CMC Profile
ADCPL9	Maintain CMC User Status Setup
ADEX	Order-material transfer posting
ADFSHM01	Flight Scheduling: Aircraft Types
ADFSHM010	Flight Scheduling: Flight Status
ADFSHM011	Flight Scheduling: Flight Route
ADFSHM012	Flight Scheduling: Terminals
ADFSHM013	Flight Scheduling: Maintain profiles
ADFSHM014	Maintain fields fields for profile
ADFSHM02	Flight Scheduling: Aircraft Category
ADFSHM03	Flight Scheduling: Airline Code
ADFSHM04	Flight Scheduling: Airport Master
ADFSHM05	Flight Scheduling: Bays
ADFSHM06	Flight Scheduling: Flight Category
ADFSHM07	Flight Scheduling: Mode of Operation
ADFSHM08	Flight Scheduling: Flight Type
ADFSHM09	Flight Scheduling: Flight Sectors
ADFSH_CUST	Flight scheduling view maintenance
ADIP	SPEC 2000: Initial Provisioning
ADMSP_CIFCUST	MSP CIF Customizing
ADPMPS	PM/PS Integration
ADPMPS2	PM/PS Integration
ADPRCP	Copy Partner Profiles for SPEC 2000
ADPT	Component Maintenance Cockpit
ADRE	ORF: Results Report
ADRF	ORF: Stock Calculation
ADS2KARCH	SPEC2000 IP Data Archiving
ADS2KIPUPL_CUST	SPEC2000 IP Upload: Gen. Customizing
ADS2KIP_PROF	User Profile
ADS2KSTAT	Update IP status after creating mast
ADS2KUPL	SPEC2000 Initial Provisioning Upload
ADS2KUPL1	Resume Upload
ADSPCIP	SPEC 2000: File Upload To ERP
ADSPCIP_EXCELMAP	SPEC2000: Settings to RSPL File
ADSPCIP_RSPL	SPEC2000:RSPL File Upload

SAP Transaction Codes – Volume One

ADSUBCON	SUBCONTRACTING Monitor
ADTBOS01	Maintenance: SD-SRV Valid Reports
ADWP_HELP	ADWP Additional Functions
AD_SPC_MOI	Customizing: Model ID Codes
AD_SPC_S1S	Customizing: Doc. Type f. Stock Inq.
AEAN	Trigger Group Message Determination
AEUB	Limit transaction types
AFAB	Post depreciation
AFABN	Post Depreciation
AFAF	Assets with errors
AFAMA	View Maint. for Deprec. Key Method
AFAMD	View Maint. Declining-Bal. Method
AFAMH	Maintain Maximum Amount Method
AFAMP	View Maint. Period Control Method
AFAMR	View Maintenance Base Method
AFAMS	View Maint. Multi-Level Method
AFAMSK	Method: Levels in Calendar Years
AFAM_093B	View Default Values for Valuation
AFAM_093C	Company Code Default Values
AFAR	Recalculate Depreciation
AFBN	Include New Depreciation Area
AFBP	Create depreciation posting log
AFO_AP_GT_CRE_UPD	Create/Update FO for Generic Trans.
AFO_AP_LOAN_MMIG	FO Integration: Loans - Migration
AFO_AP_LOAN_MUPD	FO Integration: Loans - Mass Proc.
AFO_AP_POS1_MMIG	FO Int.: Class Pos.in SA - Migration
AFO_AP_POS1_MUPD	FO Int.:Class Pos.in SA - Mass Proc.
AFO_AP_POS2_MMIG	FO Int.: Class Pos.in FA - Migration
AFO_AP_POS2_MUPD	FO Int.:Class Pos.in FA - Mass Proc.
AFO_AP_TRTM_MUPD	FO Integ.: Open TRTM - Mass Process.
AFO_CFUPDATE	Update Cash Flow Management
AFO_FOI_DER_DERIVA	FO Integ.: Derivation - Derivatives
AFO_FOI_DER_EXP	FO Integ: Derive – Operational Expos
AFO_FOI_DER_FAZ	FO Int.: Derivation from Facilities
AFO_FOI_DER_FX	FO Integration: Derivation - Forex
AFO_FOI_DER_LOAN	FO Integration: Derivation - Loans
AFO_FOI_DER_MONEY	FO Integ.: Derivation - Money Market
AFO_FOI_DER_POS1	FO Int.: Deriv. - Class Pos. in SA
AFO_FOI_DER_POS2	FO Int.: Deriv. - Class Pos. in FA
AFO_FOI_DER_ST	FO Integ: Derive - Security Trans
AFO_FOI_FIELD_EXPT	FO Integ.: Exceptions for Character.
AFO_FOI_PD	FO Integration - Log Display
AFO_FOI_PP	FO Integration: Postprocessing
AFO_FOI_RULE_DERIVA	Derivatives: Maintain Rule Entries
AFO_FOI_RULE_EXP	Operational Exp: Maintain Rule Entry
AFO_FOI_RULE_FAZ	Facility: Maintain Rule Entries
AFO_FOI_RULE_FX	Forex: Maintain Rule Entries
AFO_FOI_RULE_LOAN	Loans: Maintian Rule Entries
AFO_FOI_RULE_MONEY	Money Market: Maintain Rule Entries
AFO_FOI_RULE_POS1	Class Pos. in SA: Define Rule Values
AFO_FOI_RULE_POS2	Class Pos. in FA: Define Rule Values
AFO_FOI_RULE_ST	Security Tran: Maintain Rule Entries
AFO_PA_LOAN_MUPD	FOI PA Part for Loan - Mass Process.
AFO_PA_TRTM_MUPD	Edit Fin. Object for Fin. Trans.

SAP Transaction Codes – Volume One

AFO_UPDSAVE_DEL	Delete Admin. Data for Night Run
AFO_UPDSAVE_SHOW	Display Admin. Data for Night Run
AFO_WORK_SHOW	Display Worklist for Fin. Object
AFO_WP_CONV	Conversion of Financial Objects
AFWA	Create Maintain Analysis Structures
AFWBM	Edit Master Data for Benchmark
AFWBMPH	Assign Benchmark to PH Nodes
AFWFL	AFWCH: Filter Maintenance
AFWFLT	AFWCH: Filter Maintenance
AFWKF_MD	Master Data Reporting for RDB
AFWKF_PA	Key Figures and Eval. Procedures
AFWKF_RA	Key Figures and Eval. Procedures
AFWO1	Single Records Procedure: Monitoring
AFWO2	Final Results Procedure: Monitoring
AFWOBM	Final Results Procedure: Monitoring
AFWPH	Portfolio Hierarchies
AFWPHD	Portfolio Hierarchies (Display)
AFWS	Maintain Segment Level Characterist.
AFW_ACT1	Anal. Struct.: Activ.Sample Settings
AFW_ACT2	Anal. Struct: Activate Customizing
AFW_BP1	BP Conversion: Field Catalog Entries
AFW_BP2	BP Conversion: Portfolio Hierarchies
AFW_BP3	BP Conversion: Character.Hierarchies
AFW_BP4	BP Conversion:: Encode PH Value
AFW_BP5	BP Conv. with Ident.Numbers: BPMIG=3
AFW_BP6	Set Status to "Completed"
AFX_ACT_SNUM	Number Range Maint.: AFX_ACT Object
AFX_CUST_CHECK	Check: Archiving Customizing
AFX_CUST_DEPL	Distribute Global Ctrl Customizing
AFX_FMOD	AFX Function Modules
AFX_GLOBAL_CTRL	Control Archiving: Check Table
AFX_GLOBAL_CUST	Archiving Control: Settings
AFX_GLOBAL_PBP	Archiving Ctrl: Package Form. Procs
AFX_MONITOR	Archiving Monitor
AFX_OBJDATA_KEY	Key Terms for Runtime Data
AFX_OBJDATA_TYP	Cat. Values (Items) for Runtime Data
AFX_PSED_GLOBAL_CTRL	Global Control from WB: Control
AFX_PSED_GLOBAL_CUST	Global Control from WB: Settings
AFX_PSED_GLOBAL_PBP	Package Formation Procedures from WB
AFX_PSED_PP_APPLREL	Maintain Locks: PP Application Types
AFX_PSED_PP_JOBDISTR	Maintain Job Distribution for PP
AFX_TEXTPOOL	Text Pool for Program Templates
AFX_TREEDEF	Hierarchy Tree Definition
AFX_WB	Archiving Workbench
AFX_WZ_ARCHOBJ	Call Up AOBJ from Wizard
AFX_WZ_PPDEF	Call Up PP Customizing from Wizard
AIAB	AuC Assignment of Dist. Rule
AIAO	C AM Maint. list vers. gen. line itm
AIAZ	Display Dist. Rule Allocation
AIBU	Transfer Asset under Const.
AIDMM	Create Material Master Data IDocs
AIDNR	Create EPC Number Range IDocs
AIDNR_MASTER	Define EPC Serial Number Ranges
AIIO	C AM Maintain List Version AuC

AISF	FX Exposure
AISFSS	Single Value Analysis: FX Exposure
AISGENKF	Key Figure Analysis
AISGENKF_LAYOUT_DEF	SVA: Define Key Figure Layout
AISPL	Einzelwertanalyse: Gewinn & Verlust
AISS	Single Val. Analysis - Sensitivities
AIST	Reverse Settlement of AuC
AIS_FORMULA_DEF	Define Formulas for AIS
AIS_LAY_DEF	Define Initial Layout
AIS_STDREP	Standard Reporting on Results DB
AJAB	Year-End Closing
AJRW	Fiscal Year Change
AKAB	List purchasing arrangements
AKE1	Create Condition
AKE10	Transfer Prices: Display Overhead
AKE2	Change Condition
AKE3	Display Condition
AKE4	Copy Condition
AKE5	PCA Transfer Prices: Create Prices
AKE6	PCA Transfer Prices: Change Prices
AKE7	PCA Transfer Prices: Display Prices
AKE8	Transfer Prices: Create Overhead
AKE9	Transfer Prices: Change Overhead
AKKO	Promotion pur. pr. conditions
AKOF	C FI Maintain Table TAKOF
AKVA	List sales arrangements
AKVK	Promotion sales price conditions
AL08	Users Logged On
AL11	Display SAP Directories
AL11_OLD	Display SAP Directories
AL12	Display table buffer (Exp. session)
AL13	Display Shared Memory (Expert mode)
AL15	Customize SAPOSCOL destination
ALM99	JBALMCTRL Control Tables
ALM_01	ALM: Assign CF Type to CF Indicator
ALM_ME_DEBUG	MAM Debugging Settings
ALM_ME_GENERAL	Smartsync Settings
ALM_ME_INVENTORY	Inventory Management Profile
ALM_ME_NOTIF	Notification Processing Profile
ALM_ME_ORDER	Order Processing Profile
ALM_ME_ORDER_STATUS	Change Mobile Status for Order
ALM_ME_PUSH	MAM PUSH Control
ALM_ME_SCENARIO	Mobile Asset Management Scenario
ALM_ME_USER	User-specific settings
ALO1	Determine ASH/DOREX Relationships
ALRTCATDEF	Editing Alert Categories
ALRTCATDEF_SEL	Define Alert Category
ALRTDISP	Display Alerts
ALRTINBOX	Alert Inbox
ALRTMON	Alert Monitor
ALRTPERS	Personalize Alert Delivery
ALRTPROC	Process Alerts
ALRTSUBSCR	Subscribe to Alert Categories
ALVIEWER	ArchiveLink Viewer in the Web

AM04	Changes to Asset Classes
AM05	Lock Asset Class
AMADEUS	Amadeus Direct
AMEN	ABAP Tools Menu
AMRP	Send Stock/Requirements List
ANA_STRUCT_GEN	OLTP Metadata Repository
ANA_STRUCT_GEN_ALM	OLTP Metadata Repository
ANA_VAR	Table Analysis: Analysis Variants
ANHAL	Maintain Cutoff Value Key
ANK0	Ch.-of-Depr.-Dep. Asset Class Data
ANK1	Ch.-of-Depr.-Dep. Control Specif.
ANK2	Ch.-of-Depr.-Dep. Allocations
ANK3	Ch.-of-Depr.-Dep. Net Worth Valuat.
ANK4	Ch.-of-Depr.-Dep. Insurance Data
ANKA	Directory of asset classes
ANKL	Generate Asset Classes
ANKL_OLD	Create Asset Classes from Accounts
ANNETTE	Check Archiving Documentation
ANSICHT	Maintain Asset Views
ANSICHT00	Assignment Trans.Group - Asset View
ANVEST	Maintain Investment Support Measures
ANZARCH	Display Reloaded Structures
AO11	Assign number range
AO21	Screen layout for deprec. areas
AO25	Unit-of-prod. depreciation
AO31	Specify Depreciation Area
AO32	Assign net worth tax area
AO33	Net worth tax field selection
AO41	Add to insurance specifications
AO42	Insurance field selection
AO51	Leasing field selection
AO52	Add to leasing entries
AO61	Assign user fields
AO67	Define Transaction Type
AO68	Define Transaction Type
AO69	Account assignmt. KTNAIB
AO71	Document type for posting deprec.
AO72	Specify posting procedure
AO73	Define Transaction Type
AO73_INV	Define Transaction Type
AO74	Define Transaction Type
AO75	Define Transaction Type
AO76	Define Transaction Type
AO77	Define Transaction Type
AO78	Define Transaction Type
AO79	Define Transaction Type
AO80	Define Transaction Type
AO81	Define Transaction Type
AO82	Define Transaction Type
AO83	Define Transaction Type
AO84	Define Transaction Type
AO85	Account assignmt Acquisitions
AO86	Account assingmt. Retirements
AO87	Acct. Assignmt Revaluation on APC

AO88	Acct.Assignmt for Investment Support
AO89	Acct.assmt. not to curr ac.as.share
AO90	Account assignmt Acquisitions
AO90_OLD	Account assignmt Acquisitions
AO91	Specify field group authorization
AO92	Logical field groups
AO93	Ord. Depreciation Acct Assignment
AO94	Special Depreciation Acct Assignment
AO95	Acct. assgnmt. Unplanned deprec.
AO96	Acct. assgnmt. Transfer of reserves
AO97	Acct. assgnmt. Reval. of deprec.
AO98	Acct. assignment Interest
AO99	Acct. assgnmt. Derived dep. areas
AO99_OLD	Acct. assgnmt. Derived dep. areas
AOBJ	Archiving object definition
AOBJ_DOCU	Display Archiving Object Docu.
AOBK	Depreciation areas/Reduction rules
AOBV	Maint. of rules for delivery costs
AOCO	Cost center check (across co.codes)
AOLA	Master Data Tab
AOLAPOST	Tabstrip Posting Transactions
AOLK	Tab Layout for Asset Master Data
APB_CALL_IS_QUERIES	Call Infoset Queries
APB_LPD_CALL_RW_REP	Start Report Writer Reports
APB_LPD_CALL_TRANS	APB_LPD_CALL_TRANSACTION
APER_RESET	Reset Periodic Posting Run
APOLLO	Apollo Bypass
APPCHANGE	Reporting Options for Appraisals
APPCREATE	Create Appraisal
APPDELETE	Delete Appraisal
APPDISPLAY	Display Appraisal
APPSEARCH	Reporting Options for Appraisals
APPTAKEBACK	Reset Appraisal Status to 'Active'
AR01	Call Asset List
AR02	Call Up Asset History Sheet
AR03	Call Up Depreciation List
AR04	Call Up Depreciation + Interest List
AR05	Call Up Asset Acquisition List
AR06	Call Up Asset Retirement List
AR07	Call Up Asset Transfer List
AR08	Call Up Depreciation Compare List
AR09	Call Up Property List
AR10	Call Up Insurance List
AR11	Investment Grants
AR11N	Investment Grants
AR12	Call Up Asset Directory
AR13	Call Up Prim. Cost Plan. Dep./Int.
AR14	Call Up Manual Depreciation List
AR15	Changes to Master Record
AR16	Changes to Asset Classes
AR17	Call Up Leasing Liability List
AR18	Call Up Depr.Simulation
AR19	Call Up List of Origins
AR20	Retirement comparison

AR21	Mid-quarter Alert Report
AR22	Analysis of retirment revenue
AR23	Italy: Asset register
AR24	Italy: Assets at 3rd party
AR25	Depreciation posted
AR26	Call up special reserve list
AR27	Call up: Group asset list
AR28	Call up asset history
AR29	Re- and New Valuation of Assets
AR29N	Re- and New Valuation of Assets
AR30	Display Worklist
AR31	Edit Worklist
AR32	Call Create Worklist
AR32N	Call Create Worklist
ARAL	Display Application Log
ARCHGUIDE	Data Archiving Guide
ARCH_PROT	Archiving Logs
ARCU_COIT1	Residence Times for CO Line Items
ARKO	KOBRA: Archiving
ARMO	Schedule Monitor: Asset Accounting
ARQ0	FIAA - Ad hoc reports
ARRAY_CREATE	Generate Column Group
ART0	FIAA - Information System
ARTE	Replace Articles in Layout Modules
AR_CUST	Archiving Engine - Configurator
AR_DISPLAY_AIS	Display AIS
AR_ENGINE	Archiving Engine
AR_FACTORY	Archiving Factory
AR_HDS	Assignment of Residence Times
AR_METRIC	Definition of Residence Time
AR_TEST	Test Archiving
AS01	Create Asset Master Record
AS02	Change Asset Master Record
AS03	Display Asset Master Record
AS04	Asset Changes
AS05	Block Asset Master Record
AS06	Delete Asset Record/Mark for Delet.
AS08	Number Ranges:Asset Number
AS100	Legacy Data Transfer using Excel
AS11	Create Asset Subnumber
AS11_FMIM	Create AuC Subnumber
AS21	Create Group Asset
AS22	Change Group Asset
AS23	Display Group Asset
AS24	Create Group Asset Subnumber
AS25	Block group asset
AS26	Mark group asset for deletion
AS81	Create Old Group Assets Data
AS82	Change old group asset
AS83	Display old group asset
AS84	Create legacy group asset subnumber
AS91	Create Old Asset
AS92	Change Old Asset
AS93	Display Old Asset

AS94	Create Legacy Asset Subnumber
ASACT	Activate Application Stat. Types
ASCC	Assets on My Cost Center - GUI Vers.
ASCC_GUI	Assets on My Cost Center
ASEM	My assets
ASEM_GUI	My Assets - GUI Version
ASIM	Simulation of asset posting
ASKB	Periodic Asset Postings
ASKBN	Periodic APC Posting Run
ASMN	Asset Master Menu
ASOKEY	Definition of SAP Function OPENKEY
AS_ADMIN	SAP AS: Administration
AS_AFB	Archive File Browser
AT01	Create Asset Master Record (old)
AT02	Change Asset Master Record (old)
AT03	Display Asset Master Record (old)
AT11	Create Asset Subnumber (Old)
AT21	Create Group Asset (old)
AT22	Change Group Asset (old)
AT23	Display Group Asset (old)
AT24	Create Group Asset Sub-Number (old)
AT81	Create Old Group Asset (old)
AT82	Change Old Group Asset (old)
AT83	Display Old Group Asset (old)
AT84	Display Old Group Asset Sub-No.(old)
AT91	Create Old Asset (old)
AT92	Change Old Asset (old)
AT93	Display Old Asset (old)
AT94	Create Old Asset Sub-Number (old)
ATP01	Cancel/Delete Prod. Avail. Req.
ATPC01	Maintain number range for PAR
ATPS	ATP Check: Send Customizing
ATRA	ABAP Objects Runtime Analysis
ATRANSGRP	Transaction Group Maintenance
ATRA_E2E	ABAP Objects Runtime Analysis
AUFW	Maintain Revaluation Measures
AUN0	FI-AA Asset Summary
AUN1	FI-AA Asset Summary
AUN10	FI-AA Asset Summary
AUN11	FI-AA Asset Summary
AUN2	FI-AA Asset Summary
AUN3	FI-AA Asset Summary
AUN4	FI-AA Asset Summary
AUN5	FI-AA Asset Summary
AUN6	FI-AA Asset Summary
AUN7	FI-AA Asset Summary
AUN8	FI-AA Asset Summary
AUN9	FI-AA Asset Summary
AUT01	Configuration of Logging
AUT02	Configuration of Navigation Help
AUT03	Display Configuration
AUT04	Configuration of Long Text Logs
AUT05	Deletion of Long Texts
AUT10	Evaluation of Audit Trail

SAP Transaction Codes – Volume One

AUTH_ASSISTANT   Role Authorization Assistant
AUTH_DISPLAY_OBJECTS   Display Active Authorization Objects
AUTH_SWITCH_OBJECTS   Switch on/off authorizations
AUVA   FI-AA Incomplete Assets
AW01   Asset Explorer
AW01N   Asset Explorer
AW01_AFAR   Asset Explorer
AW01_OLD   Asset Master Rec: Display Val.Fields
AWUW   Assignment LIS except/BOR event
AXPD   Progress Tracking Evaluations
AXTEXT   Extensibility Registry
AXTOBJ   Extensibility Generation Registry
AXTREG   Extensibility Registry
AXTSHOW   Display and analyze Extensions
AXTSYS   Extensibility Tool System Info
B1B2   Create Magnetic Media files
BA01   Table T005BU
BA10   Subsystem Configuration
BA11   Config. Transceiver / Upload Files
BALA   ALE Application menu
BALD   ALE Development
BALE   Area Menu for Administration
BALM   ALE Master data
BANK_CUS_CHDOC   Customer Setting Change Doc. Tool
BANK_CUS_CHDOC_DEV   Developer Setting Change Doc. Tool
BANK_CUS_JC   Definition of Job Nets
BANK_CUS_PP   Settings for Parallel Processing
BANK_CUS_PPC   Settings for Parallel Processing
BANK_JC_OVRVW   Overview + Control of Job Nets
BANK_JC_START   Start of a Job Net
BANK_PP_APPLREL   Relationships betw. Applic. Types
BANK_PP_CHECK   Check Customizing for Parall. Proc.
BANK_PP_GEN   Generate Application Type
BANK_PP_MONITOR   Call PPF Monitor
BANK_PP_OVRVW   Overview of Current Mass Runs
BANK_PP_SETTINGS   Current Settings for Par. Processing
BAPI   BAPI Explorer
BAPI45   BAPI Browser
BAPIPPLAN   Test Tool for Payment Plan BAPIs
BAPIW   BAPI Explorer
BASIS_CL01   Call CL01 (if it exists)
BASIS_CL02   Call CL02 (if it exists)
BASIS_O1CL   Call O1CL (if it exists)
BATCHMAN   Transfer of External CO Data
BAUP   Bank Data Transfer
BBPS   EBP Order Status Tracking
BBP_ES_ANALYZE   Analyze RFC Data from E-Sourcing
BBP_ES_CUST_DOWNLOAD   Download Customizing Settings for ES
BBP_ES_RFC_DELETE   Delete RFC Data Submitted from ES
BBP_ES_SEARCH   Search for ES-Related Documents
BC01   Business Partner: Form of Address
BC03   Business Partner: Marital Status
BC04   Business Partner: Property Regime
BC05   Business Partner: Employee Group

BC06	Business Partner: Rating
BC07	Business Partner: Cred. Rat. Instit.
BC08	Business Partner: Legal Form
BC09	Business Partner: Legal Entity
BC10	Business Partner: Loan to Manager
BC11	Business Partner: Employment Status
BC12	Business Partner: GBA Information
BC13	Business Partner: Partner Grouping
BC14	Business Partner: Address ID
BC15	No. Range Maint.: BP_PARTNR Partner
BC16	Business Partner: Function
BC17	Business Partner: Department
BC18	Business Parnter Release Parameters
BC19	Business Partner: Release Activat.
BC20	Business Partner: Salutation
BC50	Business Partner: Role Type
BC51	Business Partner: Role Category
BC52	Business Partner: BP View
BC53	Business Partner: Relationship Cat.
BC54	Business Partner: Screen
BC55	Business Partner:Screen-View Assign.
BC56	Business Partner: Relationship Type
BC57	Business Partner: BP Grouping
BC60	Business Partner: Role Category View
BC61	Business Partner: Application
BC62	Business Partner: Applicat.Role Cat.
BC63	Business Partner: Phonetic Search
BC64	Business Partner: Role Csat. Text ID
BC65	Business Partner: Field Groups
BC66	Business Partner: Link Act. category
BC67	Business Partner: Link Role Category
BC68	Business partner: Field-Fld Grp Ass.
BC69	Business Partner: View-Fld Grp Ass.
BC70	BP: Field Modification Activated
BC71	Business Partner: Field Mod.Role Cat
BC72	Business Partner: Notes (Role)
BC73	Business Partner: Notes (general)
BCA0	BP: Business Partner - Applic.Cust.
BCABA	BC ABAP Programming
BCA_CONDIND_REL01	Customizing Release Procedure
BCA_CONDSTD_REL01	Customizing Release Procedure
BCA_CUS_AK	Determine Rate Type - Currency Swap
BCA_CUS_BK	Bal. Sheet Accts for Currency Swap
BCA_CUS_CC	Determine Rate Cat. - Currency Swap
BCA_CUS_REL_PROC	Customizing Release Procedure
BCA_CUS_REL_WF_RULES	AM Release WF: Rule Customizing
BCA_CUS_RP_WF_LINKS	Link Between Release Procedure & WF
BCA_US_CD_NO	Number range maintenance: BCA_US_CD
BCA_US_COMP	BCA: Activate US/Canada Component
BCA_US_DEA1	Dormancy and Escheat Accounts Report
BCA_US_DS_BC	Display Bank Checks
BCA_US_DS_HOLD	Create a Detailed Hold Report
BCA_US_F971	Account Blocks (US specific)
BCA_US_ISS_BC	Issue Bank Checks

SAP Transaction Codes – Volume One

BCA_US_ISS_CC	Issue Certified Checks
BCA_US_OD_ANAL	Overdraft protection Analyze & print
BCA_US_OD_PLAN	Maintain Overdraft Plan
BCA_US_OD_PROC	Overdraft protection (US)
BCA_US_OD_PR_LOG	Overdraft protection (US) - view log
BCA_US_OD_REL	Maintain Account Relationship
BCA_US_OD_SETUP	BCA: Maintain Overdraft Protection
BCA_US_RE_BC	Reprint Bank Check
BCA_US_RV_BC	Reverse Bank Check
BCA_US_TDA1	Time Deposit - Create
BCA_US_TDA3	Time Deposit - Display
BCA_US_TDRO1	Time deposit rollover - Mass run
BCA_US_TDRO2	Time deposit rollover - Single run
BCA_US_TDROLG	App log time deposit rollover
BCG0	Bar chart: Maintain field definition
BCG1	Bar chart: Maintain form definition
BCG2	Bar chart: Maintain graphic profile
BCG3	Bar chart: Maintain form assignment
BCG4	Bar chart: Maintain option profile
BCG5	Bar chart: Maintain color assignment
BCG6	Bar chart: Maintain color definition
BCG7	Bar chart: Call model graphic
BCG8	Bar chart: Maintain graphic element
BCG9	Bar chart: Maintain chart
BCGK	Maintain employee group to sub-group
BCMK	Maintain employee sub-group
BCT0	Create Contact
BCT1	Change Contact
BCT2	Display Contact
BCTM	Business Partner Contacts
BCTNUM	Number Range Maintenance: BCONTACT
BCT_SARA	Archiving of Customer Contacts
BC_DATA_GEN	Create Data for Flight Data Model
BC_GLOBAL_SBOOK_CREA	Create SBOOK Records
BC_GLOBAL_SBOOK_DISP	SBOOK Record Display
BC_GLOBAL_SBOOK_EDIT	Changing SBOOK records
BC_GLOBAL_SCUST_CREA	Creating SCUSTOM records
BC_GLOBAL_SCUST_DISP	Display SCUSTOM records
BC_GLOBAL_SCUST_EDIT	Change SCUSTOM records
BC_GLOBAL_SFLGH_CREA	Create SFLIGHT records
BC_GLOBAL_SFLGH_DISP	Display SFLIGHT records
BC_GLOBAL_SFLGH_EDIT	Change SFLIGHT records
BC_GLOBAL_STRAV_CREA	Creating STRAVELAG records
BC_GLOBAL_STRAV_DISP	Display STRAVELAG records
BC_GLOBAL_STRAV_EDIT	Change STRAVELAG records
BD10	Send Material
BD100	IDoc display object channel view
BD101	Consistency check
BD102	Outbound registry
BD103	Inbound registry
BD104	maintain tbd53
BD105	Maintain Supported Business Objects
BD11	Get Material
BD12	Send customer

BD13	Get customer
BD14	Send vendor
BD15	Open vendor
BD16	Send Cost Center
BD17	Get Cost Center
BD18	Send General Ledger Account
BD19	Get General Ledger Account
BD20	IDoc passed to application
BD21	Select change pointer
BD22	Delete change pointers
BD23	Delete serialization data
BD24	Send Cost Elements
BD25	Send Activity Type
BD26	Get Activity Type
BD27	Send cost center activity prices
BD28	Send obj/cost element control data
BD30	Distribute material object list
BD31	Distribute document object list
BD32	Distribute plant allocations(matBOM)
BD33	Distribute material variants (ALE)
BD34	Distribute order BOM
BD35	Send Business Process Groups
BD36	Send Business Processes
BD37	Send Business Process Price
BD40	Read change pointer for group
BD41	Dispatch IDocs for group
BD42	Check IDocs for group
BD43	Post IDocs for group
BD44	Assign Message Types to Serlz. Group
BD47	Dependencies between methods
BD48	Dependency method - message
BD50	Activate Change Ptrs for Mess. Type
BD51	Maintain function modules (inbound)
BD52	Activ.change pointer per chng.doc.it
BD53	Reduction of Message Types
BD54	Maintaining Logical Systems
BD55	Maintain IDoc Conversion
BD55OLD	Maintain IDoc Conversion
BD56	Maintain IDoc Segment Filters
BD57	Maintain link and serialization ty.
BD58	Convert organizational units
BD59	Allocation object type -> IDoc type
BD60	Additional data for message type
BD61	Activate Change Pointers - Generally
BD62	Define Segment Conversion Rule
BD62OLD	Define Segment Conversion Rule
BD63	Transport ALE Tables of Message Type
BD64	Maintenance of Distribution Model
BD65	Maintain IDoc type required fields
BD66	IDoc type field -> change doc.field
BD67	Maintain methods (inbound)
BD68	Maintain Lists
BD68OLD	Maintain Lists
BD69	Assignment of Message Type to IDoc

SAP Transaction Codes – Volume One

BD70	Synchronize Number Ranges
BD71	Define FM for dependent bus. object
BD72	Activate Events
BD73	Reposting of IDocs (ALE)
BD75	Convert IDoc Status
BD77	Distribution of control data
BD78	Monitoring control data distribution
BD79	Maintain IDoc Conversion Rules
BD79OLD	Maintain IDoc Conversion Rules
BD81	Filter objects parameter filtering
BD82	Generate Partner Profiles
BD83	Send IDocs after an ALE error
BD84	Post IDocs after ALE error
BD85	Consistency check for transfer
BD86	Consistency check for sales
BD87	Status Monitor for ALE Messages
BD89	Control data model. - initial screen
BD91	Send Characteristic
BD92	Send Class
BD93	Send Classification
BD95	Specify ALE object types
BD96	filter objects of receiver determin.
BD97	Assign RFC dest. to Logical Systems
BD98	Consistency Check Workflow Connectn.
BD99	Message type dependencies
BDA1	Call RSARFCEX
BDA4	Specify ALE object types
BDA5	Distribute documents
BDBG	Create ALE Interface for BAPI
BDBP	Hierarchy maintenance of BAPI param.
BDBR	Register BAPI for Data Transfer
BDBS	Generate coding for mapping
BDC5	Consistency of Customizing Data
BDCCC	Check Center: ALE Basis Cust. Data
BDCCV	Maintain Items
BDCONTACTS	Comments created in Biller Direct
BDCP	Number Range Maintenance: ALE_CP
BDCPMIG	Migrate Change Pointers
BDCUPDATE	Test Update in Batch Input
BDD5	Application Consistency Check
BDFDF	Request Fund
BDFDS	Send fund
BDFG	ALE Interfaces from Function Module
BDLR	Registration of transfer program
BDLS	Convert Logical System Names
BDLSC	Objects for Special Treatment
BDLSM	Definition of Conversion Matrix
BDLSS	Conversion of Logical System Names
BDLST	Start Conversion Process
BDM2	Monitoring: IDocs in Receiving Sys.
BDM5	Technical Consistency Check
BDM6	Monitor: Check input workflow
BDM7	ALE Audit: statistical analyses
BDM8	ALE Audit: Sending the confirmations

BDM9	Reorganizing the audit database
BDMC	Upload info structures
BDMO	ALE CCMS Group Administration
BDMONIC	ALE CCMS Monitoring Objects (Detail)
BDMONIC2	ALE CCMS Monitor Objects (General)
BDMONIC3	ALE CCMS Monitor Branch
BDR1	Display application log for recovery
BDR2	Reorganization of recovery data
BDRC	ALE: Determine Recovery Objects
BDRL	ALE: Process recovery objects
BDTP	Business Process- Maintain Templates
BDT_COMPARE	Compare Control Table Entries
BDT_DC_BUPA	BDT-DC for BUPA
BDWE02	Call we02
BDWE02_2	Empty Input Field in SE38
BDXA	Distribution of Distribution Groups
BDXD	Import of ALE Requests
BDXE	Generation of ALE Requests
BDXI	Model Display (Specific)
BDXJ	Maintenance of Distribution Groups
BDXK	Convert CONDAT Objects in Dist.Group
BDXL	Forward ALE Requests
BDXM	Analysis of Log Table
BDXN	Analyze Inbound Log Table
BDXQ	IMG Display of Distribution Groups
BD_GEN_GRCP	General Recipe Distribution
BD_GEN_SRCP	Replicate Site Recipe
BERE	Business Event Repository
BERP	Business Processes
BERPC	Business Processes
BF01	P&S BTEs
BF02	Bus. Events: Assignment of app.comp.
BF03	Business Event Repository: Overview
BF05	Process BTEs
BF06	Processes: Allocation of appl.comp.
BF07	Process Interfaces: Overview
BF11	BTE Evaluation Criteria
BF12	Partners
BF21	SAP Application Products
BF22	Business Framework: Partner Products
BF23	Activate Partner Products
BF24	Customer Products
BF31	Application modules per Event
BF32	Partner Modules per Event
BF34	Customer Modules per Event
BF41	Application Modules per Process
BF42	Partner Modules per Process
BF44	Customer Modules per Process
BFST	Attibutes for Selection of Events
BG00	Number Range Maintenance: BGMK_NR
BGM1	Create Master Warranty
BGM2	Change Master Warranty
BGM3	Display Master Warranty
BGM6	Warranty Entry for Technical Object

BGMN	Warranty Processing
BH05	Maiantain personnel area
BIBS	Examples of User Interface Design
BIC	Transfer Bank Data from BIC Database
BICBH03	Display Batch History
BKDR	Maintain transfer rules
BKDS	Sender Structure Maintenance
BKK_ACCNT_REACTN	Account Reactivation
BKK_CLOS_REL01	Release tool cust for Accnt closure
BKK_CLS_PRENOTIF	Account Closure Prenotification
BKK_CORR_LOG	Application log: mature report
BKK_COR_REQ_PRINT	Correspondence Print Start
BKK_FWDORD_REL01	Customize release tool Forward Ord
BKK_MASS_ACCNT_CLS	Mass Account Closure
BKK_PAYITEM_REL01	Customize release tool Payment Item
BKK_PAYMORD_REL01	Customize release tool Payment Ord
BKK_PLANITEM_REL01	Customize release tool Planned Item
BKK_PPO_CHANGE	Edit Postprocessing Order
BKK_PPO_DISPLAY	Edit Postprocessing Order
BKK_SINGLE_ACCNT_CLS	Single Account Closure
BKK_STORD_REL01	Customize release tool Standing Ord
BKK_STORD_VAR_REL01	Customize release tool Variable SO
BLOG	Overview of BRE Run
BM00	Batch Management
BMA1	Maintain Prop./Prod. Units
BMA2	Percentage proportion calculation
BMA3	Prop./prod. quant. from base quant.
BMA4	Base quant. from prop./prod. quant.
BMAA	Batch Archiving Runs
BMBC	Batch Information Cockpit
BMC1	Create Class (Class Type 'BATCH')
BMC2	Change Class (Class type 'BATCH')
BMC3	Display Class (Class Type 'BATCH')
BMCC	Integrity Check for Batch Classif.
BMCHCL	Batch Class Conversion
BMOBPRO	Original Batches in Production
BMOBPUR	Original Batches in Procurement
BMSM	Update the standard features
BMUW	Assign Worklist Folder
BMUWT	Maintain Worklist Cat. f. Batches
BMV0	Manage Data Transfers
BMVN	Number Range Maintenance: DI_JOBID
BNK_APP	Approve Payments
BNK_BATCH	Create Batches
BNK_BNK_COM_REL01	Assign Release Object to Release Pro
BNK_BNK_INI_REL01	Payment approval-First step
BNK_INCMNG_MSG_MONI	Incoming status message monitor
BNK_LG_SGN	Digital Signature Logs for Approval
BNK_MERGE_RESET	Reset a Payment Media Batch run
BNK_MONI	Batch and payment monitor
BNK_MONIA	Batch Approver list
BNK_MONIP	Payment status (batching)
BNK_MSG_TYPE	Define default rule currency
BNK_PAYMED_OPT	Define paymedium creation options

BNK_POWL_APPR_LST	Bank payment approver list
BNK_POWL_BUPA	Bank payment business partner
BNK_POWL_BUPA_FK03	Business partner
BNK_POWL_CLRD_ITEMS	Bank payment cleared items
BNK_POWL_FILE	Bank payment batch file
BNK_POWL_MSG	Bank payment incoming message
BNK_POWL_REL_HIST	Bank payment release history
BNK_POWL_STAT_HIST	Bank payment status history
BNK_POWL_WF_ATTMT	Bank payment workflow attatchments
BNK_RULE_CURR	Global data
BNK_RUL_CUST	Rule customizing
BNK_SET_HMAC_KEY	Set HMAC Key
BNK_SIGN_CONFIRM	Confirm signature user
BNK_SIGN_MAINTAIN	Maintain signature user
BNK_STATUS_DISP	Status Dispaly
BNK_STAT_MSG	Incoming status message
BNR	Number Range Maintenance: ISU_DBRE
BORC1	Maintenance of User Groups
BORGR	GR Automotive
BORGR_B	GR Automotive: Posting
BORGR_C	GR Automotive: Clearing
BORGR_V	GR Automotive: Preliminary Entry
BOS02	SD: Service Entry - Web Transaction
BOS02_WAP	Service Entry Sheet: WAP Transaction
BOSECP	Costing: Costs -> Conditions
BOSMM	Subcontractor/Vendor Processing
BOSPR	Create Subcontractor Pur. Req.
BOSPS01	BOS: Project Cost Transfer Program
BOSPS02	BOSPS Batch Processing
BOSPS_REV1	BOS/Project- Plan/Actual Revenue
BOSSC	Subcontracting COND-copying control
BOSSH	Procedure for Surcharge and Discount
BP	Maintain Business Partner
BP0	Business Partner, Initial Screen
BPACC	Line derivation budgeting documents
BPACCR	Acc Derivation Budget Entry Document
BPAR_ARCH	Business Partner: Conversion to CBP
BPAR_ARCHW	Fin. transaction: Create archive
BPAR_ARCH_W	Business Partner: Create Archive
BPB1	Evaluation of Business Partner/Roles
BPB2	Evaluation of Business Parter Data
BPB4	Evaluation of Partner Relationships
BPC1	Create Business Partner
BPC2	Change Business Partner
BPC3	Display Business Partner
BPC4	Create Bus. Partner Using Reference
BPC5	Change Business Partner - Copy
BPCA	Partner:Change Documents - Addresses
BPCD	Business Partner: Change Documents
BPCF	TRGP: Change Documents
BPCG	TRGP: Change Documents Addresses
BPCONTACTCHECK	BP<->Customer Cont check transaction
BPCUSTCHECK	BP<->Customer check transaction
BPH	Business Partner Group Hierarchy

BPH_TYPE	Maintain Hierarchy Categories
BPMD	Master Data Tab
BPMDCS	Master Data Tab
BPMDFI	Customer Company Code Master Data
BPMDGD	Master Data Tab
BPMDSD	Customer Company Code Master Data
BPOMEAS	BPO Application Measurement
BPS0	Business Planning
BPSHOW00	Analysis report: Bdgting/Overall pl.
BPS_DOWN	Load Model Files to PC
BPS_EXCEL	Excel Interface Builder
BPS_INFO	Hidden
BPS_RM	Reminder Report STS
BPS_STAT0	BPS Single Record Statistics
BPS_STAT1	BPS Single Record Status Evaluation
BPS_STS_START	Start STS Execution
BPS_TC	Maintain Status and Tracking System
BPS_TRACE	Trace for API in SEM-BPS
BPS_TRANS	Transport Planning Customizing
BPS_WB	Web Interface Builder
BPS_WEBSTART	Start Web Interfaces
BPS_WIF0	Start Web Interface
BPVENDCHECK	BP<->Vendor check transaction
BP_FMCA_CUSTOMER	Maintain Contract Partner/Customer
BP_FMCA_VENDOR	Maintain Contract Partner/Vendor
BP_LOCA	Example: Business Partner Locator
BP_SETS_1	Create Budget Period Group
BP_SETS_2	Change Budget Period Group
BP_SETS_3	Display Budget Period Group
BRECLEAR	BRE: Reorganisation or Deletion
BREE	BRE Execution
BRF	Business Rule Framework - Workbench
BRFACS01	BRF: Create Abstract Action
BRFACS02	BRF: Change Abstract Action
BRFACS03	BRF: Display Abstract Action
BRFACT01	BRF: Create Concrete Actions
BRFACT02	BRF: Change Concrete Actions
BRFACT03	BRF: Display Concrete Actions
BRFAPC01	BRF: Create Features for Appl.Class
BRFAPC02	BRF: Change Features for Appl. Class
BRFAPC03	BRF: Display Features for Appl.Class
BRFAPL01	BRF: Create Application Class
BRFAPL02	BRF: Change Application Class
BRFAPL03	BRF: Display Application Class
BRFCTX01	BRF: Create Context
BRFCTX02	BRF: Change Context
BRFCTX03	BRF: Display Context
BRFEVT01	BRF: Create Event
BRFEVT02	BRF: Change Event
BRFEVT03	BRF: Display Event
BRFEXP01	BRF: Create Expression
BRFEXP02	BRF: Change Expression
BRFEXP03	BRF: Display Expression
BRFIMC01	BRF: Create Impl. Class

BRFIMC02	BRF: Change Impl. Class
BRFIMC03	BRF: Display Impl. Class
BRFRLS01	BRF: Create Rule Set
BRFRLS02	BRF: Change Rule Set
BRFRLS03	BRF: Display Rule Set
BRFRUL01	BRF: Create Rule for Event
BRFRUL02	BRF: Change Rule for Event
BRFRUL03	BRF: Display Rule for Event
BRFU01	BRF: Compare SAPscript Texts
BRF_FILL_TBRF185	Automatic Population of TBRF185
BRF_OVERVIEW	Overview of BRF Objects
BRPL1	Accounts Receivable Ledger (Norway)
BRP_ICON_UPLOAD	Load SAP-ICONS into BDS
BS02	Maintain status profiles
BS03	Display status profiles
BS12	Maintain object types
BS13	Display object types
BS22	Maintain system status
BS23	Display system status
BS32	Maintain processes
BS33	Display processes
BS42	Maintain Status Selection Profiles
BS43	Display status selection
BS52	Maintain authorization key
BS53	Display authoriztaion key
BSMO	Object type control in Mass Change
BSMV	Transaction control in Mass Change
BSP_DLC_SDESIGN	SAP Design Objects
BSP_DLC_SDESIGN_DISP	Copy SAP Design Objects
BSP_DLC_SDESIGN_DL	SAP Design Obj. (per Obj. Type)
BSP_DLC_SDESIGN_GEN	SAP Ref. Design Objects
BSP_DLC_SDESIGN_GENL	SAP Ref. Design Obj.(Obj. Type)
BSP_DLC_SDESIGN_GENS	SAP Generic UI Object Types
BSP_DLC_SDESIGN_KM	Design Object maint. (for SAP KM)
BSP_DLC_SDESIG_DL	SAP Design Obj. (per Obj. Type,mass)
BSP_DLC_SDESIG_GENL	SAP Ref. Design Obj.(Obj. Type,mass)
BSP_WD_CMPWB	BSP WD Component Workbench
BSP_WD_CMPWB_NEW	BSP WD Component Workbench
BSP_WD_CMPWB_OLD	BSP WD Component Workbench
BSP_WD_WORKBENCH	IC WebClient Workbench
BSV1	Where-used list for transaction
BSV2	Where-used list for system status
BSV3	Where-used list for object type
BSV4	Status Profile Overview
BSVV	Parameterizable status workflow evnt
BSVW	Linkage Status Update-Workflow Event
BSVX	System Status Events
BSVY	System/User Status Events
BSVZ	System/User Status Events
BTREE	Overview of BRE Programs
BUA1	Create contact person
BUA2	Change contact person
BUA3	Display contact person
BUB1	BuPR: Create BP relationship

BUB2	BuPR: Change BP relationship
BUB3	BuPR: Display BP relationship
BUB4	BuPR: Create BP role definition
BUB5	BuPR: Change BP role definition
BUB6	BuPR: Display BP role definition
BUB9	BuPR: No. range maintenance: BP rel.
BUBA	BuPR: Relationship Categories
BUBASSTRATENVCOPY	Copy Strategy (With Text): Initial
BUBASSTRATENVDELETE	Delete Strategy: Initial
BUBB	BuPR: Role definition category
BUBD	BuPR: Applications
BUBE	BuPR: Views
BUBF	BuPR: Sections
BUBG	BuPR: Screens
BUBH	BuPR: Screen Seq. Variants
BUBI	BuPR: Events
BUBJ	BuPR: GUI Standard Functions
BUBK	BuPR: GUI Additonal Functions
BUBL	BuPR:Assgn Scr.Field->Database Field
BUBL_DI	BP: Allocate DI Field -> DB Field
BUBM	BuPR: Tables
BUBN	BuPR: Field Groups
BUBO	BuPR: Field Grouping (Criteria)
BUBP	BuPR: Field Grping Using Rel. Cat.
BUBQ	BuPR: Field Grp. Using Role Def.Cat.
BUBR	BP: Field Grpg Via Activity (Cust)
BUBS_FRG	BP: Field Grpg for Ext.Applications
BUBT	BP: Role Definition Types
BUBU	BP: Relationship Types
BUBV	BP: Maintenance Without Dialog
BUBW	BP: Generate Test File (DI)
BUBX	BP: Activities
BUBY	BP: Field Grpg via Activity (Ctrl)
BUBZ	BP: External Applications
BUC0	BP Cust: Forms of Address
BUC1	BP Cust: Address Type
BUC2	BP Cust: Groupings
BUC3	BP Cust: Data Origin
BUC4	BP Cust: BP Role->Address Type
BUC5	BP Cust: Academic Titles
BUC6	BP Cust: Aristocratic Title
BUC7	BP Cust: Name Affixes
BUC8	BP Cust: Legal Form of Organization
BUC9	BP Cust: Legal Entity Organization
BUCA	BP Cust: Industry
BUCC	BP Cust: Group Types
BUCD	BP Cust: Business Partner Type
BUCF	BP Cust: Number Ranges
BUCG	BP Cust: BP Role Field Grouping
BUCH	BP Cust: Field Grouping Activity
BUCI	BP-Cust.: Field Grpng.: Partner Type
BUCJ	BP Cust: Authorization Types
BUCK	BP Cust: Marital Status
BUCL	BP Cust: Occupation/Group

BUCM	BP Cust: Legitimation Type
BUCN	BP Cust: Field Grps f. Authorization
BUCO	BP-Cust: Screen Configuration
BUCP	BP-Cust: Fld.modif.exter.application
BUCQ	BP-Cust: Evaluation Tables
BUCS	BP-Cust: Notes on Roles
BUCT	BP-Cust: Define Note Views
BUCU	BP Cust: Where-Used List
BUCV	BP Cust. Field Grouping Appl.Object
BUCW	BP Cust: Trans. f. Address Determin.
BUCX	BP Cust: Assign Trans.->Address Type
BUC_IDCATEGORY	BP Cust: ID Categories
BUC_IDTYPE	BP Cust: ID Types
BUG1	Create Business Partner, General
BUG2	Change Business Partner, General
BUG3	Display Business Partner, General
BUG4	Bus. partner general deletion flag
BUI1	Create Prospect
BUI2	Change Prospect
BUI3	Display Prospect
BUKFBATCH	Key Figures - Batch Processing
BUM1	Create Employee (BP)
BUM2	Change Employee (BP)
BUM3	Display Employee (BP)
BUMR	BP Relationships: Config. Menu
BUN2	Change student (in role grouping)
BUN3	Display student (in role grouping)
BUNA	Number Range Maintenance: BP_PADRNR
BUP0	BDT, Multiple Call (Funct. Grp BUSS)
BUP1	Create Business Partner
BUP2	Change Business Partner
BUP3	Display Business Partner
BUPAARCH	Business Partner Archiving
BUPAARCHBDT	BDT Business Partner Archiving
BUPABWST	Gen. DataSource for BW Status Obj.
BUPADELE	Delete Business Partner
BUPADELEBDT	BDT Delete Business Partner
BUPA_ARCH	Fin. transaction: Create archive
BUPA_BIP_FILE_EXPORT	BIP: Cleansing Export
BUPA_BIP_FILE_IMPORT	BIP: Cleansing - Import
BUPA_BIP_NOHIT_SHOW	BIP: Cleansing: Show imported NoHits
BUPA_CALL_FU	FM Activation for BP Data Exchange
BUPA_CLEAR	SAP BP: Data Cleansing
BUPA_DEL	Deletion without Archiving
BUPA_EVENTS	BP Events
BUPA_IFC_CALL_FU	Determining FMs for Data Exchange:BP
BUPA_PRE_DA	Flag Business Partner for Deletion
BUPA_SEND	Send Partners and Relationshps to XI
BUPA_TAXNUMTYPE	Maintain Relevant Tax No. Categories
BUPMASS	BP Customizing: Mass Changes
BUPT	Business Partner Configuration Menu
BUR0	BuPR: Contact Person Departments
BUR1	BuPR: Contact Person Functions
BUR2	BuBR: Contact Person Authority

SAP Transaction Codes – Volume One

BUR3	BuPR: Contact Person VIP Indicator
BUR4	BP: Marital property regime
BURC_LAYOUT	Custom. Rel.Category -> Log. Group
BUS0	BDT: Application Objects
BUS1	BDT: Applications
BUS10	BDT: Search Help
BUS11	BDT: Assgn BAPI Field to Field Group
BUS2	BDT: Field Groups
BUS23	BP Tax: Data Sets
BUS3	BDT: Views
BUS4	BDT: Sections
BUS5	BDT: Screens
BUS6	BDT: Screen Sequences
BUS7	BDT: Events
BUS8	BDT: GUI Standard Functions
BUS9	BDT: GUI Additional Functions
BUSB	BDT: Assign Screen Field->DB Field
BUSB_DI	BDT: Assign DI Field->DB Field
BUSC	BDT: Field Grouping Criteria
BUSD	BDT: BP Views
BUSE	BDT: BP Role Groupings
BUSF	BDT: Application Transactions
BUSG	BDT: Tables
BUSH	BDT: External applications
BUSI	BDT: Activities
BUSJ	BP Control: FuncMod. Activity (Ctrl)
BUSM	BDT: Differentiation Types
BUSN	BDT: Activity Categories
BUSO	BP Cust: BP Cat. Field Grouping
BUSP	Generate Screen Containers
BUSRO	BP-CUST: Entry Via Search Screen
BUSSA	Transaction Entry Via Search Screen
BUSWU01	BP Control: Where-Used List,Struct.
BUSWU02	BP Control: Where-Used List, Views
BUSWU03	BP Control: Where-UL, Trans->View
BUSWU04	BP Control: Where-UL, Trans->View
BUSWU11	BP Addresses: Where-UsedL, Structure
BUSWU21	BP Bank Details: Where-UL,Structure
BUSWU31	BP PaytCard: Where-UsedL, Structure
BUSWU41	BP Rel.Addr.:Where-UsedL, Structure
BUSWU61	BP Roles: Where-Used List, Structure
BUSWU62	BP Roles: Where-Used List, Views
BUSWU63	BP Roles:Where-Used Lst S.Org ->View
BUSWU64	BP Roles:Where-Used Lst S.Org ->View
BUS_CALL	BDT: Call BDT, Complete LUW
BUS_HDRID	BP Tax: Header IDs
BUT021_INS	Update BUT021 from BUT021_FS
BUTI	Update Without Dialog
BUTJ	Generate Test File (DI)
BV01	BAV Transfer/Securities Init. Screen
BV02	BAV Transfer / Loans Initial Screen
BV03	BAV Trnsfr / Real Estate Init.Screen
BV11	BAV Display / Securities Init.Screen
BV12	BAV Display / Loans Initial Screen

SAP Transaction Codes – Volume One

BV13	BAV Display/ Real Estate Init.Screen
BVW_BC_SFLIGHT	Business View Flight Database
BW01_DISP	GBT: Document Display for Miniapp
BW03MAST	Generate general DataSources
BW03MASTER	Generate summ.table trans. structure
BW07	BW20PI: Gen. SET Hierarchies for BW
BW09	BW20PI: Product Hierarchy for SAP BW
BW10	BW20PI: Log. Gen. Hierarchy for BW
BWCA	SAPoffice: Internet Calendar
BWCCMS	CCMS Monitor for BW
BWFS_AB_DATUM_SET	Date from Which Data is Read
BWFS_INFOSOURCE_DELT	Maintain InfoSources for Delta Pos.
BWFS_INFOSOURCE_INIT	Maintain InfoSources for Pos. Init.
BWFS_INIT_DATE_SET	Date of Position Initialization
BWFS_PROT	BW Extraction Log
BWFS_TIMESTAMPS_DELA	Deletes Time Stamp Per InfoSource
BWMSSPROCS	Transaction for MSS SP Maintenance
BWOM01	BCT-CO: Change Report Row Hierarchy
BWOM02	BCT-CO: Displ/Check Report Row Hier.
BWP0	Date: Maintain Key Figure
BWP1	Date Event
BWP2	Date Origin
BWP3	Duration: Maintain Key Figure
BWP4	Dates: Assgn. of Table to Value Type
BWP5	Duratn: Assg. of Table to Value Type
BWP6	Float: Maintain Key Figure
BWP7	Float: Assg. of Table to Value Type
BWS1	Assign System Status to BW Status
BWS2	Assign User Status to BW Status
BWSP	SAPoffice: WWW
BWST	Gener. DataSource for BW Status Obj.
BWWF_WI_DECI	Execute User Decisions
BWWI_EXECUTE	Executing a work item (WEBgui)
BYPASS	Bypass for All Reservation Systems
C000	Overhead Cost Controlling
C201	Create Master Recipe
C202	Change Master Recipe
C203	Display Master Recipe
C210	Delete Costing Ind. for Operations
C211	Delete "Flexible Duration" Ind. Oper
C223	Maintain Production Versions
C223_D	Display Production Version
C251	Print Master Recipes
C252	Print Production Versions
C260	Recipe Development on Time Basis
C261	Change Document Display Master Rec.
C298	Delete Master Recipes
C299	Archive Master Recipes
C2N2	Number ranges master recipe
CA00	Routing Menu
CA01	Create Routing
CA02	Change Routing
CA03	Display Routing
CA10	Std. Text for Task List/Order

SAP Transaction Codes – Volume One

CA11	Create Reference Operation Set
CA12	Change Reference Operation Set
CA13	Display Reference Operation Set
CA21	Create Rate Routing
CA22	Change Rate Routing
CA23	Display Rate Routing
CA31	Create Reference Rate Routing
CA32	Change Reference Rate Routing
CA33	Display Reference Rate Routing
CA51	Print Rtg/Ref.Op.Set, Fields Fixed
CA60	Changes in Routings/Ref. Op. Sets
CA61	Change Documents for Routing
CA62	Documents for Ref. Op. Sets
CA63	Change documents for rate routings
CA64	Change documents for ref. rate rtgs
CA70	PRT Where-Used Lists
CA72	PRT Where-used Lists: EquipTL Types
CA73	Standard Networks for PRT
CA75	Mass Replace PRT
CA75N	Mass Change:Production Resource/Tool
CA77	Bulk Replacemt PRT: Equip.TL Type
CA78	PRT Mass replacemt. in libr.networks
CA80	Use of Work Center in Task Lists
CA81	Master recipe usage and resources
CA82	Where-used Lists EQUI Work Center
CA83	Standard Networks for Work Center
CA85	Replace Work Center in Task Lists
CA85N	Mass replacement: work center
CA86	Master recipe: replace resources
CA87	Mass Replace EQUI Work Center
CA88	Mass replace wrk. cntr. in lib.netwk
CA90	Use of Ref. Op. Set in Routings
CA95	Replace Ref. Op. Set in Task Lists
CA95N	Mass Change:Ref.OperationSet Ref.
CA96	Update material master
CA97	Mass scheduling using mat. master
CA97N	Material Master Update - New
CA98	Deletion of task lists
CA99	Archiving of task lists
CAA0	Process instr. usage in recipes
CAA1	Create Contract Account
CAA2	Change Contract Account
CAA3	Display Contract Account
CAA5	Mass replace proc.instr. in mst.rcp.
CAAT	Foreign Trade Atrium
CAC0	Master recipe menu
CAC1	Time Sheet: Maintain Profiles
CAC2	Time Sheet: Field Selection
CAC3	Time Sheet: Rejection Reasons
CAC4	CATS: Profile Authorization Groups
CAC5	Define Customer Fields
CAC6	Allowed Print Reports
CAC7	Number Range Maintenance: CATS
CAC8	Number Range Maintenance: CATS_INTRN

CACC	Master recipe: Update settings
CACH	BP Cust: Field Grouping Activity
CACI	BP Cust.: Screen Configuration
CACJ	BP Cust: Field Grouping Activity
CACP	Transfer C tables to routing
CACS	Commission System: Main Menu
CACSACC	Remuneration Inquiry for BusPartner
CACSACC1	Remun.Inquiry BP or Selection Screen
CACSACC1N	Remun.Inquiry BP or Selection Screen
CACSACCN	Remuneration Inquiry for BusPartner
CACSAPPLWIZARD	Application Wizard
CACSAPPLWIZARDX	Application Wizard
CACSB001	Display Pending Cases
CACSB002	Edit Pending Cases
CACSBDT	BDT: Task Level Menu
CACSBDTI	BDT: Task Level Menu
CACSCA1	Additional Commission Case
CACSCA1_LOG	Log: Additional Commission Case
CACSCA2	Addit.Commission Case - Resetting
CACSCA2_LOG	Log: Reset Additional Comm.Case
CACSCG_01	Poss. Constellation and Def.
CACSCG_02	Poss. Roles of Comn Recip. in CommTA
CACSCG_CONS	Poss. Constellation and Def.
CACSCG_ROLE	Poss. Roles of Comn Recip. in Trans
CACSCOND0001	V_T681F for A V
CACSCOND0002	Condition Table: Create (Price Comn)
CACSCOND0003	Condition Table: Change (Price Comn)
CACSCOND0004	Condition Table:Display (Price Comn)
CACSCOND0005	Condition Types: Remuneration
CACSCOND0006	Access: Edit (Remuneration)
CACSCOND0007	Procedure Maintenance: Remuneration
CACSCOND0011	Commissions: V_T681F for A V
CACSCOND0012	Condition Table: Create (Valuation)
CACSCOND0013	Condition Table: Change (Valuation)
CACSCOND0014	Condition Table: Display (Valuation)
CACSCOND0015	Condition Types: Valuation
CACSCOND0016	Access: Edit (Valuation)
CACSCOND0017	Comn: Schedule Maintenance Valuation
CACSCOND0021	V_T681F for A PC
CACSCOND0022	Condition Table: Create (Price Comn)
CACSCOND0023	Condition Table: Change (Price Comn)
CACSCOND0024	CondTable: Display (Price Liability)
CACSCOND0025	Condition Types - Liability
CACSCOND0026	Access: Edit (Liability)
CACSCOND0027	Edit Procedure (Liability)
CACSCOND0028	Short text
CACSCOND007C	Procedure for A P
CACSCONDAUTH	Comn: Quantifying Authorization
CACSCONDBTCI_MAP	Create Conditions BDC Session
CACSCONDBTCI_OUT	Create Conditions Seq. File Out
CACSCONDLA	Create Pricing Report
CACSCONDLB	Change Pricing Report
CACSCONDLC	Display Pricing Report
CACSCONDMAINT	Edit Conditions (Remuneration)

CACSCONDMAINT01	Condition Maintenance
CACSCONDMAINTB	Edit Conditions (Valuation)
CACSCONDMAINTC	Condition Maintenance (Liability)
CACSCONDTIME	Edit Conditions (Remuneration)
CACSCRDRECHECK	Credentials Check
CACSCS1	Correspondence Print
CACSCS1_LOG	Log: Correspondence Print
CACSCTRTACC	Contract Account Display
CACSCTRTREP	Contract Account Display
CACSDBS_DEL	Delete Database Statistics
CACSDBS_DET	Generate Database Statistics
CACSDBS_DSP	Display Database Statistics
CACSDESIGN	Construction Tool (NEW)
CACSDOCRE	Doc. Display for Remun. & Liability
CACSDOCSE	Document Display for Due Dates
CACSDOCVA	Document Display for Valuation
CACSFA_DET_ACRFA	AccntAssgnmt Types Remun. FI-CA
CACSFFLTGC	Garb.Collector; Old Primary Entries
CACSFFLTPN	Primary Entry Run for Fulf.Lvls
CACSFIREP	Contract Account Display
CACSFPPCS1	Correspondence Print
CACSFPPFR1	Parallel Processing for Flat Rates
CACSFPPGU1	Parallel Processing for Guarantees
CACSFPPRO1	Parallel Processing of Retention
CACSFPPSE1	Parallel Processing of Settlement
CACSFPP_UI_START_2	Correspondence Printing
CACSFR1	Calculate Flat Rate
CACSFR1_LOG	Log: Calculate Flat Rate
CACSFR2	Reset Flat Rate
CACSFR2_LOG	Log: Reset Flat Rate
CACSGENERATOR	CACS Generator
CACSGU1	Calculate Guarantee
CACSGU1_LOG	Log: Calculate Guarantee
CACSGU2	Resetting of Guarantees
CACSGU2_LOG	Log: Reset Guarantee
CACSIB002	Object Log Table (cacsmenue)
CACSIMG	IMG Commission Systems
CACSIMGFIND	IMG Activity of Determination Proc.
CACSIMGNUM	IMG Activity Number Ranges
CACSIMGOPT	IMG Commission Systems
CACSIMGVAL	IMG Activity Complex Valuation
CACSIMGVALPROSTAT	IMG Activity Commission Case Status
CACSIMGX	ICM S-Table Maintenance
CACSLOCCOPY	Compare Copies with Originals
CACSLOG	Message Display
CACSLOGDIS	Display Application Logs
CACSLOGDIS_GEN	Navigate to Direct Log
CACSMD001	Create Commission Contract Partner
CACSMD002	Change Commission Contract Partner
CACSMD003	Display Commission Contract Partner
CACSMD101	Create Commission Contract
CACSMD102	Change Commission Contract
CACSMD103	Display Commission Contract
CACSMD201	Create Standard Contract

CACSMD202	Change Standard Contract
CACSMD203	Display Standard Contract
CACSMD301	Create Commission Clerk
CACSMD302	Change Commission Clerk
CACSMD303	Display Commission Clerk
CACSMD401	Create Contract Bundle
CACSMD402	Change Contract Bundle
CACSMD403	Display Contract Bundle
CACSMD500	Create Commission Case
CACSMD501	Create Commission Case
CACSMD502	Change Commission Case
CACSMD503	Display Commission Case
CACSMD504	Reset Commission Case
CACSMD505	Reactivate Commission Case
CACSMD510	Create Document
CACSMD511	Create Document
CACSMD512	Change Document
CACSMD513	Display Document
CACSMD514	Cancel Document
CACSMD531	Create Commission Case
CACSMD533	Display Commission Case
CACSMD601	Create Agent
CACSMD602	Change Agent
CACSMD603	Display Agent
CACSMD6101	Create Commission Contract
CACSMD6102	Change Commission Contract
CACSMD6103	Display Commission Contract
CACSMD6401	Create Contract Bundle
CACSMD6402	Change Contract Bundle
CACSMD6403	Display Contract Bundle
CACSMD6510	Create Document
CACSMD6513	Display Document
CACSMD6514	Cancel Document
CACSMD701	Create Contract Assignment
CACSMD702	Maintain Contract Assignment
CACSMD703	Display Contract Assignment
CACSMD800	Maintain Segment
CACSMIGTIME	Migration: Individual Agreements
CACSMWB	Commission Desktop
CACSNEWAPPL	Create New Application
CACSNO1	Forward Run: Commission Notification
CACSNO2	Resetting Commission Notification
CACSNSC1	Analysis of Locked Tables
CACSNSC2	Preparation of Namespace Conversion
CACSOBJTYPES	Define Object Types
CACSPACK	Select CACS Packages From Applicatn
CACSPACK_ALV	Select CACS Packages From Applicatn
CACSPY10	Close Flate Rates and Guarantees
CACSPY11	Settlement
CACSPY12	Display Settlement Run Overview
CACSPY13	Lift Payment Locks
CACSPY14	Reversal Closing
CACSPY15	Reset Settlement
CACSPY20	Settlement Schedule Run

CACSPY21	Reset Settlement Schedule Run
CACSPY22	OBSOLETE!Delete Settlement Schedules
CACSRCPCASE	RCP: Call Commission Case Admin.
CACSRCPFRAME	RCP: Call Commission Case Admin.
CACSRCPWORKLIST	RCP: Call Worklist Administration
CACSRECHAPPLCP	Comn: Drilldown Application Copier
CACSREMDIS	Remuneration Inquiry
CACSRO1	Offset Retention
CACSRO1_LOG	Log: Offset Retention
CACSRO2	Reset Retention
CACSRO2_LOG	Log: Reset Retention
CACSRO3	Edit Retention
CACSRO3_LOG	Log: Edit Retention
CACSRO4	Display Retention
CACSSCALTIME	Personalize Scales
CACSSE1	Settlement
CACSSE1_LOG	Log: Settlement
CACSSE2	Resetting of Settlement
CACSSE2_LOG	Log: Reset Settlement
CACSSE54	Test to Transfer se11 Parameters
CACSSEDIS	Settlement Inquiry
CACSSESDIS	Settlement Schedule Display
CACSSUMRE	Totals Display for Remun. & Liab.
CACSSUMSE	Totals Display for Due Dates
CACSSUMVA	Object Totals Display for Valuation
CACSTGKW01	Maintain Values - Complex Tgt Type
CACSTGKW02	Display Values - Complex Tgt Type
CACSTGKW03	Simulate Values - Complex Tgt Type
CACSTGKW04	Maintain Correction Values
CACSTGKW05	Display Correction Values
CACSTGKW06	Maintain Values -Elementary Tgt Type
CACSTGKW07	Display Values - Elementary Tgt Type
CACSTR10	Close Additional Commission Case
CACSTR11	Reverse Additional Commission Case
CACSTRU	Target Agreements: Edit Target Rules
CACSUSER	Individual settings
CACS_0	Execute Report
CACS_1	Create Report
CACS_2	Change Report
CACS_3	Display Report
CACS_4	Create Form
CACS_5	Change Form
CACS_6	Display Form
CACS_7	Maintain Authorization Obj. Present.
CACS_8	Display Authorization Obj.Presentatn
CACS_A	Access Report Tree
CACS_ADJ_HR_PARTNER	Compare BP with HR Staff
CACS_APPL_01	Call VC_TCACS_ROLE
CACS_APPL_02	Call V_ACTGRP_ACT
CACS_APPL_03	Call VC_TCACS_OFFS
CACS_APPL_04	Call VC_TCACS_CDINTF
CACS_APPL_05	Call VC_TCACS_ACCAS
CACS_APPL_06	Call VC_TCACS_RESP
CACS_APPL_07	Call VC_TCACS_INPLAN

CACS_APPL_08	Call VC_CTRTST_STI
CACS_APPL_09	Call V_CTRT_PROL
CACS_APPL_10	Call V_TCACS_ROLCON
CACS_APPL_11	Call V_TCACS_STDREP
CACS_APPL_114	Call VC_TCACS_SE_TYPE
CACS_APPL_12	Call V_v_TCACS_CTRTP
CACS_APPL_13	Call V_TCACS_CTRTP1
CACS_APPL_14	Call VC_TCACS_STMTY
CACS_APPL_15	Call V_AGR_STCACT
CACS_APPL_16	Call V_AGR_VAL_SGN
CACS_APPL_17	Call VC_CACS_STCAGR
CACS_APPL_18	Call V_MAX_RULE_GRP
CACS_APPL_19	Call V_TCACS_ITITLE
CACS_APPL_20	Call V_TCACS_CTRCH
CACS_APPL_21	Call V_TCACS_BUSOBJ
CACS_APPL_22	Call V_TCACS_BUSCAS
CACS_APPL_23	Call V_TCACS_BUSINESS
CACS_APPL_24	Call V_TCACS_EDT
CACS_APPL_25	Call V_TCACS_EDT
CACS_APPL_26	Call V_TCACSFA
CACS_APPL_27	Call V_TCACSFD
CACS_APPL_28	Call V_APRP3_VAL
CACS_APPL_29	Call V_SPV_SGVR_AV
CACS_APPL_30	Call V_AGR_ROLSTC
CACS_APPL_31	Call V_STSGRSTSTMRU
CACS_APPL_31_SL	call V_STAGRSETTLCK
CACS_APPL_32	Call V_TCACSF
CACS_APPL_33	Call V_TCACS_CASRAN
CACS_APPL_34	Call V_TCACS_OBJRAN
CACS_APPL_35	Call VC_TCACS_ORG
CACS_APPL_36	Call V_TCACS_DOCRAN
CACS_APPL_37	Call V_TCACS_PAYSER
CACS_APPL_38	Call V_TCACS_TRISYS
CACS_APPL_39	Call V_TCACS_REMCLA
CACS_APPL_40	Call V_COMB_CASSGN
CACS_APPL_41	Call V_REM_FORM_TYPE_01
CACS_APPL_42	Call v_REM_FORM_TYPE_02
CACS_APPL_43	Call V_REM_FORM_TYPE_03
CACS_APPL_44	Call Up V_TCACS_ASSGN1
CACS_APPL_45	Call V_TCACS_APRP3
CACS_APPL_46	Call V_TCACS_STMCOM
CACS_APPL_47	Call V_TCACS_NRRCT
CACS_APPL_48	Call V_TCACS_CVGRP
CACS_APPL_49	Call V_TCACS_CVHDL
CACS_APPL_50	Call V_TCACS_CVOGRP
CACS_APPL_51	Call V_TCACS_AVAD1
CACS_APPL_53	Call V_TCACS_AUT04
CACS_APPL_54	Assign Authorization Groups
CACS_APPL_55	Call Up V_TCACS_FITYP
CACS_APPL_56	Call VC_CACS_STCAGR3
CACS_APPL_57	Call V_TISIS_CNT_TYPE
CACS_APPL_58	Call V_TISIS_APPL
CACS_APPL_59	Maintain Period Rules
CACS_APPL_60	Call VC_BUSCLIAM

CACS_APPL_61	Call VC_TCACS_INVREL
CACS_APPL_62	Call VC_TOOL_SERV_MET
CACS_APPL_63	Call VC_RULE_RULING
CACS_APPL_64	Call V_TCACS_AUT08A
CACS_APPL_65	Call V_TCACS_AUT08B
CACS_APPL_66	Call V_TCACS_AUT08C
CACS_APPL_67	Call VC_TCACS_UPD
CACS_APPL_68	Call VC_TCACS_RESULT
CACS_APPL_69	Call V_TCACS_PROCSU
CACS_APPL_70	Call VC_GLOBAL_RULING
CACS_APPL_71	Call VC_SEL_METH
CACS_APPL_72	Call VC_OFFGRPRULE
CACS_APPL_73	AuCall VC_CLC_METH
CACS_APPL_74	Call VC_SERVICE
CACS_APPL_75	Call VC_TOOLS
CACS_APPL_76	Call V_TCACS_KOART
CACS_APPL_77	Call V_TCACS_AC
CACS_APPL_78	Call V_TCACS_ADD
CACS_APPL_79	Call V_TCACS_SENDTYPE
CACS_APPL_80	Call V_TCACS_DISWAY
CACS_APPL_81	Call Up V_TCACS_CSD001
CACS_APPL_82	Call VC_TCACS_STCAGR
CACS_APPL_83	Call VC_TCACS_TRCAS
CACS_APPL_85	Call Up V_TCACS_CATT11
CACS_APPL_86	Call Up VC_TCACS_MAP_VA
CACS_APPL_87	Call Up VC_TCACS_MAP_re
CACS_APPL_88	Call Up VC_TCACS_MAP_LI
CACS_APPL_89	Call Up VC_TCACS_FILTER2
CACS_APPL_90	Call VC_TCACS_REMNAL
CACS_APPL_91	Call V_TCACS_bdltp
CACS_APPL_92	Call V_TCACS_BDRCH
CACS_APPL_93	Call V_TCACS_CVGRB
CACS_APPL_94	Call V_TCACS_cvgrb
CACS_APPL_95	Call V_TCACS_CVOGRB
CACS_APPL_96	Call V_TCACS_FLDCHG
CACS_APPL_97	Call V_TCACS_OTHPOS
CACS_APPL_98	Call Up VC_TCACS_ACTFILT
CACS_APPL_99	Call Up VC_TCACS_REMFILT
CACS_APPL_AA	Call V_TCACS_BDLSET
CACS_APPL_AB	Call VC_TCACS_ARCHIV
CACS_APPL_AC	Call VC_TCACS_ARCHIV_D
CACS_APPL_AD	Call V_TCACS_OTHPOB
CACS_APPL_AE	Call V_TCACS_FLDCHB
CACS_APPL_AF	Call VC_TCACS_VAL_LOS
CACS_APPL_AG	Maintain Waiting Periods
CACS_APPL_AH	Maintain Exit for Date Check
CACS_APPL_AI	Maintain Archiving Indicators
CACS_APPL_AJ	Call V_TCACS_CONVG_OK
CACS_APPL_AK	Call V_TCACS_OBJMETH
CACS_APPL_AL	Call VC_TCACS_OBJMETH
CACS_APPL_AM	Call V_TCACS_DELPB
CACS_APPL_AN	Call V_TCACS_DELPV
CACS_APPL_AO	Call V_TCACS_INDDIC
CACS_APPL_AP	Call VC_TCACS_REM_LOS

CACS_APPL_AQ	Call VC_TCACS_INPLAN_LOS
CACS_APPL_AR	Call VC_TCACS_RESP_LOS
CACS_APPL_AS	Call V_TCACS_CONVEXIT
CACS_APPL_AT	Call V_TCACS_NRRBD
CACS_APPL_AU	Call VC_TCACS_SEL_LOS
CACS_APPL_AV	Call VC_TCACS_CLC_LOS
CACS_APPL_AW	Call VC_TCACS_OBJ_LOS
CACS_APPL_AX	Call VC_TCACS_OBT_LOS
CACS_APPL_AY	Call VC_TCACS_CATT
CACS_APPL_AZ	Call VC_TCACS_STM_Los
CACS_APPL_BA	Call V_TCACS_MSG
CACS_APPL_BB	Call VC_TCACS_DOCPOST
CACS_APPL_BC	Call Up VC_TCACS_ASSGN2
CACS_APPL_BD	Lock Agent for Settlement
CACS_APPL_BE	Call Up VC_TCACS_SEGTYP
CACS_APPL_BF	Call Up VC_TCACS_ASGRL
CACS_APPL_BH	Call up V_TCACS_UPD_MO
CACS_APPL_BI	Call Up VC_TCACS_segtyp
CACS_APPL_BJ	Call Up V_TCACS_asgrl
CACS_APPL_BK	Call up V_TCACS_TMPL_Ex
CACS_APPL_BL	Call up V_TCACS_TMPL_Eb
CACS_APPL_BM	Call Up VC_TCACS_OBT_SEG
CACS_APPL_BN	Call VV_TCACS_070F
CACS_APPL_BO	Call V_TCACS_BUSOBJ1
CACS_APPL_BP	Process Release Types
CACS_APPL_BP_27	Process Release Types
CACS_APPL_BQ	Process Payment Release Rule
CACS_APPL_BR	Process Std Agrmnt for Pymnt Release
CACS_APPL_BS	Call View Cluster VC_CACS_STSESRU
CACS_APPL_BT	Call View Cluster VC_TCACS_SES_LOS
CACS_APPL_BU	Call View Cluster VC_TCACS_SESRU
CACS_APPL_BV	Call View V_TCACS_Proccom
CACS_APPL_BW	Call View Cluster VC_CACS_stcagr_25
CACS_APPL_BX	Call View Cluster VC_TCACS_PRAGRRU
CACS_APPL_BY	Call View V_TCACS_RGRPAD
CACS_APPL_BZ	Call VC_TCACS_PARCON
CACS_APPL_CA	Call VC_TCACS_MAP_32
CACS_APPL_CB	Call VC_TCACS_PCMET
CACS_APPL_CC	FOA: Generate User Interface
CACS_APPL_CD	FOA: Generate Process Workflow
CACS_APPL_CE	Call VC_TCACS_PS_DS
CACS_APPL_CF	Call VC_TCACS_PS_SPL
CACS_APPL_CG	Call VC_TCACS_PS_CUS1
CACS_APPL_CH	Call VC_TCACS_OARUA
CACS_APPL_CI	Call VC_TCACS_ELTRU
CACS_APPL_CJ	Call VC_TCACS_ELTREM
CACS_APPL_CK	Call V_TCACS_LVRS
CACS_APPL_CL	Call VC_TCACS_RGOA
CACS_APPL_CM	Call VC_TCACS_PROA
CACS_APPL_CN	Call V_tcacs_ps_splm
CACS_APPL_CO	Call V_TCACS_WFMG
CACS_APPL_CP	Call V_TCACS_WFAGD
CACS_APPL_CQ	Call V_TCACS_WFMGCM
CACS_APPL_CR	Call V_TCACS_WFMGCS

SAP Transaction Codes – Volume One

CACS_APPL_CS	Field Transports for Copy Service
CACS_APPL_CT	Display and Maintain Period Rules
CACS_APPL_CU	Display and Maintain Process Types
CACS_APPL_CV	Display and Maintain Period Rules
CACS_APPL_CW	Display and Maintain Period Rules
CACS_APPL_CX	Display and Maintain Period Rules
CACS_APPL_CY	Display and Maintain Process Types
CACS_APPL_D1	Agreement Types for Each Application
CACS_APPL_D2	Agreemnt Types for Each Contr.Type
CACS_APPL_D3	Std Contract for Each Application
CACS_APPL_D4	Structure of Transportable Object
CACS_APPL_D5	Implementing Classes By Context
CACS_APPL_D6	Implementing Classes By Context
CACS_APPL_D7	Implementing Classes By Context
CACS_APPL_D8	Event for Each Agreement Type
CACS_APPL_D9	Call V_TCACS_LOS_FUTI
CACS_APPL_F2	Maintain valuation formula
CACS_APPL_FHDINT	Call V_TCACS_SESRAN
CACS_APPL_FITINT	Call V_TCACS_SESRAN
CACS_APPL_NO1	Notification Rule
CACS_APPL_NO2	For VC VC_CACS_NOTRIG
CACS_APPL_P1	Call V_TCACS_PORTREM
CACS_APPL_P2	Call V_TCACS_PORTREMF
CACS_APPL_PE	Edit Periods
CACS_APPL_RO01	Retention: Retention Types
CACS_APPL_SESINT	Assign No.Ranges to SttSchedule
CACS_APPL_SET	Set Commission Application
CACS_APPL_SET_DUMMY	Set Application
CACS_APPL_STATUS	Status Information on Application
CACS_APPL_T1	Call VC_CACS_STCAGR26
CACS_APPL_T10	Call VC_TCACS_TGSV
CACS_APPL_T11	Call VC_TCACS_TGA
CACS_APPL_T12	Call CACS_COMPLEX_VALUATION_MAINT
CACS_APPL_T2	Call VC_TCACS_TGT
CACS_APPL_T20	Portal: Hide Complex Target Types
CACS_APPL_T3	Call VC_TCACS_TGC
CACS_APPL_T4	Call VC_TCACS_TGCLC
CACS_APPL_T5	Call VC_TCACS_TGCLT
CACS_APPL_T6	Call VC_TCACS_TGTCLA
CACS_APPL_T7	Call VC_TCACS_TGS
CACS_APPL_T8	Call VC_TCACS_TGPR
CACS_APPL_T9	Call VC_TCACS_VALAS
CACS_ARCHCT1	Archiving: Liability Period Check
CACS_ARCHCT2	Archiving: Exit for Date Check
CACS_ARCHCT3	Archiving: Maintain Exits
CACS_ARCH_CTRT	Set Archive Flag For Contracts
CACS_B	Maintain Batch Variants
CACS_BDTI_SEL_01	Create Commission Case Selection
CACS_BDTI_SEL_02	Change Commission Case Selection
CACS_BDTI_SEL_03	Display Commission Case Selection
CACS_BDTI_SEL_04	Reset Commission Case Selection
CACS_BDTI_SEL_07	Reactivate Commission Case Selection
CACS_BDTI_SEL_1	Create Commission Case Selection
CACS_BDTI_SEL_2	Change Commission Case Selection

CACS_BDTI_SEL_3	Display Commission Case Selection
CACS_BDTI_SEL_4	Reset Commission Case Selection
CACS_BDTI_SEL_7	Reactivate Commission Case Selection
CACS_BUCAGNR	Number Range for Ind. Agreement
CACS_BUILD	Package Builder for ICM Applications
CACS_BUPA_CREATE_CP	HR Link Through Central Person
CACS_C	Manage Comments for Commissions
CACS_CAS_ARCH	Archiving: Commission Case
CACS_CAS_LIST	Commission Case Display
CACS_CLONE	Application Cloner
CACS_CLONE_SHOW	Application Cloner: Process Steps
CACS_CN01	Number Ranges for Commission Cases
CACS_COI	Mass Resetting
CACS_COM_DOC0	Maintain Rule Set
CACS_COM_DOC1	Maintain Test Groups
CACS_COM_DOC2	Compare Test Groups
CACS_COM_DOC3	Comparison by Selection Criteria
CACS_CORR_HIST	Display Correspondence History
CACS_CSB0001	CSB Control: Applications
CACS_CSB0002	CSB Control: Field Groups
CACS_CSB0003	CSB Control: Views
CACS_CSB0004	CSB Control: Sections
CACS_CSB0005	CSB Control: Screens
CACS_CSB0006	CSB Control: Screen Sequences
CACS_CSB0007	CSB Control: Time-Spots
CACS_CSB0008	CSB Control: CUA Standard Function
CACS_CSB0009	CSB Control: CUA Additional Function
CACS_CSB0010	CSB Control: Search Help
CACS_CSB0011	CSB Ctrl: Assign Scrn Fld-> DB Field
CACS_CSB0012	CSB Control: Field Modific. Criteria
CACS_CSB0013	CSB Control: Roll Categories
CACS_CSB0014	CSB Control: Role Category Group
CACS_CSB0015	CSB Control: Application Transaction
CACS_CSB0016	CSB Control: Tables
CACS_CSB0017	CSB Control: External Applications
CACS_CSB0018	CSB Control: Activities
CACS_CSB0019	CSB Control: FM, Activity, Control
CACS_CSB0023	CSB Control: Datasets
CACS_CSB0100	CSB Cust: Field Modification Acty
CACS_CSB0103	CSB-Cust: Field Groups for Author.
CACS_CSB0104	CSB Cust: Screen Configuration
CACS_CSB0105	CSB-Cust: Field Modific. Ext. Appl.
CACS_CSBCHGRS	Field Modific.: Contract Bundle Type
CACS_CSBCTRTP	CSB Cust: Field Modific. Bundle Type
CACS_CSBCVGRB	CSB-Cust:Grp def.-Version comparison
CACS_CSBCVHDB	CSB-Cust:RegisterObj.forVersComparis
CACS_CSBCVOGRB	CSB-Cust: GroupForVersionComparison
CACS_CSBDELPB	CSB-Cust:FM to Delete Parked Version
CACS_CSBFLDCH	CSb-Cust: Fields w. Special Handling
CACS_CSBLTP	CSB-Cust: Contract Bundle Type
CACS_CSBNRRBL	CSB-CUST: Assign Number Ranges
CACS_CSBOTPOB	CSB-Cust: FM for Importing Ext. Item
CACS_CSBOTPOS	CSb-Cust: FM for importing ext.items
CACS_CSC0001	CSC Control: Applications

CACS_CSC0002	CSC Control: Field Groups
CACS_CSC0003	CSC Control: Views
CACS_CSC0004	CSC Control: Sections
CACS_CSC0005	CSC Control: Screens
CACS_CSC0006	CSC Control: Screen Sequences
CACS_CSC0007	CSC Control: Events
CACS_CSC0008	CSC Control: GUI Standard Functions
CACS_CSC0009	CSC Control: GUI Additionl Functions
CACS_CSC0010	CSC Control: Search Helps
CACS_CSC0011	CSC Control: Assign ScrFld->DB Field
CACS_CSC0012	CSC Control: Field Grouping Criteria
CACS_CSC0013	CSC Control: Role Types
CACS_CSC0014	CSC Control: Role Type Grouping
CACS_CSC0015	CSC Control: Application Transaction
CACS_CSC0016	CSC Control: Tables
CACS_CSC0017	CSC Control: External Applications
CACS_CSC0019	CSC Control: FGroupng Activ.Control
CACS_CSC0023	CSC Control: Datasets
CACS_CSC0100	CSC Cust.: Field Grouping Activity
CACS_CSC0103	CSC-Cust: Field Groups for Author.
CACS_CSC0104	CSC Cust.: Screen Configuration
CACS_CSC0105	CSC Cust.: Field Grouping Ext. Appl.
CACS_CSCBDLSET	CSB-Cust: More Settings...
CACS_CSCCHGRS	CSC-Cust: Field Grouping Cont Type
CACS_CSCCNR	CSC CUST: Number Range for Contract
CACS_CSCCTRTP	CSC-Cust: Field Grouping Cont Type
CACS_CSCCTRTP1	CSC Cust: Contract Type
CACS_CSCCVGRP	CSC Cust.: Def. of Grp for Vers Comp
CACS_CSCCVHDB	CSC Cust.: Reg. Obj for Versn Comp.
CACS_CSCCVHDL	CSC Cust.: Reg. Obj for Versn Comp.
CACS_CSCCVOGRP	CSC Cust.: Grouping for Versn Comp.
CACS_CSCDELPV	CSC-Cust:FM to delete parked version
CACS_CSCFLDCH	CSC-Cust: Special Processing Fields
CACS_CSCITITLE	CSC Cust.: Internal Title
CACS_CSCNRRCT	CSC Cust.: Assign Number Ranges
CACS_CSCOTPOS	CSC-Cust: FM for Importing Items
CACS_CSCTERMD	CSC Cust.: Cancellation Date
CACS_CSCTOFN	CSC Cust.: Period of Notice
CACS_CSCWORKA	CSC CUST.: Work District
CACS_CSD0001	CSD Control: Applications
CACS_CSD0002	CSD Control: Field Groups
CACS_CSD0003	CSD Control: Views
CACS_CSD0004	CSD Control: Sections
CACS_CSD0005	CSD Control: Screens
CACS_CSD0006	CSD Control: Screen Sequences
CACS_CSD0007	CSD Control: Events
CACS_CSD0008	CSD Control: GUI Standard Functions
CACS_CSD0009	CSD Control: GUI Additional Functns
CACS_CSD0010	CSD Control: Search Helps
CACS_CSD0011	CSD Control: Assgmt ScrnFld->DB Fld
CACS_CSD0012	CSD Control: Field Modific. Criteria
CACS_CSD0013	CSD Control: Role Categories
CACS_CSD0014	CSD Control: Role Cat. Grouping
CACS_CSD0015	CSD Control: Application Transactn

CACS_CSD0016	CSD Control: Tables
CACS_CSD0017	CSD Control: External Applications
CACS_CSD0018	CSD Control: Activities
CACS_CSD0019	Maintain Datasets
CACS_CSD0020	CSC Control: Role Types
CACS_CSD0100	CSD Cust.: Field Grouping Activity
CACS_CSD0105	CSD Cust: Fld Grouping Ext. Applictn
CACS_CSI0001	CSI Control: Applications
CACS_CSI0002	CSI Control: Field Groups
CACS_CSI0003	CSI Control: Views
CACS_CSI0004	CSI Control: Sections
CACS_CSI0005	CSI Control: Screens
CACS_CSI0006	CSI Control: Screen Sequences
CACS_CSI0007	CSI Control: Events
CACS_CSI0008	CSI Control: GUI Standard Functions
CACS_CSI0009	CSI Control: GUI Additionl Functions
CACS_CSI0010	CSI Control: Search Helps
CACS_CSI0011	CSI Control: Assign ScrnFld->DBField
CACS_CSI0012	CSI Control: Field Grouping Criteria
CACS_CSI0013	CSI Control: Role Categories
CACS_CSI0014	CSI Control: Role Category Groups
CACS_CSI0015	CSI Control: Application Transactns
CACS_CSI0016	CSI Control: Tables
CACS_CSI0017	CSI Control: External Applications
CACS_CSI0018	CSI Control: Activities
CACS_CSI0023	CSI Control: Data Sets
CACS_CSI0100	CSI Cust.: Field Grouping Activity
CACS_CSI0105	CSI Cust: Field Grpng Ext. Applictns
CACS_CTRT_ARCH	Archiving: Commission Contract
CACS_CUSTCOPY_APPL	Copy General Customizing
CACS_CUSTCOPY_CLNT	Copy Client-Specific Customizing
CACS_D	Distribute Report
CACS_D1	Execute data mining report
CACS_D2	Create Data Mining Report
CACS_D3	Change Data Mining Report
CACS_D4	Display Data Mining Report
CACS_D5	Data Mining: Create Form
CACS_D6	Data Mining: Change Form
CACS_D7	Data Mining: Display Form
CACS_D8	Display Results of Data Mining
CACS_DD	Distribute Report
CACS_DET	Customizing for Generated Tables
CACS_DET_ACC	Define Access Type
CACS_DET_ACCAS	Customizing for Generated Tables
CACS_DET_ACCAS_30	Call Generated Tables/Views
CACS_DET_ACCST	Customizing for Generated Tables
CACS_DET_ACR01	Cust.Acct.Ass.Types Remun.Cust.Syst.
CACS_DET_ACRCD	Account Assignment Types Remun.FS-CD
CACS_DET_ACRFI	Account Assignment Types Remun.FI
CACS_DET_ACRHR	Account Assignment Types Remun. PY
CACS_DET_ACS01	Cust.Acct.Ass.Types Sett.Cust.System
CACS_DET_ACSCD	Account Assignment Types Remun.FS-CD
CACS_DET_ACSFA	AccntAssgnmt Types Remun. FI-CA
CACS_DET_ACSFI	Account Assignment Types Settlmnt FI

CACS_DET_ACSHR	Account Assignment Types Sttlmnt PY
CACS_DET_AFL	Maintenance of View "V_TCACS_DETAFL"
CACS_DET_ANALYSIS	Determination: Analysis
CACS_DET_COT	Edit Calculating Object Type
CACS_DET_ETA	Determination: Agreement/Entry Point
CACS_DET_ETC	Edit Entry Point Check
CACS_DET_ETP	Edit Entry Point
CACS_DET_ETU	Maintenance of View "V_TCACS_DETETU"
CACS_DET_PROC	Edit Process Settings
CACS_DET_VAMMAP	Customizing for Generated Tables
CACS_DET_WUL_COMB	Determ: Where-Used List(Combination)
CACS_DET_WUL_RESULT	Determ.: Where-Used List (Result)
CACS_DISPHRBPCREATE	Display HR-BP Link Logs
CACS_DISPHRLOG	Comparison Log with HR Data
CACS_DISPREASSIGN	Logs for Manual HR-GP Linking
CACS_DISPTRFLOG	Logs for Transfer to BP System
CACS_DN01	Number Ranges for Commission Docs
CACS_DOC_ARCH	Archiving: Commission Case
CACS_EDT_MENUE	External Data Transfer
CACS_ELTC01	ELT: Set Application in Std Delivery
CACS_END_CTRT	Automat.End CommCtrct on Eff.to Dte
CACS_ERASE	Delete Program for ICM Applications
CACS_EURO_FIRST_STEP	Transf. Conversion Info to Gen. Appl
CACS_EURO_SUM_BUILD	Rebuilding Totals Tables
CACS_EURO_SUM_INIT	Initialization of Totals Tables
CACS_FDU	Number ranges for imp. variants
CACS_FFLHD	Number Range Maintenance: CACSFFLHD
CACS_FFLIT	Number Range Maintenance: CACSFFLIT
CACS_FHDRAN	Process Assignment NROB->FFLTHD
CACS_FILE_COPY	Copying a File
CACS_FITRAN	Process Assignment NROB->FFLTHD
CACS_FROM_TRAPPL_C	Copy Client Customizing from TRAPPL
CACS_FTAPPROVAL	Fast Track Approval
CACS_FTA_DISPLAY	Fast Track Approval Display
CACS_G	Comn Report Characteristics Groups
CACS_GENTEXT	Generate from RK2FVPCA -> RK2FGPCA
CACS_GETSOURCE	Commissions: Goes to Source Text
CACS_H	Maintain hierarchy
CACS_INFO_VIEW	Info on Cluster/View/View variants
CACS_INPUT_VIEW	Commissions: Calling the View
CACS_INVORG	Maintain Evaluation Paths
CACS_J	Maintain Hierarchy Nodes
CACS_K	Maintain Key Figures
CACS_LCC_CHECKS	Comm. Appl. consistency checks
CACS_LCC_MATCH_LOG	LCC: Matching process log
CACS_LCC_SUM_BUILD	LCC: Sum Rebuild
CACS_LOGCASE	Display Logs for The Commission Case
CACS_LOGCASECOMP	Display Log: Commn Case Comparison
CACS_LOGCLOSE	Displ. Logs: Closing Flat-Rates/Guar
CACS_LOGCLOSEREV	Disp Log:Reverse Clsg Flat-Rate/Guar
CACS_LOGCOPY	Display Logs for Generator
CACS_LOGDOCS	Display Logs for Commission Document
CACS_LOGGEN	Display Logs for Generator
CACS_LOGPRINT	Display Log: Printout Correspondence

CACS_LOGSTMT   Display Logs for Settlement
CACS_LOGSTMTREV   Display Logs for Settlement Reversal
CACS_LOGTEMP   Display Temporary Logs
CACS_LOGTRICASE   Display Logs for Add. Commn Case
CACS_LOGTRICASEREV   Display Logs Reversal Add. CommCases
CACS_LOS_INVOKE_VIEW   Logical Service: Invoke Param. View
CACS_LPD_CUST_SCA   Customizing LPD SCA
CACS_M   Test Monitor Drilldown Commissions
CACS_MRU   Mass Updating
CACS_O   Transport Reports
CACS_OA01   FOA: Create Process
CACS_OA02   FOA: Change Process
CACS_OA03   FOA: Display Process
CACS_OA05   FOA: Release Process Step
CACS_OA11   FOA: Create Worklist
CACS_OA12   FOA: Change Worklist
CACS_OA13   FOA: Display Worklist
CACS_OA14   FOA: Delete Worklist
CACS_OA20   FOA: Worklist Mass Deletion
CACS_OA21   FOA: Process Mass Deletion
CACS_OA30   FOA: Schedule Proc.Step Processing
CACS_OA35   FOA: Schedule Worklist Processing
CACS_OAC01   FOA: Generate User Interface
CACS_OAC02   FOA: Generate Process Interface
CACS_OAC03   FOA: Create Worklist UI Variant
CACS_OAC04   FOA: Create Process UI Variant
CACS_OAC11   FOA: Generate Process Workflow
CACS_OAC31   FOA: Worklist Number Range
CACS_OAC32   FOA: Process Number Range
CACS_OBJ   Number Ranges for Triggering Objects
CACS_P   Transport Forms
CACS_PAY   No. Range Ref. in Payment System
CACS_PERNRBP   Assigning Personnel Number -> BP
CACS_PRINT_ICM1   Mass Printing
CACS_PROTOKOLLFLAG   Call Report Name Range
CACS_PSSPLNO   Number Range for Partnerships
CACS_PS_CALL_VIEW   Call View for Selection Criteria
CACS_PS_MDCU_CHECK   Call Program cacs_ps_mdcu_check
CACS_Q   Import Reports from Client 000
CACS_R   Import Forms from Client 000
CACS_RANK_REMMNT   Ranking: Allowed Remuneration Types
CACS_RANK_VALMNT   Ranking: Allowed Valuation Types
CACS_RCPNO   Number Range for Partnerships
CACS_REPTYPE   CACS: Table/View -> Drilldown
CACS_RESET   Reset Copy Services
CACS_S   Display Structure
CACS_SARA   Archiving: Generated Objects
CACS_SEGAG   Number Range Maintenance: CACS_SEGAG
CACS_SESINT   Number Ranges for SttSchedule
CACS_SE_43_BDL   CACS Area Menu (Bundle)
CACS_SE_43_BP   CACS Area Menu (Business Partner)
CACS_SE_43_CAS   CACS Area Menu (Case)
CACS_SE_43_CTR   CACS Area Menu (Contract)
CACS_SE_43_DOC   CACS Area Menu (Document)

CACS_SHOW_MASSLOG   Display Logs for Mass Processing
CACS_STARTREP   Starts a Drilldown Report
CACS_START_DOC   Starts Document Display
CACS_START_SUM   Starts Totals Display
CACS_STMT   Number Ranges for Settlement Run
CACS_T   Translation Tool - Drilldown
CACS_TFW   ICM Test Framework
CACS_TFW_MC   Model Consistency
CACS_TFW_UC   ICM Test Framework
CACS_TIME_CLONE   Application Cloner
CACS_TO_TRAPPL_C   Copy Client Customizing to TRAPPL
CACS_TRG1EXEC   FOA Connection: Commission Contract
CACS_U   Convert drilldown reports
CACS_UPGRADE   ICM: Upgrade of Application
CACS_UPGRADE_CHECK   Check If Switch Upgrade Successful
CACS_USAGE   ICM System Data Measurement
CACS_USAGE_BATCH   ICM System Data Measurement (Batch)
CACS_V   Maintain Global Variable
CACS_VIEWCALL   Call View Call
CACS_VTCACSF   Maintenance View for Field Catalog
CACS_W   Maintain Currency Translation Type
CACS_WARRALLO   Closing Guarantee Offsetting
CACS_WFCASTRIG   Workflow for Case: Evaluate EDT
CACS_X   Reorganize Drilldown Reports
CACS_Y   Reorganize Report Data
CACS_Z   Reorganize Forms
CACT   Field Grpg Crit: Contract Acct Cat.
CAC_XT1   Number Range Maintenance: CATS_XTEND
CADE   CATS: Delete Transaction Data
CADO   Time Sheet: Display Data
CADT   Downtime for Capacity Category
CALL_BLKCLM   Call View Column Attributes
CALL_BLKHDL   Call View V_T706FORM_BLKHD
CANCDIS01   Collective Processing Distribution
CANINVDOC   Call transaction MR8M from Portal
CANM   Number range maintenance: ROUTING_M
CANMATDOC   Tcode for MIGO cancel from Portal
CANR   Number range maintenance: ROUTING_R
CAOR   Display Report (Structure-Related)
CAPP   CATS: Object-Related Approval
CAPS   Approve Times: Master Data
CARH   BP Control: External Applications
CARP   BP Cust: Fld. Mof. Ext. Application
CAS1   CA Control: Application
CAS2   CA Control: Field Groups
CAS3   CA Control: Views
CAS4   CA Control: Sections
CAS5   CA Control: Screens
CAS6   CA Control: Screen Sequence Variants
CAS7   CA Control: Events
CAS8   CA Control: CUA Standard Functions
CAS9   CA Control: CUA Additional Functions
CASA   BP Control: Match Codes
CASB   BP Control: Asn.Scrn.Fld->DB Field

SAP Transaction Codes – Volume One

CASC	CA Control: Field Grouping Criteria
CASD	CA Control: Role Types
CASE	CA Control: Role Type Grouping
CASF	CA Control: Application Transaction
CASG	BP Control: Tables
CASH	Branch to Cash Management
CASI	BP Control: Activities
CASK	CA Control: Datasets
CASN	FI-CA Cust: Field Groups for Auth.
CAT2	Time Sheet: Maintain Times
CAT2_ISCR	CATS: Maintain Times (Init. Screen)
CAT3	Time Sheet: Display Times
CAT3_ISCR	CATS: Display Times (Initial Screen)
CAT4	CATS: Approve Data
CAT5	Data Transfer CATS -> PS
CAT6	Transfer External -> Time Management
CAT7	CATS: Transfer Data to CO
CAT8	Time Sheet: Document Display
CAT9	Data Transfer CATS -> PM/CS
CATA	Transfer to Target Components
CATC	Time Sheet: Time Leveling
CATI	CATS: Cross-Application Time
CATM	Selection From Time Recording
CATP	CATS: Cross-Application Time
CATR	Reorganize Interface Tables
CATS	CATS: Cross-Application Time
CATSARCH	Archiving Time Sheet Data
CATSWF	CATS Workflow
CATSXC	Customizing: CATS for Service Prov.
CATSXC_CHECK	Check Customizing
CATSXC_COMP_DTL	CATSXT: Maintain Component Details
CATSXT	CATS for Service Providers
CATSXT_ADMIN	CATS for Service Providers (Admin.)
CATSXT_DA	Display Work Time and Tasks
CATSXT_DTL	Work Times: Detail Display
CATS_APPR	Approve Working Times (Poweruser)
CATS_APPR_LITE	Approve Working Times
CATS_DA	Display Working Times
CATS_SELVIEW	Maintain Selection View HRCATS
CATW	Record Working Time
CAUSE	Causes: Check Solution Path
CAVC_TEST	Configurator API test
CAWM	Business Partner Configuration Menu
CB23	Download of Master Tables for CC5
CB25	Upload Request CC5
CB32	Initial Download of Orders via CC3
CB33	Download of Master Tables via CC3
CB34	Delta Download of Orders via CC3
CB35	Upload request for CC3
CB37	Initial Download of Activities CC4
CB38	Master data download CC4
CB39	Delta download of activities CC4
CB40	Upload request for CC4
CB42	Initial Download of Orders via CC2

SAP Transaction Codes – Volume One

CB43	Transfer of master data via CC2
CB44	Delta Download of Orders via CC2
CB45	Upload request for CC2
CB85	Maintain print control process order
CBCACT	Maintenance CBP planning actions
CBCAT	Maintenance CBP Problem Categories
CBCBRG	Maintenance of v_cbp_brg
CBCF	Maintenance CBMRP flags
CBCMLGMRP	Maintenance defaults (MRP)
CBCMLGSOP	Maintenance defaults (SOP)
CBCMLS	Assign infostructure
CBCMOD	Maintain SCP model
CBCMSV	Activate versions
CBCMTG	Maintenance general technical data
CBCONFMRP	Maintenance startup parameters
CBCONFSOP	Maintenance startup parameters (SOP)
CBCPAR	Maintenance step parameters
CBCS	Activate system status
CBCSTEP	Maintenance steps
CBDE	PDC records with system errors
CBGL_CD03	EHS: Display Change Documents
CBGL_CL02	EHS: Edit Customer-Specific Labels
CBGL_CL03	EHS: Display Customer-Spec. Labels
CBGL_CS01	EHS: Transfer GLM Printers
CBGL_CS02	EHS: Adopt SAP Spool Printer
CBGL_GLMRECN	EHS: No. Range Maintenance GLM_RECN
CBGL_LS02	EHS: Edit Label Stock
CBGL_LS03	EHS: Display Label Stock
CBGL_MP01	EHS: Manual Print Dialog
CBGL_MP01_ITS	EHS: Manual Print Dialog for ITS
CBHR11	EHS-INT: Create External Person
CBHR12	EHS-INT: Change External Person
CBHR13	EHS-INT: Display External Person
CBHR21	EHS-INT: Create Authority
CBHR22	EHS-INT: Change Authority
CBHR23	EHS-INT: Display Authority
CBIH00	Industrial Hygiene and Safety
CBIH02	EHS: Edit Work Area
CBIH03	EHS: Display Work Area
CBIH12	EHS: Edit Risk Assessment
CBIH13	EHS: Display Risk Assessment
CBIH14	EHS: Amount Overview
CBIH42	EHS: Edit Pattern
CBIH43	EHS: Display Pattern
CBIH50	EHS: Information on Permitted Status
CBIH51	EHS: Call Question Catalog
CBIH52	EHS: Call General Questionnaire
CBIH72	EHS: Change Injury/Illness Log Entry
CBIH73	EHS: Display Inj./Illness Log Entry
CBIH82	EHS: Change Inc./Acc. Log Entry
CBIH83	EHS: Display Inc./Acc. Log Entry
CBIH88	EHS: Data Transfer for Amounts
CBIH89	EHS: Injury/Illn.Log Data Transfer
CBIH92	Agent Workbench

CBIH92OLD	EHS: Edit Agent (Substance)
CBIH93OLD	EHS: Display Agent (Substance)
CBIHB0	EHS: Incident/Accident Log No. Range
CBIHB1	EHS: Accident Report Number Range
CBIHB2	EHS: Injury/Illn. Log Number Range
CBIHB3	EHS: Work Area Number Range
CBIHB4	EHS: Number Rnge Spec. Questionnaire
CBIHB5	EHS: Number Range Measurement Proj.
CBIHB6	EHS: Number Range Measurement
CBIHCH1	Change Documents Work Area
CBIHCH2	Change Documents Risk Assessment
CBIHCH3	Change Documents Inc./Acc. Log
CBIHCH4	Change Documents Injury/Illness Log
CBIHM2	EHS: Edit Measurement Projects
CBIHM3	EHS: Display Measurement Projects
CBIHMR01	EHS: Agents with Measured Values
CBIHMR02	EHS: Buildings with Measured Values
CBIHMR03	EHS: Measurements with Meas. Values
CBIHMR04	EHS: Persons with Measured Values
CBIHMR05	EHS: Monitoring Dates
CBIHMR06	EHS: Measurements w. Analysis Values
CBIHMR07	EHS: Statistics for Measurements
CBIHMR08	EHS: Statistics for Measured Agents
CBIHMR09	EHS: Details of Measured Values
CBIHR01	EHS: Personal Exposure Log
CBIHSR01	EHS: SARA Reporting
CBIHT0	EHS: RFC - PA20 HR Master Data
CBIHT1	RFC - CBHR11 Create External Person
CBIHT12	RFC - CBHR12 Change External Person
CBIHT13	RFC - CBHR13 Display External Person
CBIHT2	RFC - EHSBP11 Create Physician
CBIHT22	RFC - EHSBP12 Change Physician
CBIHT23	RFC - EHSBP13 Display Physician
CBIHT3	RFC - EHSBP31 Create Health Center
CBIHT32	RFC - EHSBP32 Change Health Center
CBIHT33	RFC - EHSBP33 Display Health Center
CBIHT4	EHS: RFC - PB20 Applicant Master
CBIHT5	RFC - CBHR21 Create Authority
CBIHT52	RFC - CBHR22 Change Authority
CBIHT53	RFC - CBHR23 Display Authority
CBIHT6	RFC - EHSBP41 Create Laboratory
CBIHT62	RFC - EHSBP42 Change Laboratory
CBIHT63	RFC - EHSBP43 Display Laboratory
CBIHT7	RFC - EHSBP51 Create Extern. Company
CBIHT72	RFC - EHSBP52 Change Extern. Company
CBIHT73	RFC - EHSBP53 Display Ext. Company
CBMRP	CBP requirements planning
CBP	Constraint Based Planning Workbench
CBP1	MRP master data download
CBP2	MRP transactional data download
CBP3	SOP master data download
CBP4	Start ininitialization (MRP)
CBP5	Display ext. Planning Log SOP
CBP6	Start SOP ext. Planning Model Init

SAP Transaction Codes – Volume One

CBP7	Update SOP ext. Planning
CBPRO	Maintenance of v_tcbp_soprof
CBPV	Uploading PDC messages
CBRC01	Only Rep.: Ext. Business Partners
CBRC02	Only Rep.: Int. Business Partners
CBRC03	Imported By
CBRC04	Bonded Warehouse
CBRC10	Substance Volume Tracking: Appl. Log
CBRC11	Regulation Check: Blocked Orders
CBRC12	Regulation Check: TSCA12b Output
CBRC13	Regulation Check: Application Log
CBRC20	Subs. Volume Tracking: Monitoring
CBRC21	Subs. Volume Tracking: Blocked Docs
CBRC22	Output Customer List
CBRC23	SVT: Monitor Average Quantities
CBWA00	Area Menu Waste Management
CBWABDT	BDT Configuration Menu Waste Mgmt
CBWAMD	Waste Management Master Data
CC00	Engineering Change Management Menu
CC01	Create Change Master
CC02	Change Change Master
CC03	Display Change Master
CC04	Display Product Structure
CC04P	Parameter Transaction for CC04
CC05	Change overview
CC06	Flip trace protocoll for user
CC07	Engineering Change Mgmt information
CC11	Create Material Revision Level
CC12	Change Material Revision Level
CC13	Display Material Revision Level
CC15	Change Document Revision Level
CC16	Display Document Revision Level
CC22	Change Object Management Records
CC23	Display Object Management Record
CC31	Create Change Request
CC32	Change Change Request
CC33	Display Change Request
CC60	Browser hierarchy
CC62	Conversion of change packages
CC90	Number Ranges for Change Numbers
CC92	Distribute change number
CC93	Number Range Maintenance: TECHS
CCA1	Initial screen for archiving
CCAA	Change tables for archiving
CCAC	Reset Set-Get Parameter CAC
CCAD	Delete archived change tables
CCAR	Read archived data
CCF1	Create Message: Error Management
CCF2	Change Message: Error Management
CCF3	Display Message: Error Management
CCM2	Configuration Control Workbench
CCMONITOR_F4	Start F4
CCMONITOR_RRIF	Start Report/Report Interface
CCMON_DOC_CALL	Call Doc. Display for CCtr Monitor

CCMP_RABOX   Remote Action Box via SAPGui for HTM
CCPPL   CCP: Execute Planning Folders
CCPPM   CCP: Edit Plannng Folders
CCPPMD   CCP: Display Planning Folders
CCPX   CCP: Planning Folders, Direct Start
CCR   Customizing Check Report
CCR_EMERGENCY   Customizing Check for Old Op. VA
CCS   Cost Component Split
CCSECA   Admin. of Key Versions for PAYCRV
CCSECM0   Migration to SSF Application PAYCRV
CCSECM1   Execute Conversion
CCSECV_DATA_DEL   Deletion of Credit Card Data
CCSEC_LOG_DEL   Delete Payment Card Log
CCSEC_LOG_SHOW   Evaluate Payment Card Log
CCSEQ_CSGUPD   Update Change Sequence Graph
CCSEQ_CUST   Activate Change Sequence Graph
CCSEQ_CYCLE   Display Cycles
CCTM   Maintain Standard Variant
CCUNDO   Undo Changes
CCV2   Change Output: Document Management
CCW1   Task-specific Workflow Customizing
CCZU   Allocation: Material to Valid.Prof.
CC_MIGRATION   Migration of Credit Cards
CD   IMG for FS-CD
CDESK   CAD Desktop
CDESK_CUS   Customizing CAD Desktop
CDESK_DEL_DBTRACE   CAD Desktop: Delete Trace
CDESK_READ_DBTRACE   CAD Desktop: Analyze Trace
CDESK_SAVE_DBTRACE   Save Database Trace
CE00   Menu: CAPP-based calc. of std.values
CE01   CEP: View
CE02   CEP: Transfer
CE03   CEP: Review
CE11   Create standard value formula
CE12   Change standard value formula
CE13   Display standard value formula
CE16   Use of CAPP elements (single-level)
CE21   Create standard value method
CE22   Change standard value method
CE23   Display standard value method
CE31   Create standard value process
CE32   Change standard value process
CE33   Display standard value process
CE41   Simulate calculation of std. values
CEMN   Cost Element Accounting
CEPC   Display Table CEPC
CEP_CUST_WF   Maintain Distibution Workflows
CEP_IAC_PO   ITS Transaction Project Overview
CEP_R3_MON   SAP Transaction: Monitoring
CEP_SA_DEFCLAS   Default Classes
CEP_SA_DOCBOM   Document 2 BOM
CEP_SA_DOCDOC   Document 2 Document
CEP_SA_ICONDEF   Icon Definition for Documents
CERTMAP   Certificate Assignment

CERTREQ	Certificate enrollment
CES1	Create Set (Resource Planning)
CES2	Change Set (Resource Planning)
CES3	Display Set (Resource Planning)
CES4	Delete Set (Resource Planning)
CEV1	Create value variable(res. planning)
CEV2	Change value variable (res.planning)
CEV3	Display value variable(res.planning)
CEV4	Delete value variable (res.planning)
CEVC	Copy custom. tab. for std.val. calc.
CEVF	Number ranges for CAPP formulas
CEVM	Number ranges for CAPP methods
CEVP	Display CAPP tables
CEVV	Number ranges for CAPP processes
CEWB	PP: Engineering Workbench
CEWO	CE: Structure of product folder
CE_CL_EXTRACT	Extract Class Database
CF00	Prod. Resources/Tools Master Menu
CF01	Create Production Resource/Tool
CF02	Change Production Resource/Tool
CF03	Display Production Resources/Tools
CF10	PRT: Use of PRT master in prod.order
CF11	PRT: Use of material in prod. order
CF12	PRT: Use of document in prod. order
CF13	PRT: Use of equipment in prod. order
CF15	PRT: Use of PRT master in network
CF16	PRT: Use of material in network
CF17	PRT: Use of document in network
CF18	PRT: Use of piece of equip. in netw.
CF20	PRT: Use of PRT master in orders
CF21	PRT: Use of material in orders
CF22	PRT: Use of document in orders
CF23	PRT: Use of pc. of equip. in orders
CF25	PRT: PRT Master Usage in PM Order
CF26	PRT: Material Usage in PM Orders
CF27	PRT: Document Usage in PM Orders
CF28	PRT: Equipment Usage in PM Order
CFC01	cFolders Backend Integr. Customizing
CFC02	Mapping of Attributes
CFC1	Maintain Operating Mode ADC
CFC2	Customizing Parameters
CFC3	CIF: Initial Transfer for Block Size
CFC4	Maintenance of Object Infos
CFC6	Configuration of CIF Application Log
CFC7	RFC Destination Maintenance
CFC8	Number Range Parallelization
CFC9	Target-System-Ind. Settings in CIF
CFC91	Activate/Deactivate bgRFC for CIF
CFCAO	Customizing: Application object
CFCP	PRT: Copy C-Tables
CFCS	Clarification worklist - Customizing
CFCSS	CFC: Maintain status information
CFCSTART	Start clarification controller
CFCSTARTBOR	Start CFC with Obj. Key from BOR Mth

CFDS	Customizing - MRP based DS(APO)
CFE01	Export Documents to cFolders
CFE02	Export Objects to cFolders
CFE03	Export iPPE Objects to cFolders
CFG1	Display CIF Application Log
CFG3	Find in Application Log
CFGD	Delete Application Log Entries
CFG_TRACE_NAV	VMC RFC Trace Navigator
CFG_USER_EXIT_DEV	Variant Function Development
CFI01	Import Documents from cFolders
CFI02	Import Objects from cFolders
CFI03	Import iPPE Objects from cFolders
CFL1	Current Settings
CFM1	Create Integration Model
CFM2	Manually Activate Integration Models
CFM3	Activate Integration Models (Bkgd)
CFM4	Display Integration Models
CFM5	Integration Model Object Search
CFM6	Modify Integration Model
CFM7	Delete Integration Models
CFMALMART	Maintain ALM Valuation Type
CFMCK	Client Copy Customizing
CFMCSVK	Client Copy Customizing
CFMCSVUK	Client Copy Customizing
CFMCUK	Client Copy Customizing
CFMEVAL	Maintain Evaluation Type
CFNA	Maintain PRT number range: FHM_CRFH
CFO1	Production Sched. Profile APO CIF
CFO3	Scheduling Parameters in APO CIF
CFP1	Analyze and Send Changes
CFP2	Analyze and Send Changes
CFP3	CIF: PPM Transfer of Data Changes
CFP4	Delete PPM Change Pointer
CFQ1	Display qRFC Monitor
CFS0	Display Serialization Channels
CFS1	Serialization Channels Display (Prg)
CFS2	Display All Today's TRFCs
CFSRMPO	SRM PO Transfer Customizing
CG00	Basic Data Environment
CG02	Substance Workbench
CG02BD	Specification Workbench
CG05	Distribute Specification
CG12	Edit Phrases
CG13	Display Phrases
CG1B	Edit Phrase Sets
CG1C	Display Phrase Sets
CG2A	Create Generation Variant
CG2B	Edit Generation Variant
CG2C	Display Generation Variant
CG31	Import Phrases
CG32	Import Sources
CG33	Import Specifications
CG34	Import Report Template
CG35	Import Property Tree

CG36	Import Reports
CG36VEN	Import Single Report
CG37	Edit Worklist
CG3A	Check Source Export
CG3B	Check Phrase Export
CG3C	Check Specification Export
CG3D	Check Property Tree Export
CG3E	Check Report Template Export
CG3F	Check Source Import
CG3G	Check Phrase Import
CG3H	Check Specification Import
CG3I	Check Property Tree Import
CG3J	Check Report Import
CG3K	Check Report Template Import
CG3L	Check Import Log
CG3Y	Download file
CG3Z	Upload file
CG42	Edit Report Templates
CG43	Display Report Templates
CG4B	Edit Cover Sheet Template
CG4C	Display Cover Sheet Template
CG4D	Edit Acknowl. of Receipt Template
CG4E	Display Acknowl. of Receipt Template
CG50	Edit Report
CG54	Report Information System
CG55	Validate Report
CG56	Release Report
CG57	Assign Report Versions
CG58	Set Report to Historical
CG59	EHS: manual entry WL generation
CG5A	EHS: manual entry WL generation
CG5B	EHS: manual entry WL generation
CG5Z	EHS: WWI server monitor
CGA1	EHS: Maintain Specification Type
CGA2	EHS: Val.Asg.Type/Specification Type
CGA3	EHS: Authorization Object
CGA4	EHS: Identification Category
CGA5	EHS: Value Assignment Text Type
CGA6	EHS: Value Assignment Assessment
CGA7	EHS: Maintain component category
CGA8	EHS: Characteristic rating
CGA9	EHS: Phrase Library
CGAB	EHS: Edit Phrase Set-Attrib. Assgmt
CGAC	EHS: Display Phrase Set-Attr. Assgmt
CGB1	EHS: Number Range for Spec. Key
CGB2	EHS: No. rng. maintenance record no.
CGB3	EHS: Number range record counter
CGB4	EHS: Number range phrase key
CGB5	EHS: No. range maint.: SAP_CLASSR
CGB6	EHS: No. range maint.: SAP_CHARCR
CGB7	EHS: Char,Class,PropTree,ClientCopy
CGBB	EHS: Initial generation of phr. sets
CGBC	EHS: Load XLS Macro Spec Info System
CGC1	EHS: Validity area

CGC2	EHS: Usage profile
CGC3	EHS: Property Tree
CGC4	EHS: Identification listing
CGC5	EHS: Report Symbol Group
CGC6	EHS: Report Symbol
CGC7	EHS: Report Syntax
CGC8	EHS: Report environment
CGC9	EHS: Syntax graph definition
CGCL	EHS: Customizing - sources
CGCL2	Dangerous Goods Workbench
CGCNIMPEXP	EHS:No.Range Maintenance Imp./Export
CGCNOHORD	EHS: Number Range ESN_OHORD
CGCNRCNGRP	EHS: No. Range Maint. Group Admin.
CGCNSESSID	EHS: No. Range Maint. Session ID
CGCNWWIACL	EHS: Number Range ESN_WWIACL
CGCNWWIDOC	EHS: Number Range ESN_WWIDOC
CGCNWWIORD	EHS: Number Range ESN_WWIORD
CGCO	EHS: Customizing - Regulatory Lists
CGCV	EHS: Customizing - usage profile
CGCZ	Match Up Master Data
CGD1	EHS: Phrase languages
CGE2	Packaging Workbench
CGK1	EHS: Namespaces for characteristics
CGQM	Specify QM Interface
CGSADM	WWI and EH&S Expert Server Admin.
CGVAI01	EHS: Value Asst Type Entry Function
CGVAI02	EHS: Initial Filling TCG11_VAI
CGVERSION	EHS: Product Information
CHANGERUNMONI	Call Change Run Monitor
CHARGE	Charge API
CHECKFM	Check Correction Modules
CHECKMAN	Check Manager: Display Check Results
CHECKMAN_A	CheckMan: Administration
CHECKMAN_E	Check Manager: Check Exceptions
CHECKMAN_F	CheckMan for Final Assembly
CHECKMAN_O	CheckMan Online Object Check
CHECK_ANCHOR	Inconsistency Check:MK -MatMstr-CoEs
CHECK_PA	Test Tool Decoupled PA Infotypes
CHGOBJ1	Number range maint: CHGCOMPS
CHKPT	Call Up Checkpoint Maintenance View
CHPV1	Spec.Syst: Assignment class template
CI01	Create CIAP Document
CI02	Change CIAP Document
CI03	Display CIAP Document
CI10	Cust: Select Techn. Param. for Comm.
CI11	PDC Groups
CI12	Deviation Record.-Selection Variants
CI21	Communication parameters for KANBAN
CI23	Download master data for Kanban
CI25	Upload Request in KK5
CI31	Communication parameters for PM
CI32	Init. transfer of operations for PM
CI33	Transfer of master data for PM
CI34	Delta transfer of operations for PM

CI35	Generate Upload Request CC3
CI36	Communication parameters for PS
CI37	Init. transfer of operations for PS
CI38	Transfer of master data for PS
CI39	Delta transfer of operations for PS
CI40	Generate Upload Request CC4
CI41	Communication parameters for PP
CI42	Init. transfer of operations for PP
CI42N	PP-PDC: Download Operations
CI43	Transfer of master data for PP
CI44	Delta transfer of operations for PP
CI45	Generate Upload Request CC2
CI45N	Generate Upload Request CC2
CI50	Transfer production requirements
CI51	Transfer production commitments
CIB2	Update CC2 PDC messages
CIB3	Update CC3 PDC messages
CIB4	Update CC4 PDC messages
CIB5	Update CC5 PDC messages
CIC0	Customer Interaction Center
CIC1	Scripting: Assign Texts
CIC2	Scripting: Variable Maintenance
CIC3	Sales Summary
CIC4	Archiving Logging
CIC5	Archiving Infostore
CIC7	Maintain Scripting Profile
CIC8	CIC Customizing Menu (Temporary - Lo
CIC9	Maintain scripts
CICA	Maintain Activities in CIC
CICAA	Callback Queue Maintenance
CICAB	Callback Queue Assignment
CICAC	Callback Component Configuration
CICAD	BDC name and Transaction Code
CICAE	Input Step Mapping
CICAF	Constant Source
CICAG	Container Source
CICAH	Function Call Source
CICAI	BDC Field Destination
CICAJ	Parameter ID Destination
CICAK	Output Mapping
CICAL	CIC Compoent Variants
CICAM	Assignment of Visible Components
CICB	Detail Keys for Activities in CIC
CICC	Maintain CIC Framework ID
CICD	Assign Components to Framework ID
CICE	Assignment of Visible Components
CICF	CIC Component Definition
CICG	Call Center Profile Maintenance
CICH	CTI Telephony Buttons
CICI	Profile for Telephony Controls
CICJ	Maintain Logging Profile
CICK	Maintain Scripting Profile
CICL	CIC Profile Definition
CICM	Component Profile Type Definition

CICN	Customizing Toolbar Maintenance
CICO	CIC Profile Definition
CICP	Contact Search Configuration
CICQ	Assign Hidden Components to Framewrk
CICS	Customer Interaction Center
CICU	Toolbar Profile Maintenance
CICV	CTI Queue Maintenance
CICW	CTI Queue Assignment Maintenance
CICX	Component Container Maintenance
CICY	CTI Administration
CICZ	DNIS mapping
CIC_PPOCE	Create CIC Organizational Plan
CIC_PPOME	Change CIC Organizational Plan
CIC_PPOSE	Display CIC Organizational Plan
CIF	APO Core Interface
CIFPUCUST	Customizing CIF External Procurement
CIFPUCUST01	CIF Source of Supply Determination
CIFPUCUST02	CIF External Procurement Orders
CIP2	CC2: Update PDC messages
CIP3	CC3: Update PDC messages
CIP4	CC4: Update PDC messages
CIP5	CC5: Update PDC messages
CIPV	Posting PDC records
CISV	CIS Vendor Verification Process
CISVU	Update Vendor master
CIS_VENDOR	Vendor Master Data Update
CITI_VENTAS	CITI VENTAS REPORT
CI_IMPORT	Import Device Properties
CJ00	Find Digital Signatures
CJ01	Create Work Breakdown Structure
CJ02	Change Work Breakdown Structure
CJ03	Display Work Breakdown Structure
CJ06	Create Project Definition
CJ07	Change Project Definition
CJ08	Display Project Definition
CJ11	Create WBS Element
CJ12	Change WBS Element
CJ13	Display WBS Element
CJ14	Display WBS Element (From DMS)
CJ20	Structure planning
CJ20N	Project Builder
CJ21	Change Basic Dates
CJ22	Display Basic Dates
CJ23	Change Forecast Dates
CJ24	Display Forecast Dates
CJ25	Change Actual Dates
CJ26	Display Actual Dates
CJ27	Project planning board
CJ29	Update WBS (Forecast)
CJ2A	Display structure planning
CJ2B	Change project planning board
CJ2C	Display project planning board
CJ2D	Structure planning
CJ30	Change Project Original Budget

SAP Transaction Codes – Volume One

CJ31	Display Project Original Budget
CJ32	Change Project Release
CJ33	Display Project Release
CJ34	Project Budget Transfer
CJ35	Budget Return from Project
CJ36	Budget Supplement to Project
CJ37	Budget Supplement in Project
CJ38	Budget Return in Project
CJ3A	Change Budget Document
CJ3B	Display Budget Document
CJ40	Change Project Plan
CJ41	Display Project Plan
CJ42	Change Project Revenues
CJ43	Display Project Revenues
CJ44	Act. overhd: Projects, ind. process.
CJ45	Act. ovhd: Projects, coll. process.
CJ46	Plnd ovrhd: Projects, ind. process.
CJ47	Pld Overhead: Projects, Coll.Procssg
CJ48	Change Payment Planning: Init.Screen
CJ49	Display Payment Planning: Init.Scrn
CJ70	Maintain Project Settlement LIs
CJ72	Project: Act. amt. line item settlmt
CJ74	Project Actual Cost Line Items
CJ76	Project Commitment Line Items
CJ7E	Plan Data Transfer: Projects
CJ7G	Plan Data Transfer: Projects
CJ7M	Project Plan Cost Line Items
CJ7N	Maint. DRG inv.projects for retmt.
CJ80	Availability Control - Overview
CJ81	Update Report List
CJ88	Settle Projects and Networks
CJ8A	Act.-setlmt: Proj. retirmt. from IM
CJ8G	Actual Settlement: Projects/Networks
CJ8V	Period Close for Project Selection
CJ91	Create Standard WBS
CJ92	Change Standard WBS
CJ93	Display Standard WBS
CJ9B	Copy WBS Plan to Plan (Collective)
CJ9BS	Copy WBS Plan to Plan (Indiv.)
CJ9B_OLD	Copy Project Cost Planning (old)
CJ9C	Copy WBS Actual to Plan (Collective)
CJ9CS	Copy WBS Actual to Plan (Indiv.)
CJ9C_OLD	Copy Project Revenue Planning (old)
CJ9D	Copy Plan Versions
CJ9E	Plan Settlement: Projects
CJ9ECP	Project System: Easy Cost Planning
CJ9F	Copy Project Costing (Collective)
CJ9FS	Copy Project Costing (Indiv.)
CJ9G	Plan Settlement: Projects
CJ9K	Network Costing
CJ9L	Forecast Costs: Individual Projects
CJ9M	Forecast Costs: Coll.Project Proc.
CJ9Q	Integrated Planning for Ntwks(Coll.)
CJ9QS	Integrated Planning for Ntwks (Ind.)

97

SAP Transaction Codes – Volume One

CJA1	Proj.Rel.Order Receipts: Coll.Proc.
CJA2	Proj.Rel. Order Receipts: Ind.Proc.
CJAL	Send project
CJB1	Generate Settmt Rule: Coll.Proc.
CJB2	Generate Settmt Rule: Indiv.Proc.
CJBBS1	Planning Board Report Assignment
CJBBS2	Structure Overview Report Asst
CJBN	Reconstruct Availability Control
CJBV	Activate Project Availabilty Control
CJBW	Deactivate Project Availabilty Cntrl
CJC1	Maintenance Dialog for Stat.by Per.
CJC2	Maintain Planned Status Changes
CJCD	Change documents: WBS
CJCF	Carry Forward Project Commitments
CJCO	Carry Forward Project Budget
CJCS	Standard WBS
CJE0	Run Hierarchy Report
CJE1	Create Hierarchy Report
CJE2	Change Hierarchy Report
CJE3	Display Hierarchy Report
CJE4	Create Project Report Layout
CJE5	Change Project Report Layout
CJE6	Display Project Report Layout
CJEA	Call Hierarchy Report
CJEB	Background Processing, Hier.Reports
CJEC	Maintain Project Crcy Trans.Type
CJEK	Copy Interfaces/Reports
CJEM	Project Reports: Test Monitor
CJEN	Reconstruct: Summarized Proj.Data
CJEO	Transport Reports
CJEP	Transport Forms
CJEQ	Import Reports from Client
CJET	Translation Tool - Drilldown
CJEV	Maintain Global Variable
CJEX	Reorganize Drilldown Reports
CJEY	Reorganize Report Data
CJEZ	Reorganize Forms
CJF1	Create Transfer Price Agreement
CJF2	Change Transfer Price Agreement
CJF3	Display Transfer Price Agreement
CJF4	Transfer Price Agreement List
CJFA	Analysis of Data Trans. into PS Cash
CJFN	CBM Payment Converter
CJG1	Enter Transfer Price Allocation
CJG3	Display Transfer Price Allocation
CJG4	Enter Trsfr Price Allocation: List
CJG5	Cancel Transfer Price Allocation
CJH1	Reconstruct Project Inheritance
CJH2	Project Inheritance Log
CJI1	Project Budget Line Items
CJI2	Budget Line Items: Document Chain
CJI3	Project Actual Cost Line Items
CJI4	Project Plan Cost Line Items
CJI5	Project Commitment Line Items

CJI8	Project Budget Line Items
CJI9	Project Struct.Pld Costs Line Items
CJIA	Project Actual and Commt Paymt LIs
CJIB	Project Plan Payment Line Items
CJIC	Maintain Project Settlement LIs
CJID	Display Project Settlement Line Itms
CJIE	Projects: Retirement LI Settlement
CJIF	Projects: Profitability Analysis LI
CJIG	Display PS Cash Documents
CJK2	Change Statistical Key Figures
CJK3	Display Statistical Key Figures
CJL2	Collective Agreement
CJN1	Reval. ACT: Projects Ind.Pro.
CJN2	Reval. ACT: Projects Col.Pro.
CJNO	Number range maintenance: FMCJ_BELNR
CJO8	Overhead COMM: Projects Ind.Pro.
CJO9	Overhead COMM: Projects Col.Pro.
CJP1	Create Project Plan Adjustment
CJP2	Change Project Plan Adjustment
CJP3	Display Project Plan Adjustment
CJP4	Delete Project Plan Adjustment
CJPN	Number Range Maintenance: Proj.Items
CJPU	Execute Project Plan Adjustment
CJR2	PS: Change plan CElem/Activ. input
CJR3	PS: Display plan CElem/Activ. input
CJR4	PS: Change plan primary cost element
CJR5	PS: Display plan primary cost elem.
CJR6	PS: Change activity input planning
CJR7	PS: Display activity input planning
CJR8	PS: Change revenue type planning
CJR9	PS: Display Revenue Element Planning
CJS2	PS: Change stat. key figure planning
CJS3	PS: Display stat. key fig. planning
CJS4	PS: Change stat. key figure planning
CJS5	PS: Display stat. key fig. planning
CJSA	Data Transfer to SAP-EIS
CJSB	Select Key Figure and Characteristic
CJSG	Generate WBS Element Group
CJSN	Number Range Maintenance: Projects
CJT2	Project Actual Payment Line Items
CJV1	Create project version (simulation)
CJV2	Change project version (simulation)
CJV3	Display Project Version (Simulation)
CJV4	Transfer project
CJV5	Delete simulation version
CJV6	Maintenance: Version administration
CJV7	Display transfer log
CJVC	Value Category Checking Program
CJW1	EURO: Adjust Project Budget
CJZ1	Act. Int Calc.: Projects Coll. Proc.
CJZ2	Actual Int.Calc.: Project Indiv.Prc.
CJZ3	Plan Int.Calc.: Project Indiv.Prc.
CJZ5	Plan Int.Calc.: Project Coll.Prc.
CJZ6	Actual Int.Calc.: Indiv.CO Order Prc

CJZ7	Planned Int.Calc: Indiv.CO Ord.Proc.
CJZ8	Actual Int.Calc.: Coll.CO Order Prc.
CJZ9	Plan Int.Calc.: Coll.CO Order Prc.
CK00	Product costing initial screen
CK11	Create Product Cost Estimate
CK11N	Create Material Cost Estimate
CK13	Display Product Cost Estimate
CK13N	Display Material Cost Estimate
CK22	Organizational Measure
CK24	Price Update with Cost Estimate
CK31	Print Log of Costing Run
CK32	CK BATCH: Print logs
CK33	Comparison of Itemizations
CK40N	Edit Costing Run
CK41	Create Costing Run
CK42	Change Costing Run
CK43	Display Costing Run
CK44	Delete Costing Run
CK45	Delete Costing Run in Background
CK51	Create Order BOM Cost Estimate
CK51N	Create Order BOM Cost Estimate
CK53	Display Order BOM Cost Estimate
CK53N	Display Order BOM Cost Estimate
CK55	Mass Costing - Sales Documents
CK60	Preselection for Material/Plant
CK61	CK Batch Processing
CK62	Find Structure: BOM Explosion
CK63	CK Batch Processing
CK64	Run: Cost Estimate of Objects
CK65	CK Batch Processing
CK66	Mark Run for Release
CK68	Release Costing Run
CK74	Create Additive Costs
CK74N	Create Additive Costs
CK75	Change Additive Costs
CK75N	Change Additive Costs
CK76	Display Additive Costs
CK76N	Display Additive Costs
CK77N	Create Additive Costs
CK79_99	Material: Itemization Comparison
CK80	Flexible Cost Component Report
CK80_99	Material: Cost Components
CK81	Overview of Reports
CK82	Select Cost Estimates
CK83	Print Cost Estimates in Background
CK84	Line Items in Cost Est for Product
CK84_99	Material: Itemization
CK84_99_COST_ELEMENT	Cost Elements
CK85	Line Items in Cost Est for Order
CK85_99	Sales Document: Itemization
CK85_99_COST_ELEMENT	Cost Elements
CK86	Costed Multilevel BOM
CK86_99	Material: Multilevel BOM
CK87	Costed BOM Sales Orders

CK87_99	Sales Document: Multilevel BOM
CK88	Partner Cost Component Split
CK88_99	Material: Partner Cost Comp. Split
CK89	Flexible Cost Comp. Report SaleOrder
CK89_99	Sales Document: Cost Components
CK90	Mixed Costing
CK91	Create Procurement Alternatives
CK91N	Edit Procurement Alternatives
CK92	Change Procurement Alternatives
CK93	Display Procurement Alternatives
CK94	Change Mixing Ratio
CK95	Display Mixing Ratios
CKA1	Std Cost Est to Profitability Anal.
CKAPP01	Materials To Be Costed
CKAPP03	Sales Order Item to be Costed
CKAV	Check availability
CKC1	Check Costing Variant
CKCM	Costing Model
CKECP	Ad Hoc Cost Estimate
CKECP1	Easy Cost Planning: Central Access
CKECPCP	Ad Hoc Cost Estimate for cProjects
CKECPCP_DIR	Ad Hoc Cost Est cProjects (Direct)
CKECPEWT	Ad Hoc Cost Estimate
CKECPINT	Easy Cost Planning
CKECP_AR	Write Archive
CKM3	Material Price Analysis
CKM3N	Material Price Analysis
CKM3OLD	Material Price Analysis
CKM3VERYOLD	Display Material Ledger Data
CKM9	Show Customizing Settings for Plant
CKMACD	Value Flow Display f. Activity Types
CKMADJUST	Reconcil. with Bal. Sheet Acct in FI
CKMARCHBEL	Archive Document
CKMARCHDAT	Archive Period Records
CKMARCHIDX	Archive Index Entries
CKMARCHSPL	Archiving Actl Cost Comp. Split Recs
CKMARCHWIP	Archive WIP for Actual Costs
CKMATCON	Selection List Maintenance Dialog
CKMATSEL	Selection List
CKMB	Display Material Ledger Document
CKMB_RUN	Create Basic List for Costing Run
CKMC	Consistency Check for a Material
CKMCCC	Manual Change: Act. Cost Comp. Split
CKMCCD	ManChang: Display Actual CC Split
CKMCCS	Display Actual Cost Component Split
CKMC_RUN	Set Costing Sequence
CKMD	Transactions for a Material
CKMDISPACT	Technical Activity Type View
CKMDISPDOC	Technical View ML Document
CKMDISPPOH	Technical View of Order Development
CKMDISPTAB	Technical View of ML Master Data
CKMDUVACT	Distribution of Activity Differences
CKMDUVMAT	Distribution of Inventory Diffs
CKMDUVREC	Enter Activity Differences

CKMDUVSHOW   Display Inventory and Activity Diff.
CKME   Activation of Planned Prices
CKMF   Allow Price Determination
CKMF_RUN   Allow Price Determination for Run
CKMG   Allow Closing Entries
CKMG_RUN   Allow Closing Entries for Run
CKMH   Single-Level Price Determination
CKMH_RUN   Single-Level Price Det.for Costg Run
CKMI   Post Closing
CKMI_RUN   Post Closing for Costing Run
CKMJ   Display Organizational Measures
CKMJ_RUN   Organizational Measures for Run
CKMK   Control of Information System ML
CKML   Actual Costing/Material Ledger
CKMLAVREXP   AVR Erklärungstool
CKMLAVRPERD   Display period values
CKMLBB_AGGREGATE   Calculate Periodic Receipt Values
CKMLBB_FIFO_CALCULAT   Calculate FIFO Prices
CKMLBB_PERIODS_LIST   Display Periodic Receipt Values
CKMLBB_PRICES_CHANGE   Price Change with Alternat. Prices
CKMLBB_PRICES_LIST   Display Alternative Prices
CKMLCP   Cockpit Actual Costing
CKMLCPAVR   Alternative Valuation Run Cockpit
CKMLCPMLBF   Material Ledger Budget Cockpit
CKMLCPW   Actual Costing for Reporting Periods
CKMLDC   Debit/Credit Material
CKMLDM   Debit or Credit Material
CKMLLA   Prices in the Material Ledger
CKMLLACHANGE   Display ActvPrices, Change NO_SETTLE
CKMLLACREATE   Create ML-AT Master Data Manually
CKMLLANOSETTLE   Ind.'Do Not Consider Price'
CKMLLASHOW   Display Activity Prices
CKMLMAT   Display Material List
CKMLMVCHECK   Quantity Structure Consistency
CKMLMV_CA   Edit Controlling Level
CKMLMV_MCA_N   Mass Maintenance: Controlling Levels
CKMLOH   PO History/Multiple Currencies
CKMLPC   Price Change
CKMLPOH   Order History Display
CKMLPROT   Delete Logs
CKMLQS   Valuated Quantity Structure(M-level)
CKMLRUNCUMDEL   Delete costing run cumulation
CKMLRUNDEL   Delete Costing Run (Actual Costing)
CKMLRUNREORG   Reorganization of Costing Runs
CKMLRUNWDEL   Delete Runs for Weekly Act. Costing
CKMLSTATUS   Materials by Period Status
CKMLWIPDEACT   Check Report: WIP Deactivation
CKMLXPRA46A   Postprocessing Report for 46A-XPRA
CKML_FPR1   Create Production Process
CKML_FPR1N   Edit Production Process
CKML_FPR3   Display Production Process
CKML_PRICES_SEND   Send Material Prices
CKML_SURF   Edit Prcrmnt / Cnsmptn Alternatives
CKMM   Change Price Determination

SAP Transaction Codes – Volume One

CKMM_RUN	Multilevel Pr. Deter. for Cstg Run
CKMPCD	Display Price Change Document
CKMPCSEARCH	Price Change Documents for Material
CKMPROTDIS	Display Log
CKMPRP	Maintain Planned Prices
CKMPRP2	Maintain Future Prices by Profile
CKMPRPN	Price Maintenance
CKMR	Report Selection Material Ledger
CKMREDWIP	Value Flow Display for Reduced WIP
CKMREP	Repair Program for ML Tables
CKMS	Material Ledger Docs for Material
CKMSTART	Production Startup of Mat. Ledger
CKMTOPPRICEDIF	Mat. with Highest MAP Difference
CKMTOPSTOCKVAL	Materials w/ Highest Inventory Value
CKMVAPP	Data Transfer: Val. Production Plan
CKMVFM	Value Flow Monitor
CKMVFM_DEL	Delete Extract
CKM_CURRENCIES_LIST	Currency and Val.types in ML, FI, CO
CKNR	Maintain Number Ranges: KALK
CKR1	Reorganization in Product Costing
CKR3	Write Archive
CKR5	Reorganize in Background
CKRA	Archive: Create and Remove Index
CKRU00	Create ML Costing Run
CKRU01	ML Costing Run, Create Profile
CKRU02	ML Costing Run, Change Profile
CKRU03	ML Costing Run, Display Profile
CKRU04	Display Selection
CKRU05	Display ML Costing Run
CKRU06	Delete ML Costing Run
CKRU07	Plants in Costing Runs
CKRU08	Display Levels
CKSBX	Administration Shared Buffer
CKTC	Concurrent Costing -XiPPE Dialog
CKU1	Update Material Price
CKUC	Multilevel Unit Costing
CKVF	Show Whether Marking/Release Allowed
CKW1	Create Production Lot Cost Est.
CKW3	Display Production Lot Cost Est.
CKW4	Activate Production Lot Cost Est.
CKWE	Determine Value Added
CL00	Classification Menu
CL01	Create Class
CL02	Classes
CL03	Display Class
CL04	Delete Class
CL20	Assign Object to Classes
CL20N	Object Assignments
CL21	Display Object in Classes
CL22	Allocate Class to Classes
CL22N	Assign Class to Superior Classes
CL23	Display Class for Classes
CL24	Assign Objects to One Class
CL24N	Class Assignments

SAP Transaction Codes – Volume One

CL25	Display Objects in Class
CL26	Mass Release of Assignments
CL2A	Classification Status
CL2B	Class Types
CL30	Find Objects in Classes
CL30N	Find Objects in Classes
CL31	Find Object In Class Type
CL6A	Class List
CL6AN	Class List (ALV)
CL6B	Object List
CL6BN	Object List (ALV)
CL6C	Class Hierarchy
CL6D	Classes Without Superior Class
CL6E	Copy DIN Standard
CL6F	Copy DIN Characteristic Data
CL6G	Create Material w. DIN Char. Data
CL6H	Classes: Reassign/Split/Merge
CL6K	Delete Characteristic (Class w. Obj)
CL6M	Delete Class (with Assignments)
CL6O	Plus-Minus Object Display
CL6P	Where-Used List for Classes
CL6Q	Where-Used List for Classes
CL6R	Direct Input for Classes
CL6T	Copy Text for Classes
CLABAP	Display ABAP class library
CLB1	Batch Input for Classification
CLB2	Direct Input for Classification
CLB3	Display Classification File
CLBOR	Display BOR library
CLCO	2.1A Copy Tables for Classes
CLCP	Copy Classification C Tables
CLD0	Distr. Configuration Profile (Netwk)
CLD1	Distr. Configuration Profile (Matl)
CLD2	Distribute Global Dependencies
CLD3	Distr. Variant Tables (Structure)
CLD4	Distr. Variant Tables (Data)
CLEAR	Start Data Cleansing Tool
CLEAR_INT	Start Data Cleansing Tool (Internal)
CLEAR_INT2	Data Cleansing: Direct
CLGT	Set Up Tables for Search
CLHI	Distribution of Class Hierarchies
CLHP	Graphical Hierarchy Maintenance
CLIST	Configuration Ctrl.: Component List
CLIST_UPD_RESB	Internal TCode for CLIST Reservation
CLJP	Specify Japanese calender
CLM1	Create Claim
CLM10	Claim Overview
CLM11	Claim Hierarchy
CLM2	Change Claim
CLM3	Display Claim
CLMM	Mass Change for Assigned Values
CLNA	Namespace f. Classes/Characteristics
CLNK	Number Ranges for Class Maintenance
CLOCO	Closing Cockpit - Execution

SAP Transaction Codes – Volume One

CLOCOC	Closing Cockpit - Customizing
CLOCOS	Closing Cockpit - Aggregated View
CLOCOS_MY	Closing Cockpit - Aggregated View
CLOCO_ACE	Closing Cockpit - Accrual Engine
CLOCO_MIG	Closing Cockpit - Migration
CLOI	Production Optimization Interface
CLST	Create Class Statistics
CLUNDO	Undo Changes (CA-CL)
CLVL	Maintain Variable Lists
CLW1	Allocate Material Group Hierarchy
CLW2	Display Material Group Hierarchy
CLWA	Create Material Group (MMS)
CLWB	Change Material Group (MMS)
CLWC	Display Material Group (MMS)
CLWD	Delete Material Group (MMS)
CLWE	Create Characteristic Profile (MMS)
CLWF	Change Characteristic Profile (MMS)
CLWG	Display Characteristic Profile (MMS)
CLWH	Delete Characteristic Profile (MMS)
CLWJ	Change Generic Article (MMS)
CLWK	Display Generic article (MMS)
CLWL	Delete Generic Article (MMS)
CLWM	Create MMS Material Group Hierarchy
CLWN	Change MMS Material Group Hierarchy
CLWO	Display MMS Material Group Hierarchy
CLWP	Delete MMS Material Group Hierarchy
CM01	Cap. planning, work center load
CM02	Capac. planning, work center orders
CM03	Capac. planning, work center pool
CM04	Capac. planning, work center backlog
CM05	Capacity plan.:Work center overload
CM07	Cap. planning: Variable access
CM0X	Capacity planning
CM10	Capacity leveling
CM11	Maintain flow control
CM21	Capacity leveling SFC planning table
CM22	Capacity leveling:SFC planning table
CM23	Capacity leveling: SFC orders tab.
CM24	Capacity leveling: PM indiv. tab.
CM25	Capacity leveling: Variable
CM26	Capacity Leveling: Proj.View Tabular
CM27	Capacity level.: SFC indiv.cap.graph
CM28	Capac.level.: SFC indiv.cap. tab.
CM29	Capacity leveling: PI planning table
CM30	Cap. leveling: PM indiv.cap.graph.
CM31	Cap. leveling: SFC orders graphical
CM32	Cap. leveling: PS graph.
CM33	Cap.leveling: PM work cntr. graphic
CM34	Cap.leveling: PM work cntr. tab.
CM35	Capacity leveling: PI work cntr.tab.
CM36	Capacity leveling: PI order graphic.
CM37	Capacity leveling: PI order tab.
CM38	Capacity leveling L-T planning
CM40	Capacity leveling in the background

CM41	Evaluation of leveling in background
CM50	Capacity level.: SFC work cntr list
CM51	Cap.level.: SFC individual.cap. list
CM52	Cap.leveling: SFC orders list
CM53	Capacity leveling: PS elem/version
CM54	Capacity leveling: PS list via vers.
CM55	Cap.leveling: PS list WCntr/version
CM56	Capacity leveling: PI resource list
CM57	Capacity leveling: PI orders list
CM99	Generate basic capacity load
CMAC_FEE_CALC	Fee Calculation Report
CMAP0	Configurable Semantic Mapping
CMATRANGE	Add CWD Material Range
CMC0	
CMCE	Copy Table Contents ResourcePlanning
CMCH	Check overall profile
CMCMT	Claim Control Maintenance
CMCY	Copy table entries, capacity planng.
CMD1	Create Output: Direct Procurement
CMD2	Change output: Direct procurement
CMD3	Display Output: Direct Procurement
CMECUST	CME Customizing
CME_CHAR_DSCOPE	Assign Definition Scope to Char.
CMFN	Number Range Maint: CMF_PROTOK (SAP)
CMIG	iPPE Migration Tool
CMMAP01	Planning Hierarchy frm Master Data
CMMAP02	Maintain FM for Master Data Hier.
CMMAP03	Display FMs for Master Data Hier.
CMMAP04	Maintain FMs for Master Data Attribs
CMMAP05	Display FMs for Master Data Attribs
CMOD	Enhancements
CMP2	Workforce Planning: Project View
CMP3	Workforce Planning: Work Center View
CMP9	Workforce Planning - Reporting
CMPC	Workforce Planning Profile
CMPC1	Cond.: Field Cat. Campaign Determin.
CMPC2	CondTab: Create (Campaign Determ.)
CMPC3	CondTab: Change (Campaign Determ.)
CMPC4	CondTab: Display (Campaign Determ.)
CMPC5	Access: Maintain (Campaign Determ.)
CMPC6	Condition Types: Campaign Determ.
CMPC7	Procedure: Campaign Determination
CMPC8	Optimize Accesses (Campaign Deter.)
CMPC9	Determine Proced. Campaign Determ.
CMPDS1	Customize multiple PDS
CMPERS_CALL	Edit User Settings
CMPERS_MAINTAIN_SGL	Maintain Personalization Data
CMPERS_MM	Personalization: Collective Maint
CMPERS_TEST	Test User Settings
CMPP	Workforce Planning
CMPRO	Category Management:Project Mainten.
CMP_CHECK	Code Composer Template Check
CMP_CUST	IMG Campaign Determination
CMP_PROCESSING	Complaints Processing

CMP_REASON	Customizing for Complaints Reasons
CMRP	MRP
CMS1	Create set (PPC)
CMS2	Change Set
CMS3	Display Set
CMS4	Delete Set
CMSORG	Organizational Unit in CMS
CMS_ACG_01	Coverage Gap
CMS_ACG_02	Coverage Gap
CMS_ACG_03	Coverage Gap
CMS_AST_01	Create Asset
CMS_AST_02	Change Asset
CMS_AST_03	Display Asset
CMS_BCM	Coverage gap monitoring
CMS_BCM_ACG_DISPLAY	Display BCM Res. with Appr. Cov. Gap
CMS_BCM_DEL	Delete Coverage gap results
CMS_BCM_DISPLAY	Display BCM results for Specific Run
CMS_BII_CUS_01	Maintain Extraction Process Type
CMS_BII_DEX_PR_START	CMS Data Extraction Process
CMS_CAG_01	Create Collateral Agreement
CMS_CAG_02	Change Collateral Agreement
CMS_CAG_03	Display Collateral Agreement
CMS_COR_REQ_PRINT	Start correspondence print
CMS_CREATE_CHG_PTR	Create chg ptr for entities in const
CMS_CS	Collateral Sheet
CMS_CUS_01	Object Systems
CMS_CUS_02	Credit Systems
CMS_CUS_03	Risk Codes
CMS_CUS_04	Document Types
CMS_CUS_05	Business Partner Roles
CMS_CUS_06	Transactions
CMS_CUS_07	BDT Field Grouping for Asset Type
CMS_CUS_08	BDT Field Grouping for CAG Type
CMS_CUS_09	BDT Field Grouping for a Product
CMS_CUS_11	Asset Types
CMS_CUS_12	Collateral Agreement Types
CMS_CUS_13	Products
CMS_CUS_14	Product Sets
CMS_CUS_ACG_BDT_001	CMS Control: Applications
CMS_CUS_ACG_BDT_002	CMS Control: Field Groups
CMS_CUS_ACG_BDT_003	CMS Control: Views
CMS_CUS_ACG_BDT_004	CMS Control: Sections
CMS_CUS_ACG_BDT_005	CMS Control: Screens
CMS_CUS_ACG_BDT_006	CMS Control: Screen Seq.
CMS_CUS_ACG_BDT_007	CMS Control: Events
CMS_CUS_ACG_BDT_008	CMS Control: GUI Standard Functions
CMS_CUS_ACG_BDT_009	CMS Control: GUI Addl Functions
CMS_CUS_ACG_BDT_015	CMS Control: Appl. Transactions
CMS_CUS_ACG_BDT_018	CMS Control: Activities
CMS_CUS_ACG_REL	Assign Rel Object to Rel Procedure
CMS_CUS_ASSET_NR	Number range maintenance: CMS_ASSET
CMS_CUS_BDT_001	CMS Control: Applications
CMS_CUS_BDT_002	CMS Control: Field Groups
CMS_CUS_BDT_003	CMS Control: Views

CMS_CUS_BDT_004	CMS Control: Sections
CMS_CUS_BDT_005	CMS Control: Screens
CMS_CUS_BDT_006	CMS Control: Screen Seq.
CMS_CUS_BDT_007	CMS Control: Events
CMS_CUS_BDT_008	CMS Control: GUI Standard Functions
CMS_CUS_BDT_009	CMS Control: GUI Addl Functions
CMS_CUS_BDT_011	CMS Control: Asn.scrn.fld->dbase fld
CMS_CUS_BDT_012	CMS Control: Field Grp. Criteria
CMS_CUS_BDT_013	CMS Control: BP Roles
CMS_CUS_BDT_014	CMS Control: BP Role Groupings
CMS_CUS_BDT_015	CMS Control: Appl. Transactions
CMS_CUS_BDT_016	CMS Control: Tables
CMS_CUS_BDT_017	CMS-Control: External applications
CMS_CUS_BDT_018	CMS Control: Activities
CMS_CUS_BDT_019	CMS Control: FuncMod. Activity(Ctrl)
CMS_CUS_BDT_020	CMS Control: Search Help
CMS_CUS_BDT_021	CMS control: Assign.DI field->DB fld
CMS_CUS_BDT_022	CMS Control: Where-Used List Struct.
CMS_CUS_BDT_023	CMS Tax: Data Sets
CMS_CUS_BDT_100	CMS Cust: Field Grouping Activity
CMS_CUS_BDT_101	CMS Cust: BP Role Field Grouping
CMS_CUS_BDT_102	CMS Cust: Authorization Types
CMS_CUS_BDT_103	CMS Cust: Field Grps f.Authorization
CMS_CUS_BDT_104	CMS-Cust: Screen Configuration
CMS_CUS_BDT_105	CMS-Cust:Fld.modif.exter.application
CMS_CUS_BDT_106	CMS-Cust: Notes on Roles
CMS_CUS_BDT_107	CMS Cust: Where-Used List
CMS_CUS_CAG_NUMRANGE	Number range maintenance: CMS_CAGMT
CMS_CUS_COM_NR	Number range maintenance: CMS_MOV
CMS_CUS_INS_BDT_001	CMS Control: Applications
CMS_CUS_INS_BDT_002	CMS Control: Field Groups
CMS_CUS_INS_BDT_003	CMS Control: Views
CMS_CUS_INS_BDT_004	CMS Control: Sections
CMS_CUS_INS_BDT_005	CMS Control: Screens
CMS_CUS_INS_BDT_006	CMS Control: Screen Seq.
CMS_CUS_INS_BDT_007	CMS Control: Events
CMS_CUS_INS_BDT_008	CMS Control: GUI Standard Functions
CMS_CUS_INS_BDT_009	CMS Control: GUI Addl Functions
CMS_CUS_INS_BDT_011	CMS Control: Asn.scrn.fld->dbase fld
CMS_CUS_INS_BDT_012	CMS Control: Field Grp. Criteria
CMS_CUS_INS_BDT_015	CMS Control: Appl. Transactions
CMS_CUS_INS_BDT_016	CMS Control: Tables
CMS_CUS_INS_BDT_018	CMS Control: Activities
CMS_CUS_INS_BDT_019	CMS Control: FuncMod. Activity(Ctrl)
CMS_CUS_INS_BDT_104	CMS-Cust: Screen Configuration
CMS_CUS_LIQ_BDT_001	CMS Control: Applications
CMS_CUS_LIQ_BDT_002	CMS Control: Applications
CMS_CUS_LIQ_BDT_003	CMS Control: Applications
CMS_CUS_LIQ_BDT_004	CMS Control: Applications
CMS_CUS_LIQ_BDT_005	CMS Control: Applications
CMS_CUS_LIQ_BDT_006	CMS Control: Applications
CMS_CUS_LIQ_BDT_007	CMS Control: Applications
CMS_CUS_LIQ_BDT_008	CMS Control: Applications
CMS_CUS_LIQ_BDT_009	CMS Control: Applications

CMS_CUS_LIQ_BDT_011	CMS Control: Applications
CMS_CUS_LIQ_BDT_012	CMS Control: Applications
CMS_CUS_LIQ_BDT_015	CMS Control: Applications
CMS_CUS_LIQ_BDT_016	CMS Control: Applications
CMS_CUS_LIQ_BDT_018	CMS Control: Applications
CMS_CUS_LIQ_BDT_100	CMS Control: Applications
CMS_CUS_LIQ_BDT_103	CMS Control: Applications
CMS_CUS_LIQ_BDT_104	CMS Control: Applications
CMS_CUS_LIQ_BDT_105	CMS Control: Applications
CMS_CUS_LOC_01	Search Application Customizing
CMS_CUS_OMS_BDT_001	CMS Control: Applications
CMS_CUS_OMS_BDT_002	CMS Control: Field Groups
CMS_CUS_OMS_BDT_003	CMS Control: Views
CMS_CUS_OMS_BDT_004	CMS Control: Sections
CMS_CUS_OMS_BDT_005	CMS Control: Screens
CMS_CUS_OMS_BDT_006	CMS Control: Screen Seq.
CMS_CUS_OMS_BDT_007	CMS Control: Events
CMS_CUS_OMS_BDT_008	CMS Control: GUI Standard Functions
CMS_CUS_OMS_BDT_009	CMS Control: GUI Addl Functions
CMS_CUS_OMS_BDT_011	CMS Control: Asn.scrn.fld->dbase fld
CMS_CUS_OMS_BDT_012	CMS Control: Field Grp. Criteria
CMS_CUS_OMS_BDT_013	CMS Control: BP Roles
CMS_CUS_OMS_BDT_014	CMS Control: BP Role Groupings
CMS_CUS_OMS_BDT_015	CMS Control: Appl. Transactions
CMS_CUS_OMS_BDT_016	CMS Control: Tables
CMS_CUS_OMS_BDT_017	CMS-Control: External applications
CMS_CUS_OMS_BDT_018	CMS Control: Activities
CMS_CUS_OMS_BDT_019	CMS Control: FuncMod. Activity(Ctrl)
CMS_CUS_OMS_BDT_020	CMS Control: Search Help
CMS_CUS_OMS_BDT_021	CMS control: Assign.DI field->DB fld
CMS_CUS_OMS_BDT_022	CMS Control: Where-Used List Struct.
CMS_CUS_OMS_BDT_023	CMS Tax: Data Sets
CMS_CUS_OMS_BDT_100	CMS Cust: Field Grouping Activity
CMS_CUS_OMS_BDT_101	CMS Cust: BP Role Field Grouping
CMS_CUS_OMS_BDT_102	CMS Cust: Authorization Types
CMS_CUS_OMS_BDT_103	CMS Cust: Field Grps f.Authorization
CMS_CUS_OMS_BDT_104	CMS-Cust: Screen Configuration
CMS_CUS_OMS_BDT_105	CMS-Cust:Fld.modif.exter.application
CMS_CUS_OMS_BDT_106	CMS-Cust: Notes on Roles
CMS_CUS_OMS_BDT_107	CMS Cust: Where-Used List
CMS_CUS_PCN_ASTC_REL	Assign Rel Object to Rel Procedure
CMS_CUS_PCN_AST_REL	Assign Rel Object to Rel Procedure
CMS_CUS_PCN_CAGC_REL	Assign Rel Object to Rel Procedure
CMS_CUS_PCN_CAG_REL	Assign Rel Object to Rel Procedure
CMS_CUS_PCN_OMSC_REL	Assign Rel Object to Rel Procedure
CMS_CUS_PCN_OMS_REL	Assign Rel Object to Rel Procedure
CMS_CUS_RBL_NUMRANGE	Number range maintenance: CMS_RBL
CMS_CUS_RE_BDT_001	CMS-RE Control:Applications
CMS_CUS_RE_BDT_002	CMS-RE Control: Field Groups
CMS_CUS_RE_BDT_003	CMS-RE Control: Views
CMS_CUS_RE_BDT_004	CMS-RE Control: Sections
CMS_CUS_RE_BDT_005	CMS-RE Control: Screens
CMS_CUS_RE_BDT_006	CMS-RE Control: Screen Seq.
CMS_CUS_RE_BDT_007	CMS-RE Control: Events

CMS_CUS_RE_BDT_008	CMS-RE Control:GUI Standard Function
CMS_CUS_RE_BDT_009	CMS-RE Control:GUI Addl Function
CMS_CUS_RE_BDT_011	CMS-RE Control:Asn scrn fld->DB fld
CMS_CUS_RE_BDT_012	CMS-RE Control: Field Grp. Criteria
CMS_CUS_RE_BDT_013	CMS-RE Control: BP Roles
CMS_CUS_RE_BDT_014	CMS-RE Control: BP Role Grouping
CMS_CUS_RE_BDT_015	CMS-RE Control: Appl Transactions
CMS_CUS_RE_BDT_016	CMS-RE Control: Tables
CMS_CUS_RE_BDT_017	CMS-RE Control: External Application
CMS_CUS_RE_BDT_018	CMS-RE Control: Activities
CMS_CUS_RE_BDT_019	CMS-RE Control:FuncMod. Activity
CMS_CUS_RE_BDT_020	CMS-RE Control: Search help
CMS_CUS_RE_BDT_021	CMS-RE Control:Asn DI fld->DB fld
CMS_CUS_RE_BDT_022	CMS-RE Control:Where used-list
CMS_CUS_RE_BDT_023	CMS-RE Tax: Data Sets
CMS_CUS_RE_BDT_100	CMS-RE Cust: Fld Grouping Activity
CMS_CUS_RE_BDT_101	CMS-RE Cust: BP Role Fld Grouping
CMS_CUS_RE_BDT_102	CMS-RE Cust: Authorization types
CMS_CUS_RE_BDT_103	CMS-RE Cust: Fld Grouping Auth.
CMS_CUS_RE_BDT_104	CMS-RE Cust: Screen Configuration
CMS_CUS_RE_BDT_105	CMS-RE Cust:Fld Mod ext application
CMS_CUS_RE_BDT_106	CMS-RE Cust: Notes on rules
CMS_CUS_RE_BDT_107	CMS-RE Cust: Where used list
CMS_CUS_RE_OBJECT_NR	Number range maintenance: CMS_RE_OBJ
CMS_DEL_CAG_RBL	Deletion of invalid cag-rbl links
CMS_DEL_SUBAST_MOV	Delete wrong subassets for Movables
CMS_DEL_SUBAST_RE	Delete wrong subassets for RE
CMS_DEL_SUBAST_SEC	Delete wrong subassets for Sec acc
CMS_INS_01	Insurance Create
CMS_INS_02	Insurance Maintain
CMS_INS_03	Display Insurance
CMS_LIQ_01	Create Liquidation
CMS_LIQ_02	Change Liquidation
CMS_LIQ_03	Display Liquidation Measure
CMS_LIQ_CFL	Maintain Liq. Cash Flows (Rel 3.0)
CMS_LIQ_MOV	Liquidation Measure: MOV handle
CMS_LIQ_RE	Liquidation Measure:RE handle
CMS_LIQ_RIG	Liquidation Measure: RIG handle
CMS_LR_DE_CHANGE	Change German Land Register
CMS_LR_DE_CREATE	Create German Land Register
CMS_LR_DE_DISPLAY	Display German Land Register
CMS_LR_DE_MAINTAIN	Maintain Land Register
CMS_OVER	Collateral Overview
CMS_RBL_01	Create Receivable
CMS_RBL_02	Change Receivable
CMS_RBL_03	Display Receivable
CMS_RBL_SYNC	Synchronize receivables
CMS_REP_CAG_VLDT_01	Collateral Expiry Report
CMS_REP_TSK_LIST_01	Task List
CMS_RE_CHANGE	Change real estate
CMS_RE_COPY	Create real estate
CMS_RE_CREATE	Create real estate
CMS_RE_DISPLAY	Display real estate
CMS_SEC_ISIN	Maintain class master data for ISINs

CMS_SEC_ISIN_PRICE	Maintain price data for ISINs
CMS_WB	CMS Workbench
CMTCUS01	CM application: General settings
CMTCUS11	Maintaining life cycle profile
CMTCUS21	Configuration definition
CMTCUS22	Maintain number range for CM product
CMTCUS31	Configuration folder: Gen. settings
CMTCUS32	Maintain number range for CM folder
CMTCUS41	Baseline: General settings
CMTCUS42	Maintain number ranges for Baseline
CMTCUSEX	Maintain explosion profile
CMTCUSMEM	CM Application: General Settings
CMV1	Create variable
CMV2	Change variable
CMV3	Display variable
CMV4	Delete value variable
CMWO	Configuration Management Workbench
CMWODISP	CM Workbench - Display transaction
CMX01	XSteps: Application Registration
CMX02	XSteps: Define BAdI Filter Values
CMX03	XSteps: Services Registration
CMX04	XSteps: Release Namespaces
CMX05	XSteps: BADI Monitor
CMX10	XSEditor:Maintain BAdI Filter Values
CMX20	SXS Repository: Authorization Groups
CMX21	SXS Repository: Customizing
CMXSV	Standard XStep Repository
CMX_XS_ARC	XSteps: Generate Archive Files
CMX_XS_ARCHIVE	Archiving XSteps
CMX_XS_DEL	XSteps: Start Delete Program
CMX_XS_MANAGE	XSteps: Management
CM_CUST	IMG Retail
CM_TEST_0	Control Tests (Internal)
CM_TEST_1	Test for Single IO Test
CM_TEST_2	Test Program for KW Document Bridge
CM_TEST_3	Demo Program for Composite Control
CM_TEST_4	Test for single IO test
CN01	Create Standard Network
CN02	Change Standard Network
CN03	Display Standard Network
CN04	Edit PS Text Catalog
CN05	Display PS Text Catalog
CN06	MPX Download: Standard Network
CN07	MPX Upload: Standard Network
CN08	Allocate material -> stand. network
CN09	Allocate material -> stand. network
CN11	Create standard milestone
CN12	Change standard milestone
CN13	Display standard milestone
CN19	Display Activity (From DMS)
CN20	Dsply network/act.bsc data init.scrn
CN21	Create Network
CN22	Change Network
CN23	Display Network

CN24	Overall Network Scheduling
CN24N	Overall Network Scheduling
CN25	Confirm Completions in Network
CN26	Display Mat.Comp/Init: Ntwk,Acty,Itm
CN26N	Display Mat. Components (From DMS)
CN27	Collective Confirmation
CN28	Display Network Confirmations
CN29	Cancel Network Confirmation
CN2X	Confirm Completions in Network
CN30	Processing PDC error records
CN33	PDM-PS interface
CN34	Maintain release table TCNRL
CN35	Control stock / account assignment
CN36	BOM Transfer Profile
CN37	BOM Allocation Field Selection
CN38	Maintain Flexible Reference Point
CN40	Project Overview
CN41	Structure Overview
CN41N	Project structure overview
CN42	Overview: Project Definitions
CN42N	Overview: Project Definitions
CN43	Overview: WBS Elements
CN43N	Overview: WBS Elements
CN44	Overview: Planned Orders
CN44N	Overview: Planned Orders
CN45	Overview: Orders
CN45N	Overview: Orders
CN46	Overview: Networks
CN46N	Overview: Networks
CN47	Overview: Activities/Elements
CN47N	Overview: Activities/Elements
CN48	Overview: Confirmations
CN48N	Overview: Confirmations
CN49	Overview: Relationships
CN49N	Overview: Relationships
CN50	Overview: Capacity Requirements
CN50N	Overview: Capacity Requirements
CN51	Overview: PRTs
CN51N	Overview: PRTs
CN52	Overview: Components
CN52N	Overview: Components
CN53	Overview: Milestones
CN53N	Overview: Milestones
CN54N	Overview: Sales Document
CN55N	Overview: Sales and Dist. Doc. Items
CN60	Change Documents for Projects/Netw.
CN61	Standard network
CN65	Change documents order /network
CN70	Overview: Batch variants
CN71	Create versions
CN72	Create Project Version
CN80	Archiving project structures
CN81	PS: Archiving project - preliminary
CN82	PS: Archiving project structures

CN83	PS: Archiving project - Info System
CN84	PS: Archiving project - admin.
CN85	PS: Delete operative structures
CN98	Delete Standard Networks
CN99	Archiving Standard Networks
CNACLD	PS ACL Deletion Program transaction
CNB1	Purchase requisitions for project
CNB2	Purchase orders for project
CNC4	Consistency checks for WBS
CNC5	Consistency checks sales order/proj.
CNE1	Project Progress (Individual Proc.)
CNE2	Project Progress (Collective Proc.)
CNE5	Progress Analysis
CNFOWB	Forecast Workbench
CNG1	Netw./Hier.: Maintain frame types
CNG2	Netw./Hier.: Maintain form def.
CNG3	Netw./hier.: maintain color definit.
CNG4	Netw./Hier.: Maintain graph. profile
CNG5	Netw./Hier: Maintain options profile
CNG6	Netw./hier.: Maintain node type
CNG7	Netw./Hier.: Maintain link types
CNG8	Netw./Hier.: Maintain field def.
CNG9	Graph. Cust. Netw./Hierarchy Graph.
CNL1	Create delivery information
CNL2	Change delivery information
CNL3	Display delivery information
CNLDSTINIT	Initialization: Lang.-Dep.Short Txts
CNMASS	Mass Changes in Project System
CNMASSPROT	Display log f. mass changes PS
CNMM	Project-Oriented Procurement
CNMT	Milestone Trend Analysis
CNN0	Number Range for Library Network
CNN1	Number range maint.: ROUTING_0
CNPAR	Partner Overview
CNPAWB	Progress Analysis Workbench
CNPRG	Network Progress
CNR1	Create Work Center
CNR2	Change Work Center
CNR3	Display Work Center
CNS0	Create deleivry from project
CNS40	Project Overview
CNS41	Structure Overview
CNS42	Overview: Project Definitions
CNS43	Overview: WBS Elements
CNS44	Overview: Planned Orders
CNS45	Overview: Orders
CNS46	Overview: Networks
CNS47	Overview: Activities/Elements
CNS48	Overview: Confirmations
CNS49	Overview: Relationships
CNS50	Overview: Capacity Requirements
CNS51	Overview: PRTs
CNS52	Overview: Components
CNS53	Overview: Milestones

CNS54	Overview: Sales Document
CNS55	Overview: Sales and Dist. Doc. Items
CNS60	Change Documents for Projects/Netw.
CNS71	Create versions
CNS83	PS: Archiving project - Info System
CNSE5	Progress Analysis
CNSKFDEF	SKF defaults for project elements
CNS_CP_DELETE	Delete Change Pointers
CNS_CP_MONITOR	Display Change Pointers
CNVCDMCCA_GET_EXITS	Get Programs linked to User Exits
CNVCDMCCA_UPLD_EXITS	Upload Programs linked to User Exits
CNVCDMC_EXTRACT_KB	Transaction to Extract RIB content
CNVCDMC_IMPORT_KB	Transaction to Import RIB content
CNVL	Variable Overviews
CNV_CDMC	Custom Develop. Management Cockpit
CNV_CDMC_IMGDEF	CDMC Source Projects Definition
CNW1	WWW: Confirmation
CNW4	Project Documents
CO00	
CO01	Create production order
CO01S	Adding simulation order
CO02	Change Production Order
CO02S	Change simulation order
CO03	Display Production Order
CO03S	Display simulation order
CO04	Print Production Orders
CO04N	Print Production Orders
CO05	Collective Release of Prod. Orders
CO05N	Release Production Orders
CO06	Backorder Processing
CO07	Create order without a material
CO08	Production order with sales order
CO09	Availability Overview
CO0DS	Delete Simulation Order
CO10	Production order with project
CO11	Enter Time Ticket
CO11N	Single Screen Entry of Confirmations
CO12	Collective Entry of Confirmations
CO13	Cancel confirmation of prod. order
CO14	Display confirmation of prod. order
CO15	Enter Production order Confirmation
CO16	Conf.: Postprocessing error records
CO16N	Reprocessing Confirmation
CO17	Enter confirmation with reference
CO19	Enter Time Event
CO1F	Create confirmation of prod. order
CO1L	Confirmation: List of requests
CO1P	Predefined confirmation processes
CO1V	Confirmation: Fast entry of time tkt
CO20	Orders acc. to Order Numbers
CO21	Orders for Material
CO22	Orders for MRP Controller
CO23	Orders for the production scheduler
CO24	MissingPartsInfoSyst

SAP Transaction Codes – Volume One

CO26	Order information system
CO27	Picking list
CO28	Choose indiv. object lists
CO30	Standard trigger points
CO31	Create standard trigger point
CO32	Change standard trigger point
CO33	Display standard trigger point
CO40	Converting Planned Order
CO41	Coll. Conversion of Planned Orders
CO42	Act. Overhead: Prod.Ordr Ind.Pro.
CO43	Act. Overhead: Prod.Ordr Col.Pro.
CO44	Mass processing of orders
CO46	Order progress report
CO47	Change comparison
CO48	Conv.plan.ord.to prod.ord.part.redct
CO51	Send Process Messages
CO52	Evaluate Process Data
CO53	Control Recipe Monitor
CO53XT	Monitor Control Instructions/Recipes
CO53_BJS	Send Control Instructions/Recipes
CO54	Message Monitor
CO54XT	Monitor for Process Messages
CO54_BJS_PD	Send Process Messages (Plant-Dep.)
CO54_BJS_PI	Send Process Messages (Plant-Indep.)
CO55	Worklist for Maintaining PI Sheets
CO56	Display PI Sheet
CO57	Create Message Manually
CO58	Maintain PI Sheet
CO59	Delete PI Sheet
CO60	Find PI Sheet
CO60D	PI Sheet: Display
CO60XT	Find Work Instructions
CO60_VM	ALV Variant Maint. PI Sheet Worklist
CO62	Delete Process Messages
CO63	Evaluate Deletion Logs
CO64	Worklist for Completing PI Sheets
CO67	Worklist for Checking PI Sheets
CO68	MiniApp PI Sheet Mon -> List
CO69	Create Message Automatically
CO78	Archiving orders
CO80	Number range maintenance: AUF_RUECK
CO81	Number assignment: routing to order
CO82	Number ranges for orders
CO83	Number range maintenance: RESB
CO84	No. Range for ReqmtsTrackgNo. (KBED)
CO86	Field Selection for PP Confirmations
CO88	Act. Settlment: Prod./Process Orders
CO8A	Presett. Co-Products, Postprocessing
CO8B	Presett. Co-Products, Postprocessing
CO99	Set Status "Closed"
COA1	PP: Archiving orders - preparation
COA2	PP: Archiving orders
COA3	PP: Archiving orders - retrieval
COA4	PP: Archiving order - administration

COA5	Proc.Order: Archiving Prep. Program
COA6	Process Order: Archiving
COA7	Process Order: Retrieval - Archive
COA8	Process Order: Archive Management
COA9	PP: Archiving delete orders
COAA	Simulate Order Record
COAC	Process Order: Archive Database
COAD	Process Order: Delete Archiving
COAL	Read Order Record from Archive
COAT	COAT
COATE	COAT: Extract
COATR	COAT: Repository
COAT_CUST	COAT Customizing of Attributes
COAT_CUST_SAP	COAT Customizing of SAP Attributes
COA_TEST	Cost_object_analyzer
COB1	Create batch search strategy - prod.
COB2	Change batch search strategy - prod.
COB3	Display batch search strategy- prod.
COC0	
COCB	Process Management
COCM	OCM - Initiating object
COCM1	OCM - Procurement
COCM2	OCM - Picking
COCPCPR	Cockpit for Controlling Integration
COCPCPRE	Cockpit for Controlling Integration
COCR_NUM	Early Number Assignment for XStep
COCR_PROF	Assign Standard XStep Profile
COCS	Batch Record: Signature Strategy
COCT	Tab.transfer Tab.contents Confirm
COCU1	Batch Record: Document Profile
COCU2	Batch Record: L-Profile, Dev.Anal.
COCU3	Batch Record: Signature Strategy
COCU4	Batch Record: Cover Page
COCUSDIS	Display Customizing Settings
CODC	Change Documents for Network
CODE_SCANNER	Scans Report/Funct. Group/Class Code
COEBR	Batch Record
COF1	Filter prof. - maintain prod. order
COF4	Maintain filter profs.for proc.order
COFC	Reprocessing Errors Actual Costs
COFI	Command File Creation
COGI	Postprocess Faulty Goods Movements
COHV	Mass Processing Production Orders
COHVOMPRINT	Print Production Orders
COHVOMRELEASE	Release Production Orders
COHVPI	Mass Processing: Process Orders
COIB	As-Built for Serialized Material
COID	Select Object Detail Lists in PP-PI
COIF	Production Memos
COIK	Picking list
COINTCOCP	Cockpit for Controlling Integration
COINT_TP	Controlling Integration: Reposting
COINT_TP_CUST	CO Integration: Link to Customizing
COINT_TP_MAINT	CO Integration: Reposting Maint.

COINT_TP_MAINT_S   CO Integration: Reposting Maint.
COINT_TP_S   CO Integr.: Reposting - Indiv. Procg
COIO   Order Info System for PP-PI
COIS   Order info system: customizing
COISC   Editable Fields Mass Processing
COISF   Field Settings in Info System
COISL   List Types in Information System
COISN   Order info system: customizing
COMAC   Collective Availability Check
COMCMATERIALID   Number Range Maintenance: MATERIALID
COMCPRAUTHGROUP   Authorization Groups
COMCPRD_BSP_ID   Number Range Maintenance: PRD_BSP_ID
COMCPRFORMAT   Format of the Product ID
COMCPRLOGSYS   Prod.ID: Storage Type in Log. System
COMCPRMSG   Configure Customer-Specific Messages
COMCPRTYPENRO   Number Assignment Control
COMCSERVICEID   Number Range Maintenance Materials
COMC_CATEGORY_SCHEME   Define Category Numbering Schemes
COMC_DIFF_BSP   Number Range Maintenance: PRDDIFFBSP
COMC_LOGSYS_MAP   Assignment of Logical Systems
COMC_MATERIALID_ALL   Number Range Maintenance Materials
COMC_PRAPPLCAT   Assign Hierachies to Applications
COMC_PRODUCT_IDX   Activate Index Table for Products
COMC_PR_ALTID   Alternative Product IDs
COMC_PR_ALTID_BSP   Alternat. ID Type Profile for PC-UI
COMC_PR_OBJ_FAM   Define Object Families
COMC_PR_OBJ_FAM1   Define Object Families
COMC_PR_RFCDEST   Maintenance of Table COMC_PR_RFCDEST
COMC_SERVICEID_ALL   Number Range Maintenance Service
COMC_TRADEITEMID_ALL   No. Range Maintenance Trade Item
COMLI   Post WIP Closing for Activities
COMLWIPARCH   Archive WIP Quantities Document
COMLWIPDISP   Trans. For Prog. Display_WIP_OBJ_M
COMLWIPDOC   Display WIP Quantities Document
COMMAND_NR   Number Range Maintenance: COMMAND_NR
COMMPR01   Product Workbench
COMMPR02   Collective Proc.of Inactive Products
COMMPR03   Maintain Views
COMMPR05   Maintain Numbering Scheme
COMMPR06   Collective Proc.of Inactive Products
COMMPR_PCUI   Set Types Generation in PC-UI PRD
COMM_ATTRIBUTE   Maintain Set Types and Attributes
COMM_ATTRSET   Maintain Set Types and Attributes
COMM_ATTR_UPD_PME   Update PME
COMM_CAT_TEXT_UPG40   Convert Category Short Texts (4.0)
COMM_CAT_TRANS   Transport Category
COMM_DEL_PRWB_USER   Reset User Settings
COMM_EXTRSET   Extraction Individual Objects
COMM_HIERARCHY   Maintain Categories and Hierarchies
COMM_HIER_CAT_GUID   GUIDs for Hierarchy/Category
COMM_IOBJ_RECATEG   Recategorize Indivdual Objects
COMM_LH_KEY_GEN   Key Types - Generic Link Handler
COMM_MSG01   Customer Settings for Messages
COMM_PRAPPLCAT   Assign Hierarchies to Applications

COMM_PRDARC   Display Products from Archive
COMM_PROD_RECATEG   Recategorize Products
COMM_SETTYPE   Maintain Set Types and Attributes
COMP   Customizing Missing Parts Info Syst.
COMPDAT   BRE: Determine Planned Billing Date
COMPXPD   Progress Tracking for Components
COM_BUPA_CALL_FU   Determining FMs for Data Exchange:BP
COM_BUPA_MAPBUGROUP   Table Maintenance CRMBP_MAP_BUGRP
COM_CAT_UPG30   Check Duplicate Categ., Hierarchies
COM_CFG_SUPPORT   entry point for support tools
COM_CLEAR_NUM   Number Range Maintenance: COM_CLEAR
COM_MDF   Master Data Framework
COM_PR_MDCHECK   Consistency Check Product Master
COM_SE_ADMIN   Search Engine Service: Admin
COM_SE_NRO_CP   Number Range Maintenance: COM_SE_CP
COM_SE_NRO_CP2   Number range maintenance: COM_SE_CP2
CON1   Actual Reval.: Prod.Ordr Ind.Pro.
CON2   Actual Reval.: Prod.Ordr Col.Pro.
CONC   No.Range for CtrlRecipes: COCB_CRID
COND_POWL_CUS1   Condition: POWL Variant (Header)
COND_POWL_CUS2   Condition: POWL Variant (Item)
COND_POWL_START   Condition Information: Start POWL
COND_POWL_TEST   Condition Info.: Test Object Types
COND_TABLE_CRM_FG   Condition Tables for Free Goods
COND_TABLE_CRM_PD   Condition Tables for Product Determ.
COND_TYPE_CRM_FG   Condition Types for Free Goods
COND_TYPE_CRM_PD   Condition Types for Product Determ.
CONM   No.Range for Proc.Messages:COCB_MSID
CONV01   Converter: Display application log
CONV02   Convert document
CONV03   Convert a BOM assembly
CONV04   Convert Document Structure
CONV12   Conversion: Location Dependency
CONV20   Reset Converter(s) Status(es)
CON_FAIC01   Act. of Texts After Language Import
CON_FAIC02   Maintain Price Types
COOIS   Production Order Information System
COOISPI   Process Order Information System
COOPC   OPC Test Environment
COOPC1   Define Settings for SAP ODA
COOPCI   Define OPC Items
COOPCS   Define OPC Servers
COP1   Plan HUs - General
COP11   Plan HUs Without Sales Order
COP12   Plan HUs for Sales Order
COP13   Plan HUs for Delivery
COP14   Plan HUs for Purchase Order
COP2   Pack HUs - General
COP21   Pack HUs - Without Sales Order
COP22   Pack HUs for Sales Order
COP23   Pack HUs for Delivery
COP24   Pack HUs for Purchase Order
COPA   Archive Order Record
COPAWA   Pack components for order

COPCDATEN
COPD   Print Process Order
COPI   Print Process Order ShopFloor Papers
COPOC   Process Manufacturing Cockpit
COPP1   PackDemandMgt for ProdOrd. : Plan
COPP2   PackDemandMgt for ProdOrd. : Pack
COR1   Create Process Order
COR2   Change Process Order
COR3   Display Process Order
COR4   Customizing Process Order RecTypePar
COR5   Collective Process Order Release
COR6   Single Process Order Confirmation
COR6N   Single Screen Entry of Confirmations
COR7   Convert Planned Order to Proc. Order
COR7_PC   Part.Conv.: Plnned Ord. to Proc.Ord.
COR8   Coll.Conv.: Plnned Ord. to Proc.Ord.
COR9   Material Types for Master Recipe
CORA   Process Order: Schedule Ext. Relshps
CORC   Search Proc. for Batch Determ. PP-PI
CORD   Batch Record: Type of DMS Used
CORK   Process Order Confirmations (Total)
CORM   Mass Processing
CORN   Order Types Process Order
CORO   Create Process Order w/o Material
CORP   Control Parameters for Proc. Orders
CORR   Collective Entry of Confirmations
CORRHIST   Display Correspondence History
CORR_MAINTAIN   Maintain correlations for all instr.
CORS   Cancel Process Order Confirmation
CORT   Display Process Order Confirmation
CORU   Maintain prod. scheduler group
CORW   Prod. Scheduling Profiles/Batches
CORX   Cust.:Scheduling Type Process Orders
CORY   Cust.:Production Scheduling Profiles
CORZ   Process Order: Time Event Confirmat.
COS1   Sort profiles - maintain prod. order
COS4   Sort profiles - maintain proc. order
COSS   Transport of C Tables
COTB   Transport table contents SFC
COTF   Comm. File Missing Parts Info System
COW1   Production Order Workplace
COWBHUWA   GI HU for Production Order
COWBHUWE   GR HU for Production Order
COWBPACK   Packing in production orders
COWF1   Task Customizing (Production Order)
COX1   Create Order (Internally)
CO_ITEM_WR   Archive CO Line Items
CP01   Create Business Process
CP02   Change Business Process
CP03   Display Business Process
CP04   Delete Business Process
CP05   Process: Display Changes
CP06   CO-ABC Planning: Activity Inputs
CP07   CO-ABC Planning: Display Act. Inputs

CP12	Edit Business Processes
CP13	Business Processes: Master Data Rep.
CP14	Delete Business Processes
CP20	Business Alloc Structure Display
CP26	CO-ABC Planning: Quantities & Prices
CP27	CO-ABC Planning: Display Qty/Price
CP30	Business Process: Change Management
CP46	CO-ABC Planning: Stat. Key Figures
CP47	CO-ABC Planning: Display Stat. KF
CP65	Create ABC Planning Layout (ActInpt)
CP66	Change ABC Planning Layout (AcInput)
CP67	Display ABC Planning Layout (AcInpt)
CP75	Planning Layout: Create Qtys/Prices
CP76	Planning Layout: Change Qtys/Prices
CP77	Planning Layout: Display Qtys/Prices
CP85	Create ABC Planning Layout (St.KF)
CP86	Change ABC Planning Layout (St.KF)
CP87	Display ABC Planning Layout (St.KF)
CP97	Copy Planning for Business Processes
CP97_OLD	Business Processes: Copy Plan
CP98	Copy Planning for Business Processes
CP98_OLD	Business Process: Copy Act. to Plan
CPAE	Actl. Template Alloc: Prof. Analysis
CPAR	Archiving Business Processes
CPAS	Act. Template Alloc.: Bus. Processes
CPB1	Business Processes: Act. Line Items
CPB9	Planning Report for Bus. Processes
CPBA	Run Selected Reports
CPBB	Select Reports
CPBL	Bus. Processes: Planning Overview
CPBP	Business Processes: Plan Line Items
CPBT	Bus. Process.: Activity Price Report
CPC1	Create Actual Indirect Acty Alloc.
CPC1N	Create Actual Indirect Acty Alloc.
CPC2	Change Actual Indirect Acty Alloc.
CPC2N	Change Actual Indirect Acty Alloc.
CPC3	Display Actual Indirect Acty Alloc.
CPC3N	Display Actual Indirect Acty Alloc.
CPC4	Delete Actual Indirect Acty Alloc.
CPC4N	Delete Actual Indirect Acty Alloc.
CPC5	Execute Actual Indirect Acty Alloc.
CPC6	Overview actual ind. activity alloc.
CPC6N	Act. Indirect Acty Alloc.: Overview
CPC7	Create Indirect Activity Alloc. Plan
CPC7N	Create Indirect Activity Alloc. Plan
CPC8	Change Indirect Activity Alloc. Plan
CPC8N	Change Indirect Activity Alloc. Plan
CPC9	Display Indirect Acty Alloc. Plan
CPC9N	Display Indirect Acty Alloc. Plan
CPCA	Delete Indirect Activity Alloc. Plan
CPCAN	Delete Indirect Activity Alloc. Plan
CPCB	Execute Plan Indirect Acty Alloc.
CPCC	Indirect Acty Alloc. Plan: Overview
CPCCN	Indirect Acty Alloc. Plan: Overview

CPFX	Predistrib. of Fixed Costs:Processes
CPH1	Create Business Process Group
CPH2	Change Business Process Group
CPH3	Display Business Process Group
CPH4	Change Standard Hierarchy (BusProc)
CPH4N	Change Standard Hierarchy
CPH5	Display bus. process std. hierarchy
CPH5N	Display Std Hierarchy/Business Proc.
CPI1	Enter Statistical Key Figures
CPII	Price calc. in actl: process
CPK1	Create Task Cost Data
CPK2	Change Task Cost Data
CPK3	Display Task Cost Data
CPMA	Target=Actual-IAA: process
CPMB	ABC: Plan Reconciliation
CPMN	Activity-Based Costing Menu
CPP1	Create Actual Assess. for Processes
CPP1N	Create Actual Assess. for Processes
CPP2	Change Actual Assess. for Processes
CPP2N	Change Actual Assess. for Processes
CPP3	Display Actual Assess.for Processes
CPP3N	Display Actual Assess.for Processes
CPP4	Delete Actual Assess. for Processes
CPP4N	Delete Actual Assess. for Processes
CPP5	Execute Actual Assess.for Processes
CPP6	Actual Assess. Processes: Overview
CPP6N	Actual Assess. Processes: Overview
CPP7	Create Plan Assess. for Processes
CPP7N	Create Plan Assess. for Processes
CPP8	Change Plan Assess. for Processes
CPP8N	Change Plan Assess. for Processes
CPP9	Display Plan Assess. for Processes
CPP9N	Display Plan Assess. for Processes
CPPA	Delete Plan Assessment for Processes
CPPAN	Delete Plan Assessment for Processes
CPPB	Execute Plan Assess. for Processes
CPPC	Plan Assess. for Processes: Overview
CPPCN	Plan Assess. for Processes: Overview
CPPE	Plan Templ. Alloc.: Results Analysis
CPPI	Iter. plan act. price calc. (CO-ABC)
CPPS	Plan Template Allocation: Process
CPS1	Variance Calculation: Processes
CPS2	Actual Cost Splitting: Processes
CPSP	Split Plan Costs
CPT1	Create Template
CPT2	Change Template
CPT3	Display Template
CPT4	Delete Template
CPT6	Formula Plan for Bus. Processes
CPTA	Actual Template Allocation: Order
CPTB	Actual Template Allocation: Orders
CPTD	Actual Template Alloc.: Prod. Orders
CPTE	Actual Template Alloc.: Run Sched.
CPTG	Actual Templ. Allocation: Cost Obj.

CPTH	Actual Templ. Allocation: Cost Obj.
CPTJ	Actl Template Alloc.: Cust. Orders
CPTK	Actual Template Allocation: Project
CPTL	Actual Template Allocation: Projects
CPUA	Plan Template Allocation: Order
CPUB	Plan Template Allocation: Orders
CPUK	Plan Template Allocation: Project
CPUL	Plan Template Allocation: Projects
CPV1	Create Actual Process Distribution
CPV1N	Create Actual Process Distribution
CPV2	Change Actual Distribution Process
CPV2N	Change Actual Distribution Process
CPV3	Display Actual Process Distribution
CPV3N	Display Actual Process Distribution
CPV4	Delete Actual Process Distribution
CPV4N	Delete Actual Process Distribution
CPV5	Execute Actual Process Distribution
CPV6	Actual Process Distribution Overview
CPV6N	Actual Process Distribution Overview
CPV7	Create Plan Process Distribution
CPV7N	Create Plan Process Distribution
CPV8	Change Plan Process Distribution
CPV8N	Change Plan Process Distribution
CPV9	Display Plan Process Distribution
CPV9N	Display Plan Process Distribution
CPVA	Delete Plan Process Distribution
CPVAN	Delete Plan Process Distribution
CPVB	Execute Plan Process Distribution
CPVC	Plan Process Distribution Overview
CPVCN	Plan Process Distribution Overview
CPZI	Actual overhead calc.: process
CPZP	Plan Overhead: Business Processes
CQ85	Maintain prt control for insp. order
CR00	Resource Planning Menu
CR01	Create Work Center
CR02	Change Work Center
CR03	Display Work Center
CR04	Test Work Center Formulas
CR05	Work Center List
CR06	Work Center Assignment to Cost Ctr
CR07	Work Center Capacities
CR08	Work Center Hierarchy
CR09	Task list reference text
CR0C	Work centers current settings
CR10	Work center change documents
CR11	Add Capacity
CR12	Change capacity
CR13	Display Capacity
CR15	Capacity where-used
CR21	Create Hierarchy
CR22	Change Hierarchy
CR23	Display Hierarchy
CR24	Create Resource Network
CR25	Change Resource Network

CR26	Display Resource Network
CR31	Create Hierarchy
CR32	Change Hierarchy
CR33	Display Hierarchy
CR40	Work center usage in deleted object
CR41	Archiving work centers
CR60	Work center information system
CRA1	PP: Archiving work centers
CRA2	PP: Archiving delete work centers
CRA3	PP: Archiving work cntr maintenance
CRAA	Display Work Center
CRAF	Archive Data File
CRAH	Create Work Center
CRAM	Archive Card Master Records
CRAV	Change Work Center
CRC1	Create Resource
CRC2	Change Resource
CRC3	Display Resource
CRC4	Change Default Resource
CRCC	Current Settings - Resources
CRDCS1	Credentialing Correspondence Print
CRDIMG	Credentialing Implementation Guide
CRDSNROASID	Number Range Maintenance: CRD_AS_ID
CRD_APPL_01	Call VCRD_TYPE
CRD_APPL_02	Call VCRD_CDEFT
CRD_APPL_03	Call VCRD_CassgT
CRD_APPL_04	Call VCRD_SDEF
CRD_APPL_05	Call VCRD_SDEF
CRD_APPL_06	Call VCRD_SDEF
CRD_APPL_07	Call VCRD_SDEF
CRD_APPL_08	Configure Requirement Types
CRD_APPL_09	Simple Requirements
CRD_APPL_10	Define Requirements
CRD_APPL_11	Configure Combined Requirements
CRD_APPL_12	Call VCRD_REQATT
CRD_APPL_SET	Set Credentialing Application
CRD_DET_AF	Referencing Descriptions
CRD_DET_AFAL	Referencing Descriptions All Vers.
CRD_DET_CRD	Credential Descriptions
CRD_DET_CRDAL	Credential Descriptions All Versions
CRD_RQMNT_DETAIL	Credentialing (Internal Usage)
CRD_SEND_AS	Send Credential and Appointment Info
CRD_TEST	Credentialing: Test
CREATE_CRM_Q	Create CRM Qualifications
CRF1	Credit Cards: Read Original Data
CRF2	Credit Cards: Delete Standard File
CRF3	Credit Cards: Edit Standard File
CRF4	Credit Cards: Edit Log
CRIT	Call the Criteria Manager
CRK1	Create Card Document
CRK2	Change Card Document
CRK3	Display Card Document
CRMBS02	Maintain Status Profiles
CRMBS03	Display Status Profiles

CRMBS42	Maintain Status Selection Profiles	
CRMBS43	Display Status Selection Profile	
CRMBS52	Maintain Authorization Keys	
CRMBS53	Display Authoriztaion Key	
CRMBWST	Genertd DataSource for BW Status Obj	
CRMCFSPRODID	Number Range Maintenance: FS_PRODID	
CRMC_BLUEPRINT	Maintenance for BSP Blueprint	
CRMC_BLUEPRINT_C	IMG Call	
CRMC_BL_CHECK	Check Blueprint Tables	
CRMC_BL_COPY_QUERIES	Copy Report for Delivery Queries	
CRMC_BSP_ANALYZE	Starts CRMC_BSP_FRAME: Analysis Mode	
CRMC_BSP_CT	Customizing Tool	
CRMC_BUT_CALL_FU	Determining FMs for Data Exchange:BP	
CRMC_CIC_WSP0	CIC Component Definition	
CRMC_CUST_APPLLAYOUT	ViewCluster Mtnce CRMV_APPLLAYOUT	
CRMC_EXEC_BAB	CRM: Start Business Applic. Builder	
CRMC_EXEC_BAB_C	CRM: Start BAB in Customer Mode	
CRMC_EXEC_BAB_D	CRM: BAB in Customer Designer Mode	
CRMC_EXEC_BAB_S	CRM: Start BAB in SAP Mode	
CRMC_IC_ACPROF	Define Activity Clipboard Profiles	
CRMC_IC_ACTIONPROF	Copy/Delete Launch Transactions	
CRMC_IC_ACTIONWZ	Configure Transaction Launcher	
CRMC_IC_ACTPROF	Activity Clipboard Technical Profile	
CRMC_IC_ALERTMODELER	Define Alerts and Alert Profiles	
CRMC_IC_BOLBOR	Define BOL/BOR Mapping	
CRMC_IC_BROAD	IC WebClient Broadcast Customizing	
CRMC_IC_CHAT	Define Chat Profiles	
CRMC_IC_EMAIL	Define E-Mail Profiles	
CRMC_IC_EMAIL_BAS	Define E-Mail Profiles	
CRMC_IC_EVENTING	Define Event Classes	
CRMC_IC_FROMGRP	Define Outgoing Address Groups	
CRMC_IC_HEARTBEAT	Define Heartbeat Check Profile	
CRMC_IC_KSPROF	Define Knowledge Search Profiles	
CRMC_IC_LTX_URLS	Define URLs and Parameters	
CRMC_IC_MAIN	Define IC WebClient Profiles	
CRMC_IC_MCM_CCPRO	Define Com Mgmt Software Profiles	
CRMC_IC_NAVBAR_PERM	Define Navigation Bar Profiles	
CRMC_IC_PMASTER	Define Function Profiles	
CRMC_IC_RESPNGRP	Define Standard Response Groups	
CRMC_IC_RTFRAMEWORK	IC Runtime Framework Customizing	
CRMC_IC_SCRIPT	Maintain Interactive Scripting Prof	
CRMC_IC_TLBBTN	Define Toolbar Buttons	
CRMC_IC_TLBPROF	Define Toolbar Profiles	
CRMC_ISE_GRP	Define Script Authorization Groups	
CRMC_LAYOUTC_GENE	Generation of Customer Table Layout	
CRMC_LAYOUT_GENERATE	Generation of Layout Table	
CRMC_PCUITOOLS	Tools for PC UI	
CRMC_SAF_ADV	SAF: Advanced customizing for saf	
CRMC_SAF_ADV_APP	SAF: Customizing for applications	
CRMC_SAF_ADV_CLIENT	SAF: Advanced customizing for saf	
CRMC_SAF_ICKB	Knowledge search attachment	
CRMC_SAF_NR_FEEDBACK	SAF: Number range CRM_EIFDBK	
CRMC_SAF_TOOL	SAF Diagnosis Tool	
CRMC_SAF_WZ_APP	SAF: Wizard for applications	

CRMC_SAF_WZ_COMPILE	SAF: Wizard for compilation service
CRMC_SAF_WZ_KB	SAF: Wizard BAdI Knowledge Base
CRMC_SAF_WZ_LE	SAF: Wizard for learning engine
CRMC_SAF_WZ_RFC	Configure RFC Destinations
CRMC_SAF_WZ_SE	SAF: Wizard for seach engine
CRMC_SKIN_WB	CRM THTMLB Skin Workbench
CRMC_UI_ACTIONWZ	Configure Transaction Launcher
CRMC_UI_BI	Define BI Reports for CRM UI
CRMC_UI_CLIP	Activitiy Clipboard
CRMC_UI_COMPONENTS	Component definitions
CRMC_UI_CONF_KEY	Define Role Config Keys
CRMC_UI_DC_PARAM	Define data context parameters
CRMC_UI_LAYOUT	CRM UI Application Context Layout
CRMC_UI_NBCOMP	Define navigation components
CRMC_UI_NBLINKS	Define NavBar Profile
CRMC_UI_OBJ_MAPPING	Define Object Mapping
CRMC_UI_PARAMETERS	Define Paramters
CRMC_UI_PMASTER	Define Function Profiles
CRMC_UI_PROFILE	Define Business Roles
CRMC_UI_TPROFILE	Technical Profile Definition
CRMC_UI_WA_COMP_REP	Define Work Area Components
CRMC_XMLEDITOR	Start XML Editor for Spice
CRMM_BCB_ADM	Maintain Connections
CRMM_IC_GFS	IC Global Framework Settings
CRMM_IC_MCM_CCADM	Maintain System Settings
CRMM_IC_MCM_CCLNK	Assign Profiles
CRMM_IC_SPHQ	CCS SAPphone Queue Maintenance
CRMM_IC_SPHQA	CCS SAPphone Queue Assignment Maint
CRMOST_MON	Web Service Tool Monitoring
CRMOST_TRANS	Transport of Design Layer Settings
CRMSRVCOCP	Cockpit for Controlling Integration
CRMS_IC_CHECK	Check System Settings and Status
CRMS_IC_CROSS_SYS	Transaction Launcher Logical Systems
CRMS_UI_OBJ_MAPPING	Define Object Mapping
CRMS_UI_TLINK	Define Technical Links
CRM_AC	Check Appntmnt Rule f. Data Exchange
CRM_BSP_DELETE_QUERY	Delete Old and Unused Queries
CRM_BSP_STATE_ERASE	Erases the specified PCUI state.
CRM_BSP_VCLS_APPL	Call CRMV_APPLLAYOUT
CRM_BSP_VCLS_APPLSET	Call CRMV_APPLSET
CRM_BSP_VCLS_FLDGRP	Call CRMV_FIELDGRPOUP
CRM_BSP_VCLS_MLTGRP	Call CRMV_MULTIGROUP
CRM_BSP_VCLS_RGTAB	Call CRMV_REGTAB
CRM_BSP_VCLS_SEARCH	Call CRMV_SEARCHGROUP
CRM_BSP_VCLS_SHOW	Display view cluster
CRM_BSP_VCLS_STEPGRP	Call CRMV_STEPGROUP
CRM_BSP_VCLS_TLBAR	Call CRMV_TOOLBAR
CRM_BSP_VCLS_VIEWGR	Call CRMV_VIEWGROUP
CRM_BSP_VCLS_VSETGRP	Call CRMV_VSETGROUP
CRM_BSP_VIEW_APPLOBJ	Call CRMV_APPL_OBJT
CRM_BSP_VIEW_BLAPPL	Call CRMV_BL_APPL
CRM_BSP_VIEW_BLBY	Call CRMV_BL_BY
CRM_BSP_VIEW_BLPRNTC	Call CRMV_BLUEPRNTC
CRM_BSP_VIEW_BLSHOW	Call CRMV_BL_SHOW

CRM_BSP_VIEW_BLVIEW	View CRMV_BL_VIEW
CRM_BSP_VIEW_EVENT	Call CRMV_BSP_EVENT
CRM_BSP_VIEW_EVENTGR	Call CRMV_EVENTGRE
CRM_BSP_VIEW_EVENT_R	Call CRMV_BSP_EVENT_R
CRM_BSP_VIEW_F4REC	Call CRMV_F4MAPREC
CRM_BSP_VIEW_F4RECC	Call CRMV_F4MAPRECC
CRM_BSP_VIEW_F4SND	Call CRMV_F4MAPSND
CRM_BSP_VIEW_F4SNDC	Call CRMV_F4MAPSNDC
CRM_BSP_VIEW_FLDGRC	Call CRMV_FIELDGRPC
CRM_BSP_VIEW_FLDGRE	Call CRMV_FIELDGRE
CRM_BSP_VIEW_MLTGRP	Call CRMV_MULTIGRPE
CRM_BSP_VIEW_MLTGRPC	Call CRMV_MULTIGRPC
CRM_BSP_VIEW_MLTGRPE	Call CRMV_MULTIGRP
CRM_BSP_VIEW_MSGGRP	Call CRMV_BSP_MSG_GRP
CRM_BSP_VIEW_MSGS	Call CRMV_BSP_MSGS
CRM_BSP_VIEW_PROC	Call CRMV_BSP_PROC
CRM_BSP_VIEW_PROCC	Call CRMV_BSP_PROCC
CRM_BSP_VIEW_PROCE	Call CRMV_BSP_PROCE
CRM_BSP_VIEW_SEARGRE	Call CRMV_SERCHGRE
CRM_BSP_VIEW_SEARVAC	Call CRMV_SEARCHVAC
CRM_BSP_VIEW_SHOW	Call Maintenance Dialog for View
CRM_BSP_VIEW_SOURCE	Call CRMV_BL_SOURCE
CRM_BSP_VIEW_STEPGRC	Call CRMV_STEPGRC
CRM_BSP_VIEW_STEPGRE	Call CRMV_STEPGRE
CRM_BSP_VIEW_TABGRC	Call CRMV_RGTABGRC
CRM_BSP_VIEW_TABGRE	Call CRMV_RGTABGRE
CRM_BSP_VIEW_TLBRGRC	Call CRMV_TOOLBARGC
CRM_BSP_VIEW_TLBRGRE	Call CRMV_TLBARGRE
CRM_BSP_VIEW_VIEWGRE	Call CRMV_VIEWGRE
CRM_BSP_VIEW_VSETGRC	Call CRMV_VSETGRC
CRM_BSP_VIEW_VSETGRE	Call CRMV_VSETGRE
CRM_CIC_RABOX	Remote Action Box via SAPGui for HTM
CRM_ES_CC	CRM_ES_CLIENTCOPY_TEMPLATES
CRM_ES_CHK	CRM_ES_COMPARATOR
CRM_ES_MT	CRM_ES_ALL_MODEL_TRANSFER
CRM_ES_SGEN	Structure generation for search
CRM_ES_TR	CRM_ES_CUST_TRANSPORT
CRM_ES_WB	CRM ES Modeling Workbench
CRM_F4MULTIDEF	Call CRMV_F4MULTIDEF
CRM_F4MULTIDEFC	Call CRMV_F4MULTIDEFC
CRM_GENIL_WSC	Web Service Consumption Tool
CRM_ICI_TRACE	trace selection and display for ICI
CRM_INIT_APPLSET_REL	Application Set: Assignment Tables
CRM_PRODUCT_LOG	Display Product Verification Log
CRM_PRODUCT_STA	Display Product Status
CRM_ROLE_CHECK	Admin Tools: Role Check
CRM_ROLE_COPIER	Role Copier (Portal Administration)
CRM_ROLE_MAP_ADDER	Admin Tools: Role Mappings Adder
CRM_TAX_VALIDATE_BP	Customizing Report for BP in OLTP
CRM_UI	Start CRM WebClient
CRM_UI_DBG	Start CRM WebClient (Debug mode)
CRM_URL_CONSIST_CHK	Consistency Check (Portal Admin.)
CRM_VARIANT_DESCRP	Call CRM_BSP_VARIANT_DESCRIPTION
CRNA	Number Range Maintenance: CR_ARBPL

SAP Transaction Codes – Volume One

CRNH	Number range maintenance: CR_HIERAR
CRNK	Number Range Maintenance: CR_KAPA
CRO0	Display Card Types
CRO1	Maintain Card Types
CRO2	Display Field Control
CRO3	Maintain Field Control
CRO4	Display Selection Codes
CRO5	Maintain Selection Codes
CRQ1	Create work center
CRQ2	Change work center
CRQ3	Display work center
CRR1	Evaluate Card Master Records
CRR2	Evaluate Card Documents
CRR3	Evaluate Log File
CRS1	Create Credit Card Master Record
CRS2	Change Credit Card Master Record
CRS3	Display Credit Card Master Record
CRT0	Copy C Tables Work Center
CRT1	Work Center Options in Rel. 2.1A
CRT2	Settings Work Center Rel. 2.2a
CRT3	Upload C Tables Resource 3.0a
CRT4	Field selection transfer settings
CRTD	Payment Card: Create Example File
CRTGDSREC	Tcode for MIGO entry from Portal
CRTRETDELDOC	Tcode MIGO return delivery Portal
CRTSUBDELDOC	Tcode MIGO subsequent deliver Portal
CRWBD	Replication Workbench
CRWBD_GENBASELINE	Test of Transfer Inside WF
CS00	BOM Menu
CS01	Create Material BOM
CS02	Change Material BOM
CS03	Display Material BOM
CS05	Change Material BOM Group
CS06	Display Material BOM Group
CS07	Allocate Material BOM to Plant
CS08	Change Material BOM - Plant Alloc.
CS09	Display Allocations to Plant
CS11	Display BOM Level by Level
CS12	Multilevel BOM
CS13	Summarized BOM
CS14	BOM Comparison
CS15	Single-Level Where-Used List
CS20	Mass Change: Initial Screen
CS21	Mass Material Change: Initial Screen
CS22	Mass Document Change: Initial Screen
CS23	Mass Class Change: Initial Screen
CS25	Archiving for BOMs
CS26	BOM deletion
CS27	Retrieval of BOMs
CS28	Archiving for BOMs
CS31	Create class BOM
CS32	Change class BOM
CS33	Display class BOM
CS40	Create Link to Configurable Material

CS41	Change Material Config. Allocation
CS42	Display Material Config. Assignment
CS51	Create standard BOM
CS52	Change standard BOM
CS53	Display standard BOM
CS61	Create Order BOM
CS62	Change Order BOM
CS63	Display Order BOM
CS71	Create WBS BOM
CS72	Change WBS BOM
CS73	Display WBS BOM
CS74	Create multi-level WBS BOM
CS75	Change multi-level WBS BOM
CS76	Display multi-level WBS BOM
CS80	Change Documents for Material BOM
CS81	Change Documents for Standard BOM
CS82	Change documents for sales order BOM
CS83	Change documents for WBS BOM
CS84	Change documents for class BOM
CS90	Material BOM Number Ranges
CS91	Number Ranges for Standard BOMs
CS92	Number Ranges for Sales Order BOMs
CSA1	Enqueue test for dialog RFC
CSA2	Current settings
CSAB	Browse Sales Order BOM
CSADMIN	Content Server Administration
CSC5	Single-Level Class Where-Used List
CSCPMCL	Maintain material completion levels
CSCPPLPA	Maint. routing param with materials
CSD5	Single-Level Doc. Where-Used List
CSK1	Sales order BOM multi-lev. explosion
CSK2	Multi-level sales order BOM
CSK3	Sales order BOM - summarized BOM
CSKB	Start order Browser
CSMB	Start material BOM browser
CSMONITOR	Knowledge Provider Monitor
CSP1	Multi-level WBS BOM explosion
CSP2	WBS BOM multi-level BOM
CSP3	WBS BOM - summarized BOM
CSPB	Start WBS BOM browser
CSPC	Customer Specifications
CSRC_TRACE	Switch for BOM Recursion Trace
CT01	Create Characteristic
CT02	Change Characteristic
CT03	Display Characteristic
CT04	Characteristics
CT05	Create Characteristic
CT06	Display Characteristic
CT10	Characteristics List
CT11	CT12
CT12	Where-Used List for Char.Environment
CT21	Batch Input for Characteristics
CT22	Maint. Seq. File for Characteristics
CT23	Display Chars for Change Number

SAP Transaction Codes – Volume One

CT24	Display Change Numbers Used
CT25	Where-Used List of Chars in Deps
CTBW	Table Maint. for BW and Classes
CTBW_META	Generating Metadata
CTCP	Copy C tables for characteristics
CTCX	Table entries for scheduling
CTEW	TEW For Catt
CTNK	Number Ranges for Characteristics
CTOB	Object overview: Table entries
CTU6	Function Tree with Tree Control
CTW_PFAC_IMP_ADM	Maintain Responsibilities
CU00	
CU01	Create Dependency
CU02	Change Dependency
CU03	Display Dependency
CU04	Dependency List
CU05	Dependency Where-Used List
CU10	Dependency Maintenance - Statuses
CU11	Dependency Maintenance - Groups
CU12	Dependencies - Objects
CU13	Dep. Maint. - allowed dep. types
CU14	Maintenance Auths for Dependencies
CU15	Maintenance Auths for Dependencies
CU16	Configuration Paramters: Statuses
CU17	Configuration Parameters: Objects
CU18	Configuration Paramters: Default
CU19	Organizational Areas
CU21	Create Dependency Net
CU22	Change Dependency Net
CU23	Display Dependency Net
CU31	Create Knowledge Base Object
CU32	Change Knowledge Base Object
CU33	Display Knowledge Base Object
CU34	Create Runtime Version for SCE
CU35	Change Runtime Version for SCE
CU36	Display Runtime Version for SCE
CU37	Create SCE Database Schema
CU41	Create Configuration Profile
CU42	Change Configuration Profile
CU43	Display Configuration Profile
CU44	Material Configuration Overview
CU45	Standard Network Config. Overview
CU50	Material Config. Simul./Modelling
CU51	Order BOM
CU51E	CE: Order BOM (eoASL)
CU52	Display Order BOM
CU52E	CE: Display Order BOM
CU55	CE: WBS BOM (eoPSL)
CU59	Transfer Variant Table Contents
CU60	Table Maintenance
CU60E	MS Excel Upload of Variant Tables
CU61	Create Table Structure
CU62	Change Table Structure
CU63	Display Table Structure

129

CU64	Table Structure List
CU65	Create Function
CU66	Change Function
CU67	Display Function
CU68	Function List
CU70	Create Sort Sequence
CU71	Change Sort Sequence
CU72	Display Sort Sequence
CU80	Configurable Mat. Characteristics
CUAL	Distribution of SCE Knowledge Bases
CUCBASEINFO	CBase Entries
CUCHECK	Check Reports for LO-VC
CUCK	Copy Config. Material
CUD2	Distr. Conf. Prof. for GM Task List
CUD3	Distr. Conf. Prof. for Mod. Specs
CUFD	Distribute Variant Functions
CUID	Distribution of Interface Designs
CUK2	Distribute Dependency Nets
CULL_TRACEFILTER	Filter Param. Low-Level Conf.Trace
CULL_TRACE_DISPLAY	Display Low-Level Trace
CUMODEL	Transaction for Displaying Model
CUNI	Units of measure
CUNK	Number Ranges for Dependencies
CUNR	Number Range Maintenance: CU_INOB
CURTO_CREATE	PDS Transfer (ERP System)
CURTO_CREATE_BOM	PDS Transfer (BOM Only)
CURTO_CREATE_FOCUS	Transfer of Order/Project Status
CUSC	Customize Country Version
CUSTMON1	Objects in Customer Namespace
CUSTSELDEF_FIAA	Selection Tool Default Criteria /CUS
CUSTSELDEF_IM_FA_IA	Selection Tool Default Criteria /CUS
CUSTSEL_FIAA	Customizing of Selection Tool
CUSTSEL_IM_FA_IA	Customizing of Selection Tool
CUS_FLEET_01	Field Selection Fleet Fields Equipmt
CUS_ORIGLANG	Original Languages in Customizing
CUTABLEINFO	CBase Entries
CUTRACE	Extended Dependency Trace
CUTRC	Start of Message Handling Trace
CUUPDMV	Update Material Variants
CV00	Document Management
CV01	Create Document Info Record
CV01N	Create Document
CV02	Change Document Info Record
CV02N	Change Document
CV03	Display Document Info Record
CV03N	Display document
CV04	List Document Info Records
CV04N	Find Document
CV11	Create Document Structure
CV12	Change Document Structure
CV13	Display Document Structure
CV130	TEST_CV130
CV15	Change Document BOM Group
CV16	Display Document BOM Group

SAP Transaction Codes – Volume One

CV22	Change Frontend Type
CV30	Display Transfer Log
CV31	Find CAD Interface Errors Online
CV80	Change Documents for Doc. Structure
CV90	Number ranges for documents
CV91	Number Ranges for Doc. Structures
CVAD	Initial Screen for Archiving
CVAR	Archive DMS Tables
CVAW_CUST	Customizing for CVAW
CVD1	Edit Report Shipping Orders
CVD2	Edit Report Recipient
CVD3	EHS: Maintain report recipient (P)
CVD5	Edit Data Provider
CVI0	Document distribution
CVI1	Create recipient list
CVI2	Change recipient list
CVI3	Display recipient list
CVI4	All recipients of a document
CVI6	Display documents of recipient
CVI7	Start distribution with rec. list
CVI8	Start document distribution
CVI9	Log for distribution orders
CVII	Display Initial Order on Classific.
CVIX	Activate event type linkage
CVIY	Task-specific Customizing
CVI_CUST_CHECK	Check of the CVI customizig
CVLO	Delete Archived DMS Table Entries
CVRC1AVGE1	RC1AVGE1 - Authorization Test
CVRC1AVGE2	RC1AVGE2 - Authorization Test
CVRC1WWIDP	RC1WWIDP - Authorization Test
CVRC1WWIWP	RC1WWIWP - Authorization Test
CVRCVDCREO	Export of EH&S Documents
CVRCVDDISP	RCVDDISP - Authorization Test
CVRCVDEVEN	RCVDEVEN - Authorization Test
CVRCVDRFSH	RCVDRFSH - Authorization Test
CVRE	Read Archived Tables
CVSE_CUSTOMIZING	Customizing for SE document search
CVSE_MAINTAIN	Find and process document(s)
CVSE_SEARCH	Find document with search engine
CVSE_VERIFY	Documents in the search engine index
CVSNUMDDBID	Edit Number Range: CVD_DDBID
CVSNUMDDOID	Edit Number Range: CVD_DDOID
CVSNUMDDPID	Edit Number Range: CVD_DDPID
CVSNUMEVENT	Edit Number Range: CVD_EVENT
CVSNUMEXPORT	EHS Number Range: CVD_EXPORT
CVSNUMJOBID	Edit Number Range: CVD_JOBID
CVSNUMLOGID	Edit Number Range: CVD_LOGID
CVSNUMPARID	Edit Number Range: CVD_PARID
CVSNUMRECN	Edit Number Range: CVD_RECN
CVW1	Internet scenario for doc. search
CVW2	Index search DMS in WWW
CVW3	Find documents in the World Wide Web
CVW3A	Find documents in the World Wide Web
CVW4	Display document lists in WWW

CVW4A	Display document lists in WWW
CVWD	WWW access:Distribtution order pack.
CVWEB_DOCLIST_SHOW	Find documents in the World Wide Web
CVWG	DMS: Test for up/download ActiveX
CWBQM	QM: Engineering Workbench
CWVT	Merchandise Distribution
CX00	SAP Cons.: Application Menu
CX00N	SAP Cons.: Application Menu
CX01	SAP Cons: General Configuration Menu
CX01N	SAP Cons.: Configuration Menu
CX0A1	Edit Characteristics
CX0A2	Edit Field Groups
CX0A3	Generate Master Data Maint. Modules
CX0A4	Reorg.View Maintenance (master data)
CX0A5	Maintain Characteristic Values
CX0A6	Display Characteristic Values
CX0A7	Maintain Characteristic Values
CX0A8	Display Characteristic Values
CX0AA	Maintain Default Values
CX0AB	Display Default Values
CX0AC	Attrib for CU: Maint. Char. Values
CX0AD	Attrib for CU: Displ. Char. Values
CX0AE	Subassign.: Maintain Char Values
CX0AF	Subassign.: Display Char Values
CX0C00	Check Ref. Integrity Customizing
CX0C10	Display Chg.Log - MasterData/Custom.
CX0T9	Export Transaction Data
CX0TA	Import Transaction Data
CX0TC	Transport of ECCS Customizing
CX0UD	Copy Customizing Between Dimensions
CX0UM	EC-CS: Migration from FI-LC
CX0UN	Copy Document Number Ranges
CX0US	EC-CS: Copy Sets
CX10	Create cons charts of accounts
CX11	Change cons charts of accounts
CX12	Display cons charts of accounts
CX13	Create FS items
CX14	Change FS items
CX15	Display FS items
CX16	Edit Item Hierarchy
CX16_OLD	Edit Item Hierarchy
CX17	Display Item Hierarchy
CX17_OLD	Display Item Hierarchy
CX19	CU / Financial Data Type Assignments
CX1A	Create Breakdown Categories
CX1B	Change Breakdown Categories
CX1B0	List Master Data: Cons Units
CX1B1	Upload Methods - Cons Units
CX1B2	Upload Consolidation Units
CX1B4	Consistency Check Transaction Data
CX1C	Display Breakdown Categories
CX1C0	List Master Data: Cons Groups
CX1C1	Upload Methods for Cons Groups
CX1C2	Upload Consolidation Groups

SAP Transaction Codes – Volume One

CX1C3	Copy Cons Group Hierarchies
CX1D	Create subitem categories
CX1E	Change subitem categories
CX1F	Display subitem categories
CX1G	Create subitems
CX1H	Change subitems
CX1H0	Where-used List for CG/CU
CX1H1	FS Items Where-Used List
CX1I	Display subitems
CX1I0	Upload Methods for FS Items
CX1I1	List Master Data: FS Items
CX1I2	Upload FS Items
CX1I3	Mass Change: FS Items
CX1I4	Breakdown Categories
CX1I5	Copy Item Sets
CX1J	Create dimensions
CX1K	Change Dimensions
CX1L	Display dimensions
CX1M	Create consolidation units
CX1N	Change Consolidation Units
CX1N1	Set Cons Units Inactive
CX1O	Display Consolidation Units
CX1P	Create consolidation group
CX1Q	Change consolidation group
CX1R	Display consolidation group
CX1S	Create Hierarchy
CX1S0	Upload Methods for Subitems
CX1S1	List Master Data: Subitems
CX1S2	Upload Subitems
CX1S3	Display subitem category/subitem
CX1S4	Change subitem category/subitem
CX1T	Change Hierarchy
CX1U	Display hierarchy
CX1X	Edit Cons Group Hierarchies
CX1XN	Edit Cons Group Hierarchies
CX1X_OLD	Edit Cons Group Hierarchies
CX1Y	Display CG Hierarchy
CX1YN	Display CG Hierarchy
CX1Y_OLD	Display CG Hierarchy
CX1Z_CONGR	Hierarchy Variants for Cons Groups
CX1Z_ITEM	Hierarchy Variants for FS Items
CX20	Consolidation Monitor
CX21	Enter Additional Financial Data
CX22	Display Additional financial data
CX23	Default Values for Activity Entry
CX24	Preparation for Divestiture
CX25	Upload Reported Financial Data
CX26	Apportionment
CX27	List of Last Change of Task Status
CX2V1	Customize Version
CX30	General download
CX31	Specific download
CX32	Upload Financial Data, Offline Entry
CX33	Upload IPI AFD, Offline Data Entry

CX34	Database list of totals
CX34A	DB List of Totals - Cons Logic
CX35	Centralized entry of reported data
CX36	Display reported financial data
CX37	Create data entry layout
CX38	Change data entry layout
CX39	Display data entry layout
CX3A	Translate Data Entry Layout
CX3B	CG: Assign Valid. and CU recordable
CX3D	Cons: Import Data Entry Layout
CX3D1	Download Reported Financial Data
CX3E	Cons: Transport Data Entry Layout
CX3E0	Extract from Step Consolidation
CX3F0	Upload Methods - Chgs in Investments
CX3F1	Upload Methods - Changes in Equity
CX3F2	Upload Methods - Equity Holdings Adj
CX3F3	Upload Changes in Investments
CX3F4	Upload Changes in Investee Equity
CX3F5	Upload Equity Holdings Adjustments
CX3F6	Method for uploading inventory data
CX3F7	Method for uploading supplier data
CX3F8	Upload Inventory Data
CX3F9	Upload Supplier Data
CX3FA	Upload Methods-Fair Value Adjs(Cust)
CX3FB	Upload FVAs (Master data)
CX3FC	Upload Meths: Fair Value Adjs(Value)
CX3FD	Upload Fair Value Adjustments(Value)
CX3FE	Upload Methods, Product Groups
CX3FF	Upload Product Groups
CX3FG	Upload Methods for Breakdown Cats
CX3FH	Upload Breakdown Categories
CX3FI	Upload Methods for Goodwill
CX3FJ	Upload Goodwill
CX3FY	Flexible Upload (generic)
CX3FZ	Flexible Upload (generic)
CX3L1	DB List of Totals Recs/Jrnl Entries
CX3O0	Online Entry: Reorg File Descript.
CX3O1	Scaling Factor for Online Entry
CX40	Currency translation
CX50	Enter posting document
CX51	Change posting document
CX52	Display posting document
CX53	Number range maintenance
CX54	Intercompany elimination
CX55	Validate documents
CX56	Database list of journal entries
CX56A	DB List of Jrnl Entries - Cons Logic
CX57	Consolidation of investments
CX58	Journal Entry Report
CX59	Journal Entry Layouts
CX5A	Cons: Number Ranges - FS Items
CX5B	Cons: Number Ranges - Cons Units
CX5C	Cons: Number Ranges - Activity No's
CX5D	Cons: Number Range - Documents

CX5E	Delete Held Documents
CX5F	Display Held Documents
CX5G	Display Held Document
CX5H	Cons: Number Range Maintenance Log
CX5I1	Customizing of Interunit Elimination
CX5J1	Reconcile Totals with Jrnl Entries
CX5J2	Reconcile/Update Totals-Jrnl Entries
CX5P1	Inventory Data
CX5P2	Supplier Data
CX5R1	Customizing of Reclassifications
CX5T0	Custom Tasks
CX5T1	IMG: Tasks for Manual Posting, DM
CX5T2	IMG: Tasks for Manual Posting, CM
CX5T3	IMG: Tasks for Reclassifications, DM
CX5T4	IMG: Tasks for Reclassifications, CM
CX5T5	IMG: Tasks for Prep/CG Change, DM
CX5T6	IMG: Tasks for Prep/CG Change, CM
CX5T7	IMG: Tasks for Elim. of P/L in Inv.
CX5T8	Tasks for apportionment
CX5T9	Copy Tasks
CX5TA	Cons Groups to be Copied
CX5TB	Tasks without Settings
CX5TC	Cons Units to be Copied
CX5TD	Edit Consolidation Cycles
CX5TE	Assign Cons Cycles to Versions
CX5U0	Elim. of IU Profit/Loss in Inventory
CX5U1	Product Groups & Inventory Items
CX5U2	IPI: Product Group Posting Items
CX5U3	IPI: Inventory Item-Dep. Posting Itm
CX5U4	IPI: Offsetting items
CX5U5	IPI: Items for translation diff.
CX5U6	IPI: Item for reclass.of distr.costs
CX5UA	IPI: Item for distribution costs
CX5UB	Elim.IU P/L Inv: Subassign, Inv.Item
CX5UC	Global Settings for Elim.of IPI
CX5UD	Customizing Listing: IU P/L in Inv.
CX60	Enter changes in investments
CX61	Display changes in investments
CX62	Enter Changes in Investee Equity
CX63	Display Changes in Equity
CX64	Group shares
CX65	Changes in investments
CX66	Changes in investee equity
CX67	Amortization of goodwill
CX68	Equity Holdings Adjustments
CX69	Value Changes: Goodwill in LC
CX6C1	Customizing of Cons. of Investments
CX6C2	Subitems for Equity Aging Report
CX6C3	Check Customizing of Cons of Investm
CX6F0	Goodwill Amortization/Writeup
CX6F1	Match Activity Numbers f. Inv./Eqty
CX6F2	Fair Value Adjustments
CX6F3	Reporting Fair Value Adjustment Data
CX6F4	Rptd Data, FVA: Reporting

CX6F5	Changes to Eliminated Fair Value Adj
CX6F6	Fair Value Adjustments
CX70	Rollup
CX71	Generation of cons group sets
CX72	Number ranges for set generation
CX73	Rollup batch processing
CX7B0	Read Customizing Data from SAP BW
CX7B1	Data transfer initialization
CX7B2	Comparison data slice BCS and BW
CX7B3	Read from InfoCube
CX7F0	List of Ownership
CXA0	Mass reversal
CXA1	FS item hierarchies
CXA2	Item Categories
CXA3	CU: Assign validation groups
CXA4	CG / Validation Group Assignments
CXA5	HI: Assign cons tasks
CXA6	CU/CG: Assign contact person
CXA7	Positions of contact persons
CXA8	Fiscal year variants
CXA9	Reasons for Inclusion
CXAA	Hierarchy levels
CXAB	Assign hierarchy levels
CXAC	Assign hierarchy levels
CXAD	Organizational elements
CXAE	Char. Values of Org. Elements
CXAF	Org. Element Relationships
CXAG	HI levels with general structure
CXAH	Hierarchy Level Relationships
CXAO	CU / Translation Method Assignments
CXAP	Cons Unit/Tax Rate Assignments
CXAQ	Cons: CU: Validation Assignment
CXAR	Mass Changes - Cons Units
CXAS	Mass Changes - Cons Groups
CXB1	Versions
CXB2	Consolidation frequencies
CXB3	Global System Settings
CXB4	Generate Authorizations for CGs
CXB5	Central maintenance of master data
CXBCS20	BCS Session Manager Menu
CXBW0	Initial Data Transfer
CXBW1	Comparison of Data Slice
CXC0	Selection criteria FICDOW20
CXC2	Data Entry Groups
CXC4	Data entry profiles
CXC5	Cons: Selection parameters FICDOW00
CXC6	Cons: Selection parameters FICDOW10
CXC8	Assign PC Pathname to CG/CU
CXC9	Period Categories
CXCA	Financial data types
CXCC	Upload Methods: Reported Fin. Data
CXCD	Data Monitor
CXCD_WEB	Data Monitor for SAPGUI for HTML
CXCE	Data Monitor for a Cons Unit

SAP Transaction Codes – Volume One

CXCF	Cons Monitor for a Cons Group
CXCK	Copy Totals Records
CXCL	Cons: Item Substitution/Ret.Earnings
CXCR	Delete Totals Records
CXCX	Report Selection
CXCY	Customizing of Report Selection
CXD1	Currency translation methods
CXD2	Exchange Rate Indicators
CXD3	Cur.Trl.aff.Earnings: FS Items
CXDL	Delete trans. data in Cons ledger
CXDL1	Delete trans. data in Cons ledger
CXDT_EXT	Translation: Decentral Texts
CXDT_INT	Translation: Miscellaneous Texts
CXDT_T884M	Translation: Cur.Translation Methods
CXDT_TF100	Translation: FS Items
CXDT_TF103	Translation: Breakdown Categories
CXDT_TF105	Translation: FS Item Categories
CXDT_TF110	Translation: Subitems
CXDT_TF115	Translation: Subitems
CXDT_TF120	Translation: Cons Charts of Accounts
CXDT_TF130	Translation: FS Item Hierarchies
CXDT_TF150	Translation: Dimensions
CXDT_TF160	Translation: Cons Units
CXDT_TF170	Translation: Positions of Contacts
CXDT_TF173	Translation: Reasons for Inclusion
CXDT_TF180	Translation: Cons Groups
CXDT_TF190	Translation: Hierarchies
CXDT_TF195	Translation: Hierarchy Levels
CXDT_TF200	Translation: Versions
CXDT_TF202	Translate: Versions of Structures
CXDT_TF204	Translate: Versions of Data Entry
CXDT_TF206	Translate: Versions of CT Methods
CXDT_TF208	Translate: Versions of Exch. Rates
CXDT_TF210	Translate: Versions of Ledgers
CXDT_TF212	Translate: Versions of Selected Itms
CXDT_TF214	Translation: Tax Rate Versions
CXDT_TF216	Translation: C/I Method Versions
CXDT_TF218	Translation: Investment Versions
CXDT_TF220	Translation: Equity Capital Versions
CXDT_TF222	Translation: Hidden Reserve Versions
CXDT_TF224	Translation: Elim.Hidden Res.Version
CXDT_TF226	Translation: Earnings Versions
CXDT_TF228	Translation: Goodwill Versions
CXDT_TF230	Translation: Task Versions
CXDT_TF232	Translation: Reclassification Vers.
CXDT_TF234	Translation: Versions for Elim. IPI
CXDT_TF236	Translation: Versions for Attributes
CXDT_TF240	Translation: Cons Frequencies
CXDT_TF310	Translation: Data Entry Groups
CXDT_TF320	Translate: Financial Data Types
CXDT_TF325	Translation: Period Categories
CXDT_TF380	Translation: Upload Methods
CXDT_TF400	Translation: Cur.Translation Methods
CXDT_TF420	Translation: Exchange Rate Ind.

CXDT_TF500	Translation: Document Types
CXDT_TF515	Translation: Journal Entry Layouts
CXDT_TF530	Translation: Task Groups
CXDT_TF540	Translation: Tasks
CXDT_TF550	Translation: Consolidation Methods
CXDT_TF665	Translation: Scope for Equity Method
CXDT_TFIN003	Translation: Consolidation Types
CXE0	Task groups
CXE0P	Assignment Archiving Log
CXE1	Document Types
CXE2	Consolidation task groups
CXE3	Consolidation tasks
CXE5	Post selected items
CXE6	Tasks for IU Elimination
CXE7	Methods for Interunit Elimination
CXE8	Tasks for IU Elimination
CXE9	IMG
CXE9N	Start IMG for SAP Cons (internal)
CXEA	Tasks for Reclassification
CXEB	Methods for Reclassification
CXEC	Reclassification
CXED	Tasks for Prep.for Cons Group Change
CXEE	Cons: Contra Items / Ret. Earnings
CXEF	Cons: Rollup Standardized Fin. Data
CXEG	IMG: Doc.Types for Man.Posting - DM
CXEH	IMG: Doc.Types for Reclassific. - DM
CXEI	IMG: Doc.Types for Prep/CG Chgs - DM
CXEJ	IMG: Doc.Types for Man.Posting - CM
CXEK	IMG: Doc.Types for Reclassific. - CM
CXEL	IMG: Doc.Types for Prep/CG Chgs - CM
CXEM	IMG: Doc.Types for IU Elimination
CXEN	IMG: Doc.Types for Cons of Investmts
CXEO	IMG: Doc. Types for Realtime Update
CXEP	IMG: Document types for EIPI
CXEU1	ECCS EURO: Populate Euro Units
CXEU2	ECCS EURO: Maintain Euro Units
CXEU3	ECCS EURO: Select Ledger
CXEU4	ECCS Euro: Status Management
CXEU5	ECCS EURO: Selected Items
CXEUA	ECCS EURO: Reconcile Totals Records
CXEUB	ECCS EURO: Additional Financial Data
CXEUC	ECCS Euro: Integration
CXG1	Integrated Entry from Invest./Equity
CXGP	Global parameters
CXGWMIG	Migration of Goodwill Entries
CXH1	Minority Interest Items
CXH2	Appropriation Items for the Group
CXH3	Minority Appropriation Items
CXH4	Statistical Equity Capital
CXH5	Other Comprehensive Income
CXHA	Distribution of Dividends
CXHB	Director's Bonus
CXI0	Global Settings for C/I
CXI1	Consolidation of investments tasks

CXI2	C/I system utilization
CXI3	C/I Activities: Default Sequence
CXI4	Consolidation of investments methods
CXI5	Activity/Method Type: Asgn Doc.Types
CXI9	Selected Items for C/I
CXIA	Consolidation tasks
CXIB	Cons Tasks: Assign Document Type
CXJ1	Equity Method: Scope of Rptd Data
CXJ2	Reported Items for Equity Method
CXJ3	Posted Items in Equity Consolidation
CXJ4	Reported items for investments
CXJ5	Reported Items for Changes in Equity
CXL1	Create Ledger
CXL2	Change Ledger
CXL3	Display Ledger
CXL4	Delete Ledger
CXLP1	Display Archived Audit Trail
CXLP2	Delete Archived Logs
CXM0	Migrate Master Data EC-CS - SEM-BCS
CXM01	Migration EC-CS - SEM-BCS: Mapping
CXM1	Edit Method Hierarchies
CXM2	Display method hierarchies
CXMF	Changeover to Physical File Names
CXN0	Map Secondary Cost Elements
CXN001	Delete Docs from Realtime Updates
CXN01	Maintain Transaction Types of Cons
CXN011	Define Profit Center Groupings
CXN013	Integr. Cons Units - PrCtr Cons
CXN023	Integr. Cons Groups - PrCtr Cons
CXN1	Map Charts/Accts to Cons Charts/Acct
CXN2	Compare G/L Charts and Cons Charts
CXN3	Rules for ID Combination
CXN4	Convert Collection of CU Master Data
CXN41	Realtime Update: Ledger Selection
CXN5	Assign Company Codes/Business Areas
CXN6	Cons Type and Dimension Assignments
CXN7	Download Rollup-related Data
CXN8	Upload Rollup-related Data
CXNA	Download PCA Hierarchies
CXNB	Download Business Areas/Companies
CXNC	EC-PCA Trx.Data: Cost Elem./Activity
CXND	EC-PCA Trx.Data: Partner Info
CXNE	List CO Cost Elements by Category
CXNF	Assign G/L chart and Cons chart
CXNG	Integrated Cons Units
CXNH	Display Integrated Cons Units
CXNI	Display Items from Integration
CXNJ	Display Subitems from Integration
CXNL	Cons: Download PrCtr Master/Hier.
CXNM	Follow-up pstng FI-Doc. (Tot. table)
CXNN	Write Periodic Extract
CXNN1	Totals Record Display
CXNO	Delete Realtime-Updated Documents
CXNP	Copy Group Accounts to FS Items

CXNQ	Display Transferred Documents
CXNR	Reconc. totals record General/ConsSL
CXNT	Subsequent Integration of Org Units
CXNU	Maintain Field Movement/Real.Update
CXNV	Maintain Group Acct in G/L Account
CXNW	Subseq.Posting of FI Docs->ConsPrep.
CXNX	Reconcile FI/Cons at Document Level
CXNX1	Reconcile Trans. of G/L with Cons.
CXNY	Set/Display Lock Mode for Rollup
CXNZ	Reconciliation Totals Consolidation
CXOC1	Organizational Change Numbers
CXOC2	Top Groups, Organizational Changes
CXP0	Call Log Display
CXP01	Migration EC-CS - SEM-BCS: Log
CXP1	Assign Task groups
CXP2	Tasks for Carryforward
CXP3	Tasks for Data Collection
CXP4	Tasks for Validation of Rptd Data
CXP5	Tasks for Manual Posting
CXP6	Tasks for Currency Translation
CXP7	Tasks for Valid.of Standardized Data
CXP8	Tasks for Rollups
CXP9	Tasks for Valid.of consolidated data
CXPGW1	Reported Items for Push-down Method
CXPGW2	Posting Items for Push-down Method
CXPGW3	List of Reported Push-down Data
CXR0	Run drilldown report
CXR1	Create drilldown report
CXR2	Change drilldown report
CXR3	Display drilldown report
CXR4	Form for creating reports
CXR5	Form for changing reports
CXR6	Form for displaying reports
CXRA	Maintain Variant Groups
CXRB	Maintain Variants
CXRC	Schedule Variant Groups
CXRD	Create Variant Groups
CXRE	Reorganization of Variant Groups
CXRF	Characteristic Group Maintenance
CXRH	Hierarchy Maintenance
CXRI	Overview of Reports
CXRK	Maintain Key Figures
CXRM	Test monitor - drilldown reports
CXRO	Transport reports
CXRP	Transport forms
CXRQ	Import Reports from Client
CXRR	Import Layouts from Client
CXRT	Translation Tool - Drilldown Reports
CXRU	Cross-table translation keys
CXRV	Maintain global variables
CXRW	Convert Drilldown Reports
CXRX	Reorganize Drilldown Reports
CXRY	Reorganize report data
CXRZ	Reorganize Forms

CXS1	Carry Forward Balances
CXS3	Carryforward Items
CXS4	Non-carryforward Items
CXSA	Display Set Maintenance
CXSB	Change Set Maintenance
CXSC	Create Set Maintenance
CXSD	Delete Set Maintenance
CXSTPMIG	C/I: Migration of Stat. Postings
CXSTPMIG2	C/I: Reclass. of Stat. GW Items
CXV1	Validation
CXV2	Create Validation
CXV3	Change Validation
CXV4	Display Validation
CXV5	Maintain equivalency relationship
CXVM	Call View Maintenance
CY00	Engineering Menu
CY38	Resource planning format
CY39	Sort layout key maintenance
CY40	Planning table sort key maintenance
CZ48_1	PS-CM: Create Planning Layout
CZ48_2	PS-CM: Change Planning Layout
CZ48_3	PS-CM: Display Planning Layout
CZ48_4	Transport Planning Layouts
CZ48_5	Import Planning Layouts
DA_CONTROL	Data Archiving Control
DA_SARA	Cross-Archiving-Object Check/Delete
DB01	Analyze exclusive lockwaits
DB02	Tables and Indexes Monitor
DB02OLD	old DB02DB02
DB02_MSS	Db02 for MS SQL Server
DB03	Parameter changes in database
DB05	Analysis of a table acc. to index
DB11	Create Database Connection
DB12	DBA Backup Logs
DB12OLD	DBA Backup Logs (OLD)
DB12_MSS	DB12 Multiconnect transaction
DB13	DBA Planning Calendar
DB13C	Central DBA Planning Calendar
DB13COLD	Central DBA Planning Calendar (OLD)
DB13OLD	DBA Planning Calendar (OLD)
DB14	Display DBA Operation Logs
DB14OLD	Display DBA Operation Logs (OLD)
DB15	Data Archiving: Database Tables
DB16	Display DB Check Results
DB16ORA	Display DB Check Results: Oracle
DB17	Configure DB Check
DB17ORA	Configure DB Check: Oracle
DB2	DB2 z/OS: Select Database Activities
DB20	Update DB Statistics
DB20ORA	Update DB Statistics: Oracle
DB21	Configure DB Statistics
DB24	Administrative Database Operations
DB26	DB Profile:Monitor and Configuration
DB26ORA	DB Profile Maintenance: Oracle

DB2B	DB2 z/OS: Buffer pool tuning
DB2BW	BW Analysis Tool
DB2C	DB2 z/OS: Catalog Browser
DB2D	DB2 z/OS - Deadlock Monitor
DB2J	DB2 z/OS: Manage JCL Jobs
DB2T	DB2 z/OS - Timeout Monitor
DB2U	DB2 z/OS: Long Running Transactions
DB2W	DB2 z/OS: Workload Manager Monitor
DB2X	DB2/390: database check
DB2_IXFIX	DB2-z/OS: index fix (padded, codepg)
DB33	DB System check (configure, IFMX)
DB34	Dbspace extension (IFMX)
DB36	DB6: Alert Configuration
DB37	DB6: Alert Message Log
DB4COCKPIT	iSeries: Cockpit for CCMS Transact.
DB4DB12	iSeries: Backup and Recovery
DB4DGN	Diagnostics
DB4LCK	Lock Monitor
DB4PTFCHK	PTF Check
DB50	SAP DB Assistant
DB50N	Database Assistant
DB59	MaxDB/liveCache System Overview
DB6BACKHIST	DB6: DBA Planning Calendar
DB6CLP	DB6: Command Line Processor
DB6COCKPIT	DB6: DBA Cockpit
DB6CST	DB6: Analyze Cumulative SQL Trace
DB6CST_LST	DB6: Analyze Cumulative SQL Trace
DB6DB21	DB6: RUNSTATS Control
DB6DBALOG	DB6: DBA Log Viewer
DB6DBM	DB6: Database Manager Configuration
DB6DBP	DB6: Database Configuration
DB6EXL	DB6: Analyze Exclusive Lock Waits
DB6EXPLAIN	DB6: Explain SQL Statement
DB6FSC	DB6: File System Configuration
DB6PARHIS	DB6: Show Parameter History
DB6PERF	DB6: DB2 UDB Cockpit Performance
DB6PLAN	DB6: DBA Planning Calendar
DB6SPACE	DB6: Space Analysis
DB6SQC	DB6: Analyze SQL Cache
DB6STATS	DB6: Run Single Statistics
DB6SYSCFG	DB6: System Registration
DB6TAC	DB6: Analyze Table Snapshot
DB6TRC	DB6: Trace Status
DBACOCKPIT	Start DBA Cockpit
DBACOCKPIT_ITS	Start DBA Cockpit
DBACOCKPIT_NWA	Start DBA Cockpit
DBACOCKPIT_SOLMAN	Start DBA Cockpit
DBCO	Database Connection Maintenance
DBG_ABAP_EDITOR	Debugger -> ABAP Editor
DBG_BROWSER	Debugger -> Repository Browser
DBG_MEMORY_DIFFTOOL	Debugger: Call Memory Inspector
DBG_SCREEN_PAINTER	Debugger -> Screen Painter
DBG_TABLE_TO_EXCEL	ABAP Debugger: Table as Excel File
DC10	Define document types

DC20	Define data carrier
DC30	Define workstation application
DCSWI	Document Browser Switch
DCSWITCH	Browser and ACL switch
DDCHECK	Classification of DDIC Structures
DECK	Cash Holding Years
DEDT	Define Downtime
DELETE_COL_SETTINGS	Delete Column Configuration
DELETE_FACTS	Delete from the fact table
DELETE_MDT_SETTINGS	Delete Manager's Desktop Settings
DELETE_NF_SETTINGS	Delete Framework Settings
DELETE_OM_SETTINGS	Delete Object Manager Settings
DELG1	Edit Outbound Delivery Groups
DEMO_OO_METHOD	OO Trans. for Local Instance Method
DEMO_REPORT_TRANSACT	Report Transaction with SelScrn 500
DEMO_SCREEN_FLOW	Demonstration for Screen Sequences
DEMO_SELSCREEN_DYNP	Selection Screen as Initial Screen
DEMO_TABSTRIP	Test Tabstrip
DEMO_TCD	DEMO of a TCD Recording
DEMO_TRANSACTION	Demonstration Transaction
DEVBOOK	Project management
DEVICE_CONFIG	Device Configuration
DEV_DA_CONTROL	DEV Entries Control DA
DEXP	Expediting
DGA1	DG: Activation DG Checks
DGA10	Assign DG check schema/SD documents
DGA2	DG-Check Schema-Determ. Routine
DGA3	DG - Check Methods
DGA4	Usage Profile DG Check Routines
DGA5	DG: Countries en Route
DGA6	DG: Alloctn Chk Schema/Chk Methods
DGA7	Usage Context DG Check Schema
DGA8	DG-CheckSchemaDetRoutineShipmentDoc
DGA9	Allocate DG-CheckSchema/ShipmentDoc
DGAA	DG: Output Cond. for MatMast Fields
DGAB	DG: Profile for DG Ind. in Del. Head
DGAC	DG: Controlling EDI Processing
DGC2	DG: Specify Transport Type
DGC4	DG: Define DG Classes
DGC5	DG: Define Water Pollution Classes
DGC6	DG: Specify Danger Label
DGC8	Text IDs standard/user-defined texts
DGC9	DG: Dialog type for ident. no.
DGCA	DG: Hazard Notes
DGCB	DG: Labels for Printing
DGCC	DG: Hazard Identification Numbers
DGCD	DG: Hazard-Inducing Substances
DGCE	DG: VbF Classes
DGCF	DG: Storage Hazard Classes
DGCG	DG: Processing Status
DGCH	DG: Maintain indicator profile
DGCI	DG: Date Determination
DGCK	Txt names for DG MatMast ind. txts
DGCL	DG: Primary and Secondary Languages

DGCM	DG: Assign check list
DGCN	DG: Assign check list (pack.)
DGCR	DG: Regulations
DGCS	Texts for mode of transport cats.
DGCV	DG UN Number and Description
DGD1	Maint. and Assign Regulation Profile
DGD2	Assignmt Regul. Profile/Indic. Cat.
DGD3	Checkbox Struc. for T/O-T Materials
DGE4	First database via DGP1
DGE5	DG Filling from Spec. Management
DGE6	DG Simul. of Filling from Spec. Mgmt
DGP0	Basic Data: Environment
DGP1	Create Dangerous Goods Master
DGP10	Generate Phrase Sets
DGP2	Change Dangerous Goods Master
DGP3	Display Dangerous Goods Master
DGP5	Report for sending dangerous goods
DGP5S	Report to Simulate Sending
DGP7	Display import logs
DGP8	Delete import logs
DGP9	Activate phrase library
DGPEX2	Exceptions to DG Regulations:
DGPEX3	Exceptions to DG Regulations:
DGPEX5	Init.Distr. of Exceptions to DG Regs
DGPREL	Dangerous Goods Product Release
DGR1	Displaying DG master data
DGR2	Dangerous goods: Change document
DGR3	Display DG Packaging Data
DGR4	Display DG Packaging Data
DGSD	Display Report Logs
DGTD	DG: Maintain mat-dependent texts
DGTU	DG: Maintain mat-independent texts
DGU0	DG: Conversion of Customizing Tables
DGU1	DG: Conversion of DG Reg. tables
DGU2	DG: Conversion Texts/Descriptions
DGU3	DG: Converting the DG Descriptions
DGUC	DG: Test refer. integrity regulation
DGUD	DG: Test ref. integrity of C tables
DGUM	DG: Convert field LWDG to MasterData
DIACLC1	Logbook: counter type definition
DIACLC2	Customizing for cntr upd in Logbook
DIACLC3	Logbook: Dig. signature customizing
DIACLC4	Log Entry Type customizing
DIACL_CUST_LBK_SMODE	Set logbook sync mode
DICTIONARY	Terminology and Glossary Maintenance
DIOHFWC1	Application definition (cust.)
DIOHFWC2	Node type specification (Customizing
DIOHFWC3	Hierarchy definition (customizing)
DIOHFWC4	Fcode definitions (customizing)
DIS01	Collective Processing Distribution
DIS05	Cost Distribution: Overview
DIWPSC2	Custom. of Time Interval in MEB
DIWPSC3	Customizing of Fleet for the MEB
DIWPSC4	Customizing of Revision Type

DIWPS_REVNR	Number range maintenance: WPS_REV
DIWPS_REVNRS	Number Range Maintenance: WPS_REV
DI_0MVTPM	Movement Types for PM/CS Orders
DI_0PCS1	SN Criteria in Sales Documents
DI_0PCS2	Stock Determ. Rule PM/CS Orders
DI_0PCS3	Customizing Stock Determ. in PM/CS
DI_PCS1	Stock Det. Rules for Special Stock
DI_SCCOUNT	Meas.Point for Subcontracting
DL10	Download
DL11	Create download profile
DL12	Change condition download profile
DL13	Display condition download profile
DLC2	Comparison of Delivery Confirmations
DLCN	Delivery Confirmation Matching
DLOG	BRE: Overview of Extract Generation
DMC	Start DMC Interface
DMCAPP	Maintain Applications in DMC Tool
DMCCONF	DMC Configuration
DMCDIGEN	Generate Runtime Objects for DI-2
DMCGEN1	Generate Runtime Object
DMCGUI	DMC_L_GUI
DMCISB	Maintain Direct Input 2
DMCRULE	Maintain Global Transfer Rules
DMCUMSCHL	DMC: Recoding
DMCWB	Workbench for DMC Development
DMEE	DMEE: Format Tree Maintenance Tool
DMEE1	DMEE: Format Tree Maintenance Tool
DMEE1_DEBUG	DMEE: Format Tree Expert Mode
DMEE_DEBUG	DMEE: Format Tree Expert Mode
DMLCUST	Customizing for MDF Objects
DMLCUSTOBJTYPE	Customizing for MDF Object Types
DMS_FOLDER1	Find favorites
DMWB	Document Modeling Workbench
DNOTIF	Basic Notification
DNOTIFREP	Basis Notification Reporting
DNOTIFWL	Basic Notifications Worklist
DNOTIFWL_EWT	Basic Notifications Worklist
DNOTIF_EWT	Basic Notification
DNOTIF_FCT	Basic Notification
DNOTIF_FCT_EWT	Basic Notification
DNO_CUST01	Settings for Notification Type
DNO_CUST02	Settings for Partner Types
DNO_CUST03	Settings for Note Types
DNO_CUST04	Basic Notification: User Settings
DNO_CUST05	Subscreen Control
DNO_NOTIF	Number Range Maintenance
DNO_UPDATE	Manual Adjustment
DOCCHG_FB05	Post with Clearing
DP101	Reset Billing Plan Date
DP60	Change Accounting Indicator in LI
DP70	Conversion of Individual Orders
DP80	SM: Resource-Related Quotation
DP81	PS: Sales Pricing
DP82	PS: Sales Pricing Project

DP90	CS: Resource-Related Billing Doc.
DP91	SD: Resource-Related Billing Doc.
DP93	Res.-Rel. Billing Btwn Comp. Codes
DP95	Resource-Rel. Billing, Coll.Processg
DP96	Res-Rel.Billing Collect.Proc - Sales
DP97	Res-Rel. Billing Collect. Proc.-Srvc
DP98	Resource for Billing Request
DP99A	Doc.Flow Reporting - Res.-Rel. Bill.
DP99B	Doc.Flow for Res.-Rel. Bill. - SD
DP99C	Doc.Flow for Res.-Rel. Bill.-Service
DPCOMMON_BUPAUI	Determine BUPA User Interface
DPCOMMON_MAP_P_S	DPCOMMON: Partner to System Mapping
DPCOMMON_MAP_S_R	DPCOMMON:System to RFC Mapping
DPCOMMON_MAP_U_P	DPCOMMON: User to Partner Mapping
DPRL	Change Material When Profile Deleted
DPRV	Change Material When Profile Changed
DPWTY_IMG	IMG Dealer Portal Warranty
DRAIRPORT	Display Airport Data
DRAW_RES	Display Reserve Fields
DRBBOOK	Display Company Booking
DRBOOK	Display Booking
DRB_SHOW_CALL_DUMMY	DRB Call for Layout Maintenance
DRC1	Create Cond. Table: Deriv. Recipient
DRC2	Create Cond. Table: Deriv. Recipient
DRC3	Create Cond. Table: Deriv. Recipient
DRC4	Conditions: V_T681F for R DR
DRC5	Access Sequences: Deriv. Recipient
DRC6	Strategy Types: Derivation Recipient
DRC7	Search Proc.: Derivation Recipient
DRCARR	Display Carrier
DRCONN	Display Connection
DRCOUNTRY	Display Country
DRCUSTOM	Booked Flights for Customer
DRE	Delivery-Related Analyses
DRFLIGHT	Display Flight Data
DRP0	Network Graphic
DRP4	Network Graphic/Quotas View
DRP8	Maintain Materials Deployment
DRP9	Maintain Plant Categories
DRPA	Definition of DRP Planning Run
DRPB	Deployment: Background Processing
DRPBOOK	Display Private Booking
DRPLANETYPE	Display Aircraft Type
DRPM	Deployment for Material
DRPO	Deployment for Material
DRPS	Calculate Safety Stock
DRPW	Deployment for Plant
DSA	Service Session Workbench
DSADEV_OLD	Service Development Workbench
DSAL	Digital Signature Logs
DSA_ITS	DSVAS: ITS start transaction
DSA_SESSION_OPEN	Open the Service Assistant session
DSC1	Create CondTables: Derivation Sender
DSC2	Create CondTables: Derivation Sender

SAP Transaction Codes – Volume One

DSC3	Create CondTables: Derivation Sender
DSC4	Conditions: V_T681F for R DS
DSC5	Access Sequences: Derivation Sender
DSC6	Strategy Types: Derivation Sender
DSC7	Search Procedures: Derivation Sender
DSETGEN	BRE: Create Error Extract from Log
DSINA	Display Backlog Entry in Extract
DSLOG	Signature Tool: Log Display
DTR0	Enter Downtimes
DUMMY_MASS_EINE	Dummy transaction for mail execution
DUMMY_MASS_EKKO	Dummy transaction for mail execution
DUMMY_MASS_MARC	Dummy transaction for mail execution
DUMMY_MASS_VENDOR	Load programs global data
DVC1	Derivation: No. Range f. Deriv. No.
DVC2	Derivation: No. Range f. Cond. Recds
DVC8	Assignmt of Search Procedure to Evnt
DVCO	Condition Records Via Bill of Mat.
DVDC	Delete Extended Batch Where-Used Lst
DVDL	Delete Derivation Log
DVMAN	Perform Manual Derivation
DVMO	Monitor
DVR1	Create Derivation Recipient Record
DVR2	Change Derivation Recipient Record
DVR3	Display Derivation Recipient Record
DVS1	Create Derivation Sender Record
DVS2	Change Derivation Sender Record
DVS3	Display Derivation Sender Record
DVSA	Shipping Approval
DVSP	Set Up Derivation
DWDM	Development Workbench Demos
DXCF	DARTX Field Catalog
DXCS	DARTX Segment Catalog
DXEV	DARTX Extract Administration
DXVW	DARTX Data View Administration
DXX01	DARTX Maintain Authorization Groups
DXX02	DARTX Segment Maintenance
DXX03	DARTX Maintain SAP Segment Control
DXX04	DARTX Maintain MasterData Indicators
DXX05	DARTX Application Maintenance
DXX06	DARTX Reference Table Maintenance
DXX07	DARTX Data Set/Segment Assignments
DXX08	DARTX Data Set Maintenance
DXX09	DARTX Global Settings Maintenance
DXX10	DARTX Maintain Segment Relationships
DXX11	DARTX Maintain Sel.Parameter Display
DXX12	DARTX Directory Group Maintenance
DXX13	DARTX Maintain Customer Seg. Control
DXX14	DARTX Maintain Reference Crcy/Qty
DXXV	DARTX Define Data Extract Views
DXXVW	Execute Data View
DZ00	Introduction to decentr.systems
E1DY	Create/Rep. Dynamic Schedule Records
E25M	Extend Budget Billing Plan
E25T	Select BillOrder/Uninvoiced BillDocs

E2DY	Change/Display Dyn. Schedule Records
E2E_PROGRAM_RUNNER	Run prog in param E2E_PROGRAM_TO_RUN
E2E_TESTING_AGENT_ST	Self-Test
E309	Define Air Pressure Areas
E3DY	Delete Dynamic Schedule Records
E40A	Display Sched. Recs
E40B	Change Sched. Recs
E41A	Display Portion
E41B	Create Portion
E41C	Change Portion
E41D	List of Sched. Master Recs
E41E	Delete Portion
E41F	Display MR Units
E41G	Change MR Unit
E41H	Create Meter Reading Unit
E41I	Delete MR Unit
E41J	Maint. Portion
E41L	List of MRUs Alloc. to Main MRU
E42A	Display Parameter Recs
E42B	Create Parameter Recs
E42C	Change Parameter Recs
E42D	List of Parameter Recs
E42F	Delete Parameter Rec
E43A	Generate Sched. Recs for Rec Types
E43B	Generate SRs of all MRUs of Portion
E43C	List of Sched. Recs
E43D	List of all MRUs of a Portion
E43E	Activate Meter Reading Units
E4DY	Delete Dynamic Schedule Records
E61CD	Delete Correspondence Data
E61D	Delete Budget Billing Plan
E61K	Maintain Defaults for BB Procedure
E61L	Charges Plan Active for Div. Cat. 06
E61M	Adjust BB Plans Automatically
E61PSD	Stop Payment Scheme
EA00	Test Billing of a Contract
EA04	Maintain Specifs for PayMeth.Determ.
EA05	Display and Release Outsortings
EA10	Document Invoicing
EA10_AGGRBILL	Create Aggregated Bill
EA10_COLL	Create collective bill
EA11	Budget Billing Invoicing
EA12	Request Budget Billing Amounts
EA12IC	Request Budget Billing Amounts
EA13	Print/Billing Document Reversal
EA14	Print/Billing Document Reversal
EA15	Reversal of Invoicing Documents
EA16	Create Manual Backbilling
EA17	Change Manual Backbilling
EA18	Display Manual Backbilling
EA19	Create Bill (Individual Creation)
EA20	Reverse Billing Document
EA21	Adjustment Reversal Billing Docs
EA22	Display Billing Document

EA22_TOOL	Billing Tool
EA24	Delete Adj. Reversal frm Bill.Order
EA25	Create Partial Bill (Individual)
EA26	Mass Processing: Create Bill
EA27	Mass Processing: Create Partial Bill
EA28	Mass Process.: Request BB Amounts
EA29	Mass Processing: Bill Printout
EA29_AGGRBILL	Print Aggregated Bill
EA30	Create Rate
EA31	Change Rate
EA32	Display Rate
EA33	Mass Processing: Bill Reversal
EA34	Mass Processing: Full Reversal
EA35	Create Schema
EA36	Change Schema
EA37	Display Schema
EA38	Mass Activity: Billing
EA39	Mass Activity: Billing Simulation
EA40	Display Print Document
EA43	Generate SRs of a Record Type
EA44	Delete Sched. Recs
EA44M	Mass Deletion of Schedule Records
EA45	Create Consumption and Partial Bill
EA46	Create Consumption and Partial Bill
EA47	Crt. Discount/Surcharge
EA48	Chg.Discount/Surcharge
EA49	Displ.Discount/Surcharge
EA50	Create Operand
EA51	Change Operand
EA52	Display Operand
EA53	Create Rate Cat.
EA54	Chg. Rate Cat.
EA55	Display Rate Cat.
EA56	Maint. Rate Type
EA57	Create Budget Billing Change Doc.
EA58	Mass Activity: Coll. Bill Printout
EA59	Print Collective Bill (Old)
EA60	Print Invoicing Document
EA61	Create BB Plan
EA61EX	Budget Billing Change
EA61IC	Create Down Payment Request
EA61PS	Create Payment Scheme
EA62	Change BB Plan
EA62IC	Change Down Payment Request
EA62PS	Change Payment Scheme
EA63	Display BB Plan
EA63IC	Display Down Payment Request
EA63PS	Display Payment Scheme
EA64	Print collective bill
EA65	Portion Change
EA65PS	Create Payment Scheme Requests
EA66PS	Mass Run: Create PS Requests
EA67	Settings for BB Plan
EA68	Maint. Specifs in Posting Area R007

EA70	Create Billing Cal. Value
EA71	Change Billing Cal. Value
EA72	Display Billing Cal. Value
EA73	Create Gas Procedure
EA74	Change Gas Proced.
EA75	Display Gas Procedure
EA76	Create Cal. Value Proced.
EA77	Change Calorific Value Procedure
EA78	Display Cal. Value Proced.
EA79	Create Vol. Corr. Fact. Proc.
EA80	Change Vol. Corr. Fact.Proc.
EA81	Display Vol. Corr. Fact. Proc.
EA85	Maintain Burning Hour Calendar
EA86	Copy Burng Hr Calendar for One Year
EA87	Rate Determination
EA88	Maintain Variant
EA89	Create Price
EA90	Change Price
EA91	Display Price
EA92	Maintain Price Adjustment Clause
EA97	Evaluation 1: Variants R/2 <-> ERP
EA98	Evaluation 2: Variants R/2 <-> ERP
EA99	Eval. of Variants
EABBP	Archive Budget Billing Plans
EABI	Billing/Invoicing log display
EABICO	Bill Correction
EABIH	Archive Billing Document Headers
EABIL	Archive Billing Document Line Items
EABR	IS-U Billing
EACCBAL	Acct Balnce Display for Deregulation
EACCMAIN	Manual Acct Maintenance for Supplier
EACOLLREV	Select Reversed Documents (SR)
EADYN	Define Dynamic Period Control
EAFACTS	Archive Installation Facts
EAIN	Billing/Invoicing log display
EALOGBI_1	Detail display: MiniApp EMAP_LOGBI
EALOGIN_1	Detail display MiniApp EMAP_LOGIN
EALZ	Logical Register Numbers
EAMABI	Mass Billing
EAMACB	Consumption History from Inv. Line
EAMACF	Consumption History from Inst. Facts
EAMACH	Mass Overall Check
EAMASI	Mass Billing Simulation
EAMS00	Mass Billing of Simulation Indexes
EAMS01	Mass Act.: Billing of Sim. Indexes
EAMS10	Create Simulation Indexes
EAMS11	Monitoring of Mass Simulation
EAMS12	Statisics for Simulation Indices
EAMS13	Delete Simulation Indexes
EAMS20	Define Simulation Periods
EAMS21	UIS Version: Create for Mass Simul.
EAMS22	Statistics for Billing-Rel. Proc.
EAN1	Create GTIN Mapping
EAN2	Change GTIN Mapping

SAP Transaction Codes – Volume One

EAN3	Display GTIN Mapping
EAN4	Create GTIN Mapping with Template
EANC1	Cond.: Field Cat. GTIN Mapping
EANC2	CondTab: Create (GTIN Mapping)
EANC3	CondTab: Change (GTIN Mapping)
EANC4	CondTab: Display (GTIN Mapping)
EANC5	Access sequences: GTIN Mapping
EANC6	Condition types: GTIN Mapping
EANC7	Procedure: GTIN Mapping
EANC8	Determine Procedure GTIN Mapping
EANC9	Customizing GTIN Variant Types
EANCONSISTENCYCHECK	Change Materials Regarding EAN Attr.
EANGLN	Maintain: Global Location Number
EANPROCESS	IO Processes to be Mapped for EAN
EANSIMULATE	Simulate GTIN Mapping
EANUG	EAN.UCC (UoM Grouping criteria)
EANVENDOR	Maintain Vendor EANs
EAOUT	Display Outsourcing for Bill/Inv.
EAOUTL	Cross-Contract Billing
EAOUT_1	Detail display MiniApp EMAP_OUTBIIN
EAPDH	Archive Print Document Headers
EAPDL	Archive Print Document Line Items
EARDISP01	Display Archive: Print Doc. Header
EARDISP02	Display Archive: Print Document Itms
EARDISP03	Display Archive: Billing Document
EARDISP04	Display Archive: Budget Billng Plans
EARDISP05	Display Archive: Billing Doc. Lines
EARDISP06	Display Archive: MR Results
EARDISP07	Display Archive: Inspection List
EARDISP08	Display Archive: EDM Profile Values
EARELINVOICE	Release Billing in Background
EARETPER	Define retention period
EAROUND	Accts for Rounding Amnt Gross Price
EAR_CHECKER	Verify legal rep. cust. consistency
EASIBI	Create Individual Bill
EASICH	Individual Overall Check
EASIM	Simulation Scenarios
EASIM01	Simulation f. Backbill. and PE Bill.
EASISI	Create Individ. Simulation
EASY	Tool:Search For/Call-Up Transactions
EASYDMS_CUS	Customizing Easy Document Management
EATAXROUND_JP	Amount Rounding for Jap. Tax Calcul.
EATR	Mass Activity: Create Bill/Part.Bill
EAXX	IS-U Billing
EA_DOWNLOAD	Download Billing Master Data
EA_TRANSPORT	Complete Transport of Master Data
EA_UPLOAD	Upload Billing Master Data
EBAA	Connection object overview
EBO1	Create boleto for bills
EBPP	EBPP - Demo
EBPP_APAR_SUPPORT	Support Transaction for Bill. Direct
EBPP_AR_CONTACTS	EBPP: Remarks Created
EBPP_AR_MATCH	EBPP: Assignmt of User to Accounts
EBPP_AR_T042ICC	Account Determination Payment Cards

SAP Transaction Codes – Volume One

EBPP_AR_T042ZEBPP	EBPP: Maintain EBPP Payment Methods
EBPP_CREATE_USER	Create a new user
EBPP_CUST_CHNG	Change Notification Data
EBPP_CUST_DISP	Display Notification Data
EBPP_LOG_CUST	Customizing for Log Categories
EBPP_LOG_DISP	Display of Log Categories
EBPP_LOG_ORGA	Reorganize Log Entries
EBPP_RI	Biller Direct Bill Receipt
EBPP_RIC	Biller Direct Bill Receipt: Settings
EBPP_RICONN	Biller Direct Bill Receipt: Links
EBR_CATCFOP	CFOP Category Determination -ISU
EBR_COMPROVRET	Yearly discounted IRPJ by customer
EBR_DAICMS	ICMS Report (DAICMS)
EBR_LIVICMS	Update EBRLIVICMS table for Brazil
EBR_MATCATCFOP	Mat Categ Determination CFOP - ISU
EBR_TE011BR	Quantity dependent tax determination
EBR_VALRETIR	Monthly discounted IRPJ - Customers
EBW_DQ_CS	Marketing: Consumpt. -> Delta Queue
EBW_DQ_SS	Sales Statistics -> BW Delta Queue
EC01	Org.Object Copier: Company Code
EC02	Org.Object Copier: Plant
EC03	Org.Object Copier: Controlling Area
EC04	Org.Object Copier: Sales Organizatn
EC05	Org.Object Copier: Distribution Chnl
EC06	Org.Object Copier: Division
EC07	Org.Object Copier: Shipping Point
EC08	Org.Object Copier: Shipping Point
EC09	Org.Object Copier: Warehouse Number
EC10	Org.Object Copier: Personnel Area
EC11	Org.Object Copier: Personnel Subarea
EC12	Org.Object Copier: Employee Subgroup
EC13	Org.Object Copier: Purchasing Org.
EC14	Org.Object Copier: Storage Location
EC15	Org.Object Copier: Material Type
EC16	Org.Object Copier: Controlling Area
EC20	IS-U Front Office
EC25	IS-U navigator
EC30	Maintain rate data
EC31	Display Rate Data
EC50	Create Move-In Doc.
EC50E	Create Move-In Document
EC51	Change Move-In Document
EC51E	Change Move-In Document
EC52	Display Move-In Doc.
EC52E	Display Move-In Document
EC53	Reverse Move-In Documnt
EC53E	Reverse Move-In Document
EC55	Create Move-Out Doc.
EC55C	Tabstrip- ISU - Move-Out
EC55E	Move-Out
EC56	Chg. Move-Out Doc.
EC56E	Change Move-Out
EC57	Display Move-Out Doc.
EC57E	Display Move-Out

SAP Transaction Codes – Volume One

EC58	Reverse Move-Out Doc.
EC58E	Reverse Move-Out
EC60	Initial Processing: Move-In/Out
EC6F	Initial Processing: Move-In/Out
EC70	Accel.Entry: Move-In / Out / In/Out
EC85	Create Disc. Doc.
EC86	Change Disc. Doc.
EC87	Display Disc. Doc.
ECBWPP	Prepare Extrapolation Indexes
ECENV_BP	Data environ. for business partner
ECENV_CO	Data environ. for connection object
ECENV_DV	Data environment for device
ECHE	Assignment of Visible Components
ECH_DEFLT_RESOL_SAP	SAP Default Resolution Strategy
ECH_RESOL	Define Resolution Strategy
ECH_RESOL_COMP	Define Resolution Strategy
ECH_RESOL_COMP_SYS	Define SAP Resolution Strategy
ECH_RESOL_SYS	Define SAP Resolution Strategy
ECICACC	Konfiguration Autocall & Config
ECLP1	Create Loyalty Account
ECLP2	Change Loyalty Account
ECLP3	Display Loyalty Account
ECMCUST	Customizing for ECM
ECMO	Overview of ECOs
ECMR	Overview of ECRs
ECNC	IS-U Navigator: Customizing
ECOBJFILL	E&C Portal: Batch Proc ECP_OBJFILL
ECON1	Maintain Concession Eligibility
ECON2	Display Concession Eligibility
ECOP	Main Program for Entity Copier
ECP_CT04	Change Characteristics
ECP_CT05	Create Characteristics
ECP_FUNCT_TYPE	Maintain iView function types
ECRD1	Create Redemption
ECRD2	Change Redemption
ECRD3	Display Redemption
ECRD4	Mass Printout of Redemption Vouchers
ECRMREPL	Error Handling Replication CRM/IS-U
ECRMREPLM	Error Handling Replication CRM/IS-U
ECRM_OBJ_TEMPL	Master Data Templates for CRM TO
ECRM_PROD_TEMPL	MD Templates for CRM Products
ECVBP02	Customer Data Overview
ECVCO00	Connection object overview
ECVE	Export Resources from Web Repository
ECVM	Generate Language Version Cust. Info
EC_TUTORIAL_SAPGUI	eCATT Tutorial: SAPGUI Command
EC_TUTORIAL_TCD	eCATT Tutorial: TCD Command
EC_TUTORIAL_TESTDATA	eCATT: Demo for Test Data Management
EDATEXAGGR	Export Aggregated Messages
EDATEXAGGRMON	Monitor Aggregated Messages
EDATEXDELETE	Delete Data Exchange Task
EDATEXEVENTDUE	Monitoring of Due Date of Task
EDATEXEXECUTE	Execute Data Exchange Tasks
EDATEXGEN	Generate Data Exchange Tasks

SAP Transaction Codes – Volume One

EDATEXMON01	Monitoring of Data Exchange Tasks
EDATEXREVGEN	Generation Reversal of D.Exch. Tasks
EDATEXSEND	Send Data for Due Tasks
EDEREG_ANALYSE	Analyses for POD/Service Provider
EDEREG_PODGROUP_GEN	Generate Point of Delivery Groups
EDIT	Juergen's Editor
EDM1	Monitor Profile Import
EDX_DEL	EDX: Delete Messages (Test)
EDX_DUMP	EDX: Save Messages with Errors
EDX_LINK	EDX: Link Document to Attachments
EDX_LIST	EDX: Message Overview
EDX_PROCESS	EDX: Create IDOCs
EDX_RESET	EDX: Reset Message Status
EDX_SEND	EDX: Send Messages
EDX_TRACE	EDX: Display Trace Messages
EE25	Budget Billing Amounts
EE52	IS-U: Change Notification
EE53	IS-U: Display Notification
EE72	IS-U: Change Work Order
EE73	IS-U: Display Work Order
EE73_WM_NOTIF_1	Detail Display for MiniApp WM_NOTIF
EE73_WM_ORDER_1	Detail display for MiniApp WM_ORDER
EEAK	Employment equity - Canada
EEDM00	EDM Frame
EEDM01	Maintain Profile
EEDM02	Display Profile
EEDM04	Maintain Profile Allocation
EEDM05	Display Profile Allocation
EEDM06	Create Profile Header
EEDM07	Change Profile Header
EEDM08	Display Profile Header
EEDM09	Create Point of Delivery
EEDM10	Change Point of Delivery
EEDM11	Display Point of Delivery
EEDM12	Operand - Profile Role Allocation
EEDMCALCWB	EDM Calculation Workbench
EEDMCOPY01	Copy a file with profile values
EEDMCOPY02	Copy File with Internal Data
EEDMEXP01	Download profile values via PoD
EEDMEXP02	Download Profile Values by Prof. No.
EEDMFACTORCALC	Calculate Dynamic Modif. Factor
EEDMFICALC01	Start Formula Instance Calculation
EEDMFICALC02	Monitor Formula Instance Calculation
EEDMFICALC03	Compress Temporary Trigger
EEDMFICALC04	Analyze/Delete Calculation Run Info.
EEDMIDESERVPROV01	Create Service Provider
EEDMIDESERVPROV02	Change Service Provider
EEDMIDESERVPROV03	Display Service Provider
EEDMIDE_GRID01	Create Grid
EEDMIDE_GRID02	Change Grid
EEDMIDE_GRID03	Display Grid
EEDMIMP01	Upload Profile Values via PoD
EEDMIMP02	Upload Profile Values by Profile No.
EEDMPODCONSGEN	Generation of Consumption History

EEDMRTPCODE	Generate Codes for RTP Components
EEDMSENDPRO01	Send Profiles
EEDMSENDPRO02	List of Sent Profiles
EEDMSETTLANALYSE	Display Settled PoDs for Document
EEDMSETTLANALYSEPOD	Documents for PoD Display
EEDMSETTLCHANGE	Change Settlement Document
EEDMSETTLCREATE	Create Settlement Document
EEDMSETTLDISP	Display Settlement Document
EEDMSETTLPARA_WZ	Wizard: Check and Create Parameters
EEDMSETTLST	Start/Stop Settlement Run
EEDMSETTLUNIT01	Create Settlement Unit
EEDMSETTLUNIT02	Change Settlement Unit
EEDMSETTLUNIT03	Display Settlement Unit
EEDMSETTLVAR01	Create Selection Variant
EEDMSETTLVAR02	Change Selection Variant
EEDMSETTLVAR03	Display Selection Variant
EEDM_CMP01	Create RTP Component
EEDM_CMP02	Change RTP Component
EEDM_CMP03	Display RTP Component
EEDM_FRM01	Create RTP Formula
EEDM_FRM02	Change RTP Formula
EEDM_FRM03	Display RTP Formula
EEDM_RTP01	Create RTP Interface
EEDM_RTP02	Change RTP Interface
EEDM_RTP03	Display RTP Interface
EEDM_SETTLPROFILE	Profile Template for Settlmnt Params
EEDM_SETTLUNIT_GEN	Generation of Settlement Units
EEFO_CREDIT_CREATE	Front Office: Create Credit Memo
EEFO_INSTMNTPLN_CREA	Front Office: Create Installmt Plan
EEFO_PAYMENT	Pay Bills
EEIS1	Output Unbilled Contracts
EEIS2	Ouput Contr.Accts w/o BB Amounts
EEIS3	Output Portion w/o BB Amount
EERCH_DEL	Only Relevant for DE
EERCH_EXP	Billing Document Extraction - Export
EERCH_IMP	Only relevant for Germany
EERD_DATA_DEL	Delete Print Document Extracts
EERD_DEL	Only Relevant for DE
EERD_EXP	Print Document Extracts - Export
EERD_EXTR	Extracts: Export Print Documents
EERD_IMP	Only relevant for Germany
EEWB	Easy Enhancement Workbench
EEWC	System Data Maintenance
EEWM_CU_ANALYSIS	Analyze Operations in Task Lists
EEWM_ILCH	Change Inspection List
EEWM_ILCR	Create/Extend Inspection List
EEWM_ILDI	Display Inspection List
EEWM_INOC	Create Insp. Orders/Notifications
EEWM_SHIFTLOG	shift management
EEWZ1	Maintain Application Group Data
EEWZ2	Use for Extension Fields
EEWZ3	Additional Extension Definition
EEXTSYNPROF	Maint. View for Ext. Synth. Prof. ID
EE_CRM_CLASS_GENER	Generate class for set type

EFAK	IS-U Invoicing
EFAKTOR	Number Range Maintenance: ISU_FAKTOR
EFCC	Print Workbench Mass Processing
EFCM	Print Workbench Form Class Processg
EFCS	Print Workbench: Form Class
EFGM	Print Workbench Mass Processing
EFGN	Print Workbench: Mass Activation
EFRM	Print Workbench: Application Form
EFTP	Print Workbench Mass Processing
EFTR	Print Workbench: Generate Trans.List
EFTRADM	Translation of Application Forms
EFTRADMLANGUS	Print Workbench Mass Processing
EFTRLANGVEC	Language Transport Form Objects
EFTRSL	Print Wbench Trans. for Translation
EFTT	Print Workbench: Transl. Worklist
EFUD	Print Workbench: Application Form
EG01	Create Device Category
EG02	Change Device Category
EG03	Display Device Category
EG04	Create Register Group
EG05	Change Register Group
EG06	Display Register Group
EG07	Create Input/Output Group
EG08	Change Input/Output Group
EG09	Display Input/Output Group
EG14	Create Command
EG15	Change Command
EG16	Display Command
EG17	Create Command Group
EG18	Change Command Group
EG19	Display Command Group
EG27	Create Device Group
EG28	Change Device Group
EG29	Display Device Group
EG30	Full Replacement
EG31	Full Installation
EG32	Full Removal
EG33	Technical Installation
EG34	Billing-Related Installation
EG35	Billing-Related Removal
EG36	Technical Removal
EG41	Change device info record
EG42	Device modification
EG43	Display device info record
EG44	Create device info record
EG50	Inst./Removal/Repl.: Reversal
EG51	Installation Reversal
EG52	Reverse Technical Replacement
EG53	Reverse Technical Removal
EG60	Maintain Logical Register
EG61	Display Logical Register
EG70	Maintain Rate Data
EG71	Display Rate Data
EG72	Maintain Device Allocation

EG73	Display Device Allocation
EG75	Create Register Relationships
EG76	Change Register Relationships
EG77	Display Register Relationships
EG7A	Maint. Basic Cat. Desc. and SortSeq.
EG7B	Maintain Inspection Points
EG80	Create Sample Lot
EG81	Change Sample Lot
EG82	Display Sample Lot
EG83	Compile Sample Lot
EG84	Determine Lot Devices
EG85	Draw Sample Devices from Lot
EG88	Create Periodic Replacement List
EG89	Display Periodic Replacement List
EG8A	Compile Sample Lot: Report
EG8B	Sampling procedure B/NL
EG8C	Combine Sample Lots
EG8D	Draw Sample Devices from Lot
EG90	Create repl. orders/notifications
EG97	Perform Certification
EGCONTRACT	Number Range Maintenance: ISU_GCONTR
EGMN	IS-U Device Management
EGPB	Assign Breakpoint to User
EGR	Number Range Maintenance: ISU_DGEN
EGW1	Create Winding Group
EGW2	Change Winding Group
EGW3	Display Winding Group
EHIL	IS-U Tools
EHQL	EH&S-QM: Display Logs
EHQMC1	EH&S-QM: Maintain Types of Chars.
EHQMNUMCODE	EHS: Maintain Number Range for Codes
EHQMNUMGRP	EHS: Maintain No.Range for Code Grps
EHQMNUMSLST	EHS:Maintain No.Range for Phrase Set
EHSAMBTAET	Medical Services
EHSAMED	Occupational Health
EHSASSIGN	Assignment Protocol to Person
EHSASSLTA	Assignment LTA Rating from Work Area
EHSASSPERS	Person list for protocol assignment
EHSBC02	Edit Brief Consultation
EHSBP11	Create physician
EHSBP12	Change physician
EHSBP13	Display physician
EHSBP31	Create Health Center
EHSBP32	Change Health Center
EHSBP33	Display Health Center
EHSBP41	Create Laboratory
EHSBP42	Change Laboratory
EHSBP43	Display Laboratory
EHSBP51	Create External Company
EHSBP52	Change External Company
EHSBP53	Display External Company
EHSB_D_RC_01	Internal: Start Compliance Check
EHSB_D_RC_02	Number Range for Application Log ID
EHSCALPROX	Enter Substitutes for Calender

EHSCBER	Customizing Consultations
EHSCDCT	Customize Diagnosis Types
EHSCMAS	Customizing Measures
EHSDATIMP	Import Medical Data
EHSDIAGSL	EH&S: Diagnosis Key
EHSEVAL00	Occupational Health Report Tree
EHSEXIST0	Existing objects
EHSH_C_NR_EXA_CO	Number Ranges Examination ID
EHSH_C_NR_NEWPER	Number Ranges Internal Personnel No.
EHSH_C_NR_RECN	Number Ranges Occup. Health Rec. No.
EHSH_C_NR_VAC_ID	Number Ranges Vaccination ID
EHSH_D_PCP	Planning Cockpit
EHSK_D_ACTION_STATUS	Information for IHS Measures
EHSK_D_ASSPERSPROT	Info.for Health Surveillance Protocl
EHSK_D_GEN_SERVERS	Informationen for Generation Servers
EHSK_D_IAL	Information: Incident/Accident Log
EHSK_D_REP_GEN_QUEUE	Information for Generation Queue
EHSK_D_REP_REQUESTS	Information for Report Request
EHSK_D_RISK_ASSESS	Information for Risk Assessment
EHSK_D_SHIP_ORDERS	Information: Report Shipping Order
EHSMQUEST	Completing Questionnaires
EHSMQUEST01	Number Range Maint. Questionnaire
EHSPERSHC1	Assign Persons to Health Center
EHSPP01	Exposure Groups
EHSPRANZ	Display Med. D. Import Logs
EHSPRLOE	Delete Med. D. Import Logs
EHSQCATOH	Question catalog
EHSQEVAL01	Evaluate Completed Questionnaires
EHSQUESTOH	General questionnaire
EHSSCAN	Scan Questionnaire
EHSSERV	Medical Service Results / Sign-Off
EHSSERV01	Open Medical Service
EHSSERV11	Number Range Maint. Medical Service
EHSSERV30	Display Appointment List
EHSSERV50	Logical Database Selection Screen
EHSSTRU00	Existing objects
EHSSUGGP	Proposal list person<->prot.
EHSTERM01	Scheduling medical service
EHSVA02	Edit Vaccinations
EHSVU01	Edit Health Surveillance Protocol
EHSVU11	Edit Examination
EHSVU21	Edit Physical Tests
EHSVU31	Edit lab. tests
EHVD	HTML Customer Overview: Select Data
EI01	UIS: Activate Update
EI03	UIS: Change Communication Structure
EI10	UIS: Execute Evaluation
EI11	UIS: Create Evaluation
EI12	UIS: Change Evaluation
EI13	UIS: Display Evaluation
EI14	UIS: Settings for Standard Analysis
EI18	UIS: Create Field Catalog
EI19	UIS: Change Field Catalog
EI1B	UIS: Maintain Requirements

EI1F	UIS: Maintain Formulas
EI20	UIS: Display Field Catalog
EI21	UIS: Create Info Structure
EI22	UIS: Change Info Structure
EI23	UIS: Display Info Structure
EI24	UIS: Create Update
EI25	UIS: Change Update
EI26	UIS: Display Update
EI27	UIS: Create Evaluation Structure
EI28	UIS: Change Evaluation Structure
EI29	UIS: Display Evaluation Structure
EI30	UIS: Simulate Document Update
EI31	UIS: Statistics Update
EI32	UIS: Setup of Statistical Data
EI35	Set up stock statistics
EI44	UIS: Rate Statistics Selection
EI45	UIS: Rate Statistics Selection
EI72	CO-PA: Statistical Update
EI80	Check Document transfer COPA/BW/UIS
EIDECOM1	Communication on Basis of Serv.Prov.
EIDECOM2	Communication on Basis of Serv. Type
EIDESERV1	Define Service Types
EIDESERV2	Define Process Control
EIDESERV3	Define Own Billable Services
EIDESERV4	Define Third Party Billable Services
EIDESERV5	Define Non-Billable Services
EIDESP1	Allocate Operational Area
EIDESP2	Allocate Rate Categories
EIDESP3	Allocate Certification Status
EINF	IS-U Information System
EIS1	UIS: Current Settings
EJOBSCHEDULER	Job Scheduler
EK01	Acct Determ.: IS-U Receiv. Accounts
EK02	Acct Determ.: IS-U Rev. Accts
EK03	IS-U Argentinian Tax Determination
EK04	Activ.Code Distrib.Type in Argentina
EK05	Activ.Code Distrib.Type in Argentina
EK06	Defaults for Acct Display BB Amounts
EK07	Defaults for Acct Disp BB Amnts CIC
EK08	IS-U Account Display: Specifications
EK09	Define Specifications for Loans
EK11	Specifs: Source Item Charges in IP
EK12	Down Payment Specifications
EK13	Down Paym./Rec. Clearing Information
EK14	C FI Maintain Table TFK022A/B
EK15	Dunning Charge Specif.in Invoicing
EK16	Document Type: GI and VAT Perception
EK17	Specif. for Migration of Payments
EK20	Activate 2-Level Tax Determ. Code
EK21	Maintain 2-Step Tax Determ. Ident.
EK22	Payment Migration: Specifications
EK23	Down Payment Request Payment Proc.
EK25	Create Loan
EK26	Change Loan

EK27	Display Loan
EK70	Cust. Item Ind. -> Payment Block
EK71	Cstmzng: Aggr. Posting of Inbnd Bill
EK72	Transactions for Aggregated Posting
EK73	Aggr. Bill: Trans. -> Offsetting Tr.
EK74	Dereg. - Maintain Factory Calendar
EK75	Conversion Int./Ext. Transaction
EK78	FI-CA: Interest on Cash Sec. Deposit
EK79	Default values for cash deposit int.
EK81	Account Determ.: IS-T Receiv. Accnts
EK82	Account Determ.: IS-T Revenue Accnts
EK92	Create Payment Plan
EK93	Change Payment Plan
EK93C	Combined Change of Payment Plans
EK93M	Adjust Payment Plans Automatically
EK94	Display Payment Plan
EK94C	Combined Display of Payment Plans
EK95	Manual History for Payment Schedule
EK96	Adjust Balance-Forward Amount
EK96_DEFAULT	Default Adjustm. of Difference Amnt
EKND	IS-U Customer Service
EKS1	PURCHIS: Statistics Update: Item Lvl
EKSR	Remove BBP from Collective Bill
EK_M100	Defaults for Payment Medium ID
EK_R017	Doc. Type for Stat. Fee in Argentina
EK_R100	Def. Info. for Payment Medium ID
EK_R200	Def. Info. for Security Dep. Transf.
EK_R201	Def. Info for Sec.Dep.Trans. Revers.
EK_R202	Bollo Specifications (Italian Tax)
EK_SURS	Charge Request for Mass Activity
EL01	Execute Order Creation
EL06	Execute Mass Order Creation
EL09	Execute Order Creation
EL16	Execute Order Output
EL18	Execute Estimation
EL20	Fast Entry
EL22	Fast Entry With Correction
EL27	Correction of Implausible Results
EL27_MRUNIT	Correct Implausible MRs for MR Unit
EL28	Single Entry
EL29	Correction of Plausible Results
EL30	Estimate Meter Reading Results
EL31	Manual Monitoring
EL32	Automatic Monitoring
EL35	Meter Reading Order Output
EL37	Reverse Meter Reading Order Creation
EL37_WO_MRUNIT	Reverse MRRs w/o Order Creation
EL40	Maintain Street Route
EL41	Display Street Route
EL42	Display Meter Reading Units
EL43	Device Overview
EL50	Create Meter Reading Group
EL51	Change Meter Reading Group
EL52	Display Meter Reading Group

EL56	Change Periodic Consumption
EL57	Display period consumption
EL59	Mass Change Meter Reading Units
EL59P	Define Parameter Group
EL60	Activation EB for Individ. Install.
EL61	Activation EB for Amount of Install.
EL62	Deactivation of EB for Ind. Install.
EL70	List of Implausible MR Results
ELDM	Monitoring of IDocs Processed
ELEU	Upload of Meter Reading Results
ELMU	Upload
ELOC	Manage Container Location
ELSIG00	Signature Strategy
ELSIG01	Authorization Grp Digital Signatures
ELSIG02	Digital Signature
ELSIG03	Signature Method for Signat. Object
ELSIG03N	Signature Method for Signat. Object
EL_MA_MRIDOC	Process IDocs with errors
EM10	Goods Movement via Serial Numbers
EMAIL	SAPconnect Easy EMail
EMASN	IDoc Monitor for Inb. Ship. Notific.
EMFOR	Monitor for Forecast/JIT Del.Sched.
EMIGALL	IS-U Migration
EMIGCMP	IS-U Migration Company Maintenance
EMIGCNV	IS-U Mig: Maintain Conversion Obj.
EMIGCOM	Compare with migration Customizing
EMIGFLD	IS-U Migration: Maintain Fields
EMIGFVA	Fixed Value Maintenance
EMIGIMP	IS-U Migration: Data Import
EMIGJOB	IS-U Migration: Job Scheduler
EMIGKSV	IS-U Migration: Maintain KSM
EMIGMASSRUN	Mass Import Monitor: IS Migration
EMIGMASSRUNGROUP	Group Import IS Migration
EMIGOBJ	Maintain migration object
EMIGPROJECT	IS-U Migration: Maintain Project
EMIGSTAT	Display Stats Record: IS-U Migration
EMIGSTR	Maintenance of autom. data structure
EMIGUSR	IS-U migration user maintenance
EMJIT	IDoc Monitor for JIT Calls
EMMA	Log Analysis and Case Creation
EMMAC1	Create Case
EMMAC2	Change Case
EMMAC3	Display Case
EMMACAP	Run Automatic Processes for Cases
EMMACC	Cust. Tab. Add. Data in Transaction
EMMACCAT1	Create Case Category
EMMACCAT1M	Create Case Category from Message
EMMACCAT2	Change Case Category
EMMACCAT3	Display Case Category
EMMACCAT4	Delete Case Category
EMMACCAT5	Transport Case Category
EMMACL	Clarification List
EMMACLGEN	Generate Case List Program
EMMACLS	Case List with Shortcut Keys

EMMAIDOCLOG	IDoc log via EMMA
EMMAJ3	Display Job
EMMAJL	Job List
EMMAJOBLOG	Job log via EMMA
EMMAJP	Process Job
EMMALOG	Display Application Log
EMMA_NR_CASE	Number Range Maintenance: EMMA_CASE
EMMA_NR_JOB	Number Range Maintenance: EMMA_RUNID
EMMA_OLD	Monitor mass activity
EMORD	IDoc Monitor for SD Orders
EMSG	Maintenance of Message Groups
EMU1	Convert Loans to EURO
EMU2	Reset Conversion to EURO
EN00	Number Range Maintenance: ISU_ERDK
EN01	Subscreens for Simple Notification
EN03	No. Range Maint.: ISU_EHAU
EN04	Number Range Maint.: ISU_EVBS
EN05	No. Range Maint.: ISU_EDCN
EN06	No. Range Maint.: ISU_EANL
EN07	Number Range Maintenance: ISU_ETRF
EN08	Number Range Maintenance: ISU_EWAOBJ
EN09	Number Range Maintenance: ISU_IDOC
EN10	Number Range Maintenance: ISU_EWAORD
EN11	No. Range Maint.: ISU_EZWG
EN12	No. Range Maint.: ISU_EKOG
EN13	No. Range Maint.: ISU_EEAG
EN15	No. Range Maint.: ISU_EABL
EN17	Number Range Maintenance: ISU_EVER
EN18	Number Range Maintenance: ISU_CREFNO
EN19	Number Range Maintenance: ISU_IDEPRO
EN20	Number Range Maintenance: ISU_IDETRA
EN22	No. Range Maint.: ISU_EDSC
EN23	Number Range Maintenance: ISU_EPREI
EN25	No. Range Maint.: ISU_EABP
EN27	No. Range Maint.: ISU_DEVGRP
EN40	Number Range Maintenance: ISU_IDCDOC
EN41	Number Range Maintenance: ISU_IDCDCI
EN43	No. Range Maint.: ISU_EKON
EN50	No. Range Maint.: ISU_EEIN
EN55	No. Range Maint.: ISU_EAUS
EN70	Number Range Maintenance: ISU_PRDOC
EN80	No. Range Maint.: ISU_TE271
EN99	General Foreign Trade Processing
ENBI	Number Range Maintenance: ISU_BIRUN
ENCLEAN	Number Range Maintenance: ISU_ECLEAN
ENCO	Printing / Communication
ENDELIVER	Number Range Maintenance: EWAEL_DELI
ENEDMCR	Number Range Maintenance: ISU_EDM_CR
ENEDMFI	Number Range Maintenance: ISU_EDM_FI
ENEDMIB	Number Range Maintenance: ISU_EDM_IB
ENEDMPRO	Number Range Maintenance: ISU_EDMP
ENEDMPROT	Number Range Maintenance: ISU_EDMPT
ENEDMSC	Number Range Maintenance: ISU_EDM_SC
ENEDMSD	Number Range Maintenance: ISU_EDM_SD

SAP Transaction Codes – Volume One

ENEDMUS1	Number Range Maintenance ISU_EDM_U1
ENEDMVN	Number Range Maintenance: ISU_EDM_VN
ENER	No. Range Maint.: ISU_ERCH
ENFO	Foreign Trade/Customs: Init. Screen
ENGK	Legal control
ENGR	Periodic Declarations
ENIDESWD	Number Range Maintenance: ISU_IDESWD
ENIN	Number range maint. ISU_INDEXN
ENKOMCOTM	Test
ENLO	Documentary Payments
ENLP	Number Range Maintenance: ISU_LOGLPR
ENNR	No. Range Maint.: ISU_LOGINR
ENPA	FT: Enjoy: Period-end Closings
ENPR	Preference Handling
ENPS	No. Range Maint.: ISU_EABP
ENRD	Number Range Maintenance: ISU_ERDMP
ENROB	Number Range Maintenance: ISU_EWAROB
ENROUTE	Number Range Maintenance: ISU_EROUTE
ENSAMPLE	Number Range Maintenance: EWAEL_SMPL
ENSL	Cockpit: Sanctioned Party List
ENSV	Foreign Trade Data Maintenance
ENVD	CIC: Data Environment Maintenance
ENVOUCHER	Number Range Maintenance: EWAWA_PGR
ENWDPL	Number Range Maintenance: EWAEL_WDPT
ENWDPPROC	Number Range Maintenance: EWAEL_WDPP
ENWEIGH	Number Range Maintenance: EWAWA_WPNR
ENWEIGHOFL	Number Range Maintenance: EWAWA_WONR
ENWK	No. Range Maint.: ISU_EWIK
ENZD	Customs Objects: Documentation/Info.
ENZW	No. Range Maint.: ISU_LOGIZW
EOLA	Master Data Tab
EP01	Customizing: Transaction Statistics
EP02	Customizing: Stock Statistics
EPA1	Create Print Action Record
EPA2	Change Print Action Record
EPA3	Display Print Action Record
EPAR	List Print Action Records
EPDHIER	Display Hierarchy of MDT Category
EPDTYPE	IS-U MD Generator: MDT Categories
EPERS	IS-U Report Var. Maint. for MiniApps
EPLOT	Repayment on Account
EPMC	Customizing: Plant Manager
EPM_REPORT_START	Start Report With Variant
EPODSRVC1	Create point of delivery services
EPODSRVC2	Change point of delivery services
EPODSRVC3	Display point of delivery services
EPPM	Number Range Maintenance: ISU_PREPAY
EPRACT	Number Range Maintenance: ISU_PRACT
EPREPAY	Amount Mgmt of Prepayment Meter
EPREPAYFREE	Release locked PPM entries
EPREPAY_RELEASE	Release locked PPM entries
EPRODCUST	IS-U MD Template: Customizing
EQ01	Field Selection: Contract (IMG)
EQ02	Field Sel: Connection Object (IMG)

EQ03	Field Selection: Premise (IMG)
EQ04	Field Selection: Installation (IMG)
EQ05	Field Sel: Device Location (IMG)
EQ06	Field Sel: Initial Screen - Move-Out
EQ07	Field Sel: Move-In - Contract1 (IMG)
EQ08	Field Sel: Move-In Contract 2 (IMG)
EQ09	Field Sel: Owner Allocation (IMG)
EQ10	Field Selection for Property (IMG)
EQ30	Search Help for Parameter Recs (IMG)
EQ31	Search Help for Portions (IMG)
EQ32	Search Help for MR Units (IMG)
EQ33	Search Help for Contracts (IMG)
EQ34	Search Help for Conn. Objects (IMG)
EQ35	Search Help for Premises (IMG)
EQ36	Search Help for Installations (IMG)
EQ37	Search Help for Device Locs (IMG)
EQ38	Search Help for Register Grps (IMG)
EQ39	Search Help for I/O Groups (IMG)
EQ40	Search Help for Command Groups (IMG)
EQ42	Search Help for Winding Groups (IMG)
EQ43	Search Help for Device Categs (IMG)
EQ44	Search Help for Devices (IMG)
EQ45	Search Help for Lots (IMG)
EQ46	Search Help for Rates (IMG)
EQ47	Search Help for Schemas (IMG)
EQ48	Search Help for Rate Categs (IMG)
EQ49	Search Help for Discs/Surchgs (IMG)
EQ50	Search Help for Franchise Cont.(IMG)
EQ51	Search Help for Print Docs (IMG)
EQ52	Search Help for BB Plans (IMG)
EQ53	Search Help for Billing Docs (IMG)
EQ54	Search Help for Move-In Docs (IMG)
EQ55	Search Help for Move-Out Docs (IMG)
EQ56	Search Help for Disconn. Docs (IMG)
EQ57	Search Help for Cleaning Obj. (IMG)
EQ58	Search Help for Surfaces (IMG)
EQ59	Search Help for Routes (IMG)
EQ60	Search Help for Cont. Location (IMG)
EQ61	Srch Help for BP for Cont.Loc. (IMG)
EQ62	Srch Help for Guarantor Cntrct (IMG)
EQ80	Check Sub-Transactions for Rates
EQ81	Display Migration Handbook (IMG)
EQ82	Billing Master Data Transport (IMG)
EQ83	Check Rates (IMG)
EQ84	Check Activities (IMG)
EQ85	Check Statistics Groups (IMG)
EQ90	Task Customizing for IS-U (IMG)
ER30	Maintain Poli. Reg. Struc. Hierarchy
ER31	Maintain Political Regional Struct.
ER32	Display Political Regional Structure
ER3D	Display Poli. Reg. Struct. Hierarchy
ERCH_EXTR	Extracts: Export Billing Docuemnts
EREC01	Transfer to FI- single cont. mode
EREC02	Transfer to FI invoicing 3rd party

EREC03	Aggregated Posting to Contract Acc.
EREG	IS-U Regional Structure
ERN1	No. Range Maint.: ISU_TE227
EROD	Transfer Master Data to Route Plan.
ERONEW	Maintain Service Frequency
EROUTE	Route
ES20	Create Contract
ES20C	Tab Strip for IS-U Contract
ES21	Chg. Contract
ES22	Display Contract
ES27	Multiple Contract Maint.
ES28	Multiple Contract Display
ES30	Create Installation
ES30CONTAIN	Tabstrip: Reference Values
ES30HEAT	Tabstrip: Reference Values
ES30LIGHT	Tabstrip: Reference Values
ES30REFVAL	Tabstrip: Reference Values
ES31	Change Installation
ES32	Display Installation
ES43	Create Franchise Contract
ES44	Change Franchise Contract
ES45	Display Franchise Contract
ES50	Number Range Maintenance: ISU_EPROP
ES51	Create Ownership
ES52	Change Ownership
ES53	Display Ownership
ES54	Reverse Property
ES55	Create Connect. Object
ES56	Change Connect. Object
ES57	Display Connect. Object
ES60	Create Premise
ES61	Change Premise
ES62	Display Premise
ES64	Change Connection Object
ES65	Create Device Loc.
ES66	Change Device Loc.
ES67	Display Device Loc.
ESALES_SVOFFERS	Maintain Settings for File Table
ESARA01	IS-U Archiving: Print Docmt Header
ESARA02	IS-U Archiving: Print Document Items
ESARA03	IS-U Archiving: Billing Document
ESARA04	IS-U Archiving: Budget Billing Plans
ESARA05	IS-U Archiving: Billing Doc. Lines
ESARA06	IS-U Archiving: MR Results
ESARA07	IS-U Archiving: Inspection List
ESARA08	IS-U Archiving: EDM Profile Values
ESARA09	IS-U Archiving: Prepayment Documents
ESARA10	IS-U Archiving: Usage Factors
ESARA11	IS-U: Archiving: Settlement Docs
ESARA12	IS-U Archiving: Routes
ESARA13	IS-U Archiving: Waste Disposal Order
ESARA14	IS-U Archiving: Installation Facts
ESARA15	IS-U Archiving: Switch Documents
ESARJ01	Activate AS for print doc. header

ESARJ02	Activate AS for print doc. line itms
ESARJ03	Archive IS bill.doc.header is active
ESARJ04	Activate AS for budget billing plan
ESARJ05	Arch.Info.Struct.:Bill.Doc.Lines Act
ESARJ06	ArchInfrastr. ME Results Active
ESARJ07	ArchInfStructure InspectList Active
ESARJ08	ArchInfStruc: EDM Prof.Values Active
ESARJ09	ArchInfStructure: Prepayment Active
ESARJ10	Arch.Inf.Struct.: Act. Waste Order
ESARJ11	Arch.Inf.Structure: Activate Routes
ESARJ12	Arch.Inf.Str.: Archive Install.Facts
ESARJ13	Arch.Inf.Structure: Settlement Doc.
ESARJ14	Arch.Info.Structure: Usage Factors
ESARJ15	Activ. ArchInfoStruc. f. Switch Docs
ESD1	IS-U Business Master Data
ESD2	IS-U Technical Master Data
ESDF	Maint. of Add. Field Descriptions
ESDP	Maintain Tolerance Profile
ESFUTIL	ESF Utility
ESH_ADM_TREX_DEST	Set TREX destination
ESH_COCKPIT	Enterprise Search Cockpit
ESIMD	IS-U Archiving: Reorg. Sim. Docs
ESI_ADD_MAP	ESI Add mapping
ESI_BO_TEST_TOOL	ESI Testtool for Business objects
ESI_MAPPING	ESI Mapping
ESI_MAPPING_DB	ESI Mapping
ESOA_ENGINEER	SAP Enterprise Tomograph
ESOA_INTRO	Enterprise Introspector
ESPLOG	Display IDoc STOACT Log
ESPLOGD	Delete IDoc STOACT Log
ESWTMON01	Monitoring of Switch Documents
ETHI	Aggr. Posting Serv. Prov. CA
ETHIM	Mass Act. Aggr. Posting for ServProv
ETHIM_REV	Mass Activity Rev. Aggr. Posting SP
ETHIM_TAX	Aggregated Posting for SP with Tax
ETHI_DIS	Evaluation of DFKKTHI Entries
ETP_DELETE_TASKS	Deleting tasks
ETRANSF	Mass Activity - Aggregated Posting
ETRANSF_DIS	Display Transfer Data
ETRM	IS-U Scheduling
EUNLD	Delete Unneeded Billing Doc. Lines
EUPTSP	GP Content Transport
EVAL	BRE Statistics PARALLEL Mass Billing
EVKK	IS-U Contract Accounts R/P
EW00	Conversions for the Euro
EW01	EMU Conversion: Package Overview
EW04	EMU Conversion: Field-Rel. Control
EW06	EMU Conv.: Form Routines per Package
EW07	EMU Conv.: Form Routines per Table
EW08	EMU Conv.: Acct Determination in FI
EW09	EMU Conv.: Document Type/Posting Key
EW10	EMU: Load Organization Objects
EW11	EMU: Load CO-PA Objects
EW13	EMU: Load Conversion Info for LIS

EW14	EMU: Load Conversion Info for EIS
EW16	Records No. of Largest Tables
EW17	Determine Required Database Memory
EW18	EMU: Load Depreciation Areas
EW28	EMU: Load CO Objects
EW29	EMU: Load Tables for FI-SL
EW30	FI Previous Open Item Reconciliation
EW35	FI Previous Clearing Procedures
EW36	FI Documents/Trans.Figures Analysis
EW38	EMU Conversion: MM Stock Value List
EW38_HIERARCHY	Chge List Proc. for Ord.Hierarchies
EW39	FI Open Item Selection
EW39_HIERARCHY	Disp. List Proc. for Ord. Hierarchs.
EW3Z	Currency Select.f.Changeover Package
EW40_HIERARCHY	Multi-level List Proc.for Ord.Hier.
EW45	FI D/C G/L Accts Analysis bef.Conv.
EW46	MM Edit Contract Release Order Docu
EW47	Create Standard Package
EW48	MM Display Archived Purchasing Docs
EW49	MM MM --> FI Balance Comparison
EW4Z	Currency Select.f.Changeover Package
EW50	MM Post Adjustment Documents
EW51	FI S/L-G/L Reconciliation Analysis
EW53	FI Check Customizing
EW55	FI Adjust D/C G/L Accounts
EW57	EMU Conv: Start Postprocess.Programs
EW58	EMU Conv.: Conversion Programs Start
EW59	EMU Conv.: Start Preprocess.Programs
EW61	EMU Conv.: CO Credit w.Settl.Tables
EW62	EMU Conv.: CO Settlmnt Tables Recon.
EW63	EMU Conv.: CO Commt Totals Structure
EW64	EMU Conv.: CO Dwn Pmnt Totals Struc.
EW65	EMU: CO-AA Comparison for Investmnts
EW67	EMU: AA Summary Records Selection
EW68	EMU: AA Balance Adjustment
EW69	AA Transaction Figure Reconciliation
EW72	FI Subsequent Open Item Selection
EW73	Investment Programs Adjustment
EW74	FI Subseq.Open Item Reconciliation
EW75	FI Subsequent SL/GL Reconciliation
EW76	FI Docs/Trans.Figures Reconciliation
EW77	FI Docs/Transaction Figures Adjustmt
EW80	MM Totals Comparison MBEW
EW82	MM Stock Value List
EW84	List MM Differences
EW93	EMU: Load Conversion Info for FI-SL
EW94	EMU: Tables RESTART FLAG
EW95	EMU Conversion: Tables and Programs
EW96	EMU Conv.: Check Conversion Table
EW98	EMU Conv.: Check Conversion Program
EW99	Overview of all Packages
EWA0	EMU Conv: RE Load CO Objects
EWA1	FI-AA: Analysis of assets w/errors
EWA2	FI-AA: Asset before&after comparison

EWA3	Reconcil. of critical FI-AA documts
EWA6	Lock AA Transaction Types
EWA7	AA Totals Record Reconciliation
EWA8	AA Balances Reconciliation
EWA9	AA Asset Status Reconciliation
EWABILL	Valuate Waste Billing Category
EWABULKY	Create Bulk Waste Order
EWAC	Action Manager: Customizing
EWACAL	Maintain Calendar
EWACAPAB	Daily Capacity
EWACLEAN	Property
EWACONTS	Container Transport
EWAEL01	Delivery Locks
EWAEL02	View Control
EWAEL03	Reserve Sample
EWAEL04	Waste Disp. Installation Management
EWAEL05	Transaction Group
EWAEL06	Procedures Within Facility
EWAEL07	Operations Log
EWAELOCEO_INIT	Structure Container Loc. Allocations
EWAFAKTOR	Waste Billing Factor
EWAGG	Guarantor Contract
EWAORDALL	Create Waste Disposal Order
EWAORDDEL	Delete Waste Disposal Order
EWAORDER	Change/Display Waste Disposal Order
EWAORDERDOWN	Output Waste Disposal Order
EWAORDRESL	Confirmation
EWAPLAN	Planning
EWAROB	Cleaning Object
EWAROBTYP	Maintain Cleaning Object Category
EWAS	IS-U Waste Management
EWAWA01	Accelerated Weight Entry
EWAWA02	Weighing Procedure
EWAWA03	General Cargo Entry
EWAWA04	Offline Weighing
EWAWAT001	Hardware Profile
EWAWAT002	Profile Control
EWAWAT003	Profile Group
EWA_AAT_CHECK	Consistency Check for Billing
EWBC	Customizing: Front Office Processes
EWBE	Customizing: Editor Step
EWB_WEBGUI	FOPs for Web GUI
EWC0	RKAABR01: Order Settlement Analysis
EWC1	CO-PA Reports Translation
EWC2	CO Reconciliation Ledger
EWC4	Reconciliation of Parked Docs FM
EWCF	Confirm Euro Currency Customizing
EWCK	Currency Check BKPF, KONV
EWCM	Maintain Currency Tables for Euro
EWCT	Currency Test Converter
EWEBIAC_1_PAY	ISS Pay Bills
EWEBIAC_ACCT_INFO	ISS Accounts Information
EWEBIAC_A_PAY	ISS Direct Debit Mandate
EWEBIAC_A_PAY_CIC	ISS Direct Debit Mandate as ESS

SAP Transaction Codes – Volume One

EWEBIAC_CALLBACK	ISS Initiate Callback
EWEBIAC_CH_MD	ISS Change Bill Address
EWEBIAC_CH_MD_CIC	ISS Change Bill Address ESS
EWEBIAC_CONSUMP_HIST	ISS Consumption Overview
EWEBIAC_CONS_HIS_CIC	ISS Consumption Overview in CIC
EWEBIAC_CONTINUE	Dummy Entry for Service Usage
EWEBIAC_CPUSER	Customer Portal - User
EWEBIAC_ENROLLMEN	ISS Initial Data Creation
EWEBIAC_ENROLLMENT	ISS Initial Data Creation
EWEBIAC_ENROLL_CIC	ISS Initial Data Creation as ESS
EWEBIAC_HTMLBILL	ISS Bill
EWEBIAC_INFO	ISS Accounts Information
EWEBIAC_INFO_CIC	ISS Account Information ESS
EWEBIAC_LOGIN	ISS Internet Account
EWEBIAC_METER_CIC	ISS Meter Reading Entry from CIC
EWEBIAC_METER_READ	ISS Meter Reading Entry
EWEBIAC_MOVEOUT	ISS Move-Out
EWEBIAC_MOVE_IN	ISS Move-In
EWEBIAC_PASSWD	ISS Change Internet Password
EWEBIAC_PASSWD_NEW	ISS Password Forgotten
EWEBIAC_PREMISE_SEL	ISS Premise Selection
EWEBIAC_PREM_SEL_CIC	ISS Premise Selection
EWEBIAC_SHOW_PROFIL	ISS Display Profile Values
EWEBIAC_TEMPLATE	ISS Template
EWF1	Display FI/AA Adjustment Differences
EWF2	Display Open Item Total at Key Date
EWF3	Display Critical Documents
EWF4	Display Clearing Proced.Adjustment
EWF7	Delete Table EWUFI_SOP
EWF8	Compare Index w.Transaction Figures
EWF9	Compare Index w.Transaction Figures
EWFC	IS-U Front Office Configuration
EWFC0	Action Box Configuration
EWFC1	Action Config. for HTML Operation
EWFG	Add Up Totals Records
EWFM	Find Open Dunning Runs
EWFS	Check for Balances in Local Currency
EWFZ	Find Open Payment Runs
EWG5	Consolidation Staging Ledger
EWHV	Generic IAC for Cluster Objects
EWIC	LCC: Provider
EWK0	Customer Development: Find Fields
EWK1	Cust.Development: Curr.in Report Txt
EWK2	Cust.Development: Curr.on Screen
EWK3	Customer Development: Assign Rule
EWK4	Customer Development: Save Selection
EWM1	MM Fill Fields in EBAN
EWM3	Match MM Sales Values
EWM4	MM Purchase Order History Adjustment
EWM6	Reconcile GR/IR Clearing Account
EWMA	IS-U Work Management
EWS1	EMU Conv.: Check Analysis Program
EWS2	Evaluate Archived Data
EWS3	List of Critical Archives

SAP Transaction Codes – Volume One

EWSH	EMU Procedure Monitor
EWT0	Change Plan Year for Chngover Pckge
EWT1	Set Ability to be Restarted
EWT2	Activate a Changeover Package
EWT3	Start Forecast
EWTF	Table Selection for RESTART/NO VIEW
EWUD	EMU mass conversion in cust. master
EWUL	Currency conversion vendors
EWUM	Conversion Sequence/Server Assignmnt
EWUO	Transaction data for EMU conversion
EWUS	Maintain Largest Tables
EWUT	EMU: TA currency changeover FX/MM/DE
EWWA	Currency Select.f.Changeover Package
EWWB	Determining Ratios & Exchange Rates
EWX1	FI Analyze: Open Items
EWX2	FI Analyze: Open Items
EWX3	FI Analyze: Belegaufteilung Anpass.
EWX5	FI Analysis: Cost Element Check
EWX7	FI Post: Post Documents Subsequently
EWZ5	Lock Users
EWZ6	Unlock System
EWZA	Confirm System Settings
EXAMPLE_FLOW_M	EXAMPLE_FLOW_M
EXEORGCHEARM	Parameter transaction for TG01000008
EXPD	Expediting
EXPD_STNUM	Number Range Status Information
EXPG	Agent Determination
EXPO_ANA	Analysis of a FOX Folder
EXPO_READ	Read & Visualize FOX Storage
EXPO_TEST	Text explosion FOX with PLM objects
EXP_CUST	Express Planning Customizing
EXP_CUST_KFPRICE	Prices of Statistical Key Figs
EXP_INSTANCE_CREATE	Create Instance
EXP_INSTANCE_DISPLAY	Create Instance
EXP_INSTANCE_EDIT	Create Instance
EXTID_DN	External Identification Type DN
EXTID_ID	External Identification Type ID
EXTSDL	Administer the External Scheduler
E_DEREG_SYST	Deregulation: System Settings
E_JBP_CUST	Customizing JBP
E_JBP_SYST	SAP System Settings for JBP
F-01	Enter Sample Document
F-02	Enter G/L Account Posting
F-03	Clear G/L Account
F-04	Post with Clearing
F-05	Post Foreign Currency Valuation
F-06	Post Incoming Payments
F-07	Post Outgoing Payments
F-18	Payment with Printout
F-19	Reverse Statistical Posting
F-20	Reverse Bill Liability
F-21	Enter Transfer Posting
F-22	Enter Customer Invoice
F-23	Return Bill of Exchange Pmt Request

SAP Transaction Codes – Volume One

F-25	Reverse Check/Bill of Exch.
F-26	Incoming Payments Fast Entry
F-27	Enter Customer Credit Memo
F-28	Post Incoming Payments
F-29	Post Customer Down Payment
F-30	Post with Clearing
F-31	Post Outgoing Payments
F-32	Clear Customer
F-33	Post Bill of Exchange Usage
F-34	Post Collection
F-35	Post Forfaiting
F-36	Bill of Exchange Payment
F-37	Customer Down Payment Request
F-38	Enter Statistical Posting
F-39	Clear Customer Down Payment
F-40	Bill of Exchange Payment
F-41	Enter Vendor Credit Memo
F-42	Enter Transfer Posting
F-43	Enter Vendor Invoice
F-44	Clear Vendor
F-46	Reverse Refinancing Acceptance
F-47	Down Payment Request
F-48	Post Vendor Down Payment
F-49	Customer Noted Item
F-51	Post with Clearing
F-52	Post Incoming Payments
F-53	Post Outgoing Payments
F-54	Clear Vendor Down Payment
F-55	Enter Statistical Posting
F-56	Reverse Statistical Posting
F-57	Vendor Noted Item
F-58	Payment with Printout
F-59	Payment Request
F-60	Maintain Table: Posting Periods
F-62	Maintain Table: Exchange Rates
F-63	Park Vendor Invoice
F-64	Park Customer Invoice
F-65	Preliminary Posting
F-66	Park Vendor Credit Memo
F-67	Park Customer Credit Memo
F-90	Acquisition from purchase w. vendor
F-91	Asset Acquis. Posted w/Clearing Acct
F-92	Asset Retire. frm Sale w/ Customer
F.01	ABAP Report: Financial Statements
F.02	Compact Journal
F.03	Reconciliation
F.04	G/L: Create Foreign Trade Report
F.05	Foreign Currency Valuation
F.06	Foreign Currency Valuation:G/L Assts
F.07	G/L: Balance Carryforward
F.08	G/L: Account Balances
F.09	G/L: Account List
F.0A	G/L: FTR Report on Disk
F.0B	G/L: Create Z2 to Z4

F.10	G/L: Chart of Accounts
F.11	G/L: General Ledger from Doc.File
F.12	Adv.Retrn for Tax on Sales/Purchases
F.13	Automatic Clearing without Currency
F.14	ABAP/4 Report: Recurring Entries
F.15	ABAP/4 Report: List Recurr.Entries
F.16	ABAP/4 Report: G/L Bal.Carryforward
F.17	ABAP/4 Report: Cust.Bal.Confirmation
F.18	ABAP/4 Report: Vend.Bal.Confirmation
F.19	G/L: Goods/Invoice Received Clearing
F.1A	Customer/Vendor Statistics
F.1B	Head Office and Branch Index
F.20	A/R: Account List
F.21	A/R: Open Items
F.22	A/R: Open Item Sorted List
F.23	A/R: Account Balances
F.24	A/R: Interest for Days Overdue
F.25	Bill of Exchange List
F.26	A/R: Balance Interest Calculation
F.27	Periodic Account Statements
F.28	Customers: Reset Credit Limit
F.29	A/R: Set Up Info System 1
F.2A	A/R Overdue Int.: Post (Without OI)
F.2B	A/R Overdue Int.: Post (with OI)
F.2C	Calc.cust.int.on arr.: w/o postings
F.2D	Customrs: FI-SD mast.data comparison
F.2E	Reconciliation Btwn Affiliated Comps
F.2F	Management Acct Group Reconciliation
F.2G	Create Account Group Reconcil. G/L
F.2I	Document Assignment User Settings
F.2K	Manage Templates for Notifications
F.30	A/R: Evaluate Info System
F.31	Credit Management - Overview
F.32	Credit Management - Missing Data
F.33	Credit Management - Brief Overview
F.34	Credit Management - Mass Change
F.35	Credit Master Sheet
F.36	Adv.Ret.on Sls/Pur.Form Printout(DE)
F.37	Adv.rept.tx sls/purch.form print (BE
F.38	Transfer Posting of Deferred Tax
F.39	C FI Maint. table T042Z (BillExcTyp)
F.40	A/P: Account List
F.41	A/P: Open Items
F.42	A/P: Account Balances
F.44	A/P: Balance Interest Calculation
F.45	A/P: Set Up Info System 1
F.46	A/P: Evaluate Info System
F.47	Vendors: calc.of interest on arrears
F.48	Vendors: FI-MM mast.data comparison
F.4A	Calc.vend.int.on arr.: Post (w/o OI)
F.4B	Calc.vend.int.on arr.: Post(with OI)
F.4C	Calc.vend.int.on arr.: w/o postings
F.50	G/L: Profitability Segment Adjustmnt
F.51	G/L: Open Items

F.52	G/L: Acct Bal.Interest Calculation
F.53	G/L: Account Assignment Manual
F.54	G/L: Structured Account Balances
F.56	Delete Recurring Entry Documents
F.57	G/L: Delete Sample Documents
F.58	OI Bal.Audit Trail: fr.Document File
F.59	Accum.Clas.Aud.Trail: Create Extract
F.5A	Accum.Clas.Aud.Trail: Eval.Extract
F.5B	Accum.OI Aud.Trail: Create Extract
F.5C	Accum.OI Audit Trail: Display Extr.
F.5D	G/L: Update Bal. Sheet Adjustment
F.5E	G/L: Post Balance Sheet Adjustment
F.5F	G/L: Balance Sheet Adjustment Log
F.5G	G/L: Subseq.Adjustment(BA/PC) Sp.ErA
F.5I	G/L: Adv.Rep.f.Tx on Sls/Purch.w.Jur
F.61	Correspondence: Print Requests
F.62	Correspondence: Print Int.Documents
F.63	Correspondence: Delete Requests
F.64	Correspondence: Maintain Requests
F.65	Correspondence: Print Letters (Cust)
F.66	Correspondence: Print Letters (Vend)
F.70	Bill/Exchange Pmnt Request Dunning
F.71	DME with Disk: B/Excha. Presentation
F.75	Extended Bill/Exchange Information
F.77	C FI Maintain Table T045D
F.78	C FI Maintain Table T045B
F.79	C FI Maintain Table T045G
F.80	Mass Reversal of Documents
F.81	Reverse Posting for Accr./Defer.Docs
F.90	C FI Maintain Table T045F
F.91	C FI Maintain Table T045L
F.92	C FI Maintain T012K (Bill/Exch.)
F.93	Maintain Bill Liability and Rem.Risk
F.97	General Ledger: Report Selection
F.98	Vendors: Report Selection
F.99	Customers: Report Selection
F/LA	Create Pricing Report
F/LB	Change pricing reports
F/LC	Display pricing reports
F/LD	Execute pricing reports
F00	SAPoffice: Short Message
F000	Accounting
F010	ABAP/4 Reporting: Fiscal Year Change
F01N	Debit Position LO Single Reversal
F01O	Vacancy RU single reversal
F01P	Accruals/deferrals single reversal
F01Q	Debit position MC single reversal
F01R	MC settlement single reversal
F01S	Reversal of Periodic Postings
F01T	Reverse General Contract Accr./Def.
F04N	Vendor Foreign Currency Valuation
F05N	Customer Foreign Currency Valuation
F06N	Foreign Currency Val. (G/L Accounts)
F101	ABAP/4 Reporting: Balance Sheet Adj.

173

F103	ABAP/4 Reporting: Trnsfr Receivables
F104	ABAP/4 Reporting: Receivables Prov.
F107	FI Valuation Run
F107_A2MT	Assign Transaction Types to Actions
F107_MT2A	Assign Transaction Types to Actions
F107_PROV	FI Provisions
F107_PROVMETH	FI Provision Calculation Methods
F107_PROV_RP	FI Discounting: Receivables/Payables
F110	Parameters for Automatic Payment
F110S	Automatic Scheduling of Payment Prog
F111	Parameters for Payment of PRequest
F11CS	Config.TR Display Payment Program
F11CU	Config.TR Maintain Payment Program
F13E	Automatic Clearing With Currency
F13L	Autom. Clearing Spec. to Ledger Grp
F15	F15 Interface
F150	Dunning Run
F48A	Document Archiving
F53A	Archiving of G/L Accounts
F53V	Management of G/L Account Archives
F56A	Customer Archiving
F58A	Archiving of Vendors
F61A	Bank archiving
F64A	Transaction Figure Archiving
F66A	Archiving of Bank Data Storage
F8+0	Display FI Main Role Definition
F8+1	Maintain FI Main Role Definition
F8+2	Display FI Amount Groups
F8+3	Maintain FI Amount Groups
F8+4	Maintain Account Assignment Groups
F8+5	Maintain General Role Definition
F801	Create Payment Request
F802	Change Payment Request
F803	Display Payment Request
F804	Changes to Payment Requests
F805	Delete Payment Request
F806	Create Payment Request
F807	Change Posted Payment Request
F808	Post Payment Request
F809	Post exchange rate differences
F810	Number Ranges Payment Request
F811	Create Collective Payment Request
F812	Change Collective Payment Request
F813	Delete Collective Payment Request
F814	Reverse Collective Payment Request
F815	Display Collective Payment Request
F816	Reset Reversal Coll. Payt Request
F817	Release Collective Payment Request
F820	Coll. Payment Request Number Ranges
F821	Default Doc. Type for Request Type
F822	Set Automatic Payment Block
F823	Revenue Type/Object Class Assignment
F824	Print Request
F831	Create Recovery Request

F832	Change Recovery Request
F833	Display Recovery Request
F835	Delete Recovery Request
F836	Create Recovery Request
F837	Change Posted Recovery Request
F838	Account Grp/Revenue Type Assignment
F839	Number Range Maintenance: PSOOB
F840	Display Object
F841	Change Object
F842	Create Object
F843	Object Classes
F844	Define Summary Keys
F845	Close Posting Day
F846	Target and Actual Daily Closg Bals
F847	Define Permitted Posting Days
F848	Define Posting Day
F849	Group Responsibility
F850	G/L Account Determination (FM)
F851	Fiscal Year Identification (FM)
F852	Assign Fiscal Year Identification FM
F853	Posting Variants (FM)
F854	Assign Company Code Groups (FM)
F855	Acct Determination Characteristcs FM
F856	Posting Key According to D/C, etc.
F857	Accounts to be Proposed: Requests
F858	Number Range Maintenance: LOTNO
F859	Assign Request Cat. to Number Range
F860	Revenue Types
F861	Revenue Types/Company Code
F862	Revenue Types/Commitment Items
F863	Functions
F864	Processor
F865	Main and Secondary Revenue Types
F866	Activate Check Digits (Cust./Vend.)
F867	Deduction reasons
F868	Define Regions
F869	Where-used list
F870	Posting a Parked Request
F871	Create Payment Request (Local Auth.)
F872	Change Payment Request
F873	Display Payment Request
F874	Release Payment Request
F875	Delete Payment Request
F879	Create Payment Deduction Request
F880	Reverse Deferral
F881	Create Acceptance Request
F882	Change Acceptance Request
F883	Display Acceptance Request
F884	Release Acceptance Request
F885	Delete Acceptance Request
F886	Defer Acceptance Request
F887	Waive Acceptance Order Temporarily
F888	Waive Acceptance Request
F889	Create Acceptance Deduction Request

F890	Reverse Temporary Waiver
F891	Create Clearing Request
F891B	CR Transfer Between Different Funds
F892	Change Clearing Request
F893	Display Clearing Request
F894	Release Clearing Request
F895	Delete Clearing Request
F896	Create Blanket Remainder Clean Up
F899	Bundle Requests
F899R	Bundle FI Documents to Request
F8B1	C FI Maintain Table TBKBC
F8B2	C FI Maintain Table TBKCB
F8B3	C FI Maintain Table TBKCR
F8B4	C FI Maintain Table TBKDC
F8B5	C FI Maintain Table TBKLA
F8B6	C FI Maintain Table TBKPD
F8B6N	C FI Maintain Table TBKPV
F8B7	C FI Maintain Table TBKSP
F8B8	C FI Maintain Table TBKSR
F8B9	C FI Maintain Tables TBKRL, TBKRLT
F8BA	C FI Maintain Append to Table BNKA
F8BB	C FI Maintain Include to Table T012K
F8BC	C FI Maintain Table TBKFK
F8BD	C FI Maintain Table TBKZW
F8BE	FI Table Maintenance TBKS, TBKST
F8BF	C FI Maintain Table T042Y
F8BG	Maintain Global Data for F111
F8BH	Inconsistencies T042I and T042Y
F8BI	C FI Maintain Table T012-VPAST
F8BI1	Create Variant for RFBIBLK0
F8BJ	Maintain Clearing Accts (Rec.Bank)
F8BK	Maintain ALE-Compatible Pmnt Methods
F8BL	C FI Maintain Table TBKWT
F8BM	Maintain numb.range: Payment request
F8BN	Corr.Acctg Documents Payment Block
F8BO	Payment request archiving
F8BR	Levels for Payment Requests
F8BS	Detail display of payment requests
F8BT	Display Payment Requests
F8BU	Create payment runs automatically
F8BV	Reversal of Bank-to-Bank Transfers
F8BW	Reset Cleared Items: Payt Requests
F8BX	Online Payment
F8BZ	F111 Customizing
F8M1	Calculate Penalty Surcharge
F8O0	Delete Assignment Cust./Obj/Rev.Type
F8O1	Master Data Objects: Delete Data
F8O2	Control Different Functions
F8O3	Assignment Rounding Units CoCd Var.
F8O4	Document Type/Request Type Assgt
F8O5	Automatic Approval/Posting Control
F8O7	Prepare Archiving of Temp. Waiver
F8O8	Define Workflow Variant AO
F8O9	Assign Workflow Variant

F8P0	Spplt Dnng Proc. Assgt to Dnng Area
F8P1	Change Dnng Proc. Asst to Dnng Area
F8P2	Dunning Block in Customer Line Items
F8P3	Delete Assignment Cust./Rev.Type
F8P4	Delete Customer Execution Data
F8P5	Delete Subldgr Account Preprocessing
F8P6	Assign SL acct to SL prep. program
F8Q1	Create Recurring Payment Request
F8Q2	Create Recurring Acceptance Request
F8Q3	Change Standing Request
F8Q4	Display Standing Request
F8Q5	Release Standing Request
F8Q6	Delete Standing Request
F8Q7	Post Standing Request
F8Q8	Create Posting Documents
F8Q9	Requests from Down Payments
F8R1	Additional Setting Dunn.Procd.for FM
F8R2	Assgmt Dnng Procedure/Dunning Area
F8R3	Display Addtl Sttng Dnnn Prd. FM
F8REL	Release of Payment Requests
F8REV	Cancellation of Payment Requests
F8V1	Export execution data
F8XX	Payment Request No. Ranges KI3-F8BM
F902	Current Settings BCA
F90ABKST	Archiving Bank Statements
F90ACFBAL	Archiving Balance Carry Forwards
F90AINCAL	Archiving Account Balancing Details
F90AITEM	Archiving Payment Items
F90AORDER	Archiving Payment Orders
F90APECAL	Archiving Account Balancing Data
F90ASTORD	Archiving Standing Orders
F90ATOTAL	Archiving Value Date Trans. Figures
F90_PAR_NUMRG_GENER	Set Up Number Range Intervals
F90_PAR_REALLOCATE	Program to Create Interval Table
F91LTC	Call Fixed-Term Deposits
F92LTC	Collection of Fixed-Term Deposits
F93LTC	Postprocessing Fixed-Term Deposits
F94LTC	Restart Fixed-Term Deposits
F95LTC	Pre-notification of Maturity
F960	Application Log Cash Concentration
F961	Application Log FI Transfer
F962	Application Log Balance Sheet Prep.
F963	Appl. log bal.sh. prep.(backdated)
F970	Account Balances
F970_VAL	Balance List on Key Date
F971	Account Locks
F972	Overdraft List
F973	Display reconcil. balance list 1
F974	Display reconcil. balance list 2
F975	Compensation statememt daily status
F976	Overview Interest Accrual/Deferral
F977	Correction parked payment items
F978	Reconcil. List: FI Documents
F97A	Overview of BCA Reconciliation Keys

F97A1	Reconciliation key detail display
F97AT	Audit trail
F97C	Internal Reference Accts
F97CURR	Acct List for Currency Changeover
F97CX	External Reference Accts
F97E	Recon. to reconciliation key
F97G	Statement FI Document/BCA Posting
F97I	Reconciliation BCA /SAP FI Balances
F97J	Appl. log bal.sh. prep.(backdated)
F980	Interest Acc/Def Individ. Statement
F982	Edit general conditions
F983	Display General Conditions
F984	Release General Conditions
F984_DR	Release Deleted Conditions
F985	Edit Interest Conditions
F986	Display Interest Conditions
F987	Release Interest Conditions
F988	Edit Charge Conditions
F989	Display Charge Conditions
F98A	Release Charge Conditions
F98B	Edit Value Date Conditions
F98C	Display Value Date Donditions
F98D	Release Value Date Conditions
F98E	Edit Condition Assignment
F98F	Display Condition Assignment
F98G	Release Condition Assignment
F98R	Retroactive Condition Change
F98RK	Retroactive Condition Change
F98TM	Application Log for Term Control
F98TMAT	Application log: mature report
F98TMCOLL	Application log: collection report
F98TMPRE	Application Log for Pre-notification
F98X	Transact./Charge Transact.Assignment
F98Y	Transact./Charge Transact.Assignment
F98Z	Transact./Charge Transact.Assignment
F991	Mass Acct. Balancing (Int./Charges)
F992	Application Log Account Balancing
F992EX	Application Log Acct Balancing EDT
F993	Accrual/Deferral for General Ledger
F994	Application Log Accrual/Deferral
F995	Restart Account Balancing
F996	Single Acct. Balancing (Int./Charge)
F997	Early Mass Account Balancing
F997S	Early Individual Account Balancing
F999	Interest scale
F99C	Restart Interest Acc./Def.
F99D	Preparation Early Account Balancing
F99E	Closing: Settled Accounts
F99F	Single Acct. Balancing: Restart
F99G	Check Account Balancing Ext. Data
F99R	Create Basic Setting - Conditions
F99S	Change Basic Setting Conditions
F99X	Display Basic Setting Conditions
F9A0	BCA: Block Checks

SAP Transaction Codes – Volume One

F9A1	Create Check
F9A10	Edit Lock
F9A11	Delete Check
F9A12	Creat Check Stack
F9A13	Request Check Stack (Customer)
F9A16	BCA: Delete Stack Creation
F9A18	BCA: Request Checks from Location
F9A19	BCA: Release Check Stack
F9A20	Display Check Stack
F9A21	BCA: Block Check Stack
F9A23	Lift Block
F9A25	BCA: Location Maintenance Pos. Mgmt
F9A26	BCA: Stack Location Settings
F9A4	BCA: Request Check
F9A5	Number Range Maintenance: BCA_ACC_EX
F9A50	Change Check Status
F9A7	BCA: Revoke Check Block
F9A8	Check Locks
F9A9	BCA: Display Checks
F9AUTH	Maintain Authorization Groups
F9B1	BCA: Posting cut-off paym. transact.
F9B2	Posting Cut-Off Pay. Trans. Batch
F9B3	User Log Currency Changeover
F9B4	BCA: Report Currency Conversion
F9BA	BCA: Authorization Group Items
F9BB	BCA: Authorization Group Order
F9BENCH0	Benchmark Payment Transactions
F9BENCH1	Benchmark Account Balancing
F9BENCH10	Benchmark Payt Transactions Online
F9BENCH2	Benchmark Bank Statement
F9BENCHG1	Generate Settings
F9BENCHG2	Generate Pay. Trans. Master Data
F9BENCHG3	Generate Acct. Balanc. Master Data
F9BENCHG4	Generated Postings for Balancing
F9BENCHG4Q	Generate Trans.Figures for Balancing
F9BENCHG5	Generate Postings for Online Entry
F9BENCHM0	Monitor Benchmark: Paym. Transaction
F9BENCHM1	Monitor Benchmark: Posted Data
F9BENCHU0	Benchmark: Delete Blocked Items
F9BENCHU1	Benchmark: Reset Account Balancing
F9BENCHU3	Benchmark: Change BKKM2 for Restart
F9BENCHU4	Benchmark: Collect Statistics
F9BENCHU5	Reset Benchmark
F9BENCHV0	Maintain Number Range Parameters
F9BENCHV1	Maintain Global Benchmark Parameters
F9BTEINFO	BCA: BTE Info System (P&S)
F9C%	Job Distribution on Server
F9C&	Interval Size / Balanc. Parall. Mode
F9C(	Change Trans.Type Category Assignmt.
F9C)	Display Trans.Type Categ. Assignmt.
F9C+	Bank State. Dispatch Type Mainten.
F9C0	Current Account Groupings
F9C0_PAR_DETAIL	Par.Process. Item Postings: Detail
F9C0_PAR_MODE	Par.Process. Item Postings: General

F9C1	BCA: Blocking Reasons for Checks
F9C10	Maintain Business Transaction Code
F9C11	Maintain Reports End of Day Process.
F9C12	Scheduling Reports End of Day Proc.
F9C2	Position Types Maintenance
F9C3	Number Range Maintenance: BCA_PAORN
F9C4	Authorization types
F9C6	BCA: Field Modification Account Type
F9C7	BCA: Field Modification Activity
F9C9	Condition Groups Per Account Type
F9C=	Create Transaction Type Category
F9C?	Change Transaction Type Category
F9CA	Account Status Enhancements
F9CAA	Create Transaction Type Category 2
F9CAB	Change Transaction Type Category 2
F9CAC	Display Transaction Type Category 2
F9CAD	Create Trans. Type Category 2 Assgmt
F9CAE	Change Trans. Type Category 2 Assgmt
F9CAF	Display Trans. Type Category 2Assgmt
F9CAPPLREL	Relationships Betw. Applic. Types
F9CARCPERIODS	Retention Periods
F9CB	Old:Allowed Acct.Types per Bank Area
F9CC1	Authorizations for Field Groups
F9CC2	Screen Configuration
F9CCHGRCV	Recipient in A-Sentence
F9CD	Crete Cond.Cat.<->Diff. Type
F9CE	Display Cond.Cat.<-> Diff.Type
F9CF	Change Cond Type<->Diff Type
F9CG	Create Bank Condition Categories
F9CH	Change Bank Condition Categories
F9CI	Display Bank Condition Categories
F9CICC	Change Compensation Methods
F9CICD	Change Compensation Methods
F9CJ	Create Differentiation Types
F9CK	Change Differentiation Types
F9CL	Display Differentiation Types
F9CM	Create Condition Group
F9CN	Change Condition Groups
F9CO	Display Condition Groups
F9COGR1	Create Condition Group
F9COGR2	Edit Condition Group
F9COGR3	Display Condition Group
F9COL1	Correction of SubFinPayt Balance
F9CORRDISPMAP	Corresp: Bank Stat Dispatch Mapping
F9CORRMIGRATE	Migrate BKK45 Entries
F9CP	Create Limit Categories
F9CPP	Settings for Parallel Processing
F9CQ	Change Limit Categories
F9CR	Display Limit Categories
F9CS	Create reference limits
F9CSA	BCA Ref. Interest Rate Maintenance
F9CSO00	SO: Field Modification Activity
F9CSO01	SO: Field Modification Trans. Type
F9CSO02	SO: Authorization Types

SAP Transaction Codes – Volume One

F9CSO03	SO: Authorizations for Field Groups
F9CSO04	SO Cust: Screen Configuration
F9CSO1	SO Control: Applications
F9CSO2	SO Control: Field Groups
F9CSO3	SO Control: Views
F9CSO4	SO Control: Sections
F9CSO5	SO Control: Screens
F9CSO6	SO Control: Screen Sequence
F9CSO7	SO Control: Events
F9CSO8	SO Control: CUA Standard Functions
F9CSO9	SO Control: CUA Additional Functions
F9CSOB	SO Ctrl: Assig. ScrnFld->DBfld
F9CSOC	SO Control: Field Modificat.Criteria
F9CSOD	SO Control: Products
F9CSOE	SO Control: Product Group
F9CSOF	SO Control: Applic. Transactions
F9CSOH	SO Control: Tables
F9CSOI	SO Control: Activities
F9CSOJ	SO Control: FM per Activity
F9CT	Change reference limits
F9CTRNSTYP	Maintain Transaction Types
F9CTXTKEY	BCA: Maintain Text Key
F9CU	Display reference limits
F9CV	Principle of Dual Control Limits
F9CX	Field Control - Conditions
F9CZ	BCA: Guarant. Amounts for Posit.Type
F9C[	Authorization Types for Condiitons
F9C]	Position: Authorization Types
F9C`	Display Transaction Type Category
F9C{	Authorization Types Payment Items
F9C}	Authorization Types Payment Orders
F9D1	Messages
F9DDCC	Currency Conversion Dir. Debit Order
F9FOCC	Forward Order Currency Changeover
F9FOLLOWUP	Account Resubmission
F9G1	Create acct holder
F9G2	Change acct holder
F9G3	Display Account Holder
F9G4	Create Authorized Drawer
F9G5	Change Authorized Drawer
F9G6	Display Authorized Drawer
F9G7	Create Account Holder
F9G8	Change Account Holder
F9G9	Display Account Holder
F9GA	Create Bank Statement Recipient
F9GB	Change Bank Statement Recipient
F9GC	Dispaly Bank Statement Recipient
F9GL	Display All BP Roles
F9H0	Account Hierarchy Change History
F9H1	Create Account Hierarchy
F9H2	Change Account Hierarchy
F9H3	Display Account Hierarchy
F9H4	Cash Concentration: Single Run
F9H5	Cash Concentration: Restart

F9H6	Cash Concentration: Mass Run
F9H7	Number Range Maintenance: BKK_HYRAR
F9HA	GL Variants
F9HB	General Ledger Transaction
F9HC	General Ledger Group
F9HC4	GL Acct Assgmt, Indiv.Value Adjustmt
F9HC5	GL Acct Assgmt, Indiv.Value Adjustmt
F9HD	GL Transfer Posting Group
F9HE	GL Acct. Assignment, CA Posted
F9HEWB1	Create Individual Value Adjustment
F9HEWB2	Change Individual Value Adjustment
F9HEWB3	Display Individual Value Adjustment
F9HEWB4	Post Loss on Receivables
F9HG	Assignment Trans.Type-GL Transaction
F9HH	GL Account Assignment, Parked
F9HI	Transfer BCA - GL
F9HIST_KOND_INDIV	History of Individual Conditions
F9HIST_KOND_STAND	History of Standard Conditions
F9HIST_KOND_ZUORD	History of Condition Assignment
F9HJ	GL Acct. Assignment, Int. Acc./Def.
F9HL	Bal.Sheet Prep. BCA - GL
F9HLDAUTH	BCA: Authorization Amts for Holds
F9HLDREL	Release Holds requiring Dual Control
F9HO	GL Control for Legacy Data
F9HRVA	Post Individual Value Adjustment
F9HRVA_MT	Indiv. Val. Adjst. Proposal List
F9H_GLCUST	Check General Ledger Customizing
F9H_GLDATA	Comparison of FI Data with BCA
F9H_GL_OLD	GL Control for Legacy Data
F9I1	Create Payment Order - External
F9I1PLAN	Create Planned Order Externally
F9I2	Create Payment Order - Internal
F9I2PLAN	Create Planned Order Internally
F9I3	Display Payment Order
F9I3PLAN	Display Planned Order
F9I4	Create Payment Item
F9I7	Display Payment Item
F9I8	Postprocess Payment Item
F9I9	Edit Payment Order (General)
F9I9PLAN	General Processing of Planned Order
F9IA	Release Payment Order
F9IAPLAN	Release Planned Payment Order
F9IB	Release Payment Item
F9IC	Create Payment Order Former Account
F9ID	BCA: CpD Editing of Payment Item
F9IE	Create Payment Item Former Account
F9IF	BCA: CpD Display of Payment Item
F9IG	Reverse Payment Item
F9IH	BCA: Maintain Trans. Type Offsett.Ps
F9II	Return Payment Item
F9IJ	Edit Payment Item
F9IK	Create Return Payment Order
F9IL	Create Planned Item
F9IM	Delete Planned Item

SAP Transaction Codes – Volume One

F9IN	Display Planned Items
F9INDCOND	Release Individual Conditions
F9INDCONDDELREL	Release Individual Conditions
F9INDCONDDISP	Display Individual Conditions
F9INDIV	Display Individual conditions
F9IO	Post Planned item
F9IP	Planned items
F9IQPLAN	Delete Planned Order
F9ITAUTH	BCA: Amount Authorization for Item
F9IUPLAN	Post Planned Orders
F9IVPLAN	Planned Orders - Application Log
F9J0	Display Application Log
F9J1	Reconcile with Legacy System
F9JENQSHOW	Display BKKITENQ
F9K1	Create Account
F9K2	Change account
F9K3	Display Account
F9KAC	Release Account Closure
F9KD	Account Closure
F9KE	Application Log Account Closure
F9KG	Release Limits
F9KGDEL	Delete Limits
F9KGDISP	Limit Overview
F9KH	Release Currency Changeovers
F9KHDEL	Delete Currency Changeovers
F9KMOC	Change business partner
F9KOVRDISP	Tolerated Overdraft: Display
F9KOVRN	Tolerated Overdraft: Notification
F9KOVRN_DUPL	Tol.Ovrdft: Duplicate Notification
F9KOVRR	Tolerated Overdraft: New Run
F9KY	Close Account
F9L!	Display Assignm- Bank Area-Cond.Area
F9L(	Change Function-Trans.Type Assignm.
F9L)	Display Function-Trans.Type Assign.
F9L+	Display Condition Area Settings
F9L,	Master Data Settings
F9L.	Customizing: IMG Bank Customer Accts
F9L0	Settings for Additional Development
F9L1	Create Posting Category Assignment
F9L2	Change Posting Category Assignment
F9L3	Display Posting Category Assignment
F9L4	Posting Date for Closing in Dialog
F9L5	Create Transaction Type Categories
F9L6	Change Transaction Type Categories
F9L7	Display Transaction Type Categories
F9L8	Create Medium Categories
F9L9	Change Medium Categories
F9L=	Create Condition Area Settings
F9L?	Change Condition Area Settings
F9LA	Display Medium Categories
F9LB	Create Item Counters
F9LBDT	Development in BDT Environment
F9LC	Change Item Counters
F9LD	Display Item Counters

F9LE	Create Transaction-Category Assignm.
F9LF	Change Transaction-Category Assignm.
F9LG	Dsiplay Transaction-Category Assign.
F9LH	Create Medium-Category Assignment
F9LI	Change Medium-Category Assignment
F9LJ	Display Medium-Category Assignment
F9LK	Create Item Counter Determination
F9LL	Change Item Counter Determination
F9LM	Display Item Counter Determination
F9LN	Transact.-Interest Trans. Assignment
F9LO	Transact.-Interest Trans. Assignment
F9LP	Transact.-Interest Trans. Assignment
F9LQ	Create Dispatch Expense Counter
F9LR	Change Dispatch Expense Counter
F9LS	Display Dispatch Expense Counter
F9LT	Country Setting for IBAN
F9LTC	Fixing Fixed-Term Deposits
F9LU	Payment Notes for Returns
F9LV	Bank Area-Independent Settings, Text
F9LW	Create Trivial Amount
F9LX	Change Trivial Amount
F9LY	Display Trivial Amount
F9LZ	Create Bk.Area-Cond.Area Assignment
F9M01	S Table: Field Status Maintenance
F9M02	Table: Function Variant Maintenance
F9M03	Assign Function Variants
F9M04	Field Groups per Object
F9M05	Field Status per Activity
F9M06	Field Status per Document Type
F9M1	Bank Customer Accounts: Settings
F9M2	Business Partner: Settings
F9M3	Relationships: Settings
F9M4	Settings Payment Transactions
F9M5	Condition Settings
F9MA	Check Digit Procedure
F9MAA	Default Value Transaction Type
F9MAB	Default Media
F9MAC	Default Payment Methods
F9MAD	Alternative Currency Key
F9MARCH	Archiving: Period Maintenance
F9MB	Bank Area
F9MBC	Currency changeover
F9MBD	Currency changeover
F9MBENCH	Performance BCA
F9MBP	Permitted Products per Bank Area
F9MC	Assignment of Check Digit Procedure
F9MD	Parameters for Modulo Procedure
F9ME	Assignm. Check Dig.Proced.->Bank Key
F9MEMPOBJM	Table Mainten. Obj.Meth. Empl.Accts.
F9MF	Bank Area: Accounts Payment Trans.
F9MG	To Delete: Blocking Functions
F9MH	Settings for Hierarchies (General)
F9MHCC	Settings for Cash Concentration
F9MI	Formats for Application of Funds

F9MJ	Assignment Inverse Trans. Type
F9MJUMP	Table Maintenance Jump
F9MK	Notification of Returns
F9ML	Open BCA Events
F9MM	Assignm. Medium/Pay.Meth. to Process
F9MMETHOD	Table Maintenance Methods
F9MN	Bank Customer Accounts
F9MO	Bank Area-Independent Settings
F9MOBJECT	Table Maintenance Objects
F9MOBJMETH	Table Mainten. Obj.-Meth. Assignment
F9MP	Media Maintenance
F9MPAYM	External Payment Transactions
F9MQ	Maintain functions
F9MR	Transaction Types Maintenance
F9MREPOBJM	Table Maint. Object Meth.Perio.Tasks
F9MS	Function Groups Maintenance
F9MT	Locking Reasons Maintenance
F9MU	Acct.Type->Funct.Groups Maintenance
F9MV	Document Type Maintenance
F9MX	S Table: Field Status Maintenance
F9MY	S Table: Transaction Maintenance
F9MZ	S Table: Buttons to Hide Maintenance
F9N1	Create Bank Statements
F9N10	Overview End of Day Processing
F9N11	Start End-of-Day Processing
F9N12	Overview of Current Mass Runs
F9N13	Accts. Blocked by Single Balancing
F9N14	Duplicate Creation Bk.State. Restart
F9N15	Duplicate Creation Single Run
F9N16	Balance Notification Mass Run
F9N17	Balance Notification Single Run
F9N18	Restart Balance Notification
F9N19	Balance Notification Application Log
F9N2	Change Definition Posting Categories
F9N3	Application Log Bank Statement
F9N4	Restart - Bank Statement
F9N6	Posting Date for Balancing as Batch
F9N7	Bank Statement - Single Account
F9N8	List of Accounts in End of Day Proc.
F9N9	Bank Statement - Duplicate Creation
F9NA	S Table: Funct. Variant Maintenance
F9NARCH	Archiving Bank Statements
F9NB	Text Symbol Maintenance
F9NC	Processes in BCA
F9NCHAIN	Start End-of-Day Processing
F9ND	Assgmt Processes -> GL Processes
F9NTC4	Amount Notice: Mass Release
F9NTC5	Correct Available Balance Series
F9NTC_LOG_RELEASE	Application Log Notices
F9OO1	Create stand. order
F9OO2	Change stand. order
F9OO3	Display Standing Order
F9O43	Release Standing Order
F9O6	Delete stand. order

F9O61	Confirm Standing Order Deletion
F9OA	Standing Order: Display Applic. Log
F9OF	Create Foreign Payment Order
F9OFPLAN	Create Plannned Order - Foreign
F9OG	Post Standing Order
F9OGPAR	Post Standing Order Packages
F9OH	Postprocess Payment Order
F9OI	Reverse Payment Order
F9PEXDE1	Create EFT
F9PEXDE4	Application Log of Outgoing PT
F9PEXDE5	EFT File Overview of Incoming PT
F9PI06	Delete Payment Item
F9PICC	Planned Item Currency Changeover
F9PINDE1	Import EFT
F9PINDE2	Restart: Import EFT
F9PINDE3	Reversal Run for Incoming PT
F9PINDE4	Application Log for Incoming PT
F9PINDE5	EFT File Overview of Incoming PT
F9PO06	Delete Payment Order (General)
F9POAUTH	BCA: Authorization Group Order
F9POWFCU	Assign Workflow Tasks Acct Mgmt
F9S1	CA Control: Applications
F9S18	CA Control: Activities
F9S19	CA Control: Field Mod. per Activity
F9S2	CA Control: Field Groups
F9S3	CA Control: Views
F9S4	CA Control: Sections
F9S5	CA Control: Screens
F9S6	CA Control: Screen Sequences
F9S7	CA Control: Events
F9S8	CA Control: CUA Standard Functions
F9S9	CA Control: CUA Additional Functions
F9SA	CA Control: Matchcode
F9SB	CA Control: Assign. Scr.Field->DBFld
F9SC	CA Control: Field Modific. Criteria
F9SD	CA Control: Products
F9SE	CA Control: Product Group
F9SEPA_CR1	Create Mandate for Ordering Party
F9SEPA_CR2	Change Mandate for Ordering Party
F9SEPA_CR3	Display Mandate for Ordering Party
F9SEPA_DB1	Create Mandate for Recipient Party
F9SEPA_DB2	Change Mandate for Recipient Party
F9SEPA_DB3	Display Mandate for Recipient Party
F9SF	CA Control: Application Transactions
F9SH	CA Control: Tables
F9SI	PAIT Control: Field Groups
F9SIMMINDEP	Min. Deposit Maint.: Term-Independt
F9SJ	Condition Control: Field Groups
F9SK	Cond.Control: Assign.Sc.Fld.->DB Fld
F9SL	Cond.Control: Assign. Table<->FuMod.
F9SM	Position Control: Field Groups
F9SN	PAIT Control: Scrn.Fld. <-> DB Field
F9SO	Position Control: Scrn.Fld.->DB Fld.
F9SOAUTH	BCA: Authorization Group Order

SAP Transaction Codes – Volume One

F9SOCC	Standing Order Currency Changeover
F9SP	Position Control: Table <-> Fun.Mod.
F9SQ	PAIT Control: Table <-> Fun.Mod.
F9SR	PAOR Control: Field Groups
F9SS	PAOR Control: Scrn.Fld.<-> DB Field
F9SS1	Qualifier of Payment Notes
F9SSNRKREIS	Number Range Maintenance: BKK_PYNOT
F9ST	PAOR Control: Table <-> Func. Mod.
F9SX	BCA Control: External Applications
F9T0	Archiving Payment Orders
F9T1	Delete payment orders
F9T2	Reloading Payment Orders
F9T3	Reading Payment Order Archives
F9T4	Managing Payment Order Archives
F9T5	Archiving Standing Orders
F9T6	Deleting Standing Orders
F9T7	Reloading Standing Orders
F9T8	Reading Standing Order Archives
F9T9	Administration Stand.Order Archives
F9TA	Archiving Payment Items
F9TB	Deleting Payment Items
F9TC	Reloading Payment Items
F9TD	Reading Payment Item Archives
F9TE	Admin.of Payment Items Archives
F9TF	Archiving Account Balancing Data
F9TFASTENTRY1	Create: Fast Entry of Fixed Deposit
F9TFASTENTRY2	Change: Fast Entry of Fixed Deposit
F9TFASTENTRY3	Display: Fast Entry of Fixed Deposit
F9TG	Deleting Account Balancing Data
F9TH	Reloading Account Balancing Data
F9TI	Reading Act. Balancing Data Archive
F9TJ	Admin. of Acct.Bal.Data Archives
F9TK	Archiving Acct.Bal.Detail Data
F9TL	Deleting Acct.Bal.Detail Data
F9TM	Reloading Acct. Bal. Detail Data
F9TN	Reading Acct.Bal.Det.Data Archives
F9TO	Admin. of Acct.Bal.Det.Dat. Archives
F9TP	Archiving Value Date Trans. Figures
F9TQ	Deleting Value Date Trans. Figures
F9TR	Reloading Value Date Trans. Figures
F9TRMMINDEP	Min. Deposit Maint.: Term-Dependent
F9TS	Reading Val.Date Trans.Figs.Archives
F9TT	Admin.of Val.Dt.Trans. Figs.Archives
F9TU	Archiving conditions
F9TV	Deleting conditions
F9TW	Reloading Conditions
F9TX	Reading Condition Archives
F9TY	Admin. of Condition Archives
F9VS	Assignment of Interest Pen. TA Type
F9VU	Assignment of Interest Pen. TA Type
F9VW	Preparation of Currency Changeover
F9Z1	Changing Default Values
FA39	Call up report with report variant
FAA_GENMAP	Generate Mapping Methods

FAGL21	Create General Ledger Rollup
FAGL22	Change General Ledger Rollup
FAGL23	Display General Ledger Rollup
FAGL24	Delete General Ledger Rollup
FAGL25	Execute General Ledger Rollup
FAGL3KEH	General Ledger: Default Profit Ctr
FAGLB03	Display Balances
FAGLB03A	Display Balances
FAGLBW01	Generate Gen. Ledger Extract Struct.
FAGLBW03	Assign Gen. Ledger DataSource/Ledger
FAGLCOFIFLUP	Repost CO->FI from Worklist
FAGLCOFIIMG	Customizing for CO->FI Update
FAGLCOFILOGDISP	Display Application Log
FAGLCOFITRACEADMIN	Administr. of Trace for OnlineUpdate
FAGLCOFITRACEDEL	Deletion of Trace Data for Update
FAGLCOFITRACEOFF	Deactivate Trace for Online Update
FAGLCOFITRACEON	Activate Trace for Online Update
FAGLCOFITRACESHOW	Display Trace for Online Update
FAGLCOFITRNSFRCODOCS	Transfer CO Doc. into Ext.Accounting
FAGLCOFIWRKLSTDISP	Display Worklist
FAGLCOFIWRKLSTEDIT	Edit Worklist
FAGLCOFIWRKLSTTRACE	Display Worklist and Trace Data
FAGLCORC	CO - FI Reconciliation
FAGLF03	Reconciliation
FAGLF101	Sorted List/Regrouping
FAGLGA11	General Ledger: Create Act. Assessmt
FAGLGA12	General Ledger: Change Act. Assessmt
FAGLGA13	Gen. Ledger: Display Act. Assessment
FAGLGA14	Gen. Ledger: Delete Act. Assessment
FAGLGA15	Gen. Ledger: Execute Act. Assessment
FAGLGA16	Gen. Ledger: Act. Assessmt Overview
FAGLGA27	Gen. Ledger: Create Plan Assessment
FAGLGA28	Gen. Ledger: Change Plan Assessment
FAGLGA29	Gen. Ledger: Display Plan Assessment
FAGLGA2A	Gen. Ledger: Delete Plan Assessment
FAGLGA2B	Gen. Ledger: Execute Plan Assessment
FAGLGA2C	Gen. Ledger: Plan Assessmt Overview
FAGLGA31	Gen. Ledger: Create Act.Distribution
FAGLGA32	Gen. Ledger: Change Act.Distribution
FAGLGA33	Gen. Ledger:Display Act.Distribution
FAGLGA34	Gen. Ledger: Delete Act.Distribution
FAGLGA35	Gen. Ledger:Execute Act.Distribution
FAGLGA36	Gen. Ledger: Act. Distrib. Overview
FAGLGA47	Gen. Ledger:Create Plan Distribution
FAGLGA48	Gen. Ledger:Change Plan Distribution
FAGLGA49	Gen. Ledger:Display PlanDistribution
FAGLGA4A	Gen. Ledger:Delete Plan Distribution
FAGLGA4B	Gen. Ledger:Execute PlanDistribution
FAGLGA4C	Gen. Ledger: Plan Distrib. Overview
FAGLGCLE	Activation of Plan Line Items
FAGLGP52	Copy Model Plan
FAGLGVTR	G/L: Balance Carried Forward
FAGLL03	G/L Account Line Items (New)
FAGLP03	Display Plan Line Items

FAGLPLC	Gen. Ledger: Change Planning Layout
FAGLPLD	Gen. Ledger: Display Planning Layout
FAGLPLI	Gen. Ledger: Create Planning Layout
FAGLPLSET	Gen. Ledger: Set Planner Profile
FAGLSKF	Post Statistical Key Figures(Actual)
FAGLSKF1	Post Statistical Key Figures (Plan)
FAGLSKF3	Stat. Key Figures: Period Evaluation
FAGLSKF4	Stat. Key Figures: Document Display
FAGLSKF5	Stat. Key Figures: Document Reversal
FAGLSKF6	Stat. Key Figs: Post CO Subsequently
FAGLSKF7	Stat. Key Figs: Post FI Subsequently
FAGLSKF8	Stat. Key Figs:Post PCA Subsequently
FAGLSKFR	Stat. Key Figures: Rev. doc. list
FAGLSL25	Execute General Ledger Rollup
FAGL_104	Reserve for Bad Debt: Gross (New)
FAGL_ACTIVATE_IT	Activate Line Item Display
FAGL_ACTIVATE_OP	Activation of Open Item Management
FAGL_ACTIVATION	Activation of New G/L Accounting
FAGL_ACTIV_SPLIT_CC	Activation of Document Splitter
FAGL_BELNR	Number Range Maint. for Source Doc.
FAGL_BELNR_LD	Doc. Types for Source Docs in Ledger
FAGL_CHECK_ACCOUNT	Check G/L Accounts for Doc.Splitting
FAGL_CHECK_DOC_TYPE	Check Doc. Types for Doc. Splitting
FAGL_CHECK_LINETYPE	Check Bus. Transaction for Documents
FAGL_CHECK_OBJ	Analysis of Obj. No. Inconsistencies
FAGL_CLOCO_CALLTRANS	Start of Transactions and Programs
FAGL_CLOCO_CALLWDAPP	Start of Transactions and Programs
FAGL_CLOCO_DISPEXT	Display Basic List
FAGL_CLOCO_DISPJOB	Display Job Log
FAGL_CLOCO_DISPSPOOL	Display Spool Log
FAGL_CL_MIG_OB	Opening Balance in the Cash Ledger
FAGL_CL_MIG_OB_DISP	Display Opening Balance
FAGL_CL_MIG_RESET	Reset Migration of Cash Ledger
FAGL_CO_01	FAGL_YEC_POSTINGS Columbia
FAGL_CO_02	FAGL_YEC_POSTINGS_EHP4 Colombia
FAGL_CO_PLAN	Transfer CO Plan Documents in ERP GL
FAGL_DEL	Delete Transaction Data from Ledger
FAGL_DOCNR	Number Range Maint. for Doc. Number
FAGL_DOCNR_LD	Doc. Types for New G/L Doc. Numbers
FAGL_EHP4_T001B_COFI	Open and Close Posting Periods
FAGL_FC_TRANS	Currency Translation of Balances
FAGL_FC_VAL	Foreign Currency Valuation
FAGL_FLEXGL_IMG	IMG for New General Ledger
FAGL_GINS	G/L installation
FAGL_IT_01	FAGL_YEC_POSTINGS Italy
FAGL_IT_02	FAGL_YEC_POSTINGS_EHP4 Italy
FAGL_MIGDS_REST_ALL	Reset Migration Completely
FAGL_MIGDS_REST_OP	Reset Migration for Open Items
FAGL_MIGDS_REST_RP	Reset Migration for Documents
FAGL_MIGPS	Migrate a ledger from FM to PS
FAGL_MIG_ACTIVATE	Start Migration
FAGL_MIG_ADJUST	Log of Document-Specific Adjustments
FAGL_MIG_CRESPLIT	Process Open Items for Doc.Splitting
FAGL_MIG_CRESUM	Generate Bal.Carryforward:Open Items

FAGL_MIG_FICHAN	Subsequent Posting: FI Docs (Update)
FAGL_MIG_FICHAT	Subseq. Posting: FI Docs (Selection)
FAGL_MIG_FINISH	Complete Migration
FAGL_MIG_GCAC	Compare Against Backup Copy
FAGL_MIG_OPFILL	Worklist for Open Items
FAGL_MIG_REPORT_SUM	Generated Entries: Totals Table
FAGL_MIG_REPOST	Subsequent Posting in Migration
FAGL_MIG_REPOST_OP	Transfer Open Items to New GL
FAGL_MIG_RESTORE_ALL	Reset Migration Completely
FAGL_MIG_RESTORE_OP	Reset Migration for Open Items
FAGL_MIG_RESTORE_RP	Reset Migration for Documents
FAGL_MIG_RPFILL	Worklist for Migration Documents
FAGL_MIG_SELECT	Determine Migration Objects
FAGL_MIG_SHOW_SPL	Display Document Splitting Result
FAGL_MIG_SIM_SPL	Simulation of Document Splitting
FAGL_MIG_SPLIT	Subsequently Post Split Information
FAGL_MIG_STATUS	Analysis: Migration Status
FAGL_OBH1	C FI Doc.No.Range: Copy Company Code
FAGL_OBH2	C FI Doc.No.Range: Copy Fiscal Year
FAGL_PLAN_ACT_SEC	Integ.Planning for Sec. CostElements
FAGL_PLAN_VT	Balance Carryforward: Plan Data
FAGL_PL_LC	Number Range Maint. for Plan Docs
FAGL_PRCTR_AUTH	Activation of PrCtr Auth. Check
FAGL_PT_01	FAGL_YEC_POSTINGS Portugal
FAGL_PT_02	FAGL_YEC_POSTINGS_EHP4 Portugal
FAGL_REORG_CUST1	Restrictions at Plan Level
FAGL_REORG_CUST2	Restrictions at Package Level
FAGL_REORG_CUST3	Specify Doc. Type for Trans. Posting
FAGL_RMIGR	Report Trnsfr: EC-PCA to FI-GL (New)
FAGL_RMIGR_LOG	Transfer of PCA Reports: Log
FAGL_RO_01	FAGL_YEC_POSTINGS Romania
FAGL_RO_02	FAGL_YEC_POSTINGS_EHP4 Romania
FAGL_RPACK	Edit Reorganization Package
FAGL_RPLAN	Edit Reorganization Plan
FAGL_RREASSIGN_MD	Reorganization: Reassign Master Data
FAGL_RREPOST	Reorganization: Transfer
FAGL_RRI_CUST	Report Interface: Customizing FI-CO
FAGL_RSNAP	Reorganization: Snapshot
FAGL_RSNAPSHOW	Reorganization: Display Snapshot
FAGL_SCENARIO	Scenario Maintenance in New G/L
FAGL_SCENARIO_ASS	Scenario Assignment in New G/L
FAGL_SCENARIO_ASSIGN	Scenario Assignment for Ledger
FAGL_SK_01	FAGL_YEC_POSTINGS Slovakia
FAGL_SK_02	FAGL_YEC_POSTINGS_EHP4 Slovakia
FAGL_TRGT_LDGR	Assgnmnt:Acctg Principle to Ldgr Grp
FAGL_TR_01	FAGL_YEC_POSTINGS Turkey
FAGL_TR_02	FAGL_YEC_POSTINGS_EHP4 Turkey
FAGL_UPL_CF	G/L: Upload of Balance Carryforward
FAGL_VALIDATE	Validation of A/c Assignmt Combinat.
FAGL_VAL_LOG	Analysis: Validation Log
FAGL_WZ_NEW_RULE	Wizard: New Document Splitting Rule
FAGL_WZ_SPLIT_CONF	Wizard: Configuration of DocSpitting
FAIB01	Rule Administration
FAIB02	Build Intermediate Layers

SAP Transaction Codes – Volume One

FAIB03	Balance Sheet Valuation
FAIB04	Market Prices
FAIB05	Balance Sheet Values by Account
FAIB06	Display Intermediate Layers
FAIB07	Display Current Rules
FAIC03	Substitution of Account Assignments
FAIP04	GR/IR Clearing
FAIP05	Calculation of Actual Overhead
FAIP06	WIP Clearing
FAIP07	Target Cost Calculation
FAIP08	Revaluation Costs of Sales
FAIQS01	Create Actual Quantity Structure
FAIR01	Inventory Accounting: Line Items
FAIR02	Inventory Accounting: Line Items
FAIR03	Inventory Accounting: Document Displ
FAIR04	Inventory Accounting: Document Displ
FAIR05	Reconciliation Inv. Ledger - G/L
FAIR06	Plan/Tgt/Actual Comparison - Orders
FAIR07	Overview: Valuated Inventory
FAIV01	Price Release
FAIV02	Change material prices
FAIV03	Display Material Prices
FAIV04	Price Comparison
FAIV05	Display History for Material Prices
FAIV06	Debit/Credit Material
FAIWQ1	Worklist
FAKA	Config.: Show Display Format
FAKP	Config.: Maintain Display Format
FAR1	S FI-ARI Maint. table T061A
FARA	S FI-ARI Maint. table T061P/Q
FARB	C FI-ARI Maint. table T061R
FAREA_MODE	Setting: Determination of Funct.Area
FARI	AR Interface: Third-party applicatns
FARY	Table T061S
FARZ	Table T061V
FB00	Accounting Editing Options
FB01	Post Document
FB01L	General Posting for Ledger Group
FB02	Change Document
FB03	Display Document
FB03L	Document Display : G/L View
FB03S	Display Split Documents
FB03Z	Display Document/Payment Usage
FB04	Document Changes
FB05	Post with Clearing
FB05L	Post with Clearing for Ledger Group
FB05_OLD	Post with clearing
FB07	Control Totals
FB08	Reverse Document
FB08S	Reverse Split Document
FB09	Change Line Items
FB09D	Display Line Items
FB10	Invoice/Credit Fast Entry
FB11	Post Held Document

FB12	Correspondence Request
FB13	Release for Payments
FB15	Assign Items
FB16	Assign Items
FB16EA	Assign Items
FB17	Open Item Assignmnt: Check from List
FB18	Maintain Standard Mail Texts
FB1D	Clear Customer
FB1K	Clear Vendor
FB1S	Clear G/L Account
FB1SL	Clear G/L Account for Ledger Group
FB21	Enter Statistical Posting
FB22	Reverse Statistical Posting
FB2E	Reconciliation btwn affiliated comps
FB31	Enter Noted Item
FB41	Post Tax Payable
FB50	G/L Acct Pstg: Single Screen Trans.
FB50L	Enter G/L Account Doc for Ledger Grp
FB60	Enter Incoming Invoices
FB65	Enter Incoming Credit Memos
FB70	Enter Outgoing Invoices
FB75	Enter Outgoing Credit Memos
FB99	Check if Documents can be Archived
FBA1	Customer Down Payment Request
FBA2	Post Customer Down Payment
FBA3	Clear Customer Down Payment
FBA6	Vendor Down Payment Request
FBA7	Post Vendor Down Payment
FBA7_OLD	Post Vendor Down Payment
FBA8	Clear Vendor Down Payment
FBA8_OLD	Clear Vendor Down Payment
FBB1	Post Foreign Currency Valn
FBBA	Display Acct Determination Config.
FBBCX	Post Document with Currency Exchange
FBBP	Maintain Acct Determination Config.
FBBRVO	Vendor Operation
FBCB	Balance Carryfwd for Ledger Group
FBCJ	Cash Journal
FBCJ3	Display Cash Journal
FBCJC0	C FI Maintain Tables TCJ_C_JOURNALS
FBCJC1	Cash Journal Document Number Range
FBCJC2	C FI Maint. Tables TCJ_TRANSACTIONS
FBCJC3	C FI Maintain Tables TCJ_PRINT
FBCJC5	Maintain Numb. Groups for Cash Docs
FBCJC6	Number range maintenance: CAJO_DOC3
FBD1	Enter Recurring Entry
FBD2	Change Recurring Entry
FBD3	Display Recurring Entry
FBD4	Display Recurring Entry Changes
FBD5	Realize Recurring Entry
FBD9	Enter Recurring Entry
FBDF	Menu Banque de France
FBE1	Create Payment Advice
FBE2	Change Payment Advice

FBE3	Display Payment Advice
FBE6	Delete Payment Advice
FBE7	Add to Payment Advice Account
FBF1	C80 Reporting Minus Sp.G/L Ind.
FBF2	Financial Transactions
FBF3	Control Report
FBF4	Download Documents
FBF5	Reports Minus Vendor Accounts
FBF6	Document Changes
FBF7	C80 Reports Minus Sp.G/L Ind.
FBF8	C84 Reports
FBFT	Customizing BDF
FBIC001	Check Assignment of Accounts
FBIC002	Automatically Assign Accounts
FBIC003	Create Additional Fields
FBIC004	Activate Transaction Data Tables
FBIC005	Create Additional Fields
FBIC006	Create Additional Fields
FBIC008	Companies to be Reconciled
FBIC009	Companies to be Reconciled
FBIC010	Reconciliation Process Attributes
FBIC011	Auxiliary Programs
FBIC012	Reconciliation: Delete Data
FBIC013	Reconciliation: Recalculate Totals
FBIC014	Reconciliation: Delete Data
FBIC015	Reconciliation: Recalculate Totals
FBIC016	Reconciliation: Documents
FBIC017	Reconciliation: Totals Records
FBIC018	Reconciliation: Totals Records
FBIC019	Reconciliation: Documents
FBIC020	Reconciliation: Status
FBIC021	Reconciliation: Status
FBIC022	Reconciliation: Status
FBIC023	Reconciliation: Delete Data
FBIC024	Reconciliation: Recalculate Totals
FBIC025	Reconciliation: Documents
FBIC026	Reconciliation: Totals Records
FBIC027	Activate Process Tables
FBIC028	Activate Process Tables
FBIC029	Activate Process Tables
FBIC030	Activate Process Tables
FBIC031	Activate Process Tables
FBIC032	Companies to be Reconciled
FBIC033	Download Contact Person Data
FBIC034	Upload Contact Person Data
FBIC035	Define Companies
FBICA1	GL Open Items: Document Assignment
FBICA2	GL Accounts: Document Assignment
FBICA3	Customer/Vendor: Document Assignment
FBICC	ICR: Generate Default Customizing
FBICD1	Open Items: Differences Development
FBICD2	GL Accounts: Differences Development
FBICD3	Open Items: Differences Development
FBICIMG	Cross-System IC Reconciliation

FBICIMG3	Cross-System IC Reconciliation
FBICR1	GL Open Items: Reconcile Documents
FBICR2	GL Accounts: Reconcile Documents
FBICR3	Customer/Vendor: Reconcile Documents
FBICR3L	Intercompany Reconciliation (Local)
FBICRC_SNRO	No. Range Maintnce: FBICRC_REF
FBICS1	GL Open Items: Select Documents
FBICS2	GL Accounts: Select Documents
FBICS3	Customer/Vendor: Select Documents
FBIC_SNRO_DOC	Number range maintenance: FBICRC_DOC
FBKA	Display Accounting Configuration
FBKF	FBKP/Carry Out Function (Internal)
FBKP	Maintain Accounting Configuration
FBL1	Display Vendor Line Items
FBL1N	Vendor Line Items
FBL2	Change Vendor Line Items
FBL2N	Vendor Line Items
FBL3	Display G/L Account Line Items
FBL3N	G/L Account Line Items
FBL4	Change G/L Account Line Items
FBL4N	G/L Account Line Items
FBL5	Display Customer Line Items
FBL5N	Customer Line Items
FBL6	Change Customer Line Items
FBL6N	Customer Line Items
FBM1	Enter Sample Document
FBM2	Change Sample Document
FBM3	Display Sample Document
FBM4	Display Sample Document Changes
FBMA	Display Dunning Procedure
FBME	Banks
FBMP	Maintain Dunning Procedure
FBN1	Accounting Document Number Ranges
FBN2	Number Range Maintenance: FI_PYORD
FBO1	Mass act: Create Boleto from OI
FBO1C	Boleto: Mass cancellation
FBO1S	Boleto: Single Boleto from OI
FBOL2	Create Boleto DME File
FBOL3	Display boleto
FBOLBANK	Boleto: Bank selection by percentage
FBOLCODE	Boleto: Instruction code and keys
FBOLINST	Boleto: Instruction code/keys
FBOLNR	Number range maintenance: FKK_BOLETO
FBOLXT	Number range maintenance: FKK_BOLXT
FBP1	Enter Payment Request
FBPM	Payment medium program of PMW
FBPM1	Cross-Payment Run Payment Medium
FBPM2	Status Report
FBR1	Post with Reference Document
FBR2	Post Document
FBRA	Reset Cleared Items
FBRC	Reset Cleared Items (Payment Cards)
FBRC001	Maintain Message Templates
FBRC002	Maintain Placeholders

FBRC003	Set Up Reconciliation Display
FBRC004	Define Sets
FBRC005	Define Rules for Document Assignment
FBRC006	Define Possible Status for Documents
FBRC007	Reconciliation Process Attributes
FBRC008	Maintain Field Catalogs
FBRC009	Set Up Display Categories
FBRC010	Contact Database Maintenance
FBRC011	Application ID Maintenance
FBS1	Enter Accrual/Deferral Doc.
FBS_SE_TCT_FIN_MDM_A	Testplan Financial MDM
FBTA	Display Text Determin.Configuration
FBTP	Maintain Text Determin.Configuration
FBTR	VAT Refund
FBU2	Change Intercompany Document
FBU3	Display Intercompany Document
FBU8	Reverse Cross-Company Code Document
FBV0	Post Parked Document
FBV1	Park Document
FBV2	Change Parked Document
FBV3	Display Parked Document
FBV4	Change Parked Document (Header)
FBV5	Document Changes of Parked Documents
FBV6	Parked Document $
FBVB	Post Parked Document
FBW1	Enter Bill of Exchange Pmnt Request
FBW2	Post Bill of Exch.acc.to Pmt Request
FBW3	Post Bill of Exchange Usage
FBW4	Reverse Bill Liability
FBW5	Customer Check/Bill of Exchange
FBW6	Vendor Check/Bill of Exchange
FBW7	Bank file to file system (for FBWD)
FBW8	File to Bank (for Transaction FBWD)
FBW9	C FI Maintain Table T045DTA
FBWA	C FI Maintain Table T046a
FBWAPI0	FI Internet: Vendor Line Items
FBWAPI0EA	FI Internet: Vendor Line Items
FBWARI0	FI Internet: Customer Line Items
FBWARI0EA	FI Internet: Customer Line Items
FBWD	Returned Bills of Exchange Payable
FBWD2	Parameter Transaction for FBWD
FBWE	Bill/Exch.Presentatn - International
FBWO	Discounting of Orbian Credits
FBWO1	Maintenance View: Orbian Links
FBWQ	C FI Maintain Table T045T
FBWR	C FI Maintain Table T045W
FBWS	C FI Maintain Table T046s
FBZ0	Display/Edit Payment Proposal
FBZ1	Post Incoming Payments
FBZ2	Post Outgoing Payments
FBZ3	Incoming Payments Fast Entry
FBZ4	Payment with Printout
FBZ5	Print Check for Payment Document
FBZ8	Display Payment Run

FBZA	Display Pmnt Program Configuration
FBZA_OLD	Display Pmnt Program Configuration
FBZG	Failed Customer Payments
FBZP	Maintain Pmnt Program Configuration
FBZP_OLD	Maintain Pmnt Program Configuration
FC038	Compare Test Groups
FC039	Comparison by Selection Criteria
FC10	Financial Statements Comparison
FC11	Data Extract for FI Transfer
FC80	Document C80
FC82	Document C82
FCAA	Check Archiving
FCBOL	Boleto: mass cancellation
FCC1	Payment Cards: Settlement
FCC2	Payment Cards: Repeat Settlement
FCC3	Payment Cards: Delete Logs
FCC4	Payment Cards: Display Logs
FCCR	Payment Card Evaluations
FCH1	Display Check Information
FCH2	Display Payment Document Checks
FCH3	Void Checks
FCH4	Renumber Checks
FCH5	Create Check Information
FCH6	Change Check Information/Cash Check
FCH7	Reprint Check
FCH8	Reverse Check Payment
FCH9	Void Issued Check
FCHA	Check archiving
FCHB	Check retrieval
FCHD	Delete Payment Run Check Information
FCHE	Delete Voided Checks
FCHF	Delete Manual Checks
FCHG	Delete cashing/extract data
FCHI	Check Lots
FCHK	Check Tracing Initial Menu
FCHN	Check Register
FCHR	Online Cashed Checks
FCHT	Change Check/Payment Assignment
FCHU	Create Reference for Check
FCHV	C FI Maintain Table TVOID
FCHX	Check Extract - Creation
FCIWCU00	Generate DataSources
FCKR	International cashed checks
FCMM	C FI Preparations for consolidation
FCMN	FI Initial Consolidation Menu
FCOACTIV	Activate Failure Cost Processing
FCOACTIV_REM	Activate Failure Cost Processing
FCOACTIV_SFC	Activate Failure Cost Processing
FCODOC	Display Failure Cost Documents
FCOEX	Start Additional Expense Posting
FCOMENU	Menu Tree for Failure Costs
FCOM_ALERT_CBL	Cost Center Monitor Rule Evaluation
FCOM_ALERT_CBV	Cost Center Monitor Rule Evaluation
FCOM_ALERT_CCL	Cost Center Monitor Rule Evaluation

FCOM_ALERT_CCV	Cost Center Monitor Rule Evaluation
FCOM_ALERT_CDL	Cost Center Monitor Rule Evaluation
FCOM_ALERT_CDV	Cost Center Monitor Rule Evaluation
FCOM_ALERT_CL	Cost Center Monitor Rule Evaluation
FCOM_ALERT_CV	Cost Center Monitor Rule Evaluation
FCOM_ALERT_IBV	Investment Program Rule Evaluation
FCOM_ALERT_IMV	Investment Program Rule Evaluation
FCOM_ALERT_OBL	Order Monitor Rule Evaluation
FCOM_ALERT_OBV	Order Monitor Rule Evaluation
FCOM_ALERT_OCL	Order Monitor Rule Evaluation
FCOM_ALERT_OCV	Order Monitor Rule Evaluation
FCOM_ALERT_OL	Order Monitor Rule Evaluation
FCOM_ALERT_OV	Order Monitor Rule Evaluation
FCOM_ALERT_OYV	Order Monitor Rule Evaluation
FCOM_ALERT_OZV	Order Monitor Rule Evaluation
FCOM_ALERT_PBL	Profit Center Monitor Rule Evaluatio
FCOM_ALERT_PBV	Profit Center Monitor Rule Evaluat.
FCOM_ALERT_PCL	Profit Center Monitor Rule Evaluatio
FCOM_ALERT_PCV	Profit Center Monitor Rule Evaluatio
FCOM_ALERT_PDL	Profit Center Monitor Rule Evaluat.
FCOM_ALERT_PDV	Profit Center Monitor Rule Evaluat.
FCOM_ALERT_PL	Profit Center Monitor Rule Evaluatio
FCOM_ALERT_PML	Profit Center Monitor Rule Evaluatio
FCOM_ALERT_PMV	Profit Center Monitor Rule Evaluatio
FCOM_ALERT_PV	Profit Center Monitor Rule Evaluatio
FCOM_ALERT_RBV	Projects Rule Evaluation
FCOM_ALERT_RCV	Projects Rule Evaluation
FCOM_ALERT_RMV	Projects Rule Evaluation
FCOM_EQM_COST	Equipment Monitor Rule Evaluation
FCOM_LINE_SYNC_CBL	Delete Line Items CL
FCOM_LINE_SYNC_CCL	Deletion of Line Item CCL
FCOM_LINE_SYNC_CDL	Deletion of Line Item CCL
FCOM_LINE_SYNC_CL	Delete Line Items CL
FCOM_LINE_SYNC_OBL	Deletion of Line Item OCL
FCOM_LINE_SYNC_OCL	Deletion of Line Item OCL
FCOM_LINE_SYNC_OL	Delete Line Items OL
FCOM_LINE_SYNC_PBL	Delete Line Items PL
FCOM_LINE_SYNC_PCL	Deletion of Line Item PCL
FCOM_LINE_SYNC_PDL	Deletion of Line Item PCL
FCOM_LINE_SYNC_PL	Delete Line Items PL
FCOM_LINE_SYNC_PML	Delete Line Items PL
FCOM_RULE_CBL	Rule for Cost Center Line Items
FCOM_RULE_CBV	Rule for Cost Center Variances
FCOM_RULE_CCL	Rule for Cost Center Line Items
FCOM_RULE_CCV	Rule for Cost Center Variances
FCOM_RULE_CDL	Rule for Cost Center Line Items
FCOM_RULE_CDV	Rule for Cost Center Variances
FCOM_RULE_CL	Rule for Cost Center Line Items
FCOM_RULE_CV	Rule for Cost Center Variances
FCOM_RULE_IBV	Rule for Investment Prog. Variances
FCOM_RULE_IMV	Rule for Investment Prog. Variances
FCOM_RULE_OA	Rules for Equipment Monitor
FCOM_RULE_OBL	Rule for Internal Order Line Items
FCOM_RULE_OBV	Rule for Internal Order Variances

FCOM_RULE_OCL	Rule for Internal Order Line Items
FCOM_RULE_OCV	Rule for Internal Order Variances
FCOM_RULE_OL	Rule for Internal Order Line Items
FCOM_RULE_OV	Rule for Internal Order Variances
FCOM_RULE_OYV	Rule for Annual Order Budget
FCOM_RULE_OZV	Rule for Annual Order Budget
FCOM_RULE_PBL	Rule for Profit Center Line Items
FCOM_RULE_PBV	Rule for Profit Center Variances
FCOM_RULE_PCL	Rule for Profit Center Line Items
FCOM_RULE_PCV	Rule for Profit Center Variances
FCOM_RULE_PDL	Rule for Profit Center Line Items
FCOM_RULE_PDV	Rule for Profit Center Variances
FCOM_RULE_PL	Rule for Profit Center Line Items
FCOM_RULE_PML	Rule for Profit Center Line Items
FCOM_RULE_PMV	Rule for Profit Center Variances
FCOM_RULE_PV	Rule for Profit Center Variances
FCOM_RULE_RBV	Rule for Project Variances
FCOM_RULE_RCV	Rule for Project Variances
FCOM_RULE_RMV	Rule for Project Variances
FCOM_RULE_USER_CBL	Display Rule for a User
FCOM_RULE_USER_CBV	Display Rule for a User
FCOM_RULE_USER_CCL	Display Rule for a User
FCOM_RULE_USER_CCV	Display Rule for a User
FCOM_RULE_USER_CDL	Display Rule for a User
FCOM_RULE_USER_CDV	Display Rule for a User
FCOM_RULE_USER_CL	Display Rule for a User
FCOM_RULE_USER_CV	Display Rule for a User
FCOM_RULE_USER_IBV	Display Rule for a User
FCOM_RULE_USER_IMV	Display Rule for a User
FCOM_RULE_USER_OBL	Display Rule for a User
FCOM_RULE_USER_OBV	Display Rule for a User
FCOM_RULE_USER_OCL	Display Rule for a User
FCOM_RULE_USER_OCV	Display Rule for a User
FCOM_RULE_USER_OL	Display Rule for a User
FCOM_RULE_USER_OV	Display Rule for a User
FCOM_RULE_USER_OYV	Display Rule for a User
FCOM_RULE_USER_OZV	Display Rule for a User
FCOM_RULE_USER_PBL	Display Rule for a User
FCOM_RULE_USER_PBV	Display Rule for a User
FCOM_RULE_USER_PCL	Display Rule for a User
FCOM_RULE_USER_PCV	Display Rule for a User
FCOM_RULE_USER_PDL	Display Rule for a User
FCOM_RULE_USER_PDV	Display Rule for a User
FCOM_RULE_USER_PL	Display Rule for a User
FCOM_RULE_USER_PML	Display Rule for a User
FCOM_RULE_USER_PMV	Display Rule for a User
FCOM_RULE_USER_PV	Display Rule for a User
FCOM_RULE_USER_RBV	Display Rule for a User
FCOM_RULE_USER_RCV	Display Rule for a User
FCOM_RULE_USER_RMV	Display Rule for a User
FCOM_SNI_BUA	Settings for Hierarchy Display
FCOREP_EXCESS	Additional Expense in FCO
FCOREP_NOTIF	Quality Notification in FCO
FCOREP_RESPCC	Responsible Cost Center

SAP Transaction Codes – Volume One

FCOREP_REW	Rework in Failure Cost Processing
FCOREP_REWCO	Rework Costs in Failure Cost Proc.
FCOREP_SCRAP	Scrap Costs in Failure Cost Proc.
FCOSETTINGS	Settings in Failure Cost Processing
FCOST	Start Failure Cost Processing
FCOVALU	Valuation of Failure Cost Documents
FCRD	Credit Cards
FCV1	Create A/R Summary
FCV2	Delete A/R Summary
FCV3	Early Warning List
FCZZ	Maintain commodity master data
FC_BW_BEX	Business Explorer Analyzer
FC_BW_RSA1	Administrator Workbench
FC_BW_RSZDELETE	Delete BW Query Objects
FC_BW_RSZV	Maintain BW Variables
FD-1	Number range maintenance: FVVD_RANL
FD01	Create Customer (Accounting)
FD02	Change Customer (Accounting)
FD02CORE	Maintain customer
FD03	Display Customer (Accounting)
FD04	Customer Changes (Accounting)
FD05	Block Customer (Accounting)
FD06	Mark Customer for Deletion (Acctng)
FD08	Confirm Customer Individually(Actng)
FD09	Confirm Customer List (Accounting)
FD10	Customer Account Balance
FD10N	Customer Balance Display
FD10NA	Customer Bal. Display with Worklist
FD10NET	Customer Balance Display
FD11	Customer Account Analysis
FD15	Transfer customer changes: send
FD16	Transfer customer changes: receive
FD24	Credit Limit Changes
FD32	Change Customer Credit Management
FD33	Display Customer Credit Management
FD37	Credit Management Mass Change
FDCU	Loans customizing menu
FDFD	Cash Management Implementation Tool
FDI0	Execute Report
FDI1	Create Report
FDI2	Change Report
FDI3	Display Report
FDI4	Create Form
FDI5	Change Form
FDI6	Display Form
FDIB	Background Processing
FDIC	Maintain Currency Translation Type
FDIK	Maintain Key Figures
FDIM	Report Monitor
FDIO	Transport Reports
FDIP	Transport Forms
FDIQ	Import Reports from Client 000
FDIR	Import Forms from Client 000
FDIT	Translation Tool - Drilldown Report

SAP Transaction Codes – Volume One

FDIV	Maintain Global Variable
FDIX	Reorganize Drilldown Reports
FDIY	Reorganize Report Data
FDIZ	Reorganize Forms
FDK43	Credit Management - Master Data List
FDKTRANS	Transport User Actions FI_AP/AR
FDKUSER	Internet: User Action Assignment
FDMN	
FDM_AUTO_CREATE	Create Dispute Cases Automatically
FDM_COLL01	Collections Management
FDM_COLL_SEND01	Send Data
FDM_CREATE_PROPOSAL	Proposal for Automatic Assignment
FDM_CUST00	Activate Dispute Management
FDM_CUST01	Create Default Vals for Dispute Case
FDM_CUST02	Permit References in Dispute Case
FDM_CUST03	Settings for Dispute Case Write-Off
FDM_CUST05	Case Type for Promise to Pay
FDM_CUST06	Values for Dispute Case in FSCM-BD
FDM_CUST07	Dispute Case Reasons in FSCM-BD
FDM_CUST08	Activation of Collections Management
FDM_CUST10	Activate Assignment of Credit Memos
FDM_CUST13	Dispute Case Default Values (TPM)
FDM_CUST15	Maintain Active Company Codes
FDM_CUST16	Maintain Relevant Fields
FDM_CUST17	Harmonize Dunning Levels
FDM_CUST18	Automatic Change of Document Fields
FDM_CUST20	Cust.-Disp. Objects in Dispute Cases
FDM_CUST22	CCM Special G/L Indicators
FDM_CUST23	CCM Reason Codes
FDM_CUSTOMIZING	FSCM-DM Process Integration
FDM_JUDGE	Valuation of Promise to Pay
FDM_LDDB_DISP	Display of Changes to Documents
FDM_LDDB_EXEC	Execute Changes to Documents
FDM_LDDB_REORG	Reorganization of Changes
FDM_P2P_CONFIRM	Confirmation of Promise to Pay
FDM_PROCESS_PROPOSAL	Processing of Assignment Proposal
FDM_SAVE	Save Case during CALL DIALOG
FDOO	Borrower's notes order overview
FDTA	TemSe/REGUT Data Administration
FDTT	Treasury Data Medium Administration
FDT_HELPERS	Helper report to exec report or txn
FDT_RESERVED	Reserved ID Patterns
FDT_SHOW_DB	BRFplus - Show Object DB Entries
FDT_TRANS_EMEX	BRF+: Emergency Transport Attribute
FDT_WD_ADMIN_TOOL	BRFplus: AdminTool (WD ABAP)
FDT_WORKBENCH	FDT WD: Workbench
FDUNN	Dunning Loans
FEBA	Postprocess Electronic Bank Statmt
FEBAN	Bank statement postprocessing
FEBAN_BROWSER	Displays the Note to Payee
FEBA_ACCOUNT_BALANCE	Display Account Balance
FEBA_BANK_STATEMENT	Postprocessing Bank Statement
FEBA_CHECK_DEPOSIT	Postprocessing Check Deposit Trans.
FEBA_LOCKBOX	Display Account Balance

SAP Transaction Codes – Volume One

FEBC	Generate Multicash format
FEBMSG	Display Internet Messages
FEBOAS	Request Account Statement via OFX
FEBOFX	OFX Functions
FEBOFXN	OFX Functions
FEBP	Post Electronic Bank Statement
FEBSTS	Search String Search Simulation
FEC14	Clearing groups
FEC6	Regulatory indicator assignment
FEC7	Regulatory indicators
FEC8	CO transaction type handling
FECA	Customizing Archiving
FECC	Control of messages by the user
FECG	General regulatory parameters
FECJ	Create job for multiple periods
FECM	Online manual
FECP	Copy regulatory parameters
FECV	Clearing cost element variants
FEOD	Drill down (Old version)
FEOT	Flow of cost trace (Old version)
FEP4	Plan versions
FEP5	Fiscal year dep. version parameters
FEP6	Plan versions
FEP7	Fiscal year dep. version parameters
FER0	Standard cost adjustment
FER1	Trace flow of primary costs
FER2	Post primary costs
FER3	Post variance allocations
FER4	Direct postings
FER5	Prepare drill down
FERA	Administration
FERC	Regulatory reporting
FERD	Drill down
FERE	Transport periodic parameters
FERH	Processing history
FERN	Release notes
FERO	Process actuals for current period
FERP	Process plan for current period
FERQ	Process plan
FERR	Reverse regulatory procedure
FERS	Process actual
FERT	Flow of cost trace
FERV	Validate regulatory configuration
FESA	Summarized final objects
FESR	Import of ISR File (Switzerland)
FEUB	Adjust VIBEPP after EURO conversion
FEUI	Real Estate Implementation Guide
FEV1	Controlling area dependent parameter
FEV10	Secondary cost elem. to be ignored
FEV11	Regulatory indicator assignmnt field
FEV13	Clearing cost elements
FEV13A	Cost element variants
FEV2	Company code dependent parameters
FEV3	Regulatory accounts for traced costs

FEV3A	Regulatory indicator variants
FEV4	Specific Std. Cost. Adj. assignments
FEV5	Specific clearing COEl assignments
FEV6	Regulatory indicator assignments
FEV9	Regulatory accounts for direct post.
FEVF6	Organizational assignment of objects
FF$3	Send planning data to central system
FF$4	Retrieve planning data
FF$5	Retrieve transmission results
FF$6	Check settings
FF$7	Check all external systems
FF$A	Maintain TR-CM subsystems
FF$B	Convert Planning Group
FF$C	Convert planning level
FF$D	Convert business areas
FF$L	Display transmission information
FF$S	Display transmission information
FF$X	Configure the central TR-CM system
FF-1	Outstanding Checks
FF-2	Outstanding Bills of Exchange
FF-3	Cash Management Summary Records
FF-4	CMF Data In Accounting Documents
FF-5	CMF Records fr.Materials Management
FF-6	CMF Records from Sales
FF-7	Planned Item Journal
FF-8	Payment Advice Journal
FF-9	Journal
FF.1	Standard G/L Account Interest Scale
FF.3	G/L Account Cashed Checks
FF.4	Vendor Cashed Checks
FF.5	Import Electronic Bank Statement
FF.6	Display Electronic Bank Statement
FF.7	Compare Payment Advices
FF.8	Print Payment Orders
FF.9	Post Payment Orders
FF.D	Generate payt req. from advices
FF/1	Compare Bank Terms
FF/2	Compare value date
FF/3	Archive advices from bank statements
FF/4	Import Electronic Check Deposit List
FF/5	Post electronic check deposit list
FF/6	Deposit/loan mgmt analysis/posting
FF/7	Deposit/loan management int accruals
FF/8	Import Bank Statement into Cash Mgmt
FF/9	Compare Advices with Bank Statement
FF63	Create Planning Memo Record
FF65	List of Cash Management Memo Records
FF67	Manual Account Statement
FF68	Manual Check Deposit Transaction
FF69	Cash Mgmt: Totals Record Correction
FF6A	Edit Cash Mgmt Pos Payment Advices
FF6B	Edit liquidity forecast planned item
FF70	Cash Mgmt Posit./Liquidity Forecast
FF71	Cash Position

FF72	Liquidity forecast
FF73	Cash Concentration
FF74	Use Program to Access Cash Concntn
FF7A	Cash Position
FF7B	Liquidity forecast
FF:1	Maintain exchange rates
FFA1	Compare Advices with Bk.Stmt Advices
FFB4	Import Electronic Check Deposit List
FFB5	Post electronic check deposit list
FFCD	Cash deconcentration
FFL_OLD	Display Transmission Information
FFS_OLD	Display Transmission Information
FFTL	Telephone list
FFW1	Wire Authorization
FFWR	Post Payment Requests from Advice
FFWR_REQUESTS	Create Payment Requests from Advice
FFZK	C FI Maintainence Table T018Z
FF_1	Standard G/L Account Interest Scale
FF_3	G/L Account Cashed Checks
FF_4	Vendor Cashed Checks
FF_5	Import Electronic Bank Statement
FF_6	Display Electronic Bank Statement
FG99	Flexible G/L: Report Selection
FGI0	Execute Report
FGI1	Create Report
FGI2	Change Report
FGI3	Display Report
FGI4	Create Form
FGI5	Change Form
FGI6	Display Form
FGIB	Background Processing
FGIC	Maintain Currency Translation Type
FGIK	Maintain Key Figures
FGIM	Report Monitor
FGIO	Transport Reports
FGIP	Transport Forms
FGIQ	Import Reports from Client 000
FGIR	Import Forms from Client 000
FGIT	Translation Tool - Drilldown Report.
FGIV	Maintain Global Variable
FGIX	Reorganize Drilldown Reports
FGIY	Reorganize Report Data
FGIZ	Reorganize Forms
FGL6	IRE: One Time Posting - Gen. Contr
FGM0	Special Purpose Ledger Menu
FGRP	Report Painter
FGRW	Report Writer Menu
FGSODN_IT1	Number range maintenance: FIN2_IT
FI01	Create Bank
FI02	Change Bank
FI03	Display Bank
FI04	Display Bank Changes
FI06	Set Flag to Delete Bank
FI07	Change Current Number Range Number

FI08	Distribution of the Bank Master Data
FI09	Distribution of IBANs
FI12	Change House Banks/Bank Accounts
FI12CORE	Change House Banks/Bank Accounts
FI12_OLD	Change House Banks/Bank Accounts
FI13	Display House Banks/Bank Accounts
FI13_OLD	Display House Banks/Bank Accounts
FIAAHELP	FI-AA Utility Programs
FIAAHELP_DARK	FI-AA Utility Programs Dispatcher
FIBAN	Maintain IBAN
FIBB	Bank chain determination
FIBC	Scenarios for Bank Chain Determin.
FIBD	Allocation client
FIBF	Maintenance transaction BTE
FIBHS	Display bank chains for house banks
FIBHU	Maintain bank chains for house banks
FIBL0	Origin Indicator Definition
FIBL1	Control Origin Indicator
FIBL2	Assign Origin
FIBL3	Group of House Bank Accounts
FIBL4	Bank Clearing Account for HR Payment
FIBLAPOP	Vendors - Payment Request
FIBLAROP	Customers - Payment Request
FIBLFFP	Free Form Payment
FIBPS	Display bank chians for partners
FIBPU	Maintain bank chains for partner
FIBS	Input House Bank in Payment Request
FIBTS	Dis. bank chains for acct carry fwds
FIBTU	Main. bank chains for acctCarry over
FICAAOLA	Master Data Tab
FICAARCHBDT	BDT Contract Account Archiving
FICADELE	Contract Account Deletion
FICADELEBDT	BDT Contract Account Deletion
FICAIMG	IMG for Contract AR/AP
FICD	Cash deconcentration
FICOBDT	Financial Conditions
FICOBDT01	FICO Config. - BDT - Applications
FICOBDT0104	FICO Config - BDT - Screen Config.
FICOBDT013	FICO Config. - BDT - Roles
FICOBDT014	FICO Config. - Role Category Groups
FICOBDT02	FICO Config. - BDT - Field Groups
FICOBDT023	FICO Config. - BDT - SETS
FICOBDT03	FICO Config. - BDT - Views
FICOBDT04	FICO Config. - BDT - Section
FICOBDT05	FICO Config. - BDT - Screens
FICOBDT06	FICO Config. - BDT - Screen Sequence
FICOBDT07	FICO Config. - BDT - Event
FICOBDT08	FICO Config.- BDT - GUI Std Funct.
FICOBDT09	FICO Config.- BDT - GUI Add. Funct.
FICOBDT10	FICO Config.- BDT - Matchcodes
FICOBDT100	FICO Config - BDT - Fmod per Acct
FICOBDT102	FICO Config. - BDT - Authoriz. type
FICOBDT103	FICO Config - BDT - Fld Grp Authoriz
FICOBDT105	FICO Config. BDT -Fmod Ext. Applic.

SAP Transaction Codes – Volume One

FICOBDT11	FICO Config - BDT - ScrnFld ->DB Fld
FICOBDT12	FICO Config. - BDT - Fmod. Criteria
FICOBDT15	FICO Config. - BDT - Appl. Transact.
FICOBDT16	FICO Configuration - BDT - Tables
FICOBDT17	FICO Config.- BDT -Ext. Applications
FICOBDT18	FICO Config. - BDT - Activities
FICOBDT19	FICO Config. - BDT - Authoriz. Type
FICOBDT20	FICO Config. - BDT - Auth Fld Grps
FICOBDT_31	Define Condition Type
FICOMAIN	Menu for New Conditions Log
FICO_123	Create Basic Setting - Conditions
FICO_124	Create Basic Setting - Conditions
FICO_CG	Define Condition Group Type
FICO_CUS_LIST_BCA	Customizing for Condition Group Type
FICO_FOBU_OPERATOR	Define Formula Operators
FIEH01	Process Contracts with Errors
FIHB	In-house bank
FIHB0	Number Range Maintenance
FIHB1	Assignment of Bnk Statement to IHB
FIHB4	Assignment of IHB to Bookkeeping
FIHB5	Data for Automatic Payments
FIHB6	Assignment of Bnk Statement to IHB
FIHB7	Reversal of IHC Payment Requests
FIHB8	Transfer Recipient Items
FIHBC	Settings for In-House Bank
FIHC	Create In-House Cash Center
FILAACETRANS	Transfer ACE Documents to Accounting
FILAADJ	Manual Changes to Value ID Contents
FILAADJREV	Reverse Value ID Change
FILAADMN	Process Processing Initial Screen
FILACHECK	List Available Help Programs
FILACUS	List Available Help Programs
FILAEXAM	Lease: Process Analysis
FILAEXAMX	Processing of Process (Enhanced)
FILAEXPL	Display Lease
FILAFIRECON	Accrual Engine / FI Reconciliation
FILAHELP	List Available Help Programs
FILASTRUC_LVS_PARAM	Validation Parameter
FILASYST	Jump to IMG for System Customizing
FILATEST	Process Processing Initial Screen
FILAUF_WF_CUST	Store Order: Workflow Customizing
FILAVSRDEF	Substitution/Validation Determinat.
FILAVSRDEF_CLASS	Check Sequences f. Financ. Classif.
FILAVSRDEF_CRMC	Check Sequences f. Pricing Classif.
FILAVSRDEF_VALID	Validation Determination
FILAVSRDEF_VALUE	Determ. f. Val.Determ. Substitution
FILA_LC_TEST	Lease Classification
FILA_RE_C_CAT	Define Refinancing Categories
FILA_RE_C_CAT_C	Assign Tax ID and Clearing Accounts
FILA_RE_C_CHGPR	Assign Change Processes to Clusters
FILA_RE_C_EVENT	Assign Processes
FILA_RE_C_RFF	Generate Forfaiting Payment Schedule
FILA_RE_C_VAL	Assign Value Identifier to Ref. Cat.
FILA_RE_DOC_FLOW	Display DocFlow for Refinancing

SAP Transaction Codes – Volume One

FILA_RE_MASTER   Edit Refinancing Program
FILA_RE_NR1   Number Range Maint: Refinancing
FILA_RE_RETURN   Create Return Transaction Tranche
FILA_RE_SELECT   Create Refinancing Tranche
FILA_RE_TRANCHE   Edit Refinancing Tranche
FILA_RE_TRANCHE_PO   Post Refinancing Tranche
FILA_RE_TRANCHE_PR   Post Return Transaction Tranche
FILA_RE_TRANS_POST   Repost Customer/Vendor G/L Accounts
FILA_WRITE_DOWN   Adjustment of Residual Value
FILA_WRITE_DOWN_UNDO   Undo Adjustment of Residual Value
FILE   Cross-Client File Names/Paths
FILEEDIT   File Editor
FILINV_WF_CUST   Store Inventory:Workflow Customizing
FIMA   Financial Calculations
FIMA_TEST_DI   FiMa Test for Daily Interest
FIMA_TRACE   User Dialog for FIMA Trace
FINB_ACCO   Activation of All Configuration
FINB_ACINST_CHANGE   Change/Set Accounting Instance
FINB_CCD_ADD   Classes for Customizing Dispatcher
FINB_CONF_AFTER_NOTE   Rework after SAP Note Implementation
FINB_CONF_START_IMG   Define Configuration (SAP)
FINB_CONF_WB   Maintain Configuration Aspect
FINB_GN_TRACE   Activate Generator Trace
FINB_MSG_LG1   Analyze Application Log
FINB_PR_SHOW   Display Persistence Objects
FINB_TR_CAT   Catalog of Transport Objects
FINB_TR_CATA   Attributes of Transport Objects
FINB_TR_CATAL   Local Attributes
FINB_TR_CCM   Client Copy - Protection
FINB_TR_CCM1   Client Copy - Administration
FINB_TR_CCO   Client Copy - Object Status
FINB_TR_CC_CD   Copy Transaction Data
FINB_TR_CC_LOG   Client Copy-Postprocessing Log
FINB_TR_CUST   FINB Transport Tool: Customizing
FINB_TR_DEST   Destination for Transport Methods
FINB_TR_DISPLAY   Transport Container Display
FINB_TR_EXEC_AI   Postprocessing of Client Copy
FINB_TR_IMG   Transport Tool - Development
FINB_TR_REORG   Transport Container Reorganization
FINB_TR_TCATO   Obsolete Transport Objects
FINB_TR_U1   Copy a Transport Request
FINB_TR_U2   Prepare Delivery
FINB_TR_WZ   RFC Connection Wizard
FINB_VIEW_TO_CONFIG   Connection to Configuration
FINDR0   ParameterTransaction Derivation Tool
FINF   Info System Events
FINL_9000_SHOW   Display
FINP   Info System Processes
FINR3_CPROJECTS_CUST   cProjects IMG in Plug-In for ERP
FINT   Item Interest Calculation
FINTAP   Item Interest Calculation Vendors
FINTSHOW   Overview of Int. Runs for Item. Int.
FIN_ACCDOCNO_MAINT   Number Ranges for Document Numbers
FIN_GLACCT   Maintain G/L Accounts

FIN_GLTRATYPE	Maintain Transaction Type
FIN_PRCVARIANT	Maintain Price Variant
FIOA	Interest on Arrears - Consumer Loans
FIOR	Create Orbian Bank
FIOTPKOFIMAINTAIN	Maintain Derivation Rule Entries
FIOTP_NRIV	One-Time PostingsNumber Range Maint.
FIPAY_BDGTS01	Subsequent SPL Screening
FIPAY_CUST01	Maintenance View V_FIPAY_T042_GTS
FIPOS	Create Commitment Items
FIPRB01	FIPR Control: Applications
FIPRB02	FIPR Control: Field Groups
FIPRB03	FIPR Control: Views
FIPRB04	FIPR Control: Sections
FIPRB05	FIPR Control: Screens
FIPRB06	FIPR Control: Screen Sequences
FIPRB07	FIPR Control: Business Trans. Events
FIPRB08	FIPR Control: CUA Standard Function
FIPRB09	FIPR Control: CUA Addit. Functions
FIPRB100	FIPR Control: Matchcode
FIPRB101	FIPR Control: Matchcode
FIPRB102	FIPR Control: Matchcode
FIPRB103	FIPR Control: Matchcode
FIPRB11	FIPR Control: Assgt Scrn->DB Field
FIPRB12	FIPR Control: Field Modif. Criteria
FIPRB13	FIPR Control: Products
FIPRB14	FIPR Control: Product Group
FIPRB15	FIPR Control: Applic. Transactions
FIPRB16	FIPR Control: Tables
FIPRB18	FIPR Control: Activities
FIPRB19	FIPR Control: FB per Activity
FIPRC1	Maintain Attribute Type
FIPRC10	Fields Maintenance
FIPRC11	Feature Maintenance
FIPRC12	Field Values Maintenance
FIPRC13	Two Dimensional Field Value Mainten.
FIPRC2	Product Category Maintenance
FIPRC3	Maintain Attributes
FIPRC4	Maintain Key Prefix
FIPRC5	Field Grouping Activity
FIPRD1	Create Product
FIPRD2	Change Product
FIPRD3	Display Product
FIPRD4	Copy Product
FIP_CALL_MM03	Call the MM03 Transaction
FIP_CALL_MM43	Call the MM43 Transaction
FIP_CALL_RP_WL_DELE	Call transaction FIP_RP_WORKLIST_DEL
FIP_CALL_RP_WL_DISP	Call transaction FIP_RP_WORKLIST_DIS
FIP_CALL_WF30	Call wrapper program for WF30
FIP_CALL_WSUBST_CTAB	Call transaction WSUBST_CONTAB
FIP_CALL_WSUBST_WL	Call transaction WSUBST_WORKLIST
FIP_MD	Buffer Report for Master Data
FIP_RP_WORKLIST_DELE	Delete Worklist Replacement GR
FIP_RP_WORKLIST_DISP	Display Worklist Replacement GR
FIP_SD	Buffer Report for Statistical Data

FIP_TD	Buffer Report for Transactional Data
FIRPGR	Repetitive Code Groups Maintenance
FISPLOGCUST	Customizing for Log Categories
FISPLOGDISP	Display of Log Entries
FISPLOGORGA	Reorganize Log Entries
FITP_RESPO	Contact Partner Responsibilities
FITP_SETTINGS	Settings for Travel Planning
FITP_SETTINGS_TREE	Tree Maintenance Current Settings
FITVFELD	Tree
FITVFELD_WEB	Tree
FI_APAR_SEPA_CONV	Create SEPA Mandates in Mass Run
FI_APAR_SEPA_CUST	FI General Settings for SEPA
FI_APAR_SEPA_FIELDS	FI Changeable Fields for SEPA
FI_DRILLDOWN	GT Documents for FI Document
FJA1	Inflation Adjustment of G/L Accounts
FJA2	Change Last Adjustment Dates
FJA3	Balance Sheet/P&L with Inflation
FJA4	Infl. Adjustment of Open Items (FC)
FJA5	Infl. Adj. of Open Receivables (LC)
FJA6	Infl. Adj. of Open Payables (LC)
FK01	Create Vendor (Accounting)
FK02	Change Vendor (Accounting)
FK02CORE	Maintain vendor
FK03	Display Vendor (Accounting)
FK04	Vendor Changes (Accounting)
FK05	Block Vendor (Accounting)
FK06	Mark Vendor for Deletion (Acctng)
FK08	Confirm Vendor Individually (Acctng)
FK09	Confirm Vendor List (Accounting)
FK10	Vendor Account Balance
FK10N	Vendor Balance Display
FK10NA	Vendor Balance Display
FK10NET	Vendor Balance Display
FK15	Transfer vendor changes: receive
FK16	Transfer vendor changes: receive
FK59	C FI-CA Table maintenance TFK044A
FKCB	FI-CA Dunning - Customizing
FKCJ	BP Control: Activities
FKCUMTAX	Summarize Tax Lines UK
FKEXMA	Monitor Tax Exemptions
FKI0	Execute Report
FKI1	Create Report
FKI2	Change Report
FKI3	Display Report
FKI4	Create Form
FKI5	Formular ändern
FKI6	Display Form
FKIB	Background Processing
FKIC	Maintain Currency Translation Type
FKIK	Maintain Key Figures
FKIM	Report Monitor
FKIO	Transport Reports
FKIP	Transport Forms
FKIQ	Import Reports from Client 000

FKIR	Import Forms from Client 000
FKIT	Translation Tool - Drilldown Report.
FKIV	Maintain Global Variable
FKIX	Reorganize Drilldown Reports
FKIY	Reorganize Report Data
FKIZ	Reorganize Forms
FKJOCMDR	Job Commander Standalone
FKJOCMDR1	Job Commander from FuMo (List)
FKJOCNT	Job Container
FKJOXTR	Job Container
FKKBIXBIT02_TRANS	Transfer Raw Data to Billable Items
FKKBIXBIT02_TRANS_MA	Transfer Raw Data to Billable Items
FKKBIXBIT4_DEL	Delete Billed Billable Items
FKKBIXBIT4_MON	Analysis of Billed Items
FKKBIXBITB_MON	Analysis of Billable Items
FKKBIXBITR_MON	Analysis of Raw Data
FKKBIXBIT_CONF	Config. of Billable Item Classes
FKKBIXBIT_GEN	Generate Billable Item Classes
FKKBIX_M	Mass Billing
FKKBIX_MA	Billing
FKKBIX_S	Individual Billing
FKKBI_BA_MON	Monitor Billing Accounts
FKKBI_BILLPROC_LOG	Log Billing Procedures
FKKBI_BILL_REV_M	Mass Reversal of Billing Document
FKKBI_BILL_REV_S	Single Reversal of Billing Document
FKKBI_BI_MA	Billing
FKKBI_BT_BILL	Execute Billing Orders
FKKBI_BT_CRT	Create Billing Orders
FKKBI_BT_DEL	Delete Billing Orders
FKKBI_BT_MON	Monitor Billing Orders
FKKBI_BW_MA	BI Extraction EDRs
FKKBI_BW_MON	Analysis of BW Extraction Orders
FKKBI_EDRRJ_MON	Monitor Provisionally Rejected EDRs
FKKBI_EDRWO_MON	Monitor Permanently Rejected EDRs
FKKBI_EDR_CLEAN	Clean Up Transfer Period
FKKBI_EDR_MON	Monitor Billable EDRs
FKKBI_EDR_RELOAD	Reload Provisionally Rejected EDRs
FKKBPCL	Process BP Duplicates
FKKBPCLCLAR	Clarification of BP Duplicates
FKKBPCLDISP	Display of BP Duplicates
FKKBPCLIMP	Import of BP Duplicate
FKKBRFCIMP	BRF: Copy Implementing Classes
FKKBRFTRANS	BRF:Transport of Application Classes
FKKCLERK_CM_CUAGENT	Responsiblity Maintenance for Clerk
FKKCLERK_CM_CUCENTER	Maintain Department Responsibilities
FKKCLERK_CM_CUDUNN	Simulate Responsibility for WorkItem
FKKCLERK_CM_CUUNIT	Maintain Unit Responsibilities
FKKCLERK_CU_BUSACH	Maintain Posting Responsibilities
FKKCLERK_CU_MASACH	Maintain Dunning Responsibilities
FKKCLERK_RESP	Assign Responsibilities
FKKCOLL_MONI	Monitor of Collections Services
FKKCRM_AUTH_CHECK	Dummy: FCC Authorization Check
FKKCRM_INFO_MOD	Assign Info Module to Profiles
FKKCRM_INFO_PROF	Define Information Module

FKKEXC_AGENT Post Agent Receivable
FKKEXC_MONI Monitor for Ext. Cash Desks via XI
FKKEXC_RETRY Post External Payments (Retry)
FKKINVBILL_ARCH Archive Billing Documents
FKKINVBILL_ARCH_CUS1 Retention Period: Arch. Billing Docs
FKKINVBILL_ARCH_CUS2 Retention Period: Arch. Billing Docs
FKKINVBILL_ARCH_DEL Delete Archived Billing Documents
FKKINVBILL_ARCH_READ Display Archived Billing Documents
FKKINVBILL_A_DEL Delete Billing Additional Data
FKKINVBILL_DISP Display Billing Document
FKKINVBILL_NUM Number Range for Billing Documents
FKKINVBILL_REV_M Mass Reversal of Billing Document
FKKINVBILL_REV_S Single Reversal of Billing Document
FKKINVBILL_REV_S_NEW Single Reversal of Billing Document
FKKINVBILL_SIM_DEL Delete Simulated Billing Documents
FKKINVDOC_ARCH Archive Invoicing Documents
FKKINVDOC_ARCH_CUS1 Retention Prd of Archived Inv.Doc.
FKKINVDOC_ARCH_CUS2 Retention Prd of Archived Inv.Doc.
FKKINVDOC_ARCH_DEL Delete Archived Invoicing Documents
FKKINVDOC_ARCH_READ Display Archived Invoicing Documents
FKKINVDOC_DISP Display Invoicing Document
FKKINVDOC_NUM Number Range for Invoicing Documents
FKKINVDOC_SIM_DEL Deletion of Simulated Invoicing Docs
FKKINV_BW_MA BI Extraction of Invoicing Documents
FKKINV_BW_MON Analysis of BW Extraction Orders
FKKINV_BW_SIM Individ. Simulation of BW Extraction
FKKINV_CFC Clarification Processing: Invoicing
FKKINV_CFCNUM Number Range Maintenance: FKKINVCFC
FKKINV_M Mass Invoicing
FKKINV_MA Invoicing
FKKINV_MON Analysis of Invoicing Orders
FKKINV_REV_M Mass Reversal
FKKINV_REV_MA Invoicing Reversal
FKKINV_REV_S Ind. Reversal
FKKINV_S Individual Invoicing
FKKORD1 Edit Requests
FKKORD1_APPR Check Requests
FKKORD1_EXT Display Requests
FKKORD2 Edit Standing Requests
FKKORD2_APPR Approve Standing Requests
FKKORD2_EXT Display Standing Requests
FKKORD2_YEAREND Create EF for Standing Request
FKKORD3 Edit General Requests
FKKORD3_APPR Check General Requests
FKKORD3_EXT Display General Requests
FKKORD4 Edit Request Templates
FKKORDA Approve Request
FKKORDM Create Documents from Requests
FKKORDNR Number Range Maintenance: FKK_ORD
FKKRCD1 Display Change Documents Requests
FKKS Contract A/R + A/P
FKKSNEW Contract A/R + A/P
FKK_BRF Configure BRF
FKK_CORRSPND_CUS Customizing Object CORRSPND

FKK_CORRSPND_DELETE	Correspondence: Delete Requests
FKK_CORRSPND_PROF	Correspondence: Package Prof. Creatn
FKK_CORRSPND_SARA	Archive Administration for CORRSPND
FKK_CORR_ARCHIVEINFO	Activate Archive IS for Corr. Arch.
FKK_CORR_HISTORY	Display Correspondence History
FKK_EBS_ARC	Link Documents with External Bills
FKK_EBS_ARC_E	Postprocessing Run: Link Bills
FKK_EBS_MRD	Reversal of Bills from Billing Sys.
FKK_EBS_MRD_E	Postprocessing Run: External Reversa
FKK_EBS_POI	Create Additional Information
FKK_EBS_POI_E	Postprocessing Run: Additional Info.
FKK_EBS_TOI_COPA	Transfer Doc./CO-PA Characteristics
FKK_EBS_TOI_COPA_E	Postprocessing Run: Transfer Docs
FKK_PAYMENTRELEASE	Install Payment Release Workflow
FKLOCK01	Check Conditional Locks
FKLOCK2	Set Processing Locks
FKMN	
FKMT	FI Acct Assignment Model Management
FKPC	Payment card processing
FKR8	Report: Stock Transfer Tax
FKR9	Initializing STT Position
FLB1	Postprocessing Lockbox Data
FLB2	Import Lockbox File
FLBFILE	Generate a Test Lockbox File
FLBP	Post Lockbox Data
FLBPC1	Create BP from Vendor
FLBPC2	Link BP to Vendor
FLBPD1	Create BP from Customer
FLBPD2	Link BP to Customer
FLCC1	Create Customer
FLCC2	Change Customer
FLCC3	Display Customer
FLCU1	Create Customer
FLCU2	Change Customer
FLCU3	Display Customer
FLEXBRE	BRE: Parallel Execution of BRE
FLEXFIN	Update Obselete Backlog Entries
FLEXLOG	Total Log of Parallel BRE Run
FLOREO	Customizing of Logical Doc. Reorg.
FLQAB	Assignment from Bank Statement Info.
FLQAC	Assignment from FI Information
FLQAD	Assignment from Invoices
FLQAL	Assignment from Invoices
FLQAM	Manual Assignment
FLQC1	Liquidity Items
FLQC10	Regenerate Flow Data
FLQC11	Query Sequences (Invoice)
FLQC12	Settings for Invoice Exit
FLQC13	Settings for FI Mechanisms
FLQC14	FI Assignment Analysis
FLQC15	Query Sequences
FLQC16	Tables for Conditions in Queries
FLQC2	Global Data
FLQC3	Company Code Data

FLQC4	Other Actual Accounts
FLQC5	Query Sequences (Bank Statement)
FLQC6	Assignment: Sequences - Bank Accts
FLQC7	G/L Accounts Relevant for Query
FLQC8	Query Sequences (FI Information)
FLQC9	Delete Flow Data
FLQCUST	Menu for Liquidity Calc. Settings
FLQHIST	Line Item History
FLQINFACC	G/L Accounts w/ Liquidity Item Info
FLQLACC	G/L Accounts List
FLQLGRP	List of Query Sequences
FLQLI	Line Item List
FLQLQR	List of Queries
FLQLS	Totals List
FLQMAIN	Liquidity Calculation
FLQQA1	Edit Query (General)
FLQQA3	Display Query (General)
FLQQA5	Queries for Sequences
FLQQB1	Edit Query (Bank Statement)
FLQQB3	Display Query (Bank Statement)
FLQQB5	Queries for Seq. (Bank Statement)
FLQQB7	Test Request (Bank Statement)
FLQQC1	Edit Query (FI Information)
FLQQC3	Display Query (FI Information)
FLQQC5	Queries for Sequences (FI Info.)
FLQQC7	Test Query (FI Payment Document)
FLQQD1	Edit Query (Invoice Information)
FLQQD3	Display Query (Invoice Information)
FLQQD5	Query Sequences (Invoices)
FLQQD7	Test Query (Other FI Document)
FLQREP	Payment Report
FLQT1	Create Transfer Posting
FLQT1B	Create Transfer with Batch Input
FLQT2	Change Transfer Posting
FLQT3	Display Transfer
FLQTRCBPOS	Commitment Item Derivation
FLQTRFIPOS	Liquidity Items for Commitment Item
FLQUPGRP	Upload Query Sequence (Assignment)
FLQUPINFAC	Upload Info Accounts (Application)
FLQUPQR	Upload Queries
FLT02	Flight Scheduling: Generate Details
FLVN1	Create Vendor
FLVN2	Change Vendor
FLVN3	Display Vendor
FM+0	Display FM Main Role Definition
FM+1	Maintain FM Main Role Definition
FM+2	Display FM Amount Groups
FM+3	Maintain FM Amount Groups
FM+4	Display FM Budget Line Groups
FM+5	Maintain FM Budget Line Groups
FM+6	Display FM Document Classes
FM+7	Maintain FM Document Classes
FM+8	Display FM Activity Categories
FM+9	Maintain FM Activity Categories

FM+A	Display Doc.Class->Doc.Cat. Assgmt
FM+B	Maintain Doc.Clase->Doc.Cat.Assgmt
FM03	Display FM Document
FM03A	Display FM Document with Archive
FM2BL_DERIVE	Derive FM totals transfer to BL
FM2BL_DERIVE1	Derive FM totals transfer to FI
FM2BL_DERIVER	CO-PA Rule for FM transfer to BL
FM2BL_DERIVER1	CO-PA Rule for FM transfer to FI
FM2E	FM: Change Budget Document
FM2F	FM: Display Budget Document
FM2G	Field Contents in Funds Centers
FM2M	Index of Funds Centers
FM3G	Commitment Item Hierarchy
FM3M	Index of Commitment Items
FM3N	Commitment Items for G/L Accounts
FM48	Change Financial Budget: Initial Scn
FM48_1	PS-CM: Create Planning Layout
FM48_2	PS-CM: Change Planning Layout
FM48_3	PS-CM: Display Planning Layout
FM49	Display Financial Budget: Init.Scrn
FM4G	Budget Structure Element Hierarchy
FM4M	Directory of Functional Areas
FM5I	FIFM: Create Fund
FM5M	Index of Funds
FM5S	FIFM: Display Fund
FM5U	FIFM: Change Fund
FM6I	FIFM: Create Application of Funds
FM6M	Index of Application of Funds
FM6S	FIFM: Display Application of Funds
FM6U	FIFM: Change Application of Funds
FM71	Maintain Cover Pool
FM72	Assign FM Acct Asst to Cover Pool
FM73	Create Cust. for Distr.inCollec.Exp.
FM78	Charact.Groups for Cover Pools
FM79	Grouping Chars for Cover Pool
FM7A	Indiv. Processing of CE Rules
FM7B	Flag FMAA as Eligible for Cover
FM7C	Generate Cover Pools from Rules
FM7G	Edit rules
FM7K	Copy Cover Eligibility Rules
FM7K_N	Copy Cover Pools with Funds Centers
FM7L	Delete Cover Eligibility Rules
FM7M	Directory of Funded Programs
FM7P	Indiv. Processing of Assgt to Cvr E.
FM7S	MassMaintenac. Rules-CoverEligibilty
FM7U	Multiple Processing of Assgts to CE
FM80	Budget Incr. Rev. Maint. - Display
FM81	Budget Incr. Rev. Maint. - Update
FM9B	FM: Copy Budget Version
FM9C	Plan Data Transfer from CO
FM9D	FM: Block Budget Version
FM9E	FM: Unblock Budget Version
FM9K	FIFM: Change Budget Structure
FM9L	FM: Display Budget Structure

FM9M	FM: Delete Budget Structure
FM9N	FM: Generate Budget Object
FM9O	Copy Supplement Budget
FM9P	Reconstruct Budget Distrbtd Values
FM9Q	FM: Total Up Budget
FM9QBTP	Reconstruct Budget per Budget Type
FM9QBUD	FM: Reconstruct Budget
FM9QRIB	FM: Reconstr. of Additional Revenues
FM9R	Loc.Auth.: Change Budget Structure
FM9S	HHM: Generate Net Vote Objects
FM9T	Check Assignment Object
FM9TBUD	Check budget objects
FM9U	FM: Checking Budget Consistency
FM9W	Adjust Funds Management Budget
FM9X	FM: Delete Budget 1 Commitment Item
FM9Y	FM: Copy BS - Year-Dependent StD.
FM9Z	FM: Transfer Budget Structure
FM9ZA10	Budget Structure Mass Processing
FMA1	Matching: Totals and Balances (CBM)
FMA2	Matching: CBM Line Items and Totals
FMA3	Matching: FI Line Items (CBM)
FMA4	Matching: FI Bank Line Items (CBM)
FMAA	Matching: Line Items and Totals (FM)
FMAB	Matching: FI FM Line Items
FMABPDERIVE	Auto. Budget Postings - Customizing
FMABPDERIVER	Auto. Budget Postings - Customizing
FMABP_COR	Re Post ABP to BCS
FMABP_COR_AWORG	ABP cor. for follow on document
FMAD	Leveling: FI-FM Totals Records
FMADB_CREATE_FYV	Create Period Variant on Daily Basis
FMADB_CUSTOM	Average Daily Balances: Customizing
FMADB_POST	Average Daily Balances: Allocation
FMAF	Level Line Items and Totals Items
FMAO	Requests Journal
FMARC	Initial Archiving Run
FMARC_BATCH	Initial Archiving Run
FMAR_AT	Archive Totals Records f. Cmmt/Act.
FMAR_BCS_ED	Archive Budget Entry Documents (BCS)
FMAR_BCS_LI	Archive Budget Line Item (BCS)
FMAR_BCS_TT	Archive Budget Totals Records (BCS)
FMAR_BE	Archive Budget Entry Documents
FMAR_BH	Archive Budget Hierarchy Documents
FMAR_BT	Archive Budget Totals Records
FMAR_CO	Archive CO Line Items
FMAR_FI	Archive FI Line Items
FMAR_OI	Archive Commitment Line Items
FMAVC1	Prepare Cross Assignments Clearing
FMAVCCD	FM AVC change document number ranges
FMAVCCUST01	Display Control Ledger Customizing
FMAVCCUSTDEF	Check AVC Customizing (FM)
FMAVCDERIACTG	Derivation of Activity Groups
FMAVCDERIAO	Derivation of control object (ACO)
FMAVCDERIAOCPY	Copy strategy for derivation of ACO
FMAVCDERIAODEL	Delete strategy for deriving ACO

SAP Transaction Codes – Volume One

FMAVCDERIAOPREDEF   Add predefined steps (AFMA)
FMAVCDERIAOR   Derivation of control object (ACO)
FMAVCDERICH   Derivation of checking horizon
FMAVCDERICHR   Deriv. Rules, Deriv. of Checkng Hor.
FMAVCDERITPROF   Derivation of tolerance profile
FMAVCDERITPROFCPY   Copy strategy for derivation of TolP
FMAVCDERITPROFDEL   Delete strategy for deriving TolProf
FMAVCDERITPROFR   Derivation of tolerance profile
FMAVCLDGRCPY   Copy AVC ledger (FM)
FMAVCR01   Display Annual Data of Control Obj.
FMAVCR02   Display Overall Data of Control Obj.
FMAVCREINIT   Re-Initialize AVC Ledger
FMB0   CO Document Transfer
FMBB   Budgeting Workbench
FMBBC   Create Entry Document
FMBELI   Processing list
FMBG1   Input tax adjustmnt(monthly) for PCO
FMBG2   Input tax adjustmnt (yearly) for PCO
FMBG3   Display input tax adjustments
FMBGCP   Copy acc. assignment allocations
FMBGD   Cash Dis. and Backdated Tax Calculn
FMBGJ   Execute Annual Adjustments
FMBGKONT   Assign FM Account Assgnts to PCOs
FMBGM   Execute Monthly Adjustments
FMBGU   Reset Input Tax Adjustment
FMBGUL   Sales Tax List PCOs
FMBGV   Calculate Input Tax Deduction Rate
FMBI   Posting Line-Based Budget Increase
FMBLBASIC   BL Account classification
FMBLCLASS   BL Account classification
FMBLCOAD   Colombia budgetary ledger derivation
FMBLCOADR   Colombia budgetary ledger derivation
FMBLCORR   Budgetary Ledger Correction
FMBLEXCLWASHOUT   BL Account classification
FMBLEXT   BL Accounts for Extensions
FMBLEXT0   Set account balance to zero
FMBLEXTR   CO-PA BL Account Rule for Extensions
FMBLYRCL1   Year End Acc. Ass. derivation
FMBLYRCL2   US BL federal government derivation
FMBOSTAT   Maintain budget object & status
FMBPD   Budget Period: Maintain
FMBPD_D   Budget Period: Display
FMBPD_DELETE   FM: Delete Budget Periods
FMBPD_LIST   FM: Budget Period Report
FMBPD_MASS   FM: Mass assignment of BPs to funds
FMBPLOGSHOW   Display Retraction Log
FMBPLOGSHOW_BCS   Display Retraction Log
FMBPNO   Number Range Maintenance: FM_BPREPBW
FMBPQV   Create Query Variant
FMBPQV_BCS   Create Query Variant
FMBPRET   Budget data transfer
FMBPRET_BCS   Budget data transfer
FMBPREVERSE   Cancel Retractor Run
FMBPREVERSE_BCS   Cancel Retractor Run

215

FMBPRRC   Change Derivation Strategy
FMBPRRC_BCS   Maintain Derivation Rules BCS
FMBPRRC_COMMON   Change Derivation Strategy
FMBPRRI   Create Derivation Strategy
FMBPRRI_BCS   Create Derivation Strategy BCS
FMBPRRI_COMMON   Create Derivation Strategy
FMBPRRS   Display Derivation Strategy
FMBPRRS_BCS   Display Derivation Strategy
FMBPRRS_COMMON   Display Derivation Strategy
FMBSBO   Change Budget Addresses
FMBSBOHIS   Change History of Budget Addresses
FMBSBOHISDEL   Delete Change History of Budg. Addr.
FMBSBOS   Dispay Budget Addresses
FMBSBO_DATA   Budget data on invalid objects
FMBSBO_DEL   Delete budget objects
FMBSBO_GEN   Generate budget objects from budget
FMBSBO_HIE_MULT   Maintain Hierarchical Budget Address
FMBSBO_INCON_DEL   Delete Inconsistent Budget Address
FMBSBO_MULT   Maintain budget objects
FMBSCPY   Copy budget structure objects
FMBSDERIBO   Derivation of Budget Address
FMBSDERIBOCPY   Copy strategy for deriving bud. addr
FMBSDERIBODEL   Delete strategy for budget addresses
FMBSDERIBOPREDEF   Add predefined steps (BSAC)
FMBSDERIBOR   Deriv. Rules, Deriv. of Budget Addr.
FMBSIDX_INCON   Display index inconsistencies
FMBSIDX_RECON   Reconstruct budget structure index
FMBSPO   Change Posting Addresses
FMBSPOHIS   Change History of Posting Addresses
FMBSPOHISDEL   Delete Change History of Post. Addr.
FMBSPOS   Display Posting Addresses
FMBSPO_DATA   Actual/Commitment on invalid objects
FMBSPO_DEL   Delete posting objects
FMBSPO_GEN   Generate posting objects from data
FMBSPO_HIE_MULT   Maintain Hierarchical Posting Addr.
FMBSPO_INCON_DEL   Delete Inconsistent Posting Address
FMBSPO_MULT   Maintain posting objects
FMBS_STAT   Budget Structure Settings
FMBTB   Transfer Budget Totals to FI-BL
FMBUD001   Export ISPS Budget Data
FMBUD002   Import ISPS Budget Data
FMBUD003   Export from Local Auth. Budget Data
FMBUD004   Import from Local. Auth. Budget Data
FMBUD007   Export of Financial Results
FMBUD008   Import Financial Results
FMBUDACT   Budget/Actuals allowed for BL
FMBV   FM: Activate Availability Control
FMBY1   Budget Period Control: Applications
FMBY100   BP Ctrl: Field Grouping per Activity
FMBY101   BP Ctrl: Field Grouping per Role
FMBY108   BP Ctrl: Field Grouping per Appl Obj
FMBY11   BP Ctrl: Assign Scrn Field to DB
FMBY12   Budget Pd Ctrl: Field Group Criteria
FMBY13   Budget Pd Ctrl: Role Categories

SAP Transaction Codes – Volume One

FMBY14	Budget Pd Ctrl: Role Category Grpng
FMBY15	Budget Pd Ctrl: Appltn Transactions
FMBY16	Budget Period Control: Tables
FMBY17	Budget Pd Ctrl: External Applicatns
FMBY18	Budget Period Control: Activities
FMBY19	BP Ctrl: Fld Grpng for Each Activity
FMBY2	Budget Period Control: Field Groups
FMBY23	Budget Period Control: Data Sets
FMBY3	Budget Period Control: Views
FMBY4	Budget Period Control: Sections
FMBY5	Budget Period Control: Screens
FMBY6	Budget Period Ctrl: Screen Sequences
FMBY7	Budget Period Control: Events
FMBY8	Budget Pd Ctrl: GUI Stand. Functions
FMBY9	Budget Pd Ctrl: GUI Addtnl Functions
FMB_A01	Budget Consumption View
FMB_B01	Budget View by Document Type
FMB_B02	Budget View by Process
FMB_PL01	Budget Lines Vs. Commt./Actual Line
FMB_PT01	Budget Totals Vs. Commt./Actual Tot.
FMC2	Customizing in Day-to-Day Business
FMCAALOT	Approval Write-Off
FMCABILL	Public Sector Billing
FMCABILLI	Object-Based Tax Billing
FMCABILLM	Object-Based Tax Billing
FMCABP	B. Partner Asset w. Duplicate Search
FMCABP1	B. Partner Asset w. Duplicate Search
FMCABRFCIMP	BRF: Copy Implementation Classes
FMCABRFGEN	BRF: Generate Expressions
FMCABRFTRANS	BRF: Transport Application Classes
FMCAC1	Create Contract Partner & Customer
FMCAC2	Change Contract Partner & Customer
FMCAC3	Display Contract Partner & Customer
FMCACOLLAG	Derivation Cllction Agncy - Custom.
FMCACOLLAGE	Derivation Cllction Agncy - Mainte.
FMCACOV	Business Partner Overview
FMCACOVP	Business Partner Overview
FMCADERIVE	FM Deriv. Transactions - Customizing
FMCADERIVE2	FM Derivation Trans. - Distributor
FMCADERIVER	FM Deriv. Transactions - Maintenance
FMCADLOT	Resubmission Write-Off
FMCADOCA	Approval List for Doc. Changes
FMCAFOBI	Form-Based Tax Bill
FMCAFOBIS	Form-Based Tax Bill
FMCAGTRINVBILL_DISP	Display Grantor Billing Doc. (PSCD)
FMCAGTRINV_M	Mass Invoicing (Grantor)
FMCAGTRINV_S	Single Invoicing (Grantor)
FMCAILOT	Approval Installment Plan
FMCAINCOC	Generate Inbound Correspondences
FMCAINCOH	Process Inbound Correspondence
FMCAINVH	Invoice History
FMCAM1	Generate Inbound Correspondences
FMCAM1_OLD	Generate Inbound Correspondence
FMCAM2	Generate Invoices

217

FMCAOGRM	Generate Docs from General Requests
FMCAORDNR2	Number Range Maintenance: FMCA_ORD
FMCAPFPF	Mass Activity for Form Process
FMCASKV	Differences in Cash Discount Clearng
FMCAV1	Create Contract Partner & Vendor
FMCAV2	Change Contract Partner & Vendor
FMCAV3	Display Contract Partner & Vendor
FMCA_AIH	IS-PS-CA Archiving Invoice History
FMCA_BRF	Configure BRF
FMCA_CHECK_INCORR	Check Custom. for Enh. Inbd Corresp.
FMCA_COUPON	Generate Coupon Books
FMCA_EHVD	Customer Overview - Data Selection
FMCA_GRANT_FICA_ACT	Activate the use of Grant for FICA
FMCA_P050	Estimation Posting for Ind Cor. Req.
FMCA_P052	Deactivate Enhanced Inbnd Corresp.
FMCA_P053	Settings for Enh. Inbound Corresp.
FMCA_P673	Maintain Exception List Messages
FMCA_PT_REISPL	Information System: Parcels
FMCA_TRM_OBN_BP	OBN for Contract Object
FMCA_TRM_OBN_CO	OBN for Contract Object
FMCA_TRM_OBN_ICR	OBN for Creating Enhanced EKA
FMCA_TRM_OBN_INV	OBN for Invoicing Document
FMCA_TRM_OBN_OA	OBN for Optical Archive
FMCA_TRM_REL_LINKS	Configure Useful Links
FMCA_TRM_YOUCANALSO	Configure Other Options
FMCB	Reassignment: Document Selection
FMCC	Reassignment: FM-CO Assignment
FMCCA	Def. of FM CC - Address based
FMCCAVCCUSTDEF	Check AVC Customizing (FMCC)
FMCCAVCDERIACTG	Derivation of Activity Group
FMCCAVCDERIACTGR	Derivation of Activity Groups
FMCCAVCDERIAO	Derivation of Control Object
FMCCAVCDERIAOR	FMCC Derivation control object (ACO)
FMCCAVCDERICH	Derivation of Control Object
FMCCAVCDERICHR	FMCC Derivation of check horizon
FMCCAVCDERITPROF	Derivation of Activity Group
FMCCAVCDERITPROFR	FMCC Derivation of tolerance profile
FMCCAVCOVERVIEW	Overview of FM Cash cntrl AVC Values
FMCCAVCREINIT	Re-Initialize FM CC AVC Ledger
FMCCAVC_F110	F110 for FMCCAVC exclusively
FMCCD	Def. of FM CC - Document based
FMCCOVR	FM Obligation Closeout
FMCCR01	Consistency Check Report
FMCD	Reassignment: Delete Work List
FMCECPYCG	Copy Cover Groups
FMCECVGPNR	Maintain No.Range Intvl for Cvr Grps
FMCEDELCG	Delete CE Rules
FMCEGENCG	Generate CE Rules
FMCEHISCG	Change History of CE Rules
FMCEHISDEL	Delete Change History Records for CE
FMCEMON01	Overview of Automatic Cover Groups
FMCERG	Strategy for Generating CE Rules
FMCERGR	Derivation Rules in CE Rule Strategy
FMCERULE	Process Single CE Rule

SAP Transaction Codes – Volume One

FMCG	Reassignment: Overall Assignment
FMCG_CHAIN	Reassignment: Full Selection(Chains)
FMCIA	Edit Commitment Item
FMCIC	Display commitment item
FMCID	Change Commitment Item: Hierarchy
FMCIE	Display Commitment Item: Hierarchy
FMCIH	Commt Items: Alternative Hierarchy
FMCI_COPY_NEXT_YEAR	Copy Cmmt Items into Following Year
FMCI_FYC	Copy Cmmt Items into Following Year
FMCI_REPLACE_HIVARNT	Replace Hierarchy Variant Assignment
FMCJ	Maintain cash journal
FMCL	FM Closeout of Obligations
FMCN	Reassignment: Supplement.Acct Assgt
FMCP_EF_CLOSE	Close Earmarked Funds for Contracts
FMCP_EF_CREATE	Create Earmarked Funds for Contracts
FMCR	Reassignment: Display Work List
FMCT	Reassignment: Transfer
FMCUDERIVAL	Derivation strategy to create line
FMCUDERIVDALE	Derivation strategy for ALE distribu
FMCUDERIVMIG	Derivation strategy for migration
FMCUDERIVMIGED	Derivation strategy for migration
FMCUDERIVSUB	Derivation strategy for substitution
FMCYCOPI_BW	Transfer of SAP BW PlanData to BCS
FMCYCOPI_CO	Transfer of CO Planning Data to BCS
FMCYDOC	Copy Budget Documents
FMCYFREEZE	Copy budget data (freeze)
FMCYFREEZEN	Copy budget data (freeze)
FMCYLOAD	Copy budget data (load)
FMCYLOADN	Copy budget data (load)
FMCYPREP	Copy budget data (preparation)
FMCYRESET	Reset budget data (preparation)
FMCYTEXT	Copy Budget Text
FMD1	FM: Change Carryforward Rules
FMD2	FM: Display Carryforward Rules
FMD7	FM: Change Supplement Budget Plan
FMD8	FM: Display Supplement Budget Plan
FMD9	FM: Change Suppl. Coll. Expend. Plan
FMDA	FM: Change Budget Plan
FMDAOPA	Clear Down Payments
FMDB	FM: Display Budget Plan
FMDC	FM: Change Collect. Expend. Planning
FMDD	FM: Display Collect. Expnd. planning
FMDE	FM: Loc. Auth.: Change Fin. Result
FMDEBT_RESCHEDULE	Reschedule debt
FMDERIVATIONANALYSIS	Analysis Report on FM Derivations
FMDERIVE	FM Object Assignment - Customizing
FMDERIVER	FM Object Assignment - Maintenance
FMDF	FM: Loc. Auth.: Display Fin. Result
FMDG	FM: Loc. Auth.: Change FR in CE
FMDH	FM: Loc. Auth.: Display FR in CE
FMDI	FM Loc. Auth.: Copy Budget Version
FMDI01	Data Transfer in Direct Input
FMDJ	FM: Transfer Financial Result
FMDK	FM Loc. Auth.: Change Net Voting

FMDL	FM Loc. Auth.: Display Net Voting
FMDM	Monitor Closing Operations
FMDMR1	Display Assignment Rules for Process
FMDMR2	Display Assignmt. Rules for Val.Type
FMDN	FM: Integration in Balance Hierarchy
FMDO	FM: Loc. Auth.: Transfer Bdgt Values
FMDO1	FM: Revaluate Original Budget
FMDO2	FM: Revaluation of Supplement
FMDOCREV	Mass reversal of FM documents
FMDPEF	Create Down Paym. with EF reference
FMDPEF_DET	Create Down Paym. with EF reference
FMDPREF	Create Down Paym. Req. with EF ref.
FMDPREF_DET	Create Down Paym. Req. with EF ref.
FMDS	Copy Carryforward Rules
FMDT	Display Carryforward Rules
FMDV	FM: Residual Budget Data Transfer
FMDW	FM: Financ. Result CE Data Transfer
FMDX	FM: Coll. Expend. Plan Data Transfer
FMDY	FM: Financial Result Data Transfer
FMDZ	FM: Budget Planning Data Transfer
FME1	Import Forms from Client 000
FME2	Import Reports from Client 000
FME3	Transport Forms
FME4	Transport Reports
FME5	Reorganize Forms
FME6	Reorganize Drilldown Reports
FME7	Reorganize Report Data
FME8	Maintain Batch Variants
FME9	Translation Tool - Drilldown
FMEB	Structure Report Backgrnd Processing
FMECDERIVE	FMEUF Object Assignment -Maintenance
FMECDERIVER	FMEUF Object Assignment -Maintenance
FMEDANALYZER	Analyzis of possible Duplicated Docs
FMEDD	Display Entry Document
FMEDDW	Drilldown for Budget Entry Documents
FMEDFAMNR	FM document family number ranges
FMEDHISTDEL	Delete history of Entry Document
FMEDHISTDIS	Display history of Entry Document
FMEDNR	FM entry document number ranges
FMEH	SAP-EIS: Hierarchy maintenance
FMEK	FMCA: Create Drilldown Report
FMEL	FMCA: Change Drilldown Report
FMEM	FMCA: Display Drilldown Report
FMEN	FMCA: Create Form
FMEO	FMCA: Change Form
FMEP	FMCA: Display Form
FMEQ	FMCA: Run Drilldown Report
FMER	FMCA: Drilldown Tool Test Monitor
FMEUFDD	Display Original Document
FMEUFFINTYP	Display Financing Source Type
FMEUFINTERV	Define Intervention
FMEUFLEVELS	Define Levels
FMEUFLP1	Set Up Launchpad for Cert. Manager
FMEUFLP2	Set Up Launchpad for Cert. Accountnt

SAP Transaction Codes – Volume One

FMEUFPROC	Display Certification Procedure
FMEUFRCODE	Maintain Regional Codes
FMEUFTAXHAND	Display Certification Procedure
FMEUF_CUST	Expenditure Certification Custom.
FMEURO05	Delete Euro FM Area
FMEURO1	Create Euro FM Area
FMEURO2	Refresh Euro Master Data
FMEURO3	Display Euro FM Areas
FMEURO4	Deactivate Euro FM Area
FMEV	Maintain Global Variable
FMF0	Payment Selection
FMF1	Revenue Transfer
FMFA_0001	FMFA: Applications
FMFA_0002	FMFA: Field Groups
FMFA_0003	FMFA: Views
FMFA_0004	FMFA: Sections
FMFA_0005	FMFA: Screens
FMFA_0006	FMFA: Screen Sequences
FMFA_0007	FMFA: Events
FMFA_0008	FMFA: GUI Standard Functions
FMFA_0009	FMFA: GUI Additional Functions
FMFA_0011	FMFA: Assign Screen Field->DB Field
FMFA_0012	FMFA: Field Grouping Criteria
FMFA_0013	FMFA: Role Categories
FMFA_0015	FMFA: Application Transactions
FMFA_0016	FMFA: Tables
FMFA_0018	FMFA: Activities
FMFA_0104	FMFA: Applications
FMFA_0106	FMFA: Assign Object Part --> Note ID
FMFA_0108	Edit Funct. Area Field Sel. String
FMFEE	Calculate Fees for US Federal
FMFGAPAAC	Acc. Property account assignment cat
FMFGAPCON	Acc. Property Main Settings
FMFGAPCR	Accountable Property program
FMFGAPMT	Accountable Property Movement Types
FMFGAPTR	Acc. Property Transaction Types
FMFGBUTYPE	Budget Type attributes
FMFGCCRLIST	CCR List
FMFGCCRLISTN	CCR Vendor List
FMFGCCRUPDATE	Update CCR data using data file
FMFGCCRUPLOAD	Upload Initial CCR Data File
FMFGCCRVENDORCREATE	Create Vendor Master from CCR Data
FMFGCCRVENDORUPDATE	Update Vendor Master from CCR Data
FMFGCCR_CREATE	PSM-FG: Create/Update CCR Vendors
FMFGCCR_UPDATE	PSM-FG: Update CCR Vendors
FMFGDRVCOCKPIT	Federal Extension Derivation Data
FMFGDRVCOCKPIT_IMG	Federal Extension Derivation Access
FMFGDRVTRACE	Display US Federal derivation trace
FMFGF2_ATTRIBUTES	Configure Attributes
FMFGRCN_DEF_RULE	Reconciliation Rule Definition
FMFGRCN_DEF_SLICE	Reconciliation Slice Definition
FMFGSUBTOT	Reconciliation Subtotal Texts
FMFGTCL	Congressional Limitations (St. Fund)
FMFGYEFIELDS	Collected fields year end

FMFG_ACC_CLOSEOUT   Closeout of the Residual Accounts
FMFG_AUTO_TC   Treasury Confirmation - Automated
FMFG_CANCELED_AP   Canceled Fund for Account Payable-FI
FMFG_CANCELED_AP_MM   Canceled Fund for Account Payable-MM
FMFG_CANCELED_AR   Canceled Fund for Acct Receivable-FI
FMFG_CANCEL_FUND   A/R Cancel Fund Automatic Posting
FMFG_DIT_FBT   Maintain List of DIT/FBT Accts
FMFG_DOCT_ADJ   Document types for adjustments
FMFG_EF_POST   Post parked Earmark fund documents
FMFG_EXCLUDE_INVOICE   Exclude Invoice from PPA Calculation
FMFG_E_1099_C   Tax Form 1099-C
FMFG_E_BR1   Statement of Budgetary Resources
FMFG_E_BS1   Balance Sheet
FMFG_E_CA1   Statement of Custodial Activities
FMFG_E_CF   budget carry forward with subtypes
FMFG_E_CL0   Preclosing Rollup
FMFG_E_CL1   Preclosing rollup: fund type rules
FMFG_E_CL2   Preclosing rollup: fund rules
FMFG_E_FI1   Statement of Financing
FMFG_E_FMS1219   FMS 1219/1220 Accountability Reports
FMFG_E_NET_COST   Statement of Net Cost
FMFG_E_NP1   Statement of Changes in Net Position
FMFG_E_RB1   Reclassified Balance Sheet
FMFG_E_RC1   Reclassified Statement of Net Cost
FMFG_E_REL   Release Budget
FMFG_E_RLAYOUT   Tool Program for Reporting Layout(s)
FMFG_E_RP1   Reclassified Stmt of Net Position
FMFG_E_SF1081   US Federal SF1081 - Voucher process
FMFG_E_SF132   SF-132
FMFG_E_SF133   SF-133
FMFG_E_SF224   SF-224 Statement of Transactions
FMFG_E_SF224_ALC_CHG   SF-224: Maintain ALC GWA Master Data
FMFG_E_SF224_ALC_GWA   SF-224: Display ALC GWA Master Data
FMFG_E_SF224_DERIVE   SF-224 - Customizing
FMFG_E_SF224_DERIVER   SF-224 - Customizing
FMFG_E_SF224_TS   Treasury Subclasses
FMFG_E_TP1   Trial Balance Tie-Points
FMFG_E_TRANS_REG   Transaction Register
FMFG_E_YFITRG02   Document Listing
FMFG_E_ZFZALI00   Payment Settlement List
FMFG_E_ZOPAC   Online Payment and Collection System
FMFG_F2_TRANS   Maintain Transfer Agency and Account
FMFG_FP_REL_LIV   Release Blocked Fast Pay Invoices
FMFG_FUNDS_AVAIL_BCS   5-Column Status of Funds in BCS
FMFG_FUNDS_AVAIL_SPL   5-Column Status of Funds in FI-SL
FMFG_HELD_INVOICES   List for Parked and Held Documents
FMFG_IMPROP_REASONS   Reason code maintenance
FMFG_INVCANCEL   Cancel Invoice and Subsequent Docs
FMFG_INVSTAT   Maintain Invoice Statuses
FMFG_INV_STAGES   FMFG: Invoice Stages Activation
FMFG_IPAC   US Federal IPAC Interface Process
FMFG_IPACED   US Federal IPAC Interface Process
FMFG_IPACED_DERIV   US Fed IPACed Derivation Tool
FMFG_IPACED_FLAG   US Fed IPACed Cust/Vend Flag

SAP Transaction Codes – Volume One

FMFG_IPACED_REVERSE	IPACed Bulk File Confrm. Reverse Pro
FMFG_IPAC_CNFRM	IPAC Confirmation Process
FMFG_IPAC_REGENERATE	Regenerate previous produced bulk fi
FMFG_IPAC_REVERSE	IPAC Bulk File Reverse Process
FMFG_IPAC_SNUM	Number range maintenance: IPAC_DOCR
FMFG_MAN_RFC_CONFIRM	Treasury Confirmation
FMFG_MM_PENDING	PO Pending Changes Report
FMFG_PMT_TYPE	Maintain Pmt Method to Pmt Type map
FMFG_PO_HISTORY	Purchase Order History
FMFG_PO_POST	Post the held PO's
FMFG_PPA_TO_VENDOR	Transfer PPA Flag to Vendor
FMFG_PP_CLEAR	Federal Payment Program Clearing
FMFG_PROG_REPT_CODE	Program Report Category - FACTS II
FMFG_PR_POST	Post the held PR's
FMFG_RCN_DERIVE1	Reconciliation: Derivation cust.
FMFG_RCN_DERIVE2	Reconciliation: Derivation cust.
FMFG_RCN_DERIVE3	Reconciliation: Derivation cust
FMFG_RCV	Report on Receivables From Public
FMFG_REASON_CODE	Improper Reason Code Report
FMFG_RFC_REGE	Regenerate IPAC file Using PMW
FMFG_RPTA_DERIVE	Reporting Attributes - Customizing
FMFG_RPTA_DERIVER	Reporting Attributes - Customizing
FMFG_RPT_E_UNFILLED	Close Out Unfilled Orders
FMFG_SF108_CONFRM	SF1081/80 Confirmation/Cash Check
FMFG_SF108_REPRNT	SF1081/80 Reprint Output
FMFG_SF108_REV	SF1081/80 Reversal Confrmed Doc
FMFG_SF108_REV_UNCON	SF1081/80 Reverse Unconfirmed Doc
FMFG_SO_HISTORY	Sales Order History
FMFG_SPS_SUMM	SPS Summary File Creation
FMFG_SS_APPROVAL	Payment Sampling Approval Process
FMFG_SS_BATCH	Payment Statistical Sampling - Invoi
FMFG_SS_CERTIFY	Payment Sampling Certification Proce
FMFG_SS_STATUS	Payment Sampling Process Status Repo
FMFG_SS_USERS	Statistical Sampling Clerk/Superviso
FMFG_TC_REVERSE	Treasury Confirm Reverse Process
FMFG_TC_REV_CHECKS	US Fed. TC Schedule Reversal - check
FMFG_TC_REV_SCHEDULE	US Fed. TC Schedule Reversal - Sched
FMFG_TREASURY_CONFIR	Treasury Confirmation
FMFG_WAREHOUSE	Prompt Payment Analysis
FMFG_YEAR_END_CLOSE	Year End close open balance
FMFG_YEC_LOAD_RULES	Year End Close Load Rules
FMFG_YRCL	Year end closing rules
FMFI	Execute program RFFMCJFI
FMFPCOPY	Copy Assgmt of Cmmt Item to Rev Type
FMFUDERI	Fund and Function Derivation
FMFUDERIR	Fund and Function Derivation: Rules
FMG1	Create Budget Structure Template
FMG2	Change Budget Structure Template
FMG3	Display Budget Structure Template
FMG4	Delete Budget Structure Template
FMG5	Generate BS Object from BS Template
FMGL	Maintain Text for Grouping
FMGL_COFIMONITOR	Monitor Balancing CO-FI Postings
FMGL_PERIOD_CONTROL	Posting Periods for Gnral Ldr Fields

FMGR	Maintain Texts for Grouping
FMGX	Commitment Item Issue to UNIX-File
FMGY	Create Commitment Items via UNIX
FMHC	Check Bdgt Structure Elements in HR
FMHG	Generate Bdgt Struc Elements in HR
FMHGG	Generate BS Elements f. Several Fnds
FMHIE_CHANGE	Process Hierarchy
FMHIE_CHKINCONDATA	Check MBS Data for Inconsistencies
FMHIE_CHKINCONDISTR	Check Distr. for Inconsistencies
FMHIE_COPY	Copy hierarchical budget structure
FMHIE_DELETE	Delete hierarchical budget structure
FMHIE_DISPLAY	Display hierarchical budget structur
FMHIE_GENERATION	Generate Generate Hierarchy
FMHIE_HIEID	Create/Assign Sub-Hierarchy ID
FMHIST	Apportion Document in FM
FMHK	Copy Control Data
FMHV	Budget Memo Texts
FMIA	Indiv. Processing of Revs Incr. Bdgt
FMIB	Posting Line-Based Budget Increase
FMIC	Generate Additional Budget Incr.Data
FMIF	Correction Report for RIB-FB
FMIK	Copy Rules for Revs Incr. the Budget
FMIL	Delete Rules for Revs Incr. Budget
FMIP	Edit Revenues Increasing Bdgt Rules
FMIPCT	Payment Transfer: Customizing
FMIR	Detail Maintenance of Open Int Rules
FMIS	Display Rules for Revs.Incr.Budget
FMIT	Totals-Based Distribution Procedure
FMITPO	Payment Transfer
FMIU	Maintain Rules for Revs.Incr.Budget
FMJ0	Manual Zero Carryforward
FMJ2	Year-End Closing: Carryfwd Cmmts
FMJ2_D	Carryfwrd Cmmt Accrd. to Entry Date
FMJ3	Reverse Commitments Carryforward
FMJA	Budget Year-End Closing: Prepare
FMJB	Budget Year-End Closing: Determine
FMJC	Budget Year-End Closing: Carry Fwd
FMJD	Reverse Fiscal Year Close: Budget
FMJM	Maintain residual budget application
FMJN	Display residual budget application
FMJO	Maintain residual budget approval
FMJP	Display residual budget approval
FMJ_ANZ	Carry Forward Down Payments
FMJ_APP	Approval Step Cmmt Carryforward
FMJ_DISPLAY	Display FM Commt Carryforward Docs
FMJ_FICA	Transfer Open Items from FI-CA
FMKFDEF	FM Definition of Key Figures
FMKFR01	Display budget data
FMKO_RFFMKHPL	Budget plan
FMKUDELDATA	Delete BCS database tables
FMKUDOCRESET	Reset BCS Entry Documents
FMKUMIGDOC	Migrate FB Documents to BCS
FMKUMIGTEXT	Migration FB Budget Text to BCS
FMKUMIGTOT	Migrate FBS totals to BCS totals

FMKUTOTCOL	Collect Budget Totals
FML1	Create FI-SL Customizing Ledger
FML2	Change FI-SL Customizing Ledger
FML3	Display FI-SL Customizing Ledger
FML4	Delete FI-SL Customizing Ledger
FMLD	Ledger Deletion
FMLF	Classify Movement Types
FMLGD_H_CUST	Clearing Control
FMLGD_H_ELKO	Basic Settings Elctr. Bank Statement
FMLID	Display Change Document
FMLIDW	Drilldown for Change Documents
FMLINR	FM line item document number ranges
FMMACGPERC	Edit percentage per cover group
FMMC	FM Obligation Closeout
FMMDAUTO	FM: Auto. Creation of Master Data
FMMDCICOPY	Copy commitment item substrings
FMMDFCCOPY	Copy funds center substrings
FMMDFDCOPY	Copy fund substrings
FMMDFNCOPY	Copy functional area substrings
FMMD_SETGEN	Generate Substring Groups
FMME1	Funded Program Control: Applications
FMME10	Funded Program Control: Search Help
FMME100	FPC: Field Group per Activitiy
FMME101	FPC: Field Group per Role
FMME102	FPC: Authorization Types
FMME103	FPC: Field Groups for Authorizations
FMME104	Funded Program Control: Screen confi
FMME105	FPC: Field Group for Ext.Application
FMME106	FPC: Note View for Role Category
FMME107	FPC: Where-Used View
FMME108	FPC: Client-Wide Field Grouping
FMME109	Field Group Criteria by FM Area
FMME11	FPC: Assign Screen Field to Database
FMME12	FPC: Field Group Criteria
FMME13	Funded Program Control: BP Roles
FMME14	Funded Program Ctrl: BP Role Groupin
FMME15	FPC: Application Transaction
FMME16	Funded Program Control: Tables
FMME17	Funded Program Control: External App
FMME18	Funded Program Control: Activities
FMME19	FPC: Function Module Activities
FMME2	Funded Program Control: Field Groups
FMME20	Funded Program Ctrl:Differentiation
FMME200	Funded Progr. Contr: Change doc list
FMME21	Funded Program Ctrl: Activity type
FMME22	Funded Program Ctrl: Cat. Fld Grp
FMME23	Funded Program Control: Data sets
FMME24	Funded Progr. Where used list define
FMME25	Where used list - process to view
FMME26	FPC: Assign BAPI Flds to Field Grps
FMME27	Funded Program DI to Table fields
FMME3	Funded Program Control: Views
FMME4	Funded Program Control: Views
FMME5	Funded Program Control: Views

FMME6	Funded Program: Screen Sequence
FMME7	Funded Program: Events
FMME8	Funded Program Ctrl: GUI Std Functio
FMME9	Funded Program Ctrl: GUI Addl Func.
FMMEASURE	Funded Program: Maintain
FMMEASURED	Funded Program: Display
FMME_SET_C	Funded Program Groups Create
FMME_SET_CH	Funded Program Groups Change
FMME_SET_D	Funded Program Groups Display
FMMI	Mass Maintenance of Open Intervals
FMMIGCE	Migrate FBS cover pools and rules
FMMPCEBAL	Balancing Automatic Cover Groups
FMMPCOVR	Carry over residual budget
FMMPCOVRN	Carry over residual budget
FMMPCOVR_BT	Carry over residual budget obsolete
FMMPPCLO	Pre-close: Transfer Residual Budget
FMMPRBB	Increase Budget from Revenues
FMMPRELE	Release data
FMMPRELEN	Release data
FMMPROLLUP	Rollup budget obsolete
FMMPSTAT	Generate Statistical Budget Data
FMMPTRAN	Transfer postings
FMMPTRAN_BT	Transfer to cons.budget type obsolet
FMN0	Subsequent Posting of FI Documents
FMN0_PAY	Reconstruction of Payment Docs
FMN3	Transfer Purchase Req. Documents
FMN3N	Reconstruction of Purch. Requisition
FMN4	Transfer Purchase Order Documents
FMN4N	Reconstruction of Purchase Orders
FMN5	Transfer Funds Reservation Documents
FMN5N	Reconstruction of Earmarked Funds
FMN8	Simulation Lists Debit Position
FMN9	Posted Debit Position List
FMNA	Display CBA Rules
FMNB	CBA Budget Objects
FMND	Actual Distribution in CBA
FMNG	CE: Actual Distr. and Integration
FMNI	Integration with the Budget
FMNK	Copy Collective Expenditure
FMNL	Delete Collective Expenditure Rules
FMNM	Budget Transfer in CBA
FMNO	Number range maintenance: FMCJ_BELNR
FMNP	Maintain CBA Rules
FMNR	Assgt of SN-BUSTL to Coll. Expend.
FMNS	Display CBA Rules
FMNSD	Rebuild FM Open Item of SD Orders
FMNSDN	Reconstruction of Sales Orders
FMNU	Maintain CBA Rules
FMNV	Fast Data Entry Distribution Basis
FMOD	Override FM Update Date
FMOPER	Open Budgeting Periods
FMP2	Delete Financial Budget Version
FMPAYCORR	FM Payment lines correction program
FMPAYD	Process Payment Distribution

FMPEBADJ	Tax Adjustments
FMPEBTIL	Document Statement
FMPEBTTL	Tax Totals
FMPEP	Multiple Budget Entry
FMPF	Change Chart of Commitment Items
FMPG	Change Chart of Cmmt Items Assgmt
FMPLADM	FI-FM: Planner Profile Maintenance
FMPLCPD	FI-FM: Change Plan Data
FMPLDPD	FI-FM: Change Plan Data
FMPLLC	FI-FM Change Planning Layout
FMPLLD	FI-FM Display Planning Layout
FMPLLI	FI-FM Create Planning Layout
FMPLSET	FI-FM: Set a Planner Profile
FMPLUP	FI-SL: Excel Upload of Plan Data
FMPO	Payment Directives: Create
FMPOPDERIVE	Principle of Prudence - Customizing
FMPOPDERIVER	Principle of Prudence - Maintenance
FMPOWLEF	POWL for Earmarked Funds
FMPP	Partial Payment by GL-Entities
FMPP_CONTROL	Partial Payment by Fund:Customizing
FMPSO001	Reverse Overdue Deferrals
FMPSO002	Funds Commits.from Standing Rqsts
FMPSO50	Check Mass Deferral Requests
FMPSOSA	Process Petty Amounts
FMPU_R_MIG_ODB_ANA	Analysis of Open Document Bundle
FMPU_R_MIG_ODB_DISP	Display Worklist
FMPU_R_MIG_ODB_RP	Reconstruct Open Document Bundle
FMR0	Reconstruct Parked Documents
FMR1	Actual/Commitment Report
FMR2	Actual/Commitment per Company Code
FMR3	Plan/Actual/Commitment Report
FMR4	Plan/Commitment Report w.Hierarchy
FMR5A	12 Period Forecast: Actual and Plan
FMR6A	Three Period Display: Plan/Actual
FMRA	Access Report Tree
FMRB	Access Report Tree
FMRBCD	FM RIB change document number ranges
FMRBCPY	Copy RIB Rules
FMRBDEL	Delete Master Data for RIB
FMRBDERIMD	Assign Proposal for RIB Master Data
FMRBDERIMDR	Deriv. Rules, Strat. for RIB Rules
FMRBDERIRO	Derive RIB Object From Budget Addr.
FMRBDERIROR	Derivation Rules, Deriv. of RIB Obj.
FMRBGENMD	Generate Master Data for RIB
FMRBIDXREC	Reconstruct Index for RIB
FMRBMON01	Overview of RIB Values
FMRBREINIT	Re-Initialize RIB Ledgers
FMRBRULE	Edit Single Rule for RIB
FMRBRULEHIS	Display Change History for RIB Rules
FMRBRULEHISDEL	Delete Change History for RIB Rules
FMRC	Reason codes for penalties (report)
FMRC21	Reconciliation of Earmarked Funds
FMRC22	Reconciliation of Purchase Orders
FMRC23	Reconciliation of Purch. Requisition

FMRESV_EF_COMP	Earmarked funds set to complete
FMRESV_EF_CREATE	Create Earmarked funds for Mat. Res.
FMREW	Earmarked Funds: Enhancement Wizard
FMRE_ARCH	Archive Earmarked Funds
FMRE_EWU01	Earmarked Funds: Euro Preprocessing
FMRE_EWU02	Earmarked Funds: Euro Postprocessing
FMRE_KERLK	Close Earmarked Funds
FMRE_SERLK	Close Earmarked Funds
FMROD	Recurring Obligations Overdue Check
FMROP	Post Recurring Obligations
FMRP18	Clear Subsequent Postings
FMRPKFCHECK	Comparison of Key Figures(Reporting)
FMRPWT	Revenue Posting from Withholding Tax
FMRP_2FMB4001	Commitments/Actuals
FMRP_2FMB4002	Assigned Funds
FMRP_3FMB4001	Annual Budget
FMRP_3FMB4002	Overall Budget
FMRP_3FMB4003	Budget: Period Display
FMRP_3FMB4004	Assigned Funds (Annual Budget)
FMRP_3FMB4005	Assigned Funds (Overall Budget)
FMRP_3FMB4006	Assigned Fds (Releases, Annual Bdgt)
FMRP_3FMB4007	Assigned Fds (Releases,Overall Bdgt)
FMRP_CI_SET_HIER	Create CI Set Hier. from Master Data
FMRP_FC_SET_HIER	Create FC Set Hier. from Master Data
FMRP_RFFMAV01X	Annual Budget
FMRP_RFFMAV02X	Overall Budget
FMRP_RFFMAV03X	Budget Deficits with Expenditures
FMRP_RFFMAV04X	Budget Deficits for Revenues
FMRP_RFFMAV05X	Cross Assignments and Outside Usages
FMRP_RFFMBWBM	BW: Text-Upload
FMRP_RFFMCE01	Monitor for Cover Eligibility
FMRP_RFFMCE11	Overview of Cover Pools with FMAA
FMRP_RFFMCE12	Overview of Cover Pools
FMRP_RFFMCE13	Overview Revenue Cover Pool
FMRP_RFFMCE21	FMAA Subj. to Cvr to FMAA Ent.to Cvr
FMRP_RFFMCE22	Ent. to Cvr to Subj. to Cvr FMAA
FMRP_RFFMCE23	Subj. to cover to Expend. Cover Pool
FMRP_RFFMCE31	Rules f. Revenues Increasing Budget
FMRP_RFFMCE32	Rules for Revenues Cover Pools
FMRP_RFFMCE41	Collective Expenditure FM Acct Asgts
FMRP_RFFMEP1AX	All Postings
FMRP_RFFMEP1BX	Annual Budget
FMRP_RFFMEP1CX	CO Postings
FMRP_RFFMEP1FX	FI Postings
FMRP_RFFMEP1GX	Yr End Closing: Cmmts/Bdgt Carrd Fwd
FMRP_RFFMEP1OX	Commitments and Funds Transfers
FMRP_RFFMEP2AX	PBOF - Commts/Actuals Line Items
FMRP_RFFMEP2BX	Overall Budget
FMRP_RFFMEP30X	PBOF - Annual Bdgt vs Cmmts/Acts LIs
FMRP_RFFMEP31X	PBOF - Overall Bgt vs Cmmts/Acts LIs
FMRP_RFFMEP3GX	Year-End Clsg: Preselected Budget
FMRP_RFFMEP4BX	Periodical Display
FMRP_RFFMTO10X	Commitment/Actual Totals Records
FMRP_RFFMTO20X	Additional Revenues

FMRP_RFFMTO30X	PBOF - Ann.Bdgt vs Cmmts/Acts Totals
FMRP_RFFMTO31X	PBOF - Ovrl Bgt vs Cmmts/Acts Totals
FMRP_RFFMTO50	Annual Budget: List
FMRP_RW_BUDCON	Budget Consumption Report
FMRP_RW_BUDGET	Budget Report
FMRP_RW_BUDVER	Budget Version Comparison
FMRP_RW_COVRGRP	Budget Consumption in Cover Groups
FMRP_RW_EFFYEAR	Budget Overview by Year of Cash Eff.
FMRULES	FM Objects: Predefined Rules
FMRW	Budget Entry Documents
FMRY	Annual budget
FMRZ	Overall Budget
FMSA	Create Funds Center in FM Area
FMSB	Change Funds Center in FM Area
FMSC	Display Funds Center in FM Area
FMSD	Change Funds Ctr/Hierarchy Variant
FMSE	Display Hierarchy Variant/Funds Ctr
FMSF	Change Funds Ctr Hierarchy Variant
FMSG	Change Assignment Fnds Ctr Hier.Var.
FMSGDERIVE	Fund message: customizing
FMSGDERIVER	Fund message: customizing
FMSGLBL	Customize US BL SGL
FMSGLCLASS	SGL Account classification
FMSHERLOCK	Processing Clarification Cases
FMSHERLOCK_ADD_D	Clarification WL: Add Documents
FMSK	Commitment Item Check
FMSL	Change Cmmt Item: Mass Processing
FMSPDERIVE	Account Distributions derive: steps
FMSPDERIVER	Account Distributions derive: values
FMSPLITMAINT	Maintain Acct Asst Distribtn Rules
FMSPLIT_EXPRESS_INST	Quick installation FI-SL
FMSPLIT_TABLE_INST	Maintain FI-SL tables
FMSRCICHNG	Reassign Standing Request
FMSS	Display Status Assignment
FMST	Statistical report for PPA
FMSU	Change Status Assignment
FMSX	Output of Funds Center to UNIX file
FMSY	Create Funds Center Using UNIX
FMTB	Transfer Commitment/Actuals to FI-BL
FMTEXT	Budget Text Organizer
FMTFDERIVE	FM Object Assignment - Customizing
FMTFDERIVER	G/L Acct Deriv. Rules - Maintenance
FMTFR	HHM Object Assignment - Maintenance
FMTR	FM budgetary ledger trace
FMU0	Display Funds Reservation Doc.Types
FMU1	Maintain Funds Reservation Doc.Types
FMU2	Display Funds Reservtn Fld Variants
FMU3	Maintain Funds Resvtn Field Variants
FMU4	Display Funds Reservation Fld Groups
FMU5	Maintain Funds Reservatn Fld Groups
FMU6	Display Funds Reservtn Field Selctn
FMU7	Maintain Funds Resvtn Field Selctn
FMU8	Display Template Type for Fds Resvtn
FMU9	Maintain Template Type for Fds Resvn

SAP Transaction Codes – Volume One

FMUA	Dispay Fds Res.Template Type Fields
FMUB	Maintain Fds Res.Template Type Flds
FMUC	Display Funds Res. Reference Type
FMUD	Maintain Funds Res.Reference Type
FMUE	Display Funds Res.Ref.Type Fields
FMUF	Maintaine Fds Rsvtn Ref.Type Fields
FMUG	Display Reasons for Decision
FMUH	Maintain Reasons for Decisions
FMUI	Display Groups for Workflow Fields
FMUJ	Maintain Groups for Workflow Fields
FMUK	Display Fields in Groups for WF
FMUL	Maintain Fields in Groups for WF
FMUM	Display Field Selctn ->Variant/Group
FMUN	Display Field Seln->Variant/Group
FMUSFG1	USFG Derivation - Customize
FMUSFG2	USFG Derivation - Maintain
FMUV	Funds Resvtn Field Status Var.Asst
FMV1	Create Forecast of Revenue
FMV2	Change Forecast of Revenue
FMV3	Display Forecast of Revenue
FMV4	Approve Forecast of Revenue
FMV5	Change FM Acct Asst in Fcst of Rev.
FMV6	Reduce Forecast of Revenue Manually
FMVA01	Collective Prcssng Value Adjustments
FMVABD	Define Funds Management Validation
FMVPM1	Create Forecast of Rev. Value Adjmt.
FMVPM2	Change Forecast of Rev. Value Adjmt.
FMVPM3	Display Forecast of Rev. Value Adjmt
FMVPM4	Approve forecast of rev. value adjmt
FMVT	Fund Balance Carryforward
FMW1	Create Funds Block
FMW2	Change Funds Block
FMW3	Display Funds Block
FMW4	Approve Funds Blocking
FMW5	Change FM Acct Asst in Funds Blkg
FMWA	Create Funds Transfer
FMWB	Change Funds Transfer
FMWC	Display Funds Transfer
FMWD	Approve Funds Transfer
FMWE	Change FM Acct Asst in Funds Trsfr
FMWHEREUSED	Where-Used FM Assignments
FMWPM1	Create Fund Block for Value Adjustmt
FMWPM2	Change Fund Block for Value Adjustmt
FMWPM3	Display Funds Block for Value Adjst.
FMWPM4	Approve Fund Block for Value Adjust.
FMX1	Create Funds Reservation
FMX2	Change Funds Reservation
FMX3	Display Funds Reservation
FMX4	Approve Funds Reservation
FMX5	Change FM Acct Asst in Funds Resvn
FMX6	Funds Reservation: Manual Reduction
FMXPM1	Funds Reservation: Create Value Adj.
FMXPM2	Funds Reservation: Change Value Adj.
FMXPM3	Funds Reservation: Displ. Value Adj.

FMXPM4	Funds Reserv.: Approve Value Adjust.
FMY1	Create Funds Commitment
FMY2	Change Funds Commitment
FMY3	Display Funds Precommitment
FMY4	Approve Funds Precommitment
FMY5	Change FM Acct Asst in Funds Prcmmt
FMY6	Reduce Funds Precommitment Manually
FMYC	Funds Management Control
FMYC02	Reassignment for canceling Funds
FMYC03DERIVE	FM Object Assignment - Customizing
FMYCDERIVE	FM Object Assignment - Customizing
FMYCR	HHM Object Assignment - Maintenance
FMYC_ASSIGN	Assign Derivation Strategy
FMYC_CFBCOM	Closing Operations: Cmmt Budget (CB)
FMYC_CFBPAY	Clsg Operations: Bdgt for Cmmt (PB)
FMYC_CFCCOM	FM Closing Operations: Cmmt (CB)
FMYC_CFCPAY	FM Closing Operations: Cmmt (PB)
FMYC_CFPARAM	Closing Ops: Carryforward Parameters
FMYC_CFPCOM	Closing Ops: Residual Commt Budget
FMYC_CFPPAY	Closing Ops: Residual Payment Budget
FMYC_CFRULES	Closing Commt: Assign Carryfwd Par.
FMYC_DEFAULT	FM Closing Operations: Default
FMYC_DELWF	Reset Workflow (Earmarked Funds)
FMYC_VA	Amount Adjustment of Document Chains
FMYC_VA_REV	Undo Value Adjustment for Chains
FMYPM1	Funds Precmmt: Create Value Adjust.
FMYPM2	Funds Precmmt: Change Value Adjust.
FMYPM3	Funds precmmt: Display value adjust.
FMYPM4	Funds Precmmt: Approve Value Adjust.
FMZ1	Create Funds Commitment
FMZ2	Change Funds Commitment
FMZ3	Display Funds Commitment
FMZ4	Approve Funds Commitment
FMZ5	Change FM Acct Asst in Funds Commt
FMZ6	Reduce Funds Commitment Manually
FMZBVT	Carry Forward Balance
FMZK	Day-End Closing Correction User
FMZPM1	Funds commit.: Create value adjust.
FMZPM2	Funds commit.: Change value adjust.
FMZPM3	Funds Cmmt: Display Value Adjustment
FMZPM4	Funds commit: Approve value adjust.
FMZT	Assigning Clsng Op. Grp - FM Areas
FMZZ	Revalue Earmarked Funds
FM_CHECK_VERRECHNUNG	Check Customizing Clearing Control
FM_CISUB_SET1	Create Cmmt Item Substrings Group
FM_CISUB_SET2	Change Cmmt Item Substrings Group
FM_CISUB_SET3	Display Cmmt Item Substrings Group
FM_CLEAR_ACC	Clarification Worklist - FM AcctAsgt
FM_CM_EXCLUDE	Exclude Credit Memo for Pmt Offset
FM_CM_EXCLUDE_CLR	Reset Credit Memo for Payment Offset
FM_DLFI	Deletes FI Documnts Transferred from
FM_DLFM	Deletes all FM Data (fast)
FM_DLOI	Deletes Cmmts Transferred from FM
FM_DLPF	Reconstruct Document Bundle

FM_ENH_FMDERIVE_SETS	Update of FM derivation rules
FM_EURO	Reconciliation After Euro Conversion
FM_EURO_M	Parameter Maintenance for Euro Conv.
FM_FCSUB_SET1	Create Fds. Cntr. Substrings Group
FM_FCSUB_SET2	Change Fds. Cntr. Substrings Group
FM_FCSUB_SET3	Display Fds. Cntr. Substrings Group
FM_FDSUB_SET1	Create Fund Substrings Group
FM_FDSUB_SET2	Change Fund Substrings Group
FM_FDSUB_SET3	Display Fund Substrings Group
FM_FKBER_ACTIVATE_GL	Functional Area as GL Characteristic
FM_FNSUB_SET1	Create Func. Area Substrings Group
FM_FNSUB_SET2	Change Func. Area Substrings Group
FM_FNSUB_SET3	Display Func. Area Substrings Group
FM_FUNCTION	FM: Functional Area
FM_FUNCTION1	FM: Functional Area
FM_FUNCTION2	FM: Functional Area
FM_HHM_ACTIVATE	Activate/Deactivate Funds Management
FM_LGD_H_BSU	Search Help for Bank Turnover
FM_LGD_H_EST	Posting Statistic for Acct Statement
FM_LGD_H_MCE	Multi-Cash Editor
FM_MRP_PR	Update MRP PR's to FM
FM_RC07	Reconcile FI Paymts-> FM Line Items
FM_REVALUATION_PO	Revaluate Purchase Orders
FM_SD07	Display Worklist
FM_SETS_FICTR1	Create Funds Center
FM_SETS_FICTR2	Change Funds Center Group
FM_SETS_FICTR3	Display Funds Center Group
FM_SETS_FIPEX1	Create Commitment Item Group
FM_SETS_FIPEX2	Change Commitment Item Group
FM_SETS_FIPEX3	Display Commitment Item Group
FM_SETS_FUNCTION1	Create Functional Area Group
FM_SETS_FUNCTION2	Change Functional Area Group
FM_SETS_FUNCTION3	Display Functional Area Group
FM_SETS_FUND1	Create Fund Group
FM_SETS_FUND2	Change Fund Group
FM_SETS_FUND3	Display Fund Group
FM_SETS_FUNDPRG1	Create Fund Group
FM_SETS_FUNDPRG2	Change Fund Group
FM_SETS_FUNDPRG3	Display Fund Group
FN-1	No.range: FVVD_RANL (Loan number)
FN-4	Number range maintenance: FVVD_PNNR
FN-5	Number range maintenance: FVVD_SNBNR
FN-6	Number range maintenance: FVVD_RPNR
FN09	Create Borrower's Note Order
FN11	Change borrower's note order
FN12	Display borrower's note order
FN13	Delete borrower's note order
FN15	Create borrower's note contract
FN16	Change borrower's note contract
FN17	Display borrower's note contract
FN18	Payoff borrower's note contract
FN19	Wthdrw/Red. Borrower's Note Contract
FN1A	Create other loan contract
FN1V	Create other loan contract

FN20	Create borrower's note offer
FN21	Change borrower's note offer
FN22	Display borrower's note offer
FN23	Delete borrower's note offer
FN24	Activate borrower's note offer
FN2A	Change other loan application
FN2V	Change other loan contract
FN30	Create policy interested party
FN31	Change policy interested party
FN32	Display policy interested party
FN33	Delete policy interested party
FN34	Policy interested party in applic.
FN35	Policy interested party in contract
FN3A	Display other loan application
FN3V	Display other loan contract
FN40	Create other loan interested party
FN41	Change other loan interested party
FN42	Display other loan interested party
FN43	Delete other loan interested party
FN44	Other loan interest.party in applic.
FN45	Other loan interested prty in cntrct
FN4A	Wthdrw/Reduce Other Loan Application
FN4V	Withdraw/Reduce Other Loan Contract
FN5A	Other loan application in contract
FN5V	Payoff other loan contract
FN61	Create collateral value
FN62	Change collateral value
FN63	Display collateral value
FN80	Enter manual debit position
FN81	Change manual debit position
FN82	Display manual debit position
FN84	Change waiver
FN85	Display Waiver
FN87	Change Write-Off Debit Position
FN88	Display Write-Off Debit Position
FN8A	Manual Entry: Unscheduled Repayment
FN8B	Manual Entry: Other Bus. Operations
FN8C	Enter Single Postings
FN8D	Post Planned Records
FN8X	Business Operations: Workplace
FNA0	Policy application in contract
FNA1	Create Mortgage Offer
FNA2	Change Mortgage Offer
FNA3	Display Mortgage Loan Offer
FNA4	Mortgage Offer Withdrawal
FNA5	Mortgage Offer in Contract
FNA6	Create Policy Offer
FNA7	Change Policy Offer
FNA8	Display Policy Offer
FNA9	Policy Offer Withdrawal
FNAA	Reactivation of Deleted Mort. Offer
FNAB	Reactivation of Deleted Mort.Applic.
FNAC	Reactivate deleted mortgage contract
FNAD	Reactivation of Deleted Policy Offer

FNAE	Reactivation of Deleted Policy Appl.
FNAG	Reactvtn of Deleted Other Loan Offer
FNAH	Reactivate del. other loan int.party
FNAI	Reactivate deleted other loan cntrct
FNAK	Select File Number
FNAL	Reactivate deleted BNL contract
FNAM	Reactivate deleted policy contract
FNARCADMIN	Archiving Administration
FNARCANALYZE	Check Whether Docs Can Be Archived
FNARCEXCL	Set /Delete Archiving Lock
FNARCHIVING	Loan Document Archiving
FNARCSTATUS	Display Archiving Status
FNASL	Loans: Account Analysis
FNASSIGN_COND_X	Workplace: Condition Assignment
FNASSIGN_INL_COND_X	Workplace Cond. Assgnmnt Inst. Loan
FNASSIGN_LOC_COND_X	Workplace Condition Assignment (LoC)
FNB1	Transfer to a Loan
FNB2	Transfer from a Loan
FNB3	Document Reversal - Loans
FNB8	BAV Information
FNB9	BAV transfer
FNBD	Loans-Automatic bal.sheet transfer
FNBG	Guarantee charges list
FNBT	Balance Sheet Transfer
FNBU	DARWIN- Loans accounting menu
FNCD	Transfer Customizing for Dunning
FNCL	Consumer Loan
FNCL_ADMIN	Consumer Loan Administration
FNCL_DISPLAY	Display Consumer Loan
FNCL_EDIT	Change Consumer Loan
FNCNCL	Delete Rescission Indicator
FNCOT_CHNG	Change Condition Table
FNCOT_CREA	Create Condition Table
FNCOT_DISP	Display Condition Table
FNCOT_INL_CHNG	Change Condition Table
FNCOT_INL_CREA	Create Condition Table
FNCOT_INL_DISP	Display Condition Table
FNCOT_LOC_CHNG	Change Condition Table
FNCOT_LOC_CREA	Create Condition Table
FNCOT_LOC_DISP	Display Condition Table
FNCOT_LOS_CHNG	Change Condition Table
FNCOT_LOS_CREA	Create Condition Table
FNCOT_LOS_DISP	Display Condition Table
FNCP1	Generate Change Pointers Manually
FNCP3	Display change pointers
FNCP4	Reorganize change pointers
FNCW1	Responsibilities for Agent Assgnment
FNCW2	Administrative Responsibility
FNCW3	Assign Agents to Tasks
FNCW4	Activate/Deactivate Workflow
FNDD	Convert Dunning Data in Dunn.History
FNDEF_PAST_DUE	Display Open Items After Due Date
FNDOCSSHOW	Display Individual Documents
FNEN	Create Loan

FNENALG	Create General Loan
FNENHYP	Create Mortgage Loan
FNENPOL	Create Policy Loan
FNENSSD	Create Borrower's Note Loan
FNESRIN01	CML: Invoice Printing
FNESRNRR	Number Range Maint.: FVVD_ESRIN
FNESRTDT049E	CML Corr.: Posting Area - Part. No.
FNESRTDTZB0A	CML Corr.: Seq. Invoice Printing
FNETSCA2	Customer: Change Address
FNETSCB1	Customer: Create Bank Details
FNETSCB2	Customer: Change Bank Details
FNETSCB6	Customer: Delete Bank Details
FNETSVA2	Vendor: Change Address
FNETSVB1	Vendor: Create Bank Details
FNETSVB2	Vendor: Change Bank Details
FNETSVB6	Vendor: Delete Bank Details
FNEXP	Export Interface Loans
FNEXP_DET_DATA	CML: Loans Pooling for Synd Mgmt
FNF1	Rollover: Create file
FNF2	Rollover: Change file
FNF3	Rollover: Display file
FNF4	Rollover: Fill file
FNF9	Rollover: Evaluations
FNFO	ISIS: Create file
FNFP	ISIS: Change file
FNFQ	ISIS: Display file
FNFR	ISIS: Fill file
FNFT	Rollover: File evaluation
FNFU	Rollover: Update file
FNG2	Total Loan Commitment
FNG3	Loan Commitment
FNGEN_PRODUCT_ATTR	Processing Attrib. for Loans General
FNGEN_PRODUCT_CHNG	Changing Products for Loans General
FNGEN_PRODUCT_CREA	Creating Products for Loans in Genrl
FNI1	Create mortgage application
FNI2	Change mortgage application
FNI3	Display Mortgage Loan Application
FNI4	Mortgage Application Withdrawal
FNI5	Mortgage application to offer
FNI6	Mortgage application in contract
FNIA	Create inquiry
FNIB	Change inquiry
FNIC	Display Inquiry
FNID	Deactivate Interested Party
FNIE	Reactivate Interested Party
FNIH	Decision-making
FNIJ	Create credit standing
FNIK	Change Credit Standing
FNIL	Display Credit Standing
FNIN	Create collateral value
FNINL	Edit Installment Loan
FNINL_DISPLAY	Display Installment Loan
FNINL_EDIT	Change Installment Loan
FNINL_PRODUCT_ATTR	Process Attribs for Install. Loans

FNINL_PRODUCT_ATTR_D	Display Attributes for Inst. Loans
FNINL_PRODUCT_CHNG	Changing Products for Instllmt Loans
FNINL_PRODUCT_COMP	Compare Products for Install. Loans
FNINL_PRODUCT_COMP_C	Comp. Products Instlmt Loans by Clnt
FNINL_PRODUCT_CREA	Create Products for Install. Loans
FNINL_PRODUCT_DEL	Delete Installment Loan Products
FNINL_PRODUCT_DISP	Display Products for Install. Loans
FNINV_ACC_DISP	Display Investor Contract
FNIO	Change collateral value
FNIP	Display collateral value
FNK0	Multimillion Loan Display (GBA14)
FNK1	Loans to Managers (GBA15)
FNKO	Cond.types - Cond.groups allocation
FNKWGFLAG	Maintain GBA Reporting Indicator
FNL1	Rollover: Create Main File
FNL2	Rollover: Change Main File
FNL3	Rollover: Displ. Main File Structure
FNL4	New business
FNL5	New business
FNL6	New business
FNLOC_PRODUCT_ATTR	Process Attributes for LoC
FNLOC_PRODUCT_ATTR_D	Display Attributes for LoC
FNLOC_PRODUCT_CHNG	Change Products - Lines of Credit
FNLOC_PRODUCT_COMP	Compare Products - Lines of Credit
FNLOC_PRODUCT_COMP_C	Compare Products - LoC Using Client
FNLOC_PRODUCT_CREA	Create Products - Lines of Credit
FNLOC_PRODUCT_DEL	Delete Products - Lines of Credit
FNLOC_PRODUCT_DISP	Display Products for Lines of Credit
FNLOS_PRODUCT_ATTR	Proc. of Attrs for Aquisition Syst.
FNLOS_PRODUCT_ATTR_D	No. of Attrib. for Aquisition System
FNLOS_PRODUCT_CHNG	Change Products for Aquisition Syst.
FNLOS_PRODUCT_COMP	Compare Products for Aquisition Syst
FNLOS_PRODUCT_COMP_C	Compare Prod. for Aqu. Using Client
FNLOS_PRODUCT_CREA	Create Products for Aquisition Syst.
FNLOS_PRODUCT_DEL	Delete Products in Aquisition System
FNLOS_PRODUCT_DISP	No. of Products for Aquisition Syst.
FNLS_ACTM	Set Status Actual Completed
FNLS_CONTS	Reset Planned Completed to Contract
FNLS_PLANM	Set Status Planned Completed
FNLS_PLANS	Set Status Planned Completed
FNM1	Automatic Posting
FNM1P	Automatic Posting (Parallel.)
FNM1S	Automatic Posting - Single
FNM2	Balance sheet transfer
FNM3	Loans reversal module
FNM4	Undisclosed assignment
FNM5	Automatic debit position simulation
FNM6	Post Interest on Arrears
FNMA	Partner data: Settings menu
FNMD	Submenu General Loans
FNME	Loans management menu
FNMEC	Loans Management Menu
FNMH	Loans management menu
FNMI	Loans information system

FNMO	Loans Menu Policy Loans
FNMP	Rollover
FNMS	Loans Menu Borrower's Notes
FNMULTIARC	Archive Document Data
FNN4	Display General File
FNN5	Edit general file
FNN6	Display general main file
FNN7	Edit general main file
FNN8	Display general main file
FNN9	Edit general overall file
FNO1	Create Object
FNO2	Change Object
FNO3	Display Object
FNO5	Create collateral
FNO6	Change collateral
FNO7	Display collateral
FNO8	Create Objects from File
FNO9	Create Collateral from File
FNP0	Edit rollover manually
FNP4	Rollover: Display file
FNP5	Rollover: Edit File
FNP6	Rollover: Display main file
FNP7	Rollover: Edit main file
FNP8	Rollover: Display overall file
FNP9	Rollover: Edit overall file
FNQ2	New Business Statistics
FNQ5	Transact.type - Acct determinat.adj.
FNQ6	Compare Flow Type/Account Determin.
FNQ7	Generate flow type
FNQ8	Automatic Clearing for Overpayments
FNQ9	Int. adjustment run
FNQF	Swiss interest adjustment run
FNQG	Swiss special interest run
FNR0	Loans: Posting Journal
FNR6	Insur.prtfolio trends - NEW
FNR7	Totals and Balance List
FNR8	Account Statement
FNR9	Planning List
FNRA	Other accruals/deferrals
FNRB	Planned Record Update
FNRBP	Update Planned Records (Parallel.)
FNRB_WORKLIST	Update Planned Records from Worklist
FNRC	Accruals/deferrals reset
FNRD	Display incoming payments
FNRE	DO NOT USE:Reverse Incoming Payments
FNRELOADING	Reload Archived Documents
FNRI	Portfolio Analysis Discount/Premium
FNRLZ	Statement of Remaining Terms
FNRS	Reversal Accrual/Deferral
FNS1	Collateral number range
FNSA	Foreign currency valuation
FNSARACUST	Customizing Loan Archiving CML
FNSB	Master data summary
FNSFP	Contracts for the Finance Project

FNSIM_CORR   Simulate Backdated Condition Change
FNSL   Balance reconciliation list
FNSTA   Processing Characteristics
FNT0   Loan correspondence (Switzerland)
FNT1   Automatic Deadline Monitoring
FNT2   Copy text modules to client
FNTDPRODPROFILE   Assign Profiles to Products
FNUB   Treasury transfer
FNV0   Payoff policy contract
FNV1   Create mortgage contract
FNV2   Change mortgage contract
FNV3   Display mortgage contract
FNV4   Contract Full / Partial Recission
FNV5   Disburse Contract
FNV6   Create policy contract
FNV7   Change policy contract
FNV8   Display policy contract
FNV9   Policy Contract WIthdrawal
FNVA   Create paid off contracts
FNVCOMPRESSION   Loans: Document Data Summarization
FNVCOMPREXCL   Set /Delete Archiving Lock
FNVD   Disburse Contract
FNVD_REPAY   Loan Payoff
FNVD_TRL   Disburse Contract
FNVI   Loans: General Overview
FNVM   Change Contract
FNVR   Reactivate Contract
FNVS   Display Contract
FNVW   Withdraw or Reduce Contract
FNV_CSPRD   Credit Spreads for Loan
FNWF   WF Loans Release: List of Work Items
FNWF_REP   Release Workflow: Synchronization
FNWO   Loans: Fast Processing
FNWS   Housing statistics
FNX1   Rollover: Create Table
FNX2   Rollover: Change Table
FNX3   Rollover: Display Table
FNX6   Rollover: Delete Table
FNX7   Rollover: Deactivate Table
FNX8   Rollover: Print Table
FNXD   TR-EDT: Documentation
FNXG   List of Bus. Partners Transferred
FNXU   List of Imported Loans
FNY1   New Business: Create Table
FNY2   New Business: Change Table
FNY3   New Business: Display Table
FNY6   New Business: Delete Table
FNY7   New Business: Deactivate Table
FNY8   New Business: Print Table
FNZA   Account Determination Customizing
FN_1   Table maint. transferred loans
FN_2   Table maintenance transf. partner
FN_AUTODRAFT_PROCESS   Create Auto Debit Files
FN_BILLNUM   Number Range Maintenance Bill Number

SAP Transaction Codes – Volume One

FN_BILL_DISPLAY	Display Bills
FN_BILL_NUM	Number Range Maintenance: FVVD_BILL
FN_BILL_PROCESS	Create Bills
FN_BILL_REPRINT	Print Bills
FN_CBR_INFO	Display Files for Credit Bureau
FN_CBR_PROCESS	Create Files for Credit Bureau
FN_CL_PRODUCT_ATTR	Process Attributes: Consumer Loans
FN_CL_PRODUCT_ATTR_D	Display Attributes: Consumer Loans
FN_CL_PRODUCT_CHNG	Change Products: Consumer Loans
FN_CL_PRODUCT_COMP	Compare Products - Consumer Loans
FN_CL_PRODUCT_COMP_C	Comp.Prods.- Cons.Loans Using Client
FN_CL_PRODUCT_CREA	Create Products: Consumer Loans
FN_CL_PRODUCT_DEL	Delete Products - Consumer Loans
FN_CL_PRODUCT_DISP	Display Products: Consumer Loans
FN_CORR_MASS	Create Annual Interest Statement
FN_DAILY_ACCRUAL	Daily Interest Accrual Display
FN_DERI_COMPANY_CODE	Derivation Rules for Company Code
FN_DERI_CONDITION	Derivation Rules for Condition Table
FN_DERI_ORIGINATOR	Derivation Rules for Originator
FN_DERI_PRODUCT	Derivation Rules for Product
FN_DERI_SALES_ORG	Derivation Rules for Org. Unit
FN_LOANUNITA_ARC_ADM	Archiving Administration LOANREF_A
FN_LOANUNITV_ARC_ADM	Archiving Administration LOANREF_V
FN_LOANUNIT_ARC	Archive Loan Reference Units
FN_LOANUNIT_RELOAD	Reload Loan Reference Units
FN_MIG_CMS	Deletion of Data After Migration CMS
FN_PAY_PROCESS_SUSP	Generate PPO Error Messages
FN_PAY_PROC_PAYOFF	Create Payoff from Overpayment
FN_PAY_STOP	Create Lockbox Stop File
FN_POST_INL	Post Planned Records from Worklist
FN_PPO2	Edit Postprocessing Order
FN_PPO3	Display Postprocessing Order
FN_PPO_CUS_VIEWCALL	PPO Customizing with Component
FN_PPO_VIEWCALL	PPO Customizing with Component
FN_PRODUCT_BAS_ATTYP	Assign Attribute Types
FN_PRODUCT_BAS_CUSAT	Table/Struct.Name f.Cust. Attributes
FN_PRODUCT_BAS_PTYP	Options for Supported Product Cats.
FN_PRODUCT_BAS_TAPT	Assign Trans.to Prod.Cat.& Cond.Type
FN_PRODUCT_KEYP_WORK	Change Key Prefix for Product Key
FN_RULE_COMPANY_CODE	Rule Entries for Company Code
FN_RULE_CONDITION	Rule Entries for Condition Table
FN_RULE_ORIGINATOR	Rule Entries for Loan Originator
FN_RULE_PRODUCT	Rule Entries for Product
FN_RULE_SALES_ORG	Rule Entries for Org. Unit
FN_STOP_ADMIN	Manage Stops
FN_TRLE_CHECK_CUST	Check Cust. for Parallel Posit. Mgmt
FN_TRLE_CML_TRL	Comp. CML-BO and Parallel Pos. Mgmt
FN_TRLE_INIT_VCLASS	Initialization of General Valn Class
FN_TRLE_TEST_INIT	REP: rfvd_test_distributor_init
FN_UPD_FELDAUSW	Update Program for Field Selection
FO/E	Create exception real estate
FO/F	Maintain exception real estate
FO/G	Display exception real estate
FO/H	Create groups except. real estate

FO/I	Change groups except. real estate
FO/J	Display groups except. real estate
FO01	Real estate management leasing
FO03	
FO04	
FO05	
FO08	Reversal input tax distribution
FO10	Reserved for real estate
FO11	Number range maintenance: Land reg.
FO12	Field status: Management contract
FO13	Activate Settlement Unit
FO13U	Activate Settlement Unit
FO14	Land register: Display
FO15	Land register: Change
FO16	Land Register: Create
FO18	Land register: Parameters via MEM ID
FO19	Land register: Parameter trnsfr test
FO1B	Create expert report
FO1C	Change expert report
FO1D	Display expert report
FO1E	Owner Settlement
FO1F	Owner Account Settlement Reversal
FO1G	Correction Items Retirement
FO1I	Post-generate settlement particip.
FO1I_MV	Post-Generate Settlement Particip.
FO1J	Corr.item transfer within asset
FO1K	Reverse CI transfer within asset
FO1L	Repost Input Tax Adjustments
FO20	Reserved for real estate
FO21	Create business entity
FO22	Change business entity
FO23	Display business entity
FO24	Follow-up post. inc.pmnt rejections
FO25	Number Range for Business Entity
FO27	Number Range for Property
FO28	Number Range for Building
FO29	Reset transaction block
FO30	Maintain lease-out
FO31	Create property
FO32	Change property
FO33	Display property
FO35	Create building
FO36	Change building
FO37	Display building
FO38	Change RA: Conds of Active Contracts
FO3B	Selection real.est.obj. for CO sett.
FO3C	Real estate CO settlement
FO3K	Maintain automatic postings accounts
FO3L	Read lease-out flow archive
FO40	Reserved for real estate
FO49	Check index for real estate
FO4B	Stand.settings rental agreemnt analy
FO4C	Stand.settings rental agreemnt analy
FO4D	Stand.Settings Bus.Entity Analysis

SAP Transaction Codes – Volume One

FO4E	Standard settings property analysis
FO4F	Standard settings building analysis
FO4G	Reporting tree VI12
FO4H	Reporting tree VI13
FO4I	Reporting tree VI14
FO4J	Reporting tree VI15
FO4K	VI16 report tree
FO4L	Mainten.curr.conversion type TMR
FO4M	Translation Tool - Drilldown Report
FO4N	Number range maint.: RE_INVOICE
FO4O	Stand.settings partner analysis
FO4P	Partner analysis-new selection
FO4Q	Std settings land register analysis
FO4W	Test monitor - Real Estate reports
FO4Y	Read lease-out archive
FO5G	Real Estate report list
FO5O	Import reports
FO5P	Generate reports
FO5Q	Rental Units Standard Analysis
FO5R	Real Estate report layouts
FO5T	Lease-Out Analysis: New Selection
FO5V	Print New LO Number Correspondence
FO60	Reserved for real estate
FO61	Create settlement unit
FO61U	Create Master Settlement Unit
FO62	Change settlement unit
FO62U	Change Master Settlement Unit
FO63	Display settlement unit
FO63U	Display Master Settlement Unit
FO65	Overview of Settlement Units
FO66	Overview cost collectors for SU
FO67	SU Overview for Rental Unit
FO6A	Real estate field status application
FO6B	Display real est. applic.fld select.
FO6C	Rental request field status
FO6D	Set delete flag for CU
FO6E	Change co-applicant field selection
FO6F	Display co-applicant field selection
FO6G	No.range maintenance: FVVI_VWVTR
FO6H	Field Status: Rental Request
FO6I	Reporting tree VI11
FO6J	Maintain Real Estate Report Tree
FO70	Reserved for real estate
FO77	Number Range Maintenance: FVVI_NKSET
FO79	Maintain Rent Adjustm.History
FO7P	Property Standard Analysis
FO7Q	Buildings Standard Analysis
FO7R	Reporting tree VI10
FO7S	Maintain Batch Variants
FO7T	Rental unit analysis user settings
FO7U	Rntl agrmnt analysis user settings
FO7V	Standard analysis land register
FO7W	Reorganize Report Data
FO7Y	Tenant acct evaluation

FO80	RA debit positions - Log
FO81	Display Rent Adjustm.History
FO82	Create Management Contract
FO83	Change Management Contract
FO84	Display management contract
FO85	Simulate debit position/man.contract
FO86	Change active admin.contract fees
FO87	Change cond.act.cntrcts for bckgrnd
FO88	Management contract debit position
FO8A	Real est. trans.records accr./defer.
FO8B	RealEstate accr./defer.- Reversal
FO8C	Real Estate CO Indiv. Settlement
FO8D	Report: Displ.inp.tax distributions
FO8DA	Input Tax Distribution
FO8DB	Input Tax Distribution Posting
FO8DM	Input Tax Distribution Reversal
FO8DN	Input Tax Distribution Log
FO8E	Create admin.contract event
FO8F	Change admin.contract event
FO8G	Display admin.contract event
FO8H	Admin.costs acct sttlmnt simulation
FO8I	Management Costs Settlement
FO8J	No.range maintenance:FVVI_VWEVT
FO8K	Carry out real estate accr./defer.
FO8L	Changed Option Rate Ratios
FO8N	OptRte-Relevant Changes RU / LO
FO8P	Reset D tape data
FO8Q	Incoming payments by posting date
FO8R	Reset delete flag for SU
FO8S	Create measurement doc.
FO8T	Change Measurement Document
FO8U	Display Measurement Document
FO8V	Collective Entry of MeasDocuments
FO8W	Change Measurement Documents
FO8X	Display Measurement Documents
FO8Y	Collective Entry of MeasDocuments
FO8Z	Change Measurement Documents
FO91	VICP report tree
FO94	Number range maintenance:FVVI_BEBE
FO95	Create correction items
FO96	Change correction items
FO97	Display correction items
FO98	Delete correction items
FO9A	Display Measurement Documents
FO9B	Create measurement doc.
FO9C	Change Measurement Document
FO9D	Display Measurement Document
FO9E	Collective Entry of MeasDocuments
FO9F	Call reporting tree VI01
FO9G	Call reporting tree VI02
FO9H	Call reporting tree VI03
FO9I	Call reporting tree VI04
FO9J	Call reporting tree VI05
FO9K	Import Reports from Client

FO9L	Import Forms from Client 000
FO9M	Transport reports
FO9N	Transport Forms
FO9O	Overview of Reports
FO9P	Real estate: Create select.version
FO9Q	Real estate: Change select. version
FO9R	Real estate: Display select.version
FO9S	Real estate: Schedule select.version
FO9T	Selection Version Tree Real Estate
FO9U	User-Spec. Sel.Vers.Tree Real Estate
FO9V	Reporting tree VI06
FO9W	Reporting tree VI07
FO9X	Maintain report selection
FO9Y	Business Entities Standard Analysis
FO9Z	Reporting tree VI09
FOA0	Simulate Index Rent Adjustment
FOA1	Calculate rent adjustment: Index
FOA2	Rent adjustemnt: Display logs
FOA3	Calculate rent adjustment: CH
FOA4	Rent Adjustment - Reserved
FOA5	Activate rent adjustment: Index
FOA6	Rent adjustment letter: Index
FOA7	Rent adjustment logs: Index
FOA8	Dispay rent adjustments: Index
FOAA	Calculate rent adj.: Comp.apartment
FOAB	Assign RU to comparative group
FOABG	General contract accrual/deferral
FOAC	Activate rent adjustment: Comp.aprt.
FOAD	Display rent adjustment: Comp.apart.
FOAE	Simulate rent adjust.: Comp.apartmnt
FOAF	Comparative rnt rnt. adj. coll.print
FOAG	Rent adj. logs: Comparative apart.
FOAH	Calculate rent adj.: Free adj.
FOAI	Activate rent adj.: Free adjustment
FOAIMMO	Maintain AIMMO Indicator
FOAJ	Display rent adj.: Free adjustment
FOAK	Rent adjustment letter: Free adj.
FOAL	Display rent adjustment: Free adj.
FOAM	Simulate rent adjustment: Free adj.
FOAN	Activate rent adjustment: All methds
FOAO	Reverse rent adjustment: All methods
FOAP	Display rent adjustment logs
FOAPCUST00	Activation of Application FI-CDA
FOAPLOG01	Analyze Application Log
FOAPLOG02	Analyze Application Log
FOAPPROC01	Transfer Credits and Payments
FOAPPROC02	Clear Invoices
FOAQ	Calculate rent adj.: Rep. rent list
FOAR	Simulate rent adj.: Rep. rent list
FOAR00	Business Partner Configuration Menu
FOAR01	REAR: Applications
FOAR02	REAR: Field Groups
FOAR03	REAR: Views
FOAR04	REAR: Sections

FOAR05	REAR: Pictures
FOAR06	REAR: Screen Sequences
FOAR07	REAR: Events
FOAR08	REAR: GUI Standard Functions
FOAR09	REAR: GUI Additional Functions
FOAR0A	Create Rental Request
FOAR0B	Change Rental Request
FOAR0C	Display Rental Request
FOAR10	Application archiving
FOAR100	Management contract archiving
FOAR101	Management of mgt contract archives
FOAR103	Mngt contract archiving prep.prog.
FOAR11	Management of application archives
FOAR12	REAR: Field Modification Criteria
FOAR13	REAR: Activities
FOAR14	REAR: Field Assignment Screen->DB
FOAR15	REAR: Application Transactions
FOAR16	REAR: Tables
FOAR18	REAR: Activity Field Modification
FOAR1A	Transfer Rental Units into Offers
FOAR1B	Offer Overview
FOAR1C	Overview of Requests
FOAR20	Offer archiving
FOAR21	Management of offer archives
FOAR25	REAR: Authorization Types
FOAR26	REAR: Field Groups for Authorization
FOAR27	REAR: Search
FOAR2A	Rental Request -> Find Offer Object
FOAR2B	Offer Object -> Find Rental Request
FOAR30	Flow archiving
FOAR30R1	Read Lease-Out Flow Archive
FOAR31	Management of flow archives
FOAR33	Flow archiving preparatory program
FOAR40	Rental agreement archiving
FOAR40R1	Read lease-out archive
FOAR41	Management of rntl agrmnt archives
FOAR43	Rntl agrmnt archiving prep.program
FOAR45	LO archiving index creation
FOAR46	LO archiving index deletion
FOAR50	Archiving rental units
FOAR51	Managing rental unit archives
FOAR53	Rental unit archiving prep.program
FOAR60	Building archiving
FOAR61	Managing building archives
FOAR63	Building archives prep. program
FOAR70	Property archiving
FOAR71	Managing property archives
FOAR73	Property archiving prep.program
FOAR80	Archiving business entities
FOAR81	Managing business entity archives
FOAR83	Business entity archiving prep.prog.
FOAR90	Settlement unit archiving
FOAR91	Managing settlement unit archives
FOAR93	Settlement unit archiving prep.prog.

FOARBW	Rental Request Number Range
FOARNOTE	Rental Request: Notes
FOAROF	Offer Number Range
FOART0	RE: REsearch RE Market Place
FOART1	REsearch: Concordance Eval. Test
FOART2	REsearch: Administration Web-User
FOAS	Activate RLR Rent Adjustment
FOAT	Display Active RLR Rent Adjustment
FOAU	Rep.rnt list rnt increase coll.print
FOAV	Display RLR Rent Adjustment Log
FOAW	Print apartment valuatn Netherlands
FOAY	Balance List by Real Estate Object
FOAZ	Display Active Rent Adj. ALL
FOB0	Number range maintenance:FVVI_SOID
FOB1	Lease-Out One-Time Postings
FOB4	Check Real Estate Acct Determination
FOB9	Rent Adj. - Reminder Print ALL
FOBA	RE archive residence times
FOBB	Rent Adj. - Reminder Print CGP
FOBC	Real estate: Delete transaction data
FOBC72	Business partner: Notes (role)
FOBC73	bc73
FOBD	Rent Adj. - Simulate Amount Transfer
FOBE	Rent Adj. - Calculate Amount Transf.
FOBF	Rent Adj. - Activate Amount Transf.
FOBG	Rent Adj. - Reverse Amount Transfer
FOBH	Rent Adj. - Display Amount Transfer
FOBI	Rent Adj.- Display Amnt Transfer Log
FOBJ	Rent Adj. - Reminder Print RLR
FOBK	Copy real estate company codes
FOBL	Rent Adj. - Reminder Print EXP
FOBM	Rent Adj. - Reminder Print CEA
FOBN	Rent Adj. - Reminder Print MOD
FOBO	Rent Adj. - Reminder Print IND
FOBP	Properties: Usage type acc. dev.plan
FOBT	Rent Adj. - Reminder Print FAC
FOBW	Rent Adj. - Reminder Print SCS
FOBX	Rent Adj. - Reminder Print FAR
FOBY	Rent Adj. - Reminder Print GAR
FOBZ	Rent Adj. - Reminder Print ACO
FOCNOI	Real Estate: BDN - CN Templates
FOCORRITEM	Correction Items Report
FOCPTL	Overview of Letters and Text Modules
FOCP_COLLATERAL	Print Rental Collateral for LO
FOCP_COLLATERAL_VAL	Corr. Differ. Char: Deposit Types
FOCP_RADJ_ADJMOD_VAL	Corr. Differ. Char: Rent Adj. Modus
FOCP_RADJ_DUNMOD_VAL	Corr. Differ. Char: Rent Adj. Dun.
FOCP_RC_TYPE_VAL	Corr. Differ. Char: LO Type
FOD0	Copy Customizing Cross-IS
FOD1	Copy Real Estate Customizing
FOD2	Copy Customizing for Related Applic.
FOD9	CustDarwinRealEst:Create ac.sttl.var
FODA	Cust.darwinRealEst:Chnge ac.sttl.var
FODB	Cust.darwinRealEst: Disp.ac.sttl.var

FODC	Cust.darwinRealEst:Delete ac.stl.var
FODU	Customizing View T_TZS13 Real Estate
FODZ	Cust. object type status profile
FOE1	Create: Rental Unit
FOE2	Change: Rental Unit
FOE3	Display: Rental Unit
FOE5	Number range maintenance: MIETEINH
FOE6	Run drilldown report
FOE7	Create drilldown report
FOE8	Change drilldown report
FOE9	Display drilldown report
FOEBKA	Display account statement
FOEBL1	Lockbox total report
FOED	Maintain global variable
FOEP	Cust.ISIS Alloc. external roles TZR4
FOEP0001	Actual: Line Items
FOEP0002	Commitment line items
FOEP0003	Line Items - Plan
FOEPA001	Settlement unit actual line items
FOEPA002	Sett. unit commitment line items
FOEPV001	Management contr. actual line items
FOEPV002	Mgt contract commitment line items
FOEPV003	Mgt contract plan line items
FOEU	Create form for real estate report
FOEV	Change form for real estate report
FOEW	Display form for real estate report
FOF9	VIFI report tree
FOFI	Real Estate Management master data
FOFO	Mass release
FOFV	Real estate third-party mgmnt
FOG1	Create Provis. Agreement
FOG2	Change Provis. Agreement
FOG3	Display Provis. Agreement
FOG4	Supplement Provis. Agreement
FOG8	Sign provisional agreements
FOG9	Activate Commercial Lease-Outs
FOGEDI	Building: Direct Input
FOGEGN	Building: Generate Data File
FOGESH	Building: Change Data File
FOGH	Transfer offer to commer.lease-out
FOGRDI	Property: Direct Input
FOGRGN	Property: Generate Data File
FOGRSH	Property: Change Data File
FOGS	Property
FOH1	Create Heating System
FOH2	Change Heating System
FOH3	Display Heating System
FOH9	Management contract: Fee list
FOHA	Import A-tape
FOHB	Post external acct sttlmnt result
FOHBKID	Maintain House Bank Accounts
FOHD	Import D-tape
FOHL	Write M/L-tape
FOHS	Simulate Settlement Result

FOHX	Overview of Extern. Heating Expenses
FOI0	RE Contract: Development Menu
FOI0SCS	RE Contract: Development/Customizing
FOI1	RECN-BDT: Applications
FOI10	RECN-BDT: Search Help
FOI2	RECN-BDT: Field groups
FOI3	RECN-BDT: Views
FOI4	RECN-BDT: Sections
FOI5	RECN-BDT: Screens
FOI6	RECN-BDT: Screen Sequences
FOI7	RECN-BDT: Times
FOI8	RECN-BDT: GUI Standard Functions
FOI9	RECN-BDT: GUI Additional Functions
FOIA	RECN-BDT: Matchcodes
FOIB	RECN-BDT: Field Assignm. Screen->DB
FOIC	Real Estate Management master data
FOID	RECN-Cust: Contract Type -> Adjust.
FOIE	RECN-BDT: Field Modif. Criteria
FOIF	RECN-BDT: Application Transactions
FOIG	RECN-BDT: Tables
FOIH	RECN-Cust: Field Modification Activ.
FOII	RECN-Cust: Field Modific.ContrType
FOIJ	RECN-BDT: Generate Test File (DI)
FOIK	RECN-BDT: Update w/o Dialog
FOIL	RE Contract: Resubmission
FOIM	RE Contract: Create
FOIO	RE Contract: Change
FOIP	RE Contract: Display
FOIQ	RE Contract: Periodic Postings
FOIR	RECN Cust: Screen Configurations
FOIS	Information system
FOIT	Acct Assign. for RE General Contract
FOIU	RECN Cust: User Field Accnt Determ.
FOIV	RECN Cust: Contract Type
FOIW	RECN Cust: Authorization Types
FOIW21	Create PM Notifications in RE
FOIX_NR	Number Range Maintenance: FVVI_RECN
FOIY	RECN Cust: Resubmission Rule
FOIZ	RECN Cust: Field Groups for Author.
FOJ0	Contract: Application Menu
FOJ1	Maintain Comparative Group
FOJ2	Display Comparative Group of Apartm.
FOJ3	Real Estate Implementation Guide
FOJ4	Cash Flow Generator General Contract
FOJ5	Display Contingencies
FOJ6	Correction of VISLID Entries
FOJ7	Correction of T033F Entries
FOJ8	RECN-Cust: Object Part
FOJA	Maintain participation ID
FOJB	Display participation ID
FOJC	RECN Cust: Resubmission Rules
FOJD	RECN-Cust: Contr.Type -> Obj.Type
FOJE	RECN-BDT: Activities
FOJF	RECN-Cust: Acct Determin. Values

FOJF0	LO: Account Determination Values
FOJF1	MC: Account Determination Values
FOJG	RE Contract One-Time Posting
FOJI	RECN Cust: Validation Times
FOJJ	RECN-Cust: ContrTyp Preassignments
FOJK	RECN Cust: Substitution Times
FOJL	RECN Cust: Periods of Notice
FOJM	RECN Cust: Notice Dates
FOJN	RECN Cust: Notice Reasons
FOJO	RECN Cust: Notice Rejection Reasons
FOJP	RECN-BDT: BDT Data Client Copy
FOJQ	RE Contract: Create CN (Legacy Data)
FOJR	RE Contract: Periodic Postings Log
FOJS	RE Customer: Renewal Options
FOJSCS1	Condition Type-> Service Charge Key
FOJSCS10	Change Service Charge Settlement
FOJSCS11	Display Service Charge Settlement
FOJSCS2	Service charge keys
FOJSCS20	RE Contract:Overview of Act. Revenue
FOJSCS21	RE Contract:Overview of Plan Revenue
FOJSCS22	Overview of Missing Sales Reports
FOJSCS25	Missing Sales Report: Correspondence
FOJSCS3	Apportionment Units
FOJSCS30	RE:Rent Adj.-Index Contract Forecast
FOJSCS4	Apportionment Unit <-> Area Type
FOJSCS5	Apprtion. Unit With Extra Attributes
FOJSCS6	Cred. SC Key -> Deb. SC Key
FOJSCS7	Properties of Service Charge Key
FOJSCS8	Maintain Settlement Categories
FOJSCS9	Assign of Plan Index to Actual Index
FOJT	RE Customer: Renewal
FOJU	RE Contract: Maintain Sales Reports
FOJUN	RE Contract: Maintain Sales Reports
FOJUNS	Enter Sales with Condition Types
FOJV	RE Contract: Create Defaults
FOJW	RE Contract: Display Sales Reports
FOJWN	RE Contract: Display Sales Reports
FOJWNS	Display Sales with Condition Types
FOJX	RE Contract: Change Defaults
FOJY	RE Contract: Display Defaults
FOJZ	RE Contract: Contract Data Reporting
FOK0	Maintain key figures
FOK1	Notice of rental agreement
FOK2	Edit Rental Deposit Release
FOK3	Display rental deposit release
FOK4	Edit rental unit inspection
FOK5	Display rental unit inspection
FOK6	Print sec.dep.sttl. for dep.release
FOK7	Mass Notice on Lease-Out
FOKA	RE: Import Planning Layout
FOKB	RE: Transport Planning Layouts
FOKC	Create Cost Element Planning Layout
FOKD	Change Cost Element Planning Layout
FOKE	Display Cost Element Planning Layout

SAP Transaction Codes – Volume One

FOKF	Create Stat. KF Planning Layout
FOKFP	Copy Cash Flow to Plan Version
FOKG	Change Stat. KF Planning Layout
FOKH	Display Stat. KF Planning Layout
FOKIP	Copy Actual->Plan for Real Estate
FOKN	RE: Displ.Planning Stat.Key Figs
FOKO	Check conditions/flow types
FOKOBA	Acct Determination for Cond.Type
FOKOTCH	Check Internal Condition Categories
FOKP	RE: Change Plan.Cost El./Act.Inpt
FOKPP	Copy Plan->Plan for Real Estate
FOKQ	RE: Displ.Plan.Cost Elem/Act.Inpt
FOKR	RE: Change Plan.Prim.Cost Elements
FOKS	RE: Displ.Plan.Primary Cost Elements
FOKT	RE: Change Planning Activ.Input
FOKU	RE: Display Planning Activ.Input
FOKV	RE: Change Plan.Revenue Elements
FOKW	RE: Display Plan.Revenue Elements
FOKX	RE: Change Plan.Stat.Key Figures
FOKY	RE: Display Plan.Stat.Key Figures
FOKZ	RE: Change Plan.Stat.Key Figures
FOL1	LIREM: Report RFVILICL
FOL2	LIREM: Report RFVILICB
FOL3	LIREM: Report RFVILICF
FOL5	LIREM: Report RFVILIRL
FOL6	IRE: one-time postings lease-out
FOL7	IRE: Change record indicator
FOLA	Bulk Print. Resid.Lease-Out
FOLB	Mass Print. Bank Guarantee for LO
FOLC	Mass Print. Garage LO Correspondence
FOLD	Bulk Print. Garage Lease-Out
FOLE	Bulk Print. LO Personal Guarantee
FOLF	Bulk print. resid.RA-correspondence
FOLG	Bulk print.adv.notice of const.chngs
FOLH	Bulk print.rnt incr.due const.chngs
FOLI	Resid. and Garage LO Bulk Printing
FOLJ	FVVI Pop-up for rntl agrmnt printing
FOLK	FVVI Pop-up for addit.letter print.
FOLL	FVVI Pop-up for print of oth.letters
FOLM	Cust. FVVI letters
FOLN	Cust.FVVI letter-module relationship
FOLQ	FVVI RA-Connect.to optical archive
FOLR	FVVI Client copy text modules
FOLS	FVVI Maintain text objects
FOLT	FVVI Maintain text ID's
FOLU	Archive and Corresp.Parameters
FOLW	Allocate application/corr.activity
FOLX	Real estate Alloc. CA -> Letter/role
FOLY	Real estate correspond. activities
FOLZ	Rent adjust.CH:Int.rate per location
FOM4	Maintain rent reaductios
FOM5	Display rent reductions
FOMA	Create modernization measure
FOMAFC	RE:Rent Adj.-Index Contract Forecast

FOMAFCC	RE:Rent Adj.-Index Contract Forecast
FOMASS	Number Range for Mass Changes
FOMB	Change modernization measure
FOMC	Display modernization measuer
FOMC_1	Electr. Account Statement: Test Data
FOMC_2	Electr. Acct Statement: Gen. File
FOMD	Delete modernization measure
FOME	Rntl unit attribute selection (cust)
FOMF	OI list by business entity
FOMG	Repeat run invoice printout
FOMH	Evaluation log invoice printout
FOMKB	Tenant Account Sheet
FOMS	Swiss representative rent list
FOMS1	Maint.Rep.List of Rents (Basic Data)
FOMS2	Maint.Rep.List of Rnts (Value Table)
FOMU	OI Transfer Posting on Tenant Change
FOMY	REst. manual incom.pmnt fast entry
FOMZ	Real Estate Incoming Payments
FON1	Simulate full acct settlement: OC
FON2	Execute service charge settlement:OC
FON3	Execute full acct settlement: HC
FON4	Execute full acct settlement: OC+HC
FON5	Simulate full acct settlement: HC
FON6	Simulate full acct settlement: OC+HC
FON7	Reverse full acct settlement: OC
FON8	Reverse full acct settlement: HC
FON9	Reverse full acct settlement: OC+HC
FONA	Real Estate Management master data
FONH	Reverse External Heating Exp. Sett.
FONK	Number range for SC settlement
FONN	Correspondence SCS/Rntl Agreement
FONU	Serv.charge stt. apportionable costs
FONZ	Tenant account maintenance
FOO1	Reassign Correction Items
FOO7	Cust.heat.costs data medium exchange
FOOA1	Change Object Availability
FOOA2	Display Object Availability
FOOA3	Object Availability - Mass Change
FOOBJECTBROWSER	RE Object Browser
FOOF	Reverse debit pos.management contr.
FOOG	Reverse settl.management contract
FOOH	Invoice / Credit memo owner
FOOL	Maintain heat.oil supply
FOOPTRATES	Option Rate Report
FOOZ	Incoming Pymnts with Residual Items
FOP2	Change Real Estate planning
FOP3	Display Real Estate planning
FOP5	Simulate flat-rate adjustment
FOP6	Calculate flat-rate adjustment
FOP7	Activate flat-rate adjustment
FOP8	Flat-rate adjustment correspondence
FOPA	OI Clearing on Rental Agreements
FOPB	Condition types with acc./def. ID
FOPCBU	Connect User and Person

SAP Transaction Codes – Volume One

FOPCR_MAINTAIN	Settings for Improved Performance
FOPCS_SHM_CUST	Shared Memory Customizing
FOPC_AISLANGUAGE	Import AIS Report Names
FOPC_AIS_CO_REPORT	Import AIS Report Names
FOPC_AS_REORG	Administration Programs
FOPC_CASECUST_CHECK	Case Management Customizing
FOPC_CONSIST_CHECK	Consistency Check on Validity Period
FOPC_CUST_PERS_RESP	Set Logic for Responsible Persons
FOPC_DEFIC_ANA_COPY	Copy Issues for Deficiency Analysis
FOPC_DOC_MONITOR	MIC Documents
FOPC_HR_DEL	Deletion of HR Table Entries
FOPC_HR_LINKS_MIGRAT	Conversion of Links in KPro
FOPC_HR_REBUILD	Rebuild HR Object List
FOPC_SIGNOFF_NOTE	Maintain Note for Sign-Off
FOPC_SOD_CHECK	Segregation of duties check
FOPC_STR_CHANGE	Change MIC
FOPC_STR_CREATE	Create MIC
FOPC_STR_DISPLAY	Display MIC
FOPC_WF_SLG1	Analyze Applicat. Log for Scheduling
FOPD	Check acc./def. reference flow types
FOPE	Copy reference flow types
FOPF	List of reference flow types
FOQ0	Number Range Maintenance: VERGLWOHN
FOQ1	FVVI: Create Ext. Compara. Apartment
FOQ2	FVVI: Change Ext. Compara. Apartment
FOQ3	FVVI: Display Ext. Compara.Apartment
FOQ4	FVVI: Delete Ext. Compara. Apartment
FOQ5	RE: Simulate CH rent adj.
FOQ6	RE: Activate CH rent adjustment
FOQ7	Real estate: CH rent adj: Disp.res.
FOQ8	RE: Display CH rent adj.log
FOQ9	RE: Rent adj. - display CH
FOQA	RE: Calculate GAR rent adj.
FOQB	RE: Activate GAR rent adj.
FOQC	RE: Display active GAR rent adj.
FOQD	Free garage adj.:Tenant letter
FOQE	RE: Display GAR rent adj. log
FOQF	RE: Simulate GAR rent adj.
FOQG	Print rent adjustment Switzerland
FOQH	RE: Calculate FAR rent adj.
FOQI	RE: Activate FAR rent adj.
FOQJ	RE: Display active FAR rent adj.
FOQK	Free resid. adj.: Letter to tenant
FOQL	RE: Display FAR rent adj. log
FOQM	RE: Simulate FAR rent adj.
FOQN	RE: Calculate rent adj. AnyCond.
FOQO	RE: Activate rent adj. Any.Cond.
FOQP	RE: Display act.rent adj.AnyCond.
FOQQ	Adj. surcharges: Letter to tenant
FOQR	RE: Display rent adj.log Any.Cond
FOQS	RE: Simulate rent adj. AnyCond.
FOQU	RE: Simulate MOD rent adj.
FOQV	RE: Activate MOD rent adj.
FOQW	RE: Display active MOD rent adj.

FOQX	RE: Display MOD rent adj. log
FOQY	RE: Reverse MOD rent adj.
FOQZ	RE: Calculate MOD rent adj.
FOR1	Rooms: Maintain
FOR2	Rooms: Display
FOR3	Number range maintenance:FVVI_SRAUM
FOR5	Maintain common rooms in building
FOR6	Display common rooms in building
FOR7	Maintain rooms in RU via building
FOR8	Display rooms in RU via building
FORA	RE: Rent adj. - Calc.expert opin.
FORALSR	Process Returned Debit Memo
FORB	RE: Activate EXOP rent adj.
FORC	RE: Display act.EXOP rent adj.
FORD	RE: Display EXOP rent adj. log
FORE	RE: Simulate EXOP rent adj.
FORF	Rnt adj. as res.of exp.rep.corresp.
FORG	RE: Reverse EXOP rent adj.
FORH	RE: Rent adj. - Simulate CEA
FORI	RE: Rent adj. - Calculate CEA
FORJ	RE: Rent adj. - Activate CEA
FORK	RE: Rent adj. - Reverse CEA
FORL	RE: Rent adj. - Display CEA
FORM	RE: Rent adj. - CEA log
FORN	Rent Adj. - Print CEA
FORN1	Change Renewal Option for Contract
FORN2	RE: Change CN Renewal Option
FOROZ	VI01 reporting tree (IPD)
FORQ	RE: Rent adj. - Simulate area
FORS	RE: Rent adj. - Calculate area
FORS1	Maintain Resubmission
FORS2	Display Resubmission
FORS3	RE: Generate Resubmission Dates
FORT	RE: Rent adj. - Activate area
FORV	RE: Rent adj. - Reverse area
FORW	RE: Rent adj. - Display area
FORX	RE: Rent adj. - Area log
FORY	RE: Rent adj. - Print area
FOS1	Internal document entry
FOS8	Single Document Reversal
FOSA	Execute debit position
FOSB	Debit position simulation
FOSC	Debit position reversal
FOSE	Account determination list
FOSF	Maintain Dunning Procedure
FOSG	Display Dunning Procedure
FOSH	Vacancy debit position
FOSI	Debit pos. unoccup.status simulation
FOSJ	RU-Unoccupied:Reverse debit position
FOSK	Vacancy Debit Position - Log
FOSL	General Real Estate Posting Log
FOSM	General Real Estate Posting Log
FOSN	Real Estate - Posting
FOSO	Number Range Maintenance: FVVI_RWINT

FOSR	Replaced by transaction FVIESR
FOST	Real Estate Management master data
FOT1	Current Vacancies
FOTA	Rental units: Create data file
FOTB	Change data file rental units
FOTC	Direct input rental units
FOTD	Lease-outs: Create data file
FOTE	Change data file lease-outs
FOTED1	Electr. Data Transmission Settings
FOTED2	Elec. Data Transmission Parameter(s)
FOTF	Direct input lease-outs
FOTI00	Tenant Information - Config. Menu
FOTI01	RETI: Activities
FOTI02	RETI: Applications
FOTI03	RETI: Screen Layout Field Groups
FOTI04	RETI: Screen Layout Views
FOTI05	RETI: Screen Layout Sections
FOTI06	RETI: Screen Layout Screens
FOTI07	RETI: Screen Sequence
FOTI08	RETI: Times
FOTI09	RETI: Tables
FOTI0A	Tenant Information
FOTI10	RETI: GUI Functions - Standard
FOTI11	RETI: GUI Functions - Additional
FOTI12	RETI: Matchcode ID's
FOTI13	RETI: Assign Screen->DB Field
FOTI14	RETI: Field Modifications - Criteria
FOTI15	RETI: ApplicTransactions
FOTI16	RETI: Field Modification Activity
FOTI17	RETI: Authorizations-Author.Groups
FOTI18	RETI: Field Group Authorization
FOTIOI	RE BDN - TI Templates
FOTP	Create Electr. Special Advance Payt
FOTV	Admin. Report Data Transmission
FOTY	Error Message
FOU1	RFVI: Rent adj. due to EURO Convers.
FOU2	Maintain sales reports
FOU2N	Maintain Sales Reports
FOU2NS	Enter Sales with Condition Types
FOU3	Display sales reports
FOU3N	Display sales reports
FOU3NS	Display Sales with Condition Types
FOU4	Reverse sales-based settlement
FOU4N	Reverse Sales-Based Settlement
FOU5	Sales settlement selection
FOU6	List of sales reports per year
FOU7	List of sales reports per month
FOU8	Overview of Missing Sales Reports
FOUA	Calculate sales settlement
FOUAN	Calculate Sales Settlement
FOUB	Display sales settlement history
FOUBN	Display Sales Settlement History
FOUC	RE: Activate sales-based rent adj
FOUD	RE: Display act.sales-based rnt adj

FOUE	Simulate sales settlement
FOUEN	Simulate Sales Settlement
FOUF	RE: Activate USER rent adj.
FOUG	RE: Reverse USER rent adj.
FOUH	RE: Display active USER rent adj.
FOUI	RFVI: Simulate Rent Adjustment USER
FOUJ	RFVI: Calculate rent adjustment USR
FOUK	RE: Simulate Meth.Comp. rent adj.
FOUL	RE: Calculate Meth.Comp. rent adj
FOUM	Convers. of rep.list of rents texts
FOUP	RE: Reverse CH rent adj.
FOUQ	RE: Reverse IND rent adj.
FOUR	RE: Reverse CGP rent adj.
FOUS	RE: Reverse FAC rent adj.
FOUT	RE: Reverse RLR rent adj.
FOUU	RE: Reverse GAR rent adj.
FOUV	RE: Reverse FAR rent adj.
FOUW	RE: Reverse rent adj. AnyCond
FOUX	RE: Reverse sales-based rent adj.
FOV0	Rental agreement number range
FOV1	Create Lease-Out
FOV2	Change Lease-Out: Master Data
FOV3	Display Lease-Out
FOV4	Supplement Lease-Out
FOV6	Activate advance payment adjustment
FOV7	Call Lease-Out
FOV8	Activate Residential Lease-Outs
FOV9	Activate Provisional Agreements
FOVA	Determination of option rates
FOVB	Real Est.: Update of LO Cash Flow
FOVC	Manual input tax treatment
FOVD	Input tax trtmnt: Monthly postings
FOVE	Create Lease-Out Offer
FOVF	Change Lease-Out Offer
FOVG	Display Lease-Out Offer
FOVH	Transfer offer to lease-out
FOVI	Post trivial amnts to prior period
FOVIM	Migration: Post Trivial Amt to Prior
FOVITAXD	Analysis - VITAXD
FOVJ	Reverse input tax treatment run
FOVK	Print general rent adjustment
FOVL	Overview of Lease-Outs
FOVN	Invoice (CH) on basis of cash flow
FOVO	Print owner settlement
FOVP	Repeat invoice (cash flow)
FOVQ	OIs from FI already invoiced
FOVS	Assign Collective LO for Act. LO
FOVTIV11	Overview adjustment methods
FOVU	Print sales settlement
FOVV	Lease-out renewal
FOVX	Mass Processing of Offers
FOVZ	Rental Agreement Offer Number Range
FOW0	Real Estate application number range
FOW1	Real est. comm. application: Create

FOW2	Real est. comm. application: Change
FOW3	Real est. comm. application: Display
FOW4	Real est. priv. application: Create
FOW5	Real est. priv. application: Change
FOW6	Real est. priv. application: Display
FOW7	Overview of Rental Requests
FOW8	Rent requests evaluation
FOWB92	Rent Adj.acc. to CEA: Correspondence
FOWE	Business entity
FOWEDI	BE: Direct Input
FOWEGN	BE: Generate Data File
FOWESH	BE: Change Data File
FOWU	Display simplif.cost effic.analysis
FOWV	Change Simplif.Cost Effic.Analysis
FOWW	Create simplif.cost effic.analysis
FOWX	Create Cost Efficiency Analysis
FOWY	Change Cost Efficiency Analysis
FOWZ	Displ.Cost Efficiency Analysis
FOXA	Create broker
FOXB	Change broker
FOXC	Display broker
FOXD	Create owner
FOXE	Change owner
FOXF	Display owner
FOXG	Create tenant
FOXH	Change tenant
FOXI	Display tenant
FOXJ	Create
FOXK	Change
FOXL	Display
FOXX	Real estate current settings
FOYA	Real Estate IXS Incid.Expens.Sttlmnt
FOYB	Invoice for Rent: First Print
FOYC	Invoice for Rent: Repeat Print
FOYS	Status- and transaction control
FOZ0	Number Range Maintenance: FVVI_ZAEHL
FOZ1	Rental unit: Applications allocation
FOZ2	Rent request allocation
FOZA	Acct determ. for LO
FOZB	Customiz.Real Est.post.interface
FOZC	Customizing post.interface REstMgmt
FOZD	Change Payment Method, Bank Details
FO_ANCO_01	Analysis and Correction VITAXA
FO_ANCO_02	Analysis/Correction VIBEBE/VIBEOS
FO_ANCO_03	Analysis/Correction Program VITAXD
FO_BELEGE	Document Analysis Doc. Database BRF
FO_BELEGE_RETAX	Doc. Analysis for RETAX Documents
FO_FVVI_BUKRS	Basic Settings for RE Company Codes
FO_NKA_BUP	SCS Follow-up Posting
FO_NRIV_IMKNT	Number Range Interval: FVVI_IMKNT
FO_PRINT_NOTICE	Notice / Confirmation of Notice
FO_RFVIAB30	Correction Item Flows
FO_RFVIITLBZX	Enter Date of Service
FO_SAD9	Transfer Rental Request

FO_SETS	Generate Sets from RE Objects	
FO_USE_OF_ACCOUNTS	Accounts Used in RE Account Determ.	
FO_VIBEOS	Option Rates: Correction Items	
FO_VIOB05	Option Rates: Buildings	
FO_VIOB06	Option Rates: Properties	
FO_VIOB07	Option Rates: Business Entities	
FO_VTIV8A	Accounts for Directly Assigned Costs	
FO_V_ANKA_VI	Asset Classes - Real Estate	
FO_V_TIV65	Non-Deductible Input Tax Accounts	
FO_V_TIV79A	Input Tax Correction Accounts	
FO_V_TIV79K	Non-Deduct.Input Tax Default Account	
FO_V_TIV80	Clearing Accounts for Cost Accounts	
FO_V_TIV84	Revenue Acct Non-Ded.Inp.Tx Rev.Acct	
FO_V_TIVA1	Accounts for rounding differences	
FP00	Determine Appl. Component	
FP02R	Change Repayment Request	
FP02RC	Reset Check Reason in Repymt Request	
FP03	Submission to External Coll. Agency	
FP03D	Submit Receivables to Coll. Agency	
FP03DM	Mass Act.: Submission to Coll.Agency	
FP03DML	Logs of Submissions for Collection	
FP03E	Release of Items for Collection	
FP03EC	Submit Items for Internal Collection	
FP03F	Read Collection Agency File	
FP03H	History of Collection Items	
FP03I	Process Info fr.Ext.Collect.Agencies	
FP03L	List of Collection Items	
FP03M	Mass Run: Release for Collection	
FP03P	Process Info fr.Ext.Collect.Agencies	
FP03R	Display Repayment Request	
FP03U	Call Back Receivables fm Coll.Agency	
FP04	Write Off	
FP04H	Display Write-Off History	
FP04HP	Write-Off History Public Sector	
FP04M	Mass Run: Write-Off	
FP04P	Write-Off with Authoriz. Wrt-Off Rsn	
FP04_APPROVE	Approve Item Write-Off	
FP05	Process Payment Lot	
FP05ARC	Create Archive Index for Payment Lot	
FP05BNKD	Clarification Case Transfer	
FP05CLE	Process Payment Lot	
FP05CLE_CALL	Clarification proc. via CALL TRANS	
FP05DIS	Display payment lot item	
FP05FIK	Change Reconcil. Key for Payment Lot	
FP05_PROP	Exception Accts for Clarif. Proposal	
FP06	Account Maintenance	
FP07	Reset Clearing	
FP08	Reverse Document	
FP08M	Mass Reversal	
FP09	Returns	
FP09ALV	Returns Lot Overview	
FP09FIK	Change Recon. Key for Returns Lot	
FP09FS	Field Selection Returns Lot Header	
FP09FSL	Field Selection Returns Lot List	

FP18	Reverse Repayment Request
FP20	FI-CA Check Deposit List
FP22	Mass Reversal of Documents
FP25	Process Check Lot
FP27	Prior Period Posting to Clarif. Acct
FP2P	Valuation of Promises to Pay
FP2P1	Process Promise to Pay
FP2P2_WF	Promise to Pay: Approval
FP2P3	Display Promise to Pay
FP30	Find Payment
FP30C	Find Clarification Cases
FP31	Find Payment (fromm Payment Run)
FP35	Process Credit Card Lot
FP40	Transfer
FP45	Process Payment Order Lot
FP50	Manual Outgoing Checks Lot:
FP50FIK	Man. Check Lot: New Recon. Key
FP51	Data Transfer: Man. Outgoing Checks
FP52	Postproc.Tfr of Man. Issued Checks
FP53	Clarif.Process. of Cashed Checks
FP54	Transfer Encashment Data to Clarif.
FP55	DunSch - Customer Structure Generat.
FP60A	Aggregated Distribution Information
FP60BW	Revenue Distribution: BI Extraction
FP60G	Change Distribution Periods
FP60M	Mass Activity: Revenue Distribution
FP60P	Post Revenue Distribution
FP60PM	MassAct. Post Distribution Documents
FP60P_OLD	Post Revenue Distribution
FP60R	List of Distributed Revenues
FP60R1	Rev. Dist.: Analysis of Dist. Docs
FP60R2	Evaluation of Revenue Distribution
FP60R_NEW	Rev. Dist.: Analysis of Orig. Docs
FP60R_OLD	List of Distributed Revenues
FP70	Returns Lot: Incorrect Bank Data
FPAC	Maintain document types-runtimes
FPAC01	Maintain Correspondence Runtimes
FPAC02	Activate AS for Document Archiving
FPAC03	Activate AS for Paymt Lot Archiving
FPAC04	Activate AS for Returns Lot Arch.
FPAC05	Activate AS for contract acct arch.
FPAC06	Activate AS for Correspondence arch.
FPACTEN	Create Customer Notifications
FPAGENT	Additional Collections Specialist
FPAR	FI-CA Document Archiving
FPAR01	FI-CA Official Number Archiving
FPAR02	FI-CA: Request Archiving
FPAR02A	FICA Runtime for Archiving Requests
FPAR02B	Activate AS for Archiving Requests
FPAR03	FI-CA: Revenue Distribution Archivg
FPAR03B	Activate AS for Revenue Distribution
FPAR03C	Activate AS for Enhanced Rev.Distrib
FPAR04	FI-CA: Gen. Tax Reporting Archiving
FPAR05	FI-CA: Gen. Revenue Reporting Arch.

FPAR06	FI-CA: Gen. Tax Reporting Arch.
FPAR07	Delete Tax Reporting Data
FPAR08	Delete Reporting Data for Revenues
FPAR09	FI-CA: Foreign Currency Valuation
FPAR10	FI-CA: Clearing History Archive
FPAR11	FI-CA: Doubtful Receivables
FPAR12	FI-CA: Invoicing by Third Party
FPAR2	FI-CA Correspondence Archiving
FPARBGA0	FI-CA: Life of Tax Info. for Com.Ops
FPARBGA1	Archiving of Tax for Commercial Ops
FPARBGA2	Activate AS for Tax for Commerc. Ops
FPARBP	FI-CA: Business Partner Archiving
FPARCASE0	FI-CA: Item List Runtime
FPARCASE1	Archiving of Item List in Cases
FPARCASE2	Activate AS for Item List in Cases
FPARCJ0	FI-CA: Cash Journal Runtime
FPARCJ1	Cash Journal Archiving
FPARCJ2	Activate AS for Cash Journal
FPARCOLD0	FI-CA: Ext. Collections Resid.Time
FPARCOLD1	Archiving of External Collections
FPARCOLD2	AS External Collection
FPARCOLL0	FI-CA: Collection Agency Runtimes
FPARCOLL1	Collection Agency Archiving
FPARCOLL2	Activate AS for Collection Agency
FPARCR0	FICA Check Deposit Archiving Runtime
FPARCR1	FI-CA: Check Deposit Archiving
FPARDMS1	Archiving of Management Data for DMS
FPARDMS2	Activate AS Management Data for DMS
FPARDRE0	FI-CA: Evt-Bsd Def.Revenues Runtime
FPARDRE1	Archiving of Event-Bsd Def.Revenues
FPARDRE2	AS Event-Based Deferred Revenues
FPAREXC0	FICA: Life of External Payment Info
FPAREXC1	Archiving of External Payment Info
FPAREXC2	AS:Activate Totals Recs for Ext.Pyts
FPAREXCJ0	FI-CA: Cash Journal (Inb. Services)
FPAREXCJ1	Archiving Cash Journal (Inb. Serv.)
FPAREXCJ2	AS Cash Journal (Inbound Services)
FPAREXCS0	FICA:Life of Totals Recs for Ext.Pyt
FPAREXCS1	Archiving: Totals Recs for Ext.Payts
FPAREXCS2	AS:Activate Totals Recs for Ext.Pyts
FPARINDPAY0	Runtime of Payment Specifications
FPARINDPAY1	Payment Specification Archiving
FPARINDPAY2	Activate AS for Payment Specificatns
FPARINF0	FI-CA: Information Container Life
FPARINF1	Archiving of Information Container
FPARINF2	Activate Information Container AS
FPARIP0	FICA: Life of Payment Specifications
FPARIPL0	FI-CA: Inst.Plan Key Date Resid.Time
FPARIPL1	Archiving Key Date Record. Inst.Plan
FPARIPL2	AS Key Date Recording of Instal.Plan
FPARM0	Define FICA Dun. Archiving Runtime
FPARM1	FI-CA: Dunning History Archiving
FPARMDOC0	FI-CA: Sample Docs (General) Life
FPARMDOC1	Archiving of Sample Documents

FPARMDOC2	Activate AS for Sample Documents
FPAROB1	FI-CA Official Doc. Number Archive
FPARPCARD0	FICA: Pmt Card Supplement Resid.Time
FPARPCARD1	Archiving of Payment Card Supplement
FPARPCARD2	Activate Payment Card Supplem. AS
FPARPNBK0	FI-CA: Prenofitication Runtime
FPARPNBK1	Prenotification Archiving
FPARPNBK2	Activate Archive IS Prenotification
FPARPP0	FI-CA: Promise to Pay Life
FPARPP1	Archiving of Promises to Pay
FPARPP2	Activate Promise to Pay AS
FPARR0	FICA Returns Archiving Runtime
FPARR1	FI-CA: Returns Archiving
FPARR2	Returns History Archiving Runtime
FPARR3	FI-CA Returns History Archiving
FPARS1	Delete Totals Records
FPARSTPY0	FICA: Life for Pymts Sub. to StampTx
FPARSTPY1	Archiving of Pymts Subj. to Stamp Tx
FPARSTPY2	Activate AS for Stamp Tax Payments
FPARSUM0	FICA: Reconciliation Key Resid.Time
FPARSUM1	Archiving of Reconciliation Key
FPARSUM2	Activate Reconciliation Key AS
FPARTHI2	Activate AS for Convergent Invoicing
FPARTHP1	Archiving of Convergent Bill.(FI-AP)
FPARTHP2	Activate AS for Conv. Billing FI-AP
FPARTHPF1	Arch.of Convergent Billing (FI-CA)
FPARTHPF2	Activate AS for Convergent Billing
FPARV1	FI-CA: Contract account archiving
FPARWL0	FI-CA: Collection Worklist Runtime
FPARWL1	Archiving of Collection Worklist
FPARWL2	Activate Collection Worklist AS
FPARWLI0	FI-CA: Collection Work Item Life
FPARWLI1	Archiving of Collection Work Item
FPARWLI2	Activate Collection Work Item AS
FPARZ0	FI-CA: Payment Lot Archiving
FPARZ1	Define Payment Lot Period
FPAS00	Display Archived Payment Lot
FPAS01	Displ.FICA Pymt Lot ArchivInfoStruct
FPAS02	Displ.FICA Docs Archiv.Info.Struct.
FPAS04	Display FICA Returns Lot Archive
FPAV	FI-CA: Payment Advice Note
FPAVDEL	Delete Payment Advice Note
FPAVI	FI-CA: Pymt Advice Note fm CollAgeny
FPAWM	Processing of Report File
FPAWM_ALV	Foreign Trade Report - ALV List
FPAWM_CORR	Update Report File
FPAY1A	Create Payment Specification
FPAY1B	Create Payment Specification
FPAY2	Change Payment Specification
FPAY3	Display Payment Specification
FPAY8	Reverse Payment Specification
FPAY9	Reverse Item Preselection
FPAYR01	Payment Specifications: List
FPAYR02	Payment Specifications:Preselections

FPAYR03	Payment Specifications: Items
FPB0	Post Payment
FPB1	Document Transfer
FPB10	Paymt Lot Transfer - Cust.Struct.Gen
FPB11	ReturnsLotTransfer - Cust.Struct.Gen
FPB12	Check Register Transfer
FPB13	Check Reg. Transfer - Error Proces.
FPB14	Check Reg. Tfr - Cust. Struct. Gen.
FPB17	Transfer MultiCash File (FI-CA)
FPB2	Process Document Transfer Errors
FPB20	Payment Advice Note Transfer
FPB21	Pymt Advice Tfr - Error Processing
FPB22	Advice Note Tfr - Generate Cust.Str.
FPB3	Payment lot transfer
FPB4	Payment Lot Transfer Error Process.
FPB5	Returns Lot Transfer
FPB6	RL Transfer: Error Processing
FPB7	Transfer from Elect. Acct Statement
FPB8	Acct Stmt Transfer: Error Processing
FPB9	Doc.Transfer-Cust.Struct.Generator
FPBCD	FI-CA Data Transfer Changes
FPBL_GET	Get Locked Partners and Countries
FPBMC	Select MultiCash Conversion Program
FPBN	Process Balance Notifications
FPBPCR	Prep. Master Data Change fm Ext.Sys.
FPBPCU	Proc. Master Data Change fm Ext.Sys.
FPBRBOLO	Boleto: payment medium creation
FPBW	BW Extraction of Open Items
FPBWCINT	Maintain FICA Extraction Intervals
FPBWD	Delete Held Jobs
FPBWS	OI Selection for Extraction - Admin.
FPBW_EXTRACT	Update Delta Queue
FPB_BUA_CONF	Set Up BP for BUA
FPB_CALL_IS_QUERIES	Call Infoset queries for APB Launchp
FPB_CALL_RW_REPORT	AC Report Call for Launchpad
FPB_CALL_TRANSACTION	Transaction from Launchpad
FPB_CHANGE_APPLFIELD	Change Comb. of applid fieldnam
FPB_DELETE_PERS_DATA	Delete Selected Personalization Data
FPB_EXP_CLIENT_COPY	Copy Scenario from Client
FPB_FILL_PERS_CC	Fill for Personalization, Cost Ctrs
FPB_FILL_PERS_PC	Fill for Personalization,Profit Ctrs
FPB_LAUNCHPAD_CUST	Customizing of Report Launchpad
FPB_LINE_SYNC	Delete Line Items
FPB_LP_ASR_HRA_CUST	Report List for Role ASR
FPB_LP_ASR_HRU_CUST	Report List for Role ASR
FPB_LP_BUA_PLA_CUST	BUA Planning Report Customizing
FPB_LP_BUA_REP_CUST	BUA Reporting Report Customizing
FPB_LP_BUY_REP_CUST	Maintain Report List for Buyer
FPB_LP_EXP_CUST	Report Lists for Express Planning
FPB_LP_ISR_REP_CUST	Maintain Report List for Role ISR
FPB_LP_IVC_REP_CUST	Maint. Report List for Invoice Verif
FPB_LP_MSS_REP_CUST	MSS Reporting Report Customizing
FPB_LP_MT_REP_CUST	MT Reporting Report Customizing
FPB_LP_PM_REP_CUST	Maintain Report List for Role PM

FPB_LP_PSS_REP_CUST	PSS Reporting Report Customizing
FPB_LP_PS_REP_CUST	Maintain Report List for Role PS
FPB_LP_QI_REP_CUST	QI Reporting Report Customizing
FPB_LP_SUP_REP_CUST	Maintain Report List for Vendor
FPB_MAINTAIN_DIALOG	Personalization: Dialog Maintenance
FPB_MAINTAIN_HIER	Personalization: Hierarchy Maint.
FPB_MAINTAIN_PERS_M	Collective Processing of Pers. Data
FPB_MAINTAIN_PERS_S	Individual Processing of Pers. Data
FPB_MIGRATE_RULES	Migrate Rules of Monitors
FPB_MON_LINE	Evaluation for Line Items
FPB_MON_VAR	Evaluation for Critical Variance
FPB_MYB_CONF	Set up BP for MSS (myBudget)
FPB_RULE_ADMIN	Rule Administration
FPB_RULE_ADMIN_FRONT	Front End Rule Maintenance
FPB_RULE_USER	Display Rule for a User
FPB_SHOW_PERS_DATA	Display Personalization Data
FPB_SNI_CUST	Set Hierarchy Navigation
FPC1	FI-CA Dunning - Cust.Dunn. Procedure
FPCB	Collective Bill
FPCC	Display Cash Desk Closing
FPCC0002	Create Account Statements
FPCC0026	Balance Notification Account Creatn
FPCC0029	Create Business Partner Statement
FPCC0034	Generate Write-Off Notification
FPCCMD	Master Data f. Challenger Strategies
FPCCR	Clarification of Cashed Checks
FPCCT	FI-CA: Test Series - Coll.Strategies
FPCD	Post Payment
FPCD_PREP	selection items before cash journal
FPCF	Transfer Data to Cash Management
FPCFDEL	Delete Completed Clarification Cases
FPCG	Maintenance of Master Data Groups
FPCGA	Display Master Data Groups
FPCGB	Update of Contact Persons
FPCH1	Online Check Printing
FPCHA	Assign Payment Document to Check
FPCHESCHC	Clarification of Check Escheatment
FPCHESCH_CHANGE	Change Check Escheatment Data
FPCHESCH_DISP	Display Check Escheatment Data
FPCHESCH_ESCH	Execute Check Escheatment
FPCHESCH_START	Start Check Escheatment Process
FPCHL	List of Issued Checks
FPCHN	Create Check in Register
FPCHO	Maintain Owner of Check Forms
FPCHP	Check Assignment for Payment Run
FPCHR	Check Management
FPCHS	Document Reversal after Check Lock
FPCHV	Voiding of Checks from Payment Run
FPCHX	Check Extract for Report Files
FPCI	Information for Collection Agencies
FPCIBW	BW Extraction of Cleared Items
FPCIBWFC	Set Fields for CI Extraction
FPCJ	Cash Journal
FPCJM	Edit Cash Object

FPCJM_EX   Process External Cash Desk Object
FPCJM_IN   Define Cash Desk Structure
FPCJR   Cash Desk Evaluation
FPCJ_MAINTAIN_RESP   Maintain Cash Journal Responsibilits
FPCLBW   Extraction of Collection Items
FPCL_CUSTOMIZING   Payment Release List (France)
FPCM1   Transfer of Credit Data
FPCM2   Replication of Score
FPCMCAP   Capacity Planning
FPCNR   Clarif. Incorr. Bank Data Changes
FPCODU   Correspondence Dunning
FPCODUH   Correspondence Dunning History
FPCOHIST   Display Correspondence History
FPCOLLAG   Derivation Cllction Agncy - Custom.
FPCOLLAGP   Derivation Cllction Agncy - Mainte.
FPCOLLHIST   Display Collection History
FPCOPARA   Correspondence Printing
FPCPL   Clarification Processing: Pmnt Lot
FPCPL_ALERT   Clarification Processing: Pmnt Lot
FPCPR   Clarif. Processing: Payment Run
FPCR1   Display Creditworthiness
FPCR2   Change Creditworthiness
FPCRL   Clarification Processing: Returns
FPCRPO   Clarification Processing: Credit
FPCRPO_DET   Create Credit List
FPCR_ACTIVATE   Applic.: Activate Garnishment Reg.
FPCR_CUSTOMIZING   Garnishment Register
FPCR_NUMBERRANGE   Number Range Maintenance: FPCRCASEID
FPCS   Payment Card Billing
FPCUM   Write-Off fm Clarification Worklist
FPCVS   Clarification Processing:
FPCVS_CLAR   Confirm Payments
FPCVS_CONF   Confirm Reported Payments
FPCVS_EXAM   Monitoring of Third Party Payments
FPD1   Security Deposit Statistics Report
FPD2   Overview of Security Deposits
FPDDA2   Change Debit Memo Notification
FPDDA3   Display Debit Memo Notification
FPDDAX   Debit Memo Notification
FPDE   Document Extracts: Overview
FPDEC_DEL   Customizing Extr. - Deletion of Ext.
FPDEC_EXP   Customizing Extracts - Export
FPDEC_IMP   Customizing Extracts - Import
FPDEP_DEL   Partner Extracts - Del. of Extract
FPDEP_EXP   Partner Extracts - Export
FPDEP_IMP   Partner Extracts - Import
FPDE_AEXP   Doc. Extracts - Export fm Archive
FPDE_DEL   Doc. Extracts - Deletion of Extract
FPDE_EXP   Document Extracts - Export
FPDE_EXTR   Doc. Extracts - Export Extr. Docs
FPDE_IMP   Document Extracts - Import
FPDKCPR   Denmark : CPR / CVR No
FPDM00   Display Dispute Cases
FPDM01   Create Coll. Cases after Dunn. Run

SAP Transaction Codes – Volume One

FPDMS	Manage Documents
FPDMS1	Add Documents
FPDMS2	Determine Image of Documents
FPDMS3	Assign Business Partner
FPDMS4	Delete Images of Documents
FPDOC	Display missing FI-CA document
FPDP_ACTIVATE	Application: Activate Down Payments
FPDP_CREATE	Down Payments with Purchase Orders
FPDP_CUSTOMIZING	Down Payments
FPDP_MESSAGE	Customizing Messages
FPDR	Trans.Postg Run for Deferred Revenue
FPDR_BY_EVENT	Transfer Run (Event-Based Def.Rev.)
FPDR_BY_EVENT_CORR	Evt-Based Def.Revenues Adjustmt Run
FPDUDC	Create Docs from Standing Requests
FPDUN_REPAIR	Delta Update
FPDUTL	Dunning Telephone List
FPE1	Post Document
FPE1S	Post Sample Document
FPE2	Change Document
FPE2C	Reset Check Reason in Document
FPE2M	Mass Document Change
FPE2S	Change Sample Document
FPE3	Display Document
FPE3S	Display Sample Document
FPE4	Display Document Changes
FPEMMA	Log Analysis for Mass Runs
FPEMMACGEN	Mass Act.: Clarification Case Gen.
FPEMMAMA	EMMA: Mass Activities
FPEMMAPREP	EMMA: Mass Activity for Job Analysis
FPEW1	Euro: Reconcile with G/L
FPEW2	Euro: Status of Mass Runs
FPEW3	Euro: Conversion of FI-CA Documents
FPEW3A	EURO: Balance Determin. in FI G/L
FPEW4	EURO: Conv. Inst.Plan and Coll. Bill
FPEW5	Euro: Display Critical Documents
FPEW6	Euro: Adjust FI Reconciliation Accts
FPEW7	Euro: Check Adjustment Posting
FPEW8	Log Data on Euro Differences
FPEWG	EURO: Determin. of GLT0 Conv.Prog.
FPEWS	EURO: FI-CA Document Balances
FPEXC	Ext. Cash Desk Servs: Transfer OIs
FPEXC_TR	Turkey: Open Item selection
FPF1	Create Reconciliation Key
FPF2	Change Reconciliation Key
FPF3	Display Reconciliation Key
FPFMDY	Executn of Subsequent FM Activation
FPG0	Maintain Alternative Posting Data
FPG1	Transfer Posting Totals to G/L
FPG1M	General Ledger Transfer - Mass Run
FPG2	Reconcile with General Ledger
FPG2M	Check G/L Documents - Mass Run
FPG3	Transfer to CO-PA
FPG3M	COPA Transfer - Mass Run
FPG4	Close Reconcil. Keys Automatically

FPG5	FI-CA Docs to FI-GL Docs
FPG7	Check CO-PA Documents
FPG7M	Check CO-PA Documents - Mass Run
FPG8	Reverse General Ledger Transfer
FPI1	FI-CA: Calc. Interest Individually
FPI2	FI-CA: Interest on Cash Sec. Deposit
FPI3	FI-CA: Overdue Interest Inst.Plan
FPI4	FI-CA: Display Interest Calculation
FPI5	Loan Calculation: Test Transaction
FPINFCO1	Information Container: Send Data
FPINFCO2	Display Information Container
FPINFCO3	Information Container: Reset Send
FPINTHDEL	Delete Interest History
FPINTM1	Interest Run
FPINTM2	Cash Security Dep. Interest Run
FPIN_CUSTOMIZING	Penalty Interest
FPIN_LIST	Enter Arrears Days for Penalty Int.
FPIPBW	Installment Plan Extraction
FPIPKEY	Installment Plans for Key Date
FPK1	Item Processing
FPL9	Display Account Balance
FPL9S	Account Balance: Internal Call
FPLC	Acct Balance: Fullscreen Chronology
FPLKA	Evaluate Processing Locks
FPLKDEL	Delete Mass Locks Set
FPLOGADMI	Log Administration Form Processing
FPM3	Display Dunning History
FPM3_RELEASE	Release Dunning Notices
FPM4	Display Returns History
FPMA	Automatic Clearing
FPMANAGER	Additional Collections Manager
FPMO	FI-CA: Application monitor
FPN1	Number Range Maintenance: FKK_BELEG
FPN10	Number Range Maintenance: FKKINDPAY
FPN2	Maintain Number Range: FKK_ACCOUNT
FPN3	Number Range Maintenance: FKK_ZAUFT
FPN4	Number Range Maintenance: FKKPYFORM
FPN5	Number Range Maintenance: FKK_UMB
FPN6	Number Range Maintenance: FKK_EXTDOC
FPN7	Number Range Maintenance: FKKPYORDER
FPN8	Number Range Maintenance: FKK_TXINV
FPN9	Number Range Maintenance: FKKPYANNMT
FPNORMBP	Normalized BP for Duplicate Search
FPNP2P	Number Range Maintenance: FKK_P2P
FPNRPT	Number Range Maintenance: FKK_REPT
FPN_AGGRF	Number Range Maintenance: FKKDREGAGG
FPN_AUBID	Number Range Maintenance: FKKD_AUBID
FPN_DISPUTE	Number Range Maintenance: FKKDISPUTE
FPN_EXTDOC_IT	No. Range Maintnce: FKKEXBL_IT
FPO1	FI-CA: OI List per Key Date
FPO1P	OI List for Key Date (Parallel)
FPO1_ACC	FI-CA Key Date-Specific OI List(Acc)
FPO2	Reconciliation of OI's in G/L
FPO4	Item Evaluation

FPO4P	OI List for Key Date (Parallel)
FPO6	Evaluation of Report Totals
FPO7	Analysis of Extracted Open Items
FPO7F	Display Non-Resident Customers
FPOITR	Outbound Interface: BP Postings
FPOP	Update of BP Delta Queue
FPOPDEL	Delete Trigger for BP Delta Queue
FPOR2	Change Payment Order
FPOR3	Display Payment Order
FPOR8	Reverse Payment Order
FPOR8M	Mass Reversal of Payment Orders
FPP	Framework for Parallel Processing
FPP1	Create Contract Partner
FPP2	Change Contract Partner
FPP2A	Activate Planned Changes
FPP3	Display Contract Partner
FPP4	Maintain Payment Data
FPP7	Create Installer
FPP8	Change Installer
FPP9	Display Installer
FPPARDEL	Delete Parameter Records
FPPARHID	Hide Parameter Records
FPPARMV	Move Parameter Records
FPPARUNHID	Reactivate Parameter Records
FPPCAI	PCARD: Items in card account
FPPCAS	PCARD: Invoiced items
FPPCBP	PCARD: Business partner with cards
FPPCDL	PCARD: Delete logs
FPPCDS	PCARD: Perform invoicing
FPPCLI	PCARD: Log (paid items)
FPPCLP	PCARD: Log (payments)
FPPCSF	PCARD: Display invoicing file
FPPCSL	Payment cards: Display log
FPPCTS	PCARD: Items to be invoiced
FPPN5	Postprocess Prenotification Return F
FPPNH	Display Prenotification History
FPPNO	Prenotification file outgoing
FPPNR	Process Prenotification Return
FPPNU	Change Prenotif. Processing Status
FPPST	Denmark: Stop payment
FPP_2	Parallel Processing Initial Screen
FPP_2_SAMPLE	Example - Parallel Processing
FPP_SAMPLE	Framework for Parallel Processing
FPP_SAMPLE_ENTRY	Framework for Parallel Processing
FPP_STMT	Parallel Processing of Settlement
FPP_STMT_ENTRY	Framework for Parallel Processing
FPR1	Create Installment Plan
FPR2	Change installment plan
FPR3	Display installment plan
FPRA	Display Adjusted Receivables
FPRB	Prepare Valuation Areas for DE
FPRD	Installment Plan Printing
FPRECL	Post Reclassifications
FPREPT	Receipt Management

FPREPTM	Mass Receipt Printing
FPREPZM1	Initialization of EC Sales List
FPREPZM2	Act. of EU Tax No. for EC Sales List
FPRES_CON	Summarization of Reserve Postings
FPRETBW	Extraction of Returns
FPRH	Display Installment Plan Histories
FPRL	Release Cash Security Deposit
FPRL_ACTIVATE	Activate Payment Release List
FPRL_CLEAR_DI	Define Approval Levels
FPRL_CUSTOMIZING	Payment Release List
FPRL_DOC_DI	Define Approval Levels
FPRL_F110	F110 for PRL exclusively
FPRL_LEVELS	Define Approval Levels
FPRL_LIST	Payment Release List
FPRL_SET_APPLIC	Set Payment Release List Application
FPRS	Open Repayment Requests
FPRU	Overview of Repayment Requests
FPRV	Transfer Post Adjusted Receivables
FPRVD	Display Adjusted Items
FPRW	Adjust Receivables According to Age
FPR_PLCL	Clarification Account - Itemization
FPR_RLCL	Clarification Account - Itemization
FPS1	Load of Polling Data to Bank Buffer
FPS2	Generate Payment Advice from Polling
FPS3	Intraday Statement
FPSA	CA Selection
FPSC	Display Day-End Closing
FPSCHEDULER	Execute Mass Activity
FPSEC0	Number Range Maintenance: FKK_SEC
FPSEC1	Create Security Deposit
FPSEC2	Change Security Deposit
FPSEC3	Display Security Deposit
FPSELP	Selections for Evaluations
FPSELP1	Layout for Evaluations
FPSELPLOCK	Locks according to Preselection
FPSEPA	Creation of SEPA Mandates
FPSEPA1	Change SEPA Mandates
FPSEPA_AR1	SEPA Archiving
FPSEPA_AR2	Activate AIS SEPA
FPSNAP	Account Bal.: Creation of Snapshots
FPSNAP_CUST	Account Bal.: Partner for Snapshot
FPSNAP_DEL	Account Bal.: Deletion of Snapshots
FPSO	Post Charge After Payment
FPSP	BP Selection
FPST	Preselection by Transaction Data
FPS_RFKKBELJ00	Document Journal
FPS_RFKKPYOD	Delete Payment Orders
FPS_RFKKPYOL	List of Payment Orders
FPS_RFKPYD00	Delete Payment Data
FPT1	Check Totals Tables
FPT1M	Check Totals Records - Mass Run
FPT3	Alternative Period Transfer
FPT4	Analyze Status of Transfer
FPT5	Display documents for reconcil. key

SAP Transaction Codes – Volume One

FPT6	Recreate Totals Records
FPT7	Statement Posting Totals
FPT8	Acct Assgt Stmt for Single Docs
FPTCRPO	Credit Processing
FPTL1	Country specific fiscal reports
FPTRACE	Display Log
FPTX1	Select Country-Specific Tax Report
FPU1	Maintenance of regrouping accounts
FPU2	Tfr Posting to Other Company Code
FPU5	Transfer Documents to Another Acct
FPU6	History of Transfer
FPVA	Dunning Proposal
FPVB	Dunning Activity Run
FPVBUND	Adjustment to Percentage of Ownersh.
FPVBUND1	Maintenance of VBUND History
FPVC	Mass Reversal of Dunning Notices
FPVT	Transfer Dunning Telephone List
FPVT1	Entries in Dunning Telephone List
FPVV	Valuation of Dunnings
FPVZ	Maintain Agreed Payment Amounts
FPW1	Foreign Currency Valuation
FPW2	Log Records for For. Crcy Valuations
FPW3	Event-Controlled Inverse Posting
FPWLM	Manage Worklists
FPY1	Payment Run / Debit Memo Run
FPY1A	Analysis Tool for Payment Runs etc.
FPYE1	Year-End Postings
FPYS	Payment Run (Direct Payers)
FPZD	Reorganize Payment Documents
FPZP	Payment Form Items Overview
FPZW	Receivables correction
FPZWH	Evaluate Adjusted Receivables
FP_DEL_DFKKQSR	Delete Withhold. Tax Reporting Data
FP_DEL_DFKKREP01	Deletion of Tax Rep. Data (Belgium)
FP_DEL_DFKKZP_ARCIND	Delete Indexes for Arch. Payment Lot
FP_DEL_REPZM	Delete EC Sales List Data
FP_NOTE_CUST	Not to Payee Analysis - Customizing
FP_NOTE_TEST	Note to payee Analysis - Test
FP_PD01	Report RFKKPD01
FP_PD02	Report rfkkpd02
FP_PD03	Report rfkkpd03
FP_REG	Subscriptions for Clearing
FP_REG_DEL	Delete Obsolete Subscriptions
FQ00	FI-CA Technical Settings
FQ0015	Account Assignment of Other Taxes
FQ0025	Tax Specifications
FQ0061	FI-CA: Late Payment Surcharge
FQ0090	FI-CA: Specifications for Bundling
FQ01	C FI Maintain Table TFK022A/B
FQ0111	FI-CA: Returns Specifications
FQ02	C FI Maintain Table TFK022C
FQ0200	FI-CA: Withholding Tax Outgoing Payt
FQ0201	FI-CA: Addtl Withholding Tax OutPayt
FQ0210	FI-CA: Withholding Tax Incoming Payt

FQ0211	FI-CA: Addtl Withholding Tax IncPayt
FQ03	C FI Maintain Table TFK022D
FQ0300	FI-CA: Segment for G/L Item
FQ0301	FI-CA: Segment for Bus. Partner Item
FQ0310	Add. Acct Assignments for Down Pmts
FQ04	C FI Maintenance Table TFK000U
FQ05	FI-CA Maintenance Table TFK061A
FQ06	FI-CA Maintenance Table TFK062A
FQ07	FI-CA Maintenance Table TFK063A
FQ1031	FI-CA: Incoming Pmnt Specifications
FQ1032	FI-CA: Post Payment Order Specs
FQ1033	FI-CA: Credit Card Lot Specs
FQ1035	FI-CA: Specs for Man. Checks Lot
FQ1036	FI-CA: Specs for Check Encashment
FQ1037	FI-CA: Specs for Check Encashment
FQ1038	FI-CA: Specs for Check Encashment
FQ1039	Check Encashment Exp./Rev. Accounts
FQ1041	FI-CA: Returns Clarification Account
FQ1042	Enter Check Escheatment Specificat.
FQ1062	Specifications for Transerring Items
FQ1130	Setting of Debt Recvery Score
FQ1131	Clearing Accts for Collect.Agencies
FQ1132	Specific. for Coll.Agency Postings
FQ1297	Activate Valuation Area
FQ1310	FI-CA: Main/Sub for Official Charges
FQ1311	FI-CA: Doc. Type for Official Chrges
FQ1320	Settings for Credit Clarification
FQ1321	Settings for Credit Clarification
FQ1322	Assign Authorization in Credit Proc.
FQ1378	Requirement from Invoicing
FQ1379	Enhanced Revenue Distribution
FQ1380	Settings for Revenue Distribution
FQ1381	Posting Specs: Revenue Distribution
FQ1382	Spec. Posting Specs: Rev. Distrib.
FQ1384	Distrib. Groups Transaction Determ.
FQ1600	BP Duplicates: Transfer Specifictns
FQ2000	Fund Accounting Settings FI-CA
FQ2001	Acct Determination f. Fund Clearing
FQ2010	FM Acct Assgt for Subseq. FM Activtn
FQ2101	FI-CA: Document Type for Perception
FQ2102	FI-CA: Tax Determ. Code - Argentina
FQ2110	Tfr Pstg to Resp. Company Code
FQ2600	Document Types for Invoicing Docs
FQ2605	Maintain Doc. Types for Posting Docs
FQ2606	Calculation Rules for Scheduling
FQ2610	Acct Assgt of General Ledger Items
FQ2611	Acct Assgt of Business Partner Items
FQ2612	Summarization Trans for BPtnr Items
FQ2613	Transf. Posting Proc. for Offsetting
FQ2617	Assign Charge/Discount Key
FQ2618	Base Amount Determ. Charges/Discnts
FQ2620	Calculatn of Interest on Open Items
FQ2622	Calc. of Int. on Cash Sec. Deposits
FQ2623	Release Cash Security Deposit

FQ2625	Item Selectn: Statistical Open Items
FQ2627	Preselect Items for Activation
FQ2628	Activation in Invoicing
FQ2630	Account Maintenance in Invoicing
FQ2635	Subitems in Invoicing
FQ2637	Flag Document for Invoicing List
FQ2640	Trans. Deter. for Billing Doc. Items
FQ2641	Determine Tax Code
FQ2642	Determine Tax Condition Type
FQ2643	Add. Acct Assignment Billing Docs
FQ2645	Document Types for Billing Documents
FQ2671	Assign Check to Invoicing Document
FQ2672	Assign Check to Source Document
FQ2673	Maintain Exception List Messages
FQ2680	Determination of Application Form
FQ2685	Invoicing: Payment Method/Form
FQ2686	Assign Key for Invoice Rounding
FQ8000	Mapping EDR for Operand
FQ8106	Calculation Rules for Scheduling
FQ8110	Documtent Types of Billing Document
FQ8115	Aggregation of Billable Items
FQ8120	Define Account Assignments
FQ8121	Define Transactions
FQ8123	Assign Tax Codes
FQ8124	Specifications for Ext. Tax Transfer
FQ8125	Tax Type for Other Taxes
FQA1	Archiving of FI-CA documents
FQAT02	Follow-Up: Variants for Act. Type 2
FQAT03	Follow-Up: Variants for Act. Type 3
FQAT04	Follow-Up: Variants for Act. Type 4
FQAUTH	FI-CA Special Authorizations
FQB1	Correspondence Data Fields
FQB10	FI-CA: Bollo Specifications
FQB2	Correspondence Data Fields
FQB4	FI-CA Corresp. - Application Forms
FQB9	FI-CA: Ital. Stamp Tax Returns,Specs
FQC0	C FKK Acct Determination (General)
FQC1	C FKK Account Determination */0010
FQC1005	Prefix for Lot IDs-Acct Stmt Transfr
FQC1071	C FKK Account Determination */1071
FQC1091	Acct Determination */1091
FQC1200	Acct Determination */1200
FQC1210	Acct Determination */1200
FQC1215	C FI-CA Contract Postings
FQC1350	C FKK Account Determination */1350
FQC1351	Spec. for Posting Reclassifications
FQC1400	Acct Determ. IDOC Receivables Items
FQC1401	Account Determ. IDOC Revenue Items
FQC1402	Document Type Determination
FQC1403	Determination of Posting Data
FQC1404	Determination of Posting Transacts
FQC1405	Tax IDs for IDOC Data
FQC1410	Data for Reversing IDOC Documents
FQC1500	Receipt Management Specifications

FQC1510	Credit Specif. from Follow-Up Acts
FQC2	C FKK Account Determination */0020
FQC2120	Receipt Management Specifications
FQC3	C FKK Account Determination */0030
FQC40	C FKK Account Determination */0040
FQC5	C FKK Account Determination */0050
FQC6	C FKK Account Determination */0060
FQC7	C FKK Account Determination */0070
FQC700	Collective Bill Specifications
FQC8	C FI-CA Account Determination */0071
FQC900	Acct Determination */0900
FQCALLID	Maintenance of Table TFKCALLID
FQCC	Maintain Bank Sel. IDs for Pymt Run
FQCE	Acct Determination: Error Analysis
FQCF	User ID for Bank Transactions
FQCFCC1071	Buchungsdaten für Gutschriften
FQCG	C FI-CA Dunning Grouping */0400
FQCODU	Cont A/R + A/P - Cust. Dunn. Proced.
FQCR	Account Determination: List
FQCR600	C FKK Account Determination */R600
FQCVS	CVS Bank Clearing Account
FQC_R404	Diff.Accts for Cons.Ports Prev. Year
FQC_R410	Assign Summarization Subtransactions
FQD1	Productive Start - Delete Test Data
FQD2	Synchronization - Maintain Variants
FQDM0	Posting Area 3000
FQDM1	Posting Area 3001
FQDM2	Posting Area 3002
FQEVENTS	Events
FQEXC1	Define Specifns for Agent Posting
FQEXC2	Doc. Types for Posting for Framework
FQEXC3	Clearing Acct for Payt Lot for ExtCD
FQEXC4	Enter Specif. for Agent Commissions
FQEXC6	Specif. for Posting Cash Desk Diff.
FQEXC7	Deposit and Withdrawal Accounts
FQFUND	Activation Status Fund Accounting
FQGRP	Balances Groups
FQH0	Specifications for Diff. Postings
FQH1	Specifications for Diff. Postings
FQH2	Spec. for Document Type Payment Cat.
FQH4	Cash Desk/Cash Journal: CD Accounts
FQH5	Specifications for Diff. Postings
FQH6	Specif. for Dep./Withdrawal Posting
FQI1	Maintain Interest Keys
FQI2	Display Interest Keys
FQI3	Maintain spec. for int. on inst.plan
FQI4	Maintain Interest Entries
FQI4Z	Interest: Additional Functions
FQI5	Maintain Cash Sec.Deposit Entries
FQI6	Maintain Mass Activity: Interest
FQI7	Maintain Mass Activ: Cash Sec. Dep.
FQI8	Specifications-Interest on Arrears
FQI9	Processes for witholding tax code
FQK1	TFK021R (account balance: Search)

SAP Transaction Codes – Volume One

FQK2	TFK021R (account balance: Select)
FQK3	TFK021R (account balance: Sort)
FQK5	TFK021R (account balance: Add.field)
FQK50	Derivation of Credit Segment
FQK51	Maintain Credit Segment
FQK52	Central Credit Management Setting
FQK53	Derivation of Credit Segment
FQK6	TFK021R (posting totals: Search)
FQK8	TFK021R (posting totals: Sort)
FQKA	Document: Central Settings
FQKB	Document: User Settings
FQKL	Existing settings contract A/R & A/P
FQKP	Config.: Maintain Display Format
FQKPA	Modifiable Fields in Account Maint.
FQKPB	Broker Report: Line Layout Variants
FQKPD	Document Processing: Variants
FQKPH	Man. Issued Checks: Line Layout
FQKPI	Payment Specification: Line Layout
FQKPK	Document: Line Layout Variants (G/L)
FQKPM	Account Balance:Line Layout Variants
FQKPN	Bank Report: Line Layout Variants
FQKPO	OI Processing: Line Layout Variants
FQKPP	Document: Line Layout Variants (OI)
FQKPS	Posting Totals: Line Layout Variants
FQKPT	Broker Report: Item Entry
FQKPZ	Payment Lot: Line Layout Variants
FQKS	Account Balance: Sort Variants
FQKX	TFK021L(Acct Balance: List Cats)
FQM0	FI-CA Dunning - Cust.Dunn.Groupings
FQM1	FI-CA Dunning - Cust.Dunn.Procedures
FQM2	FI-CA Dunning - Cust. Dunning Levels
FQM3	FI-CA Dunning: Cust.Min/Max Amounts
FQM4	FI-CA Dunning-Cust.Dun. Charges Type
FQM5	FI-CA Dunning - Cust.Dunn.Groupings
FQM6	FI-CA Dunning-Cust.Dunn.Block Reason
FQM7	FI-CA Dunning - Cust.Dun.Level Types
FQM8	FI-CA Dunning - Cust.Dunn.Proc.Types
FQM9	FI-CA Dunning - Cust. Charges
FQMASS	Mass Activities
FQOGRM	Post Gen. Request Specification Docs
FQORD1	Request: Doc. Generation Specificats
FQP1	Define Payment Methods
FQP2	Item Indicator
FQP3	Payment Medium Formats
FQP4	Company Code Details for Payment
FQP5	Payment medium formats:Note to payee
FQP6	Settings for Check Creation
FQP6A	Assign Internal Check Numbers
FQP7	Maintain Instruction Key
FQP8	User ID for Bank Transactions
FQP9	DME Foreign Payment Transactions
FQR1	FI-CA Returns - Reason Settings
FQR2	FI-CA Returns - AcctDet Settings
FQR3	Returns - Allocate Return Reason

FQS1	Fast Entry: Item List
FQS2	Fast Entry: G/L Item List
FQS3	Fast Entry: Payment Lot
FQSE1	Security Deposit: Clearing
FQSEC	Security Deposit: Special Parameters
FQTAXMIN	C FI-CA Maintenance Table TFKTAXMIN
FQTFK020C	FI-CA Maintenance Table TFK020C
FQU1	FI-CA: Transfer Posting: Addl Specs
FQU2	Transfer Items: Trans. Determination
FQUD	Customer Queries
FQUK	Vendor Queries
FQUS	G/L Account Queries
FQV160	BP Duplicates: PH Change Specs
FQVAR	Balances Variants
FQVBUND	Doc. Type for VBUND Adjustment Pstg
FQVI01	Agency Coll.: Coll. Default Values
FQVI02	AgencyColl: Third-Party Default Vals
FQVI03	AgencyColls: Agency Postings on Acct
FQVI04	AgencyColl: Cust. Postings on Acct
FQVI05	AgencyColl: Deposits/Withdrawals
FQVI06	AgencyColl: Deposits/Withdrawals
FQVI07	AgencyColl: Clarification Code
FQVI08	AgencyColl: Internal Temp. Coll.
FQVI09	AgencyColl: External Temp. Coll.
FQVI10	AgencyColl: TransPost CGT
FQVI11	AgencyColl: TransPost 3rd-P. Comm.
FQVI12	AgencyColl: Payt Meths AgencyPaytRun
FQVI13	AgencyColl: Specs Shares Insurance
FQVI14	Agency Collections: Transactions
FQVI15	AgencyColl: Internal Temp. Coll.
FQVI16	Agency Collections: Document Types
FQVI17	Agency Coll: On Acct Transactions
FQVI18	Agency Coll: On Acct Clarifctn Code
FQVI19	AgencyColl: Reversal Specifications
FQVI20	Agency Coll: On Acct Clarif. Code
FQVI21	AgencyColl: Specs Shares Insurance
FQVI22	AgencyColl.: Payt Lock Subcomm.
FQXI01	Derivations for Down Payment Request
FQZ01	FI-CA: Acct Det-Alt. Acct Reversal
FQZ01F	Alt. Accts for Aperiodic Invoicing
FQZ02	FI-CA: Charge-Off Specs
FQZ02A	FI-CA: Charge-Off Specs
FQZ03	FI-CA: Mass Write-Off Specifications
FQZ03A	FI-CA: Mass Write-Off Specifications
FQZ04	FI-CA: G/L Acct Det Write Off
FQZ04A	FI-CA: Write-Off Acct Determination
FQZ04B	Maintain Table TFK048AB
FQZ04M	Mass W/Off: Specif. and Default Vals
FQZ04S	Write-Offs: Specif. and Default Vals
FQZ04T	Write-Off without Tax Adjustment
FQZ04U	Alterna. Expense and Revenue Account
FQZ04W	External System for Tax Calculation
FQZ04X	Transactions for Ext. Tax Calculat.
FQZ05	FI-CA: Acct Det - Autom. Clearing

FQZ06	FI-CA: Installm.Plan Inact. Dunn.Run
FQZ07	FI-CA: Default Vals Receivable Valtn
FQZ08	FI-CA: Acct Det.-Doubtful Items
FQZ09	FI-CA: Acct Det - Deferred Revenues
FQZ09A	FI-CA: Acct Det - Deferred Revenues
FQZ1	FI-CA: Account Balance Line Layout
FQZ10	FI-CA: Default Vals Delayed Revenues
FQZ1072	Biller Direct: Overpayment Specifs
FQZ1073	Biller Direct: Overpayment Reversal
FQZ1074	BD: Overpayment Clearing Account
FQZ11	FI-CA: Acct Det.-Ind.Val.Adjustment
FQZ12	Tax Calculation Typ Indiv.Value Adj.
FQZ13	FI-CA Maintenance Table TFKZGR
FQZ14	FI-CA Maintenance Table TFKZRGR
FQZ15	FI-CA: Coll. Agency Specifications
FQZ16	FI-CA: Acct Det. - G/L Transfer
FQZ17	Maintain Table TFKZVAR
FQZ18	Maintain Table TFKZMETH
FQZ19	Maintain Table TFKZGRME
FQZ1A	FI-CA: Acct Det.-Ind.Val.Adjustment
FQZ2	FI-CA: OI Processing Line Layout
FQZ20	FI-CA: AcctDet - Indiv. Val. Adj. CZ
FQZ21	FI-CA: Collection Agency Pstg Specs.
FQZ22	FI-CA: Callback Data Specifications
FQZ23	FI-CA: Information to Coll. Agency
FQZ24	FI-CA: Document Type for VAT Percep.
FQZ25	FI-CA: Information to Coll. Agency
FQZ26	Collection Agencies
FQZ2A	Maintain Table TFKZWEX
FQZ2B	Maintenance of Table TFKZVARI
FQZ3	FI-CA: Posting Totals Line Layout
FQZ4	FI-CA: Screen Var. B/P Item Posting
FQZ5	FI-CA: Screen var.for post.G/L items
FQZ6	FI-CA: Payment Lot Screen Variants
FQZ7	FI-CA: Returns Lot Screen Variants
FQZ8	FI-CA: Acct Det. - Output Tax
FQZ9	FI-CA: AcctDet - Tax Clearing/Dwnpmt
FQZA	FI-CA: AcctDet - CoCode Clearing
FQZB	FI-CA: AccDet - Charges Rec. Revenue
FQZBW	Activate Valuation Area
FQZC	FI-CA: Account Det. - Cash Discount
FQZD	FI-CA: AcctDet - Exchange Rate Diff.
FQZE	FI-CA: Acct Det. - G/L Transfer
FQZF	FI-CA: Acct Det. - Returns
FQZG	FI-CA: AccDet - Down Pmnt/Charge
FQZH	FI-CA: Acct Maint. Default Entries
FQZH2	FI-CA: Credit Memo Clearing (EBPP)
FQZI	FI-CA: Incoming Pmnt Specifications
FQZJ	FI-CA: Clariftn Acct Incmg Paymnts
FQZK	FI-CA: Reverse Doc. Default Entries
FQZL	FI-CA: Payment Program: Bank Accts
FQZM	FI-CA: Doc Posting: Default Entries
FQZN	FI-CA: Act Det.-Inc.Pmnt Refund Acct
FQZO	FI-CA: AcctDet- Reset Clrd Itms Def.

FQZP	FI-CA: AcctDet.- Reset Clrg: New OI
FQZQ	FI-CA: Doc Posting: Default Entries
FQZS	FI-CA: Returns: Default Entries
FQZT	FI-CA: Check Deposit Clearing
FQZU	FI-CA: AcctDet-Inst. plan charges
FQZU1	Install.Plan Surcharge Enh. Active
FQZU2	Installment Plan:Exclude HVORG/TVORG
FQZV	FI-CA: Payment Cards: Acct Determ.
FQZX	FI-CA: Payment Cards: Acct Determ.
FQZY	FI-CA: Dunning: Defaults
FQZZ	FI-CA: Instal.Plan Interest Spec.
FQ_ENH_BROKR	Create Enhancement: Broker
FQ_ENH_CCARD	Create Enhancement: Payment Cards
FQ_ENH_OPORD	Create Enhancement: Classificatn Key
FQ_ENH_RDI	Create Enhancement: Revenue Distrib.
FQ_FPCJ_ACTIVITIES	Role-Specific Activities
FQ_FPCJ_NC	Normal Clerk
FQ_FPCJ_NC_462	Normal Clerk
FQ_FPCJ_NC_GT_462	Normal Clerk
FQ_FPCJ_SC	Clerk with Special Tasks
FQ_FPCJ_SC_462	Clerk with Special Tasks
FQ_FPCJ_SC_GT_462	Clerk with Special Tasks
FQ_FPCJ_SU	Branch Office Manager
FQ_FPCJ_SU_462	Branch Office Manager
FQ_FPCJ_SU_GT_462	Branch Office Manager
FR01	Change original commitments
FR02	Display original commitments
FR04	Change original payments
FR05	Display original payments
FR07	Change Release for Commitment Bdgt
FR08	Display Release Commitments
FR10	Change Release for Payment Bdgt
FR11	Display Release Payments
FR15	Change Supplement Commitments
FR16	Display Supplement Commitments
FR19	Change Supplement Payments
FR20	Display Supplement Payments
FR23	Change Return Commitments
FR24	Display Return Commitments
FR27	Change Return Payments
FR28	Display Return Payments
FR50	Enter Original Budget
FR51	Enter Release
FR52	Enter Supplement
FR53	Enter Return
FR54	Distribute Original Budget
FR55	Distribute Release
FR56	Distribute Supplement
FR57	Distribute Return
FR58	Post
FR59	Change document
FR60	Display Document
FR61	Park Original Budget
FR62	Park Release

FR63	Park Supplement
FR64	Park Return
FR65	Park Original Budget Distribution
FR66	Park Release Distribution
FR67	Park Supplement Distribution
FR68	Park Return Distribution
FR69	Park Transfer
FR70	Post Parked Document
FR71	Cancel Parked Document
FR72	Display Parked Document
FR73	Change Parked Document
FR81	Loc.Auth.: Budget Reduction
FR86	Loc.Auth.: Enter Residual Budget
FR87	Distribute Budget Types with Release
FR88	FM: Loc.Auth.: Mass Release
FR89	Reverse Document
FR90	Loc.auth: Distribute budget types
FR91	Loc.Auth.: Transfer with auto. rel.
FR92	Reconstruction of Release Groups
FRACTIV	Activate Subdivision
FRC0	Display Profit Center -> FM AcctAss.
FRC1	Maintain Cost Element -> FM Act Asgt
FRC2	Display Cost Element -> FM Acct Asgt
FRC3	Maintain Cost Center -> FM Act Asgmt
FRC4	Display Cost Center -> FM Acct Asgmt
FRC5	Maintain Order -> FM Acct Assgmnt
FRC6	Display Order -> FM Acct Assgmnt
FRC7	Maintain WBS Element -> FM Act Asgmt
FRC8	Display WBS Element -> FM Acct Asgmt
FRC9	Maintain Profit Center -> FM ActAsgt
FRCA	Settlement calendar
FRCISUB1	Process Substring1 Commitment Item
FRCISUB1_SET	Create Cmmt Item Substring1 Group
FRCISUB2	Process Substring2 Commitment Item
FRCISUB2_SET	Create Cmmt Item Substring2 Group
FRCISUB3	Process Substring3 Commitment Item
FRCISUB3_SET	Create Cmmt Item Substring3 Group
FRCISUB4	Process Substring4 Commitment Item
FRCISUB4_SET	Create Cmmt Item Substring4 Group
FRCISUB5	Process Substring5 Commitment Item
FRCISUB5_SET	Create Cmmt Item Substring5 Group
FRD1	Maintain G/L Account -> Commt Item
FRD2	Display G/L Account -> Commt Item
FRE01	Initial transmission of Data to F&R
FRE02	Transfer changed data to F&R
FRE03	Transfer Time Series Data
FRE04	Transfer Open Orders to F&R
FRE05	Transfer changed sal. price to F&R
FRE06	Processing of Order Inbound Buffer
FRE10	Transfer Reference Site to F&R
FRE11	Initial DIF occurrence transmission
FRE12	Delta DIF occurrence transmission
FRE13	Delete admin.data for DIF occurrence
FRE14	Transfer of reference assignm data

FRE15	Deletion of reference data
FRE16	InitTrnsfr. DIF Occur. for No. Sites
FRE17	DeltTrnsfr. DIF Occur. for No. Sites
FRE18	Delete DIF Occ. for No. Sites
FRE19	Trans. P.Org + P.Org Assgn. to F&R
FRE20	Update procurement cycles
FRE21	Upd. assignment of initial buy check
FRE22	Upd. assignment of central PO cal.
FRE23	upd. repl. block. after cust. change
FRE24	Logistical Rounding Delta
FRE25	Processing Methods Delta
FRE27	Transfer structured Materials to F&R
FRE30	Maintenance of Table FRE_MD_PRODUCT
FRE31	Maintenance of Interface Tables MD4
FRE32	Calculate planned delivery time
FRE33	Deletion of consumption data
FRE34	Maintenance of Table FRE_OP_PO_KEY
FRE35	Reo Change Pointer Stock Consumption
FRE50	Send Switchover Information
FRE51	Reorganization Switchover Info
FRE80	No. Range Maintnce: FRE_PROCYC
FRE81	No. Range Maintnce: FRE_DIFREF
FRE83	Number Range Maintenance: FRE_DIF2
FRE_C1	Check Master Data
FRE_C2	Check Supply Net Data
FRE_C3	Check layout module
FRE_C4	Check Order data
FRE_C5	Reorganization F&R Control Tables
FRE_UI	User Interface for F&R Messages
FRFCSUB1	Process Substring1 Fund Center
FRFCSUB1_SET	Create Funds Center Substring1 Group
FRFCSUB2	Process Substring2 Fund Center
FRFCSUB2_SET	Create Funds Center Substring2 Group
FRFCSUB3	Process Substring3 Fund Center
FRFCSUB3_SET	Create Funds Center Substring3 Group
FRFDSUB1	Process Substring1 Fund
FRFDSUB1_SET	Create Fund Substring1 Group
FRFDSUB2	Process Substring2 Fund
FRFDSUB2_SET	Create Fund Substring2 Group
FRFNSUB1	Process Substring1 Functional Area
FRFNSUB1_SET	Create Func. Area Substring1 Group
FRFNSUB2	Process Substring2 Functional Area
FRFNSUB2_SET	Create Func. Area Substring2 Group
FRFNSUB3	Process Substring3 Functional Area
FRFNSUB3_SET	Create Func. Area Substring3 Group
FRFT	Rapid Entry with Repetitive Code
FRFT2	Repetitive fast entry form
FRFT_B	Repetitive Codes: Payment to Banks
FRFT_TR	Repetitives: Payment Treasury Partnr
FRH1	Loc.Auth.: Enter Budget Release
FRH2	Loc.Auth.: Enter Local Block
FRH5	No longer used
FRH6	Create Release Group Profile
FRH7	Transfer of Residl Bdgts from CoverP

FRHU2	Random creation of HUs
FRML02	Edit Formula
FRML03	Display Formula
FRML04	Formula Information System
FRMLC01	Customizing: Formula Level Assignmt
FRMLC02	Customiz.: Formula Conversion Assig.
FRMLC03	Custom.: Check Function/Level Assig.
FRMLC04	Custom.: General Environment Param.
FRMLC05	Customizing: Composition Display
FRMLC06	Customizing for Units of Measurement
FRMLC07	Customiz.: Substance Types per View
FRMLC08	Customizing Status
FRMLC13	Specify Field Attributes
FRMLC30	Customizing Formula Tables Layout
FRMLC35	Customizing for Key Figures
FRMLC43	Set/Activate Customizing Views
FRMLC47	Customizing Assignmt ChkMod./ F.Lev.
FRMLC49	Roles for Events
FRMLC50	Roles for Events (Explosion)
FRMLC51	Customizing Component for Event
FRMLC52	Set Parameters for Formula View
FRMLC53	Parameters for Explosion Scope
FRMLC60	Customizing User Exits OPEN / CLOSE
FRMN	Credit Management
FRSTRID	Define Subdivision
FRSUBDIV	Define Substrings
FS00	G/L acct master record maintenance
FS00001	Create Business Partner
FS00002	Change Business Partner
FS00003	Display Business Partner
FS00101	Create Business Partner Customer
FS00102	Change Business Partner Customer
FS00103	Display Business Partner Customer
FS01	Create Master Record
FS02	Change Master Record
FS02CORE	Maintain G/L account
FS03	Display Master Record
FS04	G/L Account Changes (Centrally)
FS05	Block Master Record
FS06	Mark Master Record for Deletion
FS10	G/L Account Balance
FS10N	Balance Display
FS10NA	Display Balances
FS15	Copy G/L account changes: Send
FS16	Copy G/L account changes: Receive
FSAA	Display Address for Bal.Confirmatns
FSAP	Addresses for Balance Confirmations
FSAV	Balance Confirmations: Reply View
FSBP_TC_CUST_CHECK	Check Consistency of Customizing
FSBP_TC_SHOW	Display Total Commitment
FSBP_TC_STATUS	Change Status of Total Commitment
FSCD	Change Document List
FSCDEXPIRY1	Create Expiry Notes
FSCPAR01	FI-CA: Bal. Int. Calc. Archiving

FSCPBAC	Acct Balance Interest Notification
FSCPBAH	Balance Interest Calculation History
FSCPI1	Balance Interest Calculation Run
FSCQAR01A	FI-CA Bal. Int. Cal. Arch. Runtime
FSCQAR01B	Activate AS for Bal. Int. Cal. Arch.
FSCQS000	Acct Determ. for Receivables Accts
FSCQS001	Acct Determination: Revenue Accounts
FSCQS082	Specifs for Bal. Int. Calculation
FSCQS100	Payment Media ID for Appl. Forms
FSCQS400	Specs for Bal. Int. Calc. Reset
FSE2	Change Financial Statement Version
FSE3	Display Financial Statement Version
FSE5N	Maintain Planning
FSE6N	Display Planning
FSE7	Maint.Fin.Statemnt Forgn Lang.Texts
FSE8	Display Forgn Lang Fin.Statmnt Texts
FSE9	Automatic Financial Statement Form
FSEPA_M1	SEPA: Create Mandate
FSEPA_M2	SEPA: Change Mandate
FSEPA_M3	SEPA: Display Mandate
FSEPA_M3_LUW	SEPA: Display Mandate (in new LUW)
FSEPA_M4	SEPA: List Mandates
FSF1	Financial Calendar
FSH01	Flight Scheduling : Master Data
FSH01N	Flight Scheduling : Master Data
FSH02	Flight Scheduling : Detail Data
FSH02N	Flight Scheduling : Detail Data
FSI0	Execute report
FSI1	Create Report
FSI2	Change Report
FSI3	Display Report
FSI4	Create Form
FSI5	Change Form
FSI6	Display Form
FSIB	Background processing
FSIC	Maintain Currency Translation Type
FSIG	Balance Sheet Reports Criteria Group
FSIK	Maintain Key Figures
FSIM	Report Monitor
FSIO	Transport reports
FSIP	Transport forms
FSIQ	Import reports from client 000
FSIR	Import forms from client 000
FSIT	Translation Tool - Drilldown Report.
FSIV	Maintain Global Variable
FSIX	Reorganize Drilldown Reports
FSIY	Reorganize report data
FSIZ	Reorganize forms
FSK2	Maintain Sample Rules
FSK2_OLD	Maintain Sample Rules
FSL_EVALUNR	Number Range Maintenance: SL_EVALU
FSL_VALU_NR	Number Range Maint.: SL Valuation
FSM1	Create Sample Account
FSM2	Change Sample Account

FSM3	Display Sample Account
FSM4	Sample Account Changes
FSM5	Delete Sample Account
FSMN	
FSO2	Change Finan.Statement Vers. (old)
FSO3	Display Finan.Statement Vers. (Old)
FSP0	G/L acct master record in chrt/accts
FSP1	Create Master Record in Chart/Accts
FSP2	Change Master Record in Chart/Accts
FSP3	Display Master Record in Chart/Accts
FSP4	G/L Account Changes in Chart/Accts
FSP5	Block Master Record in Chart/Accts
FSP6	Mark Mast.Rec.for Del.in Chart/Accts
FSRD	Loans Regulatory Reporting CH
FSRG	Money Mkt Regulatory Reporting CH
FSRW	Securities Regulatory Reporting CH
FSS0	G/L account master record in co code
FSS1	Create Master Record in Company Code
FSS2	Change Master Record in Company Code
FSS3	Display Master Record in Comp.Code
FSS4	G/L Account Changes in Company Code
FSSA	Display Bal.Confirmatns Sel.Criteria
FSSP	Change Bal.Confirmatns Sel.Criteria
FST2	Maintain Account Name
FST3	Display Account Name
FS_BUT021	Data Transfer to but021_fs
FT10002	Create Treasury partner
FT10003	Create Treasury partner
FTB01001	Create Principal Loan Partner
FTB01002	Change Principal Loan Partner
FTB01003	Display Principal Loan Partner
FTB01501	Create Issuer
FTB01502	Change issuer
FTB01503	Display issuer
FTB01511	Create Counterparty
FTB01512	Change Counterparty
FTB01513	Display Counterparty
FTB01521	Create Depository Bank
FTB01522	Create Depository Bank
FTB01523	Create Depository Bank
FTB01531	Create Paying Bank
FTB01532	Create Paying Bank
FTB01533	Create Paying Bank
FTB01541	Create Beneficiary
FTB01542	Create Beneficiary
FTB01543	Create Beneficiary
FTB02001	Create Guarantor
FTB02002	Display Guarantor
FTB02003	Display Guarantor
FTB02021	Create Different Settler
FTB02022	Display Different Settler
FTB02023	Display Different Settler
FTBP1	Create business partner
FTBP2	Create business partner

FTBP3	Create business partner
FTEX	Exp.bill.doc.analysis
FTE_BSM	Bank Statement Monitor
FTE_BSM_CUST	Customizing: Bank Statement Monitor
FTE_POWL_LINE_ITEMS	line items display for powl
FTE_POWL_POSTPROC	postprocessing
FTE_POWL_STMT_DISP	bank statment display for POWL
FTE_POWL_STMT_LAST	last bank statment display for POWL
FTGR	Import Gds Receipt Analysis
FTIM	Import Order Analysis
FTLC_TBSCOP	SAPscript: Standard Texts
FTR01	Maintain Number Ranges
FTR02	Bill of Exchange List
FTR03	Bill of Exchange Transactions
FTR04	Reversal of Bill Transactions
FTR05	Printout of Transaction Records
FTR06	Inflation Adj. of Monetary Items
FTRCL	Closing of Expense Accounts
FTREX1	Raw Exposure Maintenance
FTREX12	Exposure Position List
FTREX13	Exposure Flows Display
FTREX2	Raw Exposures Display
FTREX21	Process Unmatched Transactions
FTREX7	Maintain Commodity Split
FTRSL	G/L Account Balances
FTRSLK	Expense Account Balances
FTRUE	Cost of Sales Statement
FTRV_CONFIG	Define Correspondence Profile
FTRV_MAPPING_CONF	Define Mapping Rules
FTR_00	Collective Processing
FTR_ALERT	Financial Transaction: Alert Monitor
FTR_ALRTCATDEF	Alerts (TRM)
FTR_ALRT_BTCH	CO Alert in batch mode
FTR_ARCHIVE_CUST00	Min. retent. period FTR CoCd depend.
FTR_ARCHIVE_CUST01	Min.ret.period FTR per product type
FTR_ARCH_W	Fin. transaction: Create archive
FTR_BAPI	BAPI Test Program
FTR_BP_ASSIGN	TCOR Assign BP
FTR_BP_BIC	Maintain BIC/Account for BP
FTR_COCD	Change Documents: Correspondence
FTR_COCREATE	Create manual correspondence object
FTR_COMATCH	Match unmatched correspondences
FTR_COMONI	Correspondence monitor
FTR_COSEND	Execute Unsent Correspondences
FTR_CO_ARCHIVE	For archiving of co objects
FTR_CREATE	Create a Transaction (TR-TM)
FTR_CSPRD	Credit Spread for OTC Transactions
FTR_CTY01	Create Commodity Forward
FTR_CTY02	Change Commodity Forward
FTR_CTY03	Display Commodity Forward
FTR_CTY04	Reverse Commodity Forward
FTR_CTY05	Settle Commodity Forward
FTR_CTY06	Commodity Forward History
FTR_CTY76	Commodity Forward History

SAP Transaction Codes – Volume One

FTR_C_MENU	Transaction: Task Menu
FTR_DEALPOS	Dealer Position
FTR_DERIVE_EXP_FIELD	Derivation of Exposure Fields
FTR_DISPLAY	Transaction Display
FTR_DISVARIANT_DEF	TCO: Define display variants
FTR_EDIT	Process a Treasury Transaction
FTR_EXT_ASSIGN	Maint.Profile & BPG ass. to Ext.Rec
FTR_HMLOG_ARCH_W	Hedge Mgmt Log: Create Archive
FTR_IMPORT	Import Incoming Messages
FTR_INB_ASSIGN	Maintain BP group for inbound format
FTR_INB_FUNC	Assign inbound function to partner
FTR_INT_ASSIGN	Maint.Profile & BPG ass. to Int.Rec
FTR_NR_CO	Define number ranges for CO ID
FTR_NR_MATCH	Define number ranges for Match ID
FTR_OPEN_TRTM_INIT	Update: Open TRTM Components
FTR_SAT_ACTVT	Correspondence Activities for SAT
FTR_SAT_ALRT	Maintain alert cat for sec. accounts
FTR_SHOW	Display Treasury Tables
FTR_SI_DERIVE	TCOR Derive Settlement Instruction
FTR_TRD_ADJUST	Adjust
FTR_TRM_COR_REL01	Customizing correspondence release
FTR_TRM_EM_REL01	Customizing of the Release Tool
FTR_XI_MAP_FXLEG	Mapping for Gen. Transaction Data
FTR_XI_MAP_FXOPTION	Mapping for Gen. Transaction Data
FTR_XI_MAP_FXSWAP	Mapping for Gen. Transaction Data
FTR_XI_MAP_GEN	Mapping for Gen. Transaction Data
FTUS	Foreign Trade: Maintain User Data
FTW0	Tax data retention and reporting
FTW1A	Extract Data
FTWA	Extract data
FTWB	Retrieve archived data
FTWC	Merge extracts
FTWCF	Field catalog
FTWCS	Segment catalog
FTWD	Verify data extract checksums
FTWE	Verify control totals (FI documents)
FTWE1	Verify all FI control totals
FTWF	Data extract browser
FTWH	Data view queries
FTWI	Create background job
FTWJ	Clear data retrieved from archives
FTWK	Delete extracts
FTWL	Display extract log
FTWM	Rebuild data extract
FTWN	Display view query log
FTWP	Settings for data extraction
FTWQ	Configure data file data segments
FTWQMD	Number range maintenance: TXW_SN_MD
FTWQTD	Number range maintenance: TXW_SN_TD
FTWR	File size worksheet
FTWS	Transport configuration and logs
FTWSCC	DART: Settings for Company Codes
FTWW	List segment information
FTWX	Data file view authority groups

FTWY	Maintain data file view
FTWYR	DART: Maintain Segment Relationships
FTXA	Display Tax Code
FTXP	Maintain Tax Code
FT_PULL_FILES	Upload Customs Data
FV02	Reverse Correction Items
FV08	Reverse input tax treatment run
FV11	Create condition
FV12	Change condition
FV13	Display condition
FV50	Park G/L Account Items
FV50L	Park G/L Acct Doc. for Ledger Group
FV53	Display Parked G/L Account Document
FV60	Park Incoming Invoices
FV63	Displayed Parked Vendor Document
FV65	Park Incoming Invoices
FV70	Enter Outgoing Invoices
FV73	Display Parked Customer Document
FV75	Park Outgoing Credit Notes
FVBTEP	BTE Process Text Module for RE
FVCP	Copy Program for Form Variants
FVD_CORR_DOCFINDER	FS CML - Document Finder
FVD_CORR_HISTORY	Display Correspondence History
FVD_CORR_PRINT_LOG	Appl. Log for Correspond. Print Run
FVD_CORR_PRINT_START	Start Correspondence Print Run
FVE3	Foreign Exchange Valuation
FVE4	Quotation Currency Conversion
FVE7	Reverse Forex Valuation
FVI5	Electronic rent collection
FVIESR	RE: Import POR data (Switzerland)
FVIQ	Legacy data transfer of compos.rates
FVIR	Legcy Data Trnsfr:Reset Option Rates
FVOE	Edit Transfer Table. Opt.Rates
FVOI	Create Transfer Table Opt.Rates
FVOP	Transfer Opt.Rates to Prod.System
FVVC	Transfer input tax correct.values
FVVD	Lgcy Data Reset Inp.Tax.Correct.Val.
FVVE	Data Transfer Input Tax Correction
FVVOZ	Balance Interest Calc. Ins. Object
FVZA	Inflow/outflow list report
FW	FW.. reserved for VV-Securities
FW-1	Number Range Maintenance: FVVW_ANLA
FW-2	Number Range Maintenance: FVVW_BEKI
FW-3	Number range maint.: FVVW_ORDER
FW-4	Number Range Maintenance: FVVW_PNNR
FW-5	Number range maintenance: FVVW_KMNR
FW-6	Number range maintenance: FVVW_KMNR
FW-7	Number Range Maintenance: FVVW_PODOC
FW-8	Number range maintenance: FVVW_KOBJ
FW17	Maintain security price
FW18	Display security price
FW20	Create sec.acct
FW21	Display securities account
FW22	Create CoCd Position Indicators

FW22A	Create Sec. Acct Position Indicators
FW23	Change CoCd Position Indicators
FW23A	Change Sec. Acct Position Indicators
FW24	Display CoCd Position Indicators
FW24A	Display Sec.Acct Position Indicators
FW26	Change sec.acct
FW27	Maintain index
FW28	Maintain index status
FW29	Maintain Index Type
FW43	Customizing Currency Swap Accounts
FW44	Customizing portfolio items
FW45	Customizing lock flags
FW46	Customizing holding share
FW47	Customizing tax rates
FW48	Customizing dealers
FW49	Customizing reservation reasons
FW51	Customizing valuation principles
FW52	Customizing valuation classes
FW53	Customizing valuation in CoCd
FW54	Customizing ref.prod.type/repmnt typ
FW55	Customizing: Ref.prod.type/sec.class
FW56	Customizing user-specific loan key
FW57	Customizing user-specific loan key
FW59	Customizing secondary index
FW60	Customizing sec.class relation.types
FW61	Customizing valuation principles
FW62	Customizing valuation principles
FW63	Customizing rate type
FW84	Customizing security type
FW85	Customizing funds type
FWAA	Execute Amortization
FWAB	Securities accruals/deferrals
FWACR	Reverse Amortization
FWAR	Securities accr/defer. reset
FWAS	Reverse accrual/deferral
FWBA	BAV Transfer/Securities Init. Screen
FWBC	BAV Info. - Securities Init. Screen
FWBJ	Posting journal
FWBK	Balance sheet transfer
FWBS	Manual Posting
FWCP	Calculate Position
FWDG	Class information
FWDP	Securities account list
FWDS	Reverse Securities Account Transfer
FWDU	Securities Transfer
FWER	Exercise Security Rights
FWER_DRAWING	Drawable Bonds: Mass Processing
FWER_STORNO_NEU	Reversal Rights
FWIW	Securities information
FWK0	Edit corporate action
FWKB	Post corporate action
FWKS	Reverse corporate action
FWLL	Proportion of Equity and Voting Rept
FWMY	Securities management

FWO0	Display Flows from Oper. Valn Area
FWO1	Create order
FWO2	Change order
FWO3	Display order
FWO4	Create order execution
FWO5	Change order execution
FWO6	Display order execution
FWO7	Create order settlement
FWO8	Change order settlement
FWO9	Display order settlement
FWOA	Execute order
FWOB	Settle order execution
FWOC	Settle order
FWOE	Reverse Posting
FWOEZ	Reverse Debit Position
FWOF	Change transaction
FWOG	Display transaction
FWOH	Settle transaction
FWOI	Display posted order settlement
FWOK	Display reversed settlement
FWOP	Update Flows from Oper. Valn Area
FWOS	Reverse order settlement
FWPA	Period-end closing
FWPA_EMERGENCY	Old Period-End Closing - Emergencies
FWPL	Display Last Period-End Closing
FWPR	Reset Period-End Closing
FWR1	Customizing Acct Assignm. Refer.(Mod
FWSB	Rate/price valn
FWSO	Automatic debit position
FWSS	Reverse Rate/Price Valuation
FWSU	Reverse Balance Sheet Transfer
FWTU	Securities Deadline Monitoring
FWUP	Update Planned Records
FWZA	TR Securities: Account Determination
FWZB	Treasury: Acct Deter. SEC Transact.
FWZE	Manual debit position
FWZZ	Class Master Data
FW_CSPRD	Credit Spread for Securities
FXI0	Execute Report
FXI1	Create Report
FXI2	Change Report
FXI3	Display Report
FXI4	Create Form
FXI5	Change Form
FXI6	Display Form
FXIB	Background Processing
FXIC	Maintain Currency Translation Type
FXIK	Maintain Key Figures
FXIM	Report Monitor
FXIO	Transport Reports
FXIP	Transport Forms
FXIQ	Import Reports from Client 000
FXIR	Import Forms from Client 000
FXIT	Translation Tool - Drilldown Report.

SAP Transaction Codes – Volume One

FXIV	Maintain Global Variable
FXIX	Reorganize Drilldown Reports
FXIY	Reorganize Report Data
FXIZ	Reorganize Forms
FXMN	Call Additional Components (FDMN)
FXXX	Processes for witholding tax code
FY01	FI Transport T060* in Client <> 000
FY02	EB: Transfer acct assignment + T028D
FY03	EB: Transfer acct stmt (T028H/I)
FY04	EB: Transfer checks recd (T028H/I)
FYMN	Call Additional Components (IMG)
FZ-1	Number Range Maintenance: FVV_DEBIT
FZ-2	Number Range Maintenance: FVV_PARTNR
FZ-3	Number Range Maintenance: FVV_VORG
FZ-4	No.range maintenance:FVV_ADRNR
FZ-5	Number Range Maintenance: FVV_OBJNR
FZ-6	No.range maintenance:FVV_PARTID
FZ-7	Customizing contract.prty relationsh
FZ-8	Customizing cntrct.prty rel.-App.4
FZ-9	Customizing coll.sec.name-Append.4
FZ02	BAV Data ANL, AEN, ANZ
FZ03	BAV Data ANL, AEN, ANZ Real Estate
FZ05	BP customizing: Loan default values
FZ06	BP customizing: REst. default values
FZ10	Loans: Circular R5/97
FZ11	Securities: Circular R5/97
FZ12	Circular R5/95 Real Estate
FZ12_BADI	Circular R5/95 Real Estate
FZ13	Money Market: Circular R5/97
FZ14	Access PRF-0 for Eq.-Linked Life.Ins
FZ19	Customizing Release Object Active ID
FZ20	Customizing Number Components
FZ23	Customizing BAV group 101/201/600
FZ30	Customizing restraint on disposal
FZ31	v-tzv04
FZ32	Cust. Stock Indicator BAV (Display)
FZ33	Customizing tax office stock indic.
FZ34	Cust. Stock Indicator BAV (Change)
FZ35	Customizing Stock ID Valuation Areas
FZ37	Customizing conversion extern.roles
FZ41	Customizing Internal Partner Role
FZ42	Customizing customer applicatn type
FZ43	Customizing Address Type
FZ44	Customizing Object Type
FZ45	Customizing Partner Install. Param.
FZ46	Customizing Partner Forms of Address
FZ47	Customizing Partner Letter Addr.Frms
FZ48	Customizing Partner Relationships
FZ49	Customizing Partner Reference Relat.
FZ50	Customizing Legal Form
FZ51	Customizing Finan.Acctng Asset Group
FZ52	Customizing Reasons for Reversal
FZ53	Customizing PRF- Number
FZ54	Customizing PRF - Subsection

FZ55	Customizing Insurance Branch
FZ56	Customizing Balance Sheet Indicator
FZ57	Customizing BAV 4/77
FZ58	Customizing Acct Assignm. Refer.- DD
FZ59	Customizing BAV Group 101 (Secur.)
FZ5A	AWV statement Z5 and Z5a
FZ60	Customizing BAV Group 101 (Loans)
FZ61	Customizing BAV Group 101 (Real Est)
FZ62	Customizing BAV Group 102
FZ63	Customizing BAV Group 102 (Secur.)
FZ64	Customizing BAV Group 102 (Real Est)
FZ65	Customizing PRF-Number
FZ66	Customizing PRF number (Real est.)
FZ67	Customizing Sub-section (Securit.)
FZ68	Customizing Sub-section (Real Est.)
FZ69	Customizing BAV Group 501 (Loans)
FZ70	Customizing BAV Group 501 (Secur.)
FZ71	Customizing BAV Group 501 (Real Est)
FZ73	Customizing Sub-section Relationship
FZ74	Customizing BAV Group 501 Relatnship
FZ75	Customizing BAV Group 201 (Loans)
FZ76	Customizing BAV Group 201 (Secur.)
FZ77	Customizing BAV Group 201 (Real Est)
FZ78	Customizing BAV Group R11/76 (Loans)
FZ79	Customizing BAV Group 11/76 (Secur.)
FZ80	Customizing BAV Grp R11/76 (RealEst)
FZ81	Customizing BAV Group R2/87 (Loans)
FZ82	Customizing BAV Group R2/87 (Secur.)
FZ83	Customizing BAV Grp R2/87 (Real Est)
FZ84	Cust. Stat.reporting asset type
FZ85	Customizing Asset Type DV3/DV8 (Sec)
FZ86	Cust. Asset Type DV3/DV8 (Real Est)
FZ87	Customizing acct assignment ref. DW
FZ88	Customizing acct assignment ref.- DI
FZ89	Customizing SCB Asset Group
FZ91	Customer input per product type
FZ92	Customizing default-ProdTyp/CoCd(DW)
FZ93	Customizing Default-ProdTyp/CoCd(DI)
FZ94	Customizing Default Value PART (DD)
FZ95	Customizing Default Value PART (DW)
FZ96	Customizing Default Value PART (DI)
FZ97	Customizing Search + Replace Strings
FZ98	Customizing Par. 18 GBA
FZ99	Customizing Int. Item
FZA0	Customizing Int. Indicator 1
FZA1	Customizing Int. Indicator 2
FZA2	Customizing Int. Indicator 3
FZA3	Customizing Int. Indicator 4
FZA4	Customizing Int. Indicator 5
FZA5	Customizing Int. Indicator 6
FZA6	Customizing Int. Indicator 7
FZA7	Customizing Int. Indicator 8
FZA8	Customizing Int. Indicator 9
FZA9	Customizing Int. Indicator 10

FZAB	Cust. appl./role categ./dunn.param.
FZB0	Customizing Int. Indicator 11
FZB4	List of trustees
FZB5	Statements
FZB6	Control Parameters for BAV Statement
FZB7	Statements
FZB8	BAV-Lists Securities Control
FZB9	Control prem.reserve fund lists DA
FZBA	Transact. types relationship tab.-DD
FZBB	Transact.types relationship tab.-DW
FZBC	Transact types relationship tab. -DI
FZBD	Alloc. prog. transaction types - DD
FZBE	Alloc. prog. transaction types - DW
FZBG	Ratio Table for For.Exch Rate Conver
FZBH	Exchange Rate Calculation Indicator
FZBI	BAV Reporting - Real Estate
FZBK	Debit form type FVV/DD
FZBL	Form Line Items FVV/DD
FZBM	Darwin Real Estate Objects FVV
FZBN	BAV Control of Cost Elements
FZBO	Classification of Contracting Party
FZBP	Contracting Party/Class Relatnships
FZBR	Cust. trns types per post.appl.-DD
FZBU	Customizing Status Transfer
FZBV	Selection for status transfers - DD
FZBW	Selection for status transfers - DW
FZBX	Customizing status definit. D:D,W,I
FZBY	Selection for status transfers - DI
FZBZ	BAV Stat.reporting PRF-12
FZC4	Maintain Ratings
FZC5	Maintain Legal Entity
FZC6	Maintain Product Types-DW (Gen.data)
FZC7	Maintain Product Types-DW(CoCd data)
FZC8	Maintain Changes in Net Assets
FZC9	Maintain Valuation Types
FZCA	Maintain Ownership Share
FZCB	Flow types relationship keys
FZCC	Maintain VV Status Definition
FZCD	Maintain Int. Status Delivery Matrix
FZCE	Maintain Condition Type (DW)
FZCF	Maintain Condition Type (DD)
FZCG	Maintain Condition Group (DW)
FZCH	Maintain Condition Group (DD)
FZCJ	Maintain Product Types-DD (Gen.data)
FZCK	Maintain Product Types-DD(CoCd Data)
FZCN	Status Definitions
FZCO	Customizing Status Transfer
FZCP	Selection for Status Definitions -DD
FZCQ	Selection for Status Definitions -DW
FZCR	Selection for Status Definitions- DI
FZCS	Transaction type - DD
FZCT	Transaction type - DW
FZCU	Customizing Initial Transaction
FZCV	Transaction type - DI

FZCX	Special Indicator for Loans
FZCY	Determine Special Interest
FZD4	VV Plausibility Checks
FZFD	Assign planning levels
FZID	Number Range Maintenance: FVVZ_IDENT
FZKB	Clear Trivial Amnts for Cons. Loans
FZKL	Account Clearing Loans
FZLR	VV Returned debit memos
FZM4	Treasury Mgmt information system
FZMN	Treasury Management basic functions
FZNB	Payment Postprocessing
FZP0	
FZP1	Create Natural Person
FZP2	Create Legal Person
FZP3	Change Partner
FZP4	Display Partner
FZP5	Choose Partner
FZP6	Create Legal Person
FZPA	Create Partner in Role
FZPB	Change Partner in Role
FZPC	Display Partner in Role
FZPD	Edit bus.partner in role
FZPE	Change customer (hidden)
FZPF	Partner payment details
FZR1	Create Rating Agency
FZR2	Change Rating Agency
FZR3	Display Rating Agency
FZUA	Auto. Process Unscheduled Repayment
FZW0	Resubmission of Application Area
FZW1	Create Messages / MAILS
FZW2	Change Messages / MAIL
FZW3	Display Messages / MAIL
FZW4	Delete Messages / MAIL
FZW5	Maintain Text Objects: Table TTXOB
FZW6	Maintain Text IDs: Table TTXID
FZW7	Dates Overview
FZW9	Display monitoring table
FZXR	Flow types per posting application
FZZB	Cust.: Sort criteria selection
FZZC	Customizing: Sort criteria values
FZZD	Customizing: Planned item-search
FZZE	Custzomizing: IPD-transaction types
F_71	DME with Disk: B/Excha. Presentation
F_72	Mass Bill/Exch.Liability Maintenance
F_75	Extended Bill/Exchange Information
F_76	Extended Bill of Exchange List (ALV)
F_77	C FI Maintain Table T045D
F_79	C FI Maintain Table T045G
F_90	C FI Maintain Table T045F
F_CO_01	Report RFSUMB00 Colombia
F_IT_01	Report RFSUMB00 Italy
F_PT_01	Report RFSUMB00 Portugal
F_RO_01	Report RFSUMB00 Romania
F_SK_01	Report RFSUMB00 Slovakia

F_TIBAN_WO_ACCNO	Maint. View TIBAN_WO_ACCNO (Modif.)
F_TR_01	Report RFSUMB00 Turkey
GA11	Create FI-SL Actual Assessment
GA11N	Create FI-SL Actual Assessment
GA12	Change FI-SL Actual Assessment
GA12N	Change FI-SL Actual Assessment
GA13	Display FI-SL actual assessment
GA13N	Display FI-SL Actual Assessment
GA14	Delete FI-SL Actual Assessment
GA14N	Delete FI-SL Actual Assessment
GA15	Execute FI-SL actual assessment
GA16	Actual Assessment Overview
GA1D	Delete allocation line items
GA27	Create FI-SL Planned Assessment
GA27N	Create FI-SL Planned Assessment
GA28	Change FI-SL Planned Assessment
GA28N	Change FI-SL Planned Assessment
GA29	Display FI-SL Planned Assessment
GA29N	Display FI-SL Planned Assessment
GA2A	Delete FI-SL Planned Assessment
GA2AN	Delete FI-SL Planned Assessment
GA2B	Execute FI-SL Planned Assessment
GA2C	Plan Assessment Overview
GA31	Create FI-SL actual distribution
GA31N	Create FI-SL Actual Distribution
GA32	Change FI-SL actual distribution
GA32N	Change FI-SL Actual Distribution
GA33	Display FI-SL actual distribution
GA33N	Display FI-SL Actual Distribution
GA34	Delete FI-SL actual distribution
GA34N	Delete FI-SL Actual Distribution
GA35	Execute FI-SL actual distribution
GA36	Actual Distribution Overview
GA47	Create FI-SL Planned Distribution
GA47N	Create FI-SL Planned Distribution
GA48	Change FI-SL Planned Distribution
GA48N	Change FI-SL Planned Distribution
GA49	Display FI-SL Planned Distribution
GA49N	Display FI-SL Planned Distribution
GA4A	Delete FI-SL Planned Distribution
GA4AN	Delete FI-SL Planned Distribution
GA4B	Execute FI-SL Planned Distribution
GA4C	Plan Distribution Overview
GAL1	Update Assignment Table EDIMAP
GAL2	Generate Export/Import
GAL3	Export of G/L acct transactn figures
GALILEO	Galileo Bypass
GALILEO_SYNCH	Synchronization of Galileo PNRs
GALILEO_VPNR	Galileo Bypass VPNR
GAOV	Cycle Overview FI-SL
GAR1	Create Archive
GAR5	Display Structure of Local DBs
GAR8	RW/RP Reports for FI-SL Archives
GAR9	Generate FI-SL Archive/DB Reports

GB01	Document Entry for Local Ledgers
GB02	Number Range Maint.for Local Ledgers
GB03	Number Range Maint.f.Global Ledgers
GB04	Number Range Maint.for Local Ledgers
GB05	Number Range Maint.f.Global Ledgers
GB06	Reverse Local FI-SL Actual Documnts
GB11	Document Entry for Global Ledgers
GB16	Reverse Global FI-SL Actual Docmnts
GBC1	GBC: Method Repository
GBC2	GBC: Task Definition
GBC3	GBC: Field and Value Allocations
GBC4	GBC:No.Range Maintenance(ISU_GBCCON)
GBC5	GBC:No.Range Maint. (ISU_GBCLNK)
GBCA	GBC: Link Log
GC01	Call GS01 for LC
GC10	FI-LC: Print Companies
GC11	Create Company Master Record
GC12	Change Company Master Record
GC13	Display Company Master Record
GC14	Delete Company Master Record
GC16	Create Subgroup Master Record
GC17	Change Subgroup Master Record
GC18	Display Subgroup
GC19	FI-LC: Print Subgroups
GC21	Enter Individual Fin.Statement Data
GC22	Display Individual Fin. Stmt Data
GC23	FI-LC: Document Entry
GC24	FI-LC: Display Document
GC25	Maintain Consolidation Number Ranges
GC26	FI-LC: Journal Entry Report
GC27	FI-LC: Customize Journal Entry Reprt
GC28	Status Display
GC29	Status Management
GC30	FI-LC: Mass Reversal
GC31	FI-LC: Customize Curr. Translation
GC32	FI-LC: Customizing Consolidation
GC33	FI-LC: Financial Data Table Maint.
GC34	FI-LC: Reported Data Table Display
GC35	FI-LC: Transport Table Entries/Sets
GC36	Transport connection: Cons.Inv.Cust.
GC38	Data transfer
GC39	Change Local Valuation Data
GC41	GLT3 - Maintain GLT3 sub-assignments
GC44	Send Financial Statement Data
GC45	Delete Subgroup
GC4P	FI-LC Print Step-Consolidated Group
GC50	Report Selection
GC51	Report Selection
GC60	Data for elim. of IC profit/loss
GC61	Export of Transaction Data
GC62	Import of Transaction Data
GC63	Liability Method
GC99	Consolidation Test Data
GCA1	FI-SL: Field Usage for Assessment

GCA2	FI-SL: Data Control for Assessment
GCA3	FI-SL: Allocations: Data fld descr.
GCA4	FI-SL: Allocation Field Grp Texts
GCA5	FI-SL: Allocation Table Information
GCA6	FI-SL: Field Usage for Distribution
GCA7	FI-SL: Data Control for Distributn
GCA8	Sender-Receiver Relationship
GCA9	Check allocation customizing
GCAC	Ledger comparison
GCAE	Ledger comparison w/diff. clearing
GCAG	Generate FI-SL Archiving
GCAN	Analysis of FI-SL Database Contents
GCAR	Ledger Comparison Remote
GCB1	Change FI-SL Customizing Comp. Code
GCB2	Display FI-SL Customizing Comp.Code
GCB3	Copy FI-SL Customizing Company Code
GCB4	FI-SL: Delete Company Code
GCBA	FI-SL: Valid Document Types
GCBE	Texts for Document Types
GCBR	Document Types for Rollup
GCBT	Texts for Document Types
GCBW1	Generate TransStruct. for Totals Tbl
GCBW2	Generate summ.table trans. structure
GCBX	FI-SL: Valid Document Types
GCCG	Generate Code for FI-SL
GCD1	FI-SL Customizing: Diagnosis Tool
GCD2	List of FI-SL Direct Posting Tables
GCD3	Graphical Navigation in FI-SL
GCD4	Check General Ledger
GCD5	Check Currencies in FI-SL
GCD6	Graphic Display of FI-SL Tables
GCDE	Delete FI-SL Transaction Data
GCDF	Delete FI-SL Transaction Data
GCDH	G/L diagnosis
GCE1	Maintain User
GCEA	Maintain FI-LC ledgers
GCEB	Maintain FI-LC ledgers for conversn
GCEC	Maintain companies for conversion
GCED	Make special settings for conversion
GCEE	FI-LC: Reconcil. of bal. carried fwd
GCEF	FI-LC: Reconcil. of fin. data tables
GCEG	Ingeration: Euro transaction types
GCEH	Make settings for integration
GCEJ	Suggest FI-LC package assignment
GCEK	Reconcil. integration < _ > CF FILCT
GCEL	Item substitution/Ret. earn. (CF)
GCEM	Post extract in carryforward period
GCEN	Check whether balance carried fwd
GCEP	Delete period values for current yr
GCEQ	KONS-EURO: End Package
GCEU	Item can be Included in Bal.Sheet
GCF1	Create FI-SL Customizng Fld Assign.
GCF2	Change FI-SL Customizng Fld Assign.
GCF3	Display FI-SL Customizng Fd Assign.

GCF4	FI-SL: Delete Field Assignment
GCG1	Create FI-SL Customizing Glob.Comp.
GCG2	Change FI-SL Customizing Glob.Comp.
GCG3	Display FI-SL Customizing Glob.Comp
GCG4	Copy FI-SL Customizing Global Comp.
GCG5	FI-SL Customizing: Delete Companies
GCGE	Activate Global Plan Line Items
GCGG	Generation of GLU1
GCGR	Activity Groups
GCGS	Reconciliation of Total Line Items
GCGV	C FI Maintain Table T009
GCI1	Installation of FI-SL Tables
GCI2	FI-SL: Installation of Object Tables
GCI3	FI-SL Table Directory
GCI4	FI-SL Fixed Field Movements
GCIN	Maintain FI-SL tables
GCIQ	Quick installation FI-SL
GCJU	Diagnosis: Direct Access to Function
GCL1	Create FI-SL Customizing Ledger
GCL2	Change FI-SL Customizing Ledger
GCL3	Display FI-SL Customizing Ledger
GCL4	Delete FI-SL Customizing Ledger
GCL6	FI-SL: Copy Ledger
GCLE	Activate Local Plan Line Items
GCM1	Conversion
GCP1	FI-SL: Local Posting Periods
GCP2	FI-SL Customizing: T001C
GCP3	FI-SL: Local Fisc.Yr-Dep.Vers.Param
GCP4	FI-SL: Global Fisc.Yr-Dep.Vers.Para
GCP5	FI-SL: Local Plan Periods
GCP6	FI-SL: Global Plan Periods
GCR1	Rollup: Create Field Assignment
GCR2	Rollup: Change Field Assignment
GCR3	Rollup: Display Field Assignment
GCR4	FI-SL: Rollup Substitution
GCR5	FI-SL: Rollup Substitution
GCR6	FI-SL Customizing:Del.Rollup Fld.A.
GCR7	Rollup: Direct Access
GCR8	Rollup: Direct Access
GCRB	Report Selection
GCRE1	Activate drilldown rep. for SL table
GCRE2	Deactivate drilldown rep. - SL table
GCRF	Translation Factors
GCRS	Languages for Report Writer
GCS1	FI-SL: Master Data T800D
GCS5	Balance Carr. Forward Fld Movements
GCS6	Global Standard Accounts
GCS7	Bal.Carr.Forward: Global Std Accts
GCT0	Transport of Substitutions
GCT1	Transport Ledger
GCT2	FI-SL Activation
GCT3	Control Information
GCT4	Transport Rollup
GCT5	Transport: Planning Parameters

SAP Transaction Codes – Volume One

GCT6	Transport Distribution Key
GCT7	Transport: Cycles
GCT8	Transport: Document Types
GCT9	Transport of Validations
GCTA	Transport Rules
GCTR	Transport from Report Writer objects
GCTS	Transport of sets and variables
GCU0	Customizing FI-GLX Menu
GCU1	Data Transfer from FI
GCU1N	Data Transfer from FI
GCU2	Generate G1U2
GCU3	Transfer Data From CO
GCU4	Subsequent Posting of Data From MM
GCU5	Subsequent Posting of Data frm Sales
GCU6	CO plan doc subs. posting to FI-SL
GCU9	Delete Transaction Data
GCUP	Subsequently posting CO data to FISL
GCUT	Maintain user tables
GCV1	FI-SL: Create Activity
GCV2	Change FI-SL Customizing Activity
GCV3	Display FI-SL Customizing Activity
GCV4	FI-SL Customizing: Delete Activity
GCVB	Update Type in FI-SL
GCVI	FI-SL: Actual Versions
GCVO	Preparation for FI-SL Customizing
GCVP	FI-SL: Plan Periods
GCVV	FI-SL Validation / Local
GCVW	FI-SL Validation / Global
GCVX	FI-SL Substitution / Local
GCVY	FI-SL Substitution / Global
GCVZ	Rule Maintenance
GCW1	Versions for Currency Translation
GCW2	Local Translation Methods
GCW3	Global Translation Methods
GCW4	Sp.Purpose Ldgr Currency Translation
GCW5	FI-SL: Historical Curr. Translation
GCW6	FI-SL: Exchange Rates
GCW7	Transport Currency Translation Mthd
GCW8	Exchange Rate Types
GCW9	Methods for Currency Translation
GCWU	Assign tables to translation methods
GCX1	FI-SL: Client-independent user exits
GCX2	FI-SL: Client-dependent user exits
GCZ3	Generate Report Groups
GC_GR_NV	Indirect call of GCD3
GD00	Report Selection
GD02	FI-SL line item plan documents
GD12	Flex.G/L: Totals Record Display
GD13	Totals Record Display
GD20	Start Selectin FI-SL Line Items
GD21	Flexible G/L: Document Selection
GD22	Flex. G/L: Actual Document Display
GD23	FI-SL: Local Actual Document Display
GD33	FI-SL: Global Actual Doc. Display

GD42	Flex. G/L: Plan Document Display
GD43	FI-SL: Local Plan Document Display
GD44	FI-SL: Global Plan Document Display
GD51	Enter Local FI-SL Master Data
GD52	Change Local FI-SL Master Data
GD53	Display Local FI-SL Master Data
GD54	Delete Local FI-SL Master Data
GD60	Create Code Combinations
GD61	Maintain Code Combinations
GD62	Display Code Combinations
GD63	Code combinations activation
GD64	Code combinations deactivation
GDS_MATERIAL_EXTRACT	Extraction of Materials for GDS
GENC	Generate Source Code
GENEPXML	Generate Enterprise Portal Navb. XML
GENIL_BOL_BROWSER	Browser for Business Object Layer
GENIL_MODEL_BROWSER	Model Browser forGen.IL Applications
GEN_EBPP_CREATE_USER	Create New User
GEN_US_2	Activate/deactivate US enhancements
GFSRFW	Fastsearch Replication Monitor
GFSWB	Generic Fast Search Workbench
GFTR_C0001	FTTR: Applications
GFTR_C0002	TR-TM: Define Field Groups
GFTR_C0003	FTTR: Views
GFTR_C0011	TR-TM: Screen Field <--> DB Field
GFTR_C0012	TR-TM: Field Modification Criteria
GFTR_C0023	FTTR: Data Sets
GFTR_C0101	GFTR: Field Modification Prod. Cat.
GFTR_C0102	TR Transaction Mgmt: Field Selection
GFTR_C0200	Customizing Field Selection Process
GFTR_CATTR	Treasury Sample Transactions
GFTR_C_MENU	Transaction: Task Menu
GGB0	Validation Maintenance
GGB1	Substitution Maintenance
GGB3	Maintain Boolean Class
GGB4	Analysis tool for valid./subst.
GJ01	Net Cash Call to Equity Group
GJ02	JV Gross Cash Call To Equit Group
GJ03	JV Net Cash Call To Project
GJ04	JV Gross Cash Call To Project
GJ05	JV Non-operated cash call to eq grp
GJ06	JV Non-Operated Cash Call to Project
GJ09	Joint Venture detailed information
GJ0A	Non-Operated Billing by Operator V.2
GJ0B	Non-Operated Billing by Venture V.2
GJ10	Yearly balance shifting
GJ11	Joint Venture master data catalog
GJ12	Billing Ledger Extract
GJ13	Joint Venture Ledger Extract
GJ14	Hard Copy Billing
GJ15	Billing Schedule Manager
GJ16	EDI Billing
GJ17	Suspense Project / Equity Group
GJ18	Partner Suspense Clearing

GJ19	Equity Adjustments
GJ20	Venture Bank Account Switching
GJ21	Recovery indicator
GJ22	Internal recovery indicator
GJ23	Change JV partners
GJ24	Venture classes
GJ25	Cutback rules / accounts
GJ26	Cutback rules / accounts
GJ27	Cutback rules / cost centers
GJ28	Cutback rules / cost centers
GJ29	Cutback rules / projects
GJ2A	Display JV partners
GJ2B	Maintain JV partners
GJ30	Cutback / project intercompany code
GJ31	Cutback tables / orders
GJ32	Cutback rules / orders
GJ33	Equity types
GJ34	JV project in suspense
GJ35	Bank accounts
GJ36	Funding groups
GJ37	Funding group assignment
GJ39	JV Billing indicator
GJ3A	Display JV project in suspense
GJ3B	Cutback rules / intercompany assets
GJ3C	Cutback rule: Networks
GJ3D	Cutback - Intercompany networks
GJ3R	Reconsile Intercompany Mapping
GJ40	Accounts for supplemental billing
GJ41	JV Projects for supplemental billing
GJ42	JV Material Batch-Cond code x-ref
GJ44	Net profit interest groups
GJ45	JVA functions / function item types
GJ47	Billing methods
GJ49	Billing method posting rules
GJ4A	Periodic updates for company code
GJ4A_MCC	Periodic updates for company code
GJ50	JV Posting rule detail customizing
GJ51	Bank accounts for cash call print
GJ52	Non-operated billing forms
GJ53	Non-operated billing form lines
GJ54	JOA detailed information
GJ55	JV valuation area
GJ56	Accounts for exchange differences
GJ57	JIB/JIBE classes
GJ58	JIB/JIBE subclasses
GJ59	JV Conditional code
GJ60	EDI Outbound Base Configuration
GJ61	JV Clearing billing indicator
GJ62	JV Bi.Meth./CompCd. assignment
GJ63	JV Project types
GJ64	JV Cost center types
GJ65	JV Order types
GJ66	JIB master data
GJ67	JIB account mapping

SAP Transaction Codes – Volume One

GJ68	JIB class/account mapping
GJ69	JIB class/subclass/account mapping
GJ70	JOA-maintenance
GJ72	JOA classes
GJ73	Special cost elements
GJ74	Stepped rate rules
GJ75	JV stepped rate thresholds
GJ76	Partner process groups
GJ77	Drilling statistical ratios
GJ78	Producing statistical ratios
GJ80	JIB account mapping for AFE
GJ81	JV Billing structure
GJ82	Create BTCI Sessions for Cash Calls
GJ83	JV Automatic posting
GJ84	JVA NPI/CI Netting (without CI Grp)
GJ85	JV Automated Postings (Cost Calcs)
GJ86	Customize report selection
GJ87	Display summary ledger totals
GJ88	Display billing ledger totals
GJ89	Automatic Adjust of Overhead Rates
GJ90	JV Realized exchange differences
GJ91	JV Unrealized exchange
GJ92	JV Goods receipt expense orders
GJ93	JV Goods receipt inventory orders
GJ94	International Cost Calculations
GJ95	North American Overhead Calculations
GJ96	Payroll Burden Clearing
GJ97	Compare FI with JV document
GJ97N	JV Document Comparison
GJ98	North America Overhead Detail Report
GJ99	EDI mapping
GJA1	Create joint operating agreement
GJA2	Change joint operating agreement
GJA3	Display joint operating agreement
GJA4	JOA master data catalog
GJA5	Display changes for Joint Op. Agreem
GJA8	JV JOA screen
GJAA	JOA Master Transaction
GJAC	Activate JVA in a Client
GJB1	BI for supplemental detail
GJB2	Account for supplemental detail
GJB3	Project type for supplemental detail
GJB4	Cost center type for suppl. detail
GJB5	Order type for supplemental detail
GJB6	SDS protocol
GJBA	Balance sheet accounts for splitting
GJBM	GJ BAPI parameter mapping
GJBR	Billing reconciliation
GJBS	Assign substitution to JV company
GJBT	Billing threshold check
GJBV	Assign Validation to JV Company
GJC1	Activate company in JV
GJC2	Deactivate company in JV
GJCA	Housebank switching

GJCB	JV Cutback Program
GJCB_REV	Cutback Reversal
GJCC	Copy configuration from company code
GJCG	Carried interest groups
GJCM	Change message control for JVA
GJCN	Convenience netting
GJCS	JV settlement manipulation rules
GJCU	Cutback Ledger Update
GJCUST	JV Customizing
GJDA	Delete JOA
GJDC	Dunning
GJDE	Delete Joint Venture Data
GJE0	EDI invoice service codes
GJE2	JV Customize EDI Suppl Seg Drivers
GJE3	JV Customize EDI Segment Components
GJE4	EDI JIBE condition codes
GJE5	JV EDI Communications Code
GJE6	JV EDI Bill Ind to Svc Code mapping
GJE7	JV EDI Outbound: Company Config.
GJE8	JV EDI Terms of Payment
GJE9	JV EDI Contact Function Codes
GJEA	EDI inbound: company configuration
GJEB	JV EDI Outbound: Control Processed
GJEC	Pre-Cutback Equity_Change Management
GJED	JV EDI Inbound: Sender's JIBE No
GJEE	JV EDI Inbound: Property Table
GJEF	EDI inbound: withhold code
GJEG	EDI inbound: mapping qualifier
GJEH	JV EDI Inbound: Cost Object Mapping
GJEI	JV EDI Inbound: 819 CO Ref
GJEJ	JV EDI Inbound: 819 CO Ref+Class
GJEK	JV EDI Inbound: 819 CO Ref+Class+Sub
GJEL	JV EDI Inbound: 819 CO Class
GJEM	JV EDI Inbound: 819 CO Class+Sub
GJEN	JV EDI Inbound: Memo AFE
GJEO	EDI inbound: 819 account mapping
GJEP	EDI inbound: 819 acc class mapping
GJEQ	EDI inbound: 819 acc class+sub
GJER	JV EDI Inbound: 810 CO Mapping
GJES	JV EDI Inbound: 810 CO Service Code
GJET	EDI inbound: 810 account mapping
GJEV	Process history
GJEW	EDI inbound: Receiver's JIBE/PASC no
GJEX	JV mapping: Material - Service code
GJEY	JIB/JIBE Tubular Sub-Accounts
GJEZ	JIB/JIBE Non-Tubular Sub-Accounts
GJF1	Create JV assessment cycle - actual
GJF2	Change JV assessment cycle - actual
GJF3	Display JV assessment cycle - actual
GJF4	Delete JV assessment cycle - actual
GJF5	Execute JV assessment - actual
GJF6	Overview JV assessment
GJF7	Create JV assessment cycle - plan
GJF8	Change JV assessment cycle - plan

GJF9	Display JV assessment cycle - plan
GJFA	Print Allocation Information
GJFARM_0	view maintenance FARM
GJFARM_1	Farm in/out: JVTO1 and Cutback
GJFARM_2	Farm in/out: JVTO1 and Cutback
GJFARM_3	FarmIn/Out Cash Call redetermination
GJFARM_4	FarmIn/Out Cash Call correction
GJFB	Execute JV assessment - plan
GJG1	Create JV distribution cycle -actual
GJG2	Change JV distribution cycle -actual
GJG3	Display JV distribution cycle-actual
GJG4	Delete JV distribution cycle -actual
GJG5	Execute JV distribution - actual
GJG6	Overview distribution - actual
GJG7	Create JV distribution cycle -plan
GJG8	Change JV distribution cycle - plan
GJG9	Display JV distribution cycle-plan
GJGA	Display JOA graphically
GJGB	Document Entry for Local Ledgers
GJGO	Driver transaction for customizing
GJGP	Document Entry for Local Ledgers
GJGR	Graphical Navigation JVA
GJIS	Install JV standard reports
GJJ1	Generate JADE audit file
GJJ2	Billing extracts
GJJ3	JADE file description
GJJA	JV Load Balancing
GJJE	Joint venture event maintenance
GJL2	C JVA Change Ledger
GJL3	C JVA Display Ledger
GJL7	Plan Data Transfer by Documents
GJL8	Company code (global data)
GJLB	Load Balancing Distribution
GJLI	Summary ledger line items
GJLI2	Billing ledger line items
GJLV	Line item report list variants
GJM1	Mark Prepaid Inventory
GJM2	Display Prepaid Inventory
GJNO	Non open item unreal. exchange diff.
GJNR	JV Number range customizing
GJOI	Open line items for cost objects
GJP1	JVA NPI/CI Netting (with CI Grp)
GJPA	Partner regional addresses
GJPC	Penalty categories
GJPD	Determine CRP pricing procedure
GJPE	Display Documents for re-posting
GJPN	Partner Netting
GJPTS	Payment term schema
GJQ0	CRP Customising Menu
GJQ1	Conditions: Procedure for A CR
GJQ2	Condition Types: SD Pricing
GJQ3	Maintain Access (Sales Price)
GJQ4	V-T681F: Index Field Catalog
GJQ5	Create Conditions (CRP)

GJQ6	Change Conditions (CRP)	
GJQ7	Display Conditions (CRP)	
GJQ8	Create Conditions (Purchasing)	
GJQ9	Maintain Recover Ind determination	
GJQA	Change Condition Table (CRP)	
GJQB	Change Condition Table (CRP)	
GJR1	Summary Ledger Reporting	
GJR2	Billing Ledger Reporting	
GJR3	JV EDI Inbound: IDOC Status Report	
GJR4	EDI: Invoice and Operating Statement	
GJR5	JV EDI Inbound: Unusual Expenditure	
GJR6	JV EDI Inbound: Memo AFE Projects	
GJR7	JV EDI Inbnd: Expenditure Comparison	
GJR8	810/819 Mapping Report	
GJR9	810/819 Property Error	
GJRC	Cash Call Reclass	
GJRCN	Cash Call Reclassification	
GJRD	JV Recovery indicator determination	
GJRG_5J1A	Gross bill./all by venture/account	
GJRG_5J1B	Gross billable / all by cost object	
GJRG_5J1C	Gross bill/partner net by cost obj.	
GJRG_5J1D	Gross bill./all by cost obj. F.Curr	
GJRG_5J1E	Gross billable/partner net for JIB	
GJRG_5J1F	Remaining cutback by cost object	
GJRG_5J1G	Posted suspense overview	
GJRG_5J1H	Gross non-operated by cost object	
GJRG_5J2A	Venture/EG/Billing indicator	
GJRG_5J2B	Partner/Billing indicator	
GJRG_5JCA	Cost centers: overview actuals	
GJRG_5JCB	Internal orders: overview actuals	
GJRG_5JCC	WBS elements: overview actuals	
GJRG_5JCD	Cost centers: actual/plan gross/net	
GJRG_5JCE	Int. orders: actual/plan gross/net	
GJRG_5JCF	WBS elements: actual/plan gross/net	
GJRS	Configure report selection	
GJRT	Overhead burden rate type	
GJRX	Bericht auswählen	
GJS1	Create account set	
GJS2	Change account set	
GJS3	Display account set	
GJSX	Call set maintenance	
GJT0	Reverse AM/MM Transfer document	
GJT1	JV Transfer Asset to Asset	
GJT1_OLD	JV Transfer Asset to Project/Order	
GJT2	JV Transfer Asset to Asset	
GJT2_OLD	JV Transfer Asset to Asset	
GJT3	JV Transfer Asset to Asset	
GJT3_OLD	Retirement of Venture Owned Assets	
GJT4	JV Transfer Asset to Asset	
GJT4_OLD	Sale of Venture owned assets	
GJT5	JV Transfer Asset to Asset	
GJT5_OLD	Transfer Proj./Order to Proj./Order	
GJT6	JV Transfer Asset to Asset	
GJT6_OLD	Transfer Project/Order to Asset	

GJTA	Depreciation area update by RI
GJTB	Transaction Type Subst. for Cutback
GJTD	Transaction types per line
GJTE	Equity change asset transact. types
GJTF	Fields to be copied to new assets
GJTG	Maintain TransTypeGroup JV Prop.
GJTR	C FI Month End Advance Tax Return
GJTX	Maintain Field Transfers rules for
GJU1	Customizing groups
GJU2	Customizing group definition
GJU3	Processes for authorization
GJV0	
GJV1	Create Joint Venture Master
GJV2	Change Joint Venture Master
GJV3	Display Joint Venture Master
GJV4	Joint Venture Customizing Menu
GJV5	Display Change Documents JV-Master
GJV6	
GJVA	Advance Tax Report
GJVB	JV Billing formats
GJVC	IS-OIL: Joint Venture Accounting con
GJVD	Joint Venture Deletion
GJVE	List Venture / Equity Groups
GJVF	Bank Acct Switch - Maintain Data
GJVG	Bank Acct Switch - Create Data
GJVL	JV layout sets
GJVP	IS-OIL: Joint Venture Accounting pro
GJVS	JV Supplemental detail
GJVV	Joint Venture Master Transaction
GJW1	Create JV-Pricing archive
GJW2	Delete archived JV-Pricing Data
GJW3	JV-Pricing Archive-Administration
GJX1	Conditions: Procedure for A CR
GJX2	Condition Types: SD Pricing
GJX3	Maintain Access (Sales Price)
GJX4	V-T681F: Index Field Catalog
GJXC	JV cross company reconciliation
GJY01	Create JV bank account archive
GJY02	Delete archived JV bank account data
GJY03	Reload JV bank account data
GJY04	JV bank archive administration
GJY1	Create JV-Cutback archive
GJY11	Create JVA event
GJY12	Delete archived JV event data
GJY13	Reload archived JVA event data
GJY14	JVA event archive administration
GJY2	Delete archived JV-Cutback Data
GJY3	Reload JV-Cutback Archives
GJY4	JV-Cutback Archive-Administration
GJY5	Reporting on JVA-Archives
GJY6	RW/RP Reports for JVA-Archives
GJZ1	Create JV-Billing archive
GJZ2	Delete archived JV-Billing Data
GJZ3	Reload JV-Billing Archives

GJZ4	JV-Billing Archive-Administration
GJZ5	Reporting on Billing-Archives
GJZ6	RW/RP Reports for Billing-Archives
GJZA	Company code (global data)
GJZC	Company code (corporate information)
GJZD	Company code (detailed data)
GJ_GD13	Display JVA and JV-Billing totals
GJ_GD20	JVA and JV-Billing items
GJ_SUS_CC	JV cost centers in suspense
GJ_SUS_CC_DISP	Display JV cost centers in suspense
GJ_SUS_ORD	JV orders in suspense
GJ_SUS_ORD_DISP	Display JV orders in suspense
GJ_SUS_VE	Ventures in suspense
GJ_SUS_VE_DISP	Display Ventures in suspense
GL10	Flexible G/L: Transaction figures
GL20	Number Ranges FI-SL Rollup
GL21	Create rollup
GL22	Change rollup
GL23	Display rollup
GL24	Delete rollup
GL25	Execute rollup
GL26	Reverse rollup
GLA1	Activate flexible G/L
GLAREP	Flex. G/L:RW/RP reports for archives
GLARI1	Flex. GL: Line item archiving
GLART1	Flex. GL: totals archiving
GLBW	Foreign Currency Valuation:G/L Assts
GLC1	Flexible G/L: Currencies
GLC2	Flex.G/L: Activate local ledger
GLCF	Blnce carrd fwrd: Summ for P&L accts
GLDE	Deletion of Flex G/L transactn data
GLFLEXCUS	New General Ledger Accounting
GLFLEXIMG	Flexible G/L Customizing
GLFLEXSPL	New General Ledger Accounting
GLGCA1	Flexible G/L: Field use assessment
GLGCA2	Flexible G/L: Data control assessmt
GLGCA3	Flexible G/L: Data field allocation
GLGCA4	Flexible G/L: Field group texts
GLGCA5	Flexible G/L: Table information
GLGCA6	Flexible G/L: Field use distribution
GLGCA7	Flexible G/L: Data control distrib.
GLGCA8	Sender-receiver relationship
GLGCA9	Check allocation customizing
GLGCS1	General Ledger: Master Data Check
GLGCU1	Subsequently Post Docs to ERP GL
GLGCU2	Copy transaction figures
GLGVTR	Flexible G/L: Balance carry forward
GLL1	Create ledger
GLL2	Change ledger
GLL3	Display ledger
GLL4	Delete ledger
GLLI	Activate Local Plan Line Items
GLN1	Flexible G/L:Actual Document Types
GLN2	Flexible G/L: Plan Document Types

GLOBAL_TEMPLATES   Global authorization templates
GLP2   Flexible G\L: Versions
GLPA   Offsetting account determination
GLPCA   Display Table GLPCA
GLPCP   Display Table GLPCP
GLPCT   Display Table GLPCT
GLPLADM   FI-SL: Planner Profile Maintenance
GLPLANZ   FI-SL: Display Profile Maintenance
GLPLC   FI-SL Change Planning Layout
GLPLD   FI-SL Display Planning Layout
GLPLDEL   Delete Generated Programs
GLPLI   FI-SL Create Planning Layout
GLPLIMPORT   Import Layouts
GLPLINST   Installation of summary tables
GLPLINSTALL   Install all summary tables
GLPLSET   FI-SL: Set a Planner Profile
GLPLTOOL   FI-SL: Planning Tool
GLPLTRANS   FI-SL: Transport Layouts
GLPLUP   FI-SL: Excel Upload of Plan Data
GLPV   Flexible G\L: Versions
GLR1   Flex. G/L: Create rollup ledger
GLR2   Flex. G/L: Change rollup ledger
GLR3   Display flex. G/L rollup ledger
GLR4   Flex. G/L: Delete rollup ledger
GM01   Warranty categories
GM02   Warranty types
GM03   Initial transactions
GM04   Warranty counter categories
GMAACT   Calculate and Post Accruals
GMABILLING   Set Accrual Method by Billing Rule
GMABUKRS   Set Accr. Calculation by Company
GMAGRANT   Set Accrual Method by Grant
GMAPOST   Transfer ACE Docs to Accounting
GMAPSADCONT01   Acct Determntn: Maintn Entry Step 01
GMAPSADCONT02   Acct Determntn: Maintn Entry Step 02
GMAPSADMETA01   Acct Determntn: Define Rule Step 01
GMAPSADMETA02   Acct Determntn: Define Rule Step 02
GMAPSADMETASGL   Acct Detrmn: Define Single-Step Rule
GMAPSDOCITEMS   Display Line Items in the Acc. Eng.
GMAPSITEMS   Display Total Values in the Acc.Eng.
GMARECONCILE   Reconcile Acc. Eng. with Accounting
GMAREVERS   Reversal of Periodic Accrual Runs
GMAR_DOC_AC   Arch: Actual/Commitment Documents
GMAR_DOC_BD   Archiving Budget Documents
GMAR_DOC_TT   Archiving Total Records
GMAR_MD_GR   Archiving Grant
GMAR_MD_GS   Archiving Sponsor
GMATRANSFER   Transfer Grants to Accrual Engine
GMATREE03   Display Accrual Objects
GMAVCCUSTDEF   Check AVC Customizing (GM)
GMAVCDERIACTG   GM Derivation of Activity Groups
GMAVCDERIACTGR   Derivation of Activity Groups
GMAVCDERIAO   GM Derivation control object (ACO)
GMAVCDERIAOR   GM Derivation control object (ACO)

SAP Transaction Codes – Volume One

GMAVCDERICH	GM Derivation of check horizon
GMAVCDERICHR	GM Derivation of check horizon
GMAVCDERITPROF	GM Derivation of tolerance profile
GMAVCDERITPROFR	GM Derivation of tolerance profile
GMAVCDIFF	GM AVC display discrepancies
GMAVCLDGRCPY	Copy AVC ledger (GM)
GMAVCOVRW	Overview of GM AVC Values
GMAVCREINIT	Re-Initialize AVC Ledger
GMA_ACEARCHPREP	Preparation of the Archiving Run
GMA_ACEPS_ACEDOCNR	Number Range Maintenance: ACEPSDOCNR
GMA_ACEPS_APPLLOG	Number Range Maintenance: ACEAPPLLOG
GMA_ACEPS_AWREF	Number Range Maintenance: ACE
GMA_ACEPS_RUNID	Number Range Maint: ACE Posting Run
GMBDGTOVIEW	GM Budget Overview
GMBDGTOVIEWD	GM Budget Overview Direct
GMBUNR	GM change document number ranges
GMCLASS	GM Sponsored Class Master Data
GMCLAUTH	Class Authorization Groups
GMDERIVE	GM Assignment - Customizing
GMDERIVER	GM Assignment - Maintenance
GMEDNR	GM entry document number ranges
GMGAAPPOST	Post Grants Manangement GAAP Accrual
GMGRANT	Grant Master - Single Screen
GMGRANTD	Grants Master - Display Only
GMGRANTWF	Approve Grant
GMGRAUTH	Grant Authorization Groups
GMIDCPOST	Calculate GM Indirect Cost
GMLDBW	GM Special Ledger BW Extractors
GMMPRBB	Increase Budget from Revenues
GMNRG	Set Not Relevant Grant
GMPRAUTH	Program Authorization Groups
GMPROGRAM	GM Sponsored Program Master Data
GMRBDERIMD	GM: Assign Proposal for RIB Master D
GMRBDERIRO	GM: Derive RIB Object From Posting
GMRBGENMD	Generate Master Data for GM RIB
GMRBIDXREC	Reconstruct Index for GM RIB
GMRBRULE	Edit Single Rule for RIB Object
GMRELATIONSHIPS	Maintain Grant Relationships
GMREPCLASS	Define GM Report Class
GMREPORTRULE	Define GM Report Rule
GMS1	GM BDT Applications
GMS100	GM BDT field group per activity
GMS101	GM BDT field group per role category
GMS102	GM BDT Authorization Types
GMS103	GM BDT Field Groups Authorization
GMS104	GM BDT Visual Screen Tool
GMS105	GM BDT Field Groups Ext. Application
GMS106	GM BDT Note View for Role Categories
GMS107	GM BDT Where-Used Views
GMS108	GM BDT Field Grouping ApplicationObj
GMS11	GM BDT Assign Scrn Flds to DB Fields
GMS12	GM BDT Field group criteria
GMS13	GM BDT Role Categories
GMS14	GM BDT Role Groupings

GMS15	GM BDT Application Transactions
GMS16	GM BDT Tables
GMS17	GM BDT External Applications
GMS18	GM BDT Activities
GMS19	GM BDT Function Module Activity
GMS2	GM BDT Field Groups
GMS20	GM BDT Differentiation Types
GMS200	GM BDT Change document lists
GMS21	GM BDT Activity Category
GMS22	GM BDT Where-Used List:
GMS23	GM BDT Data sets
GMS24	GM BDT Where used list define view
GMS25	GM BDT Where-used process to view
GMS26	GM BDT BAPI Fields to Field Groups
GMS3	GM BDT Views
GMS4	GM BDT Sections
GMS5	GM BDT Screens
GMS6	GM BDT Screen Sequence
GMS7	GM BDT Events
GMS8	GM BDT GUI Std Functions
GMS9	GM BDT GUI Addl Functions
GMSCHEDULERULE	Define GM Schedule Rule
GMTEXTID	GM Text ID maintenance
GMTRANSLATE1	Translation: Initial Screen
GMWHEREUSED	Where-Used GM Assignments
GM_AWARD_TYPE	Maintain award types
GM_BDGT_COPY_VERSION	Copy GM Document between Versions
GM_BDGT_DEL	Delete GM Budget Documents
GM_BDGT_DOC_TYPE	Budget Document Types
GM_BDGT_RANGES	Number range maintenance: GRANT_BDGT
GM_BDGT_REASON_CODES	Plan/Budget Reason Codes
GM_BDGT_RELEASE	GM Budgeting Release Process
GM_BDGT_TRANSFER_FM	Budget Transfer to Funds Management
GM_BDGT_VERSION	Plan/Budget Versions
GM_BILLING_RULES	Configure Billing Rules
GM_BILL_PLAN_STATUS	Unblock Billing Plan Status
GM_BLOCK_STATUS	Block Billing Status
GM_BP_ACC_1	Account Group Assignment
GM_BP_ACC_2	Sponsor/Customer Details
GM_CC_SETTINGS	Maintain Company Code Settings
GM_CFDA	GM: Define CFDA codes
GM_COA	Maintain chart of account settings
GM_CREATE_BUDGET	Create GM Budget Entry Document
GM_CS_RULES	Configure Cost Sharing Rules
GM_DISPLAY_BUDGET	Display GM Budget Entry Document
GM_E_4GBA	Overall Budget vs. Commitment/Actual
GM_GAAP	Maintain chart of account settings
GM_GAAPVT	Maintain chart of account settings
GM_GRANT_TYPE	Maintain grant types
GM_IDC_RULES	Configure IDC Rules
GM_LD_CODES	Configure Legislative Codes
GM_LOC	GM: Define Letters of Credit
GM_MAINT_NR	Maintain Number Ranges for Grants
GM_MLST	Billing Plan

GM_MODIFY_BUDGET   Modify GM Budget Entry Document
GM_OBJ_MAPPER   GM Object Mapper
GM_PAYMENT_RULE   Maintain payment rules
GM_RECON_CO   GM:Reconciliation of CO Documents
GM_RECON_EF   GM:Reconciliation of Earmarked Funds
GM_RECON_FI_DEL   Delete GM Actual Line Items
GM_RECON_FI_REP   Transfer FI Documents to GM Ledger
GM_RECON_MM_REP   Transfer MM Documents to GM Ledger
GM_RECON_PK   GM:Reconciliation of FI Parked Doc.
GM_RECON_PO   GM:Reconciliation of Purchase Orders
GM_RECON_PR   GM:Reconciliation of Purchase Req.
GM_RESP   Maintain grant responsibilities
GM_REVAL   Revaluation of currency in GM
GM_REV_SETTINGS   Default FM account assignments
GM_RM_BUPA   Business Partner integration to RM
GM_RRB_IND   GM Billing (Single Processing)
GM_RRB_MASS   GM Billing (Mass Processing)
GM_SETS_GRANT1   Create Grant Group
GM_SETS_GRANT2   Change Grant Group
GM_SETS_GRANT3   Display Grant Group
GM_SETS_SPCLASS1   Create Sponsored Class Group
GM_SETS_SPCLASS2   Change Sponsored Class Group
GM_SETS_SPCLASS3   Display Sponsored Class Group
GM_SETS_SPPROG1   Create Sponsored Program Group
GM_SETS_SPPROG2   Change Sponsored Program Group
GM_SETS_SPPROG3   Display Sponsored Program Group
GM_SPLIT_RULES   Configure Splitting Rules
GM_UPD_SETTINGS   Maintain Update Settings
GM_VALUETYPES   Maintain Value Types
GM_WF_DEF_BUDGET   Definition of GM Workflow for Budget
GM_WF_DEF_MASTERDATA   Definition of GM WF for Grant Master
GP12N   FI-SL: Change Plan Data
GP12NA   FI-SL: Display Plan Data
GP30   Maintain Distribution Keys
GP31   Create Distribution Key
GP32   Change Distribution Key
GP33   Display Distribution Key
GP34   Delete Distribution Key
GP41   Create Planning Parameters
GP42   Change Planning Parameters
GP43   Display Planning Parameters
GP44   Delete Planning Parameters
GP52   Local Source Data to Plan
GP62   Global Source Data to Plan
GP82   Flexible G/L: Enter plan values
GP83   Flexible G/L: Display plan values
GPSHAD_NEW   Preparation of Shadow Table
GPSHAD_UPDATE   Update of Shadow Table
GR11   Create Standard Layout
GR12   Change Standard Layout
GR13   Display Standard Layout
GR14   Delete Standard Layout
GR17   Export standard layouts
GR18   Import standard layouts

GR19	Copy standard layouts from client
GR1L	Directory: Standard Layout
GR21	Create Library
GR22	Change Library
GR23	Display library
GR24	Delete library
GR27	Export libraries
GR28	Import libraries
GR29	Copy libraries from client
GR2L	Catalog: Libraries
GR31	Create report
GR32	Change Report
GR33	Display report
GR34	Delete report
GR37	Export reports
GR38	Import reports
GR39	Copy reports from client
GR3L	Catalog: Reports
GR51	Create report group
GR52	Change Report Group
GR53	Display report group
GR54	Delete report group
GR55	Execute Report Group
GR57	Export report groups
GR58	Import report groups
GR59	Copy report groups from client
GR5G	Generate report groups
GR5L	Directory: Report groups
GRAL	Calling SAP Graphics demos
GRCT	Report Writer: Control Tables
GRE0	Report Writer: Extract Management
GRE1	Report Writer: Display Extracts
GRE5	Report Writer: Delete Extracts
GRE6	Report Writer: Print Extracts
GRE7	Report Writer: Validity of Extracts
GRE8	Extracts: User Settings
GRE9	Extracts: User settings, coll.maint.
GRLV	List variants for line items
GRM1	Display Grouping WBS Elem Assign.
GRM2	Display MRP Group Assignments
GRM3	Colective Processing: Assignments
GRM4	Change Grouping Element Assignments
GRM5	Maintain MRP group assignments
GRM6	Grouping Consistency Check
GRM7	Display Grouping WBS Elem Assign.
GRMG	Generic Request and Message Gen.
GRM_WRAPPER	Generic Role Manager: Wrapper
GRP1	Report Writer: Display Extracts
GRP5	Report Writer: Delete Extracts
GRP6	Report Writer: Print Extracts
GRP7	Report Writer: Validity of Extracts
GRPCRTA_CLOG	Capture Change log data
GRPCRTA_PC	GRC Process Control
GRPE	Editor callup for FI/CO program

GRR1	RW: Create Row/Column Structure
GRR2	RW: Change formula
GRR3	RW: Display formula
GRR4	Create model
GRR5	Change model
GRR6	Display model
GRR7	Export models
GRR8	Import models
GRR9	Copy models from client
GRRT	Report Painter: Translate reports
GRW_PORTAL_LAUNCH	Start Report Group from Portal
GRW_PORTAL_LAUNCHNEW	Start Report Group from Portal
GS01	Create set
GS02	Change Set
GS03	Display Set
GS04	Delete set
GS07	Exports sets
GS08	Import sets
GS09	Copy sets from client
GS11	Create Variable
GS12	Change Variable
GS13	Display Variable
GS14	Delete Variable
GS17	Export variables
GS18	Import variables
GS19	Copy variables from client
GS32	Create/Change Key Figures
GS33	Display Key Figures
GSCD	Activate change documents
GSFNR	Document Display for a GSFNR
GSP_CD	Maintain constants
GSP_KD	Maintain account determination
GSP_KD1	Maintain acct deter: 0 balance
GSP_KD2	Maintain acct deter: Additional rows
GSP_LD	Define item type
GSP_LZ1	SAP internal item cat. assignment
GSP_LZ2	Allocation: acct number - item type
GSP_MD	Define Splitting Method
GSP_PD	Define business process
GSP_RD	Define Split Rule
GSP_VD	Define business process variant
GSP_VZ1	Transaction->process var. assignment
GSP_VZ2	MM movem. type->process var. assgmt
GSP_VZ3	FI doc type->process var. assignment
GSTA	Subsequent Pstng of Stat.Key Figures
GTABKEY	GTABKEY - Home
GTABKEY_SETUP	Setup of GTABKEY
GTDIS	General Table Display
GTRBILLDOC_ARCH	Archive Grantor Billing Doc. (AP/AR)
GTRBILL_DISP	Display Grantor Billing Doc. (AP/AR)
GTRBILL_NR	Maintain Number Range: GTRBILL
GTRDERIVE	GTR Object Assignment - Customizing
GTRDERIVER	GTR Object Assignment - Maintenance
GTRINV_MULTI_BP_S	Grantor Invoicing (multiple BP rec.)

GTRINV_S	Individual Grantor Invoicing
GT_DL	Upload Inbound File from GT
GT_DLN	New Upload Inbound File from GTS
GT_UL	Create Outbound File for GT
GT_ULN	New Create Outbound File for GTS
GUIBIBS	BIBS for GUI Tests
GUIT	GUI Test
GVAR	Maintenance of Fiscal Year Variants
GVTR	FI-SL: Balance Carry Forward
GVTR_NACC	FI-SL: Balance Carry Forward
GWUG	FI-SL: Global Currency Translation
GWUL	FI-SL: Local Currency Translation
GZZG	Generate FI-SL completely
HAP_TAB_CONF	Start Tab and Process Configuration
HB01	Create Business entity
HB02	Change Business entity
HB03	Display Business entity
HB11	Create Building
HB12	Change Building
HB13	Display Building
HB18	Sales mode building display
HB21	Create Sales units
HB22	Change Sales units
HB23	Display Sales units
HB28	Sales display "Sales units"
HB31	Create Lot
HB32	Change Lot
HB33	Display Lot
HB38	Sales driven display lot
HBA2	Change affected building list
HBA3	Display affected building list
HBAG	Master data generation for re-scm
HBCX	Order cancellation for RE-SCM
HBF2	Change Fit-List
HBF3	Display Fit-List
HBIS1	Building List Report
HBIS2	Business entity List report
HBIS3	Sales unit List report
HBIS4	Lot List report
HBPF	Pre-Sales Browser (no splash)
HBPS	Pre-Sales Browser
HBR2	Change Rules
HBR3	Display Rules
HBS0	(old) Create RE-SCM Sales Order
HBS1	(old) Create RE-SCM Inquiry
HBS2	(old) Create RE-SCM Quotation
HB_CO44	Enhanced project scheduling
HCMWAOKOPL1	Cost Planning
HCMWAOROOM1	Book Room
HDS	Initial Screen - HDS
HDS2	HDS: Alternative Initial Screen
HDS_HELP	HDS Implementation Aids
HDS_OVERVIEW	HDS: Overview of HDS Trees
HDS_START_DIRECT	HDS Start for Parameter Transaction

SAP Transaction Codes – Volume One

HER1	Branch to Money Market Structure
HER2	Branch to Foreign Exchange Structure
HER3	Branch to Derivatives Structure
HERB	Structure call TRGF
HIER	Application Hierarchy Maintenance
HMC2	DG: Specify Transport Type
HMC4	DG: DG Classes and Letters
HMC6	DG: Dialog Danger Label
HMC7	DG: Dialog DG Reg-Spec PackagingCode
HMC9	DG: Dialog Packaging Regulation
HMCA	EHS DGM: Hazard Inducer Types
HMCC	DG: Hazard Identification Numbers
HMCG	DG: Define Processing Status
HMCJ	DG: Risk Potentials
HMCR	DG: Dangerous Goods Regulation
HMU1	Convert Haz.-Inducers to Substances
HMU2	Convert Hazard-Inducing Substances
HMU3	Convert Dangerous Goods Descriptions
HMU4	Convert Non-DG Indicators
HMXD	DG: Hazard-Inducing Substances
HMXV	DG UN Number and Description
HMY1	Converting Phrases in Table Fields
HOSH	Maintenance View for Table ADMI_CRIT
HPAYBR_DISP_LOG	View Legal Reports Logs
HR00	HR Report Selection
HR99B00_HRCSW_NFWOF	Switch Output with Form Framework
HR99S00_DAQVIEW	DAQ viewer
HR99S00_TEMSE_VIEWER	Temse Viewer
HRALEX_PROTOCOL	Log Extended ALE Distribution
HRASR00_WFC_COMP	Interactive Components
HRASR00_WFC_DRAFT	Draft for Process Start
HRASR00_WFC_DRAFTERR	Draft for Process Start with Error
HRASR00_WFC_EXCPTHND	Exception Handling: Asynchron. Call
HRASR00_WFC_PROC	Workflow Template for Sample Process
HRASR00_WFC_PROC_VP	Workflow Template for Sample Procs.
HRASR00_WFC_WITHDRAW	WF Customizing - Withdraw Process
HRASR00_WFC_WITHD_VP	WF Customizing - Withdraw Process
HRASR00_WFC_XIACPSEL	WF Cust. XI: Respons. for Proc. Sel.
HRASR00_WFC_XIACPSTR	WF Cust. XI: Respons. for Proc.Start
HRASR00_WFC_XIFOLWUP	WF Cust. XI: Followup for Process
HRASR00_WFC_XISELPRO	Start Process for XI Data
HRASRPROCESS_UTILITY	Admin Utility for Process Instances
HRASRREF_NUM	HR Admin: Process Reference Number
HRASR_CALL_TX_ATTCH	Display Attachments
HRASR_CALL_TX_PASR	Start of Transaction PASR
HRASR_CALL_TX_PDPF	Start Personnel File
HRASR_CHK_FSCN_CUST	Check Consistency of Form Scenarios
HRASR_CHK_PROC_CUST	Check Consistencies of Processes
HRASR_DT	Design Time
HRASR_DT_HIDE_INFO	Hide Info About New Design Time
HRASR_EXEC_TX_ATTCH	Start Personnel File
HRASR_EXEC_TX_PASR	Start of Transaction PASR
HRASR_EXEC_TX_PASR_W	Start of Transaction PASR
HRASR_EXEC_TX_PDPF	Start Personnel File

HRASR_FSCN_CUST	Manage Form Scenario
HRASR_FSCN_MSGMAP	Form Scenario-Specific Msg. Override
HRASR_GS_INFO	Information About Generic Services
HRASR_LPA_HRA	Reporting LPA: EE Dependent
HRASR_LPA_HRU	Reporting LPA: EE Independent
HRASR_MSGMAP	Message Mapping
HRASR_SWN_EXUSER_UPD	Determine User To Be Excluded
HRASR_TEST_PROCESS	Test Process Execution
HRAUTH	Authorization Workbench
HRBAS_CHECK_INFTY	Test Decoupled Infotypes
HRBEN0000	Benefits Application Menu
HRBEN0001	Enrollment
HRBEN0003	Participation Monitor
HRBEN0004	EOI Monitor
HRBEN0005	Enrollment Form
HRBEN0006	Benefits Participation Overview
HRBEN0009	Benefits - Plan Overview
HRBEN0012	Automatic Plan Enrollment
HRBEN0013	Default Plan Enrollment
HRBEN0014	Termination of Participation
HRBEN0015	Confirmation Form
HRBEN0041	Jump from IMG into Maintenance Views
HRBEN0042	Configuration Consistency Check
HRBEN0043	Copy Benefit Area
HRBEN0044	Delete Benefit Area
HRBEN0045	Benefit Area Currency Conversion
HRBEN0046	Cost summary
HRBEN0047	Check Actual Working Hours
HRBEN0049	Currency Conversion Benef. Infotypes
HRBEN0050	Copying templates in BDS
HRBEN0051	Maintenance of templates in BDS
HRBEN0052	IDoc Data Transfer
HRBEN0053	Copy Benefit Plan
HRBEN0054	Delete Benefit Plan
HRBEN0055	Overview Adjustment Permissions
HRBEN0056	Standard Plans Overview
HRBEN0071	Eligible Employees
HRBEN0072	Participation
HRBEN0073	Health Plan Costs
HRBEN0074	Insurance Plan Costs
HRBEN0075	Savings Plan Contributions
HRBEN0076	Vesting Percentage
HRBEN0077	Changes in Benefits Elections
HRBEN0078	FSA Contributions
HRBEN0079	Change of Elibility Status
HRBEN0081	Employee Demographics
HRBEN0083	Change in general benefits
HRBEN0085	Costs/Contributions for Misc. Plans
HRBEN0086	Stock Purchase Plan Contributions
HRBEN0087	Benefit Election Analysis
HRBEN0088	Contribution Limit Check
HRBEN0089	Enrollment Statistics
HRBEN00ADJRSN	Create adjustment reasons
HRBEN00CEWB	Conc. Employment Benefits Workbench

HRBEN00ENSTATUS	COBRA Employer Notice
HRBEN00GENSTATUS	Status of General Notice
HRBEN00PAYRQ	Create Payment Requests
HRBEN00RETIDOCIN	Retirement plan data transfer: in.
HRBEN00RETIDOCOUT	Retirement plan data transfer out
HRBEN00RETPAYCUM	Payroll cumulations retirement plans
HRBEN00RETSRV	Service calculation retirement plans
HRBEN00TERMSTATUS	Status Report for Termination
HRBEN00UNASTATUS	Status of Unavailibility Notice
HRBENUS02	FSA claim
HRBENUSCOB01	Collect COBRA Events
HRBENUSCOB02	Create COBRA Letters
HRBENUSCOB03	COBRA Participation
HRBENUSCOB04	COBRA Payments
HRBENUSCOB05	COBRA Cost Overview
HRBENUSCOB06	COBRA Enrollment Form
HRBENUSCOB07	COBRA Election Period
HRBENUSCOB08	COBRA Invoice
HRBENUSCOB09	COBRA Confirmation Form
HRBENUSCOB10	COBRA Data Transfer to Provider
HRBENUSCOBERASSIS	COBRA Employer Premium Assistance
HRBENUSCOBOVERDUE	COBRA overdue payments
HRBENUSCOBREGEND	COBRA end of max. cov.cont. period
HRBENUSFSACLM	FSA Claims Monitor
HRBPS0001	Generate benefit point account(IT717
HRBPS0002	Display general request information
HRBPS0003	Create obligatory request
HRCCEAU_CADV	Display of Advance pay results
HRCCEAU_PU01	Delete Advance pay results AU (Q4)
HRCLM0001	Claims processing data entry
HRCLM0002	Record Claims
HRCLM0010	Jump from IMG to maintenence views
HRCLM0015	Display Entitlements and Claims
HRCLM0020	Enroll into Benefit Claims Plan
HRCMP0000	Compensation management
HRCMP0001	Compensation Administration
HRCMP0001C	Change Compensation Adjustment
HRCMP0001D	Display Compensation Adjustment
HRCMP0001_A	Compensation Adj. Reasons (Tree)
HRCMP0002	Comp. Adjustment over Org. Structure
HRCMP0003	Compensationi Adj.: Employee Selec.
HRCMP0004	Submit Compensation Adjustments
HRCMP0005	Approve Compensation Adjustments
HRCMP0006	Reject Compensation Adjustments
HRCMP0007	Activate Compensation Adjustments
HRCMP0010	Compensation Management: Budgeting
HRCMP0011	Budget Structure Maintenance: Create
HRCMP0012	Budget Structure Maintenance: Displ.
HRCMP0013	Budget Structure Maintenance: Change
HRCMP0014	Budget Administration: Display
HRCMP0015	Budget Administration: Change
HRCMP0016	Initialize Compensation Budget
HRCMP0020	Report selection
HRCMP0021	HR PA-CM: Access Ad Hoc Query

HRCMP0022	HR PA-CM: SAP Query Access
HRCMP0030	Change Matrix Catalog
HRCMP0031	Display Matrix Catalog
HRCMP0041	Pay scale Increase
HRCMP0042	Pay Scale Reclassification
HRCMP0043	Pay Scale Reclassification by Hours
HRCMP0050	Job Pricing
HRCMP0051	Maintain Job (Compensation Mgmt)
HRCMP0052	Maintain Position (Comp. Mgmt)
HRCMP0053	Display Salary Survey Data
HRCMP0060	Long-term incentives: granting
HRCMP0060C	Change award granting
HRCMP0060D	Display award granting
HRCMP0061	Long-term incentives: Exercising
HRCMP0061C	Change award exercising
HRCMP0061D	Display award exercising
HRCMP0061ESS	Exercising Employee Options
HRCMP0062	Life events for long-term incentives
HRCMP0063	Expiration/forfeiting of ltis
HRCMP0064	Cancellation of long-term incentives
HRCMP0065	Stock Split
HRCMP0070	Workflow Custom. Comp. Adjustment
HRCMP0071	Workflow Custom. Awards Exercising
HRCMP0072	Workflow Custom. Award expiration
HRCMP0073	Workflow Customizing Life Events
HRCMP0080	Display Total Compensation Statement
HRCMP0080ESS	Display Total Compensation Statement
HRCMP0081	Print Total Compensation Statement
HRCMTUNCLEAR_RETRO	HUNUCMT_CLEAR_RETRO_TAB
HREFI_UPDATE	E-filing Update Infotypes
HREIC	Start Employee Interaction Center
HREIC_ADJCUST	Customizing Synchronization for EIC
HREIC_AUTHQUERY	Define Authentication Query
HREIC_CATALOG_EIC	EIC:Catalog for Evaluation Forms
HREIC_CATEGORY	EIC: Maintain Category Catalog
HREIC_CATEG_COPY	EIC: Maintain Category Catalog
HREIC_WF_EMAIL	Customizing Workflow EIC E-Mail
HREIC_WF_EMAIL_VP	Customizing Workflow EIC E-Mail
HREIC_WF_FOLUP	Customizing Workflow EIC FollowUpAct
HREIC_WF_FOLUP_VP	Customizing Workflow EIC FollowUpAct
HREIC_WF_REQUEST	Customizing Workflow EIC Request
HREIC_WF_WEBREQ_VP	Customizing Workflow EIC Request
HRESSCA_TFR	Tax Form Reprint
HRESSDE_ATZ	ESS: Semiretirement Simulation
HRESSDE_AVST	CPS: Status of Future Pension Rights
HRESSDE_CNET	HR-ESS-DE: Monthly Net Income
HRESSHK_IR56B	End of Tax Year Form
HRESSHK_IR56F	Ceased to be Employed Form
HRESSHK_IR56G	Employee Departing Hong Kong Form
HRESSIN_F16	Display Form 16
HRESSMY_EA	EA Form
HRESSMY_PCB2	PCB 2(II) Form
HRESSPT_IID	Individual income declaration
HRESSSG_IR21	Tax form IR21

HRESSSG_IR8A	Tax form IR8A
HRESSSG_IR8E	Tax form 8E
HRESSSG_IR8S	Tax form IR8S
HRESS_PAYSIMU	HR-ESS: Payroll Simulation (Demo)
HREXP_RHEXPUPD	Synchro LDAP Data with ExpertProfile
HREXP_RHEXPUPDVAL	Synchro.Value Table w.Expert Profile
HRFBN0001	Enrollment
HRFBN0012	GB Flexbens Core Plan Enrolment
HRFBN0013	GB Flexbens Standard Plan Enrolment
HRFBN0014	Termination of Participation
HRFBN0041	Jump from IMG into Maintenance Views
HRFBN0072	Participation
HRFBN0073	Flexible Health Plan Costs
HRFBN0074	Fleible Insurance Plan Costs
HRFBN0085	Flexbile Costs/Contr for Misc. Plans
HRFBN0087	Flexbile Benefit Election Analysis
HRFBN0089	Enrollment Statistics(FlexBen)
HRFBN00ADJRSN	Create adjustment reasons
HRFBN00GRPENROL	Flexible Benefit Group Enrolment
HRFBNEENOTI	Send Notification to Employees
HRFBNFLEXSALARY	Flexible salary
HRFBNHOLIDAY	Holiday Report for Flexible Benefits
HRFBNPROVIDER	Provider Report for Flexible Benefit
HRFBNREMIND	Employee Enrolment Reminder Report
HRFORMS	HR Forms Workplace
HRFORMS_METADATA	HR Metadata Workplace
HRFPMCHG01	Allowed Period for Changes
HRFPM_CUST_DIAGNOSE	Check Customizing
HRFPM_DEL_WI	Deletion of Unnecessary Work Items
HRFPM_DIFF_ORG	Personnel Cost Savings per Org.
HRFPM_DOC_DISP	Display PBC Documents
HRFPM_ERLK	Adjust completed Indicator
HRFPM_EXTEND_OM	Enhancement of Org. Structure
HRFPM_FEATURE_PM200	Charac. Maintenance Charac. PM200
HRFPM_FINANCE_CHECK	Persons with Missing Financing
HRFPM_FIN_ORG	Budget and Financing per Org.
HRFPM_FM_BUD	Number Range Maintenance: FPM_FM_BUD
HRFPM_FTE_CHK	Check of Staff Assignment Rules
HRFPM_INC_TOOL	Process Inconsistencies
HRFPM_NR_BLK	No. Range Maintenance: FPM_FM_BLK
HRFPM_NR_COM	Number Range Maintenance: FPM_FM_COM
HRFPM_NR_PRE	Number Range Maintenance: FPM_FM_PRE
HRFPM_NR_RUNID	Number Range Maintenance: FPM_RUNID
HRFPM_OCC_CHK	Check of Financing Rules
HRFPM_PBCDOCBU_DISP	Budget Journal
HRFPM_PBCDOC_DISP	Financing Journal
HRFPM_SALSA_DISP	Display Personnel Cost Savings
HRFPM_START_AWB	Start run administrator workbench
HRFPM_VACANCY_DISP	Create Personnel Cost Savings
HRGPBSSNORHR_GB_HEID	Number range maintenace HR_GB_HEID
HRGPBSSNORP08_HESA	Number range maintenace P08_HESA
HRGPBS_HESA_NISR	HESA NISR
HRGPBS_HESA_NISR_C01	HESA NISR new records conversion
HRGPBS_HESA_NISR_C02	Batch input for HESA NISR

HRGPBS_IN1   CLASS Interface (TemSe or Database)
HRGPBS_IN3   CLASS Interface (House-keeping)
HRGPBS_ME_CHECK   Check ME Payroll Data is consistent
HRGPBS_NFI   National Fraud Initiative
HRGPBS_SMP_SSP_CHECK   Check ME SMP/SSP Data is consistent
HRGPBS_SNRO   Number Range Maintenance
HRGPBS_SNRO_HESA   Number Range for HESA Staff ID
HRGPBS_SWF   School Work Force Annual Census
HRGPBS_TEMSE_TO_PC   Public Sector GB (TemSe to PC)
HRGPBS_TPS   Teachers' Pensions Annual Return
HRGPBS_TPS_ARCH   TPS Modification of archive data
HRGPBS_TPS_SNRO   Number Range Maintenance
HRLDAP_MAP   Assign Query Field -> LDAP Attribute
HRMGE0010   Offer Letter for global employees
HRMGE0020C   Change Items List
HRMGE0020D   Display Items List
HRMGE0030   Compensation Overview (GECCO)
HRMGE0050   Customize Office templates
HRMGE0060   Generate Compensation Packages
HRMGE0070   Check Compensation Packages
HRMGE0080   Mass Activation
HRMGE0090   Merge and Split of Global Assignment
HRMGE00DOC   Business documents navigator (BDS)
HRMGE00POL   Policy tracking
HROBJ   Customizing HR
HROM   Organizational Management reports
HRPADJP_BP_ASNPRD   Assignment period generation for BP
HRPADJP_BP_PNTASN   Tool: Retire. benefit Point Assign.
HRPADJP_BT_BOTAX   Business Office Tax List
HRPADJP_CP_ASNPRD   Assignment period generation for CP
HRPADJP_CP_BNCHK   Tool: Benefit Eligibility Check
HRPADJP_CP_BRCAL   Tool: Benefit Resrce Calc. and Updt
HRPADJP_CP_FOREI_EMP   Foreigner Employment Status
HRPADJP_CP_PAMNR   Participant Status Monitor
HRPADJP_CP_PRCAL   Tool: Premium calculation and update
HRPADJP_CP_REVPRD   Revision period generation for CP
HRPADJP_CP_STCHK   Tool: Participant Eligibility Check
HRPADJP_JU_DEPINF   Update Dependents' Information
HRPADJP_LA_TIMEOFF   Time Off from Overtime
HRPADJP_LV_LINJ0   LINC File Import Report
HRPADJP_LV_LINJ1   LINC File Export Report
HRPADKRCUSTWF0001   Workflow customizing Korea
HRPADRUKLADRCHECK   KLADR - Check
HRPADRUKLADRDELETE   KLADR - Delete
HRPADRUKLADRLOAD   KLADR - Load
HRPADRUPFR   Pension Fund of Russia - SZV-6-1/2
HRPADRUPFRMANAGER   Package manager for pension fund
HRPADRUPFR_1   Form (The questionnaire ADV-1)
HRPADRUPFR_11   ADV-11 Insurance payments list
HRPADRUPFR_2   ADV-2 - the exchangeable
HRPADRUPFR_3   Pension fund of Russia
HRPADRUPFR_62   Form ADV-6-2
HRPADRUT2_2004   Personal Card T-2
HRPADRUT7RUN   T7RUN-tables tools

HRPADRU_AVNEDIT	RPLNFLY0
HRPADRU_AVP1	Insurance payments of pension paym.
HRPADRU_AVP2	Tax return calc. on unifom soc. tax
HRPADRU_AVP4	Obligatory pension insurances decl.
HRPADRU_DSV1	Form DSV-1
HRPADRU_DSV3	Form DSV-3
HRPADRU_HR33Y	Number range of tax document (RU)
HRPADRU_HRULT3	List of members of staff (Form T3)
HRPADRU_HRULTAB0	Report T-13
HRPADRU_HRYP298	Number Range of Administrative Order
HRPADRU_RSV1	Form RSV-1
HRPADRU_RUFROMS	Maintaining special RU-Forms
HRPADRU_T2	Ò-2 Employee's personal card
HRPADRU_T53	T-53 Payroll sheet
HRPADRU_T7	T-7 Vacation schedule
HRPADRU_T7RUOKSO	OKSO - Load
HRPADUNEDGR	Education Grant Maintenance
HRPADUNEDGRCOP	Copy Education Grant Records
HRPADUNEDGRSTAT	Education Grant Statistics
HRPADUNEGPYMNT	Create EG Advance Payment
HRPADUNEVE	Entitlement Validation Engine
HRPADUNEXM_NR	Number Range Maint.: HR_UN_EG
HRPADUN_AAP_CLEANUP	Delete existing PAAP records
HRPADUN_AAP_CONSDEMO	Personal actions approval console
HRPADUN_AAP_CONSOLE	Personal actions approval console
HRPADUN_AAP_CONS_ADM	Personal actions approval console
HRPADUN_AAP_CONS_ALL	Personal actions approval console
HRPADUN_AAP_CONS_OFF	Personal actions approval console
HRPADUN_AAP_UPD0001	XPRA for Customer field IT0001
HRPAYCA_ROESW	HRDC Software Attributes Update
HRPAYCA_ROEWB	Record of Employment (ROE) Workbench
HRPAYCA_ROEWB_CE	ROE Workbench for CE
HRPAYCA_ROE_CONVERT	ROE: Convert data fr. T5KSN to T5KR0
HRPAYDEBSA	Constr. Ind.: Display Constr. Sites
HRPAYDEBSP	Constr. Ind.: Maintain Constr. Sites
HRPAYJP_COMMUTER	Commuting allowance management
HRPAYJP_COMMUTER_DIS	Commuting allowance management dis.
HRPAYJP_CP_APRCAL	Total Premium Calculation
HRPAYJP_CP_DTFTM	Datafile generation for CP
HRPAYRUT7RUN	T7RUN-tables tools
HRPAYRU_HRUCEDT0	Remuneration Statements
HRPAYRU_HRUCKTO0	Lohnkonten
HRPAYRU_HRUCLJN0	Payroll Journal - Russia
HRPAYRU_HRULAVP02004	HRULAVP0_2004
HRPAYRU_HRULAVP12004	HRULAVP1_2004
HRPAYRU_HRULAVP22003	Soc. Ins. Contributions Declaration
HRPAYRU_HRULAVP42002	Declaration on insurance payments
HRPAYRU_HRULAVR0	Preliminary employees average number
HRPAYRU_HRULAVR1	Employees average number counting
HRPAYRU_HRULICO0	RPLICOY0
HRPAYRU_HRULNDFL	Income Tax (2-NDFL)
HRPAYRU_HRULTX12	Tax reestr (form N 12)
HRPAYRU_IMG_P0_011	Garnishmetn Document Category
HRPAYRU_SET_MOLGA	HR-RU Set molga

HRPAYUNJSPF	UN Joint Staff Pension Fund
HRPAYUNJSPF_MI	UNJSPF - Monthly Interface
HRPAYUN_OH11	NPO: wage type maintenance
HRPAYUN_PU30	UN: wage type maintenance
HRPBCBC	Evaluate Total Number of Positions
HRPBCBC_FORM	Evaluate Position Overview (PDFform)
HRPBCC	Create Position Plan
HRPBCCOR	Business distribution plan
HRPBCEXT	Carry Forward Position Plan
HRPBCM	Change Position Plan
HRPBCM_DYNACT	Change Position Plan
HRPBCS	Display Position Plan
HRPBCSTA	Change Budget Status
HRPBC_2FC	Reconciliation of Docs in Accounting
HRPBC_AVC	Availability Control
HRPBC_BPREP	Collection of BPREP Data
HRPBC_BPREP_MAINT	Edit Planning Data
HRPBC_BULIST	Position Analysis
HRPBC_BULIST_FORM	Position Analysis as PDF Form
HRPBC_CREATE_EARMARK	Decoupled Update in PBC
HRPBC_DATES	Monitoring of Tasks
HRPBC_DIFF_REORG	Reorganize Personnel Cost Savings
HRPBC_DIFF_SOLVE	Remove Funds Block
HRPBC_ENGINE_CHNGLOG	Objects with Flag
HRPBC_ENGINE_FS	Commitment Creation - Free Selection
HRPBC_ENGINE_INIT	Start Initial Commitment Creation
HRPBC_ENGINE_INIT_FS	Initial Cmmt Creat. - Fr. Selection
HRPBC_ENGINE_P	Commitment Creation for Persons
HRPBC_ENGINE_PCH	Commitment Creation for Org. Objects
HRPBC_ENGINE_PNP	Commitment Creation for Persons
HRPBC_ENGINE_START	Directly Start Commitment Run
HRPBC_FINLIST	Financing Analysis
HRPBC_FIN_CHK	Check of Financing Rules
HRPBC_HCP_01	Maintain Planning Results
HRPBC_IMG	Call IMG PBC
HRPBC_INIT_1514	Convert 1501 to 1005 and 1514
HRPBC_LIFI	Financing Overview
HRPBC_LOG	Display Log for Commitment Run
HRPBC_LOG_BPREP	Log for Running Planning Act.
HRPBC_LOG_BUDGET	Log for Budget Creation Run
HRPBC_MAIL01	Definition of e-mail texts
HRPBC_MDIR	Direct Infotype Maintenance
HRPBC_MOVECUST1509	Convert Customizing for IT 1509
HRPBC_MOVEINFTY1509	Convert Infotypes: 1505 to 1509
HRPBC_ORIG	Creation of Original Budget
HRPBC_PCHK	Check Violation of Earmarking
HRPBC_QUERY_EXEC	Execution of a Query
HRPBC_RC_DOC	Match Single/Totals Records
HRPBC_RC_FUND	Compare Fund/Commitment
HRPBC_RC_REQ	Compare Requirement/Commitment
HRPBC_REQ	Determine Financing Requirement
HRPBC_ROLL1520	Adjustment of Original Budget
HRPBC_SCHEDMAN	Schedule Manager
HRPBC_START	Message overview PBC

SAP Transaction Codes – Volume One

HRPBC_STOV	Evaluation of FTE Limits
HRPBC_STRUC_VIEW	Structure Overview
HRPBC_VAC	Display Vacant Positions
HRPBSBE_BAPAY	Evolution of IT0008 with seniority
HRPBSBE_CADRE	PS-BE "Cadre"
HRPBSBE_PAYSC	Generate Pay Scales
HRPBSBE_SEN12	PS-BE seniority calculation
HRPBSDENV	Retroactive Pension Insurance Admin.
HRPBSDEVA	Pension Administration
HRPBSDEVA_PRUEFER	Pension Administration (Approver)
HRPBSINGENCORRLETTER	Generate Correspondence Letters
HRPBSININFOUPDT	Infotype Update in R/3
HRPBSINLISTREQ	Claims / Advance Requests
HRPBSINOFFPAY	Start Off-Cycle Payroll-Claims
HRPBSINRESOLVERR	Resolve Infotype Update error
HRPBSIN_AC_ACRP	Advanced Claim: Display Records
HRPBSIN_AC_INFU	Advanced Claim: Infotype Update
HRPBSIN_CRCT_ASSIGN	Correct the assignments of a Roster
HRPBSIN_CUR_STAF	Current Staffing
HRPBSIN_LEAVEREQLIST	List Leave Encashment Request
HRPBSIN_LEENCASH_OFF	Start Off-cycle & Follow-up Activit
HRPBSIN_LEG_UPLD	Rosters upload from Legacy System
HRPBSIN_LENCH_RESERR	Resolve Errors for Leave Encashment
HRPBSIN_LOANUPDINFTY	Update Infotype for Approved Loan
HRPBSIN_LVENC_INFTY	Update Infotype for Approved Request
HRPBSIN_LVENC_UPSTAT	Update Request Status
HRPBSIN_NEWHIRES	New Hires with Military Status
HRPBSIN_NMBRNG	Number range maintenance: HRIPSCLAIM
HRPBSIN_NMBRNG_LE	Number range maintenance: HRIPSLE
HRPBSIN_NMBRNG_LOAN	Number range maintenance: HRIPSLOAN
HRPBSIN_ROS_CRT	Create - Roster transaction
HRPBSIN_ROS_DIS	Roster display transaction
HRPBSIN_ROS_MNT	Roster maintenance transaction
HRPBSIN_RSTRPT_CRT	Create Roster Points for a Roster
HRPBSIN_RSTR_CHNG	Chnages in Rosters in a time frame
HRPBSIN_SALARY_INCRT	Report for Salary Increment
HRPBSIN_SIMUL_RCRT	Simulate Recruitment
HRPBSIN_TRG_APV_WF	Trigger Approval Workflow
HRPBSIN_UPD_STATUS	Update Advance/Claim request status
HRPBSUSACTION	Nature of Actions
HRPBSUSACTIONCONFIG	Nature of Action Configuration (4.7)
HRPBSUSDRUG_ADDR	HR Public Sector: maintain address
HRPBSUSEEOC_ADDR	HR Public Sector: maintain address
HRPBSUSERRCONFIG	Crediting Plan Configuration for ERR
HRPDV00REPORT0001	Maintained Qualifications
HRRCF_ACT_CREATE	Workflow Customizing:CREATE ACTIVITY
HRRCF_ACT_CREA_2	Wflow Customizing Follow-Up Activity
HRRCF_ADJ_ENTRY	Workflow Customizing ADJUST ENTRY
HRRCF_APPROVE_POS	Workflow Customizing for Approvals
HRRCF_APPROVE_REQ	Workflow Customizing for Approvals
HRRCF_APPROVE_REQ_2	Workflow Customizing: Approvals (WD)
HRRCF_CAND_DERIG	Workflow Customizing: DEREGISTER
HRRCF_OBJECT_CREATE	Workflow Customizing: CREATE OBJECT
HRRCF_RECREATE_SP	Recreate Search Profile

HRRCF_RECREATE_SPSES	Recreate Search Profile
HRRCF_SEND_PASSWORD	Workflow Customizing: SEND PASSWORD
HRRCF_STATUS_CHANGE	Workflow Customizing: STATUS CHANGE
HRRCF_STATUS_CHG_2	Workflow Customizing Status Change
HRRSM00FBA	External HR Master Data
HRRSM00IMG	Customizing RSM (Internal)
HRRSM00NUMKR	Maintain Number Range: HRSM_SEQNR
HRRSM00PAR	External HR Master Data Parameters
HRTMC_CATALOG_TMC	TMC Catalog for Appraisal Forms
HRTMC_CONF_ASSESS	Start WD Application
HRTMC_PPOC	Create Succession Planning and Org.
HRTMC_PPOM	Change Succession Planning and Org.
HRTMC_PPOS	Display Succession Planning and Org.
HRTMC_PROCESS_TML	Start WD Application
HRTMC_SET_KEY	Determine Key Positions
HRTMC_TRANSPORT_PROC	Transport Process Customizing
HRTNM00_ACTIVATE	Activate Training Needs Management
HRTNM00_BATCH_DEL	TNM batch: update table _ab table
HRTNM00_BATCH_QUOTA	Gest. BF : gest. conting. batch inp.
HRTNM00_BATCH_STAT	TNM batch: update table _ab table
HRTNM00_BATCH_STAT_E	TNM batch: update table _ab table
HRTNM00_REPCRE	TNM Transaction : Create Mode
HRTNM00_REPDIS	TNM Transaction : Display mode
HRTNM00_REPMOD	TNM Transaction : Modify mode
HRTNM00_SNAP	TNM Reporting : Snapshot
HRTNM00_TN_ASSIGN	TNM: TN assignment report
HRUA_MIGRAWARDS	Migration of Awards Data
HRUA_MILITARY_LIST	Military Status List
HRUA_MILITARY_STATUS	Military Status Management
HRUA_T54	Form T-54a
HRUCDTF0	DME: Cancel Transfers
HRULCALCSEN	Results of Seniority Calculation
HRULICO0	Flexible Payroll Evaluation
HRULSICK	Sickness Certificates Register
HRULSTAT	Statistical Data Preparation
HRULSTAT_VIEW	Statistical Data Processing
HRULT530	Payroll Sheet (Form T-53)
HRULXTV0	Generate XML Files from TemSe Files
HRUSER	Set Up and Maintain ESS Users
HRUU0267	Mass Generation of IT 0267 Records
HRUU294T	Status Review for Employment Book
HRUULSP1	Convert Working Conditions
HRUUPKM1	Package Manager
HRUUSAMT	Migration of State Awards
HRWAOCOMP	EWT: Compensation
HRWAOHEAD	EWT: Headcount Plan
HRWAOSTATUSQUO	Status Quo Reporting
HRWFD_EM	WFD - HCM Employee Maintenance
HRWF_SETVACANCY	Maint. WF 01000040: Create Vacancy
HRWPC_CMP_WORKFLOW	Workflow Custom. Comp. Adjustment
HRWPC_FC_EXEC	Execute F Code in MSS
HRWPC_OADP_MIGRATION	Migration from OADP Customizing
HRWTT00MAIN	Wage type tool
HR_LSO_AD_HOC_QUERY	SAP LSO: Ad Hoc Query (Courses)

HR_NAMESPACE	Query HR Namespace
HSMC01	Activate Hazardous Substance Checks
HSMD	EHS: Hazardous Substance
HSMR01	EHS: Fill Hazardous Substance Master
HSMR02	EHS: Distribute Haz. Subs. Master
HSMR03	EHS: Change Doc. Haz. Subs. Master
HSMR04	EHS: Activate Phrases
HSMR05	EHS: Generate Phrase Sets
HSMR06	EHS: Display Filling Log
HSMR07	EHS: Delete Filling Log
HU00	Handling units
HU02	Creating and Changing Handling Units
HU03	Display of HUs
HU04	Creation of HUs with stock
HU05	Display of HUs for object
HUCANC	Matl Doc. Cancellation of HU Gds Mvt
HUCOWA	Display Staged HUs
HUCOWE	Display Manufactured HUs
HUDIFF	Adjustment of HU Stocks
HUEX	Number Range Maintenance: HU_VEKP
HUGO	Settings for Travel Planning
HUIBD	Handling Units for Inbound Delivery
HUIND	Database Indexes for Handling Units
HUINV01	Create HU Phys. Inventory Documents
HUINV02	Change HU Phys. Inventory Document
HUINV03	Enter Counted Qty for HU Phys. Inv.
HUINV04	Analysis of HU Phys. Inv. Documents
HUINV05	Post HU Phys. Inventory Differences
HUINV06	Delete Inventory Status for HUs
HUINV07	Display HU Phys. Inv. Documents
HUMAT	Handling Units Related to Matl Doc.
HUMO	HU Monitor
HUNK	Number range maintenance: LE_HU
HUNKUMP	Number range maintenance: LE_HU_UMP
HUOBD	Display HUs for Outbound Delivery
HUP1	HU creation in production
HUP10	Stock: Plan HUs - General
HUP11	Stock: Plan HUs Without Order
HUP12	Stock: Plan HUs for Order
HUP13	Stock: Plan HUs for Delivery
HUP14	Stock: Plan HUs for Purchase Order
HUP30	Stock: Pack HUs - General
HUP31	Stock: Pack HUs Without Order
HUP32	Stock: Pack HUs for Order
HUP33	Stock: Pack HUs for Delivery
HUP34	Stock: Pack HUs for Purchase Order
HUPAST	Packing Station
HUPASTW	Packing Station
HUPAST_C	Customizing -Packing Station Profile
HUPP1	Packing Program for Stock: Plan
HUPP3	Packing Program for Stock: Pack
HUTRA	Display HUs for Shipment
HUVTRF	Assign HUs to a Shipment
I009	Location/AccAsst No. Range (ILOA)

I18N	Internationalization
IA00	
IA01	Create Equipment Task List
IA02	Change Equipment Task List
IA03	Display Equipment Task List
IA04	Display PM/SM Task List (A,E,T)
IA05	Create general task list
IA06	Change General Maintenance Task List
IA07	Display General Task List
IA08	Change PM Task Lists
IA09	Display Task Lists
IA10	Display Task Lists (Multilevel)
IA11	Create FunctLoc Task List
IA12	Change FunctLoc Task List
IA13	Display FunctLoc Task List
IA15	Task List Original Change Docs
IA16	Cost Maintenance Task Lists
IA17	Print Maintenance Task Lists
IA18	Display Task Lists by Class Search
IA19	Change Task Lists by Class Search
IA21	Evaluate Task List Change Documents
IA24	Archiving of PM Task Lists
IA25	Deletion of PM Task Lists
IAC_FLIGHT	Flight Example Program
IAOCPRA	Log Entries for Cockpit (cProjects)
IAOCPRB	Marking of Errors Manually
IAOCPRC	Delete and Clean Up
IAOM0	Business Scenario Translator
IAOM1	Maintain Controlling Scenario
IAOM2	Maintain Controlling Integration
IAOM3	Bus. Scen. Grp Acct. Assgt Manager
IAOM4	Business Scenario Extension
IAOMA	Log for Account Assignment Manager
IAOMA_DB	Acc.Assgn.Man. Log w.Test Run Debug.
IAOMB	Delete Acc. Assignment Manager Log
IAOMC	Object Link Analysis Acct Management
IAOMD	Logbook Parameters
IAOME	Check and Correct Contr.Type Determ.
IAOMF	Acct Assgmt Manager Logbook Analysis
IAOMG	Display Master Data Extension
IAOM_BEMOT	Settlement:Activate Accntng Indicat.
IAOM_SOURCE	CRM Assgnmnt of Settlement Receiver
IB01	Create Equipment BOM
IB02	Change Equipment BOM
IB03	Display Equipment BOM
IB05	Change Equipment BOM Group
IB06	Display Equipment BOM Group
IB07	Assign Equipment BOM to Plant
IB08	Change Equipment BOM - Plant Alloc.
IB09	Display Equipment BOM Plant Alloc.
IB11	Create Functional Location BOM
IB12	Change Functional Location BOM
IB13	Display Functional Location BOM
IB15	Change FunctLocation BOM Group

IB16	Display FunctLocation BOM Group
IB17	Create FunctLoc. BOM Plant Assignmnt
IB18	Change FunctLoc. BOM Plant Alloc.
IB19	Display FunctLoc. BOM Plant Alloc.
IB51	Create IBase
IB52	Change IBase
IB53	Display IBase
IB54	Change Two Installed Bases
IB55	Display Two Installations
IB56	Expand IBase
IB61	Create Installed Base with Reference
IB80	Change Documents for Equipment BOM
IB81	FunctLocation BOM Change Documents
IB90	Equipment BOM Number Ranges
IB91	FunctLocation BOM Number Ranges
IBANMD	Generate IBAN
IBI2	Plant Maintenance Batch Input
IBIP	PM: Batch Input Utility
IBIPA	Transaction for BAL of IBIP
IBNR	Processing IBNR Reserves
IBR01	Enter Broker Report
IBR02	Broker Collections Acct Bal. Display
IBR03	Broker Desktop
IBR04	Clarify Broker Report
IBR05	Display Broker Report History
IBR06	Display Customers For Broker
IBR07	Search/List Broker Report Items
IBR08	Broker Report New Reconciliation Key
IBR09	Broker Report Reversal
IBR10	Number Range Maintenance: BRO_STMH
IBR23	Broker Report Clearing Account
IBR24	Interim Account Broker Report
IBR25	Default Values Broker Report
IBR27	Broker Summary Posting Default Vals
IBR28	Configure Clarification Codes
IBR30	Activities for Clarification Codes
IBR31	Broker Hierarchy Selection
IBR32	Assign Item Cat/Broker Report Cat
IBR33	Clarif. Account for Clarif. Code
IBR34	Broker Report Selection Categories
IBR35	Customizing: Broker Report Grouping
IBR36	Customizing: Account Det. Tolerance
IBR37	Customizing: Prfx Reconciliation Key
IBR40	Create Broker Account Statement
IBR50	Create Broker Report
IBR51	Broker Report Transfer
IBR52	Broker Report Transfer Error Proc.
IBR53	Broker Report Transfer - File Change
IBR54	Broker Report Transfer - File Gen.
IBR55	BrokRepTransfer - Cust. Struct. Gen.
IBR60	Request Broker Report
IBR70	Create Broker Dunning Status
IBR75	Dunning Status History
IBR80	Auto. Broker Report Postprocessing

SAP Transaction Codes – Volume One

IBR81	Specs for Auto. Brok. Rep. Postproc.
IBR85	Post Broker Report After Inc. Payt
IBR90	Create Broker Balance
IBRBAPITEST	Test Transaction BAPIs Broker Coll.
IBRO	Broker Collections Area Menu
IBSPI_RFCDEST	RFC Destination IBS-PI Functions
IBSSI_RFCDEST	RFC Destination for IBS Functions
IB_COM_CUST_01	IBase: Customizing IBase Category
IC00	
IC37	SM37 for Incremental Conversion Jobs
ICKF	Customer-Specific Key Figures
ICLAPPTOPC	File from Appl.Server to Frontend
ICLARCH	Archive Claim Data
ICLBP101	Create Retailer
ICLBP102	Change Retailer
ICLBP103	Display Retailer
ICLBP11	Create Repair Shop
ICLBP12	Change Repair Shop
ICLBP13	Display Repair Shop
ICLBP21	Create Auto Rental
ICLBP22	Change Auto Rental
ICLBP23	Display Auto Rental
ICLBP31	Create Appraiser
ICLBP32	Change Appraiser
ICLBP33	Display Appraiser
ICLBP51	Create Towing Service
ICLBP52	Change Towing Service
ICLBP53	Display Towing Service
ICLBPS1	FS-CM: Find Policyholder
ICLBPSRCHGEN	Generate Business Partner Search
ICLCCSRCHGEN	Generate Claim Bundle Search
ICLCDC01	Create Claim (Expert Mode)
ICLCDC02	Change Claim (Expert Mode)
ICLCDC03	Display Claim (Expert Mode)
ICLCDCN1	Initial Screen Claims Data Capture
ICLCDINFO	ISCD Information on a Payment
ICLCHECKNO	Delivers Free Check Numbers for User
ICLCLOSE	Close Claim (Dark)
ICLCLSRCHGEN	Generate Claim Search
ICLCUST003	ICL: CDC: Customizing Int.Claim Type
ICLCUST1	ICL: CDC: Customizing Claim Type
ICLCUST2	ICL: CDC: Customizing Subclaim Type
ICLCUST3	ICL: CDC: Roles
ICLCUST4	ICL: CDC: Cause of Loss
ICLCUST5	ICL CDC:Assign Claim Type/Loss Cause
ICLCUST50	Reserve Types
ICLCUST51	Reserve Categories
ICLCUST52	Reserve Change Reasons
ICLCUST53	Assignm. Subclaim Type-Reserve Type
ICLCUST54	Benefit Types
ICLCUST55	Assignm. Subclaim Type-Benefit Type
ICLCUST57	Reserve Types
ICLCUST58	Reserve Types
ICLCUST59	Reserve Types

ICLCUST60	Reserve Types
ICLCVERM003	Configure Internal Claim Type
ICLCVERM160	Define Benefit Type Tree
ICLCVERM320	Define Policy Products
ICLC_NR	Number Range Maintenance: ICL_CLAIM
ICLDIAGIMPORT	Import Diagnoses
ICLE1	BDT-Event: Applications
ICLE10	BDT-Event: Matchcode
ICLE100	BDT-Event: Fld Grouping (Activity)
ICLE101	BDT-Event: Fld Gouping (Role Cat.)
ICLE102	BDT-Event: Authorization Type
ICLE103	BDT-Event: Field Groups (Authoriz.)
ICLE104	BDT-Event: Screen Configuration
ICLE11	BDT-Event: Assign ScrnFld-> DBFld
ICLE12	BDT-Event: Field Grouping
ICLE13	BDT-Event: Role Categories
ICLE14	BDT-Event: Role Category Grouping
ICLE15	BDT-Event: Application Transactions
ICLE16	BDT-Event: Tables
ICLE18	BDT-Event: Activities
ICLE2	BDT-Event: Field Groups
ICLE23	BDT ICLE: Data Sets
ICLE3	BDT-Event: Views
ICLE4	BDT-Event: Sections
ICLE5	BDT-Event: Screens
ICLE6	BDT-Event: Screen Sequences
ICLE7	BDT-Event: Events
ICLE8	BDT-Event: Standard GUI Functions
ICLE9	BDT-Event: Additional GUI Functions
ICLEACCEVT	Search for Accident Event
ICLEACCEVT01	Accident Event: Create
ICLEACCEVT02	Accident Event: Change
ICLEACCEVT03	Accident Event: Display
ICLEBLKINV01	Collective Invoice: Create
ICLEBLKINV02	Collective Invoice: Change
ICLEBLKINV03	Collective Invoice: Display
ICLEBLKSBR01	Coll.Subrogation: Create
ICLEBLKSBR02	Coll.Subrogation: Change
ICLEBLKSBR03	Coll.Subrogation: Display
ICLECMCMT	Claim Control Maintenance
ICLECU1	ICL Event Custom.: Claim Bundle Type
ICLECU2	ICL Event Custom.: Clm BundleSubtype
ICLEEXPERT	Claim Bundle Search
ICLEEXPERT_OLD	Initial Screen Claim Handler
ICLET01	Claim Bundle: Create
ICLET02	Claim Bundle: Change
ICLET03	Claim Bundle: Display
ICLEUSR	Maintain User Settings
ICLEVCT	Claim Bundle Cust.: Screen Config.
ICLEWM	Claim Bundle Work Menu
ICLEWM104	BDT-FNOL: Screen Configuration
ICLEWM20	BDT ICLE: BDT Search Help
ICLEXPERT	Claim Search
ICLEXPERT_OLD	Claim Search

ICLE_EVENT	BP Events
ICLE_EVENTS	BP Events
ICLE_NR	Number Range Maintenance: ICL_EVENT
ICLE_TOUCH_MASS	Mass Processing for Claim Bundle
ICLFNOL01	Create Notice of Loss
ICLFNOL03	View Notice of Loss
ICLFNOL2CLAIM	Convert Notice of Loss to Claim
ICLFNOLSAP1	Notice of Loss from SAP User
ICLFNOLSAP3	Display Notice of Loss from SAP User
ICLIBNR01	Calculation of Suppl. Reserves
ICLIBNR840	Reserve Group / Indicatives
ICLIBNR841	Reserve Group / Indicatives
ICLIBNR843	Reserve Group Cluster
ICLIBNR848	Reserve Group / Indicatives
ICLIBNR849	Reserve Group / Indicatives
ICLIBNR850	Selection Screen Reserve Allocation
ICLIBNR851	Selection Screen Reserve Allocation
ICLIBNR852	Loss/Expense Ratio
ICLIBNR860	ResGrp -> Version
ICLIBNR861	Define Reserve Group
ICLIBNR861_HEALTH	Define Reserve Group
ICLIBNR862	Reserve Group Category
ICLIBNR863	Define Reserve Group
ICLIBNR865	Expense Calculation Rule
ICLIBNR867	Reserve Group Cluster
ICLIBNR867_HEALTH	Reserve Group Cluster
ICLIBNR867_X	Reserve Group Cluster
ICLIBNR869	Define Versions for Res.Gp Cluster
ICLIBNR873	Edit Process Sequence
ICLIBNRCLASS	Calculation of Suppl. Reserves
ICLIBNRCOMP	Comparison of Two IBNR Versions
ICLIBNRDIRECT	Selection: Direct IBNR Reserving
ICLIBNREDITRESULT	IBNR Determination of Reserves
ICLIBNREDITSTATISTIC	IBNR Determination of Reserves
ICLIBNRLE	Calculation of Suppl. Reserves
ICLIBNRPROCESS	IBNR Determination of Reserves
ICLIBNRPROCESSHEALTH	IBNR Determination of Reserves
ICLIBNRRESLOT	IBNR Determination of Reserves
ICLIMG	Go Directly to FS-CM IMG
ICLINS01	Create Insurer
ICLINS02	Change Insurer
ICLINS03	Display Insurer
ICLINVMASS01	Invoice Mass Entry
ICLINVNOT01	Single Entry of Invoice
ICLINVSG01	Invoice Mass Entry
ICLMYCLAIMS	Claim Handler: My Claims
ICLNOT01	Create Claim (Notification Mode)
ICLNOT02	Change Claim (Notification Mode)
ICLNOT03	Display Claim (Notification Mode)
ICLNOTE1	Create Note (Overview Mode)
ICLNT01	ICL FNOL: Create
ICLNT02	ICL FNOL: Change
ICLNT03	ICL FNOL: Display
ICLNWM	FS-CM: First Notice of Loss: Dialog

ICLN_NR	Number Range Maintenance: ICL_NOTICE
ICLOPENACT	Claim Handler: Pending Tasks
ICLOVER03	Display Claim (Overview Mode)
ICLPARTWCDI	DI for WCOMP Partner
ICLPAY01	Create Payment (Overview Mode)
ICLPAY03	Approve Payment (Overview Mode)
ICLPAYAUTH	Display of Payment Authorizations
ICLPCTOAPP	File from Frontend to Appl. Server
ICLPICUPLOAD	Upload and Save Picture Files
ICLPOLDISP	Display All Policies in ICLCLAIM
ICLQCL01	Create Quick Claim
ICLQCL02	Change Quick Claim
ICLQCL03	Display Quick Claim
ICLREASSIGN	Reassign Payment (Overview Mode)
ICLRES02	Change Reserve (Overview Mode)
ICLRIDATA	Report Data to RI
ICLRPDMNT	Repetitive Payment
ICLR_NR	Number Range Maintenance: ICL_RESLOT
ICLSALV01	Create Salvage (Overview Mode)
ICLSCEXPERT	Benefits Catalog Search
ICLSCT01	Create Catalog Item
ICLSCT02	Change Catalog Item
ICLSCT03	Display Catalog Item
ICLSCWM	FS-CM Task Level Menu Benefit Catelg
ICLSCWM1	BDT ICLB: Applications
ICLSCWM10	BDT ICLB: Matchcodes
ICLSCWM100	BDT ICLB: Fld Modif. per Activ.Cat.
ICLSCWM102	BDT ICLB: Authorization Types
ICLSCWM103	BDT ICLB: Fld Grp for Authorization
ICLSCWM104	BDT ICLB: Screen Configuration
ICLSCWM11	BDT ICLB: Assignment Scrn->DB Field
ICLSCWM12	BDT ICLB: Field Modificatn Criteria
ICLSCWM15	BDT ICLB: Application Transactions
ICLSCWM16	BDT ICLB: Tables
ICLSCWM18	BDT ICLB: Activities
ICLSCWM2	BDT ICLB: Field Groups
ICLSCWM20	BDT Search
ICLSCWM23	BDT ICLB: Data Sets
ICLSCWM3	BDT ICLB: Views
ICLSCWM4	BDT ICLB: Sections
ICLSCWM5	BDT ICLB: Screens
ICLSCWM6	BDT ICLB: Screen Sequences
ICLSCWM7	BDT ICLB: Events
ICLSCWM8	BDT ICLB: GUI Standard Functions
ICLSCWM9	BDT ICLB: GUI Additional Functions
ICLSUP800	ResGrp -> Version
ICLSUP801	Reserve Group / Indicatives
ICLSUP802	Reserve Group / Method
ICLSUP803	Create/Change Method
ICLSUP804	Calculation of Suppl. Reserves
ICLSUP805	Create/Change Application Method
ICLSUP806	Reserve Group -> Application Method
ICLSUP807	Application Suppl. Reserves
ICLSUP808	Comparison of Two Res. Calculations

ICLSUP809	Calculation of Suppl. Reserves
ICLSUP814	ResGrp -> Version
ICLSUP820	Product Group
ICLSUP821	Line of Insurance
ICLSUP822	Suppl. Reserves: Coverage
ICLSUP823	Statutory State
ICLSUP824	Regional Office
ICLSUP825	Company Code
ICLSUP826	Company Code
ICLSUP827	Company Code
ICLSUP860	ResGrp -> Version
ICLSUPPL01	Define Evaluation Criteria
ICLSUPPL02	Select Evaluation Criteria
ICLTOUCH	ICLTOUCH
ICLUL_NR	Number Range Maintenance: ICL_ULAEDB
ICLUSR	Maintain User Settings
ICLVCT	Claim Customizing:Scrn Configuration
ICLVEHCATALOGUPLOAD	Catalog Import for Damage Category
ICLWC01	Create Catalog Item
ICLWC02	Change Catalog Item
ICLWC03	Display Catalog Item
ICLWM	Work Menu FS-CM
ICLWM1	BDT ICL: Applications
ICLWM10	BDT-FNOL: Matchcodes
ICLWM100	BDT-FNOL: Fld Grouping (Activity)
ICLWM101	BDT-FNOL: Field Grouping (Role)
ICLWM102	BDT-FNOL: Authorization
ICLWM103	BDT-FNOL: Field Groups (Authoriz.)
ICLWM104	BDT-FNOL: Screen Configuration
ICLWM107	Where-Used List: Views
ICLWM11	BDT FNOL: Assign.ScreenFld->DBField
ICLWM12	BDT-FNOL: Field Grouping Criteria
ICLWM13	BDT-FNOL: Roles
ICLWM14	BDT-FNOL: Role Categories
ICLWM15	BDT ICL: Application Transactions
ICLWM16	BDT-FNOL: Tables
ICLWM18	BDT-FNOL: Activities
ICLWM2	BDT ICL: Field Groups
ICLWM20	BDT ICL: BDT Search Help
ICLWM22	Where-Used List
ICLWM23	BDT ICL: Data Sets
ICLWM3	BDT ICL: Views
ICLWM4	BDT ICL: Section
ICLWM5	BDT ICL: Screens
ICLWM6	BDT ICL: Screen Sequences
ICLWM7	BDT-FNOL: Events
ICLWM8	BDT-FNOL: Standard GUI Functions
ICLWM9	BDT-FNOL: Additional GUI Functions
ICLWWW01	Create Claim (WWW Mode)
ICLWWW02	Display Claim (WWW Mode)
ICLWWW03	Change Claim (WWW Mode)
ICLWWW09	Display Claim Status (Customer View)
ICL_ACCOUNT_MAINTAIN	Call FKK_ACCOUNT_MAINTAIN
ICL_BAPI_SMOD_EDIT	Create/Change CI Incl. f.AcctAssgnmt

ICL_BPCALL	Call Business Partner	
ICL_BRF_AC	Definition of BRF Actions	
ICL_BRF_EV	Definition of BRF Events	
ICL_BRF_EX	Definition of BRF Expressions	
ICL_BRF_RL	Definition of BRF Expressions	
ICL_BRF_RL_SHOW	Display All ICL Rule Lines	
ICL_BRF_RS	Definition of Rule Sets	
ICL_CASE_RESERVE2LOT	Call ICL_CF_CASE_RESERVE2LOT	
ICL_CAT2	BBP for Claim	
ICL_CHEAT_SHEET	Display Claim Memo Pad	
ICL_CI_SUPRES_MODIFY	Modify Incl. CI_ICLSUPRESERVE_COLL	
ICL_CMC_EV_CR	FS-CM: BTE (Publish & Subscribe)	
ICL_CMC_PR_CR	FS-CM: BTE (Process Interfaces)	
ICL_COPY_RULES	Copy Rules for New Maintenance	
ICL_EVENTS	BP Events	
ICL_IBNRRESULT_MODFY	Create/Change Incl. CI_IBNR_RESULT	
ICL_IBNRTOTAL_MODIFY	Modify Incl. CI_ICLINBNRQUART	
ICL_IBNR_NR	Number Range Maintenance: ICL_IBNR	
ICL_ICLBDT1	FS-CM: Data Set -> Claim Subobj.Cat.	
ICL_ICLBDT2	FS-CM: Assgnmnt BDT ScrnFlds -> Int.	
ICL_ICLIBNRQUART_MOD	Modify Incl. CI_ICLINBNRQUART	
ICL_LOT2GL	Call ICL_CF_LOT2GL	
ICL_MAINTAIN_TICL130	Maintenance of Table TICL130	
ICL_PAYMENTS2CD	Post Payments to Coll./Disbursements	
ICL_PAYMENT_REPORT	Evaluation of Documents/Payments	
ICL_PI_NR_BENTREE	Number Range Maintenance: ICL_BENTRE	
ICL_PI_NR_BENTYPE	Number Range Maintenance: ICL_BENTYP	
ICL_PI_NR_COVTYPE	Number Range Maintenance: ICL_COVTYP	
ICL_PI_NR_POLPROD	Number Range Maintenance: ICL_POLPRO	
ICL_RBP_MASS_CHANGE	Mass Change Performer Assignment	
ICL_RECOVERY_FETCH	Call ICL_CF_RECOVERY_FETCH	
ICL_REPREIMB	Call ICLH_REPREIMB_GENERATE	
ICL_SET_USER_GROUP	Assign Claim Handler Group	
ICL_STRU_ACC_EDIT	Create/Change CI Incl. f.AcctAssgnmt	
ICL_STRU_IUACC_EDIT	CI Incl. f. IBNR/ULAE Acct Assgnmnt	
ICL_STRU_ULACC_EDIT	Create/Change CI Incl. f.AcctAssgnmt	
ICL_TEXTMOD_MAINTAIN	Manage Text Modules	
ICL_TOUCH_MASS	ICL_TOUCH_MASS	
ICL_ULAE2LOT	Call ICL_CF_ULAE2LOT	
ICL_ULAEPEREDIT	Edit Reserve Parts Manually	
ICL_ULAERESALLOCATE	Distribution of ULAE Reserves	
ICL_ULAERESEDIT	Edit CF Factors Manually	
ICL_ULAERESUPLOAD	Read Input Data from Appl. Server	
ICL_WCOMP_RULES	Overview - Workers Comp Rules	
ICM1COND	Change Condit.Maint. of Remuneration	
ICM1CONDB	Change Condit.Maint. of Valuation	
ICM1CONDC	Create Condit.Maint. of Liability	
ICM2COND	Change Condit.Maint. of Remuneration	
ICM2CONDB	Change Condit.Maint. of Valuation	
ICM2CONDC	Change Condit.Maint. of Liability	
ICM3COND	Display Condit.Maint. of Remunerat.	
ICM3CONDB	Display Condit.Maint. of Liability	
ICM3CONDC	Display Condit.Maint. of Liability	
ICNV	Incremental Conversion	

ICON   Display Icons
IC_LTX   IC integration
IC_LTXE   IC integration
IDBK   Maintain Books
IDCP   Printout on Prenumbered Forms
IDCZ_VATDOCDP   VAT Document for Down Payment
IDDH   Used Prenumbered Forms Report
IDLB   Maintain Document Lots and Books
IDMX_MONTHREPORT   Monthly Invoice Report (Mexico)
IDOC   IDoc: Repair and check programs
IDPH1   Currency Diffs for Partial Payments
IDVD   Void Unused Prenumbered Forms
IDX1   Port Maintenance in IDoc Adapter
IDX2   Meta Data Overview in IDoc Adapter
IDX5   IDoc Adapter - Monitoring
IDXP   Monitor for Message Packages
IDXPW   IDoc Package Wizard
IE00
IE01   Create Equipment
IE01_ISU_C   Create Equipment
IE02   Change Equipment
IE03   Display Equipment
IE05   Change Equipment
IE06   Change Equipment
IE07   Equipment List (Multi-level)
IE08   Create Equipment
IE10   Multiple Equipment Entry
IE20   Replacement Equipment Search
IE25   Create Production Resource/Tool
IE31   Create Fleet Object
IE36   Display Vehicles
IE37   Change Vehicles
IE4N   Equipment Installation and Dismant.
IE4NCGP   Maintain General Settings for IE4N
IE4NORG   User-Group-Specific Settings
IE4NUSR   User-Specific Settings
IECS   Technical Objects
IEQCM1   Change of Equipment History
IF00   Production Resources/Tools
IFCU   Consumption Transaction
IGN1   Create Policyholder
IGN2   Change Policyholder
IGN3   Display Policyholder
IGN_SEARCH_APPLIC01   Create Search Application
IGN_SEARCH_APPLIC02   Change Search Application
IGN_SEARCH_APPLIC03   Display Search Application
IGN_SEARCH_CONCAT02   Change Logical Operators
IGN_SEARCH_CONCAT03   Display Logical Operators
IGN_SEARCH_MAINTAIN   Maintain Search
IGN_SEARCH_TEST   Test Search
IGN_SEARCH_TYPE02   Change Search Categories
IGN_SEARCH_TYPE03   Display Search Categories
IH01   Functional Location Structure
IH02   Reference Location Structure

IH03	Equipment Structure
IH04	Equipment Structure
IH05	Material Structure
IH06	Display Functional Location
IH07	Display Reference Location
IH08	Display Equipment
IH09	Display Material
IH10	Display Equipment
IH11	Display Functional Location
IH12	FunctLocation Structure
IH18	Ref. Location List (Multi-Level)
IH20	Where-Used List Time
IH22	Where-Used List Time Interval
IHB0101	Account Holder In-House Cash: Create
IHB0102	Account Holder In-House Cash: Change
IHB0103	Account Holder In-House Cash:Display
IHC0	Payment Order Browser
IHC01	Cross-Bank Area Orders
IHC02	Reverse Additional POs from Currency
IHC1ED	Create External Payment Order
IHC1EP	Create External Payment Order
IHC1ID	Create Internal Payment Order
IHC1IP	Create Internal Payment Order
IHC1IP_MUL	Manual Int. PO for several recipient
IHC2	Change Payment Order
IHC3	Display Payment Order
IHCCM0	Setup IHC Financial Status
IHCCM1	Transfer IHC Financial Status to CM
IHCCM2	IHC Financial Status Online
IHCCM3	Consistency Check for Customizing
IHCFX	FX netting with In House Cash
IHCLOGBASTA	Logs for Account Statement Postings
IHCLOGRVS	Display Logs for IHC Reversals
IHCN1	Number Range Maintenance: IHC_LOG
IHCN3	Number Range Maintenance: IHC_NRO_PN
IHCRT	IHC: Set of Rules Def. for Route Det
IHCRVS	Reversal of IHC Payment Orders
IHCWTKA	Reversal of Crcy Conv.-Pymt Orders
IHC_AUTH	Amount Group in IHC
IHC_INB_CUST	Customizing IHC IDoc Incoming
IHC_MAIN_CUST	Customizing IHC Clearing
IHC_PI_INB_CUST	Customizing IHC Inbound IDOC
IHC_REFERENCE	Display Reference Document
IHC_WORKFLOW	IHC Workflow Customizing
IK01	Create Measuring Point
IK01R	Create Reference Measuring Point
IK02	Change Measuring Point
IK02R	Change Reference Measuring Point
IK03	Display Measuring Point
IK03R	Display Reference Measuring Point
IK04	Create Measuring Points for Object
IK04R	Create Ref. Measuring Points for Obj
IK05	Change Measuring Points for Object
IK05R	Change Ref. Measuring Points for Obj

IK06	Display Measuring Points for Object
IK06R	Display Ref Measuring Points for Obj
IK07	Display Measuring Points
IK07R	Display Reference Measuring Point
IK08	Change Measuring Points
IK08R	Change Reference Measuring Point
IK09	Maintain Number Range for Table IMPT
IK10R	Transfer Data from Ref Measuring Pnt
IK11	Create Measurement Document
IK12	Change Measurement Document
IK13	Display Measurement Document
IK14	Collective Entry of MeasDocuments
IK15	Take Up Measurement Reading Transfer
IK16	Collective Entry of MeasDocuments
IK17	Display Measurement Documents
IK18	Change Measurement Documents
IK19	Maintain Number Range for Table IMRG
IK21	Collective Entry of MeasDocuments
IK22	Collective Entry of MeasDocuments
IK31	Create MeasReading Entry List
IK32	Change MeasReading Entry List
IK33	Display MeasReading entry list
IK34	Collective Entry of MeasDocuments
IK41	Display MeasDocs From Archive
IK51	MeasReading Transfer Structure
IK52	MeasReading Transfer History
IK71	Create Meas. Document in Internet
IKA1	IKA
IKKW	Valuation Variant Generic Object
IKKZ	Costing Variant Generic Object
IL01	Create Functional Location
IL02	Change Functional Location
IL03	Display Functional Location
IL04	Create FunctLocation: List Entry
IL05	Change Functional Location
IL06	Data Transfer From FunctLocation
IL07	Funct. Location List (Multi-Level)
IL08	Create Functional Location
IL09	User Profile for Labeling
IL10	Reusability of Historical Labels
IL11	Create Reference Location
IL12	Change Reference Location
IL13	Display Reference Location
IL14	Create RefLocation: List Entry
IL15	Change Reference Location
IL16	Data Transfer from RefLocation
IL17	Take up Data Transfer
IL18	Data Transfer From Equipment
IL20	Change Functional Location
IL21	Heal from INHB
ILM_C_APPL	Define Applications
ILM_C_CON	Configure Segments
ILM_C_C_CON	Configure Customer-Specific Segments
ILM_C_OBJECTS	Define Archiving Objects

SAP Transaction Codes – Volume One

ILM_C_RAOB	Register Archiving Objects
ILM_C_RAOB_TAB	Register Archiving Objects Tables
ILM_C_RELA	Relation between segments
ILM_C_SOEX	Define Segments to Extract
ILM_C_STRC	Define Structures
ILM_EQM1	Create Equipment
ILM_EQM2	Change Equipment
ILM_EQM3	Display Equipment
ILM_E_DISPLAY	Display Archive Files
ILM_E_SELECT	Run Archiving for ILM
ILM_WOC1	Create Notification
ILM_WOC2	Change Notification
ILM_WOC3	Display Notification
IM00	Investment programs
IM01	Create Investment Program
IM02	Change Investment Program
IM03	Display Investment Program
IM05	Reassign Measures/Approp.Requests
IM11	Create Investment Program Position
IM12	Change Investment Program Position
IM13	Display Inv. Program Position
IM20	Ongoing settings for inv. program
IM22	Change Investment Program Structure
IM23	Display Investment Program Structure
IM24	Create Investment Program
IM25	Create Investment Program
IM27	IM: Open new approval year
IM27_CLOSE	IM: Close old approval year
IM27_REPEAT	IM: Open New Approv. Yr- Repeat Run
IM28	Copy investment program
IM30	Change Supplement to Inv.Prog.Pos.
IM31	Display Supplement to Inv.Prog.Pos.
IM32	Change Budget of Inv. Prog. Position
IM33	Display Budget of Inv.Prog.Position
IM34	Determining Default Plan Value IM
IM35	Change Plan on Inv. Program Position
IM36	Display plan on prog. position
IM38	Change return on program position
IM39	Display return on program position
IM40	Change supplement on operative objs
IM41	Display suppmt on operative objects
IM42	Change budget operative objects
IM43	Display budget operative objects
IM44	Determining Default Budget Value IM
IM48	Change return on operative objects
IM49	Display return on operative objects
IM52	Process budget distribution
IM53	Display budget distribution
IM54	Investment Program Reorganization
IM64	Transfer from Old Investment Program
IMA0	Appropriation Requests
IMA1	Create appropriation request
IMA11	Individual Processing
IMA12	Individual Processing (Planner)

IMA13	Individual Processing (Web Trans.)
IMA1N	Create Appropriation Request
IMA2	Change appropriation request
IMA20	Ongoing settings for app. request
IMA2N	Change Appropriation Request
IMA3	Display appropriation request
IMA3N	Display Appropriation Request
IMA4	Delete appropriation request
IMA4N	Delete Appropriation Request
IMA6	Copy version assignmt to measure
IMAI	CI Management Info System
IMAM	Mass maintenance of approp.requests
IMAMB	Automatic Mass Change
IMAMP	Blanket Change to Plan Values
IMAN	Number range maintenance: IMAK
IMAP	Change plan for appropriation req.
IMAPL	Overview Planning (Planner)
IMAPL2	Overview Planning
IMAPL3	Overview Planning (Easy Web)
IMAQ	Display plan for appropriation req.
IMAR	Plan investment portion of app.req.
IMAS	Display plan: Appropriation request
IMAV	Change plan revenues
IMAW	Display plan revenues
IMB0	IM Summariz: Replicate hierarchy
IMB1	IM Summariz: Replicate curr. values
IMB2	IM Summariz: Replicate entities
IMB3	IM Summariz: Current values in file
IMB4	IM Summariz: Entities in file
IMB5	IM Summariz: Values from file
IMB6	IM Summariz: Entities from file
IMB7	IM Summarization: Copy values
IMB8	IM Summariz: Summarized val. in file
IMBC	IM Summariz: Settings in file
IMBD	IM Summariz: Delete values/hierarchy
IMBE	IM Summarization: Delete entities
IMBM	IM Summarization: Monitor
IMBPUP	Plan/Budget Rollup
IMC0	IM Summarization: Execute Report
IMC1	IM Summarization: Create report
IMC2	IM Summarization: Change report
IMC3	IM Summarization: Display report
IMC4	IM Summarization: Create form
IMC5	IM Summarization: Change form
IMC6	IM Summarization: Create form
IMC8	IM Summarization: Client copy report
IMC9	IM Summarization: Client copy form
IMCAOV	Budget Carryfwd for Inv.Programs
IMCB	IM Summarization: Background report
IMCBR3	Mass Budget Release for Projects
IMCC	IM Summarization: Curr. transl. type
IMCCP1	Copy Plan -> Budget (Inv.Prog)
IMCCP2	Transfer App.Req. Plan -> Meas. Plan
IMCCP3	Copy Plan -> Budget (Projects)

IMCCP4	Copy Plan -> Budget (Orders)
IMCCV1	Copy Plan Vers. -> PlanVers(InvProg)
IMCDISPATCH	Forward IMC Event
IMCG	Summariz. IM: Gen. User-Def. Char.
IMCK	IM Summariz: Calculated key figures
IMCM	IM Summariz: Test monitor f. reports
IMCO	IM Summarization: Transport reports
IMCOC1	Consistency Check (Inv.Prog.)
IMCOC3	Consistency Check (Projects)
IMCOC4	Consistency Check (Orders)
IMCP	IM Summarization: Transport forms
IMCRC1	Currency Reacalculation (Inv.Prog.)
IMCRC2	Currency Recalculation (App.Req.)
IMCRC3	Currency Recalculation (Projects)
IMCRC4	Currency Recalculation (Orders)
IMCT	IM Summar: Translation of drilldowns
IMCTST	IMC Test Monitor
IMCTX	Intermode Communication
IMCU	Config. menu Investment Management
IMCV	IM Summarization: Global variables
IMCX	IM Summarization: Reorg. reports
IMCY	IM Summarization: Reorg. report data
IMCZ	IM Summarization: Reorg. forms
IMD0	App.req: Execute report
IMD1	App.req: Create report
IMD2	App.req: Change report
IMD3	App.req: Display report
IMD4	App.req: Create form
IMD5	App.req: Change form
IMD6	App.req: Display form
IMD8	App.req: Client copy report
IMD9	App.req: Client copy form
IMDB	App.req: Execute report in backgrnd
IMDC	App. req: Currency translation key
IMDG	Generate User-Defined Characteristic
IMDK	App.req: Calculated key figures
IMDM	App.req: Test monitor report
IMDO	App. req: Transport reports
IMDP	App. req: Transport forms
IMDT	App. req: Translate drilldown
IMDV	App. req: Global variables
IMDX	App. req: Reorganization reports
IMDY	App. req: Reorganization report data
IMDZ	App. req: Reorganization of forms
IME0	Execute Inv. Program Report
IME1	Create cap.inv.program report
IME2	Change cap.inv.program report
IME3	Display cap.inv.prog. report
IME4	Create layout set for inv.prog. rep.
IME5	Change layout set for inv.prog. rep.
IME6	Display layout set for inv.prog.rep.
IME8	Client transport-inv. prog.reports
IME9	Client transport of forms
IMEB	Background processing of reports

SAP Transaction Codes – Volume One

IMEC	Maint. of currcy.conv. type inv.prg.
IMEG	Generate User-Defined Characteristic
IMEK	Maintain ratios
IMEM	Test monitor - inv. prog. reports
IMEO	Transport inv. prog. reports
IMEO1	Create Inv.Program in Enterprise Org
IMEO2	Change Inv.Program in Enterp. Org.
IMEO3	Display Inv.Program in Enterp. Org.
IMEO_GEN	Generate Inv.Program frm Ent.Organiz
IMEP	Transport forms for inv. program
IMEQ	Import inv.prog. rep. frm client 000
IMER	Import forms from client 000
IMET	Transl. tool - Dr.-down rep. inv.prg
IMEU	Euro conversion: IM postproces.prog.
IMEV	Maintain global variables
IMEX	Reorganize invest. program reports
IMEY	Reorganize inv. prog. report data
IMEZ	Reorganize forms for inv.prog.report
IMI0	CI Management Info System
IMIG	Incremental Migration
IMKBUD	Original Budget = Current Budget
IML1	Define Long Text Templates
IML1W	Define Long Text Templates - Word
IMLX	Define Long Text Templates
IMLXW	Define Long Text Templates - Word
IMP	Start of Mass Processing
IMPBA3	Plan/Budget Adjustment (Projects)
IMPBA4	Plan/Budget Adjustment (Orders)
IMP_CUST	Maintenance Mass Processng Customzng
IMP_MANAGER	IMP: Manager
IMP_TRIGGER_NUMBERS	Number Range Maintenance: IMP001
IMR1	Values for Capital Investment Prog.
IMR3	Delete Whole Capital Investment Prg.
IMR4	App.Req. w/o Distrib., w/o Variants
IMR5	App.Req. w/ Distrib., w/o Variants
IMR6	App.Req. w/o Distrib., w/ Variants
IMR7	App. Request w/ Distrib. w/ Variants
IMR8	Non-Assigned Measures/App.Req.
IMR9	Check of Inheritance in Inv.Program
IMR_PREINV	Recalculate preinv. analysis figures
IMSL	Set language for text
IMV1	Changes to Investment Programs
IMV2	Changes to CI Program Positions
IM_ARCR	Archiving of Approp. Requests
IM_ARDE	Delete Archived App. Requests
IM_ARMA	Admin. of App. Request Archives
IM_LKZS	Set Deletion Indicator
IN01	Create object link
IN02	Change object link
IN03	Display object link
IN04	Create FunctLoc Object Link
IN05	Change FunctLoc Object Link
IN06	Display FunctLoc Object Link
IN07	Create Object Link for Equipment

IN08	Change Object Link for Equipment
IN09	Display Object Link for Equipment
IN15	Change FunctLoc Object Network
IN16	Display Object Network for FunctLoc
IN18	Change Object Network for Equipment
IN19	Display Object Network for Equipment
IN20	Object link number ranges
INEX	Initial Data Entry of ExtractINSTSET
INOT	Create SM/PM Notification IDoc
INSO	Area Menu for Insurance in BDT
INSO0001	BDT Control: Applications
INSO0002	BDT Control: Field Groups
INSO0003	BDT Control: Views
INSO0004	BDT Control: Sections
INSO0005	BDT Control: Screens
INSO0006	BDT Control: Screen Sequences
INSO0007	BDT Control: Times
INSO0008	BDT Control: CUA Standard Funct.
INSO0009	BDT Control: CUA Addit. Funct.
INSO0011	BDT Control: Assign ScrnFld->DB Fld
INSO0012	BDT Control: Field modif. criteria
INSO0013	BDT Control: Role Categories
INSO0014	BDT Control: Role Categories Grpg
INSO0015	BDT Control: Application Transaction
INSO0016	BDT Control: Tables
INSO0017	BDT Control: External Applications
INSO0018	BDT Control: Field Modif. Activities
INSO0019	BDT Ctrl: Field Mod. IO Categories
INSO0020	BDT Control: Authorization Types
INSO0021	BDT Control: Ass. DI Field->DB Field
INSOARCH	FS-CD: Insurance Object Archive
INSOCHANGE	Change Insurance Object
INSOCREATE	Create Insurance Object
INSODISP	Display Insurance Object
INSONR	Number Range Maint.: INSOBJECT
INSOSN	Cust: Field Groups for Authorization
INTERV	Installn Interval for Backlog Set
INT_BAPI	BAPI Browser
INVADV01	Payment Advice Note Dialog
INVDOC01	Bill Dialog
INVDOC02	Bill Dialog - Sales Tax Statement
INVMASSPROC	Mass Act: Bill/Paym.Adv.Note Proc.
INVMON	Inbound Bill Monitoring
INVRETPER	Define Retention Period
INVSARA01	Archiving: Bill Documents
INVSARA02	Archiving: Transfer Lines
INVSARJ01	Activate ArchInfStruct. for Bill Doc
INVSARJ02	Activate ArchInfStruct f. TrnsfrLine
INV_DISPLAY_MAT	Display Material Master/Price Analys
IOBJWM	ICL: CDC: Dialog
IOCI_FCON2	OCI:Convert HTML Field Values
IOCI_FCONV	OCI: Convert HTML - SAP Field
IOCI_FUNCM	OCI: Conversion Functions
IOCI_ORGU	OCI: Assign Catalogs to Order Type

SAP Transaction Codes – Volume One

IORD	Create SM/PM Order IDoc
IP00	Maintenance Planning Menu
IP01	Create Maintenance Plan
IP02	Change Maintenance Plan
IP03	Display Maintenance Plan
IP04	Create Maintenance Item
IP05	Change Maintenance Item
IP06	Display Maintenance Item
IP10	Schedule Maintenance Plan
IP11	Maintain Maintenance Strategies
IP11Z	Maintain Cycle Set
IP12	Display Maintenance Strategies
IP12Z	Display Cycle Set
IP13	Package Order
IP14	Where-Used List by Strategy
IP15	Change Maintenance Plan
IP16	Display Maintenance Plan
IP17	Change Maintenance Item
IP18	Display Maintenance Item
IP19	Maintenance scheduling overview
IP20	Maintenance plan number assignment
IP21	Maintenance item number assignment
IP22	Maintain number range: OBJK_NR
IP24	Scheduling overview list form
IP25	Set deletion flag for maint. plans
IP30	MaintSchedule Date Monitoring
IP31	Maintenance Plan Cost Display
IP40	Add Service Plan for Purchasing
IP41	Add single plan
IP42	Add strategy-controlled plan
IP43	Add multiple counter plan
IP50	Create ref. for maint. contract item
IP51	Maintenance contract item lists
IP62	Material Where-Used List: Task Lists
IPCS	Maintenance Planning
IPM2	Change Permit
IPM3	Display Permit
IPMACT	Calculate and Post Accruals
IPMADCONT01	Accrl Acct Detmn: Mntn Entry Area 01
IPMADMETASGL	Act Dtmn: Define Simple Set of Rules
IPMARCHPREP	Preparation of the Archiving Run
IPMCARRYFORWARD	Balance Carryforward
IPMCRMITEM	Display CRM Contract Data
IPMD	Maintain/Display Permits
IPMDSITEMS	Reporting Accrual Objects IPM
IPMDSPARAMS	Reporting ACE Object Parameter IPM
IPMFIRECON	Accrual Engine / FI Reconciliation
IPMFISCYEAR	Open/Lock Fiscal Years in ACE
IPMIMG	IMG for CRM Accruals
IPMOACT	Calculate and Post Provisions
IPMOADCONT01	Accrl Acct Detmn: Mntn Entry Area 01
IPMOADMETASGL	Act Dtmn: Define Simple Set of Rules
IPMOARCHPREP	Preparation of the Archiving Run
IPMOCARRYFORWARD	Provisions OR: Balance Carryforward

IPMODSITEMS	Reporting: Accrual Objects: IPMO
IPMODSPARAMS	Reporting: ACE Object Parameter IPMO
IPMOFIRECON	Accrual Engine / FI Reconciliation
IPMOPSDOCITEMS	Display Posting Line Items IPMO
IPMOPSITEMS	Display Posting Totals Values IPMO
IPMOREVERS	Reversal of Periodic Accrual Runs
IPMOTRANSFER	Transferral of ACE Docs to Accnting
IPMOTREE03	Display / Change OR Accruals
IPMPSDOCITEMS	Display Line Items in IPM
IPMPSITEMS	Display Totals Values in IPM
IPMREVERS	Reversal of Periodic Accrual Runs
IPMTRANSFER	Transferral of ACE Docs to Accnting
IPMTREE01	Create IPM Accruals
IPMTREE03	Display/Change IPM Accruals
IPM_CR_REPOST_PAYM	TransfPstng of Pymnts After Revision
IQ01	Create Material Serial Number
IQ02	Change Material Serial Number
IQ03	Display Material Serial Number
IQ04	Create Material Serial Number
IQ08	Change Material Serial Number
IQ09	Display Material Serial Number
IQ10	Change UII
IQ11	Display UII
IQM1	Create cond. records qual.notificatn
IQM2	Change cond.records qual.notificatn
IQM3	Display cond.records qual.notificatn
IQM_CM_CONFIG	IQM Information Consistency
IQS1	Create Notification - Extended View
IQS12	Process Task
IQS12_EWT	Process Task
IQS13	Display Task
IQS13_EWT	Display Task
IQS2	Change Notification - Extended View
IQS21	Create Notif. - Simplified View
IQS21_EWT	Creating Notifications
IQS21_W	Creating Notifications from ISR
IQS22	Process Notif. - Simplified View
IQS22_EWT	Notification Processing
IQS23	Display Notif. - Simplified View
IQS23_EWT	Display Notification
IQS3	Display Notification - Extended View
IQS8	Worklist: Notifications (General)
IQS8WP	IQS8 - Call from Workplace/MiniApp
IQS8_EWT	Notification Worklist
IQS9	Worklist: Tasks (General)
IQS9WP	IQS9 - Call from Workplace/MiniApp
IQS9_EWT	Tasks Worklist
IQSP	Split software license
IR00	PM Resource Planning Menu
IR01	Create Work Center
IR02	Change Work Center
IR03	Display Work Center
IRF2	Optimal Rotable Float: Initial scree
IRF4	ORF: Maintain Ess. Code Table

IRF5	ORF: Batch Processing
IRF6	Batch Processing Report
IRFC1	Profiles for Single Item Calculation
IRFC2	Profiles for Batch Processing
IRM_CAT	IRM Policies
IRM_CUST	IRM Customizing
IS00	Number range maintenance: ISMP
IS01	Solution DB - Create/Display/Change
IS02	Text Indexing for Solution Database
IS03	Number range maintenance: ISOL
ISAESCR86EKES	Aggregate Vendor Confirmations
ISAESCRME84MD07	Start MD07 via Report
ISAUTO_MRNB	Automotive Revaluation
ISAUTO_OMRM	ERS Customer-Specific Notifications
ISAUTO_SICASN1	Create Inbound Delivery (Web)
ISAUTO_SICASN2	Update Inbound Delivery (Web)
ISAUTO_SICASN3	Display Inbound Delivery (Web)
ISAUTO_SICASN4	Tracking Inbound Delivery (Web)
ISAUTO_SICBC	Communication settings for SWP (Web)
ISAUTO_SICCO	Display Purchasing Pricing (Web)
ISAUTO_SICDDL1	Delivery due list
ISAUTO_SICENG	Engineering Information (Web)
ISAUTO_SICIV	Display Settlement Status (Web)
ISAUTO_SICJIT	Display Sequenced JIT Calls (Web)
ISAUTO_SICPDI	Display Purchase Document Info (Web)
ISAUTO_SICPH	Disp. Inbound Delivery History (Web)
ISAUTO_SICPI	Display Packing Instructions (Web)
ISAUTO_SICRL	Packaging accounts / postings (Web)
ISAUTO_SICRLRD	RL: Postings for Ref. Document (Web)
ISAUTO_SICRPM	Display APO-Matrix (Web)
ISAUTO_SICSR	Display Schedule Releases (Web)
ISA_CAT_REPLICATION	ISA: Product catalog replication
ISA_CAT_REPL_DELETE	ISA: Delete replicated indices
ISA_ERSLIST	ERS Collective Settlement List
ISA_ESCR_QDP	Quantity Difference Profile
ISA_SICALERT	Display MRP Alerts (Web)
ISA_SICKANBAN	KANBAN
ISBROK_ACTBAL	Broker Balance Display
ISCA	Define Symptom Type
ISCB	Define Solution Type
ISCC	Define Symptom Categories
ISCD	Define Solution Categories
ISCDTOOL12	Internal: Payt Plan Simulation Test
ISCDTOOL13	Internal: Payt Plan Tables Display
ISCE	Define Application Areas
ISCF	Define Validation Categories
ISCG	Define BO Types for Symptoms
ISE0	Funds Management
ISHN1	Create Shift Note
ISHN2	Change Shift Note
ISHN3	Display Shift Note
ISHN4	List Shift Notes for Tech. Objects
ISHR1	Create Shift Report for Techn. Obj.
ISHR2	Change Shift Report for Techn. Obj.

SAP Transaction Codes – Volume One

ISHR3	Display Shift Report for Techn. Obj.
ISHR4	List Shift Reports for Tech. Objects
ISHRN	IMG Shift Report and Shift Note
ISIPI_CP	Consignment processing (Web)
ISIPI_CS	Display current schedules (Web)
ISIPI_ESP	External Service Provider Service
ISIPI_OEPM	Ordering packaging material (Web)
ISIPI_POD	Proof of Delivery
ISIPI_PUL	Display current pickup sheets (WEB)
ISIPI_SM	Supplier Address maintenance
ISIPI_SUMJIT	Display Summarised JIT calls(web)
ISIPI_TRACK	Inbound shipment tracking (Web)
ISISMN	Insurance Applications
ISIT_PR	Testing Printing of SWP
ISI_BCI	Message inbound via BC and SWP
ISI_BCO	Message outbound via SWP and BC
ISI_POD	Analysis of the POD View Flag
ISI_PR	Maintain settings for SWP printing
ISJP_CR	Invoice Summary Processing
ISJP_MD	Master Data for Invoice Summary
ISJP_PR	Invoice Summary Printing
ISJP_SNRO	Number Range for Invoice Summary
ISJP_STR	Invoice Summary Status Report
ISJP_VA	Maintenance of Virtual Accounts
ISMCA00	Account Assgt for Main Transaction
ISMCA01	Account Assgt for Sub-Transaction
ISMCA03	Derive Transaction from IS-M
ISMCA04	Derive Document Type from IS-M
ISMCA05	Derive Document Type from IS-M
ISMCA06	Derive Document Type from IS-M
ISMCA07	Derive Document Type from IS-M
ISMCA08	Control Incoming Payment for Subs
ISMCA10	Default Settgs for IS-M Acct Display
ISMCA700	Record Doc. Type for Revenue Accrual
ISNR	Number range maintenance: ISDB
ISP4	Text
ISSR_DSUMB	Transfer Stat. Rep. Data
ISSR_GEN_TOPINCL	Transaction to generate top include
IST01	Generate Phone Number Reconnect File
ISTCA00	Account Determ.: IS-T Receiv. Accnts
ISTCA01	Account Determ.: IS-T Revenue Accnts
ISTCA10	IS-T Account Display: Specifications
ISTCA31	Cash Desk: Specifications
ISTCA32	Cash Desk: Specifications
ISTCA40	Data for IS-T collective bill
ISTCAFHIST	Disconnec.and Reconnec.File History
ISTCAXT900	Mass Generate Tel. No. Reconn. File
ISTCAXT910	Generate Reconnection File
ISTCA_T100	Def. Info. for Payment Medium ID
ISTMFCA	IS-U Contract Accounts R/P
ISTMMF1	IS-T Business Master Data
ISTMNET	IS-T Network Manag.
ISTMREG	IS-T Regional Structure
ISTMSRV	IS-T Customer Service

ISTMTLS	IS-T Tools
ISTNBTDOC	Number Range Maintenance: IST_BTDOC
ISTNBTELNR	Number Range Maintenance: IST_BTELNR
ISTUNLT930	Reconn./Disconn. Services Using XI
IST_EBS_ARC	Link Documents with External Bills
IST_EBS_ARC_E	Postprocessing Run: Link Bills
IST_EBS_MRD	Reversal of Bills from Billing Sys.
IST_EBS_MRD_E	Postprocessing Run: External Reversa
IST_EBS_POI	Create Additional Information
IST_EBS_POI_E	Postprocessing Run: Additional Info.
IST_EBS_TOI	Transfer Documents from Billing Sys.
IST_EBS_TOI_COPA	Transfer Doc./CO-PA Characteristics
IST_EBS_TOI_COPA_E	Postprocessing Run: Transfer Docs
IST_EBS_TOI_E	Postprocessing Run: Transfer Docs
IST_EVAL	Evaluate Reconnection Proposals
IST_TDATA_DELETE	Delete Terminated Telephone Nos
ISUBDMARK	Configuration marker function
ISUCC	CIC customizing menu
ISU_CRM_IL_REMOTE	Dummy for Remote IL Access
ISU_PPM_JOB_NR	Number Range Maintenance: PPM_JOB_NR
ISU_SALES_ORDER	Create Order for Utility Products
ISU_SALES_QUOTATION	Create Quotation for Utility Prods
IT00	Test IAC
IT01	Maintain IDES path for Internet
IT03	Test IAC: internal development
IT12	Test IAC language-dependent
IT13	Test IAC: language-independ template
IT18	Test IAC: start service via call TA
IT19	Test IAC: Call Trans Skip Screen
IT50	IAC Test Includes
IT5200	ITS Test Transaction with S Message
ITAGCYCALL	Call Agency Coll. with Activity
ITAGCYCOINS	Agency Collections: Coins Shares
ITAGCYCOMMCTRL	Agency Coll.: Commission Monitoring
ITAGCYCOSTCTRL	Agency Collections: Cost Control
ITAGCYCUST	IMG Activities for Agency Coll.
ITAGCYSUBCOMMCLR	Agency Coll.: Clear Stat. Comm.
ITAGCY_NO	Number Range Maintenance: BRO_CONTH
ITMOBILE00	Test Transaction for Mobile Devices
ITMOBILE01	Test Transaction for Mobile Devices
ITMOBILE02	Test Transaction for Voice Input
ITRBX	Test IAC for sapjulep Rabaxes
ITSR00	Foreign Trade Declaration (Generic)
ITSR02	FTRD Customizing Check Report
ITS_DOCU	ITS SAP Script Documentation
ITVAT_D	VAT report for Italy: detailed list
ITVAT_M	Monthly VAT report for Italy
ITVAT_Q	VAT quarterly report for Italy
ITW5200	Wrapper for it5200
IUEEDPPLOTAALC2	Distribute Aggr. Paymnt from Billing
IUEEDPPLOTAALC3	Allocate Payment to Distr. Lot
IUEEDPPLOTAALC4	Process Distr. Lot (Rev. + Reset)
IUEEDPPLOTAALC5	Process Distribution Lot
IUID_STATUS_BOARD	IUID Status Board

IW00	
IW12	Document flow list
IW13	Material Where-used List
IW20	Quality Notification No. Assignment
IW21	Create PM Notification - General
IW22	Change PM Notification
IW23	Display PM Notification
IW24	Create PM Malfunction Report
IW25	Create PM Activity Report
IW26	Create Maintenance Request
IW27	Set deletion flag f. PM notification
IW28	Change Notifications
IW29	Display Notifications
IW29WP	IW29 - Call from Workplace/MiniApp
IW30	Notification List (Multi-Level)
IW31	Create Order
IW32	CHANGE ORDER
IW33	Display PM Order
IW34	PM Order for PM Notification
IW36	Create PM Sub-Order
IW37	Change Operations
IW37N	Change Orders and Operations
IW38	Change PM Orders
IW39	Display PM orders
IW39_PM_ORDER1	Detail Display for Mini-App PM_ORDER
IW39_PM_ORDER2	Variant Maint. for Mini-App PM_ORDER
IW39_WP	IW39 - Call from Workplace/Mini-App
IW3D	Print Order
IW3K	Change order component list
IW3L	Display Order Component List
IW3M	List of Goods Movements for Order
IW40	Display Orders (Multi-Level)
IW41	Enter PM Order Confirmation
IW42	Overall Completion Confirmation
IW43	Display PM Order Confirmation
IW44	PM Order Collective Confirmation
IW45	Cancel PM Order Confirmation
IW46	Postprocessing of PDC Error Records
IW47	Confirmation List
IW48	Confirmation using operation list
IW49	Display Operations
IW49N	Display Orders and Operations
IW51	Create Service Notification-General
IW52	Change Service Notification
IW53	Display Service Notification
IW54	Create Service Notification-Malfn.
IW55	Create Activity Report
IW56	Create service request
IW57	Set Deletion Flag For Notification
IW58	Change Service Notifications
IW59	Display Service Notifications
IW61	Create Historical PM Order
IW62	Change Historical Order
IW63	Display Historical PM Order

IW64	Change Activities
IW65	Display activities
IW66	Change Tasks
IW67	Display Tasks
IW68	Change Notification Items
IW69	Display Notification Items
IW70	Orders Overall Network Scheduling
IW72	Change Service Order
IW73	Display Service Order
IW74	Change Contract for Serviceable Item
IW75	Display Serviceable Item Contract
IW81	Create Refurbishment Order
IW8W	Goods Receipt f. Refurbishment Order
IWBK	Material availability information
IWCS	
IWP01	Work Package Handling
IWP_AREA	Define Audit Area
IWP_BORKEY_DEFINE	Define BOR-Keys
IWP_CALLBACK_DEFINE	Define Callback destination
IWP_DATA_TRANSFER	Transfer Data
IWP_IMG	IMG of Retention Warehouse
IWP_LOG_DISPLAY	Display Logs from Generation
IWP_OBJECTS_GENERATE	Generate Objects
IWP_QUERY_EXPORT	Export Query Results
IWP_REUSE_DEFINE	Define infoobjects to be reused
IWP_VIEWLOG	Data View Files
IWP_VPROV_CREATE	Create a virtual Provider
IWP_VPROV_DEFINE	Define Content of VirtualProvider
IWP_WP_DELETE	Delete Content of a Work Package
IWP_WP_GENERATE	Generate Content for a Work Package
IWR1	Create / Change Revision
IWR2	Display Revision
IWWW	Create Service Notification (WWW)
I_GRAPH_MONITOR	Monitor for Jobs
J&00	IS-M: Views/Clusters for Cond.Tech
J&S0	IS-M: Create Output
J&S1	IS-M: Create Output w/Reference
J&S2	IS-M: Change Output
J&S3	IS-M: Display Output
J-01	Update Maintenance for MDIS
J-02	Std Analyses Std Settings MDIS
J-03	Media Info System: Mtn.Requirements
J-04	Media Info System: Maintain Formulas
J-05	MDIS: Overview of Field Catalogs
J-20	MDIS: Update Settings
J-31	IS-M: Access Std Analyses for MDIS
J-33	IS-M: Var.Std Analyses - User MDIS
J-34	IS-M: Perform Eval.of Info System
J-35	IS-M: Create Eval.of Info System
J-36	IS-M: Change Eval.of Info System
J-37	IS-M: Display Eval.of Info System
J-38	IS-M: Create Evaluation Structure
J-39	IS-M: Change Evaluation Structure
J-40	IS-M: Display Evaluation Structure

SAP Transaction Codes – Volume One

J-50	IS-M: Exception Analysis MDIS
J-61	IS-M: Create Selection Version MDIS
J-62	IS-M: Change Selection Version MDIS
J-63	IS-M: Display selection version MDIS
J-64	IS-M: Sel.Vers.: Schedule Job MDIS
J-6A	IS-M: Selection Version Tree MDIS
J-6B	IS-M: User-Spec.Sel.Vers.Tree MDIS
J-A1	IS-M/SD: Customer Anal. - Selection
J-A4	IS-M/SD: Sales Off.Anal. - Selection
J-A7	IS-M/SD: Product Anal. - Selection
J-AA	IS-M/SD: Plant/Ctry Anal. -Selection
J-AD	IS-M/SD: Sales Agent Anal. - Sel.
J-AG	IS-M/SD: Promotion Anal. - Selection
J-AJ	IS-M/SD: AR Cat.Analysis - Selection
J-AM	IS-M/SD: Carrier Route Anal.-Sel.
J-C1	IS-M/SD: Std Settgs f.Customer Anal.
J-C2	IS-M/SD: Std.Sett.f.Sales Off.Anal.
J-C3	IS-M/SD: Std.Sett.f.Product Analysis
J-C4	IS-M/SD: Std.Sett.f.Plant/Ctry Anal.
J-C5	IS-M/SD: Std.Sett.for Sales Ag.Anal.
J-C6	IS-M/SD: Std.Sett.for Prom.Analysis
J-C7	IS-M/SD: AR Category Statistics
J-C8	IS-M/SD: Std.Sett.f.Carr.Route Anal
J-F1	IS-M/SD: Reorg.LIS Data f.Sales Ord.
J-F2	IS-M/SD: Reorg.LIS Data for CorrOrd.
J-F3	IS-M/SD: Update LIS Delivery Data
J-F4	IS-M/SD: Reorg.LIS Data for Billing
J-FA	IS-M/SD: LIS Upd.Simul.f.Sales Order
J-FB	IS-M/SD: LIS Update Sim.Corr.Order
J-FC	IS-M/SD: LIS Update Sim.for Delivery
J-FD	IS-M/SD: LIS Update Sim.for Billing
J-FL	IS-M/SD: Reorg.LIS Data for Delivery
J-FU	IS-M/SD: Indicator Delivery Updated
J-IX	IS-M/SD: Initialize Gen.LIS Data
J-K1	IS-M/AM: Business Partner Analysis
J-K2	IS-M/AM: Order Simulation
J-K3	IS-M/AM: Restructure Order Update
J-K5	IS-M/AM: Analyse BU, Cont.Component
J-K6	IS-M/AM: Maintain TJHMC1
J-K7	IS-M/AM: Maintain TJHMC3
J-K8	IS-M: Order Sales Agent Assignment
J-K9	IS-M/AM: LIS Restructure Billing
J-L1	IS-M: LIS Billing Simulation Update
J-M1	Media information system
J-M2	Media information system
J/43	Create cond.table for comm.settlemt
J/44	Change cond.table for comm.settlemt
J/45	Display cond.table for comm.settlemt
J/63	Create cond.table for HDel.settlemt
J/64	Change cond.table for HDel.settlemt
J/65	Display cond.table for HDel.settlemt
J/72	IS-M: Output processing from NAST
J/73	Message Overview
J/H1	Create pricing report COA scale

J/H2	Change pricing report COA scale
J/H3	Display pricing report COA scale
J/H4	Execute pricing report COA scale
J/H5	Create Condition List Prices JA
J/H6	Change Condition List Prices JA
J/H7	Display Condition List Prices
J/H8	IS-M: Execute Condition List JA
J/LA	Create Condition List
J/LB	Change Condition List
J/LC	Display Condition List
J/LD	Execute Condition List
J/LE	IS-M/SD: Create Pr.Report- Post.Chrg
J/LF	IS-M: Change Pr.Report f.Post.Sett
J/LG	IS-M/SD: Display Pr.Rept f.Post.Chgs
J/LH	IS-M: Pr.Report for Postal Charges
J/P0	Create cond.table for postal settlmt
J/P1	Change cond.table f.postal settlemt
J/P2	Display cond.table f.postal settlemt
J1A3	MM goods issue revaluation
J1A5	MM Warehouse stock report (Arg.)
J1A6	Modify Official Document Number
J1A7	Average cost valuation
J1AANIV	AFIP Response File Upload
J1AB	Number range maintenance: J_1AOFFDOC
J1ACAE	Argentina Electronic Invoice
J1AH	Creating Way Bills
J1AI	Asset Revaluation (Inflation)
J1AJ	Print Way Bill Document
J1AP	Nummernkreispflege: J_1APRNTCH
J1APAC01	Create/Change Print Authoriz. Code
J1APAC02	Display Print Authoriz. Code
J1AQ	Display Index definition
J1AR	Display Index Data
J1AS	Display Composite Index
J1AX	Market price determination program
J1AZ	MM index adjustment program
J1B1	Create Nota Fiscal (Writer)
J1B1N	Create Nota Fiscal (Writer) - Enjoy
J1B2	Change Nota Fiscal
J1B2N	Change Nota Fiscal - Enjoy
J1B3	Display Nota Fiscal
J1B3N	Display Nota Fiscal - Enjoy
J1BBST	Balance Sheet Transfer Loans: Brazil
J1BBSTNEW	Balance Sheet Transfer Loans (New)
J1BE	Nota Fiscal Document Number Range
J1BECD	Electronic Accouting File (Brazil)
J1BECD_NUM	ECD Execution Number Range
J1BF	Create Entries for Output Type
J1BG	Change Entries for Output Type
J1BH	Display Entries for Output Type
J1BI	Nota Fiscal Number Range
J1BICLTAX	Intercompany loan tax calculation
J1BI_NFE	Nota Fiscal Number Range
J1BJ	Maintain Output Processing Programs

J1BK	Maintain Access Sequences (N.Fiscal)
J1BL	Maintain Output types (N.Fiscal)
J1BM	Maintain Procedures (N.Fiscal)
J1BNFE	Monitor for Electronic Nota Fiscal
J1BO	Output CondTable/Create Nota Fiscal
J1BP	Output CondTable/Change Nota Fiscal
J1BQ	Output CondTable/Display Nota Fiscal
J1BR	Conditions: V_T681F for B NF
J1BTAX	Tax Manager's Workplace
J1BTRMFME	Month End Tax Calculation for Funds
J1BTRMFSAL	Tax Calculation on the Sale of Fund
J1BTRMFTS	Sale-Transaction Creation for Funds
J1BTRMSTAX	Swap Tax Calulation
J1B_LB01	Modelo 1
J1B_LB02	Modelo 2
J1B_LB03	Modelo 3
J1B_LB07	Physical Inventory Overview
J1B_LB07N	Modelo 7 new
J1B_LB08	Modelo 8
J1B_LB12	Modelo 12
J1B_LBIS	Registro ISS
J1B_LFA1	Arquivo Magnético/Convênio ICMS
J1B_LFB1	IN68: Master Data, Files, and Tables
J1B_LFB10	IN68- Accounting-Related File 1.2
J1B_LFB2	IN68: Cadastros
J1B_LFB3	IN68: Nota Fiscal Files
J1B_LFB4	IN68: Tabelas
J1B_LFB5	IN68: FI Files
J1B_LFB6	IN68: MM Files
J1B_LFB6B	IN68: Files - Material Inventory
J1B_LFB7	IN68
J1B_LFB8	IN68: Files - Asset Accounting
J1B_LFB9	IN68 - Vendor/Customer Data
J1B_LFC1	IN86 Einstieg
J1B_LFC10	Kunden- und Lieferantenstammdaten
J1B_LFC11	Zusätzliche Tabellen
J1B_LFC12	Außenhandelsdaten
J1B_LFC2	IN86: Finanzbuchhaltungsbelege
J1B_LFC3	Sachkontenstamm Verkehrszahlen
J1B_LFC4	Einkaufs- und Verkaufsprozesse
J1B_LFC5	Nota Fiscal bezogene Dateien
J1B_LFC6	Materialbewegungen
J1B_LFC7	Materialbestände
J1B_LFC8	Stücklisten
J1B_LFC9	Anlagenbuchhaltung
J1B_LFD1	IN359-Magnetic file on Notas Fiscais
J1B_LFDI	DIRF
J1B_LFZF	Issued Notas Fiscais
J1I0	Customizing wizard
J1I2	Sales Tax Register
J1I3	Modvat utilzation in batch
J1I5	Register creation for RG23 and RG1
J1I57AE	New Monthly Returns Report Rule 57AE
J1I6	Modvat forecast

J1I7	Query Excise invoices
J1I8	TDS Challan Update
J1I9	Number ranges for excise invoice
J1IA	Excise Invoice Details
J1IA101	Excise Bonding ARE-1 procedure
J1IA102	Excise Bonding ARE-1 procedure
J1IA103	Excise Bonding ARE-1 procedure
J1IA104	Excise Bonding ARE-1 procedure
J1IA301	Deemed Exports ARE-3 Procedure
J1IA302	Deemed Exports ARE-3 Procedure
J1IA303	Deemed Exports ARE-3 Procedure
J1IA304	Deemed Exports ARE-3 Procedure
J1IANX18	Pro Forma of Running Bond Account
J1IANX19	Export of Excisable Goods
J1IARE_AGE	Aging Analysis for ARE Documents
J1IB	Excise Verification And Posting
J1IBN01	Create Excise Bond
J1IBN02	Change Excise Bond
J1IBN03	Display Excise Bond
J1IBN04	Cancel Excise Bond
J1IBN05	Close Excise Bond
J1IBONSUM	Bond Summary Report
J1IC194C	Annual Return under section 194c
J1IC194D	Annual Return under section 194d
J1IC194I	Annual Return under section 194i
J1IC194J	Annual Return under section 194J
J1ICANCINV	Cancel Invoice
J1ICCAN	Certificate cancel (Classical)
J1ICCERT	Certificate Print -Regular Vendors
J1ICOTV	Certificate Print-One time vendors
J1ICREP	Certificate Reprint(Classical)
J1ID	Rate maint & amend open po's/so's
J1IDEPOTSTOCK1	Depot stock with balances
J1IDEPOT_VAL	Depot Balance stock duty
J1IDOCFLOW	Excise document flow
J1IDUELIST	Billing document due list for modvat
J1IE	Number range maintenance: J_1ITDSNO
J1IEX	Incoming Excise Invoices
J1IEX_BO	Outgoing Excise Invoices for Exports
J1IEX_C	Capture Incoming Excise Invoices
J1IEX_P	Post Incoming Excise Invoices
J1IEX_SFAC	Incoming Exc Inv Field Selection
J1IF	Subcontracting
J1IF01	Subcontracting Challan : Create
J1IF11	Subcontracting Challan : Change
J1IF12	Subcontracting Challans : Display
J1IF13	Challan Complete/Reverse/Recredit
J1IFQ	Challan : Reconcile Quantity
J1IFR	Subcontracting Challan Listing
J1IG	RG23D register receipt at depot
J1IGA	Additional Excise Entry at Depot
J1IGAD	Additional Excise at Depot Display
J1IGR	List of GR's without gate pass
J1IH	Create Excise JV

J1IHBK	Copy House Bank ID from Invoice
J1IIEXCP	Sales Excise Invoice Exceptions
J1IIN	Outgoing Excise Invoice
J1IJ	Excise invoice selec. at depot sale
J1IK	Selection of Excise Invoice - Common
J1IL	India Localization
J1ILIC01	License : Capture
J1ILIC02	License : Change
J1ILIC03	License : Display
J1ILIC04	License : Cancel
J1ILIC05	License : Close
J1ILICSUM	Deemed Export License Summary
J1IM	Maintain Excise Number Range
J1IME2W	Open Orders- PO & Scheduling Agrmnt
J1IME3M	Open Orders- Contract
J1IN	India Version Tax Deduction at Sourc
J1INAR	Annual Returns
J1INBANK	Bank challan updation
J1INC	Tax Deduction at Source: Classic
J1INCAL	Customizing for calendar Id
J1INCANC	Certificate Cancellation
J1INCC	Print Customer WH Tax Certificates
J1INCCERT	Customer Certificate
J1INCCREP	Customer Certificate Reprint
J1INCERT	Print Vendor WH Tax Certificates
J1INCHLC	Challan Number Updation - Customers
J1INCHLN	Challan Number Updation
J1INCRT	Customizing for Certificate Printing
J1INCT	Num.Range for EWT Certificate India
J1INCTNO	Certificate Numbers
J1INCUS	Customizing for Customer Certificate
J1INCUST	Enter WH Tax Cert. from Customer
J1INDUE	Customizing for Payment Due Dates
J1INHC	Health check for migration to EWT
J1INJV	Enter Journal Voucher
J1INMIG	Data Migration Tool to EWT
J1INMIS	Withholding Tax Information System
J1INO	Customizing Table for Challan no ran
J1INPP	Update Business Place in FI document
J1INPR	Provisions for Taxes on Services
J1INQEFILE	Quarterly E-returns (India)
J1INREP	Reprint Vendor WH Tax Certificates
J1INREV	Challan reversals
J1INSUR	Surcharge Table for EWT India
J1INSUR1	Surcharge Table for EWT INDIA
J1INUM	Number Group for Internal Challan No
J1INUMBER	Number range for Internal Challan.
J1INUT	Utilise Withholding Tax on Provision
J1IO	Retrospective price amendments
J1IP	Excise invoice print
J1IQ	Year-End IT Depreciation Report
J1IR	Data Download
J1IREJECTION	Post rejected invoices
J1IS	Excise invoice for other movements

J1ITDUE	Payment Due date customising
J1IU	Forms capture
J1IUN	Forms tracking
J1IV	Excise post & print for others mvmts
J1IW	Excise Invoice without PO
J1IX	Excise Invoice Verification WO PO
J1IY	Maintain W.taxcode and Section .
J1IZ	Maintain W. Tax Section info.
J1S!	IS-M: CH/F: VAT Payment Types
J1S$	IS-M: CH: WEMF-Spec. Cat.Processing
J1S(	IS-M: CH: PTT Settlement Check
J1S)	IS-M: CH: Daily WEMF Update
J1S+	IS-M: CH/L: Item Cat.f.PTT Settlemt
J1S/	IS-M: CH: Weight Groups for Post Tax
J1S0	IS-M: Interm.Dataset for Postal Upgr
J1S1	IS-M: CH/S: Basic Postal Codes
J1S2	IS-M: CH/S: Preposition Code
J1S4	Create Operating System Files
J1S5	IS-M: CH/S: Conversion Processing
J1S6	IS-M: CH/F: Maintain Dunning Levels
J1S7	IS-M: CH/S: Customer-Spec.Streets
J1S8	IS-M: CH/J: Retail Return Assignmts
J1S9	IS-M: CH/V: Max.Weight for Postman
J1S:	IS-M: CH/V: PCode-Prod.Seq.Assignmt
J1S<	IS-M: CH/V: Manual ZEBU CH Version
J1S=	IS-M: CH: Spec.Category Default
J1S?	IS-M: CH/F: Monthly Sales Tax List
J1SA	IS-M: CH/V: Maint.PCd-ProdSeq.Assgt
J1SAVER	IS-M: Print Postal Dispatch List
J1SB	IS-M: CH/V: Displ.PCd-ProdSeq.Assgt
J1SC	IS-M: CH/V: Maintain ZEBU Data
J1SD	IS-M: CH/V: Display ZEBU Data
J1SE	IS-M: CH/F: Format POR Data
J1SF	IS-M: CH/F: POR Billing Doc.Release
J1SG	IS-M: CH/F: LSV Billing Doc.Release
J1SI	IS-M: CH/F: Dunning Run
J1SJ	IS-M: CH/S: Prepare PCode Data
J1SK	IS-M: CH/V: Display Prod.Sequence
J1SL	IS-M: CH/S: DMK Dummy Entry CH
J1SM	IS-M: CH/S: Change PCode Data
J1SN	IS-M: CH/S: Prepare Carrier Data
J1SNB	Data Transfer: Carriers
J1SNO	Data Transfer: City
J1SNP	Data Transfer: Postal Code
J1SNS	Data Transfer: Streets
J1SO	IS-M: CH/V: Display Prod.Sequence
J1SP	IS-M: CH/S: Change Street Data
J1SPTAX00	IS-M: CH: Edition Data Postal Tax
J1SPTAX01	IS-M: Postal Charge Forecast CH
J1SPTAX02	IS-M: Postal Charge Reporting CH
J1SPTAXL	IS-M: CH: Country Grp. f.Postal Tax
J1SPTAXREPAUL	IS-MSD-CH/S: Postal Charge Rept List
J1SPTAXZ	IS-M: CH: Ctry Grp.Asgt for Post Tax
J1SPUP	Maintenance View J_1SVPUPBESTAND

J1SQ	IS-M: CH/S: Change Carrier Data
J1SR	IS-M: CH/V: ZEBU Setup Part 1
J1SS	IS-M: CH/V: ZEBU Setup Part 2
J1SSUP	Maintenance View J_1SVSUPBESTAND
J1ST	IS-M: CH/V: Check Program ZEBU CH
J1SU	IS-M: CH/V: Copy ZEBU Variant
J1SV	IS-M: CH/S: Postal Charge Reporting
J1SW	Number Plan for PPacking and Sacking
J1SX	IS-M: CH/S: Num.Range.Maint.J_1S_ORT
J1SY	IS-M: CH/V: Foreign PPack Addresses
J1SZ	IS-M: CH: CH Specifications
J1S[	IS-M: CH: Monthly WEMF Update
J1S]	IS-M: CH: Annual WEMF Update
J2I0	Asset Installation
J2I5	Extract
J2I6	Print Utility
J2I7	CIN: SAPScript reporting customizing
J2I8	Avail.of subs credit for Cap Goods
J2I9	New Monthly Returns Report Rule 57AE
J2IB	Service tax challan
J2IC	Service tax returns
J2ID	Archive TDS documents
J2IE	View Archived TDS documents
J2IER1	Monthly er1 report
J2IF	Display document flow
J2IN	New RT-12 Report
J2IR23D	Register RG23D
J2IRAP1	Print RG23A Part1
J2IRAP2	Print RG23A Part2
J2IRCP1	Register RG23C part1
J2IRCP2	Register RG23C Part2
J2IRG1	Register RG1
J2IRPLA	Register PLA
J2IU	Fortnightly Utilization
J2IUN	Monthly utilization
J3G#	Field Selection - Operator's Report
J3G$	Create PBE Document
J3G&	Field Selection Equi. Insurance Data
J3G(	Create Tax/Insurance Data
J3G)	Change Tax/Insurance Data
J3G.	Transaction Calls for Joint Ventures
J3G/	Display Tax/Insurance Data
J3G1	Create Owner/Administrator
J3G2	Change Owner/Administrator
J3G3	Display Owner/Administrator
J3G=	Analysis - CO Object Determination
J3G?	ETM Function Calls
J3GARCH	ETM Archiving Number
J3GF	Maintain User Fields for ETM
J3GH	Create Shipping Documents
J3GI	Change Shipping Documents
J3GJ	Display Shipping Documents
J3GK	Shipping Docs - Change EndUsagePerd
J3GK01	Create Catalog Record

J3GK02	Change Catalog Record
J3GK03	Display Catalog Record
J3GLIAL	Catalogs - List of Characteristics
J3GN	Postproc. Input Sales Orders
J3GO	Number Assignment for ETM Documents
J3GORV	ETM No. Range Interval SD Documents
J3GORVL	ETM Settlement Run Number
J3GP	Define No. Range f. PriceLstDtrmntn
J3GPAKET1	Create Package
J3GPAKET10	List of Packages
J3GPAKET15	Manage Equipment in Packages
J3GPAKET16	Manage Material in Packages
J3GPAKET2	Change Package
J3GPAKET3	Display Package
J3GSL01	Create Catalog BOM
J3GSL02	Change Catalog BOM
J3GSL03	Display Catalog BOM
J3GSTL	Number Range Object BOMs
J3GU	Stock List for Equipment
J3GW	Stock List for Material
J3GWKAT	Display Catalog Entries
J3GZ	Create SD Orders Job Split (INPUT)
J3G]	Screen Modification - Shipping Doc.
J3G`	Overview of Stock with History
J3G{	Create PBE Document
J3G|	List of Insurance Data
J3G}	Display PBE Document
J3RALFAO1	Advance Report
J3RALFFATAXLIST	Asset Taxes
J3RALFFMCHECK	Check New Version of Inventory Card
J3RALFGEN	Russian Legal Form Generator
J3RALFINV1	Inventory of Fixed Assets
J3RALFINV11	Prepaid Expense Inventory
J3RALFINV18	Collation Statement
J3RALFINV19	Difference List for Stock
J3RALFINV1A	Inventory of Intangible Assets
J3RALFINV3	Physical Inventory List
J3RALFNRNG	Number range maintenance: J3RFORMS
J3RALFOS1	Capitalization Act of Fixed Assets
J3RALFOS14	Record for Acceptance of Equipment
J3RALFOS1A	Capitalization Act of Buildings
J3RALFOS1B	Capitalization Act of Asset Groups
J3RALFOS2	Waybill for Asset Internal Transfer
J3RALFOS3	Acceptance Act of Modernized Assets
J3RALFOS4	Deactivation Act of Fixed Assets
J3RALFOS4A	Deactivation Act of Vehicles
J3RALFOS4B	Deactivation Act of Asset Groups
J3RALFOS6	Fixed Assets Inventory Card
J3RALFOS6A	Inventory Card for Asset Groups
J3RALFOS6B	Inventory Book for Fixed Assets
J3RALFPTAXCALC	Property Tax Calculation
J3RALFPTAXDECL	Property Tax Return
J3RALFTORG10	Bill of Lading
J3RALFTORG10AFS	Bill of Lading (AFS)

J3RALFTTAXCALC	Transport Tax Calculation
J3RALFTTAXDECL	Transport Tax Return
J3RCALD	Automatic Clearing, FI-AR (Russia)
J3RCALK	Automatic Clearing, FI-AP (Russia)
J3RCREV	Clear Reversed Invoices (Russia)
J3RFAB08	FI-AA reversal documet posting
J3RFASD	Customer Balance Notification
J3RFASK	Vendor Balance Notification
J3RFBAL01	Balance Sheet Analysis (Russia)
J3RFBALANCE	Balance Sheet Key Figures (Russia)
J3RFBS5	Balance Sheet Supplement N5 (FI-AA)
J3RFCASH15	Cash Journal Reports (Russia)
J3RFDEPRBONUS	Depreciation Bonus Calculation
J3RFDSLD	Customer Turnover Balance Sheet
J3RFF2	P&L Statement, Main Section (Russia)
J3RFF2RS	P&L Statement, Explanations (Russia)
J3RFF3	Changes in Equity, Main Section
J3RFF3RZ	Changes in Equity, Reserves
J3RFF3S1	Changes in Equity, Explanations
J3RFF3S2	Changes in Equity, Explanations
J3RFF4	Cash Flow Statement (Russia)
J3RFF4V	Define Cash Flow Statement Versions
J3RFFCHA	Changes in Equity, Explanations
J3RFINVTARG	Redetermination of Invoices (Russia)
J3RFKSLD	Vendor Turnover Balance Sheet
J3RFLVMOBVED	Stock Overview (Russia)
J3RFNEGP	Negative posting partial payment(RU)
J3RFNKSPIR	Verification of Costs (Russia)
J3RFNKSREGISTR	Asset Registration (Russia)
J3RFNKSSTARTUP	Verification of Invoices (Russia)
J3RFNKSTAX	Validation of Goods Issues (Russia)
J3RFOS6	Asset Inventory Cards (Russia)
J3RFPCR	Vendor Payment Analysis (Russia)
J3RFPDE	Customer Payment Analysis (Russia)
J3RFPROPTAX	Property Tax Report (Russia)
J3RFPURB	Purchase Ledger (Russia)
J3RFRATECALC	Down Payments in Foreign Currency
J3RFREGINVD	Customer Invoice Journal (Russia)
J3RFREGINVK	Vendor Invoice Journal (Russia)
J3RFREVAL	Fixed Asset Revaluation for Russia
J3RFREVSTOR	FixedAssetRevaluation ReversePosting
J3RFSELB	Sales Ledger (Russia)
J3RFT53A	Form T-53A
J3RFTAXAMTEST	Tax Depreciation Report (Russia)
J3RFTAXFINREZLIST	Gains and Losses (Russia)
J3RFUM26	Secondary Events (Russia)
J3RFZDBPDF	Print Payment Orders (Russia)
J3RFZKRPDF	Print Payment Orders (Russia)
J3RF_AN_BALAN	Balance report for anlysis Russia
J3RF_BALANCE	Balance report for Russia
J3RF_F2	Profit and loss report Russia (F.2)
J3RF_F2RS	Decoding for some profits and losses
J3RF_F3	Capital flow
J3RF_F3RZ	Reserve

SAP Transaction Codes – Volume One

J3RF_F3S1	References (net wealth)
J3RF_F3S2	References (was received)
J3RF_FCHA	Net wealth calculation
J3RKACT	Interpretation algorithms
J3RKAID	Account priorities
J3RKAVI	Register of Amounts Posted (Russia)
J3RKBOOL	Rule Maintenance
J3RKGLK	General Ledger Report (Russia)
J3RKKRD	Determine Offsetting Accounts
J3RKKRL	Account Balances, LC (Russia)
J3RKKRN	Prohibited correspondences customiz.
J3RKKRS	Automatic Account Determination
J3RKKVL	Accounts Balances, FC (Russia)
J3RKNID	Unprocessed Accounting Documents
J3RKOBS	Account Balance Comparison (Russia)
J3RKOBX	Account Balance Comparison (Russia)
J3RKPAC	Account priorities
J3RKPAI	Priorities for pairs of accounts
J3RKSORT	Sorting rules
J3RKSPLIT	Splitting rules
J3RLFNPOSTR	Notification of Postal Money Transf.
J3RLFNPOSTRHR	Notification of Postal Money Transf.
J3RPBU18DP	Posting tax differences to GL
J3RPBU18DT	Transfer tax differences to FI-SL
J3RPBU18RA	Rates and accounts for PBU18 setting
J3RPBU18SC	Set Classes Assignment
J3RSEXPORT	Create Secondary Events for Exports
J3RTAX21	VAT Return (Russia)
J3RTAXAE	Assign Tax Hierarchy to CC/ledger
J3RTAXAS	Assign Tax Hierarchy to CC
J3RTAXCD	Tax chain definition
J3RTAXCE	Execute tax chain
J3RTAXCS	Create FI-SL settings
J3RTAXDC	Profit Tax Reporting (Russia)
J3RTAXDD	Provision for Doubtful Receivables
J3RTAXDE	FI-SL selective deletion utility
J3RTAXDP	Electronic Tax Format Maintenance
J3RTAXDR	Tax declaration rows
J3RTAXGR	Maintain FI-SL activity groups
J3RTAXHR	Tax Hierarchy Maintanance
J3RTAXID	Tax hierarchy assignment ID
J3RTAXIN	Table group install.for tax account.
J3RTAXJR	Tax journal
J3RTAXLA	List accounts used in hierarchy
J3RTAXRL	Hierarchy rollup creation
J3RTAXST	Selective field transfer parameters
J3RTAXTB	Maintain table links
J3RTAXTEST	Print Sample VAT Returns (Russia)
J3RTAXTR	Tax hierarchy transport
J3RTAXUC	Maintain unclassified objects
J3RTAXUL	Unclassified transactions listing
J3RTUPD	Transport Tax Recalculation (Russia)
J3RTVEH	Transport Tax Report (Russia)
J4G1	Check Settlement Data for Recipient

J4G2	CEM - Master Data
J4GA	ETM: Create Conditn Table (PrcList)
J4GB	ETM: Change Conditn Table (PrcList)
J4GC	ETM: Display Conditn Table (PrcList)
J4GD	ETM: Create Condition Record-PrcLst
J4GE	ETM: Change Condition Record-PrcLst
J4GF	ETM: Display Condition Record-PrcLst
J4GG	Records Released from Settlmnt Cal.
J4GH	Enter Settlement Calendar
J4GI	Release Settlement Calendar
J4GJ	Create PBE Calendar
J4GK	Fill PBE Reports
J4GL	Current Stock for Equipment
J4GM	Current Stock for Material
J4GN	Post PBE Reports
J4GO	Location Stock
J4GON	Location Stock (ALV)
J4GP	Enter Settlement Calendar
J4GQ	Document List for PBE
J4GT	ETM: Display Condition Record-PrcLst
J4GV	Archive Lists
J4GW	Movements Between Locations
J4GWN	Movements Between Locations List
J4GX	Hour Evaluation for PBE
J4GY	Display PBE Document
J4GZ	Equipment and Tools Management (ETM)
J4I0	DMC setup menu
J4I1	Default Owners DMC / Create
J4I2	Default Owners DMC / Change
J4I3	Notes Tickler/Query
J4I4	Default Owners DMC / Display
J4I6	User Master Record DMC / Create
J4I7	User Master Record DMC / Change
J4I8	User Master Record DMC / Display
J4I9	Mass Print for Action Notes
J4IA	Reporting Tree for Notes Tickler
J7L0	REA Article: Display References
J7L1	Create REA Article: Initial Screen
J7L2	Change REA Article: Initial Screen
J7L3	Display REA Article: Initial Screen
J7L4	REA Annual Prepaid Declaration
J7L5	Create REA Packaging: Initial Screen
J7L6	Change REA Packaging: Initial Screen
J7L7	Display REA Packaging:Initial Screen
J7L8	REA Info Cost Analysis: Article
J7L8_FISCH	REA Cost Analysis: Article (Old)
J7L9	REA Article: Collective Maintenance
J7LB	REA Cust.: Adjust Conditions
J7LC	REA Cust.: General Controls
J7LCD	REA Cust.: Data Filter Key
J7LDA	REA General Interface
J7LE	REA Display recycling partner
J7LF	REA Number Range Maint.: Declaration
J7LG	REA Display Packaging Group

J7LH	REA Help
J7LIGEB	REA: Fraction Charge Overview
J7LIKO	REA Condition Analysis
J7LIKU	REA Info systems customer analysis
J7LIPAA	REA Info System: ArtclPricing Analys
J7LIPAV	REA Info System:Packaging Pric.Anlys
J7LISA	REA Infosystem Article Master Data
J7LISF	REA Info System Fraction Master Data
J7LISP	REA Infosystem Price List Master
J7LISR	REA Infosystem Re.Partner Master
J7LISV	REA Infosystem Packaging Master Data
J7LIZAF	REA Infosystem Article-Fraction Asgt
J7LIZAR	REA Infosystem Article-Partner Assig
J7LIZARF	REA Infosystem Art.-RP-Fract. Asgmt
J7LIZAV	REA Infosystem Article-Pack. Assign.
J7LIZAV2	REA Info System RePartAsgmt Art-Pckg
J7LIZFA	REA Infosystem Fraction-Article Asgt
J7LIZFR	REA Infosystem Fraction-RePart.Asgmt
J7LIZFV	REA Infosystem Fraction-Packag.Asgmt
J7LIZRF	REA Infosystem RePart-Fraction Asgmt
J7LIZRV	REA Infosystem RPart-Pack. Assignm.
J7LIZVA	REA Infosystem Pack-Article Assign.
J7LIZVF	REA Infosystem Packag.-Fract. Asgmt
J7LIZVR	REA Infosystem Pack-R.Part.Assign.
J7LIZVV	REA Infosystem Pack-PackGrp Assign.
J7LK	REA Customizing: Condition Types
J7LKC	Article Consistency Check
J7LKCV	Packaging Consistency Check
J7LM	REA Article Field Changes
J7LMN	REA Article Field Changes
J7LMS	REA Declaration System
J7LN	REA Number Range: Declaration Key
J7LN1	REA Number Ranges: Declaration Key 1
J7LN2	REA Number Ranges: Declaration Key 2
J7LN3	REA Number Ranges: Data Filter
J7LO	REA Customizing: Fractions
J7LP	REA Display Price Lists: Init.Screen
J7LPUB	REA Period Overview
J7LR	REA Recycling Administration
J7LRKPD11000186	IMG Activity: J_7L_REA_LOGFILE
J7LRKPD11000187	Data Filter Assgmt Access Seq. Vend.
J7LRKR0	REA Accruals Analysis/Correction
J7LRRE711000110	IMG Activity: J_7L_REA_STEUERUNG
J7LRRE711000111	IMG Activity: J_7L_REA_NUMKREISE
J7LRRE711000112	IMG Activity: J_7L_REA_BUCHUNGSKR
J7LRRE711000113	IMG Activity: J_7L_REA_GEMBUCHKR
J7LRRE711000114	IMG Activity: J_7L_REA_LAENDGRUP
J7LRRE711000115	IMG Activity: J_7L_REA_FRAKTIONEN
J7LRRE711000116	IMG Activity: J_7L_REA_ABGRMELD
J7LRRE711000117	IMG Activity: J_7L_REA_AENDFELD_MM
J7LRRE711000118	Number Ranges Rec. Declaration Keys
J7LRRE711000119	IMG Activity: J_7L_REA_MATERIALART
J7LRRE711000120	Data Filters Item Ctgry Sales Doc.
J7LRRE711000121	Data Filters Material Type Packaging

J7LRRE711000122	Data Filters BOM Usage
J7LRRE711000123	Data Filters Item Ctgry BOM
J7LRRE711000124	IMG Activity: J_7L_REA_VERPARTEN
J7LRRE711000126	IMG Activity: J_7L_REA_VERPEBENEN
J7LRRE711000132	IMG Activity: J_7L_REA_ALLG_SCHNIT
J7LRRE711000136	Data Filters Customer's Industry Key
J7LRRE711000137	REA Change Condition Types
J7LRRE711000139	REA Display Condition Types
J7LRRE711000140	REA Splitting Filters
J7LRRE711000141	REA Weighting Factors
J7LRRE711000142	Number Ranges Rec. Declaration Keys
J7LRRE711000143	Number Ranges Rec. Declaration Keys
J7LRRE711000144	IMG Activity: J_7L_REA_FAKTURAART
J7LRRE711000145	IMG Activity: J_7L_REA_VERTRBER
J7LRRE711000146	IMG Activity: J_7L_REA_PRODHIER
J7LRRE711000147	IMG Activity: J_7L_REA_VORGART
J7LRRE711000148	IMG Activity: J_7L_REA_BEWEGARTEN
J7LRRE711000149	IMG Activity: J_7L_REA_MATBELARTEN
J7LRRE711000150	REA Customer-Specific Enhancements
J7LRRE711000151	Groups for Material Characteristic
J7LRRE711000152	Data Filters Def. Data Filter Types
J7LRRE711000153	Number Range Data Filter Keys
J7LRRE711000154	Display Data Filters
J7LRRE711000155	Data Filters Field Definition
J7LRRE711000156	Plants Assigned to CoCd for BOM
J7LRRE711000158	Data Filters Access Seq. Hierarchy
J7LRRE711000161	Data Filters Access Sequence Asgmt
J7LRRE711000162	REA Data Filters Trade Level Comb.
J7LRRE711000164	Data Filters Transaction Keys
J7LRREN11000156	IMG Activity: Form Groups Decl.Syst.
J7LRREN11000157	IMG Activity: Form Group Routines
J7LRREN11000158	IMG Activity: Interface Control
J7LRREN11000159	IMG Activity: Field Control DME
J7LRREN11000160	IMG Activity: J_7L_REA_KONDITIONEN
J7LRREN11000161	IMG Activity: J_7L_REA_WARENGRUP
J7LRREN11000162	IMG Activity: J_7L_REA_MELDESCHL1
J7LRREN11000163	IMG Activity: J_7L_REA_MELDESCHL2
J7LRREN11000164	IMG Activity: Accruals Correction
J7LRREN11000166	IMG Activity: Activate Auto.AccrCorr
J7LRREN11000167	IMG Activity: Assign Conditions
J7LRREN11000168	IMG Activity: Accrual Corr. Analysis
J7LRREN11000169	IMG Activity: Document Flow Filters
J7LRREN11000170	IMG Activity: Single Access Doc.Flow
J7LRREN11000171	IMG Activity: Document Flow Path
J7LRREN11000172	IMG Activity: Doc. Flow Access Seq.
J7LRREN11000173	IMG Activity: Document Eval. Asgmt
J7LRREN11000175	IMG Activity: J_7L_REA_SOKOA
J7LRREN11000176	IMG Activity: J_7L_REA_TEXT_KOND
J7LRREN11000177	IMG Activity: Consistency Check
J7LS	REA Customiz.: Data Filter Splitting
J7LSTO	REA Document: Cancellation
J7LTSL	REA Document: Process Test Run
J7LU	REA Material Master Field Changes
J7LUTILITY1	J_7LTMC6

J7LUTILITY10	J_7L_CORRECT_ART_FIELDS
J7LUTILITY11	J_7L_PACK_VERSIONING
J7LUTILITY12	J_7L_ART_VERSIONING
J7LUTILITY13	J_7L_ART_DATA_MIGRATION
J7LUTILITY14	J_7L_PACK_DATA_MIGRATION
J7LUTILITY15	J_7L_CREATE_DEC_KEY
J7LUTILITY16	J_7L_CORRECT_CONDITION_BUKRS
J7LUTILITY17	J_7L_CORRECT_VRKME
J7LUTILITY18	J_7L_PACK_MATTYPE_DATA
J7LUTILITY19	J_7L_PACK_PARTNER_DATA
J7LUTILITY2	J_7L_ABLSKO_AUT_EXECUTION
J7LUTILITY20	Delete REA Article
J7LUTILITY21	Delete REA Packaging
J7LUTILITY22	Delete REA Partners
J7LUTILITY3	J_7L_ANALYSE_VERSION
J7LUTILITY4	J_7L_CHANGE_ENTNR
J7LUTILITY5	J_7L_CORRECT_CONDITION_RECORDS
J7LUTILITY6	J_7L_CORRECT_PACK2ART_ASSIGN
J7LUTILITY7	J_7L_CORRECT_V03_VPART_HDLST
J7LUTILITY8	J_7L_EAR_NETGEW_TRANSFER
J7LUTILITY9	J_7L_MOVE_VPART_V01_V03
J7LV11	Create REA Document
J7LV13	Display REA Document
J7LV14	Cancel REA Document
J7LV15	REA Document: Create Test Run
J7LVERSION	REA Version Information
J7LW	REA Inf. Cost Analysis: Packaging
J7LX	REA General Field Changes
J7LXN	REA General Field Changes
J7LY	Number Range Maintenance: J_7LFKEY
J7LZ	REA Packaging Field Changes
J7LZN	REA Packaging Field Changes
JARC	IS-M: Archiving Development
JB02	Bank Single Transaction Costing
JB04	Bank Risk Management
JB05	IS-B: Bank regulatory reporting
JB06	Bank RM Configuration Menu
JB07	IS-B: Settings menu - bank reg.rep.
JB08	Bank STC Configuration Menu
JB09	Maintain Bank Products
JB0A	Maintain Sender Programs
JB0B	Maintain Financial Conditions
JB0C	Maintain Product Type
JB0J	Treasury Master Data
JB0K	Costing Call
JB0K_VT_OLD	IS-B: Costing Call VT (Old)
JB0N	Display Bank Products
JB0O	Copy Company Code
JB0P	Display and Delete Logs
JB0R	Backdating
JB0R_VT_OLD	IS-B: Back-Dated Transaction:VT(Old)
JB0U	Maintain Product Variants
JB0V	Display Product Variants
JB0W	Change Transaction Differentiation

JB0X	Display Transaction Differentiation
JB12	Limit Management
JB121	Definition
JB16	Costing Rule List
JB18	Display Req./Opt.Control
JB19	Asset/Liability Management
JB1C	Display Product Type
JB1E	Display Financial Conditions Types
JB1F	Maintain Bank Product Assign.
JB1G	Display Bank Product Assignmnt
JB1K	Update costing
JB20	Maturity Pattern
JB21	Maturity Pattern - Volume Assignment
JB22	Calculate Core Deposits
JB2X	Securities
JB3M	List of curr. supported field names
JB3P	Maintain variant groups
JB3Q	Maintain Variants
JB3R	Schedule variant group
JB3S	Define variant group
JB41	Create SD Condition
JB42	Change SD Condition
JB43	Display SD Condition
JB46	Maintain Costing Sheet
JB47	Maintain SD Condition Types
JB48	Maintain Access Sequence
JB49	Create SD Condition Table
JB4A	Change SD Condition Table
JB4B	Display SD Condition Table
JB4C	Create SD Condition using Template
JB4L	Create List of Conditions
JB4N	Change List of Conditions
JB4O	Display List of Conditions
JB4Q	Execute List of Conditions
JB4X	Money market
JB5X	Forex
JB68	Interpolate yield curves
JB69	Maintain Int. Rates for Yield Curves
JB69T	TimeOFday dep. IR's for Zcurves pfl
JB6X	Derivatives
JB72	Display int.rates for ref.int.rate
JB72T	IR's for timeOFday dep. ref. int.
JB73	Display int. rates for date
JB73T	TimeOFday dep. IR's for date
JB81	Maintain account
JB88	Maintain Output Fields
JB91	Maintain Aggregation
JB92	Display Aggregation Value Fields
JB99	Test Menu ONLINE Integration
JBA1	Maintain Base Portfolio
JBA2	Maintain Cash Flow Type
JBA3	Maintain balance type
JBA4	Maintain Maturity Scenario
JBA5	Maintain summarization rule

JBA6	Assign Summarization Rule to CF Type
JBA7	Assign Summ. Rule to Balance Type
JBA8	Maintain RM-FIMA Costing Rule
JBA9	Assign RM-FIMA to Cash Flow Type
JBAA	Assign RM-FIMA to Balance Type.
JBAB	Maintain Settings for Maturity Scen.
JBAC	Maintain Risk Hierarchy
JBAD	Risk hierarchy node
JBAE	RM Maintain Risk Factors
JBAF	Maintain Characteristics for View
JBAI	Load saved Dataset
JBAJ	Risk hierarchy node
JBAL	Overview of Analysis Structures
JBAN	Update Field Catalog
JBAO	Allocate Index to Securities ID
JBAP	Create Maintain Analysis Structures
JBAS	Save Dataset
JBAT	Report Selection
JBAX	Delete Saved Dataset
JBAY	Maintain Beta Factor Type
JBAZ	Maintain Beta Factors
JBA_US_MD_NIPL	ALM - Master Data Maint.
JBB0	Create Position Object
JBB1	Change Position
JBB2	Display Position
JBB3	IS-B. Edit Position Values
JBB4	Display Position Values
JBB5	Edit characteristics
JBB6	Edit Value Fields
JBBA	Position Generation - Securities
JBBB	Position Determ.-Stock Ex.Der.
JBBD	Forex Position Determination
JBBE	Valuation Setting
JBBEW	Maintain Position Changes
JBBEWE1	Valuation Setting
JBBG	Position Groups
JBBG1	Define Position Groups
JBBM	Positions
JBBPU	Reorg.of Field Cat.for BP Conversion
JBBW	Customize Valuation in Company Code
JBC0	Sample Customizing - Organization
JBC1	Sample Customizing - Basis Data
JBC2	Sample Customizing - Treasury
JBC3	Sample Customizing - Basis
JBC4	Sample Customizing - Money Market
JBC5	Sample Customizing - Forex
JBC6	Sample Customizing - Derivatives
JBC7	Sample Customizing - Securities
JBC8	Sample Customizing - Loans
JBC9	Sample Customizing - Accounts
JBCA	Sample Customizing - Services
JBCAPAACT	BCA: FO Integration of Prof. Anal.
JBCB	Sample Customizing-Non-Int.Positions
JBCBCA	Customizing BCA Accts Non-Critical

JBCC	Delta Customizing - Derivatives
JBCD	Delta Customizing - Loans
JBCDLI	Display Condition Lists
JBCDLITY	Display List Types for Cond. Lists
JBCDPERTY	Assign Cond. Types to List Types
JBCE	Delta Customizing - Securites
JBCF	Maintain Condition Type
JBCFTRANSAKTION	Maint. Trans. Cash Flow Transaction
JBCG	Sample Customizing - Process Costs
JBCH	Delta Customizing - Accounts
JBCI	Delta Customizing - Loans
JBCJ	Delta Customizing - Derivatives
JBCK	Delta Customizing: ABC 4.02
JBCL	Delta Cust.: Basic Data 4.02
JBCM	Delta Cust.: Loans 4.02
JBCN	Delta Cust.: Money Market 4.02
JBCO	Sample Customizing: Volumen Costing
JBCP	Customizing: Vol. Cost. Not Critical
JBCQ	Customizing: Var.Trans. Not Critical
JBCR	Goto currency redemption
JBCS	Flow Type
JBCT	Customize Flow Type
JBCTVT_NEBP	Assign New Bank Products
JBCTVT_NEBPVR	Assign Bank Product Variant
JBDAC_DEL	Deletion of Account Master Data
JBDBALCOST	Volume Cost. Costing Rule Derivation
JBDCD	Delete Change Pointers
JBDCPNUM	No. Range Maint.: Object JBD_CPID
JBDCR	Change Relevance
JBDDRBCA1	BCA: Maintain Derivation Strategy
JBDDRBCA2	BCA: Maintain Rule Entries
JBDDRDERIV1	Derivatives: Maintain Deriv. Strat.
JBDDRDERIV2	Derivatives: Maintain Rule Entries
JBDDRFGDT1	Gen. Trans: Maintain Deriv. Strat.
JBDDRFGDT2	Gen. Trans: Maint. Rule Entries
JBDDRFX1	Forex: Maintain Derivation Strategy
JBDDRFX2	Forex: Maintain Rule Entries
JBDDRLOAN1	Loans: Maintain Derivation Strategy
JBDDRLOAN2	Loans: Maintain Rule Entries
JBDDRMM1	Money Market:Maintain Deriv.Strategy
JBDDRMM2	Money Market: Maintain Rule Entries
JBDDRORD1	Order: Derivation Strategy
JBDDRORD2	Order: Maintian Rule Entries
JBDDRSTX1	Positions: Maintain Deriv. Strategy
JBDDRSTX2	Positions: Maintain Rule Entries
JBDDRVT1	Variable Transaction: Deriv. Strat.
JBDDRVT2	Var. Trans: Maintain Rule Entries
JBDEA	Export Settings
JBDEM	Overview of Change Pointers
JBDER	Export Relevance
JBDERH	Main Setting for Export Relevance
JBDEX	Start Export
JBDFOAC_DEL	Deletion of Accnt Financial Objects
JBDFOLN_DEL	Deletion of Loan Financial Objects

JBDFOSV_DEL	Deletion of FO for Services
JBDFOVT_DEL	Deletion of Financial Objects of VT
JBDFTP	FTP Update in PC Accounting
JBDIL02	Initial Load: Security Class Data
JBDIL03	Initial Load: Security Order
JBDIL04	Initial Load: Listed Derivatives
JBDIL05	Initial Load: Loans
JBDIL07	Initial Load: Forex Transactions
JBDIL08	Initial Load: Business Partner
JBDIL09DETR	Initial Load: Listed Der. Positions
JBDIL09FX	Initial Load: Forex Positions
JBDIL09SETR	Initial Load: Security Order Positns
JBDIL11	Initial Load: Position Change
JBDIL12	Initial Load: Fixed-Term Deposit
JBDIL13	Initial Load: Commercial Paper
JBDIL14	Initial Load: FRA
JBDIL15	Initial Load: Swap
JBDIL16	Initial Load: Variable Transactions
JBDIL18	Initial Load: Generic Transactions
JBDIL19	Initial Load: Facilities
JBDIL20	Initial Load: Collateral
JBDIL21	Initial Load: Security Prices
JBDIL22	Initial Load: Exchange Rates
JBDIL23	Initial Load: Interest Rates
JBDIL24	Initial Load: Indexes
JBDIL25	Initial Load: Limits
JBDIL30	Initial Load: BP Relationship
JBDIL31	Initial Load: Security Volatilities
JBDIL32	Initial Load: Index Volatility
JBDIL33	Initial Load: Currency Volatility
JBDIL34	Initial Load: Interest Volatility
JBDK	Customize Exchange Rate Type
JBDLN_DEL	Deletion of Loan Master Data
JBDM	IS-B: Loans
JBDO	Financial Object
JBDO_VT_OLD	Old Initial Screen in FO f. VT (Old)
JBDRDARL	Bank Product from Loan
JBDRVATR	Bank Product from Variable Trans.
JBDSV_DEL	Deletion of Services
JBDVT_DEL	Deletion of Master Data of Var.Trans
JBD_AFX_ACT	No. Range Maintenance Object:AFX_ACT
JBD_AFX_CUST_DEPLOY	Use Global Control
JBD_COLL_ARCH_CUS	Customizing Object COLL_ARCH
JBD_DEL_PROT	Display of Deletion Logs
JBD_FCTY_ARCH_CUS	Customizing Object FCTY_ARCH
JBD_FOBJ_ARCH_CUS	Customizing Object FOBJ_ARCH
JBD_FOCF_ARCH_CUS	Customizing Object FOCF_ARCH
JBD_GAP_ARCH_CUS	Customizing for Object GPAN_ARCH
JBD_GETR_ARCH_CUS	Customizing Object GETR_ARCH
JBD_GTVS_ARCH_CUS	Customizing Object GTVS_ARCH
JBD_LOAN_ARCH_CUS	Customizing Object LOAN_ARCH
JBD_VTBA_ARCH_CUS	Customizing Object VTBA_ARCH
JBD_VTMD_ARCH_CUS	Customizing Object VTMD_ARCH
JBD_VTTO_ARCH_CUS	Customizing Object VTTO_ARCH

SAP Transaction Codes – Volume One

JBD_VT_OLD_CUST	Customizing: Variable Trans. (Old)
JBFR	Customize Function per Register
JBFS	Maintain Due Date Scenario
JBG0	CO-PA Bank: Edit Operating Concern
JBG0O	CO-PA Bank: Edit Operating Concern
JBGK	Maintain Yield Curve Types
JBHTL	Translate Characteristic Hierarchies
JBHTR	Transport Characteristic Hierarchies
JBI1	PA transfer structure CO
JBIR	Goto reference interest rates
JBIRM	Goto ref. int. rate maintenance
JBIRMTD	Goto time-dependent int. rate. maint
JBJJ	Display Assgmt of Bal.Type>Cost.Rule
JBJK	Change Assgmt of Bal.Type>Cost.Rule
JBK1	Preliminary Costing: Create Form
JBK2	Preliminary Costing: Change form
JBK3	Preliminary Costing: Display Form
JBKA	SAP Banking: Costing Sheet Analysis
JBKR	Customize Account Assignment Ref.
JBKW	Actual Process Allocation: Fin. Obj.
JBL7	Current Settings Market Risk
JBLDC	Var. Transaction Ledger Dimensions
JBLF	Determine Log Number
JBLM	Block Size for EDT
JBLS	Bank Profit.Analysis - Curr.Settings
JBLZ	Maturity band
JBLZB1	Maturity band
JBLZB2	Maturity band
JBM0	Maintain Eval.Types (Addition)
JBM1	Maintain Eval Types - Value Fields
JBM10	Euro Reversal: Variable Transaction
JBM2	Maint. Transact. Disbursements
JBM3	SAP Banking: EURO Log Administration
JBM4	SAP Banking: EURO Conversion Lo/FT
JBM5	EURO Conversion: Current Accounts
JBM6	EURO Conv.: Current Accnts (Reverse)
JBM7	EURO Conversion Security
JBM8	EURO Conversion Security (Cancel)
JBM9	Euro Conversion: Variable Transact.
JBMK	Required/Optional Fields
JBMS	Set filter for messages
JBMT	Multitasking Maintenance
JBMT1	Evaluation Categories in SEM
JBMT2	Parallel Processing Settings
JBMU	Display Required/Optional Fields
JBMVT	Business Partner Configuration Menu
JBMVTWORK	Business Partner Configuration Menu
JBMVTWORK2	Business Partner Configuration Menu
JBNPV	Maintain NPV
JBPB	Define Period Block
JBPD	Update Character. for Process Costs
JBPERIOD	Period values
JBPF	Customize Portfolio Data
JBPH	Portfolio hierarchy

SAP Transaction Codes – Volume One

JBP_CUS_DIST_DER1   Derivation Strategy DIS1 (Distrib.)
JBP_DIST_TRO   Distribution (Treasury Offset)
JBR0   Maintain Market Data Shifts
JBR0_OLD   Maintain Market Data Shifts
JBR1   Check Selected Settings
JBR10   RM: Maintain External Key Figures
JBR10EXT   External Key Figures for FO
JBR10S   RM: Display External Key Figures
JBR10U   RM: Maintain External Key Figures
JBR2   Display Saved Data
JBR3   Assign Flow Type to Cash Flow Indic.
JBR4   Delete Portfolio Hierarchies
JBR4E   Deactivate Portfolio Hierarchies
JBR5   Update Portfolio Hierarchy
JBR6   Delete View
JBR7   Display Maturity Band
JBR8   Adjust Portfolio Hierarchy
JBR9   Report for Aggr. Base Portfolio Data
JBRA   Assign Product Type -> Eval. Type
JBRALMART   Maintain ALM Valuation Type
JBRB1   Summarization Rule - Default Setting
JBRB2   Summarization Rule - Spec. Settings
JBRBP   Reorganize Base Portfolios
JBRBPC   Bond Price Calculator
JBRCPAACT   GT: FO Integration for PA
JBRCT   RM: Transport of Char. Values
JBRCU   Edit Characteristic Values
JBRCV   Maintenance of Characteristic Values
JBRDELSVGP   Deletion of Gap Results
JBRDG   Generate Program for Char.Derivation
JBRDR   Settings for Char. Derivation
JBRDV   Maintain Derivation of Rule Entries
JBRE   Customize Register
JBREVAL   Maintain Evaluation Type
JBRF0   Collective Processing of FOs
JBRF0_VT_OLD   Collective Processing of FOs
JBRFG   Edit field groups
JBRG0   Default Settings for Gap Analysis
JBRG1   Spec. Eval. Control for Gap Analysis
JBRGE   Generate Program Env.for A.Structure
JBRGV   Reorganize Maintenance Modules
JBRI   Risk Management: Grid Analysis
JBRIN   Initialize view
JBRJ   Risk Mgmt: Sensitivity Analysis
JBRK   Display Portfolio Hierarchies
JBRKA   Display Portfolio Hierarchy (old)
JBRLZB   Maintain Maturity Band
JBRM   Valuation Rules - Evaluation Type
JBRMP0   Logs for Financial Object
JBRMP1   Logs for Portfolio Hierarchies
JBRN   Restructuring per View
JBRNR   Number Range Administration
JBRN_VT_OLD   Restructuring per View
JBROZ   RM Gap Calc. of TP using Costing

JBROZPROT	Log of TP Determination
JBRP	Customize Report Functions
JBRP0	Update Portfolio Hierarchy (Experts)
JBRPLANV	Maintenance of Planning Variables
JBRQ	Valuation Rules
JBRR	Maintain Risk Hierarchy
JBRT	ALM Simulation
JBRTOBJ	ALM Single Value Analysis
JBRTOBJ_CFM	ALM Single Value Analysis for TRM
JBRTUP	Update Saved Gap Results
JBRTUPPROT	Information on Saved Gap Results
JBRT_CFM	ALM Simulation for TRM
JBRU	Single Value Analysis: Sensitivity
JBRUD	Banking Reuse Library Display
JBRUM	Banking Reuse Library Maintenance
JBRW	Generate Portfolio Hierarchy
JBRX	Single Value Analysis: NPV
JBRY	Single Value Analysis: Hist. Sim.
JBRZ	Maintain Derivation Strategy
JBR_GPTP_ARCH_CUS	Customizing Object GPTP_ARCH
JBSTCOND	Maintain Standard Conditions
JBSV	Maintain Service
JBSY	IS-B: Treasury Master Data
JBT1	Maintain Costing Rule
JBTA	Costing Rule for Node Costing
JBTLSVORMERK	Maintain LS Selection Table
JBTLSVORMERKVERARB	Edit LS Selection Table
JBTM	SAP R/3 Top Menu
JBTZ	Maintain Cash Flow
JBT_RECONC_LOAN_PAFO	Reconciliation: Fin. Obj. and Loans
JBUB	Non-Int. Bearing Positions: Maintain
JBV0	Maintain Master Data of Volatilities
JBV61	Assign Ref. Int. Rates to Vol. Names
JBV62	Assign Currency Pair to Vol. Names
JBV63	Assign Sec.ID No. to Volatility Name
JBV64	Assign Index to Volatility Name
JBVL	Volatilities
JBVT	Activity Category Customizing
JBVT0001	VT Control: Application
JBVT0002	VT Control: Field Groups
JBVT0003	VT Control: Views
JBVT0004	VT Control: Sections
JBVT0005	VT Control: Screens
JBVT0006	VT Control: Screen Sequence
JBVT0007	VT Control: Business Trans. Events
JBVT0008	VT Control: CUA Standard Functions
JBVT0009	VT Control: CUA Additional Functions
JBVT0010	VT Control: Matchcode
JBVT0011	VT Control: Screen Fld -> DB Field
JBVT0013	VT Control: Role Categories
JBVT0014	VT Control: Role Category Groupings
JBVT0015	VT Control: Application Transactions
JBVT0016	VT Control: Tables
JBVT0018	VT Control: Activities

SAP Transaction Codes – Volume One

JBVT0019	VT Control: Field Mod. per Activity
JBVTCH	Change Variable Transaction
JBVTCR	Create Variable Transaction
JBVTDEL	Delete Variable Transaction
JBVTPAACT	Var. Trans.: FO Integ. Prof. Anal.
JBVTSH	Display Variable Transaction
JBW0	Execute Report
JBW0_MONITOR	Display Selection of Frozen Data
JBW1	Create Report
JBW2	Change Report
JBW3	Display Report
JBW4	Create Form
JBW5	Change Form
JBW6	Display Form
JBW7	Maintain authorization obj. present.
JBW8	Display authorization obj.presentatn
JBWA	Access Report Tree
JBWB	Maintain Batch Variants
JBWC	Comments Management: Treasury
JBWG	Characteristic Groups for RM
JBWH	Maintain hierarchy
JBWK	Maintain key figures
JBWM	Test Monitor: RM Drilldown Reporting
JBWO	Transport Reports
JBWP	Transport forms
JBWPORD	Securities Order Maint. Transaction
JBWPORD_ANZ	Display Securities Order Directly
JBWPR	RM: Display Interface Programs
JBWQ	Import reports from client 000
JBWR	Import Forms from Client 000
JBWS	Display structure
JBWT	Translation Tool - Drilldown Report.
JBWU	Convert drilldown reports
JBWV	Maintain Global Variable
JBWW	Mainten.curr.conversion type TMR
JBWX	Reorganize Drilldown Reports
JBWY	Reorganize Report Data
JBWZ	Reorganize Forms
JBW_AM_COA_1	IS-M: Determine BW Classificat.Again
JBW_AM_COA_2	IS-M: Unload Contracts from BW
JBYC	Overview/Maintenance of Yield Curves
JBZK	Assign Condition Types->Cond. Groups
JC9A	IS-M: Condition Master Data
JC9B	IS-M: Condition Master Data - Sales
JC9C	IS-M: Condition Master Data
JC9D	IS-M: Condition Master Data
JCIC_INWAIT_POPUP	IS-M: CIC, INWAIT Dialog Box
JCP4	IS-M: Master Data f.Postal Charges
JCR0	IS-M/SD: Postal Charges, Gen.BI Sess
JCR1	IS-M/SD:Postal Charges, Display Data
JCR2	IS-M/SD: Extract Postal Charges
JCS0	IS-M: Create Condition
JCS1	IS-M: Create Condition w/Reference
JCS2	IS-M: Change Condition

SAP Transaction Codes – Volume One

JCS3	IS-M: Display Condition
JD01	IS-M: Create Gen.Rule for Edition
JD02	IS-M: Change Gen.Rule for Edition
JD03	IS-M: Display Gen.Rule for Edition
JD04	IS-M: Create Gen.Rule f.Truck Route
JD05	IS-M: Change Gen.Rule f.Truck Route
JD06	IS-M: Display Gen.Rule f.Truck Route
JD10	IS-M: Create Ad Pre-Prt.(Fast Entry)
JD11	IS-M: Change Ad Pre-Prt.(Fast Entry)
JD12	IS-M: Display Ad Pre-Prt.(Fast Ent.)
JD20	IS-M: Create Gen.Rule for Media Prod
JD21	IS-M: Change Gen.Rule for Media Prod
JD22	IS-M: Display Gen.Rule for Med.Prod.
JD31	IS-M: Create Publication
JD32	IS-M: Change Publication
JD33	IS-M: Display Publication
JD34	Create Edition
JD35	Change Edition
JD36	Display Edition
JD37	IS-M: Create Issue
JD38	IS-M: Change Issue
JD39	IS-M: Display Issue
JD40	IS-M: Coll.Processing of Issues
JD41	IS-M: Collective Issue Display
JD42	Automatic Issue Generation
JD43	Issue Numbering
JD44	IS-M: Coll.Issue Proc.for Pub.Date
JD45	Move Publication Date of Issue
JD46	Log: Move Issue Publication Date
JD51	IS-M: Edit Edition Gen.Triggers
JD52	IS-M: Display Edition Gen.Triggers
JD55	IS-M: Create Issue Archiving
JD56	IS-M: Delete Issue Archiving
JD57	IS-M: Reload Issue Archiving
JD58	IS-M: Management of Issue Archiving
JD70	IS-M: Arrival Times of TP Objects
JD71	IS-M: Editions of Publications
JD72	IS-M: Displ.Edition Publ.Calendar
JD73	IS-M: Edition Overview
JD74	IS-M: Overview of Issue Weights
JD75	IS-M: Issue Overview
JD76	IS-M: Display Ad Pre-Print Pub.Cal.
JD77	IS-M: Ad Pre-Print Overview
JD81	IS-M: Edit Bundling Rule
JD82	IS-M: Display Bundling Rule
JD83	IS-M: Maintain Edit.Bundling Group
JD84	IS-M: Display Edition Bundling Group
JD85	IS-M: List Editions in Bundling Grp
JD86	IS-M: Maintain Edit.Bundling Group
JD87	IS-M: Display Edition Packing Group
JDMPS0	IS-M: Edit Media Product Master Data
JDMPS1	IS-M: Display Media Prod.Master Data
JDPOST01	Edition Postal Data
JF01	IS-M/SD: Create Billing Document

JF02	IS-M: Change Billing Document
JF03	IS-M: Display Billing Document
JF04	IS-M: Create Billing Document
JF05	Create Billing Interface
JF06	IS-M: Billing Logs
JF07	Simulate Billing Interface
JF11	IS-M: Reverse Billing Document
JF12	IS-M: Reverse Coll. Billing Run
JF2A	IS-M: Reorg.Billg Index aft.Canc.
JF2B	IS-M: Tfer Postings Bef.STax Reg.
JF61	List of Open Items and Balance
JF87	IS-M/SD: Create Rev.Acct Det.Table
JF88	IS-M/SD: Change Rev.Acct Det.Table
JF89	IS-M/SD:Display Rev.Acct Det.Table
JFAF	IS-M: Billing Document Check List
JFB2	IS-M: Data Transfer f.Bank Return
JFB3	IS-M: Reconc.List for Bank Return
JFB4	IS-M: Ords fr.Bank Rtns for Change
JFB5	IS-M: Ref.Transfer of Bank Returns
JFBF	IS-M: Billing Document Flow
JFBS	IS-M: Bank Returns by Return Reason
JFBT	IS-M: Payment Medium Germany
JFCA	IS-M/SD: Billing Doc.Authorization
JFCB	Check Payment Cards Before Billing
JFCC	Checking Log for Payment Cards
JFCO	Issue - Addit. Account Assignment
JFCO_PVA	Edition - Additional Account Assgmt
JFF1	Maintain number range: ISP_FIBU
JFFB	Doc.According to Billing Cond.Types
JFFI	FI Journal for Revenue Posting/Dist.
JFJOURNREVPER	Posting Journal for Per. Rev. Accr.
JFLI	IS-M/SD: List Billing Documents
JFM1	Media Sales + Distribution - Billing
JFNF	Set Up Indexes
JFNL	Non-Billed Deliveries
JFP2	Billing Docs not Transfd to RF/FI
JFP3	Collective Proc./Transfer Assignment
JFRA	Posting Journal for Revenue Accrual
JFRE	IS-M: Revenue Distribution Journal
JFREVENUECOCKPIT	Revenue Accrual Cockpit
JFRJ	IS-M: Outgoing Invoice Journal
JFRT	Orders Not Billed
JFSI	IS-M/SD: Simulate Billing
JFSU	IS-M: Information on Coll.Proc.
JFT1	Individual Transfer to FI
JFT2	Collective Transfer to FI
JFT3	IS-M/SD: Payment Card Transfer
JFT4	Collection Transfer for Billing
JFT5	IS-M/SD: Bank Returns Transfer
JFT6	IS-M/SD: Transfer Revenue Distrib.
JFTA	IS-M/SD: Call Up Individual Transfer
JFTB	IS-M/SD: Call Up Collective Transfer
JFTC	IS-M/SD: Call Up Field Coll.Transfer
JFTD	IS-M/SD: Access Bank Rtns.Transfer

JFTE	IS-M/SD: Access Revenue Accrual
JFTH	IS-M/SD: Data Transfer to HR
JFU1	Individual Transfer to FI
JFU2	Collective Transfer to FI
JFU3	IS-M/SD: Bank Returns Transfer
JFU4	Collection Transfer for Billing
JFUV	Transfer Issue to Financial Accounts
JFVL	Open Issue Account Assignments
JF_ITALY_VAT_01	Setting for VAT Reporting
JF_ITALY_VAT_02	VAT Reporting - Italy
JG01	IS-M: Create General Bus.Partner
JG02	IS-M: Change General Bus.Partner
JG03	IS-M: Display General Bus.Partner
JG07	IS-M/SD: Create Carrier
JG08	IS-M/SD: Change Carrier
JG09	IS-M/SD: Display Carrier
JG10	IS-M/SD: Create Service Company
JG11	IS-M/SD: Change Service Company
JG12	IS-M/SD: Display Service Company
JG16	IS-M/SD: Create Sales Customer
JG17	IS-M/SD: Change Sales Customer
JG18	IS-M/SD: Display Sales Customer
JG19	IS-M/SD: Create Retailer
JG20	IS-M/SD: Change Retailer
JG21	IS-M/SD: Display Retailer
JG34	IS-M/SD: Create Commission Recipient
JG35	IS-M/SD: Change Commission Recipient
JG36	IS-M/SD: Display Commission Recipt
JG40	IS-M/SD: Create Field Collector
JG41	IS-M/SD: Change Field Collector
JG42	IS-M/SD: Display Field Collector
JG43	IS-M/SD: Create Researcher
JG44	IS-M/SD: Change Researcher
JG45	IS-M/SD: Display Researcher
JG49	IS-M/SD: Create Forwarding Agent
JG50	IS-M/SD: Change Forwarding Agent
JG51	IS-M/SD: Display Forwarding Agent
JG55	IS-M/SD: Create Postal Data
JG56	IS-M/SD: Change Postal Data
JG57	IS-M/SD: Display Postal Data
JG58	IS-M/SD: Create Sales Cust.(Central)
JG59	IS-M/SD: Change Sales Cust.(Central)
JG60	IS-M/SD: Display Sales Cust.(Cent.)
JG61	IS-M/SD: Create Retailer (Central)
JG62	IS-M/SD: Change Retailer (Central)
JG63	IS-M/SD: Display Retailer (Central)
JG90	IS-M: Block Order/Bill.Doc. - Change
JG91	IS-M: Block Order/Bill.Doc.-Display
JG92	IS-M: Block Roles - Change
JG93	IS-M: Block Roles - Display
JG94	IS-M: Change BP Deletion Flags
JG95	IS-M: Display BP Deletion Flags
JGA0	IS-M: Maintain Address Management
JGA1	IS-MP: Display Address Management

JGA2	IS-M: Maintain Business Partner Asgt
JGA3	IS-M: Display Bus.Partner Assignment
JGA4	IS-M: Maintain Address Print Formats
JGA6	IS-M:Maint.AddPrintFormat-Env.Assgmt
JGA8	IS-M: Address Recording
JGA9	IS-M/SD: Add.Change -> Check Orders
JGAD	IS-M: Determine Address Duplicates
JGAE	IS-M: Determine Jurisdiction Code
JGAF	IS-M: BP Log in Non-SAP System
JGAS	IS-M: Screen Mod.for SD BP Transacs
JGB3	IS-M: Add.Synch. IS-M -> Standard
JGB4	IS-M: Add.Synch. IS-M -> Non-SAP
JGB5	IS-M: Transfer Customers on Hand
JGB6	IS-M: BTCI Session BP Data Transfer
JGB7	IS-M: Synch.bank conn. IS-M->FI
JGB8	IS-M: Bank con.synchronization log
JGBA	IS-M: Transfer Bank Data
JGBD	IS-M: Bank data changes
JGBDC1	Change Bank Number in Bank Details
JGBDC2	Bank Details Change: Create File
JGBDC3	Bank Details Change: Read File
JGBP_CHANGE	IS-M: Change Business Partner
JGBP_SHOW	IS-M: Display Business Partner
JGCL	IS-M: BP Classification
JGKS	IS-M: Sales Summary
JGM0	Business Partner
JGR1	IS-M/SD: SC Employee Turnover
JGR2	IS-M: Service Company Employees
JGR3	IS-M: Overview of Fwding Agents
JGV3	IS-M: Maintain Lost Time for SC EE
JGV4	IS-M: Display Lost Time for SC EE
JGV7	IS-M: Maintain Employment Relnship
JGV8	IS-M: Display Employment Relnship
JGWWWIU1	IS-M: Create Internet User
JGWWWIU2	IS-M: Change Acc.Data for Int.User
JGZ0	Check SAP BP Customizing
JGZ1	IS-M: Create Customer
JGZ2	IS-M: Change Customer
JGZ20	IS-M: Create Sales Customer
JGZ21	IS-M: Change Sales Customer
JGZ22	IS-M: Display Sales Customer
JGZ23	IS-M: Create Retailer
JGZ24	IS-M: Change Retailer
JGZ25	IS-M: Display Retailer
JGZ3	IS-M: Create Vendor
JGZ30	IS-M: Create Service Company
JGZ31	IS-M: Change Service Company
JGZ32	IS-M: Display Service Company
JGZ33	IS-M: Create Carrier
JGZ34	IS-M: Change Carrier
JGZ35	IS-M: Display Carrier
JGZ36	IS-M: Create Researcher
JGZ37	IS-M: Change Researcher
JGZ38	IS-M: Display Researcher

JGZ39	IS-M: Create Field Collector
JGZ4	IS-M: Change Vendor
JGZ40	IS-M: Change Field Collector
JGZ41	IS-M: Display Field Collector
JGZ42	IS-M: Create Commission Recipient
JGZ43	IS-M: Change Commission Recipient
JGZ44	IS-M: Display Commission Recipient
JGZ50	IS-M: Create Publisher
JGZ51	IS-M: Change Publisher
JGZ52	IS-M: Display Publisher
JGZ60	IS-M: Create Media Customer
JGZ61	IS-M: Change Media Customer
JGZ62	IS-M: Display Media Customer
JGZ70	IS-M: Create Media Sales Agent
JGZ71	IS-M: Change Media Sales Agent
JGZ72	IS-M: Display Media Sales Agent
JGZ90	IS-M: Create Household
JGZ91	IS-M: Change Household
JGZ92	IS-M: Display Household
JH00	IS-M: Condition Refs Check List
JH01	IS-M: Condition Refs Check List
JH51	Display UM for pricing
JH52	Design Ad Type: Admissibility
JH53	General Ad Type: Admissibility
JH54	UM for Ads & Pricing (Display)
JH55	Ad Type Design Admissibility (Displ)
JH56	General Ad Type Admissibility(Displ)
JH57	BU Grouping for Ad Type Admissibilty
JH60	Generate schedule lines
JH61	Display generation period
JH62	Item list according to date type
JH64	Status/char.attributes for item
JH65	Data transfer for new orders
JH66	Data transfer for old orders
JH67	Data transfer for COAs
JH68	Status/char.attributes bill.dataset
JH69	Status/Char.Attributes S.Line/Ad Spc
JH70	Status/Char.Attributes for AI SLine
JH72	Status/char.attributes for com.SLine
JH73	Status/Char.Attribute DT Sched.Line
JH75	Manual on-screen mark up check
JH76	Data trans.for new commercial orders
JH77	Status/Char.Attributes S.Line/Ad Spc
JH78	Return Actual Online Data Manually
JH84	Grouping for Fixed Spaces Planning
JH85	Fixed spaces capacity
JH86	Date-spec. capacity for fixed spaces
JH89	IS-M/AM: Order Transfer to TS Online
JH91	Create Conditions
JH92	Create conditions using template
JH93	Change Conditions
JH94	Display Conditions
JH99	Order transfer from emerg.sys.ACCESS
JHA0	IS-M: Sales Area Menu

JHA1	IS-M/AM: Create Order
JHA1N	IS-M/AM: Create Order
JHA1X	IS-M/AM: Create Order
JHA2	IS-M/AM: Change Order
JHA2N	IS-M/AM: Change Order
JHA2X	IS-M/AM: Change Order
JHA3	IS-M/AM: Display Order
JHA3N	IS-M/AM: Display Order
JHA3X	IS-M/AM: Display Order
JHA4	IS-M: Maintain Fast Entry
JHA6	IS-M/AM: Central Access
JHA7	Advertisement orders 1
JHA8	Business partner usage
JHAD	IS-M: Positioning Information
JHAE	IS-M: Error List for Tech.System
JHAF	IS-M: Todo List for Technical System
JHAG	Cam.rdy cpy with past reminder date
JHAH	IS-M: Payment Cards: Authorization
JHAI	IS-M/AM: Credit Check for Orders
JHAJ	Payment Cards:Coll.Process.Overview
JHAK	Credit Mgmt: Coll.Process.Overview
JHAORDER_OBJ_CHANGE	IS-M: Display Order
JHAORDER_OBJ_SHOW	IS-M: Display Order
JHAP	IS-M/AM Order Update Collective Log
JHAVMA	IS-M/AM: Update Orders
JHAVM_REGEN	IS-M: Generate New AM Order Items
JHAW	IS-M/AM: IAC Enter Classified Ad
JHAW_ADMIN	IS-M/AM: IAC Classified Ads Adminis.
JHAW_WEBEDITOR	IS-M/AM: Web Editor Test Transaction
JHB1	IS-M: Ad Insert Planning
JHB10	IS-M/AM: Online Planning
JHB2	IS-M: Commercial Planning
JHB3	IS-M: Commercial Planning Export
JHB4	IS-M/AM: Fixed Spaces Planning
JHB4_IAC	IS-M/AM: IAC Display Free Spaces
JHB5	IS-M/AM: Local Windows Planning
JHB6	IS-M: Display BU Hierarchy
JHB7	IS-M: Change BU Hierarchy
JHB9	IS-M: M/AM Order Qty <> M/SD Del.Qty
JHBA	Cond.Maint.Using Index: Display JC
JHBB	Cond.Maint.Via Index: Create JC
JHBC	Cond.Maint.Using Index: Display JE
JHBD	Cond.Maint.Using Index: Create JE
JHBE	Cond.Maint.Using Index: Change JC
JHBO	Cond.Maint.Using Index: Change JE
JHBW	IS-M: AI Plant Data Assignment List
JHC1	Contact Conversion
JHC2	Maintain positioning factor
JHCA	Archive
JHCB	Archive
JHCNTENT_REP_CALL	IS-M: Access Report With Variant
JHCP_CHANGE	Change Contact Person
JHCP_CONV	Media Contact: Convert Order/Contrct
JHCP_CONV_CAS	Media CP: Sales Support Conversion

SAP Transaction Codes – Volume One

JHCP_CONV_CAS_INDX	Media CP: CAS/INDX Conversion
JHCP_DISPLAY	Display Contact Person
JHD1	Create Condition Records (JA)
JHD2	Change Condition Records (JA)
JHD3	Display Condition Records (JA)
JHD4	Create Condition Records (JB)
JHD5	Change Condition Records (JB)
JHD6	Display Condition Records (JB)
JHD7	IS-M: Create Condition Table (JD)
JHD8	IS-M: Change Condition Table (JD)
JHD9	IS-M: Display Condition Table (JD)
JHDA	Create Condition List Prices JC
JHDB	IS-M: Change Cond.List Prices JC
JHDC	IS-M: Display Cond.List Prices JC
JHDD	IS-M: Execute Condition List JC
JHDE	IS-M: Create Cond.List Prices JE
JHDF	IS-M: Change Cond.List Prices JE
JHDG	IS-M: Display Cond.List Prices JE
JHDH	IS-M: Execute Condition List JE
JHE0	Account Determination: Display Table
JHE1	Account Determination: Create Table
JHE2	Account Determination: Change Table
JHE7	Dynam.cond.maint.f.pricng for c.ord.
JHEB	Account Determination: Create Table
JHEC	Account Determination: Change Table
JHED	Account Determination: Display Table
JHEF1	Sales Volume Proof Media Partnership
JHEF2	IS-M: VBOX Restructure
JHEM	IS-M: Create Media Partnership
JHEM1	IS-M: Create Media Partnership
JHEN	IS-M: Change Media Partnership
JHEO	IS-M: Display Media Partnership
JHEOBA	IS-M/AM: Update Revenue Object Docs
JHEOBA_RRREL	IS-M/AM: Convert Orders for ROD
JHF0	IS-M: Billing
JHF1	IS-M/AM: Create Billing Document
JHF2	IS-M/AM: Change Billing Document
JHF3	IS-M/AM: Display Billing Document
JHF7	IS-M/AM: Collective Billing Run
JHF8	IS-M/AM: Reverse Bill.Coll.Processng
JHF9	IS-M: Contract Settlement
JHFA	Coll.Proc.Contract Settlement Log
JHFB	IS-M/AM: Billing Overview
JHFC	IS-M/AM: Release to Accounting
JHFD	Billing Document Reversal BCat-Ind.
JHFE	IS-M/AM: Revenue Distribution
JHFK	IS-M: Cntrct Settlement Billing Doc.
JHFL	IS-M/AM: Bill.Log for Cntrct Sttlmnt
JHFP	IS-M/AM: Overview Coll.Billing Run
JHFR	IS-M/AM: Individual Release (Dialog)
JHFS	IS-M/AM: Billing - Ind.Reversal
JHFT	IS-M: General Receivables Charge-Off
JHFU	IS-M/AM: Release Customer Accounting
JHG1	Create Condition Table (JC)

371

JHG2	Change Condition Table (JC)
JHG3	Display Condition Table (JC)
JHGP	IS-M/AM: Overview Coll.Billing Run
JHGR	IS-M/AM: Individual Release (Dialog)
JHGS	IS-M/AM: CSetBill. Reverse Dialog
JHGT	IS-M: Charge Off Contract Settlement
JHH1	IS-M: Display Revenue Object Doc.
JHINSSERT_DET	Enter Series Determ.Rule Parameters
JHK1	IS-M: Pricing Proc.Det.for Pricing
JHK4	Activate Condition Index
JHK8	Condition table: Change index (JA)
JHK9	Reorganize condition indexes
JHKD	Condition table: Change index (JC)
JHKE	Condition table: Change index (JE)
JHKH	Reorganize condition indexes
JHKI	Reorganize condition indices JE
JHKJ	Condition table: Change index (JD)
JHKL	IS-M/AM: Sales Activity List
JHKM	Cond.maint.using index: Create
JHKN	Cond.maint.using index: Change
JHKO	Cond.maint.using index: Display
JHKP	Define campaigns
JHKR	Reorganize condition indices JE
JHKS	Cond.maint.using index: Create JA
JHKS2	Cond.Maint.Using Index: Create JD
JHKT	Reorganize condition indices JD
JHKU	Cond.Maint.Using Index: Change JA
JHKU2	Cond.Maint.Using Index: Change JD
JHKX	Cond.maint.using index: Display JA
JHKX2	Cond.Maint.Using Index: Display JD
JHM0	IS-M/AM: Interface Records Contents
JHM1	IS-M/AM: Data Generat.for New Order
JHM2	IS-M/AM: Generate Contract Data
JHM3	IS-M/AM: Data Gen.for Legacy Order
JHM4	File Check for Order Migration
JHN1	IS-M: Create Condition Table (JK)
JHN2	IS-M: Change Condition Table (JK)
JHN2JM	IS-M: Change Condition Table (JK)
JHN3	IS-M: Display Condition Table (JK)
JHN4	IS-M: Create Condition Records (JK)
JHN5	IS-M: Change Condition Records (JK)
JHN6	IS-M: Display Condition Records (JK)
JHO2	IS-M: Change Responses
JHO3	IS-M: Display Responses
JHO4	Number range maintenance: ISP_CHINR
JHO5	Display Box No.Resubmission Date
JHP0	IS-M: Sales Agent Settlement
JHP1	IS-M: Create Sales Agent Settlement
JHP2	IS-M: Change Sales Agent Settlement
JHP3	IS-M: Display Sales Agent Settlement
JHP7	IS-M: SlsAgent Settlement Coll.Proc.
JHP8	IS-M/AM: Reverse Coll.SlsAgnt Sett.
JHPA	Account Determination: Create Table
JHPB	Account Determination: Change Table

JHPC	Account Determination: Display Table
JHPP	IS-M/AM Evaluate Sls Agent Coll.Proc
JHPR	IS-M/AM: Individual Release (Dialog)
JHPS	IS-M:Ind.Vendor Bill.Doc.Reversal
JHPU	IS-M/AM: Release Vendor Documents
JHR0	IS-M: Contract Settlement
JHR1	IS-M/AM: Create Final Settlement
JHR2	IS-M/AM: Change Settlement
JHR3	IS-M/AM: Display Settlement
JHR4	IS-M/AM: Settlements List
JHR5	IS-M/AM: Create Interim Settlement
JHR6	IS-M: Alt.Payer in Contract Settlemt
JHRE	IS-M: Complaints List
JHSA	Evaluate Collective Processing Run
JHSP	IS-M: Collective Processing Log
JHSR	IS-M/AM: Reorganize Coll.Processing
JHT1	Create Condition Table (JA)
JHT2	IS-M: Change Condition Table (JA)
JHT3	Display Condition Table (JA)
JHT4	Create Condition Table (JC)
JHT5	Change Condition Table (JC)
JHT6	Display Condition Table (JC)
JHTB	IS-M: Create Condition Table (JE)
JHTC	IS-M: Change Condition Table (JE)
JHTD	IS-M: Display Condition Table (JE)
JHV1	IS-M: Create Contract Requirements
JHV2	IS-M: Change Contract Requirement
JHV3	IS-M: Display Contract Requirement
JHV4	Maintain number range: COA
JHV5	IS-M: Maintain Substitute Reqs
JHV6	Overview of Contract Requirements
JHVCATVASTD_SM34	IS-M: Issue Shift: Order Item Pool
JHW0	IS-M: Contract Monitoring
JHW1	IS-M: Create Contract
JHW2	IS-M: Change Contract
JHW3	IS-M: Display Contract
JHW3_IAC	IS-M/AM: Query Contract
JHW4	IS-M: Display BP Hierarchy
JHW5	IS-M: Create External Sales Volume
JHW6	Maintain number range: COA
JHW8	IS-M: Change Contract Billing Doc.
JHW9	IS-M: Display Contract Billing Doc.
JHWA	IS-M: Create Media-Mix Contract
JHWB	IS-M: Change Media-Mix Contract
JHWC	IS-M: Display Media-Mix Contract
JHWD	IS-M: Maintain Media-Mix Packages
JHWE	IS-M: Define No.Range Intervals
JHWF	IS-M: Create Media-Mix Settlement
JHWF1	IS-M: Media-Mix Interim Settlement
JHWF2	IS-M: Media-Mix Final Settlement
JHWG	IS-M: Change Media-Mix Settlement
JHWH	IS-M: Display Media Mix Settlement
JHWI	IS-M: Media-Mix Settlement Coll.Proc
JHWJ	Media-Mix Initial Screen Tree Strct.

JHWL	IS-M: Subsequent Contract Assignment
JHWM	IS-M: Select Assignments
JHWN	IS-M: Subsequent Assignment of BDst
JHWWWTEMP	Edit Order Data from the Internet
JHZ1	IS-M/AM: Number Range Obj.for Order
JH_COPY_FUNC_CALL	IS-M: Access Copying Function
JH_P	Maintain Print Parameters
JI20	IS-M: IVW Audit Report (General)
JI21	IS-M: IVW Audit Rep.for Daily Papers
JI22	IS-M: IVW Audit Report for Magazine
JI30	IS-M: Average Audit Report Qties
JI31	IS-M: Period Comparison of AR Qties
JI32	IS-M: AR Monthly Revenue Accrual
JI33	IS-M: AR Distribution Analysis
JI34	Daily CAR Statistics (w/o Hierarchy)
JI35	CAR Quantity Statement for Period
JI36	IS-M: AR Revenue Accrual per Issue
JI37	IS-M: IVW Revenue Accrual/Month
JI40	Edit PCode Area Evaluation Variants
JI41	Display PCode Area Eval.Variants
JI42	Edit Postal Code Evaluation Areas
JI43	Display Postal Code Evaluation Areas
JI44	Assign Postal Codes to Eval.Areas
JI45	Display PCode-Eval.Area Assignment
JI46	Create Geo.Hierarchy Variant
JI47	Delete Geo.Hierarchy Variant
JIA0	Update Circulation Book for ABC
JIA1	Manage Audit Reports (Period)
JIA2	Delete Circulation Book Records
JIA3	Display ABC Update Log
JIA4	Recompile Returns in Circ.Book
JIAA	IS-M/SD: Circulation Book Overview
JIAUDITREPORT_MPS	IS-M: Evaluate Audit Report for MPM
JIAUDITREPORT_MSD	IS-M: Evaluate Audit Report for MSD
JII0	Update Circulation Book for Audit
JII1	Close/Open IVW Audit Period
JII2	Delete Daily AR Statistics Data
JII3	Update Circulation Book for Audit
JIM1	IS-M/SD: Circulation Auditing
JIRECATEGORIZE	IS-M: Recategorize Subscrip. Orders
JISDCIRCCAT	IS-M/SD: Mass Maint.of Aud.Rpt Cat.
JISDSCSDORD	Audit Report Categorization SD Order
JIT0	Sequenced JIT Call - Main Screen
JIT1	JIT Call Inbound
JIT2	Change JIT Call
JIT3	Display JIT Call
JIT4	JIT Call Inbound: Simulation
JIT5	JIT Call Fast Change (1 screen)
JIT6	JIT: Action Entry (Barcode)
JIT6H	JIT: Action Entry (Barcode)
JIT6RF	Barcode Handheld 16 x 20
JIT7	JIT: Action Entry (Specified)
JIT7H	JIT: Action Entry (Specified)
JIT7RF	Barcode (Specified) Handheld 16 x 20

JITA	Component list
JITB	Reprocess Pool of Confirmations
JITC	JIT Basic Data-Individual Maint.
JITE	Emergency Monitoring
JITEMRA	Emergency Creation of Bundled SumJCs
JITF	Progress Confirmation
JITFX	Progress Confirmation (without tabs)
JITG	JIT Cockpit
JITH	Matching JIT call w.Fcst/JIT Del.Sch
JITI	IDoc List for Specified JIT Calls
JITJ	Signal Monitor
JITK	Summarized JIT Calls Due for Dely
JITL	Maintenance Dialog JIT Material
JITLOG	Display Action Log
JITLOGDEL	Delete Action Logs
JITM	JIT Monitoring
JITMAT	Create Material Table from SchedAgmt
JITMX	JIT Monitoring (Simple Selection)
JITN	Color Profile Maintenance
JITO	Check Delivery Combination
JITO1	Create/Change: Outbound Call
JITO3	Display: Outbound Call
JITO6	Bar Code Entry
JITOA	Archiving JIT Outbound
JITOE	Status Correction
JITOG	JIT Cockpit Outbound
JITOM	Monitoring JIT Outbound
JITOXML	XML-Download of Calls
JITQ	Display Action Network
JITR	Reorganisation Material Master Data
JITS	Graphic Progress Confirmation
JITT	JIT: Maintennace Dialog Lead Times
JITU	User Assignment - Display Variant
JITV	Maintain JIT Control Data
JITW	Lean JIT Monitoring
JITX	JIT Excel Download Monitoring
JITXML	XML Upload of Calls
JITY	Archiving JIT Inbound
JITZ	Display Documentation Data
JIU1	Change Edition Audit Report Type
JJ/0	IS-M: Maintain Forms
JJ/C	IS-M: Billing Print Parameters
JJ11	Create Conditions
JJ12	Create conditions using template
JJ13	Change Conditions
JJ14	Display Conditions
JJ20	IS-M/AM: Order Archiving
JJ21	IS-M/AM: Order Archiving Order-Del.
JJ23	IS-M: Archiving Order Management
JJ24	IS-M: Display Archive Orders
JJ25	IS-M/AM: Archive Display Full Run
JJ26	IS-M/AM: Archive Order Check
JJ30	IS-M/AM: Billing Archiving
JJ31	Billing Archiving - Billing-Delete

SAP Transaction Codes – Volume One

JJ33	IS-M: Billing Archiving Management
JJ34	IS-M: Display Billing Archive
JJ35	IS-M/AM: Archive Display Full Run
JJ36	IS-M/AM: Archive Billing Check
JJ40	IS-M/AM: Contract Archiving
JJ41	IS-M/AM: Contract Archiving Delete
JJ43	IS-M: Archiving Contract Management
JJ44	IS-M: Display Archive Contract
JJ45	IS-M/AM: Archive Display Full Run
JJ46	IS-M/AM: Archive Contract Check
JJ50	IS-M: Display M/AM Address Changes
JJ60	IS-M/AM: Media-Mix Archiving
JJ61	IS-M/AM: Archiving Med-Mix Delete
JJ63	IS-M: Media-Mix Archive Management
JJ64	IS-M/AM: Display Media-Mix Archive
JJ65	IS-M/AM: Archive Display Full Run
JJ66	IS-M/AM: Archive Media-Mix Check
JJA0	IS-M: Sales Support
JJA1	IS-M/AM: Create Contact Person
JJA2	IS-M/AM: Change Contact Person
JJA3	IS-M/AM: Display Contact Person
JJA4	IS-M/AM: Number Range Maint. PARTNER
JJADVSLSZ_WEEKDAYS	Define Weekdays for AdvertSalesZones
JJB1	IS-M: Create Booking Unit
JJB2	IS-M: Change Booking Unit
JJB3	IS-M: Display Booking Unit
JJB7	IS-M: Create Date-Specific BU
JJB8	IS-M: Change Date-Specific BU
JJB9	IS-M: Display Date-Specific BU
JJBB	IS-M: Create/Change Date-Specific BU
JJBC	Check BU Completeness
JJBD	Delete Individual booking units
JJBE	IS-M: Display BU Assignments
JJBF	IS-M: M/AM PCirQy <> M/SD Del.Qties
JJBG	IS-M: Copy BU Hierarchies
JJBH	Check BU Hierarchies
JJBI	Check Content Component Master Data
JJBJ	Maintain Alternative Dates
JJBK	CM_BU: Maintain content
JJBL	CM-BU: Maintain Date-Specific Cont.
JJBM	Check BU completeness new
JJBN	Check Booking Unit Content
JJBO	Distribution BU Planned Quantities
JJBO_FPLZ	IS-M: Maintain Online Fixed Spaces
JJBO_KTZHL	IS-M: Maintain Plan.Gross Impressns
JJBO_ZUO	IS-M: Maintain Online Assignments
JJBP	Check production unit content
JJBV	IS-M: Maintain AI BU Variant
JJBW	AI-BU: Maintain Date-Specific Capac.
JJBY	IS-M: Gen. Work Area for BU Hier.
JJBZ	IS-M: AI BU Admissibility
JJC1	IS-M: Ad Insert Processing Type
JJCAMPAIGN_CRM	IS-M: Campaigns With CRM Reference
JJCAMPAIGN_NOCRM	IS-M: Campaigns Without CRM Refernce

JJCP_ACT	IS-M/AM: Activate Contact Person
JJCP_CHANGE	IS-M: Change Contact Person
JJCP_CLA1	CP Class.: Fill JJCPCLASSCONV Table
JJCP_CLA2	CP Class.: Copy Classes
JJCP_CLA3	CP Class.: Copy Classifications
JJCP_CLA4	CP Class.: Delete Classification
JJCP_CONV_FS	Convert Free Subscription
JJCP_CONV_RB	Convert Responsibility
JJCP_SHOW	IS-M: Display Contact Person
JJCP_STATUS	Media Cnt: Define Conversion Status
JJD0	IS-M: Services
JJD1	IS-M: Create Service
JJD2	IS-M: Change Service
JJD3	IS-M: Display Service
JJD4	Maintain number range: ISP_DIEN
JJF2	IS-M: Change Condition Table (JF)
JJF3	IS-M: Change Condition Table (JG)
JJF5	IS-M: Change Condition Records (JF)
JJF7	IS-M: Change Condition Table (JA)
JJFK	IS-M: Requirement for output deter.
JJFM	IS-M: Change Condition Table (JH)
JJG1	IS-M/AM: Create Media Customer
JJG2	IS-M/AM: Change Media Customer
JJG3	IS-M/AM: Display Media Customer
JJG4	Maintain Telephone Barring List
JJG5	Maintain Telephone Barring List
JJG6	Display barred telephone list
JJG7	Maintain Sales Agent Pool
JJG9	Display Agent Pool
JJGA	Create Media Sales Agent
JJGB	Change Media Sales Agent
JJGC	Display Media Sales Agent
JJGD	IS-M/AM: Maintain BP Alias
JJGE	IS-M/AM: Display BP Alias
JJGK	Maintain Sales Agent ID Code
JJGL	IS-M/AM: Display Sales Agent ID Code
JJGM	Maintain Alternative Customer Number
JJGN	IS-M: Display Former Advertiser No.
JJH0	IS-M/AM: Product Hierarchy
JJH2	IS-M: Change BP Hierarchy
JJH3	IS-M: Display BP Hierarchy
JJI1	IS-M: Create Content Component
JJI2	IS-M: Change Content Component
JJI3	IS-M: Display Content Component
JJI4	IS-M: Coll.Entry of Content Comps
JJI5	IS-M: Coll.Processing of CCs
JJI6	IS-M: Coll.Display of Cont.Comps
JJI7	IS-M: Create Cont.Comp.Hierarchy
JJI8	IS-M: Process Cont.Comp.Hierarchy
JJI9	IS-M: Display Cont.Comp Hierarchy
JJIA	Content component conversion
JJIB	IS-M: Copy Content Components
JJIC	IS-M: Copy Content Comp.Hier.Parts
JJIH	IS-M: Where-Used List for CC Hier.

JJIK	IS-M: Where-Used List for CCs
JJK0	Call up dynamic condition mainten.
JJK1	Dynam.cond.maint.f.pricng for c.ord.
JJK2	Dyn.Cnd.Maint.f.Contrct Disc.Pricing
JJK3	Dynam.Cond.Maint.in Pric.for Commis.
JJK4	Dynam.cond.maint.f.pricng for c.ord.
JJK5	.
JJL2	IS-M: Standard Access Analyze Pages
JJL3	IS-M: Standard Access Analyze Pages
JJL4	Std Settings for Sales Agnt Analysis
JJP2	Generate booking unit - content
JJP3	Delete Booking Unit Content
JJP4	Generate Production Units
JJP5	Display generation status
JJP6	IS-M: Display Generated PUs
JJP7	IS-M/AM: Coll.Maintenance of PUs
JJP8	IS-M: Update PUs
JJP9	Display generation status
JJPH	IS-M/AM: Maintain product hierarchy
JJPI	IS-M/AM: Display Product Hierarchy
JJPO	IS-M: Partner Objects
JJPRDH_AV	IS-M/AM: Provis.Products Worklist
JJPRDH_AZ	IS-M/AM: Worklist Link Table
JJPRDH_DU	IS-M/AM: Duplicate Check (ProdHier.)
JJPRDH_FA	IS-M/AM: Create WL for Link Table
JJPRDH_IF	IS-M/AM: Data Transfer (Prod.Hier.)
JJPRDH_P1	IS-M/AM: Maintain Economic Sectors
JJPRDH_P2	IS-M/AM: Maintain Product Groups
JJPRDH_P3	IS-M/AM: Maintain Product Families
JJPRDH_P4	IS-M/AM: Maintain Umbrella Products
JJPRDH_P5	IS-M/AM: Maintain Products
JJPRDH_P6	IS-M/AM: Maintain Link Table
JJPRDH_PNKRS	IS-M/AM: No.Range for Prov.Products
JJPRDH_TGLOBAL	IS-M/AM: Global Setting: Prod.Hier.
JJPRDH_TPRS	IS-M/AM: Product Search (Cust)
JJPRDH_TUAG	IS-M/AM: Assign Agency Role (Cust)
JJPRDH_UK	IS-M/AM: Update Link Table
JJPRDH_UV	IS-M/AM: Update Provisional Products
JJS0	IS-M: Area Menu - Structures/Dist.
JJS1	Maintain Bank Details Barring List
JJS2	Display Bank Details Barring List
JJS3	Number Range Maintenance: ISP_SINR
JJS4	IS-M: Create Ad Insert
JJS5	IS-M: Change Ad Insert
JJS6	IS-M: Display Ad Insert
JJSI	IS-M: Ad Insert
JJSNRO_ISM_FESTPL	Number Range Maintenance: ISM_FESTPL
JJUPSELL	IS-M: Maintain Upselling Proposals
JJV002	RJJGA002
JJV003	RJJGA003
JJV1	IS-M/AM: Create Sales Agent Contract
JJV2	IS-M/AM: Change Sales Agent Contract
JJV3	IS-M: Display Sales Agent Contract
JJV4	IS-M/AM: Edit Exclusion Requirements

JJV5	IS-M: Display Exclusion Requirement
JJV7	IS-M/AM: Edit Inclusive Requirements
JJV8	IS-M: Display Inclusive Requirement
JJV9	Create Occasional Sales Agent Cntrct
JJW1	IS-M/AM: Add Sales Activity
JJW2	IS-M/AM: Change Sales Activity
JJW3	IS-M/AM: Display Sales Activity
JJWA	IS-M/AM: Edit Address List
JJWB	IS-M/AM: Create Letter
JJWM	IS-M/AM: Create Mailing
JJWT	IS-M/AM: Create Telephone Call
JJWV	IS-M/AM: Create Sales Call
JJXX	IS-M: Configurat.Reqs and Formulas
JK01	Create Subscription Order
JK01X	Create Subscription Order
JK02	Change Subscription Order
JK02X	Change Subscription Order
JK03	Display Subscription Order
JK03X	Display Subscription Order
JK04	Display Subscription Order
JK07	IS-M: Fast Entry of Subscriptions
JK11	Create retail order
JK11X	Create Retail Order
JK12	Change retail order
JK12X	Change Retail Order
JK13	Display retail order
JK13X	Display Retail Order
JK14	Display retail order
JK16	Fast Entry for Retail Purchase Qties
JK21	Create coupon order
JK21X	Create Coupon Order
JK22	Change coupon order
JK22X	Change Coupon Order
JK23	Display coupon order
JK23X	Display Coupon Order
JK24	Display coupon order
JK31	Create Gift Distribution Order
JK31X	Create Gift Distribution Order
JK32	Maintain order f.char.transfer dist.
JK32X	Maintain Order f.Char.Transfer Dist.
JK33	Display order for char.transfer dis.
JK33X	Display Order for Char.Transfer Dis.
JK34	Display order for char.transfer dis.
JK41	Create Subscription Offer
JK41X	Create Subscription Offer
JK42	Change Subscription Offer
JK42X	Change Subscription Offer
JK43	Display Subscription Offer
JK43X	Display Subscription Offer
JK44	Display Subscription Offer
JK51	Create retail offer
JK51X	Create Retail Offer
JK52	Change retail offer
JK52X	Change Retail Offer

JK53	Display retail offer
JK53X	Display Retail Offer
JK54	Display retail offer
JK61	Create xx offer - not used
JK62	Change xx offer - not used
JK63	Display xx offer - not used
JKA1	Create External Delivery Order
JKA1X	Create External Delivery Order
JKA2	Change External Delivery Order
JKA2X	Change External Delivery Order
JKA3	Display External Delivery Order
JKA3X	Display External Delivery Order
JKA4	Display third-party delivery order
JKACCNEWCURR	Currency Change for Liability Accts
JKAN	New Acct.Det.with Rev.Acct.Transfer
JKAN_ALOG	IS-M/SD: Log New Account Det.
JKB1	Create internal order
JKB1X	Create Internal Order
JKB2	Change internal order
JKB2X	Change Internal Order
JKB3	Display internal order
JKB3X	Display Internal Order
JKB4	Display internal order
JKCOMPL1	IS-M/SD: Create Customer Complaint
JKCOMPL1_FM	IS-M/SD: Create Complaint (Func.Mod)
JKCOMPL1_PRESET	IS-M/SD: Create Complaint (Defaults)
JKCOMPL1_WWWTEMP	IS-M/SD: Create Complaint (Posted.)
JKCOMPL2	IS-M/SD: Change Customer Complaint
JKCOMPL3	IS-M/SD: Display Customer Complaint
JKD0	Edit Delivery Viability Optimization
JKD1	Display Delivery Via.Optimization
JKD3	IS-M/SD: Delivery Viab.Optimization
JKD4	Publications for Address
JKFB01	IS-M/SD: Mass Incoming Payment
JKGP	IS-M: Generate Ad Pre-Print Order
JKK0	Order processing - central maint.
JKK1	Order management - central display
JKLF	IS-M: Sales, Current Settings
JKLIABACC	Liability Account Analysis
JKLIAB_REVERSE	Reverse Liability Account Transfer
JKON	IS-M: Generic Condition Maintenance
JKP1	Create Ad Pre-Print Order
JKP2	Change Ad Pre-Print Order
JKP3	Display Ad Pre-Print Order
JKR1	Create customer complaint
JKR2	Change customer complaint
JKR3	Display customer complaint
JKR4	Release customer complaint
JKR8	Release return
JKRA	Create Return
JKRAP	Update Amortization Plan
JKRB	Change Return
JKRC	Display Return
JKREX	Update Expiration Date

SAP Transaction Codes – Volume One

JKRGL   Data Transfer for Going Live
JKRGL_BUILD_AMODATA   Data Transfer for Going Live
JKRM   IS-M/SD: Subscription Monitoring
JKRM_ALOG   IS-M/SD: Subscription Monitoring Log
JKRN   IS-M/SD: Amortization
JKRNP   Display Amortization Log
JKRN_MASTER   IS-M: Amortization - Parallel Proc.
JKRN_OVERVIEW   Overview of Amortization Logs
JKRT   IS-M/SD: Liability Account Transfer
JKRTP   Log for Liability Account Transfer
JKS1   IS-PSD: Analysis of live subscrips
JKS2   Comparison of Live Subs (S/T/F)
JKS3   IS-PSD: Compare live sub.trans (all)
JKS4   IS-PSD: Transacs affecting live subs
JKS5   IS-PSD: Compare live subscr.transacs
JKS6   IS-M: Daily Retail Sales
JKS7   IS-M: Weekly Retail Sales
JKS8   IS-M: Reader Structure Ind./Occup.
JKS9   IS-M: Edition Distrib.Geo/Carr.Route
JKSA   IS-M: Dist.Rept Geo/CRoute Ret./Sub.
JKSADR   Deactivate Divert/Voucher Ship.Addr.
JKSB   IS-M: Dist.Rept Geo/CRoute DatComp.
JKSC   Subscription lifetime analysis
JKSD   IS-M: Distribution of Transfers
JKSD03   Edit Quantity Plan
JKSD04   Display Quantity Plan
JKSD05   Edit Quantity Plan for Phase Deliv.
JKSD06   Display Quantity Plan for Phase Del.
JKSD07   Edit Quantity Plan per Media Issue
JKSD07A   Display Qty Plan per Media Issue
JKSD08   Edit Quantity Plan Versions
JKSD09   Copy Quantity Plan Versions
JKSD10   Delete Quantity Plan Versions
JKSD11   Refresh Planning from BP Calendar
JKSD12   Quantity Plan from Planning Calendar
JKSD13   Process Worklist of Media Issues
JKSD13A   Display Worklist of Media Issues
JKSD14   Mass Change to SD Orders
JKSD15   Set Statuses of Media Issues
JKSD15_PROT   Log of Setting Media Issue Statuses
JKSD16   Mass Change to SD Orders
JKSD17   Copy Delivery Quantity from Product
JKSD21   Adjust Quantity Planning
JKSDADRRASS   Address Formatting
JKSDAREA01   Quantity Planning: Planning Area
JKSDAREA02   Quantity Planning: Segments
JKSDASSIGNCONTRACT   IS-M: Assigns Segments to Contracts
JKSDCA01   IS-M: Central Access
JKSDCOLLECT01   Create Collection
JKSDCOLLECT02   Create Collection - POS Closure
JKSDCOLLECTCALC   Calculate Collection Date for Issue
JKSDCOLLECTION   Determine Issues for Collection
JKSDCOLLECTIONPROT   Create Log for Return Index
JKSDCOLLECTISSUEDATE   Maintain Coll. Date for Media Issue

SAP Transaction Codes – Volume One

JKSDCOLLECTPLAN1	Plan Collection
JKSDCOLLMAINTAIN	Edit Return Index
JKSDCOMP01	Edit Product Kit Structure
JKSDCOMP02	Edit Product Kit
JKSDCOMP03	Generate Product Kit from Structure
JKSDCOMP04	Display Product Kit Structure
JKSDCOMP05	Display Product Kit
JKSDCON01	IS-M: Copy Contract Data
JKSDCON02	IS-M: Create Contracts
JKSDCON03	IS-M/SD: Copy Contract Data
JKSDCON04	IS-M/SD: Reject Contracts
JKSDCON05	IS-M/SD: Schedule Contracts
JKSDCON06	IS-M/SD: Schedule Contr. Rejections
JKSDCONTRACTFAST	Fast Entry of Customer Quantity Plan
JKSDCONTRACTINFO	Contract Monitor
JKSDCOPYFORECAST	IS-M: Replicates Reference Issues
JKSDCOPYMS	Copy Quantities (Master-Slave)
JKSDCRED1	Mark Credit Memo Req.w/Ref.to Order
JKSDCRED12	Log Credit Memos to SD
JKSDCRED1E	Mark Credit Memo Req.w/Ref.to Order
JKSDCRED2	Create Credit Memo Requests
JKSDCRED3	Mark Cred.Memo Req.w/Ref.to Contract
JKSDCRED3E	Mark Cred.Memo Req.w/Ref.to Contract
JKSDCRED4	Mark CMRs w/o Reference to Document
JKSDCRED4E	Mark CMRs w/o Reference to Document
JKSDCUST02	IS-M: Maintain Req.for Contract
JKSDCUST07	IS-M: Maintain Geo.Assignment Type
JKSDCUST11	IS-M: Audit Report Category Determ.
JKSDDELIVERY01	IS-M: Update Delivery
JKSDDELIVERY11	IS-M: Update Log
JKSDDISPLAYQUAN	IS-M: Display Quantities for Segment
JKSDDISPLAYSC01	Display Assignm. Segment - Contracts
JKSDDISPLAYSC02	Change Assignm. Segment - Contracts
JKSDEVENTEXEC	Change Quantity Plan from Events
JKSDFORECAST02	Change Reference Issues
JKSDFORECAST03	Display Reference Issues
JKSDFORECAST04	IS-M: Assign "Like" Contracts
JKSDFORECASTPLAN	Write Delivery Quantity to Contracts
JKSDFORECASTPROTOCOL	IS-M: Display Log
JKSDHORIZONDISPLAY	Display Planning Horizons
JKSDISSUEDATECREATE	Create Coll. Index for Media Issues
JKSDKNVP	Maintain Time-Dep. Partner Roles
JKSDKNVP1	Display Time-Dep. Partner Roles
JKSDKNVP2	Adjust Partner Roles in Contracts
JKSDKNVP3	Log of Partner Roles in Contracts
JKSDKNVP4	Adjust Partner Roles in Cust. Master
JKSDKNVP5	Log of Partner Roles in Cust. Master
JKSDMPMASTER01	Master-Slave Products
JKSDORDER01	Generate Orders for Contracts
JKSDORDER02	Quantity Changes to Orders
JKSDORDER03	Delete Order Items
JKSDORDER04	Modify Delivery Date
JKSDORDER05	Postedit Partially Generated Orders
JKSDORDER06	Adjust Components in Orders

JKSDORDER08	Restart Order Generation
JKSDORDER10	IS-M: Contract/Media Product Item
JKSDORDER11	Log Order Generation
JKSDORDER12	Quantity Change Log
JKSDORDER13	Log Order Item Deletion
JKSDORDER14	Delivery Date Log
JKSDORDER16	Adjust Components in Orders
JKSDORDER18	Log of Orders not Created Fully
JKSDORDERBOOK01	Process Order Quantity Planning
JKSDORDERBOOK02	Display Order Quantity Planning
JKSDORDERBOOKGEN	Initialize Purchase Order Planning
JKSDORDERBOOKGEN02	Purch.Order Planning: Initialize Mix
JKSDPORDERGEN	Generate Purchase Orders
JKSDPROTOCOL	Log
JKSDPROTOCOLDEL	Delete Log Entries
JKSDPROTOCOLID	IS-M: Display Log for ID
JKSDQEVENT	Events for Quantity Planning
JKSDQEVENTINIT	Corrected Sales Qty: Initialize
JKSDQEVENTVERIFY	Quantity Verification for Events
JKSDQEVENTVERIFYCUST	Quantity Verification for Events
JKSDQEVENT_NRKR	Number Range Maintenance: ISP_EVENTQ
JKSDQUAN01	IS-M/SD: Quantity Determination
JKSDREQUEST01	Administration Request
JKSDRETPROTOCOLID	IS-M: Display Log for ID
JKSDSEGMENT	Edit Segments
JKSDSETWERKSISSUE	Plant Assigned to Issue and Contract
JKSDTRANS01	Process Request
JKSDTRANS02	Create Transfer Documents
JKSDTRANS03	Process Request
JKSDTRANS12	Log Transfer
JKSDUNSOLD01	Process Requests
JKSDUNSOLD02	Create Request Documents
JKSDUNSOLD03	Process Requests
JKSDUNSOLD04	Process Request
JKSDUNSOLD05	Maintain Default User Settings
JKSDUNSOLD10	Edit Returns (Set-Get-Parameters)
JKSDUNSOLD11	Postprocess Single Returns
JKSDUNSOLD12	Log Request Documents
JKSDUNSOLD20	IS-M: Evaluation
JKSDUNSOLDCANCEL	Delete Docs for Return Rel. to SD
JKSDUNSOLDCANCELP	Delete Log Doc. for Return Release
JKSDWWW01	WWW Logon
JKSDWWW02	WWW Entry Screen for Returns
JKSDWWW03	Overview of Possible Returns
JKSDWWW04	Query Tool for Returns
JKSDWWW10	IS-M: Individual Order via Internet
JKSDWWW11	IS-M: Individual Order via Internet
JKSDWWW15	IS-M: Individual Order via WAP
JKSD_CONTRACT_ASSORT	Contract Generation from Assortments
JKSD_CONTRACT_AS_BAL	Log Contract Gen. for Assortments
JKSE	IS-M: Coll.Ex.Copy Del. Retail Ord.
JKSE01	Process Shipping Planning
JKSE02	Display Shipping Planning
JKSE25	Compile Index for Contract

JKSE26	Log of Contract Index	
JKSECONTRACT01	Activate Series Contract	
JKSECONTRACT02	Log of Series Contract Activation	
JKSECONTRACT03	Adjust Pricing for Billing Plan	
JKSECONTRACT04	Log of Pricing Adjustment	
JKSECREATECONTRACT	IS-M: Create Contract from Order	
JKSECREATECONTRACTP	Log Order from Contract	
JKSEORDER01	Order Generation	
JKSEORDER03	Delete Order Items	
JKSEORDER04	Complete Order Creation	
JKSEORDER08	Restart Order Generation	
JKSEORDER11	Log Order Generation	
JKSEORDER12	Adjust Pricing for Order	
JKSEORDER13	Log Order Deletion	
JKSEORDER14	Log Adjustment of Pricing for Order	
JKSEORDER18	Log Restart of Order Generation	
JKSEPLAN01	Adjust Delivery Schedules	
JKSEPLAN11	Log Delivery Schedule Adjustment	
JKSESUBPRICESET	IS-M: JKSESUBPRICESET	
JKSESUBPRICESETA	IS-M: JKSESUBPRICESETA	
JKSESUBPRICESETD	IS-M: JKSESUBPRICESETD	
JKSESUBPRICESETM	IS-M: JKSESUBPRICESETM	
JKSESUBPRICESETO	IS-M: JKSESUBPRICESETO	
JKSF	IS-M: Trial Items Longer Than N Days	
JKSG	IS-M: Suspensions Longer Than N Days	
JKSH	ISPC Returns Interface	
JKSI	IS-M: Transfer Dist.:Process Session	
JKSJ	Subscription Lifetime Statistics	
JKU1	Where-used list of BP in order	
JKU2	Orders for Carrier Route	
JKU3	Orders for geography	
JKU4	Orders for item types	
JKU5	Ad Pre-Print Orders for Carr.Route	
JKU6	Ad Pre-Print Orders for Carr.Edition	
JKU7	Generate free subscriptions	
JKU8	Incomplete order items	
JKU9	Ad Pre-Prints - Planning Overview	
JKUA	Orders with billing block	
JKUB	Orders with Monitoring Block	
JKUD	Notification from Shipping Serv. Agt	
JKUDSTATUS	Status of ND Notifications	
JKVIAC_RESTORE	Activate IAC Changes After Planning	
JKVIAC_SUSPEND	Suspend IAC Changes Before Planning	
JKVIAC_SUSPEND_OV	Overview of Suspended IAC Changes	
JKWA	IS-M: WBZ Outb.Proc., Data Carrier	
JKWB	WBZ Stock List (Record Type 119)	
JKWC	IS-M: WBZ Outbound, Manual Comm.	
JKWD	IS-M: WBZ, Delete Entries, RtnFile	
JKWE	IS-M: WBZ, Inbound Processing	
JKWF	IS-M/SD: WBZ, Overview	
JKWR	IS-M: WBZ, Create Confirmation File	
JKWT	IS-M/SD: WBZ, Cust.Number Exchange	
JKWWW01	IAC Subscription Sales	
JKWWW02	IAC Change Address	

JKWWW03	IAC Subscription Vacation Service
JKWWW04	IAC Change Payment Data
JKWWW05	IS-M/SD: IAC Create Complaint
JKWWWPROT	IS-M: Log of Internet Changes
JKWWWTEMP	Edit Order Data from Internet
JKWWWTEMP_ADR	IS-M: Edit Internet Address Change
JKWWWTEMP_COMPL	IS-M/SD: Edit Complaints
JKWWWTEMP_MONITOR	Access Internet Postediting
JKWWWTEMP_SERV	IS-M: Edit Internet Applications
JKX1	IS-M: Create Order Archive
JKX11	IS-M/SD: Read Archived Complaints
JKX2	IS-M: Delivery Archiving - Delete
JKX21	IS-M/SD: Archive Amo.Data for Acct
JKX3	IS-M: Reload Order Archive
JKX31	IS-M/SD: Archive Liability Account
JKX4	IS-M: Admin of Delivery Archive
JKY4	Transfer Subscription Changes
JKY7	Data transfer for sales docs (fMod.)
JK_RJKBST80	TI, FI Conversion Statistics
JL1D	IS-M: Transfer EE Comm.Settlement
JL1E	IS-M: Transfer SC Comm.Settlement
JL1F	IS-M: Transfer EE HDel.Settlement
JL1G	IS-M: Transfer SC Home Del.Sett.
JL2A	IS-M: Reverse Coll.Proc.EE Commiss.
JL2B	IS-M: Reverse Coll.Proc.SC Commiss.
JL2C	IS-M: Reverse Coll.Proc.EE Home Del.
JL2D	IS-M: Reverse Coll.Proc.SC Home Del.
JL3A	IS-M: Tfer Comm.Sett.to Seq.File
JL3B	IS-M: Tfer SC Commiss.to Seq.File
JL3C	IS-M: Tfer Deliv.Sett.to Seq.File
JL3D	IS-M: Transfer Del.SC to Seq.File
JL60	IS-M: Create EE Comm.Settlement
JL61	IS-M: Change EE Comm.Settlement
JL62	IS-M: Display Comm.Settlement EE
JL63	IS-M: Reverse Comm. Settlement EE
JL64	IS-M: Coll.Run for Comm.Sett EE
JL65	IS-M: Create Comm.Settlement SC
JL66	IS-M: Change Comm.Settlement SC
JL67	IS-M: Display Comm.Settlement SC
JL68	IS-M: Reverse Comm. Settlement SC
JL69	IS-M: Coll.Run for Comm.Sett.SC
JL70	IS-M/SD: Create HDel.Settlement EE
JL71	IS-M: Change HDel.Settlement EE
JL72	IS-M: Display HDel.Settlement EE
JL73	IS-M: Reverse HDel. Settlement EE
JL74	IS-M: Coll.Run for HDel.Sett EE
JL75	IS-M: Create HDel.Settlement SC
JL76	IS-M: Change HDel.Settlement SC
JL77	IS-M: Display HDel.Settlement SC
JL78	IS-M: Reverse Deliv. Settlement SC
JL79	IS-M: Coll.HDel.Settlement Run(SC)
JL80	IS-M/SD: Display Collective Runs
JL81	IS-M: Disp.Coll.Proc.EE Comm.Sett.
JL82	Display Coll.Commission Sett Run- SC

JL83	IS-M: Disp.Coll.HDel.Sett.Run - EE
JL84	IS-M: Disp.Coll.HDel.Sett.Run - SC
JLAA	IS-M: Exceps f.Transfer to HR/RP
JLAB	IS-M: Monitor Missing BP Substits
JLAC	IS-M: Transfer Lost Times to HR
JLAD	IS-M: Monitor Missing Absences
JLAK	Document by Billing Condition Types
JLAP	IS-M/SD: Settlement Transfers
JLC0	IS-M: Maintain Acct Det.Data (J0)
JLC1	IS-M: Maintain Acct Det.Data (J1)
JLC2	IS-M: Maintain Acc.Assgt Data (J2)
JLCB	Master Data on Payment Terms
JLCD	Master Data on Payment Terms for SC
JLCE	IS-M: Settlement Data for SComp.
JLCF	IS-M: Default Sett. Data for PA
JLCG	Master Data Contract Arr. Ext. Carr.
JLCH	Master Data Contract Arr. Ext. SC
JLCK	IS-M: Maintain Account Det.Data
JLI3	IS-M: Transfer Del.Sett to RP
JLI4	Tfer Del.Billing to Human Resources
JLI5	IS-M: Tfer Comm.Sett - Human Res
JLL1	Create Pricing Report
JLL2	Change Pricing Report
JLL3	Display Pricing Report
JLL4	Execute Condition List
JLLA	Create Pricing Report
JLLB	Change Pricing Report
JLLC	Display Pricing Report
JLLD	Execute Condition List
JLM1	IS-M: Home Del.Service Settlement
JLM2	IS-M: Serv.Settlement for Comm.
JLM3	IS-M: Serv.Settlement for Comm.
JLP0	IS-M: Postal Circulation of Edition
JLP1	IS-M: Determine Postal Circulation
JLPA	IS-M: Postal Charge Forecast for PDI
JLPB	IS-M: Post.Charges for Labeled PP
JLPC	IS-M: Postal Charges for RCP
JLPD	IS-M: Overv of Goods Arr.Lists PDI
JLPE	IS-M: Postal Charge Stats for PDI
JLPF	IS-M: Postal Charges - Labeled PP
JLPG	IS-M: Postal Charge Stats f.RCP
JLPH	IS-M: Overall Postal Charge Stats
JLSDHDSETTLEMENT	Interface for HDel. Settlemt Update
JLT1	IS-M/SD: Transfer EE HDel.Sett.to FI
JLT2	IS-M/SD: Transfer SC HDel.Sett to FI
JLT3	IS-M/SD: Transfer EE Comm.Sett.to FI
JLT4	IS-M/SD: Transfer SC Comm.Sett.to FI
JLTA	IS-M/SD: Access EE HDel.Sett.Transf.
JLTB	IS-M/SD: Access SC HDel.Sett.Transf.
JLTC	IS-M/SD: Access EE Comm.Sett.Transf.
JLTD	IS-M/SD: Access SC Comm.Sett.Transf.
JLTS	Settlements Not Yet Transferred
JLTT	Assign Coll.Processing to Transfer
JLU1	Commission Due Dates

JLW7	IS-M: Create Cond.Tab.-EAD HDel.
JLW8	IS-M: Change Cond.Table-EAD HDel.
JLW9	IS-M: Disp.Cond.Table for HDeliv.
JLX7	IS-M: Create Cond.Tab.f.ExpAccDet.
JLX8	IS-M: Change Cond.Tab.f.ExpAcDet.
JLX9	IS-M: Disp.Cond.Table f.ExpAccDet.
JM01	IS-M: Create Material
JM02	IS-M: Change Material
JM03	IS-M: Display Material
JN01	IS-M: Create Research
JN02	IS-M: Change Research
JN03	IS-PSD: Display Research
JN04	IS-M: Create Bank Returns Research
JN05	IS-M: Change Bank Returns Research
JN06	IS-M: Display Bank Rtns Research
JN30	Condition Master Data
JND0	IS-M: Reorg.Output Cont.(Order)
JND1	IS-M: Reorg.Output Cont.(Billing)
JND2	IS-M: Reorg.Output Cont.(Settlement)
JND3	IS-M: Reorg.Output Cont.(Dist.ErrH.)
JND4	IS-M: Reorg.Output Contr.(Research)
JND5	IS-M: Outpt Control Reorg.(Add.Chge)
JNS0	IS-M: Sales Output
JNS1	IS-M: Billing Output
JNS2	IS-M: Settlement Output
JNS3	IS-M: Complaint Output
JNS4	IS-M: Resubmission Output
JNS5	IS-M: Address Change Output
JNS6	IS-M: Dist.Error Message Output
JNS7	IS-M: Bank Returns Output
JNS8	IS-M: Research Output
JNS9	IS-M/SD: Monitoring Output
JNSB	Fast Entry of Bank Returns
JP02	Change Title Master
JP03	Display Title Master
JP20	Media Product Master Browser
JP20NEU	Media Product Master Browser
JP21	Create Media Product Family
JP22	Change Media Product Family
JP23	Display Media Product Family
JP24	Create Media Product
JP25	Change Media Product
JP26	Display Media Product
JP27	Create Media Issue
JP28	Change Media Issue
JP29	Display Media Issue
JP30	Move Media Issue Publication Date
JP31	Log: Move Publ. Date of Media Issue
JPBDCCR	Create OR Data Collector
JPBDCDL	Reset OR Data Collector
JPC1	Create Media Prod.Mast.from WBS Elmt
JPC3	Log Media Prod.Mast.from WBS Element
JPC4	Create Media Prod.Mast.from App.Req.
JPC6	Log Media Prod.Mast.from App.Req.

JPECPFE	Define Formula Element
JPECPPK	Define Pricing Key
JPECPVT	Define Valuation Templates
JPMDG1	Define Master Data Template
JPMDG2	Maintain Generation Profile
JPMDG3	Generate Media Product Master Recs
JPMDG4	Log Media Product Master Rec.Gen.
JPMG0	Edit Issue Sequence
JPMG1	Display Issue Sequence
JPMG2	Create Issues in an Issue Sequence
JPMG3	Display Generation Log
JPMG4	Use of Media Issue in Issue Sequence
JPMG5	Preassign Issue Sequences
JPMG6	Create Issues in Several Issue Seqs
JPMG7	Preassign Issue Sequences: Log
JPMGD2	Maintain Generation Profile
JPMGLEVEL	IS-M: DO NOT USE
JPMPMIG	Media Product Migration
JPMPMIG1	IS-M: Med.Prod.Migration: Check Data
JPMPMIG2	IS-M: Med.Prod.Migration: JFREVVA
JPMPMIG3	IS-M: Complete Media Prod.Migration
JPMPMIG_PROT	Logs of Media Product Migration
JPMPMIG_PROT1	Logs of Completion of Media Prod.Mig
JPMPMIG_PROT2	Logs of Checks on Media Prod.Migr.
JPMPMIG_PROT3	JFREVVA Conversion Logs (Migration)
JPS1	Create Ad Insert
JPS2	Change Ad Insert
JPS3	Display Ad Insert
JPSEPRODCOMP	Series Product Hierarchy
JPTSTARTER	Assign Basic Edition to Media Prod.
JPTSTARTERPRICE	Assign Basic Edition to Media Prod.
JR01	IS-M/SD: Create Truck Route
JR01E	IS-M/SD: Create Truck Route
JR02	IS-M/SD: Change Truck Route
JR02E	IS-M/SD: Change Truck Route
JR03	IS-M/SD: Display Truck Route
JR03E	IS-M/SD: Display Truck Route
JR04	IS-M: Create Truck Route Contract
JR05	IS-M: Change Truck Route Contract
JR06	IS-M: Display Truck Route Contract
JR07	IS-M: Create Loading/Unloading Point
JR08	IS-M: Change Loading/Unloading Point
JR09	IS-M: Display Loading/Unloading Pt
JR10	IS-M: Mass Rec.of Daily Truck Routes
JR11	IS-M: Create Daily Truck Route
JR12	IS-M/SD: Change Daily Truck Route
JR13	IS-M: Display Daily Truck Route
JR14	IS-M: Auto.Gen.of Daily Truck Routes
JR15	IS-M: Edit Gen.Trigs for Truck Rtes
JR16	IS-M: Display Gen.Trigs f.Truck Rtes
JR17	IS-M: Manual Gen.of Daily Truck Rtes
JR18	IS-M: Maintain Unloading Via.Sets
JR20	IS-M: Display Unloading Via.Sets
JR24	Copy Generation Triggers for Routes

JR25	IS-M: Maint.Unl.Via.Set (Del.Round)
JR26	IS-M:Summ.Unl.VSet maint.- spec.days
JR27	IS-M:Display Unl.Via.Set (Del.Round)
JR28	IS-M: Maintain Unloading Via.Set
JR29	IS-M: Maint.Unl.VSets for Spec.Days
JR30	IS-M: Access Unload.VSet Display
JR32	IS-M/SD: Edit Unloading Rule
JR33	IS-M: Display Unloading Rule
JR34	IS-M: Unloading Point Sequence
JR36	Display Unloading Rules
JR40	IS-M/SD: Replace Unloading Points
JR50	IS-M: Shipping Archiving - Create
JR51	IS-M: Shipping Archiving - Delete
JR52	IS-M: Shipping Archiving - Reload
JR53	IS-M: Shipping Archiving - Reload
JR54	IS-M: Delivery Archiving - Create
JR55	IS-M: Delivery Archiving - Delete
JR56	IS-M: Delivery Archiving - Reload
JR57	IS-M: Admin of Delivery Archive
JR58	IS-M: Daily Truck Route Arch.-Create
JR59	IS-M: Daily Truck Route Arch.-Delete
JR60	IS-M: Dly Truck Route Arch. - Reload
JR61	IS-M: Daily Truck Route Arch.-Manage
JRPRESHIP	IS-M: Log. Del. Type for Preshipping
JS01	IS-M: Create Geographical Units
JS02	IS-M: Change Geographical Units
JS03	IS-M: Display Geographical Units
JS04	IS-M: Edit Geographical Hierarchy
JS05	IS-M: Display Geographical Hierarchy
JS06	IS-M: Edit Carrier Route-Geo.Assgmts
JS07	IS-M: Display Carr.Route-Geo.Assgmts
JS08	IS-M: Edit Truck Route Assignments
JS09	IS-M: Display Truck Route Assgmts
JS10	IS-M: Create Postal Code
JS11	IS-M: Change Postal Code
JS12	IS-M: Display Postal Code Data
JS13	IS-M: Create Cities
JS14	IS-M: Change Cities
JS15	IS-M: Display Cities
JS16	IS-M: Create Streets
JS17	IS-M: Change Streets
JS18	IS-M: Display Streets
JS19	IS-M: Create P.O.Box Racks
JS20	IS-M: Change P.O.Box Racks
JS21	IS-M: Display P.O.Box Racks
JS22	IS-M: Edit Truck Route-Edit.Assgmt
JS24	IS-M: Display Truck Rte-Publ./Edit.
JS26	IS-M: Edit Distr.-Distr.Assignment
JS27	IS-M: Display Distr.-Distr.Assgmt
JS28	IS-M: Edit Geo.-Post Assignment
JS29	IS-M: Display Geo.-Post Assignment
JS30	IS-M: Edit Org.Structure-Geo.Unit
JS31	IS-M: Display Org Struc.-Geo.Unit
JS32	IS-M: Edit Org. Hierarchy

JS33	IS-M: Display Org.Hierarchy
JS34	IS-M: Edit Unloading Point Seq.
JS35	IS-M: Display Unloading Pt Seq.
JS40	Check Run for Change Number
JS41	Release Change Number
JS41ALOG	IS-M: Change Number Log
JS42	Analyze Change Number
JS43	IS-M: Create Gen.Change Number
JS44	IS-M: Modify Change Number
JS45	Display Change Number
JS46	IS-M: Find Change Number
JS47	IS-M: Create Daily Change Number
JS48	IS-M: Delete Change Number
JS49	IS-M: Postpone Date of Change Number
JS50	IS-M: Display Round Sequence
JS51	IS-M: Edit Round Sequence
JS54	IS-M: UPt Sequence, Reorganization
JS55	Analysis of Orders on Change Number
JS70	IS-M: Update addresses
JS71	Refresh Structures
JS72	Status of Postal Change Service
JSA1	Geo.Units in Carrier Routes
JSA2	Postal Units in Carrier Route
JSA3	Organizational Units in Carr.Routes
JSA4	Carrier Routes in Geo.Units
JSA5	Postal Units in Geo.Units
JSA6	Unloading Points in Geo.Units
JSA7	Org.Structure for Geo.Units
JSA8	Postal Units in Carrier Routes
JSA9	Postal unit for geographical units
JSAA	Postal Unit for Org.Structure
JSAB	Postal Unit for Addresses
JSAC	Org.Structure for Carrier Routes
JSAD	Org.Structure for Addresses
JSAE	Unloading Points in Carrier Route
JSAF	Editions Viable for Home Delivery
JSAG	IS-M: Display Truck Rtes in Car.Rte
JSAH	IS-M: Display Daily Truck Routes
JSB1	Split Entire Postal File
JSB2	IS-M: Postal Transfer DMun.Key
JSB3	IS-M: Transfer City Data
JSB4	IS-M: Transfer City District Data
JSB5	IS-M: Transfer Postal Code Data
JSB6	IS-M: Transfer Data on Streets
JSB7	IS-M: Transfer Data on P.O.Boxes
JSB8	IS-M: Convert Phonetic Search
JSB9	IS-M: Copy Ext.Street Directory
JSE0	Update Postal Data - Germany
JSE01	Refresh Postal Code-City Assignments
JSE02	Evaluate City References
JSE03	Evaluate Street References
JSE1	Transfer Cities, Postal Codes - USA
JSE10	Transfer Streets - Italy
JSE11	Transfer Postal Data (NL)

JSE2	Transfer Streets, P.O.Boxes - USA
JSE4	Set Origin Ind.for Street in City
JSE7	Update Cities, Postal Codes - USA
JSE8	Update Streets - USA
JSE9	Transfer Cities - Italy
JSGEOGEO	IS-M/SD: Create Geo-Geo Assignments
JSGEOPOST	IS-M/SD: Create Geo-Geo Assignments
JSM1	IS-M: Organizational structure
JUC016	BP Conversion Industries T016 TB023
JUC05	BP Conv. Occupations TJG05 TB028
JUC37	BP Conversion Grouping TJG37 TB001
JUC39	BP Conversion Role Categs TJG39 TBZ0
JUC41	BP Conversion Origin TJG41 TB005
JUC43	BP Conversion FOAs TJG43 TSAD3
JUC45	BP Conv.Marital Status TJG45 TB027
JUC535N1	BP Conv.Academic Title TJ535NU TSAD2
JUC535N2	BP Conv.Prefixes TJ535NU TSAD4
JUC535N3	BP Conv.Name Affixes TJ535NU TSAD5
JUCC1	Init. SAP BP Customizing
JUCC2	Customizing Conversion
JUCDCM	Customer and Vendor Conversion
JUCDCMLOG	Logs of Customer/Vendor Conversion
JUCM1	Change BP Control for Migration
JUCM2	Change BP Control After Migration
JUCMO	Migration Overview
JUCP1	Conversion of IS-M Partner to SAP BP
JUCP7	Display Conversion Logs
JUCVGF	BP Conv. Legal Entity TVGF TB032
JUPART	Conversion IS-M BP to SAP BP
JV01	IS-M: Create Carrier Route
JV02	IS-M: Change Carrier Route
JV03	IS-M: Display Carrier Route
JV04	Create Delivery Round-BP Assignment
JV06	Display Carr.Route-Bus.Partner Assgt
JV10	IS-M: Edit Delivery Viability Set
JV12	Display Delivery Viability Set
JV13	IS-M: Maintain BP Deliv.Via.Sets
JV15	IS-M: Display BP Delivery Via.Sets
JV17	IS-M: Deliveries/Unloading VSets
JV18	Delta Betw.Postal and ZEBU Data
JV19	Check Result
JV21	IS-M: Maintain Cont.Packing Rule
JV23	IS-M: Display Cont.Packing Rule
JV24	IS-M: Create Variants
JV26	IS-M: Display Variants
JV27	IS-M: Edit Shipping Schedule
JV28	IS-M: Container/Postal Pack Numberg
JV29	IS-M: Display Shipping Schedule
JV2SD01	Synchronize Unloading Pts to SAP BP
JV2SD02	Create Contract Items for LES
JV2SD03	Synch. Drop-Offs for Purch. Qty Plan
JV30	IS-M: Bundling
JV31	IS-M: Container Packing
JV34	IS-M: Import Changes into ZEBU

JV37	IS-M: Set Order Deadline
JV38	IS-M: Init.Transfer of ZEBU Data
JV40	IS-M: List Shipping Problem Messages
JV41	IS-M: Create Shipping Prob.Message
JV42	IS-M: Change Shipping Prob.Message
JV43	IS-M: Display Shipping Prob.Message
JV44	IS-M: Evaluate Shipping Prob.Message
JV45	Postprocess Shipping Chars f.Deliv.
JV46	Display Shipping Chars f.Delivery
JV47	Edit Settlement Data f.Deliveries
JV48	Display Settlement Data f.Deliveries
JV50	IS-M: Edit ZEBU File
JV51	IS-M: Display ZEBU File
JV55	Create agent district
JV56	Change agent district
JV57	Display agent district
JV59	IS-M: Update Daily Delivery Stats
JV60	IS-M: Shipping Preparation for TMC
JV61	IS-M: Edit Planning Trigger
JV62	IS-M: Display Planning Trigger
JV63	IS-M: Copy Trigger Interval
JV64	IS-M: Completeness Check f.Plannng
JV65	IS-M: Regen.Plannng f.CircPlanning
JV66	Start Coll.Netchange Run Manually
JV67	IS-M: Shipping Prep.f.Insertion
JV68	IS-M: Shipping Prep.f.Distribution
JV69	Display Planning Trigger List
JV72	IS-M: Maintain ShDoc.Destinations
JV73	IS-M: Display ShDoc.Destinations
JV74	IS-M: Maintain ShDoc.Type Usage
JV75	IS-M: Display ShDoc.Type Usage
JV76	IS-M: Edit Shipp.Doc.Control Data
JV80	IS-M: Maint.ShDoc.Dest.Search Seq.
JV84	IS-M: Create Shipping Documents
JV85	IS-M: Shipping Document Printing
JV86	IS-M: Carrier List
JV90	IS-M: Edit Order Deadline
JV91	IS-M: Display Order Deadline
JV92	IS-M: ShipList f.Labeled Per.Post
JV93	IS-M: Shipp.List f.Red.Charge.Pkge
JV94	IS-M: Check Del.Round-BP Assignment
JV99	Edit ZEBU Manual
JVA0	IS-M/SD: Goods Arr.List -Period.Post
JVA1	IS-M: Move Goods Arrival List No.
JVA2	IS-M: Ship.List f.Periodical Post
JVA3	IS-M: Plant Data for Del.Record
JVA4	IS-M: Alt.Init.Sales Date f.Del.Rec
JVA5	IS-M: Start Report for Del.Record
JVA6	IS-M: Goods Arrival List for RCP
JVA7	IS-M: Copy Trigger in Past
JVB1	Display Planned Circ.for Carr.Route
JVB2	Edit Planned Circ.for Carrier Route
JVC1	Number Range Maintenance: ISP_GP_ERS
JVFM	IS-M: Maintain Driver Notification

JVG1	Display Planned Circ.for Geo.Unit
JVG2	Edit Planned Circ.for Geo.Unit
JVLA	IS-M: Deliveries for Order
JVLF	IS-M: Sales, Current Settings
JVM4	IS-M: Distribution
JVM5	IS-M: Shipping Schedule
JVM6	IS-M: Shipping Preparation
JVM7	IS-M: Shipping
JVNC	Execute Netchange Order by Order
JVP1	IS-M: Prod.Sequence (Prod.Data)
JVP2	IS-M: Production Procedure
JVP3	IS-M: Procedure Det.for Prod.Proced.
JVP4	IS-M: Subs.Proced.for Prod.Data
JVP5	IS-M: Elements of Prod.Grouping
JVP6	IS-M: Create Production Data
JVP9	IS-M: Production Paper Usage
JVPC	IS-M: Production Group
JVPE	IS-M: Create Production Data
JVPH0	IS-M/SD: Maintain Geo.Usage Type
JVPH1	IS-M/SD: Display Geo.Usage Type
JVPH10	Initialize Ordering Schedule: Phases
JVPH2	Edit Phase Model
JVPH3	Display Phase Model
JVPH4	Edit Phase Shipping Dates
JVPH5	Display Phase Shipping Dates
JVPH8	IS-M/SD: Monitor Phase Shipping
JVPH9	IS-M/SD: Create Phase Shippg Orders
JVRULE_COP	IS-M: Maintain Packing Rule f.Copies
JVRV	IS-M: Deliveries for Backdated Subs.
JVSD01	IS-M/SD: Edit Media Issue Mix
JVSD04	IS-M: Generate Media Issue Mixes
JVSD05	IS-M/SD: Create Media Issue Mixes
JVSD06	IS-M/SD: Change Media Issue Mixes
JVSD07	IS-M/SD: Display Media Issue Mixes
JVSD08	Assign Inserts to Contracts
JVSD10	Initialize Delivery Quantities
JVSD11	Update Delivery Quantities
JVSD12	Interactive Insert Planning
JVSD13	Copy Insert Booking
JVSD14	Business Partner Insert Groups
JVSD15	Edit Quantities for Deliv.Priorities
JVSD2MSD	Transfer SD Orders to IS-M/SD
JVSDAD01	Ad Inserts from AI Orders
JVSDCUST05	SAP BP Insert Groups
JVSDCUST06	Insert Groups
JVSDGEO1	Ambiguity Check
JVSDHD0	ISM: Maint. HDel.Schedule for Mat.
JVSDHD1	ISM: Display HDel. Schedule for Mat.
JVSDHD3	Edit Ref. Edition for SD Home Del.
JVSDHD4	Display Ref.Edition for SD Home Del.
JVSDHD_COLLECT	ISM: HDel.Planning: Select SD Orders
JVSDHD_HEADER_DELETE	ISM: HDel.Planning: Delete Header
JVSDHD_RELEASE	ISM: HDel.Planning: Home Del. Data
JVSDHD_RELEASE_DEL	ISM: HDel.Planning: Delete HDel.Data

SAP Transaction Codes – Volume One

JVSDHD_VDAT_SHIFT ISM: HDel.Planning: Move Shippg Date
JVSDHSHIFT IS-M: Move Horizon
JVSDMIXLOG IS-M: Mix Creation Logs
JVSDPG Define Packaging Characteristics
JVSDPL01 Weekday-Dependent Plant Determ.
JVSDPR0 Packaging Rules for Media Issues
JVSDPR0I Packaging Rule for Media Issue
JVSDPR0M Packaging Rule Material
JVSDPR1 Packaging Rules for Media
JVSDPR1I Packaging Rule for Media Issue
JVSDPR1M Packaging Rule Material
JVSDPR2 Copy Packaging Rules
JVSDPR3 Edit Media Issue for Packing Char.
JVSO1 Create Shipping Order
JVSO10 Display Edition and Ref.Edition
JVSO11 Monitor Shipping Order
JVSO12 Full Import Assistant
JVSO13 Delta Import Assistant
JVSO14 Ship. Order Archiving: Write Archive
JVSO15 Sh. Order Archiving: Delete Archive
JVSO16 Sh. Order Archiving: Reload Archive
JVSO17 Ship. Ord. Archiving: Manage Archive
JVSO2 Change Shipping Order
JVSO3 Display Shipping Order
JVSO4 Delete Shipping Order
JVSO5 Generate Deliveries for Shipp.Orders
JVSO6 Delete Deliveries for Shipping Order
JVSO7 Check Shipping Date for Shipp.Order
JVSO8 Error List for Shipping Orders
JVSO9 Edit Edition and Reference Edition
JVSOCOMPL1 IS-M/SD: Create Ship.Order Complaint
JVSOCOMPL1_PRESET IS-M/SD: Create Issue Compl.(Def.)
JVSOCOMPL2 IS-M/SD: Change Ship.Order Complaint
JVSOCOMPL3 IS-M/SD: Display Ship.Order Complt
JVSOCOMPL_EXPORT Export File for Shipp. Order Compl.
JVSOCOMPL_IMPORT Import File: Import Ship.Ord.Compl.
JVSOCOMPL_LIST Shipping Order Complaint Overview
JVTMCP_EXCL_STRU IS-M: TMCP Exclusion CRte/GUnit
JVTMCP_GEN IS-M: TMCP: Generate Shipping Orders
JVTMCP_GEN_PROT IS-M: TMCP: Log of Shipp. Order Gen.
JVTMCP_PLANNING IS-M: TMCP: Planning for Ship.Orders
JVTMC_HH Maintain Household Parameters
JVTT Joint Venture Test Tool
JVU1 IS-M: Drop-Off Overview
JVU2 IS-M: Key Date Comparison: Drop-Off
JVU3 IS-M: Circ.of Carriers and Inserts
JVU4 IS-M: Carr.Circulation f.ShipDate
JVU5 IS-M: Check Draw Against Del.Qty
JVU6 IS-M: Production Stats for Bundles
JVU7 IS-M: Shipping Overview
JVV1 IS-M: Generate Issue Splits
JVV2 IS-M: Gen.Delivery for Ad Insert TMC
JVV3 IS-M: Gen.Delivery for AI Distrib.
JVV4 Edit Deliveries for AI Distribution

JVV5	Display Delivery for AI Distribution
JVV6	Edit Deliveries for Ad Insert TMC
JVV7	Display Delivery for Ad Insert TMC
JVV8	Assign Issue Splits to Deliveries
JVV9	Display Issue Splits in Deliveries
JVVA	IS-M: Generate Issue Splits
JVVB	IS-M: Qty Comp.SD/AM AI Insertion
JVVR	IS-M: Qty comp.SD/AM Ad Insert TMC
JVVV	IS-M: Qty Comp.SD/AM AI Distribution
JVX1	IS-M: Display Sales Offices
JVZAEM0	IS-M: Generate Std Deliv.Exception
JVZM	IS-M: Maintain Carrier Notification
JW25	IS-M/SD: Create Sales Promotion
JW26	IS-M/SD: Change Sales Promotion
JW27	IS-M/SD: Display Sales Promotion
JW34	IS-M/SD: Create Campaign Framework
JW35	IS-M/SD: Change Campaign Framework
JW36	IS-M/SD: Display Campaign Framework
JWM1	IS-M: Promotion Master Data
JWU1	IS-M/SD: Std Letter for Sales Prom.
JWU10	Standard Letter By Classification
JWU2	Print Labels for Free Gifts
JWU3	IS-M/SD: Orders for Gift
JWU4	IS-M/SD:Sales Activities in Geo.Unit
JWU5	Sales Activities for Bus.Partner
JWU6	IS-M/SD: Compare Sales Activities
JWU7	IS-M/SD: Shipped/Reserved Gifts
JWU8	IS-M: Update Sales Promotions
JWW1	IS-M/SD: Create Sales Activity
JWW2	IS-M/SD: Change Sales Activity
JWW3	IS-M/SD: Display Sales Activity
JX01	Maintain Types of Geo.Units
JX02	Maint.Hierarchy Type in Geo.Unit
JX57	SM30 Maintenance of IS-M Acct Group
JX67	SM30 Maintenance of Stats Groupings
JX72	SM30 Maint. Counter Restart DTrsfer
JX74	SM30 Maint.Search Seq.f.Std Packing
JX75	SM30 Maint.Search Seq.f.Std Packing
JX82	SM30: Edit Advertising Media
JX83	SM30 Maint.: Display Advertisg Media
JXA8	SM30 Display Edition Rept Grping 2
JXAD	IS-M: Maintain Odd Bundle Group
JXAE	IS-M: Display Edit-OddBdleGrp.Assgmt
JXAJ	SM30 Maint.of Stats Grp f.Sales Doc.
JXAK	SM30 Maint.of Update Grp Header
JXAL	SM30 Maint.of Update Grp for Item
JXAM	SM30 Maint.of UpdGrp for Delivery
JXAN	Sm30 Maint.of Stats Grp per Ord.Type
JXAO	SM30 Maint.Stats Grp per OType/I.Ass
JXAP	SM30 Maint.Stats Grp per Billg Type
JXAQ	SM30 Maint.UpdGrp f.Del.-Ord.Assgmt
JXBD	IS-M/SD: Maintain Odd Bundle Group
JXBDSD	IS-M: Maintain Comm.Odd Bundle Group
JXBE	IS-M: Maint.Edit.-Odd Bdle Grp Asgt

JXBESD	IS-M: Maint.Edit.-Odd Bdle Grp Asgt
JXG8	Assign ctry grping to shipping sch.
JXG9	Country Grouping for Shipping Sched.
JXVA	IS-M: Display Post.Packing Rule Det.
JXVB	IS-M: Edit Post.Packing Rule Determ.
JXVZ	IS-M: Consist.Check for Purch.Org.
JY10	IS-M: Formulas and Requirements
JY20	Condition Master Data
JY81	IS-M: Test - TOA01
JYA1	IS-M: Create Deliv.Sett Archive
JYA2	IS-M: Delete Deliv.Sett Archive
JYA3	IS-M: Reload Del.Sett Archive
JYA4	IS-M: Create Deliv.Sett Archive
JYA5	IS-M: Display Home Del.Sett Archive
JYA6	IS-M: Display Comm.Sett Archive
JYA9	Number Range Maintenance: ISP_ABUEB
JYB1	IS-M: Create Billing Archive
JYB2	IS-M: Delete Billing Archive
JYB3	IS-M: Reload Del.Sett Archive
JYB4	IS-M: Mgmt of Billing Archive
JYB5	Check Archivability of Billing Docs
JYBOREXECUTE	Execute BOR Method
JYC1	Maintain number range doc.conditions
JYD1	Maintain number range: ISP_DRER
JYD2	Maintain number range: ISP_VA
JYD3	Number range maintenance: ISP_VASYNC
JYE1	Create Archive for Commiss.Billing
JYE2	IS-M: Comm.Sett.Archive: Delete
JYE3	IS-M: Comm.Sett.Archive: Reload
JYE4	Comm.Sett.Archive: Administration
JYF1	Maintain number range: ISP_FSAMMG
JYF2	Maintain number range: ISP_FUEBL
JYF3	Maintain number range: ISP_FAKBL
JYF5	Number Range Maintenance: ISM_FICOL
JYF6	IS-M: Display Billing Archive
JYG1	Maintain number range: ISP_GP_NR
JYG2	Maintain number range: ISP_ADRNR
JYG4	Number range maintenance: ISP_BV
JYG5	Maintain number range: Logs
JYI1	IS-M/SD: Number Ranges for Circ.Book
JYITSWAIT	ITS Waiting
JYK1	Maintain number range: ISP_BELEG
JYK2	Number Range Maint. for Research
JYK4	Maintain number range: ISP_PROSP
JYKWWW	Number Range Maintenance: ISM_SESSNO
JYL1	Maintain number range: ISP_LSAMMG
JYL2	Maintain number range: ISP_ABRCHN
JYL3	Maintain number range: ISP_JKONV
JYM1	Maintain number range: ISP_MAT
JYN2	Number range maintenance: ISP_RECHDR
JYPO	IS-M: Print Param.f.Outpt Control
JYR1	Maintain number range: ISP_ROUPVA
JYR2	Maintain number range: ISP_ROUTE
JYR3	Maintain number range: ISP_RVERT

SAP Transaction Codes – Volume One

JYRA	Number Range Maintenance: ISP_ABLRGL
JYRB	IS-M: Install Specific Report Tree
JYRT	IS-M: Choose Report Tree
JYRZ	Maintain report trees for pub.system
JYS1	IS-M:
JYS2	IS-M: Number Ranges for Geo.Units
JYS3	Maintain number range: ISP_GEOPST
JYS4	Maintain number range: ISP_LAUFLI
JYSC	Number Range Maintenance: ISP_ORT
JYSS	Maintain number range: ISP_STR
JYTCODEEXECUTE	Execute Transaction
JYV1	IS-M: Num.Range Object - Drop-Off
JYV2	Maintain number range: ISP_NCAEND
JYV3	IS-M: Maint.Carrier Route No.Range
JYV4	IS-M: Num.Range Maint.for Post.Packs
JYV5	IS-M: Number Range for Containers
JYV7	Maintain number range: ISP_LFNGNR
JYV8	Maintain number range: ISP_JVTFV
JYV9	Maintain number range: ISP_BEABST
JYVA	IS-M: Num.Range Ship.Schedule Var.
JYVB	IS-M: Num.Range Shipping Schedule
JYVC	Number range maintenance: ISP_PAKET
JYVL	Maintain number range: ISP_LFBAR
JYVS	Maintain Number Range: ISM_JVSOH
JYW0	IS-M: Currency Change
JYW2	Number Range Maintenance: ISM_PROMO
JYWW	Maintain number range: ISP_WEKONR
JYX1	IS-M: Edit Order Deadline Status
JZ06	Maintain BU hierarchy
JZ25	Maintain settlement calendar - agent
JZ26	Maintain number range: ISP_FAKT
JZ27	Maintain agt det.proc. for media agt
JZ30	Number Range Maintenance: ISP_BELEIN
JZ31	Number range maintenance: ISP_INHAKO
JZ33	Maintain date combination (fixed)
JZ34	Number Range Maintenance: ISP_VERMV
JZ38	IS-M: Maintain Sales Agent Types
JZ39	Number range maintenance: ISP_PE
JZ40	Maintain number range: ISP_SAMMG
JZ41	Copy pricing procedure and cnd.types
JZ43	Maintain Date Combination (Flexible)
JZ44	Number Range Maintenance: ISP_EV
J_03	Cond.Table: Create (Sales Price)
J_04	Cond.Table: Change (Sales Price)
J_05	Cond.Table: Display (Sales Price)
J_1BEFD	Creation of SPED Digital Archive
J_3RSEXP	Maintain Secondary Event Numbers
J_CLBALTAX	Balance Sheet for Tax (Chile)
J_CLBS	Balance sheet (Chile)
J_CLML	Material Ledger (Chile)
J_DEV2	IS-M: Dev
KA01	Create Cost Element
KA02	Change Cost Element
KA02CORE	Maintain Cost Elements

KA03	Display Cost Element
KA03CORE	Display Cost Elements
KA04	Delete cost element
KA05	Cost element: display changes
KA06	Create Secondary Cost Element
KA10	Cost Center Master Data
KA12	CO Totals Records
KA16	CO Line Items
KA18	Archive admin: assess., distr., ...
KA23	Cost Elements: Master Data Report
KA24	Delete Cost Elements
KAB9	Planning Report: Orders
KABL	Order: Planning Overview
KABP	Controlling Documents: Plan
KAFD	External Data Transfer
KAFL	Delete All Costs Transferred w. KAFD
KAH1	Create Cost Element Group
KAH2	Change cost element group
KAH3	Display cost element group
KAID	Delete ALE-COEP(L) Line Items
KAK2	Change statistical key figures
KAK3	Display Statistical Key Figures
KAL1	Reconcil. Ledger Follow-Up Posting
KAL2	Create Archive for Reconcil. Ledger
KAL3	Delete Data After Archiving
KAL7	Overview of Cost Flows
KAL7N	Overview of Cost Flows
KAL8	Generate Reconcil. Ledger Reports
KALA	Activate Reconciliation Ledger
KALB	Deactivate Reconciliation Ledger
KALC	Cost Flow Message
KALCN	Reconciliation Posting
KALD	Reset Reconciliation Ledger
KALE	Reconcil.Ledger: Display Totals Rec.
KALE1	RCL: Parameter Transaction for GD13
KALF	Start Background Report RKAKALBT
KALG	Change Reconcil. Ledger Report List
KALH	Change Rules for Reconcil. Posting
KALI	Import Reconcil. Ledger Reports
KALK	Create Rules for Reconcil. Posting
KALM	Display Reconcil. Ledger Report Tree
KALN	Report Tree: Maint. Reconcil. Ledger
KALNRCHECK	Consist. Check for Costing Run Nos.
KALNRREORG	Reorg. of Old Costing Number Entries
KALO	Export Reconcil. Ledger (Rollup)
KALR	Reconciliaton Ledger: CO Line Items
KALS	Reverse Reconciliation Posting
KALSN	Reconciliation Posting: Reverse
KALX	Fill Original Units in CO Document
KALY	Convert Reconc. Ledger Documents
KAMN	Menu for Internal Orders
KANK	Number range maint.: RK_BELEG
KAUM	Display Conversion Milestones
KAVA	Send Cost Center Totals Records

KAVB	Send Cost Center Group
KAVC	Send Cost Element Group
KAVD	Send Activity Type Group
KB11	Enter Reposting of Primary Costs
KB11N	Enter Manual Repostings of Costs
KB11NP	Enter Manual Repostings of Costs
KB13	Display Reposting of Primary Costs
KB13N	Display Manual Repostings of Costs
KB13NP	Display Manual Repostings of Costs
KB14	Reverse Reposting of Primary Costs
KB14N	Reverse Manual Repostings of Costs
KB14NP	Reverse Manual Repostings of Costs
KB15	Enter Manual Allocations
KB15N	Enter Manual Allocations
KB15NP	Enter Manual Allocations
KB16	Display Manual Allocations
KB16N	Display Manual Allocations
KB16NP	Display Manual Allocations
KB17	Reverse Manual Allocations
KB17N	Reverse Manual Allocations
KB17NP	Reverse Manual Allocations
KB21	Enter Activity Allocation
KB21N	Enter Direct Activity Allocation
KB21NP	Enter Direct Activity Allocation
KB22	IAA via Internet
KB23	Display Activity Allocation
KB23N	Display Direct Activity Allocation
KB23NP	Display Direct Activity Allocation
KB24	Reverse Activity Allocation
KB24N	Reverse Direct Activity Allocation
KB24NP	Reverse Direct Activity Allocation
KB27	IAA Enter Other Periods
KB31	Enter Statistical Key Figures
KB31N	Enter Statistical Key Figures
KB31NP	Enter Statistical Key Figures
KB33	Display Statistical Key Figures
KB33N	Display Statistical Key Figures
KB33NP	Display Statistical Key Figures
KB34	Reverse Statistical Key Figures
KB34N	Reverse Statistical Key Figures
KB34NP	Reverse Statistical Key Figures
KB41	Enter Reposting of Revenues
KB41N	Enter Manual Repostings of Revenue
KB43	Display Reposting of Revenues
KB43N	Display Manual Repostings of Revenue
KB44	Reverse Reposting of Revenues
KB44N	Reverse Manual Repostings of Revenue
KB51	Enter Activity Posting
KB51N	Enter Sender Activities
KB51NP	Enter Sender Activities
KB53	Display Activity Posting
KB53N	Display Sender Activities
KB53NP	Display Sender Activities
KB54	Reverse Activity Posting

KB54N	Reverse Sender Activities
KB54NP	Reverse Sender Activities
KB61	Enter Reposting of CO Line Items
KB63	Display Reposting of CO Line Items
KB64	Reverse Reposting of CO Line Items
KB65	Enter Indirect Acty Alloc.Reposting:
KB66	Display Indir. Acty Alloc. Reposting
KB67	Reverse IAA Reposting
KB71	JV-Transfer Postings
KBC0	Maintain list of screen variants
KBC1	Cost Transfer Layout Variants
KBC2	Int. Cost Alloc. Screen Variants
KBC3	Screen Variants: Stat. Key Figures
KBC4	Transfer Revenue Screen Variants
KBC5	Non-alloc. Activity Screen Variants
KBC6	CO-ABC: Manual Actual Price
KBC7	CO-ABC: Display manual actl. price
KBEA	Trsfr Price Docs: Set Del.Indicator
KBEB	Trsfr Price Docs: Generate Archive
KBEC	Trsfr Price Docs: Manage Archive
KBH1	Create statistical key figure group
KBH2	Change statistical key figure group
KBH3	Display statistical key figure group
KBK6	CO-CCA: Manual Actual Price
KBK7	CO-CCA: Display manual actl price
KBXXN_CUST	Define Posting Variants
KC7R	EDT: Maintain Transfer Rules
KCA0	SAP-EIS: Edit aspect
KCA1	Reorganize aspect tables
KCA2	Edit field groups
KCA5	Edit characteristics
KCA6	Edit basic key figures
KCAB	Change Allocation Process Assessment
KCAL	Change Indirect Activity Allocation
KCAM	Change Indirect Activity Allocation
KCAN	Derivation
KCAP	Change Allocation Transfer Posting
KCAR	Change Allocation Resource Assessm.
KCAU	Change Allocation Assessment
KCAV	Change Allocation Distribution
KCB0	Execute report
KCB1	Create report
KCB2	Change report
KCB3	Display report
KCB4	Create report class
KCB5	Change report class
KCB6	Display report class
KCB7	Create user group
KCB8	Change user group
KCB9	Display user group
KCBA	Report class overview
KCBB	Set user group
KCBH	Report portfolio data transfer
KCBW	EC-EIS/BP: Generate DataSource

KCC0	Maintain currency translation key
KCC1	Currency translation sender program
KCC2	Cross-table translation key
KCCO	EC-EIS/BP: Manage comment tables
KCDI	Divide report
KCDR	Reorganization document flag T242B
KCDU	Structure of summ. level of SAP-EIS
KCDV	Maintain summarization levels
KCE1	Display transaction data
KCE2	Delete transaction data
KCE3	SAP-EIS: Choose Collection Program
KCE4	Change transaction data (EIS/BP)
KCE5	Display transaction data (EIS/BP)
KCE6	Individual record entry
KCE7	EIS: Single record display
KCE8	EC-BP: Change plan data
KCE9	EC-BP: Display plan data
KCEA	Set planner profile
KCED	Define Flexible Excel Upload
KCEE	Flexible Excel Upload to SAP-EIS
KCF0	Import File
KCF1	Import master data file
KCF2	Import comments file
KCF3	Change revaluation factors
KCF4	Display revaluation factors
KCFR	EDT: Maintain Transfer Rules
KCH1	Create Profit Center Group
KCH2	Change profit center hierarchy
KCH3	Display profit center hierarchy
KCH4	EC-PCA: Create Standard Hierarchy
KCH5	EC-PCA: Change standard hierarchy
KCH5N	EC-PCA: Change Standard Hierarchy
KCH5NX	EC-PCA: Change Stand.Hier. EO Active
KCH6	EC-PCA: Display standard hierarchy
KCH6N	EC-PCA: Display Standard Hierarchy
KCH6NX	EC-PCA: Disp. Stand.Hier. EO Active
KCHA	CCA Allocation: Data Field Descript.
KCIB	CCA: Field Use, Process Assessment
KCIF	CCA: Field Use, JV Assessment
KCIG	CCA: Field Use, JV Distribution
KCIL	CCA: Field Use, Ind. Acty Alloc.
KCIP	CCA: Field Use, Periodic Reposting
KCIU	CCA: Field Use, Assessment
KCIV	CO-OM-CCA: Distribution Field Use
KCJ0	EIS/BP: Hierarchy node maintenance
KCJ1	EC-EIS/EC-BP: Hierarchy maintenance
KCJ2	EC-EIS: Copy reference hierarchies
KCJ3	Hierarchy Maintenance
KCJB	CCA: Data Control, Proc. Assessment
KCJF	CCA: Data Control, JV Assessment
KCJG	CCA: Data Control, JV Distribution
KCJL	CCA: Data Control, Ind. Acty Alloc.
KCJP	CCA: Data Control, Period. Reposting
KCJU	CCA: Data Control, Assessment

KCJV	CCA: Data Control, Distribution
KCK0	Key figures
KCK1	Display key figure
KCKB	Formulas for basic key figures
KCLA	EDT: Automatic File Split
KCLF	External Data Transfer
KCLF001	SAP Banking EDT Financial Object
KCLF002	SAP Banking EDT Period Values
KCLF009	EDT Loans
KCLF024	EDT Financial Object
KCLFS	Sender Structures
KCLI	ALE Interface for EDT
KCLJ	EDT: Execute Transfer
KCLJ015	External Data Transfer Type 15 (BP)
KCLJ090	External Data Transfer Type 90 (BPR)
KCLJ120	Authorizations for Insurance Object
KCLJ121	DI Payt Plan Items Authorizations
KCLL	EDT: Generate Sender Structure
KCLP	Logs
KCLR	RFC Call
KCLS	Type
KCLT	EDT: Create Test Data
KCLU	EDT: Maintain Transfer Types
KCLV	EDT: Delete Obsolete Programs
KCMA	CCA Allocation: Field Group Texts
KCO1	Comments on transaction data
KCP0	Automatic Planning
KCP1	Validation logs data entry
KCP2	Automatic Planning: Forecast
KCP22	Automatic Planning: Forecast
KCP3	Currency translation key entry/main.
KCP4	Create entry form
KCP5	Change entry form
KCP6	Display entry form
KCP7	Create planning layout
KCP8	Change planning layout
KCP9	Display planning layout
KCPA	Automatic Planning: Copy
KCPA2	Copy
KCPB	Batch jobs aut. planning
KCPD	Delete plan data with key fig. sel.
KCPE	EC-BP: object-dependent revaluation
KCPF	EC-BP: object-dependent distribution
KCPG	EC-BP: object-dependent forecast
KCPL	Automatic Planning: Change
KCPL2	Automatic Planning: Change
KCPT	Automatic planning: top-down distr.
KCPT2	Automatic Planning: Top-Down
KCPU	Display Forecast Profile EC
KCPV	EC: Change forecast profile
KCPW	EC: Display weighting groups
KCPX	Change Weighting Groups
KCPZ	Segment-Specific Planning Functions
KCR0	Run Drilldown Report

SAP Transaction Codes – Volume One

KCR01_TEST	Test Calculation of CO Resource
KCR04_TEST	Cost Resource: Test Environment
KCR1	Create Drilldown Report
KCR2	Change drilldown report
KCR3	Display Drilldown Report
KCR4	Create form
KCR5	Change form
KCR6	Display form
KCR7	Maintain authorization obj. present.
KCR8	Display authorization obj.presentatn
KCRA	Maintain variant table
KCRB	Maintain variable groups
KCRC	Print/actualize reports
KCRD	Maintain Variants RKCBATCH
KCRE	Maintain Global Variables
KCRF	Maintain Char.Grps for SAP-EIS Rep.
KCRG	Maint.view for curr.transl./fld cat.
KCRH	Maint.view for curr.transl./key fig.
KCRMCO_CRM_DET	Analyze Service Contract
KCRMCO_CRM_SEL	Service Process Analysis
KCRMCO_CSCEN	Extended Service Process Analysis
KCRMCO_GENERIC	Generic Call RKKBALV1
KCRMCO_GENERIC_DET	Generic Detailed Report
KCRP	Maintain variant groups
KCRQ	Maintain Variants
KCRR	Report selection
KCRS	Schedule Variant Group
KCRT	Define Variant Group
KCRU	Convert drilldown reports
KCS0	Maintain master data
KCS2	SAP-EIS: Delete char. values
KCS3	SAP-EIS: Maintain character. values
KCS4	SAP-EIS: Display character. values
KCS5	Maintain characteristics (view)
KCS6	Display characteristics (view)
KCS7	Maintain fiscal year
KCSA	Send structure output fields default
KCSE	Sending structure output fields
KCT0	EC-EIS/EC-BP: Comment management
KCT1	EC-EIS/EC-BP: Reorganize comments
KCUA	Display Transfer Log
KCUU	Report Data Reorganization
KCV0	Maintain Distribution Keys
KCV1	Create Distribution Key
KCV2	Change distribution key
KCV3	Display distribution key
KCV4	Delete distribution key
KCVA	EIS/BP: Maintain validations/rules
KCVC	EIS/BP: Copy validations/rules
KCVD	Overview of Reports
KCVL	Variable list element in basic rep.
KCVV	Reorganization Reports
KCW0	Testmonitor reporting SAP-EIS
KCW1	Generations SAP-EIS

KCW2	Logs SAP-EIS
KCWA	Maintain Currency Translation Type
KCWW	Reorganize forms
KCXX	Reorganization of Variant Groups
KCZ1	EC-EIS/BP: Archive transaction data
KDH1	Create Account Group
KDH2	Change Account Group
KDH3	Display Account Group
KDTT	Display incorrect report
KE0B	Archiving: CO-PA
KE0C	CO-PA Distribution: Initial Supply
KE0D	CO-PA Distribution: Reconciliation
KE0E	CO-PA Distribution: Installation
KE0F	CO-PA Distribution: Activate
KE0G	CO-PA Distribution: Roll-up
KE0H	Archiving: CO-PA
KE0I	CO-PA Archiving: Customizing
KE11	Change plan data
KE12	Display plan data
KE13	Upload from Excel
KE13N	Upload from Excel
KE13P	Log: Flexible Excel Upload
KE14	Create Planning Layout
KE15	Change Planning Layout
KE16	Display Planning Layout
KE17	Maintain Planning Authorization Obj.
KE18	Display planning authorization obj.
KE19	Reorganize Planning Layouts
KE1A	Copy complete plan
KE1B	Process complete plan
KE1C	Delete Plan Data
KE1D	Forecast Plan Data
KE1E	Transfer Plan Data to SOP
KE1F	Complete Plan Management
KE1FN	Admin.: Logs for Overall Planning
KE1G	Top-Down Complete Plan
KE1H	CO-PA Planning: Set Planner Profile
KE1I	Maintain Ratio Scheme
KE1K	Transfer to LIS
KE1L	Create Plan Structure
KE1M	Change Plan Structure
KE1N	Display Plan Structure
KE1O	Maintain User Exits for Planning
KE1Q	Reorganize Long Texts
KE1R	Change Weighting Group
KE1S	Display Weighting Group
KE1T	Change Forecast Profile
KE1U	Display Forecast Profile
KE1V	Transfer to EC-PCA
KE1W	Transfer of CO-PA Plan Data to FI-GL
KE1XO	Ext. Data Transfer to CO-PA Planning
KE1Y	Transfer of CO-PA Plan Data to FI-SL
KE1Z	Transfer CO-PA Plan Data to GL (New)
KE21	Create CO-PA line item

KE21N	CO-PA Line Item Entry
KE21S	CO-PA Valuation Simulation
KE23	Display CO-PA line item
KE23N	CO-PA Line Item Display
KE24	Line Item Display - Actual Data
KE25	Line Item Display - Plan Data
KE26	Repost Accounting Document
KE27	Periodic valuation
KE27S	Reversal of KE27 Delta Line Items
KE28	Create top-down distribution
KE29	Management
KE29A	Administration: All Logs
KE29N	Administration: Logs
KE2B	Correction to Incoming Orders
KE2C	Delete records from error file
KE2D	Display Error File
KE2K	CO-PA: Maintain Key Figures
KE2S	Summarize Actual Data
KE2T	CO-PA: Assign IDoc Fields
KE2U	CO-PA: Display Segment Types EDIMAP
KE30	Execute profitability report
KE31	Create profitability report
KE32	Change Report
KE33	Display Report
KE34	Create form
KE35	Change form
KE36	Display form
KE37	Maintain Report Authorization Object
KE38	Display report authorization objects
KE39	CO-PA: Reorganize report data
KE3A	CO-PA: Reorganize reports + data
KE3B	Print and actualize reports
KE3C	Reorganize Forms
KE3D	Reorganize Line Item Layouts
KE3E	Maintain Global Variables
KE3F	Create line item layout
KE3G	Change Line Item Layout
KE3H	Display line item layout
KE3I	CO-PA: Transport tool
KE3J	Import
KE3K	Maintain hierarchy
KE3L	Split report
KE3M	Overview of Reports
KE3P	Maintain Variant Groups
KE3Q	Maintain Variants
KE3R	Schedule Variant Group
KE3S	Define Variant Group
KE3T	Reorganization of Variant Groups
KE3U	Maintain variants (RKEBATCH)
KE3X	Customize Application Tree
KE3Y	Report selection
KE3Z	Convert profitability report
KE40	Maintain view V_TKEVA03
KE41	Create condition

SAP Transaction Codes – Volume One

KE42	Change condition
KE43	Display condition
KE45	Maintain View V_T258I_KO
KE46	Maintain costing sheet
KE47	Maintain condition types
KE48	Maintain access sequences
KE49	Create Condition Table
KE4A	Change condition table
KE4B	Display condition table
KE4C	Copy Condition
KE4D	Maintain external str. in ABAP Dict.
KE4E	Maintain View V_T258W_KE
KE4F	Post Incoming Orders Subsequently
KE4G	Maintain View V_TKEVG
KE4H	Maintain view V_TKEVA03A
KE4I	View maintenance VV2_T258I_V
KE4IEX	Assignment of CRM Conditions
KE4IM	Maintain View VV_T258I_M
KE4J	Maintain view V_TKEVA03M
KE4L	Pricing report
KE4M	Maintain view V_T258M
KE4MS	Assign CO-PA Standard Quantity
KE4N	Change Pricing Report
KE4O	Display Pricing Report
KE4Q	Execute Pricing Report
KE4R	Maintain view V_TKEVA04
KE4S	Post billing documents to CO-PA
KE4S00	CO-PA: Reversal of Line Items
KE4SCRM	Subsequent.Post CRM Billing to CO-PA
KE4SFI	CO-PA: Post Subsequently from FI
KE4SMM	CO-PA: Post Material Documents Subs.
KE4ST	Simulation billg docs transfer CO-PA
KE4T	Set Up Transfer of Incoming Orders
KE4TS	Simulate Doc. Transfer from Orders
KE4U	Maintain view cluster V_TKEVAx
KE4V	Control table for ext. data transfer
KE4W	Reset value fields
KE4XO	Transfer External Data to CO-PA
KE4Z	Maintain view V_T258Z_KE
KE50	
KE51	Create Profit Center
KE52	Change Profit Center
KE53	Display Profit Center
KE54	Delete Profit Centers
KE55	Mass Maintenance PrCtr Master Data
KE56	EC-PCA: Mass Maintenance CCode Assgt
KE57	EC-PCA: Mass Maintenance CCode Assgt
KE59	EC-PCA: Create Dummy Profit Center
KE5A	EC-PCA: Call up report
KE5B	EC-PCA: Copy Balance Sheet Acct Grps
KE5C	EC-PCA: Account Master Data (CO/FI)
KE5T	Compare G/L Accounts FI <-> EC-PCA
KE5U	Compare and Reconcile G/L Accounts
KE5X	Profit Center: Master Data Index

KE5Y	Profit Center: Plan Line Items
KE5Z	Profit Center: Actual Line Items
KE61	EC-PCA: Cost group CCSS to GLTPC
KE62	EC-PCA: Copy Data to Plan
KE71	Archive Management
KE72	Archive Administration: Line Items
KE73	Archive Administration: Totals Recs
KE75	EC-PCA: ALE Get profit centers
KE77	EC-PCA: ALE send profit centers
KE78	EC-PCA: Execute ALE Rollup
KE79	EC-PCA: Send ALE Hierarchies
KE80	EC-PCA: Execute Drill-Down Report
KE81	EC-PCA: Create Drill-Down Report
KE82	EC-PCA: Change Drill-Down Report
KE83	EC-PCA: Display Drill-Down Report
KE84	EC-PCA: Create Form
KE85	EC-PCA: Change Form
KE86	EC-PCA: Display Form
KE87	RW/RP Reports for EC-PCA Archives
KE8B	EC-PCA: Drill-Down Reporting, Bckgd
KE8C	EC-PCA: Maintain Currency Transl.
KE8D	Overview of Reports
KE8I	Copy Report-Report Interface/Report
KE8K	Maintain Key Figures
KE8L	EC-PCA: Reorganize Reports
KE8M	EC-PCA: Test Monitor for Drill-Down
KE8O	Transport Reports
KE8P	Transport Forms
KE8Q	Import Reports
KE8R	Import Form from Client
KE8U	Reorganize Report Data
KE8V	EC-PCA: Maintain global variables
KE8W	EC-PCA: Reorganize Forms
KE91	Create Line-Item-Based Report
KE94	Create form
KE95	Change Form
KE96	Display Form
KE97	Maintain Report Authorization Object
KE98	Display Report Authorization Objects
KE9D	Reorganize Line Item Layouts
KEA0	CO-PA: Maintain Operating Concern
KEA0O	CO-PA: Maintain Operating Concern
KEA5	Maintain Characteristics
KEA6	Edit Value Fields
KEAD01	Assign Account to Value Field
KEAE	Generate Proc. Template Environment
KEAF	Value Field Analysis
KEAI	Value Flow FI -> SD / CO -> CO-PA
KEAL	Change Allocation IAA Result
KEAS	Selection Characteristics CO-PA/ABC
KEAT	Reconcile CO-PA <-> SD <-> FI
KEAU	Change Allocation Assessment Result
KEAV	Valuation
KEAW	Reconciliation Make-to-Order Prod.

KEB0	Create CO-PA DataSource
KEB1	CO-PA Hierarchy DataSource
KEB2	Display Dtld Info on CO-PA DataSrce
KEB3	Activate Debugging Support
KEB4	Debugging Support Hierarchies
KEB5	Reduce Data Volumes for Test
KEBA	Display operating concern
KEBC	Change operating concern
KEBD	Set Operating Concern
KEBI	Set operating concern (batch-input)
KEC0	Maintain curr. transl. type (CO-PA)
KEC3	Cross-table translation key CO-PA
KECA	Copying Transaction Data (Actual)
KECB	CO-PA Company Code Line Items
KECC	Copy Transaction Data (Plan)
KECD	Valuation of Overhead Cost Transfer
KECM	CO-PA: Customizing Monitor
KECO	Transfer of Cost Component Split
KECP	Copy Operating Concern
KECRM_0KEL	PCA: Substitutions CRM Integration
KECT	Maintain Environ. Dyn. Process Alloc
KED0	Derivation: Initial Screen
KED5	Data Mining: Create Form
KED6	Data Mining: Change Form
KED7	Data Mining: Display Form
KEDA	Export Summarization Level
KEDB	Deletion of Test Data in CO-PA
KEDD	COPA Char. Derivation Overview ALV
KEDE	Maintain Derivation Rule Entries
KEDF	CO-PA: Fill Summ. Levels (Expert)
KEDJ	CO-PA: Fill Summ. Levels (Expert)
KEDP	Maintain CO-PA Account Determination
KEDR	Maintain Derivation Strategy
KEDRA	COPA Customizing via ALE
KEDR_CHACO	Derivation When OpConc. Implemented
KEDT	Log Summarization Logs
KEDU	CO-PA: Build Summarization Levels
KEDUS	CO-PA: Period Build of Summ. Levels
KEDUSM	CO-PA: Monitor Build for Summ. Lvls
KEDV	CO-PA: Maintain Summarization Levels
KEDVP	Default for Summarization Levels
KEDVPD	Proposal for Summ. Levels (Analysis)
KEDVS	Maintain Old Storage Summ. Levels
KEDW	CO-PA: Fill Summ. Levels (Expert)
KEDX	CO-PA:Fill Summ.Lev. from Summ. Lev.
KEDZ	Read Interface for CO-PA Log
KEE0	PCA: Generate Line Item Difference
KEEU	CO-PA EIS/BP: Generate transfer
KEF1	Change Revaluation Keys
KEF2	Display revaluation indices
KEF3	Time-Dependent Revaluation Factors
KEF4	Display Events
KEFA	Maintain Sender Structures
KEFB	Maintain Rules

KEFC	CO-PA External Data Transfer
KEFD	Maintain Rules
KEG1	Create Indirect Actual Acty Alloc.
KEG1N	Create Indirect Actual Acty Alloc.
KEG2	Change Indirect Actual Acty Alloc.
KEG2N	Change Indirect Actual Acty Alloc.
KEG3	Display Indirect Actual Acty Alloc.
KEG3N	Display Indirect Actual Acty Alloc.
KEG4	Delete Indirect Actual Acty Alloc.
KEG4N	Delete Indirect Actual Acty Alloc.
KEG5	Execute Indirect Actual Acty Alloc.
KEG6	Indirect Actual Acty Alloc.:Overview
KEG6N	Indirect Actual Acty Alloc.:Overview
KEG7	Create Indirect Plan Acty Alloc.
KEG7N	Create Indirect Plan Acty Allocation
KEG8	Change Indirect Plan Acty Alloc.
KEG8N	Change Indirect Plan Acty Allocation
KEG9	Display Indirect Plan Acty Alloc.
KEG9N	Display Indirect Plan Acty Alloc.
KEGA	Delete Indirect Plan Acty Alloc.
KEGAN	Delete Indirect Plan Acty Allocation
KEGB	Execute Indirect Plan Acty Alloc.
KEGC	Indirect Plan Acty Alloc.: Overview
KEGCN	Indirect Plan Acty Alloc.: Overview
KEGD	Overview Actual IAA Cycles
KEGE	Overview Plan IAA Cycles
KEGS	Business Transactions in CO-PA
KEGV	Generate Variant from KEPM Environmt
KEH5	Change Form
KEHIER1	Maintain CO-PA Customiz. Hierarchies
KEI1	Maintain PA Transfer Structure
KEI2	Maintain PA Transfer Structure
KEI3	Maintain PA Transfer Structure
KEICO	Value Field Assignment CO-Interface
KEIH	CO-PA Allocation: Data Field Descr.
KEII	CO-PA Assessment: Field Usage
KEIJ	CO-PA Assessment: Data Control
KEIK	CO-PA: Field Usage, Int. Cost Alloc.
KEIL	CO-PA: Data Control,Int. Cost Alloc.
KEIM	CO-PA Allocation: Field Group Texts
KEIT	CO-PA Allocation: Table Information
KEK0	Test Key Figure Transaction
KEKE	CO-PA: Activation Indicator
KEKF	Transfer Incoming Sales Orders
KEKG	Active Indicator for Prof.Ctr Update
KEKK	Maintain view V_TKA01_ER
KEKW	Maintain Process Template Determin.
KEL0	Assign CRM Cost Element Group
KELC	BW/CO-PA Retraction: Customizing
KELR	BW/CO-PA Retraction: Execute
KELS	BW/CO-PA Retraction: Cancel
KELU	BW/CO-PA Retraction: Overview
KELV	BW/CO-PA Ret: Variant Query Variable
KEMDM	Profit Center Master Data Maint.

KEMN	Profitability Analysis appl. menu
KEMO	Profitability report: Test monitor
KEN1	Maintain Number Range: COPA_IST
KEN2	Maint. number ranges: CO-PA planning
KEND	Realignments
KEO1	Create Enterprise Organization
KEO2	Change Enterprise Organization
KEO3	Display Enterprise Organization
KEOA1	Activate Cost Centers
KEOA2	Activate Profit Centers
KEOA3	Activate Processes
KEOAP2	Change Altern. Profit Center Struct.
KEOAP3	Display Alter. Profit Center Struct.
KEOC1	Settings for EntOrg Cost Centers
KEOC2	Settings for EntOrg Profit Center
KEOC2AP	Altern. Profit Center Struct. Active
KEOD1	Reset Inactive Cost Centers
KEOD2	Reset Inactive Profit Centers
KEOD3	Reset Inactive Business Process
KEOG1	Generate Standard Hierarchy
KEOG2	Generate Alternative Hierarchy
KEOG3	Replace Standard Hierarhcy
KEOP1	Print Standard Hierarchy
KEOP2	Print Enterprise Organization
KEOV	CO-PA: Cycle Overview
KEP0	Assign value fields (Dir.post. FI)
KEP1	Maintain record types
KEP5	Maintain operating concern
KEP6	Maintain characteristics
KEP7	Display characteristics
KEP8	Operating concerns
KEP9	Value field assignment
KEPA	Char. Groups for Actual and Planning
KEPC	Flexible Callup of Cost Estimates
KEPD	Characteristic groups for reports
KEPE	Segment-Specific Revaluation Keys
KEPF	Segment-Specific Distribution Keys
KEPG	Segment-Specific Forecast Profiles
KEPH	Segment-Specific Events
KEPI	Maintain Rule Values for Revaluation
KEPJ	Maintain Rule Values for Distrib.
KEPK	Maint. Rule Values for Forcast Prof.
KEPL	Maintain Rule Values for Events
KEPM	CO-PA Planning
KEPMU	Create Planning Level from Layout
KEPM_W	Sales & Profit Planning in the WWW
KEPM_WAO	CO-PA Planning Framework
KEPP	Check plan structure
KEPV	Plan Settlement: Assign Version
KEPZ	Segment-Specific Planning Functions
KEPZ_E	Access of Segment-Specific Events
KEPZ_P	Access of Segment-Specific Forecast
KEPZ_U	Access of Segment-Specific Revaltn
KEPZ_V	Access of Segment-Specific Distr.Key

KEQ3	Maintain Charact. for Segment Level
KEQ4	Maintain Segment-Lvl Chars ALE
KEQ5	Maintain View for Defined Op.Concern
KEQ6	View Maint. with Preset Op. Concern
KER1	Maintain Key Figure Scheme
KES1	CO-PA Maintain Characteristic Values
KES2	Customizing: Display characteristics
KES3	Maintain Characteristics Hierarchy
KES4	Transfer Customer Rebate Agreements
KESF	Maintain View V_TKEPPI
KETE	CO-PA: Operating Concern Templates
KETR	CO-PA Translation Tool
KEU1	Create Actual Transfer of CCtr Costs
KEU1N	Create Actual Transfer of CCtr Costs
KEU2	Change Actual Transfer of CCtr Costs
KEU2N	Change Actual Transfer of CCtr Costs
KEU3	Display Actl Transfer of CCtr Costs
KEU3N	Display Actl Transfer of CCtr Costs
KEU4	Delete Actual Transfer of CCtr Costs
KEU4N	Delete Actual Transfer of CCtr Costs
KEU5	Perform act. cost-ctr cost transfer
KEU6	Actl Transfer of CCtr Costs,Overview
KEU6N	Actl Transfer of CCtr Costs,Overview
KEU7	Create Plan Transfer of CCtr Costs
KEU7N	Create Plan Transfer of CCtr Costs
KEU8	Change Plan Transfer of CCtr Costs
KEU8N	Change Plan Transfer of CCtr Costs
KEU9	Display Plan Transfer of CCtr Costs
KEU9N	Display Plan Transfer of CCtr Costs
KEUA	Delete Plan Transfer of CCtr Costs
KEUAN	Delete Plan Transfer of CCtr Costs
KEUB	Perform plan cost-ctr cost transfer
KEUC	Plan Transfer of CCtr Costs,Overview
KEUCN	Plan Transfer of CCtr Costs,Overview
KEUD	Overview Actual Assessment Cycles
KEUE	Overview Plan Assessment Cycles
KEUG	Set up cost-center cost transfer
KEUH	Maintain Key Figures for Allocations
KEUU	Reorganize data
KEV0	Maintain Distribution Keys
KEV1	Create distribution key
KEV2	Change distribution key
KEV3	Display distribution key
KEV4	Delete distribution key
KEVF	CO-PA Planning: Value Field Assignm.
KEVFG	CO-PA Value Field Groups
KEVG	Record Types for Process Costs
KEVG2	Assign Characteristic Group
KEVG3	Assign Value Field Groups
KEVG4	Assign char. grp to plan cycles
KEVG5	Assign char. grp to actual cycles
KEVG6	PA Transfer Schema: Overhead ACTUAL
KEVG7	PA Transfer Schema: Overhead PLAN
KEVP	CO-PA Planning: Distribution Profile

KEWUSL	Where-Used List for Cycles (PA)
KEWW	Reorganize forms
KEX9	Reorganize planning layouts
KEZ5	Execute Distribution
KE_CHACO_1	Convert ProfSegments in Sender Table
KE_CHACO_2	Convert CO Obj,Acct-Based PrAnalysis
KE_CHACO_3	Convert ProfSegments in Sender Table
KE_CHACO_4	Convert ProfSegments in Sender Table
KFM_REPORT_DETAIL	Detail Display for Key Figure
KFTP	R/2 - R/3 - Link: File Transfer
KGBC	Copy CMP Client
KGF4	Maintain overhead dependencies
KGI2	Act. Overhead: Int.Order Ind.Pro
KGI4	Actual Overhead:Int.Ord. Coll. Proc.
KGO2	Overhead Commt: Int.Orders Ind.Pro.
KGO4	Overhead Commt: Int.Orders Col.Pro.
KGP2	Overhead Plan.: Int.Orders Ind.Pro.
KGP4	Overhead Plan.: Int.Orders Col.Pro.
KGST	Control Tables: Consistency Check
KGT5	Overhead: Field catalog
KIMS	R/2 - R/3 - Link: IMS Systems
KIS6	Segment Adjustment: Overview
KIS6N	Segment Adjustment: Overview
KISR	Execute Actual Segment Adjustment
KJCCSJ3BI01	Customizing for Estimation Procedure
KJH1	Create WBS Element Groups
KJH2	Change WBS Element Groups
KJH3	Display WBS Element Groups
KK01	Create Statistical Figure
KK02	Change Statistical Figure
KK03	Display Statistical Key Figures
KK03DEL	Delete Statistical Key Figures
KK04	Stat.Key Figures: Master Data Report
KK05	Create Cond. Table (Price Overhead)
KK06	Change Cond.Table (Price Overhead)
KK07	Display Cond.Table (Price Overhead)
KK11	Create Condition
KK12	Change Condition
KK13	Display Condition
KK14	Create Condition with Reference
KK16	CO-COC Plng: Change Costs/ActyInput
KK17	CO-COC Plng: Display Costs/ActyInput
KK46	CO-COC Plng: Change Stat. Key Fig.
KK47	CO-COC Plng: Display Stat. Key Fig.
KK65	COC Create Planng Layt Cost/ActInput
KK66	COC Change Plnng Layt Cost/ActvInput
KK67	COC Display Plnng Layt Cost/ActvInpt
KK87	Actual settmt: prodn cost collector
KK88	Actual Settlement: Cost Objects
KK89	Actual Settlement: Cost Objects
KK95	COC Create Planning Layout Stat. KF
KK96	COC Change Planning Layout Stat. KF
KK97	COC Display Planning Layout Stat. KF
KKA0	Maintain Cutoff Period

KKA0P	Maintain Cutoff Period
KKA1	Order Results Analysis and WIP Calc.
KKA1P	Order Results Analysis and WIP Calc.
KKA2	Project Results Anal. and WIP Calc.
KKA2P	Project Results Anal. and WIP Calc.
KKA3	Sales Document Item Results Analysis
KKA3P	Sales Document Item Results Analysis
KKA4	Create Res. Analysis Data for Order
KKA5	Create RA Data for WBS Element
KKA6	Create RA Data for Sales Order
KKA7	Delete Results Anal. Data for Order
KKA7P	Delete Results Anal. Data for Order
KKA8	Delete RA Data for WBS Element
KKA8P	Delete RA Data for WBS Element
KKA9	Delete RA Data for Sales Order
KKA9P	Delete RA Data for Sales Order
KKAA	Sales Document Line Items Res.Anal.
KKAB	Run Selected Reports
KKAC	Sales Order Hierarchy Display
KKAD	Order List for Make-to-Order
KKAE	Results Analysis: Display Worklist
KKAF	Results Analysis: Delete Worklist
KKAG	WIP: Display Worklist
KKAH	Sales Order Selection
KKAI	Actual Results Analysis: Orders
KKAIP	Planned Results Analysis: Orders
KKAJ	Actual Results Analysis: WBS Elem.
KKAJP	Plan Results Analysis: WBS Elements
KKAK	Actual Results Analysis: Sales Ordrs
KKAKP	Plan Results Analysis: Sales Orders
KKAL	Results Analysis: Display Log
KKAM	Make-to-order
KKAN	Results Analysis: Delete Log
KKAO	WIP Calc.: Collective Processing
KKAQ	Display WIP - Collective Processing
KKAS	WIP Calc. for Product Cost Coll.
KKAT	WIP Display for Product Cost Coll.
KKAV	WIP Calculation for Cost Object Hier
KKAW	WIP Display Cost Object Hierarchy
KKAX	WIP Calculation for Order
KKAY	WIP Display for Order
KKB0	Control Parameters for Info System
KKB0N	Control Parameters for Info System
KKB1	Costing Items for Sales Document
KKB2	Costing Items for Cost Object
KKB3	Costing Items for WBS Elements
KKB4	Itemization for Base Planning Obj.
KKB5	Costing Items for Material
KKB6	Configure Report Trees
KKBB	Report Call CM
KKBB_ORD_46C	Target/Actual Comparison for Orders
KKBC	Main Tree for CO-PC Info System
KKBC_BPR	Analyze Business Process
KKBC_HOE	Analyze Summarization Object

KKBC_KST	Analyze Cost Center
KKBC_KTR	Analyze Cost Object
KKBC_KUN	Analyze Sales Order
KKBC_MAT	Analyze Material Cost Estimate
KKBC_ORD	Analyze Order
KKBC_ORD_INT	Analyze Internal Order
KKBC_PKO	Analyze Product Cost Collector
KKBD	Order Selection Without Variances
KKBE	Order Selection with Variances
KKBF	Order Selection (Classification)
KKBG	Generate Report Group
KKBH	Planning report: Cost objects
KKBI	Import/Generate FI/CO Report Groups
KKBO	Report Tree
KKBU	Cost Object: Planning Overview
KKBZ	Display Hierarchy List
KKB_RLISE	Report List (Single-Level)
KKB_RLISH	Report List (Hierarchical-Sequent.)
KKB_RLISP	Report List (Data Check Only)
KKC1	Create Cost Object
KKC2	Change Cost Object
KKC3	Display Cost Object
KKC4	Create Cost Object Planning
KKC5	Change Cost Object Planning
KKC6	Display Cost Object Planning
KKC7	Create Product Group
KKC8	Change Product Group
KKC9	Display Product Group
KKCA	Cost Objects: Variance Line Items
KKCP	Cost Object Line Items - Plan
KKCS	Cost Objects: Line Items - Actual
KKCV	Var. Cost Obj. Line Items Config.
KKDV	CO-PC: Summarization level maint.
KKE1	Add Base Planning Object
KKE2	Change Base Planning Object
KKE3	Display Base Planning Object
KKE4	List Base Planning Objects
KKE5	Delete Test Data for Base Object
KKE6	Analyze Unit Cost Est Base Plan Obj
KKE7	Report Tree Base Planning Object
KKE8	Archive Base Planning Objects
KKEB	Revaluate Base Planning Objects
KKEC	Compare Base Object - Unit Cost Est
KKED	BOM for Base Planning Objects
KKF1	Create CO Production Order
KKF2	Change CO Production Order
KKF3	Display CO Production Order
KKF4	Change CO-FA Plan Values
KKF5	Display CO-FA Plan Values
KKF6	Create Production Cost Collector
KKF6M	Create Multiple Product Cost Coll.
KKF6N	Maintain Product Cost Collector
KKF7	Change Production Cost Collector
KKF8	List Production Cost Collector

KKF9	Find CO Orders
KKFB	RS Header: Line Items Variance
KKG0	Display Cutoff Period
KKG0P	Display Cutoff Period
KKG1	Create Cost of Sales: Order
KKG2	Create Cost of Sales: Project
KKG3	Create Cost of Sales: Sales Order
KKH1	Create Cost Object Group
KKH2	Change Cost Object Group
KKH3	Display Cost Object Group
KKML0	Run Drilldown Report
KKML1	Create Drilldown Report
KKML2	Change Drilldown Report
KKML3	Display Drilldown Report
KKML4	Create Form
KKML5	Change Form
KKML6	Display Form
KKML7	Maintain Key Figures
KKML8	Background Processing of Reports
KKMLH	Transport of Reports
KKMLI	Transport of Forms
KKMLJ	Client Copy of Reports
KKMLK	Client Copy of Forms
KKMLM	Test Monitor Object Record Reports
KKMLN	Reorganization of Report Data
KKMLO	Reorganization of Reports
KKMLP	Reorganization of Forms
KKMLV	Maintain Global Variable
KKMN	Product costing application area
KKN1	Actual Reval.: Cost.Obj. Ind.Pro.
KKN2	Actual Reval.: Cost Obj. Col.Pro.
KKO0	Run Drilldown Report
KKO1	Create Drilldown Report
KKO2	Change Drilldown Report
KKO3	Display Drilldown Report
KKO4	Create Form
KKO5	Change Form
KKO6	Display Form
KKO7	Maintain Key Figures
KKO8	Background Processing of Reports
KKOB	Basic Functions of Cost Object Contr
KKOG	Characteristic Groups for Costing
KKOH	Transport of Reports
KKOI	Transport of Forms
KKOJ	Client Copy of Reports
KKOK	Client Copy of Forms
KKOM	Test Monitor Object Record Reports
KKON	Reorganization of Report Data
KKOO	Reorganization of Reports
KKOP	Reorganize Forms
KKOR	Report Selection
KKOT	Split Report
KKOV	Maintain Global Variable
KKOW	Maintain Currency Translation Type

SAP Transaction Codes – Volume One

KKP1	Create Hierarchy Master Record
KKP2	Change Hierarchy Master Record
KKP3	Display Hierarchy Master Record
KKP4	Display Cost Object Hierarchy
KKP5	Cost ObjHier: Indiv. Proc. Variances
KKP6	Cost Object: Analysis
KKPA	Create Cost Est w/o Qty Structure
KKPAN	Create Cost Est. w/o Qty Structure
KKPB	Change Cost Est w/o Qty Structure
KKPBN	Change Cost Est. w/o Quantity Struct
KKPC	Display Cost Est w/o Qty Structure
KKPCN	Display Cost Est. w/o Qty Structure
KKPD	Order List for Process Manufacturing
KKPDN	Create Cost Est. w/o Qty Structure
KKPE	Report Selection for Process Mfg
KKPG	Graph. Cost Object Hierarchy Maint.
KKPH	Collective Entry
KKPHIE	Cost Object Hierarchy
KKPJ	Actual OHead: Cost Obj Collec Proc.
KKPK	Collective Entry
KKPM	Process costing menu
KKPN	Material Assignment
KKPQ	Create Cost Object Archive
KKPT	Cost Obj Hier: Coll. Proc. Variances
KKPU	User's List of Reports
KKPV	Delete Transaction Data
KKPX	Actual Cost Distribution: Cost Obj.
KKPY	Actual Cost Distribution: Cost Obj.
KKPZ	Actual Overhead: Cost Obj Individ.
KKR0	CO Summarization: Hierarchy Maintena
KKR1	CO Summarization: Summ. Object Types
KKR2	CO Summarization: Summ. Characterist
KKRA	Order Summarization
KKRC	Summarization: CO Object
KKRO	Data Collection: Product Drilldown
KKRP	Project Summarization
KKRS	Summarization: Repetitive Mfg (COC)
KKRV	Data Collection Product Drilldown
KKRZ	Summarization: Process Mfg (COC)
KKS1	Variances - Product Cost by Lot (C)
KKS1N	Variances - Product Cost by Lot (C)
KKS2	Variances - Product Cost by Lot (I)
KKS3	Scrap - Product Cost by Lot (C)
KKS4	Scrap - Product Cost by Lot (I)
KKS5	Variances - Product Cost by Per. (C)
KKS6	Variances - Product Cost by Per. (I)
KKS7	Scrap - Product Cost by Period (C)
KKS8	Scrap - Product Cost by Period (I)
KKSB	Start Selected Reports
KKSD	Order List for Order-Related Prod.
KKSM	Product Cost Ctrllg: Make-to-Stock
KKSP	Variances - Engineer-to-Order (C)
KKSQ	Variances - Engineer-to-Order (I)
KKSR	Scrap - Engineer-to-Order (C)

KKSS	Scrap - Engineer-to-Order (I)
KKST	Variances - Cost by Sales Order (C)
KKSU	Variances - Cost by Sales Order (I)
KKSV	Scrap - Cost by Sales Order (C)
KKSW	Scrap - Cost by Sales Order (I)
KKV1	View Maint. Sel. Production Orders
KL01	Create Activity Type
KL02	Change Activity Type
KL02CORE	Maintain Activity Types
KL03	Display Activity Type
KL03CORE	Display Activity Types
KL04	Delete Activity Type
KL05	Activity type: Display changes
KL13	Activity Types: Master Data Report
KL14	Delete Activity Types
KL20	Templ. Alloc. Struct. CCTR/Acty Type
KLABL	Derivation of the Default Risk Rule
KLABL_ACP	Deriv. of DRR for Class Pos.Sec.Acct
KLABL_BCA	Derivation of DRR for BCA
KLABL_DE	Derivation of DRR for Derivative
KLABL_FAZ	Derivation of DRR for Facilities
KLABL_FX	Derivation of DRR for Foreign Exch.
KLABL_LO	Derivation of DRR for Loan
KLABL_MM	Derivation of DRR for Money Market
KLABL_RC	Derivation of DRR for Risk Object
KLABL_ST	Derivation of DRR for Security Trans
KLABL_VT	Derivation of DRR for Var. Trans.
KLAU	Change Allocation Assessment Ledger
KLAV	Change Alloc. Distribution Ledger
KLCCTOEU	Log Admin for Facilities+Collateral
KLCOCUMIG	Initial Loading Assignmt Crcy->Cntry
KLEH	Display Logs
KLEXT	Display Active External Transactions
KLFZ0001	Facilities Control: Application
KLFZ0002	Facilities Control: Field Groups
KLFZ0003	Facilities Control: Views
KLFZ0004	Facilities Control: Sections
KLFZ0005	Facilities Control: Screens
KLFZ0006	Facilities Control: Screen Sequence
KLFZ0007	Facilities Control: Time
KLFZ0008	Fac. Cntrl: GUI Standard Functions
KLFZ0009	Fac. Cntrl: CUA Additional Functions
KLFZ0010	Facilities Control: Matchcode
KLFZ0011	Fac. Cntrl: Assign Scrn fld->DBfield
KLFZ0013	Facilities Control: Role Categories
KLFZ0014	Facilities Ctrl: Role cat. groupings
KLFZ0015	Facilities Ctrl: Application trans.
KLFZ0016	Facilities Control: Tables
KLFZ0018	Facilities Control: Activities
KLFZ0019	Fac. Cntrl: FldModif./Activity(Cntl)
KLFZ01	Facilities: Create
KLFZ02	Facilities: Change
KLFZ03	Facilities: Display
KLFZCCTOEU	Currency Conversion for Facility

SAP Transaction Codes – Volume One

KLFZDT01	Detail Reporting for Facilities
KLFZDT02	Detail Reporting for Facilities
KLFZMD01	Facilities: Master Data Reporting
KLFZMD03	Facilities: Master Data Reporting
KLGPUPDLR	Mass Processing of Financial Objects
KLH1	Create Activity Type Group
KLH2	Change Activity Type Group
KLH3	Display Activity Type Group
KLLE	Overview: Exceeded Limits
KLLE_DELETE	Deletion of Exceeded Limits
KLMAP	Assign Accounts to Business Partner
KLMASSPRT	Display Logs
KLMASSUPD	Mass Processing of Financial Objects
KLMASSUPD_VT_OLD	Mass Processing of Financial Objects
KLMAXLIMIT	Change Limit for Product/Trans. Type
KLNACHT	Attributable Amount Determination
KLNACHT1	Old: Postprocess Data Pool Trans.
KLNACHT2	Postprocessing of Mass Data
KLNAEG01	STChk for Datapool Transactions
KLNK	Number Range Maintenance: ISB_KL
KLNR	Number Range Maintenance: ISB_KL
KLONL	Online Check
KLREL_LIMIT	Reporting for Relative Limits
KLREL_LIMIT_ASS	Assign Rel. Limits to Portfolio Node
KLSDC1	Single Transaction Check: New
KLSDC2	Single Transaction Check: Change
KLSDC3	Single Transaction Check: Deactivate
KLSDC4	Display Transactions
KLSDCPDEF	Define STC Products
KLSDCPROTS	STC Log Generation: Control
KLSI01	Create Collateral Provision
KLSI01_CFM	Create Collateral Provision
KLSI02	Change Collateral Provision
KLSI02_CFM	Change Collateral Provision
KLSI03	Display Collateral Provision
KLSI03_CFM	Display Collateral
KLSICCTOEU	Currency Changeover for Collateral
KLT1	Credit Limit: Global Settings
KLTEV01	Credit Limit: Global Settings
KL_ARR_RC	Assign Risk Object
KM1V	Cost Center Selection Variants
KM3V	Select. Variants for Bus. Processes
KM5V	Selection Variants: Cost Elements
KM7V	Activity Type Selection Variants
KNMA	Target=Actual-IAA: cost centers
KO01	Create Internal Order
KO02	Change Order
KO03	Display Internal Order
KO04	Order Manager
KO08	Data Transfer for Order Master Data
KO09	Sender Structures for Trans. Data
KO12	Change Order Plan (Overall, Year)
KO12N	Overall Planning for Orders: Change
KO13	Display Order Plan (Overall, Year)

KO13N	Overall Planning for Orders: Display
KO14	Copy Planing for Internal Orders
KO14N	Set planner profile
KO14_OLD	Copy Order Plan Version (old)
KO15	Copy Actual Int.Order Data to Plan
KO1ECP	Internal Orders: Easy Cost Planning
KO22	Change Order Budget
KO23	Display Order Budget
KO24	Change Order Supplement
KO25	Display Order Supplement
KO26	Change Order Return
KO27	Display Order Return
KO2A	Change budget document
KO2B	Display budget document
KO30	Activate Orders Availability Control
KO31	Reconstruct Order Availability Cntrl
KO32	Deactivate Order Availability Cntrl
KO88	Actual Settlement: Order
KO8A	Act.-setlmt: Order retmt. from IM
KO8B	Display Settlement Document
KO8G	Act. Settlment: Int.-/Maint. Orders
KO8N	No. Ranges for Settlement Document
KO9E	Plan Settlement: Internal Order
KO9G	Plan Settlement: Internal Orders
KOA1	Send Internal Order
KOAA	Archive Settlement Documents
KOAB	Order Types: Budget Profile
KOAI	Order Types: Default Int. Planning
KOAK	Order Types: Classification
KOAL	Order Types: Settlement Profile
KOAM	Order Types: Model Order
KOAO	Order Types: Commitment Update
KOAP	Order Types: Plan Profile
KOAR	Archive CO Orders
KOB1	Orders: Actual Line Items
KOB2	Orders: Commitment Line Items
KOB3	Orders: Variance Line Items
KOB4	Orders: Budget Line Items
KOB5	Orders: Maint. Line Item Settlement
KOB6	Orders: Settlement Line Items
KOB7	Orders: Line Item Settlement Retirem
KOB8	Orders: WIP/Results Anal. Line Items
KOBP	Orders: Plan Line Items
KOC2	Run Selected Reports
KOC4	Cost Analysis
KOCF	Carry Forward Order Commitments
KOCM	Conversion Classification: AUFK
KOCO	Budget Carryforward for Orders
KOH1	Create Order Group
KOH2	Change Order Group
KOH3	Display Order Group
KOH9	Change Order Group
KOK2	Collective Proc. Internal Orders
KOK3	Collective Disp. Internal Orders

KOK4	Aut. Collect. Proc. Internal Orders
KOK5	Master Data List Internal Orders
KOK6	Collect. Printing of Internal Orders
KOL1	Order List (Master Data)
KOM1	Create CO model order
KOM2	Change CO Model Order
KOM3	Display CO model order
KOMM	Customizing pick list
KON1	Actual Reval.: Int.Orders Ind.Pro.
KON2	Actual Reval.: Int.Orders Col.Pro.
KONK	Maintain Order Number Ranges
KOP1	Create Orders for Plan Revaluation
KOP2	Change Orders for Plan Revaluation
KOP3	Display Orders for Plan Revaluation
KOP4	Delete Orders for Plan Revaluation
KOPA1	Overall Plan., Orders: Create layout
KOPA2	Overall Plan., Orders: Change Layout
KOPA3	Overall Plan., Orders: Displ. Layout
KOPU	Execute Orders for Plan Revaluation
KOR2	_
KORI	Job Selection
KORJ	Job Selection (Output)
KOSL	Incompleteness FT Data BOM
KOSRLIST	Collective Displ.: Settlement Rules
KOSRLIST_OR	Internal Orders: Coll. Displ. SettRu
KOSRLIST_PP	Prod. Orders: Coll. Displ. SettRules
KOSRLIST_PR	Projects/Nets: Coll. Displ.SettRules
KOSRLIST_RE	Real Estate: Coll. Displ. Sett.Rules
KOSRLIST_VB	Sales Doc.: Coll. Displ. Sett. Rules
KOT2	Maintain Order Types - All Categs.
KOT2_FUNCAREA	Functional Area Order Types (CO)
KOT2_OPA	Order types for internal orders
KOT2_OPA_STSMA	Order Types for Internal Orders
KOT2_PAUF	Check Order Type-Manufacturing Ord.
KOT2_PKOSA	Check Order Type-Prod.Cst Collector
KOT2_TP	Maintain Order Types - All Categs.
KOT3	Display Order Types
KOT3_OPA	Order types for internal orders
KOTZ	Costing Items for Order
KOUPD	Analysis Tool for Condition Update
KOV2	Maintain Transaction Grps for Orders
KOV3	Display Transaction Grps for Orders
KOW1	Create Periodic Reposting
KOW1N	Create Periodic Reposting
KOW2	Change Periodic Reposting
KOW2N	Change Periodic Reposting
KOW3	Display Periodic Reposting
KOW3N	Display Periodic Reposting
KOW4	Delete Periodic Reposting
KOW4N	Delete Periodic Reposting
KOWEB_CREATE_OR	Create Order Master Data (Web)
KOWEB_EDIT_OR	Edit Order Master Data (Web)
KP04	Set Planner Profile
KP06	Change CElem/Activity Input Planning

KP07	Display Planning CElem/Act. Input
KP16	Change Plan Data for Primary Costs
KP17	Display Plan Data for Primary Costs
KP26	Change Plan Data for Activity Types
KP27	Display Plan Data for Activity Types
KP34	CO Maintain Planner Profile
KP34BP	Maintain CO Planner Profiles
KP34ER	Maintain CO Planner Profiles
KP34PC	Maintain CO Planner Profiles
KP34PS	Maintain CO Planner Profiles
KP35	Display CO Planner Profile
KP36	Change Secondary Cost Plan Data
KP37	Display Secondary Costs Plan Data
KP46	Change Stat. Key Figure Plan Data
KP47	Display Stat. Key Figure Plan Data
KP56	Change Revenue Plan Data
KP57	Display Revenue Plan Data
KP65	Create Cost Planning Layout
KP66	Change Cost Planning Layout
KP67	Display Cost Planning Layout
KP75	Create Activity Type Planning Layout
KP76	Change Activity Type Planning Layout
KP77	Display Activ. Type Planning Layout
KP80	Maintain Distribution Keys
KP81	Create Distribution Key
KP82	Change Distribution Key
KP83	Display Distribution Key
KP84	Delete Distribution Key
KP85	Create Stat. KF Planning Layout
KP86	Change Stat. KF Planning Layout
KP87	Display Stat. KF Planning Layout
KP90	Delete Planned Costs
KP90NI	Delete Planned Costs
KP91	Delete Planned Costs
KP91NI	Delete Planning Data
KP95	Revaluate Manual Planning
KP96	Activate L. Items and Int. Planning
KP97	Copy Planning for Cost Centers
KP98	Copy Actual to Plan for Cost Centers
KP9R	Copy CO Resource Prices
KP9S	Revaluate CO Resource Prices
KPA6	Change Primary Cost Element Planning
KPA7	Display Primary Cost Elem. Planning
KPAS	Actl. Templ.-Alloc.: CCTR/Acty Type
KPB6	Change Activity Type Plan Data
KPB7	Display Activity Type Plan Data
KPC6	Change Activity Input Planning
KPC7	Display activity input planning
KPD6	Change Stat. Key Figure Plan Data
KPD7	Display Stat. Key Figure Plan Data
KPE6	Change Revenue Element Planning
KPE7	Display Revenue Element Planning
KPEP	Log: Flexible Excel Upload
KPEU	Flexible Upload for Excel Planning

KPF6	Change CElem/Activity Input Planning
KPF7	Display CElem./Acty Input Planning
KPG1	Create Planning Parameters
KPG2	Change Planning Parameters
KPG3	Display Planning Parameters
KPG4	Delete Planning Parameters
KPG5	Create Cost Planning Layout
KPG6	Change Cost Planning Layout
KPG7	Display Cost Planning Layout
KPH0	Maintain Distribution Keys
KPH1	Create Distribution Key
KPH2	Change Distribution Key
KPH3	Display Distribution Key
KPH4	Delete Distribution Key
KPH5	Create Stat. KF Planning Layout
KPH6	Change Stat. KF Planning Layout
KPH7	Display Stat. KF Planning Layout
KPHR	Transfer HR Costs to CO
KPI6	Change Stat. Key Figure Plan Data
KPI7	Display Stat. Key Figure Plan Data
KPPS	Allocation Templ. Plan: CCtr/ATyp
KPR1	Callup View Maintenance With COArea
KPR2	Maintain Resources Master Record
KPR3	Display Resource Master Record
KPR4	Maintain CO Resource Price Types
KPR5	Display CO Resource Price Types
KPR6	Maintain CO Resource Prices
KPR7	Maintain CO Resource Prices
KPR8	CO Res.: Maintain Valuation Variants
KPR9	CO Res.: Display Valuation Variants
KPRA	CO Resources: Maint. Price Strategy
KPRB	CO Resources: Display Price Strategy
KPRC	Maintain Costing Sheet for CO Res.
KPRD	Display Costing Sheet for CO Res.
KPRF	Settings Cost Obj Contr Process Mfg
KPRI	Define Price Tables
KPRK	Define Access Sequences
KPRN	Copy Resource Planning
KPRO	KPRO Administration
KPRW	Evaluate resources used
KPRZ	Depend.Planning: Recalculation
KPSI	CO-CCA Plan Reconciliation
KPSR	Execute Plan Segment Reversal
KPT6	Execute Formula Planning
KPU1	Create Plan Revaluation
KPU2	Change Plan Revaluation
KPU3	Display Plan Revaluation
KPU4	Delete Plan Revaluation
KPUB	Revaluate Plan in Background
KPY1	Create Planning Parameters
KPY2	Change Planning Parameters
KPY3	Display Planning Parameters
KPY4	Delete Planning Parameters
KPZ2	Change Cost Center Budget

KPZ3	Display Cost Center Budget
KR01	Create Summarization
KR02	Change Summarization
KR03	Display Summarization
KR04	Delete Summarization
KR05	Execute Summarization
KRMI	Run Sched. Header: Line Items Actual
KS01	Create cost center
KS02	Change cost center
KS02CORE	Maintain Cost Centers
KS03	Display Cost Center
KS03CORE	Display Cost Centers
KS04	Delete cost center
KS05	Cost Center: Display Changes
KS07	Execute rough entry of cost center
KS08	Execute list editing of cost center
KS12	Change Cost Centers
KS13	Cost Centers: Master Data Report
KS14	Delete Cost Centers
KS30	Cost Centers: Change Management
KSA3	Actual Accrual for Cost Centers
KSA4	Execute actual accrual
KSA8	Plan Accrual for Cost Centers
KSA9	Execute Plan Accrual
KSAG	Maintain condition tables
KSAH	Display condition tables
KSAI	Accrual Calc.: Maintain Actual Data
KSAJ	Accrual Calc.: Maintain Tgt=Act Cred
KSAP	Accrual Calc.: Maintain Plan Data
KSAQ	Maintain surcharge conditions
KSAR	Display Overhead Conditions
KSAZ	Accrual: Maintain Overhead Structure
KSB1	Cost Centers: Actual Line Items
KSB2	Cost Centers: Commitment Line Items
KSB5	Controlling Documents: Actual
KSB9	Planning Report: Cost Centers
KSBB	Run Selected Reports
KSBL	Cost centers: Planning overview
KSBP	Cost Centers: Plan Line Items
KSBT	Cost centers: Activity prices
KSC1	Create Actual Indirect Acty Alloc.
KSC1N	Create Actual Indirect Acty Alloc.
KSC2	Change Actual Indirect Acty Alloc.
KSC2N	Change Actual Indirect Acty Alloc.
KSC3	Display Actual Indirect Acty Alloc.
KSC3N	Display Actual Indirect Acty Alloc.
KSC4	Delete Actual Indirect Acty Alloc.
KSC4N	Delete Actual Indirect Acty Alloc.
KSC5	Execute Actual Indirect Acty Alloc.
KSC6	Act. Indirect Acty Alloc.: Overview
KSC6N	Act. Indirect Acty Alloc.: Overview
KSC7	Create Indirect Activity Alloc. Plan
KSC7N	Create Indirect Activity Alloc. Plan
KSC8	Change Indirect Activity Alloc. Plan

KSC8N	Change Indirect Activity Alloc. Plan
KSC9	Display Indirect Acty Alloc. Plan
KSC9N	Display Indirect Acty Alloc. Plan
KSCA	Delete Indirect Activity Alloc. Plan
KSCAN	Delete Indirect Activity Alloc. Plan
KSCB	Execute Plan Indirect Acty Alloc.
KSCC	Indirect Acty Alloc. Plan: Overview
KSCCN	Indirect Acty Alloc. Plan: Overview
KSCF	Carry Forward Cost Center Commitment
KSCK	Find CCtrs in Cycles and Segments
KSCP	Find Processes in Cycles / Segments
KSCYC3	Display Cycle/Segment Objects
KSES	CO: Alloc. Structure for Assessment
KSEX	Allocations: Extracts
KSFX	Predistribute fixed costs: cctr
KSH1	Create Cost Center Group
KSH2	Change Cost Center Group
KSH3	Display Cost Center Group
KSI4	Actual Overhead: Cost Centers
KSII	Actual Price Determination: CCtrs
KSMN	Actual Menu
KSO9	Commitment Overhead: Cost Centers
KSOP	CO-OM-ABC: Transfer SOP/LTP
KSOV	Cycle Maintenance/Overview (CCA,ABC)
KSP4	Plan Overhead: Cost Centers
KSPI	Iterative Plan Price Calculation
KSPP	Transfer Planning From Logistics
KSPU	Execute Plan Revaluation
KSR1_ORC	Strategies for Internal Orders
KSR1_ORI	Maintenance Order Strategies
KSR1_PRN	WBS Element Strategies
KSR1_VBP	Strategies for sales order item
KSR2_NPH	Strategy Sequences for WBS Elements
KSR2_ORC	Strategy Sequences: Internal Orders
KSR2_ORI	Strategy Sequences for PM-Orders
KSR2_PRN	Strategy Sequences for WBS Elements
KSR2_VBP	Strat. sequences f. sales order item
KSR3_ORC	Strategy Seq. - Order Cat.: Internal
KSR3_ORI	Strategy Sequence - Ordtyp PM-Orders
KSR4	User-Defined Strategies
KSRT	Allocations: Runtime Analysis
KSS1	Variance Calculation: Cost Centers
KSS2	Actual Cost Splitting: Cost Centers
KSS3	Calculate Target Costs
KSS4	Split Plan Costs
KSU1	Create Actual Assessment
KSU1N	Create Actual Assessment
KSU2	Change Actual Assessment
KSU2N	Change Actual Assessment
KSU3	Display Actual Assessment
KSU3N	Display Actual Assessment
KSU4	Delete Actual Assessment
KSU4N	Delete Actual Assessment
KSU5	Execute Actual Assessment

KSU6	Actual Assessment: Overview
KSU6N	Actual Assessment: Overview
KSU7	Create Plan Assessment
KSU7N	Create Plan Assessment
KSU8	Change Plan Assessment
KSU8N	Change Plan Assessment
KSU9	Display Plan Assessment
KSU9N	Display Plan Assessment
KSUA	Delete Plan Assessment
KSUAN	Delete Plan Assessment
KSUB	Execute Plan Assessment
KSUC	Plan Assessment: Overview
KSUCN	Plan Assessment: Overview
KSV1	Create Actual Distribution
KSV1N	Create Actual Distribution
KSV2	Change Actual Distribution
KSV2N	Change Actual Distribution
KSV3	Display Actual Distribution
KSV3N	Display Actual Distribution
KSV4	Delete Actual Distribution
KSV4N	Delete Actual Distribution
KSV5	Execute Actual Distribution
KSV6	Actual Distribution: Overview
KSV6N	Actual Distribution: Overview
KSV7	Create Plan Distribution
KSV7N	Create Plan Distribution
KSV8	Change Plan Distribution
KSV8N	Change Plan Distribution
KSV9	Display Plan Distribution
KSV9N	Display Plan Distribution
KSVA	Delete Plan Distribution
KSVAN	Delete Plan Distribution
KSVB	Execute Plan Distribution
KSVC	Plan Distribution: Overview
KSVCN	Plan Distribution: Overview
KSW1	Create Periodic Reposting
KSW1N	Create Periodic Reposting
KSW2	Change Periodic Reposting
KSW2N	Change Periodic Reposting
KSW3	Display Periodic Reposting
KSW3N	Display Periodic Reposting
KSW4	Delete Periodic Reposting
KSW4N	Delete Periodic Reposting
KSW5	Execute Actual Periodic Reposting
KSW6	Periodic Repostings: Overview
KSW6N	Periodic Repostings: Overview
KSW7	Create Plan Periodic Reposting
KSW7N	Create Plan Periodic Reposting
KSW8	Change Plan Periodic Reposting
KSW8N	Change Plan Periodic Reposting
KSW9	Display Plan Periodic Reposting
KSW9N	Display Plan Periodic Reposting
KSWA	Delete Plan Periodic Reposting
KSWAN	Delete Plan Periodic Reposting

SAP Transaction Codes – Volume One

KSWB	Execute Plan Periodic Reposting
KSWC	Plan Periodic Repostings: Overview
KSWCN	Plan Periodic Repostings: Overview
KSWUSL	Where-Used List: Cycles in CCA
KTPF	View Maint.: Find Template
KVA0	Maintain Assignment Cost Ctr./KF
KVA1	Display Plan Assignment CCtr/KF
KVA2	Maintain Actual Assignment CCtr/KF
KVA3	Display Actual Assignment CCtr/KF
KVA4	Transfer Plan Statistical Key Figure
KVA5	Transfer Actual Stat. Key Figure
KVA6	Copy Assignment CCtr/KF
KVB0	Maintain Plan Assignment Process/KF
KVB1	Display Plan Assignment Process/KF
KVB2	Change Actual Assignment Process/KF
KVB3	Display Actual Assignment Process/KF
KVB4	PROZ: Copy Plan Stat. Key Figures
KVB5	PROZ: Copy Actual Stat. Key Figures
KVB6	Copy Assignment Processes/KF
KVBI	Sales Documents: Line Items Actual
KVBO	Sales Documents: Commit. Line Items
KVC0	Change Plan Assignment CObj/KF
KVC1	Display Plan Assignment CObj/KF
KVC2	Change Actual Assignment CObj/KF
KVC3	Display Actual Assignment CObj/KF
KVC4	KSRTG: Copy Plan Stat. Key Figures
KVC5	KSRTG: Copy Actual Stat. Key Figures
KVC6	Copy Assignment Cost Object/Key Fig.
KVD0	Maintain Plan Assignment ATyp/KF
KVD1	Display Plan Assignment ATyp/KF
KVD2	Change Actual Assignment ATyp/KF
KVD3	Display Actual Assignment ATyp/KF
KVD4	LSTAR: Copy Plan Stat. Key Figures
KVD5	LSTAR: Copy Actual Stat. Key Figures
KVD6	Copy Assignment ActType/Key Figure
KW3P	WWW: Internal Price List
KWSTAT	KW Statistics Functions
KXH1	Create Group (Hierarchical)
KXH2	Change Group (Hierarchical)
KXH3	Display Hierarchy (Hierarchical)
KZA1	Select Overhead
KZB2	Maintain Calculation Base
KZB4	Calculation Base Cost Ctr/Activ.Type
KZE2	Maintain Credit
KZM2	Maintain quantity-based overhead
KZO2	Maintain Basis of Output Quantity
KZS2	Maintain Costing Sheet
KZZ2	Maintain Percentage Overhead
LACCS	CO_ML_DISPLAY
LAS1	Sequencing in Background Job
LAS2	Change Sequence Schedule
LAS3	Display Sequence Schedule
LAS4	Change Sequence Sched. Interactively
LAST_SHORTDUMP	Display Last Short Dump

SAP Transaction Codes – Volume One

LAUNCH_CRW	Start of Crystal Report Designer
LB01	Create Transfer Requirement
LB02	Change transfer requirement
LB03	Display Transfer Requirement
LB10	TRs for Storage Type
LB11	TRs for Material
LB12	TRs and Posting Change for Mat.Doc.
LB13	TRs for Requirement
LBK1	Logbook Application
LBW0	Interface LIS Information Structures
LBW1	Update Activation LIS/BW
LBW2	Version Copier LIS/BW
LBWE	LO Data Ext.: Customizing Cockpit
LBWF	Log for Logistics Extract. Structure
LBWG	Delete Newly Reorg. BW Data
LBWQ	Logistics Queue Overview
LBWR	Reconstruct Extraction Queue
LC10	liveCache Assistant
LC11	Creating the liveCache connection
LCA01	Read LCA Object Tracing
LCA02	LCA Object Tracing
LCA03	Standard liveCache Test
LCA04	Display the Current LCA Version
LCA13	liveCache and LCA Objects Analysis
LCA20	Profiling
LCO1	Set Up Warehouse Co/Material Docs.
LCO2	Set Up Warehouse Co/Transport Orders
LCRCHECK	Test LCR Connection
LCRHTMLGUI	Start LCR GUI in Browser
LCRSERVADDR	Maintain Landscape Directory Server
LD00	Line Design
LDA2	Change Takt Time
LDA3	Display Takt Time
LDAP	LDAP Customizing and Test
LDAPEXTRACT_LOG	Log For Displaying the Extractor Log
LDAPLOG	Analyze LDAP Log
LDAPMAP	Maintain LDAP Attribute Assignment
LDB1	Create Line Hierarchy
LDB2	Change Line Hierarchy
LDB3	Display Line Hierarchy
LDD1	Create Line Balance
LDD2	Change Line Balance
LDD3	Display Line Balance
LDE1	Work Instruction for Routing
LDE2	Work Instruction for Line Hier.
LDGRP	Definition of Ledger Groups (FI-SL)
LEAN	Request long-term VendDecl. (vendor)
LECI	Register Means of Transport/Visitor
LECIFORM	Form Maintenance at Check-in
LECIW	Register Means of Transport/Visitor
LECMOFF	Deactivate Change Management
LEER	Create long-term VenDecl. (customer)
LEMA	Dun long-term vendor decl. (vendor)
LEPA	Activate Determination Log

LEPD	Deletion of INDX Records
LEPS	Display Determination Log
LH01	Assign Pick-HU to TO
LH03	Assign Pick-HU to TO Display
LI01	Create System Inventory Record
LI01N	Create System Inventory Record
LI02	Change System Inventory Record
LI02N	Change System Inventory Record
LI03	Display System Inventory Record
LI03N	Display System Inventory Record
LI04	Print System Inventory Record
LI05	Inventory History for Storage Bin
LI06	Block stor.types for annual invent.
LI11	Enter Inventory Count
LI11N	Enter Inventory Count
LI12	Change inventory count
LI12N	Change inventory count
LI13	Display Inventory Count
LI13N	Display Inventory Count
LI14	Start Inventory Recount
LI15	Evaluation of quant inventory
LI16	Cancel Physical Inventory Doc. Item
LI20	Clear Inventory Differences WM
LI21	Clear Inventory Differences in MM-IM
LICC	Cycle Counting per Quant
LICENSE_ADMIN	License Administration Workbench
LICENSE_ATTRIBUTES	Maintain License Attributes of Roles
LISH	LIS Standard Analyses: Hierarchies
LISK	LIS: Data Collection in R/2
LISTCUBE	List viewer for InfoCubes
LISTSCHEMA	Show InfoCube schema
LK01	Create consumer
LK02	Change consumer
LK03	Display consumer
LL01	Warehouse Activity Monitor
LLDEL	Delete application logs
LLVS	WM Menu
LM00	Logon RF
LM01	Dynamic Menu
LM02	Select by SU -Put Away
LM03	Put Away - by TO
LM04	Put Away -System Guided
LM05	Picking by TO ID
LM06	Picking - by Delivery ID
LM07	Picking - System Guided
LM09	Put Away by Delivery ID
LM11	Posting Changes
LM12	Material Inquiry
LM13	Put Away Clustered
LM18	Handling Unit Inquiry
LM19	Handling Unit - Pack
LM22	Handling Unit - Unpack
LM24	Packing HU by Delivery
LM25	Unpack HU by Delivery

LM26	Picking by Delivery - W/O sel scree
LM27	Put Away by Delivery - W/O sel scree
LM30	Load Control - Load by Shipment
LM31	Load Control - Load by Delivery
LM32	Load Control - System Guide Load
LM33	Load Control - UnLd by Shipment.
LM34	Load Control - UnLd by Delivery
LM35	Load Control - Detail by Shipping Un
LM36	Load Control - Detail by Delivery
LM37	Load Control - Detail by Shipment
LM45	Pick and Pack
LM46	Pick and Pack by Delivery
LM47	nested handling units
LM50	Count Inventory By System Guided
LM51	Count Inventory By User Selection
LM55	Print Storage Bin Labels
LM56	Select by SU - Interleaving
LM57	System Guided Putaway - Interleaving
LM58	Sys. guided dynamic inventory count
LM59	User initiated dynamic invent. count
LM60	User guided dynamic invent. count
LM61	Goods Issue by Delivery
LM62	Goods Issue by MS area
LM63	Goods Issue by Shipment
LM64	Goods Issue by ALL
LM65	Goods Issue by Group
LM66	Goods Issue by HU
LM71	Goods Receipt by Delivery
LM72	Goods Receipt by MS area
LM73	Goods Receipt by Shipment
LM74	Goods Receipt by ALL
LM76	Goods Receipt by HU
LM77	Queue Assignment
LM80	Serial number capture
LMFO_GEN_PD	FO Integration - Log Display
LMFO_LO_MUPD	FO Integr. Loan - Mass Data (Limit)
LMFO_POS_MUPD	FO-Int. Cl. Pos. Sec. Act - Mass Lim
LMFO_TRTM_MUPD	FO-Int. Cl. Pos. Sec. Act - Mass Lim
LMIBKKA	BCA Account: FO Integr. act./inact.
LMIFGDT	Risk Object: FO Integr. act./inact.
LMIJBVT	Var. Trans.: FO Integr. act./inact.
LMIKLFZ	Facility: Activate/Deactivate FO Int
LN01	Number Ranges for Transfer Requirem.
LN02	Number Ranges for Transfer Orders
LN03	Number Ranges for Quants
LN04	Number Ranges for Posting Changes
LN05	Number ranges physical inventory
LN06	Number Ranges for Group Number
LN07	Number Ranges for WM Communic.Rec.
LN08	Number range maintenance: LVS_LENUM
LN09	Number Range Maintenance: LVS_LBELN
LNRMS	Number range maintenance: TRM_MSGSEQ
LNRRQ	Number range maintenance: TRM_REQEST
LNRRS	Number range maintenance: TRM_RSRC

LNRTK	Number range maintenance: TRM_TASK
LOCA	Locator Demo
LOCA_APPL	Locator Applications
LOCA_CUST	Locator Customizing
LP00	Mobile Presentation
LP10	Direct picking for PO
LP11	WM staging of crate parts
LP11W	WM Staging for Crate Parts (IAC)
LP12	Staging release order parts (WM-PP)
LP21	WM replenishment for fixed bins
LP22	Replenishm. Planning for Fixed Bins
LP24	WM Replenishment for Random Whse
LPCONFIG	Maintain Logical Ports
LPD_CUST	Launchpad customizing
LPD_CUST_BUA_PLA	Customizing for Role BUA / PLA
LPD_CUST_BUA_REP	Customizing for Role BUA /REP
LPD_CUST_PARAM	Start Launchpad parametrized
LPD_MP_REP_CUST	MP Report Launchpad Customizing
LPD_MS_REP_CUST	MS Report Launchpad Customizing
LPD_MT_REP_CUST	MT Report Launchpad Customizing
LPD_QI_REP_CUST	QI Reporting Customizing (ABAP)
LPIN	Info: Material Stock WM-PP
LPINW	Info Transaction (IAC)
LPK1	Create Control Cycle for WM
LPK2	Change Control Cycle for WM
LPK3	Display Control Cycle for WM
LPK4	Create Contr.Cycles for Rel.Ord.Part
LPRO	Material Forecast Menu
LPSC	RF Screen Conversion Tool
LPVAS	VAS Management
LPYRD	Yard Management
LQ01	Transfer Posting in Invent. Mgmt
LQ02	Transfer Posting in Invent. Mgmt
LRF1	RF Monitor, Active
LRF2	RF Monitor, Passive
LRFMD	Maintain RF user master data
LROUT	Creation or adjustement of routes
LRSW	Resource element maintenance wizard
LS01	Create Warehouse Master Record
LS01N	Create Warehouse Master Record
LS02	Change Warehouse Master Record
LS02N	Change Warehouse Master Record
LS03	Display Warehouse Master Record
LS03N	Display Warehouse Master Record
LS04	Display Empty Storage Bins
LS05	Generate Storage Bins
LS06	Block Storage Bins
LS07	Block Quants
LS08	Block Storage Bins by Aisle
LS09	Display Material Data for Stor.Type
LS10	Generate Storage Bins
LS11	Change several stor.bins simultan.
LS12	Block stor.type
LS22	Change Quants

LS23	Display Quants
LS24	Display Quants for Material
LS25	Display Quants per Storage Bin
LS26	Warehouse stocks per material
LS27	Display quants for storage unit
LS28	Display storage units / bin
LS32	Change storage unit
LS33	Display storage unit
LS41	List of control cycles for WIP loc.
LS51	Create Batch Search Strategy - WM
LS52	Change Batch Search Strategie - WM
LS53	Display Batch Search Strategy - WM
LSET_BIN_COORDINATES	Maintain Storage Bins by selection
LSMW	Legacy System Migration Workbench
LSOTACITEM	Item Statistics
LSO_ACTIVATE	SAP Learning Solution On/Off
LSO_ETCHANGE	Reset Access Counter
LSO_EVAL_ADMIN	Administrator: Appraisal Document
LSO_EVAL_CATALOG	Evaluation Catalog
LSO_EVAL_CHANGE	Edit Appraisal Document
LSO_EVAL_CREATE	Create Appraisal
LSO_EVAL_PREPARE	Prepare Appraisal
LSO_EVAL_SEARCH	Find Appraisal
LSO_FLUP	Follow Up Participation w/o Date
LSO_LOCAL_CONTENT	Locally Available Course Content
LSO_MMA_ADM	Manage Required Courses
LSO_MMA_MGR	Manage Required Courses
LSO_OORT	Create Resource Type
LSO_PADBOOK	Database Conversion SAP LSO600
LSO_PP40	Manual Output
LSO_PSV1	Dynamic Participation Menu
LSO_PSV2	Dynamic Course Menu
LSO_PSV3	Dynamic Information Menu
LSO_PSV5	Info: Participation
LSO_PSV6	Information: Courses
LSO_PSV7	Reporting: Resources
LSO_PSV8	Create Participant
LSO_PSV9	Change / Display Participant
LSO_PSVI	User-Defined Settings
LSO_PSVO	Change / Display Training Provider
LSO_PSVP	Dynamic Planning Menu
LSO_PSVQ	Create Training Provider
LSO_PSVR	Dynamic Resource Menu
LSO_PSVT	Dynamic Tool Menu
LSO_PUBLISHER	Display Publisher Database
LSO_PV00	Book Participation
LSO_PV01	Rebook Participation
LSO_PV02	Prebook Participation
LSO_PV03	Replace Participation
LSO_PV04	Cancel Participation
LSO_PV05	Book List: Participants/Courses
LSO_PV06	Prebook List: Participants
LSO_PV07	Book List: Participants
LSO_PV08	Book List: Courses

LSO_PV10	Create Course with Resources	
LSO_PV11	Create Course Without Resources	
LSO_PV12	Firmly Book/Cancel Course	
LSO_PV14	Lock/Unlock Course	
LSO_PV15	Follow Up Course	
LSO_PV16	Prebook List: Course Types	
LSO_PV17	Billing	
LSO_PV18	Activity Allocation	
LSO_PV19	Activity Allocation for Instructors	
LSO_PV1A	Change Course	
LSO_PV1B	Display Course	
LSO_PV1C	Cost Transfer Posting	
LSO_PV1D	Price Proposal	
LSO_PV1M	Materials Procurement	
LSO_PV33	Create Appraisal	
LSO_PVCT	Master Data Catalog	
LSO_PVDC	Edit Curriculum Type	
LSO_PVDCEL	Curriculum Type Elements	
LSO_PVEC	Edit Curriculum	
LSO_PVEC_CREATE	Access: Create/Change Curriculum	
LSO_PVEK	Manage Course Program	
LSO_PVK0	Correspondence History	
LSO_PVSEARCH_ADM	Administer Search Engine	
LSO_RHABLAUF_OLD	Course Schedule	
LSO_RHPPROGRS	Completion Progress of Learner	
LSO_RHRBEL00	Resource Reservation	
LSO_RHREFDOC0	Reference Document Reporting	
LSO_RHSEMI60	Course Information	
LSO_RHSSREF0	Instructor Information	
LSO_RHXBUCH0	Bookings per Participant	
LSO_RHXCGRP0	Course Hierarchy	
LSO_RHXERES0	Resource List per Course	
LSO_RHXEVALV_OLD	Course Appraisals	
LSO_RHXKBED0	Course Demand	
LSO_RHXKBRO0	Course Brochure	
LSO_RHXKBRO1	Course Dates	
LSO_RHXKBRO2	Course Prices	
LSO_RHXKURS2	Participation Statistics	
LSO_RHXKURS3	Participation and Sales Statistics	
LSO_RHXKVOR0	Participation Prerequisites	
LSO_RHXMARP0	Material Requirements per Course	
LSO_RHXORES1	Resources Not Yet Assigned / Course	
LSO_RHXORES2	Resources Not Yet Assigned/Res. Type	
LSO_RHXQANF0	Prerequisites Matchup	
LSO_RHXRBEL1	Graphical Resource Reservation	
LSO_RHXRESO0	Resource Reservation Statistics	
LSO_RHXSTOR0	Cancellations per Course	
LSO_RHXSTOR1	Cancellations per Participant	
LSO_RHXTEILA	Attendance List	
LSO_RHXTEILN	Participant List	
LSO_RHXTHIST	Participant's Training History	
LSO_RHXUMBU0	Participants for Rebooking	
LSO_RHXVORM0	Prebookings per Course Type	
LSO_RHXVORM1	Prebookings per Participant	

LSO_SCORM_CONVERT	Convert SCORM 1.2 to SCORM 2004
LSO_SCORM_REPORT	Report of SCORM Data
LSO_SMM	Stopmark Manager
LSO_SUBSCRIBE_CP	Subscribe to Course Program
LSO_TAC_ITEMSTAT	Results Overview: Item Statistics
LSO_TAC_PART_RESULT	Results Overview: Participant
LSO_TAC_TRAIN_RESULT	Results Overview: Course
LSO_TP_C	LS: Participation Document
LSO_WD_CRP_CHANGE	Change Correspondence Request (WD)
LSO_WD_CRP_PREVIEW	Correspondence Request Preview (WD)
LT01	Create Transfer Order
LT02	Create TO for Inventory Difference
LT03	Create TO for Delivery
LT04	Create TO from TR
LT05	Process Posting Change Notice
LT06	Create TO for Material Document
LT07	Create TO for mixed storage unit
LT08	Manual Addition to Storage Unit
LT09	ID point function for storage units
LT0A	Pre-plan storage units
LT0B	Putaway Pre-Picked Handling Units
LT0C	Removal of Pre-Picked HUs from Stock
LT0D	Transfer of Existing Handling Units
LT0E	Create Removal TO for 2-Step Picking
LT0F	Create TO for Inbound Delivery
LT0G	Return delivery to stock
LT0H	Putaway/Stock Transfer of HUs
LT0I	Removal of Handling Units from Stock
LT0J	Put Away Handling Unit
LT0R	Request replenishment manually
LT0S	Create TO for multiple deliveries
LT10	Create Transfer Order from List
LT11	Confirm Transfer Order Item
LT12	Confirm transfer order
LT13	Confirm TO for storage unit
LT14	Confirm preplanned TO item
LT15	Cancelling transfer order
LT16	Cancelling TO for storage unit
LT17	Single Entry of Actual Data
LT1A	Change Transfer Order
LT1B	Confirm TO-Item Pick
LT1C	Confirm TO-Item Transport
LT1D	Confirm Transfer Order Pick
LT1E	Confirm Transfer Order Transport
LT1F	Confirm TO for SU Pick
LT1G	Confirm TO for SU Transport
LT21	Display Transfer Order
LT22	Display Transfer Order / Stor. Type
LT23	Display Transfer Orders by Numbers
LT24	Display Transfer Order / Material
LT25	Display Transfer Order / Group
LT25A	Display Transfer Order / Group
LT25N	Confirm Transfer ORder / Group
LT26	Transfer orders for storage bin

LT27	Transfer order for storage unit
LT28	Display Transfer Order / Reference
LT31	Print TO Manually
LT32	Print transfer order for stor.unit
LT343XYZ	Copy Storage Bin Definition Rules
LT343XYZA	Maintain Bins by Definition Rule
LT41	Prepare TRs for Multiple Processing
LT42	Create TOs by Multiple Processing
LT43	Forming groups for deliveries
LT44	Release for Multiple Processing
LT45	Evaluation of reference numbers
LT51	Maintain Preallocated Stock
LT63	Control: Single Entry of Actual Data
LT64	Single Entry of Actual Data
LT72	Determine 2-step relevance
LT73	Display 2-step
LTRA	TRM Alert Monitor
LTRCC	TRM Customization Consistency Check
LTRL	TRM Log Reports
LTRMS	TRM Monitor
LU01	Create Posting Change Notice
LU02	Change Posting Change Notice
LU03	Display Posting Change Notice
LU04	Selection of Posting Change Notices
LVASA	VAS Alert Monitor
LVASDVC	Maintain Presentation Devics for VAS
LVASEXIT	Exit stock from Work Center
LVASM	VAS Monitor
LVASNR	Number range maintenance: LXVAS_VOID
LVAST01	Create VAS Template
LVAST02	Modify VAS Template
LVAST03	Display VAS Template
LVASUSR	Define RF Users for VAS
LVASWC02	LXVAS work center operation - Update
LVASWC03	LXVAS work center operation - Displa
LVASWOR	Create VAS Order w/o reference
LX01	List of Empty Storage Bins
LX02	Stock list
LX03	Bin Status Report
LX04	Capacity load utilization
LX05	Block Bins in Bl.Storage w.Time Lim.
LX06	Fire Department Inventory List
LX07	Check storage
LX08	Accident Regulations List
LX09	Overview of All Transf.Requirements
LX10	Activities per Storage Type
LX11	Document overview
LX12	Document Overview: Landscape Format
LX13	Analysis of differences
LX14	Matl mvmt frequency
LX15	Selection of Bins for Annual Invent.
LX16	Selection of Bins for Continuous Inv
LX17	List of Inventory Differences
LX18	Statistics of Inventory Differences

LX19	Inventory Data Takeover by Btch Inp.
LX20	Generate interim storage bins
LX21	Pick List for Several Transfer Ord.
LX22	Process Inventory from Overview
LX23	Stock comparison IM - WM
LX24	Display of hazardous mat.numbers
LX25	Inventory Status
LX26	Inventory in WM via cycle counting
LX27	Stock levels by shelf life exp.date
LX28	Relevant TO item for ext.system
LX29	Fixed bin supervision
LX30	Overview of WM messages ext.system
LX31	Analysis of print control tables
LX32	Archived transfer orders
LX33	Archived transfer requirements
LX34	Archived posting change notices
LX35	Archived system inventory records
LX36	Archived Inventory Histories
LX37	Linked objects
LX38	Check Report Customizing Strategy K
LX39	Evaluation Reference No. for 2-S.Pck
LX40	Material Situation Prod. Storage Bin
LX41	Bin Status Report WM/PP Interface
LX42	Evaluation PP Order from WM View
LX43	Consistency Check for Control Cycles
LX44	Inward and outward movements
LX45	Verification Field in Storage Bin
LX46	Transmission WM perform. data to HR
LX47	Analysis of Delayed Delivery Update
LXDCA	Cross Docking Alert Monitor
LXDCK	Cross-Docking Monitor
LXDNR	Cross-Docking Decision Number Range
LXE_MASTER	Translation Environment
LYACT	Yard activities number ranges
LYCHP	Check-in / Check-out transaction
LYLDP	Load & unload transaction
LYRDA	Yard Alert Monitor
LYRDM	Yard Monitor
LYSCH	Yard Scheduling Chart
LYVHC	Yard Inventory
M-01	Create Vendor
M-02	Create goods vendor
M-03	Create payment recipient
M-04	Create invoicing party
M-05	Create carrier
M-06	Create ordering address
M-07	Create one-time vendor
M-12	Create hierarchy nodes
M-51	Create vendor
M-52	Create goods vendor
M-53	Create payment recipient
M-54	Create invoicing party
M-55	Create carrier
M-56	Create ordering address

M-57	Create one-time vendor
M-62	Create hierarchy nodes
M/03	Create Conditions Table (Purchasing)
M/04	Change Conditions Table (Purchasing)
M/05	Displ. Conditions Table (Purchasing)
M/06	Condition Type: (Purchasing)
M/07	Access: Maintain (Price Purchasing)
M/08	Conditions: Schema for Purchasing
M/10	Condition Type: Services
M/11	Access: Maintain (Price Services)
M/12	Conditions: Schema for Services
M/13	Create Condition Table (Service)
M/14	Change Condition Table (Services)
M/15	Display Condition Table (Services)
M/16	Conditions: Var. Schema for Service
M/25	Condition type: Short txt for cust.
M/32	Maint. Message Determ. Schema: RFQ
M/36	Maintain Message Determ. Schema: PO
M/42	Maintain Message Schema: Del. Sched.
M/48	Maintain Access Sequences: RFQ
M/50	Maintain Access Sequences: PO
M/52	Maint. Access Sequences: Outl. Agmt.
M/54	Maint. Access Sequences: Del. Sched.
M/56	Messages: Create Cond. Table: RFQ
M/57	Messages: Change Condition Table
M/58	Messages: Display CondTab: RFQ
M/59	Messages: Create CondTab: Pur. Order
M/60	Messages: Change CondTab: Pur. Order
M/61	Messages: Disp. CondTab: Pur. Order
M/62	Messages: Create CondTab: Del. Schd.
M/63	Messages: Change CondTab: Del. Schd.
M/64	Messages: Disp. CondTab: Del. Sched.
M/65	Messages: Create CondTab: O. Agmt.
M/66	Messages: Change CondTab: O. Agmt.
M/67	Messages: Disp. CondTab: Outl. Agmt.
M/68	Maintain Message Schema: Outl. Agmt.
M/70	Messages: Create CondTab.: Entry Sh.
M/71	Messages: Change CondTab.: Entry Sh.
M/72	Messages: Disp. CondTab.: Entry Sh.
M/73	Maintain Access Sequences: Entry
M/74	Maintain Access Sequences: Entry
M/75	Maintain Messages: Serv. Entry Sheet
M/76	Display Messages: Entry
M/77	Maintain Message Schema: Entry Sheet
M/78	Disp. Message Determ. Schema: Entry
M/N1	Maintain accesses (fr.gds - purch.)
M/N2	Create free goods table
M/N3	Display free goods table
M/N4	Free goods types - purchasing
M/N5	Free goods: Procedure for purchasing
M/N6	Free goods pricing procedure
M703	Output: Create Conditions Table
M704	Output: Change Condition Table
M705	Output: Display Conditions Table

M706	Maintain Output Types: Inv. Mgmt
M708	Output Determination: Procedure
M710	Output Determ.: Access Sequences
M802	Message Requirements (IV)
M804	Message Processing Program (IV)
M806	Message Types (Invoice Verification)
M808	Message Schema (Inv. Verification)
M810	Message Access Sequence (Inv. Ver.)
M811	Create Message Condition Table (IV)
M812	Change Message Condition Table (IV)
M813	Display Message Condition Table (IV)
MAHD1	Load Alternative Historical Data
MAHD2	Change Alternative Historical Data
MAHD3	Display Alternative Historical Data
MAHD4	Delete Alternative Historical Data
MAL1	Create material via ALE
MAL2	Change material via ALE
MAP1	Create contact person
MAP2	Change contact person
MAP3	Display contact person
MAPREVACC	Mapping Revenue Account
MASS	Mass Change
MASSD	Mass Maintenance
MASSOBJ	Maintain Mass Maintenance Objects
MASSS2V	Copy System Variant as Variant
MASSV2S	Copy Variant as System Variant
MASSVAR	Display variants
MASSVAR_S	Display System Variants
MASS_EINE	Inforecord Mass Maintenance
MASS_EKKO	PO mass maintenance
MASS_MARC	Logistic/Replenishment Mass Maint.
MASS_VENDOR	Vendor Mass Maintenance
MATGRP01	Create Article Hierarchy
MATGRP02	Change Article Hierarchy
MATGRP03	Display Article Hierarchy
MATGRP04	Delete Article Hierarchy
MATGRP05	Activate Article Hierarchy
MATGRP06	Article Hierarchy: Copy Nodes
MATGRP07	Deactivate Article Hierarchy
MA_DD_REPORT	Start a Drilldown Report
MA_WM_IDOCMO_P	Personalization: IDoc Monitor
MB00	Inventory Management
MB01	Post Goods Receipt for PO
MB02	Change Material Document
MB03	Display Material Document
MB04	Subsequ.Adj.of "Mat.Provided"Consmp.
MB05	Subseq. Adjustmt: Act.Ingredient Mat
MB0A	Post Goods Receipt for PO
MB11	Goods Movement
MB1A	Goods Withdrawal
MB1B	Transfer Posting
MB1C	Other Goods Receipts
MB21	Create Reservation
MB22	Change Reservation

MB23	Display Reservation
MB24	Reservation List
MB25	Reservation List
MB26	Picking list
MB31	Goods Receipt for Production Order
MB51	Material Doc. List
MB52	List of Warehouse Stocks on Hand
MB53	Display Plant Stock Availability
MB54	Consignment Stocks
MB55	Display Quantity String
MB56	Analyze batch where-used list
MB57	Compile Batch Where-Used List
MB58	Consgmt and Ret. Packag. at Customer
MB59	Material Doc. List
MB5A	Evaluate Batch Where-Used Archive
MB5B	Stocks for Posting Date
MB5C	Pick-Up List
MB5D	Delete Docs of Batch Where-Used File
MB5E	Create Batch Where-Used Archive
MB5K	Stock Consistency Check
MB5L	List of Stock Values: Balances
MB5M	BBD/Prod. Date
MB5OA	Display Valuated GR Blocked Stock
MB5S	Display List of GR/IR Balances
MB5T	Stock in transit CC
MB5TD	Stock in Transit on Key Date
MB5U	Analyze Conversion Differences
MB5V	Manage Batch Where-Used Archive
MB5W	List of Stock Values
MB90	Output Processing for Mat. Documents
MB9A	Analyze archived mat. documents
MBAD	Delete Material Documents
MBAL	Material Documents: Read Archive
MBAR	Archive Material Documents
MBAV	Manage Material Document Archive
MBBM	Batch Input: Post Material Document
MBBR	Batch Input: Create Reservation
MBBS	Display valuated special stock
MBC1	Create MM Batch Search Strategy
MBC2	Change MM Batch Determ. Strategy
MBC3	Display MM Batch Determ. Strategy
MBGR	Displ. Material Docs. by Mvt. Reason
MBLB	Stocks at Subcontractor
MBMENUS	Process MM-IM Inconsistencies
MBN1	Free goods - Create (Purchasing)
MBN2	Free goods - Change (Purchasing)
MBN3	Free goods - Display (Purchasing)
MBNK	Number Ranges, Material Document
MBNL	Subsequent Delivery f. Material Doc.
MBPM	Manage Held Data
MBRL	Return Delivery for Matl Document
MBSF	Release Blocked Stock via Mat. Doc.
MBSI	Find Inventory Sampling
MBSL	Copy Material Document

MBSM	Display Cancelled Material Docs.
MBST	Cancel Material Document
MBSU	Place in Stor.for Mat.Doc: Init.Scrn
MBVR	Management Program: Reservations
MBW1	Special stocks via WWW
MBWO	Error Correction: Subs. Value Calc.
MBXA	Printout of XAB Documents
MC$0	PURCHIS: PurchGrp PurchVal Selection
MC$2	PURCHIS: PurchGrp Freqs. Selection
MC$4	PURCHIS: Vendor PurchVal Selection
MC$6	PURCHIS: Vendor DelRelblty Selection
MC$8	PURCHIS: Vendor QtyRelblty Selection
MC$:	PURCHIS: Vendor Freqs. Selection
MC$<	PURCHIS: MatGrp PurchVal Selection
MC$>	PURCHIS: MatGrp PurchQty Selection
MC$A	PURCHIS: MatGrp DelRelblty Selection
MC$C	PURCHIS: MatGrp QtyRelblty Selection
MC$E	PURCHIS: MatGrp Freq. Selection
MC$G	PURCHIS: Material PurchVal Selection
MC$I	PURCHIS: Material PurchQty Selection
MC$K	PURCHIS: Material DelRelib Selection
MC$M	PURCHIS: Material QtyRel Selection
MC$O	PURCHIS: Material Freqs. Selection
MC(A	SIS: Customer,Inc.Orders - Selection
MC(B	SIS: Variant Configuration
MC(E	SIS: Material,Inc.Orders - Selection
MC(I	SIS: SalesOrg. Inc.Orders Selection
MC(M	SIS: Sales Office, Inc.Orders Selec.
MC(Q	SIS: Employee, Inc.Orders Selection
MC(U	SIS: Shipping Point Deliveries Sel.
MC+2	SIS: SalesOrg.Invoiced Sales, Selec.
MC+6	SIS: SalesOrg.Credit Memos Selection
MC+A	SIS: Customer Returns, Selection
MC+E	SIS: Customer, Sales - Selection
MC+I	SIS: Customer Credit Memos - Selec.
MC+M	SIS: Material Returns, Selection
MC+Q	SIS: Material, Sales - Selection
MC+U	SIS: Material Credit Memos, Selec.
MC+Y	SIS: Sales Org. Returns, Selection
MC-0	SIS: Shipping Point Returns, Selec.
MC-A	SIS: Sales Office Returns, Selection
MC-E	SIS: Sales Office - Sales Selection
MC-I	SIS: Sales Office Credit Memos Selec
MC-M	SIS: Employee - Returns, Selection
MC-Q	SIS: Employee - Sales, Selection
MC-U	SIS: Employee - Credit Memos, Selec.
MC.1	INVCO: Plant Anal. Selection: Stock
MC.2	INVCO: Plant Anal.Selection, Rec/Iss
MC.3	INVCO: Plant Anal.Selection,Turnover
MC.4	INVCO: Plant Anal.Selection,Coverage
MC.5	INVCO: SLoc Anal. Selection, Stock
MC.6	INVCO: SLoc Anal. Selection: Rec/Iss
MC.7	INVCO: SLoc Anal. Selection,Turnover
MC.8	INVCO: SLoc Anal.Selection, Coverage

MC.9	INVCO: Material Anal.Selection,Stock
MC.A	INVCO: Mat.Anal.Selection, Rec/Iss
MC.B	INVCO: Mat.Anal.Selection, Turnover
MC.C	INVCO: Mat.Anal.Selection, Coverage
MC.D	INVCO: MRP Cntrllr.Anal.Sel. Stock
MC.E	INVCO: MRP Cntrllr Anal.Sel. Rec/Iss
MC.F	INVCO: MRP Cntlr Anal.Sel. Turnover
MC.G	INVCO: MRP Cntlr.Anal.Sel. Coverage
MC.H	INVCO: Business Area Anal.Sel. Stock
MC.I	INVCO: Bus. Area Anal. Sel. Rec/Iss
MC.J	INVCO: Bus. Area Anal. Sel. Turnover
MC.K	INVCO: Bus. Area Anal. Sel. Coverage
MC.L	INVCO: Mat.Group Analysis Sel. Stock
MC.M	INVCO: Mat.Group Anal. Sel. Rec/Iss
MC.N	INVCO: Mat.Group Anal. Sel. Turnover
MC.O	INVCO: Mat.Group Anal. Sel. Coverage
MC.P	INVCO: Division Analysis Sel. Stock
MC.Q	INVCO: Division Anal. Sel. Rec/Iss
MC.R	INVCO: Division Anal. Sel. Turnover
MC.S	INVCO: Division Anal. Sel. Coverage
MC.T	INVCO: Mat.Type Anal.Selection Stock
MC.U	INVCO: Mat.Type Anal.Sel. Rec/Issues
MC.V	INVCO: Mat.Type Anal.Sel. Turnover
MC.W	INVCO: Mat.Type Anal.Sel. Coverage
MC/1	Create Exception: EWS/INVCO
MC/2	Maintain exception: EWS/INVCO
MC/3	Display exception: EWS/INVCO
MC/4	Create groups exception: INVCO
MC/5	Change groups exception: INVCO
MC/6	Display exception: INVCO
MC/7	Create job for exception: INVCO
MC/8	Change jobs exceptions: INVCO
MC/9	Display jobs exceptions: INVCO
MC/B	Schedule jobs: Exceptions INVCO
MC/E	Create Exception: EWS/PURCHIS
MC/F	Maintain exception: EWS/PURCHIS
MC/G	Display exception: EWS/PURCHIS
MC/H	Create groups exception: PURCHIS
MC/I	Change groups exception: PURCHIS
MC/J	Display exception: PURCHIS
MC/K	Create job for exception: PURCHIS
MC/L	Change jobs exceptions: PURCHIS
MC/M	Display jobs exceptions: PURCHIS
MC/N	Schedule jobs exceptions: PURCHIS
MC/Q	Create exception: EWS/SIS
MC/R	Maintain exception: EWS/SIS
MC/S	Display exception: EWS/SIS
MC/T	Create groups exception: SIS
MC/U	Change groups exception: SIS
MC/V	Display exception: SIS
MC/W	Create job for exception: SIS
MC/X	Change Jobs: Exceptions SIS
MC/Y	Display Jobs: Exceptions SIS
MC/Z	Schedule Jobs: Exceptions SIS

MC00	Logistics Information System (LIS)
MC01	Key Figure Retrieval Via Info Sets
MC02	Key Fig.Retrieval Using Text Strings
MC03	Key Fig Retrieval via Classification
MC04	Create Info Set
MC05	Change Info Set
MC06	Display Info Set
MC07	Create Key Figure
MC08	Change Key Figure
MC09	Create Field Catalog
MC0A	Number Range Maintenance: Key Figs.
MC0C	Number Range Maintenance: Info Sets
MC1!	RIS: Maintain Requirements
MC1$	RIS: Display Formulas
MC1%	External Data: Maintain Requirements
MC1&	External Data: Display Requirements
MC1(	External Data: Display Formulas
MC1+	RIS: Display Requirements
MC1/	External Data: Maintain Formulas
MC10	Perform Analysis
MC11	Create Evaluation
MC12	Change Evaluation
MC13	Display Evaluation
MC14	TIS: Maintain requirements
MC15	TIS: Maintain formulas
MC16	LIS: Delete Evaluation Structure
MC18	Create Field Catalog
MC19	Change Field Catalog
MC1A	Maintain Formulas/Requirements
MC1AT	Maintain Formulas/Requirements
MC1B	SIS: Maintain Requirements
MC1BT	TIS: Maintain requirements
MC1C	SIS: Display Requirements
MC1CT	TIS: Display requirements
MC1D	SIS: Maintain Formulas
MC1DT	TIS: Maintain formulas
MC1E	SIS: Display Formulas
MC1ET	TIS: Display formulas
MC1F	PURCHIS: Maintain Requirements
MC1G	PURCHIS: Display Requirements
MC1H	PURCHIS: Maintain Formulas
MC1I	PURCHIS: Display Formulas
MC1J	SFIS: Maintain Requirements
MC1K	SFIS: Display Requirements
MC1L	SFIS: Maintain Formulas
MC1M	SFIS: Display Formulas
MC1N	INVCO: Maintain Requirements
MC1O	INVCO: Display Requirements
MC1P	INVCO: Maintain Formulas
MC1Q	INVCO: Display Formulas
MC1R	Display Formulas/Requirements
MC1S	QMIS: Maintain Requirements
MC1T	QMIS: Display Requirements
MC1U	QMIS: Maintain Formulas

SAP Transaction Codes – Volume One

MC1V	QMIS: Display Formulas
MC1W	PMIS: Maintain Requirements
MC1X	PMIS: Display Requirements
MC1Y	PMIS: Maintain Formulas
MC1Z	PMIS: Display Formulas
MC1§	RIS: Maintain Formulas
MC20	Display Field Catalog
MC21	Create Info Structure
MC22	Change Info Structure
MC23	Display Info Structure
MC24	Create Update
MC25	Change Update
MC26	Display Update
MC27	Create Evaluation Structure
MC28	Change Evaluation Structure
MC29	Display Evaluation Structure
MC30	Update Log
MC31	Create Planning
MC35	Create Rough-Cut Planning Profile
MC36	Change Rough-Cut Planning Profile
MC37	Display Rough-Cut Planning Profile
MC38	Number range maintenance: MC_ERKO
MC3V	U3 update
MC40	INVCO: ABC Analysis of Usage Values
MC41	INVCO: ABC Analysis of Reqmt Values
MC42	INVCO: Range of Coverage by Usg.Val.
MC43	INVCO: Range Of Coverage By Reqmts
MC44	INVCO:Analysis of Inventory Turnover
MC45	INVCO: Analysis of Usage Values
MC46	INVCO: Analysis of Slow-Moving Items
MC47	INVCO: Analysis of Reqmt Values
MC48	INVCO: Anal. of Current Stock Values
MC49	INVCO: Mean Stock Values
MC50	INVCO: Analysis of Dead Stock
MC59	Revise Planning Hierarchy
MC60	Maintain SOP Plant
MC61	Create Planning Hierarchy
MC62	Change Planning Hierarchy
MC63	Display Planning Hierarchy
MC64	Create Event
MC65	Change Event
MC66	Display Event
MC67	Init.graphics screen: genl.plg.hier.
MC6A	Sales and Operations Planning
MC6B	Sales and Operations Planning
MC70	Maintain Capacity Planning (SOP)
MC71	Evaluation: Product Group Hierarchy
MC72	Evaluation: Product Group Usage
MC73	Evaluation: Material Usage, Prod.Grp
MC74	Transfer Mat. to Demand Management
MC75	Transfer PG to Demand Management
MC76	Disaggregation: Planning
MC77	Disaggregation: Display Planning
MC78	Copy SOP Version

MC79	User Settings for SOP
MC7A	Plant Distribution
MC7B	Information Structure: Units
MC7C	Key Figure Parameters: Info Struct.
MC7D	Planning Parameters: LIS
MC7E	ALE Configuration for Info Structure
MC7F	Planning Parameters
MC7M	Methods maintenance
MC7N	Price Band Prices
MC7O	Characteristic Fields for Info Str.
MC7P	COPA Profile
MC7Q	Characteristic Assignment
MC7R	Key Figure(s) Assignment
MC80	Delete and activate versions
MC81	Sales and Operations Planning
MC82	Sales and Operations Planning
MC83	Sales and Operations Planning
MC84	Create Product Group
MC85	Display Product Group
MC86	Change Product Groups
MC87	Sales and Operations Planning
MC88	Sales and Operations Planning
MC89	Sales and Operations Planning
MC8A	Create Planning Type
MC8B	Change Planning Type
MC8C	Display Planning Type
MC8D	Mass Processing: Create Planning
MC8E	Mass Processing: Change Planning
MC8F	Delete Entry in Planning File
MC8G	Schedule Mass Processing
MC8H	Maintain User Methods
MC8I	Mass Processing: Check Planning
MC8J	Reprocess Mass Processing
MC8K	Copy/Delete Planning Versions
MC8L	Calculate Proportions: SOP
MC8M	Read Opening Stocks
MC8N	Delete forecast versions
MC8O	Reset Generation Time Stamp
MC8P	Standard SOP: Generate Master Data
MC8Q	Aggregate Copy
MC8R	RESET: Status for Planning Objects
MC8S	Transfer Profiles
MC8T	Activities
MC8U	Calculate Proportional Factors
MC8V	LIS Planning: Copy Versions
MC8W	LIS Planning: Delete Versions
MC8X	SOP: Distribution Scenario - Select
MC8Y	SOP: Distribution Scenario - Display
MC8Z	SOP => Key Figure Assignments
MC90	Tsfr.to Dm.Mgmt.: Mat.from any IS
MC91	Initial Graphic: Product Groups
MC92	Initial: Product Groups, Hierarchies
MC93	Create Flexible LIS Planning
MC94	Change Flexible LIS Planning

MC95	Display Flexible LIS Planning
MC96	Maintain Table 440P
MC97	Number Range Maintenance: MC_SAUF
MC98	Maintain Planning Objects
MC99	Display Planning Objects
MC9A	Flexible Planning: Gen. Master Data
MC9B	Calc. Proportions as in Pl.Hierarchy
MC9C	Reports for Flexible Planning
MC9D	Maintain Copy Profiles
MC9E	Info Structure: Add to General Char.
MC9F	Info Structure: Delete All Charact.
MC9K	Maintain Available Capacity
MC9M	Process IDOC Mapping
MC9V	Define MRP Elements in Key Figure
MC:1	Create exception: EWS/RIS
MC:2	Maintain exception: EWS/RIS
MC:3	Display exception: EWS/RIS
MC:4	Create exception group: RIS
MC:5	Change groups exception: RIS
MC:6	Display exception: RIS
MC:7	Create job for exception: RIS
MC:8	Change jobs exceptions: RIS
MC:9	Display jobs exceptions: RIS
MC:B	Schedule jobs exceptions: RIS
MC=1	Create exception: EWS/SFIS
MC=2	Maintain exception: EWS/SFIS
MC=3	Display exception: EWS/SFIS
MC=4	Create groups exception: SFIS
MC=5	Change groups exception: SFIS
MC=6	Display exception: SFIS
MC=7	Create job for exception: SFIS
MC=8	Change jobs exceptions: SFIS
MC=9	Display jobs exceptions: SFIS
MC=B	Schedule jobs exceptions: SFIS
MC=E	Create exception: EWS/PMIS
MC=F	Maintain exception: EWS/PMIS
MC=G	Display exception: EWS/PMIS
MC=H	Create groups exception: PMIS
MC=I	Change groups exception: PMIS
MC=J	Display exception: PMIS
MC=K	Create job for exception: PMIS
MC=L	Change jobs exceptions: PMIS
MC=M	Display jobs exceptions: PMIS
MC=N	Schedule jobs exceptions: PMIS
MC=Q	Display exception: EWS/QMIS
MC=R	Maintain exception: EWS/QMIS
MC=S	Display exception: EWS/QMIS
MC=T	Display groups exception: QMIS
MC=U	Change groups exception: QMIS
MC=V	Display exception: QMIS
MC=W	Create job for exception: QMIS
MC=X	Change Jobs: Exceptions QMIS
MC=Y	Display Jobs: Exceptions SIS
MC=Z	Schedule Jobs: Exceptions QMIS

MC?0	WFIS: Schedule Jobs - Exceptions
MC?1	WFIS: Create Exception
MC?2	WFIS: Maintain Exception
MC?3	WFIS: Display Exception
MC?4	WFIS: Create Exception Group
MC?5	WFIS: Change Exception Group
MC?6	WFIS: Display Exception Group
MC?7	WFIS: Create Jobs - Exceptions
MC?8	WFIS: Change Jobs - Exceptions
MC?9	WFIS: Display Jobs - Exceptions
MCA7	INVCO: Execute Evaluation
MCAA	WFIS: Maintain Requirements
MCAB	WFIS: Display Requirements
MCAC	WFIS: Maintain Formulas
MCAD	WFIS: Display Formulas
MCAE	WFIS: Activate Updating
MCAF	WFIS: Standard Analyses
MCAG	WFIS: Customizing, Standard Analyses
MCAH	WFIS: Organization View - Selection
MCAI	WFIS: Process View - Selection
MCAJ	WFIS: Object View - Selection
MCAK	WFIS: Group View - Selection
MCAL	WFIS: Sample Scenario - Selection
MCAM	WFIS: Append Structure
MCAN	WFIS: Selection Program
MCAO	WIS: Application PM/QM/SM Selection
MCAP	WIS: Delete Data
MCAQ	WIS: Correct Data
MCAR	WIS: Transfer Data
MCAT	WFIS: Display Evaluation Structure
MCAU	WFIS: Change Evaluation Structure
MCAV	WFIS: Create Evaluation Structure
MCAW	WFIS: Display Evaluation
MCAX	WFIS: Change Evaluation
MCAY	WFIS: Create Evaluation
MCAZ	WFIS: Execute Evaluation
MCB%	INVCO: Set up stats. for parm. anal.
MCB&	INVCO: Set up statis. for stck/reqt
MCB)	INVCO: Long-Term Stock Selection
MCB0	Maintaining Transactn Key BW Transf.
MCB1	Inventory Controlling
MCB2	INVCO: Create Evaluation Structure
MCB3	INVCO: Change Evaluation Structure
MCB4	INVCO: Display Evaluation Structure
MCB5	INVCO: Create Evaluation
MCB6	INVCO: Change Evaluation
MCB7	INVCO: Display Evaluation
MCBA	INVCO: Plant Analysis Selection
MCBC	INVCO: Stor. Loc. Analysis Selection
MCBE	INVCO: Material Analysis Selection
MCBG	INVCO: MRP Cntrlr Analysis Selection
MCBI	INVCO: Business Area Anal. Selection
MCBK	INVCO: MatGrp Analysis Selection
MCBM	INVCO: Division Analysis Selection

MCBO	INVCO: Mat.Type Analysis Selection
MCBR	INVCO: Batch Analysis Selection
MCBV	INVCO: Parameter Analysis Selection
MCBZ	INVCO: Stck/Reqt Analysis Selection
MCB_	Determine Industry Sector
MCC1	Inventory Controlling
MCC2	Inventory Information System
MCC3	Set Up INVCO Info Structs. from Docs
MCC4	Set Up INVCO Info Structs.from Stock
MCD	MI:Process Mobile Component
MCD7	PURCHIS: Create Eval. Structure
MCD8	PURCHIS: Change Eval. Structure
MCD9	PURCHIS: Display Eval. Structure
MCDA	PURCHIS: Create Evaluation
MCDB	PURCHIS: Change Evaluation
MCDC	PURCHIS: Display Evaluation
MCDG	PURCHIS: Execute Evaluation
MCE+	PURCHIS: Reporting - Subseq. Settlmt
MCE0	Purchasing Information System
MCE1	PURCHIS: PurchGrp Analysis Selection
MCE2	PURCHIS: Update Diagnosis Purch.Doc.
MCE3	PURCHIS: Vendor Analysis Selection
MCE5	PURCHIS: MatGrp Analysis Selection
MCE7	PURCHIS: Material Analysis Selection
MCE8	PURCHIS: Service Analysis Selection
MCE9	Purchasing Information System
MCEA	PURCHIS:Long-Term Plg Vend.Analysis
MCEB	PURCHIS:Lng-Term Plg Mat.Gr.Analysis
MCEC	PURCHIS:Long-Term Plg Mat. Analysis
MCER	PURCHIS: Service Purch.Qty-Selection
MCES	PURCHIS: Service Purch.Val-Selection
MCF9	PURCHIS: Quantity Grid - Maintain
MCFA	PURCHIS: Grid for Dates - Maintain
MCFB	PURCHIS: Display Pattern, QtyRel
MCFC	PURCHIS: Display Pattern On Schedule
MCG1	Rough-Cut Planning Profiles
MCG2	Var. standard anal. def. sett. IS-R
MCG3	Call Self-Defined Analyses: Retail
MCGC	RIS: Season: Mvmts + Stk - Selection
MCGD	RIS: POS: Sales - Selection
MCGE	RIS: POS: Matl Aggr. POS - Selection
MCGF	RIS: POS: Cashier - Selection
MCGG	RIS: Cust./Material Grp - Selection
MCGH	RIS: Customer/Material - Selection
MCGJ	RIS: POS: POS Balancing - Selection
MCGK	RIS: Matls w/ additionals- Selection
MCGL	RIS: Sales data: Customers- Sel.
MCH+	RIS: Display Evaluation Structure
MCH0	Retail Information System
MCH01	Mass Maintenance of Maint. Plans
MCH02	Log of Mass Changes
MCH03	Delete Variant
MCH1	RIS: Execute Evaluation
MCH2	RIS: Create Evaluation

MCH3	RIS: Change Evaluation
MCH4	RIS: Display Evaluation
MCH6	Update Maintenance: RIS
MCH7	RIS: Update Diagnosis, SP Change Doc
MCH8	RIS: Perishables - Selection
MCH9	RIS: Inventory Controlling - Stores
MCH:	RIS: STRPS/Mvmts + Stock - Selection
MCHA	RIS: Till Receipt/Matl - Selection
MCHB	RIS: Till Receipt - Selection
MCHC	Companion sales
MCHD	Maintain Dynamic IS Read Rules
MCHG	RIS: Purchasing: Mvmt+Stck-Selection
MCHP	RIS: Material: Mvmt+Stck - Selection
MCHS	RIS: Promotion - Selection
MCHV	RIS: Material/Add-On - Selection
MCHY	RIS: Create Evaluation Structure
MCHZ	RIS: Change Evaluation Structure
MCH_	Activate IS-R Enhancement for RIS
MCI0	Plant Maintenance Information System
MCI1	PMIS: Object Class Analysis
MCI2	PMIS: Manufacturer Analysis
MCI3	PMIS: Location Analysis
MCI4	PMIS: Planner Group Analysis
MCI5	PMIS: Object Damage Analysis
MCI6	PMIS: Obj.Statistic.Analysis
MCI7	PMIS: Breakdown Analysis
MCI8	PMIS: Cost Evaluation
MCIA	PMIS: Customer Notification Analysis
MCIS	Call Up PM Standard Analyses
MCIZ	PMIS: Vehicle Consumption Analysis
MCJ1	PMIS: Create Evaluation
MCJ2	PMIS: Change Evaluation
MCJ3	PMIS: Display Evaluation
MCJ4	PMIS: Execute Evaluation
MCJ5	PMIS: Create Evaluation Structure
MCJ6	PMIS: Change Evaluation Structure
MCJ7	PMIS: Display Evaluation Structure
MCJB	MTTR/MTBR for Equipment
MCJC	FunctLoc: Mean Time Between Repair
MCJE	PMIS: Info System
MCK0	Plant Maintenance Information System
MCK1	Create Hierarchy
MCK2	Change hierarchy
MCK3	Display hierarchy
MCK4	Change SAP OIW Hierarchy
MCK5	Display SAP OIW Hierarchy
MCK6	Create Customer OIW Hierarchy
MCK7	Change Customer OIW Hierarchy
MCK8	Display Customer OIW Hierarchy
MCK9	Maintain Customer OIW Info Catalog
MCKA	OIW Metadata
MCKB	TIS selection version tree
MCKC	User-spec. TIS select. version tree
MCKH	Selection version tree: Sales

MCKI	Selection version tree: Purchasing
MCKJ	Selection version tree: Stock
MCKK	Selection version tree: Production
MCKL	Selection version tree: Quality
MCKM	Selection version tree: Plant Maint.
MCKN	Selection version tree: Retail
MCKO	Selection version tree: General
MCKP	User-spec. selec. vers. tree: Sales
MCKQ	User-spec. sel. vers. tree: Purchase
MCKR	User-spec. sel. vers. tree: Stock
MCKS	User-spec. sel. vers. tree: Product.
MCKT	User-spec. sel. vers. tree: Quality
MCKU	User-spec. sel. vers. tree: PM
MCKV	User-spec. sel. vers. tree: Retail
MCKW	User-spec. sel. vers. tree: General
MCKY	WFIS: Selection Versions (User-Spec)
MCKZ	WFIS: Selection Versions (General)
MCL1	WMS: Stck Placemt.+Remov. Selection
MCL5	WMS: Flow of Quantities Selection
MCL9	WM: Material Plcmt/Removal:Selection
MCLD	WM: Material Flow - Selection
MCLH	WM: Movement Types - Selection
MCLIMAN	MultiClient Manager
MCM%	RIS: Create Selection Version
MCM+	WFIS: Create Selection Version
MCM-	WFIS: Change Selection Version
MCM/	WFIS: Display Selection Version
MCM0	INVCO: Change selection version
MCM1	SIS: Create selection version
MCM10	TIS: Create selection version
MCM11	TIS: Change selection version
MCM12	TIS: Display selection version
MCM13	TIS: Selection Version: Schedule Job
MCM2	SIS: Change selection version
MCM3	SIS: Display selection version
MCM4	SIS: Selec. version: Schedule job
MCM5	PURCHIS: Create selection version
MCM6	PURCHIS: Change selection version
MCM7	PURCHIS: Display selection version
MCM8	PURCHIS: SelectVers: Schedule job
MCM9	INVCO: Create selection version
MCM?	RIS: Schedule Selection Version
MCMA	INVCO: Display selection version
MCMB	INVCO: SelecVers: Schedule job
MCMC	PPIS: Create selection version
MCMD	PPIS: Change selection version
MCME	PPIS: Display selection version
MCMF	PPIS: SelectVers: Schedule job
MCMG	QMIS: Create selection version
MCMH	QMIS: Change selection version
MCMI	QMIS: Display selection version
MCMJ	QMIS: Selection Version:Schedule Job
MCMK	PMIS: Create selection version
MCML	PMIS: Change selection version

MCMM	PMIS: Display selection verison
MCMN	PMIS: SelectVers: Schedule job
MCMO	Create selection version
MCMP	Change selection version
MCMQ	Display selection version
MCMR	Selection Version: Create Variant
MCMS	Selection Version: Change Variant
MCMT	Selection Version: Display Variant
MCMV	Selection version: Schedule job
MCMX	RIS: Change Selection Version
MCMY	RIS: Display Selection Version
MCMZ	RIS: Selection Version: Schedule Job
MCNB	BW: Initialize Stock Balances
MCNR	Number Range Maintenance: MCLIS
MCO1	RIS: OTB - Selection
MCO2	OTB: Copy Planning Type
MCO4	Create OTB Planning
MCO5	Change OTB Planning
MCO6	Display OTB Planning
MCO7	Create OTB Planning
MCO8	Change OTB Planning
MCO9	Display OTB Planning
MCOA	QMIS: Cust. analysis, Lot overview
MCOB	QMIS: General Results for Customer
MCOC	QMIS: Cust. Analysis Quant. Overview
MCOD	QMIS: Quantitative Results for Cust.
MCOE	QMIS: Customer Analysis Q Score
MCOG	QMIS: Customer Analysis Lot Counter
MCOI	QMIS: Customer Analysis Quantities
MCOK	QMIS: Customer Analysis Expense
MCOM	QMIS: Customer Analysis Level/Disp.
MCOO	QMIS: Customer analysis - insp. lots
MCOP	QMIS: Cust. Analysis Item Q Not.
MCOV	QMIS: Cust. Anal. Overview Q Not.
MCOX	QMIS: Customer Analysis Defects
MCP0	Shop Floor Information System
MCP1	SFIS: Operation Analysis Selection
MCP3	SFIS: Material Analysis Selection
MCP5	SFIS: Material Analysis Selection
MCP6	Goods rcpt analysis: repetitive mfg
MCP7	SFIS: Work Center Analysis Selection
MCP8	Goods rcpt analysis: repetitive mfg
MCP9	SFIS: Select Run Schedule
MCPB	Operation analysis: Dates
MCPD	Production order analysis: Dates
MCPE_CUS	Commodity Pricing Customizing for MM
MCPE_DOC	Commodity Pricing in MM Documents
MCPE_FA_ACC_SEQ	Access Sequence for Formula Assembly
MCPE_FA_COND_TYPE	Condition Types for Formula Assembly
MCPE_FA_CT	Cond. Tables for Formula Assembly
MCPE_FA_DET_PROC	Det. Procedure for Formula Assembly
MCPE_FA_FC	MM Field Catalog
MCPE_FA_GCM	Formula Master Data Maintenance
MCPE_MD	Commodity Pricing Master Data for MM

MCPE_WB	CPE Formula Workbench for MM
MCPF	Material analysis: Dates
MCPH	Work center analysis: Dates
MCPI	Menu: Production Info System
MCPK	Operation analysis: Quantities
MCPM	Production order anal.: Quantities
MCPO	Material analysis: Quantities
MCPQ	Work center analysis: Quantities
MCPS	Operation analysis: Lead time
MCPU	Production Order Analysis: Lead Time
MCPW	Material analysis: Lead time
MCPY	Work center analysis: Lead time
MCQ.	SFIS: Kanban analysis selection
MCQA	Call Up QM Standard Analyses
MCR1	SFIS: Create Evaluation
MCR2	SFIS: Change Evaluation
MCR3	SFIS: Display Evaluation
MCR4	SFIS: Execute Evaluation
MCR7	SFIS: Create Evaluation Structure
MCR8	SFIS: Change Evaluation Structure
MCR9	SFIS: Display Evaluation Structure
MCR:	Std Analyses: User Settings, CALL
MCRA	LIS Layout Reports
MCRB	LIS: Generate Evaluations
MCRC	Charact. Texts for Eval. Structures
MCRE	Material Usage Analysis: Selection
MCRG	Change Settings: PPIS
MCRH	Display Settings: PPIS
MCRI	Product Cost Analysis: Selection
MCRJ	Prod. Cost Analysis: Repetitive Mfg
MCRK	Prod. Cost Analysis: Repetitive Mfg
MCRM	Reporting Point Stats.: Selection
MCRO	Matl consumptn anal.: repetitive mfg
MCRP	Matl consumptn anal.: repetitive mfg
MCRQ	Call Standard Analyses: PP-IS
MCRT	LIS Readings for Internal Numbers
MCRU	PP-PI: Operation Analysis Selection
MCRV	PP-PI: Process Order Analysis
MCRW	PP-PI: Resources Selection
MCRX	PP-PI: Material Usage Analysis
MCRY	PP-PI: Product Cost Analysis
MCS$	Info Structure Data: Process Archive
MCS%	Info Structure Data: Manage Archive
MCS&	Info Structure Data: Reload Archive
MCS/	Mass Generation: Info Struct./Update
MCS1	Standard Analyses; General Logistics
MCS2	Routine LIS Settings
MCS3	Routine SIS Settings
MCS4	Routine INVCO Settings
MCS5	Routine PURCHIS Settings
MCS6	Routine PPIS Settings
MCS7	SIS: Create Evaluation Structure
MCS8	SIS: Change Evaluation Structure
MCS9	SIS: Display Evalaution Structure

SAP Transaction Codes – Volume One

MCS=	Info Structure Data: Create Archive
MCSA	SIS: Create Evaluation
MCSB	SIS: Change Evaluation
MCSC	SIS: Display Evaluation
MCSCHECK	Check Utility - Logistic Infosystem
MCSD	Routine PMIS Settings
MCSE	Routine QMIS Settings
MCSF	Routine RIS Settings
MCSG	SIS: Execute Evaluation
MCSH	Call Std. Analyses of Customer Appl.
MCSI	Call Standard Analyses of Sales
MCSJ	Call Standard Analyses of Purchasing
MCSK	Call Standard Analyses of Stocks
MCSL	Call Shop Floor Standard Analyses
MCSM1	TIS: Create evaluation
MCSM2	TIS: Change evaluation
MCSM3	TIS: Display evaluation
MCSM4	TIS: Execute evaluation
MCSM5	TIS: Create evaluation structure
MCSM6	TIS: Change evaluation structure
MCSM7	TIS: Display evaluation structure
MCSO	Current Settings: TIS
MCSR	Standard Analyses External Data
MCSS	Display Log: Gen. Info Structure
MCST	Display Log: Gen. Updating
MCSV	Call View V_TMC6P_D
MCSW	Archiving of Selection Versions
MCSX	Archive Statistical Data
MCSY	Reset Time Stamp: LIS Generation
MCSZ	Convert LIS Statistical Data
MCT0	Initial SIS Screen
MCT1	Standard SDIS Analyses
MCT2	Initial SIS Screen
MCTA	SIS: Customer Analysis - Selection
MCTC	SIS: Material Analysis - Selection
MCTE	SIS: Sales Org. Analysis - Selection
MCTG	SIS: Sales Office Analysis Selection
MCTI	SIS: Sales Empl. Analysis Selection
MCTK	SIS: Shipping Pt. Analysis Selection
MCTV01	SIS: Sales Activity - Selection
MCTV02	SIS: Sales Promotions - Selection
MCTV03	SIS: Address List - Selection
MCTV04	SIS: Address Counter - Selection
MCTV05	SIS: Customer Potential Analysis
MCU0	Transportation Info System (TIS)
MCU1	Create LIS Unit
MCU2	Delete LIS Unit
MCU3	Call Standard Analyses: Transportatn
MCUA	TIS: Shpt analysis
MCUB	TIS: Shipment Analysis: Routes
MCUC	TIS: ShipmentAnaly: MeansOfTransport
MCUD	TIS: Shipment Analysis: Shipping
MCUE	TIS: Shipment Analysis: Stages
MCUF	TIS: Shipment Analysis: Material

MCV0	Purchasing Information System
MCV1	QMIS: Vendor analysis - insp. lot
MCV3	QMIS: Material analysis - insp. lot
MCV5	Call Up Price List w.Stepped Display
MCV6	Call Up Indiv. Customer Prices List
MCV7	Call Up List of Price Groups
MCV8	Call Up Material/MatPrcGroup List
MCV9	Call Up List of Incomplete Documents
MCVA	QMIS: Vendor Analysis Lot Overview
MCVB	QMIS: General Results for Vendor
MCVC	QMIS: Vendor Analysis - Qty Overview
MCVCHECK01	SIS: Update Group Check
MCVCHECK02	SIS: Header STAFO Check
MCVCHECK03	SIS: Item STAFO Check
MCVD	QMIS: Quant. Results for Vendor
MCVE	QMIS: Vendor Analysis Quality Score
MCVG	QMIS: Vendor Analysis - Lot Numbers
MCVI	QMIS: Vendor Analysis - Quantities
MCVK	QMIS: Vendor Analysis - Effort
MCVM	QMIS: Vendor Analyis - Level & Disp.
MCVO	Vendor Analysis - Lots Overview
MCVP	QMIS: vendor analysis items Q notif.
MCVQ	Quality Management Info System QMIS
MCVR	SIS: update diagnosis - order
MCVS	TIS: Update Diagnosis: Transportatn
MCVT	SIS: update diagnosis - delivery
MCVV	SIS: update diagnosis - billing doc.
MCVVK	SIS: Updating - Sales Activities
MCVW	INVCO: Update Diagnosis MatDoc
MCVX	QMIS: Vendor analysis defects
MCVY	INVCO: Update Diagnosis AcctngDoc
MCVZ	QMIS: Ven. Analysis- Q Not. Overview
MCW1	PURCHIS: Evaluate Payment Header
MCW2	PURCHIS: Evaluate Payment Item
MCW3	PURCHIS: Evaluate VBD Header
MCW4	PURCHIS: Evaluate VBD Item
MCW5	Payment: Simulate Updating
MCW6	LIS Setup for Agency Documents
MCWIS	FK Simulation Inventory Document
MCWRP	FK Simulation Invoice Document
MCW_AA	IMG Retail
MCW_AA_APP	Maintain Analytical Applications
MCW_AA_METH	Maint. Methods for Analytical Apps
MCW_AA_QUERY	Maint. Queries for Analytical Apps
MCW_AA_TEST	Test Remote Execution of Queries
MCX1	QMIS: Create Evaluation
MCX2	QMIS: Change Evaluation
MCX3	QMIS: Display Evaluation
MCX4	QMIS: Execute Evaluation
MCX7	QIS: Create Evaluation Structure
MCX8	QIS: Change Evaluation Structure
MCX9	QIS: display evaluation structure
MCXA	QMIS: Material Analysis-Lot Overview
MCXB	QMIS: General Results for Material

MCXC	QMIS: Matl Analysis - Qty Overview
MCXD	QMIS: Quant. Results for Material
MCXE	QMIS: Matl Analysis - Quality Score
MCXG	QMIS: Matl Analysis - Lot Numbers
MCXI	QMIS: Material Analysis - Quantities
MCXK	QMIS: Material Analysis - Effort
MCXM	QMIS: Matl Analysis - Level & Disp.
MCXP	QMIS: Matl. Analysis - Q Notif. Item
MCXV	QMIS: mat. analysis overview Q not.
MCXX	QMIS: Material analysis defects
MCY1	Create Exception EWS/LIS
MCY2	Maintain Exception EWS/LIS
MCY3	Display Exception (EWS/LIS)
MCY4	Create Group Exception
MCY5	Change Group Exception
MCY6	Display Exception
MCY7	Create Job For Exception
MCY8	Change Jobs: Exceptions
MCY9	Display Jobs: Exceptions
MCYA	Delete Jobs: Exceptions
MCYB	Plan Jobs: Exceptions
MCYG	Exception Analysis INVCO
MCYH	Exception Analysis: PURCHIS
MCYI	Exception Analysis: SIS
MCYJ	Exception Analysis: PP-IS
MCYK	Exception Analysis: PM-IS
MCYL	Exception Analysis: QM-IS
MCYM	Exception Analysis: Retail IS
MCYN	Exception Analysis: LIS-General
MCYO	Exception analysis: TIS
MCYO0	Schedule Jobs: Exceptions: TIS
MCYO1	Create Exception: EWS/TIS
MCYO2	Maintain Exception: EWS/TIS
MCYO3	Display Exception: EWS/TIS
MCYO4	Create Exception Group: TIS
MCYO5	Change Exception Group: TIS
MCYO6	Display Exception: TIS
MCYO7	Create Job for Exception: TIS
MCYO8	Change Jobs: Exceptions: TIS
MCYO9	Display jobs: Exceptions SIS
MCYY	WFIS: Exception Analysis
MCZ1	Create LIS Inbound Interface
MCZ2	Change LIS Inbound Interface
MCZ3	Display LIS Inbound Interface
MD00	MRP : external procurement
MD01	MRP Run
MD02	MRP - Single-item, Multi-level -
MD03	MRP-Individual Planning-Single Level
MD04	Display Stock/Requirements Situation
MD05	Individual Display Of MRP List
MD06	Collective Display Of MRP List
MD07	Current Material Overview
MD08	Reorg. MRP Lists
MD09	Pegging

MD11	Create Planned Order
MD12	Change Planned Order
MD13	Display Planned Order
MD14	Individual Conversion of Plnned Ord.
MD15	Collective Conversion Of Plnd Ordrs.
MD16	Collective Display of Planned Orders
MD17	Collective Requirements Display
MD19	Firm Planned Orders
MD20	Create Planning File Entry
MD21	Display Planning File Entry
MD25	Create Planning Calendar
MD26	Change Planning Calendar
MD27	Display Planning Calendar
MD40	MPS
MD41	MPS - Single-item, Multi-level -
MD42	MPS - Single-item, Single-level -
MD43	MPS - Single-item, Interactive -
MD44	MPS Evaluation
MD45	MRP List Evaluation
MD46	Eval. MRP lists of MRP controller
MD47	Product Group Planning Evaluation
MD48	Cross-Plant Evaluation
MD4C	Multilevel Order Report
MD50	Sales order planning
MD51	Individual project planning
MD61	Create Planned Indep. Requirements
MD62	Change Planned Indep. Requirements
MD63	Display Planned Indep. Requirements
MD64	Create Planned Indep.Requirements
MD65	Change Standard Indep.Requirements
MD66	Display Standard Indep.Requirements
MD67	Staggered Split
MD70	Copy Total Forecast
MD71	Copy Reference Changes
MD72	Evaluation; Charac.Plnng Techniques
MD73	Display Total Indep. Requirements
MD74	Reorganization: Adapt Indep.Reqmts
MD75	Reorganization: Delete Indep.Reqmts
MD76	Reorg: Delete Indep.Reqmts History
MD79	PP Demand Mngmt - XXL List Viewer
MD81	Create Customer Indep. Requirements
MD82	Change customer indep. requirement
MD83	Display Customer Indep. Requirements
MD85	List Customer Indep. Requirements
MD90	Maintain Number Range for MRP
MD91	Maintain No. Range for Planned Order
MD92	Maint.No.Range for Reserv/Dep.Reqmt
MD93	Maintain Number Range: MDSM
MD94	Number range maint.: Total reqs
MDAB	Planning File - Set Up BATCH
MDAC	Execute Action for Planned Order
MDBA	BAPI planned order processing
MDBS	MPS - total planning run
MDBT	MRP Run In Batch

MDC6	Start of MD06 via Report
MDC7	Start MD07 by using report
MDDISPONENT	MRP Controller Workflow
MDDO	Evaluation Report RoCs Online
MDDS	Evaluation Report Ranges of Coverage
MDEX	MRP Data Extractor
MDF_ATTRSET	Maintain Set Types and Attributes
MDHI	Master Data and Hierarchy
MDL1	Create Production Lot
MDL2	Change Production Lot
MDL3	Display Production Lot
MDLD	Print MRP List
MDLP	MPS
MDM1	Mail To Vendor
MDM2	Mail to Vendor
MDM3	Mail to Customer
MDM4	Mail to MRP Controller
MDM5	Workflow: Mail to MRP Controller
MDMC	Send Customers (MDM)
MDMGX	MDM Generic Extraction Framework
MDMGXC0	Transaction for MDMGXC0
MDMGXC1	Transaction for MDMGXC1
MDMGXC2	Transaction for MDMGXC2
MDMGXMOBJ	Maintain Object Types
MDML	Calculation of Multilevel Delay
MDMV	Send Vendors (MDM)
MDM_CLNT_EXTR	Local Extraction
MDM_FSBP_TEST	Tests MDM Scenarios for FSBP
MDP0	Independent Requirements
MDP1	Create combination structure
MDP2	Change combination structure
MDP3	Display combination structure
MDP4	Maintain combinations
MDP6	Modeling
MDPH	Planning Profile
MDPP	Demand Management
MDPV	Planning variant: Initial screen
MDRD1	Determine Delivery Relationship
MDRD2	Change Delivery Relationship
MDRD3	Display Delivery Relationship
MDRD4	Delete Delivery Relationship
MDRE	Checking Plnng File In BCKGRND Mode
MDRP	Distribution Resource Planning
MDSA	Display Serial Numbers
MDSP	Change BOM Explosion Numbers
MDS_COMPARE_TOOL	Compare Tool for Master Data Sync.
MDS_CONSISTENCY_TOOL	Consistency check Tool for MDS
MDS_LINKS	Get the Mapped Cust/Vend/BP
MDS_LOAD_COCKPIT	Synchronization Cockpit
MDS_PPO2	PPO for Master Data Synchronization
MDUM	Convert Planned Orders into PReqs
MDUP	Maintain Project New Key Assignment
MDUS	Assign New Key to WBS Elements
MDVP	Collective Availability Check PAUF

SAP Transaction Codes – Volume One

MDW1	Access MRP control program
MDXTEST	MDX Test Panel
ME00	
ME01	Maintain Source List
ME03	Display Source List
ME04	Changes to Source List
ME05	Generate Source List
ME06	Analyze Source List
ME07	Reorganize Source List
ME08	Send Source List
ME0M	Source List for Material
ME11	Create Purchasing Info Record
ME12	Change Purchasing Info Record
ME13	Display Purchasing Info Record
ME14	Changes to Purchasing Info Record
ME15	Flag Purch. Info Rec. for Deletion
ME16	Purchasing Info Recs. for Deletion
ME17	Archive Info Records
ME18	Send Purchasing Info Record
ME1A	Archived Purchasing Info Records
ME1B	Redetermine Info Record Price
ME1E	Quotation Price History
ME1L	Info Records per Vendor
ME1M	Info Records per Material
ME1P	Purchase Order Price History
ME1W	Info Records per Material Group
ME1X	Buyer's Negotiation Sheet for Vendor
ME1Y	Buyer's Negotiat. Sheet for Material
ME21	Create Purchase Order
ME21N	Create Purchase Order
ME22	Change Purchase Order
ME22N	Change Purchase Order
ME23	Display Purchase Order
ME23N	Display Purchase Order
ME24	Maintain Purchase Order Supplement
ME25	Create PO with Source Determination
ME26	Display PO Supplement (IR)
ME27	Create Stock Transport Order
ME28	Release Purchase Order
ME29N	Release purchase order
ME2A	Monitor Confirmations
ME2B	POs by Requirement Tracking Number
ME2C	Purchase Orders by Material Group
ME2COMP	Component Consumption History
ME2DP	Down-Payment Monitoring for PO
ME2J	Purchase Orders for Project
ME2K	Purch. Orders by Account Assignment
ME2L	Purchase Orders by Vendor
ME2M	Purchase Orders by Material
ME2N	Purchase Orders by PO Number
ME2O	SC Stock Monitoring (Vendor)
ME2ON	Subcontracting Cockpit
ME2S	Services per Purchase Order
ME2SCRAP	Scrap Analysis (Component Consump.)

ME2V	Goods Receipt Forecast
ME2W	Purchase Orders for Supplying Plant
ME308	Send Contracts with Conditions
ME31	Create Outline Agreement
ME31K	Create Contract
ME31L	Create Scheduling Agreement
ME32	Change Outline Agreement
ME32K	Change Contract
ME32L	Change Scheduling Agreement
ME33	Display Outline Agreement
ME33K	Display Contract
ME33L	Display Scheduling Agreement
ME34	Maintain Outl. Agreement Supplement
ME34K	Maintain Contract Supplement
ME34L	Maintain Sched. Agreement Supplement
ME35	Release Outline Agreement
ME35K	Release Contract
ME35L	Release Scheduling Agreement
ME36	Display Agreement Supplement (IR)
ME37	Create Transport Scheduling Agmt.
ME38	Maintain Sched. Agreement Schedule
ME39	Display Sched. Agmt. Schedule (TEST)
ME3A	Transm. Release Documentation Record
ME3B	Outl. Agreements per Requirement No.
ME3C	Outline Agreements by Material Group
ME3J	Outline Agreements per Project
ME3K	Outl. Agreements by Acct. Assignment
ME3L	Outline Agreements per Vendor
ME3M	Outline Agreements by Material
ME3N	Outline Agreements by Agreement No.
ME3P	Recalculate Contract Price
ME3R	Recalculate Sched. Agreement Price
ME3S	Service List for Contract
ME41	Create Request For Quotation
ME42	Change Request For Quotation
ME43	Display Request For Quotation
ME44	Maintain RFQ Supplement
ME45	Release RFQ
ME47	Create Quotation
ME48	Display Quotation
ME49	Price Comparison List
ME4B	RFQs by Requirement Tracking Number
ME4C	RFQs by Material Group
ME4L	RFQs by Vendor
ME4M	RFQs by Material
ME4N	RFQs by RFQ Number
ME4S	RFQs by Collective Number
ME51	Create Purchase Requisition
ME51N	Create Purchase Requisition
ME52	Change Purchase Requisition
ME52N	Change Purchase Requisition
ME52NB	Buyer Approval: Purchase Requisition
ME53	Display Purchase Requisition
ME53N	Display Purchase Requisition

ME54	Release Purchase Requisition
ME54N	Release Purchase Requisition
ME55	Collective Release of Purchase Reqs.
ME56	Assign Source to Purch. Requisition
ME57	Assign and Process Requisitions
ME58	Ordering: Assigned Requisitions
ME59	Automatic Generation of POs
ME59N	Automatic generation of POs
ME5A	Purchase Requisitions: List Display
ME5F	Release Reminder: Purch. Requisition
ME5J	Purchase Requisitions for Project
ME5K	Requisitions by Account Assignment
ME5R	Archived Purchase Requisitions
ME5W	Resubmission of Purch. Requisitions
ME60	Screenpainter Test
ME61	Maintain Vendor Evaluation
ME62	Display Vendor Evaluation
ME63	Evaluation of Automatic Subcriteria
ME64	Evaluation Comparison
ME65	Evaluation Lists
ME69	List non confirmed WEB releases
ME6A	Changes to Vendor Evaluation
ME6B	Display Vendor Evaln. for Material
ME6C	Vendors Without Evaluation
ME6D	Vendors Not Evaluated Since...
ME6E	Evaluation Records Without Weighting
ME6F	Print
ME6G	Vendor Evaluation in the Background
ME6H	Standard Analysis: Vendor Evaluation
ME6Z	Transport Vendor Evaluation Tables
ME80	Purchasing Reporting
ME80A	Purchasing Reporting: RFQs
ME80AN	General Analyses (A)
ME80F	Purchasing Reporting: POs
ME80FN	General Analyses (F)
ME80R	Purchasing Reporting: Outline Agmts.
ME80RN	General Analyses (L,K)
ME81	Analysis of Order Values
ME81N	Analysis of Order Values
ME82	Archived Purchasing Documents
ME83	Remove Scheduling Agreement Releases
ME84	Generation of Sched. Agmt. Releases
ME84A	Individual Display of SA Release
ME85	Renumber Schedule Lines
ME86	Aggregate Schedule Lines
ME87	Summarize PO History
ME88	Set Agr. Cum. Qty./Reconcil. Date
ME89	Release of Stopped SA Releases
ME91	Purchasing Docs.: Urging/Reminding
ME91A	Urge Submission of Quotations
ME91E	Sch. Agmt. Schedules: Urging/Remind.
ME91F	Purchase Orders: Urging/Reminders
ME92	Monitor Order Acknowledgment
ME92F	Monitor Order Acknowledgment

SAP Transaction Codes – Volume One

ME92K	Monitor Order Acknowledgment
ME92L	Monitor Order Acknowledgment
ME97	Archive Purchase Requisitions
ME98	Archive Purchasing Documents
ME99	Messages from Purchase Orders
ME9A	Message Output: RFQs
ME9E	Message Output: Sch. Agmt. Schedules
ME9F	Message Output: Purchase Orders
ME9K	Message Output: Contracts
ME9L	Message Output: Sched. Agreements
MEAN	Delivery Addresses
MEB0	Reversal of Settlement Runs
MEB1	Create Reb. Arrangs. (Subseq. Sett.)
MEB2	Change Reb. Arrangs. (Subseq. Sett.)
MEB3	Displ. Reb. Arrangs. (Subseq. Sett.)
MEB4	Settlement re Vendor Rebate Arrs.
MEB5	List of Vendor Rebate Arrangements
MEB6	Busn. Vol. Data, Vendor Rebate Arrs.
MEB7	Extend Vendor Rebate Arrangements
MEB8	Det. Statement, Vendor Rebate Arrs.
MEB9	Stat. Statement, Vendor Rebate Arrs.
MEBA	Comp. Suppl. BV, Vendor Rebate Arr.
MEBABW	Delta Init for BI-Extraction
MEBB	Check Open Docs., Vendor Reb. Arrs.
MEBC	Check Customizing: Subsequent Sett.
MEBE	Workflow Sett. re Vendor Reb. Arrs.
MEBF	Updating of External Busn. Volumes
MEBG	Chg. Curr. (Euro), Vend. Reb. Arrs.
MEBH	Generate Work Items (Man. Extension)
MEBI	Message, Subs.Settlem. - Settlem.Run
MEBJ	Recompile Income, Vendor Reb. Arrs.
MEBK	Message., Subs. Settlem.- Arrangment
MEBM	List of settlement runs for arrngmts
MEBOR	Work Center Conversion
MEBR	Archive Rebate Arrangements
MEBS	Stmnt. Sett. Docs., Vend. Reb. Arrs.
MEBT	Test Data: External Business Volumes
MEBV	Extend Rebate Arrangements (Dialog)
MECCM	Send Purchasing Data to Catalog
MECCP_ME2K	For Requisition Account Assignment
MEDL	Price Change: Contract
MEER	Mass Act: Create Electronic Bill
MEI1	Automatic Purchasing Document Change
MEI2	Automatic Document Change
MEI3	Recompilation of Document Index
MEI4	Compile Worklist for Document Index
MEI5	Delete Worklist for Document Index
MEI6	Delete purchasing document index
MEI7	Change sales prices in purch. orders
MEI8	Recomp. doc. index settlement req.
MEI9	Recomp. doc. index vendor bill. doc.
MEIA	New Structure Doc.Ind. Cust. Sett.
MEIS	Data Selection: Arrivals
MEK1	Create Conditions (Purchasing)

MEK2	Change Conditions (Purchasing)
MEK3	Display Conditions (Purchasing)
MEK31	Condition Maintenance: Change
MEK32	Condition Maintenance: Change
MEK33	Condition Maintenance: Change
MEK4	Create Conditions (Purchasing)
MEKA	Conditions: General Overview
MEKB	Conditions by Contract
MEKC	Conditions by Info Record
MEKD	Conditions for Material Group
MEKE	Conditions for Vendor
MEKF	Conditions for Material Type
MEKG	Conditions for Condition Group
MEKH	Market Price
MEKI	Conditions for Incoterms
MEKJ	Conditions for Invoicing Party
MEKK	Conditions for Vendor Sub-Range
MEKL	Price Change: Scheduling Agreements
MEKLE	Currency Change: Sched. Agreements
MEKP	Price Change: Info Records
MEKPE	Currency Change: Info Records
MEKR	Price Change: Contracts
MEKRE	Currency Change: Contracts
MEKX	Transport Condition Types Purchasing
MEKY	Trnsp. Calc. Schema: Mkt. Pr. (Pur.)
MEKZ	Trnsp. Calculation Schemas (Purch.)
MEL0	Service Entry Sheet
MELB	Purch. Transactions by Tracking No.
MEM1	Replacement for Purchase Order Item
MEMASSCONTRACT	Mass Changing of Contracts
MEMASSIN	Mass-Changing of Purch. Info Records
MEMASSPO	Mass Change of Purchase Orders
MEMASSRQ	Mass-Changing of Purch. Requisitions
MEMASSSA	Mass Changing of Sched. Agreements
MEMON_CUST	Activating monitoring for RC-monitor
MEMPADELIM	Maintain Delimiters for Message
MENU_MIGRATION	Menu Migration into New Hierarchy
MEPA	Order Price Simulation/Price Info
MEPB	Price Info/Vendor Negotiations
MEPO	Purchase Order
MEQ1	Maintain Quota Arrangement
MEQ3	Display Quota Arrangement
MEQ4	Changes to Quota Arrangement
MEQ6	Analyze Quota Arrangement
MEQ7	Reorganize Quota Arrangement
MEQ8	Monitor Quota Arrangements
MEQB	Revise Quota Arrangement
MEQM	Quota Arrangement for Material
MER4	Settlement re Customer Rebate Arrs.
MER5	List of Customer Rebate Arrangements
MER6	Busn. Vols., Cust. Reb. Arrangements
MER7	Extension of Cust. Reb. Arrangements
MER8	Det. Statement: Cust. Rebate Arrs.
MER9	Statement: Customer Reb. Arr. Stats.

SAP Transaction Codes – Volume One

MERA	Comp. Suppl. BV, Cust. Rebate Arrs.
MERB	Check re Open Docs. Cust. Reb. Arr.
MERE	Workflow: Sett. Cust. Rebate Arrs.
MEREP_BWAFDEL	delivery of BWAFMAPP entries
MEREP_DISP_DQ	display download data
MEREP_DISP_UQ	display upload data
MEREP_EMULATE	Calls the Report MEREP_EMULATOR
MEREP_EX_REPLIC	Execute Replicator
MEREP_GEN_ALL	Transaction to generate all
MEREP_LOG	Activity Log
MEREP_MBL	deletion of obsolete mobile ids
MEREP_MIG	Migration
MEREP_MON	Mobile Monitor
MEREP_PD	Profile Dialog
MEREP_PURGE	Purge Tool
MEREP_REPAIR	Repair critical tables in MI
MEREP_SBUILDER	SyncBO Builder
MERF	Updating of External Busn. Volumes
MERG	Change Curr. (Euro) Cust. Reb. Arrs.
MERH	Generate Work Items (Man. Extension)
MERJ	Recomp. of Income, Cust. Reb. Arrs.
MERS	Stmnt. Sett. Docs. Cust. Reb. Arrs.
METAL	Transaction Starter Purchasing
MEU0	Assign User to User Group
MEU2	Perform Busn. Volume Comp.: Rebate
MEU3	Display Busn. Volume Comp.: Rebate
MEU4	Display Busn. Volume Comp.: Rebate
MEU5	Display Busn. Volume Comp.: Rebate
MEW0	Procurement Transaction
MEW1	Create Requirement Request
MEW10	Service Entry in Web
MEW2	Status Display: Requirement Requests
MEW3	Collective Release of Purchase Reqs.
MEW5	Collective Release of Purchase Order
MEW6	Assign Purchase Orders WEB
MEW7	Release of Service Entry Sheets
MEW8	Release of Service Entry Sheet
MEWP	Web based PO
MEWS	Service Entry (Component)
ME_RTRACE	Client Trace Settings
ME_SWP_ALERT	Display MRP Alerts (Web)
ME_SWP_CO	Display Purchasing Pricing (Web)
ME_SWP_IV	Display Settlement Status (Web)
ME_SWP_PDI	Display Purchase Document Info (Web)
ME_SWP_PH	Display Purchasing History (Web)
ME_SWP_SRI	Display Schedule Releases (Web)
ME_WIZARD	ME: Registration and Generation
MF00	Run Schedules
MF02	Change Run Schedule Header
MF03	Display Run Schedule Header
MF12	Display Document Log (With ALV)
MF20	REM Cost Controlling
MF22	Versions: Overview
MF23	Linking Versions Graphically

MF26	Display Reporting Point Quantity
MF27	Update Stats for Planned Quantities
MF30	Create PrelimCostEst - ProdCostColl.
MF36	C RM-MAT MD Create Planning IDs
MF37	C RM-MAT MD Linking Versions
MF3A	Document Archiving
MF3D	Delete Archived Document
MF3E	Evaluate Archived Document
MF3M	Manage Archived Documents
MF3R	Reload Archived Document
MF41	Reverse Backflush (With ALV)
MF42	Collective Backflush
MF42N	New Collective Entry
MF45	Reprocessing Components: Rep.Manuf.
MF46	Collective Reprocessing, Backflush
MF47	Open Reprocessing Records / Pr.Line
MF4R	Resetting Reporting Points
MF50	Planning Table - Change
MF51	Print Production Quantities
MF52	Planning Table - Display
MF53	Maintaining Variants-Production List
MF57	Planning Table - By MRP Lists
MF60	Pull List
MF63	Staging Situation
MF65	Stock Transfer for Reservation
MF68	Log for Pull List
MF70	Aggregate Collective Backflush
MFBF	Backflushing In Repetitive Mfg
MFHU	Backflushing In Repetitive Mfg
MFI2	Actual Overhead: Run Schedule Header
MFN1	Actual Reval.: PrCstCol. Ind.Pro.
MFN2	Actual Reval.: PrCstCol. Col.Pro.
MFP1	REM: Plan HUs - General
MFP11	REM: Plan HUs Without Order
MFP12	REM: Plan HUs for Order
MFP13	Rep. Manuf.: Plan HUs for Delivery
MFP14	Rep. Man.: Plan HUs for Purch. Order
MFP2	REM: Pack HUs - General
MFP21	REM: Pack HUs Without Order
MFP22	REM: Pack HUs for Order
MFP23	Rep. Manuf.: Pack HUs for Delivery
MFP24	Rep. Man.: Pack HUs for Purch. Order
MFPP1	PackDemandMgt Repetitive Mfg: Plan
MFPP2	PackDemandMgt Repetitive Mfg: Pack
MFPR	Process Inspection Lot for Versions
MFS0	LFP: Change Master Plan
MGMT	Device Configuration
MGMT_ADMIN	Device Configuration
MGMT_AUTHORITY	Edit Authorizations
MGMT_CUSTOMIZING	Screen Control for Device Config.
MGMT_DEV_IDTXT	Assign Text to Device ID
MGMT_PARA	Assign Configuration Parameters
MGMT_PARA_COND	Parameter Conditions
MGMT_PARA_PATT	Set Device Configuration Parameters

SAP Transaction Codes – Volume One

MGMT_PARA_PROP	Get Parameter Properties
MGMT_SERVICE	Assign Agents to Monitoring Function
MGMT_TYPES	Device Configuration - Types
MGVEXTOBJ	Maintain Mass Maintenance Objects
MGV_CORRECT	Checks + Corrects Quantity Structure
MGV_MAPALE	Mapping externa/internal number ALE
MGV_OMSL	Maintain TMCNV for long material no.
MGW0	Create Components for Set Material
MGW1	Display Components for Set Material
MGW2	Create Components for Display Matl
MGW3	Display Components for Display Matl
MGW4	Create Components for Prepack Matl
MGW5	Display Components for Prepack Matl
MGW6	Create Components for Full Product
MGW7	Display Components for Full Product
MGW8	Change Components for Set Material
MGW9	Change Components for Display Matl
MGWA	Change Components for Prepack
MGWB	Change Components for Full Product
MI00	Physical Inventory
MI01	Create Physical Inventory Document
MI02	Change Physical Inventory Document
MI03	Display Physical Inventory Document
MI04	Enter Inventory Count with Document
MI05	Change Inventory Count
MI06	Display Inventory Count
MI07	Process List of Differences
MI08	Create List of Differences with Doc.
MI09	Enter Inventory Count w/o Document
MI10	Create List of Differences w/o Doc.
MI11	Recount Physical Inventory Document
MI12	Display changes
MI20	Print List of Differences
MI21	Print physical inventory document
MI22	Display Phys. Inv. Docs. f. Material
MI23	Disp. Phys. Inv. Data for Material
MI24	Physical Inventory List
MI31	Batch Input: Create Phys. Inv. Doc.
MI32	Batch Input: Block Material
MI33	Batch Input: Freeze Book Inv.Balance
MI34	Batch Input: Enter Count
MI35	Batch Input: Post Zero Stock Balance
MI37	Batch Input: Post Differences
MI38	Batch Input: Count and Differences
MI39	Batch Input: Document and Count
MI40	Batch Input: Doc., Count and Diff.
MI9A	Analyze archived phy. inv. docs
MIAD	Delete Phys. Inv. Documents
MIAL	Inventory Documents: Read Archive
MIAR	Archive Phys. Inv. Documents
MIAV	Manage Phys. Inv. Doc. Archive
MIBC	ABC Analysis for Cycle Counting
MICN	Btch Inpt:Ph.Inv.Docs.for Cycle Ctng
MIDO	Physical Inventory Overview

SAP Transaction Codes – Volume One

MIE1	Batch Input: Phys.Inv.Doc. Sales Ord
MIGO	Goods Movement
MIGO_GI	Goods Movement
MIGO_GO	Goods Movement
MIGO_GR	Goods Movement
MIGO_GS	Subseq. Adjust. of Material Provided
MIGO_TR	Transfer Posting
MIGR1	KW: Conversion of enh./rel. (global)
MIGR2	KW: Conver. of Enh/Rel/Origin (sel.)
MIGR_TEST	Test Menu for Migration
MIK1	Batch Input: Ph.Inv.Doc.Vendor Cons.
MILES	Infrastructure Navigator
MILL_00	IS Mill Products
MILL_CUT	Cutting Stck Trans. and Confirmation
MILL_CUT_CO	Cutting Confirmation
MILL_CUT_LBA	Confirmation DNP Processing
MILL_CUT_TR	Cutting Stock Transfer
MILL_OC	Create Order Combination
MILL_OMI4	MRP Lot-Sizing Procedures
MIM1	Batch Input: Create Ph.Inv.Docs RTP
MIMD	Tansfer PDC Physical Inventory Data
MINING_IBM	Communictn with Data Mining Software
MIO1	Batch Input: Ph.Inv.Doc.:Stck w.Subc
MIQ1	Batch Input: PhInvDoc. Project Stock
MIR4	Call MIRO - Change Status
MIR5	Display List of Invoice Documents
MIR6	Invoice Overview
MIR7	Park Invoice
MIRA	Fast Invoice Entry
MIRCMR	Material Reconciliation
MIRO	Enter Incoming Invoice
MIRO_WORKFLOW	Customizing for Log. IV: Workflow
MIRU_WORKFLOW_FREIG	Customizing for Log. IV: Workflow
MIRU_WORKFLOW_VERV	Customizing for Log. IV: Workflow
MIS1	Create Sample-Based Phys. Inv. - ERP
MIS2	Change Inventory Sampling
MIS3	Display Inventory Sampling
MIS4	Create Inventory Sampling - R/2
MIS5	Create Inventory Sampling - Other
MISS	Extract: Check Solution Paths
MIV1	Batch I.:PhInDoc f.Ret.Pack.at Cust.
MIW1	Batch I.;PhInDoc f. Consigt at Cust.
MI_ALBACK	Back Up CCMS Alerts for MI
MI_ALMON	Alert Monitor for MI Alerts
MI_CLOGMON	Client Log Analysis
MI_CONFIG_CLIENTS	Configuration of MI Client
MI_MCD	MI:Process Mobile Component
MI_MSD	MI:Process Mobile Component
MI_SYNEWS	MI SystemNews
MK01	Create vendor (Purchasing)
MK02	Change vendor (Purchasing)
MK03	Display vendor (Purchasing)
MK04	Change Vendor (Purchasing)
MK05	Block Vendor (Purchasing)

MK06	Mark vendor for deletion (purch.)
MK12	Change vendor (Purchasing), planned
MK14	Planned vendor change (Purchasing)
MK18	Activate planned vendor changes (Pu)
MK19	Display vendor (purchasing), future
MKH1	Maintain vendor hierarchy
MKH1N	Display/Maintain Vendor Hierarchy
MKH2	Display vendor hierarchy
MKH2N	Display Vendor Hierarchy
MKH3	Activate vendor master (online)
MKH4	Activate vendors (batch input)
MKK	Mass Contract Invoicing
MKOP	Call Up Material Master-Copier
MKVG	Settlement and Condition Groups
MKVZ	List of Vendors: Purchasing
MKVZE	Currency Change: Vendor Master Rec.
ML01	Create Standard Service Catalog
ML02	Maintain Standard Service Catalog
ML03	Display Standard Service Catalog
ML05	Purchasing Object for Service
ML10	Create Model Service Specifications
ML100	Calculate Taxes at Service Level
ML11	Change Model Service Specifications
ML12	Display Model Service Specifications
ML15	List of Model Service Specifications
ML20	Create Conditions
ML30	Create Vendor Conditions
ML31	Change Vendor Conditions
ML32	Display Vendor Conditions
ML33	Create Vendor Conditions
ML34	Change Vendor Conditions
ML35	Display Vendor Conditions
ML36	Create Vendor Conditions
ML37	Change Vendor Conditions
ML38	Display Vendor Conditions
ML39	Create Vendor Conditions
ML40	Change Vendor Conditions
ML41	Display Vendor Conditions
ML42	Create Service Conditions
ML43	Change Vendor Conditions
ML44	Display Vendor Conditions
ML45	Display Service Conditions
ML46	Change Service Conditions
ML47	Display Service Conditions
ML48	Create Conditions
ML49	Change Conditions
ML50	Display Conditions
ML51	Create Conditions
ML52	Change Conditions
ML53	Create Conditions
ML60CK	Release Procedure Checks
ML81	Maintain Service Entry Sheet
ML81N	Service Entry Sheet
ML82	Display Service Entry Sheet

ML83	Message Processing: Service Entry
ML84	List of Service Entry Sheets
ML85	Collective Release of Entry Sheets
ML86	Import Service Data
ML87	Export Service Data
ML89	Definition of Formulas
ML90	Field Selection for Services
ML91	Stand. Values f. Ext.Services Mgmt.
ML92	Entry Sheets for Service
ML93	Purchasing Object for Service
ML94	External Services Mgmt.: Direct Call
ML95	List Display: Contracts for Service
ML96	Purchase Requisitions for Service
ML97	Recompile Index
ML98	Std. EKORG Values f. Ext. Srv. Mgmt.
ML99	Formula Variable IDs
MLCCSPD	Cost Components for Price
MLRP	Periodic Invoicing Plans
MLS5	Import Standard Service Type
MLS6	Report for Standard Service Catalog
MLV1	Conditions: Services
MLV2	Create Total Price (PRS)
MLV3	Create Total Price (PRS)
MLV4	Create Total Price (PRS)
MLV5	Change Currency (Contracts)
MLV6	Create Other
MM00	
MM01	Create Material &
MM02	Change Material &
MM03	Display Material &
MM04	Display Material Change Documents
MM06	Flag Material for Deletion
MM11	Schedule Creation of Material &
MM12	Schedule Changing of Material &
MM13	Activate Planned Changes
MM14	Display Planned Changes
MM15	Display Changes (Migration)
MM16	Schedule Material for Deletion
MM17	Mass Maintenance: Indus. Matl Master
MM18	Activate Planned Changes
MM19	Display Material & at Key Date
MM41	Create Material &
MM42	Change Material &
MM43	Display Material &
MM44	Display Change Documents
MM46	Mass Maintenance: Retail Matl Master
MM50	List Extendable Materials
MM60	Materials List
MM70	Sel. Materials Flagged for Deletion
MM71	Reorganize Materials
MM72	Display Archive of Materials
MM73	Special Stocks: Preparation
MM74	Archive Special Stocks
MM75	Display Archive of Special Stocks

SAP Transaction Codes – Volume One

MM90	Analyze ALE Appl. Log for MatMaster
MM91	Delete ALE Appl. Log for Matl Master
MMAM	Change Material Type
MMB1	Create Semifinished Product &
MMBE	Stock Overview
MMBE_OLD	Stock Overview
MMCL	Stock Overview by Characteristic
MMD1	Create MRP Profile
MMD2	Change MRP Profile
MMD3	Display MRP Profile
MMD6	Delete MRP Profile
MMD7	Display MRP Profile Usage
MMDE	Delete All Materials
MMF1	Create Finished Product &
MMG1	Create Returnable Packaging &
MMH1	Create Trading Goods &
MMI1	Create Operating Supplies &
MMK1	Create Configurable Material &
MML1	Create Empties &
MMLS	Logistic Switch (Not Released)
MMM1	Create Message: Material Master
MMN1	Create Non-Stock Material &
MMNR	Define Material Master Number Ranges
MMP1	Create Maintenance Assembly &
MMPI	Initialize Period
MMPURPAME21N	Create Purchase Order from Portal
MMPURPAMEPO	Call MEPO from Portal
MMPURPAMEREQ	Call MEREQ from Portal
MMPURPAMIGO	Call MIGO from Portal
MMPURPAMIRO	Call MIRO from Portal
MMPURUICALLMD03	Wrapper for transaction MD03
MMPURUICALLME28	Wrapper for transaction ME28
MMPURUICALLME29N	Wrapper for transaction ME29N
MMPURUICALLME49	Wrapper for transaction ME49
MMPURUICALLME54N	Wrapper for transaction ME54N
MMPURUICALLME55	Wrapper for transaction ME55
MMPURUIME21N	Wrapper transaction for ME21N
MMPURUIML81N	Call ML81N
MMPURUIPRCREQ	Create PO from Requisition
MMPUR_ME41	RFQ Transaction
MMPV	Close Periods
MMR1	Create Raw Material &
MMRV	Allow Posting to Previous Period
MMS1	Create Service &
MMSC	Enter Storage Locations Collectively
MMSC_MASS	Maintain Storage Locations Coll.
MMSRVAC03	Display Service Master from Portal
MMSRVCRTSES	Create SES from Portal
MMSRVENTRY	Call transaction ML81N from Portal
MMSRVSES	Call SES from Portal
MMSRVSESINV	Call transaction MIRO from Portal
MMU1	Create Non-Valuated Material &
MMV1	Create Packaging &
MMVD	Change Decentr. for Decentr.Shipping

MMVH	Create Centrally: Decentral.Shipping
MMVV	Change Centr. for Decentr. Shipping
MMW1	Create Competitor Product &
MMZ1	Create Material, General (Old MM01)
MMZ2	Change Material (Old MM02)
MMZ3	Display Material (Old MM03)
MN01	Create Message: RFQ
MN02	Change Message: RFQ
MN03	Display Message: RFQ
MN04	Create Message: PO
MN05	Change Message: PO
MN06	Display Message: PO
MN07	Create Message: Outline Agreement
MN08	Change Message: Outline Agreement
MN09	Display Message: Outline Agreement
MN10	Create Message: Schd. Agmt. Schedule
MN11	Change Message: Schd. Agmt. Schedule
MN12	Displ. Message: Schd. Agmt. Schedule
MN13	Create Message: Service Entry Sheet
MN14	Change Message: Service Entry Sheet
MN15	Display Message: Service Entry Sheet
MN21	Create Condition: Inventory Mgmt
MN22	Change Condition: Inventory Mgmt
MN23	Display Condition: Inventory Mgmt
MN24	Create Message: Shipping Notif.
MN25	Change Message: Shipping Notif.
MN26	Display Message: Shipping Notif.
MN27	Create message: rough goods receipt
MN28	Change message: rough goods receipt
MN29	Display message: rough goods receipt
MNKR	Number range maintenance: W_EREIGNIS
MNTB	Table Maintenance for PSO48
MNTF	Table Maintenance for PSO49
MOALL	Delete Agent Allocation
MOKA	CAP: Calculation Restitution
MOKS	CAP: Calculation Simulation
MP00	Material Forecast Menu
MP01	Maintain AMPL Records
MP02	Display AMPL Records
MP11	Create message for direct production
MP12	Change Message for direct production
MP13	Display message - direct production
MP30	Execute Material Forecast
MP31	Change Material Forecast
MP32	Display Material Forecast
MP33	Reprocess material forecast
MP38	Total Forecast Run
MP39	Print
MP80	Create Forecast Profile
MP81	Change Forecast Profile
MP82	Delete Forecast Profile
MP83	Display Forecast Profile
MP90	Maintain No. Range: Forecast Param.
MP91	Maintain No. Range: Forecast Values

MPACONTACT   MPA with MEREP_CONTACT (sample app.)
MPAD   Delete archived materials from AMPL
MPAMSGTEMPL   Maintain Message Template
MPAR   Archive final issue materials
MPAV   Manage archive for maufacturer parts
MPA_REPLY_CUST   MPA Reply Handling
MPBT   Total Forecast In BATCH Mode
MPD   Maintenance Program Definition
MPDR   Print in BATCH Mode
MPD_MAP   MPD: Data Mapping
MPE1   Create buyer
MPE2   Change buyer
MPE3   Display buyer
MPLT   Test Appl. for Interface to iPPE WB
MPN01   MPN Conversion Reconcilation
MPND   Field Synchronization, Interch.Parts
MPN_V_V2   MPN and SuS Rescheduling
MPOCCMONALERT   Write Extracts for CC Monitor
MPOCCPOSALERT   Write Extracts for Line Items
MPOILVALERT   Write Extracts for IAA Monitor
MPOORDALERT   Write Extracts for ORDMonitor
MPOORDPOSALERT   Extracts of Critical Line Items ORD
MPO_ADMIN   Administration of Rule Maintenance
MPO_APPREQ   Services for Request Types
MPO_CCMONITOR_F4   Start F4
MPO_CCMONITOR_RRIF   Start Report/Report Interface
MPO_CCMON_DOC_CALL   Call Doc. Display for CCtr Monitor
MPO_ILV   Rule Maintenance for IAA Monitor
MPO_LINE   Rule: Unusual Postings - Orders
MPO_MON   Rule Maintenance for CCtr Monitor
MPO_ORD   Rule Maintenance for Order Monitor
MPO_PERS_DATA_DELETE   Delete User's Personalization Data
MPO_PERS_FILL_CC   Fill for Personalization, Cost Ctrs
MPO_PERS_FILL_PC   Fill for Personalization,Profit Ctrs
MPO_POS   Rule Maint. for Unusual Postings
MPR1   Forecast Adopted from External Data
MPR2   Deletion of Forecast Data
MPSD_CA_CE_001   Maintain table for grouping reason
MR00   Invoice Verification
MR01   Process Incoming Invoice
MR02   Process Blocked Invoices
MR03   Display Inv. Verification Document
MR08   Cancel Invoice Document
MR11   GR/IR account maintenance
MR11SHOW   Account Maint.Docu.Display-Reversal
MR11_OLD   Old GR/IR account maintenance
MR21   Price Change
MR22   Material Debit/Credit
MR32   Change Material Layer (LIFO)
MR33   Display Material Layer (LIFO)
MR34   Change FIFO Data
MR35   Display FIFO Data
MR39   Display Documents (LIFO)
MR41   Park Invoice

MR42	Change Parked Invoice
MR43	Display Parked Invoice
MR44	Post Parked Document
MR51	Material Line Items
MR8M	Cancel Invoice Document
MR90	Messages for Invoice Documents
MR91	Messages for Invoice Documents
MRA1	Archive Invoice Documents
MRA2	Delete Archived Invoice Documents
MRA3	Display Archived Invoice Documents
MRA4	Manage Invoice Document Archive
MRBE	Valuation
MRBP	Invoice Verification in Background
MRBR	Release Blocked Invoices
MRBWNEU	Recompilation
MRCHVW	Batch mgmt with reconciliation
MRDC	Automatic Delivery Cost Settlement
MRER	Auto. ERS Automotive
MRF1	Execute FIFO Valuation
MRF2	Diplay Documents (FIFO)
MRF3	FIFO Valuation: Create Doc. Extract
MRF4	FIFO: Select Materials
MRF5	FIFO: Delete Valuation Data
MRHG	Enter Credit Memo
MRHR	Enter Invoice
MRIS	Settle Invoicing Plan
MRKO	Settle Consignment/Pipeline Liabs.
MRL1	Perform LIFO Valuation: Single Matl
MRL2	Perform LIFO Valuation: Pools
MRL3	LIFO Lowest Value Comparison
MRL4	Display LIFO Valuation: Single Matl
MRL5	Display LIFO Valuation: Pools
MRL6	Select Materials
MRL7	Display Pool Formation
MRL8	Create Base Layer
MRL9	LIFO Valuation: Create Doc. Extract
MRLA	Check Pool Formation
MRLB	Delete Layer
MRLC	Transfer Third-Party Data
MRLD	Transfer Valuation Prices
MRLE	Change Group Structure
MRLF	Create Version as Copy
MRLG	Aggregate Layer
MRLH	Change LIFO/FIFO Valuation Level
MRLI	Generate Pools
MRLJ	LIFO Data Transfer
MRLK	LIFO: Adjust Units of Measure
MRLL	LIFO: Reassign Material Layer
MRM0	Logistics Invoice Verification
MRM1	Create Message: Invoice Verification
MRM2	Change Message: Invoice Verification
MRM3	Display Message: Inv. Verification
MRM4	Number Ranges, Invoice Verification
MRN0	Deter. Lowest Value: Market Prices

MRN1	Deter. Lowest Value: Rge of Coverage
MRN1_TS	Determine Lowest Value: Rge of Cov.
MRN2	Determ. Lowest Value: Mvmt Rate
MRN3	Loss-Free Valuation
MRN8	Lowest Value: Price Variances
MRN9	Balance Sheet Values by Account
MRNB	Revaluation
MRO2	Configuration: IV Lists
MRRL	Evaluated Receipt Settlement
MRRS	Evaluated Receipt Settlement
MRTRSC01	RMS-MRTRS : RFC Destination of GR
MRTRSC02	RMS-MRTRS : Master Recipe Generation
MRTRS_START	RMS-MRTRS : Start MR Transformation
MRY0	Coll. Maint. of Phys. Inv. Prices
MRY1	Calculate Average Receipt Price
MRY2	Transfer Physical Inventory Prices
MRY3	Display Valuation Alternative
MRY4	Transfer ML Prices
MRY_SCMA	Execute via Schedule Manager
MRY_SCMO	Analyze via Schedule Manager
MRY_SLG1	Analyze Application Log
MR_BEWART	Material Reconciliation
MR_FORM	Reconciliation: Formula
MR_PARAM	Reconciliation: Formula Parameter
MS00	Long-term planning
MS01	Long-Term Planning: Total Planning
MS02	Long-term plng: single-itm, mult-lvl
MS03	Long-term plng: singl-itm, singl-lvl
MS04	Planning Scenario: Stock/Reqmts List
MS05	Long-term planning: display MRP list
MS06	Long-term plnng: collective MRP list
MS07	Long-Term Plng: Material Overview
MS08	Reorg.MRP Lists for Long-Term Plnng
MS11	LTP: Create planned order
MS12	LTP: Change planned order
MS13	LTP: Display planned order
MS20	Planning File Entry: Long-Term Plnng
MS21	Planning File Entry: Long-Term Plnng
MS22	Set Up Plg File Entries for Scenario
MS23	Delete Plng File Entries of Scenario
MS29	Calculate Sim. Initial Stock
MS31	Create planning scenario
MS32	Change planning scenario
MS33	Display planning scenario
MS44	Flexible Evaluation Long-Term Plnng
MS47	Evaluation LTP for Product Group
MS50	Make-to-order planning (LTP)
MS51	Project planning (LTP)
MS64	Create Simulation Version
MS65	Requirements Situation
MS66	Copy Simulative Dependent Reqmts
MS70	Evaluation Plng Scenario for PURCHIS
MS71	Copy info structure version to LTP
MSAB	LTP: set up plnng file entries BATCH

SAP Transaction Codes – Volume One

MSAC	LTP: delete plnng file entries BATCH
MSBT	Long-term plng:plng background job
MSC1	Create Batch
MSC1N	Create Batch
MSC2	Change Batch
MSC2N	Change Batch
MSC3	Display Batch
MSC3N	Display Batch
MSC4	Display Batch Changes
MSC4N	Display Change Documents for Batch
MSC5N	Mass Processing for Batches
MSC6	Start of MS06 via Report
MSC6N	Batch Worklist
MSC7	Start MS07 from Report
MSCUST	Maintain Due Date Scenarios
MSDO	LTP Evaluation Report RoC Online
MSDS	LTP Evaluation Report Coverages
MSE7	EKS Simulation: Material Selection
MSEX	LTP Data Extractor
MSG_TEST	Test Message
MSINA	Maintain Backlog Entry in Extract
MSJ1	Mass Maintenance in the Background
MSK1	Create Vendor Consignment Goods
MSK2	Change Vendor Consignment Goods
MSK3	Display Vendor Consignment Goods
MSK4	Display Vdr Consignment Change Docs
MSK5	Vdr Consignment: Activate Fut. Price
MSL1	Display Mass Maintenance Logs
MSL2	Delete Mass Maintenance Logs
MSLD	Print MRP List; Long-Term Planning
MSRV1	List for Service
MSRV2	Service List for Requisition
MSRV3	Service List for Purchase Order
MSRV4	Service List for RFQ
MSRV5	Service List for Contract
MSRV6	Service List for Entry Sheet
MSR_CRD	RRD for Customer Returns
MSR_INSPV	Enter Material Insp. from Vendors
MSR_INSPWH	Enter Material Insp. in Warehouse
MSR_INSP_DISPLAY	Display Inspection Results
MSR_IRD	RRD for Internal Returns
MSR_PLNCHK	Approval check related plants
MSR_RETURNS_REASON	MSR: Returns Reason Codes
MSR_RETURNS_REFUND	MSR: Returns Refund Codes
MSR_RO_PROPOSAL	MSR: PROPOSAL VALUES
MSR_RRCDEF_CRD	MSR: View for Returns Refund Code
MSR_RRCDEF_IRD	MSR: View for Returns Refund Code
MSR_SELECT	MSR: Maintain Selection Criteria
MSR_SNUM	Maintain the number range for MSR_ID
MSR_TRC_C	Tracking of Customer Returns
MSR_TRC_I	Tracking of Supplier Returns
MSR_TVAK_CMR	MSR: TVAK Credit Memo Request
MSR_TVAK_RO	MSR: TVAK Returns Order
MSR_TVLK	Def. Billing Type for IC Returns

SAP Transaction Codes – Volume One

MSR_UGROUP	Assign User to User Group
MST0	Mass changes
MSTRVAR	Transport Variants
MSTRVAR_S	Transport System Variants
MSW1	Reset Warnings (in the Foreground)
MSW2	Reset Warnings (in the Background)
MTBEC1	Customizing
MUSS	_
MVD_CUST	Cutosmizing: Material Versions LS1A
MWB1	Creating Prop./Prod. Unit Valuation
MWB2	Changing Prop./Prod. Unit Valuation
MWB3	Displaying Prop/Prod Unit Valuation
MWBC	Consistency Chck f. Prop./Prod. Unit
MWBE	Purchase order history corr. PUR
MWBK	Actv. ingr. management corr. factor
MWBQ	Purchase order history corr. QM
MWCH	Change Procurement IAC
MY01	C MM-PUR Matchcode Purchasing Doc.
MY03	C MM-PUR Matchcode Purchasing Doc.
MY04	C MM-PUR Matchcode Purchasing Doc.
MY05	C MM-PUR Matchcode Purchasing Doc.
MY06	C MM-PUR Matchcode Purchasing Doc.
MY07	C MM-PUR Matchcode Purchasing Doc.
MY08	C MM-PUR Matchcode Purchasing Doc.
MY09	C MM-PUR Matchcode Purchasing Doc.
MY10	C MM-PUR Matchcode Purchasing Doc.
MY11	C MM-PUR Matchcode Purchasing Doc.
MY12	C MM-PUR Matchcode Purchasing Doc.
MY13	C MM-PUR Matchcode Purchasing Doc.
MYB3	Bus. Volume Comparison Type Purchas.
MYB4	Bus.Vol. Tolerance Group Purchasing
MYB5	User Settings, Subsequent Settlement
M_LA	Purchasing: Condition List
M_LB	Change Condition List
M_LC	Display Condition List
M_LD	Execute Condition List
N10B	IS-H*MED: Maintain work station org.
N10C	IS-H*MED: Maint. asnmt WrkCntr-TMkr
N10D	IS-H*MED: Maint. plan.object classes
N10E	IS-H*MED: Maint. svc-based resources
N10F	IS-H*MED: Displ. svc-based resources
N10G	IS-H*MED: Display table N1NURSHIFT
N10H	IS-H*MED: Maintain table N1NURSHIFT
N10I	IS-H*MED: Maintain roll assignment
N10J	IS-H*MED: Maintain OR-service split
N10K	IS-H*MED: Display proc. instructions
N10L	IS-H*MED: Maintain proc.instructions
N10M	IS-H*MED: Maintain transfer times
N10N	IS-H*MED: Display transfer times
N10O	IS-H: Maintain Symbols for WP IDs
N10V	IS-H: Display Work Env-to-User Asgmt
N10W	IS-H: Maintain Work Env-to-User Asgt
N1A0	IS-H*MED: Create position/task
N1A1	IS-H*MED: Change position/task

N1A2	IS-H*MED: Display position/task
N1A3	IS-H*MED: Create collective entry
N1A4	IS-H*MED: Change collective entry
N1A5	IS-H*MED: Display collective entry
N1A6	IS-H*MED: Maintain employees inv.
N1A7	IS-H*MED: Display employees inv.
N1AA	IS-H*MED: Service Details
N1AB	IS-H*MED: Service Details
N1AC	IS-H*MED: Change service code
N1AD	IS-H*MED: Display service code
N1AE	IS-H*MED: Create Request Category
N1AEN	IS-H*MED: Create Request Category
N1AF	IS-H*MED: Change Request Category
N1AFN	IS-H*MED: Change Request Category
N1AG	IS-H*MED: Display Request Category
N1AGN	IS-H*MED: Display Request Category
N1AT	IS-H*MED: No.range req. categories
N1AU	IS-H*MED: Request Overview
N1B0	IS-H*MED: Create Visit Sequence
N1B1	IS-H*MED: Change org.assignment
N1B2	IS-H*MED: Display org.assignment
N1B4	IS-H*MED: Create task qualification
N1B5	IS-H*MED: Change task qualification
N1B6	IS-H*MED: Display task qualification
N1B7	IS-H*MED: Maintain nurs.profile
N1B8	IS-H*MED: Display nurs.profile
N1BA	IS-H*MED: Create service request
N1BB	IS-H*MED: Change service request
N1BC	IS-H*MED: Display service request
N1BE	IS-H*MED: Enter requests received
N1C0	IS-H*MED: Create employee position
N1C1	IS-H*MED: Change employee position
N1C2	IS-H*MED: Display employee position
N1C4	IS-H*MED: Maintain mat. consumption
N1C5	IS-H*MED: Display mat. consumption
N1COMPCON	IS-H: Maintain Component Configurat.
N1CORD	IS-H: Create Clinical Order
N1COT	IS-H: Set Up Clinical Order Types
N1CT	IS-H: Define Context Types
N1CUSTIDS	IS-H*MED: Customer-Spec. Class Types
N1D1	IS-H*MED: Maint.printer f.each inst.
N1D2	IS-H*MED: Dsply.printer f.each inst.
N1DEFVT	Prereg.Type Definition - Master Data
N1DI	IS-H*MED: Pat.Transport - Dispatcher
N1E0	IS-H*MED: Create nursing cycle
N1E1	IS-H*MED: Change nursing cycle
N1E2	IS-H*MED: Display nursing cycle
N1E3	IS-H*MED: Cycle Prioritization
N1E4	IS-H*MED: Cycle Prioritization
N1EC	IS-H*Med: Extra services
N1EXTENDTEXTEDITOR	Activate Long Text Editor for CORD
N1G1	IS-H*MED: Menu Service facility mgmt
N1GENPROC	IS-H*MED: Generate Procedures
N1GS	IS-H*MED: Menu care unit mgmt

SAP Transaction Codes – Volume One

N1IS1	IS-H*MED: Internet Service
N1K1	IS-H*MED: Maintain quota planning
N1K2	IS-H*MED: Display quota planning
N1K3	IS-H*MED: Display OUs involved
N1K4	IS-H*MED: Maintain OUs involved
N1K7	IS-H*MED: Display day sched/svc.quot
N1K8	IS-H*MED: Display day sched/svc.quot
N1KA	IS-H*MED: Medical Record Management
N1KH	IS-H*MED: hsptl structure
N1L1	IS-H*MED: Task by position
N1L2	IS-H*MED: Qualifications by task
N1L3	IS-H*MED: List task by service
N1L4	IS-H*MED: Qualifications by person
N1L5	IS-H*MED: List employee position
N1L6	IS-H*MED: Requestable org. unit
N1L7	IS-H*MED: Service range list
N1L8	IS-H*MED: Qualif.-task-employee
N1LA	IS-H*MED: Material proposal
N1LP	IS-H*MED: Nursing Worklist
N1LU	IS-H*MED: Worklist
N1LU01	IS-H*MED: Standard Worklist
N1LU02	IS-H*MED: Worklist Variant Selection
N1LUT1	IS-H*MED: Worklist w/o init. scrn.
N1LUT2	IS-H*MED: Worklist w/ Initial Screen
N1LUV1	IS-H*MED: Worklist w/o In.Scrn
N1LUV2	IS-H*MED: Work list w/ init. screen
N1M0	IS-H*MED: Maintain subseq.srvc entry
N1M1	IS-H*MED: Display subseq.srvc entry
N1M2	IS-H*MED: Maintain subseq.srvc entry
N1M3	IS-H*MED: Maintain subseq.srvc entry
N1MA	IS-H*MED: Maintain Material Asgnmnt.
N1MATV	IS-H*MED: Maintain mat. consumption
N1ME	Medication Evaluations
N1MEAM	IS-H*MED: Maintain Agents
N1MEAM1	IS-H*MED: Maintain All Agents
N1MEDSRV	IS-H*MED: Med. Service Entry
N1MEFLS	Scrap Posting f. Care Unit Store
N1MEFM	Maintain Formulary
N1MEPI	IS-H*MED: Fill List - Pick List
N1ME_AHEVT	i.s.h.med: Create Ad Hoc Event
N1ME_CO	i.s.h.med: Create Medication Order
N1ME_ESTAT	IS-H*MED: Maintain Table TN1ESTATUS
N1ME_EVT_END	i.s.h.med: End Events
N1ME_EVT_GEN	i.s.h.med: Event Generation
N1ME_IMP_AGENT	Import External Agent Catalog
N1ME_IMP_BDCC	Import External Drug Catalog
N1ME_LTYP	IS-H*MED: Maintain Table TN1LINTYP
N1ME_MELOC	IS-H*MED: Maintain Table TN1MELOC
N1ME_N1TPOU	Template / Group - OU Assignment
N1ME_N1TPUSER	Assign Template/Group to User
N1ME_N1TPUSER_ALL	Assign Template/Group to User
N1ME_OPRI	IS-H*MED: Maintain Table N1MEOPRI
N1ME_OSTAT	IS-H*MED: Maintain Table TN1OSTATUS
N1ME_OTYPE	IS-H*MED: Maintain Table TN1OTYPE

N1ME_TMPL	IS-H*MED:Medication; Create Template
N1ME_TPDIA	Templates - Diagnoses Assignment
N1ME_UNIT	IS-H*MED: Maintain Table TN1MEUNIT
N1ML	IS-H*MED: Medical unit list
N1MO	IS-H*MED Basic Data: Surgery System
N1MP	IS-H*MED: Nursing
N1MS	IS-H*MED: Basic data srvc processing
N1MZ	IS-H*MED: Display Material Assignmnt
N1N1	IS-H: Display scoring table NASCO
N1N2	IS-H: Maintain scoring table NASCO
N1NK	IS-H*MED: Number Ranges
N1OT	IS-H: Define Object Types
N1P0	IS-H*MED: Maintain service entry
N1P1	IS-H*MED: Display service entry
N1P2	IS-H*MED: Maintain service entry
N1P3	IS-H*MED: Display service entry
N1P4	IS-H*MED: Specify treatment:Maintain
N1P5	IS-H*MED: Specify treatment:Display
N1P6	IS-H*MED: Create req. profile
N1P7	IS-H*MED: Change req. profile
N1P8	IS-H*MED: Display req. profile
N1PA	IS-H*MED: Display Nrs.Pln.Prfl.Asnmt
N1PATORG	IS-H*MED: Call Patient Organizer
N1PC	IS-H: File transfers PC - SAP
N1PDNK	Number Range Interval Births
N1PE	IS-H: File Transfer PC --> R3
N1PF	IS-H*MED: Call nursing plan
N1PG	IS-H*MED: OR Schedule
N1PH	IS-H*MED: Patient History
N1PK	IS-H*MED: Worklist f. Nursing Svcs.
N1PM	PERINAT: Perinatal monitor
N1PN	IS-H*MED: OR Planning List
N1PP	IS-H*MED: Nurs.ac.evaluat.
N1PR	IS-H*MED: Maint. Nrs.Pln.Prfl.Asnmt
N1RADCLEANUP	Delete Contents of Radiolog. Table
N1RB	IS-H*MED: Evaluation of visits
N1RK	IS-H*MED: Patient Transport Service
N1RL	IS-H*MED: Service management
N1RS	IS-H*MED: Basic medical data
N1S1	IS-H*MED: Display task
N1S2	IS-H*MED: Maintain task
N1S3	IS-H*MED: Display position
N1S4	IS-H*MED: Maintain position
N1S5	IS-H*MED: Display qualifications
N1S6	IS-H*MED: Maintain qualifications
N1S7	IS-H*MED: Display srvc facility type
N1S8	IS-H*MED: Maintain srvc facil. type
N1S9	IS-H*MED: Display srvc grouping type
N1SA	IS-H*MED: Maintain srvc.gr.types
N1SB	IS-H*MED: Display service status
N1SC	IS-H*MED: Maintain service status
N1SD	IS-H*MED: Display srvc task asgnmt
N1SE	IS-H*MED: Maintain srvc task asgnmt
N1SF	IS-H*MED: Display cancel. reasons

N1SG	IS-H*MED: Maintain cancel. reasons
N1SH	IS-H*MED: Display request status
N1SI	IS-H*MED: Maintain request status
N1SJ	IS-H*MED: Display request priority
N1SK	IS-H*MED: Maintain request priority
N1SL	IS-H*MED: Display Req. Type Usage
N1SM	IS-H*MED: Maintain Req. Type Usage
N1SN	IS-H*MED: Display transport types
N1SO	IS-H*MED: Maintain transport types
N1SP	IS-H*MED: Display OU-rel.Customizing
N1SQ	IS-H*MED: Maint. OU-Rel. Customizing
N1SR	IS-H*MED: Display date interpretat'n
N1SS	IS-H*MED: Maint. date interpretat'n
N1ST	IS-H*MED: Display deg. of infection
N1SU	IS-H*MED: Maint. deg. of infection
N1SV	IS-H*MED: Display med.ext.srvc.cat
N1SW	IS-H*MED: Maintain med.ext.srvc.cat
N1SX	IS-H*MED: Maintain planned beds
N1TB	IS-H*MED: Table-Utility INT.USE ONLY
N1TR	IS-H*MED: Transport List
N1TX	IS-H*MED: Messages for Closed OU
N1TX1	IS-H*MED: Messages for Closed OU
N1US	IS-H*MED: Update Desktop Components
N1VE	IS-H: Set Up Preregistration Types
N1VK	IS-H*MED: Preregistration List
N1VL	Insur.Verification/Extension Request
N1VM	IS-H*MED Pre-registration list
N1VPP1	IS-H*MED: Display Vital Parameters
N1VPP2	IS-H*MED: Maintain Vital Parameters
N1VPPF41	IS-H*MED: Vital Parameters Inp. Help
N1VPPF42	IS-H*MED: Maint. Vital Par. Inp.Help
N1VPPOEZ1	IS-H*MED: Display Vit. Par. OU Asmnt
N1VPPOEZ2	IS-H*MED: Maint.Vital Par. OU-Assnmt
N1W1	IS-H*MED: Task-rel.employeeSrvcList
N1W2	IS-H*MED: Diagnosis-rel.srvc.eval
N1W3	IS-H*MED: List Srvc.-patient-employ.
N1W4	IS-H*MED: Patient-rel.srvc.list
N1WA	IS-H*MED: Waiting list info. funct.
N1WL	IS-H*MED: Follow-up visit list
N1WR	IS-H*MED: Waiting List
N1WSCONFIG	Configure Web Service
N201	IS-H*MED: Create Document
N202	IS-H*MED: Change Document
N203	IS-H*MED: Display document
N204	IS-H*MED: Documents List
N205	IS-H*MED: Maint. diagn. code control
N206	IS-H*MED: Display diagn.code control
N207	IS-H*MED: Create OU Diag. Hit List
N208	IS-H*MED: Maintain OU diagn.hit list
N209	IS-H*MED: Display OU diagn. hit list
N210	IS-H*MED: Display diagnosis groups
N211	IS-H*MED: Maintain diagnosis groups
N212	IS-H*MED: Display class. areas asgmt
N213	IS-H*MED: Maintain class.areas asgmt

N214	IS-H*MED: Displ. nurStd-basCat.asgmt
N215	IS-H*MED: Maint. nurStd-basCat.asgmt
N216	IS-H*MED: Displ. nurStd-serCat.asgmt
N217	IS-H*MED: Maint. nurStd-serCat.asgmt
N218	IS-H*MED: Displ.nurStd-classAr.asgmt
N219	IS-H*MED: Maint.nurStd-classAr.asgmt
N220	IS-H*MED: Displ.basCat-classAr.asgmt
N221	IS-H*MED: Maint.basCat-classAr.asgmt
N222	IS-H*MED: Maint. diagnos. doc./case
N223	IS-H*MED: Displ. diagn. doc./case
N224	IS-H*MED:Displ.serCat-class.ar.asgmt
N225	IS-H*MED: Maint.serCat-classAr.asgmt
N2AN	Number Range Ext. Data References
N2APPLOG	IS-H*MED: Application Logging
N2ASPECT_DEF	Definition of Aspects
N2AZ	IS-H*MED: Maint. task - time asgmt
N2BA	IS-H*MED: Assign empl.authoriz.cat.
N2BASEITEM	Base Item Editor
N2BN	IS-H*MED: WCA Number Range Interval
N2CATC	Process Categories
N2CA_NR	i.s.h.med: Cardiology Number Range
N2COMHIST	Transfer History
N2COMIBX	Document Inbox
N2COMLOG	Communication Log for Admin.
N2COM_DOCIN_WS	Release Web Svce for Doc. Confim.
N2COM_DOCOUT_LP	Create Logic Port for Doc. Dispatch
N2COM_DOCRESPIN_WS	Release Webservice for Doc. Dispatch
N2COM_DOCRESPOUT_LP	Logical Port for Confirm. Dispatch
N2DOKTRANS	DocCat definition transport client
N2DS_SAPFTP_CUST	Customizing for SAPFTP Cardiology
N2DU	IS-H*MED: Load and unload docdefs
N2E0	IS-H*MED: Create docCat-SvcItem asgt
N2E1	IS-H*MED: Change docCat-SvcItem asgt
N2E2	IS-H*MED:Display docCat-SvcItem asgt
N2E3	IS-H*MED: Create docCateg.- OU asgmt
N2E4	IS-H*MED: Change docCateg.- OU asgmt
N2E5	IS-H*MED: Display docCategy-OU asgmt
N2E6	Maintain OU-Related Document Profile
N2E7	Display OU-Related Document Profile
N2E8	Maintain Svce-Related Doc. Profile
N2E9	Display Svce-Related Doc. Profile
N2F4	IS-H*MED: Extern. data module maint.
N2FD	PMD: EDM Maintenance (General)
N2FN	Number Range Ext. Data References
N2G1	IS-H*MED: Menu Service facility mgmt
N2GA	Assign Pathway
N2GB	Pathway Library
N2GD	Treatment Pathway Definition
N2GL	Layout Processing Pathways
N2GL_CAT	Edit Categories
N2GM	Pathway Monitor
N2GR	pathways Evaluations
N2GU	Patient Pathway
N2HIT	Maintain Findings Hit List

SAP Transaction Codes – Volume One

N2KA	PMD: Combobox Catalogs Maintenance
N2KO	IS-H*MED: Maint. complications
N2KZ	IS-H*MED: Maint. compl.-compl. asgmt
N2L1	IS-H*MED: OU diagnoses hit list
N2LINKDEF	Definition of Link Module
N2LIZENZ	IS-H*MED: License Management
N2MD	IS-H*MED: Basic data: medical d
N2ON	IS-H*MED: Number range OR
N2OT	IS-H*MED: Maintain OR Departments
N2OW	ISH-MED DWS: Outpat Clin. Wk Stat.
N2OX	Start OR document
N2OZ	IS-H*MED: Surgery times
N2PC	IS-H*MED: admin. docum. templates
N2PRZ	IS-H*MED: Maintain Procedure HitList
N2PRZ_BASIS	IS-H*MED: SPC Hit List - Global
N2RO	IS-H*MED: Surgery System
N2RP	IS-H*MED: Nursing
N2RR	IS-H*MED: Radiologie Evaluations
N2RS	IS-H*MED: Med.basic data/documentat.
N2RW	Findings Work Station
N2S0	IS-H*MED: Create Document Element
N2S1	IS-H*MED: Change document element
N2S2	IS-H*MED: Display document element
N2SW	X-Ray Rounds
N2T5	IS-H*MED: Copy Document Category
N2T6	IS-H*MED: Create document category
N2T7	IS-H*MED: Change document category
N2T8	IS-H*MED: Display document category
N2T9	IS-H*MED: Copy Definite Design
N2TBS	Management of Text Modules
N2TL	IS-H*MED: Param. doc. tool box
N2TOOL	PMD Toolbox (New, Unreleased)
N2UX	Application Server Utility
N2VD00	Progress Entries Number Range
N2WLD	Template Management
N2ZO	Time definition
N2ZP	Time definition
N2_COM_SCHEMA_DOWNL	XML Profile Download for Doc Disp.
N2_F4_SIMPLETREE_ADM	Manage Simple Tree Maintenance
N2_FORUM	i.s.h.med Forum
NA01	IS-H: Create Billing Statistics
NA02	IS-H: Print Invoice(s)
NA03	IS-H: Cancel Invoice(s)
NA04	IS-H: Post invoices with calc.block
NA05	IS-H: Invoice List
NA07	IS-H: Bill.status of dischrged cases
NA08	IS-H: Billing Statistics by IP Types
NA10	IS-H: Revenue Accrual
NA12	IS-H: Invoice statistics by payer
NA17	IS-H: Adjust services to absence
NA18	IS-H: Revenue Accrual
NA20	IS-H: Create CASE Selection Billing
NA21	IS-H: Delete CASE Selection Billing
NA22	IS-H: Display CASE Selection Billing

NA23	IS-H: Edit Billing Document Msgs
NA24	IS-H: Copy Case Selection
NA25	IS-H: Billing selection via visits
NA26	IS-H: Inpatient Test Billing
NA30	IS-H: Case Billing
NA30N	IS-H: Case Billing
NA30OLD	IS-H: Case Billing - Old
NA31	IS-H: Change Billing Block Inpat.
NA32	IS-H: Change Billing Block Outpat.
NA33	IS-H: Cascade Bill Processing
NA35	IS-H: Billing Information Case
NA40	IS-H: Case-Related Invoice Overview
NA45	IS-H: Case monitor billing
NA46	IS-H: Compensation check BPflV '95
NA47	IS-H: Propose charges
NA48	Compare Charges
NA52	IS-H: Subsequent billing
NA55	IS-H: Process outpatient flat rates
NA60	IS-H: Export data for IFA billing
NA65	IS-H: Log transfer IFA billing
NA66	IS-H: IFA status info transf. cases
NA70	ÎS-H SG: Estimated Bill
NA90	IS-H: Create Invoice Selection
NA91	IS-H: Change Bill Selection
NA92	IS-H: Create Collective Invoice
NA93	IS-H: Print Collective Invoice
NA94	IS-H: Collective Invoice
NA95	IS-H: Provisional Invoice
NACE	WFMC: Initial Customizing Screen
NACO	Conditions for Output Control
NACP	WFMC: Define Conditions
NACQ	WFMC: Maintain Condition Tables
NACR	WFMC: Maintain Output Condition Rec.
NACS	WFMC: Assign Output Type Access Seq.
NACT	WFMC: Maintain Condition Types
NACU	WFMC: Customizing Output Types
NACV	WFMC: Partner Definition
NACW	WFMC: Maintain Processing Program
NACX	WFMC: Access Sequences
NACY	WFMC: Field Catalog
NACZ	WFMC: Procedure
NAPRKEY	Print Parameters for Output
NAS1	IS-H SG: Create Inpat. Bill
NAVCT685B	Output Types (Cluster)
NAVP_MANAGE	Manage Navigation Profiles
NAWF	Start Customizing Control Flow
NB20	IS-H: Create Organizational Unit
NB21	IS-H: Change Organizational Unit
NB22	IS-H: Display Organizational Unit
NB23	IS-H: Maintain Org. Unit Hierarchy
NB24	IS-H: Display Org. Unit Hierarchy
NB25	IS-H: Maintain Interd. B.Assgmt. OU
NB26	IS-H: Display Interd. B.Assgmt. OU.
NB27	IS-H: Maintain Statistical Beds

NB28	IS-H: Display Statistical Beds
NB29	IS-H: Collective Entry Build. Unit
NB30	IS-H: Maintain Building Units
NB31	IS-H: Change Building Units
NB32	IS-H: Display Building Units
NB33	IS-H: Maintain Bld. Unit Hierarchy
NB34	IS-H: Display Bld. Unit Hierarchy
NB35	IS-H: Maintain Bld. Unit / OU
NB36	IS-H: Display Bld. Unit /OU
NB37	IS-H: Maintain pl. charac. bld. unit
NB38	IS-H: Display Pl.Charac. Bld. Unit
NB39	IS-H: Maintain Equipment Bld. Unit
NB40	IS-H: Display Equipment Bld. Unit
NB41	IS-H: Maintain Door Coordinates
NB42	IS-H: Display Door Coordinates
NB43	IS-H: Release Build. Structure
NB44	IS-H: Set up BU identifier
NB45	IS-H: Maintain Plan. Chars Single BU
NB46	IS-H: Display Plan, Chars Single BU
NB51	IS-H: Delete Org. Structure
NB52	IS-H: Set up OU identifiers
NB53	IS-H: Release Org. Structure
NBU1	IS-H: Maint. Fixed Vals User Master
NC10	IS-H Create Message Type Copy
NC11	IS-HCM Change Message Type
NC12	IS-HCM Display Message Type
NC20	IS-H Create Message Segment Copy
NC21	IS-HCM Change Message Segment
NC22	IS-HCM Display Message Segment
NC301KK	Create §301 Message for Hlth Insurer
NCEDI	IS-H: EDI Workbench
NCH1	IS-HCO CH: Create Case-Based Orders
NCO1	IS-H: Transfer service to CCenter
NCO2	HCO: Create Case-Based Orders
NCO3	HCO: Assign Preliminary Costing
NCO4	HCO: Status Monitoring Case-Bsd Ord.
NCO7	HCO: Case-Based Order Classification
NCO8	IS-H: Stat. key figure (nursing)
NCO9	IS-H: Stat. Key Figures (Dept.)
NCOA	IS-H: Asgmt org.unit to cost centers
NCOB	IS-H: Asgmt services to act. types
NCOC	IS-H: Revenue accrual billing
NCOD	IS-H: Stat.ratio-CO stat.ratio asgmt
NCOE	IS-H: Assign Svce to Base ObjCosting
NCOF	IS-H: Settings
NCOG	IS-H: Supported characteristics
NCOH	IS-H: Order characteristics
NCOI	IS-H: Org.unit-CCtr asgmt f.rev.acct
NCOJ	IS-H: Stat. key figures (inter-dept)
NCOK	IS-HCO: Services to be Transferred
NCOL	IS-HCO: Transfer Information
NCOM	IS-H: Copy NOEK into NO2K
NCON	HCO: Stat. Key Figs (Case-Bsd Ord.)
NCOO	IS-H: Stat. Key Figs (Case-bsd ord.)

NCOP	IS-HCO: Maintain Cost Centers-OU
NCOQ	HCO: Stat. Key Figures (Coll.Order)
NCOR	HCO: Copy Collective Orders
NCOS	HCO: Determine Collective Orders
NCO_COLORD	HCO: Define Collective Orders
NCW3	IS-H: EDI Workbench
ND01	IS-H: Create medical record/document
ND02	IS-H: Maintain record/document list
ND03	IS-H: Display record/document list
ND04	IS-H: Collect.entry of returned rec.
ND05	IS-H: Return medical record/document
ND06	IS-H: Create Med. Record Reminder
ND07	IS-H: Request med. record/documents
ND08	IS-H: Borrow single rec./document
ND09	IS-H: Create record via mvmnt list
ND10	IS-H: Borrow record via mvmnt list
ND11	IS-H: Return Temp. Medical Records
ND12	IS-H: Borrow requested med. record
ND13	IS-H: Collect.Entry for Borrowed Rec
ND14	IS-H: Transfer Med.Rcrds via BorrLst
ND15	IS-H: Transfer single rec./document
ND18	IS-H: Evaluate Med. Record Archive
NDRPAT	IS-H: Bus. Partner-Patient Rlnshp
NDV1	Maintain Version Interfaces
NDV2	Maintain System Releases
NDYM	IS-H: Screen Modification
NE10	IS-H: Display Copayment
NE11	IS-H: Maintain Copayment
NE15	IS-H: Transfer Copayment
NE16	IS-H: Write off Copayment Requests
NE17	IS-H: Generate copayment
NE18	IS-H: Post copayment back
NE20	IS-H: Maintain Down Payment
NE21	IS-H: Display Down Payment
NE22	IS-H: Down Payment Overview
NE23	IS-H: Down Payment Monitor
NEDI	EDI Workbench
NEDIIN	IS-H EDI Inbound Worklist
NEDIOUT	IS-H EDI Outbound Worklist
NEDIW	EDI Worklist
NEDIWORK	IS-H EDI Worklist
NEFE	Statistical Setup: SFIS / Versions
NEO01	IS-H: Create External Order
NEO02	IS-H: Maintain External Order
NEO03	IS-H: Display External Order
NEO04	IS-H: Ext.Order- Create Order Placer
NEO05	IS-H: Ext.Order- Change Order Placer
NEO06	IS-H: Ext.Order-Display Order Placer
NEOAB	IS-H: External Order - Billing
NEODR	IS-H: External Order - Mass Print
NEOST	IS-H: Ext.Order - Cancel Billing Doc
NEWTON	Mathematical Tests
NEW_SERP	Report Tree Maintenance
NG01	IS-H: Create General Bus. Partner

NG02	IS-H: Change General Bus. Partner
NG03	IS-H: Display General Bus. Partner
NG04	IS-H: Create Bus. Partner Employee
NG05	IS-H: Change Bus. Partner Employee
NG06	IS-H: Display Bus. Partner Employee
NG07	IS-H: Create B.Partner Ins. Provider
NG08	IS-H: Change B.Partner Ins. Provider
NG09	IS-H: Display B.Partner Ins.Provider
NG10	IS-H: Create Bus. Partner Customer
NG11	IS-H: Change Bus. Partner Customer
NG12	IS-H: Display Bus. Partner Customer
NG13	IS-H: Create Bus. Partner Employer
NG14	IS-H: Change Bus. Partner Employer
NG15	IS-H: Display Bus. Partner Employer
NG16	IS-H: Create Bus. Partner Hospital
NG17	IS-H: Change Bus. Partner Hospital
NG18	IS-H: Display Bus. Partner Hospital
NG30	IS-H: Create Bus.Partner RP Employee
NG40	IS-H: Maintain Ins. Prov. Types
NG41	IS-H: Display Guarantor Types
NGLM	Customizing and Performance Monitor
NGM0	
NIAPPS	IS-H: Visit Scheduling at Web - Demo
NK01	IS-H: Maintain IV request (coll.ent)
NK02	IS-H: Display IV request (coll.ent.)
NK06	IS-H: Maintain IV Confm.(Coll.Entry)
NK19	IS-H: Print request for IV - outpt.
NK20	IS-H: Print Insurance Verif. request
NK21	IS-H: Dun Insurance Verification
NK22	IS-H: Generate outpatient ins.verif.
NK23	IS-H: Generate IV f. inpatients
NK24	IS-H: Monitoring of IV Requests
NK25	IS-H: Monitoring Insurance Verifictn
NK26	IS-H: Extend request for ins.verif.
NK30	IS-H: Maintain Pre-Approved Ins.
NK31	IS-H: Display Pre-Appr.IV Confmtn.
NK35	IS-H: Maintain IV Default Values
NK36	IS-H: Display IV Default Values
NK50	IS-H: Create IV declaration (AT)
NK51	IS-H: Change IV declaration (AT)
NK52	IS-H: Display IV declaration (AT)
NKM0	IS-H: Menu Catalogs
NKRS	IS-H: Number Ranges
NKVWS1	IS-H: Change PPA Work Station
NKVWS2	IS-H: Display PPA Work Station
NL01N	IS-H: Service Entry for all Cases
NL04N	IS-H: Service Entry - OU-Related
NL10	IS-H: Maintain Service Entry
NL10N	IS-H: Case-Related Service Entry
NL11	IS-H: Display service entry
NL11N	IS-H: Case-Related Service Display
NL20	IS-H: Maintain prelim. service entry
NL21	IS-H: Display prelim. service entry
NL22	IS-H: Maintain Prelim. Entry by OU

NL23	IS-H: Display Prilim. Entry by OU
NL28	IS-H: Transfer Svces from PE by OU
NL29	IS-H: Transfer srvs from prel. entry
NM00	
NM01	
NM02	
NM07	
NM10	
NM20	
NM30	IS-H: HCO Int.controlling area menu
NM40	IS-H Communication
NM44	IS-H: Communication Menu
NMA0	
NMCO1	IS-H MM: Transfer Matl. Consumption
NMCO2	IS-H MM: Data Transfer Matl.Consumpt
NMCOL	IS-H MM: List Material Consumptions
NMG1	IS-H*MED: Menu Service facility mgmt
NMM0	Material Requisition
NMM1	IS-H: Create Material Req. by OU
NMM2	IS-H: Maintain OU-Rel. Material Req.
NMM3	IS-H: Display Material Req. by OU
NMM4	IS-H: Collective Proc. Material Req.
NMM5	IS-H: Create Case-Rel. Material Req.
NMM6	IS-H: Display Case-Rltd Mat. Requis.
NMM7	IS-H: Maintain Case-Rel. Goods Issue
NMM8	IS-H: Display Case-Rltd Goods Issue
NMM9	IS-H: Pick List
NMMC1	IS-H MM: Maintain Matl Consumption
NMMC2	IS-H MM: Display Matl Consumption
NMMD	IS-H*MED: Basic data: medical d
NMMO	IS-H*MED Basic Data: Surgery System
NMMP	IS-H*MED: Nursing
NMMS	IS-H*MED: Basic data srvc processing
NMND	IS-H: Reset Client
NMO1	
NMO2	
NMO3	
NMO4	
NMO9	ISH: Customizing patient management
NMOA	
NMOB	
NMOC	Custom. Billing Service Entry
NMOE	
NMOF	Customizing pat. acctg. srv convers.
NMOG	
NMOH	
NMOI	ISH: Custom. Copayment Processing
NMOJ	
NMOK	IS-HCM Customizing communication
NMOL	IS-HCO: Settings link to Controlling
NMR0	
NMS1	Patient accounting
NMS2	Inpatient Management
NMS3	Outpatient Management

NMS4	Nurse Station Management
NMS5	Medical / Nursing Documentation
NMS6	Medical Record Administration
NMS7	Hospital Structure
NMS8	Service Master
NMS9	Business Partners
NMT0	IS-H: Basic data: srv. master data
NN1L	Menu Service facility management
NN2L	IS-H*MED: Menu Service facility mgmt
NNIH	IS-H NL: Customizing Dutch tables
NNL1	_
NNL2	_
NODE_TYPE_DEFINITION	Maintain Table URL_EXITS
NOM0	
NP01	IS-H: Create patient master data
NP02	IS-H: Change patient master data
NP03	IS-H: Display patient master data
NP04	IS-H: Maintain risk factors
NP05	IS-H: Display risk factors
NP06	IS-H: Merging patients
NP07	IS-H: Find Similar Patients
NP10	IS-H: Call Case Overview
NP10D	IS-H: Call Case Overview Display
NP11	IS-H: Create inpatient admiss. data
NP12	IS-H: Change inpatient admiss. data
NP13	IS-H: Display inpatient admiss. data
NP20	IS-H: Maintain delivery data
NP21	IS-H: Display delivery data
NP22	IS-H: Maintain newborn admission
NP23	IS-H: Display newborn admission
NP24	IS-H: Maintain gen. case/case asgmt
NP25	IS-H: Display gen. case/case asgmt
NP26	IS-H: Maintain comp. case/case asgmt
NP27	IS-H: Display comp. case/case asgmt
NP28	IS-H: Maintain newb. case/case asgmt
NP29	IS-H: Display newb. case/case asgmt
NP30	IS-H: Maintain companion admission
NP31	IS-H: Display companion admission
NP32	IS-H: Maintain person assignment
NP33	IS-H: Display person assignment
NP36	IS-H: Create surgery (case)
NP37	IS-H: Create surgery (visit)
NP38	IS-H: Change surgery
NP39	IS-H: Display surgery
NP40	IS-H: Create outpatient case
NP41	IS-H: Create outpatient visit
NP42	IS-H: Change outpatient visit
NP43	IS-H: Display outpatient visit
NP44	IS-H: Maintain treatment certificate
NP45	IS-H: Display treatment certificate
NP46	IS-H: Treatment certificate evaluat.
NP47	IS-H: Maintain Procedures for Case
NP48	IS-H: Display Procedures for Case
NP51	IS-H: Maintain nurs. acuity per case

NP52	IS-H: Display patient group per case
NP53	IS-H: Maintain patient group per OU
NP54	IS-H: Display patient group per OU
NP55	IS-H: Maintain case classif.per case
NP56	IS-H: Display case classif. per case
NP57	IS-H: Maintain case classif. per OU
NP58	IS-H: Display case classific. per OU
NP61	IS-H: Maintain Diagn. Doc. by Case
NP62	IS-H: Display Diagn. Doc. by Case
NP63	IS-H: Maintain Diagnosis Doc. by OU
NP64	IS-H: Display Diagnosis Doc. by OU
NP71	IS-H: Maintain medical grounds
NP72	IS-H: Display medical grounds
NP91	IS-H: Create absence
NP92	IS-H: Change leave of absence
NP93	IS-H: Display leave of absence
NP94	IS-H: Generate leave of absence
NP97	IS-H: Create discharge
NP98	IS-H: Change discharge
NP99	IS-H: Display discharge
NPDRG1	IS-H: Display DRG Data
NPDRG2	IS-H: Maintain DRG Data
NPDRG3	IS-H: DRG Grouping of Multiple Cases
NPFA	IS-H: Public List
NPFL	IS-H: Religious list
NPLNC01	IS-H: Change Statistical Occ.Chrctst
NPLNC02	IS-H: Display Statist. Occ. Chrctst
NPPR	IS-H: Nurs. Acuity Classific. Eval.
NPRT	LIS/setup/log
NR00	IS-H: Report selection
NR11	IS-H: Care Unit Overview (List)
NR12	IS-H: Care Unit Overview Graphic
NR13	IS-H: Occupancy Overview
NR14	IS-H: Outpatient Clinic Management
NR16	IS-H: Visit Scheduling
NR17	IS-H: Move Appointments
NR19	IS-H: Apptmnt Lists Outp.Clinic.Mgmt
NR20	Change Planning Object
NR21	Display Planning Object
NR22	Maintain Available Time Slots
NR23	Display Time Slots
NR24	IS-H: List Planning Objects
NR25	Create Planning Object
NR26	IS-H: Collective Print of Appts
NRAM	IS-H: Outpatient admission inquiry
NRAU	IS-H: Inpatient admission inquiry
NRBA	IS-H: Report Ctrl. Other Basic Data
NRBG	IS-H: Report Ctrl. Business Partner
NRBL	IS-H: Report Ctrl. Service Master
NRBS	IS-H: Report Ctrl. Hospital Struc.
NRC3	IS-H Report ctrl data exchange §301
NRCM	IS-H: Communication report control
NRCPB	IS-H: Information Clin.Proc. Builder
NRCQ	IS-H: Report control monitoring

NREDOMA1	Change Renewable Document Management
NREDOMA2	Display Renewable Document Mgmt
NREN	IS-H: Inquiry on discharge
NREP	IS-H: General report control
NRKV	Medical records adm. inquiry
NRMA	IS-H: Outpatient dept. mgmt. inquiry
NRMP	IS-H: Med.Nur.Evaluations Rep.Contr.
NRPA	IS-H: Patient accctg report control
NRPP	IS-H: Nurs. Acuity Classific. Eval.
NRPV	IS-H: Patient Mgmt report control
NRSM	IS-H: Nurse station managem. inquiry
NRSS	IS-H: Report contr. Other Statistics
NRST	IS-H: Report contr. govt-mandated st
NRVE	IS-H: Inquiry on transfer
NS01	IS-H: Midnight Census Statistics
NS02	IS-H: Geographics Statistics
NS03	IS-H: S1 Bed Assignment Figures
NS04	IS-H: S4 Perf. Fig. of Departments
NS10	IS-H: Data Collection Diagnoses
NT01	IS-H: Create Services in Catalog
NT02	IS-H: Change Services in Catalog
NT03	IS-H: Display Services in Catalog
NT07	IS-H: Display Service Catalog
NT08	Additional srv data Germany
NT09	IS-H: Planned Values by Service / OU
NT10	ISH: View Maint. Charge Catalog Asgm
NT11	ISH: View Maint. Charge Asgmt. (No.)
NT12	IS-H: Assign Services to SurgPrcds
NT13	IS-H: Assign SrgPrcds to Services
NT32	IS-H: Maintain Service Group
NT33	IS-H: Display Service Group
NT34	IS-H: Maintain Dynamic Srv. Groups
NT42	IS-H*MED: Create Personnel Qualif.
NT43	IS-H*MED: Change Personnel Qualif.
NT44	IS-H*MED: Display Personnel Qualif.
NT45	IS-H*MED: Maintain Material Proposal
NT46	IS-H*MED: Display Material Proposal
NT50	Maintain Billing Types
NT51	Display Billing Types
NT60	IS-H*MED: Create service spectrum
NT61	IS-H*MED: Change service spectrum
NT62	IS-H*MED: Display service spectrum
NT70	IS-H: Maintain service categories
NT75	IS-H: Maintain rules for charge prop
NT76	IS-H: Display rules for comp.prop.
NTP1	IS-H: Maintain model transaction
NTP2	IS-H: Display model transaction
NTRB	Transport Building Units
NTRL	Transport Service Master
NTRO	Transport Organizational Units
NTWXPD	Progress Tracking:Networks
NV01	IS-H: Create inpatient admission
NV02	IS-H: Change inpatient admission
NV03	IS-H: Display inpatient admission

NV04	IS-H: Create quick inpatient admiss.
NV05	IS-H: Change quick inpatient admiss.
NV06	IS-H: Display quick inpatient admis.
NV07	IS-H: Create emergency inpat. adm.
NV08	IS-H: Change emergency inpat. adm.
NV09	IS-H: Display emergency inpat. adm.
NV10	IS-H: Inpatient companion admission
NV11	IS-H: Create transfer
NV12	IS-H: Change transfer
NV13	IS-H: Display transfer
NV20	IS-H: Inpatient newborn admission
NV2000	IS-H: Clinical Process Builder
NV2000_AMB	IS-H: SAP ACM - Complete
NV2000_AMB_BG	IS-H: SAP ACM - Workers Comp.Variant
NV2000_AMB_KV	IS-H: SAP ACM - PPA Variant
NV2000_AMB_NA	IS-H: SAP ACM - Emergency Admission
NV2000_AMB_PV	IS-H: Private Insured Variant
NV2000_EMERGENCY	IS-H: Emergency Admission
NV2001	IS-H: Clinical Process Builder
NV2001_AMB	IS-H: SAP ACM - Complete
NV2002	IS-H: Clinical Process Builder
NV2003	IS-H: Clinical Process Builder
NV2004	IS-H: Clinical Process Builder
NV2005	IS-H: Clinical Process Builder
NV2006	IS-H: Clinical Process Builder
NV2007	IS-H: Clinical Process Builder
NV2008	IS-H: Clinical Process Builder
NV22	IS-H: Maintain insurance relatshp
NV23	IS-H: Display insurance relationship
NV25	IS-H: Maintain insurance relatshp
NV26	IS-H: Display insurance relationship
NV31	IS-H: Maintain insurance relatshp
NV32	IS-H: Display insurance relationship
NV33	IS-H: Maintain insurance relatshp
NV34	IS-H: Display insurance relationship
NV35	IS-H: Maintain Guarantors
NV36	IS-H: Display Guarantors
NV41	IS-H: Create outpatient admission
NV42	IS-H: Change outpatient admission
NV43	IS-H: Display outpatient admission
NV44	IS-H: Create quick outpat. admission
NV45	IS-H: Change quick outpat. admission
NV46	IS-H: Display quick outpat.admission
NV47	IS-H: Create emergency admission
NV48	IS-H: Change emergency admission
NV49	IS-H: Display emergency admission
NV50	IS-H: Outpatient companion admission
NV60	IS-H: Outpatient newborn admission
NVT0	IS-H: Display Contract. Categories
NVT1	IS-H: Maintain Contract. Categories
NVT2	IS-H: Contract Scheme - Ins. Provs
NVT3	IS-H SG: External Contract Schemes
NWBC	Launch NWBC
NWCH02	IS-H CH: Assign Post. Code to Region

NWCH03	IS-H CH: Assign Post. Code to Region
NWCH04	IS-H CH: Assign Geog. Area to Canton
NWCH05	IS-H CH: Assign Geog. Area to Canton
NWCH06	IS-H CH: Canton Tariff
NWCH07	IS-H CH: Canton tariff
NWCH08	IS-H CH: Convention
NWCH09	IS-H CH: Convention
NWCH10	IS-H CH: Code Group Pension Ins. No.
NWCH11	IS-H CH: Code Group Pension Ins. No.
NWCH12	IS-H CH: Patient Category
NWCH13	IS-H CH: Patient Category
NWCH14	IS-H CH: Patient Type
NWCH15	IS-H CH: Patient Type
NWCH16	IS-H CH: Absence Rules
NWCH17	IS-H CH: Absence Rules
NWCH18	IS-H CH: Billing Agreements
NWCH19	IS-H CH: Billing Agreements
NWCH20	IS-H CH: Determine Bill. Agreement
NWCH21	IS-H CH: Determine Bill. Agreement
NWCH22	IS-H CH: Movement Types
NWCH23	IS-H CH: Movement Types
NWCH24	IS-H CH: Patient Classes
NWCH25	IS-H CH: Patient Classes
NWCH26	IS-H CH: Service Rule Billability
NWCH27	IS-H CH: Service Rule Billability
NWCH28	IS-H CH: Svce Rule for Sve High.Val.
NWCH29	IS-H CH: Svce Rule for Sve High.Val.
NWCH30	IS-H CH: Svce Rule for Svce Breakdwn
NWCH31	IS-H CH: Svce Rule for Svce Breakdwn
NWCH32	IS-H CH: Service Generation
NWCH33	IS-H CH: Cancel Service Generation
NWCH34	IS-H CH: Assign Billing Agreement
NWCH35	IS-H CH: Determine Charge Fact. Val.
NWCH70	IS-H CH: Manage Insurance Verif.
NWCH71	IS-H CH: Manage Insurance Verif.
NWCH72	IS-H CH: Manage Insurance Verif.
NWCH73	IS-H CH: Ins. Verification Reminder
NWCH74	IS-H CH: Extend Ins. Verification
NWCH75	IS-H CH: Ins. Verif. Status Tracking
NWCH76	IS-H CH: Assign Contract Scheme (IV)
NWCH90	IS-H CH: Create Fee Recipient
NWCH91	IS-H CH: Change Fee Recipient
NWCH92	IS-H CH: Display Fee Recipient
NWCHIVT	Maint. View for Object Types Table
NWCVLICENCE	IS-H: License Mgmt Country Version
NWP1	IS-H: Clinical Work Station
NWTM	Monitoring Network Dates
NWTM01	Date type maintenance
NWTM02	Maintain ref. fields f. date types
NWTM03	Maintain date status
NWTM04	Edit profile for monitoring dates
NWTM05	Edit role for monitoring dates
NWTM06	Edit Assignment of User to Role
NZLVCON	HR New Zealand Leave Conversion

O000	C RM-MAT Menu - Classification
O005	C CL Characteristic Default Settings
O020	Record Layout for BTCI (Classes)
O021	Class Data Transfer
O023	Display Class Maintenance Data File
O024	Transfer Class Data: Direct Input
O02F	Screen Field Ctrl f. Bch Master Rec.
O02G	Screen Field Ctrl f. Bch Master Rec.
O02K	Maintain Period Indicator
O035	Country version delivery sys created
O037	HR Customizing User Parameters
O03C	Assign Target Fields to Mess. Dest.
O041	Cust. Chars: Char. Statuses
O042	Cust. Chars: Char. Groups
O043	Cust. Classes: Class Groups
O044	Cust. Chars: Template Characters
O045	Cust. Characteristics: Templates
O04C	PI: Message Control Purchasing
O050	Customizing: General Info System
O052	Set up Clients
O053	Customizing Request Management
O05C	PI: Messages Control C5
O06C	Define Process Manufacturing Cockpit
O06S	Define Process Manufacturing Cockpit
O07C	Obsolete transaction
O08C	Release Char. Grp for Proc. Messages
O09C	Release Char. Group for Proc. Instr.
O0SC	Requirement Request- Req./Confirmat.
O10C	Assig. Ctrl Rec. Dest./Proc. Instr.
O10CXT	Change Destination for XSteps
O11C	Maint. Acct.Assgnmt.Types for Order
O12A	Maintain Object Types
O12C	Assign Charact. / Proc. Instr. Cat.
O13C	MessCat./Dest./Chars./Target Fields
O15C	Overview Var.: PI Sheet Selection
O1CL	Maintain Class Types
O20C	ProcMgmt: Copy Settings betw. Plants
O21C	PP-PI: Where-Used List for Charact.
O22C	Copy SAP Messages (Standard)
O22C_VHUMI	Copy Message Cats Mat.Ident./Reconc.
O23C	Client Copy of PP-PI Characteristics
O23C_VHUMI	Copy Material Ident. Characteristics
O24C	Copy SAP Messages (Generic)
O25C	Create Charac. with PP-PI Attributes
O25X	Create Charac. with PP-PI Attributes
O26C	Change Charac. with PP-PI Attributes
O26X	Change Charac. with PP-PI Attributes
O27C	Display Charac. with PP-PI Attribute
O27X	Display Charac. with PP-PI Attribute
O285	Master Recipe/QM Data
O28C	Copy SAP Messages (Central)
O29C	Copy SAP Messages (Decentralized)
O2CL	Profile for User Settings
O300	IS-Oil Administration infosystem

SAP Transaction Codes – Volume One

O3O1	Tab:buffering allowed+optional Index
O3O2	Consistency check no. range object
O3O3	Install. component dependency check
O3A1	Create Exchange Agreement
O3A2	Maintain Exchange Agreement
O3A3	Display Exchange Agreement
O3A4	Create Netting Document
O3A5	Maintain Netting Document
O3A6	Display Netting Document
O3A7	Exchange Material Movements
O3A8	Reset Netting Document Header
O3A9	Netting Statement
O3AA	Archive Exchange Balance Records
O3AB	Exchange Abstract
O3AC	Cancel Enjoy LIA
O3AD	Display Enjoy LIA
O3AI	Create Enjoy LIA
O3AL	Execute Detail Exg Transaction Rep.
O3AQ	List Selection Qty.Schedules
O3AR	QS Partner Entitlement/Obligation
O3AU	Create LIA Transaction
O3AX	Exchanges operations
O3AY	Exchanges master data
O3A_PRP	Assign price reference plants
O3B0	Delete Netting Document
O3B1	Exchanges Create Exg Stmnt Print Req
O3B2	Exchanges Mtn. Exg Stmnt Print Req
O3B3	Exchanges Disp. Exg Stmnt Print Req
O3B4	Exchanges Del. Exg Stmnt Print Req
O3B7	Create Netting Document
O3B8	Change Netting Document
O3B9	Display Netting Document
O3BU	Display LIA transaction
O3C1	Create Oil Conversion Defaults
O3C2	Change Oil Conversion Defaults
O3D0	API Check Results Report
O3D1	Inst. Test for API C-code Rout.
O3D2	QCI:Test RFC Server Prog./Call exter
O3DEFAULTS	New Defaulttransaction
O3G5	Report Ship-to/Sold-to
O3G6	Report Ship-to/Sold-to
O3GV	Loading Master Record
O3I0	Customer Price List
O3I1	Appl./Customiz. Customer Price List
O3I2	Define Price Information for Quote
O3I3	Integrity Check for Quotation Table
O3I4	Maintain Gross/Net Rule Defaults
O3I5	Define Price Information for Quote
O3I7	Create Repository Formula
O3I8	Change Repository Formula
O3I9	Display Repository Formula
O3INT	Special interest table
O3JDCM	Document change management
O3O_ARCC	OLM container archiving

491

O3O_ARCF	OLM object flow archiving
O3O_ARCH	OLM container history archiving
O3O_ARCR	OLM returns archiving
O3O_ARCV	OLM Voyage archiving
O3O_C101	Create container
O3O_C102	Change container
O3O_C103	Display container
O3O_C104	Display container change documents
O3O_C107	Delete container
O3O_CT01	Maintain container materials
O3O_CT03	Display transport container
O3O_CT05	List containers
O3O_CT06	Display container history
O3O_CT07	List shipments for container
O3O_CTL02	Maintain container location
O3O_CTL03	Display container location
O3O_C_ACT	Maintain supply activities
O3O_C_MAIN	Maintain system parameters
O3O_C_OBJTY	Maintain document flow object types
O3O_C_SBSDC	Subsequent posting rules for returns
O3O_C_SPDRV	Maintain supply process derivation
O3O_C_SPPNR	Maintain no ranges for auto packing
O3O_C_SPROC	Maintain supply processes
O3O_GRCD	Goods receipt cross-docking
O3O_GRLG	Display goods receipt message log
O3O_GRSD	Goods receipt subsequent delivery
O3O_HD01	PM Orders by held status
O3O_HD02	PM Components by held status
O3O_HD03	Requisitions by held status
O3O_IMG	IMG Offshore Logistics
O3O_IMG_SYSTEM	IMG Offshore Logistics - System
O3O_MT01	Material tracking - PM Order
O3O_MT02	Material tracking - purchase reqn.
O3O_MT03	Material tracking - transport reqn.
O3O_MT04	Material tracking - goods receipt
O3O_MT05	Material tracking - returns
O3O_MT06	Material tracking - Project
O3O_MT07	Material tracking - WBS element
O3O_MT08	Material tracking - delivery
O3O_MT09	Material tracking - purchase order
O3O_MT10	Material tracking - transport order
O3O_MT11	Material tracking - PS Network
O3O_MT12	Material tracking - Services
O3O_MTXX	Test navigation function
O3O_MX01	Tracking extracts
O3O_PACK01	Assign containers to loading areas
O3O_PACK02	Assign containers to shipments
O3O_PACK03	Pack deliveries into loading areas
O3O_PACK04	Pack deliveries into shipments
O3O_PACK05	Move ld area containers to shipments
O3O_PACK06	Move containers between ld areas
O3O_PACK07	Move containers between shipments
O3O_RN03	Display mobilization log
O3O_RT01	Create returns document

SAP Transaction Codes – Volume One

O3O_RT02	Change returns document
O3O_RT03	Display returns document
O3O_RT04	Display changes for returns document
O3O_RT05	Returns worklist - update
O3O_RT06	Returns worklist - display
O3O_SC01	Convert transport requisitions
O3O_SC02	Convert transport requisitions
O3O_SC03	Display tr.req. conversion log
O3O_SC04	Identify isolated stock
O3O_SR02	Shipment receipt
O3O_SR03	Shipment receipt cancellation
O3O_SR10	Shipment summary
O3O_SR11	Shipment container list
O3O_SR12	Shipment container type summary
O3O_SR13	Shipment detail report
O3O_SR14	Shipment output
O3O_SR15	Deck Utilization Report
O3O_SR20	Batch stock list
O3O_SR21	Material movements by batch
O3O_VG01	Create Voyage
O3O_VG02	Change Voyage
O3O_VG03	Display Voyage
O3O_VG04	Display voyage change documents
O3O_VG05	List voyages
O3O_VL10B	OLM Purchase Orders Due for Delivery
O3O_VL10D	OLM Purch. Order Items due for Dlv
O3O_VL10F	OLM PurchOrd Sched Lines due for Dlv
O3O_VL10X	OLM VL10 for excluded items
O3QCITEST	QCI TEST Calculations
O3RA1	Display application log
O3RA2	Delete application log
O3RAM1	Maintain material handling groups
O3RAM3	Display material handling groups
O3RAPL1	Location Based Collective output
O3RAPR1	Create Print document
O3RAPR2	Change Print program
O3RAPR3	Display Print document
O3RAPRC1	Create Output: SSR output document
O3RAPRC2	Change Output: SSR output document
O3RAPRC3	Display Output: SSR output document
O3RA_ARCHIVING	SSR - Archiving customizing
O3RA_ARCH_OBJ	SSR - Archiving customizing
O3RA_EXECUTE_PROCESS	SSR - Process execution
O3RB12	Change LAA Managers
O3RB13	Display LAA Managers
O3RB16	Show User address
O3RCF000	Fuels processing
O3RCMM01	SSR Meters - Maintenance
O3RCMM02	SSR Meters - Detail report
O3RCMM03	SSR Meters - Errors (background pr.)
O3RCMM03S	SSR Meters - Errors (background pr.)
O3RCMM04	SSR Meters - Errors maintenance
O3RCMM05	SSR Meters - Clearing
O3RCMM06	SSR Meters - Rebuild aggregated data

O3RCMM07	SSR Meters - End day process
O3RCMM07I	SSR Meters - End day process (init.)
O3RCMM07R	SSR Meters - End day process (rest.)
O3RCMM08	SSR Meters - Month Quantities
O3RCMM09	SSR Meters - Invoice quantites
O3RCMM10	SSR Meters - Deleted meter readings
O3RCMM11	SSR Meters - Delete quantity reading
O3RCMMX4	SSR Meters - App. log Errors maint.
O3RCMV01	Material movem. based on meter read.
O3RCMV02	Material movem. based on dip reading
O3RCPC02	SSR - Profile maintenance (material)
O3RCPR00	SSR Pricing - Maintain column values
O3RCPR01	SSR Pricing - Group update
O3RCPR02	SSR Pricing - Group reverse
O3RCPR03	SSR Pricing - Group log archive
O3RCPR04	SSR Pricing - Price check
O3RCPR06	SSR Pricing - Network-Group report
O3RCPR2D	SSR Pricing - Price maintenance
O3RCPR2D_D	SSR Pricing - Price Deletion
O3RCPR2D_RS	SSR Pricing - Price maintenance
O3RCPR50	SSR - Price history for location
O3RCPR51	SSR - Network prices at special time
O3RCPR52	SSR - Price changes
O3RCPR53	SSR - Netw. average prices by loc.
O3RCPR54	SSR - Price changes dealer delay
O3RCPR55	SSR - Netw. average prices by date
O3RCPRCM	SSR Pricing - Price cluster maint.
O3RCPRCN	SSR Pricing - Branch cluster maint.
O3RCSM01	SSR Stocks - Maintenance
O3RCSM02	SSR Stocks - Stock corrections
O3RCSM03	SSR Stocks - Errors (background pr.)
O3RCSM04	SSR Stocks - Errors maintenance
O3RCSM05	SSR Stocks - Clearing
O3RCSM06	SSR Stocks - Review stocks
O3RCSM07	SSR Stocks - End day process
O3RCSM07I	SSR Dips - End day process (init.)
O3RCSM07R	SSR Dips - End day process (rest.)
O3RCSM08	SSR Stocks - List
O3RCSMX2	SSR Stocks - Stock corrections (D)
O3RCSMX4	SSR Stocks - App. log Errors maint.
O3RC_CLUSTER_DEF	SSR Pricing - Location cluster def.
O3RC_CLUSTER_DIFF	SSR Pricing: Cluster diff. maint.
O3RC_COMP_DIFF	SSR Pricing: Competitor diff. maint.
O3RC_END_DAY_PROCESS	SSR - End process execution
O3RC_GROUP_DIFF	SSR Pricing: Group diff. maint.
O3RC_LIST_DIFF	SSR Pricing - Differences list
O3RECH1	Create CH Settlement/Transmission
O3RECH2	change settlement/transmission
O3RECH3	Display Settlement/Transmission
O3RECH4	Assign Customer to Clearing house
O3RECH5	Payment Card Processing Daily Report
O3RECOMPL	SSR Complaint process
O3RECON1	Payment card reconciliation
O3RECON2	Reverse Paymt Card Reconciliation

SAP Transaction Codes – Volume One

O3RECON3	Display Paymt Card Reconciliation
O3REDTF00	Execute the DTF report
O3REDTF01	DTF Create
O3REDTF02	DTF Change
O3REDTF03	DTF Display
O3REDTF04	SSR Payment cards: Mass correction
O3RE_RECON	Payment Card Reconciliation
O3RH01	Transaction for Comp price Watch
O3RH31	Display of Location master data
O3RH41	SSR IAC: meter reading
O3RH51	SSR IAC: dip reading
O3RH_CHLM	Process change pointers for location
O3RH_CHPR	Process change pointers for prices
O3RH_WSGM	SSR STWB: Navigation menu IAC
O3RI01	Service Station Partner Invoicing
O3RI02	Location partner daily report
O3RI03	Reverse periodic invoices
O3UBL01_WORKPLACE	Balancing Workplace
O3UCA_DOIXREF	DOI to MP/WC Cross Reference
O3UCA_GPSS	Gas Plant Sliding Scale
O3UCA_MKGRPL	List processing for Marketing Groups
O3UCA_OSP	Owner Selective Processing Options
O3UCA_PRL	Percent Return to Producer
O3UCA_PSP	Plant Selective Processing Options
O3UCA_TRNCT	MP/WC Transporter Contract XRef
O3UCI_ARVAR	Receivable and Price Variance
O3UCI_CDEX	CDEX Workplace
O3UCI_MASS	Processing Checks in Mass
O3UCI_PDX	Purchaser to Property/DOI Xref
O3UCI_PPD	PRA Payment Posting Desktop
O3UCI_PRDX	CDEX Comapny Product Cross Reference
O3UCI_REMX	CDEX Remitter Cross Reference
O3UCI_SUSP	Suspended Line Items messages
O3UCM_BA	Integrated Business Associate
O3UCM_CONTRACT	PRA Contract Maintenance
O3UCM_T8JV	PRA Joint Venture Master Data
O3UCM_TAB_MAINT	Generic Table Maintenance
O3UCM_TAB_MAINT_003	Reclassification of Production Codes
O3UCM_TAB_MAINT_004	Material and Product Code Proc XRef
O3UCM_TAB_MAINT_005	Material Sum - Gas Plant Comp Alloc
O3UCM_TAB_MAINT_006	SPF NGL Component Allocation Basis
O3UCM_TAB_MAINT_007	SPF Wet Gas Equivalent
O3UCM_TAB_MAINT_008	Sliding Scale Methods - Dim / Materl
O3UCM_TAB_MAINT_009	PRA Partner Table from JV
O3UCM_TAB_MAINT_010	Volumetric SKF
O3UCM_TAB_MAINT_011	Setup Code and Generic Values Dated
O3UCM_TAB_MAINT_012	Reg Rpt: MP/State Assigned ID XRef
O3UCM_TAB_MAINT_013	State Agency & PRA Material XRef
O3UCM_TAB_MAINT_014	PRA JVA Companies
O3UCM_TAB_MAINT_017	Roy Rpt: Code Maintenance
O3UCM_TAB_MAINT_018	Parameters for TX Migration
O3UCM_TAB_MAINT_019	Zero Rejects for Wyoming Royalty
O3UCM_TAB_MAINT_020	MMS-2014 Date Effective Edits
O3UCM_TAB_MAINT_021	Agency/PRA Product Code XRef

SAP Transaction Codes – Volume One

O3UCP_CO2_RMV0	CO2 Removal Fee Processing
O3UCP_MKT_CST0	Contract Marketing Costs
O3UCP_TAR_RMB0	Tax and Royalty Reimbursement
O3UCW_BANK	Bank Details for Payment Processing
O3UCW_BA_EXEMPTION	BA exempt from state NRIT Withholdin
O3UCW_EXCEPTION	Exception list from Payment run
O3UCW_PAYMENT_RUN	PRA Payment Processing
O3UCW_TAX	Owner Taxes Withheld Report
O3UGT_EDITOR	Upstream Graphics Editor
O3UGT_ICON_DOWNLOAD	Download Upstream Graphics Bitmaps
O3UGT_ICON_MAINT	Bitmap/Flashform Maintenance
O3UGT_ICON_UPLOAD	Upload Upstream Graphics Bitmaps
O3UHS_CM1	Common Table Entries - Create
O3UHS_CM2	Common Table Entries - Change
O3UHS_CM3	Common Table Entries - Display
O3UHS_CM4	Common Table Entries - Delete
O3UH_1099	1099 Report
O3UH_ACCEPTED_JE	Posted Journal Entries Reports
O3UH_ACCT_CLOSE	Accounting Period Close
O3UH_AD_VAL	Ad Valorem
O3UH_ARJE	A/R Journal Entry Generation
O3UH_ARWOC	A/R Write Off Cents Report
O3UH_AR_UP	Accounts Receivable Update
O3UH_CC	Check Clearing
O3UH_CR_NA	Create Negative Amounts
O3UH_ES	Escheat Processing
O3UH_FLASH_DOWNLOAD	Download Reporting Flashforms
O3UH_FLASH_UPLOAD	Upload Reporting Flashforms
O3UH_FT	Funds Transfer
O3UH_JEPOST	JE Posting
O3UH_JEPURGE_ANN	JE Annual Purge
O3UH_JEPURGE_OFF	JE Offset Purge
O3UH_LOAD_JEINTF	Load JEINTF rec for Batch type 40&41
O3UH_NA_IN	Negative Amount Invoice
O3UH_NA_PU	Negative Amount Purge
O3UH_NP_SU	Negative Payment Suspense Report
O3UH_OUT_CDEX	Outbound CDEX
O3UH_REJECTED_JE	Rejected Journal Entries Report
O3UH_REPEX	Report Execution
O3UH_RV	Revenue Report Viewer
O3UH_TC	Treasury Check
O3UH_TP_WO	Taxes Payable Write Off
O3UH_VC_CP	Void/Cleared Check Purge
O3UH_VMC	Process Void/Manual Checks
O3UI7	Create Repository Formula
O3UI8	Change Repository Formula
O3UI9	Display Repository Formula
O3UOW_CHECKIN_JOBS	View Check In and Check Out Jobs
O3UOW_COT	Chain of Title
O3UOW_DOC	Change Owner List Processing
O3UOW_OR0	Owner Transfer/Maintenance
O3UOW_OTX	Owner Transfer Execution Report
O3UOW_OW9	DOI Tract by Owner List Processing
O3UOW_PP	Production Payment

O3UOW_SUMM_BAL	Outstanding summary balance
O3UOW_UT9	DOI Tract by Tract List Processing
O3UOW_UTP0	Unit to Tract Participation
O3UOW_UV9	Unit Venture List Processing
O3UPC_AVGRP	Availability Groupijng
O3UPC_SPADJ	Sales Point Adjustment
O3UPR_DNST9	Display DN Status
O3UPR_MPALF	Display MP Allocation Factor
O3UPR_RWC	Regulatory Reallocated WC
O3UPR_SKF	SKF Submission
O3UPR_WCALF	Display Well/WC Allocation Factor
O3UPR_WCDPS	WC Daily Pressures
O3UP_ADMIN_WORKBENCH	PDM Administrators' Workbench
O3UREP_MASTER	Regulatory Reporting Master Data
O3UREP_MMS_2014	MMS-2014 Workplace
O3UREP_MMS_2014_FORM	MMS 2014 Printable Form
O3UREP_MMS_MRTHIST	MMS Level Historic Royalty Trans Rep
O3UREP_MMS_MRTPEND	MMS Level Pending Royalty Trans Rep
O3UREP_MMS_RECOUP	MMS Indian Recoupable Report
O3UREP_MMS_REJECTS	MMS Extraction Rejects Report
O3UREP_MMS_RTHIST	Historic Extract Report
O3UREP_OPERATOR	Regulatory Reporting Setup
O3UREP_ROY_BASEDATA	Royalty base data maintenance
O3UREP_ROY_MASTER	Master Maint. for Royalty Reporting
O3UREP_ROY_MDQ	Master Data Query
O3UREP_ROY_REPORTING	Royalty Reporting
O3UREP_WYPMT_DTL	Wyoming Payment Detail,
O3URV_COMB	Combined Run Report
O3URV_DOC	Valuation Document Worklist
O3URV_SRPT	Valuation Selection Report
O3URV_SS0	Settlement Statement
O3URV_SST0	Settlement Stmnt/DOI Cross-Reference
O3UT2_FDN9	Display FDN records
O3UT2_IM0	Interface Monitor
O3UVL_GSP0	Gas Statement Profile
O3UVL_GST9	Gas Statement Report List Processing
O3UVL_MTA	Marketing Cost Tax Allowance
O3UVL_OSP0	Oil Statement Profile
O3UVL_OST9	Oil Statement Report List Processing
O3UVL_RPA0	Royalty Processing Allowance
O3UVL_RTI	Run Tickets
O3UVL_SS0	Settlement Statement
O3UVL_STR0	State Tax Rates
O3UVL_TCD0	Tax Calculation Data - Doc Concept
O3UVL_TCL0	Tax Classification
O3UVL_TCL9	Tax Classification List Processing
O3UVL_TPA0	Tax Processing Allowance
O3UVL_TTX0	Tier Tax Maintenance
O3UX1_MIGR_FINAL	Finalize tax reporting migration
O3UX1_MIGR_TRN	Migrate tax transaction data
O3UX1_TAXREP_MAIN	Tax Reporting Main
O3UX1_TAXREP_MSTR	Tax reporting master maintenance
O3UX1_TAX_ADJ	Tax adjusments transaction
O3UX2_MSTR_QUERY	master data query

O3UX3_DISP_TX_EDTERR	Texas Additional Edit Errors
O3UX3_DISP_TX_OOSWO	Display Texas OOS Write Off Info
O3UX3_DISP_TX_RPVAR	Texas Tax Variance Report
O3UX3_MIGRATION	Tax Reporting - Migration Workbench
O3UX3_MIGRATION_001	Texas Migration Workbench
O3UX3_PORTAL	Generic Portal
O3UX3_PORTAL_001	Tax Reporting Portal
O3UX3_RPT_PROF	Reporting Profile Maintenance
O3UX3_TX_ASU	Texas Auto Suspend Maintenance
O3UX3_TX_BATXID	Texas BA Tax ID Maintenance
O3UX3_TX_LEASE	Texas Lease Maintenace
O3UX3_TX_MASTER	Texas Master Data Maintenance
O3UX3_TX_OOS_WO	Texas Out Of Statute Write Off
O3UX3_TX_SOL	Texas Statute of Limitation Maint
O3UX3_TX_SOLE	Texas Statute of Limitation Exceptn
O3UX3_TX_TAXHST	Texas Up To Date Reported Trans
O3UX3_TX_TAXTXN	Display Texas Tax Transactions
O3UX3_UPD_TX_TAXHST	Texas Maintain Tax History
O3UX3_WORKPLACE	Tax 2.0 Workplace
O3UX4_OUT_BAL	TPSL/TP out of balance report
O3UX4_PORTAL_002	Taxes Payable Reconciliation Portal
O3UX4_RESP_ID	Maintain Taxes Payable Resp. ID
O3UX4_WORKPLACE	TP Summary Workplace
O3UX4_WO_SETUP	Taxes Payable Write Off Setup
O3U_APIG	API Gravity Scale Adjustments
O3U_BA	Create Business Associate
O3U_BA1	Create Business Associate
O3U_BA2	Change Business Associate
O3U_BA3	Display Business Associate
O3U_BG1	Create Bearer Group
O3U_BG2	Change Bearer Group
O3U_BG3	Display Bearer Group
O3U_BG6	Delete Bearer Group
O3U_BG9	Burden Group: List Processing
O3U_BLTMPL	CT Vol by MP Build Template
O3U_CA011	Create Marketing Group Assignment
O3U_CA012	Change Marketing Group Assignment
O3U_CA013	Display Marketing Group Assignment
O3U_CA016	Delete Marketing Group Assignment
O3U_CA021	Create Allocation Cross Reference
O3U_CA022	Change Allocation Cross Reference
O3U_CA023	Display Allocation Cross Reference
O3U_CA026	Delete Allocation Cross Reference
O3U_CA029	Allocation Cross Reference List Proc
O3U_CA031	Create CA Manual Entry
O3U_CA032	Change CA Manual Entry
O3U_CA033	Display CA Manual Entry
O3U_CA036	Delete CA Manual Entry
O3U_CA039	CA Manual Entry List Proc
O3U_CA042	Change DN Volume Allocation
O3U_CA043	Display DN Volume Allocation
O3U_CA052	Change Contract Volume by MP
O3U_CA053	Display Contract Volume by MP
O3U_CA059	Contract Volume by MP List Processin

O3U_CA061	Revised Owner Availability List
O3U_CA062	Revised Owner Availabilty - Change
O3U_CA063	Revised Owner Availabilty - Display
O3U_CA069	Revised Owner Availability List Proc
O3U_CA071	Create SPF Statement Volumes
O3U_CA072	Change SPF Statement Volumes
O3U_CA073	Display SPF Statement Volumes
O3U_CA076	Delete SPF Statement Volumes
O3U_CA079	List Processing for SPF
O3U_CA09	Allocated Volumes Inquiry
O3U_CA09A	NOT IN MENU
O3U_CA10	Entitled Volumes Inquiry
O3U_CA10A	NOT IN MENU
O3U_CA11	Contract Volumes by WC Inquiry
O3U_CHA1	Create Chemical Analysis
O3U_CHA2	Change Chemical Analysis
O3U_CHA3	Display Chemical Analysis
O3U_CHA6	Delete Chemical Analysis
O3U_CHA9	Chemical Analysis List
O3U_CPAM1	Create Custom Plant Allocation Mth
O3U_CPAM2	Change Custom Plant Allocation Mth
O3U_CPAM3	Display Custom Plant Allocation Mth
O3U_CPAM6	Delete Custom Plant Allocation Mth
O3U_CTYP1	Create Component Typification
O3U_CTYP2	Change Component Typification
O3U_CTYP3	Display Component Typification
O3U_CTYP6	Delete Component Typification
O3U_DI1	Base DOI Maintenance Create
O3U_DI2	Base DOI Maintenance Change
O3U_DI3	Base DOI Maintenance Display
O3U_DI6	Base DOI Maintenance Delete
O3U_DI9	Base DOI List Processing
O3U_DMG1	Create DN Measurement Group
O3U_DMG2	Change DN Measurement Group
O3U_DMG3	Display DN Measurement Group
O3U_DMG6	Delete DN Measurement Group
O3U_DN1	Create Delivery Network
O3U_DN11	Create Delivery Network-call from UG
O3U_DN2	Update Delivery Network
O3U_DN3	Display Delivery Network
O3U_DNAP1	CREATE DN ALLOCATION PROFILE
O3U_DNAP2	CHANGE DN ALLOCATION PROFILE
O3U_DNAP3	DISPLAY DN ALLOCATION PROFILE
O3U_DNAP6	DELETE DN ALLOCATION PROFILE
O3U_DND1	Create Delivery Network Dated
O3U_DND11	Create DN Dated - call from UG
O3U_DND2	Change Delivery Network Dated
O3U_DND3	Dialog Delivery Network Dated
O3U_DND6	Delete Delivery Network Dated
O3U_DNH1	Delivery network group create
O3U_DNH2	Delivery network group change
O3U_DNH3	Delivery network group show
O3U_DNND1	Create Delivery Netwok Link
O3U_DNND2	Change Delivery Netwok Link

O3U_DNND3	Display Delivery Netwok Link
O3U_DNND6	Delete Delivery Netwok Link
O3U_DNND9	DNND Report
O3U_DO2	DOI Owner Maintenance Change
O3U_DO3	DOI Owner Maintenance Display
O3U_DOL1	List process for DOI Interest
O3U_DOL2	Owner Interest List processing
O3U_DP1	DOI Accounting - Doc Concept
O3U_DP2	DOI Accounting Change - Doc Concept
O3U_DP3	DOI Accounting Display - Doc Concept
O3U_DP6	DOI Accounting Delete - Doc Concept
O3U_DP9	DOI Accounting List Processing
O3U_FLD1	Field Identification Create
O3U_FLD2	Field Identification Change
O3U_FLD3	Field Identification Display
O3U_FLD6	Field Identification Delete
O3U_FRML1	Create Formula Id Maintenance
O3U_FRML2	Change Formula Id Maintenance
O3U_FRML3	Display Formula Id Maintenance
O3U_FRML6	Delete Formula Id Maintenance
O3U_GAS1	Create API Gravity Adjustment Scale
O3U_GAS2	Change API Gravity Adjustment Scale
O3U_GAS3	Display API Gravity Adjustment Scale
O3U_GAS6	Delete API Gravity Adjustment Scale
O3U_JV1	Create Joint Venture
O3U_JV2	Change Joint Venture
O3U_JV3	Display Joint Venture
O3U_JV9	JV List Processing
O3U_LWGOR1	Create Lease Wide GOR
O3U_LWGOR2	Change Lease Wide GOR
O3U_LWGOR3	Display Lease Wide GOR
O3U_LWGOR6	Delete Lease Wide GOR
O3U_MAIN	Main Menu
O3U_MCCT	Maintain container categories
O3U_MDE1	Mass Data Entry MP Volumes
O3U_MEASUREMENT	Measurement system (temporary me
O3U_MECF	Maintain calculation functions
O3U_MECL	Maintain measurement classes
O3U_MEDOCC	List measurement document changes
O3U_MEDOCL	List measurement documents
O3U_MEMC	Maintain measurement calculations
O3U_MEMT	Maintain measurement types
O3U_MEMTNR	Meas.doc. number range assignment
O3U_MENU	Production Application Menu
O3U_MERT	Maintain reading types
O3U_MESC	Measurement sources
O3U_MEUMG	Maintain unit of meaure groups
O3U_MKT1	Create Internal Marketing Rates
O3U_MKT2	Change Internal Marketing Rates
O3U_MKT3	Display Internal Marketing Rates
O3U_MKT6	Delete Internal Marketing Rates
O3U_MP1	Create Measurement Point
O3U_MP11	Create MP - call from UG
O3U_MP2	Change Measurement Point

O3U_MP21	Change MP - call from UG
O3U_MP3	Display Measurement Point
O3U_MPAP1	Create MP Allocation Profile
O3U_MPAP2	Change MP Allocation Profile
O3U_MPAP3	Display MP Allocation Profile
O3U_MPAP6	Delete MP Allocation Profile
O3U_MPAP9	List Processing MP Alloc Profile
O3U_MPD1	Measurement Point Dated Create
O3U_MPD11	MP Dated Create - call from UG
O3U_MPD2	Measurement Point Dated Change
O3U_MPD21	MP Dated Change - call from UG
O3U_MPD3	Measurement Point Dated Browse
O3U_MPD6	Measurement Point Dated Delete
O3U_MPFUS1	Create MP Fuel Usage
O3U_MPFUS2	Change MP Fuel Usage
O3U_MPFUS3	Display MP Fuel Usage
O3U_MPFUS6	Delete MP Fuel Usage
O3U_MPH1	Measurement point group create
O3U_MPH2	Measurement point group change
O3U_MPH3	Measurement point group show
O3U_MPVL1	Create Measurement Point Volumes
O3U_MPVL2	Change Measurement Point Volumes
O3U_MPVL3	Display Measurement Point Volumes
O3U_MPVL6	Delete Measurement Point Volumes
O3U_MPVL9	Measurement Point Volumes List
O3U_MSP1	Create MP Meter Specifications
O3U_MSP2	Change MP Meter Specifications
O3U_MSP3	Display MP Meter Specifications
O3U_MSP6	Delete MP Meter Specifications
O3U_MWG1	Create WC & MP Measurments
O3U_MWG2	Change WC & MP Measurments
O3U_MWG3	Display WC & MP Measurments
O3U_MWG6	Delete WC & MP Measurments
O3U_MWG9	MP/WC Measurements
O3U_MWHV1	Create MP/WC Default HV Cross Ref.
O3U_MWHV2	Change MP/WC Default HV Cross Ref.
O3U_MWHV3	Display MP/WC Default HV Cross Ref.
O3U_MWHV6	Delete MP/WC Default HV Cross Ref.
O3U_MWT1	MP/WC to Transporter Xref - Create
O3U_MWT2	MP/WC to Transporter Xref - Change
O3U_MWT3	MP/WC to Transporter Xref - Display
O3U_MWT6	MP/WC to Transporter Xref - Delete
O3U_MWT9	MP/WC to Transporter Xref List
O3U_OMPMRA	M.Pt. Meas.Reading assignment
O3U_OMPMTD	M.Pt. meas.type derivation
O3U_PAM1	Create Plant Allocation Methods
O3U_PAM2	Change Plant Allocation Methods
O3U_PAM3	Display Plant Allocation Methods
O3U_PAM6	Delete Plant Allocation Methods
O3U_PC011	Create Capacity
O3U_PC012	Change Capacity
O3U_PC013	Display Capacity
O3U_PC016	Delete Capacity
O3U_PC019	Capacity List Processing

O3U_PC022	Availability - Change
O3U_PC023	Availability - Display
O3U_PC029	Availability List Processing
O3U_PC032	Multiple Sales Sourcing - Change
O3U_PC033	Multiple Sales Sourcing - Display
O3U_PC039	Multiple Sales Sourcing List Process
O3U_PC042	Change Transporter Rankings
O3U_PC043	Display Transporter Ranking
O3U_PC051	Create Daily Availability
O3U_PC052	Daily Availability - Change
O3U_PC053	Daily Availability - Display
O3U_PC059	Daily Availability List Processing
O3U_PC06	Availability Exceptions Report
O3U_PC06A	Call Validation Routine
O3U_PC07	Submit Nomination Changes
O3U_PC08	Review Nomination Changes
O3U_PC09	Availability by Owner
O3U_PC10	CA Interface
O3U_PF1	Platform Maintenance Create
O3U_PF2	Platform Maintenance Change
O3U_PF3	Platform Maintenance Display
O3U_PF6	Platform Maintenance Delete
O3U_PP2	Price maintenance
O3U_PP3	Price maintenance
O3U_PPN02	Valuation PPN Selection
O3U_PPNM01	Manual PPN: Create
O3U_PPNM02	Manual PPN: Change
O3U_PPNM03	Manual PPN: Display
O3U_RES1	Create Reservoir
O3U_RES2	Change Reservoir
O3U_RES3	Display Reservoir
O3U_RES6	Delete Reservoir
O3U_RETMPL	CT Vol by MP Refresh Template
O3U_RMAT1	Create WC/MP Reproduced Materials
O3U_RMAT2	Change WC/MP Reproduced Materials
O3U_RMAT3	Display WC/MP Reproduced Materials
O3U_RMAT6	Delete WC/MP Reproduced Materials
O3U_ROLLMP	Capacity Roll - Measurement Point
O3U_ROLLWC	Capacity Roll - Well Completion
O3U_RQST	VA/CA Allocation Request
O3U_RVT02	Set deletion flag for Val. rejects
O3U_SCM2	Maintain Gravity Scale Defintion
O3U_SCM3	Display Gravity Scale Defintion
O3U_SS1	Create Supply Source
O3U_SS2	Change Supply Source
O3U_SS3	Display Supply Source
O3U_SS6	Delete Supply Source
O3U_TCM1	DN/WC Create Theo Calc Meth
O3U_TCM2	DN/WC Change Theo Calc Meth
O3U_TCM3	DN/WC Display Theo Calc Meth
O3U_TCM6	DN/WC Delete Thoo Calc Meth
O3U_TCM9	DN/WC Theo Calc Meth List Proc
O3U_TOV1	Create Allocation Basis for MP/WC
O3U_TOV2	Change Allocation Basis for MP/WC

O3U_TOV3	Display Allocation Basis for MP/WC
O3U_TOV6	Delete Allocation Basis for MP/WC
O3U_TOV9	MP/WC Theo Override List Processing
O3U_VAFR1	Create VA Formula Rules
O3U_VAFR2	Change VA Formula Rules
O3U_VAFR3	Display VA Formula Rules
O3U_VAFR6	Delete VA Formula Rules
O3U_VCR1	Create Valuation Cross Reference
O3U_VCR2	Change Valuation Cross Reference
O3U_VCR3	Display Valuation Cross Reference
O3U_VCR6	Delete Valuation Cross Reference
O3U_VCR9	VCR List Processing
O3U_VLFR1	Create Valuation Formula
O3U_VLFR2	Change Valuation Formula
O3U_VLFR3	Display Valuation Formula
O3U_VLFR6	Delete Valuation Formula
O3U_VLFR9	Valuation Formula list processing
O3U_VPPN9	Production PPN Dialog
O3U_WC1	Create Well Completion
O3U_WC11	Create Well Completion- call from UG
O3U_WC2	Change Well Completion
O3U_WC21	Change Well Completion- call from UG
O3U_WC3	Display Well Completion
O3U_WCCO1	WC contamination Override Create
O3U_WCCO2	WC contamination Override Change
O3U_WCCO3	WC contamination Override Display
O3U_WCCO6	WC contamination Override Delete
O3U_WCD1	Create Well Completion Dated
O3U_WCD11	Create WC Dated - call from UG
O3U_WCD2	Change Well Completion Dated
O3U_WCD21	Change Well Completion Dated
O3U_WCD3	Display Well Completion Dated
O3U_WCD6	Delete Well Completion Dated
O3U_WCDC1	Create WC Downhole Commingled
O3U_WCDC2	Change WC Downhole Commingled
O3U_WCDC3	Display WC Downhole Commingled
O3U_WCDC6	Delete WC Downhole Commingled
O3U_WCDT1	Create WC Downtime
O3U_WCDT2	Change WC Downtime
O3U_WCDT3	Display WC Downtime
O3U_WCDT6	Delete WC Downtime
O3U_WCDT9	Well Completion Downtime report
O3U_WCDVL1	create wc volumes
O3U_WCDVL2	Change wc volumes
O3U_WCDVL3	Display wc volumes
O3U_WCDVL6	Delete wc volumes
O3U_WCDVL9	Well Completion Volumes List
O3U_WELLIDMAINT	Well ID Maint
O3U_WL1	Well Identification Create
O3U_WL11	Well Id Create - call from UG
O3U_WL2	Well Identification Change
O3U_WL3	Well Identification Display
O3U_WL6	Well Identification Display
O3U_WLH1	Well completion group create

O3U_WLH2	Well completion group create
O3U_WLH3	Well completion group create
O3U_WLTS1	Create Well Test
O3U_WLTS2	Well Test Change
O3U_WLTS3	Well Test display
O3U_WLTS6	Well Test delete
O3U_WLTS9	Well Test Report
O3_DIPWL	Silo Mgmt.: Worklist entries
O400	Location Management (IS-Oil MRN)
O401	Create Location Master Record
O402	Change PBL Master Record
O403	Display PBL Master Record
O404	Display Business Location Changes
O405	List of Contracts
O407	Change Business Location Type
O408	Close Business Location
O40A	Archiving - Archive Business Loc.
O40D	Archiving - Delete Business Loc.
O40R	Archiving - Reload Business Loc.
O40V	Archiving - Manage BL. archive
O41LB	Location balancing
O460	BLIS: Location Analysis - Selection
O461	BLIS: Location Incoming Orders - Sel
O462	BLIS: Location Returns - Selection
O463	BLIS: Location Invoice Sales - Sel
O464	BLIS: Location Credit Memos - Sel.
O4AA	TD Maintain Compartment Group Index
O4AB	TD Display Compartment Group Index
O4AC	TD Assign Ind. to Compartment Group
O4AD	TD Display Compartment Group Index
O4AN	TD Maintain Product Group Index
O4AO	TD Display Product Group Index
O4AP	TD Assign Ind. to Product Group
O4AQ	TD Display Indicators Product Group
O4AR	TD archiving - rack meters
O4AS	TD archiving - shipments
O4AT	TD archiving - transport units
O4AU	TD archiving - vehicle meters
O4AV	TD archiving - vehicles
O4AW	TD archiving - drivers
O4AX	Display archived shipments on screen
O4B1	Start shipment worklist
O4B2	Batch mass processing of shipments
O4B4	Shipment change history
O4B5	Vehicle change
O4B7	Report for Definition of Batch Run
O4B8	TD mass processing: display logs
O4B9	TD mass processing: display logs
O4BA	TD Maintain Customer Group Index
O4BB	TD Display Customer Group Index
O4BC	TD Assign Ind. to Customer Group
O4BD	TD Display Indicators Customer Group
O4BER	Number range maintenance: OIJ_BER
O4BT	TD Maintain Vehicle Group Index

O4BU	TD Display Vehicle Group Index
O4BV	TD Assign Ind to Vehicle Group
O4BW	TD Display Indicators Vehicle Group
O4C1	TD Create Transport Unit
O4C2	TD Change Transport Units
O4C3	TD Display Transport Units
O4C4	TD Delete Transport Unit
O4C6	Distribute Transport Units
O4D1	TD Create Driver
O4D2	TD Change Driver
O4D3	TD Display Driver
O4D4	TD Delete Driver
O4D6	Distribute Drivers
O4EDI_VEND	Assign EDI account number to Vendor
O4F1	TD Create Shipment
O4F2	TD Change Shipment
O4F3	TD Display Shipment
O4F4	TD Delete Shipment
O4F6	Distribute Shipments
O4G1	Loading confirmation
O4G2	Loading Confirmation - Display
O4H1	Delivery Confirmation
O4H2	Delivery Confirmation - Display
O4H5	Cancel material document from shpmt.
O4I1	Text Maintenance
O4J3	Two Step Transfer Tracking Report
O4K1	Create license master data
O4K2	Change license master data
O4K3	Display license master data
O4K4	Quantity License Tracking Report
O4K5	Excise Duty Rate Maintenance
O4K6	Group update for external rates tab.
O4K9	ED license change documents
O4KB	Revaluation activ check report 1/2
O4KC	Revaluation activ check report 2/2
O4KD	Excise Duty Valuation record 1/3
O4KE	Excise Duty Valuation record 2/3
O4KF	Excise Duty Stock values 1/3
O4KG	Excise Duty Stock values 2/3
O4KH	Excise Duty Stock values 3/3
O4KI	Excise Duty Valuation record 3/3
O4KT	Excise Duty Revaluation
O4K_J1B_08	Maintain Incoming Taxation Table
O4K_J1B_10	Maintain Refinery Taxation Table
O4K_J1B_11	Maintain Printing Exceptions ICMS
O4K_J1B_12	Maintain Acquisition Price Table
O4K_J1B_13	Maintain Controlled Price
O4K_J1B_16	Complement ICMS rules inside calc.
O4K_J1B_20	Maintain Post. exp. for ICMS compl.
O4K_J1B_23	Nota Fiscal for gains/losses
O4K_J1B_28	Maintain PMPF price table
O4K_LICENSE	License Master Data
O4L1	TD-F Doc Item Quantity-Create/Change
O4L3	TD-F Doc Item Quantity - Display

O4L4	TD-F Maint. miss. fields for shp.c.
O4L6	TD Create shipment cost worklist
O4L7	TD Collective run in background
O4L8	Selec.var. coll. run shipment costs
O4LB_OI	Loc Bal opening inventory calc
O4M1	TD Create Vehicle Meters
O4M2	TD Change Vehicle Meters
O4M3	TD Display Vehicle Meters
O4M4	TD Delete Vehicle Meters
O4M5	Vehicle Meter Reconciliation
O4M6	Distribute Compartment Meter
O4N0	Bulk Replenishment (IS-Oil BDRP)
O4N2	Maintain General Meter
O4N3	Display General Meter
O4N8	Maintain plant site control parms
O4N9	Maintain SOC type data
O4NA	Assign Storage Objects
O4NC	Create Nomination
O4NCN	Create Nomination
O4ND	Display Assigned Storage Objects
O4NI	Enter customer stock data
O4NJ	Customer stock overview
O4NM	Maintain Nomination
O4NR	OIL-TSW Recover Nomination
O4NS	Display Nomination
O4NSN	Display Nomination
O4NV	Change Nomination
O4NVN	Change Nomination
O4N_DIP_OC	Opening closing test calculator
O4O1	Create output: Bulk Tran. Scheduling
O4O2	Change Output:Bulk Tran. Scheduling
O4O3	Display Output:Bulk Tran. Scheduling
O4O4	Create output: Bulk Tran. Loading
O4O5	Change Output:Bulk Tran. Loading
O4O6	Display Output:Bulk Tran. Loading
O4O7	Create output: Bulk Tran. Del. Conf.
O4O8	Change Output:Bulk Tran. Del. Conf.
O4O9	Display Output:Bulk Tran. Del. Conf.
O4OA	Modify Output Det. - Scheduling
O4OB	Modify Output Det.-Sch. (Detailed)
O4OC	Modify Output Det. - Loading
O4OD	Modify Output Det.-Del. Confirmation
O4OE	TD Output from deliveries
O4P0	Terminal Automation Interface
O4P1	Create LID Master Data
O4P2	Change LID Master Data
O4P3	Display LID Master Data
O4P4	Delete Load ID
O4P5	Display released LID's
O4P7	Release LIDs
O4P8	Revise LIDs
O4P9	Transport Planning System Interface
O4PDCC	Change DCP data
O4PDCL	List DCP history

O4PDCR	Delete DCP status entries
O4PDCT	Delivery Confirmation Frontend
O4PH	Display Load information
O4PI	Show LID-Details
O4PJ	Display LID to SD-Document
O4PK	Load data pickup
O4PL	Transfer Location Master Data to TPS
O4PM	Call Flowlogic Control
O4PMN	TPI History Information
O4PN	Skip shipment inbound process
O4PO	Change order and plant
O4PP	Shipment planning
O4PQ	Distribute orders
O4PR	Selection without LID Type
O4PS	Load data shipment
O4PTPIR	Delete TPI status entries
O4PV	Driver Vehicle Assignment
O4PW	IDOC via Changepointer for OILDVA
O4PX	Shipment Planning Workbench
O4PZ	Display / Delete log table entries
O4R1	TD Create Rack Meter
O4R2	TD Change Rack Meter
O4R3	TD Display Rack Meter
O4R4	TD Delete Rack Meter
O4R5	Rack Meter Reconciliation
O4R6	Distribute Rack Meter
O4RP1	Create release profile
O4RP2	Change release profile
O4RP3	Display release profile
O4S0	Transport and Distribution
O4S1	TD Master Data
O4T0	IS-OIL TSW (Trader's & Scheduler's W
O4T3WP	3 way pegging
O4T3WPD	3 way pegging (display)
O4T5	Create records in cond table - NOM
O4T5_TKT	Create records in cond table - TKT
O4T6	Change records in cond table - NOM
O4T6_TKT	Change records in cond table - TKT
O4T7	Display records in cond table - NOM
O4T7_TKT	Display records in cond table - TKT
O4T8	Display of archived nominations
O4TAPN	Automatically process nominations
O4TB	Stock Projection Worksheet
O4TBB	Stock Projection Worksheet
O4TB_CT	Change What-if type
O4TB_CV	Copy What-if Version
O4TB_PHYS	To update physical inventory figures
O4TB_RDALV	Stock Projection Worksheet
O4TC	Generate Stock Projection
O4TCB	Generate Stock Projection for batch
O4TCN	Generate Stock Projection New
O4TD	Generate worklist entries
O4TDG	OIL TSW: Maintain deal groups
O4TDL	OIL-TSW Delete Location

O4TE	OIL-TSW: Enter movement ticket
O4TEN	Ticket create new
O4TENCORR	Correct ticket
O4TENCRPT	Terminate invalid ticket
O4TENREV	Reverse Ticket
O4TE_CORRECT	OIL-TSW: Correct ticket actualizatio
O4TE_REVERSE	OIL-TSW: Reverse ticket actualizatio
O4TF	OIL-TSW: Change ticket
O4TFN	Change ticket
O4TG	OIL-TSW: Display Ticket
O4TGN	Display Ticket
O4TG_ALV	OIL-TSW: Display Ticket ALV
O4TH	OIL-TSW: Delete movement ticket
O4THN	Delete Ticket
O4TI	TSW archiving - Tickets
O4TJ	Display archived tickets
O4TK	TSW archiving - Nomination
O4TL	TSW Delete Transport System
O4TLB_CP	Loc Bal copy schedules
O4TM	OIL-TSW: Safety stock calc. engine
O4TM_BPB	Berth Planning Board
O4TN	OIL-TSW: Planning engine
O4TO	Worklist
O4TO_LIST	Worklist
O4TP	Partner Role Parser
O4TQ	OIL-TSW Create Partner Role
O4TR	OIL-TSW Change Partner Role
O4TS	OIL-TSW Display Partner Role
O4TSCD	Display Transport System Changes
O4TSW_PD	Production data
O4TT	Create Transport System
O4TU	Change Transport System
O4TV	Display Transport System
O4TW	OIL-TSW Create Location
O4TX	OIL-TSW Change Location
O4TX_LIST	Maintain location / material list
O4TX_TREE	Drill-down planning locations
O4TY	OIL-TSW Display Location
O4TZ	OIL-TSW : Recover Tickets
O4T_EDIACC	Assign EDI account numbers to vendor
O4V1	TD Create Vehicle
O4V2	TD Change Vehicle
O4V3	TD Display Vehicle
O4V4	TD Delete Vehicle
O4V5	Vehicle Reconciliation (LOV-PTL)
O4V6	Distribute Vehicles
O4W1	WWWInterface to rapid confirmation
O4_SILO_ANA_CREATE	Create tank analysis data
O4_TIGER	Tank Management
O501	General functionality switch(On/Off)
O502	Customize message control
O503	Parameter admin. (set value)
O505	Customize message control
O50BW01	BW init. UoM group / mass changes

O541	Number Range Maintenance: OIA01
O542	Number Range Maintenance: OIA10H
O544	Maintain Exchange Stmnt. Customizing
O545	Customzing for Exchange Statement
O547	Reconciliation OIA07
O548	Reconcile Movb. Netting balance
O54E	Maintain Exchange Accounting
O54L	Set Price Ref. Plant Flag
O54N	Set reversal movement type indicator
O54R	Maintain IS-OIL User Exits
O54U	Number Range Maintenance: OIA08
O54X	Create Netting Selection Crit.
O54Y	Maintain Netting Selection Crit.
O54Z	Display Netting Selection Crit.
O581	OIB02 Conversion Mode
O588	Conversion group maintenance
O591	QCI CUSTOMIZED MESSAGE HANDLING
O5A4	Intransit store location determ
O5AA	Number range maintenance: OIG_TU
O5AB	Number range maintenance: OIG_DRIVER
O5AC	Number range maintenance: OIG_VEHMET
O5AD	Number range maintenance: OIG_VEH
O5AE	Number range maintenance: OIG_S
O5AF	Number range maintenance: OIG_RACMET
O5AM	In-transit batch/handling type
O5AW	Number range maintenance: OIG_MASSPR
O5AX	TD Customized Message Handling
O5AY	Define intransit storage location
O5BAP4	Set up application log
O5BAPR1	Number range maintenance: OIRA_PRDOC
O5BAPR2	Number range maintenance: OIRA_PRIDX
O5BAPRDE1	SSR Output Det. - Field catalog
O5BAPRDE2	Cond.table - SSR Group output
O5BAPRDE3	Maintain Condition Type - SSR Gr.Out
O5BAPRDE4	Access Sequence (SSR Group Output)
O5BAPRDE5	SSR Group Output Det.Procedure
O5BAPRDE6	Output Det. Procedure - SSR Gr.Outp.
O5BAPRDE7	Cond.table - SSR Group output
O5BAPRDE8	Cond.table - SSR Group output
O5BC08	SSR Pricing - Create LV/Cond.
O5BC09	SSR Pricing - Disp/Change LV/Cond.
O5BC19_COPY	SSR Pricing - Copy error check cust.
O5BC19_LIST	SSR Pricing - List error check cust.
O5BCNRRG	Number range maintenance: OIRC_PRUPD
O5BCPRCH	Number range maintenance: OIRC_PRCHG
O5BEAD1	V_T681F: SSR CH Object-Allowed flds
O5BEAD11	Cond.proc. for SSR CH Object
O5BEAD13	Credit card accounts
O5BEAD16	SSR Clearing House Determination
O5BEAD2	SSR CH Det. : Create tab.
O5BEAD3	SSR CH Det. : Change tab.
O5BEAD4	SSR CH Det. : Display tab.
O5BEAD5	SSR CH Object det: Acc. seq.- Create
O5BEAD8	Condition types: SSR CH Object

O5BENR	Number range maintenance: OIREDTF
O5BENR01	SSR DTF 'DUMMY' No. Range
O5BENRRECON	Number range maintenance: OIRERECON1
O5BENRRECON2	Number range maintenance: OIRERECON2
O5BEPC4	Generate DTF Objects
O5BESNR	Number range maintenance: OIRESETLNR
O5BESTAT1	Update Maintenance: IS-Oil
O5BH03	Generate CH Sttlmnt Msg Structure
O5BH04	Number range maintenance: OIRH_CHSMG
O5BINR03	Number range maintenance: OIRALINKNR
O5F5	Maintain Form and Average Exits
O5F9	Number Range Maintenance: RepForm-ID
O5K_J1B_27	Global plant business settings
O5N7	Customized Messages for BDRP
O5NX	Maintain time windows for Ref. set
O5O_CTNUM	Number range maintenance: OIO_CNTNR
O5O_PKGNR	Number range maintenance: OIO_EXIDV
O5O_RTNUM	Number range maintenance: OIO_RTDOC
O5O_VGNUM	Number range maintenance: OIO_VOYAGE
O5PC	Number range maintenance: OIK_LID
O5PL	TPI Customized Message Handling
O5R7	Number Range Maintenance: OIF_PBL
O5S1	Output - Cond.Table - Scheduling.
O5S2	Conditions: Possible fields schedul.
O5S3	Maintain Condition Type - Scheduling
O5S4	Access Sequence (Bulk Scheduling)
O5S5	Bulk Scheduling Output Det.Procedure
O5S7	Output Det. Procedure - Scheduling
O5SA	Output - Cond.Table - Change TD Load
O5SB	Conditions: Possible fields loading
O5SC	Maintain Condition Type - Loading
O5SD	Access Sequence (Bulk Tran.-Loading)
O5SE	Bulk Loading Output Det. Procedure
O5SG	Output Det. Procedure - Loading
O5SJ	Output - Cond.Table - Del. Confirm.
O5SK	Conditions: Possible Fields Del.Conf
O5SL	Maintain Condition Type-Del. Confirm
O5SM	Access Sequence (Bulk Scheduling)
O5SN	Bulk Scheduling Output Det.Procedure
O5SP	Output det.procedure del confirm.
O5T1	Number range maintenance: OIJ_WL
O5T4	Number range maintenance: OIJ_TS
O5T7	Maintain condition tables - NOM
O5T7_TKT	Maintain condition tables - Ticket
O5T8	Update fields in field catalog - NOM
O5T8_TKT	Update fields in field catalog - TKT
O5T9	Maintain Condition Type - NOM
O5T9_TKT	Maintain Condition Type - TKT
O5TA	Maintain access sequence - NOM
O5TA_TKT	Maintain access sequence - TKT
O5TB	Maintain output det procedure - NOM
O5TB_TKT	Maintain output det procedure - TKT
O5TC	Assign output det procedure - NOM
O5TE	Assign forms and programs - NOM

SAP Transaction Codes – Volume One

O5TE_TKT	Assign forms and programs - TKT
O5TG	Maintain TSW Planning Calendar
O5TNR_NOM_COMM	Number range maintenance: OIJ_NOMCOM
O5TNR_NOM_VERS	Number range maintenance: OIJ_VERS
O5TNR_OIJ_NOM	No. Range Maintnce: OIJNOM
O5TNR_OIJ_PEG	Number range maintenance: OIJ_PEG
O5TNR_OIJ_SIM	Number range maintenance: OIJ_SIM
O5TPEGT	Define Pegging type
O5UCM_SN_NR	PRA Number Range Maintenance
O5UCM_TT	Common Table Maintenance
O5UCW_CHECK_NUMBERS	Configure Check Numbers in Check Lot
O5UH_JE03	Accounting Category
O5UOW_ORQDOCN	No. Range Maintnce: OIUOW_RQDC
O5UP_SET_MONTHS	Set Data Retention Periods
O5UREP_BACKUP1	Number range maintenance: OIUREPSYS
O5UREP_COMMON	Regulatory Reporting Setup
O5UREP_MMS_TRANS_VAR	MMS-2014: Transport Suppl Rpt Vars
O5U_MEDOCN	Measurement document number ranges
O5VI	Number range maintenance: OIJ_EL_TKT
O5W10	Storage location/license number
O5W11	Config.excise duty account determ.
O5W12	ED consumpt.posting/Activ.movement
O5W13	Activ.ED postings per movement type
O5WV	Number range maintenance: OIH01
O5WW	Number range maintenance: OIH30
O5WX	Number Range Maint.: Tax Revaluation
O5Z0	TDP CUSTOMIZED MESSAGE HANDLING
O5ZZ	C FI Table T030 EXD
O5_SILO02	Silo M. Cust.: Tank storage location
O7E1	Payment advice note entry screens.
O7E3	Acnt assignment model entry screens
O7E4	Preliminary posting entry screens
O7E5	Vendor inv./cr.mem. entry screens
O7E6	G/L item fast entry screens
O7F1	Clearing field selection conditions
O7F2	Clearing field selection search
O7F3	Clearing Field Selection Sort
O7F4	Item Display Field Sel.Conditions
O7F5	Item Display Field Selection Search
O7F6	Item Display Field Selection Sort
O7F7	Item Display Field Selection Total
O7F8	Item Display Field Sel.Addit.Fields
O7F9	Paymnt Adv.Notes Field Selction Flds
O7FA	Pyt Adv.Notes Field Sel.Ext.Sel.Fld
O7FB	Auto.Pymt Fld Sel.Sort Payment
O7FC	Auto.Pymt Fld.Sel.Find Payment
O7FD	Auto.Pymt Fld.Sel.Sort Payment
O7FE	Auto.Pymt Fld.Sel.Find Line Item
O7L0	FI IMG Link
O7L1	FI IMG Link: Check Document
O7L2	Check Parked Documents
O7L3	Check Correspondence
O7L4	Check Withholding Tax
O7L5	Settings for Displaying Payments

O7L6	Settings for Displaying Line Items
O7L7	Settings for Processing Open Items
O7L8	Check Workflow Basis Settings
O7L9	Settings for Payment Release
O7R1	Item Display Totals Variants
O7R2	Item Display Master Record Info.
O7R3	Item Display Special Fields
O7S1	Pyt Medium Correspondence Sort Varnt
O7S2	Pyt Medium Line Items Sort Variant
O7S3	Credit Management Sort Variants
O7S4	General Correspondence Sort Variants
O7S5	Correspondence Int.Docs Sort Variant
O7S6	Line Item Corresp.Sort Variant
O7S7	Item Display Sort Variants
O7V1	Document Display Default Line Layout
O7V2	Item Display Default Line Layout
O7V3	Clearing Default Line Layout
O7V4	Automatic Paymnt Default Line Layout
O7V5	Auto.Pyt Line Item Dflt Line Layout
O7V6	Paymt Adv.Notes Default Line Layout
O7V7	Credit Management Dflt Line Layout
O7Z1	Document Display Line Layout
O7Z2	Document Posting Line Layout
O7Z3	Document Display Line Layout
O7Z4	Clearing Line Layout
O7Z4D	Clearing Line Layout
O7Z4K	Clearing Line Layout
O7Z4S	Clearing Line Layout
O7Z5	Auto.Payment Line Layout
O7Z6	Auto.Pyt Line Item Line Layout
O7Z7	Payment Adv.Notes Line Layout
O7Z8	External Documents Line Layout
O7Z9	Credit Management Line Layout
O851	Update settings
O984	Customizing doc converter program
OA01	Gain/loss substitution -Fixed assets
OA02	Substitution: Mass Changes to Assets
OA03	C AM Asset Class Index
OA05	C AM Maintain Table T499S
OA07	Generate C AM BALTD Record Layout
OA08	FI-AA: Maintain Country Table
OA11	C AM Asset Master Matchcode
OA13	FI-AA Legacy Data Transfer
OA14	Direct import of data
OA15	C AM Maintenance Table T094P
OA1X	Asset Data Transfer
OA50	Maint. of rules for delivery costs
OA79	C AM Maintain Ast.Hist.Sheet Defin.
OA80	C AM Maint. Asset.Hist.Sheet Defin.
OA81	Maintain Transaction Types - Expert
OA84	Generate Period Control
OA85	C FI-AA: Weighting periods
OA90	AM: Asset Register
OAA1	SAP ArchiveLink: Maint. user st.syst

OAA3	SAP ArchiveLink protocols
OAA4	SAP ArchiveLink applic. maintenance
OAAD	ArchiveLink Administration Documents
OAAQ	Take back FI-AA year-end closing
OAAR	C AM Year-end closing by area
OAAT	SAP ArchiveLink: Create ILQBATCH
OAAW	FI-AA: Memo value for asset class
OAAX	FI-AA: Asst class for grp asset only
OAAY	FI-AA: Hist. layout set-asset class
OAAZ	FI-AA: Settlement profile
OAB4	SAP ArchiveLink: Create batch job
OABA	SAP ArchiveLink: Batch job
OABC	Depreciation areas/value transfer
OABD	Depreciation areas/param. transfer
OABE	Deprec. areas/gross transfer
OABK	Delete asset class
OABL	C AM Reset Company Code
OABM	Depreciation areas/Transfer of resvs
OABN	Depreciation areas/ordinary deprec.
OABO	Displaying Open Bar Codes
OABR	Maint. of rules for delivery costs
OABS	Depreciation areas/Special deprec.
OABT	Set Up Parallel Currencies
OABT_OLD	Deprec. areas/parallel currencies
OABU	Depreciation areas/Unplanned deprec.
OABW	Depreciation areas/Replacement vals
OABX	Deppreciation areas/Investmt support
OABY	C AM Maintain Table T093Y
OABZ	Depreciation areas / Interest
OAC0	CMS Customizing Content Repositories
OAC1	C AM Leasing Types
OAC2	SAP ArchiveLink: Global doc. types
OAC3	SAP ArchiveLink: Links
OAC5	SAP ArchiveLink: Bar code entry
OACA	SAP ArchiveLink workflow parameters
OACB	Customer name for evaluation group 1
OACC	Customer name for evaluation group 1
OACCR01	Accruals/Deferrals Doc. Type Maint.
OACCR02	G/L Acct Determination for Acr./Def.
OACD	Customer name for evaluation group 1
OACE	Customer name for evaluation group 1
OACF	Customer name for evaluation group 1
OACH	SAP ArchiveLink: Link Check
OACHP	SAP ArchiveLink: Link Check
OACI	Send RFC Info (CINF)
OACK	SAP ArchiveLink: Syntax check
OACK_FRONTEND	Customizing Check Front End
OACS	C FI-AA View maint. substitutions
OACT	Maintain Categories
OACV	C FI-AA View maint. validations
OAD0	SAP ArchiveLink: Object links
OAD2	SAP ArchiveLink document classes
OAD3	SAP ArchiveLink: Link tables
OAD4	SAP ArchiveLink: Bar code types

OAD5	ArchiveLink: Customizing Wizard
OADB	Define Depreciation Area
OADB_WZ	Set Up Parallel Valuation
OADC	Depreciation Areas: Area type
OADD	ArchiveLink: Print List Display
OADFFCUST	DF Framework Customizing
OADI	Maintain KPro Distribution Tables
OADOCSP	SAP ArchiveLink Document Area
OADR	SAP ArchiveLink: Print list search
OAER	SAP ArchiveLink: Document search
OAG1	SAP ArchiveLink Basic Settings
OAG2	SAP ArchiveLink Basic Settings
OAG3	SAP ArchiveLink Basic Settings
OAG4	SAP ArchiveLink Basic Settings
OAGL	Reset posted depreciation
OAGO	ArchiveLink:Gen. Obj.Key Maintenance
OAGZ	Maintain report selection
OAHT	Send Certificate
OAI5	C FIAA Time-dependent inv. support
OAIA	Customizing Application Attributes
OAIA2	Customizing Application Attributes
OAIMC_VIEW	Document Viewer using IMC
OAK1	C AM Consist. Chart of Depreciation
OAK2	C AM Consist. Company Code
OAK3	C AM Consist. Depreciation Area
OAK4	C AM Consist. G/L Accounts
OAK5	C AM Customizng reconc. acct. contrl
OAK6	C AM Consist. G/L accounts
OAK7	Reconc. acct. as stat. cost element
OAKA	Standart texts in asset class
OAKB	Define asset for gain/loss
OAKPRO	SAP ArchiveLink KPRO Archivelink
OALO	Maintain KPro Locations
OALOGCUST	Customizing Logging
OALX	Define Long Text Templates
OAM1	ArchiveLink: Monitoring
OAM3	ArchiveLink: Monitoring
OAMK	Change Reconciliation Accounts
OAMP	C MM-PUR Purch. Maint. Blockg. Reas.
OANR	Number Range Maintenance: ARCHIVELNK
OAOA	FI-AA: Define asset classes
OAOB	FI-AA: Assign company codes
OAOH	ArchiveLink: Create Documents
OAOR	Business Document Service: Documents
OAP4	FI-AA: Description of chart of dep.
OAPL	C FI-AA: Set Chart of Depreciation
OAQI	SAP ArchiveLink: Create Queues
OAR1	SAP ArchiveLink: Request Management
OARC	Maint. of retention periods FI-AA
OARE	SAP ArchiveLink:St.syst.return codes
OARK	Archive Settings
OARM	Advanced Returns Management
OARM_ARCH_PR	Archiving Supplier Returns
OARM_ARCH_SR	Archiving Customers Returns

OARP	Call up of AM report overview
OASI	FI-AA Implementation Guide (smart)
OASV	Enter G/L Account Postings
OATASK	ArchiveLink Customizing transaction
OATB	Asgmt of dep.area to cross-sys.area
OATR	Define Report Selection
OATU	–
OAUP_LINK	Update Links
OAV5	Index figures
OAV7	C AM Change Simulation Versions
OAV8	FI-AA C Def. Eval. Group, 8 places
OAV9	C AM Asset hist. group view maint.
OAVA	C AM Eval. Group View Maintenance
OAVB	C AM View Maintenance Prop.Indicator
OAVC	C AM Manual Valuat. View Maintenance
OAVD	C AM Insurance Data View Maintenance
OAVE	C AM View Maintenance Classif.NWTax
OAVF	C AM View Maint. Insurance Companies
OAVG	C AM View Maint. Report Simul.(Dep)
OAVH	C AM View Maint. Period Control
OAVI	C AM View Maint. Sort Versions
OAVIEW_IMC	IMC Viewer for ArchiveLink
OAVJ	C AM View Maint. Trans.Type Group
OAVL	C AM View Maint. Locations
OAVM	C AM View Maint. Field Groups
OAVN	C AM View Maint. Fld.Grp. Asset Data
OAVO	C AM View Maint. Screen Control
OAVP	C AM View Maint. Deprec.Trace Texts
OAVR	C AM View Maint. Dep.Check Rules
OAVS	C AM View Maint. Period Rule
OAVT	C AM View Maint. Insurance Premium
OAVX	C AM view maint no.periods shtd f.yr
OAVZ	C AM Call up report
OAW1	Reason for investment
OAW2	Maximum base value
OAW3	Translation method
OAWD	SAP ArchiveLink: Store documents
OAWF	Assign Workflow Tasks
OAWS	Maintain presettings
OAWT	AW01- define value field texts
OAWW	ArchiveLink: Workflow Wizard
OAXB	Deprec. areas for transaction types
OAXC	Deprec. areas for transaction types
OAXD	Deprec. areas for transaction types
OAXE	Deprec. areas for transaction types
OAXF	Define Transaction Type
OAXG	Define Transaction Type
OAXH	Deprec. areas for transaction types
OAXI	Deprec. areas for transaction types
OAXJ	Deprec. areas for transaction types
OAY1	Special handling of transfer posting
OAY2	Asset class: Low value asset check
OAYA	Deprec. areas for transaction types
OAYB	Limiting transaction type groups

OAYC	Legacy data transfer: Depr. terms
OAYD	Legacy data transfer: Man. entry FC
OAYE	Legacy data transfer: Sequence
OAYF	Legacy Data Transfer: Accumul. Depr.
OAYG	Legacy data transfer: Calc.repl.val.
OAYH	Depreciation area currency
OAYI	Memo value of area
OAYJ	Net book value is changeover amount
OAYK	Low-value assets
OAYL	Individual period weighting
OAYM	Permit group asset for area
OAYN	Assign bal.sheet/inc.stmt to area
OAYO	Rounding specific. for deprec. area
OAYP	Shortening rules for shortened FY
OAYQ	Gross/net resrvs.for special deprec.
OAYR	Posting rules for depreciation
OAYS	Special treatment of retirement
OAYT	Transact.type for proportional vals
OAYU	Capitaliztn of dwn-paymnts (transfr)
OAYZ	Asset class: Depreciation areas
OAZ1	Validation Rules for Trans.Typ.Grp.
OAZ2	Substitution for trans.type group
OA_FIND	SAP ArchiveLink: Document search
OA_LOG_VIEW_DOC	Display Log of Documents
OA_LOG_VIEW_PRI	Display Log of Print Lists
OB00	C FI Maintain Table T030 (RDF)
OB01	C FI Maintain Table T691A
OB02	C FI Maintain Table T024B
OB03	C FI Maintain Table T003
OB04	C FI Maintain Table T030F
OB05	C FI Maintain Table T001S
OB06	C FI Maintain Table T031S
OB07	C FI Maintain table TCURV
OB08	C FI Maintain table TCURR
OB09	C FI Maintain Table T030H
OB10	C FI Maintain Table T049L
OB11	C FI Maintain Table T018P
OB12	C FI Maintain Table T691B
OB13	C FI Maintain Table T004
OB14	Configure Field Status Definition
OB15	C FI Maintain Table T004R
OB16	C FI Maintain Table TZUN/TZUNT
OB17	C FI Maintain Table T040
OB18	C FI Maintain Table T040S
OB19	C FI Maintain Table T059M
OB1A	C FI Maint. Table T004 (Layouts)
OB1B	C FI Maint. Table T004 (Layouts)
OB20	C FI Maintain Table T078D
OB21	C FI Maintain Table T079D
OB22	C FI Maintain Table T001A
OB23	C FI Maintain Table T078K
OB24	C FI Maintain Table T079K
OB25	C FI Maintain Table T001X
OB26	C FI Maintain Table T078S

OB27	C FI Maintain Table T008
OB28	C FI Maintain Table T001D
OB29	C FI Fiscal Year Variants
OB30	Accts Rec: Allocate flds -> fld gps
OB31	C FI Maintain Table T055G
OB32	C FI Maintain Table TBAER
OB33	C FI Maintain Table T055
OB34	C FI Maintain Table T055G
OB35	Customer Balance Confirmation
OB36	Vendor Balance Confirmation
OB37	C FI Maintain Table T001 (PERIV)
OB38	Assign Co.Code -> Cred.Cntl Area
OB39	C FI Maintain Table TRAS
OB40	C FI Maintain Table T030
OB41	Maintain Accounting Keys
OB42	C FI Maintain Table T056Z
OB43	C FI Maintain Table T015L
OB44	C FI Maintain Table T016
OB45	C FI Maintain Table T014
OB46	C FI Maintain Table T056
OB47	C FI Maintain Table T015W
OB48	C FI Maintain Matchcode SAKO
OB49	C FI Maintain Matchcode DEBI
OB50	C FI Maintain Matchcode KRED
OB51	C FI Maintain Table T024P
OB52	C FI Maintain Table T001B
OB53	C FI Maintain Table T030
OB54	C FI Maintain Table T001 (PERIV)
OB55	C FI Maintain Table TFAV
OB56	C FI Maintain Table T053
OB57	C FI Maintain Table T043
OB58	C FI Maintain Table T011/T011T
OB59	C FI Maintain Valuation Methods
OB60	C FI Maintain Table T041B
OB61	C FI Maintain Table T047M
OB62	C FI Maintain Table T001 (KTOPL + 2)
OB63	C FI Maintain Table T001 (XGJRV)
OB64	C FI Maintain Table T001 (WAABV)
OB65	C FI Maintain Table T001 (XGSBE)
OB66	C FI Maintain Table T001 (XKDFT)
OB67	C FI Maintain Table T001 (MREGL)
OB68	C FI Maintain Table T001
OB69	C FI Maintain Table T001
OB70	C FI Maintain Table T001
OB71	C FI Maintain Table T001
OB72	C FI Maintain Table T001O
OB73	C FI Maintain Table T031
OB74	C FI Maintain Table TF123
OB75	Cust.Pmnt Program: Available Amnts
OB76	C FI Maintain Table T045E
OB77	C FI Maintain Table T048/T048T
OB78	C FI Maintain Table T048B
OB79	C FI Maintain Table T048I
OB80	C FI Maintain Table T043K

OB81	C FI Maintain Table T056A
OB82	C FI Maintain Table T056U
OB83	C FI Maintain Table T056P
OB84	C FI Maintain Table T056D
OB85	C FI Maintain Table T056B
OB86	C FI Maintain Table T005 (WECHF)
OB87	C FI Maintain Table T001N
OB88	C FI Maintain Table T001
OB89	C FI Maintain Table T030
OB90	C FI Maintain Table T001R
OB91	C FI Maintain Table T001F
OB92	C FI Maintain Table T001G
OB93	C FI Maintain Table TGSBG
OB94	C FI Maintain Table T042M
OB95	C FI Maintain Table T042N
OB96	C FI Maintain Table T001F
OB97	C FI Maintain Table T059A
OB98	C FI Maintain Table T059F
OB99	C FI Maintain Table T005Q
OBA0	G/L Account Tolerance Groups
OBA1	C FI Maintain Table T030
OBA2	C FI Maintain Table T001M
OBA3	C FI Maintain Table T043G
OBA4	C FI Maintain Table T043T
OBA5	Change Message Control
OBA6	C FI Maintain Table T046
OBA7	C FI maintain table T003
OBA8	C FI Maintain Table TRERI
OBA9	C FI Maintain Table T015Z
OBAA	C FI Maintain Table T056S
OBAB	C FI Maintain Table T056Y
OBAC	C FI Maintain Table T056R
OBAD	C FI Maintain Table T005P
OBAE	C FI Maintain Table T005S
OBAF	C FI Maintain Table T048K
OBAG	C FI Maintain Table T060O
OBAH	C FI Maintain Table T060A
OBAI	C FI Maintain Table T060
OBAJ	C FI Maintain Table T060
OBAK	C FI Maintain Table T060
OBAL	C FI Maintain Table T052A
OBAM	C FI Maintain Table T052R
OBAN	C FI Maintain Table T060O
OBAO	C FI Maintain Table T060O
OBAP	C FI Maintain Table TZGR
OBAQ	C FI Maintain Table T047R
OBAR	C FI Maintain Table T077D
OBAS	C FI Maintain Table T077K
OBAT	C FI Maintain Table T055G
OBAU	C FI Maintain Table T055
OBAV	C FI Maintain Table T049E
OBAW	C FI Maintain Table T049F
OBAX	C FI Maintain Table T049A
OBAY	C FI Maintain Table T049B

OBAZ	C FI Maintain Table FEDICUS
OBB0	C FI Maintain table T030 valuatn adj
OBB1	C FI Maintain Table T001G
OBB2	C FI Maintain Table TFMC
OBB3	C FI Maintain Table TFMC
OBB4	C FI Maintain Table TFMC
OBB5	C FI Maintain Table T001
OBB6	C FI Maintain Table TGSB
OBB7	C FI Maintain Table TGSB
OBB8	C FI Maintain Table T052
OBB9	C FI Maintain Table T052S
OBBA	C FI Maintain Table T012C
OBBB	C FI Maintain Table T012A
OBBC	C FI Maintain Table T052 (Block Key)
OBBD	C FI Maintain Table T045T
OBBE	C FI Maintain Table T053R and T053S
OBBF	C FI Maintain Table TCURD
OBBG	C FI Maintain Table T005 (KALSM)
OBBH	C FI Maintain Table T001Q (Document)
OBBI	Maintain G/L Account Field Groups
OBBJ	Maintain Sample Account Field Groups
OBBK	C FI Maintain Table T055G (Banks)
OBBL	C FI Maintain Table T055 (Banks)
OBBM	C FI Maintain Table T055G (Docs)
OBBN	C FI Maintain Table T055 (Docs)
OBBO	C FI Maintain Table T010O
OBBP	C FI Maintain Table T001 (OPVAR)
OBBQ	C FI Maintain Table T044D
OBBR	C FI Table T042R Maintenance
OBBS	C FI Maintain Table TCURF
OBBT	C FI Table T030 Maintenance GLU+GLU
OBBU	C FI Maintain Table T044K List
OBBUSPRO	Business Processes
OBBV	C FI Maintain Table T030 BI2+SPACE
OBBW	C FI Maintain Table T030 BI3+A00
OBBX	C FI Maintain Table T030 BI4+SPACE
OBBY	C FI Maintain Tables T028V + T028W
OBBZ	C FI Subst. FI/0005: Activate
OBC1	C FI Maintain Table T054
OBC2	C FI Maintain Table T054A
OBC3	C FI Maintain Table TLSEP
OBC4	C FI Maintain Table T004V
OBC5	C FI Maintain Table T001
OBC6	C FI Maintain Table T001
OBC7	C FI Maintain Table T059Q
OBC8	C FI Table T001 Maintenance (TXKRS)
OBC9	External Group Number for Taxation
OBCA	C FI Maintain Table T076B
OBCB	C FI Maintain Table T076I
OBCC	C FI Maintain Table T076K
OBCD	C FI Maintain Table T076M
OBCE	C FI Maintain Table T076S
OBCF	C FI Maintain Table T007F
OBCG	C FI Maintain Table T007K

OBCH	C FI Maintain Table T007L
OBCI	C FI Maintain Table T007I
OBCJ	C FI Maintain Table T007J
OBCK	FI Table Maintenance T001 (XSTDT)
OBCL	FI Table Maint. T001 (MWSKV+MWSKA)
OBCM	C FI Maintain Table T007F
OBCN	C FI Maintain Table T007B
OBCO	C FI Maintain Table TTXD
OBCP	C FI Maintain Table TTXJ
OBCQ	C FI Table T053G Maintenance
OBCR	C FI Table T053V + T053W Maintenance
OBCS	C FI Table T053E Maintenance
OBCT	C FI Table T053A + T053B Maintenance
OBCU	C FI Table T053C Maintenance
OBCV	C FI FAKP: T021R with SL-AX
OBCW	C FI table T053D maintenance
OBCX	TTXC View
OBCY	C FI Table TTYPV Maintenance
OBCZ	C FI Maintain Table T021E
OBD1	Document parking posting date
OBD2	C FI Maintain Table T077D
OBD3	C FI Maintain Table T077K
OBD4	C FI Maintain Table T077S
OBD5	C FI Maintain Table T003B
OBD6	C FI Maintain Table TCURS
OBDA	C FI Table T059E + T059G Maintenance
OBDB	C FI Table T053R Maintenance
OBDC	C FI Maintain View Cluster V_T060K
OBDD	C FI Table T060K Maintenance
OBDE	C FI Table T060M Maintenance
OBDF	C FI Maint.view cluster V_T060o
OBDG	C FI Maintain Table T076A
OBDH	C FI Maintain Table T076E
OBDI	C FI Maintenance of Table T007Z
OBDU	Job Names for Data Transfers
OBE7	C FI Batch Input Customers
OBE8	C FI Generate Btch Input Rcrd Layout
OBEA	Maintain Convertible Reports
OBEB	Main.Table for Old Local Curr.(EURO)
OBEBGEN	Electronic Banking: General
OBEBLADR	Assign Banks to OFX partners
OBETX	Number Assignment for Ext. Tax Docum
OBF1	C FI Maintain Table TFI01/TFI01T
OBF2	C FI Maintain Table TFI02
OBF3	Bank selection, current setting
OBF4	C FI maintain table T003
OBF5	C FI Maint. Table T042OFI/T042OFIT
OBF8	C FI Batch Input Vendors
OBFA	C FI Corresp.Sort Variants/Corresp.
OBFB	C FI Corresp.Sort Variants/Documents
OBFC	C FI Corresp.Sort Variants/Lne Items
OBG1	C FI Maintain tbl T030 offsttng acct
OBG4	C FI Batch Input Documents
OBG5	C FI Batch Input G/L Accounts

OBH1	C FI Doc.No.Range: Copy Company Code
OBH2	C FI Doc.No.Range: Copy Fiscal Year
OBI1	C FI Maintain int.rules & conditions
OBIA	C FI Maintain View Cluster VC_TFAG
OBIB	Parameter Transaction for V_TFAGM
OBIC	Customizing Selection BIC
OBICACT	Follow-Up Actions: Batch Cockpit
OBICACTU	Follow-Up Actions: Assign BIC
OBICBRO	BIC: Batch-Related Objects
OBICBROT	BIC: Tables: Batch-Related Objects
OBICOBJ	Define Object Types and Parameters
OBICSEL	Enhanced Selection: Batch Cockpit
OBICSELU	Enhanced Selection: Assign BIC
OBIC_DIS	Display SAP Standard Selection BIC
OBIC_S	Customizing: SAP Selection BIC
OBJ1	C FI Year End Financial Statement
OBJ2	C FI Year End Compact Doc.Journal
OBJ3	C FI Year End Bill of Exchange List
OBJ4	C FI Year End G/L Account Balances
OBJ5	C FI Year End G/L Account List
OBJ6	Posting Totals
OBJ7	Bill of Exchange Charges Statement
OBK1	C FI Year End OI Customer List
OBK2	C FI Year End Customer Acct Balances
OBK3	C FI Year End Customer List
OBK4	C FI Year End OI Vendor List
OBK5	C FI Year End Vendor Acct Balances
OBK6	C FI Year End Vendor List
OBK7	Subledger Accts Bal.Carried Forward
OBK8	G/L Accounts Balance Carried Forward
OBK9	Payment Notices Correspondence
OBKA	Account Statement Correspondence
OBKB	Internal Documents Correspondence
OBKC	Individual Letters Correspondence
OBKD	Document Statements Correspondence
OBKE	Customer Stmnt Corresp.Account Stmnt
OBKF	Failed Payment Correspondence
OBKG	Correspondence Sel.Criteria Letters
OBKR	Maintain Number Range: FI_RECEIPT
OBKS	C FI Table T058A Maintenance
OBKT	C FI Table T058B Maintenance
OBKU	C FI Table T011A + T011B Maintenance
OBKV	C FI Table T011E + T011F Maintenance
OBKW	C FI Table T011V Maintenance
OBL1	Consistency Check: Auto.Pstg (Docu.)
OBL2	Consistency Check: Auto.Pstg (ErAny)
OBL3	Consistency Check: Sp.G/L (Docu.)
OBL4	Consistency Check: Sp.G/L (Err.Anly)
OBL5	Consistency Check: Pmnt Prog.Config.
OBL6	Consistency Check: Dunn.Prog.Config.
OBM1	C FI Month End Advance Tax Return
OBM2	C FI Month End Financial Statement
OBM3	C FI Month End Foreign Trade Regns
OBM4	C FI Month End Compact Doc.Journal

OBM5	C FI G/L Balances Monthly Report
OBM6	Posting Data Reconciliation
OBMA	Default Transaction Type for FI Acts
OBMD	C FI Selec.Variants Dunning/Dun.line
OBMK	C FI Selec.Variants Dunning/Dunn.hdr
OBML	Assgmt LO Trans Type to FI Trans Typ
OBMSG	Configurable Messages
OBN1	C FI Month End OI Customer List
OBN2	C FI Month End Financial Statement
OBN3	C FI Month End OI Vendor List
OBN4	C FI Month End Vendor Acct Balances
OBNB	Transaction Code for SAPMFKM2
OBO1	C FI FAKP Line Item Line Layout
OBO2	C FI FAKP Credit Mangmnt Line Layout
OBOB	C FI FAKP Line Item Line Layout
OBOFXBUS	OFX: Business Customizing
OBOFXTECH	OFX: Technical Customizing
OBOR1	Maintenance Profiles for GR Dialog
OBOR2	Maintenance of Function Profile
OBOR3	Maintenance of Object Profiles
OBOR4	Maintenance of Selection Profiles
OBOR5	Maintain Column Profiles
OBOR6	Maintenance of Filter Profiles
OBOR7	Maintenance of Config. Profiles
OBP1	C FI create distribution key
OBP2	C FI Change Distribution Keys
OBP3	C FI display distribution key
OBP4	C FI delete distribution key
OBP5	Delete FI planning data
OBP6	G/L: Versions
OBPE	C FI Penalty Interests
OBPL	Subsequently post CO plan.data to GL
OBPM1	Maintenance of Pymt Medium Formats
OBPM1A	Display of Pymt Medium Formats
OBPM2	Maintenance of Note to Payee
OBPM3	Payment Medium Formats (Customer)
OBPM4	Payment Medium Selection Variants
OBPM5	Cross-Payment Run Payment Medium
OBPN	C FI Penalty Interests
OBQ1	C FI Condition Compnt: Condit.Types
OBQ2	C FI Condit.Component: Access Seque.
OBQ3	C FI Condition Component: Calc.Proc.
OBR1	Delete Documents
OBR2	Delete Subledger Accounts
OBR3	C FI Maintain Table T001
OBR4	Delete Banks
OBR7	Maintain account type life
OBR8	Maintain document type life
OBRD	Customers: maintain report selection
OBRK	Vendors: maintain report selection
OBRS	G/L: maintain report selection
OBRX	Flexible G/L: Maintain Report Selec.
OBS1	C FI Create Ledger
OBS2	C FI Change Ledger

OBS3	C FI Display Ledger
OBS4	C FI Delete Ledger
OBT1	C FI Maintain Table TTXID (KNA1)
OBT10	C FI Maint. Table TTXID (DOC_ITEM)
OBT2	C FI Maintain Table TTXID (KNB1)
OBT3	C FI Maintain Table TTXID (KNKK)
OBT3Z	C FI Maintain Table TTXID (KNKA)
OBT4	C FI Maintain Table TTXID (LFA1)
OBT5	C FI Maintain Table TTXID (LFB1)
OBT6	C FI Maintain Table TTXID (SKA1)
OBT7	C FI Maintain Table TTXID (SKB1)
OBT8	C FI Maintain Table TTXID (BELEG)
OBT9	C FI Maintain Table TTXID (MR01)
OBU1	Document Type/Posting Key Options
OBUV	TxApportnmnt for Cross-Co.Cde Trans.
OBV1	C FI Int.For Dys Overdue Acct Deter.
OBV2	C FI G/L Acct Bal.Int.Calc.Acct Det.
OBV3	C FI Cust.Bal.Int.Calc.Acct Determ.
OBV4	C FI Vend.Bal.Int.Calc.Acct Determ.
OBV5	C FI Maintain Table T030Q
OBV6	C FI Maintain Table T030V
OBV7	C FI Maintain Table T001O
OBV9	C FI Act Det.Vendor Intrst on Arrs
OBVCS	C FI Display View
OBVCU	C FI Maintain View Cluster
OBVS	C FI Display View
OBVT	C FI Display Restricted View
OBVU	C FI Maintain View
OBVV	C FI Maintain Restricted View
OBVW	C FI maintain view
OBVY	C FI Maintain Table T030H
OBW1	C FI Maintain Table T001F
OBW2	C FI Maintain Table T001G
OBW3	Instructions in Payment Transactions
OBWA	C FI Table VBWF01+VBWF02 Maintenance
OBWB	C FI Table VBWF08 Maintenance
OBWC	C FI Table VBWF03 Maintenance
OBWD	C FI Table VBWF05 Maintenance
OBWE	C FI Table VBWF06+VBWF07 Maintenance
OBWF	C FI Table VBWF09+VBWF10 Maintenance
OBWG	C FI Table VBWF04 Maintenance (Cust)
OBWH	C FI Table VBWF04 Maintenance (Vend)
OBWI	C FI Table VBWF04 Maintenance (G/L)
OBWJ	C FI Table T001 Maintenance (WFVAR)
OBWK	C FI Table VBWF04 (Assets)
OBWL	C FI Maintain Tables VBWF11 + VBWF12
OBWO	C FI Withholding Tax
OBWP	Payment release by authorized person
OBWQ	Payment Release Document Types
OBWR	C FI Maintain Table FEDIWF1
OBWS	C FI Withholding Tax
OBWU	C FI Withholding Tax
OBWW	C FI Withholding Tax
OBWZ	Number Range Maintenance: WITH_CTNO

OBX1	C FI Table T030B: G/L Acct Posting
OBX2	CO-FI Table T030B Document Splitting
OBXA	C FI Table T030
OBXB	C FI Table T030
OBXC	C FI Table T030
OBXD	C FI Maintain Table T030
OBXE	C FI Table T030
OBXF	C FI Sort Bank Directory
OBXG	C FI Maintain Bank Direc.Automatic.
OBXH	C FI Table T041A/T041T
OBXI	C FI Table T030
OBXJ	C FI Table T030B
OBXK	C FI Table T030
OBXL	C FI Table T030
OBXM	C FI Table T030
OBXN	C FI Table T030 GAU/GA0
OBXO	C FI Table T030 KDW
OBXP	C FI Maintain Table T030 zaf
OBXQ	C FI Table T030 KDZ
OBXR	C FI Table T074
OBXS	C FI Table T030
OBXT	C FI Table T074
OBXU	C FI Table T030
OBXV	C FI Table T030
OBXW	C FI Table T030B Cleared Invoices
OBXY	C FI Table T074
OBXZ	C FI Table T030 G/L Accont Clearing
OBY0	C FI Copy CoCde with Ctry Chrt/Accts
OBY2	C FI Copy company code (G/L account)
OBY6	C FI Maintain Table T001
OBY7	C FI Copy Chart of Accounts
OBY8	C FI Delete Chart of Accounts
OBY9	C FI Transport Chart of Accounts
OBYA	C FI Table T030
OBYB	Maintain automatic postings accounts
OBYC	C FI Table T030
OBYD	C FI Table T030
OBYE	C FI Table T030
OBYF	Revenue Account Determination
OBYG	C FI Table T030
OBYH	C FI Table T030
OBYK	C FI Table T045W
OBYL	C FI Table T030 HRI + HRC
OBYM	C FI Table T074 Bill of Exchange
OBYN	C FI Table T074 Bill Receivable
OBYP	C FI Table T074 Check/Bill of Exch.
OBYR	C FI Table T074
OBYS	C FI Table T074 Tangible Fixed Asset
OBYT	C FI Table T030 HRI + HRD
OBYU	C FI Table T030 HRI + HRD
OBYY	C FI Table T030 Maintenance KDT/KDT
OBYZ	C FI Condition Components
OBZ1	C FI FBZP T042B
OBZ2	C FI FBZP T042

OBZ3	C FI FBZP T042Z
OBZ4	C FI FBZP T042E
OBZ4CT	Letter for Payment Correspondence
OBZ5	Maintain Bank Determination Ranking
OBZ6	C FI FBZP Consistency Check
OBZA	Reporting Selection: Global Menu
OBZB	Reporting Selection: Accts Receivble
OBZC	Reporting Selection: Accts Payable
OBZD	Reporting Selection: G/L Accounts
OBZE	Reporting Selection: Documents
OBZF	Reporting Selection: Documents
OBZG	Reporting Selection: G/L Accounts
OBZH	C FI Maintenance Table TCCFI
OBZI	C FI Maintenance Table TCCAA
OBZJ	C FI Maintenance Table T000CM
OBZK	C FI Maintenance Table T001CM
OBZL	C FI Maintain Table T001 (XCOS)
OBZM	C FI Substitution FI/0005: Create
OBZN	C FI Substitution FI/0005: Change
OBZO	Doc.Types for Single Scrn Transactns
OBZT	Single Screen Transaction Tax Code
OB_7	C FI Maint.Table T044G Val.Adj.Key
OB_8	C FI Maintain Table T044I Base Value
OB_9	C FI Maintain Table T044J: Display
OB_GLACC01	Create G/L accounts with reference
OB_GLACC11	G/L acct record: Mass maintenance 01
OB_GLACC12	G/L acct record: Mass maintenance 02
OB_GLACC13	G/L acct record: Mass maintenance 03
OB_GLACC21	Configuration G/L account record
OB_GLACC31	Assign G/L Account Change Request
OB_T001_CESSION	FI Customizing: Accts Rble Pledging
OB_VAR_FBWAPI0	FI Cust.: INet/Service Variants
OB_VAR_FBWARI0	FI Cust.: INet/Service Variants
OB_V_CESSION	FI Customizing: Accts Rble Fact.Ind.
OB_V_FDKDATES	FI Cust.: Internet/Time Frame
OC00	C FI-LC : Table T850
OC01	C FI-LC : Table T850A
OC02	C FI-LC : Table T852P
OC03	C FI-LC : Table T854
OC04	C RF-KONS : Table T854S
OC05	C FI-LC : Table T854T
OC07	C FI-LC : Table T855T
OC08	C FI-LC : Table T856
OC09	C FI-LC : Table T856T
OC10	C FI-LC : Table T857
OC11	V_T850F: Define Upload Methods
OC14	C FI-LC : Table T858
OC15	C FI-LC : Table T858T
OC16	C FI-LC : Table T859
OC17	C FI-LC : Table T859T
OC18	C FI-LC : Table T860
OC19	C FI-LC : Table T861
OC20	C RF-KONS : Table T862Q -> T862S
OC21	C RF-KONS : Table T862K -> T862T

OC22	Customizing line layout of reports
OC23	C FI-LC : Table T863
OC24	C FI-LC : Table T863T
OC25	Maintain VAlue Types
OC26	C FI-LC : Table T864
OC27	Customizing IC eliminations
OC28	C FI-LC : Table T866
OC29	C FI-LC : Table T867
OC30	C FI-LC : Table T867T
OC31	C FI-LC : Table T869
OC32	C FI-LC : Table T869T
OC33	Customize document types
OC34	C FI-LC : Table T876T
OC35	C RF-KONS: Table T866Z
OC36	C FI-LC : Table T879
OC37	C FI-LC : Table T881
OC38	C FI-LC : Table T884
OC39	C FI-LC : Table T884H
OC40	C FI-LC : Table TCURC
OC41	Maintain Exchange Rates
OC42	C RF-KONS : Table T876V
OC43	C FI : Table T850S
OC44	C FI : Table T880B
OC45	C FI-LC : Table T851
OC46	C FI : Table T871
OC47	Maintain E/R Types for Crcy Transl.
OC48	C FI-LC : Table T855
OC49	C FI-LC: Table T863I
OC50	Gain/Loss from asset retirement
OC51	C RF-KONS : Table T866Z - add.fld
OC52	Group Shares
OC53	Group Reports
OC55	Contra items/Retained earnings
OC56	Download for consolidation
OC57	Transfer chnges in invest./equity
OC58	Data transfer for affiliated co.s
OC59	Print data entry forms/audit trail
OC60	Bundle Data Entry Forms
OC61	K3 form
OC62	List of Ownership
OC63	Changes in equity
OC64	Changes in investment
OC65	Print Translation Method
OC66	Changes in hidden reserves
OC67	Investment in companies
OC68	Interactive consolidation reporting
OC69	Consolidation of investments
OC70	Print financial statement items
OC71	Listing of Totals File Records
OC72	Database list: Journal entries
OC73	Consolidation: data input via MT
OC74	Bundle Consolidation Activities
OC75	Print cons. of investments method
OC76	Data input via PC

OC77	Validate consolidation data
OC78	Copy FS items from RF Tables
OC79	Create D/E form from f/s item tables
OC80	Build Standard Report from D.E.form
OC81	Change FS Item Numbers
OC82	Validation Check: Items/DE Forms
OC83	Exchange Item Numbers:Totals Records
OC84	Renumber Lines for Data Entry Forms
OC85	Renumber Standard Report Table
OC86	Copy Totals Records
OC87	Data selection for reporting
OC88	Layout of FS Chart of Accounts
OC89	Intercompany Elimination
OC90	Reclassifications
OC91	Currency Translation (Consolidation)
OC92	Carry Forward Balances-Consolidation
OC93	Currency devaluation
OC94	Elim.of Intercompany Profit/Loss
OC95	Validation Maintenance
OC96	Exchange Item Numbers: Documents
OC97	Upload FS Items and Texts
OC98	FI-LC: Rptg line layout frm Item tbl
OC99	Totals recs: Delete (local values)
OCA0	
OCA1	C FI-LC: Equity/Earnings Adj.Table
OCA2	C FI_LC: Fidden Reserves Table
OCA3	C FI-LC: Amot.of Hidden Reserves Tbl
OCA4	C FI-LC: Asset Tfr Dep.History Tble
OCA5	C FI-LC: IC P&L Elim. - Rep.Co. Tble
OCA6	C FI-LC: IC P&L Elim. - Sup.Co. Tble
OCA7	C FI-LC: IC Asset Transfers Table
OCA8	C FI-LC: Display Cons.Methods Table
OCA9	C RF : Table T863B
OCAA	C FI-LC: Table T862K
OCAB	C FI-LC: Table T862Q
OCAC	C FI-LC: Table T862X
OCAD	C FI-LC: Display V_T862K
OCAE	C FI-LC: Display V_T862Q
OCAF	C FI-LC: Display V_T862X
OCAG	C FI-LC: Display V_T862S
OCAH	C FI-LC: Display V_T862T
OCAI	C FI-LC: Display V_T862Z
OCAJ	C FI-LC: Display V_T863W
OCAK	FI-LC: Print Transaction Types
OCAL	FI-LC: Print IC Eliminations
OCAM	FI-LC: Print Inventory Mgmt Company
OCAN	FI-LC: Print Supplying Company
OCAO	FI-LC: Print Changes in Net Income
OCAP	FI-LC: Print Hidden Reserves
OCAR	FI-LC: Print Chgs in Trfr Depreciatn
OCAS	FI-LC: Print Asset Transfer
OCAT	FI-LC: Print Versions
OCAU	FI-LC: Print Selected FS Items
OCB0	Step consolidation

OCB1	Bundle Standard Reports
OCB2	Consolidation Documents
OCB3	C FI : Table T879P
OCB4	C FI : Table T882C
OCB5	Extract Subgroup
OCB6	Totals file records
OCB7	Create set
OCB8	Create set
OCB9	Create set
OCBA	Create set
OCBB	Create set
OCBC	Create set
OCBD	C RF-KONS : Table T854S
OCBE	C RF-KONS : Table T854S
OCBF	C RF-KONS : Table T854S
OCBG	C RF-KONS : Table T854S
OCBH	C RF-KONS : Table T854S
OCBI	C RF-KONS : Table T854S
OCBJ	C FI-LC : Table T869
OCBK	C FI-LC : Table T869
OCBL	C FI-LC : Table T865
OCBM	C RF-KONS : Table T854S
OCBN	C FI-LC : Table T879
OCBO	C FI-LC: AM Trans.Types Table
OCBP	Upload extract from R/2
OCBQ	C RF-KONS : Table T854S
OCBR	C RF-KONS : Table T854S
OCBS	C RF-KONS: Per.Equity/Earn.Adj.Table
OCBT	C FI-LC: Cons.Method Assign.Table
OCBU	C RF-KONS : Table T854S
OCBV	Reconcile Extended G/L Accounts
OCBW	Consolidation: data input via MT
OCBX	FI-LC: Field Mvt for BalCarFwd Tble
OCBY	Create Corporate Chart of Accounts
OCBZ	Compare Extract / Cons.Data Base
OCC0	Central Group Table
OCC1	FI-LC: Table FGSBK
OCC2	FI-LC: Table TGSB
OCC3	FI-LC: Table TGSBG
OCC4	FI-LC: Table T880G
OCC5	FI-LC: Display Table T880G
OCC6	FI-LC: Table TLMGB
OCC7	FI-LC: Table TKMGB
OCC8	Info System: Report Selection
OCCB	Info System: Further Reports
OCCC	Maintain Group Account
OCCD	Customer: Maintain Trading Partner
OCCE	Change GL customizing company code
OCCF	Create GL Customizing Company code
OCCG	Business area for MM
OCCI	Cons. Integration Settings
OCCJ	Maintain FILCA Number range
OCCK	Vendor: Trading Partner
OCCL	FI-LC: Table T880 / read

OCCM	Reconcile G/L Accounts/Consolidation
OCCM1	Equip. BOM Settings for CC
OCCP	Print G/L account / group account
OCCS	Validate GL acct Group acct
OCCT	FS Items from Chart of Accounts
OCD2	Line layout entry form
OCD3	Line layout entry form texts
OCD4	Column layout data entry form
OCD5	D/E form column layout texts
OCD6	Line layout data entry form number
OCD7	Column layout data entry form number
OCD8	Maintain Validation groups
OCD9	Maintain Valid.group texts
OCDA	Maintain data entry form groups
OCDB	Maintain D/E form group texts
OCDC	Maintain Transaction Type Groups
OCDD	Maintain TTy Groups - Texts
OCDE	Maintain Cons. Activity Groups
OCDF	Maintain Cons.Activity Group texts
OCDG	Maintain Report groups
OCDH	Maintain Report groups - Texts
OCDI	Maintain Cons.Frequencies
OCDJ	Maintain F/S Item short texts
OCDL	Delete FI-LC Ledger Transaction data
OCDM	Hierarchy of Totals Reports
OCDN	Download MS ACCESS
OCDO	Delete FS chart of accounts
OCDT	FI-LC: V_T876B_CT (DTs for Transltn)
OCDZ	Cons stag. ledger: delete trans data
OCE1	C RF-KONS : Table T85A
OCE2	C RF-KONS : Table T85B
OCE3	C RF-KONS : Table T85C
OCE4	C RF-KONS : Table T85S1
OCE5	C RF-KONS : Table T85S2
OCE6	Additional Field Category
OCFV	Organizational area restrictions
OCH0	Batch Management
OCHA	IMG Batch Management
OCHS	Set system messages
OCI1	Maintain TCUSC
OCL1	FI-LC: Create Ledger
OCL2	FI-LC: Change Ledger
OCL3	FI-LC: Display Ledger
OCL4	FI-LC: Delete Ledger
OCL5	Extract to EIS
OCL6	Import Report definition
OCLM1	Task Customizing
OCLM2	Claim Field Selection: General
OCM1	Backgrd Job: Processing Init.Objects
OCM2	Backgd Job: Processing Proc.Elements
OCM3	Background Job: OCM Goods Movements
OCM9	Fill Partner Roles for Header Scrns
OCMAC01	Create Condition Tables
OCMAC02	Change Condition Tables

OCMAC03	Display Condition Tables
OCMAC04	Maintain Field Catalog
OCMAC05	Define Access Sequences
OCMAC06	Define Condition Types
OCMAC07	Maintain Pricing Procedures
OCMAC_01A	Create Condition Record
OCMAC_01B	Maintain Condition Record
OCMAC_01C	Display Condition Record
OCMAC_01D	Create Condition Record With Ref.
OCMAC_03C	Determine Document Currency
OCMAC_03D	Determine Fee Calculation Procedure
OCMAC_05C	Determine Contract Account Category
OCMAC_05D	Determine Document Type
OCMAC_05G	Determine G/L Account
OCMAC_05M	Determine Main and Sub Transaction
OCMAC_05T	Determine Contract Object Type
OCMAC_06C	Determine.CO Account Assignment
OCMAC_07C	Determine dunning procedure
OCMAC_07D	Determine Document Type(Grant)
OCMAC_07S	Determine St. C.O.T (Grant)
OCMAC_07T	Main Trans./Subtrans. for Grants
OCMAC_08	Define Acct. Key
OCMAC_09	Assign Acct. Key
OCMAC_FEEDOCNUM	Number Range Maintenance: CMAC_FEEC
OCMAC_GRDOCNUM	Number Ranges for Grant Documents
OCMAC_PC09	Grant Clearing Account
OCMAC_PC20	Determine Tax Code
OCMAC_PCU0	1098T: Derivation of Tuit Statement
OCMI	Import models cost elements
OCN1	FI-LC: Repost FI data
OCN2	FI-LC: Repost MM data
OCN3	FI-LC: Repost SD data
OCNG	Graphic customizing
OCNPQ1	Customizing Invoicing Plan PS
OCNRC	Search Schema for CN Batch Detmntn
OCO2	Customizing: Country Version
OCP0	PDM
OCP1	Allowed Business Objects
OCP2	Profile Names
OCP3	Field Groups per Profile Name
OCP4	Profile Sequences
OCP5	Filters for Structure Overview
OCPLM	Data Display in PLM Portal
OCPLMT	Group Descriptions for PLM Portal
OCPLMU	Data for User Groups in PLM Portal
OCPP	GG Price Protection by Sales Org.
OCPR	Maintenance of Backflush Profiles
OCR1	Payment Cards: Check Results
OCR2	Payment Cards: Check Results
OCR3	Payment Cards: Check Results
OCR4	Payment Cards: Check Results
OCRD	Number Range Maintenance: FCRP
OCU0	Customizing Menu for Variants
OCUW	Assign Worklist Folder to Users

OCV1	FI-LC: V_T854T_A (only SY-LANGU)
OCV2	FI-LC: V_T854U_A (only SY-LANGU)
OCV3	FI-LC: V_T855T_A (only SY-LANGU)
OCV4	FI-LC: V_T850A_A (SY-LANGU only)
OCV5	FI-LC: V_T879_2 (only AA='AW')
OCV6	FI-LC: V_T879_2 (only AA='PC')
OCV7	FI-LC: V_T879_2 (only AA='PL')
OCV8	FI-LC: V_T850_A (Access entry)
OCV9	FI-LC: V_T850_B (DBase entry)
OCVA	FI-LC: V_T850I_A (Access entry)
OCVB	FI-LC: V_T850I_A (Dbase entry)
OCVC	FI-LC: V_T850I_B (PC entry, other)
OCVD	FI-LC: V_T850I_C (only valid.groups)
OCVE	FI-LC: V_T850_D (only DE form group)
OCVF	FI-LC: V_T850_E (only first consol.)
OCVG	FI-LC: V_T850_F (only sort criteria)
OCVH	FI-LC: V_T852_A (only report group)
OCVI	FI-LC: V_T852V_A (only cons.group)
OCVJ	FI-LC: V_T880B_A (only transl.meth.)
OCVK	FI-LC: V_T879_A ('PL',only SY-LANGU)
OCVM	View Maintenance: initial screen
OCVN	FI-LC: V_T850I_A (from SAP System)
OCVO	FI-LC: V_T850I_A (from R/2 system)
OCVP	FI-LC: V_T881_A
OCVQ	FI-LC: V_T850I
OCVR	V_T85A Additional Fields
OCVS	V_T85S1 Assignment AddFld 1- AddFld2
OCVT	V_T85S2 Assignment AddFld2 - AddFld3
OCVU	FI-LC: V_T879_A ('K3',only SY-LANGU)
OCVV	FI-LC: V_T879_A ('AW',only SY-LANGU)
OCWS_APO	Activate Prop/Prod Quantities in APO
OCWS_MAT_APO	Define Materials
OCWT	Define Worklist Folder
OCY1	Create Totals Archive
OCY11	Create Line Item Archive
OCY6	RW/RP Reports for FI-LC Archive
OCYA	FI-LC: V_T850I_D (Access Data Entry)
OCYB	FI-LC: V_T850I_E (Dbase Data Entry)
OCYC	Assign Type of Additional Field
OCZ1	FI-SS: Create add. ledger
OCZ2	FI-SS: Change Cons Staging Ledger
OCZ3	FI-SS: Display Add. Ledger
OCZ4	FI-SS: Delete Add. Ledger
OD00	Number ranges for documents
OD01	Document Types
OD05	Data Carr./Netwk Node
OD06	Data carrier
OD07	Frontends
OD08	Text for document types
OD09	Document Status Texts
OD10	Document Status
OD11	Key Fields of Classifiable Ojbects
OD12	Maintain Number Range for Vaults
OD13	Sources for Application

OD14	Text for Object Link
OD15	Object Link
OD16	Document link text
OD20	Data Carrier Type
OD25	Application
OD30	Lab/Office
OD36	Mount Points/Log. Drives
OD37	Workstation Applications
OD40	CAD System
OD41	Global DMS Settings
OD50	DMS IAC - group definition
OD51	Control Parameters
OD52	DMS IAC - User allocation
OD55	Functions
OD56	Assign Field Sets
OD57	Field Names
OD58	Field Sets SAP->CAD
OD59	Field Sets
OD60	Exception Fields
OD65	User Functions
OD70	Create Conditions Table (DMS)
OD71	Change conditions table (DMS)
OD75	Output Types for Documents
OD77	Document Output Determ. Procedure
OD79	Document Output Access Sequence
OD81	Messages by Partner Function
OD90	Record Layout for Batch Input (Docs)
OD91	Document Data Transfer
OD92	Document Batch Input Example File
OD93	Display Document File
ODELGRP1	Number Range Maintenance: AUTO_SUEDG
ODI1	Number range for distr. order Id
ODI2	Number range for initial order Id
ODI3	Number range for dist.order pack. Id
ODI4	Number range for partial order Id
ODI5	Number range for original files
ODI6	Number range for recipient list
ODLC	Delivery Confirmation Outbound
ODLCM	Create Delivery Conf. Manually
ODOC	Activate Docmt Mgmt for Batches
ODP1	DIP Profile
ODP11	DIP Profile: Billing Plan Integratn
ODP14	Fixed Price Condition for Billing
ODP2	DIP Profile: Consistency Check
ODP2A	DIP Profile:Multiple Consist. Checks
ODP2L	DIP Profile:Consistency Check (List)
ODP3	Determine Apportionment Reason
ODP4	Determine Cost Condition
ODP5	Residence Time for DIP Sources
ODRV	Customizing for Derivation
OE00	HR Customizing: Maintenance T500C
OEH4	Field Catalog Variants V_T681F
OEH5	Define Access Sequence for Variants
OEH6	Condition Types Variant Matching

OEH7	EHS: Variant Matching Procedure
OESP	Setup for ESP procurement
OEXC	Define Expiring Currencies
OEXP	Subsequent Process in Expiring Curr.
OEXR	Expiring Currencies
OEXU	Superuser for Expiring Currencies
OEXW	Define Warning and Error Date
OF01	Maintain FM Area
OF03	Transfer Cash Holdings
OF05	Activate/Deactivate Cash Budget Mgt
OF06	Commt Item for Unassgd Revs/Exps
OF07	Cash Budget Mgt Consistency Check
OF09	Funds Management Consistency Check
OF12	FM: Maintain Budget Profile
OF14	Set Up FM Area
OF15	Maintain FM Area - Funds Management
OF16	Activate/Deactivate Funds Management
OF18	Assign Company Code to FM Area
OF19	Maintain Number Range: FM_BELEG2
OF20	FM Budget Avail.Control Tolerances
OF21	FM: Budget Versions
OF22	Financial Budgeting Versions
OF23	Availability Control Tolerances
OF24	Assign Default Funds Center
OF28	Maintain Commitment Type Profile
OF29	Settings for the Payment Transfer
OF29_EH4	Settings for the Payment Transfer
OF30	Assign FY Variant to FM Area
OF31	Assign Plan Profile to FM Area
OF32	Assign FY Variant to FM Area
OF33	Assign Number Range to FM Area
OF34	Assign Budget Profile to FM Area
OF35	Assign Status Profile to FM Area
OF36	User-Dependent Profile Maintenance
OF37	Assign FS Profile to FM Area
OF38	Assign cmmt type profile to FM area
OF39	Customized update profile
OF40	Activate Funds Management and HR
OF41	Define Default FM-PM Account Asst
OF4A	Categories
OF4B	Assign transaction/subtransaction
OF4C	Calculate Budget Surcharges
OF52	Maintain RFC Dest.for FM Pos.Mgt
OFAK	Activate/Deactivate PPA
OFB2E1	RFC Connections for IC Reconciliatn
OFB2E2	e-mail Templates for IC Reconciliatn
OFB2E3	Define Reconciliation Criteria
OFB2E_CNUM	Company IDs in External System
OFBL	Budgetary ledger account derivation
OFBLBW	Budgetary Ledger BW Extractors
OFBW	Classify Movement Types
OFC1	Assign FM Area to CO Area
OFC3	Year-Dependent Assignment
OFC4	Assign CO Transctns for FM Recording

OFCA	FM: Budget Calculation
OFCC	Cover Eligibility Restrictions
OFCL	Rules for Closing Ledger Accounts
OFCV	Settings for Cover Eligibility
OFD1	Cash Bdgt Mgt: Delete Master Data
OFD2	Cash Budget Mgt: Delete Act.Data
OFD3	Cash Budget Mgt: Delete Plan Data
OFD5	Delete Funds and Application of Fnds
OFD7	Funds Management: Delete Budget
OFD8	Delete Commitment Item From G/L Acct
OFDA	FM Areas - Year-Dependent Parameters
OFDC	Real Estate Implementation Guide
OFDE	FM: Delete Cmmt Items in FM Area
OFDF	Delete Funds Centers in FM Area
OFDG	Delete Funds Centr in Hierarchy Var.
OFDH	Funds Management: Delete CO Actuals
OFDM1	Delete Earmarked Funds by Client
OFDM2	Delete Selection of Earmarked Funds
OFDSM	Delete Status Management Entries
OFE1	Maintain Resvtn Doc.Types for HR/PM
OFED	Create Template for Commitment Items
OFES	Create Characters for Cmt Itm Templ.
OFFNUMLV	Assignment of Active Number Group
OFFP	Maxium amount limit
OFFPMG	Fast Pay material group
OFFT	Create FM fund types
OFG1	Cash Bdgt Mgt: Take Over All Docs
OFG2	Cash Budget Mgt: Take Over MM Data
OFG3	Cash Bdgt Mgt:Take Over Fds Res Data
OFG4	Cash Bdgt Mgt: Take Over Pymt Tsfr
OFG5	Funds Mgmt: Take Over All Documents
OFG6	Funds Mgmt: Take Over MM Data
OFG8	Funds Mgmt: Take Over Pymt Tfr Data
OFG9	CBM: Gradual FI Data Transfer
OFGA	CBM: FI Data Transfer in Full
OFGB	Funds Mgmt: Gradual FI Data Transfer
OFGC	Funds Mgmt: FI Data Transfer in Full
OFGD	Customize Budgeting
OFGE	Cash Holding Years
OFGG	Copy Commitment Item To G/L Account
OFGH	Sequence In Generic Arguments
OFGR	Create user groups
OFIR	(Penalty) Interest rate entries
OFIV	Invoice verification rules for PPA
OFK1	Maintain Criteria Type Cmmt. Item
OFK2	Maintain Criteria Category Group
OFK3	Assign Crit.Cat. to Crit.Cat.Group
OFK4	Maintain Criteria
OFKA	Maintain Carryfwrd Values Tot. Rec.
OFKT	Generic in Revenues Incr. Budget
OFKT2	FM Account Assignment Settings
OFM01A	Create Doc. Type and Clearing Item
OFMBG0	Activating public-owned comm. oper.
OFMBG1	Maintain PCO

OFMBG2	Maintain Input Tax Deduction Rates
OFMBG3	Maintain Global Data
OFMCA_P000	Account Determination: Rec/Pay
OFMCA_P001	Account Determination: Rev/Expense
OFMCA_P010	Derive Transactions for Acct Balance
OFMCA_P020	Ranking Order Funds Application Sel.
OFMCA_P030	Write Off Additional Specifications
OFMCA_P040	Petty Amounts for Mass Write-Off
OFMCA_P100	Paymt Medium - ID Application Form
OFMCA_P110	Switch Off Acct Assmnt on RE Contrct
OFMCA_P200	Document Interface PSM-FM =>IS-PS-CA
OFMCA_P201	Doc. Type Assgnmnt PSM-FM =>IS-PS-CA
OFMCA_P203	IS-PS-CA Clearing Account Assignment
OFMCA_P204	Document Interface PSM-FM =>IS-PS-CA
OFMCA_P205	RDCA: Settings for One-Time Customer
OFMCA_P210	Sender of XML Files to Coll. Agency
OFMCA_P220	Payments Without Mail for Coll.Agncy
OFMCA_P230	Dunning Grouping for Collections
OFMCA_PD05	Default Values: Contract Acct Cat.
OFMCA_PGIN	Default Values: Contract Acct Cat.
OFMCA_PL05	Versions for Plan and Sample Docs
OFMCA_PSOBASACT	AS for Contract Objects is Active
OFMCA_PSOBNUM	Number Range Maintenance: FMCA_PSOB
OFMFGRLAYOUT	Reporting Layout
OFMFG_ALC	Maintain Agency Location Code
OFMFG_PMS_ALC	Map Pmt Meth Supp to ALC and Pmt Off
OFMFG_PO	Maintain Payment Office
OFMG	Funds Management Message Control
OFMM	Maintain minimum & maximum penalties
OFMR0	Global Settings for Earmarked Funds
OFMR1	Earmrkd Funds: Maintain Lock Reasons
OFMR2	Earmarked fnds: Diplay block reasons
OFMR3	Maintain Acct Assgmt Transfer Rules
OFMR5	Assgt of Activities to Transfer Rule
OFMR6	Maintain Template Types
OFMRO_TKBBA	Recurring Obligation document types
OFMS	FM: +/- Sign in the Info System
OFMTOAC2	Define Debit/Credit GL in FM to AC
OFM_ACT_CCR	Activate CCR Vendor Functionality
OFM_ACT_MD_YEAR	Activate Year-Dependent Master Data
OFM_FM01_KOM	Maintain ID Number in FM Area
OFM_HSART	Maintain Commitment Item
OFNG	Maintain negative grace days
OFNM	Maintain payment term for mat. group
OFO1	OI List Per Real Estate Objects
OFP1	Maintain Transfer Price Number Range
OFP2	Access Seqs: Packing Object Determ.
OFP3	Condition types: Pack.obj.determin.
OFP4	Procedure: Pack.obj.determination
OFP5	Condition table: Pack.obj.determin.
OFP6	Condition table: Pack.obj.determin.
OFP7	Condition table: Pack.obj.determin.
OFP8	Field catalog pack.obj.determination
OFPK	FM budgetary ledger posting keys

OFPM	Change Message Control
OFPT	Maintain all PPA payment terms
OFR1	Cover Pool Number Ranges
OFR2	Assign Cover No.Range to FM Area
OFRA	Report Selection
OFRB	Report Selection
OFRC	Maintain reason codes & their texts
OFSN	Collective Expenditure Settings
OFTC	Funds Management
OFTD	Cash Management Configuration Menu
OFUC	Call Procedure
OFUD	Distribution Procedure/Line Items
OFUG	Settings for Revenues Incr. Budget
OFUN	Assign Commitment Item to Fund
OFUP	Funds Management Control
OFUR	Overwrite FM update profile
OFUT	Totals-Based Distribution Procedure
OFY5	Closing Ops for Budget: Approval
OFY6	Number Ranges Fiscal Yr Change Docs
OFY7	Number Ranges Lot Number
OFZC	Cash Holding Years
OG00	Personnel Administration Customizing
OG01	Personnel Administration Customizing
OG02	Recruitment Customizing
OG03	Generate calendar for cumulation
OG04	Customizing: Country-Spec. Features
OG05	Customizing: Dyn. Schema Selection
OG07	Current settings Time Management
OG30	HR:call SM30 subobjects individually
OG42	Customizing Tool for PA42
OGS6	Load zip codes
OGS7	Generate schema
OGS8	Delete tax table entries
OGS9	Generate ADP number ranges
OH00	Access Subset View
OH02	Call View Cluster with Subset Views
OH04	Conversion of third party remittance
OH11	Copy Wage Types
OH12	Access View for T512W
OH13	HR Customizing: Wage Type Grouping
OH14	Access Subset View for Check Table
OH16	Call RPUCTF00 with Var. SAP_OH16
OH17	HR Customizing: SI Contrib.Statement
OH18	HR Customizing: Absence Docu.
OH19	Access Transaction OH20
OH20	Maintain Payroll Constants
OH21	Supply Parameters for PE51
OH23	Enter Parameters for PUFK
OHPS	Org.Management Configuration
OHX2	Maintain wage types for remittance
OHX3	Maintain number ranges for 3PR
OHX4	Number range for 3PR
OHX5	Number range for tax reporting
OIAA	ABC Indicator

OIAB	Plant Sections
OIAC	Matchcode notifications
OIAD	Field sel. equipment-specific fields
OIAE	Field selection funct.loc/ref.loc
OIAF	Field sel. equipment/functional loc.
OIAG	Authorization Group
OIAH	Bus. transactions with auth. profile
OIAI	Maintenance Planner Groups
OIAJ	Field sel. for (ref) funct. location
OIAK	Cost key figure info system
OIAL	Field Selection for PM Notifications
OIAN	Field Selection Order Header Data
OIAO	Field Select. Ref. Obj. PM Notific.
OIAP	Maintenance Order Cost Profile
OIAS	Maintain Locations
OIAT	Object Cat. Transaction Def. Value
OIAW	Stats. Currency: Info System
OIAY	Field Selection Order Header Service
OIAZ	Field selection functional location
OIB1	Maintain inv.program budget profile
OIB3	Budget profile: proj.->invst.prg.typ
OIB4	Budg. profile order -> inv.prog.type
OIB5	Depreciation areas/value transfer
OIB9	TL list - production resource/tool
OIBC	List Task Lists (M.-Lev.) Eqpmt Data
OIBD	List Task Lists (M.-Level) Loc. Data
OIBS	Maintain Status Profiles
OIBY	List Display of Goods Movements
OICA	User-Specif. Settings f. BOMs
OICB	BOM Modification Parameters
OICC	BOM Default Values
OICD	BOM Usage
OICE	BOM Usage Default Values
OICF	DefltVals f. Copying Item Status
OICG	Valid Material Types in BOM
OICH	BOM Status
OICI	Laboratory/Office
OICJ	BOM Usage Priorities
OICK	Item Categories
OICL	BOMs with History Requirement
OICM	Variable-Size Item Formulas
OICMPD	Field Selection for Components PM/CS
OICMPL	Field selection component list PM/CS
OICN	Spare Part Indicators
OICO	Material Provision Indicators
OICP	Valid Material Types for BOM
OICQ	Application-Specific Criteria
OICS	Alternative BOM Selection
OICT	C PM BOM Application
OICX	BOM Item Object Types
OICY	Application ID for PM
OID1	Shop Papers
OID2	Shop Papers by Document Type
OID3	User-Specific Print Control

OID4	Activate Print Diversion
OID5	Print Diversion Values
OID6	Print Control Online/Update
OIDA	PM Shop Papers for Notifications
OIDB	PM Shop Papers by Notification Type
OIDC	PM Notifs - User-SpecifPrintControl
OIDD	PM Print Diversion for NotifPapers
OIDE	PM NotifPrintDivers. by FldContent
OIDF	PM Shop Papers for Orders
OIDG	PM Shop Papers by Order Type
OIDH	PM Orders - User-SpecifPrintControl
OIDI	PM Shop Paper Print Diversion
OIDJ	PM OrdPrintDivers. by FldContent
OIDP	PD Order - Define Shop Papers
OIDQ	PD Shop Papers by Order Type
OIDR	PD Order - User Specif. Print Contrl
OIDS	PD Print Diversion f. Shop Papers
OIDT	PD Order Print Diversion by FldConts
OIDU	PM Download
OIDV	Download SAP Tables into MS Access
OIDW	Download catalog profile
OIEA	Equipment Types
OIEB	Equipment Status Profile
OIEF	EquipMaster Field Selection
OIEG	Editing Types
OIEH	Usage History
OIEM	Matchcode for Equipment
OIEN	Equipment Number Ranges
OIEP	Installation at FunctLoc.
OIES	Multilingual Texts
OIET	Equipment Categories
OIEV	Allocate PartnrDetProc. to EqCateg.
OIEZ	Insert Usage Period
OIF1	Partner schema for app. request
OIF2	Maint. of plan profile f. app.req.
OIF3	Maint.- plan profile app.r. cash flw
OIFL	Vehicle List
OIGN	List Editing of Permits
OIK1	Maintenance of PM value categories
OIK2	Maint. of PM value cat. assignments
OIKS	Maintenance of Cost Estimate Version
OIL0	Number Ranges: FunctLoc.Task Lists
OIL1	Task List Status
OIL2	Standard Task List Usage
OIL3	Planner Group
OIL4	Task List Number Ranges
OIL5	Equipment number ranges
OIL6	Operation Default Value Profiles
OIL7	Operation Control Keys
OIL8	Standard Text
OILA	Wage groups
OILB	Qualification Type
OILC	Object Overviews Gen.Task Lists
OILD	Object Overview Equip.Task List

OILE	Object Overviews FunctLoc Task Lists
OILG	Standard Task List Matchcode
OILJ	User Fields
OILZ	BOM Usage Free Material Asssignment
OIM1	PM Notification Workflow Settings
OIM2	SM Notification Workflow Settings
OIM3	Order Type by NotifType
OIM6	Alloc. PartnDetermProc. to NotifType
OIM7	Response time monit. by NotifType
OIM8	Priorities by Priority Types
OIM9	Service Notif. Special Parameters
OIMD	Object Info Parameters
OIME	Edit Response Profile
OIMF	Service Window
OIMK	Catalog Types
OIML	Notification Info Window
OIMM	Operating Condition
OIMN	Customizing setting table TQSCR
OIMP	Priority Types
OIMRC	Field Selection Meas.Points & Docs
OIMW	Effects on the Function
OIMX	Define follow-up actions for tasks
OIMZ	System Status
OINI	Network ID
OINM	Object Link Medium
OINV_HU	Number Range Maintenance: HUINV
OIO1	Priority Types
OIO2	Priorities by Priority Types
OIO3	Maintenance Activity Types
OIO4	Default MAT by Order Type
OIO5	Valid MATs by Order Type
OIO6	Default Control Keys
OIO7	Operation Control Keys
OIO8	Default Current Date
OIO9	Operation Units: Duration/Work
OIOA	Maintenance Order Types
OIOB	Revisions
OIOD	Valid Order Types by PlanPlant
OIOE	Operation No. - AutoIncrement
OIOF	Costing Parameters
OIOG	Maintenance Order Status Profile
OIOH	PM Graphic and Rel. for Orders
OIOI	MatAvailCheck Control
OIOJ	Object Info Parameters f. Order Type
OIOK	Posting Rules
OIOL	Service Order Indicator
OIOM	Assign PartnDetermProc. to OrdType
OION	Order number ranges
OIOP	Order Priority Types
OIOPD	Field Selec. for Order Opertn Detail
OIOPL	Field Selec. for Order Opertn Detail
OIOR	Order Completion Confirmation
OIOS	Default Planning Indicator
OIOT	Scheduling Type

OIOV	PM Order Costing Sheet
OIP1	Maintain inv.prog. planning profile
OIPG	Maintenance of Permit Group
OIPK	FunctLocation StructIndicators
OIPL	Plant Maint./Service search help
OIPM	Matchcode for Functional Locations
OIPP	Change functional location category
OIPR	RefFunctLocation Categories
OIPSMDMAT	Field Selection for PS Components
OIPSMKMAT	Field Selection PS Component List
OIPT	FunctLocation Categories
OIPU	Alternative Indicator Syst. Settings
OIPV	Functional Location Labeling Systems
OIR0	Task lists (multi-lvl)- Test eqpmt
OIR1	FieldSel. PartnType Customer
OIR2	FieldSel. PartnType Vendor
OIR3	FieldSel. PartnType Personnel No.
OIR4	FieldSel. PartnType Contact Person
OIR5	FieldSel. PartnType OrganiznUnit
OIR6	FieldSel. PartnType Position
OIR7	FieldSel. PartnType User
OIR8	Field Selection for General Address
OIRA	Field selectn serial no. RefurbOrder
OIRB	PM Object Contracts
OIRC	Multi-Level EquipList - Permit
OIRE	Field Sel. Serial No. Product. Order
OIRE0	Field Sel. Serial No. Handling Unit
OIRE1	Field Selection Serial No. Inventory
OIRE2	Field Selection for Serial No. in PO
OIRE3	Field Selection for Serial No. in PR
OIRF	Measuring Point List
OIRG	Multi-Level Order List - Permit
OIRH	Order List (M.-Lev.) - Iss. Permits
OIRI	Location List (Multi-Level) - Permit
OIRL	Measurement Document List
OIRM	FieldSelect. Ser.No. Goods Movement
OIRN	FieldSelect. Ser.No. Delivery
OIRO	FieldSelect. Ser.No. Inspection Lot
OIRP	FieldSelect. Ser.No. Sales Order
OIRQ	FieldSelect. Ser.No. PM Order
OIRR	Field Sel. Serial No PM Notification
OIRS	Multi-level Order List: Sub-Orders
OIRT	List Task Lists (M.-Level) - Header
OIRU	List Task Lists (M.-Lev) - Operation
OIRV	List Task Lists (M.-Lev.) - Sub-Optn
OIRW	List Task Lists (M.-Lev.) - Relships
OIRX	List Task Lists (M.-Lv) - Components
OIRZ	List Task Lists (M.-Lv) - Maint.Pkg.
OIS0	Funds Management
OIS1	Global Parameters for Serial Numbers
OIS2	Maintain serial number profile
OIS3	Task Lists (Multi-lvl)- ServPackages
OIS4	Task List (Mul.lev.) - ObjectDepend.
OIS5	Archive Serial Number History

SAP Transaction Codes – Volume One

OISC	Generation of PM Orders
OISD	Generation of PM Orders from SD
OISE	SD Service Processing Active?
OISF	Generation of Orders from the WP
OISH	Customizing
OISK	Funds Management
OISM	Customizing
OISN	Number range maintenance: IRESTO
OIST	Maintain Permit Categories
OIT1	Special Character Position Coding
OIT2	Coding Masks for Inv. Prog. Position
OIT3	Program types
OIT4	Number range maint: IM_POSNR
OIT5	Assignmt of actual vals to bdgt cat.
OIT6	Inv. Programs Report Selection
OIT7	Approp. Request Report Selection
OIT8	Budget categories
OITA	Investment profile
OITB	Inv. Profile - AuC per Source Assgn.
OITD	Definition of scale
OITE	Version aspect cap.inv. FI-AA/PM
OITF	Version aspect cap.inv. IM/PS/CO-OPA
OITG	Value type aspect cap. investments
OITK	Key figure allocation for scale
OITL	Field selection for app. request
OITM1	User name for user field 1
OITM10	User name for user field 10
OITM11	User name for user field 11
OITM12	User name for user field 12
OITM13	User name for user field 12
OITM14	User name for user field 12
OITM2	User name for user field 2
OITM3	User name for user field 3
OITM4	User name for user field 4
OITM5	User name for user field 5
OITM6	User name for user field 6
OITM7	User name for user field 7
OITM8	User name for user field 8
OITM9	User name for user field 9
OITN	Assign workflow tasks
OITO	Master Data Tab
OITW	Lower value limit for scale
OIU	E&P Production Application Menu
OIUB	Field Sel. Equipment Usage List
OIUC	Equipment List - CS
OIUCI_CR	Check Input Copy/Reverse
OIUF	Functional Location List - CS
OIUG	Service Order List
OIUH_CI03	Check Layout
OIUH_CI04	Remitter/Layout Cross Reference
OIUH_CI05	Check Input - Process Rules - CI05
OIUH_CI06	Product/Property Translations
OIUH_DO08	DOI Owner Accounting Entry code
OIUH_JE01	Account Maintenance

541

OIUH_JE02	Account Entry Control
OIUH_JE04	Journal Entry Batch Control
OIUH_JE05	Manual Journal Entry
OIUH_JE07	General Ledger Query
OIUH_JE10	Miscellaneous Subledger Query
OIUH_JE11	Intercompany Subledger Query
OIUH_JE12	Owner Payable Subledger Query
OIUH_JE13	Legal Suspense Subledger Query
OIUH_JE14	Statistical Subledger Query
OIUH_JE15	Income Subledger Query
OIUH_JE16	Expense Subledger Query
OIUH_JE17	Tax Payable Subledger Query
OIUH_JE18	Accounts Payable Subledger Query
OIUH_JE19	Accounts Receivable Subledger Query
OIUH_RD02	A/R Reconciliation
OIUH_RD03	Owner Check
OIUH_RD04	Owner 1099 Information
OIUH_RD05	Owner Check Detail
OIUH_RD06	Withholding Tax Rate
OIUH_RD07	Ad Valorem Tax Recovery
OIUH_RD08	Negative Payable/Suspence
OIUH_RD09	A/R Write-off Approval
OIUH_RD10	Manual Royalty Check (RD10)
OIUH_RD14	Owner Interest Calculation
OIUH_SRDA	Responsibility Id
OIUH_TR01	Tax and Royalty Profile
OIUH_TR02	Severance Tax Master File
OIUH_TR04	Severance Tax Transaction
OIUH_TR06	Colorado Ad Valorem
OIUH_VL10	Purchaser/Remitter Cross Reference
OIUI	Order List - CS
OIUK	Order list (multi-lev.) - goods mvmt
OIUL	Order list (multi-lev.)-relationship
OIUN	Order list (multi-lev.) costs/rev.
OIUO	Func.loc.list (multi-lev)-meas.point
OIUOR	R.P. List (Multilev.)- Ref. Meas.Pt
OIUOW01_SCH_A	DOI Schedule A Report
OIUP	Func.loc.list (multi-lev)-meas.doc.
OIUQ	Equi.list(multi-lev)-measuring point
OIUR	Equi.list(multi-lev)-measuring doc.
OIUT2_PURGE	Purge Interface records
OIUX1	Eqmt List (Multilevel) - Maint.Item
OIUX2	Eqmt List (Multilevel) - Maint.Date
OIUX3	Eqmt List (Multilevel) -Maint.Pckg.
OIUX4	Eqmt List (Multilevel) - Operation
OIUX5	Func.Loc.List(Multilvl) -Maint. Item
OIUX6	Func.Loc.List(Multilvl) -Maint. Date
OIUX7	Func.Loc.List(Multilvl) -Maint. Pckg
OIUX8	Func.Loc.List (Multilvl) - Operation
OIVA	Maintenance Plan Default Order Type
OIVC	Check Report for Value Categories
OIVN	Maintenance Plan No. Ranges
OIW0	Detail Info (MaintPlan)
OIW1	Activities list display

OIW3	List of Order Confirmations
OIW5	Maintenance dates list display
OIW6	FunctLocation list - PM
OIW7	Reference location list
OIW8	Material List
OIWD	Object Networks - Objects (FL)
OIWE	Equipment Structure Display
OIWI	PM Notification List
OIWK	CS Notification List
OIWL	PM order list
OIWM	Component Structural Display
OIWO	List of PM task lists
OIWP	Functional Location Structure
OIWQ	Installed Base Structural Display
OIWR	Reference Location Structure
OIWU	PM Operation List
OIWUN	Order- and Operation List
OIWW	Maintenance plan list
OIWY	Maintenance item list
OIX0	Run Mntce Planning Plant Maintenance
OIX1	Allocn PlanPlant to MaintPlant
OIX2	Multi-Lev.FunctLocList - FunctLoc.
OIX2R	R.P. List (Multilevel) - Ref. Locat
OIX3	Multi-Lev.FunctLocList - EquipUsage
OIX4	Multi-Lev.FunctLocList - Equipment
OIX5	Multi-Lev.FunctLocList - Partners
OIX6	Multi-Lev.FunctLocList - Notifictn
OIX7	Multi-Lev.FunctLocList - Order
OIX8	Multi-Lev.FunctLocList - Class
OIX8R	R.P. List (Multilevel): Class
OIX9	Multi-Lev.FunctLocList - Chrctrstic
OIX9R	R.P. List (Multilev)- Characteristic
OIXA	Multi-Lev.FunctLocList - Document
OIXAR	R.P. List (Multilevel) - Document
OIXB	Multi-Lev.FunctLocList - Object Link
OIXC	Multi-Lev.EquipList - Equipment
OIXD	Multi-Lev.EquipList - EquipUsage
OIXE	Multi-Level EqList - FunctLocation
OIXF	Multi-Lev.EquipList - Partners
OIXG	Multi-Lev.EquipList - Notification
OIXH	Multi-Lev.EquipList - Order
OIXI	Multi-Lev.EquipList - Class
OIXJ	Multi-level EqList - Characteristic
OIXK	Multi-level EqList - Document
OIXL	Multi-level EqList - Object Link
OIXM	Multi-Level NotifList - Notification
OIXN	Notif. List (M.-Lev.) - Funct. Loc.
OIXO	Notif. List (Multi-Lev.) - Equipment
OIXP	Multi-Level NotifList - Partners
OIXQ	Notif. List (Multi-Level) - Item
OIXR	Multi-Level NotifList - Activity
OIXS	Multi-Level NotifList - Class
OIXT	Notif. List (Multi-Lev.) - Charact.
OIXU	Notif. List (Multi-Level) - Task

OIXV	Multi-Level NotifList - Order
OIXW	Multi-Level Order List - Order
OIXX	Multi-Level Order List - FunctLoc.
OIXY	Multi-Level Order List - Equipment
OIXZ	Multi-Level Order List - Notif.
OIY1	C PM Transport Table Settings
OIY2	C PM TableSettngs MaintPlanning 2.1A
OIY3	C PM PrelimTabSettngs PM Notifs 2.1A
OIY4	C PM PrelimTabSettngs PM Orders 2.1A
OIY5	C PM TableSettngs ObjectNtwrkng 2.1A
OIY6	PM PrelimTabSettngs Master Data 2.1A
OIY9	Scheduling Overview
OIYC	Equipment list
OIYG	Confirmations list for PM operations
OIYH	Serial number list
OIYJ	Object Links - Objects (EQ)
OIYL	Detail Info (Order Operation)
OIYM	Details (Order Header)
OIYP	Multi-Level Order List - Partners
OIYQ	Multi-Level Order List - Operation
OIYR	Multi-Level Order List - Component
OIYS	Multi-Level Order List - CompConf.
OIYT	Multi-Level Order List - PRTs
OIYV	Notifictn list (multi-level) - cause
OIYW	List of Tasks
OIYZ	Notification Item List
OIZ0	Specify Distribution Key
OIZ1	WrkCtrCategory. by ApplicType
OIZ2	Default Value Keys
OIZ3	PersResp. f. Work Center
OIZ4	Location
OIZ5	Operation Control Keys
OIZ6	Standard Text
OIZ7	Work Center Matchcode
OIZ8	Qualification Type
OIZ9	HR Interface Parameters
OIZA	Maintain Work Center Categories
OIZB	Wage groups
OIZD	Maintain Task List Usage
OIZE	TaskListUsage by TL Type
OIZF	Capacity Category
OIZG	Work Center Planner
OIZH	Factory Calendar
OIZI	Work Center Shift Program
OIZJ	Work Center Shift Definition
OIZK	PerfEfficRate Keys
OIZL	Formula Parameters
OIZM	Formula Definition
OIZN	Field Sel. for Confirmation PM Order
OIZO	Capacity Default Values
OIZR	PerfEfficRate Validity Area
OIZS	Maintain Transport Times Matrix
OIZU	Work Centers Screen Sequence
OIZV	Work Center Default Values

OIZX	Define distribution function
OIZY	Specify Distribution Functions
OIZZ	Specify Distribution Strategy
OJI2	JIT Call Profile
OJI3	Maintain Time Definitions
OJIN1	Maintain Cond. Table: Sum. JIT Call
OJIN2	Maintain Access Seqs: Sum. JIT Call
OJIN3	Maintain Mess. Types: Sum. JIT Call
OJIN4	Maintain Mess.Det.Schema: SumJITCall
OJIN5	Maintain Partner Role: Sum. JIT Call
OJIT0	JIT Customizing Subtree
OJIT1	Customizing JIT Actions
OJIT13	Maintenance Dialog SumJC Settings
OJIT14	JIT: Authorizations Internet
OJIT15	Number Range Maintenance
OJIT16	Number Range Maintenance: JIT_HD_01
OJIT17	Number Range Maintenance: JIT_IT_01
OJIT18	Number Range Maintenance: JIT_MA_01
OJIT2	JIT: Customizing Status
OJIT20	Number Range Maintenance: DELCONHD01
OJIT21	Number Range Maintenance: JIT_GR_01
OJIT22	JIT: Assign Operator Tasks
OJIT23	JIT: Activate Event Linkage
OJIT24	Profile Delivery Creation (JIT)
OJIT25	JIT: Maintenance Dialog Ref. Numbers
OJIT26	Maintenance of HU Profile
OJIT3	JIT: Customizing Call Control
OJIT4	JIT: Customizing Comp.Group Determn
OJIT5	JIT : Sort Variant Maintenance
OJIT50	Replenishment Strategy SumJCs
OJIT51	Replenishm Strat. SumJC Stk Transf.
OJIT52	Replenish. Strat. SeqJC Ext. Proc.
OJIT53	Scheduling Profile SumJCs
OJIT54	Determine Storage Location Vendor
OJIT55	Number Range Maintenance JITO_HD_01
OJIT56	Number Range Maintenance PABHD
OJIT57	Number Range Maintenance JITO_DLCN
OJIT58	JIT Outbound: Actions
OJIT59	JIT Outbound: Processing Statuses
OJIT6	JIT : Barcode Qualifier Maintenance
OJIT60	JIT Outbound: Action Control
OJIT61	JIT Outbound: No. Range Maintenance
OJIT62	Vendor-specific Number Ranges
OJIT63	Barcode Qualifier JIT Outbound
OJIT64	JIT Call Profile
OJIT7	JIT: Control Print Formatting
OJIT8	JIT : Ctrl Prfle Int. Warehouse Call
OJIT9	Variable JIT Messages
OJITI	Customizing JIT Inbound
OJITO	Customizing JIT Outbound
OK01	Controlling Area: Components/StKFs
OK02	Maintain Status Profiles
OK03	Display Status Profiles
OK11	Number Ranges for Cost Plg/Budgeting

OK12	Reset "Budgeted" Status
OK13	Maintain Reconcil. Ledger Nr. Ranges
OK14	Maintain Budget Manager
OK15	Maintain authorization group version
OK16	Planner Profiles: Maint. Auth.Group
OK17	Reconciliation Ledger: Acct Determ.
OK18	Maintain Authorization Groups
OK19	RW/RP Reports Reconc. Ledger Archive
OK29	Maintain SMP profile/variant
OK30	Software Maintenance Process
OK31	Execute SMP profile/variant
OK32	SMP order due list
OK34	Define push-material
OK36	SMP Log
OK60	Maintain Number Range: IRW_PFLEGE
OK70	Number Range Maintenance: EF_GROUPNB
OK91	Maintain Number Range: BP_BPDK
OKA1	Display Cost Center Types
OKA2	Maintain Cost Center Categories
OKA4	Maintain Attribute Groups
OKA5	Display Attribute Groups
OKA6	Maintain Cost Element Attributes
OKA7	Display Cost Element Attributes
OKA8	Change Primary Posting Price Var.
OKA9	Display Primary Posting Price Var.
OKB1	Transfer G/L Acct: Display Defaults
OKB2	Transfer G/L Acct: Maintain Defaults
OKB3	Batch Input for Cost Elements
OKB6	Generate Cost Center Acctg. Reports
OKB9	Change Automatic Account Assignment
OKB9N	CO Account Determination
OKB9NR	CO-Account Determination: Rule Maint
OKBA	Transfer FI Documents to CO
OKBB	Transfer MM Documents to CO
OKBC	Transfer SD Documents to CO
OKBD	Change Function Areas
OKBF	Import Planning Layouts
OKBG	Post Down Payments
OKBI	Define CO Line Item Summarization
OKC0	View maint. TKCF Text read table
OKC1	Display CO Transactions
OKC3	Delete transaction data
OKC4	Delete Cost Centers
OKC5	Delete cost elements
OKC6	Delete Activity Types
OKC7	Define Validation
OKC8	Change Currency Translations
OKC9	Define Substitution
OKCA	RKC Maintaining data area
OKCB	Time dimension of characteristics
OKCC	Maintain Sender Structures
OKCD	Transfer parameters
OKCDBC	Maintain sender structure package
OKCDBD	Create sender structure package

SAP Transaction Codes – Volume One

OKCDS	SAP-EIS: Data Slice Statistics
OKCE	SAP-EIS: Set up data collection rep.
OKCF	Maintain value types
OKCG	CO-BPC Maintain Transfer Rules
OKCH	Create key figure groups TKCKU
OKCI	Display Characteristic Values
OKCJ	Change Characteristic Values
OKCK	Generate Master Data Maint. Modules
OKCL	Sort into report portfolio T242E
OKCM	
OKCP	Reorganize EIS field catalog
OKCS	SAP-EIS character. display TKCF
OKCSL	Process Data Slices
OKCSLA	Assignment of data slices to tables
OKCSLD	Data Slices
OKCSLG	Data slice option groups
OKCSLU	Data Slices: User Assignment
OKCX	Change "All Currencies" Indicator
OKCY	Number range record no. in EIS/BP
OKD1	Export CO-CCA Reports
OKD3	Import CO-CCA Reports
OKD6	Import Individual Reports
OKE1	Display logical databank CRK
OKE10	Transport Organization Customizing
OKE2	Display logical databank CEK
OKE3	Display logical databank CIK
OKE4	Display logical databank CPK
OKE5	Transport Organization Customizing
OKE6	Transport Mater Data Settings
OKE7	Transport Planning Settings
OKE8	Transport Actual Posting Settings
OKE9	Transport Tool Settings
OKEA	Maintain Cost Center Matchcode IDs
OKEB	Display Cost Center Matchcode IDs
OKEC	Maintain Cost Element Matchcode IDs
OKED	Display Cost Element Matchcode IDs
OKEE	Maintain Activity Type Matchcode IDs
OKEF	Display Activity Type Matchcode IDs
OKEG	Change Time-Based Fields/Cost Ctrs
OKEH	Display Time-Based Fields/Cost Ctrs
OKEI	Maintain Time-Based Fields/Act.Types
OKEJ	Display Time-Based Fields/Act.Types
OKEK	Maintain Time-Based Fields/CElems
OKEL	Display Time-Based Fields/CElems
OKEM	Display logical databank SAK
OKEN	Display Standard Hierarchy
OKENN	Display Standard Hierarchy
OKENNX	Display stand.hierarchy: UO active
OKEO	Change Standard Hierarchy
OKEON	Change Standard Hierarchy
OKEONX	Change standard hierarchy: UO active
OKEP	Down Payment: Maintain Default CElem
OKEQ	Maintain Versions (General)
OKEQN	General Version Maintenance

OKER	Define Component/Switching Structure
OKES	Maintain Splitting Structure
OKET	Maintain Price Calculation Settings
OKET1	Maintain settings: plan reconciliatn
OKET2	Maintain settings: target=actl IAA
OKEU	Change Source Structure
OKEV	Maintain Versions (CO Area)
OKEV1	Change Valuation in Version 0
OKEVN	Version Maintenance in CO Area
OKEW	Splitting: Assignment KOSTL -> SCNAM
OKEX	Transport Planning Layouts
OKEY	Display Time-Dependent Field/Process
OKEZ	Change Time-Dependent Field/Process
OKF1	Change Budget Planning Profile
OKG1	Results Analysis Keys
OKG2	Results Analysis Versions
OKG3	Customizing Valuation Methods
OKG4	Update for Results Analysis
OKG5	Customizing Assignment
OKG6	No. Ranges Results Analysis CO Doc.
OKG8	Posting Rules for Res. Analysis Data
OKG9	Results Analysis Versions for WIP
OKGA	Update for WIP Calculation
OKGB	Customizing Assignment
OKGC	Customizing: WIP Valuation
OKGD	Customizing: WIP Valuation
OKGG	Customizing: SD
OKGK	Maintain Capitalization Percentages
OKGL	Versions for capitalization val.calc
OKI0	Determine activity number: entry
OKI1	Activity numbers for activity types
OKI2	Activity numbers for cost elements
OKI3	Activity numbers for stat. key fig.
OKIP	Costing variants: Simulation costing
OKIQ	Costing types simulation costing
OKIR	Movement variants simulation costing
OKK4	Valuation Variants for Prod. Costing
OKK5	Qty Structure Control for Costing
OKK6	Scheduling for Costing
OKK7	Price Factors for Costing Relevancy
OKK9	Indicator for Relevancy to Costing
OKKA	Maintain Controlling Area
OKKB	Selection Screen Maintenance
OKKC	Maintain Sel. Screens for Order-Rel.
OKKD	Maintain Sel. Screens Intern. Orders
OKKE	Valuation Variants: Base Plan Obj.
OKKI	Costing Types for Product Costing
OKKK	Maintain Costing Tables
OKKL	Transfer of Cstg Table Entries: 2.1D
OKKM	Transfer Control
OKKN	Costing Variants for Product Costing
OKKO	Costing Variants Base Planning Obj
OKKP	Maintain Controlling Area
OKKP1	Controlling Area: ALE Settings

OKKP2	Controlling Area: ALE Settings
OKKR	Costing Variants for Internal Orders
OKKS	Set Controlling Area
OKKT	Costing Variants for Projects
OKKW	Valuation Variants for Projects
OKKX	Valuation Variant f. Internal Orders
OKKY	Maintain Selection Screens for MTO
OKKZ	Maintain Selec. Screens Process Mfg
OKL1	Report Tree for CO-OPA
OKL2	Report Tree: Order-Related Prod.
OKL3	Report Tree: Sales-Order-Rel. Prod.
OKL4	Report Tree: Repetitive Mfg
OKL5	Report Tree: Unit Costing
OKL8	Report Tree: Product Costing
OKLB	Maintain ABC Report Tree
OKLF	Report Tree: Cost Objects
OKLH	Report Tree: Engineer-to-Order
OKLI	Report Tree: Process Manufacturing
OKLS	Maintain CCA Report Tree
OKM0	Display IMG Structure
OKM1	IMG Controlling: General
OKM2	IMG Controlling: General
OKMI	Import models Cost Center Accounting
OKN0	Control of CO-PC Information System
OKN2	Control Info Sys Prod Cost by Order
OKN3	Control Info Sys Prod Cost Sales Ord
OKN4	Control Info Sys Prod Cost by Period
OKN8	Control Info Sys Prod Cost Planning
OKNF	Control Info Sys Intangible Goods
OKO1	Maintain Order Matchcode IDs
OKO2	Display Order Matchcode IDs
OKO3	Maintain Hier.Std.Cost Elem.Layout
OKO5	Delete CO Orders
OKO6	Maintain Allocation Structure
OKO7	Maintain Settlement Profiles
OKO8	Maintain Processing Groups
OKO9	Maintain Settlemen Exchng. Rate Type
OKOA	Init. Screen-Customizing Settlement
OKOB	CO Orders: Budgeting profiles
OKOD	Convert Avlability Cntrl Tol.Limits
OKOG	Maintain overhead key
OKOH	Maintain Cost Element Group
OKOI	Maintain Capitalization Percentages
OKOJ	Results Analysis Key for Cap.Value
OKOL	Int.Orders: Maintain Screen Variants
OKOR	Selection Rules for Internal Orders
OKOS	Struct.Planning Profiles - CO Orders
OKOT	Transport Settlement Tables
OKOU	Substitution Rules - Internal Orders
OKOV	Select. Variants for Internal Orders
OKOZ	Maintain Overhead Tables
OKP1	Maintain Period Lock
OKP2	Display Period Lock
OKP6	Costing Variant for PM Order

OKP7	Costing Types for PM Order
OKP8	Valuation Variants for PM Order
OKPLACTRL	Transfer Plan Data from Foreign Sys.
OKPLAMDT	CCA Planning in Manager's Desktop
OKQ0	Classification Data (Summarization)
OKQ1	Classification Data for Obj. Records
OKQ2	Define Reference Characteristics
OKQ3	Define Reference Character. (Orders)
OKQ4	Define Reference Chars (Projects)
OKQ5	Maintain Hierarchy Struct. (General)
OKQ6	Maintain Characteristic Structure
OKR0	Report List for Sales Orders
OKR1	Report List for Internal Orders
OKR2	Report List for Repetitive Mfg
OKR3	Report List for Make-to-Order
OKR4	Report List for Process Mfg
OKR5	Report List for Unit Costing
OKR6	Change Report List for Cost Centers
OKR7	Report List for Projects
OKR8	Report List for Product Costing
OKRA	Summarization Hierarchy for Orders
OKRC	Report List for Run Schedule Headers
OKRD	Report List for PPC
OKRH	Table Maintenance for Report List
OKRI	Table Maintenance for Report Layouts
OKRK	Report Layouts for Sales Orders
OKRL	Report Layouts for Internal Orders
OKRM	Report Layouts for Repetitive Mfg
OKRN	Report Layouts for Make-to-Order
OKRO	Report Layouts for Process Mfg
OKRP	Report Layouts for Unit Costing
OKRS	Change Report Layouts for Cost Ctrs
OKRT	Report Layouts for Projects
OKRU	Report Layouts for Product Costing
OKRV	Report Layouts for Run Sched Headers
OKRW	Report Layouts for PPC
OKRZ	Hierarchy ID for Process Mfg
OKS0	Generate Reports for Sales Orders
OKS1	Generate Reports for Int.Ord.: Batch
OKS2	Generate Reports for Repetitive Mfg
OKS3	Generate Reports for Make-to-Order
OKS4	Generate Reports for Process Mfg
OKS5	Generate Reports for Unit Costing
OKS6	Generate Reports for Cost Ctr: Batch
OKS7	Generate Reports for Projects
OKS8	Generate Reports for Product Costing
OKS9	Generate Reports for Run Schedules
OKSA	Generate Reports for Internal Orders
OKSB	Import Reports for Repetitive Mfg
OKSC	Export Reports for Make-to-Order
OKSD	Import Reports for Make-to-Order
OKSE	Export Reports for Process Mfg
OKSF	Import Reports for Process Mfg
OKSH	Export Reports for Unit Costing

SAP Transaction Codes – Volume One

OKSI	Import Reports for Unit Costing
OKSJ	Export Reports for Product Costing
OKSK	Maintain Cost Element Group: Orders
OKSL	Import Reports for Product Costing
OKSM	Export Reports for Run Schedules
OKSN	Import Reports for Run Schedules
OKSO	Export Reports for Sales Orders
OKSP	Import Reports for Production Ctrl
OKSQ	Export Reports for Projects
OKSR	Import Reports for Projects
OKSS	Generate Reports for Run Schedules
OKST	Report Layouts for Summ. Objects
OKSU	Maintain Cost Element Group
OKSV	Maintain Cost Component Structure
OKT0	EC-PCA: Import Reports
OKT4	Define Report Writer Languages
OKT5	Cost Comp. Groups for Repetitive Mfg
OKT6	Cost Comp. Grps for Product Costing
OKT7	Report List: General Cost Objects
OKT8	Cost Elem. Groups: General Cost Obj
OKT9	Generate General Cost Object Reports
OKTA	General Cost Object Reports
OKTB	Report List for Process Mfg
OKTC	Cost Element Groups for Process Mfg
OKTD	Generate Reports for Process Mfg
OKTE	Import Reports for Process Mfg
OKTG	Generate text module
OKTH	Report List for Orders, Eng.-to-Ord
OKTI	Cst Elem Grps for Orders, Eng-to-Ord
OKTJ	Generate Rpts for Orders, Eng-to-Ord
OKTK	Import Reports for Orders,Eng-to-Ord
OKTO	Call Summariz. Hierarchy for Orders
OKTP	Call Summar. Hierarchy for Projects
OKTZ	Cost Comp. Str (View Cluster Maint.)
OKU0	Maintain variants RKCSUB00
OKU1	Maintain compound characteristics
OKU2	EC-EIS/EC-BP: Hierarchy maintenance
OKU4	Translation tool
OKU5	Print settings for WinWord
OKU7	Variables: CO-PA list element
OKU9	Variable list elements
OKUA	SAP-EIS Basic key figure aggr. TKCF
OKUB	Key figure display TKCF
OKUC	Maintain key figure subgrps TKCF
OKUD	Calculated key fig. display TKCK
OKUE	Database statistics
OKUF	Maintain calc. key fig. subgrp TKCK
OKUH	Reorganization of data transfer
OKUI	Display data structure
OKUK	Consistency test SAP-EIS
OKUL	Constants T242C
OKUM	Aspect summarization
OKUO	C FI Fiscal Year Variants
OKUP	Copy aspect from another client

SAP Transaction Codes – Volume One

OKUQ	Deactivate aspect in this client
OKUS	Exchange rates
OKUT	Exchange rate types
OKUU	Reorganize forms
OKUW	Generate aspect summarization
OKUY	Display aspect (with environment)
OKUZ	Define aspect archiving
OKV0	Variance Keys for Cost Centers
OKV1	Variance Keys for Orders
OKV2	Variance Keys for Cost Objects
OKV5	Maintain Tgt Cost Vers for Cost Ctrs
OKV6	Target Cost Versions for Orders
OKV7	Target Cost Versions for Cost Objs
OKVF	Change Variance Vrnts for Cost Ctr
OKVG	Variance Variants for Orders
OKVH	Variance Variants for Cost Objects
OKVK	Maintain Variance Tables
OKVO	Call Summariz. Hierarchy for Orders
OKVW	Default Values for Varian. Key/Plant
OKVZ	Change Variance Key in Mat. Master
OKW2	Maintain View V_CBAR_PP
OKWA	ABC Report List
OKWB	Change Report Layout Bus. Processes
OKWC	Generate ABC Reports
OKWT	Transport Planning Layouts
OKX0	Maint.sender str.for mast.data hier.
OKX1	Maintain Transfer Rules
OKX3	Where-used list
OKX4	Maintain Sender Str. for Master Data
OKX5	Sender Structure Comments
OKX6	Sender structures
OKX7	sender str. comments on trans. data
OKX8	Display Hierarchy Directory
OKX9	Maintain Hierarchy Directory
OKXB	Transport Tool
OKXC	Reorg.view maintenance (master data)
OKXE	Enter aspect in control tables
OKXF	Delete aspect from control tables
OKXG	Import tool
OKXO	SAP-EIS: Object Hier.Collector
OKXO1	CO transport collector: grouping
OKXR	Report Tree
OKXU	Function modules for doc.connection
OKY0	Val. Variants Sales Order/Prod. Cost
OKY1	Sales Order: Unit Costing
OKY2	Costing Variants CO Production Order
OKY3	Costing Variants: Cost Objects
OKY4	Costing Variants for Primary Costs
OKY5	Valuation Variants for CO Prod.Order
OKY6	Costing Variants: Cost Objects
OKY7	Val. Variants Sales Order/Unit Cstg
OKY8	Val. Variants Detail Plan Cost Ctr
OKY9	Costing Variants (Sales Order)
OKYA	Costing Types (Sales Order)

SAP Transaction Codes – Volume One

OKYB	Partner Versions
OKYC	Reference Cost Estimates
OKYD	Costing Versions
OKYE	Costing Types (Sales Order)
OKYF	Costing Variants Network Component
OKYG	Cstg Variants Network Costs Activity
OKYH	Costing Variants: Seiban
OKYI	Costing Variants Message
OKYJ	Valuation Variants Message
OKYK	Costing Types: Seiban
OKYL	Valn. Variants Network Component
OKYM	Valn. Variants Network Costs Actvy
OKYN	Valuation Variants: Seiban
OKYO	Assignment of Delivery Costs
OKYP	Costing Types Base Planning Object
OKYQ	Costing Variants: Service Line
OKYR	Valuation Variants: Service Line
OKYS	Costing Variants: Service Line
OKYT	Valuation Variant: Service Line
OKYU	Valn. Variants Appropriation Request
OKYV	Cross-Company Costing
OKYW	Cost Comp. Split Multiple Currencies
OKYY	Costing Variants (Brackets)
OKYZ	Cstg Variants Appropriation Request
OKZ1	Costing Origins
OKZ2	Maintain Overhead Groups
OKZ3	Default Values Cost Obj Controlling
OKZ4	Routing Control Key
OKZ5	Cost Object Category: Process Mfg
OKZ6	Cost Object Profile: Process Mfg
OKZ7	General Cost Object Categories
OKZ8	General Cost Object Profiles
OKZA	Base Planning Object Group
OKZZ	Message Management (Release)
OL01	Display / change LDK34 (bins)
OL02	Display / change RLPLA (bins)
OL03	Display / change LDK33 (stock)
OL04	Display / change RLBES (stock)
OL05	Display / change LDK30 (mat.whse)
OL06	Display / change LDK31 (mat.type)
OL10	Test storage bin data transfer
OL12	Data transfer stock RLBES-> B.I.
OL14	Test stock data transfer
OL15	Data transfer material whse no.view
OL16	Test mat.master data transfer (MLGN)
OL17	Data transfer material storage type
OL18	Test mat.master data transfer (MLGT)
OL19	Generate Distribution Model
OL20	Consistency Check (Centr.Processing)
OL21	Consistency Check (Decentr.Process.)
OL22	Check LE /HU Number Assignment
OLDPS	Process Sheet: Layout Management
OLE	OLE demo transaction
OLI0	C Plant Maintenance Master Data

OLI1	INVCO Stat. Setup: Material Movemts
OLI1BW	INVCO Stat. Setup: Material Movemts
OLI2	INVCO Stat. Setup: Stocks
OLI2BW	INVCO Stat. Setup: Stor. Loc. Stocks
OLI3	PURCHIS Statistical Setup
OLI3BW	Reorg.PURCHIS BW Extract Structures
OLI4	SFIS Statistical Setup
OLI4BW	Reorg. PPIS Extract Structures
OLI4KBW	Initialize Kanban Data
OLI5	PMIS Statistical Setup
OLI6	Periodic stock qty - Storage locatn
OLI6BW	Recompilation Appl. 06 (Inv. Ver.)
OLI7	SIS Statistical Setup: Orders
OLI7BW	Reorg. of VIS Extr. Struct.: Order
OLI8	Set Up SIS for Deliveries
OLI8BW	Reorg. VIS Extr. Str.: Delivery
OLI9	SIS Statistical Setup: Billing Docs
OLI9BW	Reorg. VIS Extr. Str.: Invoices
OLIA	C Maintenance Processing
OLIABW	Setup: BW agency business
OLIB	PURCHIS: StatUpdate Header Doc Level
OLID	SIS: Stat. Setup - Sales Activities
OLIE	Statistical Setup - TIS: Shipments
OLIF	SFIS: Setup-Repetitive Manufacturing
OLIFBW	Reorg. Rep. Manuf. Extr. Structs
OLIG	Reconstruct: Global Trade BW
OLIGBW	Reconstruct GT: External TC
OLIH	MRP Data Procurement for BW
OLIIBW	Reorg. of PM Info System for BW
OLIKBW	Setup GTM: Position Management
OLILBW	Setup GTM: Position Mngmt w. Network
OLIM	Periodic stock qty - Plant
OLIP	C Plant Maintenance Planning
OLIQ	Reorganization of QM info system
OLIQBW	QM Infosystem Reorganization for BW
OLISBW	Reorg. of CS Info System for BW
OLIX	Stat. Setup: Copy/Delete Versions
OLIZ	INVCO Setup: Invoice Verification
OLIZBW	INVCO Setup: Invoice Verification
OLMB	IMG Inventory Management
OLMD	Customizing For MRP
OLME	IMG View: Purchasing
OLML	IMG structure Warehouse Management
OLMR	IMG Invoice Verification
OLMRLIST	Maintain List Variant
OLMRVERDLIST	Maintain Aggregation Variant
OLMS	C RM-MAT Master Data Menu
OLMSRV	Customizing MM-SRV
OLMW	IMG Valuation/Acct Assgt
OLPA	SOP Configuration
OLPE	Sales order value
OLPF	Customizing Production Order
OLPK	Customizing for capacity planning
OLPM	Set Up: Plant Maintenance IS

SAP Transaction Codes – Volume One

OLPR	Customizing for Project System
OLPS	Customizing basic data
OLQB	QM Customizing in Procurement
OLR3_CJ20N	OLR3 Direct Entry: Project Builder
OLR3_ME2XN	Display Purchasing Document
OLS1	Customizing for Rebates
OLVD	C SD Shipping Menu
OLVF	C SD Billing Menu
OLVS	C SD Menu for Master Data
OLZSN	Leading Zeroes Customizing
OM00	Customizing KANBAN
OM01	MRP at client level
OM0A	Storage Mode for MRP Lists
OM0C	Requirements Grouping
OM0D	Period Profile for Safety Time
OM0E	Define Scope of Planning
OM0F	Convert MDVM/MDVL for MRP Areas
OM0H	MRP User Settings U444B
OM0I	Declaration Selection Rule
OM0J	Declaration Display Filter
OM0K	Define Navigation Profile
OM0L	Texts for Exception Groups
OM0M	Define MRP Views
OM0N	Activate Parallel Reading of SRL
OM0O	Evaln Profile Ranges of Coverage
OM0P	Define Extraction Mode
OM0R	Activate Material Groupings
OM11	Control Key; In-House Production
OM12	Control Key; External Procurement
OM13	Control Profile: Stock Transfer
OM14	No.Range Maintenance: PKHD
OM15	Maintain Status Short Text - Kanban
OM16	Maintain Kanban Status Sequences
OM17	Define Actions for Status Switching
OM18	Number Range Maintenance: PKKEY
OM19	Kanban Calculation Profile
OM1R	Maint. Periodic Invoicing Plan Types
OM20	Adjust Control Cycle
OM22	Field Selection Control Cycle Data
OM23	Display of Kanbans
OM24	Quick Info for Kanbans
OM25	Alternative Error Handling KANBAN
OM27	Automatic Deletion of Kanbans
OM28	LE: Storage Location Control
OM2R	Maint. partial invoicing plan types
OM3R	Maintain Date IDs
OM4R	Maint. Date Cat. for Invoicing Plan
OM5R	Default Date Category for Inv. Plan
OM6R	Maintain Dates
OM7R	Rule Table for Date Determination
OM8R	Invoicing Plan: Blocking Reasons
OM9R	Purch. Order: Reasons for Rejection
OMA0	Conditions: V_T681F for H ME
OMA1	Create Cond. Table: Batches in MM

SAP Transaction Codes – Volume One

OMA2	Change Cond.Table: Batches in MM
OMA3	Display Cond. Table: Batches in MM
OMA4	Field catalog V_T681f free goods (M)
OMA5	Field catalog V_T681 free goods (SD)
OMA6	Condition Table: Listing/Exclusion D
OMA7	Condition Table: Add Index
OMA8	Condition table: Change Index
OMAB	Definition Initial Status Batch
OMAC	Definition Initial Status Batch
OMAD	Number Ranges for Batch Numbers
OMAE	Number ranges of strategy records
OMAG	View Maintenance
OMB0	List of document types
OMB1	Dynamic Availability Check
OMB2	Create SLoc. Automatically (GI)
OMB3	Create SLoc. Automatically (GR)
OMB4	Maintain Print Indicator (GI)
OMB5	Maintain Print Indicator (GR)
OMB6	Change Manual Account Assgt.
OMB7	Test Data: Init.Entry of Stock Balcs
OMB8	Test Data: Reservations Transfer
OMB9	Change Document Lives
OMBA	Number Assgmt. for Accounting Docs.
OMBB	Batch Where-Used List
OMBC	Set Missing Parts Check
OMBD	Business Area from MM View
OMBF	Control BTCI Sessions for Goods Mvmt
OMBG	Set Stock Balance Display
OMBH	Phys. Inventory Settings in Plant
OMBI	Suggest Items Preselected GR
OMBJ	Suggest Items Preselected GI
OMBK	Suggest Items Preselected: Reservtn
OMBM	Control BTCI Sessions for Reserv.
OMBN	Defaults for Reservation
OMBO	Assign Forms and Programs
OMBP	Freeze Book Inventory Balance
OMBR	General Print Settings
OMBS	Reasons for Movements
OMBT	No. Ranges: Mat. Doc./Phys.Inventory
OMBU	Allocate Layout Sets to Reports
OMBV	Control BTCI Sessions for Phys. Inv.
OMBW	Set Screen Layout for Goods Movement
OMBX	Stock Balance Display
OMBZ	Rev. GR Despite Invoice
OMC0	Tolerance Limits for Goods Receipt
OMC1	Goods Receipt/Issue Slip Number
OMC2	Number Assignment for Reservations
OMC3	Suggest Items Preselected: Phys.Inv.
OMC4	BTCI Data Transfer: Inventory Count
OMC6	Test Data Transfer: Phys. Inventory
OMC7	BTCI Data Transfer: Inv.Count + Diff
OMC8	BTCI Data Tranfer: Inv. Doc./Count
OMC9	BTCI Data Tfr.: Inv.Doc./Count/Diff.
OMCB	Service Lists

OMCC	Generate Phys.Inv.Doc.for Goods Mvmt
OMCD	Suggest "Del. Completed" Indicator
OMCDB	Activate Documentary Batch
OMCE	Define Batch Level
OMCF	Print Label
OMCG	Search Procedures: Batch Determ. MM
OMCH	Set Manual Account Assignment (GR)
OMCI	Scope of List: Service Lists
OMCJ	Screen Layout: Goods Receipt
OMCK	Inventory Sampling Profile
OMCL	Inventory Sampling: St. Mgmt Levels
OMCM	Dynamic Availability Check: GR
OMCN	Control BTCI Sessions for Phys. Inv.
OMCO	Set Cycle Counting
OMCP	Dynamic Availability Check: GI
OMCQ	Settings for System Messages
OMCR	Inventory Sampling: St.Mgmt Lvl: WM
OMCS	Activate Batch Status Management
OMCT	Batch Definition
OMCU	Batch Status Management in Plant
OMCV	Classify Batches
OMCW	Strategy Types: Batch Determin.MM
OMCWB	Activate WIP Batch
OMCX	Access Seq. Batch Determination MM
OMCY	Search Procedures: Batch Determ. MM
OMCZ	Activate batch number allocation
OMD0	C RM-MAT MRP Controllers
OMD1	C RM-MAT MD Mat.type/MRP procedure
OMD2	C RM-MAT MD Weighting Groups
OMD3	C RM-MAT MD Exception Message T458A
OMD5	C MM MRP Element Description T457
OMD6	C RM-MAT MD Rqmts Plng Active T001W
OMD7	C RM-MAT MD Schedul.Parameters T399D
OMD8	C RM-MAT MD Control Parameters T438M
OMD9	C RM-MAT MD Spec.Procurmt.Key T460A
OMDA	C RM-MAT MD Period Split T449A
OMDB	Marking Material for MRP Termination
OMDC	C RM-MAT MD Planned Orders T436A
OMDD	C RM-MAT MD Planned Ord. Types T460C
OMDE	C RM-MAT MD Lot Sizes T439A
OMDF	C RM-MAT MD StgeCosts Lot Size T439L
OMDG	C RM-MAT MD Ord.ForecastRequmt T439P
OMDH	C RM-MAT MD Plnned Order Types T460D
OMDI	C RM-MAT MD Lot Size Texts
OMDJ	C RM.MAT MD Corr.Factors for Forcast
OMDK	C RM-MAT MD Error Allocation
OMDL	C MM-MRP User Maintenance
OMDN	C MM-MRP No.RangeInterval - PurReq.
OMDO	Create Planning File
OMDP	Check Consistency for Planning File
OMDQ	C RM-MAT MRP Types T438A
OMDR	C MD Run Time Statistics
OMDS	C MD Number of Planned Orders
OMDT	C MM-MRP External Procurement

OMDU	C MD Activate MRP
OMDV	C MD Convert Planning Run
OMDW	C MD Rescheduling
OMDX	C MD Planning Horizon
OMDY	C MD Planning Run Abend
OMDZ	C MD MRP Creation Indicator
OME1	C MM-PUR Purchasing Value Keys
OME2	C MM-PUR Terms of Payment
OME4	C MM-PUR Purchasing Groups
OME5	C MM-PUR Activate Plant: Source List
OME9	C MM-PUR Acct. Assignment Categories
OMEC	Copying Control Maintenance
OMEE	C MM-PUR Reorganization RFQ
OMEH	C MM-PUR User Maintenance
OMEI	C MM-PUR User Profiles
OMEL	C MM-PUR Certificate Categories
OMEN	C MM-PUR Reorg. Sched. Agrmnt Time
OMEO	C MM-PUR Number Ranges: Info Record
OMEP	C MM-PUR Number Ranges: Source List
OMEQ	C MM-PUR Quota Arrangement Rules
OMES	C MM-PUR Comments on Quotation
OMESCJ	Activate chargeable info records
OMET	Settings for Function Authorizations
OMEV	Determine Consgt. Valuation Prices
OMEW	C MM-PUR Requisition Processing Time
OMEX	C MM-PUR Reorganization: Requisition
OMEY	C MM-PUR Reorganization PO
OMEZ	C MM-PUR Reorg. Contract Time
OMF0	C MM-PUR Activate Cond. for Plant
OMFH	C MM-PUR Find Calc. Schema - Rebate
OMFI	Settings for Default Values
OMFJ	C MM-PUR Rec. Layout for Batch Input
OMFK	C MM-PUR Field Selection: Vendor
OMFL	C MM-PUR Transfer of Info Rec. Data
OMFM	C MM-PUR Schema Groups: Purch. Org.
OMFN	C MM-PUR Schema Groups: Vendor
OMFO	C MM-PUR Find Calculation Schema
OMFP	C MM-PUR Schema Group <-> Pur. Org.
OMFQ	C MM-PUR Scope of List: Conditions
OMFR	C MM-PUR Mkt. Price Schema: P. Org.
OMFS	CC-MM-PUR Chge.-Notice-Relev. Fields
OMFT	Message Determination Requirements
OMFZ	C MM-PUR: Stock Transfer Schema
OMG0	CS MM-PUR Item Cat./Acc. Assgt. Cat.
OMG1	C MM-PUR Commodity Code
OMG2	C MM-PUR Customs Offices
OMG3	C MM-PUR Modes of Transport
OMG4	C MM-PUR Business Transaction Type
OMG5	C MM-PUR Default Busn. Trans. Type
OMG6	C MM-PUR Import Procedures
OMG7	C MM-PUR Authorizations
OMG8	C MM-PUR Conditions/Sequence
OMG9	C MM-PUR Assignment Conditions/TCode
OMGA	C MM-PUR Texts: Creditor (Central)

OMGB	C MM-PUR Texts: Creditor (Purch.)
OMGC	C MM-PUR Weighting Keys
OMGEN	Generate Organizational Units
OMGENP	Generate Organizational Units
OMGF	C MM-PUR Output Device: Messages
OMGG	Settings for Message Determination
OMGH	C MM-PUR: Transaction/Event Keys
OMGI	C MM-PUR Main Criteria
OMGM	Settings for Subcontracting
OMGQCK	Release Procedure Checks
OMGQ_CHAR	Charact. Maint.: Release Procedure
OMGSCK	Release Procedure Checks
OMGT	Import Data
OMGU	C MM-PUR Scope of Ranking Lists
OMGV	Intrastat
OMGX	MM-PUR Form for Buyer's Neg. Sheet
OMGY	MM-PUR Buyer's Neg. Sheet Routines
OMH0	Interface to Activity Allocation
OMH6	Number Ranges for Purch. Documents
OMH7	Number Ranges for Purch. Requisition
OMH8	Number Ranges for Service Package
OMH9	Number Ranges for Entry Sheet
OMHA	Cr. Vol. Rebate Cond. Table (Purch.)
OMHB	Change Volume Rebate Table: Purch.
OMHC	Cond. Table: Display Rebate (Purch.)
OMHD	Arrangement Type: Purchasing
OMHE	Overview of Condition Type Groups
OMHF	Assign Cond. Type Group - Cond. Type
OMHG	Assign Arrangement Type - Cond. type
OMHH	Purchasing Selections
OMHI	Conditions: View Seq. F, M, Rebate
OMHJ	Purchasing: Condition Index
OMHK	Batch Input, Purchase Requisitions
OMHL	C MM-PUR Matchcode Info Record
OMHM	C MM-PUR Matchcode Requisition
OMHN	C MM-PUR Matchcode Purch. Document
OMHO	C MM-PUR Matchcode Source List
OMHP	Updating of Order Price History
OMHS	Display Info Record Transfer File
OMHT	Display Requisition Transfer File
OMHU	Example File: Batch Input Info Rec.
OMHV	Example File, Batch Input Requisn.
OMHX	Plant for company code (sbq. sttlmt)
OMI0	Error List for Intrastat Declaration
OMI1	C MD Safety Stock
OMI2	C MM-MRP Number Ranges: Mat. plg.
OMI3	C MM-MRP No. Ranges for Pld Ords
OMI4	C MD Lot Sizes
OMI5	C MD Item Numbers
OMI7	C MM-MRP No. Ranges for Pld Ords
OMI8	Plant Parameters
OMI9	PP MRP C Direct Procurement
OMIA	C MRP Range of Coverage Profile
OMIB	C MRP Start Times - Background Jobs

OMIC	MatMasterCust.:Batch Job Start Times
OMID	Maintain Number Range: Indep.Reqmts
OMIE	Maintain Number Range: Reqmts Plan
OMIG	MRP Group per Material Type
OMIH	Check. rule for updating backorders
OMII	Missing Parts Controller
OMIJ	C MRP Rounding Profiles
OMIK	Control of CO Integration
OMIL	Sel. Receipt Elements for Coverage
OMILL_CUT	Customizing for Cutting Processing
OMILL_MMCL	Maintain Selection Profile
OMILL_SE_ATNAM	Customizing Fast Entry
OMILL_SE_POSTYP	Customize Global Item Category
OMILL_T160M	Mill Products Message Control
OMILL_T160M_SD	Sales Order Versions
OMILL_VS	Sales Order Versions
OMILL_WF_SD	Customizing Workflow MILL_SD
OMIM	Maximum MRP Period
OMIN	Firming Scheduling Agreements
OMIO	Screen Seq. MRP List ; Ext.Header
OMIP	Reference Plant for MRP Master Data
OMIQ	Destinations Parallel MRP
OMIR	Storage Location MRP
OMIS	Convert Planned Order -> Prod. Order
OMIT	Start Date in the Past
OMIU	Action Code - Planned Order Control
OMIV	Action Control - Planned Order
OMIW	BOM Explosion
OMIX	Text: User Exit Planning Run
OMIY	Plng File Entries for Goods Mvmts
OMIZ	MRP area
OMJ1	Allow Negative Stocks
OMJ2	Maintain Phys.Inv.Tolrnce->Employee
OMJ3	Printer Determination Plant/SLoc.
OMJ4	Printer Determ: Plant/SLoc./User Grp
OMJ5	Exp.Date at Plant Level and Mvmt Lvl
OMJ6	Maintain No. Range for GR/GI Slips
OMJ7	Plant/Val.Area - Divis. -> Busin.Ar.
OMJ8	Create Stor. Loc. Automatically
OMJ9	Change Manual Account Assgt.
OMJA	Set Screen Layout for Goods Movement
OMJC	Generate Phys.Inv.Doc.for Goods Mvmt
OMJD	Set Missing Parts Check
OMJE	Exp.Date at Plant Level and Mvmt Lvl
OMJH	Maintain Dataset for Phys. Inventory
OMJI	Set Material Block
OMJJ	Customizing: New Movement Types
OMJK	Number Ranges for Reservations
OMJL	Maintain Print Indicator (autom.MvT)
OMJM	Comprn plnt/val.area - divis.->BusAr
OMJN	General field selection: goods mvmnt
OMJO	Convert MKOP into Consgt. Info Recs.
OMJP	Batch Input: Consignment Info Recs.
OMJQ	Deletion Flag: Consg. Price Segments

OMJR	Printer Determin.: Message Type/User
OMJS	Check expiration date at goods issue
OMJU	Gen. field selection, physical inv.
OMJV	Subsequent Calculation of Value
OMJW	Create Purchase Order Automatically
OMJX	GR Field Selection From Procurement
OMJY	GR Field Selec. Fr. Procment (Table)
OMK0	Link to PP interface
OMK1	Batch search method for Whse Mgmt
OMK2	Customer exits for strategies
OMK3	Conditions: field catalog (WM)
OMK4	CondTable: Create (Batches, WM)
OMK5	CondTable: Change (Batches, WM)
OMK6	CondTable: Display (Batches, WM)
OMK7	Batch WM..... (will be deleted)
OMK8	Services: Exclusion Indicator
OMKA	Conditions: V_T681F for A V
OMKB	Conditions: Rebate - Allowed Fields
OMKC	C MM PUR Price Marking
OMKD	C MM PUR Supply Regions
OMKE	C MM-PUR: Optimize Access
OMKF	C MM-PUR: Exlusion Indicators
OMKG	C MM-PUR: Limits
OMKH	C MM-PUR Reg. Vend. Source of Supply
OMKI	C MM-PUR Default Purchasing Org.
OMKJ	C MM-PUR P.Org. Cross-CoCode Release
OMKK	C MM-PUR Tax Indicators: Material
OMKL	C MM-PUR Tax Indicators: Acc. Assgt.
OMKM	C MM-PUR Tax Indicators: Plant
OMKN	C MM-PUR Assign Tax Inds. to Plant
OMKO	C MM-PUR Assign Tax Inds. to A. Ass.
OMKR	Search Types: Optimize Access WM
OMKT	Strategy Types: Batch Determin.WM
OMKU	Access: Maintain Batch Determin.WM
OMKV	Batch Determination: Proced.for WM
OMKW	Stock removal strategy "SLED"
OMKX	Automatic Transfer Orders
OMKY	Link to External System via ALE
OMKZ	Automatic Transfer Orders
OML1	Overview of Criticl Whse Monitor Obj
OML2	Var. Report RLLL01SE: TOs
OML3	Var. Report RLLL02SE: TR Items
OML4	Var. Report RLLL03SE: Post.Chge Doc.
OML5	Var. Report RLLL04SE: Deliveries
OML6	Var. Report RLLL05SE: Negative Stock
OML7	Var. Report RLLL06SE: Interim Stock
OML8	Var. Report RLLL07SE: Stock Product.
OML9	Customizing MOB Interface
OMLA	Putaway Near Picking Bin
OMLB	MObj.01: Critical TOs
OMLC	MObj.02: Critical TRs
OMLD	MObj.03: Critical Post. Chge Notices
OMLE	M.Obj.04: Critical Deliveries
OMLF	M.Obj.05: Negative Stocks

OMLG	M.Obj.06: Stocks Interim Stor.Bins
OMLH	M.Obj.07: Critical Stocks in Prod.
OMLI	Report Variant: Single Entry ActData
OMLJ	Movement Types for Whse Management
OMLK	Default Values for Inventory
OMLL	WM Movement Type: Clear Invent.Diff.
OMLM	Definition Empty Bin Index
OMLN	Warehouse Control Link
OMLO	Sectioning of Storage Bins
OMLP	Plan Jobs for Whse Activity Monitor
OMLQ	Stock Removal Strategy FIFO
OMLR	WM Interface to Inventory Management
OMLS	Stock Removal Strategy LIFO
OMLT	Stock Removal Strat. Partial Qty
OMLU	Stock Placement Strategy Empty Bin
OMLV	Print Control for Whse Management
OMLW	Number Ranges for Whse Management
OMLX	Confirmation
OMLY	Storage Type Search
OMLZ	Storage Section Search
OMM1	Storage Bin Type Search
OMM2	Haz.Material Stock Placement
OMM3	Stock Placement Strat.for Pallets
OMM4	Putaway Strategy for Bulk Storage
OMM5	Storage Type Definition
OMM6	Storage Type Definition
OMM7	Storage Type Maintenance
OMM8	Stock Removal Strat. Stringent FIFO
OMM9	Stock Removal Strat. Large/Small
OMMA	Print Assignment per Storage Type
OMMB	Inventory No.Ranges for Whse Mgmt
OMMC	Printer Assignment per WM Mov.Type
OMMD	Confirmation Ctrl per Storage Type
OMME	Confirmation Ctrl per Movement Type
OMMF	Number Ranges per Warehouse
OMMG	Number ranges physical inventory
OMMH	Type Search per Movement
OMMI	Section Check per Storage Type
OMMJ	Storage Unit Check per Storage Type
OMMK	Putaway Strategies
OMML	Hazardous Materials Storage Type
OMMM	Storage Type Maintenance
OMMN	Stringent FIFO Storage Type
OMMO	Consistency Check for MM-WM Tables
OMMP	Decentralized Warehouse Management
OMMQ	Pre-allocated stock
OMMR	Group numbers
OMMS	Reference Number Documents
OMMT	Reference Number Documents 2
OMMU	Link to Decentralized Unit
OMMV	Accumulation Decentralized
OMMW	Error Recovery Decentralized
OMMX	Printer Determination
OMMY	Print Code

OMMZ	Spool Parameters for WM Print Ctrl
OMN0	Control of Transaction Codes (MM-WM)
OMN1	Print Reference Number
OMN2	Stor.Type Control, Block Storage
OMN3	Storage Classes Allowed
OMN4	Storage Section Search
OMN5	Storage Units Allowed
OMN6	Storage Bin Type Search
OMN7	Storage Type Search
OMN8	Difference Indicators
OMN9	Block Sectioning
OMNA	Assignment for Bin Sectioning
OMNB	Assignment PF Status
OMNC	Control of Subsequent Screen
OMND	Field Selection for Whse Mgmt
OMNE	Control of Transactions in MM-WM
OMNF	Requirement Types for Whse Mgmt
OMNG	Queues Warehouse Management System
OMNH	APPC Interface per Warehouse Number
OMNI	Print Program per Warehouse Number
OMNJ	Link to Warehouse Control Unit
OMNK	Inventory Control per Storage Type
OMNL	Warehouse Number Maint./Inventory
OMNM	Define Mail Recipient
OMNN	Conversion Exit SU Number
OMNO	Define Mail Recipient
OMNQ	Special Movement Indicators
OMNR	TO Print Control with SU Management
OMNS	Print Code for TOs with SU Mgmt
OMNT	Printer Pool for SU Management
OMNU	Print Control with SU Management
OMNV	Number Range Intervals for Whse Mgmt
OMNW	System Parameters for Dec.Whse Mgmt
OMNX	Bulk Storage Indicators
OMNY	Access Strategy for Stor.Type Search
OMNZ	Parameters for Activity in WM
OMO!	Std Analyses: Std Settings, LO
OMO$	QMIS: Std Settings, Gen.Std Analyses
OMO,	Std Analyses: Delete Sel. Version
OMO0	Self-Def.Anal.: Std.Settings PP-IS
OMO1	Update Maintenance: SIS
OMO2	Update Maintenance: PURCHIS
OMO3	Update Maintenance: External Data
OMO6	Maintain Applications
OMO9	Update Maintenance: INVCO
OMO=	PMIS: Default Settings,Gnl.Std.Anal.
OMOA	LIS: Create Application
OMOB	LIS: Change Application
OMOC	LIS: Display Application
OMOD	Update Maintenance: SFIS
OMOE	Generate and Initialize LIL
OMOF	Update Maintenance: User-Defined App
OMOG	Maintain Update Groups
OMOH	Var.Std Analyses: Standard Settings

OMOJ	Var.Std Analyses: SIS Std Settings
OMOK	Var.Std Analyses: Ext. Std Settings
OMOL	Var.Std Analyses: PURCHIS Std Set.
OMON	Var.Std Analyses: INVCO Std Settings
OMOR	Update Maintenance: QMIS
OMOS	Update Maintenance: PMIS
OMOT	Updating maintainence: TIS
OMOU	Var. Std Analyses: TIS Std Settings
OMOY	Maintain Updating: Warehouse Mgmt
OMOZ	Update Maintenance: Logistics Genrl
OMP0	Customizing: Demand Mngmt (Menu)
OMP1	Customizing: Requirements Types
OMP2	Customizing: Versions
OMP3	Customizing: Vers. per Reqmts Class
OMP4	Customizing: Indep. Reqmts History
OMP5	Customizing: Refer.Type (Dep.Reqmts)
OMP6	Customizing: Consuming Indep. Reqmts
OMP8	Customizing: Reorganizing Indep.Req.
OMP9	Customizing: Fixing Indep. Reqmts
OMPA	Customizing: Version per Ref. Type
OMPC	Customizing:PlgInd/Cons.Indep.Reqmts
OMPD	Customizing:Indep.Reqmts Init.Screen
OMPE	Takeover Structure
OMPG	Maintain Consumption Mode
OMPH	Period Split
OMPI	Configuration
OMPJ	Reqmts Type Message Control
OMPL	Direct Input
OMPL1	Specify system messages
OMPL2	Edit MPL_C_ADAPTER
OMPL3	Edit MPL_C_DOCTYPES
OMPM	Create Example File
OMPN	C MM-PUR Purchasing Manuf. Part No.
OMPO	Maintain Requirements Classes
OMPP	Internal Number Assignment
OMPS	Maintain Period Split
OMQ1	Transfer of Purchase Orders
OMQ2	Transfer of Purchase Order History
OMQ3	Transfer of PO Texts
OMQ4	Create PO Transfer File
OMQ5	Edit PO Transfer File
OMQ6	Create PO Text Transfer File
OMQA	C MM-PUR: Take-Back Agreement
OMQK	Fine-Tuned Control: RFQ
OMQL	C MM-PUR: Supply Region for Plant
OMQM	C MM-PUR Matchcode: Entry Sheet
OMQN	Fine-Tuned Control: Purchase Order
OMQO	Fine-Tuned Control: Outl. Agreement
OMQP	Fine-Tuned Ctr.: Sch. Agmt. Schedule
OMQQ	Fine-Tuned Control: Service Entry
OMQR	Assign Schema to RFQ
OMQS	Assign Schema to Purchase Order
OMQT	Assign Schema to Outline Agreement
OMQU	Assign Schema to Sch. Agmt. Schedule

SAP Transaction Codes – Volume One

OMQV	Assign Schema to Service Entry Sheet
OMQW	Entry Aids w/o Material Master
OMQX	Default Asset Class for Mat. Group
OMR0	C MM-IV Autom. Acct. Assgt. (Simu.)
OMR0H	C MM-IV Automatic Account Assignmnts
OMR14	Define Variant Name
OMR2	C RM-MAT MR Default Incoming Invoice
OMR3	C MM-IV Default Account Maintenance
OMR4	MM-IV Doc.Type/NK Incoming Invoice
OMR5	MM-IV Doc.Type/NR Acct Maintenance
OMR6	Tolerance limits: Inv.Verification
OMR8	C RM-MAT MR PO Supplement
OMR9	C RM-MAT MR Payment Block Reasons
OMRA	C MM-IV Val.Cat./Subs.Debit/Credit
OMRAB	Maintain Settlement Profile
OMRB	C MR Tolerance Groups
OMRBW	Maintain movement type parameters
OMRC	C MR Alloc. User/Tolerance Group
OMRDC	Configure Duplicate Invoice Check
OMRE	Purchasing Document Lists Config.
OMRER_WORKFLOW	Workflow for Eval.Receipt.Settlement
OMRF	C MM_IV Activate Stochastic Block
OMRG	C MM-IV Stochastic Block Values
OMRH	C MM-IV Activate Item Amount Check
OMRI	C MM-IV Item Amount Check Parameters
OMRJ	C MM-IM NoRange RE_BELEG
OMRK	Mail to Purchasing
OMRL	Tax Version
OMRM	C MM-IV Customer-Specific Messages
OMRMA	Screen Selection Initial Screen
OMRMB	Screen Selection Header Data Screen
OMRN	C MM-IV Carry Forward Price Change
OMRO	G/L Account Auth. in Requisition
OMRP	G/L Account Auth. in Purchase Order
OMRQ	G/L Account Auth. in Contract
OMRR	Transaction/Event Key Usage
OMRS	Transaction/Event Key Usage
OMRT	Transaction/Event Key Usage
OMRU	Sender Texts, Form
OMRV	Invoice Status Change
OMRW	Treatment of Exch. Rate Differences
OMRX	Vendor-Specific Tolerances
OMRY	EDI Program Parameters
OMRZ	Runtime Invoice Document Archiving
OMS1	Units of Measure Grouping
OMS2	Maintain Material Types
OMS2OLD	C MM-BD Material Types
OMS3	Configure Industry Sectors
OMS4	C MM-BD Material Status
OMS5	C MM-BD Set Up Laboratory
OMS6	C MM-BD Storage Condition(s)
OMS7	C MM-BD Temperature Condition(s)
OMS8	C MM-BD Container Requirement(s)
OMS9	Configure Field/Screen Selection

SAP Transaction Codes – Volume One

OMSA	C MM-BD T130W Plant-Specific
OMSB	C MM-BD Special Stock Description
OMSD	C MM-BD F. Sel. Spec. T148G
OMSE	C MM-BD F. Sel. Reference T148W
OMSF	C MM-BD Material Groups
OMSFIX	Maintain Lock-Relevant Indicator
OMSG	Account Groups: Vendor
OMSH	C MM-BD Matchcode for Material
OMSI	C MM-BD Matchcode for vendor
OMSJ	C MM-BD Number Range for Vendor
OMSK	C MM-BD Valuation Classes T025
OMSL	C MM-BD Maintain TMCNV
OMSL2	Maintain table TMCNV
OMSL_DI	Maintenance Table TMCNV in DI
OMSM	CS MM Set Up Administrative Data
OMSP	C MM-BD Divisions
OMSPCUST	Maintain:Ext No Range & Rev.Type
OMSR	C MM-BD Field Groups
OMSS	C MM-BD Field Groups: Special Stocks
OMST	C MM-BD Record Layout f. BATCH INPUT
OMSU	C MM-BD Mat. Master Data Transfer
OMSV	C MM-BD Vendor Data Transfer
OMSW	C MM-BD Record Layout f. BATCH INPUT
OMSX	TCODE/Field Selection: Vendor
OMSY	C MM-BD Company Code for Matl Master
OMT0	C MM-BD Global Setting
OMT1	C MM-BD Consistency Check Updating
OMT2	Required Fields Control MM-BD ALE/DI
OMT3	Customizing for the Material Master
OMT3B	Maintain Screen Sequences
OMT3C	Copy Customer-Spec. Function Group
OMT3E	Maintain Influencing Factors
OMT3P	Maint. Status Determination Type
OMT3R	Maintain Order of Screens
OMT3U	Maintain User Settings
OMT3Z	Assign Secondary Screens
OMT4	Customizing for EAN Messages
OMT5	Auth. Group MatMaster (Inactive)
OMT6	Maintain Basic Materials Allowed
OMT8	Transfer Material Master Data by DI
OMTA	Output Program: RFQ
OMTB	Output Program: Purchase Order
OMTC	Output Program: Outline Agreement
OMTD	Output Program: Delivery Schedule
OMTE	Output Program: Service Entry Sheet
OMTF	Output Partner: RFQ
OMTG	Output Partner: Purchase Order
OMTH	Output Partner: Outline Agreement
OMTI	Output Partner: Delivery Schedule
OMTJ	Output Partner: Service Entry
OMTX	Define non-SAP system
OMUP	Forecast Schedule: Transm. Profile
OMV1	Service Category
OMV2	Org. Status, Service Category

OMW0	C MM-IV Control Valuation
OMW1	C RM-MAT MW Price Control
OMW2	C Define LIFO Pools
OMW3	C Define LIFO Valuation Levels
OMW4	C LIFO/FIFO-Relevant Movements
OMW5	C Devaluation by range of coverage
OMW5W	C Devaln by Rge of Coverage (Val.Ar)
OMW6	C Devaln by Slow/Non-Movement
OMW6W	C Devaln by Slow/Non-Mvt (Val. Area)
OMW7N	C Weighting Mat. Mvts (Mvt Rate)
OMW7R	C Weighting: Consmpts (Rge Coverage)
OMW8	C Stock Weighting (Obsolete)
OMW8N	C Stock Weighting (Mvt Rate)
OMW8R	C Stock Weighting (Rge of Coverage)
OMW9	C RM-MAT MW Doc.Type/F-u.Csts.Pr.Ch.
OMWA	C RM-MAT MW Doc.Type/F-up Csts.D/C
OMWB	C MM-IV Autom. Acct. Assgt. (Simu.)
OMWC	C MM-IV Split Material Valuation
OMWD	C RM-MAT MB Grouping Valuation Area
OMWE	C LIFO/FIFO Valuation Active?
OMWEB	Maintain C Valuation Tracks
OMWF	C MM-IV User Maintenance
OMWG	C RM-MAT MW User Profiles
OMWH	C Indicator for Materials LIFO Pools
OMWI	C Movement Types: Lowest Value
OMWJ	C Document Types: Lowest Value
OMWK	C MM-IV Authorizations
OMWL	C LIFO/FIFO Global Setting
OMWM	C MM IV Control: Accnt Determination
OMWN	MM-IM: Acct Group. Code for Mvt.Type
OMWO	C MM-PUR: Purchase Account Mgmt
OMWP	C LIFO/FIFO Methods
OMWPS1	C LIFO Pools: Splitting
OMWPS2	C LIFO Pools: Merging
OMWPS3	C LIFO: Reassign Material Layer
OMWQ	C LIFO/FIFO Sample
OMWR	C LIFO Layer Versions
OMWS	Activate Proportion/Product Unit
OMWT	C FIFO Valuation Levels
OMWU	C Constants for DB Commit
OMWV	C Movement Types: Movement Rate
OMWW	MM Account Determination Wizard
OMWW2	Old MM Account Determination Wizard
OMWX	C Mvt Types: Excptns, Rge of Cov.
OMWY	C Reduction: Sales Prices
OMWZ	C LIFO/FIFO: Company Code Parameters
OMX0	Assign ML Movement Type Groups
OMX1	ML Activation in n Valuation Areas
OMX2	Define Material Ledger Type
OMX3	ML Assignment of Valuation Area
OMX4	Number Range Maintenence: ML-DOCU.
OMX5	Dyn. Price Release Plan. Pr. Change
OMX6	Texts for Currency Types/Valuations
OMX7	Definition ML Movement Type Groups

OMX8	Assign Material Update Structure
OMX9	Define Material Update Structure
OMXA	Display Quantity Structure Type
OMXB	Define Naming Rule
OMXC	Rules for Name Formation
OMXD	Maintain Naming Structure
OMXE	Assign Naming Structure to Plant
OMXF	Activate Actual Cst Component Split
OMXG	Maintain Key Figure Scheme
OMXH	Maintain FIFO Variant
OMXL	Configure empties processing
OMXW	Activate WIP at Actual Costs
OMXX	Update Contr. Release Order Docu. MM
OMX_NLINK_DISP	Assign Contr. Level to Process Cat.
OMX_NRULE_DISP	Display Controlling Levels
OMX_UMB_ACCOUNTS	Display Accounts for Account Key UMB
OMY0	Display Material Transfer File
OMY1	Create Input File from Material
OMZE	C MM-PUR Reorg. Contract Extra
OMZN	C MM-PUR Reorg. Sched. Agrmnt Extra
ON/1	IS-H: Calc. Procedure Determination
ON01	IS-H: Control Institution
ON02	IS-H: Parameter Time-dep. Institut.
ON03	IS-H: Maintain Screen Sequence
ON04	IS-H: Screen Modification
ON05	IS-H: Control Client
ON06	IS-H: Parameters time-dep., client
ON07	IS-H: Default Service Catalog
ON08	ISH: Authorizations
ON09	ISH: User
ON10	ISH: User Profiles
ON100	IS-H: Calc.Formula for Cmp DynCaseMx
ON14	IS-H: Postal code maintenance
ON15	IS-H: Maintain Geographical Areas
ON16	IS-H: Parishes
ON17	IS-H: Addresses
ON18	IS-H: Name affixes - titles
ON19	IS-H: Parameters, time-indep.,client
ON20	IS-H: Inst-Spec., Time-Indep. Params
ON21	IS-H: Sex
ON22	IS-H: Default End Date of Services
ON24	IS-H: Certificate Status
ON25	IS-H: Name elements for search
ON26	IS-H: Marital Status
ON27	IS-H: Religious denominations
ON28	IS-H: Relationships
ON29	IS-H: Asgmt. of case type to org.cat
ON30	IS-H: Categories of case-case asgmt.
ON31	Conditions: Customizing for Pricing
ON32	IS-H: Parameter for Copymnt Request
ON33	IS-H: Parameter for Copayment
ON34	IS-H: Accident types
ON35	IS-H: Copayment Waiver
ON36	IS-H: Diagn.Coding Catalog Ctgrs

ON37	IS-H: Diagnoses Codes
ON38	IS-H: Cust.Proc. maint.Prce.Determtn
ON39	IS-H: Risk Factors
ON40	IS-H: Service Text Service Entry
ON41	IS-H: Case types
ON42	IS-H: Case-to-person asgmt functions
ON43	IS-H: Movement categories
ON44	IS-H: Movement types
ON45	IS-H: Discharge statuses
ON46	IS-H: Types of Coverage
ON47	IS-H: Causes of death
ON48	IS-H: Delivery categories
ON49	IS-H: Birth Procedures
ON4A	IS-H: Case categories
ON4B	IS-H: Assignments to Case Categories
ON4C	IS-H: Activation of Case Categories
ON50	IS-H: Organizational Categories
ON51	IS-H: Organizational Cat. Hierarchy
ON52	IS-H: Assgmt. Specialty - Department
ON54	IS-H: Departmental Key
ON55	IS-H: Down Payment Parameters
ON56	IS-H: Params. for Down Pymnt request
ON57	IS-H: R/2 screens for batch input
ON59	IS-H: Outpatient visit status
ON60	IS-H: Building Categories
ON61	IS-H: Building Category Hierarchy
ON62	IS-H: Equipment/Facilities ID code
ON63	IS-H: General Parameter Maintenance
ON64	IS-H: Blocking Reason Build. Unit
ON66	IS-H: Service-related Cat.Determntn.
ON68	IS-H: Hierarchy Bld.Cat. - Org. Cat.
ON69	IS-H: Maintain Division for Pricing
ON70	IS-H: Work org. type: ID codes/texts
ON71	IS-H: Event-work org.type: SAP value
ON72	IS-H: Event-Work Org.Type Asgmt-Cust
ON73	IS-H: Work Organ.: Keys/texts/types
ON74	IS-H Specialty categories
ON75	IS-H: Work Organizer Ctrl w/o Condit
ON76	IS-H: Work Organizer Ctrl with IPTyp
ON77	IS-H: Work org.: Form windows, elem.
ON78	IS-H: Input/output device assignment
ON79	IS-H: Assign Work Organ. to Printer
ON7A	IS-H: Work org.: With bill.t./IPType
ON7B	IS-H: Assign Work Organizers to OUs
ON7C	IS-H List of work organizer settings
ON7F	IS-H: Work Organizer-Event Filter
ON80	IS-H: Determine Billing Type
ON81	IS-H: Maintain Charge Master Type
ON82	IS-H: Charge Master Columns
ON83	IS-H: Grouping categories
ON84	IS-H: Maintain Record Types
ON85	IS-H: Maintain Record Structure
ON86	IS-H: Default values for FI data
ON87	ISH: Catalog Determination

ON88	IS-H: Charge Master Column Detn
ON89	ISH: Assgnmnt.-Service Conversion
ON90	IS-H: Certificate categories
ON91	IS-H: Certificate Types
ON92	IS-H: Service Text Parameters
ON93	IS-H: Warning f. service adjustment
ON94	IS-H: Create Copayer
ON95	IS-H: Create FI Customer
ON96	IS-H: Type of Processing Cust.Sessn.
ON97	IS-H: Def.Value Country for Bus.Part
ON98	IS-H: Def.Value Language Bus.Partner
ON99	IS-H: Default Start Date of Services
ONA0	IS-H: Routines for filling FI Cust.
ONA1	IS-H: Sort Procedure Ins.Verificatn.
ONA2	IS-H: Displ. Params. f. Copay.Requst
ONA3	IS-H: Display Copayment Parameters
ONA4	IS-H: Display Down Payment Params.
ONA5	IS-H: Display Down Paymt.Req.Params.
ONA6	IS-H: Rules for Direct Pat. Billing
ONA7	IS-H: Change Billing Block
ONA8	IS-H: Change Rules for Point Values
ONA9	IS-H: Control Billing Messages
ONAA	IS-H: Maintain Ins. Contract Type
ONAG	IS-H: IV reasons for rejection
ONAK	IS-H: Copayment amount per day
ONAV	IS-H: Variants for Inv.Restrictions
ONB0	IS-H: User groups
ONB1	IS-H: Priorities for waiting list
ONB2	IS-H: Terminal def. HC smart card
ONB3	IS-H: Activity-spec. bus.partner txt
ONB4	IS-H: Bus.partn.funct. int.-ext.cat.
ONB5	IS-H: Assign IV request to clerk
ONB6	IS-H: SAP user exits
ONB7	IS-H: Customer user exits
ONB8	IS-H: Movement reasons
ONB9	IS-H: Exclusions for service pairs
ONBA	IS-H: Define stat. key figures
ONBB	IS-H: Maintain leave of abs settings
ONBC	IS-H: Maintain Pricing Procedure
ONBD	Assign Bill.Type to Doc.PricingProc.
ONBE	IS-H: Create Condition Table
ONBF	IS-H: Create Access Sequence
ONBG	IS-H: Create Condition Type
ONBH	IS-H: Create Condition Records
ONBI	IS-H: Maintain no.range f. bill.doc.
ONBK	IS-H: Define Billing Types
ONBL	IS-H: Define Partner Functions
ONBM	IS-H: Define Document Flow
ONBN	IS-H: Define Blocking Reasons
ONBO	IS-H: Assign bill.type to bill.block
ONBP	IS-H: Maintain access seq. acct detn
ONBQ	IS-H: Maintain Acct Detn Type
ONBR	IS-H: Assessment rate rules
ONBS	IS-H: Maintain Acct Detn Procedure

ONBT	IS-H: Billing exception comments
ONBU	IS-H: Procedure Dtn. for Act. Dtn.
ONBV	IS-H: Assign Revenue Accounts
ONC0	IS-HCM: Maintain Seg. -> Seg. Asgmt.
ONC1	IS-HCM Maintain Message Type
ONC1D	IS-HCM: Delete Customer Msg. Cmpnts.
ONC2	IS-HCM: Create Partner System
ONC3	IS-HCM Maintain Message Segment
ONC4	IS-HCM: Delete Partner System
ONC5	IS-HCM Installation Check Subsystems
ONC6	IS-HCM: Maintain System Attributes
ONC7	IS-HCM Display Incorr. Incoming Msg.
ONC8	IS-HCM Maintain Message Fields
ONC9	IS-HCM Delete Incorr. Incoming Msg.
ONCA	IS-HCM Maintain Cat.-Segment-Assgmnt
ONCA1	IS-HCM: Display Msg.Type-Sgmt Asgmt
ONCB	IS-HCM Display Receipt Logs
ONCC	IS-HCM Maintain Segment-Field-Assgmt
ONCC1	IS-H: Display MsgSegment-Field Asgmt
ONCD	IS-HCM Delete Receipt Logs
ONCE	IS-HCM List of partner system sett.
ONCEDI0	EDI Procedure Basic Customizing
ONCEDI1	IS-H EDI Institution Agreements
ONCEDI2	IS-H EDI Convert int.<->ext. Code
ONCEDI3	IS-H EDI Communication Status
ONCEDI302	IS-H EDI DCP-to-Ins. Provider Asgmt
ONCEDI4	IS-H EDI Application status
ONCEDI5	IS-H EDI DCP-to-Ins. Provider Asgmt
ONCEDI6	IS-H EDI DCP-to-Ins. Prov. Coll.Asgt
ONCEDI7	IS-H EDI Display DCP-Ins.Prov. Asgmt
ONCEDI8	IS-H EDI: Message Structure Tree
ONCEDI9	IS-H Build EDI File Names
ONCEDIC0	IS-H: Control/Options for EDI
ONCEDIDE0	IS-H §301 DCP File Compare
ONCEDIDE1	IS-H P301/P302 HI Fund File Compare
ONCEDIUA	IS-H EDI: Deposit Old EDI Records
ONCEDIUA2C	IS-H Display EDI Recs.in Temp.Storag
ONCEDIZ	IS-H EDI Service <-> Room Type Asgmt
ONCF	IS-HCM: EDI Transfer System
ONCG	IS-HCM Generate SAP Structures
ONCH	IS-HCM Generate Customer Structures
ONCI	IS-HCM: Display Dispatch Options
ONCJ	IS-H: Synchronous dispatch options
ONCK	IS-HCM: Display Receipt Options
ONCL	IS-HCM: EDI - Excluded cases
ONCM	IS-HCM: Activate EDI Comm. Procedure
ONCN	IS-HCM: Number Ranges
ONCO	Customizing
ONCP	IS-HCM: Maint. Dispatch w/o Refer.
ONCQ	IS-H: Monitoring check programs
ONCR	IS-HCM Maintain Disp. w. OU Refer.
ONCS	IS-H: Synchronous dispatch
ONCSTAT	IS-HCM Table Entry Evaluations
ONCT	IS-HCM Maintain Convert. HL7 Values

ONCU	IS-HCM: EDI - Exclude Msg to InsProv
ONCV	IS-HCM Maintain Recpt. w/o Reference
ONCW	IS-HCM: DC Point Transaction Data
ONCX	IS-HCM: Display Dispatch Logs
ONCY	IS-HCM: Delete Dispatch Logs
ONCZ	IS-HCM: Maintain data coll. point
OND1	IS-H: Maintain BDT Format Versions
OND2	IS-H: Maintain BDT Format Fields
OND3	IS-H: Maintain BDT Format Rules
OND4	IS-H: Maintain BDT Fixed Vals.OU-rel
ONDT	IS-H: Planning type
ONE1	IS-H: IMG CP/EP Discount
ONE2	IS-H: Set up Direct Patient Billing
ONE3	IS-H: HCO documentation
ONE4	IS-H: HCO documentation
ONE5	IS-H: HCO documentation
ONEI0	IS
ONEIS	IS-H: Determine chars., key figs EIS
ONFCL	IS-H: Case Categorization
ONG0	IS-HCM: Maintain Message Standards
ONG1	IS-H: Maintain EDI Procedures
ONG2	IS-H: Assign Events to EDI Proced.
ONG3	IS-H: Maintain EDI Proc. Funct. Call
ONG4	IS-H EDI Procedure-to-Standard Asgmt
ONG5	IS-H: Assign Events to EDI Proced.
ONG6	IS-H: Assign Events to EDI Proced.
ONHA	–
ONHB	–
ONHC	–
ONHD	–
ONHE	–
ONHF	–
ONHG	–
ONHH	–
ONHI	–
ONHJ	–
ONHK	–
ONHL	–
ONHM	–
ONHN	–
ONHO	–
ONHP	–
ONHQ	–
ONHR	–
ONHS	–
ONHT	–
ONHV	–
ONHW	–
ONK1	ISH: Assign Application to System
ONK2	ISH: Assgn Event to Application
ONK3	IS-H: Events
ONK4	IS-H: Event/configuration assignment
ONK5	IS-H: Application Parameters
ONK6	IS-HCM: Maintain System Attributes

ONK7	IS-H: Check Configuration
ONL0	IS-H: Maintain Service Rule Types
ONL1	IS-H: Maintain Service Exclusions
ONL2	IS-H: Maintain Service Combinations
ONL3	IS-H: Maintain Service Max. Values
ONL4	IS-H: Assign rule types to events
ONL5	IS-H: Check procedure
ONL6	IS-H: Maintain compensation proposal
ONL7	IS-H: Control parameters FR/PS
ONLA	IS-H: Check Procedure - Overview
ONLA_NPROC_RULES	IS-H: Check Procedure - Overview
ONLONGTERMSVC	IS-H:
ONM1	IS-H: Borrowing reason
ONM2	IS-H: Borrower categories
ONM3	IS-H: Borrowing authorizations
ONM4	IS-H: Admin.of med.records paramet.
ONM9	IS-H: Assign Material Catalog to OU
ONMA	Define Material Catalogs
ONMB	Define Material Sets
ONMC	IS-H: Assign Material Sets to OU
ONMD	Generate Material Catalogs
ONME	Define Material Sets
ONMF	IS-H: Maintain Material Proposal
ONMG	Generate Material Catalogs
ONMH	Define Cabinets
ONMHC	Copy Closets
ONMHD	Closet List
ONN1	IS-H: Number Ranges for Org. Units
ONN2	IS-H: Number Ranges for Build. Units
ONN3	IS-H: Number Ranges Pers. Structure
ONN4	IS-H: Number Ranges Patients
ONN5	IS-H: Case Number Ranges
ONN6	IS-H: Number Ranges Business Partner
ONN7	IS-H: Number Ranges Ins.Verif./Cert.
ONN8	IS-H: Number Ranges Billing
ONN9	IS-H: Technical Number Range
ONNKTR_KV	IS-H: Create External Ins. Prov.
ONO1	Maintain flat rate type (AT)
ONO2	Determine flat rate type (AT)
ONO3	Maintain flat rate rules (AT)
ONO4	Flat rate scales (AT)
ONO5	Flat rate exclusions (AT)
ONO6	IS-H: Outpt. ind. services/ins.prov.
ONOA	IS-H: VAT assessment (Austria)
ONOC	IS-H*MED: Assign Physician - OU
ONOT	Maintain Quotation Types
ONP1	IS-H: Periods
ONP4	Create Ntwk Pl.Layout Statistical KF
ONP5	Change Ntwk Pl.Layout Statistical KF
ONP6	Display Nwk Pl.Layout Statistical KF
ONR0	IS-H: Applications report control
ONR1	IS-H: Report Control Groups
ONR2	IS-H: Report Ctrl Assgmt. User-Group
ONR3	IS-H: Report Ctrl. Assgmt. Grp.-Rep.

ONRA	IS-H: Maintain Record Types
ONRB	IS-H: Maintain Record Structure
ONRC	IS-H: Statistics: Srv valuat. factor
ONRD	IS-H: Stat. - Case class. val. form.
ONRE	IS-H: Statistics: Svce Remapping
ONRF	IS-H: Statistics - Geogr.area totals
ONRK	IS-H: Age groups for statistics
ONRL	ISH: Maintenance Statistics for NLSU
ONS1	IS-H: Maintain selection proc. (AT)
ONTNPC1	IS-H: Maintain Occup.Characteristics
ONTNREL	IS-H: Start View Maintenance TNREL
ONU0	IS-H: Client reset control
ONU1	IS-H: Import Postal Code Directory
ONU2	IS-H: Import Postal Code Directory
ONU3	IS-H: Import Postal Code Directory
ONV0	IS-H: Change CP/EP Discount
ONV1	IS-H: Maintain Treatment Category
ONV2	IS-H: Display Treatment Category
ONV3	IS-H: Maintain Case Class/Treat.Cat.
ONV4	IS-H: Display Case Class./Treat.Cat.
ONV5	IS-H: Services for Treatmnt Category
ONV6	IS-H: Display Service per Trtmt.cat.
ONV7	IS-H: Maintain Ins. Prov. Types
ONV8	IS-H: Display Guarantor Types
ONV9	IS-H: Create CP/EP Discount
ONVA	ISH: View Maintenance Institutions
ONVB	ISH: View maint. classification cat.
ONVC	ISH: View maint. classification type
ONVD	ISH: View Maint. Nurs. Acuity Class.
ONVE	IS-H: Maintain Guarantor Class
ONVF	IS-H: Display Guarantor Class
ONVI	IS-H: Nurs. acuity classif. params
ONVJ	IS-H: Cases for NAcuity CorrectProc.
ONVV	IS-H: Ins. Relat. System Parameters
ONWA	IS-H: Bad debt parties
ONWPCB	Customizing MiniApps Inpat. Billing
OO0C	Context Maintenance
OO0D	Object Description Profile
OO0O	Object Data Definition
OO0R	Relationship Data Definition
OO0T	Tool Definition
OO2S	Description: Subtypes
OO513PAPD	Appraisal Model for PA/PSA/EE-gp/sgp
OO91	SAP Org. Object Type Assignment
OO9M	Matrix Types
OOAA	Edit Recipient Groups
OOAC	HR: Authorization main switch
OOAD	Task Functions
OOAE	Settings for Appraisal Systems
OOAI	Appraisal Transfer Persons
OOAK	Selection Criteria (Detail)
OOAK_NEW	Criteria for Detailed Selection
OOALEBSIZE	T77S0: Set ALE BSIZE
OOALECOMB	HR: Distributable Relationship

SAP Transaction Codes – Volume One

OOALEINTE	T77S0: Set ALE INTE	
OOALEPCR	T77S0: Set ALE PCR	
OOALEPOPPA	T77S0: Set ALE POPPA	
OOALEPOPUP	T77S0: Set ALE POPUP	
OOALERELA	HR: Distributable Relat. Direction	
OOALEREPLI	T77S0: Set ALE REPLI	
OOALEREPPA	T77S0: Set ALE REPPA	
OOALESIN	HR: Serialization in ALE Inbound	
OOALESOUT	HR: Serialization in ALE Outbound	
OOALE_FILTER1	HR:Master Data Distribution Filter 1	
OOALE_FILTER2	HR:Master Data Distribution Filter 2	
OOAM	Change Appraisals Catalog	
OOAP	Set Active Plan Version	
OOAS	Aspects	
OOATTRCUST	Customizing General Attribute Maint.	
OOATTRCUST_DISP	Customizing General Attribute Maint.	
OOATTRCUST_TRSP	Customizing General Attribute Maint.	
OOAU	Authorizations	
OOAW	Evaluation Paths	
OOAZ	Building Address	
OOB1	Form of Appraisal	
OOB2	Assign Appraisal Model	
OOBA	Define Reservation Type	
OOBC	Pushbutton Control Batch Input	
OOBD	Cancellations	
OOBE	Budgeting Parameters	
OOBG	Reasons	
OOBI	INTERN: PA-PD Integration in Batch	
OOBS	Staffing Schedule	
OOBU	Business Events Bookings	
OOBX	Appraisal Type: Standard Input	
OOC3	PD-TEM: Master Data Catalog	
OOCA	Activity Types	
OOCB	Customer Enhancement for Master Data	
OOCC	Cost Center of Cost Object	
OOCDIST	Integration with Cost Distribution	
OOCDOC_CUST	Activate Change Documents	
OOCE	Organizational Elements	
OOCH	Consistency Check	
OOCINH	Inheritance of Contr. Area in Pos.	
OOCK	Integ. Cost Plng & Cost Accounting	
OOCM	Compensation Management Settings	
OOCM_AD	Compensation Administration Settings	
OOCM_CR	Calculation of Compa Ratio	
OOCM_JP	Job pricing parameter	
OOCM_SS	Participation in Salary Survey	
OOCM_TCS	Total Compensation Statement Para.	
OOCO	Integration HR Planning: Cost Acctng	
OOCOLFRAMCUST	Column Framework Customizing	
OOCOLFRAMCUST_DISP	Column Framework Customizing	
OOCOLFRAMCUST_TRSP	Column Framework Customizing	
OOCP	Maintain Company	
OOCR	Set up PD Transport Connection	
OOCT	Catalogs	

SAP Transaction Codes – Volume One

OOCU	Task Customizing
OOCU_PAR	Task Customizing with parameters
OOCU_PAR_HRGB	Activate workflow 'HR_GB:PrtCar'
OOCU_RESP	Customizing Responsibilities
OODA	Online Process
OODB	Data Collection
OODC	Shift Planning: Requirements Entry
OODD	Shift Planning: Lock Settings
OODE	Shift Planning: Work Center View
OODF	Shift Planning: Abbrev. Proposal
OODG	Shift Planning: Standard Shift Group
OODH	Shift Planning: Selection View
OODIFMA	Restrict to One FM Area
OODK	Shift Planning: Factory Calendar
OODL	Default Values for Output
OODM	Activate indicator for subst. types
OODN	Shift Planning: Dialog Box Cust.
OODO	Shift Planning: Different Payment
OODQ	Time Evaluation: External Access
OODR	Time Evaluation: Report Variant
OODS	Data Views
OODT	Data Transfer
OODU	Shift Planning: Report Variant
OODV	Shift Planning: Substitution Type
OODW	Shift Planning: Messages
OODX	Shift Planning: Groupings
OODY	Shift Planning: Time Types/Balances
OOEC	Change Development Plan Catalog
OOECM_AD	Administration Control Parameters
OOECM_BD	Budgeting Control Parameters
OOECM_JP	ECM Switches for Job Pricing
OOECM_MAIN	ECM Activation Switch
OOEE	Settings for Development Plans
OOEF	Firmly Book/Cancel
OOEG	Create Business Event Group
OOEP	Set Suitability Areas
OOER	Create External Instructor
OOES	Restrictions
OOET	Create Business Event Type
OOEV	Attendees: Booking Checks
OOEW	Booking Priorities
OOEX	Print Shift Plan w/Microsoft Excel
OOEY	Further Processing of Plan States
OOEZ	Define Development Plan States
OOFA	Switch for Business Event Locations
OOFD	Search Function
OOFF	Passport photo
OOFK	Factory Calendar
OOFO	Form Editing
OOFRAMEWORKCUST	Hierarchy Framework Customizing
OOFRAMEWORKCUST_DISP	Hierarchy Framework Customizing
OOFRAMEWORKCUST_TRSP	Hierarchy Framework Customizing
OOFRAMEWORKIFCUST	Hierarchy Framework Customizing
OOFRAMEWORKIFCUST_DI	Hierarchy Framework Customizing

SAP Transaction Codes – Volume One

OOFRAMEWORKIFCUST_TR	Hierarchy Framework Customizing
OOFT	Customizing Quota Planning FTE
OOFUNC_AP	Functions - Appraisals
OOFUNC_DP	Functions - Development Plans
OOGA	Designs
OOGP	Work Schedule Group Assignment
OOGT	User Assignment
OOGV	Health Examinations
OOHAP_BASIC	Basic Appraisal Template Settings
OOHAP_CATEGORY	Appraisal Category Settings
OOHAP_CAT_GROUP	Category Group Settings
OOHAP_SETTINGS_PA	PA: Settings
OOHAP_VALUE_TYPE	Standard Value Lists
OOHCP1	Basic Settings Pers. Cost Planning
OOHCP2	Data Collection Settings PersCostPl.
OOHCP3	Planning Run Settings PersCostPl.
OOHCP4	Detail Planning Settings PersCostPl.
OOHCP5	Posting Settings Pers. Cost Planning
OOHCP_MODIFY	Change Customizing Headcount Plng
OOHCP_SHOW	Display Customizing Headcount Plng
OOHP	Set Up PD - PA Integration
OOHQ	Integration: PLOG - PREL
OOHRCE_CEQUA	Switches for PAD CE
OOHRCE_CHGLP	Change Legal Person
OOHRCE_CHGPY	Allow Change of Payroll Area
OOHRCE_MAINS	Switches for PAD CE
OOHRFPM_MAXNO	Max. No. of Objects to be Checked
OOHRPBC01	Gen. Settings for Pay Scale Evaluatn
OOHRPBC02	Subtype for Reassignment Lock
OOHRPBC03	Activate Monitoring of Tasks
OOHRPBC04	Activate Basic Conversion of STA
OOHRPBC05	Value of Pay Scale Eval. in Trnf.
OOHRPBC06	Activate Basic Conversion
OOHRPBC07	Posting Date for Payroll Simulation
OOHRPBC08	Retroactive Acctg by Cmmt Processor
OOHRPBC09	General Settings
OOHRPBC_BCS	Original Budget Creation BCS
OOHRPBC_FBS	Original Budget Creation FBS
OOHRPPBC_ADT0	Switch for Main/Sub-Group
OOIF	HR: Switch for IBAN Functionality
OOIL	Integration Cost Allocation
OOIO	Initialization Object Type
OOIT	Infotypes
OOIV	Initial Business Event/Resource Type
OOKA	Incompatible Attendances/Absences
OOKB	Cost/Price Determination
OOKF	Cost Center Determination
OOKO	Resources and Authorities
OOKP	Cost Planning
OOKR	Fee Handling
OOKU	Correspondence User Groups
OOKV	Conflict Reaction
OOKY	Set up Current Year for YEA Korea
OOLA	List Entry

OOLB	Wage Elements
OOLC	Create Business Event Location
OOLE	Current Settings
OOLG	Language Sequence in Pers. Planning
OOLW	Workflow connection - Ctry Reassign.
OOMA	Mail Connection
OOMD	HR Search Function
OOME	Define Lunch Times
OOMG	Control Elements Materials Mgmt
OOML	Room Administration Mail Connection
OOMM	Integration Materials Management
OOMP	Organization Elements Materials Mgmt
OOMS	Toolboxes
OOMT	Actions
OOMV	Create Sequential File for PD
OOMW	Display Sequential File for PD
OOMWB1	MDT Scenario Maintenance
OONA	Naming
OONB	Actions for Business Event Assessmnt
OONC	No. Assignment for All Plan Versions
OONF	Note Function
OONR	Number Ranges
OONS	Name Tags
OONT	Note Function
OOOBJMANCUST	Object Manager Customizing
OOOBJMANCUST_DISP	Object Manager Customizing
OOOBJMANCUST_TRSP	Object Manager Customizing
OOOD	Data Sets
OOOE	Organizational Plan
OOOS	Functions
OOOT	Maintain object types
OOOU	Create Organizational Unit
OOPADCE_PER	Switches for PAD CE
OOPADCE_UI	Switches for PAD CE
OOPAYGP	Switch for Payroll of Global EE
OOPB	User groups
OOPC	Administration: Personnel No. Check
OOPCPWIZ1	Wizard: Personnel Cost Planning
OOPD	HR Master Data
OOPE	Organizer Types
OOPF	Define Profiles
OOPH	Set Up PA - PD Integration
OOPM	HR Planning: Search Function
OOPP	Consistency Check for Integration
OOPPOMSET	T77S0: PPOM Settings
OOPR	Authorization Profile Maintenance
OOPS	HR Master Data Integration
OOPT	Participate in Integration
OOPV	Plan Versions
OOPW	Indiv. Attendee Check Path - Company
OOQ4	Maintain Career Model
OOQ5	Copy Requirements Profile to Holder
OOQA	Change Qualifications Catalog
OOQB	Qualification Transfer: Applicants

OOQI	Transfer Qualifications - Employee
OOQM	Qual. Profile: Mass Data Maintenance
OOQU	Settings for Personnel Development
OOQ_SKILL_ESS	Root Qualification Group
OORA	Create Room
OORB	HR-TEM: Number Range Reference Doc.
OORE	Create Resource
OORP	Plan Version for Room Reservation
OORT	Create Resource Type
OORU	Shift Planning: Proposal Strategy
OORV	Strategy for Automatic Assignment
OORW	Work Schedule: Rule Values
OOSB	User (Structural Authorization)
OOSC	Define Scales
OOSD	Integration Billing
OOSE	Organizational Elements
OOSF	Search Function
OOSG	Settings for Credit Memo
OOSH	Control Elements Day-To-Day Actys
OOSK	Cost Accounting Control
OOSO	Create Organizational Unit
OOSP	Authorization Profiles
OOSQ	Create Requirements Profile
OOSR	Settings for Invoice
OOSS	Prices, Taxes, Account Assignment
OOST	Standard Assignment
OOSU	Subtypes
OOSV	Customizing for Ctry Reassg Workflow
OOSW	Create Work Center
OOT1	Shift Groups for Shift Planning
OOT2	Requirement Types per WS/Shift Group
OOT3	Requirements
OOT5	Shift Groups for Shift Planning
OOTA	Attendee Type: Print Control
OOTB	Attendee/Organizer Types Allowed
OOTG	Areas
OOTK	Integration Appointment Calendar
OOTM	Time Schedule
OOTO	Specify Appointment Types
OOTP	Create Development Plan
OOTR	Display Import Lock Table
OOTS	Breakpoints
OOTT	Attendee Types
OOTV	Prebookings
OOUA	Batch Input User Level
OOUM	Integration Cost Transfer Posting
OOUR	C. Enhancement Resource Reservation
OOUS	Maintain User
OOV1	Display Table T77S0
OOV2	Maintain Table T77S0
OOVA	Business Event Catalog
OOVACPTIME	No.of Days to Bring Forward Vacns
OOVB	Vacancy Editing
OOVC	Formatting Text Variables

SAP Transaction Codes – Volume One

OOVD	Output Sequence of Text Elements
OOVI	Notification Abbr.: Assign Event
OOVK	Relationships
OOVM	User-Specific Output Control
OOVO	Prebooking Business Event Types
OOVS	Create Notification Abbreviation
OOVW	Service for Lock
OOW1	Classification of Task Complexes
OOW2	Substitute Profile
OOW3	Substitute Profile: Class. Assignmnt
OOW4	Workflow/Org.Mgmt Prefix Numbers
OOWB	TEM-ESS : Standard values
OOWFAC	Activate Workflow Event Linkage
OOWIZ1	Wizard: Cost Transfer Posting
OOWIZ2	Wizard: Activity Allocation
OOWIZ3	Wizard: Billing
OOWIZ4	Wizard Customizing Correspondence
OOWIZ41	Form Wizard
OOWIZ42	Text Variable Wizard
OOWIZ43	Notification Abbreviation Wizard
OOWIZ5	Wizard: Cost Transfer Posting
OOZI	Dynamic Menus Additional Info
OOZO	Shift Planning: Simulate Attendences
OOZR	Target OT-Dependent Time Constraint
OOZS	Attendance Types Time Management
OOZT	Shift Planning: Employee Status
OOZW	Integration with Time Management
OO_CA_TAX_SPL	HR: Set up Canada Tax Split
OO_CENTRAL_PERSON	HR: Set Up Central Person
OO_ESS_WEB_DYNPRO	ESS Web Dynpro
OO_GB_ABS_PAY1	HR: Set up GB SSP/SMP/OSP/OMP 1
OO_GB_ABS_PAY2	HR: Set up GB SSP/SMP/OSP/OMP 2
OO_GB_DRILLDOWN	HR: Set up GB Drilldown Reporting
OO_GB_HESA_01	HR: Set up GB HESA Institution Code
OO_GB_ME	HR: Set up GB Multiple Employments
OO_GB_ME_CHECK	HR: Set up GB ME consistency check
OO_GB_ME_PAYSLIP	HR: Set up GB ME payslip aggregation
OO_GB_OSP_OMP	HR: Set up GB OSP/OMP
OO_HRALXCUSTINT	Activate Integration
OO_HRALXCUSTOBP	Data Synchronization: Org. Units
OO_HRALXCUSTPBP	Data Synchronization: Persons
OO_HRALXCUSTPER	Logging/Error Analysis
OO_HRRCF_CAT_CREATE	Set Up Categories for Questionnaires
OO_HRRCF_CAT_TRANS	Transport Categories
OO_HRRCF_CAT_UPDATE	Update Questionnaire Categories
OO_HRRCF_CHECK_SRCH	Check of Settings for Search
OO_HRRCF_CPOINTER	Clean Up Change Pointers
OO_HRRCF_CREATE_USER	Create User for E-Recruiting
OO_HRRCF_DBCDCYL_IDX	Indexing of Assignment Lists
OO_HRRCF_DEL_EXTCAND	Delete External Candidates
OO_HRRCF_IMG1	Customizing up to and including BF 1
OO_HRRCF_SYST_CUST	System Parameters in E-Recruiting
OO_HRRCF_SYST_CUST_2	System Parameters in E-Recruiting
OO_HRRCF_VIEW_SRVLOG	Display Search Query Log

SAP Transaction Codes – Volume One

OO_HRRCF_WD_BL_CUST	System Parameter Backend System
OO_HRRCF_WD_CUST	System Parameter Front-End System
OO_MGE_MAN_PATH	Master Switch for Man. of Gl. Empl.
OO_MGE_MS	Master Switch for Man. of Gl. Empl.
OO_POST_ARCHI	Archiving Function for Posting Index
OO_POST_PPMAR	Payment Posting Active AR
OO_POST_PPMAT	Payment Posting Active AT
OO_POST_PPMAU	Payment Posting Active AU
OO_POST_PPMBE	Payment Posting Active BE
OO_POST_PPMBR	Payment Posting Active BR
OO_POST_PPMCA	Payment Posting Active CA
OO_POST_PPMCH	Payment Posting Active CH
OO_POST_PPMCN	Payment Posting Active CN
OO_POST_PPMDE	Payment Posting Active DE
OO_POST_PPMDK	Payment Posting Active DK
OO_POST_PPMES	Payment Posting Active ES
OO_POST_PPMFI	Payment Posting Active FI
OO_POST_PPMFR	Payment Posting Active FR
OO_POST_PPMGB	Payment Posting Active GB
OO_POST_PPMHK	Payment Posting Active HK
OO_POST_PPMID	Payment Posting Active ID
OO_POST_PPMIE	Payment Posting Active IE
OO_POST_PPMIN	Payment Posting Active IN
OO_POST_PPMIT	Payment Posting Active IT
OO_POST_PPMJP	Payment Posting Active JP
OO_POST_PPMKR	Payment Posting Active KR
OO_POST_PPMMX	Payment Posting Active MX
OO_POST_PPMMY	Payment Posting Active MY
OO_POST_PPMNL	Payment Posting Active NL
OO_POST_PPMNO	Payment Posting Active NO
OO_POST_PPMNZ	Payment Posting Active NZ
OO_POST_PPMPH	Payment Posting Active PH
OO_POST_PPMPT	Payment Posting Active PT
OO_POST_PPMRU	Payment Posting Active RU
OO_POST_PPMSE	Payment Posting Active SE
OO_POST_PPMSG	Payment Posting Active SG
OO_POST_PPMTH	Payment Posting Active TH
OO_POST_PPMTW	Payment Posting Active TW
OO_POST_PPMUS	Payment Posting Active US
OO_POST_PPMVE	Payment Posting Active VE
OO_POST_PPMXX	Payment Posting Active XX
OO_POST_PPMZA	Payment Posting Active ZA
OO_PTSPPS_ADHVP	Additional Checks PP61
OO_PTSPPS_AKSP	Save Shift Abbreviation
OO_PTSPPS_BDV	Activate Cumulation of Requirements
OO_PTSPPS_DET	Activation of Additional Information
OO_PTSPPS_EXBDA	MS EXCEL Print Macros Reqmts Matchup
OO_PTSPPS_INCLUPD	Activate Functionality
OO_PTSPPS_MRK	Activate Special Day Marking
OO_PTSPPS_PSABG	Activate Long-Term Temp. Assignments
OO_PTSPPS_PSAPL	Direct Access to Absence Planner
OO_PTSPPS_PSASP	Result of Proposal Determination
OO_PTSPPS_PSCDO	Activate PSOLL Change Documents
OO_PTSPPS_PSDCI	Activate Background Process

OO_PTSPPS_PSDWI	Protect Employee Preferences
OO_PTSPPS_PSHID	Hide Temp. Reassigned Employees
OO_PTSPPS_PSINF	Activate Extended Info Columns
OO_PTSPPS_PSKSA	Retain Abbreviation for Availability
OO_PTSPPS_PSLVV	Delete Obsolete Substitutions
OO_PTSPPS_PSPLM	Activate Pool Management
OO_PTSPPS_PSSRT	Activate Enhanced Sorting
OO_PTSPPS_PSTAA	Maintain Info Texts for Att./Absence
OO_PTSPPS_PSTSN	Time Statement for Student Nurses
OO_PTSPPS_RFRSH	Refresh on Saving
OO_PTSPPS_SMUCD	Assgmt Proposal for Changed Days
OO_PTSPPS_SMUDR	Assgmt Proposal for Changed Days
OO_PTSPPS_TASSA	Temp. Assgmt Despite Att./Absence
OO_RCF_INIT_KPRO	Initialization of KPro Integration
OO_RCF_UPD_DOC_ATTRB	Document Attribute Index Category
OO_RCF_UPD_DOC_ATTRC	Update Document Attribute in KPro
OO_T77BW	Automatic State Management
OO_UGHR_CENTRAL_PERS	HR: Set Up Central Person
OO_USPS_CERT_RENEW	Msg Class for Cert. Renewal Code
OP00	Maintain Operation Control Key
OP01	Customizing Routing/Work Center
OP03	Factory Calendar C
OP04	Word Processing
OP07	Standard Text
OP08	Standard Text
OP09	Maintain Alternative Activity Desc.
OP10	Maintain Person Responsible
OP11	Maintain Period Pattern Key
OP12	Maintain Location
OP13	Maintain Screen Sequence
OP14	Maintain Type of Std. Value Determin
OP15	Production User Profile
OP16	Maintain Period Pattern
OP17	Formula Parameters
OP18	Maintain Setup Group/Setup Group Cat
OP19	Standard Value Key
OP20	Maintain Setup Type Key
OP21	Define Formula
OP22	Maintain Wage Groups
OP23	Maintain Location
OP24	Maintain period dependent oper. val.
OP26	Maintain suitability
OP28	Maintain Perf. Efficiency Rate Key
OP30	Maintain Move Time Matrix
OP31	Maintain Time Segment (Per. Pattern)
OP32	Maintain Capacity Category
OP34	Maintain Work Center Planner Group
OP35	Maintain Perf. Efficiency Rate Key
OP36	Maintain Capacity Default Values
OP37	Maintain Available Capacity Version
OP38	Maintain Setup Type Key
OP39	Maintain Graphics Profile
OP40	Maintain Work Center Category
OP41	Matchcode for work center

OP42	Default work center
OP43	Maintain Setup Group Categories
OP44	Maintain Task List Usage
OP45	Maintain Usage
OP46	Maintain Task List Status
OP47	Maintain PRT Usage
OP48	Maintain Planner Group
OP49	Matchcode for Routings/Ref. Op. Sets
OP4A	Maintain Shift Sequences
OP4B	Overview variant: Routing
OP4C	Overview variant: Ref. oper. set
OP4D	Overview variant: Rate routing
OP4E	Overview variant: Ref. rate routing
OP4F	Overview var.:Scheduling of routings
OP4G	Overview var.:Scheduling ref.op.set
OP4H	Overview var.:Scheduling of rate rtg
OP4I	Overview var.:Scheduling RefRateRtgs
OP50	Assign Material Types
OP51	Formula Parameters
OP52	Formula Parameters
OP53	Formula Parameters
OP54	Define Formula
OP55	Define Formula
OP56	Define Formula
OP57	Define Formula
OP58	Maintain Default Value Profiles
OP59	Formula Parameters
OP5A	Field Selection: Task List Overview
OP5B	Field Selection: Task List Header
OP5C	Field Selection: Task List Sequence
OP5D	Field Selection: Task List Details
OP5E	Field selection task list overview
OP5F	Field selection std network -> PRT
OP5H	Field sel. insp.plan characteristics
OP61	Number range maintenance: ROUTING_3
OP62	Number ranges for routings
OP63	Number Ranges for Ref.Operation Sets
OP64	Maintain Setup Group Key
OP65	Formula Parameters
OP66	Maintain Location Group
OP67	Maintain Operation Control Key
OP68	Maintain Move Time Matrix
OP69	Maintain wage type
OP70	Maintain PRT Control Key
OP71	Maintain Wage Group
OP72	PRT Control Key
OP73	PRT Authorization Group
OP74	Maintain PRT Group Key
OP76	Define suitability
OP77	Engineering Workbench for Task Lists
OP78	Maintain Type of Std. Value Determin
OP7A	Customizing matchcode for PRTs
OP7B	Define Parameters
OP80	Maintain PRT Status

OP82	Define Formula
OP84	Profiles: Default Values for Rtgs.
OP85	Profiles: Default Values for QM
OP87	Maintain Routing/Ref.Op.Set Usage
OP88	Maintain Assignmt. of Task List Type
OP8A	Maintain operation value description
OP8B	Maintain standard value texts
OP8C	Record layout for background (APL)
OP8D	Data transfer APL
OP8E	Command file task lists Rel. 2.2A
OP8F	Maintain production scheduler
OP8H	Profiles: Default Values for Rtgs.
OP91	Maintain Object Overview Version
OP95	Assign Work Center Cat. to Applicatn
OP96	Maintain Work Center Category
OP97	Maintain Performance Efficiency Rate
OP98	Maintain Validity of Perf.Effic.Rate
OPA0	Status selection profiles
OPA1	Maintain combination definitions
OPA2	Define selection profile
OPA3	Define option profile
OPA4	Define list profile
OPA5	Define graphics profile
OPA6	Define overall profile
OPA7	Define columns
OPA9	Maintain selection profiles
OPB1	Define list versions
OPB2	Define distribution function
OPB3	Specify distribution functions
OPB4	Specify distribution strategies
OPB5	Specify distribution key
OPC0	Axis representation selection
OPC1	Maintain axis representation
OPC2	Curve representation selection
OPC3	Maintain curve representation
OPC5	Max. no. of data records
OPCD	Capacity category
OPCE	Capacity planner
OPCF	Time units
OPCG	Maintain Operation Control Key
OPCH	Maintain production scheduler
OPCI	Setup group key/category
OPCL	Scheduling type
OPCM	Standard value key
OPCN	Maintain move time matrix
OPCQ	Efficiency rate
OPCR	Formula parameters
OPCS	Define formula
OPCT	Strategies
OPCU	Strategy levels
OPCW	Planned order parameters
OPCX	Formula parameters
OPCY	Define formula
OPD0	Resource planning overall profile

OPD1	Resource planning selection profile
OPD2	Capacity leveling - time profile
OPD3	Resource planning evaluation profile
OPD4	Resource planning period profile
OPD5	Flow control definition
OPD6	Flow control control table
OPD7	Flow control statuses
OPD8	Flow Control Actions
OPD9	Flow Control Messages
OPDA	Transition matrix (setup matrix)
OPDB	Capacity Leveling Strategy Profile
OPDD	Factory calendar
OPDE	Resource planning control profile
OPDF	Define requirements grouping
OPDH	Capacity leveling - list profile
OPDJ	Define layout
OPDK	Define standard overview
OPDL	Cap. plan. detailed cap.list maint.
OPDM	Define detail list (leveling)
OPDQ	Profile for planning table (tab.)
OPDR	Define layout key
OPDT	Define detail list
OPDU	Maintain perf. efficiency rate key
OPDV	Com-file (Rel-Info/OLPK) KOP. Set´s
OPDW	Com-file (Rel-Info/OLPK) KOP. Set´s
OPE0	Maintain Sort String
OPE1	Maintain Value Type
OPE2	Maintain Machine Type
OPE3	Maintain Planner Group
OPE4	Maintain Control Parameters
OPE5	Maintain rounding categories
OPE6	Maintain Rounding Category
OPE7	Maintain overhead key
OPE8	Maint. Roundg. and Add.Val.Key (Def)
OPE9	Maintain User Profile
OPEA	User selection
OPEB	Automatic selection
OPEC	PP user fields
OPENPS	Download Activities to Palm Pilot
OPF0	Maintain User
OPF1	Authorizations for CAPP
OPFA	Field selection: Work center
OPFP	Configuring the Fixed Price Version
OPFR01	RPUCORF0PBS : IMG Link
OPG0	Profile for planning table
OPG1	Chart sequence - selection
OPG2	Line representation
OPG3	Scale time axis
OPG4	Time scale profile
OPG5	Graphic obj.type sel./repr.profile
OPG6	Transition matrix setup fam.key
OPG7	Line display selection
OPG9	Graphical object type/obj.represent.
OPGD	Ref. Oper. Set-All Task Lists (PP)

OPGE	Ref. Oper. Set - Rate Routings (PP)
OPGF	Work Center - All Task Lists (PP)
OPGG	Work Center - Rate Routings (PP)
OPGH	Document PRT - All Task Lists
OPGI	Equipment PRT - All Task Lists
OPGJ	Material PRT - All Task Lists
OPGK	Misc. PRT - All Task Lists
OPGL	Resource - Master Recipes (PI)
OPGM	Process Instr. Cat. - Master Recipe
OPGN	Document PRT - Maintenance Task List
OPGO	Equipment PRT-Maintenance Task Lists
OPGP	Material PRT - Maintenance Task List
OPGQ	Misc. PRT - Maintenance Task Lists
OPGR	Work Center - Standard Network (PS)
OPGS	Document PRT - Standard Network (PS)
OPGT	Equipment PRT - Standard Network(PS)
OPGU	Material PRT - Standard Network (PS)
OPGV	Misc. PRT - Standard Network (PS)
OPH1	CO Cash Bgt Mgmt: Delete Actual Data
OPH2	PS Cash Management: Delete Plan Data
OPH3	CO Cash Bgt Mgmt: Delete Master Data
OPH4	CO Cash Bgt Mgmt: MM Data Transfer
OPH5	CO CBM: Successive FI Data Transfer
OPH6	CO CBM: Take Over FI Completely
OPH7	CO-CBM: Take Over All Data
OPI1	Maintain Value Categories
OPI2	Value Categories for Cost Elements
OPI3	Update Control: File RPSCO
OPI4	Commitment Item Value Categories
OPI5	Value Categories for Stag.Key Figs
OPI6	Activate CO Cash Budget Management
OPI8	Display Value Category
OPIA	Interest Profile for Projects
OPIB	Maintain Interest Profile
OPIC	Intrst Relevance: Cost Els/Cmmt Itms
OPIC1	Specify system messages
OPID	Proj.Int Calc: Account Determination
OPIE	Interest Indicator
OPIF	View Maintenance:Compound Int.Cont.
OPIG	View Maint.: Compound Int. Periods
OPIH	Interest Scale, General Conditions
OPIN	Number range maintnce: VHU_PINST
OPJ2	Production order stock determination
OPJ4	Schedule batch function request
OPJ6	Maintain Status Profiles
OPJ7	Maintain Routing Usage
OPJ8	Maintain Operation Control Key
OPJ9	Maintain prod. scheduler group
OPJA	Maintain setup group/group category
OPJB	Specify system messages
OPJC	Maintain Wage Groups
OPJD	Item Categories
OPJE	User Selection
OPJF	Automatic Selection

OPJG	Maintain Default Values
OPJH	Order types production order
OPJI	BOM Usage Priorities
OPJJ	Maintain Scope of Check
OPJK	Maintain Control
OPJL	Maintain Checking Rule
OPJM	Application-Specific Criteria
OPJN	Maintain Scheduling Type
OPJO	C MM-BD units of measurement
OPJP	Maint. acct.assgnm.types for orders
OPJQ	Standard Value Key
OPJR	Maintain move time matrix
OPJS	PP: Maintain reduction strategies
OPJT	Maintain Strategy Levels
OPJU	Production order control parameters
OPJV	Maintain Capacity Category
OPJW	Maintain Capa.Planr.Grp for WrkCentr
OPJX	Factory Calendar C
OPJY	Maintain perf. efficiency rate key
OPJZ	Maintain Release Periods
OPK0	Confirmation Parameters PP
OPK0T	Confirmation Parameters
OPK1	Confirmation Parameters PP-PI
OPK1T	Confirmation Parameters
OPK2	Formula Parameters
OPK3	Define Formula
OPK4	Confirmation Parameters
OPK4N	Confirmation Parameters (Extended)
OPK5	Maintain variances
OPK6	List Layout
OPK7	Accessing Customizing PDC transfer
OPK8	Maintain print control prod. orders
OPK9	Maintain Goods Receipt Valuation
OPKA	Maintain Movement Types
OPKB	Control parallel confirmation
OPKC	Control confirmation process chain
OPKD	Control confirmation process chain
OPKE	Screen Sequence for Components
OPKF	Control parallel confirmation
OPKG	Maintain Messages
OPKH	Maintain Breakpoints
OPKI	Maintain Collective Confirmation
OPKJ	Maintain PRT Control Key
OPKK	Standard Text
OPKL	Formula Parameters
OPKM	Define Formula
OPKN	Overview variant production control
OPKO	Command File for Production Orders
OPKP	Shop floor control profile
OPKQ	Customizing: Matchcode for Proc.Ord.
OPKR	Print flag
OPKS	Maintain Origins for CO Object
OPKT	Initial Screen: Settlement Structure
OPKU	Maintain Collective Confirmation

OPKV	Print Flag
OPKW	Print shop papers
OPKX	Deletion Flag/Indicator
OPKZ	Customizing Matchcode for ProdOrder
OPL1	Costing Variants: PP Prod. Order
OPL2	Maintain trigger point group
OPL3	Trigger point usage
OPL4	Profile for missing parts list
OPL5	Order type LIS parameters
OPL6	Profile for documented goods mvmts
OPL7	Order change management profile
OPL8	Order type parameters: Overview
OPL9	Parameters for order change mgmt
OPLA	Conditions: V_T682F for H CO
OPLB	CondTab: Create (batch, prod.)
OPLC	CondTab: Change (batchs, prod.)
OPLD	CondTab: Display (batches, prod.)
OPLE	Strategy types: Batch determ. (prod)
OPLF	Access: Maintain batch determ.(prod)
OPLG	Batch determ.: Procedure for prod.
OPLH	Overview variant - production orders
OPLI	Background job for goods movements
OPLJ	Job "Fast entry confirmation"
OPLK	Overall profile for order prog. rep.
OPLL	Order progress: Displayed fields
OPLM	Order progress: Displayed fields
OPLO	maintain selection profile
OPLP	Job "Convert planned order"
OPLQ	maintain filter for control keys
OPLR	Maintain filter for capacity version
OPLS	Parallel processing control
OPLT	Target System for Data Transfer
OPLV	Maintain Filter for Task List Usage
OPLW	Maintain Filter for Task List Status
OPLX	Maintain Filter for BOM Usage
OPLY	Maintain Filter for BOM Status
OPLZ	Maintain POI Planned Order Selection
OPM0	Maintain profile - field selection
OPM1	Costing Variants - Production Order
OPM2	Maintain Detail Screen Control Oper.
OPM3	Maintain Detail Scrn Control Header
OPMC	Activation of Enhancement Objects
OPMCF	PDF Form: Plant Assignment
OPMF	Field Selection - BOM Transfer
OPMI	Import models activities
OPMJ	Determine progress values
OPN0	Master Recipe Profile
OPN1	Maintain Profiles for Master Recipes
OPN2	Valuation Variants - Prod. Order
OPN3	Overv.Var.: Master Recipe Scheduling
OPN5	Field Seln: Std Network Overview
OPN6	Field Selection Standard Network Hdr
OPN7	Field Sel.:Std Ntwk Activity Detail
OPN8	Field Sel.:Std.Ntwk Comp.Overview

OPN9	Field Sel. Std Ntwk Comp.Detail
OPO1	Create Cost Element Planning Layout
OPO2	Change Cost Element Planning Layout
OPO3	Display Cost Element Planning Layout
OPO4	Create Stat. KF Planning Layout
OPO5	Change Stat. KF Planning Layout
OPO6	Display Stat. KF Planning Layout
OPO7	View Maintenance V_TCJ41_7
OPO8	View Maintenance V_TCJ41_8
OPO9	View Maintenance V_TCJ41_9
OPOA	View Maintenance V_T003O_N0
OPOB	View Maintenance V_T003O_N1
OPOC	View Maintenance V_T399X_N0
OPOD	View Maintenance V_T399X_N1
OPOE	View Maintenance T_T399X_N2
OPP1	Customizing MRP
OPP2	MPS
OPP3	Customizing Repetitive Manufacturing
OPP5	List Profile Component List
OPPA	PP/MRP Customizing Explosion
OPPB	Direct Procurement
OPPC	Period Grouping
OPPD	Customizing Planning Time Fence
OPPE	Conversion Plnnd Order -> Prod.Order
OPPE01	General iPPE Customizing
OPPE02	Define iPPE Node Type
OPPE03	Define iPPE Variant Types
OPPE04	Define iPPE Alternative Types
OPPE05	Define iPPE Relationship Types
OPPE06	Customer-Spec. Model Assgts (iPPE)
OPPE07	Time Analysis: Partner Products iPPE
OPPE11	Profiles: iPPE WB Professional
OPPE12	Tabs: iPPE Workbench Professional
OPPE13	User Assgmt: iPPE WB Professional
OPPE14	Define Reports for iPPE WB Prof.
OPPE15	Define Interface for iPPE Workbench
OPPE20	Profile Maintenance iPPE PS
OPPEACT01	Define Std Val. Determin. Type
OPPEACT02	Object Dependency in Process Struct.
OPPECHK01	Customizing: Consistency Check
OPPEDOK	Documentation
OPPEGENFILT	Generate Attribute Value Filter
OPPELUI01	Profile Definition: iPPE WB Express
OPPELUI02	User Assignment: iPPE WB Express
OPPERES01	Customizing for Production Resources
OPPESCMPV	Object Dependent Status Management
OPPESTATUS	Cross-Application Status Management
OPPF	Customizing for Order Report
OPPH	Customizing Purchase Req. Conversion
OPPI	Available Stock
OPPJ	MRP Checking Rule
OPPK	Hierarchy Element
OPPL	MRP
OPPM	Evaluation Profiles

OPPN	Layout
OPPP	Customizing Direct Procurement
OPPQ	C M MRP Plant Parameters for MRP
OPPR	C M MRP MRP Group
OPPS	Strategy
OPPT	Strategy Group
OPPU	Strategy Group for MRP Group
OPPZ	MRP Group
OPQDP02P	Define Derivation Paths
OPQDP03D	Maint. Derivation Paths for Stucture
OPQ_CORRESPONDENCE	Deter. interest key, tol. grp, clear
OPQ_DDS_OF_PSOB	Determine DDS for Contr. Object Type
OPQ_LOCK_REASON	Determine Payment Lock Reason
OPQ_PAYMENT_METHOD	Determine Payment Method and DDS
OPQ_ST_BP_SYNC	Create Business Partner for Student
OPQ_ST_SYNC_CURR	Synchronize Student Account Data
OPR1	Area of Responsibility <-> Message
OPR3	Definition of Breakpoints
OPR4_ACT	Multilevel Actual Settlement
OPR4_CK	Material Cost Estimate
OPR4_CKMC	Mass Costing - Sales Documents
OPR4_CKML	Closing and Calc. of Periodic Price
OPR4_CKPF	Price Update
OPR4_FCO	Collective Processing: Variances
OPR4_KKA	WIP Calculation
OPR4_KKP	Repetitive Mfg and Process Mfg
OPR4_KKS	Collective Processing: Variances
OPR4_KKS1	Individual Processing: Variances
OPR4_PPCO	Production Order: Cost Calculation
OPR5	Definition of Error Mgmt IDs (SAP)
OPR6	Definition of Object IDs (SAP)
OPR7	Def. of Areas of Responsibility
OPR8	Def. of Minimum Message Types (SAP)
OPR9	Def. of Reference Objects (SAP)
OPRCMFE	User-Defined Messages
OPRF	Maintain Quotation Prefixes
OPS	Customizing for Project System
OPS0	Maintain print control for networks
OPS1	Maintain User Fields
OPS2	Maintain Relationship Texts
OPS3	Maintain PS Text Types
OPS4	maintain simulation profile
OPS5	Maintain Standard Network Profile
OPS6	Maintain Project Manager
OPS7	Maintain Applicant
OPS8	Materialflow network
OPS9	Budget Management Profile
OPSA	Maintain Project Profile
OPSB	Cost Planning Profile
OPSC	Create network types
OPSCAS	Command File Payments (PS)
OPSCOS	Command File Costs (PS)
OPSD	Maintain Profile for Report Lines
OPSE	Maintain Report Groups

OPSF	Maintain Report Variations
OPSG	Order change management profile
OPSH	Maintain ctrl. key for activity (PS)
OPSI	Edit PS validation rules
OPSINS	Command File Info System (PS-F)
OPSJ	Maintain Project Coding
OPSK	Maintain Special Characters
OPSL	Project Info System Overview Maint.
OPSM	Maintain Overall Profile PS InfoSys
OPSN	Edit PS substitution rules
OPSO	Maintain Project Types
OPSP	Capacity availability check
OPSPAR1	Maintain Partner Functions
OPSPAR2	Define Lang.-Dep.Partner Functions
OPSPAR3	WBS Partner Profile
OPSQ	Intervals for Cost/Revenue Types
OPSR	Maintain milestones
OPSREV	Command File Revenues (PS)
OPSS	Maintain milestones
OPST	Network Confirmation Parameters
OPSU	Maintain Activity Control Key
OPSV	Cost object ind.
OPSW	Info System Profile
OPSX	PS: Reset "Budgeted" Status
OPT1	Maintain PS Transaction Types
OPT2	Matchcode for project definition
OPT3	Matchcode for WBS elements
OPT4	Matchcode for standard network
OPT5	Customizing matchcode for network
OPT6	Maintain std. milestone group
OPT7	Project planning board profile
OPT8	Maintain hierarchy graphic / dates
OPT9	Network parameters for PS-SD
OPTA	Command file for PS -> FI area
OPTB	Command file for WBS
OPTC	Command file for network
OPTD	Command file for standard network
OPTE	Command file for PS info system
OPTF	Command file for PS graphic
OPTG	Maintain PS Info Summztn Criteria
OPTH	PS info system maintenance
OPTI	Maintain Progrss Analysis Overview
OPTJ	Maintain PS Info Unit Conversion
OPTK	Exclude Cost Elems from Avlbty Cntrl
OPTL	Maintain PS Info Comparison Criteria
OPTM	Fincl Budgeting Profile for Projects
OPTN	Maintain priorities
OPTO	Change costing variants
OPTP	Sub-network parameters
OPTQ	Maintain WBS scheduling parameters
OPTR	Strategies for settlement rules
OPTS	Maintain project version profile
OPTT	Maint. acct.assgnm.types for orders
OPTU	Maint. PS Info System field settings

OPTV	Maint. PS Info System sort criteria
OPTW	Maint.PS Info System group. criteria
OPTX	Maint. PS Info System database set.
OPTY	Capacity leveling - Time profile/PS
OPTZ	Matchcode for standard WBS elements
OPU0	Matchcode for standard project def.
OPU3	Production order control parameters
OPU4	Maintain Capacity Planning (SOP)
OPU5	Parameter long term planning PlndOrd
OPU6	Production order control parameters
OPU7	Control parameters plant maintenance
OPU8	Overview Var.: Header Line Info Sys.
OPU9	Overview Variant: Item Line
OPUA	Field selection: Network: Header
OPUB	Field selection: Network: Overview
OPUC	Field selection: Network: Details
OPUD	Field selection:Network confirmation
OPUH	Field sel: Std. project definition
OPUI	Field selection: Std. WBS elements
OPUJ	Field selection: Project definition
OPUK	Field selection: WBS element
OPUL	PS: Maintain reduction strategies
OPUM	Maintain Subprojects
OPUN	Capacity overviews
OPUO	Project schedule overviews
OPUP	Subnetwork schedule overview
OPUQ	Overall network scheduling overview
OPUR	Info System: Structure overview
OPUS	Maintain Version Number Entry Mask
OPUT	Maintain overview variants
OPUU	Maintain Network Profile
OPUV	Network Type Parameters
OPUW	Standard Network Status
OPUX	Maintain overview variants std netwk
OPUY	Overview var.:Std.ntwrk scheduling
OPUZ	Control parameters plant maintenance
OPVC	Convert Avlability Cntrl Tol.Limits
OPVP	Collective availibility checkProfile
OQ02	Maintain Forms
OQ26	Maintain qualification type
OQ49	Routing matchcode
OQ62	Number ranges for inspection plans
OQ63	Number ranges for ref.operation sets
OQ77	Engineering Workbench for QM
OQ84	Profile def. values: Task list/gen.
OQ85	Profile def. values: Task list/char.
OQB1	Maintain control key
OQB2	Maintain certificate type
OQB3	Maintain procurement block key
OQB4	Maintain document types Q documents
OQB5	Insp. type for stat. prof. and stat.
OQB6	Number range for certificate receipt
OQB7	Maintain required QM systems
OQB8	Define QM systems

OQBA	Variants-maintain all-QINF in DB
OQBB	Activate Customizing doc. types
OQBC	Deactivate Customizing doc. types
OQCZ	Settings for Workflow Certificates
OQFA	Adapt field selection
OQGN1	Task Customizing
OQI3	Storage Data Maintenance
OQI4	Customize Lot Selection for QA32/33
OQI5	List of control charts for insp. lot
OQI6	List of control charts for task list
OQI7	Results Recording Worklist: New
OQI8	Work list variant automatic UD
OQI9	Cntrl chart lists for master charac.
OQIA	Maintain variant: Q-level evaluation
OQIC	Work list variant for results rec.
OQID	Order maint. variant for material
OQIE	Usage var. for QM order in material
OQIF	Customize Lot Selection for QVM1
OQIG	Customize Lot Selection for QVM2
OQIH	Customize Lot Selection for QVM3
OQII	Customize Lot Selection for QA16
OQIJ	Field select. maintain results hist.
OQIK	Field sel. PhysSampDraw with ref.
OQIL	Field sel. insp. lots for physSamps
OQIM	Field sel. deletion program Q-levels
OQIN	Results recording for insp. points
OQIO	Results recording for insp. lots
OQIP	Results recording for insp. charac.
OQIQ	Results recording variant for sample
OQIR	Results recording variant for equip.
OQIS	Res. recording variant for fnct. Loc
OQIT	Settings for Insp. Method List
OQIU	Settings for Master Insp. Char. List
OQIV	Results History for Task List Charac
OQIW	Results History for Task List Charac
OQIX	Test Equipment Usage List
OQIY	Test Equipment Tracking
OQIZ	Settings for Notification Workflow
OQL8	Assign origin for delivery type
OQL9	Assign Inspection Type to Del. Type
OQM1	Q-Notification Field Selection: Gen.
OQM2	Q-Notif. Field Sel: Initial Screens
OQM3	Q-Notif. Field Sel: Ref. Objects
OQM4	Q-Notif. Field Sel: Partner Screens
OQN0	Maintain notification types
OQN2	Maint. status prof. for Q-notif.type
OQN3	Maint. prio. types for notif. types
OQN5	Maintain catalogs for notif. types
OQN6	Maintain cat. profile for Q-notific.
OQN7	Start values - notification
OQNAOB	Fld Selectn Multilvl List:Assnd Obj.
OQNC	Set field selection for notif. list
OQND	Set field selection for task list
OQNE	Set field selection for item list

OQNF	Variant: Work list activities
OQNL	Field selec. multi-lvl list - notif.
OQNM	Field selec. mul.lev. list - partner
OQNN	Field selec. mul.level list - item
OQNO	Field selec. multi-lvl list - activ.
OQNP	Field selec. multi-level list - task
OQNR	Define follow-up actions
OQNU	Multi-lev. list fld selection-cause
OQNW	Settings for Notification Workflow
OQP1	Insp. plan lists
OQR0	Organize QM Archiving
OQS8	Customizing for IQS8
OQS9	Customizing for IQS9
OQZ6	Def. access seq. for cert. profile
OQZ7	Create cond. table for certificates
OQZ8	Change cond. table for certificates
OQZ9	Disp. cond. table for certificates
OQZA	Field catalog cert. profile V_T681F
OQZC	Condition types certificate profiles
OQZE	Certif. profiles search procedure
OQZN	Number ranges for quality certs.
ORA_LOCK	Oracle: Lock-Monitor
ORA_PERF	DBACockpit: Oracle - Performance
ORA_SPACE	DBACockpit: Oracle - Space Statistic
ORCP01	Recipe Customizing Status
ORCP03	Customizing for Equip. Requirements
ORCP04	Customizing for Recipes
ORCP05	Customizing for Process Stages
ORCP06	Customizing for Processes
ORCP07	Customizing for Actions
ORCP08	Customizing for Operations
ORCP09	Customizing for Units of Measurement
ORDO	Download of an Investment Program
ORET	Report Selection
ORF1	C SD TVST in Route Determination
ORF2	C SD TVLK in Route Determination
ORFA	Asset Accounting Customizing
ORFB	
ORGANIZER	Records Management
ORIS	Stat. Setup: Sales Price Revaluation
ORISBW	Reorg: BW Sls Price Revaluation Docs
ORK0	Configuration menu gen. controlling
ORK1	Customizing: Account-Based EC-PCA
ORK2	EC-PCA: Call IMG
ORKA	C CO-OPA Configuration Menu: Orders
ORKE	Display CO-PA IMG
ORKL	Reconciliation Ledger Menu
ORKS	
ORLNA	Number Range Maintenance: VHU_ACCT
ORLNC	Number Range Maintenance: VHU_CPGRP
ORLNI	Number Range Maintenance: TRMNO_INT
ORLNP	Number Range Maintenance: VHU_PSHP
ORLNR	Number Range Maintenance: VHU_REPROC
ORLNS	Number Range Maintenance: VHU_PSHPA

ORLNT	Number Range Maintenance: VHU_ACST
ORLNV	Number Range Maintenance: VHU_ACPO
ORLPT	Maintain account posting types
ORLPTA	Assign Account Posting Types
ORLRP	Residence Times for Archiving
ORLRS1	Create Condition Table
ORLRS2	Change Condition Table
ORLRS3	Display Condition Table
ORLRS4	Field Catalog for RP Acct Statement
ORLRS5	Access Sequence for RP Acct Statemt
ORLRS6	Output Types for RP Account Statemts
ORLRS7	Assign Output to Partner Roles
ORLRS8	Output Procedure for RP Acct Statemt
ORMI	Import models orders
ORMXT04	Custom.: Field Sel. for Trial Views
ORMXTNR	Maintain Number Ranges for Trials
ORMXTQMBBIDNR	Maintain Number Ranges for Trials
ORPS1	Checks for Worklists
ORPS11	Settings for Variant Selection
ORPS2	Message Type for Confirmation
ORPS3	Qty/Error Combination for Confirm.
ORPS4	Assign Quantity Layout to Plant/ID
ORPS5	Define Confirmation Layouts
ORPS6	Assign Layouts to Plant/Order Type
ORPS7	Shift Report Type
ORPS8	Shift Note Type
ORUP	Upload of an Investment Program
OS01	LAN check with ping
OS02	Operating system configuration
OS03	O/S Parameter changes
OS04	Local System Configuration
OS05	Remote System Cconfiguration
OS06	Local Operating System Activity
OS06N	Operating System Activity
OS07	Remote Operating System Activity
OS07N	Remote Operating System Activity
OS07_HOST	call OS07 with hostname
OS07_U	Remote Operating System Activity
OS11	Spare Part Indicators
OS12	Material Provision Indicators
OS13	Item Categories
OS14	Material Types Allowed in BOM Item
OS15	Variable-Size Item Formulas
OS16	BOM Item Object Type
OS17	Explosion Types
OS18	Relevancy to costing
OS20	BOM Usage
OS21	BOM Usage Default Values
OS22	Copying Defaults for Item Statuses
OS23	BOM Statuses
OS24	Material Types Allowed in BOMs
OS25	BOMs with History Requirement
OS26	Laboratory/Office
OS27	Modification Parameters for BOMs

OS28	Defaults for BOMs
OS29	User-Specific Settings for BOMs
OS30	Application
OS31	BOM Usage Priorities
OS32	Alternative BOM Determination
OS33	Alt. Determination in Inventory Mgmt
OS34	Alt. Determination in Costing
OS35	Alt. Determination in Production
OS36	Alt. Determination in SD
OS37	Alt. Determination in PM
OS38	Alt. Determination in MRP
OS40	Generate BOM Transfer File
OS41	Transfer BOM without Long Text
OS42	Process Transfer File
OS43	Copy BOM changes
OS44	Copy BOM variants
OS45	Copy BOM with description
OS46	Edit transfer file (long text)_
OS47	Field Groups: Assigned Fields
OS48	Field Groups: Definition and Descs
OS51	Change Master Statuses
OS52	Change Master Matchcode
OS53	Number Ranges for Change Master
OS54	Change Master Control Data
OS55	Material Revision Level Sequence
OS56	Change Types
OS57	Document Revision Level Sequence
OS58	Object Mgmt Record Change Types
OS59	ECM: Profile Settings
OS60	Effectivity Parameters: Definition
OS61	Effectivity Type
OS62	Effectivity parameters - popup texts
OS65	Effectivity types - texts
OS66	Effect. params - texts - headings
OS67	ECH: Effectivity Profile
OS68	ECH: History Requirement Control
OS69	Engineering Change Mgmt: release key
OS70	User-Specific List Profiles
OS71	ECH: Change Number Format
OS72	ECH: Workflow for ECR/ECO
OS73	ECH: Workflow for Object Mgmt Record
OS80	REM Planning Table (Gen. + Sched.)
OS81	REM Planning Table (Row Display)
OSC1	Appointment Type Maintenance
OSC2	Appoint. diary: Maint. destination
OSC3	Appointment Calendar:Priority Maint.
OSC4	Maintenance of Appointment Type Grps
OSC_WF_REPLY	Customizing for WF appt. replies
OSDPAPO	Distinction SDP-APO or Standard APO
OSGR	Command file for Customizing graph.
OSP1	Settings for Repet.Manufacturing
OSP2	Repetitive Mfg Profile
OSP4	Repetitive Mfg: Distribution Functn
OSP5	Repetitive Manufacturing: Cost Log

OSP6	Create Cost Collector Strategy
OSP7	Withdrawal Sequence
OSP8	Number Range for Backlogs
OSP9	Number Range for Document Log
OSPA	Customizing Distribution Function
OSPB	Customizing Production Order Type
OSPC	Customizing Goods Movements
OSPCT_CHECK_TOOL	Check Tool
OSPD	Customizing Planning Periodicity
OSPF	Repetitive Manufacturing Line Texts
OSPH	Batch Search Proced. in REM Profile
OSPI	Number Range for Backflush Discrep.
OSPJ	No.Range Maintenance f. Document Log
OSPK	Storage Location Search
OSPM	Background Job Reprocessing REM
OSPN	Background Job: Adjmt. of Dep. Reqs
OSPO	Backgr. Job - Agg. Coll. Backflush
OSPP	Customizing for Pull List
OSPR	Number Ranges in REM
OSPS	Batch Search Procedure for Pull List
OSPT	Repetitive Mfg Profile Assistant
OSPX	Customizing stock determination
OSPY	Conversion for withdrawal seq. grp
OSQ1	Customizing for Seqeuncing: Visual.
OSQ2	Customizing for Sequencing: Planning
OSS1	Logon to SAPNet
OSSC	Appt. Calendar: Appt. Type Maint.
OST1	CS Transport C Tables TCS21/TCS22
OST2	CS Transport C Tables BOM Usage
OST3	Transp. Customizing tabs T418F,T418G
OS_APPLICATION	OO Framework Application
OT01	C FI Maintain Table 001_K
OT02	C FI Maintain Table T056S
OT03	C FI Maintain Table T056A2
OT05	C FI Maintain Table T039
OT06	C FI Maintain Table T079D
OT07	C FI Maintain Table T078D
OT08	C FI Maintain Table T079K
OT09	C FI Maintain Table T078K
OT10	C FI Maintain Table T077D
OT11	C FI Maintain Table T077K
OT12	C FI Maintain Table T036
OT13	C FI Maintain Table T035
OT14	C FI Maintain Table T036
OT16	C FI Maintain Table T035D
OT17	C FI Maintain Table T038
OT18	C FI Maintain Table T038T
OT19	C FI Maintain Table T038V
OT20	Number Ranges of Memo Records
OT21	C FI Maintain Table T037
OT22	C FI Maintain Table T037A
OT23	C FI Maintain Table T036S
OT24	C FI Maintain Table T018C
OT25	C FI Maintain Table T056P

OT26	C FI Maintain Table T056R
OT27	C FI Maintain Table T018D
OT29	C FI Maintain Table 001_I
OT30	Current Account
OT31	Not Current Account
OT32	C FI Maintain Table T004F
OT33	C FI Maintain Table T056
OT34	C TD Levels for Special G/L
OT35	Purchase orders
OT36	C FI Maintain Table T056B
OT37	C FI Maintain Table T077S
OT38	C FI Batch Input Program
OT39	C FI Batch Input Program
OT40	C FI Change Customer
OT41	C FI Change Vendor
OT42	C FI Change G/L Account
OT43	C Maintain version: Man. bank stmt
OT45	C Maintain variants: check deposit
OT47	C FI Maintain Table T0350
OT48	C FT CMF Reorganization
OT49	C FI Maintain checks recd (T028D)
OT50	C Elec acct assignment /checks recd
OT51	C FI Maintain T028G
OT52	C FI Maintain T028H
OT53	C FI Maintain T028H
OT54	C FI Maintain T001F
OT55	C FI Maintain T028B
OT56	C FI Maintain manual acct (T028D)
OT57	C FI Maintain elec account (T028D)
OT58	C Elec acct determntn (manual acct)
OT59	C Elec.bkng.ac.assignment (elec.ac.)
OT60	C TR Acct determin G/L acct bal int
OT61	Program and variant selection
OT62	C acct determination dep./loan mgmt
OT63	C FI Maintain table T001F (BlExPres)
OT64	C FI Maintain table T001G (BlExPres)
OT65	C FI Maint. Table T001F (RetBlEx)
OT66	C FI Maintain table T001G (RetBlEx)
OT67	C FI Maintain table T046S
OT68	C FI Maintain table T012K (RetBlEx)
OT69	Reorganize CM data from orders
OT73	C FI Maintain Table T028M
OT74	C FI Maintain Table T028O
OT75	Reconstruct CM from Vendor Bill.Docs
OT76	Reconstruct CM from Loans
OT77	Reconstruct CM from Securities
OT78	Reconstruct FC, Money Mkt, Deriv.
OT79	Reconstruct CM from Securities
OT80	Planning levels/Treasury Management
OT81	Process Repetitive Codes
OT82	C FI Tabellenpflege T028L
OT83	Basic Settings for the El.Bank St.
OT84	Bank Stmt/Check Dep.Posting Specs
OT85	C FI Mainenance in Table T035Z

OT90	C FI Maintenance Table T028Q
OTCP	Call TR OTCO
OTC_CONV	CFM 1.0: Migration OTC Int.Rte Inst.
OTF1	Material-Freight Groups
OTF2	Forwarding Agent - Freight Groups
OTF3	Freight Code Sets
OTF4	Determine Freight Code Set
OTF5	Freight Codes
OTF6	Freight Code Determination
OTF7	Define Freight Code Index
OTLA	Report Selection
OTLD	Current Settings for Cash Management
OTPM	Define El.Bank Stmt Search String
OTR1	Number Range for Form Numbers
OTR2	Number Range for Control Numbers
OTR3	Number range for log numbers
OTR4	Number range for temse files
OTZ1	C FI Users
OTZ2	C FI Profiles
OTZ3	C FI Authorizations
OV-0	View V_TVP0, Attribute 10
OV-1	View V_TVPH, Attribute 1
OV-2	View V_TVP2, Attribute 2
OV-3	View V_TVP3, Attribute 3
OV-4	View V_TVP4, Attribute 4
OV-5	View V_TVP5, Attribute 5
OV-6	View V_TVP6, Attribute 6
OV-7	View V_TVP7, Attribute 7
OV-8	View V_TVP8, Attribute 8
OV-9	View V_TVP9, Attribute 9
OV/1	Generate Record Layout
OV/2	R V Batch Input Program
OV/3	R V Batch Input Program
OV/4	R V Batch Input Program
OV/5	R V Batch Input Program
OV/6	R V Transfer Program
OV/7	Test Data for Data Transfer
OV/8	Test Data - Transfer Data - Cond.
OV/9	Display Test Data
OV01	Access Sequence: Matl Listng/Exclsn
OV02	Condition Type: Listing/Exclusion
OV03	Procedure: Listing/Exclusion
OV04	C RV Tab. TVAK "Listing/Exclusion"
OV05	Condition Table: Listing/Exclusion A
OV06	Condition Table: Listing/Exclusion C
OV07	Condition Table: Listing/Exclusion D
OV08	Condition Table: Add Index
OV09	Condition table: Change Index
OV10	Condition Table: Display Index
OV11	Access Sequence: Matl Determination
OV12	Condition Types: Material Determin.
OV13	Procedure: Material Determination
OV14	C SD Tab. TVAK "MaterialSub"
OV16	Condition Table: Material Substit. A

OV17	Condition Table: Material Substit. C
OV18	Condition Table: Material Substit.D
OV1Z	Define Product Allocation Procedure
OV20	Condition Table: Create Rebate
OV21	Condition Table: Change Rebate
OV22	Condition Table: Display Rebate
OV23	Condition Exclusion: SD
OV24	Pricing: V_T681F for A U
OV25	V_T681F: RevAccDeter - Allowed Flds
OV26	V_T681F: MatDeterm. - Allowed Flds
OV27	V_T681F: List Excl. - Allowed Fields
OV28	V_T681F: Rebate - Allowed Fields
OV29	V-T681F: Index Field Catalog
OV2Z	Define Product Allocation Object
OV30	Condition Exclusion: ProcedAssignmnt
OV31	Maintain Exclusion Group
OV32	Maintain CondTypes for ExclusionGrp
OV33	C RV View V_TVFK_KON
OV34	View V_T687 Account Key
OV35	C RV View V_T683S_EL
OV36	Archiving Conditions V_T681H
OV3Z	Determine Prod. Allocation Hierarchy
OV40	V_T681F:Cross-Selling:PermittedFldNo
OV41	Access sequences: Cross-selling
OV42	Condition types: Cross-selling
OV43	Diagram: Cross-selling
OV46	Condition table: Cross-selling H
OV47	Condition table: Cross-selling Ä
OV48	Condition table: Cross-selling A
OV4Z	Product Allocation Control
OV50	Comparison of master data for cust.
OV51	Display of Changes for Customer
OV52	Del.Customers Pre-Production Startup
OV5Z	Maintain Consumption Periods
OV60	V_T681F: RecAccDet - Allowed fields
OV61	Recon. account det.: Create table
OV62	Rec. account det.: Change table
OV63	Rec. account det.: Display table
OV64	Account determin. - rec. accounts
OV65	Cond. proc. for rec. account det.
OV66	Cond. types: Acc. det. rec. accounts
OV67	Rec. account det.: Access sequences
OV68	Ass. billing type - rec. acc. proc.
OV71	Cash account det.: Change table
OV72	Cash account det.: Display table
OV73	V_T681f: RecAccDet - Allowed fields
OV74	Cash account det.: Access sequences
OV75	Cash account det.: Condition types
OV76	Cond.: Procedure for cash acc. det.
OV77	Account determination -Cash accounts
OV78	Assign billing type-cash acc. proc.
OV7Z	Create Characteristics for Rem.Alloc
OV80	Acc. det.- credit cards: Create tab.
OV81	Acc. det.- credit cards: Change tab.

OV82	Acc. det.- credit cards: Displ. tab.
OV83	V_T681F: Credit card -Allowed fields
OV84	Credit card acc. det: Acc. sequences
OV85	Condition types: Acc.det. cred.cards
OV86	Cond.proc. for credit cards
OV87	Credit card accounts
OV88	Assign billing type-credit card proc
OV8Z	Check Settings
OV90	COPA project: Create table
OV91	COPA project: Change table
OV92	COPA project: Display table
OV93	V_T681F: COPA project all. fields
OV94	COPA project: Access sequences
OV95	COPA project: Condition types
OV96	Pricing procedure for COPA project
OV97	Accounts COPA project
OV98	Assign billing types-COPA proj.proc.
OV9A	Card Authorization Requirements
OV9B	Copying Requirements for Deliveries
OV9C	Copying Requirements f. Billing Docs
OV9Z	Suitable Statistical Structures
OVA0	C_RV_Tab. VVVS "Status group"
OVA2	Incompletion log
OVA3	C_RV_Tab. TAUUM SlsDocType Convers.
OVA4	/nse38/nse38Schedule Usage
OVA5	C SD Tab.VHA Ord.Type Group Itm Det.
OVA6	Credit Groups for Document Types
OVA7	Credit Relevancy of Item Categories
OVA8	Automatic Credit Checks
OVA9	/nse38/Handling Errors SchedAgrs
OVAA	C SD Tab. VAG Rejection Reasons
OVAB	/nse38/Schedule Line Types
OVAC	C SD Tab VCPA "Copy Documents
OVAD	Delivery Type Assignment
OVAE	C SD Tab. VEP Orders
OVAF	C SD Tab. 184 Item Category Determ.
OVAG	C SD Tab. VAG Rejection Reasons
OVAH	/nse38/Variable Messages
OVAI	/nse38/Determine Sold-to Party
OVAJ	/nse38/Distribution Function
OVAK	Sales Order Type Assignment
OVAL	C SD Table VASP Sales Docs: Blocks
OVAM	C SD View TVKOV_AU DistChanDoc.Types
OVAN	C SD View TVKOS_AU "Div.Doc.Types"
OVAO	C SD View TVKO_AU "SlsOrgDoc.Types"
OVAP	C SD Tab. VAP Item Categories
OVAQ	C SD Tab. VAU Order Block Reasons
OVAR	C SD Tab. ROAZ Route Determination
OVAS	C SD Tab. VAST "Order: Block Reasons
OVAT	C SD Tab. TXVR Copy Document Text
OVAU	C SD Tab. VAU Other Reasons
OVAV	C SD Tab. MVFU Avail.Check Criteria
OVAW	C SD Tab. PTM Item Category Groups
OVAX	C SD Tab. VAU

OVAY	C SD Tab. 184E Sched.Line Determ.
OVAZ	C SD Tab. VAKZ Order Type/Organiz.
OVB0	Change "Billing: Document Types"
OVB1	Sales Organizations - Rebate
OVB2	
OVB3	Rebate: Reorganiz. of Billing Index
OVB5	Req. for Creating a Purch.Requisit.
OVB6	Requirement for Picking a Delivery
OVB7	Requ. for Goods Issue of a Delivery
OVB8	Criteria for Creating a Requirement
OVB9	Create Delivery Due Index
OVBA	Conditions: Views (Pricing)
OVBB	Conditions: View sequence A,V,Rebate
OVBC	Documents Value Classes
OVBD	Assign Credit Control Area
OVBE	Default Values for Display Variant
OVBF	Conditions: View sequence A,V,SDeal
OVBH	Conditions: View sequence A,V, Price
OVBI	Maintain Billing Plan Type
OVBJ	Maintain Date Category for BillPlan
OVBK	Assign Bill Plan Type to Item Catgry
OVBL	Date Category Proposal for Bill Plan
OVBM	Maintain dates
OVBN	Maintain Date IDs
OVBO	Maintain milestone billing plan type
OVBP	Assign billing plan type
OVBR	Assignment to Item Category
OVBS	Rule Table for Determining Dates
OVBT	Modification Report Billing Plan
OVBV_DIS	Requ. for Goods Issue of a Delivery
OVC1	C SD Tab. TVC1 Activity Outcomes
OVC2	C SD Tab. TVC2 Activity Reason
OVC3	C SD Tab. TVC Sales Activity Status
OVC4	C SD Tab. TVC4 Activity Outcomes
OVC5	C SD Tab. TVC5 Sales Activities
OVC6	C SD Tab. TVC6 Activity Status
OVC7	c SD Tab TVC7 Assign Activities
OVCA	C RV Tab. TVKK "NoRng Adr > Acct.
OVCB	Structure of Reporting View
OVCC	Assign View to User
OVCD	Definition of Reporting View
OVCE	Control Update of Perform.Measures
OVCF	Control Reporting - Info Blocks
OVCG	Mtn Action Box for Follow-Up Act.
OVCH	Version Change: Listing
OVCI	C SD Set Workflow Action box
OVCK	C SD Tab. TVKK Activity Types
OVCM	RVCust:TVKK:Planning:Sales Act. Type
OVCN	C RV Tab. TVKK "NoRng for sls.activ.
OVCO	C RV Tab. TVKK (SalesAct <--> STGRP)
OVCP	C SD Tab. TVCPK Activity Copying Con
OVCS	C SD Tab. TVKK Activity Types
OVCT	C RV Tab. TKSF "CAS: Statistics grp
OVCU	C RV Tab. TKSFK "CAS: Statistics seq

OVCW	C RV View V_TVKO_COM "Competit/TVKO
OVD0	/nse38/Spec.Features EDL-LS-EDI
OVD1	/nse38/Special Billing Features
OVD2	Define reference conditions
OVD3	Define tolerances for self-billing
OVD4	SD Self-Billing: General Parameter
OVD5	SD Self-Billing: EDI Partner
OVD6	SD Self-Billing: Tolerance Groups
OVD7	SD Self-Billing:Sold-To Party Params
OVD8	SD Self-Billing: Tolerances Definitn
OVDSP	Customize Subsequent Deliv. Split
OVE1	Commodity Code / Import code no.
OVE2	C SD Table T615 Customs offices
OVE3	C SD Table T618 Mode of Transport
OVE4	C SD Table T605 "Business type"
OVE5	C RV Table T605Z "Prop. for bus.type
OVE6	C RV Table T616 "Exp/Import Proced.
OVE7	C SD Table T616Z "BusTransTypeProp.
OVE8	C SD Table TVFM "MatPrGrp-Imp/Exp
OVE9	Completion check
OVELO00	Global VMS parameters
OVELO1	Define Actions
OVELO11	Define Action Controls
OVELO12	Define Vehicle Status
OVELO13	Define Availability
OVELO14	Define Vehicle Usage
OVELO18	Define Vehicle Search Areas
OVELO19	Define VMS Roles
OVELO2	Define No. Range for Int.Veh. No.
OVELO20	Define Vehicle Categories
OVELO21	Assign Vehicle Categories
OVELO27	Access Auth. During Vehicle Search
OVELO29	Define Search Views
OVELO3	Define No. Range for Act. Ctrl Det.
OVELO30	Calculation sheet profile
OVELO4	Define Addnl Data for Vehicle
OVELO5	Define External Status
OVELO6	Define Technical Data for Actions
OVELO7	Assign Own Dialog Messages
OVELO8	Define No.Range f, Config Chg Determ
OVELOL	Define Vehicle Location
OVELOM01	Maintain Condition Tables
OVELOM04	Define Field Catalog for Messages
OVELOM11	Define Access Sequences
OVELOM21	Define Message Types
OVELOM31	Define Message Determ. Procedures
OVELOM41	Assign Msge Determ. Schema to Plant
OVELOTREX	Define Columns for TREX Download
OVELOVSRINIT	Initialize Category Rule Maintenance
OVEP	Rev. recognition: Ind. Item Categ.
OVF0	C SD Table T134G Business Areas
OVF1	C SD Table TVTA Business Areas
OVF2	C SD Table TVTA Business Areas
OVF3	C_RV_Tab. VAUK "Cost Centers"

OVF4	C SD Matchcodes Billing Documents
OVF6	VAUK Dunning Areas
OVFB	C SD Tab. TVBO
OVFC	C SD Tab.TVCPF
OVFD	Forms of payment guarantee
OVFE	Payment guarantee procedure
OVFF	Control for payment guarantee proced
OVFG	Customer payment guarantee procedure
OVFH	Document payment guarantee procedure
OVFI	Assign doc. payment guarantee proced
OVFJ	Determine payment guarantee proced.
OVFK	C SD Table VFK Billing Documents
OVFL	Assign credit contrl area/sales area
OVFS	C SD Table VFS
OVFU	C SD Table VFSP
OVFV	C SD Tab.TVPR
OVG1	Redetermine subtotal
OVH1	C RV Tab. THIT Hierarchy Type
OVH2	C SD Tab. THIZU AcctGrpAssignment
OVH3	C RV Tab. THIOZ Org.assignments
OVH4	C RV Hierarchie Pricing
OVHU01	Define customizing HU check profile
OVHU2	Customizing for Pack. Transn Profile
OVHU4	Customizing HU Picking Profile
OVK1	C SD Table V_TST "Tax Catg./Country"
OVK2	C SD Table T005S "Regions"
OVK3	C SD Table TSKD "Cust.Tax Indicator"
OVK4	C SD Table TSKM "Mat.Tax Indicator"
OVK5	V Table VKM Material Acct Grp
OVK6	C SD Table T001W Plants/Countries
OVK7	C SD Table T459 "Reqt/PlanOrd.Type"
OVK8	C SD Tab. TVKT Customer Acct Grp
OVK9	Tax Records for Each Country
OVKA	SD Tab. T686C "Responsibility
OVKB	Tax Record Conditions VK11
OVKC	Tax Record Conditions VK12
OVKD	Tax Record Conditions VK13
OVKE	Tax Record Conditions VK14
OVKF	C SD Table T005E Ctry/Region/County
OVKG	C SD Table T005G Ctry/Region/City
OVKH	C SD Table TVAK Sales Document Types
OVKI	C RV Table V_TVKV "DocPricingProcdr"
OVKJ	C RV Table V_TVAK_PR "Order > Procd
OVKK	C RV Table T683V "ProcedrDeterminatn
OVKL	C RV Table TVAP "Assign Billing Itm
OVKM	C RV Table TVCPA 'Flow Order'
OVKN	C RV Table V_TVCPF "Flow Bill Doc
OVKO	C RV Table TVAP_PR "Item Pricing
OVKP	SD Table TVKD "Customer detrm procdr
OVL1	C SD Tab. VRO Transportat.Planning
OVL2	Shipping Point Determination
OVL3	Picking Location Determination
OVL5	Maintain Transit Time
OVL6	C_RV_Tab. VUVS "Status Group Dely"

OVL7	Assigning Shipping Point/Ctry/Zone
OVLA	C SD Tab T173 Shipping Types
OVLB	C SD Tab TVKOL
OVLC	C SD Tab.TVCPL
OVLD	SD Table VKN Trans.connection points
OVLE	SD Table VTR Mode of Transport
OVLF	C SD Tab TROLZ
OVLG	C SD Tab. TVLG Weight Grp/Delivery
OVLH	SD Table VRO Routes
OVLK	C SD Tab TVLK Delivery Header
OVLL	C SD Tab T630L Loading Times
OVLM	C RV Tab. TROLZ "Route determ."
OVLN	C SD Tab TVLSP Delivery Blocking
OVLO	C SD Table TVLK Route Control
OVLP	C SD View 142 Picking by Item
OVLQ	C SD Table TVLK "Picking Control"
OVLR	C SD Tab TROAL
OVLS	C SD Tab TVLS Delivery Block Reasons
OVLT	C SD Table TVST "Picking Lists"
OVLU	c_rv_tab. vro "Transit time"
OVLV	C SD Tab T630R Shipping Times
OVLW	C SD Tab.T644
OVLX	C SD Tab TVLSP Delivery Blocks
OVLY	C SD Table Scheduling Control
OVLZ	Scheduling by Shipping Point
OVM1	Controllable Error Messages Shipping
OVM2	I Messages in Mult. Processing Log
OVNA	C SD Table T685B
OVNB	C SD Tab. TVST Shipping Point Info
OVNC	C SD Tab. TNAPR Layouts
OVND	C SD Tab TNAPN Output/Part.Function
OVNE	C SD Tab. TVKO Sales Org.Information
OVNF	C SD Table T685B
OVNG	C SD Tab. TVAK Assign Ouput
OVNI	C SD Tab. TVLK Assign Output
OVNJ	C SD Tab. TVFK Assign Output
OVNK	C SD Table 077D Higher-level Output
OVNL	C SD Table T685B
OVNM	C SD Background job messages
OVNN	C SD Output Variants
OVNO	C SD Table TVKO Form for Sales Off.
OVP0	Pr. point gr. -> Organization/MatGrp
OVP1	Create price point group
OVP2	Create pricing group
OVP3	Change price point group
OVP4	Display price point group
OVP5	Assignment to VKALS/LIFEL
OVP6	Create list variant
OVP7	Pricing group -> Organization
OVP8	Assignment: fields -> list variant
OVP9	Assignment: Texts -> List field
OVPS	Document Mgmt Customizing
OVR0	SD Table 171 Sales Regions
OVR1	SD Table ZONE Transportation Zones

OVR2	c_rv_Tab. T016 "Sectors"
OVR3	C SD Tab. Customer Calendar
OVR4	C SD Tab. Billing Schedules
OVR5	C SD Tab. TBRC Industry Code (Cust.)
OVR6	C SD Tab. TVGF Legal Status (Cust.)
OVR7	C_RV_Tab. TVIP VIP ID/AP
OVRA	C SD Tab. TVSD Customer Stats Grps
OVRB	Statistical Currency per Sales Org.
OVRC	C SD Variants for Orders on Hand
OVRD	C SD Background Jobs f. Ord. on Hand
OVRE	C SD Top Cust/Mat Variants
OVRF	C SD Table TVSM Material Stats Grps
OVRG	C SD Background Jobs f. Top Cust/Mat
OVRH	C RV TAB TVAK "Sales Document Types"
OVRI	C RV Tab. TVAP "Sales Doc.Item Cat."
OVRK	C RV Tab. TVLK "Delivery Types"
OVRL	C RV Tab. TVLP "Delivery Item Categ"
OVRM	C SD Tab. TVFK BillingDoc: DocTypes
OVRN	C RV Tab. TVSF "SD:Stats"
OVRO	C RV Tab. TVSFK "Updates"
OVRP	C RV Tab. TVSFP "Updates"
OVRQ	C SD Table TVSU "Substit.Reason"
OVRT	Customizing: Routes
OVRX	SD Cust.Tble TBPROC:Business Trans.
OVRZ	C TV_Table TVST Assign Transprt Zone
OVS0	C SD Matchcodes Product Proposals
OVS1	SD Matchcodes Materials
OVS2	C SD Matchcodes Customers
OVS3	C SD matchcode for contact person
OVS4	C SD Matchcodes Vendors
OVS5	C SD Matchcodes Sales Personnel
OVS6	C SD Table TKUKL "Customer Classif."
OVS7	C SD Tab.TKUPA "PartnerGrp/Customer"
OVS8	Maintain Weight Groups
OVS9	C SD Table T151 "Customer Groups"
OVSA	C SD Table T130W "Plant Fld Selec."
OVSB	C SD Tab.T176 "Purchase Order Types"
OVSC	C SD Table TVWA "GoodsReceivingHrs."
OVSD	C SD Tab.TPRIO "Delivery Priorities"
OVSF	C SD Table TVSB "Shipping Cond."
OVSG	C SD Table TINC "Incoterms"
OVSH	C SD Table TVBO Rebate Groups
OVSI	C SD View V_T189 "Price List Categ."
OVSJ	C SD Table T178 "Mat.Cond.Group"
OVSK	C SD Table TVPR Commission Groups
OVSL	Pricing groups for customers
OVSM	C SD Table TVAV Buying Habits
OVSN	C SD Table TPFK
OVSO	C SD Table T137 "Mat.Indust.Fld Sel"
OVSP	C SD MS Material Types
OVSQ	C SD Table TSAB Departments
OVSR	C SD Table TVPV Decision Authority
OVST	C SD Table TVLG Weight Groups
OVSU	C SD Table TUMS "Material Status"

OVSV	C RV Customizing Product Hierarchy
OVSW	C SD Table TVBR Call Frequency
OVSX	C SD Table TLGR
OVSY	C SD Table TGR
OVSZ	C SD Table Field Sel.Mat.Field Grp.
OVT0	C SD Table 077D "Accnt Grp Customer"
OVT1	C SD Table 142 Storage conditions
OVT2	SD Table 143
OVT3	C SD Table 023 "Material Groups"
OVT4	C SD Valuation Classes Materials
OVT5	C SD Table 077K Vendor Account Grp
OVT6	View V_TVRL
OVTH	C SD Table T079V "Screen Selection"
OVTL	C RV Del. item cats: Transp. relev.
OVTP	C SD Table TVFK Billing Procedure
OVTR	C SD Delivery Type: Transport.Relev.
OVTS	C SD Reason for Shipment Block
OVTVT_CA	Maintain Planning for Fwdg Agents
OVTY	Transport categories
OVU0	Condition Type: Optimize Access
OVU1	Optimize Access: Revenue Acct Detrmn
OVU2	Condition Type: Optimize Access
OVU3	Condition Type: Optimize Access
OVUR	Revenue Realization: Unbilled Rec.
OVV0	C SD Tab. TVCPA Order Copying Rule
OVV1	C SD Tab.VCPL Delivery Copying Rules
OVV2	C SD Tab.TVCPF Billing copying rules
OVV3	C SD Table TVFS Billing Block
OVV4	C SD Tab. TVFSP Billing Block Reason
OVV5	C SD Tab. TVSA Collect.Doc.Parameter
OVV6	C SD Tab. TVSA Collect.Doc.Parameter
OVV7	C SD Table VSA
OVV8	VSA
OVV9	C SD Table VSA
OVVA	C SD Table VSA
OVVM	Group for Freight List
OVVR	Group for Invoice Lists
OVVX	Collective Document Types for SD
OVWA	Condition Maintenance Goods Issue
OVX1	C RV Tab. VBUR "Sales offices
OVX2	Business area->Plant/Division
OVX3	Company code -> Sales organization
OVX3N	Company code -> Sales organization
OVX4	C RV Tab. VKGR "Sales group
OVX5	C RV Tab. VKO "Sales org.
OVX6	Plants->Sales org./distr.channel
OVX6N	Plants->Sales org./distr.channel
OVX7	Loading points
OVX8	Check Report Organization Sales
OVX8N	Check Report Organization Sales
OVXA	Division -> Sales organization
OVXAN	Division -> Sales organization
OVXB	Divisions
OVXC	Shipping point -> Plant

OVXD	Shipping Points
OVXG	Define sales areas
OVXGN	Define sales areas
OVXI	Distribution channels
OVXJ	Sales group -> Sales office
OVXJN	Sales group -> Sales office
OVXK	Distrib.channels->Sales organiz.
OVXKN	Distrib.channels->Sales organiz.
OVXM	Sales office -> Sales area
OVXMN	Sales office -> Sales area
OVXN	C RV Tab. VKN
OVXT	Transportation planning points
OVXZ	C SD Table NLS "Nielsen ID
OVZ0	SD Cust.AvCh/Req forEach Sched.Line
OVZ1	C SD Tab. TMVFP Avail.check criteria
OVZ2	C SD Tab. MVF Avail. check control
OVZ3	C SD Tab. TMVFU Avail.check criteria
OVZ4	C SD Factory Calendar
OVZ6	C SD Maintain User Profile V_SD_All
OVZ7	C SD Tab TVLS Deliveries: Blocking
OVZ8	Avail.Check Procedure by SchLineCat.
OVZ9	SD Cust. Control Availability Check
OVZA	C SD Number Ranges/Product Proposals
OVZB	C SD Number Ranges/Material Master
OVZC	C SD Number Ranges/Customer Master
OVZD	C SD Inactive !!! NR contact persons
OVZE	C SD Number Ranges/Vendors
OVZF	C SD Number Ranges/Sales Personnel
OVZG	SD Customers: Requirements Classes
OVZH	SD Customizing: Requirements Types
OVZI	SD Cust: Assignment Req/Transaction
OVZJ	Default Values for Availability
OVZK	Procedure per Delivery Item Category
OW00	Default values for fields in views
OW01	Ref. plant per distribution chain
OW12	Maintain V_WEWU for 01/02
OW16	V_WEWU maintenance for 01/06
OW21	V_WEWU maintenance for 02/01
OW22	V_WEWU maintenance for 02/02
OW31	V_WEWU maintenance for 3/01
OW33	V_WEWU maintenance for 03/03
OW41	V_WEWU maintenance for 04/01
OW53	Maintain V_WEWU for 05/03
OW54	Maintain V_WEWU for 05/04
OW55	V_WEWU maintenance for 05/05
OW63	Maintain V_WEWU for 06/03
OW64	Maintain V_WEWU for 06/04
OW65	V_WEWU maintenance for 06/05
OWA1	Configuration: Generate Foll.Docs AT
OWB1	Trading contract: Status, groups
OWB10	Number range maintenance: WB2B
OWB2	Trading contract: Item categories
OWB3	Trading contract: Purchasing group
OWB4	Trading contract: Sales group

OWB5	Trading contract:Trad. contract type
OWB6	Trading Contract: Purchasing Group
OWB7	Trading contract: AppStatGroupApplSt
OWB8	Trading contract: Incompleteness
OWB9	Trading Contract: Incident.Cost Type
OWBA	Trading Contract: Inc. Costs Sales
OWBB	Trading Contract: Incid. Costs Applc
OWBC	Trading Contract: Incid. Costs Purch
OWBD	Trading contract: Locked fields
OWBE	Customizing Release Trading Contract
OWBEXPCUST	Customizing GT Expenses
OWBF	Customizing Copy Control
OWBG	Customizing Assign Exp. TC Type
OWBH	Condition Groups Sales
OWBI	Trading Contract: Open Status/Delive
OWBJ	Trading Contract: Open Status/Delive
OWBK	Trading Contract: Profit Simulation
OWBL	Trading Contract: Profit Simulation2
OWBM	Trading Contract: Profit Simulation2
OWBN	Trading Contract: Profit Simulation2
OWBO	Trading Contract: Open PO/delivery
OWBP	Trading Contract: Profit Simulation
OWB_EXP_1	Trading Contract: Incident.Cost Type
OWB_EXP_10	Grouping of Expense Classes
OWB_EXP_2	Expenses: Class
OWB_EXP_3	Expenses: Customer/Vendor
OWB_EXP_4	Expenses: Vendor Billing Doc.
OWB_EXP_5	Trading Contract: Posting Types
OWB_EXP_6	Expenses: VBD Type DetMeth
OWB_EXP_7	Expenses: Assign Classes
OWB_EXP_8	Expenses: Accounting Types
OWB_EXP_9	Grouping of Expense Classes
OWCBM	Condtn Contract: Cond. Group Purch.
OWCBV	Condtn Contract: Cond. Group Sales
OWCB_CC10	Number Range Maintenance: WCB_CC
OWD1	Maintain rounding profiles
OWEA	Output Determination, Mat. Maint.
OWEB	Delete Label Messages (GR)
OWEF	Labeling: Field Catalog
OWEK	Labeling: Conditions
OWEN	Labeling: Message Types
OWEP	Labeling: Partner Functions
OWES	Labeling: Output Determ. Procedures
OWET	Labeling: Condition Table
OWEV	Labeling: Processing Program
OWEZ	Labeling: Access Sequences
OWIA	Purchasing: Opt. PO-Based Load-Bldg.
OWKW	Group for Picking Wave
OWM1	Competitor: Price Entry
OWNA1	Change Doc. Item for Message Categ.
OWNA2	Change Doc. Item for Message Categ.
OWNA3	Change Doc. Item for Message Categ.
OWNA4	Change Doc. Item for Message Categ.
OWNA5	Change Doc. Item for Message Categ.

SAP Transaction Codes – Volume One

OWS0	Batch Management
OWS1	Assortment List: Sales Conditions
OWS2	POS Outbound: Sales Conditions
OWS3	POS Outbound: Sales Conditions
OWTEST	Test
OWTY	Customizing Warranty Processing
OWTYA01	Account Determination: Create Table
OWTYA02	Account Determination: Change Table
OWTYA03	Account Determination: Display Table
OWTYA04	Field Catalog for Warranties
OWTYA11	Access sequences
OWTYA21	Condition Types
OWTYA31	Calculation Schema
OWTYA41	Account Determination
OWTYAP	Action Profile
OWTYBT	Pushbutton Profile
OWTYCU	WTY Tabstrip Customizing
OWTYM01	Condition Table: Create (Messages)
OWTYM02	CondTab: Change (Messages)
OWTYM03	CondTab: Display (Messages)
OWTYM04	Field Catalog for Warranties
OWTYM11	Access sequences
OWTYM21	Condition Types
OWTYM31	Calculation Schema
OWTYMR	Reference Objects/Equipment for WTY
OWTYP01	Create Condition Table (SD Price)
OWTYP02	Change Condition Table (Sales pr.)
OWTYP03	Display Condition Table: (Sales Pr.)
OWTYP04	Field Catalog for Warranties
OWTYP11	Access sequences
OWTYP21	Condition Types
OWTYP31	Calculation Schema
OWTYP41	Condition Exclusion Group
OWTYP42	Condition Type for Exlusion Group
OWTYP43	Cond. Exclusion Procedure Assignment
OWTYP51	Document Type Maintenance
OWTYP61	Maintain Cond. Types per Claim Type
OWTYSC	Customizing for WTYSC
OWTYSC01	Maintain view types
OWTYSC02	Maintain document types
OWTYSCCU	Warranty workbench Layout
OWTYSC_PROF	Maintain Profile
OWV0	Customizing Pricing
OWV1	Maintain pricing document type
OWV2	Cond. types for doc index ext.supply
OWV3	Allowed pricing levels
OWV4	Cond. Types for Doc Indx Int.Supply
OWV5	Determination procedure (Purchasing)
OWV6	Determination procedure (Sales)
OWV7	Price point groups
OWV8	Texts for list fields
OWV9	Pricing strategy
OWVA	Cond. types for doc indx int.supply
OWVKP1	Selection Variant

SAP Transaction Codes – Volume One

OX01	Company Code -> Purchasing Org.
OX02	Customizing: Company Code Setup
OX03	Customizing: Business Area Setup
OX06	Controlling Area: Basic Data
OX08	Define Purchasing Organization
OX09	Customize storage locations
OX10	Customize plant
OX14	C MM-IV Valuation area - val. level
OX15	Define internal trading partner
OX16	Assignment co.code->Internl.trad.ptr
OX17	Plants -> Purchasing organization
OX18	Assignment Plants -> Company Code
OX19	Controlling Area: Assgn. to CCode
OXA1	List: Service Master Records
OXA2	Field Sel. Service Indiv. Processing
OXA3	Field Sel. Service List Processing
OXK1	Coding Block: Maintain Subscreens
OXK2	Display Coding Block Subscreens
OXK3	Coding Block: Maintain CustomerField
OXK4	Coding Block: Display CustomerField
OXT4	Extension Scenario Maintenance
OXT5	Task Type Maintenance
OXT6	Task Sequence Maintenance
OXT7	Knowledge Database Maintenance
OXT8	Postprocessing Maintenance
OXTEXT	Task Type Maintenance
OXTTASK	Task Type Maintenance
OXW1	Object to be Generated: WEB Purch.
OXW2	Catalogs per Mat. Group: WEB Purch.
OY01	Customize: set up countries
OY03	Define currencies
OY04	C Decimal Places for Currencies
OY05	Factory calendar
OY07	C Configure Countries (T005 - Basis)
OY09	Countries: Mobile Phone Properties
OY17	Countries - field checks
OY18	Table history
OY19	Customizing Cross-System Viewer
OY20	Authorizations Customizing
OY21	User profiles Customizing
OY24	Client maintenance
OY25	CS BC: Set Up Client
OY27	Create super user Customizing
OY28	Deactivate SAP* Customizing
OY29	Technical Writer
OY30	Technical writer
OYC1	C SAPcomm: Server location T164O
OYC2	C SAPcomm: Server selection T164P
OYC3	C SAPcomm: exceptions T164U
OYC4	C T005K country dialling code
OYC5	C SAPcomm: Server assignment T164C
OYC6	C SAPcomm: Inbox distributor T164Y
OYEA	IDoc administration
OYEB	Event coupling for IDoc inbound

OYEC	Delete codes for process technology
OYED	Conversion EDIS -> EDIR
OYM1	C Report Recipient
OYM2	C Reporting Country Indicator
OYM3	C Country Indicator Assignment Rules
OYS1	Maintain Number Range: EDIPORT
OYSM	Number Range tRFC Port
OYSN	Number Range IDoc
OYSO	Number Range R/2 Mailbag
OYSP	Process codes <-> standard tasks
OYSQ	Number range for R/2-R/3 linkage
OZCMLST	Cusmtomizing MiniApp Milestones
P0000_M10_CL0_PBS	Generate Qualifications/Qual. Groups
P0000_M10_CL1_PBS	Convert Certf./Lic. to Qualification
P0000_M10_CL2_PBS	Out-of-Field Report
P0000_M10_CL3_PBS	Select Certificates/Licenses
P0000_M10_CL4_PBS	Check Qualif./Certif. Consistency
P0000_M10_EEO_PBS	EEO-4 and EEO-5 Reporting
P0000_M10_ORM_PBS	Form 1042-S Printing
P0000_M10_SBT_PBS	U.S. Savings Bond Purchase
P0000_M10_SPT_PBS	Substantial Presence Test
P0000_M10_SVB_PBS	Display U.S. Savings Bond Purchase
P0000_M10_XCC_PBS	Clear Table COSTS (U.S. Pub. Sector)
P0000_M10_XFC_PBS	XDEC Conversion (U.S. Pub. Sector)
P000_M07_C224	Infotype 0224 Conversion Workbench
P000_M07_C224_BNCK	Business Number Conversion Check
P000_M07_C224_CONV	Infotype 0224 Conversion
P000_M07_C224_ITCK	Tax Framework Consistency Check
P000_M07_EEA	EEA report (Canada)
P000_M07_GHIS	Garnishment history (Canada)
P000_M07_GRVS	Grievance summary
P000_M07_GSTA	Garnishment statistics (Canada)
P000_M07_PARP	Payroll audit/reconciliation report
P000_M07_PIER	Pensionable and insurable earnings
P000_M07_ROE	Record of Employment (Canada)
P000_M07_ROH	Report on hirings
P000_M07_TXUP	New year tax update utility
P000_M10_AAPM	AAP: Movement analysis report
P000_M10_AAPT	AAP: Turnover analysis report
P000_M10_AAPW	AAP: Workforce distribution report
P000_M10_BTX	Client transp. prog. for BTX* tables
P000_M10_DEP	Benefits dependents list
P000_M10_DTTE	Delete/insert tax table entries
P000_M10_EEO	EEO-1 report
P000_M10_EER	Exemption expiration report
P000_M10_ERISA	ERISA 5500
P000_M10_GANS	Garnishment: Display answer letters
P000_M10_GCUST	Garnishment: Customizing review
P000_M10_GNOT	Garnishment: Display notice letters
P000_M10_GPAL	Garnishment: Print answer letter
P000_M10_GPNL	Garnishment: Print notice letter
P000_M10_GSTA	Garnishment statistics
P000_M10_GSUM	Grievance summary
P000_M10_HER	Employee history report

P000_M10_HIPAA	HIPAA certificate report
P000_M10_LTX	List tax amts in interface tables
P000_M10_NDT	401(k) non-discrimination testing
P000_M10_NHR	New hire report
P000_M10_OSHA1	OSHA-101 report
P000_M10_OSHA2	OSHA-200 report
P000_M10_PEHR	Pensionable earnings and hours
P000_M10_PW2	Print W-2 forms from TemSe file
P000_M10_TAUTH	Display tax authorities
P000_M10_TAUTN	Tax authorities incl. tax area
P000_M10_TMODEL	Taxability models/tax types by auth.
P000_M10_TSUM	Tax infotype summary
P000_M10_VETS	VETS-100 report
P000_M10_W4	W-4 withholding allowance report
P01A_CU01	Copy/Delete Entitlements
P01A_CU02	Copy/Delete Benefit Types
P01A_FO01	Pension Adjustment
P01A_FO02	Pre.program DME
P01A_FO02A	Mass Print/Status of Pension Rights
P01A_FO02B	General Statement
P01A_FO03A	Pre.program DME
P01A_FO03B	Display Reimbursements
P01A_FO03C	Maintain Reimbursements
P01A_FO03D	Check Reimbursements
P01A_FO03E	Delete Reimbursements
P01A_FO03F	Contribution Reimbursement with BI
P01A_M01	Payroll Germany
P01A_RBM01	Create MI01 Notifications
P01A_RBM02	Create MZ01 Notifications
P01A_RBM03	Collect Outbound Messages
P01A_RBM04	Process Inbound Messages
P01A_RBM05	Process IM01 Messages
P01A_RBM06	Review Notifications
P01A_RBM_RESET	Reset B2A Outbound
P01A_RBM_ZE99	Subsequent Display of ZE99 Files
P01A_RE01	Pension Calculation
P01A_RE02	Transfer Data to CPS Database
P01A_RE03	Display Incorrect Personnel Numbers
P01A_RE04	Delete Incorrect Personnel Numbers
P01A_TO01	Display CPS Database
P01A_TO02	Maintain CPS Database
P01A_TO03	Change Pension Status
P01A_TO04	List CPS Database
P01A_TO05	Delete Pension Determination Actions
P01A_TO06	Copy Entitlements
P01A_TO07	Copy Benefit Types
P01A_TO10	Value Type List
P01A_TO11	Conversion Report for Pension Rights
P01A_VA01	PEP: List of Court Requests
P01A_VA02	Mass Printing of Statements
P01A_VA05	Determine Distribution Proposal
P01A_VM01	Create Dataset
P01A_VM02	Display Dataset
P01A_VM03	Create Data Medium

SAP Transaction Codes – Volume One

P01A_VM04	Display Data Medium
P01A_VM05	Download Data Medium
P01A_VM06	Change Status of Notifications
P01T_TXC	Update of Tax ID
P01T_TXE	Create Query Tax ID
P06_AVGL	Pay Scale Progression
P06_AVGS	Managemnt of Promotion Process Steps
P06_IMG_SENOR_AVANC	RPUSEN20 + Variant SAP&P06P1_AVAN
P06_IMG_SENOR_STAGE	RPUSEN20 + Variant SAP&P06P1_STAG
P06_IMG_SENOR_VALABS	RPUSEN20 + Variant SAP&P06P1_VLAB
P0G1	Copy entries for garnishments
P16B	Salary packaging (web)
P16B_ADMIN	Salary packaging
P16B_TEST	Salary Packaging (test mode)
P16B_WFCUST	Workflow: Salary packaging ESS
P16_LRCAS	Labour Relations Case File
P16_LRCONF	Lab. Relations Configuration
P16_LRREP	Labour Relations Report
P16_NQFCHANGE	Change NQF Catalogue
P16_NQFDISP	Display NQF Catalogue
P16_NQFMATCH	Profile Matchup
P16_NQFPROFILE	Display NQF profile
P16_NQFSETUP	Configure NQF
P1B1	Transfer hiring data for applicant
P1B2	Transfer hiring data for applicant
P1B3	Transfer hiring data for applicant
P1B4	Transfer table T588Z, infotype 4000
P1B5	Transfer opt. archive for applicant
P1B6	Transfer hiring data for applicant
P1B7	Conversion T750B
P1OA	Transfer Settings for Opt.Archiving
P1Q0	Increment Progression
P201	Transfer T514D/V from Client 000
P2R0	Letter of appointment
P2R1	Release letter of appointment
P2R2	Accept letter of appointment
P2R3	Verify and hire applicant
P2R4	Print letter of appointment
P2R8	Display letter of appointment
P2R9	Display letter of appointment
P301	Billing Error Analysis
P301D	Billing Error Detail Analysis
P3PR	3PR Reconciliation Workbench
P4Q0	Termination & Redundancy Organiser
P5DB4	Constr. Ind.: Maintain Constr. Sites
P5P1	Addition of IT0122 to T588B
P5Q0	Obsolete: Do not use
P6Q0	Termination and redundancy workbench
PA00	Initial PA Master Data Menu
PA03	Maintain Personnel Control Record
PA03_MENUE	Access PA03 from payroll menu
PA04	Maintain PA Number Ranges
PA05	Number Range Maintenance: RP_COIFT
PA06	Number Range Maintenance: PD_SEQ_NR

PA07	Number Range Maintenance: RP_GARNEM
PA07_RP_CBSID	Maintain Number Range: RP_CBSID
PA08	Maintain Number Range: RP_GARNSUB
PA09	Number Range Maintenance: HR_MMSRV
PA0A	Number Range Maintenance: HRPERSON
PA10	Personnel File
PA20	Display HR Master Data
PA30	Maintain HR Master Data
PA40	Personnel Actions
PA41	Change Entry/Leaving Date
PA42	Fast Entry for Actions
PA48	Hiring from External System
PA51	Display Time Data
PA53	Display Time Data
PA61	Maintain Time Data
PA62	List Entry of Additional Data
PA63	Maintain Time Data
PA64	Calendar Entry
PA70	Fast Entry
PA71	Fast Entry of Time Data
PA97	Compensation administration - matrix
PA98	Compensation Administration
PA99	Compensation Admin. - Release Report
PAAH	Call Ad-Hoc Query
PAC0	PC Editor: Initial screen
PAC0001	Applications
PAC0002	Field Groups
PAC0003	Views
PAC0004	Sections
PAC0005	Screens
PAC0006	Screen sequences
PAC0007	Events
PAC0008	GUI Standard Functions
PAC0009	GUI additional functions
PAC0010	Matchcodes
PAC0011	Assignment of Screen Fields
PAC0012	Field Grouping Criteria
PAC0013	BDT: Payment Card Categories
PAC0015	Application transactions
PAC0016	Tables
PAC0018	Activities
PAC0023	Data Sets
PAC0100	Field Grouping per Activity
PAC0101	Field Control Payment Card Type
PAC0104	Screen Configuration
PAC5	Maintain HR Master Data
PACA	PF Administration
PACA_MAIN	Payment Card Master Maintenance
PACB	PF account maintenance
PACC	PF debugger
PACC1	Assign checking rule
PACC2	Maintain Payment Card Type
PACC3	Maintain payment card category
PACC4	Assignment BDT Payment Card Cat./Typ

PACC5	Maintain payment card blocks
PACE	Pension fund : Postings
PACEN	New posting maintenance
PACG	HR-CH-PF ESS-Online Simulation
PACK	HR-CH: Pension fund
PACN	Number range maint. for accounts
PACO	Account/Posting maintenance PF
PACP	Pension Fund, Interface
PACS	Applicant Evaluation PF
PACT	PC parameter maintenance
PAD_LEAVG_NOTI	Trigger for PersonelLvgNoti
PAD_LEAVG_NOTI_SETUP	Initial SetUp for PersonelLvgNoti
PAEP1	Procedure for Single Records: PA
PAEP2	Procedure for Final Results: PA
PAEPBM	Procedure for Final Results: PA
PAEPBM_RATIO	Ratio Key Figues: Final Results
PAFN	DADSU: Number range processing
PAJP	Call Reporting Tree - Japan
PAKG	Adjustments workbench
PAKY	Adjustments Workbench (excl. adjust)
PAL	Printing Assistant for Landscape
PAL1	Create Sales Representative
PAL2	Display Sales Representative
PAL3	Maintain Sales Representative
PAL4	Create Buyer
PAL5	Maintain Buyer
PAL6	Display Buyer
PAM00	Maintain Pools Using SM34
PAM01	Create Pools
PAM02	Maintain Pools
PAM03	Graphical Operational Planning (PAM)
PANP	Number Range Maintenance: HRPKBUNUM
PAR1	Flexible Employee Data
PAR2	Employee List
PARA	Print Paremeter Group
PARDB1	RDB: Archive Single Records
PARDB2	Delete Archived Single Records
PASR	HR Administrative Services (DAB)
PASRPDEL	Reorganization Single Records Proc.
PASR_AWC_RP_FILLCUST	Fill Customizing for Reports
PASR_DAB_HISTORY	Delete History Data
PASR_DPF_CREATE	Create Personnel File
PASW	Partner Inheritance Switch
PAT1	Personnel Administration Info System
PAUX	Adjustment Workbench
PAUY	Adjustment Workbench (retro proc.)
PAW1	Who is who
PA_CASHFLOW_PROPOSAL	Customizing Help for Loans PA
PA_CFTYPMAP_GE	Map PA Flow Type to CF Flow Type
PA_FILLFTYPEMATCH	Fill Assignm. Table for PA Flow Type
PA_FILLUTYPEMATCH	Proposal Generation for PA Cash Flow
PB00	Recruitment
PB04	Number Range Maintenance: RP_PAPL
PB10	Init.entry of applicant master data

PB20	Display applicant master data
PB2A	B2A Manager
PB2A_GB	GB B2A manager
PB30	Maintain applicant master data
PB40	Applicant actions
PB50	Display Applicant Activities
PB60	Maintain Applicant Activities
PB80	Evaluate vacancies
PBA0	Evaluate advertisements
PBA1	Applicant index
PBA2	List of applications
PBA3	Applicant vacancy assignment list
PBA4	Receipt of application
PBA5	Recurring tasks: Print letters
PBA6	Recurring tasks: Print letters
PBA7	Recurring tasks: Data transfer
PBA8	Recurring tasks: Transfer data
PBA9	List of planned actions
PBAA	Evaluate recruitment instrument
PBAB	Maintain vacancy assignments
PBAC	Applicant statistics
PBAD	Recurring tasks: Print letters
PBAE	Applicant pool
PBAF	Vacancy assignment list
PBAG	Screening
PBAH	Decision
PBAI	All applicants via qualifications
PBAJ	Recruitment info system
PBAK	Recurring Tasks: Print Labels
PBAL	Bulk processing
PBAM	Variable Applicant List
PBAN	Ad Hoc Query
PBAO	ABAP Query
PBAP	Internal Applicants Via Quals
PBAQ	External Applicants Via Quals
PBAT	Choose SAPscript or WinWord
PBAU	Maintain T750C
PBAV	Display T750C
PBAW	Maintain T750B
PBAX	Display T750B
PBAY	Maintain T750X
PBAZ	Display T750X
PBCX	Cust. Account Assign. Reference (MM)
PBCY	Cust. Account Assign. Reference (FX)
PBCZ	Cust. Account Assign. Reference (DE)
PBC_WIZARD_OM	Activate PBC Functions in OM
PBC_WIZARD_OM_CS	Client-Dependent Activatn PBC in OM
PBR1	Responsible persons' addresses
PBW1	Career Center
PBW2	Application Status
PBW2_TC	Application Status
PBW3	Internet scenario for applicant
PBW3_TC	Internet scenario for applicant
PBW4	Assigned Applicants: OBSOLETE

SAP Transaction Codes – Volume One

PBW5	Assigned Applicants: OBSOLETE
PBWW	Customizing standard text in WinWord
PC00_M00	Area menu - Payroll
PC00_M00_CDCP	DME Prel.Program Collective Transfer
PC00_M01	Payroll Germany
PC00_M01_A2F2	Team Data
PC00_M01_A2F4	Hostels
PC00_M01_A2FG	External data
PC00_M01_A2FH	Partners
PC00_M01_A2FQ	Technical Assignments for WCA
PC00_M01_ABS_DESTROY	Destroy Absences
PC00_M01_ANZDEUEV	List DUEVO Notifics
PC00_M01_B1A4	Wage Statement for WCA
PC00_M01_BESCH	DEUEV Statements
PC00_M01_BEWZ	HR-DBW: Manage Data Records
PC00_M01_BG_DATEI	Import PPO File
PC00_M01_BKGO	PS / Child / Standard Letter 01
PC00_M01_BV_BESCHEIN	PPO DEUEV Statements
PC00_M01_BV_DATEI	Import PPO File
PC00_M01_BWDRD0	Print Report for CPS Statements
PC00_M01_BWDRD2	Print Cyclical Entitlements CP
PC00_M01_CALC	Payroll for Germany
PC00_M01_CALC_SIMU	Payroll Simulation Germany
PC00_M01_CATAD1	Semiretirement: Minimum Net Contribs
PC00_M01_CATZGES	Legal Lump-Sum Minimum Net Amount
PC00_M01_CATZLIS	Payroll List for Semiretirement
PC00_M01_CATZTAR	Pay Scale Flat-Rate Minimum Net Amt
PC00_M01_CBKB	List BEMEL
PC00_M01_CBKC	Copy SFP Data Medium to Disk
PC00_M01_CBKD	Delete Social Fund Procedure
PC00_M01_CBKL	List Notifications for SFP
PC00_M01_CBKM	Social Fund Procedure Statements
PC00_M01_CBKR	Display TemSe Object in SFP
PC00_M01_CBKS	Statistics for Social Fund Procedure
PC00_M01_CBKT	Data Medium for Social Fund Proc.
PC00_M01_CBKU	Status Change for Social Fund Proc.
PC00_M01_CBKV	Notifications for Social Fund Proc.
PC00_M01_CBLA	Wage Compensation Calculation
PC00_M01_CBLB	Wage Compensation Table
PC00_M01_CBLG	Breakdown of Trade Tax
PC00_M01_CBLI	Contribution Statement for SFP
PC00_M01_CD3HD0_OUT	Create DEUEV Reporting Files
PC00_M01_CD3R	SI Totals Adjustment
PC00_M01_CD3VD1	Create DEUEV Notifications
PC00_M01_CD3ZD0	Delete all DEUEV notifications
PC00_M01_CDSLD0O	Administrator List Immediate Notifs
PC00_M01_CDSLD0ODIS	Display DEUEV Immediate Notifs
PC00_M01_CDSMD0	Issue Stmt for DEUEV Immed. Notifs
PC00_M01_CDSTD0	Create Data Medium (Immed. Notifs)
PC00_M01_CDSVD0	Create DEUEV Immediate Notifications
PC00_M01_CDTA	Prelim. Program Wage/Salary Transfer
PC00_M01_CDTB	Prelim. Program Advance Payment
PC00_M01_CDTFD0	DME - Reversal of Transfers
PC00_M01_CDTS	Prelim. Program Transfer to HI Fund

PC00_M01_CEDT	Remuneration Statements
PC00_M01_CELHD0_IN	Assign ELENA Inbound Notifications
PC00_M01_CELHD0_OUT	Create File with ELENA Notifications
PC00_M01_CELKD0	Query ELENA Communication Server
PC00_M01_CELLD0_IN	Process ELENA Inbound Notifications
PC00_M01_CELLD0_OUT	Process ELENA Outbound Notifications
PC00_M01_CELVD0_IN	ELENA Confirmations Process DSVV
PC00_M01_CELVD0_OUT	Create ELENA Notifications
PC00_M01_CGEWD1	Union Dues List, Data Medium
PC00_M01_CKTO	Payroll account
PC00_M01_CKUG	Benefit Records
PC00_M01_CKUL	Construction Industry RHC/WC List 01
PC00_M01_CKULD	RHC List
PC00_M01_CLJN	Payroll journal
PC00_M01_CLSTDP	Display Garn. Results (Cluster DP)
PC00_M01_CLSTDQ	Display Garnishment Dir.(Cluster DQ)
PC00_M01_CLSTR	Display Payroll Results G (RD)
PC00_M01_CNET	Net Income 01
PC00_M01_CPDRD0	Third-Party Debt Decl. Sec. 840 ZPO
PC00_M01_CPL1	Evaluation of Garnishment Results
PC00_M01_CRSVD0	Rehabilitants: Reimbursement Applic.
PC00_M01_CSDF	Tax Formulas
PC00_M01_CSTA	Employment Tax Notification (G)
PC00_M01_CSTB	Employment Tax Statement (G)
PC00_M01_CSTG	Breakdown of Trade Tax (Germany)
PC00_M01_CSTT	Display Tax Values
PC00_M01_CSTV	Tax: Average Flat-Rate Tax Rate
PC00_M01_CSVA	SI Contribution Statement (Cancel)
PC00_M01_CSVB	Contribution Statement 01
PC00_M01_CSVBD2	SI Contribution Statement (Cancel)
PC00_M01_CSVC	List of SI Supplementary Pensions
PC00_M01_CSVD1	Bank Suppl. Insurance Relief Fund
PC00_M01_CSVE	SI Suppl.Pension Press Ins. Fund 01
PC00_M01_CSVF	SI Suppl. Pens. Gen. Suppl. Pens. 01
PC00_M01_CSVG	Create EDI Notification File 01
PC00_M01_CSVHD0	Data for E-Mail Contrib. Statement
PC00_M01_CSVK	Miners' Contribution Statement 01
PC00_M01_CSVKD2	SI Contr. Statement, Miners (Cancel)
PC00_M01_CSVWD0	Calculate Disruptive Event SI-Air
PC00_M01_CTAE_DIS	Enter External Data
PC00_M01_CTAE_UPD	Enter External Data
PC00_M01_CTAL	Display Employment Tax Notifications
PC00_M01_CTAM	Print Employment Tax Notifications
PC00_M01_CTAS	Summarize Registration Data
PC00_M01_CTAV	Create Registration Data
PC00_M01_CTAW	Further Process Notification Data
PC00_M01_CTAZ	Manage Employment Tax Notifications
PC00_M01_CTX0	Generate Employment Tax Data
PC00_M01_CTX1	Create Employment Tax Statement
PC00_M01_CTXK	Correct Employment Tax Data
PC00_M01_CTXL	Display Employment Tax Data
PC00_M01_CTXM	Create Employment Tax Statement
PC00_M01_CTXM_AO	ETStmt - Display Tax Auditor
PC00_M01_CTXS	Merge Employment Tax Data

SAP Transaction Codes – Volume One

PC00_M01_CTXV	Generate Employment Tax Data
PC00_M01_CTXW	Further Process Employment Tax Data
PC00_M01_CTXZ	Manage Employment Tax Data
PC00_M01_D3RELDAT	DEUEV-Relevant Master and Time Data
PC00_M01_DEUEV	Create DEUEV Notifications
PC00_M01_DEUVDOWNLOA	Save DEUEV File
PC00_M01_DEUVSHOW	Display DEUEV Data Medium
PC00_M01_DEUV_DFUE	HR-DEUEV: Create EDI File
PC00_M01_DRHD0_RVNUM	Display Confirmation of PI Numbers
PC00_M01_DSV1D0	Documentation from HI Funds
PC00_M01_DSV2D0	Documentation on SI Calculation
PC00_M01_DSV3D0	Documentation on SI Calculation
PC00_M01_DSVCD0	Display Contribution Percentage File
PC00_M01_DTERST	DEUEV: Create Notification File
PC00_M01_DUVANZ	Display DEUEV Notifications
PC00_M01_EHAK	Labor Costs Census
PC00_M01_EHGD	Download to Diskette
PC00_M01_EHGL	Create Remuneration Survey
PC00_M01_EHVE	Quarterly Survey of Earnings
PC00_M01_EHVS	Remuneration Structure Survey
PC00_M01_FALLGRP	Audit-Relevant Case Groups (BUEVO)
PC00_M01_FFOL	Create Bank Transf. Med. - Internatl
PC00_M01_FFOU	Create Bank Transf. Med. - Domestic
PC00_M01_HRF	Wage Statement with HR Forms
PC00_M01_HRF_PAYRACC	Payroll Account with HR Forms
PC00_M01_IBLV	BI for Teams/Const.Site Substitution
PC00_M01_IJST	Batch Input for New Tax Rates
PC00_M01_IKUG	Create Red. Working Hrs Infotypes 01
PC00_M01_IPITD0	Create BI Session for Garnishment DE
PC00_M01_ISVK	Batch Input for Successor Fund
PC00_M01_ISVR	Change Maximum HI Gross Amount
PC00_M01_JAHRLICHE	Subsequent Activities Menu - Year
PC00_M01_KENNZMLDG	Indicate DEUEV Notifications
PC00_M01_LBLE	Weekly Report for Hourly Time Rec.
PC00_M01_LBLT	Time Leveling
PC00_M01_LEHA	List/Stat. Severely Challenged 01
PC00_M01_LEHB	Earnings Survey
PC00_M01_LEHD	Model: Remuneration Statistics Chem.
PC00_M01_LEHE	Model: Remuneration Statistics Metal
PC00_M01_LEROD0	Reimbursements Acc. to G131
PC00_M01_LKGO	PS/Child/Check Child Allowance 01
PC00_M01_LRZA0	Pension Information Procedure: INL
PC00_M01_LRZB0	Pension Information Procedure: BEN
PC00_M01_LSTA	Tax List Child Allow. Cert. 01
PC00_M01_LSTK	Tax Cards (Not) Submitted
PC00_M01_LSVC	Pension Payment Notifications
PC00_M01_LSVE	Check HI Annual Income Limit
PC00_M01_LSVF	Check HI Annual Income Limit
PC00_M01_LSVM	Certify Annual Remuneration
PC00_M01_LSVP	List of Employees with Private HI
PC00_M01_LSVU	Check Contribution Liability
PC00_M01_LSVWD0	Display Value Credit and SI ITD
PC00_M01_LVBA	Capital Formation Overview
PC00_M01_LWAGD0	Customizing Tool CPS

PC00_M01_OTEM	Create Master Data Export
PC00_M01_PAP	Area Menu: Subs. Activ. per Payr.
PC00_M01_PDUNABHAGIG	Area Menu: Subseq. Activities - Per.
PC00_M01_PRDBEG	Define DEUEV Start
PC00_M01_RPBZVMD2	SP Employee Statement
PC00_M01_RPCAMBD0	AVmG: List for Contribution Taxation
PC00_M01_RPCAOAD0	Employment Tax Notific. Tax Auditor
PC00_M01_RPCAOBD0	Employment Tax Statement Tax Auditor
PC00_M01_RPCAODD0	Data Access Tax Audit: Download
PC00_M01_RPCAOKD0	Payroll Account Tax Auditor
PC00_M01_RPCAOLD0	Wage Type Reporter Tax Audit
PC00_M01_RPCAOPD0	Data Access Tax Audit: Export
PC00_M01_RPCAOSD0	Info Types - Display Tay Auditors
PC00_M01_RPCAOTD0	Tax Relevant Wage Types Tax Audit
PC00_M01_RPCBIHD0	Assignment of PPO Error Confirmatns
PC00_M01_RPCBILD0	List for PPO Error Confirmations
PC00_M01_RPCBILD0_DI	Display of PPO Error Confirmations
PC00_M01_RPCBMHD0_IN	Assign PPO DEUEV Inbound Notificatns
PC00_M01_RPCBMLD0ODI	Display DEUEV Notifications (PPO)
PC00_M01_RPCBMLD0OUT	Pers. Resp. List DEUEV Notif. PPO
PC00_M01_RPCBMLD0_IN	Administrator List PPO DEUEV Inbound
PC00_M01_RPCBMTD0	Create DEUEV Data Medium for PPO
PC00_M01_RPCBMTD1	Create DEUEV Data Medium for PPO
PC00_M01_RPCBMVD0	Create Notifications for PPO
PC00_M01_RPCBOHD0	Transfer Notifications to DASBV
PC00_M01_RPCBOLD0	PPO Administrator List
PC00_M01_RPCBOVD0	Create Contribution Collection Not.
PC00_M01_RPCBVBD0	Deduction of Contribution Amt to PPO
PC00_M01_RPCBVLD0	Display PPO Contrib. Collect. Notif.
PC00_M01_RPCD3LD0_ID	Display DEUEV Inbound Notifications
PC00_M01_RPCD3LD0_O	Edit DEUEV Notifications
PC00_M01_RPCD3LD0_OD	Display DEUEV Notifications
PC00_M01_RPCDRHD0	Asst of DEUEV Inbound Notifications
PC00_M01_RPCDRLD0	Administrator List DEUEV Inbox
PC00_M01_RPCDRVD0	Process PI Number Confirmations
PC00_M01_RPCSVPD0	Query GKV Communication Server
PC00_M01_RPCZIHD0	Paying Office Report. Inb. RPCZIHD0
PC00_M01_RPCZILD0	Paying Office Report. Inb. RPCZILD0
PC00_M01_RPCZIVD0	Paying Office Report. Inb. RPCZIVD0
PC00_M01_RPCZOBD0	Paying Office Reporting RPCZOBD0
PC00_M01_RPCZOHD0	Paying Office Report. Outb. RPCZOHD0
PC00_M01_RPCZOLD0	Paying Office Report. Outb. RPCZOLD0
PC00_M01_RPCZOMD0	Paying Office Report. Outb. RPCZOMD0
PC00_M01_RPCZOVD0	Paying Office Report. Outb. RPCZOVD0
PC00_M01_RPCZSLD0	Paying Office Reporting RPCZSLD0
PC00_M01_RPCZVBD2	SP Statement of Contributions Paid
PC00_M01_RPCZVDD2	SP Data Medium Creation
PC00_M01_RPCZVDTAD2	Determination of Contributions
PC00_M01_RPCZVDTSD2	Bank Transfer of Contributions
PC00_M01_RPCZVMD2	SP Notification Creation
PC00_M01_RPDZVCD2	SP Customizing Display
PC00_M01_RPLBUZD0	List of Gross Overpayments
PC00_M01_RPLZVMD2	SP Notification Display
PC00_M01_RPUBGDD0	Import AI Master Data Files

SAP Transaction Codes – Volume One

PC00_M01_RPUBILD0	List for Non-Assigned PPO Notific.
PC00_M01_RPUBRCD0	Customizing: Construction Industry
PC00_M01_RPUD3LD0_I	Edit Unassigned DEUEV Inbound Notif.
PC00_M01_RPUSVMD0	SI: Display Certificate Lists
PC00_M01_RPUTSVD6	Paying Office Reporting Out RPUTSVD6
PC00_M01_RPUTSVD7	Files for Sending by E-Mail to PPO
PC00_M01_RPUTSVD8	Display E-Mail Ins. Contrib. Stat.
PC00_M01_RPUZILD0	Processing Unassigned Notifications
PC00_M01_RPUZVAD2	SP Notification Status/Delete
PC00_M01_RPUZVCD2	SP Data Med. Display and Comparison
PC00_M01_RPUZVDD2	SP Data Medium Administration
PC00_M01_RPUZVMD2	Grouped Data Medium Creation
PC00_M01_RPUZVTD2	SP Data Medium Download
PC00_M01_RZBS	Assign Destination to Constr. Site
PC00_M01_SKGO	Child Allowance Statistics
PC00_M01_SONSPERIOD	Area Menu: Subseq. Activ. - Other
PC00_M01_SVEO	Create Pension Recipient 01
PC00_M01_TLEA	Leave Reserve
PC00_M01_UD3MD0	Distributed Reporting for DEUEV
PC00_M01_UDDQD0	Organize Directory DQ from Clstr DP
PC00_M01_UELTD0	Display ELENA File
PC00_M01_UKGO	Child Allowance Statistics: DL TemSe
PC00_M01_URZB	Public Sector Pension Data Medium 01
PC00_M01_USTG	Import Tax Municipality Data
PC00_M01_USVAD0	Set Retro Acctg Date for HI Changes
PC00_M01_USVCD0	Comparison of Contribution Rates
PC00_M01_USVED0	Import Contribution Rate File
PC00_M01_USVMD0_FLAG	Indicate Notifications
PC00_M01_UTSV	Download Data Medium to Disk
PC00_M01_UTSVD2	Display Contrib. Statemt Data by EDI
PC00_M01_UTSVDD	Download Data Medium to Disk
PC00_M01_UVEO	Download Data Medium to Disk
PC00_M01_UWCU10	Copy/Delete Entitlements
PC00_M01_UWCU15	Customizing Tool: Cop./Del.Ben.Type
PC00_M01_UWEDDA	Transfer Ext. Data to CPS Database
PC00_M01_UWUPDB	Edit Pension Statement Element in DB
PC00_M01_ZFABZ01	Create BZ01 Notifications
PC00_M01_ZFABZ02	Create BZ02 Notifications
PC00_M01_ZFACLST	ZfA Cluster Display
PC00_M01_ZFAINBOUND	Process ZfA Inbound Directory
PC00_M01_ZFAKZ01	KZ01 - Generate Notifs
PC00_M01_ZFAKZ02	Ind. 02: Create Notifications
PC00_M01_ZFAOUTBOUND	Outbound ZfA Notifications
PC00_M01_ZFAZB01	Process ZB01 Notifications
PC00_M01_ZFAZK01	Process ZK01 Notifications
PC00_M01_ZFAZKNN	Non-Assigned ZK01 Notifications
PC00_M02	Area Menu Payroll for Switzerland
PC00_M02_CALC	Payroll Switzerland
PC00_M02_CALCCM	Scheduler for Multiple Payroll (CH)
PC00_M02_CALCCM_SM	Simu. Scheduler Multiple Payroll CH
PC00_M02_CALC_SIMU	Payroll Simulation Switzerland
PC00_M02_CASB0	Solidarity Contribution Statement
PC00_M02_CDTA	Preliminary Program for DME
PC00_M02_CDTBC0	Preprog. DTA seperate payment run

PC00_M02_CDTPC0	Preprogram: DME for NrP PS CH
PC00_M02_CEDT	Remuneration Statements
PC00_M02_CKTO	Payroll Account
PC00_M02_CKTO1	Revision of AHV/AIL Payroll Account
PC00_M02_CLJN	Payroll Journal
PC00_M02_CLSTBV	BV PCL2 Cluster Display
PC00_M02_CLSTR	Display Payroll Results (RC)
PC00_M02_CPK0C0	Calculate Bonus Wage Type
PC00_M02_DLAW2	Wage Statement 2005
PC00_M02_FFOP	Swiss Payment Medium - /SAD /BAD
PC00_M02_FFOU	Swiss Payment Medium - Bank Transfer
PC00_M02_HRF	Wage Statement with HR Forms
PC00_M02_HRF_PAYJNAL	Payroll Journal with HR Forms
PC00_M02_HRF_PAYRACC	Payroll Account with HR Forms
PC00_M02_IADUC0	Create BI for Legacy Data Transfer
PC00_M02_IPKLC0	Evaluation List with BI Folder
PC00_M02_JAHRLICHE	Area menu-Annual subsequent activity
PC00_M02_LAHV0	Employee List with AHV No. /CD
PC00_M02_LAHV1	AHV - Pay Statement
PC00_M02_LASM0	ASM - Wage and Salary Statistics
PC00_M02_LASM1	Solidarity contribution statement
PC00_M02_LBGA0	BFS Quarterly Employment Statistics
PC00_M02_LBGA1	BFS-wage level and structure
PC00_M02_LELM0	ELM - Data Extractor
PC00_M02_LERC0	Employer Statement
PC00_M02_LFAK1	Accounting of Family-Related Bonuses
PC00_M02_LFAK2	Calculation of Enhanced Fam.Rel.Bon.
PC00_M02_LFAK3	Family-Related Bonuses - Check
PC00_M02_LFAK6	Acctg of Family-Rel. Bonuses (ELM)
PC00_M02_LFAK7	Overall Monthly Report (FamRelBReg)
PC00_M02_LIKA1	IF Annual Payroll (Obsolete)
PC00_M02_LIKA2	IF Annual Payroll (AKIS-Lohn'08)
PC00_M02_LINF0	Infotype Overview for Employee
PC00_M02_LJAE0	Annual Overview of Payroll Results
PC00_M02_LKUA0	Reduced Working Hours Payroll Run
PC00_M02_LLAW0	Wage Statement for Tax Declaration
PC00_M02_LLAW1	Wage Statement from File
PC00_M02_LLAW2	Wage Statement 2005
PC00_M02_LLVG0	Salary Comparison
PC00_M02_LPFL0	Wage Type Control
PC00_M02_LPFL1	Wage Type Liabilities Tax
PC00_M02_LPFL2	WType Control - Multiple Employment
PC00_M02_LPFL3	Wage Type Liabilities AHV/AIL
PC00_M02_LPKKC0	Account evaluation
PC00_M02_LPKOC0	PF Evaluation Callup with Scheduler
PC00_M02_LPKPC0	Person Selection for Pension Fund
PC00_M02_LPKSC0	Pension Fund Universal Evaluation
PC00_M02_LPKTC0	Universal Evaluation List
PC00_M02_LQSB0	WTax Notific. of Official Assessment
PC00_M02_LQSF0	Withholding Tax Statement
PC00_M02_LQST0	Withholding Tax - Payroll
PC00_M02_LQST0_OLD	Withholding Tax - Payroll
PC00_M02_LQST1	Withholding Tax Statement Waadt
PC00_M02_LQST2	Withholding Tax Statement-St Gallen

PC00_M02_LQST4	Gross Wage Cross-Border EE France
PC00_M02_LRMC0	Maternity Pay Registration
PC00_M02_LSTM0	HR Master Data Sheet - Switzerland
PC00_M02_LSUV0	UVG Annual Accounting
PC00_M02_LUVG	Wage type capitulation
PC00_M02_LUVG2	Monthly Wage Type Recapitulation
PC00_M02_LVER0	Payroll Insurance Switzerland
PC00_M02_OTEM	Create Master Data Export
PC00_M02_PAP	Area menu-subs. activities per payr.
PC00_M02_PDUNABHAGIG	Area menu - Period-indep. subs. act.
PC00_M02_PLZC1	Read Report Municip. Codes (BFS) CH
PC00_M02_SONSPERIOD	Area menu - Subs. activities, other
PC00_M02_U45BC0	Initial Value Conversion
PC00_M02_U46AC0	Function View Conversion
PC00_M02_UA79C0	Purge IT Individual Values PF
PC00_M02_UACOC0	Create accounts
PC00_M02_UADUC0	Model Report - Legacy Data Transfer
PC00_M02_UAHV0	Import/Display Report New AHV No.
PC00_M02_UAHV1	Update IT36 with New AHV No.
PC00_M02_UIID0	ELM - Customizing Institution IDs
PC00_M02_UKASC0	Global Copier for Pension Funds
PC00_M02_UPENC0	Write Postings to Accounts
PC00_M02_UPKSC0	Conversion of Custom. Evaluations
PC00_M02_UPKUC0	Master Data & Account Conversion
PC00_M02_UQST0	Maintain Withholding Tax Tables
PC00_M02_UQST2	Read Withholding Tax BWA Diskette
PC00_M02_USICC0	Read SI Numbers for Children
PC00_M02_UVSCC0	Check for Processing Control
PC00_M02_UVSEC1	Processing Control: Schedule Editor
PC00_M02_VALC0	PC calculation for workflow
PC00_M02_XR2C0	PF Interface to Data Connect
PC00_M03	Area Menu Payroll Austria
PC00_M03_BARB	Statement of Employment
PC00_M03_CABF	Rsrvs for Severance Pay/Pension 03
PC00_M03_CALC	Payroll/Simulation
PC00_M03_CALC_SIMU	Payroll Simulation Austria
PC00_M03_CBET	Tax-company tax office 03
PC00_M03_CBGN	Social ins. StatmntContribBasesGKK
PC00_M03_CBRU	Works Council Contribution
PC00_M03_CBVA	SI Contribution Statement BVA 03
PC00_M03_CBVAA1	SI Proof of Contribution BVA (A)
PC00_M03_CBVJ	Soc. ins. statemntContibBasesBVA 03
PC00_M03_CDTA	Payroll Transfer Prlmnry Prgm DME03
PC00_M03_CEDT	Remuneration Statements 03
PC00_M03_CEFZ	Refund requests EFZG 03
PC00_M03_CGWB	Union 03
PC00_M03_CIST	Economic Statistics 03
PC00_M03_CJUB	Reserves for Anniversary Pymts 03
PC00_M03_CKSG	List-Issued Sickness Certificates 03
PC00_M03_CKSJ	Tax: Municipal Tax 03
PC00_M03_CKSM	Tax: Municipal Tax 03
PC00_M03_CKTO	Edit Wage Types for Payroll Accnt 03
PC00_M03_CL16	Payslip L16 03
PC00_M03_CLJN	Wage types-edit payroll journal 03

PC00_M03_CLPC	Absence Calendar - Country Part 03
PC00_M03_CLSTAE	Display Garnishment Result ClusterAE
PC00_M03_CLSTAF	Display Garnishment Direct. Clstr AF
PC00_M03_CLSTEF	Prcssd List Refund Requests EFZG 03
PC00_M03_CLSTKN	Display Cluster KN: First Illness
PC00_M03_CLSTLZ	Processed Lists-Payslip L16 03
PC00_M03_CLSTNS	Display Cluster NS: Heavy Labor NS
PC00_M03_CLSTRA	Display Payroll Results
PC00_M03_CMLIA0	Cash Breakdown List Payment Int.
PC00_M03_CPCN	Search: Absence Types in Calendr 03
PC00_M03_CPDRA0	Third-Party Debtor Decl. par. 301
PC00_M03_CPFA	Statement for Support Payment
PC00_M03_CPGTA0	Creditor Notific. Remaining Debt 03
PC00_M03_CPL1A0	Evaluation of Garnishment Results
PC00_M03_CSPUA0	SP Entitl.Transfer from Payr.Account
PC00_M03_CSVB	SI Contribution Statement GKK 03
PC00_M03_CUBS	Tax: ER-Dependent Vienna 03
PC00_M03_CURL	Leave Accrual 03
PC00_M03_DTBA0	PRELIM. PROGRAM DATA MEDIUM EXCH. (A
PC00_M03_FFOP	DME Transfer V3 Format
PC00_M03_FFOU	Payroll Transfer-Create DME 03
PC00_M03_HRF	Wage Statement with HR Forms
PC00_M03_HRF_PAYJNAL	Wage Statement with HR Forms
PC00_M03_IELD	Check ELDA Records
PC00_M03_IKSG	Sick.certif.-BI-sick certif fee 03
PC00_M03_IKSH	Sickness Certs-BI-Sickness Certs 03
PC00_M03_ILSK	New tax rates 03
PC00_M03_IPITA0	Create BI Session for Garnishment AT
PC00_M03_IRRVA0	Maint. Date Type Retro. Acc. IT41 BI
PC00_M03_JAHRLICHE	Area menu-Annual subsequent activity
PC00_M03_LAEBA0	Work and Remun. confirm. for SP/MP
PC00_M03_LKPH	Print Sickness Certificates 03
PC00_M03_PAP	Area menu-Subs. activities per payr.
PC00_M03_PDUNABHAGIG	Area menu - Period-indep. subs. act.
PC00_M03_SONSPERIOD	Area menu - Subs. activities, other
PC00_M03_TGEN	Generate Personal Calendar 03
PC00_M03_TNSH	Night Shift Heavy Labor 03
PC00_M03_UDAFA0	Create Direct. from Garn. Cluster AE
PC00_M03_UELD	ELDA Data Medium 03
PC00_M04	Area menu Payroll for Spain
PC00_M04_C11X	Generate employment tax reports
PC00_M04_C190	Generate employment tax reports
PC00_M04_CALC	Payroll
PC00_M04_CALC_SIMU	Payroll run simulation Spain
PC00_M04_CCRI	Deductions certificate
PC00_M04_CDEA	Delt@ - Electronic notifications
PC00_M04_CDEB	Delt@ RATSB - Accidents w/o leave
PC00_M04_CDTA	Prepare data exchange
PC00_M04_CEDT	Remuneration Statement
PC00_M04_CEDT_XE	Remuneration Statement (XE)
PC00_M04_CERT_EMP	Company certificate
PC00_M04_CKTO	Payroll Account
PC00_M04_CLJN	Payroll journal
PC00_M04_CLSTR	Display payroll results

SAP Transaction Codes – Volume One

PC00_M04_CONTR_INEM	Notification of contracts for INEM
PC00_M04_CPEF	Confirm cash payments
PC00_M04_CTCE	Social Insurance forms
PC00_M04_ERE_CALEN	Manage ERE calendars
PC00_M04_ERE_EXPED	Social Insurance contribution models
PC00_M04_FFOT	Prepare DME trasfers
PC00_M04_HRF	Remuneration statement with HR Forms
PC00_M04_HRF_PAYJNAL	Remuneration statement with HR Forms
PC00_M04_HRF_PAYRACC	Payroll account with HR Forms
PC00_M04_JAHRLICHE	Area menu-Annual subsequent activity
PC00_M04_MENS_AFI	Affiliation message
PC00_M04_MENS_FDI	FDI message
PC00_M04_OTEM	Create Master Data Export
PC00_M04_PAP	Area menu-subs. activities per payr.
PC00_M04_PDUNABHAGIG	Area menu - Period-indep. subs. act.
PC00_M04_RESP_FDI	FDI message response evaluation
PC00_M04_RESP_FRA	AFI message replies evaluation
PC00_M04_RESP_INEM	Evaluation of INEM responses
PC00_M04_RPCAFIE1	Affiliation message
PC00_M04_RPCDTBE0	Prep. data medium exchange
PC00_M04_RPCIR1E0	Mass generation of emplymt tax data
PC00_M04_RPCLJNE9	Payroll journal Spain
PC00_M04_RPCLPCE0	Display personal calendar
PC00_M04_RPCMLIE0	Cash breakdown list
PC00_M04_RPCRT2E0	Certific@2
PC00_M04_RPCSPUE0	Entitlements transfer
PC00_M04_RPCSPXE1	Automatic special payments
PC00_M04_RPIMBIE0	Estimate of taxable income
PC00_M04_RPU31G02	XPRA for conversion of IT0090
PC00_M04_RPU620E0	Conversion program for IT0062
PC00_M04_RPUCLAE0	Create and change additional clauses
PC00_M04_RPUCMWE0	Contract Management Workbench
PC00_M04_RPUFORE0	Theoretical training mgmt hours
PC00_M04_RPUP62E0	Create new record IT0062
PC00_M04_RPUP62E1	Create new record IT0062
PC00_M04_RPURT2E0	Certific@2 reply evaluation
PC00_M04_RPW001E0	Customize taxes (display)
PC00_M04_RPW003E0	Cutomize taxes (change)
PC00_M04_SONSPERIOD	Area menu - Subs. activities, other
PC00_M04_TGEN	Generate personal calendar
PC00_M04_UTMS	Display TemSe files
PC00_M05	Area menu - Payroll Netherlands
PC00_M05_B2ACHECK	Check B2A Settings
PC00_M05_CABCDA	Digital Delivery Ins. Statement ER
PC00_M05_CABCKO	Fxd-term Contr./Standby Wkrs Statem.
PC00_M05_CABCKV	Fixed-term Contract Statement
PC00_M05_CABCOV	Interrupt.Statem.(Paym.of HI Contr.)
PC00_M05_CABCV	Employer Insurance Statement
PC00_M05_CAKH	Premium Reduction Overview
PC00_M05_CALC	Payroll Netherlands
PC00_M05_CALC_SIMU	Payroll Simulation (NL)
PC00_M05_CAT	Conversion f. Relationship Managem.
PC00_M05_CBJO	Ann.Statem.GAK
PC00_M05_CCDS	SI Notification for Cadans

PC00_M05_CCJO	Ann.Statem.Cadans
PC00_M05_CDTA	Preliminary Prog. Data Exchange DME
PC00_M05_CDTB	Preliminary Prog. Data Exchange DME
PC00_M05_CEDK	Process response message
PC00_M05_CEDM	Create Day-one-announcement
PC00_M05_CEDT	Payroll - Payroll Journal
PC00_M05_CEDZ	B2A Manager
PC00_M05_CFBR	Administration Tool Flex. Benefits
PC00_M05_CFBS	FlexBen Yr-End Settlement Simulation
PC00_M05_CHSV	Change of Particip. Codes/SI Groups
PC00_M05_CJLO	Annual Statement Employment Tax
PC00_M05_CJWN	Annual Statement Employee
PC00_M05_CJWN_OUD	Employee Annual Tax Statement
PC00_M05_CKTO	Payroll Account
PC00_M05_CLAA	Close Wage Return
PC00_M05_CLAD1	Wage Return: Data Download (TemSe)
PC00_M05_CLAF	Classify Wage Return Errors
PC00_M05_CLAJ	Annual wage return
PC00_M05_CLAK	Process Response Messages
PC00_M05_CLAL	Display Wage Return Data
PC00_M05_CLAL1	Wage Return: Display Data
PC00_M05_CLAO	Set Wage Return Status to Sent
PC00_M05_CLAR	Display Response Messages
PC00_M05_CLAS	Create Wage Return File
PC00_M05_CLAV	Collect Wage Return Data
PC00_M05_CLAZ	B2A Manager
PC00_M05_CLGB	Wage Tax - Green Table Spec.Payments
PC00_M05_CLGP	Wage Tax - Green Table
PC00_M05_CLJN	Payroll Journal
PC00_M05_CLKO	Taxed Childcare Table Overview
PC00_M05_CLSTR	Display Payroll Results
PC00_M05_CLWB	Wage Tax - White Table Spec.Payments
PC00_M05_CLWP	Wage Tax (LH) - White Table
PC00_M05_CMBV	SI Notification for GAK
PC00_M05_CNET	Detailed Simulation
PC00_M05_COGB	Comp. Allwnce (OT) - Green Table SP
PC00_M05_COGP	Comp. Allowance (OT) - Green Table
PC00_M05_COWB	Comp. Allownce (OT) - White Table SP
PC00_M05_COWP	Comp. Allowance (OT)- White Table
PC00_M05_CSRH	Control Register
PC00_M05_CVZA	Create registrations/deregistrations
PC00_M05_CVZD	Download transfer file
PC00_M05_CVZP	Select persons for registration
PC00_M05_CVZU	Upload transfer file
PC00_M05_CVZZ	B2A Manager
PC00_M05_CZKML	Notif. of Sickness and Recovery
PC00_M05_EH	Final Levy
PC00_M05_EHBW	Different Rate Special EE Groups
PC00_M05_EHET	Final Levy - Single Rate (Tax Table)
PC00_M05_EHTT	Final Levy - Table Rate (Tax Table)
PC00_M05_FFOT	Payroll Transfer - Create DME
PC00_M05_HRF	Wage Statement with HR Forms
PC00_M05_HRF_MADASH	Wage Statement with HR Forms
PC00_M05_HRF_PAYRACC	Lohnkonto with HR Forms

SAP Transaction Codes – Volume One

PC00_M05_IBBL	Batch Input for Initialization P0060
PC00_M05_ICAS	Batch Input for Legal Person Entry
PC00_M05_IFBA	BMI for Creation of IT0378
PC00_M05_IFBB	BMI for Creation of IT0171
PC00_M05_IFBL	Determin. and Saving Source Amounts
PC00_M05_ITVO	Batch Input Sess.f.Ch.Tx.Cl.+Ch.OT
PC00_M05_JAHRLICHE	Area menu-Annual subsequent activity
PC00_M05_LAKH	Overview Master Data Prem. Reduction
PC00_M05_LCBS	CBS Record Salary Administration
PC00_M05_LFBC	Customizing Overview
PC00_M05_LFBI	Total Overview Indiv. Flex. Ben.Ch.
PC00_M05_LFBK	Total Overview Options Flex. Benefit
PC00_M05_LFBS	Overview of Flexible Benefits Source
PC00_M05_LFBV	Balance Overview Flexible Ben. (NL)
PC00_M05_LLAE	Overview of collective returns
PC00_M05_LLHB	Overview Master Data for Wage Tax
PC00_M05_LPLH	Employment Tax and NI Return to 2005
PC00_M05_LSPR	Overview Master Data Spec. Provision
PC00_M05_LSVZ	Overview Master Data for Social Ins.
PC00_M05_LWBA	Annual Report SAMEN
PC00_M05_LWPA	Absence Overview
PC00_M05_LWPM	PW Monitor
PC00_M05_LWPO	Poortwachter Overview
PC00_M05_LZFW	Overview HI Income Threshold
PC00_M05_OFPM	Special payroll process
PC00_M05_OTCL	Payroll driver NL for import process
PC00_M05_OTCP	Combined payroll export
PC00_M05_OTEM	Create Master Data Export
PC00_M05_OTEX	Create Gross Payroll Export
PC00_M05_OTLJ	Payroll Journal - Outsourcing
PC00_M05_OTMM	Mini master export
PC00_M05_PAP	Area menu-Subs. activities per payr.
PC00_M05_SONSPERIOD	Area menu - Subs. activities, other
PC00_M05_TFBK	Individual Options Overview
PC00_M05_UADR	Convert Addresses from T536A ->T536C
PC00_M05_UCRN	Conversion of Cluster RN (PCL2)
PC00_M05_UCSR	Change Savings Data
PC00_M05_UCVZ	Entry of De-/Registr. or Updates
PC00_M05_UEDM	Enter day-one-announcement manually
PC00_M05_UFBC	Customizing Check Flex. Benefits
PC00_M05_UFBR	Register Collectively
PC00_M05_UFBU	Customizing Copier
PC00_M05_UITW	Manual Entry of Transfer File
PC00_M05_UJWN	Start JOWN in Case of COJ
PC00_M05_ULAC	Check Customizing
PC00_M05_ULAE	Check Master Data
PC00_M05_UPSV	Transfer SI Contr. Between REPERs
PC00_M05_UTAE_DIS	Display Collective ER Data
PC00_M05_UTAE_UPD	Change Collective ER Data
PC00_M05_UTSVN0	Download TemSe Objects
PC00_M05_UTSVN1	Display TemSe Objects
PC00_M05_ZKMN0_OLD	Notification of Sickness
PC00_M05_ZKMN2	Print Sickness/Recovery Notification
PC00_M05_ZKS	Analysis of Absences Due to Sickness

PC00_M06	Payroll Menu - France	
PC00_M06_2483	Declaration 2483	
PC00_M06_CALC	Payroll France	
PC00_M06_CALC_SIMU	Payroll Simulation (France)	
PC00_M06_CDTA	Payroll transfer - pre.prgm DME	
PC00_M06_CEDT	Payroll: Remuneration Statement	
PC00_M06_CJDP	Summarized Journal	
PC00_M06_CKTO	Wage types output: payroll account	
PC00_M06_CLJN	Wage types output - payroll journal	
PC00_M06_CLSTR	Tools - payroll result	
PC00_M06_FFOT	Payroll transfer - first DME	
PC00_M06_HDL	Document status manager	
PC00_M06_HRF	Remuneration statement with HR Forms	
PC00_M06_HRF_GRN	Wage Statement with HR Forms	
PC00_M06_HRF_PAYJNAL	Remuneration statement with HR Forms	
PC00_M06_HRF_PAYRACC	Payroll account with HR Forms	
PC00_M06_ILVA	Create annual leave	
PC00_M06_JAHRLICHE	Area menu-Annual subsequent activity	
PC00_M06_LA35	Reduction salaries & fringe benefits	
PC00_M06_LAAI	ASSEDIC statement	
PC00_M06_LAAS	ASSEDIC Statement	
PC00_M06_LABS	Absence counter	
PC00_M06_LACI	Entertainers' Leave	
PC00_M06_LANC	Electors and elegible amts delegates	
PC00_M06_LASA	Pay notif. after ATT	
PC00_M06_LASI	Wage statemnt cont. interr. over 6m	
PC00_M06_LASM	Pay notif. after sick	
PC00_M06_LBIJ	SPSI Balance	
PC00_M06_LBRC	Social insurance summary URSSAF	
PC00_M06_LBS1	'Bilan Social' (FR)	
PC00_M06_LCOT2	Social insurance contributions list	
PC00_M06_LCRC	DADS suppl.pens. fnd	
PC00_M06_LDAD	Unified DADS	
PC00_M06_LDAT	ATT stmnt	
PC00_M06_LDH1	D2 challenged stmnt	
PC00_M06_LDH2	D2 challenged stmnt	
PC00_M06_LDMO	Workforce Notification	
PC00_M06_LDPE	Employ. reg. request	
PC00_M06_LDUC	C.S.S. / D.U.C.S.	
PC00_M06_LDUE	Single hiring declaration	
PC00_M06_LEPH	Labor court election	
PC00_M06_LPAB	Profit sharing overview	
PC00_M06_LPAD	Indiv. Summary of Paid PShare	
PC00_M06_LPAN	List of paid profit sharing	
PC00_M06_LPAR	Profit sharing - individual form	
PC00_M06_LPM1	Calc. Budgeting for Medals	
PC00_M06_LPR1	Calc. Retirement Budget	
PC00_M06_LRPS	Employee register	
PC00_M06_LSA1	Garnishment - Payment document	
PC00_M06_LSA2	Garnishment - Overview	
PC00_M06_LSA3	Garnishmt: Date Monitoring	
PC00_M06_LSA4	Delimit Garnishment	
PC00_M06_LTDS	DADS-TDS	
PC00_M06_MP1060BI	Batch Input IT1060	

PC00_M06_MP1600BI	MP1060BI
PC00_M06_MP1601BI	Batch Input IT1601
PC00_M06_OTEM	Create Master Data Export
PC00_M06_PAP	Area menu-Subs. activities per payr.
PC00_M06_PBS_AVEF	Pay Progression: Update Assignment
PC00_M06_PBS_IAVG	Grade Increase: Appointment
PC00_M06_PBS_LAVG	Grade Increase: Selection
PC00_M06_PBS_LDAF	PersNos List: Perm. Work Contracts
PC00_M06_PBS_PERSK	Generate Personal Calendar
PC00_M06_PDUNABHAGIG	Area menu - Period-indep. subs. act.
PC00_M06_RPCDTBF0	Preliminary Program for DME
PC00_M06_RPCLJNF9	Payroll Journal France
PC00_M06_RPCLPCF0	Display Personal Calendar
PC00_M06_RPCMLIF0	Cash Breakdown List
PC00_M06_RPCRUCF0	Cumulated Wage Type Selection
PC00_M06_RPCRUCF1	Cumulated Wage Type Selection PA70
PC00_M06_RPCRUMF0	Monthly Wage Type Selection
PC00_M06_RPLASAF1	Pay Statement
PC00_M06_RPLASMF10	Pay Statement
PC00_M06_RPLBRCF1	SI Summary Sheet
PC00_M06_RPLCTRF0	Table Check Program <->IT
PC00_M06_RPLDATF0	Preliminary Stage
PC00_M06_RPLDRCF0	DADS-U file control
PC00_M06_RPLRBSF0	Employees Who Benefit
PC00_M06_RPLTR0F0	2483 Statement
PC00_M06_RPSTRTFI	Start ADP String
PC00_M06_RPTCONF00	Employee Selection
PC00_M06_RPTCONF10	Employee Selection
PC00_M06_RPU1G1F0	Transfer contr. assess. thresholds
PC00_M06_RPUDWNF0	Retrieve PC File
PC00_M06_RPUDWNF1	Retrieve TEMSE File
PC00_M06_RPUGENF0	Convert Absence Calendar
PC00_M06_RPUGENF10	Update Absence Quotas
PC00_M06_RPUTIRF0	Generate 'cheque' Lunch Coupon File
PC00_M06_RPUTIRF1	Generate 'ticket' Lunch Coupon File
PC00_M06_RPUTIRF2	Generate 'dejeuner' Lunch Coup. File
PC00_M06_RPU_M06_FFO	RPU_M06_FFOT
PC00_M06_SONSPERIOD	Area menu - Subs. activities, other
PC00_M06_TGEN	Generate Pers. Calendar
PC00_M06_UF1C	Update TAUX table
PC00_M06_UF1G	Update ASS table
PC00_M06_UF1H	Modify Contribution Calculation Base
PC00_M06_UPAD	Profit Sharing - General Payment
PC00_M06_UPAI	Profit Sharing: Interest Payment
PC00_M06_UPAP	Profit sharing: Partial Payment
PC00_M06_UPAR	Profit Sharing: Distribution
PC00_M06_UPRO1	Calculate Reserve for Paid Leave
PC00_M07_CALC	Payroll Driver Canada
PC00_M07_CALC_SIMU	Payroll driver simulation (Canada)
PC00_M07_CBS	Canada savings bonds
PC00_M07_CCYR	Processing Year-end Reporting 07
PC00_M07_CDTA	Payroll Transfer Pre-Program DTA-07
PC00_M07_CDTB	Pre.Program Advance Payment
PC00_M07_CDTC	Advance Payment

PC00_M07_CEDT	Payroll Remuneration Statement - 07
PC00_M07_CKSB	Canada Savings Bonds
PC00_M07_CKTO	Payroll Account
PC00_M07_CLJN	Payroll Account 07
PC00_M07_CLSTR	Tools - Payroll Results - 07
PC00_M07_CPIE	Reconciliation - P.I.E.R. Report 07
PC00_M07_CROE	Record of Employment (ROE) 07
PC00_M07_CROH	Report on Hirings 07
PC00_M07_CWCA0	W.C.B. Reporting 07
PC00_M07_DPR	Display payroll results
PC00_M07_FFOC	Payroll Transfer - Check Printing 07
PC00_M07_FFOT	Create Payroll Transfer DTA 07
PC00_M07_H	Garnishments History Canada
PC00_M07_HRF	Wage Statement with HR Forms
PC00_M07_HRF_PAYJNAL	Payroll Journal with HR Forms
PC00_M07_JAHRLICHE	Bereichsmenü-Folgeaktivitäten - Jäh
PC00_M07_K500	3PR Prepare evaluation run (CA)
PC00_M07_OTCL	Payroll Driver Canada for Import
PC00_M07_OTEM	Create Master Data Export
PC00_M07_OTEX	Create Export Data
PC00_M07_OTLJ	Payroll Journal - Outsourcing
PC00_M07_PAP	Bereichsmenü-Folgeaktivitäten - Pro
PC00_M07_PCALC	Payroll driver (Canada)
PC00_M07_PDME	Pre-program DME: advance payments
PC00_M07_PDUNABHAGIG	Bereichsmenü-Folgeaktivitäten - Peri
PC00_M07_PRA	Payroll account
PC00_M07_PRJ	Payroll journal
PC00_M07_RCON	Audit report
PC00_M07_REMU	Remuneration statements
PC00_M07_RFFOAVIS	Print zero net advices
PC00_M07_RROE	Record of Employment (ROE)
PC00_M07_S	Garnishment statistics (Canada)
PC00_M07_SCAN0	Business payroll survey report
PC00_M07_SEEA	Emplmt.Equity Assessment 07
PC00_M07_SEET	Emplmt.Equity Assessment 07
PC00_M07_SONSPERIOD	Bereichsmenü-Folgeaktivitäten - Sons
PC00_M07_STDR	STD/LTD Report
PC00_M07_UKRM	Transfer to Third Gen. Form PD7A 07
PC00_M07_UNTU	Start of Year Cred/Ded. Update 07
PC00_M07_URMP	3PR Create posting run (CA)
PC00_M07_XPM	Export/transf. to process model
PC00_M07_YEAM	YE Amendment Reason report, Canada
PC00_M07_YETM	TemSe administration
PC00_M07_YEVW	Run viewer
PC00_M08	Area menu-payroll for Great Britain
PC00_M08_ABS_ENTITLE	Absence Evaluation Entitlements
PC00_M08_ABS_GO_LIVE	Generate Used Entitlement History
PC00_M08_ABS_HISTORY	Absence Evaluation History
PC00_M08_ABS_SCHEMES	Absence Evaluation Schemes
PC00_M08_AHPOC	Off-Cycle Workbench: AHP
PC00_M08_ASHE	ASHE return
PC00_M08_BCHG	SxP and OxP band changes
PC00_M08_C35C	P35 Checklist and Declaration
PC00_M08_CALC	Start payroll

PC00_M08_CALC_SIMU	Payroll simulation Great Britain
PC00_M08_CAPM	Legislative reporting APM listing 08
PC00_M08_CBSM	Actual company car trips 08
PC00_M08_CCRT	Court order dedns. 08
PC00_M08_CDTA	Payroll-transfer-prelim. prog.DTA-08
PC00_M08_CDTB	Advance payment 08
PC00_M08_CEDT	Pay.accounting remun. statement - 08
PC00_M08_CEOY	End-of-year processing
PC00_M08_CEOY_PBS	End-of-year processing (PBS)
PC00_M08_CEOY_STD	End-of-year processing
PC00_M08_CEXC	Exceptions 08
PC00_M08_CEXLN	Exclusions 08
PC00_M08_CHIST	Sickness History SSP 1 08
PC00_M08_CKTO	Payroll account 08
PC00_M08_CLEG	Legisl. rept. P14 & P60 listing 08
PC00_M08_CLJN	Payroll journal 08
PC00_M08_CLPC	Absence calendar 08
PC00_M08_CLSTR	Tools - payroll result - 08
PC00_M08_CLSTR_V02	Tools - old payroll result -08
PC00_M08_CMAG	Magnetic media driver
PC00_M08_CMPY	Maternity pay period 08
PC00_M08_CNIL	Display NI payroll results
PC00_M08_CNIR	NI rates and limits
PC00_M08_CNIT	NI contributions report
PC00_M08_CONV	SxP and OxP conversion
PC00_M08_COSTS	Absence (SxP & OxP) costs analysis
PC00_M08_CP35	P35 listing 08
PC00_M08_CP45	P45 processing 08
PC00_M08_CP45_PBS	P45 processing (PBS)
PC00_M08_CP45_STD	P45 processing 08
PC00_M08_CP46	P46 (Company Car) form
PC00_M08_CP46PEN_STD	P46PEN processing 08
PC00_M08_CP46_PBS	P46 (Company Car) form (PBS)
PC00_M08_CP46_STD	P46 (Company Car) form
PC00_M08_CPEN	Pension contribs. 08
PC00_M08_CPENNOT_STD	PENNOT processing 08
PC00_M08_CPENS	Total Pension Contribs for Tax Year
PC00_M08_CPNEY	Pension Simplification 06/07 Report
PC00_M08_CREC	Payroll Results Control Tool 08
PC00_M08_CSCO	Statement of Court Orders
PC00_M08_CSMP1	SMP 1 08
PC00_M08_CSSP1	SSP 1 08
PC00_M08_CSSP1L	SSP 1(L) 08
PC00_M08_CSTARTR	STARTER processing 08
PC00_M08_CSTARTR_PBS	STARTER processing 08
PC00_M08_CSTARTR_STD	Standard SE starter report
PC00_M08_CTXB	Taxable benefits 08
PC00_M08_DRL_COSTOBJ	Drilldown Reporting on Cost Objects
PC00_M08_DRL_PERSON	Drilldown Reporting on Employees
PC00_M08_ENTS	SxP and OxP entitlements left
PC00_M08_EXCLUSIONS	SxP exclusions
PC00_M08_FFOT	Payroll transfer-first DTA 08
PC00_M08_HIST	SxP and OxP history
PC00_M08_HRF	Remuneration Statement with HR Forms

PC00_M08_HRF_PAYJNAL	Payroll Journal with HR Forms
PC00_M08_HRF_PAYRACC	Payroll Accounts with HR Forms
PC00_M08_IP46	HR-GB: P46(Car) Archive Init. report
PC00_M08_JAHRLICHE	Area menu-Annual subsequent activiti
PC00_M08_LGPS_CLR	LGPS Pension Details Override Flag C
PC00_M08_LGPS_DET	LGPS Pension Details
PC00_M08_MSA_FACTOR	Fill MSA factor field
PC00_M08_ODOC	Off-Cycle Workbench: On Demand Paymt
PC00_M08_OTEM	Create Master Data Export
PC00_M08_OVERVIEW	Absence data overview
PC00_M08_PAP	Area menu-subsequent activities per
PC00_M08_PATTERN	Absence pattern analysis
PC00_M08_PAY_SHEET	SxP and OxP payment sheet
PC00_M08_PBS_RESIDEN	Check Residency Status
PC00_M08_PCTAB_UPD	Update the infotype 0071 with contri
PC00_M08_PCUP	Update pens.contr. 08
PC00_M08_PC_EXP	Update infotype 0071 with EE FLAG
PC00_M08_PDUNABHAGIG	Area menu-Subsequent activities, per
PC00_M08_QDP_CHECK	Check SSP QDP migration
PC00_M08_RPCDTFG0	DME Cancel Transfers
PC00_M08_RPCLJNG9	Payroll Journal
PC00_M08_RPCP45G0	P45 form (old)
PC00_M08_RPCSSPG0_SM	Statutory Maternity Pay form SMP1
PC00_M08_RPISSEG0	Batch update SSP Easement on IT0084
PC00_M08_RPPCUPG0	Batch update of IT0071 pension amts.
PC00_M08_RPPCUPG0_EX	Update infotype 0071 with EE FLAG
PC00_M08_RPPCUPG0_UP	Update the infotype 0071 with contri
PC00_M08_RPULCCG0	Bat. updt Payr-stat 4 leavers w. CC
PC00_M08_RPUTCUG0	Start-of-year tax code update 08
PC00_M08_SCHM	SxP and OxP schemes
PC00_M08_SONSPERIOD	Area menu-Subsequent activities, oth
PC00_M08_SPELLS	Absence spells analysis
PC00_M08_UCCI	Start-of-year company car update 08
PC00_M08_ULCC	Company car f.leavr 08
PC00_M08_UREC0	Recon. prep. data generation 08
PC00_M08_UREC5	Recon. prep. data display 08
PC00_M08_USS_CONTRIB	USS Contributions
PC00_M08_USS_SALARY	USS Salary Changes
PC00_M08_UTCU	Start-of-year tax code update 08
PC00_M08_UTMS	TemSe view and download program
PC00_M09	Area Menu-Payroll for Denmark
PC00_M09_CA72	Delimit Tax Infotypes
PC00_M09_CALC	Payroll for Denmark
PC00_M09_CALCNET	Payroll: Net Import
PC00_M09_CC72	Import and Create Tax Infotypes
PC00_M09_CCOR	Create Correction File Year Values
PC00_M09_CCTPM0	GenTranfrDatesForSpecialOCPeriods
PC00_M09_CDECM1	Display Export File
PC00_M09_CDMF	Create DMF statistics
PC00_M09_CEDT	Payr.accounting remun.statement - 09
PC00_M09_CFTPM2	FTP link to PBS
PC00_M09_CH22	Change training code
PC00_M09_CHED	Change training code
PC00_M09_CHWP	Change work center code

PC00_M09_CICP	Copy wage types for difference
PC00_M09_CIMP	Import Year-End Values
PC00_M09_CIMPM	Receive net from PBS 09
PC00_M09_CIT5	Create leave entitlement Denmark
PC00_M09_CKTO	Payroll Account for Denmark
PC00_M09_CL72	Tax Infotype List for Denmark
PC00_M09_CLGMM6	Difference display wage types
PC00_M09_CLGMM7	Consistency Check for Interface WTs
PC00_M09_CLGMM8	Display Imported Wage Types
PC00_M09_CLGMM9	List of Year-End Values
PC00_M09_CLJN	Payroll journal
PC00_M09_CLLM	Change of employer
PC00_M09_CLSTR	Tools - Payroll result - 09
PC00_M09_CNYCOMP	Comparison of two new year runs
PC00_M09_CNYL	New year's value list
PC00_M09_CPEX	Gross Export to PBS format
PC00_M09_CPRR	Pension overview
PC00_M09_CRPPWF1M2	Restore Payroll Statistics
PC00_M09_CRSTM0	Change Payroll Status
PC00_M09_CRSTM1	Display Payroll Status
PC00_M09_CSND	Send gross to PBS
PC00_M09_CSTEP	Refresh Payroll Status
PC00_M09_CTPM0	Generate date of transfer
PC00_M09_CYECOMP	Comparison of two year end runs
PC00_M09_DELM1	RPCDELM1
PC00_M09_DIFM0	RPCDIFM0
PC00_M09_FM2M0	Consisteny Check for PBS Wage Types
PC00_M09_FSTM0	?RPLFSTM0
PC00_M09_ICPM0	Copy Wage Types for Diff. Display
PC00_M09_IM2	Import New Year's Values
PC00_M09_ISTA	Training code Import and create 09
PC00_M09_ISTW	Import and Create Work Centercodes
PC00_M09_IT5_AGE	Create Age-Related Leave Entitlement
PC00_M09_IT5_CHARGE	Create payscale-related LveEntitlmts
PC00_M09_IT5_PRV_YR	Create LveEntitlements as Last Year
PC00_M09_IT5_SUMMER	Create Leave Entlmnts acc.to SummVac
PC00_M09_JAHRLICHE	Area menu-Annual subsequent activity
PC00_M09_MPBSCONST	Change PBS constants
PC00_M09_MPBSSAP	Display SAP-PBS Constants
PC00_M09_MSB5	Test send connection
PC00_M09_MSB6	Test receiv. conn.
PC00_M09_MSB7	Test file man. conn.
PC00_M09_MSTM0	Master data
PC00_M09_MYEC	Display Corrections for Year-End
PC00_M09_PAP	Area menu-Subs. activities - Pro
PC00_M09_PBTM0	Create Test File PBS Wage Types
PC00_M09_PDUNABHAGIG	Period-independent subs.activities
PC00_M09_PSTM	HR master data sheet
PC00_M09_PSTM0	?RPUPSTM0
PC00_M09_RPUFERM0	Find Inactive Employees
PC00_M09_SH22	Display Training Code
PC00_M09_SHED	Display Training Code
PC00_M09_SHWP	Display work center code
PC00_M09_SONSPERIOD	Subs. activities - other periods

PC00_M09_SYEC	Display corrections for year end
PC00_M09_TR22	Transport training code
PC00_M09_TRED	Transport training code
PC00_M09_TRWP	Transport work center code
PC00_M10	Bereichsmenü - Abrechnung für USA
PC00_M10_CALC	Payroll Driver USA
PC00_M10_CALC_SIMU	Simulation payroll accounting 10
PC00_M10_CDTB	Per Payroll Period - Advance 10
PC00_M10_CDTC	Payroll Transfer Prelim. Prog DTA-10
PC00_M10_CDTE	Payroll Transfer - Test Transfer 10
PC00_M10_CEDT	Payroll Remuneration Statement - 10
PC00_M10_CLAIMS	Claims processing
PC00_M10_CLJN	Payroll Journal
PC00_M10_CLMR	US Overpayment Recovery
PC00_M10_CLSTR	Tools - Payroll Results - 10
PC00_M10_CPL3U0	Garnishment Stats 10
PC00_M10_CPL5U0	Garnish. Letter - Tax Authorities 10
PC00_M10_CPL7U0	Garnish.Letter-Tax Type/Tax Auth. 10
PC00_M10_CPRS	Payroll Reconciliation (Scheduler)
PC00_M10_FFOC	Payroll Transfer - Check Printing 10
PC00_M10_FFOT	Create Payroll Transfer DTA 10
PC00_M10_HRF	Wage Statement with HR Forms
PC00_M10_HRF_PAYJNAL	Wage Statement with HR Forms
PC00_M10_HRF_PJ_ASCE	txn for US_CE, PY_JL per. ass. info
PC00_M10_HRF_PJ_PRCE	txn for US_CE, PY_JL person info
PC00_M10_IPIT0	Garnishment: Active -> inactive
PC00_M10_IPIT1	Garnishment: Pending -> active
PC00_M10_IPIT2	Garnishment: Delimit
PC00_M10_JAHRLICHE	Bereichsmenü - Jährliche
PC00_M10_OTCL	Payroll Driver US for Import Process
PC00_M10_OTEM	Create Master Data Export
PC00_M10_OTEX	Create Gross Payroll Export
PC00_M10_OTL1	Cross Year Adjustment Display
PC00_M10_OTLJ	Payroll Journal - Outsourcing
PC00_M10_OTU1	IF delete by pay period
PC00_M10_OTUR	Tax Services - Reconciliation
PC00_M10_OTUT	Tax Services
PC00_M10_OTUT_DISP	Display IF cluster tax fields
PC00_M10_OTUT_SETUP	US Tax Services Outsourcing setup
PC00_M10_OTUY	Tax Services - Yearly
PC00_M10_PAP	Bereichsmenü - Pro Abrechn.Periode
PC00_M10_PCALC	Payroll Driver (USA)
PC00_M10_PDUNABHAGIG	Bereichsmenü - Periodenunabhägig
PC00_M10_PRJ	Payroll journal
PC00_M10_REC	Payroll reconciliation report
PC00_M10_REMU	Remuneration statements
PC00_M10_RFFOAVIS	Print zero net advices
PC00_M10_SONSPERIOD	Folgeaktivitäten - Sonstige Perioden
PC00_M10_TXL_AUD	US: BSI TaxLocator Audit Report
PC00_M10_TXL_CFG	US: BSI TaxLocator Config Report
PC00_M10_U500	3PR Prepare evaluation run (US)
PC00_M10_UAUTU1	Utilities - Tax Authority Util. 10
PC00_M10_UAUTU2	Utilities - Auths. not in Area 10
PC00_M10_UBSIU7	Utilities - Cmpr.delivered auths 10

PC00_M10_UBTXU0	Utilities - Update Clients	10
PC00_M10_UTAX	Tax Reporter Util. Delete Entries	10
PC00_M10_UTMDU0	Utilities - Expand Tax Models	10
PC00_M10_WRPR_PJUSCE	Wrapper report calling Py. Jnl. USCE	
PC00_M10_XPM	Export /transfer to process model	
PC00_M11	Bereichsmenü-Abrechnung für Irland	
PC00_M11_ABSEMP	Evaluate Absence History of an Emplo	
PC00_M11_ABSENTS	Evaluate Absence Scheme Entitlements	
PC00_M11_ABSHIST	Evaluate Absence History of an Emplo	
PC00_M11_CALC_SIMU	Simulation payroll accounting 11	
PC00_M11_CDTB	Pre.program DME Advance Payment (IE)	
PC00_M11_CILC0	Income Levy Certificate	11
PC00_M11_CLJN	Payroll journal	
PC00_M11_CLSTR	Tools - payroll results - 11	
PC00_M11_CPEOY	EOY P60 and P35 returns	
PC00_M11_CVHI2	VHI Contributions	11
PC00_M11_EHECS	EHECS Form	
PC00_M11_HRF	Payroll account with HR Forms	
PC00_M11_HRF_PAYJNAL	Payroll account with HR Forms	
PC00_M11_HRF_PAYRACC	Payroll account with HR Forms	
PC00_M11_JAHRLICHE	Bereichsmenü-Subs. activities - Annu	
PC00_M11_OTEM	Create Master Data Export	
PC00_M11_P30	P30 Amounts	
PC00_M11_P46	Starter Notification	
PC00_M11_PAP	Bereichsmenü-Subs. activities - Per	
PC00_M11_PAYE	HR IE: PAYE Tax Credit Upload Report	
PC00_M11_PDUNABHAGIG	Bereichsmenü-Subs. activities - Peri	
PC00_M11_PENS	Irish Pensions Contributions Report	
PC00_M11_SIPTU	SIPTU	
PC00_M11_SONSPERIOD	Bereichsmenü-Subs. activities - Othe	
PC00_M11_WTK	Wage Type Reporter	
PC00_M12	Area menu - Payroll for Belgium	
PC00_M12_BOWA_AT	BELCOTAX - Analyze TemSe file	
PC00_M12_BOWA_CM	BELCOTAX/FINPROF - Checkmonitor	
PC00_M12_BOWA_GE	BELCOTAX - Generate TemSe file	
PC00_M12_BOWA_MG	BELCOTAX - Manage TemSe file	
PC00_M12_BOWA_PD	FICHES 281.xx - Printing documents	
PC00_M12_BOWM_AT	FINPROF - Analyze TemSe file	
PC00_M12_BOWM_EP	FINPROF - External Payments	
PC00_M12_BOWM_GE	FINPROF - Generate TemSe file	
PC00_M12_BOWM_MG	FINPROF - Manage TemSe file	
PC00_M12_BOWM_RS	BELCOTAX/FINPROF-Tool Infotype 3207	
PC00_M12_CALC	Payroll calculation	
PC00_M12_CALC_SIMU	Payroll simulation for Belgium	
PC00_M12_CC32	Edition of Unemployment Docum. C3.2	
PC00_M12_CDPE	Pension Declaration	
PC00_M12_CDTA	Prelimin.prog.- Data Medium Exchange	
PC00_M12_CEDT	Remuneration statements	
PC00_M12_CKTO	Payroll Account	
PC00_M12_CLJN	Payroll journal	
PC00_M12_CLPC	Display personal calendar	
PC00_M12_CLSTC	List Belcotax cluster directory	
PC00_M12_CLSTCW	List cluster dir. SI quart. totals	
PC00_M12_CLSTCX	List cluster direct. SI declaration	

SAP Transaction Codes – Volume One

PC00_M12_CLSTR	Display payroll results (Cluster RB)
PC00_M12_CLSTW	List Belcotax Results
PC00_M12_CLSTWW	List Cluster SI quarterly totals
PC00_M12_CLSTWX	List Cluster SI Declaration
PC00_M12_CSBA	Analyze and Print Declaration
PC00_M12_CSBG	Generate Declaration
PC00_M12_CSBU	Maintain External and Previous Year
PC00_M12_CSIB	SI Declaration Management
PC00_M12_CSIF	Printing Control List SI Declaration
PC00_M12_CSIG	Download SI declaration file
PC00_M12_CTXA	Annual preparation of Belcotax
PC00_M12_CTXB	Creation Belcotax Declaration Tape
PC00_M12_CTXC	Printing of Belcotax Documents
PC00_M12_CTXD	Deletion professional tax scales
PC00_M12_CTXE	Generation professional tax scales
PC00_M12_CTXF	Monthly preparation Belcotax
PC00_M12_CTXH	Tax help programs 12
PC00_M12_CTXI	List Professional Tax Scales
PC00_M12_DMFA_CR	DMFA consultation request
PC00_M12_DMFA_GE	Generate DMFA Temse File
PC00_M12_DMFA_MG	Manage DMFA Temse Files
PC00_M12_DMFA_MG_OLD	Manage DMFA Temse Files
PC00_M12_DMFA_SN	Digitally sign temse files
PC00_M12_DMNCONFFILE	Confirmation file processing
PC00_M12_DMNDECLPREP	Prepare DIMONA declaration
PC00_M12_DMNFILEGEN	DImona declaration generation report
PC00_M12_DMNRCPTFILE	Receipt file processing
PC00_M12_DMNSIGNDECL	Digital Signature
PC00_M12_DMNTEMSEVIE	View Dimona file
PC00_M12_DMN_DIM	Dimona: Display Reference Data
PC00_M12_DMN_DIU	Dimona: Prepare Reference Data
PC00_M12_DMN_GE	DIMONA - Generate TemSe file
PC00_M12_DMN_MG	DIMONA - Manage TemSe file
PC00_M12_DMN_PR	DIMONA - Prepare Declaration
PC00_M12_EDLE	Educational Leave Declaration
PC00_M12_FFOE	Payment medium - Foreign DME
PC00_M12_FFOT	Payment medium - Domestic DME
PC00_M12_GARN	Garnishment history
PC00_M12_HDL	Document status manager
PC00_M12_HRF	Wage Statement with HR Forms
PC00_M12_HRF_PAYJNAL	Wage Statement with HR Forms
PC00_M12_HRF_PAYRACC	Lohnkonto with HR Forms
PC00_M12_JAHRLICHE	Area menu-Annual subsequent activity
PC00_M12_MODELGPRINT	Printing of the Model G form(s)
PC00_M12_N	Notification in advance educ. leave
PC00_M12_P	Personnel Register
PC00_M12_PAP	Area menu-subs. activities per payr.
PC00_M12_PDUNABHAGIG	Area menu - Period-indep. subs. act.
PC00_M12_R	Reimbursement declar. educ. leave
PC00_M12_SOBA	Social Balance
PC00_M12_SONSPERIOD	Area menu - Subs. activities, other
PC00_M12_SRD_GE	Generate Social Risk Temse File
PC00_M12_TGEN	Generate personal calendar
PC00_M13	Bereichsmenü-Abrechnung für Australi

SAP Transaction Codes – Volume One

PC00_M13_AAFI_PS	APS Agest Fund Interface
PC00_M13_ABSR_PS	Aus. Bureau of Statistics (ABS)
PC00_M13_ADDR	Addr. Infotype Validation For IT0006
PC00_M13_AGEST_PS	AGEST Interface
PC00_M13_AP01	Payment summary mag. med. file
PC00_M13_APSED	APSED Report
PC00_M13_ATOR_PS	Employment Detail Declaration (ATO)
PC00_M13_CALC_SIMU	Simulation payroll accounting 13
PC00_M13_CCDT_PS	Continuous Contribution Details
PC00_M13_CDTB_PS	BT with extra payment
PC00_M13_CG00	2000/2001 Payment summary
PC00_M13_CG99	1999/2000 Group certificates
PC00_M13_CP01	2001/2002 Payment Summary
PC00_M13_CTO3	Termination Organizer
PC00_M13_CWTR	Wage Type Reporter
PC00_M13_EG98_PS	ETP Group Certificate 98
PC00_M13_EPDD_PS	Employment Detail Declaration (ABS)
PC00_M13_HDCS_PS	Higher Duty Cessation Report
PC00_M13_HDLT_PS	Long Term Higher Duty Report
PC00_M13_HDNA_PS	Nominal/Actual Position Report
PC00_M13_HRF	Payroll Results with HR Forms
PC00_M13_HRF_PAYJNAL	Payroll Journal with HR Forms
PC00_M13_HRF_PAYRACC	Payroll Account with HR Forms
PC00_M13_INDR_PS	Increment Due Report
PC00_M13_INHDA_PS	HDA Increment Report
PC00_M13_INPR_PS	Increment Progression Report
PC00_M13_INPW_PS	Increment Progression Workbench
PC00_M13_INPW_PS_CE	CE Increment Progression Workbench
PC00_M13_INRR_PS	Increment Register
PC00_M13_JAHRLICHE	Bereichsmenü-Folgeaktivitäten - Annu
PC00_M13_JAHRLICH_PS	Area menu
PC00_M13_LEAV	Leave Reports
PC00_M13_LG00	Payment summary listing 2000/2001
PC00_M13_LG98	Group Certs. Listing 1998/1999
PC00_M13_LG99	Group Certs. Listing 1999/2000
PC00_M13_LP01	Payment summary listing 2001/2002
PC00_M13_LVAP_PS	Leave Advance Payment
PC00_M13_LVPR_PS	Leave Provision
PC00_M13_PAP	Bereichsmenü-Folgeaktivitäten-Per Pa
PC00_M13_PAP_PS	Area menu-Subsequent activities per
PC00_M13_PAYG_PS	Pay As You Go Contribution
PC00_M13_PDUNABHAGIG	Bereichsmenü-Folgeaktivitäten - Peri
PC00_M13_PDUNABHA_PS	Area Menu-Subsequent Activities-Inde
PC00_M13_PIF_PS	PIF Interface
PC00_M13_PQGO	Maint pymnt sum / grp cert overrides
PC00_M13_PRSV_PS	Prior Service Report
PC00_M13_PS	Payroll accounting for Germany
PC00_M13_PSATO	Payment summary ATO file report
PC00_M13_PSGEN	Payment summary generation report
PC00_M13_PSLST	Payment summary listing report
PC00_M13_PSMP_PS	PSMPC Interface
PC00_M13_SEDR_PS	Superannuation Exception Data
PC00_M13_SONSPERIOD	Bereichsmenü-Folgeaktivitäten - Othe
PC00_M13_SONSPERI_PS	Area Menu-Subsequent Activities-Othe

PC00_M13_SUPH_PS	Superannuation history report
PC00_M13_SUPM	Superannuation fund maintenance
PC00_M13_SUPR	Superannuation Report
PC00_M13_SWCQ	SuperWork Choice Creation
PC00_M13_TARO_PS	Termination & Redundancy Organiser
PC00_M13_TERM_PS	Termination and redundancy workbench
PC00_M13_TERM_PS_CE	Termn and redundancy workbench CE
PC00_M13_TERM_PS_SE	Termination and redundancy workbench
PC00_M13_WGST	Wage type statement Australia
PC00_M14	Bereichsmenü-Abrechnung für Malaysie
PC00_M14_AWS	AWS accounting for Malaysia
PC00_M14_CALC	Start Payroll
PC00_M14_CALC_SIMU	Simulate Payroll
PC00_M14_CANG	Run Report for Angkasa
PC00_M14_CANN	Display Annual Payroll Results
PC00_M14_CASB	Run Report for ASB
PC00_M14_CAWS	Generate Annual Wage Supplement
PC00_M14_CBKI	Scr for BIK Text and codes: T5LBT
PC00_M14_CDTA	Payroll-transfer-prelimProg. DME-14
PC00_M14_CDTB	BT for extra payment 14
PC00_M14_CDTC	Prepare Bank Transfer
PC00_M14_CEBA	Run EPF Report for Borang A
PC00_M14_CEDT	Print Remuneration Statement
PC00_M14_CEUI	Upload EPF Initials
PC00_M14_CFAP	Generate Festival Advance Payment
PC00_M14_CHTB	Run Report for Tabung Haji
PC00_M14_CKTO	Display Payroll Account
PC00_M14_CLJN	Display Payroll Journal
PC00_M14_CLSTR	Display Payroll Results
PC00_M14_CM59	Record Receipt Number of Tax Office
PC00_M14_CS8A	Run SOCSO Report for Borang 8A
PC00_M14_CS8B	Run SOCSO Report for Borang 8B
PC00_M14_CSB2	Run SOCSO Report for Borang 2
PC00_M14_CSB3	Run SOCSO Report for Borang 3
PC00_M14_CSCL	SOCSO CheckList
PC00_M14_CT21	Run Tax Report for CP21
PC00_M14_CT22	Run Tax Report for CP22
PC00_M14_CT2A	Run Tax Report for CP22A
PC00_M14_CT39	Run Tax Report for CP39
PC00_M14_CT59	Run Tax Deduction Report for CP159
PC00_M14_CTEA	Print EA Form
PC00_M14_CTP1	TP1 Form
PC00_M14_CTP12010	TP1 Report 2010
PC00_M14_CTP2	Run Employee Tax Report for PCB2
PC00_M14_CTP3	TP3 Report
PC00_M14_CTRN	Prepare Table T5LRN for CP159
PC00_M14_CTSQ	Prepare EA Form
PC00_M14_CURN	Delete Table T5LRN Records
PC00_M14_CUSQ	Delete Table T5LSQ Records
PC00_M14_CUTC	Copy Records from T5LRN to T5LTC
PC00_M14_FAP	FAP accounting for Malaysia
PC00_M14_FFOD	Create DME (Print Payment advice)
PC00_M14_FFOM	Perform Bank Transfer
PC00_M14_HRF	Wage Statement with HR Forms

SAP Transaction Codes – Volume One

PC00_M14_HRF_PAYJNAL	Payroll Journal with HR Forms
PC00_M14_HRF_PAYRACC	Payroll Account with HR Forms
PC00_M14_JAHRLICHE	Bereichsmenü-Jährliche Folgeaktivitä
PC00_M14_LTCH	Display Tax Scale
PC00_M14_NCTEA	Print New EA Form
PC00_M14_ODS	On-demand Payroll for Malaysia
PC00_M14_PAP	Bereichsmenü-Folgeaktivitäten pro Ab
PC00_M14_PDUNABHAGIG	Bereichsmenü-Periodenunabhängige Fol
PC00_M14_SONSPERIOD	Bereichsmenü-Folgeaktivitäten sonsti
PC00_M15	Area menu-payroll for Italy
PC00_M15_730	Template 730
PC00_M15_770	Form 770
PC00_M15_ANF	Expiring personnel action report
PC00_M15_B2A	Update TemSe's B2A Status
PC00_M15_B2AMANAGER	Italian transaction for B2A Manager
PC00_M15_BSF	File per richiesta bonus famiglia
PC00_M15_CALC	Pay calculation
PC00_M15_CALC_SIMU	Simulation-payroll accounting-Italy
PC00_M15_CDTA	Preliminary DME Transfer Program 15
PC00_M15_CEDT	Remuneration statement
PC00_M15_CEDT_ME	Remuneration statement (only for
PC00_M15_CKTO	Payroll Account lists/statistic
PC00_M15_CLJN	Payroll journal lists/statistic
PC00_M15_CLSTR	Tools - Payroll Result
PC00_M15_CNTDISXCAT	Challenged employees by category
PC00_M15_CNTDISXCAZ	Challenged employees by category
PC00_M15_COMP	Italy-PS: Company transfer
PC00_M15_CRIE	Payroll Overview lists/statistic
PC00_M15_CUD	CUD form
PC00_M15_DM10	DM 10
PC00_M15_F24	Report for handling form F24 2008
PC00_M15_F24_CBI	Report for handling F24 CBI
PC00_M15_FFOT	Create DME Bank Transfer
PC00_M15_GLA	GLA form for CoCoCo
PC00_M15_HRF	Remuneration statement with HR forms
PC00_M15_HRF_PAYJNAL	Wage Statement with HR Forms
PC00_M15_HRF_PAYRACC	Lohnkonto with HR Forms
PC00_M15_IAS	Estrattore dati per IAS#19
PC00_M15_INAIL	INAIL Autoliquidazione
PC00_M15_INPDAP	DMA extractor
PC00_M15_INPSM	Monthly INPS statement
PC00_M15_JAHRLICHE	Area menu-subseq.activities annual
PC00_M15_LISDIZ	List of challenged employees
PC00_M15_O1M	Period standardization ex-O1/M
PC00_M15_O1M_SOST	Report O1m - Sost.
PC00_M15_OTEM	Create Master Data Export
PC00_M15_PAP	Menu area-activities for payr.accntg
PC00_M15_PDUNABHAGIG	Area menu-Subsequent activities-Ind.
PC00_M15_REPPAR	Parameter forms
PC00_M15_RPC10II0	Annual forms report
PC00_M15_RPC770I0	770 form
PC00_M15_RPC77LI0	Display of form 770 list
PC00_M15_RPCDMLI0	Service report for master display
PC00_M15_RPCDMVI0	Report for data check

SAP Transaction Codes – Volume One

PC00_M15_RPCDTBI0	Prelim. program for data exchange
PC00_M15_RPCF24I0	Report for F2 form management
PC00_M15_RPCI21I0	IT 21 and IT0156 Consistency Check
PC00_M15_RPCINAIL	Report for INAIL SelfSettl Extract.
PC00_M15_RPCINPI0	Protected personnel action list
PC00_M15_RPCLPCI0	Print Personal Calendar -
PC00_M15_RPCLSTLU	SB (Single Book) Cluster Viewer
PC00_M15_RPCLULI0	Output of Single Book of Work
PC00_M15_RPCO1MI0	Parameter program for 01/M form
PC00_M15_RPCSPUI0	Additional payments
PC00_M15_RPCSPXI1	RPCSPXI1
PC00_M15_RPI730I0	Batch Input
PC00_M15_RPI730I3	Batch input - Data loading for 730
PC00_M15_RPI730I4	Batch Input for 730 2007
PC00_M15_RPI730I5	Batch Input for 730 2008
PC00_M15_RPI730I6	Batch Input for 730 2009
PC00_M15_RPICARI0	File loading for Batch Input
PC00_M15_RPIINAILI0	INAIL Batch Input
PC00_M15_RPISCAI0	Batch-Input
PC00_M15_RPISCAI0_PS	Scale jump calculation
PC00_M15_RPISTDI0	Batch Input Load IT
PC00_M15_RPISTDI2	Batch Input Load IT0001
PC00_M15_RPISTDI3	Batch Input Load IT0001
PC00_M15_RPUCMNI0	Update town tables
PC00_M15_RPUCMNI1	Maintain municipal exempt tax
PC00_M15_RPUINAIL	Report for INAIL SelfSettl Extract.
PC00_M15_RPULULI0	Single Book SB cluster creation
PC00_M15_RPUTMSI0	Display of Temse Italy objects
PC00_M15_SONSPERIOD	Area menu-subseq.activities Other
PC00_M15_STATUS_HDL	Status Handler viewer
PC00_M15_TABANF	Simulation of Table ANF
PC00_M15_TFR_CONV	Subtype 3 conversion for SP
PC00_M15_UECALC	Transaction for report RPCUEMI0
PC00_M15_UECHECK	Uniemens Customizing Check tool
PC00_M15_UECLDEL	Transaction for Report RPUDELI0
PC00_M15_UECLDELAZIE	Transaction for report RPCLSTI1
PC00_M15_UECLVIEW	Transaction for report RPCLSTI1
PC00_M15_UECONS_XML	Consolidates XML as sent in backgr.
PC00_M15_UEPOST	Transaction for report RPCUEDI0
PC00_M15_UEXML	Transaction for report RPCUEXI0
PC00_M15_UE_F_MATRIC	Uniemens empl. no. data forcing
PC00_M15_USER_INPUT	Transaction for report RPUDUII0
PC00_M16	Area menu-payroll for South Africa
PC00_M16_CALC	Payroll Driver South Africa
PC00_M16_CALC_SIMU	Simulation payroll accounting 16
PC00_M16_CDTA	Payroll-transfer-prelimProg. DME-16
PC00_M16_CDTB	Advance Payment Run - South Africa
PC00_M16_CEDT	Pay.accounting remun. statement - 16
PC00_M16_CFUS	Deduction Schedule Create 16
PC00_M16_CKTO	Payroll account 16
PC00_M16_CLOW0	Loans account statement
PC00_M16_CLSTR	Tools - payroll result - 16
PC00_M16_COID	COID/WCC COID 16
PC00_M16_CPEV	Process

SAP Transaction Codes – Volume One

PC00_M16_CTCA	Tax Certificates - Administration 16
PC00_M16_CTCS	Tax Certificates - Pre-Selection 16
PC00_M16_CUIA	UIF Downloads - Administration
PC00_M16_FFOT	Payroll transfer-first.DME 16
PC00_M16_HRF	Wage Statement with HR Forms
PC00_M16_HRF_PAYJNAL	Payroll Journal with HR Forms
PC00_M16_HRF_PAYRACC	Payroll Account with HR Forms
PC00_M16_JAHRLICHE	Area menu-annual subsequent activiti
PC00_M16_LEAV	Leave entitlement 16
PC00_M16_LOBL	Leave control list 16
PC00_M16_LVEW0	RPILVEW0
PC00_M16_OVTM	Payroll overtime 16
PC00_M16_PAP	Area menu-subsequent activities per
PC00_M16_RPCEDSW0	RPCEDSW0
PC00_M16_RPCLGVW0	Wagetype statement
PC00_M16_RPCLJNW0	Payroll Journal
PC00_M16_RPCMADW0	RPCMADW0
PC00_M16_RPCMLIW0	RPCMLIW0
PC00_M16_RPCPELW0	RPCPELW0
PC00_M16_RPCPFDW0	RPCPFDW0
PC00_M16_RPCRSCW0	Regional Service Council Report
PC00_M16_RPCTAXW2	RPCTAXW2
PC00_M16_RPCTCEW0	RPCTCEW0
PC00_M16_RPCTCNW0	?RPCTCNW0
PC00_M16_RPCUMPW1	South African Social Insurance
PC00_M16_RPIALRW0	RPIALRW0
PC00_M16_RPLEAVW0	RPLEAVW0
PC00_M16_RPLERAW0	Empl. Equity: Income Differentials
PC00_M16_RPLEWAW0	Empl. Equity: Workforce Analysis
PC00_M16_RPLOBLW0	RPLOBLW0
PC00_M16_RPOVTMW0	RPOVTMW0
PC00_M16_RPUCDVW0	RPUCDVW0
PC00_M16_RPUSPAW0	Salary Package Check Utility
PC00_M16_T5W2Q	Close the tax year
PC00_M16_UAUD	Payroll audit trail 16
PC00_M17	Main menu for Venezuelan payroll
PC00_M17_CADR0	Incident report document
PC00_M17_CALC	Payroll
PC00_M17_CALC_SIMU	Payroll
PC00_M17_CARC0	AR-C form: Deduction statement
PC00_M17_CCCR0	Collective contract report
PC00_M17_CDTA0	Data medium exchange
PC00_M17_CEDT	Payslip and severance payslip
PC00_M17_CIMP0	Generate ISRL data
PC00_M17_CINE0	Worker's Contributions to INCES
PC00_M17_CINR0	Quarterly company INCES contribution
PC00_M17_CISL0	Generate ISLR file
PC00_M17_CIVS0	Consistency of Work report for IVSS
PC00_M17_CKTO	Payroll account
PC00_M17_CLGA0	Wage type statement
PC00_M17_CLJN	Payroll journal
PC00_M17_CLOF0	Loans account statement
PC00_M17_CLOG0	Employer loans overview
PC00_M17_CLOH0	Determine present value of loans

PC00_M17_CLPH0	Generate LPH list
PC00_M17_CLSTR	Display payroll results
PC00_M17_CMIN0	Juvenile workers record (cls 265)
PC00_M17_COL00	Collective vacations report
PC00_M17_CPSR0	Profit share declaration document
PC00_M17_CRAI0	RA-I form: Annual tax statement
PC00_M17_CRNR0	Update listing
PC00_M17_CSIE0	IVSS report 14-02
PC00_M17_CSIE1	IVSS report 14-03
PC00_M17_CSSR0	File for SANE system
PC00_M17_CSVB0	Loan and interest account balance
PC00_M17_CTRA1	Apprentice report (cls 270)
PC00_M17_CWHR0	Hours worked report
PC00_M17_FAOV	Movements and payments to FAOV info
PC00_M17_FFOC	Check printout 17
PC00_M17_FFOT	Create DME 17
PC00_M17_FFOV	Notice of payment 17
PC00_M17_HRF	Wage Statement with HR Forms
PC00_M17_HRF_PAYJNAL	Wage Overview with HR Forms
PC00_M17_HRF_PAYRACC	Payroll account with HR Forms
PC00_M17_INT0	OC payroll accntng for interest pymt
PC00_M17_INTR	Table of interest rates
PC00_M17_JAHRLICHE	Subsequent activities - annual
PC00_M17_PAP	Subsequent activities - by period
PC00_M17_PDUNABHAGIG	Subsequent activities - independent
PC00_M17_RNEE_MINTRA	Archive generation for MINTRA
PC00_M17_SONSPERIOD	Subsequent activities - other prds
PC00_M17_TIUNA	Archives for TIUNA system
PC00_M17_TRM0	Termination Venezuela
PC00_M17_UCVM4	Currency changeover (VE)
PC00_M17_UPSA0	Profit share payments to retired EEs
PC00_M17_VAC00	Leave payment report
PC00_M17_VINT	Interests view
PC00_M19	Payroll for Portugal
PC00_M19_ADSE_PAY_PS	ADSE Payment Guide
PC00_M19_ADSE_TRT_PS	Upload ADSE Treatment Data
PC00_M19_CAID	Annual income declaration
PC00_M19_CALC	HR-PT: payroll driver
PC00_M19_CALC_SIMU	Payroll simulation 19
PC00_M19_CDTA	HR-PT: preprog. data medium exchange
PC00_M19_CEDT	HR-PT: Editing payroll results
PC00_M19_CGAMF_PS	CGA Magnetic File
PC00_M19_CIID	Individual income declaration
PC00_M19_CIPC	Search for unposted payroll results
PC00_M19_CIPC_PNP	Check Completeness of Posting
PC00_M19_CKTO	HR-PT: Payroll accounts
PC00_M19_CLGA	Wage type statement
PC00_M19_CLGV	Wage type distribution
PC00_M19_CLJN	HR-PT: Payroll Journal
PC00_M19_CLST	Payroll results for cluster RP
PC00_M19_CLSTR	pront cluster rp
PC00_M19_CMLI	Cash breakdown list (international)
PC00_M19_COVC	HR-PT: Overtime Communication
PC00_M19_COVR	HR-PT: Overtime Record

PC00_M19_CPRS	Personnel summary
PC00_M19_CRSP	HR-PT: Remuneration Sheet (Print)
PC00_M19_CSOC	Social balance
PC00_M19_CSSM	HR-PT: Employee's Remuneration Sheet
PC00_M19_CSSP	HR-PT: Employee's Remuneration Sheet
PC00_M19_FFO	Create DME
PC00_M19_HRF	Remuneration statement w/HR forms
PC00_M19_HRF_PAYJNAL	Wage Statement with HR Forms
PC00_M19_HRF_PAYRACC	Payroll with HR Forms
PC00_M19_ICHR	Create Chr.all.payments in IT0015
PC00_M19_IVAC	Create vac.all.payments in IT0015
PC00_M19_JAHRLICHE	Subs. activities - annual
PC00_M19_LFEE	HR-PT: List of membership contribs.
PC00_M19_PAP	subs. activities - per payroll perio
PC00_M19_PBS_BDAP	Public Sector Portugal - BDAP
PC00_M19_PDUNABHAGIG	Subsequent period-independent activi
PC00_M19_PROGRSS_PS	Automatic Progression
PC00_M19_REMGD_PS	Remuneration Guide
PC00_M19_RPCDTBP0	Programmed data medium exchange
PC00_M19_RPCECSP0	HR-PT: Earnings Complementary Survey
PC00_M19_RPCGSRP0	HR-PT: Earns.Surv.+Work Sched.Surv.
PC00_M19_RPCI97P0	HR-PT: IRS tax calculation
PC00_M19_RPCLCSP0	HR-PT: Quadriennal Labor Costs Surv.
PC00_M19_RPCMLIP9	HR-PT: Cash Breakdown List
PC00_M19_RPCS97P0	HR-PT: Social Security Calculation
PC00_M19_RPCSSRP0	HR-PT: Employee's Remuneration Sheet
PC00_M19_RPCTAXP0	Tax declarations
PC00_M19_RPCU1RP0	HR-PT: Update of min.values in T5P1R
PC00_M19_RPCUNRP0	Unique Report
PC00_M19_RPLESUP0	HR-PT: Leave Annual Summary
PC00_M19_RPLWKCP0	HR-PT: List of workers commissions
PC00_M19_RPPSTMP0	Master data sheet
PC00_M19_RPSSESP0	HR-PT: Structured Employment Survey
PC00_M19_RPTSSBP0	HR-PT: Strike Statistical Bulletin
PC00_M19_RPUIRSP0	HR-PT: Load table T5P1R from file
PC00_M19_RPUVTSP0	Show and download of TemSe/XML
PC00_M19_SENIO_PS	Calculate Seniority
PC00_M19_SIAAG_PS	SIADAP: Appraisals Generation Report
PC00_M19_SIABI_PS	SIADAP Batch Input Maintain Infotype
PC00_M19_SIAHG_PS	SIADAP: Bulk Homologation
PC00_M19_SIALO_PS	SIADAP Load columns and buttons data
PC00_M19_SOCBAL_PS	Social Balance
PC00_M19_SONSPERIOD	Subsequent activities in other perio
PC00_M19_UDIR	Restore payroll results directory
PC00_M19_UTPS_PS	HR-PT-PS: TemSe Display/Download Ut.
PC00_M19_UTSV	HR-PT: TemSe Display/Download Util.
PC00_M19_VAL_PS	Calculate Basic Pay
PC00_M20	Bereichsmenü-Abrechnung für Norwegen
PC00_M20_ALT_XII	ERC integration with Altinn
PC00_M20_CALC	Payroll Driver Norway
PC00_M20_CALC_SIMU	Simulation payroll accounting 20
PC00_M20_CDTA	Überweisung Vorprogramm DTA 20
PC00_M20_CDTB	Prel. DME program, separate payment
PC00_M20_CEDT	Entgeltnachweis 20

SAP Transaction Codes – Volume One

PC00_M20_CERC	Terminrapporten, rep. tax and employ
PC00_M20_CERC_02	Terminrapporten, rep. tax and employ
PC00_M20_CGAR	Norwegian garnishment report
PC00_M20_CIND	Import tax card 20
PC00_M20_CLSTR	Werkzeuge - abrechnungsergebnis - 20
PC00_M20_CRKV	Tax info. to TemSe 20
PC00_M20_CRMB	Reimbursable payments by absences
PC00_M20_CTRM0	Extract data for forskuddsskatt ER
PC00_M20_CTRM1	Terminrep -Tax and ER contrib.
PC00_M20_EMFV	Statistsic on Self-declared Ilness
PC00_M20_FONO_D	Payment Medium (NO) - BBS
PC00_M20_FONO_T	Payment Medium (NO) - DME
PC00_M20_HRF	Remuneration Statement with HR Forms
PC00_M20_JAHRLICHE	Bereichsmenü-Subs.activities - Annua
PC00_M20_LAAM	AA-register - electronic version
PC00_M20_LEAT	Arbeidstakerreg. 20
PC00_M20_LINF	Employee master data overview
PC00_M20_LINS	Innsynsrapport 20
PC00_M20_LLON	Loan and Deposit Notification
PC00_M20_LSDI	View self-declared sicknesses
PC00_M20_LTEM	2-month rpt-Transfer to file 20
PC00_M20_LTO_5VT0	Status tax reporting
PC00_M20_LTO_CATP	Prepare reporting
PC00_M20_LTO_LATB	Kakseskatt
PC00_M20_LTO_LATF	Download tax reporting file
PC00_M20_LTO_LATK	Overview of LTO customization
PC00_M20_LTO_LATS	Print tax form
PC00_M20_OVTM	Overtime Reporting
PC00_M20_PAP	Bereichsmenü-Subs.activities - Per p
PC00_M20_PBS_510	Similar entries in T510
PC00_M20_PBS_INTE	Transfer jobcode relations from 0509
PC00_M20_PBS_SPK	Main SPK Report
PC00_M20_PBS_SPK_DEL	SPK Delete Cluster Report
PC00_M20_PBS_SPK_DIS	SPK Display Report
PC00_M20_PBS_SPK_DL	SPK Download Report
PC00_M20_PBS_SST	Main SST Report
PC00_M20_PBS_STL	Change in Job linked to a position
PC00_M20_PBS_UNI	Pay difference due to Trade Unions
PC00_M20_RMB_DEL	Report to delete cluster
PC00_M20_RMB_DIS	Report to display cluster
PC00_M20_RMB_MAIN	Main report for Reimbursement
PC00_M20_RMB_PRINT	Follow-Up report for Reimbursement
PC00_M20_RPCTAXV0	Norwegian tax table overview
PC00_M20_RPDABSV0	RPDABSV0
PC00_M20_SONSPERIOD	Bereichsmenü-Subs.activities - Other
PC00_M20_SSSB	Quarterly stats SSB statistics 20
PC00_M20_TFER	Check list vacation 20
PC00_M20_TFRV	Quarterly report "Fraværsrapport" 20
PC00_M20_UKOM	Load Municipal Codes 20
PC00_M20_UPST	Load Postal Codes 20
PC00_M20_URMB	Import Reimbursement Claim File List
PC00_M20_UTRY	Load "Trygdekontor" 20
PC00_M20_UYRK	Upload of yrkeskoder
PC00_M20_XIA_5VXI	Status of ERC data sent to Altinn

PC00_M22   Payroll accounting for Japan
PC00_M22_CACC   Display Infotype Access Log Japan
PC00_M22_CALC_ESTDEC   Start estimation of Dec. payroll
PC00_M22_CALC_ESTDES   Simulate estimation of Dec. payroll
PC00_M22_CALC_MNTH   Start monthly payroll
PC00_M22_CALC_NPSY   Start NP Shoyo payroll
PC00_M22_CALC_NPSY_S   Simulate NP Shoyo payroll
PC00_M22_CALC_PRYEA   Start provisional Y.E.A. w/ Shoyo
PC00_M22_CALC_PRYEAS   Simulate provisional Y.E.A. w/ Shoyo
PC00_M22_CALC_REPYEA   Start Repeat Y.E.A.
PC00_M22_CALC_RETALS   Simulate ret. allowance payroll
PC00_M22_CALC_RETALW   Start ret. allowance payroll
PC00_M22_CALC_RETLC   Start ret. liquid. current period
PC00_M22_CALC_RETLCS   Simulate ret. liquid. current period
PC00_M22_CALC_RETLN   Start ret. liquid. next period
PC00_M22_CALC_RETLNS   Simulate ret. liquid. next period
PC00_M22_CALC_REYEA   Start Y.E.A. recalculation
PC00_M22_CALC_REYEAS   Simulate Y.E.A. recalculation
PC00_M22_CALC_RPYEAS   Simulate Repeat Y.E.A.
PC00_M22_CALC_SIMU   Simulate monthly payroll
PC00_M22_CALC_SY   Start Shoyo payroll
PC00_M22_CALC_SY_SIM   Simulate Shoyo payroll
PC00_M22_CALC_YEA   Start Y.E.A. with monthly payroll
PC00_M22_CALC_YEACDS   Simulate Y.E.A. CoD
PC00_M22_CALC_YEACOD   Start Y.E.A. Correction of Dependent
PC00_M22_CALC_YEACOR   Start Y.E.A. Correction
PC00_M22_CALC_YEACRS   Simulate Y.E.A. Correction
PC00_M22_CALC_YEA_S   Simulate Y.E.A. with monthly payroll
PC00_M22_CBHI_NPSY   HI premium payt NP Shoyo (Obsolete)
PC00_M22_CBHI_SY   HI premium payt Shoyo (Obsolete)
PC00_M22_CDEC   Check estimated amount of Dec. pay.
PC00_M22_CDLG   Delete Access/Update Log Japan
PC00_M22_CDTA_MNTH   Prepare DME for monthly payroll
PC00_M22_CDTA_NPSY   Prepare DME for NP Shoyo
PC00_M22_CDTA_RETALW   Prepare DME for ret. allowance
PC00_M22_CDTA_RETLIQ   Prepare DME for ret. liquidation
PC00_M22_CDTA_SY   Prepare DME for Shoyo
PC00_M22_CDTA_YEA   Prepare DME for monthly with Y.E.A.
PC00_M22_CEAD_CDC   Withholding tax statement (data)
PC00_M22_CEAD_PS   Withholding tax statement (printed)
PC00_M22_CEAD_YEA   Withholding tax statement for retire
PC00_M22_CECK   Check Y.E.A. results
PC00_M22_CEDT   Remuneration statement
PC00_M22_CEDT_MNTH   Remun. state. for monthly payroll
PC00_M22_CEDT_NPSY   Remun. state. for NP Shoyo payroll
PC00_M22_CEDT_RETALW   Remun. state. for ret. allowance
PC00_M22_CEDT_RETLIQ   Remun. state. for ret. liquidation
PC00_M22_CEDT_SY   Remun. state. for Shoyo payroll
PC00_M22_CEDT_YEA   Remun. state. for Monthly w/ Y.E.A.
PC00_M22_CEIA   EI Acquisition of Qualification Form
PC00_M22_CEIB   Application Form for Continuous Empl
PC00_M22_CEIC   Certification and Application for Co
PC00_M22_CEIL   EI Loss of Qualification Form
PC00_M22_CELV   Report Certification of Leaving

SAP Transaction Codes – Volume One

PC00_M22_CEWC	Wage Certificate At The Age Of 60
PC00_M22_CEWG	Wage ledger
PC00_M22_CHAR_CHECK	Master/Cust table charcode checker
PC00_M22_CHUB	Shoyo payment form data file (HU)
PC00_M22_CHUG	GEPPEN form data file (HU)
PC00_M22_CHUS	SANTEI form data file (HU)
PC00_M22_CIDP	Life/accident ins. deduc. monthly
PC00_M22_CIDS	Life/accident ins. deduc. Shoyo
PC00_M22_CKTO	Payroll account
PC00_M22_CLIA	Fixed labor insurance fee
PC00_M22_CLJN	Payroll Journal
PC00_M22_CLJN_NPSY	Payroll journal for NP Shoyo
PC00_M22_CLJN_PPP	Payroll journal for monthly payroll
PC00_M22_CLJN_SY	Payroll journal for Shoyo
PC00_M22_CLJN_YEA	Payroll journal for monthly w/ Y.E.A
PC00_M22_CLOG	Overview of Company Loans(Japan)
PC00_M22_CLSTGJ	Santei/Geppen evaluation results
PC00_M22_CLSTR	Payroll results
PC00_M22_CLSTY	Year End Adjustement results
PC00_M22_CNRP	Non-resident payment report
PC00_M22_CPFB	Shoyo payment form data file (PF)
PC00_M22_CPFG	GEPPEN form data file (PF)
PC00_M22_CPFS	SANTEI form data file (PF)
PC00_M22_CPRT	Payment report
PC00_M22_CRES	Print Residence Tax Change
PC00_M22_CRTS	Withholding tax state. ret. allow.
PC00_M22_CRTX	Create resident tax payment datafile
PC00_M22_CSHA	Summary list of Shoyo payment form
PC00_M22_CSHB	Shoyo payment form data file (SI)
PC00_M22_CSHG	GEPPEN form data file (SI)
PC00_M22_CSHS	SANTEI form data file (SI)
PC00_M22_CSIB	Santei adjustment
PC00_M22_CSIC	Santei form
PC00_M22_CSIC_NT	Santei form August
PC00_M22_CSIC_TKO10	Santei form for October (Tokyo)
PC00_M22_CSIC_TKO8	Santei form for August (Tokyo)
PC00_M22_CSIC_TKO9	Santei form for September (Tokyo)
PC00_M22_CSID	Santei data
PC00_M22_CSIE	Geppen form
PC00_M22_CSIE_NT	Geppen form for August
PC00_M22_CSIE_NT_OT	Geppen form
PC00_M22_CSIE_TKO10	Geppen form for October (Tokyo)
PC00_M22_CSIE_TKO8	Geppen form for August (Tokyo)
PC00_M22_CSIE_TKO9	Geppen form for September (Tokyo)
PC00_M22_CSIE_TKOOT	Geppen form (Tokyo)
PC00_M22_CSIF	Geppen data
PC00_M22_CSIG	Soukatsu-hyou
PC00_M22_CSIG_IKATU	Soukatsu-hyou for August (Ikkatsu)
PC00_M22_CSIG_NT	Soukatsu-hyou for August
PC00_M22_CSIG_TKO	Soukatsu-hyou for August (Tokyo)
PC00_M22_CSIH	Create B/I file to update std. comp.
PC00_M22_CSIIJ0	Start Santei Geppen check list
PC00_M22_CSIKJ0	Start Cluster GJ modification list
PC00_M22_CSIL	Certification of Loss of SI Qualifi.

PC00_M22_CSIM	SI data matching with SI office data
PC00_M22_CSIP	Check/Update Emp. with Gep. Prntl Lv
PC00_M22_CSIS	Start Santei/Geppen evaluation
PC00_M22_CSIS_SIMU	Simulate Santei/Geppen evaluation
PC00_M22_CSIT	Evaluate Soushitsu-sya
PC00_M22_CUEM	Employement insurance applic. data
PC00_M22_CUPD	Display Infotype Update Log Japan
PC00_M22_CWTS	Summary of Withholding Tax Statement
PC00_M22_FFOT	Create payment medium - Domestic DME
PC00_M22_HRF	Wage Statement with HR Forms
PC00_M22_HRF_PAYJNAL	Wage Statement with HR Forms
PC00_M22_HRF_PAYRACC	Lohnkonto with HR Forms
PC00_M22_HRF_SKPLEDG	Wage Statement with HR Forms
PC00_M22_JAHRLICHE	Subsequent activities - annual
PC00_M22_LBENPAY	Payment order for benefits
PC00_M22_LDQA	Address change form
PC00_M22_LDQL1	Lost status form
PC00_M22_LDQO	Acquisition form
PC00_M22_LDTD	EE's Income Tax & Family Depend. Tax
PC00_M22_LFDA	Address change data file
PC00_M22_LFDL	Lost status data file
PC00_M22_LFDO	Acquisition data file
PC00_M22_LHUL	Loss of qual. form data file (HU)
PC00_M22_LHUO	Acq. of qual. form data file (HU)
PC00_M22_LLID	Run LI and Spouse Tax Declaration
PC00_M22_LLID3	Run LI and Spouse Tax Declaration
PC00_M22_LPFL	Loss of qual. form data file (PF)
PC00_M22_LPFO	Acq. of qual. form data file (PF)
PC00_M22_LRAC	Determination of ret. allow. amount
PC00_M22_LRLG	Retirement allowance amount calc.log
PC00_M22_LSHA	Addr. change form data file (SI)
PC00_M22_LSHL	Loss of qual. form data file (SI)
PC00_M22_LSHO	Acq. of qual. form data file (SI)
PC00_M22_LSIP	Social Insurance Premium Payment
PC00_M22_PAP	Subsequent activities - per payroll
PC00_M22_PDUNABHAGIG	Subsequent activities - period indep
PC00_M22_RETIRE	Retirement accounting for Japan
PC00_M22_SONSPDSI	Subsequent activities - other period
PC00_M22_SONSPERIOD	Subsequent activities - other period
PC00_M22_SYOYO	Shoyo accounting for Japan
PC00_M22_U510J0	Pay Scale Re-creation (Base-up)
PC00_M22_U510J1	Delimit IT0008 after P/S Re-creation
PC00_M22_UDELGJ	Refresh S/G evaluation results
PC00_M22_UNIIJ	Nursing Insurance Status Check
PC00_M22_USAC	Determination of Shoyo amount
PC00_M22_UTRFJ0	Automatic Pay Increase (P/S level)
PC00_M22_UTRFJ1	Pay Increase due to promotion
PC00_M22_UTRFJ2	Update P/S based on appraisal data
PC00_M22_UTRFJ3	Update P/S based on promotion ind.
PC00_M22_UTSV	Download HR TemSe object
PC00_M22_UUSC	Refresh EE's monthly std. comp. data
PC00_M22_YRENDADJ	Year-End Adjustment for Japan
PC00_M23	Bereichsmenü-Abrechnung für Schweden
PC00_M23_CALC_CE	Payroll calculation 23 CE

PC00_M23_CALC_SIMU	Simulation payroll accounting 23
PC00_M23_CALC_SIM_CE	Simulation payroll accounting 23 CE
PC00_M23_CEDT_CE	Remuneration Statement 23
PC00_M23_CKPAS0_CE	KPA Pension - Prepare Data
PC00_M23_CKU0	Annual tax statement
PC00_M23_CKU1	Annual tax statement
PC00_M23_CKU1S0_CE	Annual Tax Statement (SE-CE)
PC00_M23_CLPCS0_CE	Absence Overview and Entry Check
PC00_M23_CNORS0_CE	Nordea Bank Transfers
PC00_M23_CSPMS0_CE	SPV Monthly Pension (PA-03) - Prepar
PC00_M23_CSPP	Conversion Report for Alecta
PC00_M23_CSPYS0_CE	SPV Yearly Pension (PA-91) - Prepare
PC00_M23_CSTA	employer´s contrib. and tax cumulate
PC00_M23_CSUSS0_CE	SUS Bank Transfers
PC00_M23_CTAXS0_CE	Calculation of ER Contribution and D
PC00_M23_CVAC	Vacation and Compensation debt
PC00_M23_CVACS0_CE	Vacation and Compensation Debt
PC00_M23_HRF	Lohnkonto with HR Forms
PC00_M23_IABS	Correct absence
PC00_M23_ICS0	Sickness Statistic for Annual Report
PC00_M23_IQTRS0_CE	Transfer to New Assignment
PC00_M23_ISIF	Batch input yearly update from SIF
PC00_M23_ITAX	Batch input for taxes infotype 0273
PC00_M23_ITAXS0_CE	Batch Input for Tax Information in I
PC00_M23_JAHRLICHE	Bereichsmenü-Jährliche Folgeaktivitä
PC00_M23_LABS	Absence Adjustments
PC00_M23_LAMF	Report and file to AMF
PC00_M23_LGAX	Garnishment exceptions report.
PC00_M23_LGAXS0_CE	Garnishment
PC00_M23_LINS	Personal Data Act
PC00_M23_LKPAS0_CE	KPA Pension - Create File
PC00_M23_LLABS0_CE	Labor Protection
PC00_M23_LLAS	LAS Report
PC00_M23_LMEF	Deducted fees on a file to Metall
PC00_M23_LMER	Deducted fees local Metall union
PC00_M23_LRQT	Request tax info from CSR
PC00_M23_LRQTS0_CE	Request Tax Information from CSR
PC00_M23_LSIF	Deducted fees on a file to SIF
PC00_M23_LSPMS0_CE	SPV Monthly Pension (PA-03) - Create
PC00_M23_LSPP	SPP monthly insurance events
PC00_M23_LSPYS0_CE	SPV Yearly Pension (PA-91) - Create
PC00_M23_LTCES0_CE	Termination Certificate
PC00_M23_LUSM	SIF and Metall union fees
PC00_M23_LWTR	Wage Type Report
PC00_M23_LWTRS0_CE	Debts and Negative Bases
PC00_M23_MTRN	Report of Match Routine for Swedish
PC00_M23_PAP	Bereichsmenü-Folgeaktivitäten pro Ab
PC00_M23_PDUNABHAGIG	Bereichsmenü-Periodenunabhängige Fol
PC00_M23_REHB	Rehabilitation Report for Sweden
PC00_M23_SADT	Sickness Admin Tool report (SE)
PC00_M23_SAMKLK_CE	Economic Cycle Statistics - Municipa
PC00_M23_SAMKLL_CE	Economic Cycle Statistics - County C
PC00_M23_SAMKLS_CE	Economic Cycle Statistics - State Of
PC00_M23_SAMKSO_CE	Short Period Statistics AM KSO

PC00_M23_SAMSLK_CE	Salary Structure Statistics - Munici
PC00_M23_SAMSLL_CE	Salary Structure Statistics - County
PC00_M23_SDWL	Transfer statistics file from TemSe
PC00_M23_SINS	Report of Sick people to the Insuran
PC00_M23_SINSS0_CE	Report of Employee Sickness to the S
PC00_M23_SONSPERIOD	Bereichsmenü-Folgeaktivitäten sonsti
PC00_M23_SRFV	RFV sickness pay statistics
PC00_M23_SRFVS0_CE	Statistics on Sick Pay for SCB
PC00_M23_SSBK	SCB - Economic Cycle Statistics
PC00_M23_SSBM	SCB salary structure statistics
PC00_M23_SSBS	Short period employement statistics
PC00_M23_SSFD	SAF - Membership/partownership
PC00_M23_SSFM	SAF employee statistics file
PC00_M23_SSFT	SAF time usage statistics file
PC00_M23_SSICS0_CE	Sickness Statistics for Annual Repor
PC00_M23_T5SPP	HR-SE:Information reported to Alecta
PC00_M23_T5SVT	Manual update of VACS table T5SVT
PC00_M23_TOVT	Overtime report
PC00_M23_TOVTS0_CE	Overtime
PC00_M23_TSTAS0_CE	Time Statistics
PC00_M23_U512S0_CE	Wage-Type-Related Customizing for HC
PC00_M23_UABSS0_CE	Absence-Related Customizing for HCM
PC00_M25_AWS	Singapore Specific AWS
PC00_M25_CALC	Start Payroll
PC00_M25_CALC_SIMU	Simulate Payroll
PC00_M25_CANN	Display Annual Payroll Results
PC00_M25_CAWS	Generate Annual Wage Supplement
PC00_M25_CCPF	Run Monthly Report for CPF
PC00_M25_CCPF_PS	Run PS Monthly Report for CPF
PC00_M25_CCPY	Run Year-End Report for CPF
PC00_M25_CDTA	Prepare Bank Transfer
PC00_M25_CDTB	BT for extra payment 25
PC00_M25_CEDT	Print Remuneration Statement
PC00_M25_CFAP	Generate Festival Advance Payment
PC00_M25_CGML	Run GML Report
PC00_M25_CKTO	Display Payroll Account
PC00_M25_CLJN	Display Payroll Journal
PC00_M25_CLMS	Run Labour Survey Query
PC00_M25_CLSTR	Display Payroll Results
PC00_M25_CMIB	Run CPF Survey on Occupational Wages
PC00_M25_CNRCL	Run Employer Claim Report for NRS
PC00_M25_CNRS	Run NRS Report for MINDEF
PC00_M25_CRET	Retro Detection Utility 25
PC00_M25_CT21	Run Income Tax Report for IR21
PC00_M25_CT8A	Run Income Tax Report for IR8A
PC00_M25_CT8S	Run Income Tax Report for IR8S
PC00_M25_CVCOP	Run Vol. CPF Overpaid Report
PC00_M25_DEL8A	Deletion utility for IR8A cluster
PC00_M25_FAP	Bereichsmenü-Außerperiodisch SYOYO
PC00_M25_FFOD	Create DME (Print Payment advice)
PC00_M25_FFOT	Perform Bank Transfer
PC00_M25_HRF	Remuneration Statement with HR Forms
PC00_M25_HRF_PAYJNAL	Payroll Journal with HR Forms
PC00_M25_HRF_PAYRACC	Payroll Account with HR Forms

PC00_M25_JAHRLICHE	Area menu-annual subsequent activity
PC00_M25_MID	Bereichsmenü-Außerperiodisch SYOYO
PC00_M25_MIDP	Start Mid-Month Payroll
PC00_M25_NCT8A	Run new Income Tax Report for IR8A
PC00_M25_NNRS	Run new NRS Report for MINDEF
PC00_M25_ODS	Bereichsmenü-Außerperiodisch SYOYO
PC00_M25_PAP	Area menu-subs. activities per payr.
PC00_M25_PBS_BN	Bonus Computation SG Public Sector
PC00_M25_PBS_CCV1	CV
PC00_M25_PBS_CLVE	Leave Scheme
PC00_M25_PBS_CMED	Monthly Medisave Contribution Report
PC00_M25_PBS_CSA1	Generate PS Salary Structure
PC00_M25_PBS_CSA2	Adjustment Across Civil Service
PC00_M25_PBS_CSA3	NPVP Adjustment Across Civil Service
PC00_M25_PBS_CSA4	Planning Tool for Adjustment
PC00_M25_PBS_CSA5	NPVP Adj for Directly Valuated WT
PC00_M25_PBS_GNP	Transaction code for GNP
PC00_M25_PBS_PENS	Transaction code for Pension Program
PC00_M25_PDUNABHAGIG	Area menu - period-indep. subs. act.
PC00_M25_PS_CMED_PE	Monthly PS Medisave Contr Report
PC00_M25_RPCALCR0	RPCALCR0
PC00_M25_RPCMLIR0	H99CMLI0
PC00_M25_RPU006R0	RPU006R0
PC00_M25_RPUCONR0	RPUCONR0
PC00_M25_SDFR	Print Attendee List for SDF
PC00_M25_SONSPERIOD	Area menu-subseq. activities other
PC00_M25_SRS1	SRS Report for Singapore
PC00_M26	Payroll for Thailand
PC00_M26_CALC	Start Payroll
PC00_M26_CALC_SIMU	Simulate Payroll
PC00_M26_CAWS	Generate Annual Wage Supplement
PC00_M26_CDTB	Pay in Advance
PC00_M26_CDTC	Prepare Bank Transfer
PC00_M26_CEDT	Print Remuneration Statement
PC00_M26_CKTO	Display Payroll Account
PC00_M26_CLJN	Display Payroll Journal
PC00_M26_CLSTR	Display Payroll Results
PC00_M26_CREATE_SEQN	Create Seq. no. for Thai employee
PC00_M26_CSSD1	Print Details of Social Sec. Form
PC00_M26_CSSS1	Print Summary of Social Sec. Form
PC00_M26_CTX1A	Print Income Tax Form 1A
PC00_M26_CTX5B	Print Income Tax Form 50 BIS
PC00_M26_CTX91	Reconcile Income Tax for Form PIT91
PC00_M26_CTXF1	Run Tax Report for Income Tax Form 1
PC00_M26_FFOM	Perform Bank Transfer
PC00_M26_HRF	Remuneration Statement for HR Forms
PC00_M26_HRF_PAYJNAL	Wage Statement with HR Forms
PC00_M26_HRF_PAYRACC	Payroll Account with HR Forms
PC00_M26_JAHRLICHE	Subsequent activities TH - annual
PC00_M26_LVA0	Create Leave Entitlement
PC00_M26_PAP	subs.activities - per payroll period
PC00_M26_PDUNABHAGIG	Subs. activities TH - period-indepen
PC00_M26_SONSPERIOD	Subsequent activities TH - other per
PC00_M27	Payroll Accounting for Hong Kong

PC00_M27_CALC	Payroll Driver Hong Kong
PC00_M27_CALC_SIMU	Simulate Payroll
PC00_M27_CDTB	Prepare Bank Transfer /Extra Payment
PC00_M27_CDTC	Prepare Bank Transfer
PC00_M27_CEDT	Print Remuneration Statement
PC00_M27_CKJN	Display Payroll Journal
PC00_M27_CKTO	Display Payroll Account
PC00_M27_CLSTR	Display Payroll Result
PC00_M27_CPFB	MPF contr. medium report for Bermuda
PC00_M27_CPFC	MPF contri. medium report for HSBC
PC00_M27_CREC0	Perform Payroll Results Check
PC00_M27_CTXB	Run Employee Tax Report for IR56
PC00_M27_CTXE	Print Form IR56E
PC00_M27_CTXF	Print Form IR56F
PC00_M27_CTXG	Print Form IR56G
PC00_M27_EOY	Prepare End of Year Payment
PC00_M27_FFOT	Perform Bank Transfer
PC00_M27_HHKCLGA0	Wage Type Statement(Read Cluster HK)
PC00_M27_HHKCLST1	Payroll Results for Cluster HZ
PC00_M27_HHKCSKLE	Batch Input: Statutory Sick Leave
PC00_M27_HRF	Remuneration Statement with HR Forms
PC00_M27_HRF_PAYJNAL	Payroll Journal with HR Forms
PC00_M27_HRF_PAYRACC	Payroll Accounts with HR Forms
PC00_M27_JAHRLICHE	Subsequent activities - Annual
PC00_M27_PAP	Subsequent activities per payroll pe
PC00_M27_PDUNABHAGIG	Subsequent activities - Period-indep
PC00_M27_SONSPERIOD	Subsequent activities - Other period
PC00_M27_SSL	Create Statutory Sickness Leave
PC00_M27_UREC0	Prepare Payroll Results Check
PC00_M27_UREC5	Display Payroll Results Check
PC00_M28_CALC	Payroll (China)
PC00_M28_CALC_SIMU	Payroll simulation (China)
PC00_M28_CAWS	Process Year End Bonus
PC00_M28_CCBD	PHF/SI contribution base declaration
PC00_M28_CCBR	PHF/SI contribution base upload
PC00_M28_CDTA	Bank transfer pre.program DME China
PC00_M28_CEDT	Remuneration statement China
PC00_M28_CKTO	Payroll account - China
PC00_M28_CLJN	Payroll journal China
PC00_M28_CLSTR	Payroll result China
PC00_M28_CPHF	Public housing fund
PC00_M28_CSI	Social insurance report
PC00_M28_CTAX	Tax report
PC00_M28_CTXD	Year End IITax Declaration
PC00_M28_CTXE	Year End IITax Declaration - CN00
PC00_M28_HRF	Wage Statement with HR Forms
PC00_M28_HRF_PAYJNAL	Payroll Journal with HR Forms
PC00_M28_HRF_PAYRACC	Payroll Accounts with HR Forms
PC00_M28_JAHRLICHE	Subsequent activities - Annual
PC00_M28_LCT	Labor Contract Termination Workbench
PC00_M28_LCT_SE	Labor Contract Termination Workbench
PC00_M28_PAP	Area menu - Subsequent activities pe
PC00_M28_PDUNABHAGIG	Subsequent activities - Period-indep
PC00_M28_SONSPERIOD	Subsequent activities - Other period

PC00_M28_STCHK	Pension Status Check & Update
PC00_M28_TERM	Termination Statement (China)
PC00_M29	Area menu-Payroll acctg Argentina
PC00_M29_CALC	Payroll
PC00_M29_CALC_SIMU	Simulation payroll accounting 29
PC00_M29_CART	Third ART statement 29
PC00_M29_CCEN	ANSeS census 29
PC00_M29_CDGI0	SIJP-Interface 29
PC00_M29_CDGI1	RG 4110 interface 29
PC00_M29_CDGI2	Income Tax
PC00_M29_CDTA	Payroll-transfer to prel.prog.DME-29
PC00_M29_CDTB	Payment advances Pre-program DME 29
PC00_M29_CEDT	Payroll remunerations statement - 29
PC00_M29_CF649	Form 649 29
PC00_M29_CIMPF	Final settlement 29
PC00_M29_CKTO	Payroll account 29
PC00_M29_CLJN	Payroll journal 29
PC00_M29_CLPD	Settlement monetary payments
PC00_M29_CLSTR	Tools - payroll result - 29
PC00_M29_CLSTRA2	Display earn. final settl. results
PC00_M29_CSERV	Certification of Service
PC00_M29_CTER0	Termination
PC00_M29_CVAC0	Vacation leave 29
PC00_M29_FFOC	Intl payment methods - Cheque
PC00_M29_FFOT	Create DME 29
PC00_M29_FFOV	Intl payment method - notification
PC00_M29_HRF	Remuneration statement with HR Forms
PC00_M29_HRF_PAYJNAL	Monthly remun. statement w/HR Forms
PC00_M29_HRF_PAYRACC	Payroll account with HR Forms
PC00_M29_JAHRLICHE	Area menu-Subseq. activities Annual
PC00_M29_LIBR	Legal Payroll Payments Book 29
PC00_M29_MONATLICHE	Area menu-Subseq. activities Monthly
PC00_M29_MSIM	My Simplification
PC00_M29_MSTMS	My Simplification - Display TemSe
PC00_M29_NVAC	Leave notification
PC00_M29_OS00	Welfare Fund 29
PC00_M29_PAP	Area menu-Subs. act. Per payr. per.
PC00_M29_PDUNABHAGIG	Area menu-Subs. act. Period-indep.
PC00_M29_SI00	Unions 29
PC00_M29_SIG0	Income Tax Return simulation
PC00_M29_SONSPERIOD	Area menu-Subs. act. Other periods
PC00_M29_SSDD	Social insurance payment data
PC00_M29_SSDD_ADMIN	Social insurance payment data
PC00_M29_TAX0	Income Tax Return list
PC00_M29_TRM0	Termination driver
PC00_M29_UTMS	TemSe display 29
PC00_M32	Area menu-Payroll Mexico
PC00_M32_CAFL0	Integrated daily wage notification
PC00_M32_CAFL0_CE	Integrated daily wage notification
PC00_M32_CAGU0	Annual bonus
PC00_M32_CAGU0_CE	Annual bonus
PC00_M32_CAJD0	Adjustment of annual deferred tax
PC00_M32_CAJD0_CE	Adjustment of annual deferred tax
PC00_M32_CALC	Payroll - simulation - 32

PC00_M32_CALC_SIMU	Simulation payroll accounting 32
PC00_M32_CCRE0	Credit on wage paid in cash
PC00_M32_CCRE0_CE	Credit on wage paid in cash
PC00_M32_CCSD0	Integrated daily wage calculation
PC00_M32_CDAN0	Annual Declaration
PC00_M32_CDEM0	Multiple Electronic Documents
PC00_M32_CDEM0_CE	Multiple Electronic Documents
PC00_M32_CDIE0	HR-MX: State Tax detail
PC00_M32_CDIE0_CE	HR-MX: State Tax detail
PC00_M32_CDNT0	Delete IT 372 notification
PC00_M32_CDNT0_CE	Delete IT 372 notification
PC00_M32_CDSS0	Wages and salaries declaration
PC00_M32_CDTA	Payroll - Transf.to Pre-prog. DME-32
PC00_M32_CEDT	Payroll remuneration statement - 32
PC00_M32_CEDT_CE	Remuneration statement: Mexico
PC00_M32_CETS0	IDW limit surplus
PC00_M32_CETS0_CE	IDW limit surplus
PC00_M32_CFIC0	Theor. tax. income frm loans
PC00_M32_CFIC0_CE	Theor. tax. income frm loans
PC00_M32_CFIN0	Termination details
PC00_M32_CFNC0	FONACOT credit balances
PC00_M32_CGRB	Prepare evaluation
PC00_M32_CGRB_CE	Prepare evaluation
PC00_M32_CGRH	Garnishments 32
PC00_M32_CGRH_CE	Garnishments 32
PC00_M32_CGRI0	Deducted tax
PC00_M32_CGRI0_CE	Deducted tax
PC00_M32_CIFA0	Interest distribution Savings Fund
PC00_M32_CIFA0_CE	Interest distribution Savings Fund
PC00_M32_CINF0	FONACOT/INFONAVIT discounts made
PC00_M32_CINO0	State tax
PC00_M32_CINO0_CE	State tax
PC00_M32_CISR0	Tax formulas
PC00_M32_CISR0_CE	Tax formulae
PC00_M32_CKTO	Payroll account 32
PC00_M32_CLFA0	Savings fund settlement
PC00_M32_CLFA0_CE	Savings fund settlement
PC00_M32_CLJN	Payroll journal 32
PC00_M32_CLJN_CE	Payroll journal 32
PC00_M32_CLSTR	Tools - payroll result - 32
PC00_M32_CMCI0	Tax Methods Comparative
PC00_M32_CMCI0_CE	Tax Methods Comparative
PC00_M32_CRET0	Tax deduction statements
PC00_M32_CRET0_CE	Tax deduction statements
PC00_M32_CRFC0	RFC Notification
PC00_M32_CRFC0_CE	RFC Notification
PC00_M32_CRNS0	Wage range remuneration
PC00_M32_CRUT0	Profit sharing
PC00_M32_CRUT0_CE	Profit sharing
PC00_M32_CSDI0	Wage integration
PC00_M32_CSDI0_CE	Wage integration
PC00_M32_CSFA0	Savings Fund balances
PC00_M32_CSFA0_CE	Savings Fund balances
PC00_M32_CSSA0	HR-MX: Social Insurance Audits

PC00_M32_CSSA0_CE	HR-MX: Social Insurance Audits
PC00_M32_CSSI	IMSS contrib. report 32
PC00_M32_CSSI0	IMSS-INFONAVIT contributions
PC00_M32_CSSI0_CE	IMSS-INFONAVIT contributions
PC00_M32_CSSI_CE	IMSS contrib. report 32
PC00_M32_CSSS	IMSS related earnings 32
PC00_M32_CSSS_CE	IMSS related earnings 32
PC00_M32_CVAL0	Food vouchers magnetic format
PC00_M32_CVAL0_CE	Food vouchers magnetic format
PC00_M32_FFOC	Print check
PC00_M32_FFOT	Create DME
PC00_M32_FFOV	Payment notification
PC00_M32_FVAL0	Food voucher format
PC00_M32_FVAL0_CE	Food voucher format
PC00_M32_HRF	Salary statement with HR Forms
PC00_M32_HRF_PAYJNAL	Monthly Wage Statement with HR Forms
PC00_M32_HRF_PAYRACC	Payroll account with HR Forms
PC00_M32_JAHRLICHE	Area menu-Subseq. activities Annual
PC00_M32_MONATLICHE	Area menu-Subseq. activities Annual
PC00_M32_PAP	Area menu-Subs. act. Per payr. per.
PC00_M32_PBS_CFOV	FOVISSSTE report
PC00_M32_PBS_CFOV_CE	FOVISSSTE report
PC00_M32_PBS_CIPD	Payroll information report
PC00_M32_PBS_CREG	Report for Employee Category
PC00_M32_PBS_CSAR	SAR report
PC00_M32_PBS_CSAR_CE	SAR report
PC00_M32_PBS_CSPP	SAR Report per Payroll Period
PC00_M32_PBS_CSPP_CE	SAR report per payroll period
PC00_M32_PBS_UACT	Generation of Affiliation Trnsctions
PC00_M32_PBS_UACT_CE	Generation of Affiliation Trans.
PC00_M32_PBS_UIST	Loading of ISSSTE Discount Orders
PC00_M32_PBS_UIST_CE	Loading of ISSSTE Discount Orders
PC00_M32_PBS_USAR	Load for contribution files
PC00_M32_PBS_USAR_CE	Load for contribution files
PC00_M32_PBS_UUAH	Initial load Affiliation Trnsactions
PC00_M32_PDUNABHAGIG	Area menu-Subs. act. Period-indep.
PC00_M32_SONSPERIOD	Area menu-Subs. act. Other periods
PC00_M32_TRM0	Termination driver
PC00_M32_TRM0_CE	Termination driver
PC00_M32_TRTR0	Occupational hazard
PC00_M32_TRTR0_CE	Occupational hazard
PC00_M32_TVAC0	Vacation quota settlement
PC00_M32_TVAC0_CE	Vacation quota settlement
PC00_M32_UTRB_CE	Payroll status update: Mexico
PC00_M33_CALC	Start payroll Russia
PC00_M33_CALCM_SIM	Scheduler of Simul. Multiple Payroll
PC00_M33_CALC_SIMU	Simulation of payroll run for Russia
PC00_M33_CDTA	Preprogramm DTA
PC00_M33_CDTB	Preprogramm DTB
PC00_M33_CDTB_RFFOD	Create DTA
PC00_M33_CDT_RFFOD	Create DTA
PC00_M33_CEDT	Remuneration statement
PC00_M33_CLSTR	Display result
PC00_M33_HRF	Wage Statement with HR Forms

PC00_M33_REP_ADM_ORD   Personnel Order Management
PC00_M33_REP_STAT_AN   Payments and Deductions
PC00_M34_CALC   Start Payroll
PC00_M34_CALC_SIMU   Simulate Payroll
PC00_M34_CANN   Display Annual Payroll Results
PC00_M34_CAWS   Generate Annual Wage Supplement
PC00_M34_CDTC   Prepare Bank Transfer
PC00_M34_CEDT   Print Remuneration Statement
PC00_M34_CFRM0   Run report for Employee tax etc.
PC00_M34_CJAM   Run Monthly Report for Jamsostek
PC00_M34_CJAM1   Run Annual Report for Jamsostek
PC00_M34_CKTO   Display Payroll Account
PC00_M34_CLGA   Display Wage Type Statement
PC00_M34_CLJN   Display Payroll Journal
PC00_M34_CLSTR   Display Payroll Results
PC00_M34_CTAX1   Run Annual Report for Tax
PC00_M34_FFOD   Perform Cash Payment
PC00_M34_FFOT   Perform Bank Transfer
PC00_M34_HRF   Wage Statement with HR Forms
PC00_M34_HRF_PAYJNAL   Payroll Journal with HR Forms
PC00_M34_HRF_PAYRACC   Payroll Account with HR Forms
PC00_M37   Payroll area menu for Brazil
PC00_M37_3RDE0   List of third-party contributions
PC00_M37_AVFE   Leave Notice Notification   37
PC00_M37_AVPR   Leave Notice Notification   37
PC00_M37_CALC   Payroll for Brazil
PC00_M37_CALC_SIMU   Simulation payroll accounting 37
PC00_M37_CCED   Income Declaration   37
PC00_M37_CEDT1   Monthly remuneration statement
PC00_M37_CKTO   Financial File   37
PC00_M37_CLJN   Analytical data   37
PC00_M37_CLSTR   Tools - payroll result - 37
PC00_M37_CTER   Payroll accounting run
PC00_M37_CVTR   Transportation ticket
PC00_M37_DEPD   Dependents Declaration   37
PC00_M37_DIRF   Withholding Income Tax Decl.   37
PC00_M37_DOCS   HR Personhal Documents
PC00_M37_ETIQ   Salary Adjustment Label   37
PC00_M37_ETQF   Leave data label   37
PC00_M37_FCOL   Company vacation calculation
PC00_M37_FERI   Advance Leave Calculation   37
PC00_M37_FICH   Salaried Employee Tab Page   37
PC00_M37_GPS   Guide of Social Welfare
PC00_M37_GRFC   FGTS Termination Guide
PC00_M37_GRFP   FCGSWI-FGTS TermCollGui.Soc.Welf.Inf
PC00_M37_GRPS   Guide of Collect and Social Welfare
PC00_M37_GRR0   Guide of Collect termination   37
PC00_M37_GRRF   FCG
PC00_M37_HRF   Remuneration statement w/HR forms
PC00_M37_HRF_PAYRACC   Payroll accounts with HR Forms
PC00_M37_IN68   Normative instruction 68
PC00_M37_IN86   Normative instruction 86
PC00_M37_JAHRLICHE   Area menu-subsequent activities-anua
PC00_M37_MANAD   MANAD - standard guide digital files

PC00_M37_MENS	Payroll Monthly Report	
PC00_M37_MONATLICHE	Area menu-subsequent activities- oth	
PC00_M37_MOPR	Process Model	37
PC00_M37_OTEM	Create Master Data Export	
PC00_M37_PAP	Area menu-subsequent activities per	
PC00_M37_PDUNABHAGIG	Area menu-subsequent activities-ind.	
PC00_M37_PISC	SIP - Data Medium Registration	37
PC00_M37_QGEN	Generate legal leave entitlement 37	
PC00_M37_RAIS	Social Information Annual Report 37	
PC00_M37_RECT	Termination	37
PC00_M37_RTER	Termination Term	37
PC00_M37_SAB0	Absence and acquisiton per.control	
PC00_M37_SALC	List and Spec.of Contrib.Salaries 37	
PC00_M37_SALF	Child allowance file	
PC00_M37_SEFI	FCSWI	37
PC00_M37_SEGD	Release from Work Notification	37
PC00_M37_SONSPERIOD	Area menu-subsequent activities- oth	
PC00_M37_TEMSE	Display facsimile TemSe files	
PC00_M37_TERM	Dependents Decl.Child Allowance	37
PC00_M37_TMIF	AFD import interface	
PC00_M37_TMS5	Display TemSe files	
PC00_M37_TMSH	Punch clock mirror report	
PC00_M37_TRM0	Termination driver	
PC00_M37_TRSF	File generator punch clock	
PC00_M37_VALT	Transportation ticket	37
PC00_M37_VENF	Issue of Leave Notice	
PC00_M39_CALC	Chile Payroll	
PC00_M39_CALC_SIMU	Payroll Simulation Chile	
PC00_M39_CDTA	Payroll Transfer to prel.prog.DME-39	
PC00_M39_CEDT	Remuneration statement	
PC00_M39_FFOT	Create DME	39
PC00_M39_ITCCAF	CCAF Interface	
PC00_M39_RAFP	Statement of Pension Fund Contr.	
PC00_M39_RAPV	Statement of Vol.Pension Savings	
PC00_M39_RCCAF	Statement of Family Allowance	
PC00_M39_RCHW	Statement Heavy Work Contributions	
PC00_M39_RCPYB	Payments Book	
PC00_M39_RCRT	Income Certificate	
PC00_M39_RINE	Remuneration and Labor Cost (INE)	
PC00_M39_RINP	Statement of Contributions to INP	
PC00_M39_RISL	Statement of Contributions to Mutual	
PC00_M39_RISPR	Statement of Contributions to ISAPRE	
PC00_M39_RPRV	PREVIRED Interface	
PC00_M39_TRM0	Termination Chile	
PC00_M40_ALR	Allowance Restructuring	
PC00_M40_ANN	Payroll annual display - India	
PC00_M40_BONS	Bonus Calculation - India	
PC00_M40_BSG	Basic - General Increments	
PC00_M40_BSP	Basic - Promotions	
PC00_M40_CALC	Payroll program - India	
PC00_M40_CALC_SIMU	Payroll simulation India	
PC00_M40_CBLIST	Cash breakdownlist - India	
PC00_M40_CDTA	Payroll-transfer-prelimProg. DME-40	
PC00_M40_CDTB	BT for Aditional payments	40

PC00_M40_CEDT	Remuneration Statement - India
PC00_M40_CLSTR	Payroll Results - 40
PC00_M40_CMAP	Income Tax: Challan mapping program
PC00_M40_DAB	Batch program for Dearness Allowance
PC00_M40_DF17	Form 17 Dowanlaod Utility
PC00_M40_EPF	Provident Fund Reports - India
PC00_M40_EPN	PF Reports (Exempted Trust) - India
PC00_M40_ESIB	ESI Batch Program
PC00_M40_ESIF	ESI Form6 & Form7
PC00_M40_ESIU	Utility Program for ESI
PC00_M40_F16	Form 16
PC00_M40_F217	Form 217
PC00_M40_F24	Income Tax: Form24 for India
PC00_M40_F24C	Form 24Q: e-File consolidation
PC00_M40_F24Q	Form 24Q
PC00_M40_FFOD	Create DME (Print Payment advice)
PC00_M40_FFOM	Create.DME 40
PC00_M40_GRY	Gratuity Listing
PC00_M40_HRA	Rent receipt updation report
PC00_M40_HRF	Wage Statement with HR Forms
PC00_M40_HRF_PAYJNAL	Wage Statement with HR Forms
PC00_M40_KTO	Payroll account - India
PC00_M40_LJN	Payroll Journal - India
PC00_M40_LON1	Loans Summary Report
PC00_M40_LON2	Penal Interest Batch Program
PC00_M40_LWF	LWF Reports
PC00_M40_PFE	Provident Fund Reports - India
PC00_M40_PFY	Program For Annual PF Reports
PC00_M40_PNE	PF Reports (Exempted Trust) - India
PC00_M40_PNY	Program for Annual pension reports
PC00_M40_PTX	Professional Tax Form 5
PC00_M40_REMC	Balance Carry Forward
PC00_M40_REMP	Disbursement of claims
PC00_M40_REMS	Status for claims
PC00_M40_REMT	Balance Disbursement
PC00_M40_RIST	Update utiliy for T7INGE table
PC00_M40_S24	Batch program for Section 24
PC00_M40_S80	Batch program for Section80
PC00_M40_S88	Batch program for Section80
PC00_M40_SANL	Super annuation list
PC00_M40_SWCH	HR IN: Switch activation utility
PC00_M40_TERM	Termination
PC00_M40_TMSE	Display Form 24q TemSe data
PC00_M40_UPCF	Upload for Claims processing
PC00_M40_UTAN	TAN upload utility
PC00_M40_XLS	EXCEL (Upload / download)
PC00_M41_BEN_DED	Benefits deduction list
PC00_M41_BONUS	Bonus payroll Korea
PC00_M41_CALC	Start payroll
PC00_M41_CALC_RETIRE	Start payroll
PC00_M41_CALC_SIMU	Simulation payroll accounting
PC00_M41_CALC_SIMU_R	Simulation payroll
PC00_M41_CDTA	Prepare Bank Transfer
PC00_M41_CEDT	Print Remuneration Statement

SAP Transaction Codes – Volume One

PC00_M41_CKTO	Payroll account
PC00_M41_CLJN	Payroll journal
PC00_M41_CMIS	List for Health Insurance Lost
PC00_M41_EIAL0	List for EI Eligibility Aquired.Lost
PC00_M41_HRF	Remuneration Statement with HR Forms
PC00_M41_HRF_PAYJNAL	Payroll Jornal with HR Forms
PC00_M41_HRF_PAYRACC	Payroll Accounts with HR Forms
PC00_M41_JAHRLICHE	Subsequent activities - annual
PC00_M41_LEAVE	Leave compensation payroll
PC00_M41_LQC0	Generate leave quota compensation
PC00_M41_NP00	Grade Change BDC (SI)
PC00_M41_PAP	Area menu - Subsequent activities pe
PC00_M41_PDUNABHAGIG	Subsequent activities - period indep
PC00_M41_PTAX_RCT	Tax payment receipt
PC00_M41_RETIRE	Retirement payroll
PC00_M41_SEPARATION	Separation
PC00_M41_SEPR	Withholding separation tax receipt
PC00_M41_SIACQ	The acquired of SI eligiblity
PC00_M41_SICHG	The changed of SI eligiblity
PC00_M41_SILOS	The lost of SI eligiblity
PC00_M41_SIP0	SI premium deduction list
PC00_M41_SONSPERIOD	Subsequent activities - other period
PC00_M41_UPNP	Annual income notification (SI)
PC00_M41_UTSV	Download TemSe file
PC00_M41_YEA	Year end adjustment Korea
PC00_M41_YEA_DED	Report of Income Exemption & Deduct
PC00_M41_YEA_DON	Report of Donation Expense
PC00_M41_YEA_LST	Withholding income tax payment list
PC00_M41_YEA_MED	Report of Medical Expense
PC00_M41_YEA_RCT	Withholding income tax receipt
PC00_M42	Payroll menu for Taiwan
PC00_M42_ADV_OCRN	Advance payment using off-cycle reas
PC00_M42_ADV_REP	Advance payment using report
PC00_M42_AWS	Area menu for Bonus
PC00_M42_CALC	Payroll Driver Taiwan
PC00_M42_CALC_SIMU	Simulate Payroll
PC00_M42_CAWS	Process Year End Bonus
PC00_M42_CDTA	Prepare Bank Transfer
PC00_M42_CDTB	Prepare Bank Transfer /Extra Payment
PC00_M42_CDTF	Cancel Bank Transfer
PC00_M42_CEDT	Print Remuneration Statement
PC00_M42_CKTO	Display Payroll Account
PC00_M42_CLJN	Display Payroll Journal
PC00_M42_CLSTR	Display Payroll Result
PC00_M42_CMP0	First payment in Monthly Payroll 42
PC00_M42_CTDC	List and Update Court Deduction
PC00_M42_CTXM	Run Yearly Tax Certificate Report
PC00_M42_CTXP	Periodical salary tax summary
PC00_M42_CTXW	Tax Certificate Report (Payday)
PC00_M42_CWTR	Wage Type Reporter for Taiwan
PC00_M42_FFOT	Perform Bank Transfer
PC00_M42_HRF_PAYRACC	Lohnkonto with HR Forms
PC00_M42_HRF_PJNAL_1	Wage Statement with HR Forms
PC00_M42_HRF_PSLIP_1	Wage Statement with HR Forms

PC00_M42_HTWCMLI9	Cash Breakdown List(Read Cluster TN)
PC00_M42_HTWSI970	Social Insurance (LI/NHI) of Taiwan
PC00_M42_HTWUTXM0	Delete tax reported data
PC00_M42_JAHRLICHE	Subsequent activities TW - Annual
PC00_M42_LAM0	LI/NHI amount adjust from payroll 42
PC00_M42_LHCE	Print LI/NHI Certificate
PC00_M42_LHI0	Display/Update LI/NHI date 42
PC00_M42_LHIA	NHI legal reporting Adjustment 42
PC00_M42_LHIC	NHI legal reporting Changes 42
PC00_M42_LHID	NHI difference report
PC00_M42_LHIJ	NHI legal reporting Join 42
PC00_M42_LHIM	NHI legal reporting Medium 42
PC00_M42_LHIQ	NHI legal reporting Quit 42
PC00_M42_LIM0	3in1 (LI/NHI/NP) or 2in1 (LI/NP) med
PC00_M42_LINF	Masterdata overview 42
PC00_M42_LLIA	LI legal reporting Adjustment 42
PC00_M42_LLIC	LI legal reporting Changes 42
PC00_M42_LLIJ	LI legal reporting Join 42
PC00_M42_LLIQ	LI legal reporting Quit 42
PC00_M42_LLPD	LI & NP Data Comprison
PC00_M42_LNC0	Update infotype from T7TW1B 42
PC00_M42_NPPS	Pension and Severance payment report
PC00_M42_NPR0	New Pension DME Download Report
PC00_M42_PAP	Subs.activities - Per payroll period
PC00_M42_PDUNABHAGIG	Subs. activities TW - Period-indepen
PC00_M42_SONSPERIOD	Subsequent activities TW - Other per
PC00_M43	Area menu-payroll for New Zealand
PC00_M43_BTD0	Bank Transfer Details
PC00_M43_CAD0	Holiday pay act report
PC00_M43_CADV	Advance payment 43
PC00_M43_CALC	Payroll accounting - simulation - 43
PC00_M43_CALC_SIMU	Simulation payroll accounting 43
PC00_M43_CDAP	Delete Advance Payment 43
PC00_M43_CDTA	Payroll-transfer pre. program DME-43
PC00_M43_CEDT	HR accounting remun. statement - 43
PC00_M43_CIRC	IR Certificates 43
PC00_M43_CLEA	Leave View
PC00_M43_CLSTR	Tools - payroll result - 43
PC00_M43_CLVP	LVPAY correction report
PC00_M43_CPTQ	Ptquoded correction report
PC00_M43_CTR1	Terminations 43
PC00_M43_FFOT	Payroll transfer-first.DME 43
PC00_M43_HNZCLAB0	HNZCLAB0
PC00_M43_HNZCLAC0	HNZCLAC0
PC00_M43_HNZCLJN0	HNZCLJN0
PC00_M43_HNZCLVP0	HNZCLVP0
PC00_M43_HNZCMLI9	HNZCMLI9
PC00_M43_HNZCQULD	HNZCQULD
PC00_M43_HNZCSUP0	HNZCSUP0
PC00_M43_HNZCTAX0	HNZCTAX0
PC00_M43_HNZUCLR0	HNZUCLR0
PC00_M43_HNZUDIR0	HNZUDIR0
PC00_M43_HRF	Wage Statement with HR Forms
PC00_M43_LABQ0	Absence Quota Balance Batch Update

PC00_M43_LACC	Payroll Rpts ACC Employer report 43	
PC00_M43_LCSE	Payroll Rpts Child Support report 43	
PC00_M43_LDET	Payroll Reports Detail report 43	
PC00_M43_LEMS	EMS Report - New Zealand	
PC00_M43_LEXC	Payroll Reports Exception report 43	
PC00_M43_LKED	KiwiSaver Employee Details	
PC00_M43_LLVL	Leave Liability Report	
PC00_M43_LPRR	Payroll Rpts PAYE/ACC Recon. rpt 43	
PC00_M43_LQES	Quarterly employment survey	
PC00_M43_LREC	Payroll Reports Reconciliation rpt43	
PC00_M43_LREM	Employer deductions: Remittance cert	
PC00_M43_LSCS	Quarterly labour cost survey - super	
PC00_M43_LSUM	Payroll Reports Summary report 43	
PC00_M43_LSUP	Superannuation report 43	
PC00_M43_LXMS	Shifting of Christmas and New Year	
PC00_M43_N1DL	Display And Delete Advance Pay Resut	
PC00_M43_PAP	Area menu-subseq. activities - Per	
PC00_M43_PLRECNZ1	PLRECNZ1	
PC00_M43_QESL	QES Report -Annual Leave Entitlement	
PC00_M43_SAUPD	Update Superannuation -NZ (IT0310)	
PC00_M43_UHCU	Update Holiday Pay Bill Cluster	
PC00_M43_UKSU	Program to Upload KIWCO table	
PC00_M43_ULVP	LVPAY cluster update report	
PC00_M43_ULVR	Avg & Current rate for leave payout	
PC00_M44_ATS_DC	Data Collector Annual Tax Statement	
PC00_M44_ATS_PRES	Data Presentation for ATS	
PC00_M44_BI_TUMF	Mass Update of Union Fees via BI	
PC00_M44_CALC	Payroll driver	
PC00_M44_CALC_SIMU	Simulate payroll accounting Finland	
PC00_M44_CDTA	Prelim.Program Data Medium Exchange	
PC00_M44_CDTA_TUMF	Preliminary DME for Trade Union Fees	
PC00_M44_CEDT	Payslip	
PC00_M44_CEDT_ELETTR	Remuneration statement as eLetter	
PC00_M44_CKTO	Payroll Account	
PC00_M44_CLJN	Payroll Journal	
PC00_M44_CLJNPAYCARD	Pay Card	
PC00_M44_CLJNPAYLIST	Pay List	
PC00_M44_CLSTR	Display cluster FI (Results for SF)	
PC00_M44_CTAX	Monthly tax and social remittance	
PC00_M44_FTUM	Create Trade Union File	
PC00_M44_HPAC	Utility report to clean HPA DBtables	
PC00_M44_HPAL	Transaction for HPA with FI postings	
PC00_M44_HRF	Wage Statement with HR Forms	
PC00_M44_HRF_PAYJNAL	Payroll Journal with HR Forms	
PC00_M44_IABP0	Mass Update: Vacation Bonus Payments	
PC00_M44_LAAI0	Annual Accident Insurance Statement	
PC00_M44_LAIR	Accident Insurance Reporting	
PC00_M44_LAWT0	Annual Working Time	
PC00_M44_LCST	Labor Cost Statistics	
PC00_M44_LDED	List Deductions	
PC00_M44_LERR0	Employee Representative Report	
PC00_M44_LGAR	List employee garnishments	
PC00_M44_LHPA0	Holiday Pay Accrual	
PC00_M44_LKEL0	Kela application report	

661

PC00_M44_LLIS	Report for Low Income Support
PC00_M44_LOTR0	Overtime Report
PC00_M44_LPEN	EEs changing insurance type
PC00_M44_LSEA	Earnings statement
PC00_M44_LTALEL	LEL/TaEL announcement
PC00_M44_LTCRE	Display Tax Card Information
PC00_M44_LTEL	TEL employment and year announcement
PC00_M44_LTUM	List Trade Union Membership Fees
PC00_M44_LTVR	TVR Hours for PS Reclassification
PC00_M44_LVAC0	Finnish Vacation Planning
PC00_M44_LVAC1	Vacation Calculation
PC00_M44_LWTR	Finnish subappl. wage type reporting
PC00_M44_NISA	Calculate Seniority Allowance F&P
PC00_M44_OTEM	Create Master Data Export
PC00_M44_PU30_M940	Copy TUMF model wage type
PC00_M44_PU30_M950	Copy SPC model wage type
PC00_M44_RIP0	Raise in Pay History
PC00_M44_RIP1	Raise in Pay Comparison
PC00_M44_SPOB	Statistics on Places of Business
PC00_M44_SSTS0	Service Sector Statistics
PC00_M44_STAT	Statistical reporting
PC00_M44_STBC	Blue Collar Statistics
PC00_M44_STPR	Private sector statistics, Finland
PC00_M44_STWC	White Collar Monthly Statistics
PC00_M44_TCDOWN	Tax card download
PC00_M44_TCUP	Tax card upload
PC00_M44_TYEL0	TYEL Monthly Reporting
PC00_M44_TYEL1	TYEL Yearly Reporting
PC00_M44_UCPL	Check for locked personnel numbers
PC00_M44_UTCCP	Delimit/Copy Tax Infotype
PC00_M44_WTE1	Work time equalization year-end
PC00_M44_WTE2	Work time equalization days followup
PC00_M44_WTE3	Work time equalization predicting
PC00_M48	Bereichsmenü-Abrechnung für Philipin
PC00_M48_13MN	13th Month Calculation Program
PC00_M48_CALC_13MN	13th Month Bonus Runs
PC00_M48_CALC_BN	Off-cycle - Bonus payments
PC00_M48_CALC_MRND	Off-cycle - Multiple runs w/o ded
PC00_M48_CALC_MRWD	Off-cycle - Multiple runs w/ ded
PC00_M48_CALC_SIMU	Payroll Driver Simulation - Phil.
PC00_M48_CDTA	Bank transfer pre.program DME 48
PC00_M48_CKTO	Payroll account - Philippines
PC00_M48_CMP0	Adv pay multiple runs calc. program
PC00_M48_HRF	Lohnkonto with HR Forms
PC00_M48_HRF_PAYJNAL	Lohnkonto with HR Forms
PC00_M48_HRF_PAYRACC	Lohnkonto with HR Forms
PC00_M48_JAHRLICHE	Bereichsmenü-Folgeaktivitäten - Annu
PC00_M48_NHIP	PhilHealth Remittance Report (RF-1)
PC00_M48_PAP	Bereichsmenü-Folgeaktivitäten - Per
PC00_M48_PDUNABHAGIG	Bereichsmenü-Folgeaktivitäten - Peri
PC00_M48_REDI	SSS EDI Net
PC00_M48_RHDM	HDMF Monthly Remit.
PC00_M48_RSBR0	Display of receipt numbers
PC00_M48_RSBRU	SBR-Utility report for updation

PC00_M48_SBRU	Bank Receipt Updation Utility
PC00_M48_SONSPERIOD	Bereichsmenü-Folgeaktivitäten - Othe
PC00_M99	Area Menu - International Payroll
PC00_M99_ABKRS	Set payroll area
PC00_M99_B2AFILE	B2A: Upload/Download Files
PC00_M99_CALC	International Payroll
PC00_M99_CALC_SIMU	International Simulation Payroll
PC00_M99_CDTA	Bank transfer pre.program DME Inter.
PC00_M99_CEDT	Remuneration statement Internat.
PC00_M99_CIPC	Check Completeness of Posting
PC00_M99_CIPC_PNP	Check Completeness of Posting
PC00_M99_CIPE	Create Posting Run
PC00_M99_CIP_T_CHECK	Posting: Technical Document Trace
PC00_M99_CKTO	Payroll account - International
PC00_M99_CLGA00	Wage type statement - International
PC00_M99_CLGA09	Wage type statement (US stand.) Int.
PC00_M99_CLGV00	Wage type distribution - Internat.
PC00_M99_CLGV09	Wage type distribution (US st.) Int.
PC00_M99_CLJN	Payroll journal International
PC00_M99_CLOF	Account Statement for Company Loans
PC00_M99_CLOG	Overview of Company Loans
PC00_M99_CLOH	Calculation of Present Value
PC00_M99_CLSTPC	Absences - International
PC00_M99_CLSTR	Payroll result International
PC00_M99_CMLI0	Cash breakdown list payment Int.
PC00_M99_CMLI0_NEW	Cash breakdown list payment Int.
PC00_M99_CMLI9	Cash breakdown list payment(9) Int.
PC00_M99_CPRC	Payroll calendar - International
PC00_M99_CPYS	Payroll calendar - International
PC00_M99_CURSET	Current settings
PC00_M99_CWTR	Wage type reporter
PC00_M99_CWTR_NO_OC	Wage type reporter
PC00_M99_DKON	Assign WTS- Display G/L Accounts
PC00_M99_DLGA20	Wage type use - International
PC00_M99_FPAYM	Create Payment Medium
PC00_M99_HRF	Wage Statement with HR Forms
PC00_M99_HRF_CALL	Call HR Forms Print Report
PC00_M99_HRF_CALL01	Call HR Forms Print Report
PC00_M99_INF_BPD_ACT	Activation Infotypes for Budget Per.
PC00_M99_INF_BPD_UPD	Update Infotypes for Budget Period
PC00_M99_ITRF	Pay Scale Increase Ext. Internation.
PC00_M99_ITUM	Pay Scale Reclass. International
PC00_M99_MOLGA	Set PCG
PC00_M99_OTEM	Create Master Data Export
PC00_M99_OTLJ	Payroll Journal - Outsourcing
PC00_M99_PA03_CHECK	Check results
PC00_M99_PA03_CORR	Corrections
PC00_M99_PA03_END	Exit payroll
PC00_M99_PA03_RELEA	Release payroll
PC00_M99_PAP	Area menu - Subs. activities per PP
PC00_M99_PPM	Generate Posting Run - Payments
PC00_M99_RPIADVL0	Advance Payment-Generation Internat.
PC00_M99_TLEA	Annual leave listing International
PC00_M99_TLEA30	Annual leave update International

SAP Transaction Codes – Volume One

PC00_M99_U510	Pay scale increase International
PC00_M99_UCRT	Restructure Cumulation Tables
PC00_M99_UDEL	Report to delete CSR Recon tables
PC00_M99_UDIR	Restructure Payroll Directory
PC00_M99_URMA	3PR Acknowledgement run
PC00_M99_URMC	Run remittance completeness check
PC00_M99_URMD	3PR Undo remittance runs
PC00_M99_URME	Run remittance evaluation
PC00_M99_URML	3PR TemSe files upload/download
PC00_M99_URMP	3PR Create posting run (US)
PC00_M99_URMR	3PR Remittance reconciliation
PC00_M99_URMU	3PR Store evaluation run
PC00_M99_URMW	3PR Check processing classes
PC00_M99_UTSV	List TemSe Objects
PC00_MNA_CC_ADM	Cost Center Report - Administrator
PC00_MNA_CC_MAN	Cost Center Report - Manager
PC00_MUN_BOOK	Program HUNUCMT_BOOK
PC00_MUN_CALC	NPO Payroll
PC00_MUN_CALC_SIMU	NPO Simulation Payroll
PC00_MUN_CDTA	Bank transfer pre.program DME NPO
PC00_MUN_CEDT	Remuneration statement NPO
PC00_MUN_CIPE	Create Posting Run
PC00_MUN_CKTO	Display Payroll Account
PC00_MUN_CLJN	Payroll Journal --- NPO
PC00_MUN_HRF	Remuneration Statement with HR Forms
PC00_MUN_HRF_PAYJNAL	Payroll Jonral with HR Forms
PC00_MUN_HRF_PAYRACC	Payroll Account with HR Forms
PC00_MUN_LOADER	NPO: Loader for CMT Data in XML Form
PC00_MUN_LOGMAINT	NPO: Log Maintenance for CMT Compone
PC00_MUN_PA03_CHECK	Check results
PC00_MUN_PA03_CORR	Corrections
PC00_MUN_PA03_END	Exit payroll
PC00_MUN_PA03_RELEA	Release payroll
PC00_MUN_QTASLA	NPO: Quota Update for Sick Leave Acc
PC00_MUN_QTASLC	NPO: Quota Update for Sick Leave Acc
PC00_MUN_QTASLE	NPO: Quota Update for Sick Leave Ent
PC00_MUN_SCHGEN	NPO: XML Schema and Sample Generator
PC00_OFPM	Special payroll process model
PC00_OTBN	Create Generic Benefits Export
PC00_OTIN	Process Inbound
PC00_OTRL	Release IDocs
PC00_OTTM	Create Time Wage Type Export
PC01	Payroll Germany
PC02	Area Menu Payroll for Switzerland
PC03	Area Menu Payroll Austria
PC04	Area menu Payroll for Spain
PC05	Area menu - Payroll Netherlands
PC06	Payroll Menu - France
PC07	Bereichsmenü-Abrechnung für Kanada
PC08	Area menu-payroll for Great Britain
PC09	Area Menu-Payroll for Denmark
PC10	Bereichsmenü - Abrechnung für USA
PC11	Bereichsmenü-Abrechnung für Irland
PC12	Area menu - Payroll for Belgium

PC13	Bereichsmenü-Abrechnung für Australi
PC14	Bereichsmenü-Abrechnung für Malaysie
PC15	Area menu-payroll for Italy
PC16	Area menu-payroll for South Africa
PC17	Main menu for Venezuelan payroll
PC19	Payroll for Portugal
PC20	Bereichsmenü-Abrechnung für Norwegen
PC22	Payroll accounting for Japan
PC23	Bereichsmenü-Abrechnung für Schweden
PC25	Payroll Menu: Singapore
PC26	Payroll for Thailand
PC27	Payroll Accounting for Hong Kong
PC28	Area menu - International payroll
PC29	Area menu-Payroll acctg Argentina
PC32	Area menu-Payroll Mexico
PC34	Payroll Menu for Indonesia
PC37	Payroll area menu for Brazil
PC41	Payroll Korea
PC42	Payroll menu for Taiwan
PC43	Area menu-payroll for New Zealand
PC48	Bereichsmenü-Abrechnung für Philipin
PC99	Area menu - International payroll
PCA	Payment Cards
PCA0	Production campaign menu
PCA1	Creating a Production Campaign
PCA2	Change Prod. Camp.: Initial Screen
PCA3	Display Prod. Camp.: Initial Screen
PCA_BILA	Customizing: Bal. Sheet Accts in PCs
PCA_CHK	Check of External Encryption
PCA_DBCHK	Check Database Consistency
PCA_FB03	Display FI Document w/o Fiscal Year
PCA_MC	Mass Encryption /Decryption
PCA_SC	Server Check
PCA_VAR	Set variant
PCC0	Maintnce fam.rltd.bonuses Switz.
PCC1	Maintain Swiss Payroll Units
PCCO	Production Campaign: Costs
PCCV	Payment Card: Field Grouping
PCGC	Maintain Car Database
PCKC	Consistency Check Constants
PCKY	Consistency Check Year-End
PCM0_MAINTAIN_PBSWT	Maintain PBS wage type intervals
PCOO_M25_C3CL	3CML Report
PCP0	Edit posting runs
PCRWF	Customizing Workflow Change Requests
PC_PAYRESULT	Display Payroll Results
PDA4	Object List: Absence Events
PDD_DET_PROC	product det. procedure maintenance
PDF0	Convert form for remun.statement
PDF7	Delete form in customer client
PDF8	Copy form from SAP client
PDF9	Copy forms within customer client
PDFA	Convert payroll journal form
PDFN	DUCS : number range maintenance

SAP Transaction Codes – Volume One

PDN	Product Designer Workbench
PDNO	Number Range Maintenance: FMPD
PDO1	List of Average CA Supplements SR
PDSY	HR Documentation Maintenance
PDS_DEL	Delete Additional PDS Data
PDS_MAINT	Maintain Additional PDS Data
PDT2	HU creation in production
PDW1	Create reporting time types
PDW2	Create Quota Types for Reporting
PE00	Starts Transactions PE01, PE02, PE03
PE01	HR: Maintain Payroll Schemas
PE01N	Editor for Payroll Schemas
PE02	HR: Maintain Calculation Rules
PE02N	Editor for PC rules
PE03	HR: Features
PE04	Creates Functions and Operations
PE50	PE50
PE51	HR form editor
PE51_CHECKTAB	Check Table Maintenance HR-Forms
PECLUSTER	Process HR cluster
PECM_ADJUST_0759	Adjust Compensation Process Records
PECM_ADJ_SAL_STRU	Update of Pay Grade Amounts
PECM_CHANGE_STATUS	Change Compensation Process Status
PECM_CHK_BUDGET	Check and Release Budget
PECM_CONV_BDG_STKUN	Convert Budget Stock Unit
PECM_CONV_LTI_STKUN	Convert LTI Grant Stock Unit
PECM_CREATE_0758	Create Compensation Program Records
PECM_CREATE_COMP_PRO	Create Compensation Process Records
PECM_DEL_HIST_DATA	Delete Comp. Planning History Data
PECM_DISPLAY_BUDGETS	Display Budgets
PECM_DISPLAY_CHANGES	Display Comp. Planning Changes
PECM_DISP_PROGRESS	Display Comp. Planning Progress
PECM_EVALUATE_GRANT	Evaluate LTI Grants
PECM_EXERCISE_IDOC	Import LTI Exercise Data
PECM_GENERATE_BUDGET	Generate Budget from Org. Hierarchy
PECM_GRANT_IDOC	Export LTI Grant Data
PECM_INIT_BUDGET	Upload Budget Values from PCP
PECM_NOTIFY_MANAGERS	Notify Managers
PECM_PARTICIP_IDOC	Export LTI Participant Data
PECM_PREP_ORGUNITS	Prepare Org. Units for Comp. Plng.
PECM_PRINT_CRS	Print Comp. Review Statement
PECM_PROCESS_EVENT	Process Event for LTI Grants
PECM_QUERY_SURVEY	Data Extraction for Salary Survey
PECM_START_BDG_BSP	Start Budgeting BSP
PECM_START_JPR_BSP	Start Job Pricing BSP
PECM_SUMMARIZE_CHNGS	Summarize Comp. Planning Changes
PECM_UPD_0008_1005	Update IT0008 when IT1005 changes
PEG01	Collective Processing Pegging
PEG02	Manual Assignment Maintenance
PEG03	Breakpoint Maintenance
PEG04	Assignment of Exceptions
PEG05	Assignment Overview
PEG06	Goods Issues Overview
PEG07	Stock Overview

PEG08	Display Change Documents
PEG10	Compare Stock
PEG11	Pegging: Table Maintenance
PEG12	Filling of Pegging Worklist
PEG13	Pegging: Unassigned Replenisments
PEG14	Pegging: Intransit stock report
PEG15	Transfer Pegging Program
PEPM	Profile Matchup
PEPMEN	Task Level Menu for the PEP
PEPP	Profiles
PERSREG	Personalization object
PERS_DEFI	Define Personalization Objects
PEST	Maintenance of process model
PEST_IMG	Maintenance of process models
PEWA2	EEA2 Workforce Analysis
PEWA4	EEA4 Income Differentials
PEXP	Manage Expert Communities
PF02	Cust. Test of Value-Based IM
PF05	Number Range Maintenance: HRSOBJECT
PFAC	Maintain Rule
PFAC_CHG	Change Rules
PFAC_DEL	Delete Rule
PFAC_DIS	Display Rule
PFAC_INS	Create Rule
PFAC_RESPO	Maintain Responsibilities
PFAC_STR	Maintain Rules -> Dummy Screen
PFAL	HR: ALE Distribution HR Master Data
PFCG	Role Maintenance
PFCG_EASY	Profile Generator (Easy Version)
PFCG_EASY_NEW	saplprgn_catt
PFCG_OLD	Maintain Old Roles
PFCG_OLD_MINIAPPS	Maintain Table SSM_CUST
PFCP	Copy Workflow Tasks
PFCT	Task Catalog
PFCU	Task Customizing
PFDE	HR-PF: PC Editor
PFDESS_02PKB1	ESS Insurance Statement
PFDESS_02PKB4	ESS Simulated Leaving
PFDESS_02PKB8	ESS Advance
PFDESS_02PKM1	ESS Insurance Statement
PFDESS_02PKM4	ESS Simulated Leaving
PFDESS_02PKM8	ESS Advance
PFDESS_12PKB1	HR-PF-BE: ESS Pension Certificate
PFDESS_12PKB3	HR-PF-BE: ESS Retirement Statement
PFDF	FI Interface Pension Fund
PFDFP	HR-PF-FI: Check Customizing
PFDT	Overview of Insured Persons' Data
PFM2	Period Monitor: Log Display
PFM3	PEP CO-PC-ACT: Dummy
PFM4	Period Monitor: Log Display
PFM5	Period monitor - log display
PFOM	Maintain Assignment to SAP Org.Objs
PFOS	Display Assignment to SAP Org.Objs
PFO_CUST_ARCHINDEX	Define Archive Information Structure

PFO_CUST_COM_GO_SEG	Maintain Combinations (BusObj.)
PFO_CUST_COM_ZO_SEG	Maintain Combinations (AssgnmntObj.)
PFO_CUST_CONST	Construct New Object Type
PFO_CUST_CONST_FOA	Construct New Object Type
PFO_CUST_OBT	Maintain Object Types
PFO_CUST_ORIGIN	Maintain Origin
PFO_CUST_ROL_GZO	Maintain Assgnmnt Roles (BusObjAsst)
PFO_CUST_ROL_SZO	Maintain Assgnmnt Roles (SegmntAsst)
PFO_CUST_SGT	Maintain Segment Types
PFO_GZO	Call Report PFO_GZO
PFO_SEG	Call Report PFO_SEG
PFO_SZO	Call Report PFO_SZO
PFSE	Call Process Flow Scheduler
PFSM	Start Download of PFS Master Data
PFSO	User's Organizational Environment
PFT	Maintain Customer Task
PFTC	General Task Maintenance
PFTC_CHG	Change Tasks
PFTC_COP	Copy Tasks
PFTC_DEL	Delete Tasks
PFTC_DIS	Display Tasks
PFTC_INS	Create Tasks
PFTC_STR	Task Maintenance -> Dummy Screen
PFTG	Maintain Task Group
PFTR	Standard Task for Transaction
PFTS	Standard Task
PFUD	User Master Data Reconciliation
PFWF	Maintain Workflow Task (Customer)
PFWS	Maintain Workflow Template
PF_WLS_SUBST	Substitute inbox worklist server
PGOM	Graphical Structure Maintenance
PHAP_ADMIN	Administrator - Appraisal Document
PHAP_ADMIN_PA	PA: Administrator - Appr. Document
PHAP_ANON	Appraisal Documents - Anonymous
PHAP_CATALOG	Appraisal Template Catalog
PHAP_CATALOG_PA	PA: Catalog for Appraisal Templates
PHAP_CHANGE	Change Appraisal Document
PHAP_CHANGE_PA	PA: Change Appraisal Document
PHAP_CORP_GOALS	Co. Goals & Core Value Maintenance
PHAP_CREATE	Create Appraisal
PHAP_CREATE_PA	PA: Create Appraisal Document
PHAP_PMP_OVERVIEW	Start PMP Process Overview
PHAP_PMP_TIMELINE	Maintain Process Timeline
PHAP_PREPARE	Prepare Appraisal Documents
PHAP_PREPARE_PA	PA: Prepare Appraisal Documents
PHAP_SEARCH	Evaluate Appraisal Document
PHAP_SEARCH_PA	PA: Evaluate Appraisal Document
PHAP_START_BSP	Generate Internet Addresses
PHAP_TEAM_GOALS	Maintaining Team Goals
PHCPADCO	Post Cost Planning Data to CO
PHCPADMN	Manage Cost Planning Data
PHCPCLCO	Display Original Document (Cluster)
PHCPCLPL	Display Plan Data (Cluster)
PHCPDCDL	Delete Infotype Data

PHCPDCEM	Collect Cost Planning Data: Employee
PHCPDCOO	Collect Cost Planning Data: OrgObj
PHCPDCPY	Manage Data from Payroll
PHCPDCUI	Maintain Data Basis
PHCPDETL	Detailed planning
PHCPDETLC	Detail Planning Cent.Pers.Respons.
PHCPISCO	Display Original Documents
PHCPISCP	Compare Personnel Cost Plans
PHCPISDT	Display Plan Data Changes
PHCPISPL	Display Plan Data
PHCPPRMV	Delete Plan (All Information)
PHCPPRUN	Execute Planning Run
PHCPRELS	Release plan
PHCPSLG1	Application Log Pers. Cost Planning
PHIN_ORGANIZER2	CALL Record Management from THO
PHM01	Material types for Inv. Count IView
PI30	PP-PI Options for Release 3.0
PI50	Transfer selected R/2 orders
PI51	Transfer current R/2 orders
PI60	Transfer confirmations to R/2
PIC01	Maintain Parts Interchangeability
PIC03	Display Parts Interchangeability
PIC31	PIC : Mass maintenance for MPN Sets
PIDE	Settings for Data Exchange
PIDV	Settings for Data Exchange
PIMG	Display R/3 Plug In IMG
PIMG_HRDECI01	SAP Enhancement for Expenses
PIMG_XPSVEOD0	SAP Enhancement/Pension Recipient
PIMN	Human Resources Information System
PIQACADOFFER00	Edit Event Offerings
PIQACADOFFER00_D	Display Event Offerings
PIQACADOFFER00_DW	Display Event Offerings
PIQACADOFFER00_W	Edit Event Offerings
PIQACADOFFER01	Event Offerings for Cohorts
PIQACADOFFER01_D	Display Offerings for Cohort
PIQACSTAGEVIEW	Stage Display
PIQAGDUPDATE	Updating AGD for a List of Students
PIQAGM	Edit Transfer Regulations
PIQAGM_DT	Program RHIQ_AGM_DT
PIQAGR_ARCH	Archive Lower-Level Appraisals
PIQAGR_AS_ACT	Archive Infostructure for Appraisals
PIQAGR_CUST	Customizing Templates (Appraisal)
PIQAGR_SENDALRT	Send Alert for Missing Grades
PIQAUDF_ARCH	Archive Requirement Profile
PIQAUDF_AS_ACT	Archive Info Structure: ReqmtProfile
PIQAUDR_ARCH	Archive Audit Run
PIQAUDR_AS_ACT	Archive Info Structure: Audit Run
PIQAUDSD	Maintain Subrequirement
PIQAUDSM	Edit Subrequirement
PIQAUDTMPL_D	Display Reqmt Profile Templates
PIQAUDTMPL_M	Edit Reqmt Profile Templates
PIQAUD_MP_CP	Audit (Process-Dependent)
PIQAUD_MP_CS	Audit (Process-Independent)
PIQBKGWINDOW	Mass Assignment of Booking Windows

PIQCAM   Maintain Academic Calendar
PIQCAU1   Display Date Information
PIQCG   Edit Module Group
PIQCHKACCMASTER   Check student account master data
PIQCHKSTACC   Chk customizing for main. ST master.
PIQCHKSTMASTER   Chk customizing for main. ST master.
PIQCIP_CODE_UPLOAD   Program RHIQ_CIP_CODE_UPLOAD
PIQCMPRSTATADM   Change Process Status (Admission)
PIQCMPRSTATCMPL   Change Process Status (Completion)
PIQCOH00   Cohort Builder
PIQCONVERT_SSN   Convert Identification Number
PIQCOPY   Copy Event Offerings
PIQCOPY2   Copy Event Offerings
PIQCORADMC   Create Admission Correspondence
PIQCORADMP   Print Admission Correspondence
PIQCORRSMC   Create Module Correspondence
PIQCORRSMP   Print Module Correspondence
PIQCORRSTC   Create Student Correspondence
PIQCORRSTP   Print Student Correspondence
PIQCPDERIVE_CUST   Rules for Credit Derivation
PIQCQ   Edit Internal Qualification
PIQCW   Edit Miscellaneous Academic Work
PIQDECISION   UCAS Decisions
PIQDIPLOMA_EXTRACT   Extract Diploma Data
PIQED   Equivalency Determination
PIQEO   Edit External Organization
PIQEQ   Edit External Qualification
PIQEVALD   Display Assessments
PIQEVALM   Edit Assessments
PIQEVALREGD   Display Assessment Process
PIQEVALREGM   Edit Assessment Process
PIQEXTCHECK   Extended Booking Check Maintenance
PIQFEE_ARCH   Archive Fee Calculation Documents
PIQFEE_AS_ACT   Archive Info Structure:Fee Calc.Docs
PIQFICA_AS_ACT   Archive Infostructure for ContAccts
PIQFILECREATE   UCAS: Create Export File
PIQGD   Display Grant Master Data
PIQGGB0   Edit Validation
PIQGGB1   Edit Substitution
PIQGM   Edit Grant Master Data
PIQGRAD   Graduation per Program
PIQGRADING_FILE   Calculate Performance Indexes
PIQGRADST   Graduation per Student
PIQGRAD_FEE   Determine Graduation Request Fee
PIQLOG_SYS1   Evaluate Application Log
PIQLPDCUST_ADV_AUDR0   Configure You Can Also Links
PIQLPDCUST_ADV_AUDR1   Configure You Can Also Links
PIQLPDCUST_ADV_BPLAN   Configure Launch Pad
PIQLPDCUST_ADV_EDDSP   Configure Launch Pad
PIQLPDCUST_ADV_EDSIM   Configure Launch Pad
PIQLPDCUST_ADV_EDSTR   Configure Launch Pad
PIQLPDCUST_ADV_REP   Configure Launch Pad
PIQLPDCUST_ADV_STIC   Configure Launch Pad
PIQMN   HRIQC: Area Menu

PIQMPMODBKG	Mass Transfer of Module Bookings
PIQMPSTATTR	Set Student Attributes
PIQMPSTATUSIND	Mass Setting of Holds or Statuses
PIQMP_AGRCONVERT	Convert Grades of Incomplete to Fail
PIQMSGMAP_CUST	Message Mapping for Student Service
PIQPIUPDATE00	Mass Update of Performance Indices
PIQPREBOOK	Clean Up Prebookings
PIQPROC_ARCH	Archive Activity Documents
PIQPROC_AS_ACT	Archive Infostructure f. Acty Docs
PIQPROC_DISPLAY	Display Activity Documents
PIQPROGGR	Program Type Progression
PIQPROGRESS	Program Progression
PIQRC	Edit Rule Container
PIQRCGENERATE	Rule Container Generation
PIQREG_MASS_DEREG	Mass De-registration
PIQREPLICATE00	Learning Management Integration
PIQRLCATD	Display Requirement Catalog
PIQRLCATM	Edit Requirement Catalog
PIQRPC	Create Related Person
PIQRPD	Display Related Person
PIQRPM	Change Related Person
PIQRSTIMETAB	Room Reservation Plan
PIQRULEMODULE	Edit Rule Module
PIQRULEWB_AC	Overview of CM Rules (For Acad.Obj.)
PIQRULEWB_RC	Rule Overview
PIQSC	Edit Program of Study
PIQSELT1	Test Help for Selection Methods
PIQSM	Edit Module
PIQSMBO	Module Attendee List
PIQSMFU	Edit Appraisal
PIQSPECS_CHANGE	Change of Specialization Report
PIQST	Create Student (Old)
PIQST00	Student File
PIQST10	Student File (Extended Maint.Dialog)
PIQSTAW00	Standard Academic Work UI
PIQSTAW10	Extended Academic Work UI
PIQSTC	Create Student Master Data
PIQSTD	Display Student Master Data
PIQSTM	Maintain Student Master Data
PIQSTMD_ARCH	Archive Student Master Data
PIQSTMD_AS_ACT	Arch.Infostructure f. Student Master
PIQSTTIMETAB	Timetable of Bus. Event Attendees
PIQSTU0	Student File with Object ID
PIQSTU1	Change student number
PIQSTUDEL	Deletion Program for Student Data
PIQSTYDT_ARCH	Archive Study Data
PIQSTYDT_AS_ACT	Archive Infostructure: Study Data
PIQST_ARCH_PREP	Set Archiving Flag
PIQST_BOOKING_DEL	Delete Business Event Bookings
PIQSU	Edit External Subject
PIQSUBREQGRP	Subrequirement Group
PIQSX	Edit Exchange Program
PIQUCASAPPLICANTSTAT	UCAS: Applicant Status
PIQUCASCHECKDECISION	Show/Check Decisions on applicants

PIQUCASDECISION   UCAS: Create UCAS Transactions
PIQUCASIMPORT   Import Applicant Data From UCAS
PIQUCASIMPREFDATA   Report for Importing Reference Data
PIQUCASIN   UCAS: Export UCAS File (UFILEIN)
PIQUCASLINKAPPLOG   UCAS logs for applicant
PIQUCASLINKSHOWLOG   UCAS Link - Show Logs
PIQUCASMAKEDECISION   UCAS : Make Decision
PIQUCASMIGREP   Migration Report from MARVIN to UCAS
PIQUCASODLLIST   Get Outstanding decision list(UCAS)
PIQUCASOUT   UCAS: Import UCAS File (UFILEOUT)
PIQUCASREPROCESS   Reprocess Imported Data
PIQUCASSCHOOLDET   UCAS School Details
PIQUCASSENDDECISION   Send applicants decisions to UCAS
PIQUCASSHOWLOG   UCAS: Show Import Log (UFILEOUT)
PIQUCASSYNCDATA   Report for synchronizing aplcnt data
PIQUCASTRANSACTION   UCAS: Show/Check Transactions
PIQUCASVIEW   UCAS: Display Import File (UFILEOUT)
PIQWAITLMOVE   Waiting List Administration
PIQXML_DOWNLOAD   Download XML Files from Application
PIQ_ACCATLG   Module Catalog
PIQ_ACSTRUC   Program Catalog
PIQ_FEECALC_HIST   Fee Calculation History
PIQ_GB_UCN   Number range maintenance: PIQ_GB_UCN
PIQ_ISR_MONITOR   Application Overview
PIQ_LOG_FEECALC   Fee Calculation Application Log
PIQ_LOG_GRANT   Grant Evaluation Application Log
PIQ_MAINT_SUBSTITUTE   Maintenance of Substitutes
PIQ_MATR   Number Range Maintenance: PIQ_MATR
PIQ_MATR_Y   Number Range Maint.: PIQ_MATR_Y
PIQ_NL_CRIHO_COMPARE   Compare CRIHO Files
PIQ_NL_CRIHO_INFILE   Process CRIHO Incoming File
PIQ_NL_CRIHO_OUTFILE   Create CRIHO Outgoing File
PIQ_NL_DISPALYFAILED   Display Unsuccessful Incoming Msgs.
PIQ_NL_IBGHISTORY   Display IBG History
PIQ_NL_MESSAGE22   Send a Message to Student
PIQ_NL_MIS_INFO   Missing Information Report
PIQ_NL_REF_FILE   Update Reference Tables
PIQ_NL_SENDUNSENTMSG   Send Unsent Messages to Studielink
PIQ_REQ   Number Ranges for Rule Modules
PIQ_US_1098T   1098T: Tuition Statement Reporting
PIQ_US_COMP_MASUPD   Mass update of Composite Results
PIQ_US_IPEDS   CM : US legal Reporting IPEDS
PIQ_US_NCAACOPYLOCAL   Copy NCAA XML Files to Local Disk
PIQ_US_NCAAINTERFACE   NCAA Interface
PIQ_US_NSCH_CORE   Transaction for Core Services Report
PIQ_US_NSCH_DEGREE   Transaction for Degree Verify Report
PIQ_US_SEVIS_EVI   CM US SEVIS EV Inbound XML
PIQ_US_SEVIS_EVO   CM US SEVIS EV Outbound XML
PIQ_US_SEVIS_STI   CM US SEVIS XML INBOUND
PIQ_US_SEVIS_STO   CM US SEVIS XML OUTBOUND
PIQ_US_TESTSCRUPLOAD   Test Score Upload
PIQ_US_VETERANS   Veterans reporting
PIQ_XML00   Create XML for Academic Structure
PITC   Maintain Tax Classifications

SAP Transaction Codes – Volume One

PITM	Mapping Tax Classification
PITX	Mapping Text IDs R/3 <-> CRM
PIU1	View program example 1
PIU2	View program example 2
PIU3	View program example 3
PIVV	Filter Mode Relating to KNVV
PJ02	Change JIT Call
PJ03	Display JIT Call
PJ04	Display JIT Calls
PJNA	Message Output
PJNK1	Create Condition: JIT Call
PJNK2	Change Condition: JIT Call
PJNK3	Display Condition: JIT Call
PJWE	Goods Receipt for JIT Call
PK00	Kanban
PK01	Create Control Cycle
PK02	Change Control Cycle
PK02NR	Change Control Cycle
PK03	Display Control Cycle
PK03NR	Display Control Cycle
PK05	PP Maintain Supply Area (Kanban)
PK05S	Fast Entry Supply Area
PK06	PP Maintain Supply Area (Kanban)
PK07	Kanban Calculation
PK08	Check Kanban Calculation Result
PK10	Define Status of Kanban Board
PK11	Plant Overview: Kanban
PK12	Kanban Board: Supply Source View
PK12N	Kanban Board: Supply Source View
PK13	Kanban Board: Demand Source View
PK13N	Kanban Board: Demand Source View
PK17	Collective Kanban Print
PK18	Evaluation Control Cycle/Kanban
PK21	Change Kanban Container Status
PK22	Kanban Quantity Signal
PK23	Manual Kanban Creation
PK23L	Delete Kanbans Automatically
PK24	Enter Customer KANBAN Call
PK31	Container Correction
PK37	Supply Area Stock Correction
PK41	Backflush KANBAN Orders
PK50	Display Errors: Kanban
PK51	Error Processing PDC Kanban
PK52	Kanban Calculation Error Log
PKAL	Due Replenishment Elements
PKBC	Chnge Container Status With Bar Code
PKC1	Process cost controlling
PKG1	Copy entries for garnishment CA
PKMC	Control Cycle Maintenance
PKRF21	Kanban Signal with Radio Frequency
PKRF22	Quantity Signal with Radio Frequency
PKRF23	Event-Driven KANBAN Radio Frequency
PKRFBC	Kanban Barcode without Actual Qty
PKW1	Kanban Board WWW

PL00	Maintenance of Packing Instructions
PLMC_AUDIT	Audit Management: Customizing
PLMC_AUDIT_MAPPING	Customizing Field Assignment MS Proj
PLMC_AUDIT_RESIDENCE	Audit Comps: Define Residence Time
PLMC_AUDIT_SFAC_AQN	Field Selectn:Audit Questn List/Item
PLMC_AUDIT_SFAC_AUO	Field Selection: Audit
PLMC_AUDIT_SFAC_AUP	Field Selection: Audit Plan
PLMC_AUDIT_SFAC_COR	Field Selectn: Audit Corrective Actn
PLMC_AUDIT_SFAC_QUE	Field Selectn: Audit QuestnList Item
PLMC_AUDIT_SFAC_QUN	Field Selection: Audit Question List
PLMC_FMEA_SFAC_AQN	Field Selection: FMEA List Items
PLMC_FMEA_SFAC_COR	Field Selection: FMEA Measure
PLMC_FMEA_SFAC_FMA	Field Selection FMEA
PLMD_AUDIT	Audit Management
PLM_AUDITMONITOR	Audit Management: Evaluations
PLM_AUDIT_DISPLAY	Audit Component: Display
PLM_AUDIT_PARTNER	Classification of Audit Partners
PLM_PDN_WUI_2_SCREEN	Dialog Method Calls via ITS
PLM_PS_TRANS	Call PS Transactions
PM01	Enhance Infotypes
PM03	Maintain Features Number Range
PM10	Statements Selection
PM11	Statements - Single Entry
PM12	Statements - Fast Entry
PM13	Statements - Print
PM20	Statements with SAPscript
PM22	Copy and Delete Statement
PM23	Statements Collector
PM24	HR-DBW: Display Data Records
PM30	Statements with Interactive Forms
PMAH	HR-FPM: Access Ad Hoc Query
PMB0	Position Management Plan Version
PMB1	Change Overall Budget
PMB1I	Internet Scenario - Budget Info
PMB2	Display Overall Budget
PMBA	Position Management Report Selection
PMBC	Create Overall Budget
PMBD	Display Overall Budget
PMBF	Carry Forward Overall Budget
PMBM	Change Overall Budget
PMBP	Change Plan Status
PMBPI	Internet Scenario - Position Mgt
PMBS	Change Budget Status
PMBT	Tools for Report Selection
PMC1	Check Consistency With Org. Mgt
PMEC	Change Employee
PMED	Display Employee
PMESIM	Manual Payroll Simulation
PMEVC	Variant Configuration Modeling Envmt
PMFD	Access HR-PFM via FM Account Assgmt
PMFM	Access HR-PFM via FM Account Assgmt
PMHS	Change Budget Status
PMIC	Consistency check with Funds Mgt
PMIMG	Access Customizing HR-FPM

PMIS	HIS for HR-FPM
PMJR	Derivatives Document Journal
PMLA	Create: Portfolio List
PMLB	Change: Portfolio List
PMLC	Display: Portfolio List
PMLD	Execute: Portfolio List
PMMF	Financing workbench
PMMN	HR Funds and Position Management
PMOC	Create Organization
PMOD	Display Organization
PMOF	Position List: Listed Options/Fut.
PMOF3	Position List: Listed Derivatives
PMOF4	Flow List: Listed Derivatives
PMOM	Change Organization
PMSI	Simulate Payroll Run
PMSV	Reversal of Margin Flows
PMUS	User-Specific Settings
PMVM	Calculate variation margin
PMWIZ001	'Generation...' Enhancement
PMWIZ002	'Reconcile...' Enhancement
PMWIZ003	Activate Document Display
PMWIZ004	Define Summarizt. of Required Funds
PMWIZ005	Required Funds of Vacant Positions
PMWIZ006	Enhanced Financing Distribution
PMWIZ007	Collective Processing of Financing
PNZ3	Pay Scale Reclassification NZ
PNZ4	Pay Scale Increase NewZealand
PNZ5	Pay Scale Inc. Extended NewZealand
PO01	Maintain Work Center
PO01D	Display Work Center
PO02	Maintain Training Program
PO02D	Display Training Program
PO03	Maintain Job
PO03D	Display Job
PO04	Maintain Business Event Type
PO04D	Display Business Event Type
PO05	Maintain Business Event
PO05D	Display Business Event
PO06	Maintain Location
PO06D	Display Location
PO07	Maintain Resource
PO07D	Display Resource
PO08	Maintain External Person
PO08D	Display External Person
PO09	Maintain Business Event Group
PO09D	Display Business Event Group
PO10	Maintain Organizational Unit
PO10D	Display Organizational Unit
PO11	Maintain Qualification
PO11D	Display Qualification
PO12	Maintain Resource Type
PO12D	Display Resource Type
PO13	Maintain Position
PO13D	Display Position

SAP Transaction Codes – Volume One

PO14	Maintain Task
PO14D	Display Task
PO15	Maintain Company
PO15D	Display Company
PO16	Maintain Services
PO16D	Display Service
PO17	Maintain Requirements Profile
PO17D	Display Requirements Profile
PO18	Maintain Resource 'Room'
PO18D	Display Resource Room
PO19	Maintain External Instructor
PO19D	Display External Instructor
POART	Portfolio Types
POASS	Portfolio Determination: Access Seqs
POBJ_TESTTOOL	POBJ Generic Framework Test Tool
POD1	Start Report RPU_UPDATE_IT118_46C
POD2	Start Report RPLKGPD0PBS
POD3	Start Report RPU_FILL_IT595_46C
POD4	Start Report RPLOZPD0PBS
POD5	Start Report RPU_UPDATE_DOZUL_46C
POF1	Create Pkg Instruction Determination
POF2	Change Pkg Instruction Determination
POF3	Display Packing Instr. Determination
POFO1	Create Portfolio
POFO2	Change Portfolio
POFO3	Display Portfolio
POFO31	Portfolio: Create
POFO32	Portfolio: Change
POFO33	Portfolio: Display
POFO34	Portfolio: Create with Reference
POI1	Start Download of Master Data
POIL	View Received Data Log
POIM	Start Download of Master Data
POIT	Start Download of Transaction Data
POIU	Start Receiving Changes to Data
POP0	Maintenance of Packing Instructions
POP1	Create Packing Instruction
POP2	Change Packing Instruction
POP3	Display Packing Instruction
POP4	Deletion flag undo for pack.instr.
POP5	Determination of Pkg Instr. Use
POPC	Components in Packing Instructions
POPRO	Portfolio determination: Schema def.
POPT	Test Packing Instruction Master Data
POSTIVDOC	Call transaction MIRO from Portal
POTAB	Define Portfolio Tables
POTABC	Change Portfolio Tables
POTABD	Display Portfolio Tables
POTB	Parameters for OTB
POWL_CAT	Maintain POWL categories
POWL_EASY	Easy-POWL Feeder Builder
POWL_QUERY	Maintain POWL Query definition
POWL_QUERYR	Maintain POWL Query role assignment
POWL_QUERYU	Maintain POWL Query user assignment

SAP Transaction Codes – Volume One

POWL_TYPE	Maintain POWL Type definition
POWL_TYPER	Maintain POWL Type role assignment
POWL_TYPEU	Maintain POWL Type user assignment
PP01	Maintain Plan Data (Menu-Guided)
PP01_DISP	Display Plan Data (Menu Guided)
PP02	Maintain Plan Data (Open)
PP03	Maintain Plan Data (Action-Based)
PP03_DIRECT	Execute Action Directly
PP05	Number Ranges
PP06	Number Range Maintenance: HRADATA
PP23	Reset Password
PP25	Display Scenario Group
PP26	Plan Scenario Administration
PP27	Release plan scenario
PP28	Create Scenario (Proj.Pay)
PP29	Change Scenario Group
PP2B	Create Scenario (Basic Pay)
PP2D	Administer Payroll Results
PP2P	Create Scenario (PyrllRes.)
PP2U	Data Transfer to CO
PP30	SAP Room Reservation Management
PP32	SAP Room Reservations: Services
PP40	Correspondence
PP60	Display Shift Planning
PP61	Change Shift Planning
PP62	Display Requirements
PP63	Change Requirements
PP64	Choose Plan Version
PP65	Edit Entry Object
PP66	Shift Planning: Entry Profile
PP67	Create Requirements
PP69	Choose Text for Organizational Unit
PP6A	Personal Shift Plan
PP6B	Attendance List
PP6C	Undo Completed Target Plan
PP6D	Define Shift Abbreviation Sequence
PP6E	Substitution Types in Shift Plans
PP6F	Define Info Column
PP6G	Info Column: Main Proposal
PP6H	Info Column: Proposal List
PP6I	Temp. Assgmt List for Shift Planning
PP6J	Display Tgt Plan Changes per User
PP6K	Display Tgt Plan Changes by Person
PP6U	Conversion Add'l Data HRPADNN/PADUZ
PP70	Organizational Management
PP72	Shift Planning
PP74	Personnel Cost Planning
PP7S	Organizational Management
PP90	Set up Organization
PPAD	Display Appraisals Catalog
PPA_LOG	Display PPA application log
PPCA1	Archive
PPCA2	Delete
PPCA3	Postprocessing

PPCA4	Evaluate
PPCA5	Administration
PPCCUS1	PPC: Number Range Maintenance
PPCCUS2	PPC: Number Range for Mat. Tables
PPCCUS3	PPC: Number Range for Activity Table
PPCCUSBW	PPC: Customizing for BW Transfer
PPCGO	Backflush Execution
PPCGO2	Execute Backflush - Step 2
PPCI	Copy Infotype
PPCJ	Create Infotype
PPCK	Enhance List Screen
PPCLOG	Log Display
PPCM	Enhance Infotype
PPCO	Organisational Plan: Initial Screen
PPCP	Career Planning
PPCRPA	Reprocessing of Activities
PPCSA	Display of Production Activities
PPCSC	Display of Component Withdrawal
PPCSHOW	Displays Backflushes
PPCT	Task Catalog
PPCVAR	Enter Variances
PPDM	Detail Maintenance Planning ITs
PPDPCS	Display Development Plan Catalog
PPDPHM	Change Development Plan History
PPDPHS	Display Development Plan History
PPDPIM	Change Individual Development Plan
PPDPIS	Display Individual Development Plan
PPDPSPFP	Find Objs Who Have Completed a Plan
PPDPSPFS	Find Persons for Development Item
PPE	iPPE Workbench
PPECFP1	Transfer iPPE Changes
PPECHK	iPPE Consistency Check (Prod. Vers.)
PPECMP	Configuration Comparison
PPECMP_STTA	Control Table
PPECOLMR	Maintain Color Key
PPECS	Convert iPPE Model
PPEEVAL	Status Cockpit
PPEHDR01	Create a Production Version
PPEHDR02	Change a Production Version
PPEHDR03	Display a Production Version
PPEM	PD: Display Organizational Structure
PPEPS	iPPE PS Interface
PPETI	Configuration Mode - Select. Screen
PPETICLS	Allowed Classes for Tab. Maint. iPPE
PPEUIARCH	Display Archived iPPE Data
PPE_BAL_COUNT_WDUR	Calculation of Weighted Duration
PPF_HISTORY	Display Mass Run History
PPI0	Transfer of Table Entries
PPIS	Human Resources Information System
PPLB	Evaluate Careers
PPMDT	Manager's Desktop
PPMDTCW	Customizing wizard Manager's Desktop
PPME	Change Matrix Organization
PPMM	Personnel Planning

PPMS	Display Matrix Organization
PPO1	Change Cost Center Assignment
PPO2	Display Cost Center Assignment
PPO3	Change Reporting Structure
PPO4	Display Reporting Structure
PPO5	Change attributes
PPO6	Display attributes
PPOC	Create Organizational Plan
PPOCA	Create Attributes
PPOCE	Create Organization and Staffing
PPOCW	Create Org. and Staffing (WF)
PPOC_OLD	Create Organizational Plan
PPOM	Maintain Organizational Plan
PPOMA	Change Attributes
PPOMDETAIL	Detail screen in mini framework
PPOME	Change Organization and Staffing
PPOMW	Change Org. and Staffing (WF)
PPOM_DEL	Delete user settings
PPOM_MODE	Org. Management:InterfaceMaintenance
PPOM_OLD	Maintain Organizational Plan
PPOS	Display Organizational Plan
PPOSA	Display attributes
PPOSE	Display organization and Staffing
PPOSW	Display Org. and Staffing (WF)
PPOS_OLD	Display Organizational Plan
PPPD	Display Profile
PPPDC02	Initial and Delta Dowload PP-PDC
PPPDC03	Upload Request PP-PDC
PPPDC04	Update PDC Messages PP-PDC
PPPE	Area Menu: Personnel Development
PPPE_SEARCH_FOR_Q	Find Objects for Qualifications
PPPM	Change Profile
PPQ1	Find Objects for Qualifications
PPQ2	Find Objects for Requirements
PPQ3	Find Objects for Profile
PPQD	Display Qualifications Catalog
PPRL	Change Material When Profile Deleted
PPRP	Reporting: Personnel Development
PPRV	Change Material When Profile Changed
PPSC	Create Structure
PPSM	Change Structure
PPSP	Succession Planning
PPSS	Display Structure
PPST	Structure Evaluation
PPUP	Settings: User Parameters
PPWFBUF	Synchronize OM Workflow Buffer
PP_APL	Absence Planner: Public Sector DE
PP_MY_APP	Appraisals Where Appraisee
PP_MY_APP_CREATE	Create Appraisal
PP_MY_APP_MGT	My Appraisals
PP_MY_PROFILEMATCHUP	Profile Matchup With Own Position
PP_MY_QUALIFICATIONS	Display Qualifications Profile
PP_MY_REQUIREMENTS	Display Requirements Profile
PP_TSN_CUM	Educ/Training Time Statement: Totals

PP_TSN_DET   Educ/Training Time Statement: Detail
PQ01   Actions for Work Center
PQ02   Actions for Training Program
PQ03   Actions for Job
PQ04   Actions for Business Event Type
PQ06   Actions for Location
PQ07   Actions for Resource
PQ08   Actions for External Person
PQ09   Actions for Business Event Group
PQ10   Actions for Organizational Unit
PQ12   Actions for Resource Type
PQ13   Actions for Position
PQ14   Actions for Task
PQ15   Actions for Company
PQ17   Actions for Requirement Profiles
PQ18   Actions for Resource Room
PQ19   Actions for External Instructor
PQAH   Ad Hoc Query
PQLV   Australian Leave Processing
PQTO   Transaction for screen 2000
PQTO_CE   Termination Organiser for AU CE
PQ_FEE_CALC   Fee Calculation
PQ_GRANT_CALC   Grant Evaluation
PR00   Travel expenses
PR01   Maintain (Old) Trip Data
PR02   Travel Calendar
PR03   Trip Advances
PR04   Edit Weekly Reports
PR05   Travel Expense Manager
PR05_ESS   Travel Expense Manager via ESS
PR10   Number Range Maint.: RP_REINR
PR11   Number range maint.: HRTR_PDOC
PR12   Number Range Maint. for Posting Runs
PR20   Create Trip
PR706Z   Copy T706Z -> T706Z1
PR71   Customizing Coding Block 1701
PR72   Customizing Coding Block 1702
PR73   Customizing Coding Block 1703
PRAA   Automatic Vendor Maintenance
PRAP   Approval of Trips
PRC2   Customizing Coding Block 1200
PRC7   Customizing Coding Block 1700
PRCAT   Analysis Tools Pricing
PRCC   Import Credit Card Files
PRCCD   Display Credit Card Receipts
PRCCE   Process Incorrect Transactions
PRCCF   Generate File with Correct Trnsactns
PRCCT   Create Credit Card Clearing TestFile
PRCD   Delete/Copy Trip Countries
PRCO   Copy Trip Provision Variant
PRCR   Travel Expense PDs/FRs: Download
PRCT   Current Settings
PRCU   Check Printing USA
PRC_CONDLIMIT   maintain upper and lower limit

PRC_CONDTYPE	maintain pricing condition type
PRC_COPYTYPE	maintain copy type
PRC_EXCL_GROUP	maintain exclusion group (cond.type)
PRC_EXCL_PROC	maintain exclusion (procedure)
PRC_FIXGROUP	maintain fixation group
PRC_PRICPROC	maintain pricing procedure
PRC_PURPOSE	maintain condition purpose
PRC_SIMULATION	Pricing Simulation
PRD1	Create DME
PRDE	Delete Trip Prov.Variant
PRDH	Employees with Exceeded Trip Days
PRDX	Call Country Version DME Pre.Program
PREC	Travel Expenses Accounting Program
PREP	Import Program for Per Diems
PREX	Create expense report
PRF0	Standard Form
PRF0_PDF	Mass Printing of Standard Forms
PRF1	Summarized Form 1
PRF2	Summarized Form 2
PRFAM	Maintain Price Families
PRFI	Posting to Financial Accounting
PRFW	Income-rel.Expenses Statement
PRHD	Maximum Value Delimitation for Meals
PRHH	Scale Maximum Amounts for Meals
PRHP	Scale Per Diems for Meals
PRICAT	PRICAT: Maintain mat. as per catalog
PRICATCUS1	Pricat: Customizing for V_pricat_001
PRICATCUS2	Pricat: Customizing for V_pricat_002
PRICATCUS3	Pricat: Customizing for V_Pricat_003
PRICATCUS6	Pricat: Maint. View V_Pricat_006
PRICATCUS7	Pricat: Maint. View V_Pricat_007
PRICATLOG	PRICAT: Display application log
PRICATLOGOUT	PRICAT: Display Application Log
PRICREAT	PRICAT: BAPI outbound IDoc test data
PRKE	Evaluation Program
PRMC	Travel Expenses: Feature TRVCT
PRMD	Maintain HR Master Data
PRMF	Travel Expenses: Feature TRVFD
PRML	Set Country Grouping via Dialog Box
PRMM	Personnel Actions
PRMO	Travel Expenses: Feature TRVCO
PRMP	Travel Expenses: Feature TRVPA
PRMS	Display HR Master Data
PRMT	Update Matchcode T
PROF	Profit Center Accounting
PROT451	Evaluate Error Log (Parallel Run)
PRPBIL	Customizing print profile bill. doc.
PRPBILV	Print Profile Maintnce: Billing Doc.
PRPD	Delimitation of Per Diems for Meals
PRPDBIL	Print Prof. Customizing EWM BillDocs
PRPDBILV	Print Profile Maint. EWM BillDocs
PRPHU	Customizing Print Profiles HU
PRPHUV	Print Profile Maintenance HU
PRPL	Create Travel Plan

PRPPRO	Call Maintenance View for Print Prof
PRPR	Parameter transf. to V_LEDRUCKPROF1
PRPSHP	Custimizing print profiles shipping
PRPSHPV	Print Profile Maintenance Shipping
PRPTRA	Customizing print profile transport
PRPTRAV	Print Profile Maintenance Transport
PRPY	Transfer to External Payroll
PRP_US_EFFR_ACTUALS	EfEffort Reporting-US: Actual Report
PRP_US_EFFR_BUND_ACT	Effort Reporting-US: Actual Report
PRP_US_EFFR_BUND_DUN	Effort Reporting-US: Dunnin Report
PRP_US_EFFR_DUNNING	Effort Reporting-US: Dunning Report
PRP_US_EFFR_STRESET	Reset Status of Certification Record
PRRL	Reset Trips to 'To be Accounted'
PRRQ	Create Travel Request
PRRW	Post Accounting Data
PRSC	Record: Start Values for Trip Chain
PRSD	Display: Start Values for Trip Chain
PRST	Period Statistics
PRS_REM	Delete Job for Engagement Management
PRT3	Travel Expenses: Maintain Postings
PRTA	Overview of Travel Expense Reports
PRTC	Display Imported Documents
PRTE	Trip Details
PRTS	Overview of Trips
PRUL	Travel Expense PDs/FRs: Upload
PRVCCC_D	Dispaly V_PRV_CCC by key
PRVH	Scale Maximum Amounts for Meals
PRVP	Scale Per Diems for Meals
PRVT	VAT Recovery
PRWW	Expense Reports (Offline)
PR_CHECK	Check Customizing Settings
PR_WEB_1000	Trip Data
PR_WEB_1200	General Trip Data
PR_WEB_1300	Trip Receipts
PR_WEB_1400	Trip Deductions
PR_WEB_1500	Trip Advances
PR_WEB_1600	Trip Destinations
PR_WEB_1700	Cost Distribution: Trip
PR_WEB_1710	Cost Distribution for Receipts
PR_WEB_1720	Cost Apportionment Destinations
PR_WEB_1730	Cost Distribution: Miles/Kilometers
PR_WEB_1800	Legs of Trip
PR_WEB_1900	Check Trip
PS4S_STATUS_DEL	Delete Status Confirmation Table
PS4S_STATUS_PROC	Send Status Confirmation
PSA00	Activate PSA
PSA01	Activate Rollup for PSC
PSA02	PSA Authorities
PSA03	Configuration screens for production
PSA04	Volume Conversion Factors
PSA05	Calculation Types
PSA06	Display profile for PSC documents
PSA07	PSA Source Company Code Assignment
PSA08	PSA Currency & Exchange Rate Types

PSA09	Adjustment Reasons
PSA10	PSC Master data
PSA11	PSA Product Master
PSA12	PSC Ships
PSA13	PSA Group
PSA14	PSC Calculation Scheme and Detail
PSA15	PSA Ship Codes
PSA16	PSA Oil Types
PSA17	PSA Terminal Codes
PSA18	PSA Version Mainenance
PSA19	PSA Lifting Group Master
PSA20	Venture Assignment to PSC
PSA21	Source Assignment to Product
PSA22	Source Assignment to Calc Type
PSA30	PSA Product Assignment
PSA31	Calculation Scheme Assignment
PSA32	PSC Assignment to Terminal
PSA33	PSA Lift Group to Partner Assignment
PSA40	Populate Cost Plans
PSA41	Planned Volume Data Entry
PSA42	Copy Plan Versions
PSA45	Entitlement Plan Calculation
PSA45R	Entitlement Plan Calc. Reversal
PSA50	Acutal Rollup to PSC tables
PSA51	Volume Data Entry
PSA55	PSC Calculation Actual
PSA55R	PSC Calculation Reversal
PSA56	Manual Transfers
PSA56R	Manual Transfers Reversal
PSA57	Entitlement Transfers
PSA57R	Entitlement Transfers Reversal
PSA58	Cost Adjustments
PSA58R	Cost Adjustments Reversal
PSA59	Stock Adjustments
PSA59R	Stock Adjustments Reversal
PSA60	Balance Carry Forward
PSA70	JV Partner Entitlement
PSA71	Statement of Storage Entitlement
PSA71U	Statement of Storage Entitlement/Upd
PSA72	PSC Master Data
PSA73	Production Data with Adjustments
PSA74	Lifting Data with Prices
PSA75	Flat Prices
PSA76	Adjustment Volumes
PSA77	Partner Report
PSA78	PSA Print Entitlement
PSA79	Volumes by Volume Types
PSA80	Maintain Price by Terminal
PSA81	Maintain Daily Prices by PSC
PSA82	Maintain Production Data
PSA83	Daily Lifting Data Entry
PSA84	Maintain Adjustment Data
PSA85	PSA Open Periods
PSA86	Open PSC Periods

PSA87	Maintain Lifting Data by Terminal
PSA88	Maintain Weighted Aver Price Period
PSA89	Manual AL Weighted Average Price
PSA90	PSC Production Interface
PSA91	Arms/Non-arms Length
PSA93	PSA Malaysia Production Interface
PSA94	PSA PI Malaysia - COEP %
PSA95	PSA Split Lifting by PSC
PSA96	Lifting by Terminal (CoCd indep.)
PSANR	PSA Document Number
PSARP1	PSA document display
PSB0	Generation quart.SI declarat.periods
PSB1	Generate Tax scales (B)
PSC0	Set Plan Version Valid for Cost Plan
PSC09	PSC Conversion Factor Transaction
PSC10	PSC Master data
PSC11	PSC product
PSC12	PSC calculation type
PSC13	PSC group
PSC14	Calculation scheme
PSC15	Calculation scheme detail
PSC151	Test transaction
PSC16	Production information
PSC17	PSC source assignment
PSC20	PSC product assignment
PSC21	PSC calculation type assignment
PSC23	PSC Venture Assignment
PSC24	PSC Source Assignment
PSC25	PSC Source Master
PSC26	PSC Source Assignment to Product
PSC27	PSC Source Assignment to Calc Type
PSC28	PSC Source group Ledger Assignments
PSC29	PSC Calc Type Category
PSC30	PSC Calc Scheme and Detail
PSC35	Display profile for PSC documents
PSC40	Rule Maintenance
PSC90	PSC Volume Entry
PSC91	PSC Volume Entry
PSC93	PSC Ships
PSC94	PSC Oil Type
PSC95	PSC Production Interface
PSC96	PSC Period Opening
PSC97	PSC Periods
PSCCA	PSC calculation
PSCREV	PSC calculation reversal
PSCRP1	PSC document display
PSCRPT	psc report
PSCRU	PSC Rollup
PSCRUA	Activate Rollup for PSC
PSCTF	PSC Transfer Calculation
PSCTFREV	PSC Transfer Funds Reversal
PSC_MENU	Product Sharing Agreement
PSC_MENU_X	Product Sharing Agreement
PSEMAINT	PSE Management

SAP Transaction Codes – Volume One

PSEN_IMG_XX_CUST	Display settings
PSHLP10	Project Worklist
PSHLP20	Project Editor
PSHLP30	Draft Workbench
PSHLP90	Administrator Workbench
PSO0	Set Plan Version for OrgManagement
PSO1	Set Aspect for OrgManagement
PSO2	PS System/Database Tools
PSO3	Infotype Overview
PSO4	Individual Infotype Maintenance
PSO5	PD: Administration Tools
PSOA	Work Center Reporting
PSOB0001	BDT Control: Applications
PSOB0002	BDT Control: Field Groups
PSOB0003	BDT Control: Views
PSOB0004	BDT Control: Sections
PSOB0005	BDT Control: Screens
PSOB0006	BDT Control: Screen Sequences
PSOB0007	BDT Control: Times
PSOB0008	BDT Control: CUA Standard Funct.
PSOB0009	BDT Control: CUA Addit. Funct.
PSOB0011	BDT Control: Assign ScrnFld->DB Fld
PSOB0012	BDT Control: Field modif. criteria
PSOB0013	BDT Control: Role Categories
PSOB0015	BDT Control: Application Transaction
PSOB0016	BDT Control: Tables
PSOB0017	BDT Control: External Applications
PSOB0018	BDT Control: Activities
PSOB0023	BDT Control: Data Sets
PSOB0100	Cust: Field Mod. for each Activity
PSOB0102	Cust: Authorization Types
PSOB0103	Cust: Authorization for Each Fld Grp
PSOB0104	BDT Control: Screen Configuration
PSOB0200	BDT Change Document List
PSOBARCH	Contract Object Archiving
PSOBARCHBDT	BDT Contract Object Archiving
PSOBCHANGE	Change Contract Object
PSOBCHDOC	Display Change Document List
PSOBCREATE	Create Contract Object
PSOBDELE	Delete Contract Object
PSOBDELEBDT	BDT Delete Contract Object
PSOBDISPLAY	Display Contract Object
PSOBPCDACT	Activate Planned Changes
PSOBWORK	Edit Contract Object
PSOB_TREE_START	Edit Contract Object
PSOC	Job Reporting
PSOG	OrgManagement General Reporting
PSOI	Tools Integration PA-PD
PSOO	Organizational Unit Reporting
PSOS	Position Reporting
PSOT	Task Reporting
PSSD	Check BNL flow types
PSV0	Change / Display Resources
PSV1	Dynamic Attendance Menu

PSV2	Dynamic Business Event Menu
PSV3	Dynamic Information Menu
PSV4	Set Plan Version
PSV5	Info: Attendances
PSV6	Reporting: Business Events
PSV7	Reporting: Resources
PSV8	Create Attendee
PSV9	Change / Display Attendee
PSVA	Set Aspect
PSVB	User-Specific Settings
PSVC	Training and Events:Current Settings
PSVE	Output Filter Business Events
PSVI	User-Defined Settings
PSVL	Set Business Event Language
PSVO	Change / Display Organizer
PSVP	Dynamic Planning Menu
PSVQ	Change / Display Organizer
PSVR	Dynamic Resource Menu
PSVS	Set Access
PSVT	Dynamic Tool Menu
PSW5	Per.Repostgs in Actual for Projects
PSWB	Execute Per.Reposting Plan Projects
PT00	Time Management
PT00_M99_HRF	Time Statement
PT01	Create Work Schedule
PT02	Change Work Schedule
PT03	Display Work Schedule
PT10	Number Range Maintenance: PTM_DOCNR
PT11	Number Range Maintenance: PTM_QUONR
PT12	Number Range Maintenance: HRAA_PDOC
PT40	PDC Error Transaction
PT41	Customizing CC1 Communication Param.
PT42	Supply Personnel Data
PT43	Supply Master Data
PT44	Upload Request
PT45	Post Person Time Events
PT46	Post Working Time Events
PT50	Quota Overview
PT60	Time Evaluation
PT60_NON_CE	Time Evaluation (RPTIME00)
PT61	Time Statement
PT62	Attendance List
PT63	Personal Work Schedule
PT64	Absence List
PT65	Graphical Attendance/Abs. Overview
PT66	Display Cluster B2
PT67	Third-Party Payroll
PT68	Activity Allocation
PT69	Multiple Time Recording
PT70	Time Management Info System
PT705B	Display Features
PT71	Tool Selection for Time Management
PT80	CC1: Manager
PT90	Absences: Calendar View

SAP Transaction Codes – Volume One

PT90_ATT   Attendances: Calendar View
PT91   Absences: For Multiple Employees
PT91_ATT   Attendances: For Multiple Employees
PTARQ   Test Environment for Leave Request
PTCCX   Test Environment
PTCOR   Clock-In/Out Corrections: Test
PTE1   Generate Batch Input Session
PTE2   Process Batch Input Session
PTE3   Reorganize Interface File
PTFMLA   FMLA Workbench
PTFMLA_PROF   FMLA Workbench
PTG1   Pflegen Krankengeld-Bezahlung (GB)
PTG3   Display Qualifying Day Pattern (GB)
PTKC_ANU_PAY_FED   Federal Tax Calculator: Annual
PTKC_ANU_PAY_QC   Quebec Tax Calculator: Annual
PTKC_CAR   Car Taxable Benefit Calculator
PTKC_NONREG_PAY_FED   Fed. Tax Calculator: Regular/Bonus
PTKC_NONREG_PAY_QC   QC Tax Calculator: Regular/Bonus
PTKC_REG_PAY_FED   Federal Tax Calculator: Pay period
PTKC_REG_PAY_QC   Quebec Tax Calculator: Pay period
PTME   Time Manager's Workplace
PTME_PROF   Time Manager's Workplace
PTMW   Time Manager's Workplace
PTMW_PROF   Time Manager's Workplace
PTMW_TIME_ADMIN   Maintain Time Data
PTMW_TIME_ADMIN_GRP   Maintain Time Data for Group
PTMW_WORKLIST   Process Messages
PTRM_PLARR_DELTA_UP   Delta upload TrvPlArrgNotifcation
PTRM_PLARR_INI_UP   Intial upload TrvPlArrgNotifcation
PTRM_PLARR_SETUP   Intial setup TrvPlArrgNotifcation
PTRV_AD_HOC_QUERY   Travel Management Queries
PTRV_BSTAT   Create and Maintain Trip Statistics
PTRV_CALC   Pocket Calculator
PTRV_CATSXT   Integration Trip -> CATSXT
PTRV_CATS_APPR   Integration Trip -> CATSXT
PTRV_FILL_PERS   Personalization: Trip Approval
PTRV_FI_PAYMENT_DATE   Determine FI Payment Date
PTRV_OFFLINE   Activate Offline Travel Manager
PTRV_PAYMENT_HISTORY   Travel Expenses Payment History
PTRV_QUERY   Travel Management Queries
PTRV_RESPO   Contact Partner Responsibilities
PTRV_RTREE   Display Trav. Management Report Tree
PTRV_STAT   Customizing HR Trip Statistics
PT_55400   Examine Table T554S
PT_ABS20_ATT   Attendance/Absence Data: Overview
PT_BAL00   Cumulated Time Evaluation Results
PT_BPC00   Generate Personal Calendar
PT_BPC10   Leave Accrual and Quota Deduction
PT_CLSTB1   Temp. Time Eval. Results (ClusterB1)
PT_CLSTB2   Time Evaluation Results (Cluster B2)
PT_CLSTG1   Group Incentive Wages (Cluster G1)
PT_CLSTL1   Individual Inc. Wages (Cluster L1)
PT_CLSTPC   Cluster PC: Personal Calendar
PT_DOW00   Time Accounts

PT_DSH20	Daily Work Schedule	
PT_EDT_TEDT	Time Statement	
PT_EDT_TELU	Time Balances Overview	
PT_ERL00	Time Evaluation Messages: Analysis	
PT_FMLA_DOC_NUM	Number Range Maintenance: PT_FMLDOCN	
PT_FMLA_REQ_NUM	Number Range Maintenance: PT_FMLAN	
PT_ILVA00	Leave Accrual	
PT_LEA40_ABS	Att./Absences: Graphical Overview	
PT_LEA40_ATT	Att./Absences: Graphical Overview	
PT_LEACONV	Transfer Remaining Leave from IT0005	
PT_QABS	Absences: List	
PT_QATT	Attendances: List	
PT_QREM	Employee Remuneration Information	
PT_QTA00	Generate Absence Quotas	
PT_QTA10	Absence Quota Information	
PT_QTAL	Employee Time and Labor	
PT_REOPC	Reorg. Pers. Calender (Cluster PC)	
PT_SHF00	Generation of Work Schedules	
PT_UPD00	Revaluation of Att./Absence Records	
PT_UTPR00	Revaluate Daily Work Schedules	
PT_UWSH00	Revaluate Planned Working Time IT	
PU00	Delete Personnel Data	
PU01	Delete current payroll result	
PU03	Change Payroll Status	
PU11	Supplementary Pension: Public Sector	
PU12	Connection to Third-Party Payroll	
PU12_CONVERT	Data Export	
PU12_DOWNLOAD	Data Export	
PU12_EXPORT	Data export	
PU12_IDOC_CREATE	Create IDocs	
PU12_IDOC_PROCESS	Process IDocs	
PU12_SHOW_CLUSTER	Display Interface Results	
PU12_SHOW_FILE	Display TemSe File	
PU19	Tax Reporter	
PU22	HR Archiving	
PU23	SARA Parameters Set For PA_CALC	
PU24	SARA Parameters Set For PA_TIME	
PU25	SARA Parameters Set For PA_TRAVEL	
PU30	Wage Type Maintenance	
PU90	Delete applicant data	
PU95	HR: Maintain Log. Views & WT Groups	
PU96	HR: Maintain Wage Type Groups	
PU97	HR: Logical View Maintenance	
PU98	Assign Wage Types to Groups	
PUC0	HR-CH: Maintain MA attributes	
PUC9	Reorganization of Infotype 0279	
PUCA	PC administration for PF	
PUCE	PC editor for PF	
PUCF	PC Form Maintenance PF	
PUCF_PDF	PDF Form Maintenance PF	
PUCG	Global Funds Copier	
PUCK	Entity copier for funds	
PUCP	PC Parameter Maintenance for PF	
PUCV	Entity copier for PC objects	

PUCW	Maintenanace of HSC tasks for PF
PUFK	Form manager
PUIT_UI	Test for ITF Conversion Classes
PULT	Transport HR Tables for Logistics
PUOCBA	Off-Cycle-Batch: Subsequent Activity
PUOCBLTI	Subsequent Processes for Mass LTIs
PUOCBP	Off-cycle batch: Payroll follow-up
PUOCBR	Off-cycle batch: Replacement
PUOCLG	OC-Batch: Batch Table List
PUOCLL	OC: List of Replacements/Reversals
PUOC_07	Off-Cycle Workbench Canada
PUOC_07_CE	Off-Cycle Workbench Canada CE
PUOC_08	Off-Cycle Workbench Great Britain
PUOC_10	Off-Cycle Workbench USA
PUOC_10_CE	Off-Cycle Workbench USA CE
PUOC_11	Off-Cycle Workbench Ireland
PUOC_13	Off-Cycle Workbench Australia
PUOC_13_CE	Off-Cycle Workbench Australia CE
PUOC_16	Off-Cycle Workbench South Africa
PUOC_17	Off-Cycle Workbench Venezuela
PUOC_20	Off-Cycle Workbench Norway
PUOC_23	Off-Cycle Workbench Sweden
PUOC_23_CE	Off-Cycle Workbench Sweden CE
PUOC_25	International Off-Cycle Workbench
PUOC_27	Perform Ad Hoc Payments
PUOC_28	Perform Ad Hoc Payments
PUOC_29	Off-Cycle Workbench Argentinia
PUOC_32	Off-Cycle Workbench Mexico
PUOC_33	Off-cycle Workbench Russia
PUOC_37	Off-Cycle Workbench Brazil
PUOC_40	Off-Cycle Workbench(India)
PUOC_41	Off-Cycle Workbench for Korea
PUOC_42	Perform Ad Hoc Payments
PUOC_44	Off-Cycle Workbench Finland
PUOC_44_VAC	Off-Cycle Vacation Handling
PUOC_99	International Off-Cycle Workbench
PUOC_99_CE	Off-Cycle Workbench 99 CE
PUOC_UN	Off-Cycle Workbench United Nations
PURBL	Backlog List MM
PUST	HR Process Workbench
PUST_2	HR Process Workbench (Old)
PUST_LIM	HR Process WB (Some Processes Only)
PUST_SO	HR Process Workbench (Display)
PUU1	BSI Test Tool 5.0
PUU2	transaction of sapmpuu2
PV00	Book Attendance
PV01	Rebook Attendance
PV02	Prebook Attendance
PV03	Replace Attendance
PV04	Cancel Attendance
PV05	Book List: Attendees/Business Events
PV06	Prebook List: Attendees
PV07	Book List: Attendees
PV08	Book List: Business Events

PV09	Plan Business Events
PV0I	Display Business Event Catalog
PV10	Create Business Event with Resources
PV11	Create Business Event w/o Resources
PV12	Firmly Book / Cancel Business Event
PV14	Lock / Unlock Business Event
PV15	Follow Up Business Event
PV16	Prebook List: Business Event Types
PV17	Billing
PV18	Activity Allocation
PV19	Activity Allocation for Instructors
PV1A	Change Business Event
PV1B	Display Business Event
PV1C	Cost Transfer
PV1D	Price Proposal
PV1I	Attendee Bookings: System Users
PV1M	Materials Procurement
PV26	Prebook List: Attendees/Event Types
PV2I	Attendee Bookings (Web Users)
PV32	Create Appraisal
PV33	Business Event Appraisal
PV34	Attendee Appraisal
PV35	Appraisal Conversion Program
PV3I	Book Attendance System Users
PV4I	Book Attendance Web Users
PV5I	Cancel Attendance: System Users
PV6I	Cancel Attendance Web Users
PV7I	Training Center
PV8I	My Bookings
PVB0	Business Event Budget
PVB1	Create Business Event Budget
PVB2	Display Business Event Budget
PVB3	Change Business Event Budget
PVB6	Initialize Business Event Budget
PVBA	Training & Events: Budget Comparison
PVBB	Change / Create Development Plan
PVCT	Master Data Catalog
PVD0	Create/Change Business Event Type
PVDM	Maintain Dynamic Menus
PVERSN	Maintain Progress Version
PVF0	Create/Change Location
PVF1	Maintain Location
PVG0	Create/Change Resource
PVG1	Create/Change Room
PVG2	Lock/Unlock Resource
PVG3	Maintain Room
PVH0	Create/Change External Instructor
PVH1	Create/Change Instructor
PVH2	Maintain External Person
PVK0	Correspondence History
PVL0	Create/Change Business Event Group
PVMN	Training and Event Management
PVR0	Create/Change Resource Type
PVR1	Maintain Room Equipment

SAP Transaction Codes – Volume One

PVSEARCH_ADM	Administer Search Engine
PVU0	Create/Change Company
PVU1	Maintain Company
PVV0	Create/Change Service
PW00	Incentive Wages
PW01	Maintain Incentive Wages Data
PW02	Display Incentive Wages Data
PW03	Record Incentive Wages Data
PW41	Generate Batch Input Session
PW42	Process Batch Input Session
PW43	Reorganize Interface File
PW61	Time Leveling
PW62	Employment Percentage
PW63	Reassignment of Pay Scale Group
PW70	Recalculate Indiv. Incentive Wages
PW71	Recalculate Group Incentive Wages
PW72	Remove leaving employee from group
PW74	Delete time tickets from cluster L1
PW75	Delete time tickets from cluster G1
PW80	Incentive Wages: Current Settings
PW91	Incentive Wages: Control Parameters
PW92	Incentive Wages: User Exits
PW93	Incentive Wages: Group Parameters
PW94	Inc. Wages: Logistics Parameters
PWKC	Create Work Center Capacity IDoc
PWPC	Convert Column Framework
PWPC_CONV_MDT_TO_LPA	Convert MDT Data to MSS LPA
PW_CEDTX0_AFTER	Remuneration Statements
PW_CEDTX0_BEFORE	Remuneration Statements
PX01	Planning Area, External Plan. Tool
PX02	Planning Tool, Physical System
PX03	Planning Tool
PX04	Ext.Planning Tool: StartParam. WinNT
PX05	External Planning Tool: Lock Table
PY01	Adopt T77R* from release note 20.A
PYK0	History of year end reporting runs
PYKT	Configuration Copier
PZ00	ESS Start Menu
PZ01	Who's Who
PZ01C	ESS Customizing for ESS Who's Who
PZ01_ADD_0032	Who's Who: Authorization
PZ01_ADD_0105	Who's Who: Authorization
PZ02	Address
PZ03	Bank Details
PZ04	Time statement
PZ04_OLD	Time Statement
PZ05	Emergency Address
PZ07	Participation Overview
PZ08	Taxes
PZ09	Time accounts
PZ10	Tax Deductions Form (W-4)
PZ11	Remuneration Statement
PZ11_OLD	Payroll Results
PZ11_PDF	Remuneration Statement

PZ12	Family/Related Person
PZ13	Personal Data
PZ14	Enrollment
PZ15	New Hire Data
PZ16	Employment and Salary Verification
PZ17	Work Schedule
PZ17_OLD	Work Schedule
PZ18	Emergency Contact
PZ19	ESS Time Management
PZ20	Notification of Marriage
PZ21	Employment Opportunities
PZ21_TC	Employment Opportunities
PZ22	Application status
PZ22_TC	Application status
PZ23	My Preferences
PZ24	Who's Who
PZ25	ESS Australian Taxes
PZ26	Organizational Chart
PZ26_NEW	Org.Cart Using Tree Control
PZ27	ESS Superannuation Australia
PZ28	ESS Previous Employers
PZ29	ESS External Bank Transfer Australia
PZ30	My Photo
PZ31	Advanced HR: Access Profile Maint.
PZ31_EWT	Advanced HR: Access Profile Maint.
PZ32	Advanced HR: Profile Maintenance
PZ34	ESS Time Management
PZ35	Who's Who (Flow Logic)
PZ35_MA	ESS Who's Who MiniApp (dummy)
PZ36	ESS Change YEA (Korea)
PZ38	ESS - Medical expense for DME (KR)
PZ39	Personal ID Information
PZ40	FSA Claims
PZ41	Capital Formation Germany
PZ42	ESS Alternative Name
PZ43	Retirement Benefits
PZ49	Start ESS
PZ50	Change Who's Who Data
PZ51	ESS: Tax Thailand
PZ52	ESS Change Address
PZ53	ESS for Prior Service Public Sector
PZ54	ESS for Leave Public Sector AU
PZ56	Additional Personal Data
PZ58	Deferred Compensation Germany
PZ60	ESS benefit requests
PZ61	Benefit request query report
PZ63	Enrollment
PZ64	Participation Overview
PZ67	ESS for Commuting Allowance
PZ68	ESS for Process request management
PZ70	ESS Donation Expense (Korea)
PZ80	ESS Investment detls - IT585 -Sec80
PZ81	ESS Expense Information(Korea)
PZ88	ESS Sec 80C Deduction details- IT586

PZBBPST01	Business-to-Business Procurement
PZFOTO	ESS Photo MiniApp (dummy)
PZLE	ESS Life Event (Dummy)
PZLE_01	ESS Life Event - New Hire (Dummy)
PZLE_02	ESS Life Event - New Hire (Dummy)
PZLE_03	ESS Life Event - New Hire (Dummy)
PZLE_04	ESS Life Event - Marriage (Dummy)
PZLE_05	ESS Life Event - Birth/Adoption
PZLE_06	ESS Life Event - New Hire (Dummy)
PZLE_07	ESS Life Event - New Hire (Dummy)
PZM0	ESS Start Menu
PZM1	ESS Start Menu 1
PZM2	ESS Start Menu
PZM3_START_MA	ESS Start Menu - Authorization
PZPR	Password Reminder
PZSU53	ESS Display Authorization Errors
PZUS	ESS General Settings
PZUSFB	ESS MiniApp Photograph/Birthday
PZUSWHO	ESS Who's Who
PZWHOC	ESS Who's Who: Customizing

www.ingramcontent.com/pod-product-compliance
Lightning Source LLC
LaVergne TN
LVHW022258060326
832902LV00020B/3146